Etón E1XM AM/FM/Shortwave/XM Satellit

Building off of a 25-year tradition of manufacturing the finest high-end tabletop receivers in the world, the E1XM is designed without compromise to give you direct access to news, sports and music from around the world.

- Frequency Coverage: 100-30,000 KHz, includes shortwave, medium wave AM broadcast band and longwave; 76-90, 87-108 MHz FM broadcast band; XM Satellite Ready Radio
- Reception Modes: AM, FM-stereo, Single Sideband (selectable USB/LSB) and CW
- Digital Display: large 5.7 inch square, 240 x 320 pixel, dot matrix display. Shows all modes and selected functions
- Programmable Memories: 500 user programmable with alpha labeling plus 1200 user definable country memories, for a total of 1700
- Memory Scan Function
- Digital Phase Lock Loop (PLL) Synthesized Tuning with Direct Digital Synthesis (DDS) for drift-free frequency stability and finest tuning resolution
- Dual Conversion Superheterodyne Circuit: results in minimized interference through superior selectivity
- Excellent Sensitivity: yielding a true high-performance receiver
- High Dynamic Range: allowing for detection of weak signals in the presence of strong signals
- Selectable Bandwidths: 7.0, 4.0, 2.5 kHz for excellent selectivity
- Single Sideband Synchronous AM Detector: selectable USB/LSB or double sideband to minimize adjacent frequency interference and fading distortion of AM signals
- IF Passband Tuning: an advanced tuning feature that functions in AM and SSB. Greatly helps reject interference
- Tuning Modes: variable-rate tuning knob, direct keypad frequency entry, up/down pushbuttons and auto-tuning
- Direct Shortwave Band Entry: allows instant access to the shortwave band of choice
- Selectable AGC: fast and slow mode
- Display Backlighting: evenly lit backlight enables display viewing under all lighting conditions
- Dual Programmable Clocks With WWV Auto-Setting
- Dual-Event Programmable ON/OFF Timers: can be used for recording or 'alarm clock' function
- Superior Audio Quality via a bridged type audio amplifier, providing high output power with battery operation
- Separate, continuous bass and treble tone controls
- Headphone Jack
- Stereo Line-Level Input: allows listening to other devices such as a CD player through the E1XM
- Stereo Line-Level Output: for recording or routing the output to another device such as a home stereo
- Calibrated LCD signal strength meter
- Built-In Antenna: telescopic antenna for AM, FM and Shortwave reception
- External Antenna Connection for the addition of auxiliary antennas, e.g. professionally engineered shortwave antennas; long-wire shortwave antennas; specialized AM broadcast band antennas for enthusiasts of AM DX'ing; FM broadcast band antennas
- Power Source: 4 "D" Batteries (not included); AC Adapter (included)
- Dimensions: 13"W x 7-1/2"H x 2-1/2"D (333 x 188 x 66 mm)
- Weight: 4 lb 3 oz. (1.9 Kg)

XM Satellite Radio subscription and antenna sold separately.

etón ®
RE_INVENTING RADIO
www.etoncorp.com

2007 Passport to

World Band Radio

International Broadcasting Services, Ltd.

ISSN 0897-0157

OUR READER IS THE MOST IMPORTANT PERSON IN THE WORLD!

Editorial

Editor in Chief	Lawrence Magne
Editor	Tony Jones
Assistant Editor	Craig Tyson
Consulting Editor	John Campbell
Founder Emeritus	Don Jensen
PASSPORT REPORTS	Lawrence Magne, Dave Zantow; along with George Heidelman, George Zeller
WorldScan® Contributors	Azizul Alam Al-Amin (Bangladesh), Gabriel Iván Barrera (Argentina), David Crystal (Israel), Alok Dasgupta (India), Graeme Dixon (New Zealand), Nicolás Eramo (Argentina), Paulo Roberto e Souza (Brazil), Alokesh Gupta (India), Jose Jacob (India), *Jembatan DX*/Juichi Yamada (Japan), Anatoly Klepov (Russia), Marie Lamb (U.S.), Célio Romais (Brazil), Nikolai Rudnev (Russia), David Walcutt (U.S.)
WorldScan® Software	Richard Mayell
Laboratory	Robert Sherwood
Artwork	Gahan Wilson, cover
Graphic Arts	Bad Cat Design; Mike Wright, layout
Printing	Transcontinental Printing

Administration

Publisher	Lawrence Magne
Associate Publisher	Jane Brinker
Offices	IBS North America, Box 300, Penn's Park PA 18943, USA; www.passband.com; Phone +1 (215) 598-9018; Fax +1 (215) 598 3794; mktg@passband.com
Advertising & Media Contact	Jock Elliott, IBS Ltd., Box 300, Penn's Park PA 18943, USA; Phone +1 (215) 598-9018; Fax +1 (215) 598 3794; media@passband.com

Bureaus

IBS Latin America	Tony Jones, Casilla 1844, Asunción, Paraguay; scheditor@passband.com
IBS Australia	Craig Tyson, Box 2145, Malaga WA 6062; addresses@passband.com
IBS Japan	Toshimichi Ohtake, 5-31-6 Tamanawa, Kamakura 247-0071; Fax +81 (467) 43 2167; ibsjapan@passband.com

Library of Congress Cataloging-in-Publication Data

Passport to World Band Radio.
1. Radio Stations, Shortwave—Directories. I. Magne, Lawrence
TK9956.P27   2006   384.54'5 06-22739
ISBN 978-0-914941-63-7

Opener photo credits: M. Guha (pp. 3, 4, 10, 30); M. Wright (pp. 50, 62, 74, 84, 88, 148, 156, 176, 184, 212, 236, 296, 362, 384, 408, 420)

Printed in Canada

Who says the world is round?*

IC-PCR1500

- 0.01 ~ 3299.99 MHz**
- AM, FM, WFM, CW, SSB
- Record and Save Audio as .WAV File
- USB Cable Connection
- Optional DSP

IC-PCR2500

- 0.01 ~ 3299.99 MHz** (Main)
  50 to 1300 MHz** (Sub)
- AM, FM, WFM, CW, SSB
- Optional APCO 25 and D-STAR
- Dual Wideband Receivers
- Dual Watch PC window

Podcasting, anyone?

Icom's new black box receivers have wide spectrum coverage, USB connectivity, and .wav file recordability. Save your favorite radio programs for personal Podcasts!

IC-R1500

- 0.01 ~ 3299.99 MHz**
- AM, FM, WFM, CW, SSB
- Single Receiver
- Mobile or PC Controlled

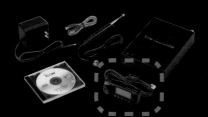

IC-R2500

- 0.01 ~ 3299.99 MHz** (Main)
  50 to 1300 MHz** (Sub)
- AM, FM, WFM, CW, SSB
- Dual Wideband Receiver
- Mobile or PC Controlled
- Optional APCO 25 and D-STAR
- Dual Receiver Diversity

THE WORLD IN YOUR HAND:

IC-R20
ADVANCED WIDE-
BAND RECEIVER
0.150 - 3304.0 MHz
(Cellular Blocked)

IC-R3
SEE & HEAR WIDE-
BAND RECEIVER
0.5 - 2450.0 MHz
(Cellular Blocked)

IC-R5
COMPACT WIDE-
BAND RECEIVER
0.5 - 1300.0 MHz
(Cellular Blocked)

For free literature:
425.450.6088 or
www.icomamerica.com

*Radio cover is actually black. World as seen from space artwork not included. **Refer to owner's manual for exact frequency specs.
©2006 Icom America Inc. The Icom logo is a registered trademark of Icom Inc. All specifications are subject to change without notice or obligation. 8789

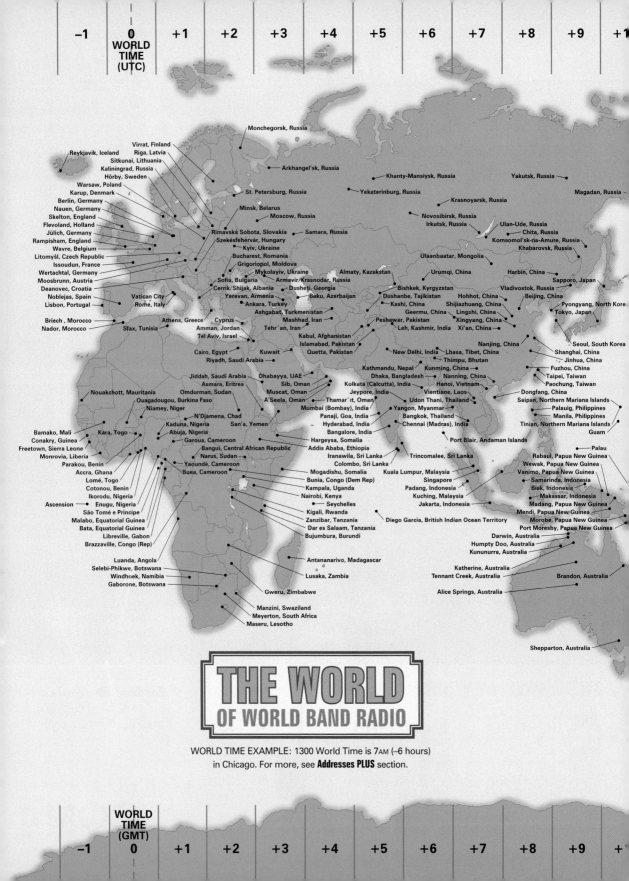

THE WORLD
OF WORLD BAND RADIO

WORLD TIME EXAMPLE: 1300 World Time is 7AM (–6 hours) in Chicago. For more, see **Addresses PLUS** section.

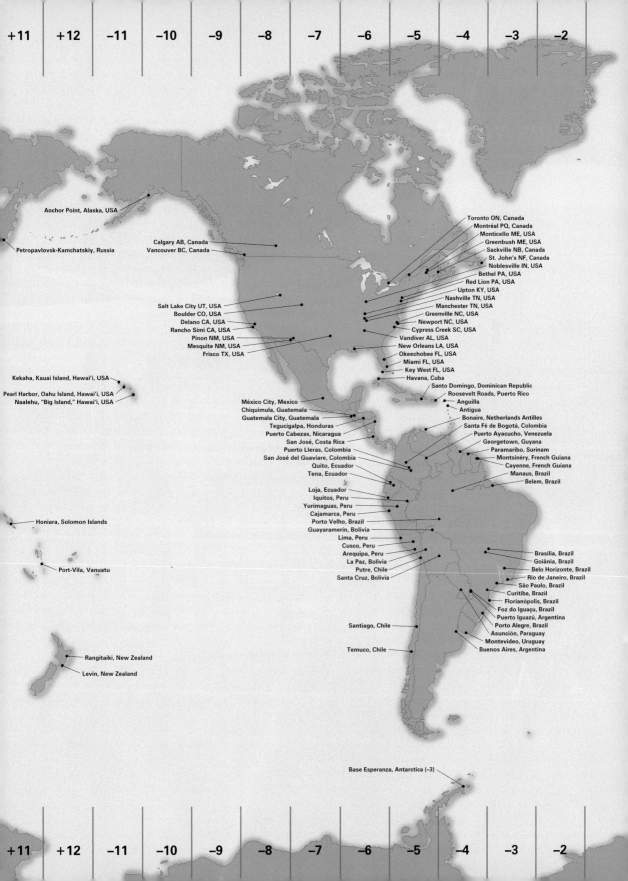

+11   +12   −11   −10   −9   −8   −7   −6   −5   −4   −3   −2

Anchor Point, Alaska, USA

Petropavlovsk-Kamchatskiy, Russia

Calgary AB, Canada
Vancouver BC, Canada

Toronto ON, Canada
Montréal PQ, Canada
Monticello ME, USA
Greenbush ME, USA
Sackville NB, Canada
St. John's NF, Canada
Noblesville IN, USA
Bethel PA, USA
Red Lion PA, USA
Upton KY, USA
Nashville TN, USA
Manchester TN, USA
Greenville NC, USA
Newport NC, USA
Cypress Creek SC, USA
Vandiver AL, USA
New Orleans LA, USA
Okeechobee FL, USA
Miami FL, USA
Key West FL, USA
Havana, Cuba

Salt Lake City UT, USA
Boulder CO, USA
Delano CA, USA
Rancho Simi CA, USA
Pinon NM, USA
Mesquite NM, USA
Frisco TX, USA

Kekaha, Kauai Island, Hawai'i, USA

Pearl Harbor, Oahu Island, Hawai'i, USA
Naalehu, "Big Island," Hawai'i, USA

México City, Mexico
Chiquimula, Guatemala
Guatemala City, Guatemala
Tegucigalpa, Honduras
Puerto Cabezas, Nicaragua
San José, Costa Rica
Puerto Lleras, Colombia
San José del Guaviare, Colombia
Quito, Ecuador
Tena, Ecuador
Loja, Ecuador
Iquitos, Peru
Yurimaguas, Peru
Cajamarca, Peru
Porto Velho, Brazil
Guayaramerin, Bolivia
Lima, Peru
Cusco, Peru
Arequipa, Peru
La Paz, Bolivia
Putre, Chile
Santa Cruz, Bolivia

Santo Domingo, Dominican Republic
Roosevelt Roads, Puerto Rico
Anguilla
Antigua
Bonaire, Netherlands Antilles
Santa Fé de Bogotá, Colombia
Puerto Ayacucho, Venezuela
Georgetown, Guyana
Paramaribo, Surinam
Montsinéry, French Guiana
Cayenne, French Guiana
Manaus, Brazil
Belem, Brazil

Honiara, Solomon Islands

Port-Vila, Vanuatu

Brasília, Brazil
Goiânia, Brazil
Belo Horizonte, Brazil
Rio de Janeiro, Brazil
São Paulo, Brazil
Curitiba, Brazil
Florianópolis, Brazil
Foz do Iguaçu, Brazil
Puerto Iguazú, Argentina
Porto Alegre, Brazil
Asunción, Paraguay
Montevideo, Uruguay
Buenos Aires, Argentina

Santiago, Chile

Rangitaiki, New Zealand

Levin, New Zealand

Temuco, Chile

Base Esperanza, Antarctica (−3)

+11   +12   −11   −10   −9   −8   −7   −6   −5   −4   −3   −2

E5
Takes You Around the World

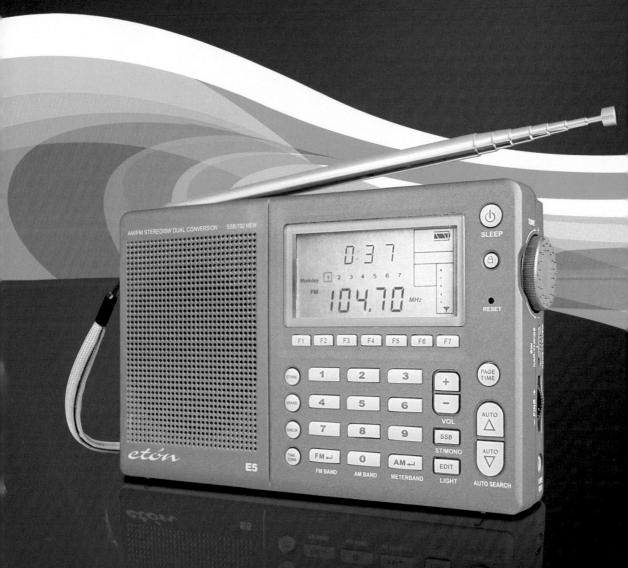

Etón E5 AM/LW/FM-Stereo/Full Shortwave Portable Radio

The E5 is the world's leading portable, multi-band and Single Side Band (SSB) enabled radio. The E5 unites performance and mobility into one compact unit, bringing the power of local and world-band radio into the palm of your hand. The ultimate in portable technology, the E5 is the latest edition to the Etón Elite range, demonstrating how form and function can work in harmony.

- Digital world-band radio
- AM/LW/FM-Stereo and Full Shortwave Coverage (1711 - 29999KHz)
- Earphones (included)
- PLL Dual Conversion
- Synthesized Tuning System
- Single Side Band (SSB) and Wide-Narrow Bandwidth Switch
- 700 Memory Programmable Presets
- Auto-Scan, Manual-Scan, Direct Key-in Entry, Tuning Buttons and Tuning Knob
- FM Station Automatic Tuning Storage (ATS) provides automatic acquisition of the strongest stations in your area
- Full-featured world time zone Clock, Sleep Timer, 4 Programmable Alarm Timers and Weekday View Display
- Station name input features allow a 4-character input of the stations call letters
- Internally recharges Ni-MH batteries (not included)
- Dimensions: 6-5/8"W x 4-1/8"H x 1-1/8"D (167 x 105 x 27 mm)
- Weight: 12.2 oz.(346 g).

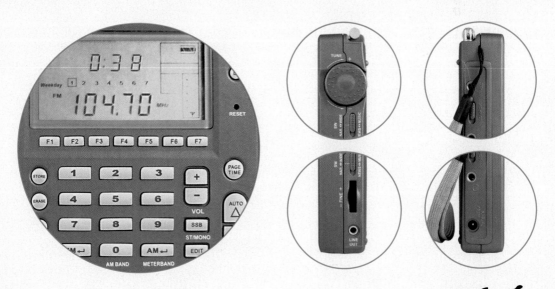

RE.INVENTING RADIO
www.etoncorp.com

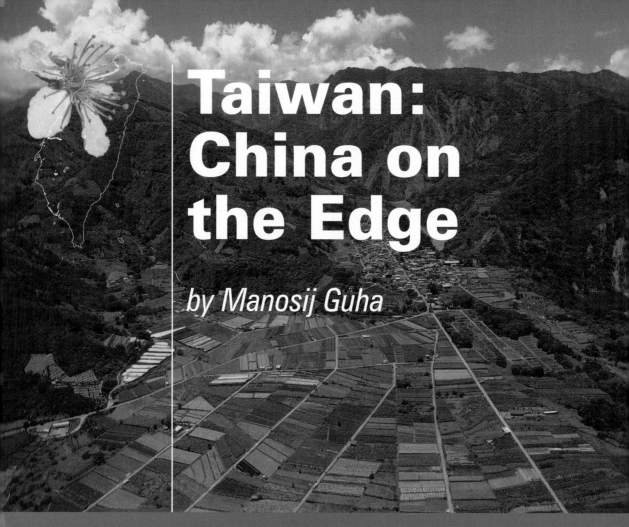

Taiwan: China on the Edge

by Manosij Guha

Dubbed *Ilha Formosa*, or beautiful island, by Portuguese seafarers, Taiwan still lives up to that name with its lush tropical landscape. Situated off the edge of the Chinese mainland, it's still regarded by some as the "other" China.

For all its lush beauty Taiwan is awash in modernity and innovation. With a population of just 23 million people in a place smaller than Denmark, it is the polar opposite of China's towering size and population.

There is even disagreement over what Taiwan is and what it should be called. To set the record straight: Taiwan is the name of the main island of a 78-island nation which calls itself the Republic of China. But the whole country is now increasingly being called Taiwan, to differentiate it from the People's Republic of China.

Independence-oriented Taiwanese, though historically of Chinese origin, regard China as a colonizing force—carpetbaggers little different from earlier European and Japanese occupiers. Having become increasingly separate in language and culture from their mainland kinsfolk, these Taiwanese would rather align with Japan than their mighty neighbor a stone's throw away.

Inhabitants Vary over Time

Taiwan's first inhabitants left no written records of their origins. Anthropological and archaeological evidence suggests that Taiwan's indigenous peoples are of proto-Malayan ancestry. Later, there took place a mass migration of Han—ethnic Chinese—from southern China in the early 1400s, then shipwrecked Portuguese appeared in 1582.

In 1622 the Dutch East India Company established a military base on the Pescadores Islands—present day Penghu—but they were forced out by China's Ming court and moved to the main island a couple of years later. With its colonial capital in Tainan in southern Taiwan, the Dutch ruled for the next 38 years.

Two years later the Spanish also made their presence felt in northern Taiwan. They built two trading outposts, but were finally expelled by the Dutch in 1642.

The Dutch generated huge volumes of mercantile trade, which made Taiwan a major transshipment center for goods to and from Japan, China, Persia, the Netherlands and Batavia—present-day Jakarta—in the Dutch East Indies, now Indonesia. Waves of settlers came from China to feed this industry and to work on Dutch plantations and farms.

Stragglers from the Ming court finally overthrew the Dutch a few decades later. In turn, they were overthrown by the Manchus in 1683, bringing Taiwan under the jurisdiction of nearby Fujian province. China

RTI's low-profile sign points to a hidden driveway. M. Guha

Taiwan's media environment is among the freest in Asia.

Rain doesn't dampen Taipei's can-do ethic. Like New York, it never sleeps. M. Guha

RTI producer Miguel Mai mixes a popular program in Cantonese. The show has fans not only in China, but also among the world's diaspora Chinese.

M. Guha

thus ruled the island for 212 years until 1895, when the Ching administration ceded Taiwan to Japan in 1895 under the Treaty of Shimonoseki.

The Japanese extensively developed Taiwan as a colony. Taiwan's infrastructure, agriculture, public health, banking, education and business all existed to support Japan's growing empire. The resulting powerhouse then served as a launching pad for Japanese forces headed to China's mainland and, later, Southeast Asia and India.

Colonial Japanese modernized harbors and also constructed 2,857 miles of rail lines and 2,500 miles of highways. They also built concrete dams, reservoirs and large aqueducts to form an extensive irrigation network so thousands of acres of marginal farmland could be brought into production.

Following Japan's August 15, 1945 wartime surrender, on October 25 Taiwan was once again ceded to China. It was officially known as the Republic of China and was ruled by Chiang Kai-shek's Nationalist Party (Kuomintang, or KMT). Given the poor administration of Taiwan, civil unrest erupted on the island two years later, climaxing in the February 28 Incident in 1947. Crowds rioted across the island, seizing police stations, arms and radio stations and killing a number of mainlanders. In succeeding months reinforcements were sent from the

mainland and the unrest was quelled. This led to the arrest and execution of thousands of reform-minded islanders.

Taiwan Stands Alone, America Helps

On October 1, 1949 the People's Republic of China was established and headed by Chiang's arch-rival Mao Zedong. This left the Republic of China as a rump state nonetheless recognized by the United Nations and most world powers. Since then Taiwan has managed to hold its own against the People's Republic of China, thanks in large part to support from the United States.

Taiwan came to the brink of war with China in August 1958 when the People's Republic began shelling the tiny and relatively barren Taiwanese islands of Quemoy and Matsu near the mainland. The attack eventually subsided by the end of October, thanks to the Eisenhower administration's diplomatic initiatives and firm stand. But the issue wouldn't fade away. It went on to become a political hot potato in the 1960 Nixon-Kennedy presidential race, with Nixon defending Eisenhower's action and Kennedy suggesting that the two islands weren't worth the risk of war.

A turning point in Taiwan's international relations came in 1971 when the United Nations switched its diplomatic recognition to the People's Republic. This went a step further in 1979, when Taiwan's strongest ally, the United States, did an about face: President Carter broke diplomatic ties with Taiwan in favor of China. Since then, China has offered various countries large economic incentives to break off diplomatic ties to Taiwan. Now, fewer than 30 continue to recognize the Republic of China as a sovereign nation.

Yet, the lack of diplomatic relations has not hampered the military and economic relationship between the United States and Taiwan. The sternest test came in 1996, when China conducted provocative missile tests in an attempt to influence Taiwan's first direct presidential election. In response, American President Clinton ordered the biggest display of American military power in Asia since the Vietnam War. A U.S. Navy flotilla was dispatched to the Taiwan Strait, sending an unmistakable message to Beijing.

China is equally adamant, and continues to regard Taiwan as a breakaway province which it wishes to retake, by massive force if necessary. Hundreds of Chinese missiles now aim across the narrow strait of water that separates them. But Taiwan argues to the contrary, that it is a sovereign country and has been so for over half a century, with its own constitution, democratically elected leaders and 400,000 troops in its armed forces.

In recent years Taiwan has made a smooth transition from an authoritarian one-party state to a fledgling democracy. It has also achieved an economic miracle, becoming one of the world's top producers of computer technology even as most nations have ceased officially recognizing its existence. Tensions and breast-beating notwithstanding, Taiwan and China enjoy healthy trade links, the mainland being the island's number one export market. By 2002 Taiwanese companies had invested more than $26.6 billion on the mainland, and up to a million Taiwanese now live there to help run factories and such.

Japanese Create First Taiwanese Station

Unlike within China, the media environment in Taiwan is now among the freest in Asia and is extremely competitive. Besides government media, there are now hundreds of privately owned newspapers and radio and television stations.

The island is home to more than 170 radio outlets, many with American-style music formats and popular phone-in programs.

The genesis of today's lively Taiwanese radio scene began over eight decades ago, when the first radio station fired up in Taipei on June 17, 1925. Known simply as Taiwan Radio, it was a mouthpiece of the colonial Japanese government. Running on a mere

Once a Dutch colonial outpost, Tainan is now home to RTI's mightiest transmitters. Towering antennas stand out against the serene coastline. M. Guha

G5
High Performance Radio Wherever You Are

GRUNDIG G5
AM/LW/FM-Stereo/Full Shortwave Portable Radio

The G5 is the world's leading portable, multi-band and Single Side Band (SSB) enabled radio. The G5 unites performance and mobility into one compact unit, bringing the power of local and world-band radio into the palm of your hand. The ultimate in portable technology, the G5 is the latest edition to the Grundig by Etón line of innovative products, demonstrating how form and function can work in harmony.

- Digital world-band radio
- AM/LW/FM-Stereo and Full Shortwave Coverage (1711 - 29999 KHz)
- Earphones (included)
- PLL Dual Conversion
- Synthesized Tuning System
- Single Side Band (SSB) and Wide-Narrow Bandwidth Switch
- 700 Memory Programmable Presets
- Auto-Scan, Manual-Scan, Direct Key-in Entry, Tuning Buttons and Tuning Knob
- FM Station Automatic Tuning Storage (ATS) provides automatic acquisition of the strongest stations in your area
- Full-featured world time zone Clock, Sleep Timer, 4 Programmable Alarm Timers and Weekday View Display
- Station name input features allow a 4-character input of the stations call letters
- Internally recharges Ni-MH Batteries (not included)
- Dimensions: 6-5/8"W x 4-1/8"H x 1-1/8"D (167 x 105 x 27 mm)
- Weight: 12.2 oz. (346 g).

The Grundig Radio Line by:

etón®
RE-INVENTING RADIO
www.etoncorp.com

The Nationalists once ran an elaborate radio network from this historic site in Nanking (Nanjing). RTI

50 Watts, it was actually part of a demonstration at an exhibition in the office of the Governor General of Formosa, as Taiwan was then known. Power was increased to 1 kW in 1927, then on November 1, 1928 a new transmitter started experimental broadcasting under the aegis of the Traffic Bureau. A permit was granted to the station and the listener's fee was waived.

By January 15, 1931 the station became the Taipei Broadcasting Station, JFAK, and power was upped to 10 kW. A listener's fee of one yen was instituted, in keeping with the custom throughout Japanese-held territories. The next few years saw a rapid expansion of the network. On April 1, 1932 another station, JFBK at 1 kW, was added in the southern city of Tainan.

June 20, 1934 saw the start of radiotelephone service between Tokyo and Taipei, as well as a world band radio service probably using the same facilities. Later that year, on September 12, an island-wide radio service was established. Like its counterparts in Manchuria and Korea, the station also began relaying NHK programs from Tokyo.

Another station, Taichung Broadcasting Station-JFCK, began in Taichung Park on May 11, 1935 with 1 kW. Starting July 16, 1937 the Taipei Broadcasting Station began an external service in Amoy. This operated

at 10 kW and was directed towards the Chinese province of Fujian across the narrow strait. It was followed a month later with a transmission to the South Pacific. In 1939 the station carried intensive broadcasts for Nationalist forces who were overrun at their capital in Nanjing and were compelled to relocate to Chungking (Chongquing).

By New Year's Day of 1941, Taiwan's rebroadcasts of NHK from Tokyo were expanded to 13 hours a day. These were carried simultaneously by stations in Manchuria and Korea for eight hours daily.

The next station to follow went on the air in Jiayi on August 31, 1942 with the call-sign JFDK and a modest 0.5 kW. A second transmitter with a whopping 100 kW was added the same year in Minxiong (see sidebar), with another service from Taipei being added on October 10. Japanese expansion in broadcasting concluded on May 15, 1944 with a tiny 100 Watt station, JFEK, in Hwalien's harbor.

Nationalist Radio Begins in Nanking

The present government radio infrastructure had its beginning on China's mainland during the rule of the Nationalist Party. Its first station was established in the then-national capital of Nanking (Nanjing) on August 1, 1928.

As Japanese forces overran the wartime capital in 1937, the station was first moved to Hankou, then to Chungking. After World War II, what had evolved into a network of 39 stations was called the China Broadcasting System (CBS), and the Broadcasting Corporation of China (BCC) was formed to manage it. When Japan surrendered unconditionally to Allied forces on August 15, 1945, nationalist leader Generalissimo Chiang Kai-shek personally visited the station to give a victory speech that was broadcast to the world.

In May 1946 the station, like the government, returned to Nanjing, the wartime capital of the nationalist government. With the communist takeover of China in 1947 and the resulting retreat of the Republic of China government to Taiwan, the BCC was left with just five stations that had survived American wartime bombing: Taipei, Taichung, Tainan, Chiayi and Hwalien.

About this time the CBS and BCC went their separate ways, with the BCC managing the national and regional radio networks. The CBS continued to operate quasi-international broadcasts beamed to the Chinese mainland and the rest of the world; programs were in domestic dialects and various foreign languages. The organizational separation was short-lived, and in 1949 the CBS was re-incorporated into the BCC in its first board meeting that year.

Name Game

On October 10, 1949 the CBS resumed international broadcasting as the Voice of Free China—a name that was to become familiar to millions in the decades to come. In order to increase broadcasting to the People's Republic, the Mainland China Broadcasting Section (MCBS) was formed in 1951. As the war of airwaves between China and Taiwan intensified, the MCBS was expanded a few years later to have its own staff and an independent budget. This continued until 1972 when the MCBS was restructured and, in time-honored fashion, called simply the China Broadcasting System. In subsequent

years the CBS transmitted to the mainland only under direct government supervision, then it was transferred to the Ministry of National Defense. The station relocated to its present premises in 1981.

Writing in *Broadcasting in Asia and the Pacific*, Taiwanese media expert Prof. Chia-shih Hsu provides a lucid understanding of Taiwanese broadcasting at that time. The Republic of China government on the mainland, before the People's Republic was founded, encouraged private media ownership. The same is still prevalent in Taiwan today—radio stations continue to be owned by the Nationalist Party, various government agencies and private enterprises.

After the Nationalists relocated to Taiwan, the largest network continued to be the BCC, divided into three networks: Voice of Free China, the overseas service; CBS, to reach the mainland; and four domestic groups. Domestic FM broadcasting began on August 1, 1968 from four locations to celebrate the BCC's 40th anniversary. Output included an educational channel and another on FM in Mandarin and Amoy that in due course was aired throughout the island from nine stations.

The Voice of Asia was added in 1979 for listeners in Southeast Asia and the Chinese mainland. It offered a lighter format, with

On August 15, 1945, Generalissimo Chiang Kai-shek broadcast news of the Japanese surrender over BCC Nanking (Nanjing). Four years later he was forced to flee to Taiwan. RTI

STATION INCLUDES RADIO MUSEUM

Located in Jiayi County, the Minxiong transmitting station has been converted into a broadcasting museum with an extensive collection of transmitter and broadcasting paraphernalia. Constructed during the Japanese era, much of its original studios and behemoth transmitter remain intact, curated by dedicated RTI employees. Its Japanese-style building has been officially designated as a historic site.

RTI's elder Minxiong site has become a must-see museum. Artifacts include a legendary bullet-ridden transmitter.   M. Guha

Station construction began in 1937, with broadcasts commencing three years later. These were beamed to China using 100 kW on 750 kHz mediumwave AM, and were an important part of the Japanese war propaganda machine. Programs were aired from 6 PM to 10 PM local time, which at those hours often generated a beefy skywave signal to China's mainland.

The transmitter, an engineering marvel, was one of three custom built by the Nippon Electric Company (NEC)—the other two went to Manchuria and Keijo (Gyeongseong), as Seoul was known then. The transmitter itself is so large that it almost fills the main hall located on the first level of the two-story building. The transmitter is cooled through a maze of ceramic tubes, drawing water from a swimming-pool-size open reservoir outside. Although the transmitter and building survived American bombing, the antenna bit the dust.

In 1952, when the CBS took over the station, the United States helped increase the power to 150 kW. The resulting massive signal became well-heard even in central China, and the transmitter remained a workhorse for more than half a century. This veteran from the Japanese occupation is still fired up regularly, making a mockery of some modern transmitters that are considered "worn out" before they've seen much more than a couple of decades of use.

Minxiong's Bulletproof Transmitter

Bullet holes left by the War can still be seen on the walls and the transmitter itself. This is a prime draw for visitors, who become transported to a different world even though peace and quiet permeates the station instead of

Minxiong engineer Chi-Ming Wang shows a 50 kW Harris transmitter.   M. Guha

bombs, sirens and gunfire. A Japanese anti-aircraft position in front of the station adds to the eerie sense that "you are there."

Yung-szu Chang was a strapping 16 year old engineering assistant at the Minxiong transmitting station 65 years ago. Despite his advanced age, he recalls the mighty transmitter as if it were yesterday.

"Looking after the transmitter tube was big job. Distilled water was passed through ceramic tubes during transmission and also during breaks. It was quite safe, as the electricity was shut off when the door to the transmitter cabinet was open."

He remembers an accident that happened under his watch. "One Japanese engineer was injured when he accidentally tripped the step-up transformer, which converts very high voltage from 3300 kW to 16000 kW. He touched the coil with his finger. There was a big spark burning half his body. He was rushed to the hospital. It was lucky that his right side was burnt; otherwise, his heart would have stopped."

In those days, programs were fed by wire to the transmitter site from NHK studios in the Shinjong Yuan area of Taipei. The Japanese administration had started construction of a major broadcasting complex there, but Japan's defeat put an end to that.

"Everybody wore uniforms. As I am of Japanese stock, I had no problems working for the Japanese government," exclaims Chang excitably though a translator, lapsing between Mandarin and his native Amoy. Chang recalls the day of Japan's surrender, August 15, 1945. "Like others we first heard it on the radio. The Japanese manager, who was also a soldier, left that day. Other staff held a brief ceremony, and they too departed leaving everything behind, taking just their personal belongings. We were sad because the Japanese were like our brothers."

It was business as usual after the Japanese handover. "The only change was that the new managers who came were not so professional as the Japanese," reminisces Chang.

Japanese-era technician Yung-szu Chang displays staff photo. M. Guha

The Minxiong National Radio Museum is now the final resting place for many old transmitters that pioneered Taiwanese broadcasting. The first to catch the eye is a Gates SHF0-5/10B; according to its plaque, its power is 10 kW and it was constructed in 1953 for the U.S. Navy. Another bears the type number FT & RCAN/FRT-6B; it is a 35 kW marine communications transmitter used by American warships on 30 crystal-controlled frequencies. Both transmitters came with 360-degree rotatable antennas, probably for ships' masts. All this was part of a larger U.S. aid package for the Kuomintang government, which in 1961 gave the transmitters to the CBS after modification for broadcast use. They were decommissioned in 1995.

Station Airs World Band

Since then Minxiong has morphed into a world band facility. The first shortwave transmitter to be added was a Gates 10 kW marine unit modified for broadcast use. This was replaced in 1991 by a 50kW Harris SW-50A feeding an 80-foot (24 meter) rhombic antenna hoisted over four towers. Operating on 7130 kHz, this configuration beams RTI programs to Japan in Japanese, as well as to Southeast Asia in Indonesian, Thai and Vietnamese.

There are two other world band sites nearby. Closest is Kuohu, with both mediumwave AM and shortwave transmitters, five manufactured by Continental Electronics. Of these, two are 250 kW for mediumwave AM, while three are 100 kW shortwave which carry news in Cantonese and Mandarin on world band.

"The transmitters are likely to be replaced by Harris transmitters soon," hopes Chi-Ming Wang who shares joint charge between the Minxiong and Kuohu stations. "These shortwave transmitter sites were established when the Japanese-era site in Panchiao, in Taipei county, was closed down due to congestion and local opposition from housing."

Another shortwave site is nearby Baozhong. Established in 1971, the station saw a major upgrade in 1991 when four 100 kW Harris SW-100B transmitters were installed, feeding curtain antennas aimed at Korea and Southeast Asia, as well as to China's mainland in Mandarin, Cantonese, Taiwanese and Amoy.

Plain and fancy: The Grand Hotel's majestic pagoda dwarfs RTI's unadorned headquarters in downtown Taipei.

M. Guha

more music and entertainment to attract a broader listenership.

More restructuring took place in 1996, when Taiwan's highest lawmaking body, the Legislative Yuan, passed a statute to merge the BCC's Overseas Department and the CBS into a single national radio station. The merged station, using the established CBS name, became a nonprofit organization supervised by the Government Information Office and with an annual budget scrutinized by the Legislative Yuan.

There was yet more restructuring in 1998, with international broadcasts split between the new Radio Taipei International and the long-running Voice of Asia. The latter was eventually terminated on December 31, 2001, although its Thai broadcast remained as a separate "Voice of Asia" program within Radio Taipei International's regular Thai service. Yet another name change occurred on July 1, 2003, when Radio Taipei International was dropped in favor of today's Radio Taiwan International.

The BCC's domestic service now consists of five networks on FM and mediumwave AM: Pop, Formosa, Music, News and Country. These transmit from multiple locations throughout the island, plus there's a separate AM747 Hakka station for Taipei. Island-wide networks are in Mandarin, Hakka and Amoy, and include music and popular phone-in shows. Interestingly, there is also the Public Radio System (PRS) that is

actually run by the national police. It offers catchy traffic reports, weather and other information.

Radio Taiwan International

Taiwan's global voice, Radio Taiwan International (RTI), is headquartered in the shadow of Taipei's imposing Grand Hotel. It beams to the island and the rest of the world in 13 languages. Most shows are produced at headquarters in 29 well-equipped studios.

Like some other government-funded radio stations around the world, RTI is not immune to shrinking budgets and staff dismissals. Each year, the RTI budget has to be passed by Taiwan's parliament, and many MPs are not supportive of international broadcasting. The annual budget is supplemented by services for outside organizations provided by RTI's staff, including program production and technical assistance.

The main ingredients on RTI's programming menu are news and music in Mandarin (Standard Chinese), various Chinese dialects and a potpourri of foreign languages. Mandarin is by far the mainstay, while the Chinese-dialect service is in Hokkien (Amoy), Hakka and Cantonese. These two streams are aimed at China's mainland, Taiwan and the worldwide Chinese diaspora.

RTI's foreign-language stream is in English, French, German, Indonesian, Japanese, Russian, Spanish, Thai and Vietnamese. Pro-

HISTORIC CITY HOUSES WORLD BAND CENTER

Tainan ranks first among historic cities in Taiwan. Located towards the island's south, it was the colonial capital of the Dutch, who constructed a fort and many other historic buildings. The Netherlanders were finally driven out by Koxinga, a warlord from the Ming court in China. Since then Tainan has always stood as one of Taiwan's foremost cities.

Tainan's shortwave center is also RTI's most important transmission facility. It was established in 1976 with two 250 kW BBC SK-53F3 transmitters, with a pair of identical transmitters added the following year. More transmitters were not scheduled to be added for another five years, but the upgrade was accelerated by one year in response to developments in Indonesia.

"Dynasty" Transmitters

The engineers have lovingly named the transmitters Tang, Ming, Han and Ching, after four main Chinese dynasties. Optimod amplitude-modulation processing is used to conserve energy.

Tainan's contemporary transmitter hall is rigorously automated, with few engineers.
M. Guha

The four transmitters feed a large antenna farm whose impressive towers and curtain arrays can be seen from miles away. The 20 antennas, standard issue, are held in place by 46 towers arranged in a 270-degree arc.

Tainan station chief Tseng Win-Sun keys in an RTI channel on his trusty Sangean portable. M. Guha

"With our eight beams, we can cover almost the whole world," beams Tseng Win-Sun, station chief, pointing to the large azimuthal map on his office wall. He is a big fan of Sangean receivers and whips one out to tune to a station from China. "Chinese programming is not good, and I don't listen to them," he says, shaking his head to underscore his disapproval.

Much transmission time not taken up by RTI's programs is devoted to rebroadcasting material supplied by foreign clients. Many are brokered by England's VT Communications, which feeds programs by satellite to Taipei. There, RTI microwave makes the final hop to the transmitter site—this is facilitated by a microwave repeater in the Yangmin mountains with a direct line-of-sight link from the capital.

Tainan's station console monitors operations.
M. Guha

E100
AM/FM/Shortwave Portable Radio

The E100 fits full-sized features into your palm or pocket. This little marvel is packed with all the latest radio features you want: digital tuning, 200 programmable memories, digital clock and alarm, plus AM/FM and Shortwave reception. And, it is small enough to fit in your coat pocket.

- Full featured Digital Tuner in extremely small size
- Shortwave – 1711-29.995 KHz
- FM 87.0 – 108.0MHz; MW 520 - 1710
- Manual and Auto-Scan Tuning
- Direct Keypad Frequency Entry
- Manual/Auto Scan to scan the preset stations
- Fine-tuning control knob
- 200 Random Programmable Memories
- Memory Page Customizing
- 9/10KHz step size selector for correct worldwide

- medium wave (AM) reception
- FM-Stereo/Signal Strength/Power Level Indicators
- Selectable 12/24 hour clock display format
- Simultaneous display of frequency and clock
- Programmable alarm
- Programmable sleep timer (10 – 90min.) functions
- LCD display light
- Built in antennas for AM, FM and SW reception
- Power Source: 2 AA Batteries or AC Adapter (not included)
- Dimensions: 5"W x 3"H x 1-1/4"D (125 x 76 x 31 mm)
- Weight: 7 oz. (201 g)

Etón E1100
AM/FM/Shortwave Radio

Small enough to fit into your pocket, yet strong enough to receive 10 Shortwave bands, the E1100 makes the perfect travel companion. Providing AM/FM and Shortwave reception, this little marvel is sure to keep you connected to both local and international news and music wherever you are.

- AM, FM-stereo and 10 Shortwave bands
- Analog tuning with digital frequency and clock
- Alarm
- Light and Snooze
- Headphone-Stereo
- AC Adapter - 3VDC, neg. polarity (not included)
- Accessories: Owner's Manual, Pouch
- Dimensions: 5.12"Wx3.15"Hx1.14"D (126mm Wx 80mm Hx 29mm D)
- Weight: 7 oz. (0.2 kg)

Etón Mini300
AM/FM/Shortwave Radio

Weighing less than 5 ounces the Mini 300PE world-band radio makes a perfect travel companion. Its oversized telescopic antenna provides great AM/FM reception for when camping, hiking, listening to sports, or just relaxing in the backyard. Also pulling in 7 shortwave bands, you'll have access to both local and international news and music wherever you go.

- AM, FM-stereo and 7 shortwave bands

- (49, 41, 31, 25, 22, 19 and 16 meters)
- Analog tuning with digital frequency readout
- Clock, alarm and sleep timer
- Digital display shows frequency, time, sleep time and symbols for sleep timer and alarm activation
- Telescopic antenna for FM and SW reception
- Internal ferrite bar antenna for AM (MW) reception
- Dimensions: 2-1/2"W x 4-1/2"H (not incl. 2-1/4" stub ant.) x 3/4"D (70 x 102 x 19 mm)
- Weight: 4.5 oz. (128 g)

etón®
RE-INVENTING RADIO
www.etoncorp.com

GS350DL
AM/FM/Shortwave Field Radio

G1100
AM/FM/Shortwave Radio

The Grundig S350DL blends the best of yesterday and today. With the look of a retro field radio sporting a rugged body and military-style controls—the Grundig S350DL also features today's innovation for excellent AM, FM, and Shortwave reception and a large, full-range speaker for clear sound.

- AM 530-1710 KHz, FM 88-108 MHz
- Shortwave – continuous Coverage from 3 to 28 MHz. This includes 13 international broadcast bands. 11, 13, 15, 16, 19, 22, 25, 31, 41, 49, 60, 75 and 90 meters
- AM/FM Frequency lock feature
- Highly sensitive and selective analog tuner circuitry
- Liquid Crystal Display, LCD, for frequency and clock
- Digital clock with selectable 12/24 hour format
- Wake-up timer (use as radio-play alarm clock)
- Power failure backup feature
- Sleep timer
- Variable RF Gain Control
- Variable, independent bass and treble control
- Left/Right line level outputs (stereo in FM)
- Stereo/mono switch
- Earphone socket
- Strap type carrying handle
- Built in telescopic antenna for FM and shortwave
- Built in ferrite bar antenna for AM
- Jacks for supplementary AM, FM and shortwave antennas
- Power Source: 4 D or AA batteries (not included) or AC Adapter (included)
- Dimensions: 12-1/2"W x 7"H x 3-1/2"D (315 x 175 x 89 mm)
- Weight: 3 lb. 4 oz. (1.48 Kg)

This little marvel receives 10 Shortwave bands. The G1100 makes the perfect travel companion. Providing AM/FM and Shortwave reception, it is bound to keep you connected to both local and international news and music wherever you are.

- AM, FM-stereo and 10 Shortwave bands
- Analog tuning with digital frequency and clock
- Alarm
- Light and Snooze
- Headphone-Stereo
- AC Adapter - 3VDC, neg. polarity (not included)
- Accessories: Owner's Manual, Pouch
- Dimensions: 5.12"Wx3.15"Hx1.14"D (126mm Wx 80mm Hx 29mm D)
- Weight: 7 oz. (0.2 kg)

grams include news, politics, economic issues, culture, education and entertainment.

Between 1998 and the first half of 2006, RTI had received 1.3 million letters—and nearly 500 thousand emails, faxes and phone calls—from listeners all over the world. These are processed by computer to help the news, programming and engineering departments in their planning.

RTI runs nine world band and mediumwave AM transmitting sites with a total output of over 15 Megawatts—a belly bustin' bowlful for such a small country. This makes Taiwan one of the largest international broadcasters in Asia and a major global influence.

Transmitting facilities are mostly along the center and south of the island on the western seaboard, thanks to China-centric beams. Locations are Baozhong (Paochung), Changchi (Changzhi), Danshui (Tanshui), Fangliao, Huwei, Kouhu, Lukang, Minxiong (Minhsiung) and Tainan. Of these, Baozhong, Huwei, Minxiong, Tainan and Danshui are only world band, while Kouhu also includes mediumwave AM. Changchi, Fangliao and Lukang are only mediumwave AM.

DEVELOPMENT LIMITS STATION EXPANSION

The shortwave transmission facility closest to Taipei is at Danshui, established in 1981 and now with 25 staffers and three 300 kW Marconi senders. Yet, it is also the smallest, as development has engulfed the once-remote site, leaving it astride a popular beach and small harbor.

"Most of our transmitters do not have spare parts. We either find compatible matches or we build it ourselves," explains deputy chief Brian Cheng, explaining the challenges of maintaining aging transmitters.

The extensive antenna farm—guarded by a high wall, watchtower and thicket of trees—is home to four Marconi curtain arrays using 50-meter masts, with back radiation limited to only 1 kW. Two antennas have fixed beams to southern China and India, while the others are trained northwards towards China's mainland. The first set relays Family Radio in English and Hindi to India some four hours a day; otherwise, the

Danshui station chief Brian Cheng explains a monitoring rack's functions.   M. Guha

station carries 17.5 hours a day of RTI programs in Mandarin, which of course are intensely jammed.

"In the beginning we used to change frequencies quite often to avoid jamming. But we realized that the Chinese jammers can find us in 15 minutes. So now we stick to the same frequency," explains Cheng. "We try to make better programs by giving the Chinese people more information on China itself," explains Wayne Wang, RTI's Chief of International Affairs.

The Family Radio feed is sent by satellite from Okeechobee, Florida, then downlinked at Oakland, California and fed to RTI by undersea cable.

Japanese-era watchtower overlooks Danshui.   M. Guha

RTI's "Gang of Four": Chairman Feng-jeng Lin (book) with International Affairs Director Wayne Wang. They are flanked by deputies Angela Huang and Lingyi Hsu.   M. Guha

As the digital era has ramped up, RTI has enhanced its online broadcasts and web design. RTI's site, www.rti.org.tw, is a portal for ten languages and e-newsletters in Chinese, English and Thai, as well as live and archived audio. RTI's website also welcomes emailed listeners' letters and world band reception reports. The station and Taiwan's Sangean Electronics (see sidebar) are also experimenting with Digital Radio Mondiale (DRM) and other over-the-air digital transmission modes.

Wayne Wang is RTI's Chief of International Affairs. He has done extensive research about Taiwanese radio broadcasting since the Japanese occupation of the island, and is a human encyclopedia of Chinese broadcasting.

He tells PASSPORT about China's broadcasts to Taiwan, "Chinese broadcasters have also become smart; they don't do direct propaganda anymore. They now generate interest among listeners in Taiwan by providing something of cultural and entertainment value, which the people can directly identify with."

Interestingly, RTI occasionally cooperates with China National Radio/CPBS in Beijing. "Our Mandarin service does actually have a program exchange during festival time with CPBS. But they always try to get their point across that Taiwan is a breakaway province

of China, making it political. At other times during breaking news and low level visits, journalists from both sides are allowed to visit, but are restricted to just the event that is being covered."

This uneasy cooperation is exemplified by a large photo at CRI's Beijing museum of a CRI reporter covering the earthquake in Taiwan.

Springboard for Free Expression

Given its strategic location and relatively modern and powerful transmitters, Taiwan has morphed into a springboard for a different kind of ideological combatant: religious broadcasters and dissident expatriate voices. These typically sow the seeds of democracy and evangelize to listeners in China and Vietnam, where religion and democracy are sharply circumscribed. Reception is limited within China's urban areas, thanks to groundwave jamming. But as skywave jamming is much less effective, particularly when there is twilight immunity, Taiwan's radio broadcasts are known to penetrate outside urban centers.

Meanwhile, RTI is profiting from these arrangements while the Chinese government is being forced to spend astronomical sums for jamming that is only partially effective. Sometimes dozens of powerful jamming

Family Radio's Terry Elders adjusts a Gates HF100 transmitter for the next operating frequency. Family Radio relays Radio Taiwan International from its mighty WYFR facility at Okeechobee, Florida.   Curtis Jarvis, WYFR

transmitters, countless staffers and a visible chunk of the nation's electrical generating capacity have to be used for each Taiwanese or Western transmitter that's being jammed.

RTI also has swap agreements with various stations to relay its service to North America and Europe. For over a decade RTI has been relayed by evangelical WYFR-Family Radio in Okeechobee, Florida. Using its 100 kW transmitters, WYFR relays RTI broadcasts to North, Central and South America, as well as to Europe.

In Europe, similar swaps have resulted in RTI's using what traditionally has been a BBC site (now operated by VT Communications) at Skelton, England, as well as Radio France International's Issoudun location. These facilities relay RTI transmissions in Chinese, English, French, German and Russian to Europe, and in English and French to Africa. RTI's Spanish programs also use a European relay: Nauen, in the eastern part of Germany.

Family Radio is overwhelmingly the largest user of RTI relay facilities, using both world band and mediumwave AM transmitters to broadcast to India, China, Russia and Southeast Asia, as well as to listeners in Taiwan. Radio France International uses RTI shortwave transmitters to broadcast in Chinese to the Chinese mainland and French to Southeast Asia.

RTI's relationship with London-based VT Communications allows a number of stations to be placed on Taiwanese transmitters, and the mix keeps changing. Besides relaying the BBC World Service on mediumwave AM, RTI also relays a host of American religious broadcasters and dissident voices on both world band and mediumwave AM: Family Radio, of course, plus Adventist World Radio, Truth for the World, Shiokaze (Sea Breeze), "Hmong Lao Radio," "Moj Them Radio," "Minghui Radio," "Voice of China," Sound of Hope, "Voice of China Reborn," "Chan Troi Moi" (New Horizon Radio) and Little Saigon Radio. Additionally, Radio Australia and Radio Free Asia are heard via Taiwanese transmitters, implying sales of airtime.

Besides having international clients, RTI provides relay facilities to domestic organizations. For example, Trans World Broadcasting Ministry is a religious broadcaster based in the southern port city of Kaohsiung. It maintains an office in the San Francisco Bay area, while it is aired in Chinese via RTI.

Yet, not all Taiwanese organizations broadcast via Taiwan. Taipei's China Radio, another religious broadcaster, is sometimes referred to as the True Light Station. It transmits to China's mainland not via RTI, but rather from leased facilities in Petropavlovsk-Kamchatskiy, Russia.

Army Counters Voice of the Strait

The Nationalists have always had a broadcasting service for the army. When the Nationalist government relocated to Taiwan, the station came under the Ministry of Defense and was re-christened Voice of Han ("Hansheng")—Han being the majority ethnic group in China that most people worldwide think of as "Chinese."

The station beams to China's mainland on 9745 kHz using a Ministry of Defense transmitter facility at Pali, near Taipei. According to the Transmitter Documentation Project, it has five 100 kW SW-100 and SW-100A Harris transmitters which were installed in 1981 and 1986, respectively.

Additionally, Voice of Han uses 15 other AM-FM transmission sites around Taiwan. Even though it is a defense broadcasting station, much content is non-military and entertaining, focusing on social issues and popular trends. It is ostensibly to counter propaganda from the PLA-controlled Voice of the Strait in Fuzhou in Fujian province, just across the narrow Taiwan Strait. Voice of Han's website www.voh.com.tw offers a host of information in English and Mandarin, along with streaming audio.

Another government agency on world band is the Fu Hsing Broadcasting Station, run by the Ministry of the Interior from Taipei. The station operates on 5995 and 9410 kHz at 0400–0600, 0800–1000, 1100–1500 and 2300–0100 World Time. Current transmitter power is unknown, although the station previously used a single transmitter of 10 kW on 15250 kHz. It offers streaming audio at www.fhbs.com.tw/broadcast.php.

Radio Helps Integrate Newcomers

Finally, at the beginning of 2006, Taiwan's government set up an island-wide radio network for certain foreign groups in Taiwan. Its purpose is to help new immigrants blend into and become an active part of Taiwanese society.

The network combines the resources of RTI and the Voice of Han. Transmissions are on FM and mediumwave AM in Vietnamese, Thai and Indonesian.

_____

Prepared in cooperation with Tony Jones.

SANGEAN PIONEERS DIGITAL RADIOS

Sangean Electronics is one of the world's leading manufacturers of affordable radio receivers, and now also manufactures leading-edge DAB and DRM digital receivers. Established in 1974, Sangean was for many years a major force in the manufacture of world band portables.

Sangean's sales of world band radios have steadily declined as competition has intensified; in 2004 it had fallen to just 20% of total turnover. "As you know after our flagship ATS-909 we did not actually develop a new advanced world receiver model," says Albert Cheng of Sangean.

In order to gain market share without costly marketing activity, Sangean has primarily manufactured for other firms: Radio Shack, Siemens, Panasonic, Braun, JVC, Grundig, Philips, Roberts and a host of others. Additionally, Sangean-branded products are offered by such electronic retailers, distributors and catalog suppliers as C. Crane, Universal Radio, Sharper Image, Hammacher Schlemmer, Haverhills, Fry's Electronics, J&R Music and the Discovery Channel.

Most Sangean production is in China, but some remains in Taiwan. Sangean

The American Red Cross
FR300 by Etón
AM/FM Radio with NOAA, TV VHF, Flashlight, and Cell Phone Charger

The American Red Cros
FR250 by Etó
AM/FM/Shortwave Radio with Flash light and Cell Phone Charger

Built-in cell phone charger

This all-in-one unit offers functionality and versatility that makes it ideal for emergencies. The ARC FR300 provides you with radio, light, and cell phone battery life when you need it most. The Hand-Crank Power Generator charges the internal rechargeable Ni-MH battery pack. With the NOAA weather channels and TV VHF channels, you can find weather forecasts or listen to TV shows when you're away from the set.

• AM and FM
• TV1 and TV2 - VHF channels 2-13
• NOAA weather – all 7 channels plus "Alert"
• 3 LED light system with emergency flash
• Emergency siren
• Cellphone charger
• Crank-charge system charges built-in rechargeable battery
• Charges rechargeable battery via AC adapter/charger (not included)
• Can be powered by 3 AA batteries
• Can be powered with all batteries removed, by continuous cranking
• Power Source: Built-In Rechargeable Ni-MH Battery Pack; 3 AA Batteries (not included); Crank power alone; AC Adapter (not included); AC Adapter recharges built-in Ni-MH battery pack
• Dimensions: 6-1/2"W x 6"H x 2-1/2"D (168 x 155 x 64 mm)
• Weight: 1 lb. 4 oz. (568 g)

Stay informed and prepared for emergencies with this s ered 3-in-1 radio, flashlight and cell-phone charger — no required. The Hand-Crank Power Generator gives you u power for AM/FM Radio, 7 International Shortwave Bands Flashlight, and cell phone battery life when you need it mos ARC FR250 is not only perfect for emergencies, but also for o hiking, or anywhere you need to stay in touch.

• Nine Band Tuning – receives AM, FM and 7 shortwave ban
• Built-in power generator recharges the internal rechargeal MH battery and cell phone batteries
• Can be powered from four different sources:
  1) From the built-in rechargeable Ni-MH battery that takes charge from the dynamo crank and from an AC adapter (AC adapter not included)
  2) From 3 AA batteries
  3) From the AC adapter alone (AC adapter not included)
  4) From the dynamo crank alone, even with no battery pack installed
• Earphone jack – 3.5mm earphone socket
• Cell-phone charger output jack 3.5mm (various cell phone plug tip
• Emergency Siren
• Can be operated on three AA size batteries
• Incorporates a fine-tuning control knob super-imposed on main tuning control knob
• Power Source: Built-In Rechargeable Ni-MH Battery Pack; 3 Batteries (not included); Crank power alone; AC Adapter (not i AC Adapter recharges built-in Ni-MH battery pack
• Dimensions: 6-1/2"W x 6"H x 2-1/2"D (168 x 155 x 64 mm)
• Weight: 1 lb. 3 oz. (539 g)

The American Red Cross Rac

American
Red Cross

etó
RE_INVENTING
www.etoncorp

The American Red Cross
FR350 by Etón
AM/FM/Shortwave Radio with Flashlight and Cell Phone Charger

The American Red Cross
FR400 by Etón
AM/FM Radio with NOAA, TV VHF, Flashlight, and Cell Phone Charger

Built-in cell phone charger

Improved technology, functionality and versatility, the ARC FR350 is ideal for emergencies. The ARC FR350 provides you with a water resistant radio, LED lights, and cell phone charger when you need it most. Using the Hand-Crank Power Generator, charge the internal rechargeable Ni-MH battery pack in times of need.

- AM/FM/Shortwave
- Water resistant body
- Hand Crank Power Generator
- 3 LED light system with emergency flash
- Emergency siren
- Built-in cell phone charger
- Power Source: Hand-Crank Power Generator with rechargeable battery pack, 3 AA batteries (not included) or AC adaptor (included)
- Dimensions: 4.5"H x 8.6"W x 2"D (114 x 220 x 50mm)
- Weight: 1.5lb (680 g)

Improved technology, functionality and versatility, the ARC FR400 is ideal for emergencies. The ARC FR400 provides you with a water resistant radio, LED lights, and cell phone charger when you need it most. Using the Hand-Crank Power Generator, charge the internal rechargeable Ni-MH battery pack in times of need. With NOAA weather channels and TV-VHF channels, you have easy access to weather forecasts and can listen to TV shows while away from the set.

- AM/FM/NOAA/TV1/TV2 - VHF channels 2-13
- Water resistant body
- NOAA weather – all 7 channels plus "Alert" function
- Hand Crank Power Generator
- 3 LED light system with emergency flash
- Can be powered from four different sources:
  1) From the built-in rechargeable Ni-MH battery that takes charge from the dynamo crank and from an AC adapter (AC adapter included)
  2) From 3 AA batteries
  3) From the AC adapter alone (AC adapter included)
  4) From the dynamo crank alone, even with no battery pack installed
- Emergency siren
- Built-in cell-phone charger
- Crank-charge system charges built-in rechargeable battery
- Charges rechargeable battery via AC adapter (included)
- Can be powered with all batteries removed, by continuous cranking
- Power Source: Built-In Rechargeable Ni-MH Battery Pack; 3 AA Batteries (not included); Crank power alone; AC Adapter (included); AC Adapter recharges built-in Ni-MH battery pack
- Dimensions: 4.5"H x 8.6"W x 2"D (114 x 220 x 50 mm)
- Weight: 1.5 lb (680 g)

The American Red Cross Radio Line By:

etón®
RE:INVENTING RADIO
www.etoncorp.com

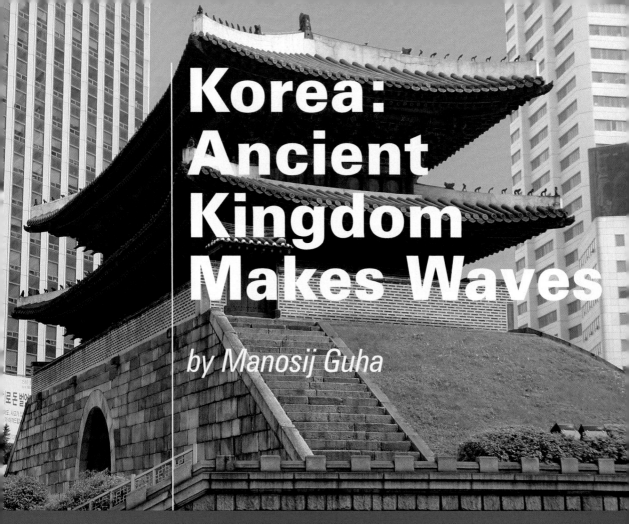

Korea: Ancient Kingdom Makes Waves

by Manosij Guha

The Korean peninsula extends from East Asia like a crooked finger, with a history dating back to the first kingdom, Gogoseon or Ko-Choson, in 2333 B.C. From then on, successive kingdoms ruled the peninsula and beyond, creating a cultural identity different from that of its overpowering neighbor, China.

The Japanese invasion of 1910 interrupted this identity, and for the next 36 years Koreans were under occupation. This finally ended when the Japanese laid down their arms at the end of World War II.

A People Torn Apart

Korea was then divided, slightly north of the 38th parallel, into the democratic South—the Republic of Korea, or ROK—and communist North Korea, officially the Democratic People's Republic of Korea (DPRK). After North Korea failed to conquer the South in the 1950–1953 Korean War, it began practicing exceptional self-reliance as set forth in the late leader Kim Il Sung's "Juche" philosophy. The results have been catastrophic, with widespread famine and disruption.

Since the mid-1990s, after decades of economic mismanagement and resource misallocation, the North has relied heavily on international aid to feed its population. At the same time it continues to lavish scarce resources on costly advanced weapons systems and an army of about one million soldiers.

More recently, North Korea's long-range missile development and nuclear research, along with its massive conventional armed forces, have caused grave concern within the international community. Despite multiparty talks with China, Japan, Russia, South Korea and the United States, resolving key issues has proved to be elusive.

Seoul Tower's antennas and restaurant have a bird's eye view.   M. Guha

I. Radio's Beginnings

Radio broadcasting began in Korea during the Japanese occupation. As early as July 1924 a flea-powered 50 watt transmitter and a special studio were installed in the Governor General's office in Keijo (Gyeongseong), as Seoul was known during the Japanese occupation. On November 29 of that year the station came on the air using the callsign J8AA.

A receiver and a speaker were in a dining room just 200 meters away from the transmitter to allow newspaper reporters to witness this technological marvel. On December 10 a "mass reception" receiver was placed on permanent public display at the Keijo (Gyeongseong) branch of Mitsukoshi, a famous Japanese department store then in the city's Honmachi neighborhood. Starting June 21, 1925, broadcasts lasting

Broadcasting sprang from nothing during Japanese occupation.

Reenactment of the changing of royal guards is a must-see during palace tours.   M. Guha

KBS distinctive complex is capped by exposed latticework and a crown of antennas. It dwarfs all other buildings in Seoul's government district.   M. Guha

several hours became a regular fixture: Tuesday and Friday in Japanese, Thursday in Korean, and Sunday in Japanese and Korean.

Cultural Station Launched

To further its cultural policies the colonial authorities decided to launch the Gyeong-seong Broadcasting Station on medium-wave AM at 1 kW with the callsign JODK. It officially commenced on February 16, 1927 using 820 kHz, following tests from December 9, 1926 onward on approximately 817 kHz. On February 1, 1930, the frequency was changed to 690 kHz, then on April 26, 1933 two program streams were created: First in Japanese on 900 kHz and Second in

Korean on 610 kHz, each using new 10 kW transmitters.

On September 17, 1935, the station's name was altered to Gyeongseong Central Broadcasting Station. On January 10, 1937 its frequencies were changed to 710 kHz for the First Program and 970 kHz for the Second, which on April 17 was boosted to 50 kW. Although some sources cite 870 kHz, this frequency was never actually used by Gyeongseong.

Two Languages, Two Audiences

There was a license fee of two yen, later cut in half, but even this was beyond most people's reach. Thus, it was mostly the more prosperous Japanese occupiers who could afford a radio, even though both Korean and Japanese alternated as official broadcast languages until 1934.

Although there was official surveillance and censorship, JODK's broadcasts did much to promote local culture. For example, the station often aired live broadcasts of popular Korean operas, theatrical events and concerts—it even had exclusive contracts with a number of Keijo (Gyeongseong) bands to provide music for the station.

Nonetheless, Japanese norms were widely disseminated. For example, on June 25, 1927 the station relayed a Japanese Imperial Theater stage play live from Tokyo. And from September 1929 onward, the Broadcasting Corporation of Japan authorized relays of major programs originating at domestic radio stations in Japan.

1930s Spurt

Ten stations were opened before the start of Japan's Pacific War: JBAK Fuzan (Pusan), JBBK Heijo (Pyongyang), JBCK Seishin (Cheongjin), JBDK Kanko (Hamheung), JBFK Riri (Iri), JBGK Taikyu (Daegu), JBHK Koshu (Kwangju), JBIK Taiden (Daejeon), JBJK Genzan (Wonsan) and JBKK Kaishu (Haeju). After the Pacific War started, four more stations were inaugurated: JBLK Shingishuu (Sinwiju), JBMK Shunsen (Chuncheon),

JBPK Joshin (Seongjin) and JBQK Seishu (Cheongju). Additionally, six auxiliary stations were set up at Koryo (Kangreung), Kaijo (Gaeseong), Moppo (Mokpo), Basan (Masan), Chozen (Jangjeon) and Zuisan (Seosan), while transmission facilities JBRK, JBNK and JBOK-3 were upgraded to broadcasting stations.

On January 10, 1937 Gyeongseong got a second channel and transmitter operating on 970 kHz with mostly Korean programs. This was boosted to 50 kW a few months later, allowing the whole country to listen even with simple receivers. Other stations getting a second transmitter and a dedicated Korean channel were, progressively, those in the cities of Heijo (Pyongyang), Kanko (Hamheung), Taiku (Daegu), Fuzan (Pusan), Seishin (Cheongjin), Koshu (Kwangju), Riri (Iri), Genzan (Wonsan), Kaishu (Haeju) and Taiden (Daejeon). In 1939 a mobile broadcast vehicle and a tape recorder—advanced technology for that period—were introduced for the first time.

Surrender Speech Aired Live

The Japanese emperor's historic August 15, 1945 acceptance of the Potsdam declaration was aired live on radio not only in Japan, but also in Korea. Thus ended World War II, but nine days later the feeder lines for live broadcasts were cut north of the

Elaborate face painting is part of an actor's makeup at the National Theater.   M. Guha

38th parallel—a harbinger of conflict that was to turn into war in 1950.

After World War II, Soviet and American forces divided the country at the 38th parallel, changing the nature of broadcasting within and to both halves. On September 9, 1945, American forces disarmed Japanese forces at the Gyeongseong Central Broadcasting Station and immediately shut down the Japanese channel of 710 kHz, leaving active only the Korean channel on 970 kHz. On October 1 that same year, all radio station call letters were changed from the Japanese-oriented JB to Korea's distinctive HL.

Many of the world's major cities include a prized historic section. This well-preserved ancient village lies in the heart of ultramodern Seoul.

M. Guha

II. Republic of Korea's Ascending Voice

Early in the Korean War, the Republic of Korea's radio broadcasting was minimal. In mid-1950, immediately following North Korea's invasion, one of the few stations known to be operating was Radio Seoul on 7933–7935 kHz with 5 kW. Later, however, radio broadcasting was expanded to ten other cities as part of the Korean Broadcasting System. Over time, KBS' domestic network extended to 25 broadcasting centers, including regional headquarters.

Use Once, Then Toss

> South Korean radio had all but vanished by 1950.

According to the Transmitter Documentation Project, a 10 kW shortwave transmitter of indeterminate make was installed at Yunhi in 1953. About the same time, a new world band transmission facility was set up at nearby Suwon, where two 50 kW shortwave units were added in 1957. As the radio wars intensified, in 1981 these were joined by another 50 kW sender from Continental Electronic Corporation of Dallas; this workhorse is still being used.

A Thomcast (now Thales) 100 kW HF transmitter was added in 1997. Remarkably, it was in operation for only one year, its duties having been taken over by newer stations at Kimjae and Hwasung.

Vigorous Postwar Growth

Commercial broadcasting has long been a major force in South Korean radio. The first private operation—Pusan Munhwa Broadcasting Station—was launched in 1959 from the southern city of Pusan. This was followed by Munhwa Broadcasting Corporation in Seoul, Dong-A

Women occupy responsible positions at Radio Korea International. The author and an RKI colleague pause with the English service's Hee Joo Han, Executive Director, and Seung Joo (Sophia) Hong, Producer.   M. Guha

 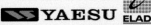

RKI's many language services feed off a central news pool. All language groups are situated next to each other in a tunnel-like production hall.

M. Guha

Broadcasting Station, Tongyang Broadcasting Company and, in 1966, the Seoul FM Station.

The next three decades were turbulent, with South Korea's nascent democracy being in and out of emergency rule. By 1973 the Korean Broadcasting System, now a publicly managed corporation, was by far the largest broadcaster. It boasted 51 stations throughout South Korea, with the key station in Seoul using high-powered 100 kW and 500 kW transmitters. The network operated two domestic services, along with an international service with three world band stations in Seoul, Suwon and Taegu.

Key players were the state-owned Korean Broadcasting System, the private Tong-Yang Broadcasting, the commercial Hankuk Munhwa Broadcasting Corporation, the omnipresent American Forces Korea Network (sidebar) and several Christian broadcasters such as the Far East Broadcasting Company. Each operated a network of low-power repeaters on mediumwave AM and FM, with some even venturing into world band.

Government Turns Nasty

Even though a legal framework was in place to keep broadcasting insulated from government meddling, in practice it was lightly enforced. As a result the state-operated networks were pretty much voices of bureaucratic officialdom. Even the private networks were not truly independent, as they were owned by vested-interest groups.

Such was the government's fear of truly independent radio that it repeatedly rejected the application for a radio network by Dong-A Ilbo—Korea's venerated independent newspaper co-published with the International Herald Tribune. In the mid-60s to the 70s, Dong-A Broadcasting finally fired up a single station in Seoul, but it suffered the displeasure of several governments, which charged its employees with seditious speech and threw them into jail. That didn't stop the station, so in 1975 its signal was jammed, then armed thugs aided by police broke in and abused workers. The station was finally forced to close.

Then in 1980 a military regime took power, after which KBS and local broadcasters faced severe government control. But by 1990 the licensing of SBS (Seoul Broadcasting System) revived diversity, allowing public and private broadcasters once again to prosper. In the provinces, privately owned broadcasting services debuted in Pusan, Daegu, Daejeon and Gwangju in 1995, and two years later in Incheon, Ulsan, Jeonju and Cheongju.

Korean public broadcasting was not intended to entertain. Instead, it served up weighty doses of news, punctuated by lighter cultural items, public service announcements, drama and music. Other, special, programs dealt with education, the armed forces and paeans to anti-communism. This stern menu was in marked contrast to popular fare being aired by private networks.

Three-Legged Network

The Broadcasting Act of December 1999 addressed issues of control and regulation—not only of radio, but also television and cable. This legislation required the Korean Broadcasting Commission to oversee program content, as well as broadcasting policies and administration that had been dispersed among various other ministries.

Radio Korea International announcer pores over her script in preparation for a newscast.   M. Guha

Today, the KBS has three national program streams relayed by scores of FM and mediumwave AM transmitters. Each is dedicated to news, commercial and non-commercial programming in a public service format.

Additionally, there are two program streams branded "Liberty," with sociocultural information for Koreans living abroad and, ostensibly, kinsmen north of the border. For better reach, KBS Radio 1 and both Liberty streams are relayed on world band by two 10 kW transmitters on 3930 kHz and one of

100 kW on 6135 kHz from the Hwasung site near Seoul.

There are also two dedicated music channels airing traditional Korean and popular music, along with Western music, nearly 24/7. These are relayed in FM stereo throughout the country.

Besides the government-controlled KBS, there are dozens of radio networks man-

Seoul is no Palo Alto. At RKI, even studio engineers at mixing consoles wear long-sleeved dress shirts and conservative ties.

M. Guha

UNCLE SAM: EARLY AIRWAVE GIANT

For 57 years the United States Army has been a major outside force in Korean broadcasting. With the onset of the Korean War in June of 1950, the American Forces Korea Network (AFKN) took the lead in broadcasting within the region.

Americans Broadcast from North Korea

Initially only an extension of the post-WW II Far East Network (FEN) in Japan, AFKN's Korean-based radio started at a U.S. Army base in Yongsan, near Seoul, in September 1950. Television was added in 1958.

John D. Harmer, today the transmitter engineer at WCOL in Columbus, Ohio, was AFKN's chief engineer. He writes in *Technician-Engineer*, " The headquarters of the then Far East Network in Korea was in Taegu, where EUSAK (Eighth Army Headquarters) was located, and consisted of five stations. Later, the network was renamed the American Forces Korea Network (AFKN) and was increased from five to nine stations. Of the original five, one was in Pusan, on the southernmost point of the peninsula, the headquarters station in Taegu, a station in Seoul, the country's capital, and two actually in North Korea at Kumwha and Inje." These last two were very close to the Demilitarized Zone (DMZ).

Stations were largely on mediumwave AM, with the majority simply operating out of trucks and shacks. Instead of call signs, stations were given colorful names such as Homesteader, Kilroy, Vagabond, Gypsy and Troubadour. Harmer explains, "The Far East Command (FEC), in addition to calls, also assigned the operating power and frequencies for the different stations in the standard broadcast band; however, all were above 1 megacycle per second [1 MHz]."

In most cases communications utility transmitters were put to use for broadcasting. The key station, Homesteader in Pusan, used a Gates BC-IF. At Taegu, Kilroy operated out of a van with two BC-610 onetime-communications transmitters. The van also held two shortwave receivers to pick up newscasts from FEN stations JKI and JKL on 19 and 25 meters out of Tokyo.

In mid-1952, with United Nations' forces advancing northwards, four more stations were established with 1 kW transmitters; the main facility was at Chunchon, South Korea, with a Gates BC-IF broadcast transmitter. In all, there were nine AFKN stations—six with Gates 1 kW broadcast transmitters and the rest with BC-610 senders.

Complementing AFKN's pattern of mediumwave AM operation, from around 1954 to early 1960 it was also heard on shortwave from Yongsan. Although its single faint world band transmitter was intended to reach audiences directly, it appears to have seconded as an affiliate feeder—much as do AFRTS' low-power shortwave transmitters today.

Currently, the American forces maintain one of the largest broadcasting infrastructures in South Korea. AFKN is also the largest United States armed forces network anywhere in the world, with 14 mediumwave AM outlets and a like number of FM repeaters.

PsyWar: Voice of the UN Command

U.S. Army PsyWar operations have played a significant role in Korea. The Army's Korean PsyWar broadcasting effort, Voice of the United Nations Command (VUNC), started with leased facilities in Japan. Eventually it was moved to Army turf in Okinawa and Seoul.

Following the North's attack the station quickly grew, adding broadcasts in Korean beamed to both Koreas. It was initially operated from August or so of 1951 to 1954 by the

U.S. Army 4th Mobile Radio Broadcasting Company of the 1st Radio Broadcasting and Leaflet Battalion. From 1954 to 1958 VUNC operations were conducted by the 14th Radio Broadcasting and Leaflet Battalion, and after that by the 14th Psychological Warfare Battalion until reorganization as the 7th PSYOP Group in 1965. Operations continued until 1975 when the 7th Group was assigned to the reserves.

The VUNC was ultimately headquartered in Machinato, Okinawa. Here, programs were written in English, then translated into Korean and tape recorded in a small studio. These were then fed to Korea by a GE 50 kW USB shortwave utility transmitter at Deragawa, Okinawa. This feed was retransmitted after having been picked up by receivers at the U.S. Army's Seoul office in the KBS building. Later, in order to overcome jamming of Okinawa's upper-sideband signal, shortwave was replaced for the feed.

The VUNC transmitted from Seoul for much of the day on 1100 kHz mediumwave AM with 5 kW. World band frequencies were 2635 and 3985 kHz, each with a DX-juicy 250 watts—thankfully, the station was an excellent verifier. By 1954 the VUNC was using a 2.5 kW transmitter in Pusan, South Korea on 4780 kHz, JBD 10 kW (later 20 kW) from Nakazi, Japan on 9505 kHz (later 6015 kHz) and JBD2 10 kW at Yamato, Japan on 9560 kHz.

After 1958 it was also on 1240 kHz with 5 kW from VUNC-B, which originally was smack on the DMZ in the Panmunjom area. After having been moved to Seoul for a brief period in the last half of 1961, VUNC-B ultimately wound up in the Chorwon Valley.

VUNC-A operated on 1270 kHz from Kangwha-do Island, also close to the DMZ, with 50 kW into a directional antenna. Also, the South Korean government's KBS eventually relayed the VUNC for 25 minutes daily on 600 kHz mediumwave AM with a thumping 500 kW.

Each day the VUNC aimed music, news, and features to upper-level political cadres, upper and middle government bureaucrats, and armed forces officers in North Korea. Programs included "Facts on Freedom" and "100,000 Questions," along with five-minute news capsules complemented each day by ten minutes of news analysis and two five-minute news commentaries.

The Voice of the United Nations Command broadcast from Seoul until 1971, when the U.S. Army's 24th PSYOP began operating it as the VOA. Tim Yoho

In 1967, according to the 7th PSYOP Group's official history, SP4 John Snell and SP5 Doug Stalker became overnight successes. The song "The Ballad of Kim," written and produced by Snell and Stalker, was aired over VUNC without any particular fanfare. Nevertheless, inquiries and requests for tapes and records of the song came flowing in from all over Korea. Copies of the tape were supplied to many local Korean stations, making it even more popular.

—Manosij Guha, Tim Yoho and Lawrence Magne.

Curtain antenna arrays beam the Republic of Korea's world band voice from a vast transmission facility at Kimjae.
M. Guha

aged by public corporations, private enterprises and religious broadcasters—Christian and Buddhist—all operating their own FM and mediumwave AM transmitters countrywide.

A new player is the government-funded Arirang Radio, which operates in English to provide tourists and expatriates with information about Korea. Originally aired only on Cheju Island, it became a national service on August 31, 2005 with the launching of digital satellite multimedia broadcasts.

Mighty Voice, Global Reach

South Korea has always given external broadcasting the highest priority. Objectives have included conveying the promise of a better Korea to the closed North, as well as cultivating a spirit of nationhood for a future reunification—the ultimate holy grail for most Koreans. So an external service, Voice of Free Korea, was established on August 15, 1953 as part of the Korean Broadcasting System. Its first foreign-language broadcast was in English for 15 minutes a day.

Since then, its role has been expanded to project an image of national development to the world. It was renamed Seoul International Broadcasting (HCLA) in July 1961,

Radio Korea in March 1973 and Radio Korea International (RKI) in August 1994; today it is known as KBS World Radio, bringing the total to five names over five decades. It provides a picture of, and news about, Korea's politics, society, culture, traditions and the economy—while also dishing up entertainment. It reaches an estimated 40 million listeners worldwide, and additionally targets the growing and influential community of Koreans living abroad.

More foreign languages were gradually added, in addition to Korean—Japanese, Russian, Chinese, Spanish, Indonesian, Arabic and German. However, Portuguese and Italian services established in the 1980s were closed down in 1994.

The present-day external service is located inside the KBS complex in the bustling Yeouido government precinct. Its swank tower, located near the Korean parliament building, is a landmark in downtown Seoul.

All language desks are located in a single large hall. They are staffed by a mix of Korean managers and native speakers, which gives the station an international feel. Almost all programs are prerecorded onto digital servers, while news and features are translated by foreign-language writers from a central Korean and English pool.

World band is the mainstay of KBS World Radio. It uses powerful transmitters not only on the peninsula, but also abroad thanks to exchange agreements. Too, much of the station's output can be downloaded from its multilingual website—early adopters, the then-RKI went on the web in November 1997.

Two Sites Cover Globe

Using 24 different frequencies—23 world band and one mediumwave AM—the station broadcasts 91 hours a day, including rebroadcasts. Asia and beyond are blanketed by high-powered mediumwave AM and shortwave transmitters at Kimjae and Hwasung.

The larger, Kimjae in North Cholla province, stands out for its size and modernity. Established in 1975, it is operated and maintained by experienced engineers drawn from the Korean Broadcasting System, KBS World Radio's parent organization. The site presently has seven shortwave transmitters—three of 250 kW and the rest 100 kW. These are mostly from the ABB Asea Brown Boveri consortium, but an original 250 kW transmitter, ca. 1975, is from Continental Electronics.

These feed a sprawling network of 17 dipole curtain array antennas switched by an elaborate transmission plan controlled entirely by computer. It's so versatile that a comprehensive switching matrix can quickly connect any transmitter to any antenna. This site also houses a 500 kW mediumwave AM transmitter aimed at neighboring counties on 1170 kHz.

In late August 2001, two older antennas were torn down to make room for replacements targeted at Indonesia, Southeast Asia and South China—new priority areas for what was then called RKI. This revised directionality is also attractive to potential clients considering exchange or leased-time arrangements.

The smaller transmitter facility is in Hwasung, a picturesque fortress town in Kyunggi province only 37 miles from Seoul. Operational since 1980, this was originally the site for Liberty broadcasts aimed at the North. With the closure of the Suwon shortwave transmitting station at the end of 1998, Hwasung became the secondary external-service transmission facility.

Its seven shortwave transmitters were installed during the late eighties and early nineties. Two are 100 kW Continentals, three are 100 kW from Brown-Boveri and the remainder are 10 kW from NEC. While the 100 kW units are predominantly for KBS World Radio broadcasts, the 10 kW senders carry a mix of KBS domestic programming, Liberty programs for the North and a few transmissions of KBS World Radio.

Relays Expand Voice

A relay exchange with Radio Canada International allows KBS World Radio to use RCI's transmitters at Sackville, New Brunswick to put a strong signal into the Americas. The April 1990 relay agreement has done wonders for reception of the station's Spanish, Korean and English broadcasts.

In May 1993 a similar agreement was reached with what is now VT Communications. This has given KBS World Radio a daily relay of five and a half hours in Korean, Russian, Arabic, German, French and English to Europe and North Africa from transmitters in Skelton and Rampisham in the United Kingdom. In return, Radio Canada International and the BBC World Service are relayed by 100 kW and 250 kW Korean shortwave transmitters at Kimjae.

New Technologies Broaden Coverage

Since August 15, 2003, KBS output in English, French, German and Russian has also been available on satellite via WRN. Formerly World Radio Network, WRN now targets audiences in Europe, Africa, North America, Asia and the Pacific.

Additionally, since September 3, 2003 a half-hour pilot DRM transmission has been aired to Europe every Friday. This puts KBS World Radio in a favorable position should a significant DRM audience materialize in due course.

AM/FM/Shortwave Radio, Flashlight, and Cell Phone Charger

AM/FM Radio with NOAA, TV VHF, Flashlight, and Cell Phone Charger

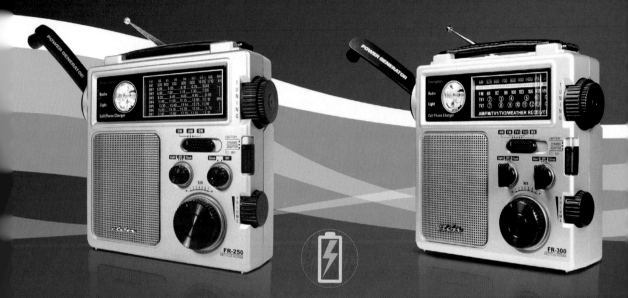

Built-in cell phone charger

Stay informed and prepared for emergencies with this self-powered 3-in-1 radio, flashlight and cell-phone charger — no batteries required. The Hand-Crank Power Generator gives you unlimited power for AM/FM Radio, 7 International Shortwave Bands, Built-in Flashlight, and cell phone battery life when you need it most. So the FR250 is not only perfect for emergencies, but also for camping, hiking, or anywhere you need to stay in touch.

- Nine Band Tuning – receives AM, FM and 7 shortwave bands
- Built-in power generator recharges the internal rechargeable Ni-MH battery and cell phone batteries
- Can be powered from four different sources:
  1) From the built-in rechargeable Ni-MH battery that takes charge from the dynamo crank and from an AC adapter (AC adapter not included)
  2) From 3 AA batteries
  3) From the AC adapter alone (AC adapter not included)
  4) From the dynamo crank alone, even with no battery pack installed
- Earphone jack – 3.5mm earphone socket
- Built-in cell-phone charger
- Can be operated on three AA size batteries
- Incorporates a fine-tuning control knob super-imposed on the main tuning control knob
- Built-in 2 white LED light source and one flashing red LED
- Emergency siren
- Pleasant audio from the 2 1/2 inch speaker
- All antennas built-in: telescopic antenna for FM and SW; internal ferrite bar antenna for AM
- Power Source: Built-In Rechargeable Ni-MH Battery Pack; 3 AA Batteries (not included); Crank power alone; AC Adapter (included); AC Adapter recharges built-in Ni-MH battery pack
- Dimensions: 6-1/2"W x 6"H x 2-1/2"D (168 x 155 x 64 mm)
- Weight: 1 lb. 3 oz. (539 g)

This all-in-one unit offers functionality and versatility that makes it ideal for emergencies. The FR300 provides you with radio, light, and cell phone battery life when you need it most. The Hand-Crank Power Generator charges the internal rechargeable Ni-MH battery pack. With the NOAA weather channels and TV VHF channels, you can find weather forecasts or listen to TV shows when you're away from the set.

- AM and FM
- TV1 and TV2 - VHF channels 2-13
- NOAA weather – all 7 channels plus "Alert"
- 3 LED light system with emergency flash
- Emergency siren
- Built-in cell-phone charger
- Crank-charge system charges built-in rechargeable battery
- Charges rechargeable battery via AC adapter/charger (not included)
- Can be powered by 3 AA batteries
- Can be powered with all batteries removed, by continuous cranking
- Power Source: Built-In Rechargeable Ni-MH Battery Pack; 3 AA Batteries (not included); Crank power alone; AC Adapter (not included); AC Adapter recharges built-in Ni-MH battery pack
- Dimensions: 6-1/2"W x 6"H x 2-1/2"D (168 x 155 x 64 mm)
- Weight: 1 lb. 4 oz. (568 g)

etón®
RE.INVENTING™ RADIO
www.etoncorp.com

FR350

AM/FM/Shortwave Radio with Flashlight, and Cell phone Charger

FR400

AM/FM Radio with NOAA, TV VHF, Flashlight, and Cell Phone Charger

Built-in cell phone charger

Improved technology, functionality and versatility, the FR350 is ideal for emergencies. The FR350 provides you with a water resistant radio, LED lights, and cell phone charger when you need it most. Using the Hand-Crank Power Generator, charge the internal rechargeable Ni-MH battery pack in times of need.

- AM/FM/Shortwave
- Water resistant body
- Hand Crank Power Generator
- 3 LED light system with emergency flash
- Emergency siren
- Built-in Cell phone charger
- Power Source: Hand-Crank Power Generator with rechargeable battery pack, 3 AA batteries (not included) or AC adaptor (included)
- Dimensions: 4.5"H x 8.6"W x 2"D (114 x 220 x 50 mm)
- Weight: 1.5 lb (680 g)

Improved technology, functionality and versatility, the FR400 is ideal for emergencies. The FR400 provides you with a water resistant radio, LED lights, and cell phone charger when you need it most. Using the Hand-Crank Power Generator, charge the internal rechargeable Ni-MH battery pack in times of need. With NOAA weather channels and TV-VHF channels, you have easy access to weather forecasts and can listen to TV shows while away from the set.

- AM/FM/NOAA/TV1/TV2 - VHF channels 2-13
- Water resistant body
- NOAA weather – all 7 channels plus "Alert" function
- Hand Crank Power Generator
- 3 LED light system with emergency flash
- Can be powered from four different sources:
  1) From the built-in rechargeable Ni-MH battery that takes charge from the dynamo crank and from an AC adapter (AC adapter included)
  2) From 3 AA batteries
  3) From the AC adapter alone (AC adapter included)
  4) From the dynamo crank alone, even with no battery pack installed
- Emergency siren
- Built-in cell-phone charger
- Crank-charge system charges built-in rechargeable battery
- Charges rechargeable battery via AC adapter (included)
- Can be powered with all batteries removed, by continuous cranking
- Power Source: Built-In Rechargeable Ni-MH Battery Pack; 3 AA Batteries (not included); Crank power alone; AC Adapter (included); AC Adapter recharges built-in Ni-MH battery pack
- Dimensions: 4.5"H x 8.6"W x 2"D (114 x 220 x 50 mm)
- Weight: 1.5 lb (680 g)

Also Available in:

III. DPRK: Roar of the Gulag

Even during the Japanese occupation, radio stations in northern Korea were scarce, being only in Pyongyang, Hamhung, Haeju, Kaesang and Wonsan. Later, during the Korean War, the American Forces Korea Network (AFKN) set up stations just north of the DMZ at Kumwha and Inje (sidebar). Of course, these were closed down when the border was redrawn.

> **North Koreans risk prison and torture to hear foreign stations.**

For the nearly 23 million people living in North Korea, radio broadcasting has been organized similarly to that of now-defunct communist nations. The Central Broadcasting Committee oversees production of all domestic broadcasting of the Central Broadcasting Station, while the Ministry of Communication provides and maintains technical facilities. "Central" is the operative word, as almost everything is controlled by the ruling Workers' Party.

Precious little is known about internal broadcasting in North Korea. Domestically, over 20 local and provincial stations relay the Central Broadcasting Station, using scores of mediumwave AM transmitters with daily programs in Korean. World band transmitters play an important role, with every major city having its own outlet. Additionally, the Pyongyang Broadcasting Station serves the capital with many FM and mediumwave AM outlets, and is also relayed on world band. Pyongyang is further saturated by a separate FM-only service that's relayed countrywide.

Preset Radios, Wired Broadcasts Numb Audience

"Most domestic broadcasts are received by a wired distribution network which extends to towns and villages, reaching about a million

Unification talks between the two Koreas can inflame passions. To keep the North appeased, anticommunist demonstrations in the South are swiftly quelled by police action. M. Guha

homes and community listening posts," wrote Professors Sunwoo Nam and John Lent in the 1974 treatise *Broadcasting in Asia and the Pacific*. Quoting a reporter, they continued, "Loudspeakers broadcast the current transmissions from Radio Pyongyang. In the 200 meter deep Bongha (Torch) station [perhaps referring to the Pyongyang Metro, the deepest subway in the world, which also doubles as a bomb shelter], a reading of Comrade Kim's works was followed by a radio play about the Korean War. The station echoed disconcertingly to the sound of battle cries, artillery and machine guns. Nobody took the slightest notice. The row of passive faces were switched right off. Perhaps that is the closest the visitor can get to the pulse of Pyongyang."

According to Reporters Without Borders' Annual Report of 2005, "In the absence of the Internet (e-mail is banned) and satellite dishes, the only way for many North Koreans to sidestep the official propaganda is to tune to the Korean-language broadcasts of foreign radio stations.

" 'You can buy radio sets in North Korea that are preset to the government radio frequency and sealed, but some people take the risk of opening them up in order to be able to tune into other frequencies,' a refugee explained. Today, radio sets are increasingly getting into the country—especially to Pyongyang—from neighboring China.

"At the end of 2003, the head of each communist party cell in neighborhoods and villages received instructions to verify the seals on all radio sets. The North Korean authorities then designated radio sets as 'new enemies of the regime' on June 13, 2004."

Classic Propaganda

After the Korean War, the North Korean government made it a priority to restore broadcast facilities which had been destroyed. They also emphasized airing propaganda to South Korea and jamming international broadcasts, especially those from the South.

Also important was the development of external broadcasts to the region and

RKI's language output is managed by an intricate playlist on a powerful server. Nevertheless, it can be overridden manually at this no-nonsense patch panel.   M. Guha

beyond—the Middle East, Europe and the Americas—to propagate the views of the Workers' Party. "The Party Bureau for the South" of the Workers' Party oversees all foreign broadcasts through the Pyongyang Broadcasting Committee.

Before 2001 the North Korean external service was called Radio Pyongyang. Now, it's the Voice of Korea in eight foreign languages, plus Korean broadcasts produced by Pyongyang Broadcasting Station and the Korean Central Broadcasting Station (KCBS).

English, the world's key language, gets front teat with ten hours a day. Although programs are less strident than in the past, they still provide listeners with plenty of opportunity to sample vintage Marxist propaganda.

RADIOS TARGET NORTH KOREA

Broadcasting in South Korea has mirrored the country's turbulence and led to propaganda broadcasts beamed to the North. In November 1972, both Korean governments agreed to desist from hostile propaganda, but the radio cease-fire was broken two years later. The South Koreans were accused of sending propaganda balloons into the North, while northerners were blamed for operating a clandestine radio station close to the demilitarized zone. To date, however, the former cacophony of broadcasting through loudspeakers at the DMZ hasn't resumed.

Even though the two Koreas have reached several agreements to cease hostile propaganda, these have never lasted long. According to clandestineradio.com and 1970s-era articles by Lawrence Magne, South Korean authorities ran black clandestine broadcasts to North Korea from Kyonggi-do.

"Echo of Hope" started on June 10, 1973 and today is on 3912 and 6348 kHz. It was then joined on June 25, 1985 by "Voice of the People," which currently uses 6600 kHz. "Voice" claims to be operated by the North Korean Workers' Union, but it is actually run by the South Korean armed forces. Before that, the same facilities appear to have been used by the former black clandestines "Voice of the East" and "Voice of Unification."

World Band Replaces Internet

On April 20, 2003, a group of North Korean defectors headed by Kim Seong-min started an Internet radio station, "Radio Free North Korea," which ran for an hour a day.

With the Internet all but nonexistent in North Korea, it was no surprise that the station eventually started regular world band transmissions in December 2005. Brokered by VT Communications in the United Kingdom, initial broadcasts were aired via a transmitter in Irkutsk, Russia. However, in April 2006 the broadcasts were switched to a transmitter in Taiwan. For now, the RFNK daily schedule is 1000–1030 on 7390 or 11750 kHz, and 1700–1730 on 5890 or 9760 kHz. The station is also reported to be using a mediumwave AM transmitter in Mongolia.

Initially, "Radio Free North Korea" and another organization, "Open Radio for North Korea," shared airtime. However, "Open Radio" eventually started its own one-hour broadcasts, reportedly using a transmitter in Central Asia, at 1500–1600 on 7470 kHz.

"Radio Free North Korea" has publicly stated that it receives indirect financial support from the U.S. Congress, while "Open Radio for North Korea" is headquartered in the state of Virginia. It is therefore likely that both stations are supported by American funding.

Aids Kidnapped Japanese

Since October 30, 2005 the "Investigation Commission on Missing Japanese Probably Related to N. Korea" has been leasing airtime brokered by VT Communications. Using a transmitter in Taiwan, the Tokyo-based group airs "Shiokaze" (Sea Breeze) in Japanese, English, Korean and Chinese to North Korea. The program's objective is to help in the rescue of up to 200 Japanese nationals believed to have been kidnapped by North Korean authorities, and includes messages from their families in Japan.

Transmissions have been vigorously jammed, almost certainly from North Korea, since May 5, 2006. However—with proper transmitter location, timing and frequency management—world band radio has the one-of-a-kind potential of sidestepping jamming in rural areas. Thus, although once on 5890 kHz, "Shiokaze" has been going to higher, then back to lower, frequencies and making time shifts to take full advantage of twilight immunity—a proven anti-jamming technique.

Paul Stettler was the last engineer at Swisscom's Schwarzenburg transmission facility, once used by Swiss Radio International. Four transmitters decommissioned from here mysteriously wound up in North Korea.

Bob Thomann

According to the Transmitter Documentation Project, there are three shortwave sites in North Korea, the oldest having five 200 kW transmitters at Kanggye near the Chinese border. Also with five 200 kW units is a newer site at Kujang, but the capital city of Pyongyang is the big enchilada with ten 200 kW senders. Almost certainly all these are of venerable Soviet design, manufactured either in China or the former USSR.

Pyongyang's Swiss Connection

That leaves North Korea's four biggest world band transmitters unaccounted for. As it turns out, these have a curious provenance originating in tiny Swiss cantons.

In 1995 Swiss Radio International's shortwave operation had come to a close, in part because of environmental concerns. This left a number of elder transmitters to be disposed of by Swisscom, which owned SRI's transmission facilities at Schwarzenburg and elsewhere. Normally, old units like these would simply be scrapped, but a more financially attractive solution was quietly devised.

As confirmed by veteran Schwarzenburg engineer Paul Stettler and former SRI host Bob Zanotti—who now produces the popular "Switzerland in Sound" (switzerlandinsound. com)—Swisscom sold four of the decom-

missioned SRI shortwave transmitters, sans antennas, to North Korea: two from Schwarzenburg and a pair from Beromünster. All are manually operated 1968 Brown-Boveri/ BBC 250 kW units—old and lacking automation, but renowned for their robustness, just as North Koreans are renowned for keeping equipment going no matter what.

The secretive North never revealed to the Swiss the intended purpose or ultimate location of this million watts of shortwave superpower. Even today, an exact location has yet to be made public. What is known is that North Korea's Ministry of Posts and Telecommunications uses these to beam hefty Voice of Korea signals to listeners all over the globe.

The station's programs attract listeners who want to sense the pulse of Marxist and Islamist movements. Reaching this audience directly is valuable to North Korea, so the station is not likely to go away anytime soon.

Prepared in cooperation with Tony Jones. Our thanks to the many helpful contributors who helped make this article possible, including Jun Sato and Toshimichi Ohtake of the Japan Short Wave Club, John D. Harmer/ Technician-Engineer, and Prof. Tim P. Yoho and historians of the U.S. Army 7th PSYOP Group.

Etón E5
AM/LW/FM-Stereo/ Shortwave Portable Radio

For the ultimate in portable technology the E5 is the latest edition to the Etón Elite range and demonstrates that form and function can work in harmony.

- AM/LW/FM Stereo and Full Shortwave Coverage (1711 - 29999 KHz)
- Single Side Band (SSB) and Wide-Narrow Bandwidth Switch
- 700 Memory Programmable Presets
- FM Station Automatic Tuning Storage (ATS) provides automatic acquisition of the strongest stations in your area
- Full-featured world time zone Clock, Sleep Timer, 4 Programmable Alarm Timers and Weekday View Display

Etón E100
AM/FM/Shortwave Radio

The E100 fits full-sized features into your palm or pocket. This little marvel is packed with all the latest radio features you want: digital tuning, 200 programmable memories, digital clock and alarm, plus AM/FM and Shortwave reception. And, it is small enough to fit in your coat pocket.

- Shortwave – 1711-29.995 KHz
- 200 Random Programmable Memories
- Memory Page Customizing
- FM-Stereo/Signal Strength/Power Level Indicators
- Built in antennas for AM, FM and SW reception

Etón S350DL
AM/FM/Shortwave Radio

The S350 DELUXE blends the best of yesterday and today. With the look of a retro field radio sporting a rugged body and military-style controls—the S350 DELUXE also features today's innovation for excellent AM, FM, and Shortwave reception and a large, full-range speaker for clear sound.

- AM/FM/Shortwave Radio reception
- Highly sensitive and selective analog tuner circuitry
- LCD for frequency and clock display
- Digital clock with selectable 12/24 hour format
- AM/SW Frequency lock
- Low-pass filter for shortwave reception
- Available in three colors, Black, Metallic Red and Silver

Etón FR400
AM/FM Radio with NOAA, TV VHF, Flashlight, and Cell-Phone Charger

Improved technology, functionality and versatility, the FR400 is ideal for emergencies. The FR400 provides you with a water resistant radio, LED lights, and cell phone charger when you need it most.

- AM/FM/NOAA/TV1/TV2 - VHF

channels 2-13
- Water resistant body
- Hand Crank Power Generator
- 3 LED light system with emergency flash
- Built-in cell-phone charger
- Emergency siren
- Crank-charge system charges built-in rechargeable battery
- Can be powered with all batteries removed, by continuous cranking
- Includes AC Adapter
- Available in: Red, Black, Silver, Yellow & Blue

Etón E1XM

The E1XM is the world's first radio to combine AM, FM, Shortwave, and XM Satellite Radio Ready technology into one ultra-high-performance unit.

Etón E1XM AM/FM/Shortwave/ XM Satellite Ready Radio

- AM/FM/Shortwave/XM Satellite Ready Radio
- 1700 station presets
- Digitally synthesized PLL tuner with synchronous detector
- Passband tuning, selectable bandwidth filters and Selectable Single Sideband (SSB) reception
- Dual Clocks and programmable timers
- Headphone jack
- Built-In Antenna: telescopic antenna for AM, FM, and Shortwave reception
- External Antenna Connection for the addition of auxiliary antennas
- Calibrated LCD signal strength meter
- XM antenna & subscription sold separately

Select Model Available at:

etón®
RE_INVENTING™ RADIO
www.etoncorp.com

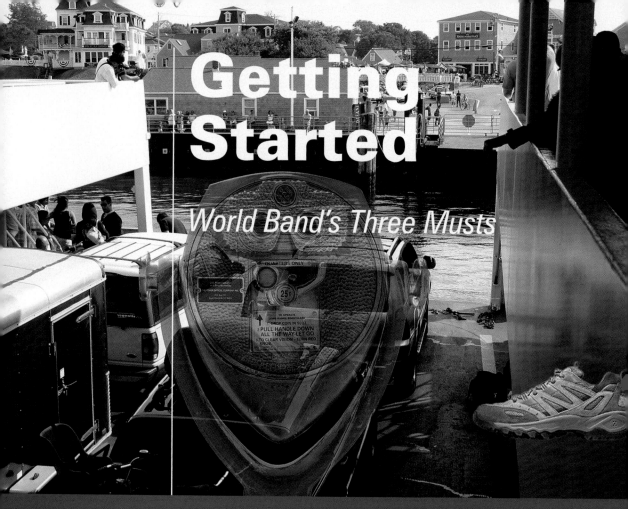

Getting Started

World Band's Three Musts

World band isn't run-of-the-mill radio—it travels freely by skywave and needs special receivers. So, here are three musts so you can master it right off.

Must #1: World Time and Day

World band schedules use a single time. World band is global, with programs aired around the clock from nearly every time zone.

Imagine the chaos if each station's schedule were given in its local time to listeners scattered all over the world.

Solution: World Time—one time zone for the entire planet.

World Time—officially called Coordinated Universal Time (UTC)—has replaced the virtually identical Greenwich Mean Time (GMT) as the global standard. It's in 24-hour format, so 2 PM is 14:00 ("fourteen hundred hours" or "fourteen hours"). Ideally, leading zeroes are shown; for example, 08:00, spoken as "oh-eight-hundred hours" or "eight hours," is more correct than 8:00. In the military, World Time (UTC) is often called Zulu or Zulu Time.

Don't forget to "wind your calendar," because at midnight a new *World Day* arrives. This can trip up even experienced listeners—sometimes radio stations, too. So if it is 9:00 PM EST Wednesday in New York, it is 02:00 hours World Time *Thursday*.

Bottom line for clocks: Purchase a radio with a 24-hour clock or buy a separate clock, then check out the sidebar "World Time: Setting Your Clock".

Oregon Scientific RM323A self-setting travel clock with world time.

Must #2: Finding Stations

PASSPORT **shows station schedules three ways: by country, time of day and frequency.** By-country is best for tuning to a given station. "What's On Tonight's" hour-by-hour format is like *TV Guide*, complete with program descriptions. The Blue Pages' quick-access grids show what you might be hearing when you're dialing around the bands.

World band frequencies are usually given in kilohertz (kHz), but some stations and radios use Megahertz (MHz). The only difference is three decimal places, so 6170 kHz is the same as 6.17 MHz, 6175 kHz equals 6.175 MHz, and so on.

FM and other stations keep the same spot on the dial, day and night—webcast URLs, too, sort of. But things are different on the international airwaves. World band radio is like a global bazaar where a variety of merchants come and go at various times of the day and night. So, where you once tuned in a French station, hours later you might find a Russian roosting on that same spot.

Or on a nearby perch. If you suddenly hear interference, it doesn't necessarily mean something is wrong with your radio—another station may have fired up on a nearby frequency. There are more stations on the air than available space, so sometimes they try to outshout each other.

World Time— one time zone for one planet.

PASSPORT'S THREE-MINUTE START

Owner's manual a yawn? Try this:

1. Night time is the right time, so listen evenings when signals are strongest. In a concrete-and-steel building put your radio by a window or on a balcony.

2. Make sure your radio is plugged in or has fresh batteries. Extend its telescopic antenna fully and vertically. Set the DX/local switch, if there is one, to DX, but otherwise leave controls at the factory settings.

3. Turn on your radio after dark. Set it to 5900 kHz and begin tuning slowly toward 6200 kHz. You should hear stations from around the world.

Other times? Read the nearby sidebar, "Best Times and Frequencies for 2007."

To cope with this, purchase a radio with superior adjacent-channel rejection—selectivity—and lean towards models with synchronous selectable sideband. PASSPORT REPORTS tests these and other features and tells you which models can hack it.

Because world band is full of surprises from one listening session to the next, experienced listeners like to stroll through the airwaves. Daytime, you'll find most stations above 11500 kHz; at night, below 10000 kHz, but there are interesting exceptions.

If a station can't be found or fades out, there is probably nothing wrong with your radio or the schedule. World band stations are located on *terra firma*, but because of the earth's curvature their signals eventually run into the sky-high ionosphere. When the ionosphere is suitably energized, it deflects these signals back down, after which they bounce off oceans or soil and sail back up to the ionosphere.

This bouncing up and down like a basketball continues until the signal arrives at your radio. However, if the ionosphere at any one "bounce point" isn't in a bouncing mood—it varies daily and seasonally, like the weather—the signal passes through the ionosphere and disappears into space.

That's great for intergalactic travelers, but for the rest of us it's the main reason a scheduled signal might be audible one hour, gone the next.

No Censorship—Even During War

World band stations cope with the ionosphere's changeability by operating within different frequency ranges, depending on the season and time of day—even the 11-year sunspot cycle. This changeability is part of the fun and lets you eavesdrop on juicy signals not intended for your part of the world.

The ionosphere is also why world band radio is free from regulation and snooping. Unlike on the Internet, nobody can know what you're hearing—world band signals don't rely on cables or satellites, just layers of heavenly gases. This makes world band the ultimate for not leaving tracks that could come back to haunt during states of national emergency, security-clearance investigations or employment checks.

The ionosphere also helps analog world band transmissions to be heard even when there's skywave jamming, the only type feasible outside urban areas. Daily jam-

WORLD TIME CLOCKS

Some radios include a digital World Time clock displayed fulltime—this is handiest, although they usually gain or lose a minute or so over time. Other radios may have World Time clocks, but to see time when the radio is on you have to press a button or turn the radio off.

The $35 MFJ-133RC atomic clock displays exact World Time. Similar clocks are available for outside North America.

World Time is in 24-hour format, so digital numbers are easier to read than analog hands. MFJ Enterprises, Sharper Image, La Crosse Technology and others offer a wide variety of clocks, some with seconds displayed numerically, from $9.95 to $79.95.

Other 24-hour clocks, targeted to professionals, can run up to two kilobucks. Pricier models display seconds and even split-seconds numerically, while many synchronize with one or another of the world's several official atomic clock standards. There are even wristwatches that give World Time in analog or digital format.

This 1935 Tefag Supertefadyn KW woodie tunes world band between 5850 and 15800 kHz. It originally belonged to the uncle of veteran Finnish radio aficionado Simo Soininen, who still fires it up regularly.

S.S. Soininen

ming is currently limited to authoritarian regimes—Cuba, Iran and China, for example. Yet, even some democratic governments have infrastructures in place to disrupt communications during emergencies. As world band radio is largely beyond their control, it can inform even during the gravest of crises.

Bottom line for tuning in: World band is almost always there, no matter what.

Must #3: The Right Radio

Choose carefully, but start affordably. If you just want to hear major stations, you'll do fine with one of the higher-rated moderately priced portables. If you want something better, a top-end portable can do surprisingly well with challenging signals and offer superior audio quality.

Tabletop supersets are aimed at experienced and demanding users. If that's you, go for it. Otherwise, pass until you're sure you want a Maserati instead of a Boxter.

Select a radio with digital frequency display. This makes digging out stations much easier—virtually all radios in PASSPORT REPORTS have this, but portables with analog

display (slide-rule tuning) still abound. Some low-cost hybrids have analog tuning with digital frequency display, but most digital-display radios use synthesized tuning. These include such handy tuning aids as presets and keypads.

Also, get a radio that covers at least 4750-21850 kHz with no significant frequency gaps. Otherwise, it may miss some juicy stations.

An exotic outside antenna isn't a must unless you're using a tabletop model—portables are designed to work quite well with their built-in telescopic antennas. If you want to enhance a portable's weak-signal sensitivity, simply clip several yards or meters of insulated wire onto that antenna, or use one of the portable active antennas evaluated in PASSPORT REPORTS.

Bottom line for buying radios: Avoid cheap models, especially with slide-rule tuning—they suffer from major defects. But don't break the bank.

_____

Prepared by Jock Elliott, Tony Jones and Lawrence Magne.

WORLD TIME: SETTING YOUR CLOCK

PASSPORT's "Addresses PLUS" lets you figure out local time in other countries by adding or subtracting from World Time. Use it to ascertain local time in a country you are hearing.

This sidebar shows the opposite: what to add or subtract from your local time to get World Time. For example, if you live near Chicago and it's 7:00 AM winter, the list below shows World Time as six hours later, or 13:00.

In the summer, with saving time in effect, World Time is only five hours later—noon, or 12:00. That's because World Time, unlike Chicago time, doesn't change with the seasons. So, once you've set your clock for World Time you won't have to fool with it again.

Many major international broadcasters announce World Time at the hour. On the Internet it's given at various sites, including time5.nrc.ca/webclock_e.shtml. For North America and vicinity, World Time is announced over official stations WWV in Colorado, WWVH in Hawaii and CHU in Ottawa. WWV and WWVH use world band frequencies of 5000, 10000 and 15000 kHz, with WWV also being on 2500 and 20000 kHz. CHU ticks away on 3330, 7335 and 14670 kHz.

WHERE YOU ARE	TO DETERMINE WORLD TIME
North America	
Newfoundland St. John's NF, St. Anthony NF	Add 3½ hours, 2½ summer
Atlantic St. John NB, Battle Harbour NF	Add 4 hours, 3 summer
Eastern New York, Miami, Toronto	Add 5 hours, 4 summer
Central Chicago, Mexico City, Nashville, Winnipeg	Add 6 hours, 5 summer
Mountain Denver, Salt Lake City, Calgary	Add 7 hours, 6 summer
Pacific San Francisco, Vancouver	Add 8 hours, 7 summer
Alaska	Add 9 hours, 8 summer
Hawaii	Add 10 hours
Central America & Caribbean	
Bermuda	Add 4 hours, 3 summer
Barbados, Puerto Rico, Virgin Islands	Add 4 hours
Bahamas	Add 5 hours, 4 summer
Cuba	Add 4 hours
Jamaica	Add 5 hours
Costa Rica	Add 6 hours

Europe

United Kingdom, Ireland, Portugal	Same time as World Time winter, subtract 1 hour summer
Continental Western Europe; parts of Central and Eastern Continental Europe	Subtract 1 hour, 2 hours summer
Elsewhere in Continental Europe: Belarus, Bulgaria, Cyprus, Estonia, Finland, Greece, Latvia, Lithuania, Moldova, Romania, Russia (Kaliningradskaya Oblast), Turkey, Ukraine	Subtract 2 hours, 3 summer
Moscow	Subtract 3 hours, 4 summer

Mideast & Africa

Côte d'Ivoire, Ghana, Guinea, Liberia, Mali, Morocco, Senegal, Sierra Leone	World Time exactly
Angola, Benin, Chad, Congo, Nigeria	Subtract 1 hour
Tunisia	Subtract 1 hour, 2 summer
Egypt, Israel, Jordan, Lebanon, Syria	Subtract 2 hours, 3 summer
South Africa, Zambia, Zimbabwe	Subtract 2 hours
Ethiopia, Kenya, Kuwait, Saudi Arabia, Tanzania, Uganda	Subtract 3 hours
Iran	Subtract 3½ hours

Asia & Australasia

Pakistan	Subtract 5 hours
India, Sri Lanka	Subtract 5½ hours
Bangladesh	Subtract 6 hours
Laos, Thailand, Vietnam	Subtract 7 hours
China (including Taiwan), Malaysia, Philippines, Singapore	Subtract 8 hours
Japan, Korea	Subtract 9 hours
Australia: *Victoria, New South Wales, Tasmania*	Subtract 11 hours local summer, 10 local winter (midyear)
Australia: *South Australia*	Subtract 10½ hours local summer, 9½ hours local winter (midyear)
Australia: *Queensland*	Subtract 10 hours
Australia: *Northern Territory*	Subtract 9½ hours
Australia: *Western Australia*	Subtract 8 hours
New Zealand	Subtract 13 hours local summer, 12 hours local winter (midyear)

GRUNDIG G5
AM/FM-Stereo and Full Shortwave Portable Radio

The G5 is the world's leading portable, multi-band and Single Side Band (SSB) enabled radio. The G5 unites performance and mobility into one compact unit, bringing the power of local and world-band radio into the palm of your hand.
• Digital world-band radio

• AM/LW/FM-Stereo and Full Shortwave Coverage (1711 - 29999 KHz)
• Synthesized Tuning System
• 700 Memory Programmable Presets
• Built-in cell-phone charger
• Auto-Scan, Manual-Scan, Direct Key-in Entry, Tuning Buttons and Tuning Knob
• Full-featured world time zone Clock, Sleep Timer, 4 Programmable Alarm Timers and Weekday View Display
• Internally recharges Ni-MH battery (not included)

GRUNDIG Mini300
AM/FM/Shortwave Radio

Weighing less than 5 ounces and small enough to fit into your pocket, the Mini 300PE world-band radio makes a perfect travel companion. Its oversized telescopic antenna provides great AM/FM reception for when camping, hiking, listening to sports, or just relaxing in the backyard.

• AM, FM-stereo and 7 shortwave bands (49, 41, 31, 25, 22, 19 and 16 meters)
• Analog tuning with digital frequency readout
• Digital display shows frequency, time, sleep time and symbols for sleep timer and alarm activation
• Rotary volume control
• Earphone socket
• Telescopic antenna for FM and SW reception
• Internal ferrite bar antenna for AM (MW) reception

GRUNDIG S350DL
AM/FM/Shortwave Field Radio

The Grundig S350 Deluxe blends the best of yesterday and today. With the look of a retro field radio sporting a rugged body and military-style controls—the Grundig S350 Deluxe also features today's innovation for excellent AM, FM, and Shortwave reception and a large, full-range speaker for clear sound.

• AM 530-1710 KHz, FM 88-108 MHz
• Shortwave – continuous coverage from 3 to 28 MHz.
• Highly sensitive and selective analog tuner circuitry
• Power failure backup feature
• Variable RF Gain Control
• Rotary volume control
• Variable, independent bass and treble control
• Low-pass filter for shortwave and AM reception
• AM/SW Frequency lock feature

Grundig Radio Line by:

etón®
RE.INVENTING RADIO
www.etoncorp.com

Together We Prepare

The American Red Cross FR300: The Definition of Necessity

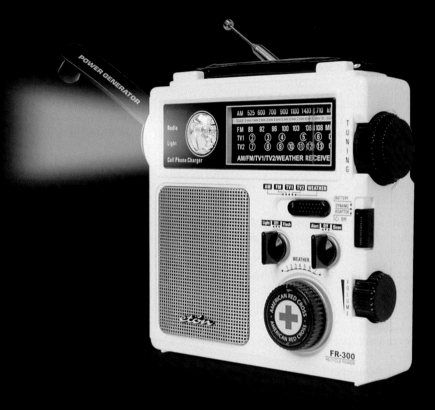

The American Red Cross

FR300

Emergency Crank Radio

- AM and FM, TV1 and TV2 - VHF channels 2-13
- NOAA weather – all 7 channels plus "Alert"
- 3 LED light system with emergency flash
- Emergency siren
- Built-in cell-phone charger
- Crank-charge system charges built-in rechargeable battery
- Charges rechargeable battery via AC adapter/charger (not included)
- Can be powered with all batteries removed, by continuous cranking
- Power Source: Built-In Rechargeable Ni-MH Battery Pack; 3 AA Batteries (not included); Crank power alone; AC Adapter (not included); AC Adapter recharges built-in Ni-MH battery pack
- Dimensions: 6-1/2"W x 6"H x 2-1/2"D (168 x 155 x 64 mm)
- Weight: 1 lb. 4 oz. (568 g)

The American Red Cross Radio Line By:

Available at:

RadioShack.

RE_INVENTING RADIO
www.etoncorp.com

American Red Cross

BEST TIMES AND FREQUENCIES FOR 2007

Dialing randomly within the full range of shortwave frequencies might get you nothing but dead air. That's because world band stations transmit on limited segments within the shortwave spectrum. Some of these are alive and kicking only by day, while others don't spring to life until night. Time of year also counts.

World band is always active, but many signals are strongest evenings because they're aimed your way. Still, lots of interesting stuff is heard outside prime time when, thanks to shortwave's scattering properties, signals beamed elsewhere are heard.

Experienced station hunters especially enjoy the hour or two on either side of dawn. Because propagation is different then, you may hear parts of the world that normally elude. Try after lunch, too—especially towards sunset. After midnight may also be interesting, especially winters.

Fine Print and Slippery Excuses: Treat this time and frequency guide like a good weather forecast: helpful, but not holy writ. Nature, as always, has a mind of its own, and world band is nature's radio.

This guide is most accurate if you're north of the African and South American continents. Even then, what you hear will vary depending on such things as your location, where the station transmits from, the time of year and your radio hardware.

☞ World band radio has fourteen official frequency segments. Nevertheless, broadcasters also operate "out of band" as legitimate secondary users, provided they don't cause harmful initial interference to such primary users as fixed-service utility stations.

☞ "Night" refers to your local hours of darkness, give or take.

Night—Very Limited Reception
Day—Local Reception Only

2 MHz (120 meters) **2300–2495 kHz**—used by a very few domestic stations, plus 2496–2504 kHz for time stations only.

Night—Limited Reception
Day—Local Reception Only

3 MHz (90 meters) **3200–3400 kHz**—overwhelmingly domestic broadcasters, but also some international stations.

World band is free from regulation and snooping.

Day and Night—Good-to-Fair in Europe and Asia except Summer Nights; Elsewhere, Limited Reception Night

4 MHz (75 meters) **3900–4050 kHz**—international and domestic stations, primarily not in or beamed to the Americas; 3900–3950 kHz mainly Asian and Pacific transmitters; 3950–4000 kHz also includes European transmitters; 4001–4050 kHz currently out-of-band.

Night—Fair Reception
Day—Regional Reception Only

5 MHz (60 meters) **4750–4995 kHz** and **5005–5100 kHz**—mostly domestic stations, plus 4996–5004 kHz for time stations only; 5061–5100 kHz currently out-of-band.

Night—Excellent Reception
Day—Regional Reception Only

6 MHz (49 meters) **5730–6300 kHz**—5730–5899 kHz and 6201–6300 kHz currently out-of-band.

> **World band is always there, whether in crisis or in calm.**

Night—Good Reception
Day—Mainly Regional Reception

7 MHz (41 meters) **6890–6990 kHz** and **7100–7600 kHz**—6890–6990 kHz and 7351–7600 kHz currently out-of-band; 7100–7300 kHz no American-based transmitters and few transmissions targeted to the Americas. The 7100 kHz lower parameter for outside the Americas shifts to 7200 kHz in March of 2009.

Day—Fair Reception Winter; Regional Reception Summer
Night—Good Recepti on Summer

9 MHz (31 meters) **9250–9995 kHz**—9250–9399 kHz and 9901–9995 kHz currently out-of-band, plus 9996–10004 kHz for time stations only.

Day—Good Reception
Night—Variable Reception Summer

11 MHz (25 meters) **11500–12200 kHz**—11500–11599 kHz and 12101–12200 kHz currently out-of-band.

13 MHz (22 meters) **13570–13870 kHz**

15 MHz (19 meters) **15005–15825 kHz**—15005–15099 kHz and 15801–15825 kHz currently out-of-band, plus 14996–15004 kHz for time stations only.

Day—Good Reception
Night—Limited Reception Summer

17 MHz (16 meters) **17480–17900 kHz**

19 MHz (15 meters) **18900–19020 kHz**—few stations use this segment.

Day—Variable Reception
Night—Little Reception

21 MHz (13 meters) **21450–21850 kHz**

Day—Rare, if Any, Reception
Night—No Reception

25 MHz (11 meters) **25670–26100 kHz**

Etón E1XM

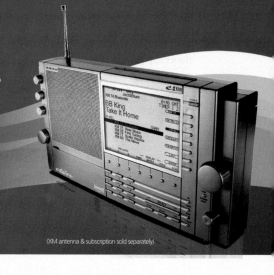

The E1XM is the world's first radio to combine AM, FM, Shortwave, and XM Satellite Radio Ready technology into one ultra-high-performance unit.

- AM/FM/SW/XM Satellite Ready Radio
- 1700 station presets
- Digitally synthesized PLL tuner with synchronous detector
- Passband tuning, selectable bandwidth filters and Selectable Single Sideband (SSB) reception
- Dual Clocks and programmable timers
- Built-In Antenna: telescopic antenna for AM, FM, and Shortwave reception
- External Antenna Connection for the addition of auxiliary antennas
- Calibrated LCD signal strength meter

(XM antenna & subscription sold separately)

Etón E5
AM/LW/FM-Stereo/ Shortwave Portable Radio

For the ultimate in portable technology the E5 is the latest edition to the Etón Elite range and demonstrates that form and function can work in harmony.

- AM/LW/FM-Stereo and Full Shortwave Coverage (1711 - 29999 KHz)
- Single Side Band (SSB) and Wide-Narrow Bandwidth Switch
- 700 Memory Programmable Presets
- FM Station Automatic Tuning Storage (ATS) provides automatic acquisition of the strongest stations in your area
- Full-featured world time zone Clock, Sleep Timer, 4 Programmable Alarm Timers and Weekday View Display

Etón S350DL
AM/FM/Shortwave Radio

The S350 DELUXE blends the best of yesterday and today. With the look of a retro field radio sporting a rugged body and military-style controls—the S350 DELUXE also features today's innovation for excellent AM, FM, and Shortwave reception and a large, full-range speaker for clear sound.

- AM/FM/Shortwave Radio reception
- Highly sensitive and selective analog tuner circuitry
- LCD for frequency and clock display
- digital clock with selectable 12/24 hour format
- Low-pass filter for shortwave reception
- AM/SW Frequency lock feature
- Available in three colors, Black, Metallic Red and Silver

Etón E100
AM/FM/Shortwave Radio

The E100 fits full-sized features into your palm or pocket. This little marvel is packed with all the latest radio features you want.

- Shortwave – 1711-29.995 KHz
- 200 Random Programmable Memories
- Memory Page Customizing
- FM-Stereo/Signal Strength/Power Level Indicators
- Built in antennas for AM, FM and SW reception

Available at:

universal radio inc.

etón®
RE_INVENTING RADIO
www.etoncorp.com

Together We Prepare

The American Red Cross FR350: The Definition of Necessity

The American Red Cross
FR350
Emergency Crank Radio

- AM/FM/Shortwave
- Water resistant body
- Hand Crank Power Generator
- 3 LED light system with emergency flash
- Emergency siren
- Built-in Cell phone charger
- Power Source: Hand-Crank Power Generator with rechargeable battery pack, 3 AA batteries (not included) or AC adaptor (included)
- Dimensions: 4.5"H x 8.6"W x 2"D (114 x 220 x 50mm)
- Weight: 1.5 lb (680 g)

Available at:

The American Red Cross Radio Line By:

etón ®
RE:INVENTING RADIO
www.etoncorp.com

First Tries: "Big Ten" Catches

Getting started? Here's a Big Ten roster of stations easily heard worldwide. All are in English and most make for interesting listening.

Times and days are in World Time (UTC). "Winter" and "summer" refer to the Northern Hemisphere, where summer is midyear—July and so on.

EUROPE
Germany

Deutsche Welle focuses heavily on local and national issues, but it's more than just a "voice of Germany." Coverage of news and culture in nearby countries also gives it a European flavor.

DW has some excellent world band shows, although it now targets fewer countries with advanced economies so it can focus elsewhere. Nevertheless, it continues to audible in "uncovered" regions, thanks to the scattering properties of shortwave.

☞ RECOMMENDED: "Arts on the Air" and "A World of Music."

North and Central America: Best for the eastern and southern United States and the Caribbean is the broadcast for West Africa at 2100–2200. Try 9615 and 11690 kHz winter, and 11865 and 15205 kHz in summer.

Europe: 0600–1000 and 1300–1600 year-round on 6140 kHz.

Southern Africa: 0400–0500 midyear on 12045 kHz; 0500–0530 winter—summer in the Southern Hemisphere—on 7225 kHz, and midyear on 9630 kHz; 1900–1930 winter on 12025 kHz, and midyear on 15620 kHz; 2000–2100 winter on 9735 and 12035 kHz, and midyear on 7130, 11795 and 15205 kHz.

East and Southeast Asia: 0000–0100 on 7345, 9900, 15320 and 15445 kHz.

Netherlands

Radio Nederland Wereldomroep—known in English as **Radio Netherlands**—makes the most of its resources. Working with a modest budget, it produces relatively few programs, opting for quality over quantity. With a strong commitment to social issues, Radio Netherlands is a thought-provoking alternative to mainstream broadcasters.

☞ RECOMMENDED: "Weekend Connection" and "Research File."

North America: (East) 1100–1200 summer on 11675 kHz; 1200–1300 winter on 9890 kHz; 1900–2100 (weekends only) on 15525 kHz winter and 17735 kHz summer; 0000–0100 winter on 6165 kHz, replaced summer by 9845 kHz; *(Central)* 1900–2100 (weekends only) on 15315

> You can often hear stations beamed elsewhere, thanks to shortwave's scattering properties.

Dr. Irene Quaile-Kersken heads Magazine Programming at Deutsche Welle's English Radio Service. She has been a major force behind DW's high program quality. DW

Vitaliy Glazunov, correspondent and host of Voice of Russia's "Guest Speaker." VoR

kHz; and 0100–0200 winter on 6165 kHz, replaced summer by 9845 kHz; *(West)* 1900–2100 (weekends only) on 17725 kHz winter and 17660 kHz summer; and 0500–0600 (one hour earlier in summer) on 6165 kHz.

Southern Africa: 1800–1900 on 6020 kHz, and 1900–2100 on 7120 kHz.

East and Southeast Asia: 1000–1100 winter on 6040, 9795 and 12065 kHz; and summer on 12065, 13710 and 13820 kHz.

Australasia: 0500–0600 winter—summer in the Southern Hemisphere—on 11710 kHz, and 0700–0800 midyear on 9700 kHz. The 1000–1100 broadcast for East and Southeast Asia is also heard within the region.

Russia

Its programs sometimes reflect official government policy, yet the **Voice of Russia** is still popular among world band listeners. With decades of exclusive archived material at its disposal, some of its cultural offerings are among the very finest.

☞ RECOMMENDED: "Jazz Show," "Folk Box" and "Songs from Russia."

Eastern North America: Winter, 0200–0400 on 7250 kHz, 0200–0600 on 7180 kHz,

0300–0600 on 7350 kHz, and 0400–0600 on 7150 kHz; summer, 0100–0200 on 7250 kHz, 0100–0500 on 9665 kHz (7180 kHz in autumn), 0200–0500 on 9860 kHz, and 0300–0500 on 9880 kHz. Winter afternoons, try frequencies beamed to Europe—some make it to eastern North America.

Western North America: Winter, 0200–0400 on 15595 kHz, 0200–0500 on 15475 kHz, 0200–0600 on 15425 kHz, and 0400–0600 on 9840 and 12010 kHz; summer, 0100–0500 on 15555 kHz, 0200–0500 on 15595 kHz, and 0300–0500 on 15425 and 15455 kHz.

Europe: Winter, 1600–1700 on 6130 and 7320 kHz; 1700–1800 on 7320 kHz; 1800–1900 on 5950 and 6175 (weekends only), 7290 and 7320 kHz; 1900–2000 on 6175 and 7290 kHz; 2000–2100 on 6145, 7290 and 7330 kHz; and 2100–2200 on 7330 and 7390 kHz. Summer, 1500–1600 on 7370, 12040 (or 9810) and 15455 (or 11980) kHz; 1600–1700 on 7370 kHz; 1700–1800 on 7370, 9890 and (weekends) 9820 and 11675 (or 7320) kHz; 1800–1900 on 7370, 9820, 9890 and 11630 (or 9480) kHz; 1900–2000 on 7195, 7310, 9890 and 12070 kHz; and 2000–2100 on 7195, 9890, 12070 and 15455 (or 11980) kHz.

Middle East: Winter, 1600–1700 on 9470 kHz, 1700–1800 on 7360 and 9470 kHz, and 1800–1900 on 7360 kHz; summer, 1500–1800 on 11985 kHz.

Southern Africa: Winter (summer in the Southern Hemisphere), 1800–1900 on 11510 kHz, and 1900–2000 on 7335 and 11510 kHz; midyear, 1700–1800 on 11510 kHz, and 1800–1900 on 9745 and 11510 kHz.

Southeast Asia: Winter, 1500–1600 on 6205, 7415 and 9660 kHz; summer, 1400–1500 on 7165, 12055 (or 6205), 15605 and 17645 kHz; and 1500–1600 on 9660 kHz.

Australasia: Winter (summer in the Southern Hemisphere), 0600–0900 on 17805 kHz, 0600–1000 on 17665 kHz, and 0800–1000 on 17495 kHz; midyear, 0500–0900 on 17635 and 21790 kHz, and 0700–0900 on 17495 kHz.

United Kingdom

The reinvented **BBC World Service** has been living off its legendary reputation for some time, now. Yet, however faded its glory, it still offers a diverse menu of programs.

☞ RECOMMENDED: "The Instant Guide" and "Heart and Soul."

North America: Summer 2006 will be remembered as the time the BBC World Service all but killed its world band broadcasts to the Americas. Only the Caribbean survived, with a threadbare service of four hours daily in English and one in Spanish. Worse, the resulting schedule left most of North America unable to receive the broadcasts for the Caribbean. The schedule is 1100–1200 on 5875 (winter), 6130 and (summer) 9660 kHz; 1200–1300 on 9660 and 9750 kHz; 2100–2200 on 9660 (winter), 11675 and (summer) 13765 kHz; and 2200–2300 winter on 5975 and 9660 kHz; and summer on 5975 and 13765 kHz.

Some frequencies for Europe, Africa and the Mideast manage to reach North America—particularly during summer. But times vary, depending on location and time of year. Early morning in western North America, the BBC's East Asia stream on 9740 kHz (1000–1600) is well heard, especially on the West Coast.

Europe: (Western) Winter, 0500–0800 on 6195 and 9410 kHz; 1500–1700 on 9410 and 12095 kHz; 1700–1900 on 6195 and 9410 kHz; and 1900–2200 on 6195 kHz. Summer, 0400–0600 on 6195 and 9410 kHz; 0600–0700 on 6195, 9410 and 12095 kHz; 1400–1700 on 12095 and 15485 kHz; 1700–1900 on 6195 (from 1800), 9410, 12095 and (till 1800) 15485 kHz; 1900–2100 on 6195 and 9410 kHz. *(Central and Southeast)* 0400–0700 and 1500–1900 (one hour earlier in summer) on 6195, 9410, 12095 and (winter) 17640 kHz (times vary for each channel).

Middle East: 0200–2000. Key frequencies—times vary according to whether it is winter or summer—are 6195 (winter), 9410, 11760, 12045 (summer), 12095, 15575 and (winter) 17640 kHz.

Southern Africa: 0300–2200 on, among others, 3255, 6005, 6190, 11765 (midyear), 11940, 12095, 15400 and 21470 kHz—times vary for each channel.

East and Southeast Asia: 0000–0300 on 6195 (till 0200), 9740 (till 0100), 15280 (or 15285), and 15360 kHz; 0300–0500 on 15280 (or 15285), 15360, 17760 (from 0200 in winter) and 21660 kHz; 0500–0800 on 11955, 15285 (winter), 15360, 17760 and 21660 kHz; 0800–1030 on 5975 (winter, from 0900) 6195, 9605 (summer, from 0900), 9740, 15285 (winter), 17760 (till 1000 winter) and 21660 kHz; 1030–1300 on 6195, 9740, (winter) 11750 and (summer) 17760 kHz; 1300–1600 on 6195, 9740 and (summer) 11750 kHz; 1600–1700 on 3915, 6195 and (summer) 7160 kHz; 1700–1800 on 3915 and (summer) 7160 kHz; 2100–2200 on 3915, 5955 (winter), 5965 and 6195 kHz; 2200–2300 on 3915 (winter) 5955 (summer), 5965, 5995, 6195, 7255 (summer) and 9740 kHz; 2300–2400 on 3915, 5965, 6195, 9740, 11850 (summer), 11945 and 11955 kHz.

Australasia: Like North America, Australasia is no longer an official target for BBC broadcasts. However, some transmissions for Southeast Asia are easily heard in Australia and New Zealand. Best are 0500–0800 on 11955 and 15360 kHz, and 0800–1600 on 9740 kHz. At 2200–2300, 9660 and 12080 kHz are also available for some parts of the region.

ASIA
China (People's Republic)

While the sun has been setting on some Western broadcasters, **China Radio International** has been taking up the slack. It is now the largest world band station, with powerful transmitters at home and abroad to ensure global coverage. CRI's English broadcasts are heard just about everywhere, from Cape Horn to Alaska.

News, current events and features are CRI's meat and potatoes. But for listeners who want something different, there's an upbeat drive-time show offered several times each

Etón E1XM
AM/FM/Shortwave/XM-Satellite Ready Radio

- Reception Modes: AM, FM-stereo, XM Satellite Single Sideband (selectable USB/LSB) and CW
- Digital Phase Lock Loop (PLL) Synthesized Tuning with Direct Digital Synthesis (DDS) for drift-free frequency stability and finest tuning resolution
- Excellent Sensitivity: yielding a true high-performance receiver
- Selectable Bandwidths: 7.0, 4.0, 2.5 kHz for excellent selectivity

(XM antenna & subscription sold separately)

Etón E5
AM/LW/FM-Stereo/ Shortwave Portable Radio

For the ultimate in portable technology the E5 is the latest edition to the Etón Elite range and demonstrates that form and function can work in harmony.

- AM/LW/FM-Stereo and Full Shortwave Coverage (1711 - 29999 KHz)
- Single Side Band (SSB) and Wide-Narrow Bandwidth Switch
- 700 Memory Programmable Presets
- FM Station Automatic Tuning Storage (ATS) provides automatic acquisition of the strongest stations in your area
- Full-featured world time zone Clock, Sleep Timer, 4 Programmable Alarm Timers and Weekday View Display
- Internally recharges Ni-MH battery (not included)

Etón E10
AM/FM/Shortwave Radio

Now, intelligence meets performance in the E10. With 550 programmable memories, manual and auto scan, precision tuning and alarm clock features, the E10 provides the sophisticated tools for listening to news, sports, and music from around the world.

- FM Frequency Range: 87 – 108 MHz (For North America); 76 – 108 MHz (For Japan)
- Shortwave Frequency Range: 1711 – 29999KHz
- SW IF SET feature, shifts the intermediate frequency to minimize interference during shortwave reception
- Direct Keypad Frequency Entry
- Digital Tuning Knob With Lock Feature
- 550 Programmable Memories

Etón E100
AM/FM/Shortwave Radio

The E100 fits full-sized features into your palm or pocket. This little marvel is packed with all the latest radio features you want.

- Full featured Digital Tuner in extremely small size
- Shortwave – 1711-29.995 KHz

- FM 87.0 – 108.0MHz; MW 520 - 1710
- Manual and Auto-Scan Tuning
- Direct Keypad Frequency Entry
- Manual/Auto Scan to scan the preset stations
- Fine-tuning control knob
- 200 Random Programmable Memories
- Memory Page Customizing
- FM-Stereo/Signal Strength/Power Level Indicators

Select Models Available at:

etón®
RE.INVENTING RADIO
www.etoncorp.com

Etón S350DL
AM/FM/Shortwave Radio

- AM/FM/Shortwave Radio reception
- Highly sensitive and selective analog tuner circuitry
- Digital clock with selectable 12/24 hour format
- Low-pass filter for shortwave and AM reception
- Available in three colors, Black, Silver and Metallic Red
- Variable, independent bass and treble control
- AM/SW Frequency lock feacture

Etón FR250
AM/FM/Shortwave Radio, Flashlight, and Cell Phone Charger

Stay informed and prepared for emergencies with this self-powered 3-in-1 radio, flashlight and cell-phone charger — no batteries required. The Hand-Crank Power Generator gives you unlimited power when you need it most.

- Nine Band Tuning – receives AM, FM and 7 shortwave bands
- Built-in power generator recharges the internal rechargeable Ni-MH battery and cell phone batteries
- Emergency siren
- Cell-phone charger output jack 3.5mm (various cell phone plug tips included)
- Incorporates a fine-tuning control knob super-imposed on the main tuning control knob

Etón FR300
AM/FM Radio with NOAA, TV VHF, Flashlight, and Cell Phone Charger

This all-in-one unit offers functionality and versatility that makes it ideal for emergencies. The FR300 provides you with radio, light, and cell phone battery life when you need it most.

- AM and FM, TV1 and TV2 - VHF channels 2-13
- NOAA weather – all 7 channels plus "Alert"
- 3 LED light system with emergency flash
- Cell-phone charger output jack 3.5mm (various cell phone plug tips included)
- Crank-charge system charges built-in rechargeable battery
- Can be powered with all batteries removed, by continuous cranking

Select Models Available at:

RE_INVENTING RADIO
www.etoncorp.com

weekday. Weekends, it's replaced by Chinese ethnic and popular music.

☞ RECOMMENDED: "China Roots" and "Voices from Other Lands."

Eastern North America: 0000–0100 on 6020 and 9570 kHz; 0100–0200 on 6005 (winter), 6020, 9570 and (summer) 9790 kHz; 0300–0400 on 9690 and 9790 kHz; 0400–0500 on 6020 (summer), 6080 (summer) and (winter) 6190 kHz; 0500–0600 on 5960 (winter), 6020 (summer) and 6190 kHz; 1000–1100 summer on 6040 kHz; 1100–1200 winter on 5960 kHz and summer on 6040 kHz; 1100–1200 summer on 11750 kHz; 1200–1300 winter on 9560 kHz; 1300–1400 on 9570, 9650 (summer), 15230 (winter) and (summer) 15260 kHz; 1400–1500 winter on 15230 kHz; 2300–2400 on 5990, 6040 (winter), 6145 (summer), 11970 (winter) and (summer) 13680 kHz.

Western North America: 0100–0200 on 6005 (winter), 9580 and (summer) 9790 kHz; 0300–0400 on 9690 and 9790 kHz; 0400–0500 on 6020 (summer), 6080 (summer) and (winter) 6190 kHz; 0500–0600 5960 (winter), 6020 (summer) and 6190 kHz; 0600–0700 winter on 6115 kHz; 1100–1200 summer on 11750 kHz; 1300–1400 on 9650 (summer), 15230 (winter) and (summer) 15260 kHz; 1400–1500 on 13740 and (winter) 15230 kHz; 1500–1600 on 13740 kHz; 2300–2400 winter on 11970 kHz, and summer on 13680 kHz.

Europe: 0000–0100 on 7130, 7345 (winter) and (summer) 9725 kHz; 0100–0200 winter on 7130 and 7345 kHz, and summer on 9410 and 9725 kHz; 0700–0900 on 11785 and 17490 kHz; 0900–1100 on 17490 kHz; 1100–1300 on 13650 (summer), 13665 (winter), 13790 (from 1200) and 17490 kHz; 1300–1400 on 13610 and 13790 kHz; 1400–1500 on 9795 (winter), 11765 (winter) 13610 and (summer) 13710 and 13790 kHz; 1500–1600 winter on 9435 and 9525 kHz, and summer on 11965 and 13640 kHz; 1600–1700 winter on 7255, 9435 and 9525 kHz, and summer on 11940, 11965 and 13760 kHz; 1700–1800 winter on 6100 and 7255 kHz, and summer on 9695, 11940 and 13760 kHz; 1800–1900 summer on 9600,

11940 and 13760 kHz; 1900–2000 summer on 11940 kHz; 2000–2200 on 5960, 7190, 7285, 9490 (winter), 9600 and (summer) 9800 kHz; 2200–2300 winter on 7170 kHz, and summer on 7175 kHz.

Middle East: 0500–0600 on 7220 (winter), 11710 (summer), 15285 (winter) and 17505 kHz; 0600–0700 on 11710 (summer), 11750 (winter), 11870 (summer), 15140 (summer), 15285 (winter) and 17505 kHz; 1900–2000 on 7295 and 9435 (or 9440) kHz; 2000–2100 on 7295 and 9440 kHz.

Southern Africa: 1400–1600 on 13685 and 17630 kHz; 1600–1800 on 6100, 9570 and 11900 kHz; 2000–2130 on 11640 and 13630 kHz.

East Asia: 0000–0100 winter on 5915 kHz, and summer on 13750 kHz; 0300–0500 winter on 9460, 13620 and 15120 kHz, and summer on 13750, 15120 and 15785 kHz; 0800–1000 winter on 9415 kHz, and summer on 11620 kHz; 1000–1100 winter on 5955, 7135 and 7215 kHz, and summer on 11610, 11635 and 13620 kHz; 1100–1600 on 5955 kHz; 2200–2300 winter on 5915 kHz, and summer on 9590 kHz; 2300–2400 winter on 11900 kHz, and summer on 11685 kHz.

Southeast Asia: 0000–0100 winter on 11650 and 11885 kHz, and summer on 11885 and 15115 kHz; 0100–0200 winter on 11650 and 11885 kHz, and summer on 15115 and 15785 kHz; 0600–0800 on 13645 (winter), 13660 (summer) and 17710 kHz; 1000–1200 on 13590 and 13720 kHz; 1200–1300 on 9730 and 11980 kHz; 1300–1400 on 9730, 9870 and 11980 kHz; 1400–1500 on 9560 (winter) and 9870 kHz; 1500–1600 on 7325 and 9870 kHz.

Australasia: 0900–1100 on 15210 and 17690 kHz; 1200–1400 on 9760 and 11760 kHz.

China (Taiwan)

Though small in comparison to its neighbor across the strait, **Radio Taiwan International** is widely heard. Powerful relay facilities in Europe and North America help it to project Taiwan and its culture to a wider overseas audience.

☞ RECOMMENDED: "Jade Bells and Bamboo Pipes."

North America: (East and Central) 0200–0300 on 5950 and 9680 kHz; *(West)* 0300–0400 and 0700–0800 on 5950 kHz.

Europe: 1800–1900 on 3965 kHz; and 2200–2300 winter on 9355 kHz, replaced summer by 15600 kHz.

Middle East: There is nothing specifically targeted to the Mideast, but try the 2200 broadcast to Europe.

Southern Africa: 1700–1800 winter on 11850 kHz, and summer on 15690 kHz.

Asia: (East) 0100–0200 on 15465 kHz, and 1200–1300 on 7130 kHz; *(Southeast)* 0100–0200 on 11875 kHz, 0300–0400 on 15320 kHz, 0800–0900 on 11610 kHz, 1100–1200 on 7445 kHz, and 1400–1500 on 15265 kHz; *(South)* 1600–1700 on 11550 kHz.

Australasia: 0800–0900 on 9610 kHz.

Taiwan may be simply an island, but Radio Taiwan International booms in worldwide. Carlson Wong hosts RTI's "Jade Bells and Bamboo Pipes." RTI

Japan

With a global network of relay transmitters, **Radio Japan** is one of the easiest stations to pick up. Its programs focus on events in East Asia, as well as Japanese life and culture.

RECOMMENDED: "Japan and the World 44 Minutes."

Eastern North America: 0000–0100 on 6145 kHz, and 1000–1200 on 6120 kHz, both via the Canadian relay at Sackville, New Brunswick.

Western North America: 0100–0200 on 17825 kHz; 0500–0600 on 6110 kHz; 0600–0700 winter on 11690 kHz, and summer on 13630 kHz; 1500–1600 on 9505 kHz; 1600–1700 summer on 9535 kHz; 1700–1800 on 9535 kHz; and 2100–2200 on 17825 kHz. Listeners in Hawaii can tune in at 0600–0700 on 17870 kHz, and 2100–2200 on 21670 kHz.

Europe: 0500–0600 on 5975 kHz; 0500–0700 on 7230 kHz; 1000–1100 on 17585 kHz; 1700–1800 on 11970 kHz; and 2100–2200 on 6055 (summer), 6090 (winter) and 6180 kHz.

Middle East: 0100–0200 on 5960 (summer), 6030 (winter) and 17560 kHz; and 1000–1100 on 17720 kHz.

Southern Africa: 1700–1800 on 15355 kHz.

Asia: 0000–0015 on 13650 and 17810 kHz; 0100–0200 on 11860, 15325, 17810 and 17845 kHz; 0500–0600 on 15195 and 17810 kHz; 0600–0700 on 11840 kHz; 0600–0700 on 11715, 11740, 11760 and 15195 kHz; 1000–1200 on 9695 and 11730 kHz; 1400–1600 on 6190 (from 1500), 7200, and (winter) 9875 or (summer) 11730 kHz. Transmissions to Asia are often heard in other parts of the world, as well.

Australasia: 0100–0200 on 17685 kHz; 0300–0400 on 21610 kHz; 0500–0700 and 1000–1100 on 21755 kHz; 1400–1500 on 11840 kHz; and 2100–2200 on 6035 kHz.

NORTH AMERICA
Canada

Radio Canada International is heard well in Europe, Asia and Africa, thanks in part to enhanced overseas relays.

Radio Canada International includes programs from its CBC parent organization. Among them is "Quirks and Quarks," where Bob McDonald illuminates science issues. RCI

Ironically, not everything from RCI is written for a foreign audience. Its most enjoyable shows often originate from the domestic networks of its parent organization, the Canadian Broadcasting Corporation.

☞ RECOMMENDED: "Quirks and Quarks" and "The Vinyl Café."

North America: The morning broadcast is beamed to the eastern, central and southern United States at 1400–1700 winter on 9515, 13655 and 17820 kHz; and 1300–1600 summer on 9515, 13655 and 17800 kHz. The evening schedule is more complicated: 2300–2400 (eastern U.S., and one hour earlier in summer) on 6100 (or 6195) kHz; 0000–0200 year-round (eastern and southern U.S.) on 9755 kHz; and 0100–0200 summer only (central and western U.S.) on 13710 kHz.

Europe: 2100–2200 winter on 5850 and 9770 kHz; and 2000–2100 summer on 5850, 7235, 11765 and 15325 kHz.

Middle East: Try 2100–2200 winter on 5850 kHz, and 2000–2100 summer on 11765 kHz.

Southern Africa: Try 1800–1900 winter (summer in the Southern Hemisphere) on 17740 kHz; and midyear on 13730 kHz.

Asia: (East) 1200–1300 winter on 7105 and 9665 kHz; summer on 9660 and 15170 kHz. *(Southeast)* 0000–0100 winter on 9880 kHz, and summer on 11700 kHz; 1200–1300 winter on 9665 kHz, and summer on 15170 kHz; *(South)* 0000–0100 on 5970, 9560 and 11780 kHz; and 1500–1600 winter on 9635, 11870 and 11975 kHz, and summer on 11675, 15360 and 17720 kHz.

United States

Few would expect an inspirational broadcaster lacking government largesse to be heard on all continents—especially in English. Yet, **Family Radio** has achieved that goal, serving as America's religious ambassador to the world. Its transmitters in Okeechobee, Florida target Europe and the Americas, while relays in Europe, the Mideast, South Africa and Asia complete its global reach.

North America: (East) 0000–0100 winter on 6085 kHz, and summer on 6065 kHz; 0100–0445 on 6065 kHz; 0400–0600 and 0700–1100 on 6855 kHz; 1000–1245 winter on 6890 kHz, and summer on 5950 kHz; 1300–1600 winter on 11855 kHz, and summer on 11910 kHz; 1400–1500 and 1600–1700 on 13695 kHz; 1700–2000 on 13690 (or 13695) kHz; *(Central)* 0000–0445 on 9505 kHz; 0600–0700 on 9680 kHz; 0700–1045 winter on 7455 kHz; 0700–1245 summer on 5985 kHz; 1100–1345 winter on 7780 kHz; 1300–1400 on 11830 and (summer) 11865 kHz; 1400–1500 summer on 11830 kHz; 1400–1645 winter on 11565 kHz; 1500–1545 on 11830 and (summer) 11865 kHz; 1800–2145 winter on 17535 kHz, and summer on 13800 kHz; *(West)* 0100–0200 summer on 11835 kHz; 0200–0300 winter on 9525 kHz; 0300–0345 summer on 11835 kHz; 0400–0500 and 0700–0800 on 9715 kHz; 0800–0845 on 5950 kHz; 0900–1145 winter on 5950 kHz, and summer on 9755 kHz; 1200–1345 winter on 11970 kHz;

1200–1645 summer on 17750 kHz; 1400–1545 winter on 17760 kHz; 1700–2145 winter on 17555 kHz, and summer on 17795 kHz.

Europe: 0400–0500 on 7780 kHz; 0500–0600 winter on 7520 kHz, and summer on 9355 kHz; 0600–0700 winter on 7780 and 11530 kHz, and summer on 7780 and 11580 kHz; 0700–0800 on 7780 kHz; 1600–1700 on 18980 and 21455 kHz; 1700–1800 on 3955 (winter), 18980 and 21455 kHz; 1900–2000 on 3955 (summer), 15565 (winter), 18930 (summer) and 18980 kHz; 2000–2100 summer on 7360, 17750 and 18980 kHz; 2000–2200 winter on 5745, 6855 and 7300 kHz; 2100–2200 summer on 7360, 11565 and 18980 kHz.

Middle East: 1800–1900 winter on 7240 and 7345 kHz, and summer on 7345 and 13780 kHz.

Southern Africa: 1900–2100 on 3230 kHz, and 2100–2200 on 6045 kHz.

Asia: (East) 0900–1100 on 9450 kHz; 1400–1500 winter on 7535 kHz, and summer on 12150 kHz; *(South)* 0100–0200 on 15195 kHz; 1300–1500 on 7155 (winter), 9415 (summer) and 11560 kHz; 1500–1600 on 6280 and (winter) 12015 or (summer) 15520 kHz; 1600–1700 winter on 12010 kHz, and summer on 11850 kHz. Some of the broadcasts for South Asia are also heard in Australia, especially to the west.

Family Radio is heard by millions worldwide, thanks in part to WYFR transmission engineer Ed Marcy and his wife Ev, the station secretary. Azimuth the guard cat saves rodents from electrocution.

Curtis Jarvis, WYFR

The **Voice of America**, once led by the likes of Edward R. Murrow, had enormous worldwide influence from World War II until the end of the elder President Bush's administration. Since then, a new generation of elected leaders and management has come into power. Raised on jukebox radio and advertising, they have chipped away at the station's core strength of credible information.

Nevertheless, this is the official voice of the world's only superpower and merits being heard. Contrary to what is often reported, it is not against the law for Americans to listen to the VOA.

☞ RECOMMENDED: "Music Time in Africa."

North America: The VOA can still be heard in North America, albeit far less than it used to be. Try the African Service at 0400–0500 on 9575 kHz; 0400–0700 winter on 6045 kHz; 0500–0630 winter on 6035 kHz; 1900–2100 winter on 15240 kHz, and summer on 15445 kHz.

Southern Africa: 0300–0430 winter on 9885 kHz; 0300–0600 on 4930 and (midyear) 15580 kHz; 1400–1600 on 4830 kHz; 1600–1800 on 4930 (till 1700 weekdays), 6080 and (winter) 15580 kHz; and 1800–2100 on 4930 (from 1830 weekdays), 6080 and (winter) 15580 kHz.

East and Southeast Asia: 1200–1300 summer on 6160 and 11750 kHz; 1200–1400 on 9645, 9760 and (winter) 11705 and 13625 kHz; 1400–1500 on 9760, 11705 (winter) and (summer) 15185 kHz; 2200–2400 on 7215 (summer), 11725 (summer), 15185, 15205 (winter), 15290 and (winter) 17740 kHz.

Australasia: 1200–1400 on 9645 kHz; 2200–2400 winter on 15185 and 17740 kHz, and midyear on 11725 kHz.

"Music Time in Africa" hosts Matthew Lavoie and Leo Sarkisian. VOA

Prepared by Tony Jones and the staff of PASSPORT TO WORLD BAND RADIO.

AM/FM/Shortwave Radio, Flashlight, and Cell Phone Charger

Stay informed and prepared for emergencies with this self-powered 3-in-1 radio, flashlight and cell-phone charger — no batteries required. The Hand-Crank Power Generator gives you unlimited power for AM/FM Radio, 7 International Shortwave Bands, Built-in Flashlight, and cell phone battery life when you need it most.

- Nine Band Tuning – receives AM, FM and 7 shortwave bands
- Built-in power generator recharges the internal recharge-able Ni-MH battery and cell phone batteries
- Earphone jack – 3.5mm earphone socket
- Emergency siren
- Built-in Cell-phone charger
- Can be operated on three AA size batteries (not included)
- Pleasant audio from the 2 1/2 inch speaker
- All antennas built-in: telescopic antenna for FM and SW; internal ferrite bar antenna for AM
- Power Source: Built-In Rechargeable Ni-MH Battery Pack; 3 AA Batteries (not included); Crank power alone; AC Adapter (included); AC Adapter recharges built-in Ni-MH battery pack
- Dimensions: 6-1/2"W x 6"H x 2-1/2"D (168 x 155 x 64 mm)
- Weight: 1 lb. 3 oz. (539 g)

Also Available in:

FR200

AM/FM/Shortwave Radio and Flashlight

FR350

AM/FM/Shortwave Radio with Flashlight, and Cell phone Charger

Without the need for batteries, this self-powered 2-in-1 radio and flashlight helps you stay informed and prepared for emergencies. The Hand-Crank Power Generator gives you power for AM/FM radio, access to 12 international Shortwave bands, and a built-in LED flashlight. So the FR200 is not only perfect for emergencies, but also for camping, hiking, traveling, or just relaxing in the backyard.

- 14 Band Tuning – receives AM, FM and 12 shortwave bands
- Built-in power generator recharges the internal rechargeable Ni-MH battery
- Earphone jack – 3.5mm earphone socket
- Incorporates a fine-tuning control knob superimposed on the main tuning control knob
- Built-in white LED light source
- Pleasant audio from the 2 1/2 inch speaker
- All antennas built-in: telescopic antenna for FM and SW; internal ferrite bar antenna for AM
- Power Source: Built-In Rechargeable Ni-MH Battery Pack; 3 AA Batteries (not included); Crank power alone; AC Adapter (not included); AC Adapter recharges built-in Ni-MH battery pack
- Dimensions: 6-1/2"W x 5-3/4"H x 2-1/4"D (168 x 147 x 56 mm)
- Weight: 1 lb. 2 oz. (511 g)

Improved technology, functionality and versatility, the FR350 is ideal for emergencies. The FR350 provides you with a water resistant radio, LED lights, and cell phone charger when you need it most. Using the Hand-Crank Power Generator, charge the internal rechargeable Ni-MH battery pack in times of need.

- AM/FM/Shortwave
- Water resistant body
- Hand Crank Power Generator
- 3 LED light system with emergency flash
- Emergency siren
- Built-in Cell phone charger
- Power Source: Hand-Crank Power Generator with rechargeable battery pack, 3 AA batteries (not included) or AC adaptor (included)
- Dimensions: 4.5"H x 8.6"W x 2"D (114 x 220 x 50 mm)
- Weight: 1.5 lb (680 g)

Also Available in:

Also Available in:

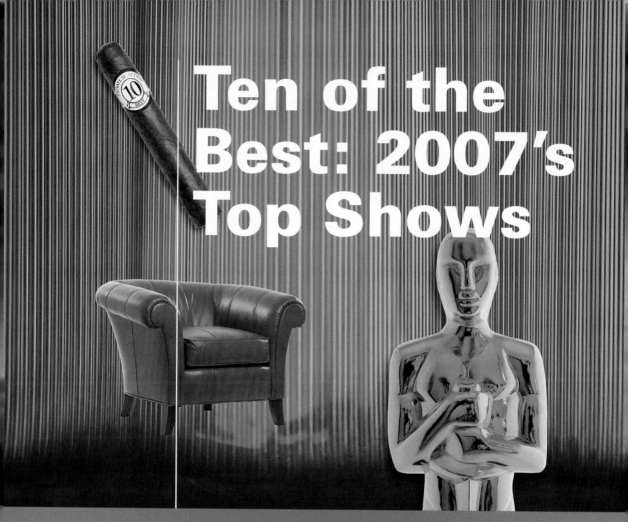

Ten of the Best: 2007's Top Shows

Unlike ordinary radio, world band offers real variety. Here are ten top teasers that you won't find anywhere else.

Times and days are in World Time (UTC). "Winter" and "summer" refer to the Northern Hemisphere, where summer is midyear—July and so on.

"Jazz Show"
Voice of Russia

Russia's thriving jazz scene includes superb musicians, but few are known abroad despite their talent. So, it's three cheers to the Voice of Russia for allowing the rest of us to appreciate them.

Variety is the soul of jazz, and that's what you get from "Jazz Show."

There's neatly timed syncopation, dusty Russian recordings of Benny Goodman, folk-jazz fusion— even a jazz version of Joaquín Rodrigo's "Concierto de Aranjuez." This is jazz pushing the boundaries, and it makes for exciting listening. Unsurprisingly, it's also the station's top-rated show.

North America: Winter, 0231 Wednesday (Tuesday evening local American date) on 7180, 7250, 15425, 15475 and 15595 kHz; summer, one hour earlier on 7250, 9665 (7180 kHz in autumn) and 15555 kHz.

Europe: Winter, 2031 Wednesday on 6145, 7290 and 7330 kHz; and 2131 Friday on 7330 and 7390 kHz; summer, 1931 Wednesday on 7195, 7310, 9890 and 12070 kHz; and 2031 Friday on 7195, 9890, 12070 and 15455 (or 11980) kHz

Middle East: Winter, 1631 Monday on 9470 kHz; summer, one hour earlier on 11985 kHz.

Southeast Asia: Winter, 1531 Wednesday on 6205 and 9660 kHz; summer, 1431 Wednesday on 7165, 12055, 15605 and 17645 kHz; and 1531 Monday on 9660 kHz.

Australasia: Winter, 0731 Wednesday on 17665 and 17805 kHz; 0831 Thursday on 17495, 17665 and 17805 kHz; and 0931 Friday on 17495 and 17665 kHz; summer, 0631 Wednesday on 17635 and 21590 kHz; and 0731 Thursday and 0831 Friday on 17495, 17635 and 21790 kHz.

> Russia's once-hidden archives abound with musical rarities.

"Heart and Soul"
BBC World Service

Any program which takes a hard look at religion and the religious has to tread lightly, but "Heart and Soul" does it with aplomb. It's not afraid

Carl Watts, host of "Jazz Show," and Elena Biryukova, editor. The program spotlights creative talent otherwise rarely heard outside Russia.   VoR

RFE-RL Chief Broadcast Engineer, Laura Mir. She came to Radio Free Asia and RFE-RL after work at the Smithsonian Institution and Victoria's Secret. Her musician/engineer husband Abner is also employed at RFE-RL Engineering.
RFE-RL

to tackle controversial topics, such as the issue of Jesus' relationship with Mary Magdalene, or dicey subjects like nuns donating their brains to science. There's also delving into legends like Gaucho Gil, the Argentinean cowboy who became an unofficial saint for seekers of justice.

All transmissions are Sunday, World Time.

North America: North America is no longer a target for the BBC World Service, but "Heart and Soul" has two slots in the service for the Caribbean: 1132 winter on 5875 and 6130 kHz, summer on 6130 and 9660 kHz; and 2232 winter on 5975 and 9660 kHz, summer on 5975 and 13765 kHz.

Europe: 0832 (one hour earlier in summer) on 6195 and 9410 kHz; 1832 winter on 6195 and 9410 kHz; and 1732 summer on 9410, 12095 and 15485 kHz.

Middle East: 0432 on 9410 and 11760 kHz; and 0832 and 1232 on 11760 and 15575 kHz (all times are one hour earlier in summer).

Southern Africa: 0832 (one hour earlier mid-year) on 6190, 11940 and (winter) 21470 kHz.

East and Southeast Asia: 0232 (one hour earlier in summer) on 6195 (summer), 15280 (or 15285) and 15360 kHz.

"Quirks and Quarks"
CBC/Radio Canada International

Science shows need to be unusually interesting to appeal to a general audience.

Few fit the bill as well as "Quirks and Quarks." Produced by RCI's parent organization, the CBC, and hosted by Bob McDonald, the show can be as irreverent as it is knowledgeable. Gay genes, running bats and ultrasonic gophers might appear to be lightweight topics, but don't be fooled—"Quirks and Quarks" takes its science seriously.

North America: Winter, 1605 Saturday on 9515, 13655 and 17820 kHz; summer, one hour earlier on 9515, 13655 and 17800

Asia: (East) 1205 Sunday, winter on 7105 and 9665 kHz, and summer on 9660 and 15170 kHz; *(Southeast)* 1205 Sunday, winter on 9665 kHz, and summer on 15170 kHz.

"China Roots"
China Radio International

"China Roots" was originally for English-speaking residents in Beijing and only aired on FM. Gradually it made its way to CRI's world band schedule, and is now heard several times on Saturday.

Some songs are instinctively pleasing to the Western ear. Yet, at other times it's ethnic music at its rawest—like spicy Szechuan food, it can take some getting used to. This makes the show a treasure chest for those interested in authentic Chinese music, while others can pick and choose.

All transmissions are aired Saturday in the target area.

North America: 1110 winter on 5960 kHz, and summer on 6040 and 11750 kHz; and 0110 (Sunday World Time) on 6020 and 9570 kHz. The 1110 winter broadcast is only for eastern North America.

Europe: 1010 on 21490 kHz; 1110 on 13650 (summer), 13665 (winter) and 21490 kHz; 1710 winter on 6100 and 7255 kHz; and summer on 9695, 11940 and 13760 kHz; and 2200 winter on 7170 kHz, replaced summer by 7175 kHz.

Southern Africa: 1710 on 6100, 9570 and 11900 kHz.

Australasia: 1010 on 15210 and 17690 kHz.

"The Instant Guide"
BBC World Service

Good things come in small quantities, and "The Instant Guide" fits the mold.

The diminished BBC World Service has become increasingly dependent on stringers, so in-depth reporting has taken a hit. Fortunately, some bright soul came up with a way to turn lemon into lemonade: a short program giving background information on one of the week's main international news stories. "The Instant Guide" explains it all in ten lean minutes.

North America: There are no specific broadcasts to *North America*, but the Caribbean has its slot at 2132 Saturday on 9660 (winter), 11675 and (summer) 13765 kHz. In western North America, try 1232 Sunday (one hour earlier in summer) on 9740 kHz, via the BBC's East Asia stream.

Europe: Winter, 1832 Saturday on 6195 and 9410 kHz; and 2050 Sunday on 6195 kHz; summer, 1732 Saturday on 9410, 12095 and 15485 kHz; and 1950 Sunday on 6195 and 9410 kHz.

Middle East: 1132 Saturday and 0732 Sunday (one hour earlier in summer) on 11760 and 15575 kHz; 1950 winter on 12095 kHz; and 1850 summer on 12045 kHz.

Southern Africa: 0732 Saturday on 6190 and 11940 kHz; 1032 Sunday on 6190, 11940 and 21470 kHz; and 1950 on 3255 and 6190 kHz. All transmissions are one hour earlier in summer.

Gudrun Heise, editor of Deutsche Welle's cultural "Arts on the Air," prepares for the next program. DW

East and *Southeast Asia:* 0432 Saturday on 15280 (or 15285), 15360, 17760 and 21660 kHz; 0732 Saturday on 11955, 15360, 17760 and 21660 kHz; and 1232 Sunday on 6195, 9740 and 11750 (or 17760) kHz. All transmissions are one hour earlier in summer.

Australasia: 0732 Saturday on 11955 kHz; and 1232 Sunday on 9740 kHz. Both transmissions are one hour earlier midyear.

"Folk Box"
Voice of Russia

The rise of interest in world music has forced much traditional folk music out of public view. Nevertheless, its embers continue to be stoked. Some of the most compelling folk music is found in Russia, so it is no surprise that the Voice of Russia's long-running "Folk Box" maintains the tradition. What may surprise is that the show remains a perennial favorite among world band listeners.

The balalaika and accordion feature prominently, but often it's the human voice which occupies center stage—from curiosities like Tuvan throat singing to songs so sublime they make the spine tingle.

North America: Winter, 0231 Tuesday (Monday evening local American date) on 7180, 7250, 15425, 15475 and 15595 kHz; and 0531 Thursday on 7150, 7180, 7350, 9840, 12010 and 15425 kHz; summer, 0131 Tuesday on 7250, 9665 (7180 kHz in autumn) and 15555 kHz; and 0431 Thursday on 9665 (7180 kHz in autumn), 9860, 9880, 15425, 15455, 15555 and 15595 kHz.

Europe: Winter, 1631 Thursday on 6130 and 7320 kHz; 2131 Thursday on 7330 and 7390 kHz; and 1831 Friday on 5950, 7290 and 7320 kHz; summer, 1531 Thursday on 7370, 12040 (or 9810) and 15455 (or 11980) kHz; 2031 Thursday on 7195, 9890, 12070 and 15455 (or 11980) kHz; and 1731 Friday on 7370, 9890 and 11675 (or 7320) kHz.

Middle East: Winter, 1631 Thursday on 9470 kHz; and 1831 Friday on 7360 kHz; summer, 1531 Thursday and 1731 Friday on 11985 kHz.

Olga Shapovalova, editor of "Folk Box." Olga was among the prize winners of the Seventh International Radio Festival held in Iran in spring 2006.   VoR

Southern Africa: Winter, 1831 Friday on 11510 kHz; summer, one hour earlier on the same frequency.

Southeast Asia: Winter, 1531 Monday on 6205 and 9660 kHz; summer, 1431 Monday on 7165, 12055, 15605 and 17645 kHz; and 1531 Thursday on 9660 kHz.

Australasia: Winter, 0731 Saturday on 17665 and 17805 kHz; 0831 Tuesday on 17495, 17665 and 17805 kHz; and 0931 Thursday on 17495 and 17665 kHz; summer, 0631 Saturday on 17635 and 21590 kHz; and 0731 Tuesday and 0831 Thursday on 17495, 17635 and 21790 kHz.

"A Good Life"
Radio Netherlands

Developing countries and areas of conflict are home territory for "A Good Life." From combat zones in rural Colombia to the urban slums of Zimbabwe, it focuses on human and social issues. Its reports can be revealing, too, as with health tourism to India caused by deteriorating social services

Anna Yeadell, producer of Radio Netherlands' "A Good Life," in Botswana. It is one of the standout programs on the air.   RN

in Europe. Well done and thought-provoking, it's one of world band's best.

North America: (East) Winter, 1227 Friday on 9890 kHz, and 0027 Saturday (Friday evening local American date) on 6165 kHz; summer, 1127 Friday on 11675 kHz, and 0027 Saturday on 9845 kHz; *(Central)* 0127 Saturday winter on 6165 kHz, and summer on 9845 kHz; *(West)* 0527 Saturday (one hour earlier in summer) on 6165 kHz.

There's nothing for *Europe* or the *Middle East*, but *Southern Africa* has three slots: 1827 Friday on 6020 kHz, 2000 Friday on 7120 kHz, and 1900 Tuesday on 6020 kHz.

Asia: (East and Southeast) 1027 winter on 6040, 9795 and 12065 kHz; and summer on 12065, 13710 and 13820 kHz; *(South)* 1430 Friday and 1500 Tuesday, winter on 9345, 12080 and 15595 kHz; and summer on 9345, 9890 and 11835 kHz.

Australasia: 0527 winter—summer in the Southern Hemisphere—on 11710 kHz, and 0727 midyear on 9700 kHz. The 1027 airing for East and Southeast Asia is also heard within the region.

"Jade Bells and Bamboo Pipes"
Radio Taiwan International

Taiwanese traditional music is pleasant and exotic, so Radio Taiwan International has long showcased it to appreciative foreign listeners.

"Jade Bells and Bamboo Pipes" is RTI's longest-running program—its most popular, too. There's plenty of variety, from aboriginal to Buddhist and beyond, so it doesn't wear thin.

All transmissions are Wednesday World Time

North America: (East and Central) 0230 (Tuesday evening local American date) on 5950 and 9680 kHz; *(West)* 0330 and 0730 on 5950 kHz.

Europe: 1830 on 3965 kHz; 2230 winter on 9355 kHz, and summer on 15600 kHz.

Southern Africa: 1730 winter on 11850 kHz and summer on 15690 kHz.

Asia: (East) 0130 on 15465 kHz; and 1230 on 7130 kHz; *(Southeast)* 0130 on 11875 kHz, 0330 on 15320 kHz, 0830 on 11610 kHz, 1130 on 7445 kHz, and 1430 on 15265 kHz; *(South)* 1630 on 11550 kHz.

Australasia: 0830 on 9610 kHz.

"Arts on the Air"
Deutsche Welle

Germany is heavily steeped in *die Kultur*, so it's hardly surprising that Deutsche Welle offers a quality arts program.

"Arts on the Air" looks at culture in general. Yet, it's at its best when delving into the past and narrating the personal lives of authors and composers. This is elite stuff, not competition for "Survivor," but culture vultures get plenty of red meat to feed on.

North America: 2130 Tuesday, winter on 9615 and 11690 kHz, and summer on 11865 and 15205 kHz. Nominally beamed to West Africa at this hour, but also heard in the eastern and southern United States and the Caribbean.

Europe: 0730, 0930 and 1430 Wednesday on 6140 kHz.

"Arts on the Air" host Breandáin O'Shea.   DW

"Songs from Russia"
Voice of Russia

"Songs from Russia" appeals more to over-40s than to tenderfoot audiences sought out by commercial radio. It spotlights music from the past, going back almost a century, and oozes nostalgia. For those who yearn for the talent and spirit of yesteryear, it's a treat that stands apart from commodity fare.

North America: Winter, 0331 Sunday (Saturday evening local American date) on 7180, 7250, 15425, 15475 and 15595 kHz; summer, one hour earlier on 9665 (7180 kHz in autumn), 9860, 15555 and 15595 kHz.

Europe: Winter, 2131 Monday on 7330 and 7390 kHz; and 1631 Friday on 6130 and 7320 kHz; summer, 2031 Monday on 7195, 9890, 12070 and 15455 (or 11980) kHz; and 1531 Friday on 7370, 12040 (or 9810) and 15455 (or 11980) kHz.

Middle East: Winter, 1631 Friday on 9470 kHz; summer, one hour earlier on 11985 kHz.

Southeast Asia: 1531 Friday, summer only, on 9660 kHz. *Australasia:* Winter, 0831 Sunday on 17495, 17665 and 17805 kHz; midyear, one hour earlier on 17495, 17635 and 21790 kHz.

> "Songs from Russia" is unabashedly for over-40s.

Prepared by Tony Jones and the staff of PASSPORT TO WORLD BAND RADIO.

"Jade Bells and Bamboo Pipes" host Carlson Wong. This multifaceted offering has long been Radio Taiwan International's most popular show.   RTI

Etón E1

The E1 is the world's first radio to combine AM, FM, and Shortwave technology into one ultra-high-performance unit.

- AM/FM/Shortwave Radio
- 1700 station presets
- Digitally synthesized PLL tuner with synchronous detector
- Passband tuning, selectable bandwidth filters and Selectable Single Sideband (SSB) reception
- Dual Clocks and programmable timers
- Built-In Antenna: telescopic antenna for AM, FM, and Shortwave reception
- External Antenna Connection for the addition of auxiliary antennas
- Calibrated LCD signal strength meter

Etón E5
AM/LW/FM-Stereo/ Shortwave Portable Radio

For the ultimate in portable technology the E5 is the latest edition to the Etón Elite range and demonstrates that form and function can work in harmony.

- AM/LW/FM-Stereo and Full Shortwave Coverage (1711 - 29999 KHz)
- Single Side Band (SSB) and Wide-Narrow Bandwidth Switch
- 700 Memory Programmable Presets
- FM Station Automatic Tuning Storage automatically selects the strongest stations
- Full-featured world time zone Clock, Sleep Timer, 4 Programmable Alarm Timers and Weekday View Display
- Internally recharges Ni-MH battery (not included)

Etón E100
AM/FM/Shortwave Radio

The E100 fits full-sized features into your palm or pocket. This little marvel is packed with all the latest radio features you want.

- Full featured Digital Tuner in extremely small size
- Shortwave – 1711-29.995 KHz
- FM 87.0 – 108.0MHz; MW 520 - 1710
- Manual and Auto-Scan Tuning
- Direct Keypad Frequency Entry
- Fine-tuning control knob
- 200 Random Programmable Memories
- Memory Page Customizing

Select Model Distributed in Europe by:

L&V Laauser & Vohl GmbH
+49 / (0)711 / 4 48 18 - 0 (Germany)

NOVIS
+43 (0) 15266660 (Austria)
+41 (0) 43 355 75 00 (Switzerland)

INTODESIGN
+46 (0) 40 916658 (Sweden)
+45 (0) 20 97 47 21 (Denmark/ Finland)

ANMI electronics
+34 (93) 300 26 18 (Spain)

HI-FI UNITED
+39 0523 716178 (Italy)

www.nevada.co.uk
+44 / (0) 2392 313090 (United Kingdom)

etón®
RE-INVENTING RADIO
www.etoncorp.com

E1100
AM/FM/Shortwave Radio

ES350DL
AM/FM/Shortwave Field Radio

Small enough to fit into your pocket, yet strong enough to receive 10 Shortwave bands, the E1100 makes the perfect travel companion. Providing AM/FM and Shortwae reception, this little marvel is sure to keep you connected to both local and international news and music wherever you are.

- AM, FM-stereo and 10 Shortwave bands
- Analog tuning with digital frequency and clock
- Alarm
- Light and Snooze
- Headphone-Stereo
- AC Adapter - 3VDC, neg. polarity (not included)
- Accessories: Owner's Manual, Pouch
- Dimensions: 5.12"Wx3.15"Hx1.14"D (126mm Wx 80mm Hx 29mm D)
- Weight: 7 oz. (0.2 kg)

The S350DL blends the best of yesterday and today. With the look of a retro field radio sporting a rugged body and military-style controls—the ES350DL also features today's innovation for excellent AM, FM, and Shortwave reception and a large, full-range speaker for clear sound.

- AM/SW Frequency lock freature
- AM 530-1710 KHz, FM 88-108 MHz
- Shortwave – continuous Coverage from 3 to 28 MHz. This includes 13 international broadcast bands. 11, 13, 15, 16, 19, 22, 25, 31, 41, 49, 60, 75 and 90 meters
- Highly sensitive and selective analog tuner circuitry
- Liquid Crystal Display, LCD, for frequency and clock
- Digital clock with selectable 12/24 hour format
- Wake-up timer (use as radio-play alarm clock)
- Power failure backup feature
- Variable RF Gain Control
- Variable, independent bass and treble control
- Left/Right line level outputs (stereo in FM)
- Stereo/mono switch
- Strap type carrying handle
- Built in telescopic antenna for FM and shortwave
- Built in ferrite bar antenna for AM
- Jacks for supplementary AM, FM and shortwave antennas
- Power Source: 4 D Batteries (not included) or AC Adapter (included)
- Dimensions: 10-3/4"W x 7"H x 3-1/2"D (272 x 175 x 89 mm)
- Weight: 3 lb. 2 oz. (1.42 Kg)

How to Choose a World Band Radio

Some electronic products are scarcely more than commodities. With a little common sense you can find what you want.

But not world band receivers, which can vary greatly from model to model. As usual money talks, but even that's a fickle barometer. Fortunately, many perform well and we rate them accordingly. Yet, even among models with comparable star ratings it helps to read the fine print.

Squeezed-in Stations

World band radio offers hundreds of channels, each shoehorned five kilohertz away from the other. That's more crowded than FM and around twice as crammed as mediumwave AM.

It gets worse: Global treks wear down signals, causing fading and reduced strength. To cope with these challenges, a world band radio has
to perform electronic gymnastics. Some succeed, others don't.

This is why PASSPORT REPORTS was created. At International Broadcasting Services we've independently tested hundreds of world band
radios, antennas and accessories since 1977. These evaluations include rigorous hands-on use by listeners, plus specialized lab tests developed over the years. These form the basis of PASSPORT REPORTS, and
for the Full Monty on various popular premium receivers and antennas
there are also Radio Database International White Papers®.

**Know what you want.
Etón's S350DL is popular
for music and news, but
not for faint rarities.**

Four-Point Checklist

✔ **Price.** Want to hear major stations, or do you prefer gentler voices
from exotic lands? Powerful evening signals, or weaker stations by
day? Decide, then choose a radio that slightly surpasses your needs—
this helps ensure against disappointment without spending too much.

Once the novelty of world band wears thin, most people give up on
cheap radios—they're clumsy to tune, often receive poorly and can
sound terrible. That's why we rarely cover analog-readout radios. Yet,
even some models with digital frequency readout can disappoint.

Most find satisfaction with digital-readout portables selling for $65–150
in the United States or £60–130 in the United Kingdom, and having a
rating of ✪✪¾ or more. If you're looking for elite performance, shoot
for a costlier portable rated ✪✪✪¾ or better. If you want bragging
rights, a five-star tabletop or a professional model is *numero uno*.

**Radios must
overcome the
beating taken by
global signals.**

✔ **Location.** Signals are usually strongest around Europe, North Africa
and the Near East; they're almost as good in eastern North America.
Elsewhere in the Americas—or in Hawaii, Australasia or the Middle
East—spring for a receiver with superior sensitivity to weak signals.
Some sort of accessory antenna helps, too.

✔ **Features.** Divide features between those for performance and
those that impact operation (see sidebars), but regard them with a
cynical eye. Radios with relatively few features sometimes outperform
those tricked out with seductive goodies.

PASSPORT'S STANDARDS

At International Broadcasting Services we have been analyzing shortwave equipment
since 1977. Our reviewers, and no one else, write and edit everything in PASSPORT
REPORTS. Our lab tests are performed by an independent laboratory recognized as the
world's leader. (For more on this, see the Radio Database International White Paper,
How to Interpret Receiver Lab Tests and Measurements.)

The review process is completely separate from equipment advertising, which is
not allowed within PASSPORT REPORTS. Our team members may not accept review
fees from manufacturers, nor may they "permanently borrow" radios. International
Broadcasting Services does not manufacture, sell or distribute world band radios or
related hardware.

PERFORMANCE FEATURES

A signal should sound pleasant, not just be audible. To help, some radios have features to ward off unwanted sounds or improve audio quality. Of course, just because a feature exists doesn't mean it functions properly, but PASSPORT REPORTS' team checks this out.

Reception "Musts"

Full world band coverage from 2300-26100 kHz is best, but 3200-21850 kHz is plenty good—even 5730-21850 kHz is usually okay. Less coverage? Look over "Best Times and Frequencies for 2007" elsewhere in PASSPORT to see what's missed.

Synchronous selectable sideband helps knock out adjacent-channel interference and reduce fading distortion. This advanced feature is found on a few portables, as well as most tabletop and professional models. PASSPORT REPORTS indicates which work well.

Especially if a receiver doesn't include synchronous selectable sideband, it benefits from having two or more *bandwidths* to reduce adjacent-channel interference. Some premium models have multiple bandwidths and synchronous selectable sideband—a killer combo.

Double (or multiple) conversion helps reject unwanted disturbances—images, unwanted growls, whistles and dih-dah sounds. Few cheaper models have it.

Spit and Polish

Tone controls are a plus, especially if continuous with separate bass and treble. For world band reception, *single-sideband* (SSB) isn't important, but is essential for utility or "ham" signals. SSB's main use for world band is to hear the American Forces Radio and Television Service.

Look for good coverage, selectivity and image rejection.

Tabletop models flush out stubborn signals, but they're for veterans and are overkill for casual listening. Look for a tunable *notch filter* to zap howls; *passband offset* (also called *passband tuning* and *IF shift*) for superior adjacent-channel rejection and audio contouring, especially in conjunction with synchronous selectable sideband; and multiple *AGC* decay rates. At electrically noisy locations a *noise blanker* is essential, although performance varies greatly.

Digital signal processing (DSP) attempts to enhance reception quality. Until recently it has been much smoke, little fire, but it's improving. Watch for more DSP receivers to appear, but don't worship at their altar.

Digital Radio Mondiale (DRM), a form of digital transmission with good and bad points, is slowly being rolled out for world band. Thus far there have been no DRM-capable receivers offered to the public, just regular receivers that feed a 12 kHz IF to a personal computer to process DRM signals. However, the first genuine DRM portables are scheduled for introduction by early 2007.

With portables an *AC adaptor* reduces operating costs and may improve weak-signal performance. Some are poorly made and cause hum or buzzing, but most are okay. With tabletop models an *inboard AC power supply* is preferable but not essential.

✔ **Where to buy?** Whether you buy in a store, by phone or on the Internet makes little difference. That's because world band receivers don't test well in stores except in the rare showroom with an outdoor antenna. Even then, long-term satisfaction is hard to gauge from a spot test, so check at different times.

One thing you can nail down in a store is ergonomics—how intuitive is the radio to operate? You can also get a thumbnail idea of world band fidelity by listening to mediumwave AM stations or a muscular world band station.

Internet purchases from foreign countries are usually hassle-free, although don't expect enforceable warranties. Too, AC voltages may be inappropriate, and packets are sometimes refused by customs because of trademark and other legal considerations.

CONVENIENCE FEATURES

To find stations quickly, look for *digital frequency readout*, found on virtually all models tested by PASSPORT REPORTS. Too, a *24-hour World Time clock* to know when to tune in; many receivers include them. The best allow time to be read while the frequency is being displayed.

If your radio doesn't include a World Time clock, there are standalone 24-hour clocks and watches. Seconds displayed numerically are a nice touch so you can be alert for station IDs.

Other handy features: direct-access tuning by *keypad* and station *presets* ("memories"); and any combination of a *tuning knob*, up/down *slewing controls* or *"signal-seek" scanning* to search for stations. A few models have handy *one-touch presets* buttons, like a classic car radio. Quick access to *world band segments* (meter bands) is another time saver.

Presets are important because world band stations don't stay on the same frequency all day. Being able to store a station's multiple frequencies makes the station easier to find. With sophisticated receivers, presets should be able to store not only frequency, but also such parameters as bandwidth, mode and AGC.

Useful but less important is an *on/off timer*. Also, look for an *illuminated display* and a good *signal-strength indicator*, either as an analog meter or a digital display.

Travelers like portables with *power-lock switches* or *recessed power buttons* so the radio won't go on by itself in luggage. ☞ The locks on some Chinese portables don't disable display illumination.

If ergonomics stand out, bad or good, PASSPORT REPORTS says so. But few controls doesn't necessarily mean handier operation. Some receivers with many controls are easier to operate than comparable receivers with few controls—especially if operation involves complex software choices.

Tabletop models can run in the four figures, but not always. Palstar's R30 costs little more than a premium portable.

Universal Radio

Portables for 2007

Portables are world band's meat and potatoes. They are handy, affordable and usually do the trick whether at home or away.

In Europe and eastern North America evening signals come in well, so virtually any well-rated portable is okay. Elsewhere or daytime, when broadcasts may be more interesting but weaker, a good portable can be boosted by an accessory antenna.

Digital Broadcasts

So far there's been only one portable for DRM digital broadcasts, but it apparently didn't go into production. Indeed, no portable is even DRM ready—equipped to receive digital world band broadcasts after being connected to a PC.

But if you're experimental, take heart. Modification instructions for some models are at drmrx.org/receiver_mods.html. You'll also need DRM software from www.drmrx.org.

A number of manufacturers plan to release the first crop of DRM portables in 2007. Presumably most will cover world band frequencies.

Three Categories

Think of pocket portables like cellphones, compacts like Palm-type handhelds and large portables like laptop PCs. You can't go wrong with a $150 compact rated at three or more stars, but lesser models can cut that in half or less.

Top end goes for five hundred dollars. That's for near-tabletop performance with satellite reception thrown in—more than you need, but for sure not more than you want.

Friendly skies? Pocket models are ideal, and their limited speaker audio can be overcome with earpieces. Yet, slightly larger "compact-compacts" sometimes perform better, sell for less and are small and light enough for most.

Longwave

The longwave band is still used for domestic broadcasts in Europe, North Africa and Russia. If you live or travel in rural areas there, long-wave coverage may be a plus. Otherwise, forget it.

Fix or Toss?

Portables aren't meant to be friends for life and are priced accordingly. The most robust models are usually not ready for the landfill until a decade or two of use, whereas pedestrian portables may give only a few years of regular service. Rarely are any worth fixing outside warranty except top end models.

If you receive a DOA portable, insist upon an immediate exchange without a restocking fee—manufacturers' repair facilities tend to have a disappointing record. If out-of-warranty service is a priority, consider a tabletop model.

> **Find major updates to the 2007 PASSPORT REPORTS at www.passband.com.**

The Etón E5 is one of several mid-priced compact portables offering solid reception. Because these perform well at home and are handy on trips, they've become popular world band choices.

• **AC adaptor.** Those provided by the manufacturer are usually best and should be free from hum and noise—those that aren't are cited under "Con." Some are multivoltage and operate almost anywhere in the world. ☞ Beware of "switching" type power supplies, as these disrupt radio signals. In principle no radio manufacturer should be offering switching power supplies for use with radios, but it sometimes happens and in California it can be the law. PASSPORT REPORTS points these out.

• **Adjacent-channel rejection—I: *selectivity, bandwidth*.** World band stations are about twice as tightly packed as ordinary mediumwave AM stations. So, they tend to slop over and interfere with each other—DRM digital broadcasts are even worse. Radios with superior selectivity are better at rejecting interference, but at a price: better selectivity also means less high-end ("treble") audio response and muddier sound. So, having more than one bandwidth allows you to choose between tighter selectivity (narrow bandwidth) when it is warranted, and more realistic audio (wide bandwidth) when it is not.

• **Adjacent-channel rejection—II: *synchronous selectable sideband*.** With powerful stations "out in the clear," this has little audible impact. However, for tough catches it improves listening quality by minimizing selective-fading distortion and adjacent-channel interference. *Bonus:* it also helps reduce distortion with fringe mediumwave AM stations at twilight and even at night.

• **Ergonomics.** Some radios are a snap to use because they don't have complicated features. Yet, even sophisticated models can be designed to operate intuitively. Choose accordingly—there's no reason to take the square root and cube it just to hear a radio station.

• **Single-sideband demodulation.** If you are interested in hearing non-broadcast shortwave signals—"hams" and utility stations—single-sideband circuitry is *de rigueur*. Too, the popular low-powered American Forces Radio-Television Service requires this.

• **Speaker audio quality.** Unlike many portatop and tabletop models, few portables have rich, full audio through their speakers. However, some are much better than others, and with a model having line output you can connect amplified PC speakers for pleasant home listening; home FM transmitters, too.

• **Tuning features.** Models with digital frequency readout are so superior to analog that these are now the only radios normally tested by PASSPORT. Look for such handy tuning aids as direct-frequency access via keypad, station presets (programmable channel memories), up-down tuning via tuning knob and/or slew keys, band/segment selection, and signal-seek or other (e.g., presets) scanning. These make the radio easier to tune—no small point, given that a hundred or more channels may be audible at a time.

• **Weak-signal sensitivity.** Sensitivity is important if you live in a weak-signal location or tune exotic or daytime stations. Most portables have enough sensitivity to pull in major stations during prime time if you're in ☞ places as Europe, North Africa or eastern North America.

• **World Time clock.** In 24-hour format, this is a "must." You can obtain these separately, but many radios have them built in; the best provide time whether the radio is on or off. However, many portable radios' clocks tend to gain or lose time if not reset periodically. In North America and beyond, the official shortwave time stations WWV on 2500, 5000, 10000, 15000 and 20000 kHz and CHU on 3330, 7335 and 14670 kHz are ideal for this; the Pacific is also served by WWVH in Hawaii on 2500, 5000, 10000 and 15000 kHz.

Shelling Out

Street prices are cited, including European and Australian VAT/GST where applicable. These vary plus or minus, so take them as the general guide they are meant to be. Shortwave specialty outlets and some other retailers usually have attractive prices, but duty-free shopping is not always the bargain you might expect.

David Heim, electronics deputy editor at *Consumer Reports* and quoted in *Reader's Digest*, suggests, "Look for stuff that's been factory refurbished." In North America refurbished Grundig and Etón portables are occasionally available—these are cited in PASSPORT REPORTS—and try pot luck if you are near a Sony outlet store.

We try to stick to plain English, but specialized terms can be useful. If you come across something that's not clear, *see* Worldly Words.

What PASSPORT's Ratings Mean

Star ratings: ✪✪✪✪✪ is best. Stars reflect overall performance and meaningful features, plus to some extent ergonomics and perceived build quality. Price, appearance, country of manufacture and the like are not taken into account. To facilitate comparison, portable rating standards are quite similar to those used for the portatop, tabletop and professional models reviewed elsewhere in this PASSPORT REPORTS.

A rating of at least ✪✪½ should please most who listen to major stations regularly during the evening. However, for casual use on trips virtually any small portable may suffice.

Passport's Choice. La crème de la crème. Our test team's personal picks of the litter—models we would buy or have bought for our personal use. Unlike star ratings, these choices are unapologetically subjective.

🅒: A relative bargain, with decidedly more performance than the price would suggest.

Tips for Using This Section

Models are listed by size; and, within size, in order of world band listening suitability. Street selling prices are cited, including VAT/GST where applicable.

Unless otherwise indicated, each model has:

- Keypad tuning, up/down slew keys, station presets and signal-seek tuning/scanning.
- Digital frequency readout to the nearest kilohertz or five kilohertz.
- Coverage of the world band shortwave spectrum from at least 3200–26100 kHz.
- Coverage of the usual 87.5–108 MHz FM band, but not the Japanese and other FM bands below 87 MHz.
- Coverage of the AM (mediumwave) band in selectable 9 and 10 kHz channel increments from about 530–1705 kHz. No coverage of the 153–279 kHz longwave band.
- Adequate image rejection, almost invariably resulting from double-conversion circuitry.

Unless otherwise indicated, each model lacks:

- Single-sideband demodulation.
- Synchronous selectable sideband. However, when it is present the unwanted sideband is rejected approximately 25 dB via phase cancellation, not IF filtering.
- If 24-hour clock included, lacks tens-of-hours leading zero that properly should be displayed with World Time (UTC).

POCKET PORTABLES

Perfect for Travel, Marginal for Home

Pocket portables weigh around half a pound, or 0.2 kg, and are between the size of an audio cassette jewel box and a handheld calculator. They operate off two to four "AA" (UM-3 penlite) batteries. These diminutive models are ideal to carry on your person, but listening to tiny speakers can be tiring. If you plan to listen for long periods or to music, opt for using headphones or earpieces, or look into one of the better compact models.

Best by far is the Sony ICF-SW100 series, but it's been discontinued and is getting harder to find. There has been nothing else like it in the history of world band radio, nor may we ever see its likes again. So, if you want this little Spook's Friend, get it while you can.

✪✪✪ (see ☞) *Passport's Choice*
Sony ICF-SW100E

Price: *ICF-SW100E:* £159.95 in the United Kingdom. €269.00 in Germany. *ACE-30 220V AC adaptor:* £24.95 in the United Kingdom. €25.50 in Germany.

Pro: Tiny, easily the smallest tested, but with larger-radio performance and features. High-tech synchronous selectable sideband generally performs well, reducing adjacent-channel interference and selective-fading distortion on world band, longwave and mediumwave AM signals, while adding slightly to weak-signal sensitivity and audio crispness (*see* Con). Single bandwidth, especially when synchronous selectable sideband is used, exceptionally effective at adjacent-channel rejection. Relatively good audio,

The scarce Sony ICF-SW100E/S portable is one of a kind. Incredible performance, James Bond package.

provided supplied earbuds or outboard audio are used (*see* Con). FM stereo through earbuds. Numerous helpful tuning features, including keypad, two- speed slew, signal-seek-then-resume scanning (*see* Con), five handy "pages" with ten station presets each. Station presets can display station name. Tunes in relatively precise 0.1 kHz increments. Good single-sideband performance (*see* Con). Good dynamic range. Worthy ergonomics for size and features. Illuminated display. Clock for many world cities, which can be made to work as a *de facto* World Time 24-hour clock (*see* Con). Timer and sleep delay. Travel power lock. Japanese FM (most versions) and longwave. Outboard passive reel accessory antenna aids slightly in weak-signal reception (*see* Con). Weak-battery indicator; about 16 hours from a set of batteries (*see* Con).

Con: Hard to find. Tiny speaker, although innovative, has mediocre sound, limited loudness and little tone shaping. Closing clamshell reduces speaker loudness and high-frequency response. Weak-signal sensitivity could be better, although included outboard active antenna helps. Expensive. No tuning knob. Clock not readable when station frequency displayed. As "London Time" is used by the clock for World Time, the summertime clock adjustment cannot be used if World Time is to be displayed accurately. Rejection of images, and 10 kHz "repeats" when synchronous selectable sideband off, could be better. In some urban locations, FM signals from 87.5 to 108 MHz can break through into world band segments with distorted sound, e.g. between 3200 and 3300 kHz. Synchronous selectable sideband tends to lose lock if batteries weak, or if NiCd cells are used. Synchronous selectable sideband alignment can vary with temperature, factory alignment and battery voltage, causing synchronous selectable sideband reception to be slightly more muffled in one sideband than the other. Batteries run down faster than usual when radio off. Tuning in 0.1 kHz increments means that non-synchronous single-sideband reception can be mis-tuned by up to 50 Hz, so audio quality varies. Signal-seek frequency scanning sometimes stops 5 kHz before a strong "real" signal. No meaningful signal-strength indicator. Mediumwave AM reception only fair. Mediumwave AM channel spacing adjusts peculiarly. Flimsy battery cover. No batteries (two "AA" required).

☞ The above star rating reflects mediocre speaker audio quality. Through earpieces, the rating rises to ✪✪✪⅛.

☞ In early production samples, the cable connecting the two halves of the "clamshell" case tended to lose continuity with extended use because of a very tight radius and an unfinished edge; this was successfully resolved with a design change in 1997. Owners of early units who encounter this problem should go to tesp.com/sw100faq.htm for repair tips.

Verdict: The ICF-SW100E's synchronous selectable sideband and effective bandwidth filter provide superior adjacent-channel rejection. Speaker and, to a lesser extent, weak-signal sensitivity keep it from being all it could have been. Yet, this Japanese-made gem rules the pocket category, and even outperforms most compact models.

This jewel among world band radios is a shoehorned wonder, but is getting harder to find anymore. Although world band radio was a priority for Sony founder Akio Morita, it no longer appears to be on the radar screen of Sony's replacement management. For now the 'SW100E continues to be available from outlets in Japan and parts of Europe (exporters as of presstime include wsplc.com and thiecom.de) but don't hold your breath.

✪✪✪ *Passport's Choice*
Sony ICF-SW100S

Price: €298.00 as available in Germany. ¥43,800 as available in Japan.

Verdict: This discontinued version, even harder to find new than the ICF-SW100E, includes an outboard active antenna, an AC adaptor that adjusts automatically to worldwide voltages, wall (mains) plugs for European and American sockets, and a high-quality travel case for the radio and accessories. Otherwise, it is identical to the Sony ICF-SW100E, above.

☞ Performance of the supplied active antenna is similar to that of the Sony AN-1 antenna reviewed elsewhere in PASSPORT REPORTS.

✪✪ ✐
Degen DE105, Kaito KA105

Price: *KA105:* $59.95 in the United States. CAD$48.00 in Canada.

Pro: Reasonably good selectivity from single bandwidth. Good voice-audio quality, with ample volume, for a small speaker (*see* Con). A number of helpful tuning features, including keypad (*see* Con), up/down slew (*see* Con) and signal-seek frequency scanning; also, 30 station presets, of which ten are for world band with others divided between FM and mediumwave AM. Above-average weak-signal sensitivity. Dual-zone 24-hour clock (*see* Con) with clock radio/alarm and sleep delay. Illuminated display via non-timed pushbutton. Clicky keys have superior feel. LCD has excellent contrast. Low battery consumption. Weak-battery indicator. Battery cover hinged to avoid loss. Travel power lock (*see* Con). FM in stereo through earbuds, included (*see* Con). Telescopic antenna swivels and rotates (*see* Con). Insertable elevation tab, attached to carrying strap, tilts radio to handy operating angle. Includes short external wire antenna accessory. *Kaito:* Tough, attractive matte

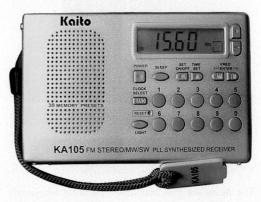

Top value in a travel companion is Kaito's KA105, sold in Asia as the Degen DE105.   D. Zantow

aluminum alloy face plate. 120V AC adaptor (*see* Con). Mediumwave AM 9/10 channel steps user-selectable. *Degen:* Available in either slate blue or silver.

Con: World band coverage of 5950–15600 kHz misses important 17 and 21 MHz (16 and 13 meter) segments, skips chunks of 6 and 15 MHz (49 and 19 meters), and omits lesser 2, 3, 4, 5, 19 and 25 MHz (120, 90, 75, 60, 15 and 11 meter) segments. Single-conversion IF circuitry results in poor image rejection. Speaker audio bereft of low-frequency ("bass") response. Audio through earbuds may be stronger in one channel at lower volume, whether in mono or stereo. No tuning knob. Keypad not in standard telephone format. Tunes world band only in 5 kHz steps and displays in nonstandard XX.XX/XX.XX$_5$ MHz format. Slow microprocessor lock time while slew tuning degrades bandscanning. Degen's quality control, once well above average, appears to have become hit-or-miss over the past year. No signal-strength indicator. Clock doesn't display when frequency is shown. Mediumwave AM coverage of 520–1620 kHz omits 1625–1705

The diminutive Etón Mini 300PE performs adequately on trips, yet it's no big deal if lost or stolen. Also sold under Grundig and Tecsun brands.

kHz. Mediumwave AM suffers slightly from LCD digital hash. FM has so-so sensitivity, mediocre capture ratio and some tendency to overload. FM audio distorted through earbuds. Because telescopic antenna exits from cabinet's side, it can't tilt to the right for optimum FM reception. Travel power lock does not disable LCD illumination. Two "AA" batteries not included. *Kaito:* Minor hum with AC adaptor.

Verdict: Except for the lack of single-sideband to hear the American Forces Radio and Television Service, this Chinese travel portable is a thrifty choice. Still, the larger Degen/Kaito siblings DE1101/KA1101 and DE1102/KA1102 cover more frequencies, perform significantly better and cost little more.

❂⅝ ✐
Etón Mini 300PE, Grundig Mini 300PE, Tecsun R-919

Price: *Mini 300PE:* $29.95 in the United States. CAD$39.95 in Canada. £24.95 in the United Kingdom. *Grundig/Lextronix Mini 300PE:* €27.95 in Germany.

Pro: Weak-signal sensitivity quite reasonable. Pleasant room-filling audio for such a small package (*see* Con). Clock/alarm-timer with sleep delay (*see* Con). FM in stereo with earbuds, included. Low battery consumption. Available in five colors. Soft carrying case affixes to belt or purse strap. Two "AA" batteries included.

Con: Analog tuned with digital frequency counter, so tunes only by thumbwheel, which is somewhat touchy. Does not tune 2, 3, 4, 5, 19, 21 and 25 MHz (120, 90, 75, 60, 15, 13 and 11 meter) segments; misses small bits of other world band segments. Single-conversion IF circuitry results in poor image rejection. Audio lacks bass response. Frequency drift with changes in temperature. Telescopic antenna does not rotate or swivel. Antenna's plastic base protrudes even when antenna collapsed. Displays in nonstandard XX.XX/XX.XX$_5$ MHz format. Display not illuminated. Minor drift when hand grasps back of cabinet. Frequency

MAKE YOUR PORTABLE "HEAR" BETTER

Regardless of which portable you own, you can boost weak-signal sensitivity on the cheap. How cheap? Nothing, for starters.

Look for "sweet spots" to place your radio: near windows, appliances, telephones, building I-beams and the like. If your portable has an AC adaptor, try that, then batteries; sometimes the adaptor works better, sometimes batteries. Places to avoid are near computers and appliances with microprocessors; also, light dimmers, non-incandescent lighting and cable TV or telephone lines. Sometimes power lines and cords can be noisy, too.

Outdoor Antenna Optional

An outdoor antenna shouldn't be needed with a portable. But it can help, especially with models lacking in weak-signal sensitivity with their built-in telescopic antennas. With compact and pocket models, simplest is often best—sophisticated or big antennas can cause "overloading." Run several meters or yards of ordinary insulated wire to a tree, then clip one end to your set's telescopic antenna with an alligator or claw clip available from RadioShack and such. It's fast and cheap, yet effective.

> **Today's portables don't require outdoor antennas.**

If you are in a weak-signal location, such as central or western North America or Australia, and want signals to be more audible, even better is to erect an inverted-L (so-called "longwire") antenna. Also sometimes called random-length antennas, they are available in the United States at RadioShack (278–758, $9.99) and world-wide at radio specialty outlets. Powerful versions can be constructed from detailed instructions in the RDI White Paper, PASSPORT *Evaluation of Popular Outdoor Antennas*. Antenna length is not critical, but keep the lead-in wire reasonably short.

Use an outdoor antenna only when required—disconnect during thunder, snow or sand storms, and when the radio is off. And don't touch any connected antenna during dry weather, as discharged static electricity might damage the radio.

Creative Indoor Solutions

All antennas work best outdoors, away from electrical noises inside the home. If your supplementary antenna has to be indoors, run it along the middle of a window with Velcro, tape or suction cups. In a reinforced-concrete building which absorbs radio signals, you can affix a telescopic car antenna so it sticks outdoors, like a wall flagpole. These are all but invisible, but work because they reach away from the building.

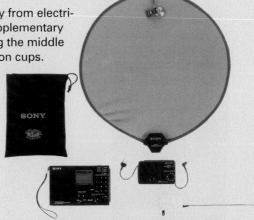

Compact amplified ("active") antennas, reviewed in this PASSPORT REPORTS, are small and handy but cost more. Many are for tabletop models, but a growing number are for portables.

The Sony AN-LP1 is the best portable antenna, but nigh impossible to find new. J. Brinker

counter noise slightly audible when finger placed over LCD during mediumwave AM reception. Some FM overloading in strong-signal environments. Clock in 12-hour format, displays only when radio off. No jack for AC adaptor, much less the adaptor itself. *North America:* Toll-free tech support.

Verdict: Best of the really inexpensive portables, even though it comes up short on daytime frequency coverage, lacks display illumination and its clock isn't in World Time format. But thanks to true pocket size, nice weak-signal sensitivity and decent audio quality it is hard to resist for casual use on trips.

✪½
Kaiwa KA-818, Tecsun R818

Price: $34.95 or less as possibly still available in the United States and elsewhere. CNY138 in China.

Pro: Reasonable weak-signal sensitivity for low-cost pocket model. Clock with timer/alarm (*see* Con).

Con: Analog tuned with digital frequency counter, so tunes only by thumbwheel, which is somewhat touchy. Does not tune important 13 and 21 MHz (22 and 13 meter) segment or lesser 2, 3, 4, 5, 19 and 25 MHz (120, 90, 75, 60, 15 and 11 meter) seg-

The hard-to-find Kaiwa KA-818, manufactured by Tecsun, is outclassed by similarly priced competition.

ments; misses bits of other world band segments. Single-conversion IF circuitry results in poor image rejection. Frequency drift with changes in temperature. Frequency counter completely omits last digit so, say, 9575 kHz appears as either 9.57 or 9.58 MHz. Clock in 12-hour format only, displays only when radio off. Display not illuminated. Mediocre speaker audio quality. Telescopic antenna does not rotate or swivel. Mediumwave AM lacks weak-signal sensitivity. Pedestrian FM, with spurious signals. On one of our new units the telescopic antenna immediately fell apart. Two "AA" batteries not included. Few vendors in America and Europe. Warranty only 90 days in United States and various other countries.

Verdict: Performance brings up the rear, but price, size and alarm make this Chinese-made model worth consideration for casual use on trips. Lots of luck trying to find one outside China.

✪¼
Sharper Image SN400

Price: $29.95 in the United States.

Pro: Helpful tuning features include up/down slew and signal-seek frequency scanning; also, world band segment selection and 30 station presets (*see* Con), of which ten are for world band with others divided between FM and mediumwave AM. Clicky keys have superior feel. Timed LCD illumination (*see* Con). Travel power lock (*see* Con). Dual-zone clock (*see* Con) with sleep delay. FM stereo through earbuds (see *Con*), included. Mediumwave AM 9/10 kHz switch. Telescopic antenna rotates and swivels. Elevation panel tilts radio to handy operating angle. Superior carrying pouch (*see* Con).

Con: Digital buzz often degrades, and sometimes obliterates, world band reception. World band coverage of 5950–15600 kHz misses important 17 and 21 MHz (16 and 13 meter) segments, skips portions of major 6 and 15 MHz (49 and 19 meter) segments, and omits lesser 2, 3, 4, 5, 19 and 25 MHz (120, 90, 75, 60, 15 and 11 meter) segments. No keypad or tuning knob. Slow microprocessor lock time while slew

tuning degrades bandscanning. Single-conversion IF circuitry results in poor image
rejection. Speaker audio bereft of low-frequency ("bass") response. Peculiar battery
replacement/AC adapter procedure to
retain memory data. Tunes world band only
in 5 kHz steps and displays in nonstandard
XX.XX/XX.XX₅ MHz format. Presets acces-
sible only serially via up/down carousel.
Mediumwave AM coverage of 520–1620
kHz omits 1625–1705 kHz. FM has so-so
sensitivity, mediocre capture ratio and some
tendency to overload. FM audio distorted
through earbuds. Audio through earbuds
may be a skosh stronger in one channel.
Both clocks only in 12-hour format and
neither displays when frequency is shown.
No signal-strength indicator. Travel power
lock does not deactivate LCD illumination
button. No AC adaptor, and no indication of
required polarity for an aftermarket adaptor.
Two "AA" batteries not included. Carrying
pouch has slight tire odor. Warranty only 90
days.

Verdict: Sharp, this Chinese radio isn't. No
low price can't justify the digital buzz that
plagues world band reception, and important world band frequencies can't be tuned.

COMPACT PORTABLES

Nice for Travel, Okay for Home

Compacts are hugely popular, and no
wonder. They offer a value mix of affordable
price, worthy performance, manageable
size and acceptable speaker audio. They tip
in at one to two pounds, under a kilogram,
and are typically sized less than 8 × 5 ×
1.5 inches, or 20 × 13 × 4 cm. Like pocket
models, they almost always feed off "AA"
(UM-3 penlite) batteries—but, usually, more
of them. They travel almost as well as pocket
models, but sound better through their larger
speakers. They can also suffice for home use.

❶❶❶¼ *Passport's Choice*
Sony ICF-SW07

Price: €389.00 in Germany. ¥46,800 in
Japan.

Sharper Image's SN400 is readily obtained and
inexpensive, but performance brings up the rear.

D. Zantow

Pro: Best non-audio performance among
travel-worthy compact portables. Attractive
and unusual styling. High-tech synchronous
selectable sideband generally performs well
and is straightforward to operate; reduces
adjacent-channel interference and selective-
fading distortion on world band, longwave
and mediumwave AM signals while adding
slightly to weak-signal sensitivity. Unusually
small and light for a compact model when
used without accessory antenna. Numerous
tuning aids, including pushbutton access
of frequencies for four stations stored on
a replaceable ROM, keypad, two-speed
up/down slew, 20 station presets (ten for
world band) and "signal-seek, then resume"

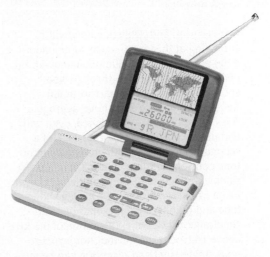

Another of Sony's fading gems is the ICF-SW07—the
best compact portable ever made.

tuning. Clamshell design aids in handiness of operation, and is further helped by illuminated LCD readable from a wide variety of angles. Hump on the rear panel places the keypad at a convenient operating angle. Comes with AN-LP2 outboard "tennis racquet" antenna, commendably effective in raising the 'SW07's weak-signal sensitivity to excellent on world band; this antenna, unlike the Sony AN-LP1 optional accessory antenna for other receivers, has automatic preselector tuning, simplifying operation. Good single sideband performance (see Con). Clock covers most international time zones, as well as UTC (see Con). Outstanding reception of weak and crowded FM stations, with limited urban FM overloading resolved by variable-level attenuator. FM stereo through earbuds, included. Japanese FM (most versions) and longwave. Above-average reception of mediumwave AM band. Travel power lock. Closing the clamshell does not interfere with speaker performance. Low-battery indicator. Presets information is non-volatile, can't be erased when batteries changed. Presets and time zone readout can be user-programmed to display six-character alphanumeric readout on LCD. Two turn-on times for alarm/clock radio. Sleep delay. Battery cover hinged to avoid loss, although AN-LP1 antenna battery cover not hinged. AC adaptor, albeit only single-voltage (e.g., 120V in version for North America).

Con: Hard to find. Only one bandwidth, surprising at this price—even some under-$100 models now provide two bandwidths. Pedestrian audio quality through small speaker, with relatively narrow audio-frequency response and above-average "hiss." Audio fidelity diminished, even with earbuds, in part because of the lack of a second, wider, bandwidth and meaningful tone control. No tuning knob. On our latest sample, the telescopic antenna would break its internal case mounting. Display shows time and tuned frequency, but not both simultaneously. Tuning resolution of 0.1 kHz above 1620 kHz means that non-synchronous single-sideband reception can be mistuned by up to 50 Hz, allowing audio fidelity to suffer. Synchronous selectable sideband

tends to lose lock if batteries weak or if NiCd cells used. Synchronous selectable sideband alignment can vary with temperature, factory alignment and battery voltage, causing synchronous selectable sideband reception to be slightly more muffled in one sideband than the other. No meaningful signal-strength indicator, an unusual shortcoming at this model's price. LCD frequency/time numbers relatively small for size of display. AN-LP2 accessory antenna has to be physically disconnected for proper mediumwave AM reception. 1621–1705 kHz portion of American AM band and 1705–1735 kHz potential public service segment are erroneously treated as shortwave, although this does not harm reception quality. Low battery indicator misleadingly shows batteries as dead immediately after fresh batteries are installed; clears up when radio is turned on. No batteries (two "AA" required for radio, two more for antenna). UTC displays as "London" time even summer during DST, when London is an hour ahead of UTC; best is to re-label "London" as "UTC" and not display that zone at DST; however, the DST key can change UTC to UTC +1 in error if user is not careful.

Verdict: Speaker audio and sticker shock aside, this Japanese-made model is still the best compact portable for travel—if you can find one. It also passes the Caribbean Palm Frond Test as an effective prop for attracting friendly strangers. Clamshell open and antenna unfurled, the Sony ICF-SW07 is a great conversation-starter, especially among the intellectually curious...or, sometimes, the curiously intellectual.

✪✪✪⅛ Ⓒ *Passport's Choice*
Sony ICF-SW7600GR

Price: *ICF-SW7600GR:* $159.95 in the United States. CAD$329.99 in Canada. £173.95 or less in the United Kingdom. €169.00 in Germany. AUD$509.00 in Australia. ¥31,800 in Japan. *MW 41-680 120V regulated AC adaptor (aftermarket, see below):* $19.95 in the United States.

Pro: One of the great values in a meaningful world band radio. Far and away the least-costly model available with high-tech synchronous selectable sideband; this generally performs well, reducing adjacent-channel interference and selective-fading distortion on world band, longwave and mediumwave AM signals (*see* Con). Single bandwidth, especially when synchronous selectable sideband is used, exceptionally effective at adjacent-channel rejection. Seemingly robust—similar predecessor had superior quality of components and assembly for price class, and held up unusually well. Numerous helpful tuning features, including keypad, two-speed up/down slew, 100 station presets and "signal-seek, then resume" tuning. For those with limited hearing of high-frequency sounds, such as some men over the half-century mark, speaker audio quality may be preferable to that of Grundig G4000A/Yacht Boy 400PE (*see* Con). Single-sideband performance arguably the best of any portable; analog clarifier, combined with LSB/USB switch, allow single-sideband signals (e.g., AFRTS, utility, amateur) to be tuned with uncommon precision, and thus with superior carrier phasing and the resulting natural-sounding audio. Dual-zone 24-hour clock with single-zone readout, easy to set. Slightly smaller and lighter than most other compact models. Outboard reel passive wire antenna accessory aids slightly with weak-signal reception. Simple timer with sleep delay. Illuminated LCD has high contrast when read head-on or from below. Travel power lock. Superior reception of difficult mediumwave AM stations. Superior FM capture ratio aids reception when band congested, including helping separate co-channel stations. FM stereo through earpieces or headphones. Japanese FM (most versions) and longwave. Superior battery life. Weak-battery indicator. Stereo line output for recording, FM home transmitters and outboard audio systems. Battery cover hinged to avoid loss. Automatically provides power for optional AN-LP1 active antenna.

Con: Audio lacks tonal quality for pleasant world band or mediumwave AM music reproduction, and speaker audio tiring for any type of FM program. Weak-signal sensitivity, although respectable, not equal to that of the top handful of top-rated portables;

The Sony ICF-SW7600GR is the #1 best buy among world band portables. Other radios with synchronous selectable sideband cost over three times as much.

helped considerably by extra-cost Sony AN-LP1 active antenna reviewed elsewhere in this edition. Image rejection adequate, but not excellent. Three switches, including those for synchronous selectable sideband, located unhandily at the side of the cabinet. No tuning knob. Slow microprocessor lock time while slew tuning degrades bandscanning. No meaningful signal-strength indicator. Synchronous selectable sideband holds lock decently, but less well on weak signals than in Sony's larger models; too, it tends to lose lock even more if batteries weak or if NiCd cells used. Synchronous selectable sideband alignment can vary with temperature, factory alignment and battery voltage, causing synchronous selectable sideband reception to be slightly more muffled in one sideband than the other. No AC adaptor included. In North America the optional Sony AC-E60A 120V AC "switching" adaptor causes serious interference to radio signals and, incredibly, is labeled "Not for use with radios"; Universal Radio offers its own MW 41-680 to remedy this, and presumably other firms will be offering something similar in due course. Reader reports indicate Sony's recommended 240V AC adaptor also causes serious interference to radio signals. Radio's adaptor socket is of an unusual size, making it difficult to find a suitable third-party AC adaptor. 1621–1705 kHz portion of American AM band and 1705–1735 kHz potential public-service segment are erroneously treated as shortwave, although this does not harm reception quality. Even though it has a relatively large LCD, same portion of display is used for clock and frequency digits; thus, clock doesn't display when frequency is shown, although pressing the EXE key allows time to replace frequency for nine seconds. No earphones or earpieces. No batteries (four "AA" needed).

Verdict: The robust Sony ICF-SW7600GR provides excellent bang for the buck, even though it is manufactured in high-cost Japan. Its advanced-tech synchronous selectable sideband is a valuable feature that other portable manufacturers have yet to engineer properly—even some professional models costing thousands of dollars still haven't got it right. To find this useful operating feature at this price is without parallel.

Top drawer single-sideband reception for a portable, too, along with superior tough-signal FM and mediumwave AM reception. But it has warts: Musical audio quality through the speaker is only *ordinaire* and Sony of America's recommended adaptors should be avoided.

New for 2007
✪✪✪ *Passport's Choice*
Etón E5, Grundig G5

Price: *E5/G5:* $149.95 in the United States. CAD$149.00 in Canada. £89.95 in the United Kingdom.

Pro: Much improved ergonomics over Degen/Kaito siblings, including dedicated volume controls and additional slewing buttons; main keypad and slewing buttons are nicely sized (*see* Con) with pleasant feel. Worthy tuning knob does not mute when turned (*see* Con). Very useful auto scanning circuit that on shortwave allows for two stop modes (scan, five-second pause, resume scan; scan, stop), with an FM-only mode for auto store to presets. 700 station presets store mode; each of 100 seven-presets "pages" can display a four-letter

alphanumeric ID tag (*see* Con). Presets nonvolatile. Two ways to quick-access individual world band segments; returns to last-tuned frequency within each segment. Two bandwidths, well chosen. Superior sensitivity, low circuit noise. Dual conversion provides adequate image rejection (*see* Con). Superior dynamic range for a compact portable; thus, radio suitable for use with outdoor wire antennas. Above average single-sideband reception, thanks in part to analog fine-tuning thumbwheel (*see* Con) and freedom from excessive drift (*see* Con). Effective LED illumination (*see* Con) stays on for 15 seconds with battery power, continuously with AC adaptor. Audio quality slightly above average for compact portable, powerful enough to drive some external speakers (*see* Con). Clock displays separately from frequency (*see* Con). Four-event alarm. Sleep delay; once its 99-minute default is changed (i.e., to something between one and 98 minutes), new setting is retained. Four-segment battery indicator. Useful five-segment signal-strength indicator. Nickel metal hydride batteries recharge inside radio (*see* Con). Telescopic antenna rotates and swivels. Travel power lock (*see* Con). Station presets and time not erased during battery charging or if batteries replaced quickly. Battery cover hinged to avoid loss. Superior FM sensitivity. Excellent FM capture ratio aids reception when band congested, including helping separate co-channel stations. FM in stereo through earbuds, included (*see* Con). Simple tone control for FM (*see* Con). Stereo line output with proper audio level for recording, home FM transmitters and outboard audio systems. Japanese FM. Longwave. Indoor wire antenna and single-voltage AC adaptor/charger (*see* ☞). Vinyl carrying case has greater protection than case for the Degen DE1103/Kaito KA1103 (*see* Con).

Con: World band and mediumwave AM audio would profit from more crispness and a tone control (tone control works only on FM, and FM audio sounds better). Just as with the Degen DE1103/Kaito KA1103, volume blasts when radio initially turned on, although there's a way around this. Although some buttons nicely sized, most are small. LCD relatively difficult to read in low ambient light without illumination. Minor chuffing when tuning, although vastly preferable to the alternative of muted audio. Image rejection, although fairly good, not all it could be for a model with enough dynamic range to handle outboard antennas. Single sideband uses fine-tuning thumbwheel instead of USB/LSB selector; thumbwheel lacks center detent. Touchy fine-tuning thumbwheel makes manual ECSS reception impractical. AGC too fast in single-sideband mode, causing distortion; too, AGC swamped by exceptionally strong signals unless single-level attenuator used. Travel lock does not disable LCD illumination. Tuning knob has only 1 kHz step, although slewing buttons complement this nicely with 5 kHz step. Individual presets do not store bandwidth or ID tag. Signal strength indicator does not work on FM. Bandwidth chosen by hard-to-select slide switch on side of cabinet. No standard or rechargeable batteries (four "AA" needed). In principle, rubbery paint on cabinet might eventually wear through. Carrying case has creosote odor, remediable by thorough airing.

Verdict: The Etón E5's and Grundig G5's worthy performance is similar to that of the Degen DE1103/Kaito KA1103. However, the Chinese-made E5/G5 clears up the '1103's seriously flawed ergonomics by, for example, including dedicated volume and slewing controls. On the other hand, the '1103 comes with rechargeable batteries, while the pricier E5/G5 doesn't.

Overall, the E5/G5 is one of the best compact portables around. What it lacks is synchronous selectable sideband, such as is found on Sony's similarly priced ICF-7600GR.

☞ Early samples of the E5 in North America included a 120V AC adaptor with a rounded back, like a tortoise, which emitted considerable "hash" on all bands, even FM. Etón eventually replaced it with a quiet, more squarish adaptor. Those with noisy adaptors should contact Etón for a free replacement.

Evaluation of New Model: In early 2005, drawings appeared on the Internet showing a proposed model DE1106 portable from

The new Etón E5, although manufactured by Degen, is superior to any Degen-branded model.

Degen, a respected young firm in China. Later that year it dropped out of sight, eventually resurfacing as the Etón E5 and Grundig G5. This represents the first time Etón-Grundig has contracted Degen rather than Tecsun for its Chinese manufacturing, although unconfirmed reports claim that Tecsun has a major equity stake in Degen.

Proven Circuitry, Upgraded Controls

Most of the E5/G5's circuitry appears to be identical to that of the kindred Degen DE1103, sold in North America as the Kaito KA1103. However, the firmware and front panel have been redesigned and significantly upgraded. For example, the '1103 has a clunky volume control shared with the tuning knob encoder, whereas the E5/G5 uses dedicated buttons to control volume—a huge improvement.

However, like the '1103, volume blasts when the receiver is first powered up out of the box—or if left without batteries or with dead batteries. But unlike with the '1103 there's a way to get around this, assuming you remember that it needs to be done: Before the radio is turned on, pre-adjust the volume by pressing the keypad or +/– volume buttons until the "Vol" numeric value drops to "0."

Other improvements include a keypad in standard telephone layout and with beefier keys; other keys remain small. Slewing buttons have been added and use steps appropriate for each band: 5 kHz for shortwave, 10/9 kHz for mediumwave AM, 3 kHz for longwave and 100 kHz for FM. The tuning knob's different rates complement this, being fixed at 1 kHz on except on FM, where it's 25 kHz.

FM's 76–108 MHz coverage includes both the conventional and Japanese bands. Longwave goes down to 150 kHz and, unlike on the '1103, can be keypad-tuned.

Scanning Works Nicely

Shortwave is scanned in appropriate 5 kHz increments. Unlike the '1103, the E5/G5 scans mediumwave AM in correct steps: 10 kHz, or 9 kHz outside the Americas. When a scan comes across an active frequency, it can either pause for five seconds or stop entirely. Also, on FM "ATS" can be selected to store to a preset. Withal, scanning performs well in all bands.

Easy Access to 700 Presets

The E5/G5 has fully 700 station presets, as opposed to 268 on the '1103. Accessing these is a snap, as they are clustered in groups of seven within each of 100 pages; once a page is selected, a preset is accessed simply by using the F1 through F7 buttons just below the LCD. Indeed, it's nearly as easy to enter a new preset as to access an existing one.

Not only is there an icon to display which of the seven presets is being used, you can attach a four-character alphanumeric ID tag to each page, even though individual presets can't be tagged.

The F1-F7 buttons have two other functions: to provide quick access to world band segments, and to set up the receiver; for example, to choose either 9 or 10 kHz mediumwave AM steps for scanning/slewing.

Various Accessories, but No Batteries

The E5/G5 comes with an AC adaptor, earbuds and an outboard world band wire antenna. Also, a nice travel pouch that's much better than those supplied by Degen/Kaito. It initially smells of creosote, but one good airing banishes this radio B.O.

The E5/G5 can recharge batteries internally, but no batteries of any sort are included. Here, the E5/G5 falls short, as the kindred '1103s comes with four rechargeable "AA" cells.

There's a travel power lock, but the lock's not very tight: It doesn't deactivate display illumination, even though the '1103's does.

Nasty Surprise, Remedied Pronto

The initial 120V AC adaptor for North America generated raucous noise on all bands, even FM. Etón eventually replaced it with a new adaptor (see ☞, above) which we tested, and it works as it should.

Useful Display with Signal-Strength Indicator

The '1103 sports an analog-looking ersatz "dial," in addition to the usual digital frequency readout. This pointless feature is absent on the E5/G5, freeing up the front panel for genuinely useful functions.

A prototype E5 we peeked at just before PASSPORT 2006 went to press used blue LEDs for display illumination. It was too dim, making the LCD exceptionally difficult to read in the dark. Thankfully, the production E5/G5's illumination has been improved, which is important because the LCD has limited contrast for reading in dim light.

The LCD's frequency digits are large and thus easy to read. Another plus over the '1103 is that the World Time clock displays separately from the frequency.

The '1103 uses a four-segment LCD signal strength indicator, but it's only marginal as it overreads. The E5/G5's indicator is much better: It adds a segment, is easier to read and is more accurate.

Worthy World Band Performance

Weak-signal sensitivity is superior whether with the telescopic rod or an external antenna; this is aided by relatively quiet circuitry. The E5/G5 also has notable dynamic range for a portable, important when a significant external antenna is used at night. Adjacent-channel rejection—selectivity—is above average, too, and flexible because there's a choice between two suitable bandwidths.

Image rejection is superior, thanks to double conversion that's rarely found around this price. Still, some exceptionally powerful stations "repeat" weakly 900 kHz down.

The E5/G5 features single-sideband demodulation to eavesdrop on, for example, the popular American Forces Radio and Television Service. It also has the necessary stability and narrow selectivity for all but serious utility/ham DXing.

For this, there is no LSB/USB switch; rather, a variable-pitch analog thumbwheel fine tunes between 1 kHz tuning increments. Alas, this vintage-technology but precise control lacks a center detent and is too touchy for everyday manual ECSS tuning. Too, the nature of the AGC's timing appears to be the cause of some single-sideband distortion.

Another sign of possible AGC limitation is that with some supersignals—local mediumwave AM or within, say, 49 meters evenings—audio weakens unless the attenuator is switched in. This is uncommon and seems to occur only when an external antenna is used.

Otherwise, speaker audio is pleasant—even if a bit more crispness and bass response would have been appreciated; too, the tone control works only on FM. A stereo line jack outputs audio at an excellent level for recording and such.

Other Bands Perform Comparably

Commendable performance isn't limited to world band—FM and mediumwave AM come across commendably, as well, even if the signal-strength indicator doesn't function on FM. FM tunes not only the usual 87–108 MHz band, but also the 76–90 MHz Japanese band. It has a superior capture ratio and weak-signal sensitivity, along with stereo audio through earbuds.

As a result, the E5/G5 performs nicely on FM in rural fringe areas, as well as in suburban locations with band congestion. There is above-average resistance to overloading near FM transmitters, making it a sensible choice for urban locations.

Mediumwave AM provides yeoman service, with long-distance reception being aided by dual bandwidths.

Almost as Good as It Gets

The Etón E5/Grundig G5 is about as good as it gets in a compact world band portable except that, unlike the Sony ICF-SW7600GR, it has no synchronous selectable sideband.

✪✪✪ ✄ *Passport's Choice*
Degen DE1102, Kaito KA1102

Price: *Kaito:* $79.95 in the United States. CAD$99.95 in Canada.

Pro: Unusually small and light for a sophisticated compact model; only a skosh larger and one ounce (28 grams) heavier than its simpler sibling '1101. Two bandwidths, both well chosen. A number of helpful tuning features, including keypad, up/down slew (1 or 5 kHz steps for world band, 1 or 9/10 kHz for mediumwave AM), carousel selector for 49–16 meter segments, and signal-seek frequency scanning (*see* Con) and memory scanning; also, ten 19-preset "pages" provide a total of 190 station presets, of which 133 can be used for shortwave (*see* Con). Auto-store function automatically stores

Best in Degen's stable is the DE1102, although single-sideband operation is clumsy. Sold in North America as the value-priced Kaito KA1102. D. Zantow

presets; works on all bands. Tunable BFO allows for precise signal phasing during single-sideband reception (see Con). No muting during manual shortwave bandscanning in 1 or 5 kHz steps, or mediumwave AM bandscanning in 1 kHz steps. PLL and BFO relatively free from drift during single-sideband operation (see Con). Above-average weak-signal sensitivity and image rejection. Little circuit "hiss." Superior speaker audio quality, intelligibility and loudness for size. Four-LED signal-strength indicator for mediumwave AM and shortwave (see Con); three-level signal-strength indicator for FM (fourth LED becomes stereo indicator). World Time 24-hour clock displays seconds numerically when radio is off; when on, time (sans seconds) flashes on briefly when key is held down; user may choose 12-hour format, instead. Unusually appropriate for use in the dark, as display and keypad illuminated by pleasant blue light which works only in dark (see Con). Clicky keys have superior feel. LCD has excellent contrast when viewed from sides or below. Alarm with sleep delay (see Con). Travel power lock. Rechargeable NiMH batteries (3 × "AA"), included, can be charged within the radio; station presets and time not erased during charging. Switchable bass boost supplements high-low tone switch, significantly improves FM audio (see Con). Low battery consumption except with FM bass boost. Battery-level indicator. Battery cover hinged to avoid loss. Superior FM weak-signal sensitivity. Excellent FM capture ratio aids reception when band congested, including helping separate co-channel stations. FM in stereo through earbuds, included (see Con). Japanese FM. Full coverage of mediumwave AM band. Includes short external wire antenna accessory, which in many locations is about the most that can be used without generating overloading. Available in black or aluminum colors. *Degen:* AC adaptor (220V). *Kaito:* AC adaptor (120V).

Con: Speaker audio, except FM, lacks low-frequency ("bass") response as compared to larger models. Bass-boost circuit, which could relieve this on world band, works only on FM. Dynamic range, although roughly average for a compact portable, not anywhere

equal to that of the sibling '1101; overloads easily with a significant outdoor antenna, although much less often with the built-in antenna or a short outboard antenna. Not so straightforward to operate as some other portables; for example, single-sideband mode works only when presets "page 9" is selected (or SSB button is held in manually), even if no presets are to be chosen (in any event, presets don't store mode); otherwise, "ERR" is displayed; manufacturer says this is to prevent its Chinese consumers, who are unfamiliar with single sideband, from turning on the BFO accidentally and thus becoming confused. Slight warble in audio with ECSS reception, varies with how many signal-strength LEDs are being illuminated; LEDs can't be turned off. Volume at earphone jack sometimes inadequate with weak or undermodulated signals; variable-level earphone jack misleadingly described as "line out." Power button activates a 99-minute sleep delay; to turn the radio on fulltime, a second key must be pressed immediately afterwards. No tuning knob. No LSB/USB switch. Displays in nonstandard XX.XX/XX.XXx MHz format. Signal-strength indicator overreads. Little-used 2 MHz (120 meter) world band segment not covered. Degen's quality control, once well above average, appears to have become hit-or-miss over the past year. Clock doesn't display when frequency is shown, although push-button allows time to replace frequency briefly. Always-on LCD/keypad illumination with AC adaptor, as described in owner's manual, did not function on test sample. LCD/keypad illumination dim and uneven. FM IF produces images 21+ MHz down.

Verdict: An exceptional price and performance winner from Degen—just don't expect much in the way of low-end audio.

❋❋❋ *Passport's Choice*

Etón G4000A, Grundig G4000A, Grundig Yacht Boy 400PE

Price: *G4000A:* $149.95 in the United States. CAD$199.00 in Canada. AUD$279.00 in Australia. *YB400PE, as available:* $129.95 in the United States. *Refurbished YB400PE, as available:* $99.95 in the United States.

Pro: Speaker audio quality tops in size category for those with sharp hearing. Two bandwidths, both well-chosen. Ergonomically superior, a pleasure to operate. A number of helpful tuning features, including keypad, up/down slew, 40 station presets, signal-seek frequency scanning and scanning of station presets. Signal-strength indicator. Dual-zone 24-hour clock, with one zone shown at all times; however, clock displays seconds only when radio is off. Illuminated display. Alarm with simple sleep delay. Tunable BFO allows for superior signal phasing during single-sideband reception (*see* Con). Outboard reel passive wire antenna accessory aids slightly with weak-signal reception. Generally superior FM performance, especially in weak-signal locations. FM in stereo through earpieces. Longwave. AC adaptor. *G4000A:* Excellent hardside leather travel case. *North America:* Toll-free tech support.

Con: Circuit noise ("hiss") can be slightly intrusive with weak signals. No tuning knob. At many locations there can be breakthrough of powerful AM or FM stations into the world band spectrum. Keypad not in telephone format. No LSB/USB switch, and single-sideband reception is below par. Battery consumption slightly above norm. No batteries (six "AA" needed).

☞ Refurbished units reportedly include gift and similar returns from department stores and other outlets where customers tend to be unfamiliar with world band radio. Everything but the radio itself is supposed to be replaced. Limited availability.

Verdict: This most popular of Grundig's digital-readout portables offers superior audio quality, ease of use and a roster of other virtues. So it's hardly surprising that this Chinese-made receiver is unusually popular for enjoying world band programs, including music. Tough FM catches, too, although single-sideband isn't all it could be.

✪✪⅞ (*see* ☞) ℰ

Degen DE1103, Kaito KA1103

Price: *Kaito:* $109.95 in the United States. CAD$109.00 in Canada.

The Etón G4000A is the latest version of Grundig's exceptionally popular compact portable.

Pro: Two bandwidths, both well chosen (*see* Con). Helpful tuning features include tuning knob (*see* Con), keypad (*see* Con), world band segment up/down carousel, signal-seek (pause, resume) frequency scanning and presets scanning; also, sixteen "pages" holding 16 presets each provide 256 station presets, plus another dozen to select among world band segments (alternatively, "pages" may be bypassed for quick-access tuning, reducing available presets to 100). Presets store mode (*see* Con). Tuning knob not muted when tuned, facilitating bandscanning (*see* Con). Scanner works better than

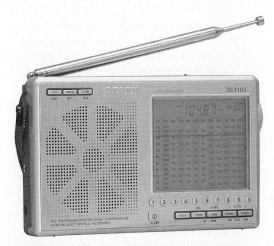

Degen's DE1103 is offered in North America as the Kaito KA1103. Hostile ergonomics make this less attractive than the cheaper Degen DE1102/Kaito KA1102.

most. Radio can return to last-tuned frequency within ten world band segments, as well as FM and mediumwave AM. Superior dynamic range for a compact portable—better than that of DE1102/KA1102, and even approaching that of DE1101/KA1102. Tunable BFO (see Con) allows for precise signal phasing during single-sideband reception. Relatively free from drift during single-sideband operation. Above-average sensitivity aided by quiet circuitry. Using dual conversion, image rejection is above average (see Con). Speaker audio quality, although limited, fairly good except during single-sideband reception (see Con). Four-level signal-strength indicator (see Con). World Time 24-hour clock (see Con). Display and keypad illumination is about as good as it gets: During battery operation, it can be switched not to go on; otherwise, it is automatically activated by any of various controls, including those for tuning, and stays on for a full 15 seconds. Clicky keys with superior feel (see Con). Sleep delay. Two-event timer. NiMH batteries (4 × "AA"), included, slowly rechargeable within radio. Travel power lock. Station presets and time not erased during battery charging or if batteries replaced quickly. Battery-level indicator. Battery cover hinged to avoid loss. Superior FM sensitivity. Excellent FM capture ratio aids reception when band congested, including helping separate co-channel stations. FM in stereo through earbuds, included (see Con). Stereo audio line output with appropriate level for recording, home FM transmitters and outboard audio systems. Japanese FM. Longwave (see Con) tunes down to 100 kHz. Elevation panel tilts radio to handy operating angle. Includes short external wire antenna accessory. Available in black or aluminum colors. *Degen:* AC adaptor (220V). *Kaito:* AC adaptor (120V).

Con: Hostile ergonomics include having to operate two controls to change volume; nonstandard single-row keypad; small keys; stiff slider controls; only one knob tuning rate (1 kHz, slow) for world band and mediumwave AM; and no center detent for fine-tuning (tunable BFO) thumbwheel. Pseudo-analog LCD "dial," a pointless gimmick that takes up space which could

have been used to display useful information and provide proper keypad layout. No up/down slew controls. No tone control except "news-music" switch that works only on FM. No LSB/USB switch. Single-sideband has audible distortion, seemingly from AGC. Image rejection, although fairly good, not all that it could be for a model with enough dynamic range to handle some outboard antennas. Slight microprocessor noise when tuning knob turned—a small price to pay to avoid bandscan limitations brought about by muting. Even though dynamic range superior, AGC seemingly swamped by exceptionally powerful signals, causing lowered volume; switching attenuator to "LO" allows volume to return to normal level. Signal-strength indicator overreads and does not operate on FM. Degen's quality control, once well above average, appears to have become hit-or-miss over the past year. Clock doesn't display when frequency is shown, although pushbutton allows time to replace frequency briefly. Presets do not store bandwidth. Longwave less convenient to access than other bands.

☞ The '1103 merits three stars for performance, but only two for ergonomics (see Evaluation).

☞ Unlike the sibling DE1101/KA1101 and DE1102/KA1102, the '1103's AC adaptor jack uses standard center-pin-positive polarity.

Verdict: Dreadful ergonomics and a wasted LCD make this a model to approach with caution. Yet, the Degen DE1103/Kaito KA1103 is a solid and versatile performer at a surprisingly low price. If you can endure its ergonomic shortcomings, the '1103 offers excellent performance value.

✪✪⅛
Sony ICF-SW55

Price: €379 in Germany.

Pro: Audio quality. Dual bandwidths. Logical controls. Innovative tuning, with alphabetic identifiers for groups ("pages") of stations; some like this approach. Weak-signal sensitivity a bit better than most.

Demodulates single-sideband signals (*see* Con). Reel-in antenna, AC adaptor, earbuds and cord for external DC power. Signal/battery strength indicator. Local and World Time clocks, one displayed separately from frequency. Snooze/alarm. Five-event (daily only) timer. Illuminated display. Longwave and Japanese FM.

Con: Page tuning system cumbersome for some. Spurious-signal rejection in higher segments not commensurate with price. Wide bandwidth rather broad for receiver lacking synchronous selectable sideband. Tuning increments of 0.1 kHz and frequency readout of 1 kHz compromise single-sideband reception. BFO pulling reportedly causes audio quavering; not found in our test units. Display illumination dim and uneven. High battery consumption.

Verdict: Overpriced, but if you like the Sony ICF-SW55's operating scheme and want a small portable with good audio quality, this discontinued veteran is a respectable performer in its size class. But this Japanese-made unit, no longer in production, is still available here and there as "new old stock." It lacks synchronous selectable sideband—a major plus found on newer Sony and Etón models.

Back from the dead is Sony's ICF-SW55. Long out of production, but new old stock recently surfaced in Germany.

in unusually precise 0.04 kHz increments without having to use a fine-tuning control, making this one of the handiest and most effective portables for listening to these signals (*see* Con). Shortwave dynamic range slightly above average for portable, allowing it to perform unusually well with an outboard antenna (*see* Con). Travel power lock. 24-hour clock shows at all times, and can display local time in various cities of the world (*see* Con). Excellent 1–10 digital signal-strength indicator. Low-battery indicator. Elevation panel tilts radio to handy operating angle (*see* Con). Clock radio feature offers three "on" times for three discrete frequencies. Sleep delay. FM sensitive

✪✪⅞
Sangean ATS 909, Sangean ATS 909W, Sangean ATS 909 "Super," Roberts R861

Price: *ATS 909:* $259.95 in the United States. CAD$299.00 in Canada. £139.95 or less in the United Kingdom. €168.00 in Germany. *ATS 909W:* €168.00 in Germany. *ATS 909+mini-antenna:* €198.00 in Germany. *ATS 909 "Super" (not tested):* $328.95 in the United States. *Multivoltage AC adaptor:* £16.95 in the United Kingdom. €30.00 in Germany. *R861:* £199.99 in the United Kingdom.

Pro: Exceptionally wide range of tuning facilities, including hundreds of world band station presets (one works with a single touch) and tuning knob. Tuning system uses 29 "pages" and alphanumeric station descriptors for world band. Two voice bandwidths. Tunes single-sideband signals

Sangean's flagship receiver, the ATS 909, is available in the U.K. as the Roberts R861.

to weak signals (see Con) and performs well overall, has RDS feature, and is in stereo through earpieces, included. Illuminated display. Superior ergonomics, including tuning knob with detents. Longwave. *ATS 909W:* Japanese FM. *ATS 909 (North American units), ATS 909 "Super" and Roberts:* Superb, but relatively heavy, multivoltage AC adaptor with North American and European plugs. ANT-60 outboard reel passive wire antenna accessory aids slightly with weak-signal reception. Sangean service provided by Sangean America on models sold under its name. *ATS 909+mini-antenna (not tested):* includes accessory travel antenna. *ATS 909 "Super," available only from C. Crane Company:* According to C. Crane, includes enhanced tuning knob operation, elimination of muting between stations when band-scanning, improved filtering, enhanced LCD visibility and added bass response.

Con: Weak-signal sensitivity with built-in telescopic antenna not equal to that of comparable models; usually remediable with ANT-60 accessory antenna (provided) or other suitable external antenna. Tuning knob tends to mute stations during bandscanning; C. Crane Company offers a "Deluxe" modification to remedy this. Larger and heavier than most compact models. Signal-seek tuning, although flexible and relatively sophisticated, tends to stop on few active shortwave signals. Although scanner can operate out-of-band, reverts to default (in-band) parameters after one pass. When entering a new page, there is an initial two-second wait between when preset is keyed and station becomes audible. Although synthesizer tunes in 0.04 kHz increments, frequency readout only in 1 kHz increments. Software oddities; e.g., under certain conditions, alphanumeric station descriptor may stay on full time. Page tuning system enjoyed by some users, but cumbersome for others. Speaker audio quality only so-so, not aided by three-level treble-cut tone control. No carrying handle or strap. The 24-hour clock set up to display home time, not World Time, although this is easily overcome by not using world-cities-time feature or by creative setup of World/Home display to London/Home. Clock does not compensate for daylight (summer) time in each displayed city. FM can overload in high-signal-strength environments, causing false "repeat" signals to appear; capture ratio average. Heterodyne interference, possibly related to the digital display, sometimes interferes with reception of strong mediumwave AM signals. Battery consumption well above average. No batteries (four "AA" required). Elevation panel flimsy.

☞ Frequencies pre-programmed into "pages" vary by country of sale. It helps to keep a couple of empty pages to aid in editing, deleting or changing pre-programmed page information.

Verdict: While many models are similar to others being offered, this compact from Sangean marches to its own drummer. Relatively high battery consumption and insufficient weak-signal sensitivity lower its standing as a portable, and our star rating reflects this. Yet, when it is used as a *de facto* tabletop connected to household current and an outboard antenna, it becomes worthy of a three-star rating—even if not as a genuine portable. In part, this is because its circuitry is more capable than those of most other compact portables in handling the increased signal load from an outboard antenna.

As a result, this feature-laden model has a visible and enthusiastic following among radio aficionados for whom portability is not *de rigueur.* Like the tabletop Icom IC-R75, it is a favorite for tuning utility and ham signals, as it offers superior single-sideband performance at an attractive price. The '909 is also the only Sangean model still made exclusively in Taiwan.

❂❂⅞
Sangean PT-80, Grundig Yacht Boy 80

Price: *PT-80:* $159.95 as available in the United States. CAD$169.99 in Canada. *YB 80:* €96.00 in Germany.

Pro: Excellent world band selectivity (*see* Con). Worthy sensitivity and image rejection. Numerous helpful tuning features, including tuning disc-type knob with raised dots (see Con); nicely located up/down slew-scan keys; 18 world band presets; 9 additional presets each for longwave, FM and mediumwave AM; "auto arrange" scanning of presets from low-to-high frequency; auto entry of presets (see Con); meter-segment selector; and selectable 5 kHz/1 kHz tuning steps on shortwave. For size, generally pleasant speaker audio in all bands (see Con). Single-sideband demodulation (see Con), with precise analog +/– 1.5 kHz fine-tuning thumbwheel. No muting with tuning disc, aids bandscanning. Unusually attractive, sheathed in tan leather. Flip-open leather case excellent at protecting front, top and rear of the receiver (see Con). Leather case affixed to receiver with snaps and magnetic catches, so nearly impossible to misplace. Frequency easy to read, with decent-sized digits and good contrast. Illuminated LCD (see Con). Travel power lock (see Con). Tuning-disc lock. Superior mediumwave AM performance. On FM, superior capture ratio and worthy sensitivity. Dual-zone clock in 12 or 24 hour format (see Con). Alarm/clock radio with sleep delay. Rubber feet on bottom to prevent slipping. Stereo indicator (see Con). Battery cover hinged to avoid loss. Keys have good feel (see Con). Low battery indicator. Outboard reel passive wire antenna accessory aids slightly with weak-signal reception. Longwave. Earbuds. *Sangean (North America):* 120V AC adaptor (see Con).

Con: During single-sideband reception, circuit "pulling" during strong modulation peaks causes annoying warbling in audio. Just enough drift at times to prompt occasional tweaking during single-sideband reception. World band and mediumwave AM audio slightly muffled; becomes clearer if station off-tuned by 1 kHz or so, which also can reduce adjacent-channel interference. Limited dynamic range; tends to overload with significant external antenna; attenuator helps, but also reduces signal considerably. (Better to skip attenuation and use the outboard reel antenna, letting out just enough wire to give good reception.) Attenuator doesn't work on mediumwave AM or longwave; however, in unusual circumstances this can be a convenience. Birdies.

The PT-80 is one of Sangean's latest. Although sibling ATS 909 is a skosh better overall, the PT-80 has more weak-signal sensitivity.

Tuning disc has some "play," and raised dots can irritate finger during lengthy bandscanning sessions. Long-stroke keys need to be depressed fully to make contact. No meaningful signal-strength indicator. Spurious signal rejection wanting; at one test location, and alone among several radios there, the PT-80 occasionally had a point-to-point voice transmission puffing away in the background throughout the entire shortwave spectrum. When radio on, displays either frequency or time, but not both at once. FM stereo indicator worked at some test locations, but not all. External antenna jack functions only on shortwave; however, this can also be a convenience. No audio line output for recording, home FM transmitters and outboard audio systems. Auto entry of presets does not function on world band. Leather case: 1) sags when used as an elevation panel; 2) has no holes for speaker on front, just on back, so audio is muffled when case closed; and 3) does not protect receiver's sides or bottom. Travel power lock does not deactivate LCD illumination key. No batteries (four "AA" required). *Sangean:* Country of origin, China, not shown on radio, manual or box. Instructions for setting clocks may confuse newcomers, as both clocks are referred to as being for "local time," not UTC, and the manual's mention of UTC mis-states it as "Universal Time Coordinated" instead of Coordinated Universal Time (however, the PT-50's manual gets it right). *Sangean (North America):* 120V AC adaptor generates minor hum.

Verdict: This entry from Sangean is pleasant performer on world band and superior on mediumwave AM and FM. Its main drawbacks: single-sideband reception with "warbling" audio, and no meaningful signal-strength indicator.

With an external antenna, the sibling Sangean ATS 909 gets the nod, mainly for superior single-sideband performance, dual bandwidths, signal-strength indicator and sophisticated presets. However, as a true portable for only occasional single-sideband listening the PT-80 holds its own, plus it doesn't mute during bandscanning and costs much less.

★★⅞ ✪ *Passport's Choice*
Degen DE1101, Kaito KA1101

Price: *Kaito:* $59.95 in the United States. CAD$79.95 in Canada.

Pro: Exceptional dynamic range for a compact portable. Unusually small and light for a compact model. Two bandwidths, both well chosen. A number of helpful tuning features, including keypad, up/down slew and signal-seek frequency scanning (*see* Con); also, 50 station presets of which ten are for 3,000–10,000 kHz and ten for 10,000–26,100 kHz; others are for FM,

The DE1101 was Degen's first serious model. Also sold as the Kaito KA1101, it still ranks as one of the great buys among compact portables.   D. Zantow

FML and mediumwave AM. Above-average weak-signal sensitivity and image rejection. Little circuit "hiss." Superior intelligibility and loudness for size. World Time 24-hour clock displays seconds numerically when radio is off; when on, time (sans seconds) flashes on briefly when key is held down. Illuminated display, works only in dark. Clicky keys have superior feel. LCD has excellent contrast when viewed from sides or below. Alarm with sleep delay (*see* Con). AC adaptor (120V Kaito, 220V Degen). Rechargeable NiMH batteries (3 × "AA"), included, can be charged within the radio; station presets and time not erased during charging. Low battery consumption. Battery-level indicator. Battery cover hinged to avoid loss. Travel power lock. Superior FM weak-signal sensitivity. Excellent FM capture ratio aids reception when band congested, including helping separate co-channel stations. FM in stereo through earbuds, included. "FML" covers Japanese FM. Line output socket (separate from earphone socket) for recording, FM home transmitters and outboard audio systems. Available in gray or aluminum colors. *Kaito:* Mediumwave AM 9/10 channel steps user-selectable, tunes up to 1710 kHz.

Con: Speaker audio quality lacks low-frequency ("bass") response as compared to larger models. Power button activates a 99-minute sleep delay; to turn the radio on fulltime, a second key must be pressed immediately afterwards. Station presets, slew and scanning require pressing bandswitch carousel button up to four times when tuning from below 10 MHz to above 10 MHz and *vice versa*. No tuning knob. Tunes world band only in 5 kHz steps and displays in nonstandard XX.XX/XX.XX$_5$ MHz format. Digital buzz under some circumstances, such as when antenna is touched. Spurious signals can appear when user's hand is pressed over back cover. With our unit, microprocessor locked up when batteries removed for over a day; resolved by pressing tiny reset button. No signal-strength indicator (what appears to be an LED tuning indicator is actually an ambient-light sensor to disable LCD illumination except when it's dark). Degen's quality control, once well above average, appears to have become hit-or-miss over the past year. Clock doesn't display when frequency is shown, although pushbutton allows time to replace frequency briefly. Little-used 2 MHz (120 meter) world band segment not covered. On Degen unit tested, FM sounded best when tuned 50 kHz above nominal frequency on LCD; this would appear to be a sample-to-sample issue. *Degen:* Upper limit of mediumwave AM tuning is 1620 kHz, rather than the 1705 kHz band upper limit in the Americas, Australia and certain other areas. Mediumwave AM tunes only in 9 kHz steps, making it ill-suited for use in the Americas.

☞ The Kaito version comes with the proper 120V AC adaptor for North America, whereas the Degen version comes with a 220V AC adaptor suitable for most other parts of the world. Both are safe when used "as is," or with a Franzus or other recognized 120V-to-220V or 220V-to-120V AC converter. However, according to unconfirmed reports, the Degen version ordered by Americans from a vendor in Hong Kong comes with a 220-to-120V AC converter that appears to pose a fire hazard.

Verdict: Radio's Sixty-Buck Chuck. The Degen DE1101, sold in North America as the Kaito KA1101, is a knockout bargain. Engineered and manufactured in China, it is one of the smallest compact models tested, and has exceptional dynamic range. It comes with an enviable grab-bag of features and accessories, right down to inboard rechargeable batteries. But if you want music-quality audio, be prepared to use earpieces.

✪✪¾
Etón E10, Tecsun PL-350, Tecsun PL-550

Price: *Etón:* $129.95 in the United States. CAD$149.95 in Canada. £69.95 in the United Kingdom. *Etón/Lextronix:* €98.00 in Germany

Pro: Superior audio quality for size. Numerous helpful tuning features include 1/5 kHz knob, 5/100 kHz up/down slew, world band segment selector (covers all 14 segments), signal-seek frequency scanning, keypad

The Etón E10 has many earmarks of a superior model. However, image rejection is not all it could be—especially when for little more you can have a sibling E5 or G4000A. D. Zantow

and 550 station presets clustered within pages. Fully 500 presets are for general use (*see* Con), including world band; the other 50 are for the "Automatic Tuning System" (ATS), which installs strong FM and mediumwave AM stations (not world band) into presets, like when setting up a VCR. Presets pages programmable to hold 10, 20, 25 or 50 presets per page. Audio muting scarcely noticeable when tuning by knob. Respectable world band and mediumwave AM sensitivity, with low circuit noise. Overloading, which can appear with a substantial external antenna, controllable by two levels of attenuation via a three-position switch. Two well-chosen bandwidths for program listening (*see* Con). Generally worthy ergonomics, including keys with positive-action feel (*see* Con). World Time clock (*see* Con) with alarm, clock radio (two on/off 30-minute timers), snooze and sleep delay (*see* Con); may also be set to 12-hour format. Clock reads out separately from frequency. Clock operates after batteries removed. LCD large and easy to read. Display illumination can either fade out in five seconds, be switched off before the five seconds have expired, or stay on fulltime when button held down more than five seconds. Five-level signal-strength indicator (*see* Con). External antenna jack for world band and FM. Novel 455/450 kHz IF control shifts images by 10 kHz (*see* Con). Elevation panel tilts radio to handy operating angle; rubber pads on bottom reduce sliding when panel in use. Worthy FM sensitivity for superior fringe reception. Japanese FM. Weak-battery indicator. Includes worthy travel pouch, stereo earbuds and outboard reel passive wire antenna. Numerous user-defined software functions, including page definitions for presets, FM frequency coverage and battery type (1.6V normal *vs.* 1.3V rechargeable). Travel power lock (*see* Con). *Etón:* 120V AC adaptor. Four "AA" nickel metal hydride cells that recharge inside radio. Stylish curved front panel, albeit silver colored. Toll-free tech support. *Tecsun (both):* Regulated 220V AC adaptor. *Tecsun PL-350:* Three "AA" nickel metal hydride cells that recharge inside radio. *Tecsun PL-550:* Four "AA" nickel metal hydride cells that recharge inside radio.

Con: Single-conversion circuitry allows for images, although these are weaker than usual even without the novel image-shifting control. Image-shifting control eliminates most image interference, but complicates operation. When image-shifting control adjusted from 455 kHz IF with wide bandwidth to the 450 kHz alternative to escape image interference, only the narrow bandwidth functions; too, when returning to the 455 kHz IF, the narrow bandwidth appears even if the wide bandwidth had originally been in use. Narrow bandwidth too broad for many DX situations. Signal-strength indicator overreads somewhat. Antenna-tuning control seems pointless: does not work with external antenna; yet, with telescopic antenna appears to require only initial tweaking—no adjusting thereafter. No audio line output for recording, home FM transmitters and outboard audio systems. Signal-seek frequency scan rate is slow and stops only at strongest stations. Entering presets data unnecessarily complicated. Some keys relatively small for large fingers. Telescopic antenna, with fixed-height base, does not allow for full vertical positioning when radio laid flat; partially remedied by elevation panel. Travel power lock does not deactivate timers or LCD illumination key. Clock when in 24-hour format does not show leading tens-of-hours zero. Power switch needs to be held down for a second for radio

to stay on fulltime; otherwise, sleep delay eventually turns off radio. FM frequency readout slightly off on one sample. *Etón:* Recessed keys not as easy as most to engage. *Tecsun PL-350:* Simplified controls.

Verdict: The Etón E10 offers unusually pleasant program listening and is loaded with useful goodies, even if it does not demodulate single-sideband signals. There are some questionable features, but the good points are significant while negatives are mainly small potatoes.

✪✪¾
Sangean ATS 606AP, Sangean ATS 606A, Panasonic RF-B55, Roberts R876, Sanyo MB-60A

Price: *ATS 606AP:* $119.95 in the United States. CAD$189.00 in Canada. €102.00 in Germany. *ATS 606A:* €95.00 in Germany. *RF-B55:* £109.95 in the United Kingdom. *R876:* £129.99 or less in the United Kingdom. *MB-60A:* R1,000.00 in South Africa.

Pro: Relatively diminutive for a compact model. Single bandwidth reasonably effective at adjacent-channel rejection, while providing reasonable audio bandwidth. Speaker audio quality better than most for size (*see* Con). Weak-signal sensitivity at least average. Various helpful tuning features, including keypad, 54 station presets, slew, signal-seek tuning and meter band selection. Keys have superior feel. Easy to operate. Longwave. Dual-zone 24-hour clock. Illuminated LCD. Alarm. Sleep delay. Travel power lock (*see* Con). Multi-level battery strength indicator; also, weak-battery warning. Stereo FM through earphones or earbuds. Above-average FM weak-signal sensitivity and selectivity. Above-average capture ratio aids reception when band congested, including helping separate co-channel stations. Memory scan. Elevation panel tilts radio to handy operating angle; rubber feet reduce sliding while panel in use. *R876 and ATS 606AP:* UL-approved 120/230V AC adaptor, with American and European plugs, adjusts to proper AC voltage automatically. *ATS 606AP:* ANT-60 outboard reel passive wire antenna accessory aids slightly with weak-signal reception. In North America, service provided by Sangean America to models sold under its name. *RF-B55:* Cabinet and controls not painted, so should maintain their appearance unusually well. Made in Taiwan, and so indicated on radio and box.

Con: No tuning knob. Speaker audio quality lacks low-frequency ("bass") response as compared to larger models. Clock not readable while frequency displayed. No meaningful signal-strength indicator. Keypad not in telephone format. Travel power lock doesn't disable LCD illumination button. No carrying strap or handle. No batteries (three "AA" needed). *ATS 606AP:* Country of manufacture (China) not specified on radio or box. *RF-B55:* No AC adaptor or outboard reel antenna included, although the owner's manual says that the radio is supposed to come with an "external antenna." Not available within the Americas.

Verdict: This classic continues to hold its own among travel-friendly compact models. Now, it is available in separate Chinese-made and Taiwanese-made versions.

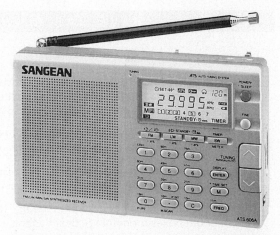

The ATS 606A/AP is a sensibly priced classic. Although manufactured by Sangean, it is also sold under other names.

LCD. Dual-zone 24/12-hour clock. Alarm with sleep delay. Modest battery consumption. Nine-level battery-reserve indicator. Travel power lock (*see* Con). FM stereo through earbuds, included. Longwave. AC adaptor. *ATS 505P:* Tape measure antenna.

Con: Bandwidth slightly wider than appropriate for a single-bandwidth receiver. Large for a compact. Only 18 world band station presets, divided up between two "pages" with nine presets apiece. Tuning knob tends

✪✪⅝
Sangean ATS 505P, Sangean ATS 505, Roberts R9914

Price: *ATS 505P:* $129.95 in the United States. CAD$159.00 in Canada. £79.95 in the United Kingdom. €105.00 in Germany. AUD$199.00 in Australia. *ATS 505:* €95.00 in Germany. *R9914:* £99.99 or less in the United Kingdom. IAC adaptor: £16.95 in the United Kingdom.

Pro: Numerous helpful tuning features, including two-speed tuning knob, keypad, station presets (*see* Con), up/down slew, meter-band carousel selection, signal-seek tuning and scanning of presets (*see* Con). Automatic-sorting feature arranges station presets in frequency order. Analog clarifier with center detent and stable circuitry allows single-sideband signals to be tuned with uncommon precision and to stay properly tuned, thus allowing for superior audio phasing for a portable (*see* Con). Illuminated

Sangean's ATS 505/P includes single-sideband reception. Otherwise, consider the cheaper ATS 606A/AP.

HAVE RADIO, WILL TRAVEL

Getting Past Airport Annie

Even in times of high alert, air travel with a world band radio is almost always trouble-free if common-sense steps are taken. To minimize the odds of delay at airport security, remember that their job is to be paranoid about you, so it's prudent to be paranoid about them.

• Answer all questions honestly, but don't volunteer information or joke around. Friendly banter can get you into the Dreaded Search corner.

• The nail that sticks out gets hammered first. Good security focuses on the unfamiliar or unusual, no matter how innocuous it may seem to you. Be gray.

• Bring a portable, not a portatop or tabletop—terrorists like big radios (they don't call them boom boxes for nothing). Best by far is a pocket or compact model.

• Stow your radio in a carry-on bag, not in checked luggage or on your person. Don't stuff it at the bottom, wrapped in clothing, like you're trying to hide something. Equally, it's usually best not to place it out in the open where it can be seen. However, if you decide to put a small radio into the manual inspection basket at the security portal, have it playing softly with earbuds or earphones attached, as though it were a Walkman you're listening to. Place any world band accessories, extra batteries, guides and instruction books in your checked luggage, or at least in a separate carry-on bag.

• Before entering the terminal, or at least before entering the security area, preset the radio to any popular FM music station, then keep batteries inside the radio so you can demonstrate that it actually works. Don't mention world band or shortwave unless queried.

• If asked what the radio is for, say for your own listening. If they persist, reply that you like to keep up with news and sports while away, and leave it at that. Don't volunteer information about alarm, snooze or other timer facilities, as timers can be components in bombs.

• If traveling in zones of war or civil unrest, or off the beaten path in parts of Africa or South America, take a radio you can afford to lose and which fits inconspicuously inside a pocket.

• If traveling to Bahrain, avoid taking a radio which has "receiver" visible on its cabinet. Security personnel may think you're a spy.

• If traveling to Malaysia, Bahrain or Saudi Arabia, don't take a model with single-sideband capability—or at the very least take steps to disguise this capability so it is not visually apparent. If things get dicey, point out that you listen to news and sports from the popular American AFRTS station, which transmits only in the single-sideband mode. (PASSPORT can be used to authenticate this.)

Theft? Radios, cameras, binoculars, laptops and other glitzy goodies are almost always stolen to be resold. The more worn the item looks—affixing scuffed stickers helps—the less likely it is to be confiscated by corrupt inspectors or stolen by thieves.

Tuning Local Stations Overseas

Mediumwave AM channel separation in the Americas is 10 kHz, elsewhere 9 kHz. When choosing a radio for traveling between these zones, try to select a model that tunes both norms. FM differs too, so Americans should select a model which can tune FM in increments of 0.1 MHz or less.

to mute stations during bandscanning by knob, especially when tuning rate is set to fine (1 kHz); muting with coarse (5 kHz) tuning is much less objectionable. Keys respond slowly, needing to be held down momentarily rather than simply tapped. Stop-listen-resume scanning of station presets wastes time. Pedestrian overall single-sideband reception because of excessively wide bandwidth and occasional distortion caused by AGC timing. Clock does not display independent of frequency. No meaningful signal-strength indicator. No carrying handle or strap. Country of manufacture (China) not specified on radio or box. Travel power lock does not deactivate LCD illumination key. No batteries (four "AA" needed).

Verdict: An okay portable that demodulates single-sideband signals.

Sony has discontinued outstanding models engineered before its corporate decline. Nevertheless, the relatively pedestrian ICF-SW35 remains.

✪✪⅝
Sony ICF-SW35

Price: $89.95 in the United States. €99.00 in Germany. AUD$269.00 in Australia. ¥16,500 in Japan.

Pro: Superior reception quality, with excellent adjacent-channel rejection (selectivity) and image rejection. Fifty world band station presets, which can be scanned within five "pages." Signal-seek-then-resume scanning works unusually well. Two-speed slew. Illuminated display. Dual-zone 24-hour clock. Dual-time alarm. Sleep delay. Travel power lock. FM stereo through earpieces, not included. Weak-battery indicator. Japanese FM (most versions) and longwave.

Con: No keypad or tuning knob. Synthesizer muting and poky slew degrade bandscanning. Speaker audio quality clear, but lacks low-frequency response ("bass"). Clock not displayed independent of frequency. LCD lacks contrast when viewed from above. No jacks for recording or outboard antenna. AC adaptor is extra and pricey. No batteries (three "AA" required).

Verdict: The Sony ICF-SW35 has superior rejection of images, which are the bane of most other under-$100 models. This Chinese-made compact lacks a keypad, which is partially overcome by a large number of station presets and effective scanning. Overall, a decent choice only if you listen to a predictable roster of stations.

✪✪½
Degen DE1105

Price: *via stores.ebay.com/radio-and-component* (see *RP2000 review for vendor specifics*): $59.90 including worldwide air shipping from China. As of presstime, not available from vendors outside China.

Pro: One thousand presets (*see* Con) within ten "pages" (*see* Con); presets do not erase if batteries removed or exhausted. Other handy tuning features include keypad, signal-seek frequency scanning, automatic tuning system (ATS) and up/down slewing. Also, a knurled wheel with un-muted variable-rate tuning shifts from slow (1 kHz) to fast (5 kHz) increments when rotated quickly (*see* Con). Worthy sensitivity and selectivity. Double conversion provides effective image rejection. Dynamic range resists overloading. Buttons have excellent feel (*see* Con). LCD and most buttons illuminate when touched or tuning wheel turned. Ten-level signal strength indicator accurate and precise for price class. Internal automatic NiMH battery recharging virtually eliminates

Although a decent performer, the Degen DE1105 has yet to be sold outside China.   D. Zantow

having to purchase batteries. Three-level battery-strength indicator, seconds as battery-charging indicator. Radio shuts down if batteries too low. Clock selectable between 12-hour and 24-hour formats; seconds displayed numerically (*see* Con). Worthwhile FM sensitivity and selectivity. FM in stereo with earpieces. Bass boost, albeit only on FM with earpieces. Japanese FM. Three alarms with sleep delay. Travel power lock. Hinged battery cover prevents loss. Includes soft carrying case, two "AA" NiMH batteries, earbuds, accessory wire antenna and 220V AC adaptor. Displays ambient (e.g., room) temperature (*see* Con).

Con: Not available outside China except via eBay and with no warranty. Potentially confusing presets "page" system and user setup. Power button activates 99-minute sleep delay bypassed only by quickly pushing another button. World band coverage from 5800 to 26100 kHz, although reasonable, misses lesser 2, 3, 4 and 5 MHz (120, 90, 75 and 60 meter) segments and 5730–5795 kHz end of important 6 MHz (49 meter) segment. Because only one (narrow) bandwidth provided, world band and mediumwave AM audio quality only fair with earpieces and internal speaker. Except for frequency/clock, LCD information small and

hard to see. Buttons undersized. Keypad not in standard telephone format. Tuning wheel operates only in slow (1 kHz) increments within many "out-of-band" frequency zones. Degen's quality control, once well above average, appears to have become hit-or-miss over the past year. Clock shares display with frequency, so you can see one or the other but not both at once. Clock setting erases when batteries removed or exhausted. Mediumwave AM sensitivity only fair. No external antenna or audio line-out jacks. Temperature only in Celsius.

Verdict: The Chinese-made Degen DE1105 is a solid performer within its price class. Size and features make it especially welcome for use on trips, but for similar money there are better choices.

✪✪½
Etón E100, Tecsun PL-200

Price: *Etón:* $99.95 in the United States. CAD$99.99 in Canada. £59.95 in the United Kingdom. *Etón/Lextronix:* €79.00 in Germany.

Pro: Handy size for travel. Very good weak-signal sensitivity. Above-average dynamic range. Superior audio for size, aided by hi/lo tone switch. Several handy tuning aids, including keypad; tuning knob in 1 kHz segments for world band/MW AM (*see* Con); 200 station presets, with eight pages where user selects how many presets per page; world band segment selector; and slew buttons (5 kHz world band increments, 9/10 kHz MW AM increments). Illuminated LCD, easy to read. World Time clock (*see* Con) with alarm, clock radio, snooze and sleep delay; may also be set to 12-hour format. Clock reads out separately from frequency. Signal-seek frequency scanning searches world band segments or preset channels (*see* Con). Five-level signal/battery strength indicator, works well. Keys have positive-action feel (*see* Con). FM stereo with earbuds, included. Japanese FM. Travel power lock. Telescopic antenna swivels and rotates. Setting to allow for optimum performance from either regular or rechargeable batteries. Elevation panel tilts radio to handy operating angle. *Etón:* Excellent hardside leather travel case. Two "AA" alkaline batteries included. Stylish curved front panel, silver colored. Toll-free tech support. Owner's manual unusually helpful for newcomers. *Tecsun:* 220V AC adaptor/battery charger and rechargeable "AA" batteries included. Softside travel case protects better than most. Choice among three colors (red, gray, silver).

Con: Single-conversion IF circuitry results in mediocre image rejection. Signal-seek frequency scanning progresses slowly. Some muting when tuning by knob or slewing, slows down bandscanning. Tuning knob has no selectable 5 kHz step option. Power button activates 90-minute sleep delay; works as full-time "on" control only if held down for two seconds, a minor inconvenience; there is an additional three seconds to boot up, so basically it takes five seconds to turn on. World band frequencies on all Etón and Tecsun samples displayed 1 kHz high. Small, cramped keys. No jacks for line output or external antenna. *Etón:* No AC adaptor included. On our early sample the tuning knob rubbed the cabinet slightly.

Verdict: A spit-and-polish offering for tuning major stations at home or away.

Etón's E100 is nicely sized for travel. Image rejection keeps performance below three stars, but ergonomics, features and audio quality are superior.

Clock readout separate from frequency display, shows whether radio on or off. Signal-seek frequency scanning searches world band segments or preset channels (*see* Con). Five-level signal/battery strength indicator, works well. FM stereo with earbuds, included. Japanese FM. Travel power lock. Telescopic antenna swivels and rotates (*see* Con). Setting to allow for optimum performance from either regular or rechargeable batteries. *YB 550PE and PL-230:* Generally pleasant audio (*see* Con). Stylish. Removable elevation panel (*see* Con) tilts radio to handy operating angle. LCD easy to

✪✪⅜
Etón YB 550PE, Grundig YB 550PE, Tecsun PL-230

Price: *YB550PE:* $79.95 in the United States. CAD$79.95 in Canada. £69.95 in the United Kingdom. *Etón/Lextronix YB550PE:* €79.00 in Germany.

Pro: Very good selectivity. Above-average dynamic range. Several handy tuning aids, including 200 station presets with eight pages where user selects how many presets per page; also, world band segment selector. For world band, slew buttons tune in 5 kHz increments, while a fine-tuning (encoder) thumbwheel tunes shortwave and mediumwave AM in 1 kHz increments. Illuminated LCD (*see* Con). World Time clock (*see* Con) with alarm, clock radio and sleep delay; may also be set to 12-hour format.

The Etón YB550PE is slotted within a highly competitive price zone, but customer support helps it stand out.

read. *PL-230:* AC adaptor/battery charger and rechargeable "AA" batteries included. *YB 550PE:* Three "AA" alkaline batteries included. *North America (Grundig YB 550PE):* Toll-free tech support.

Con: Weak-signal sensitivity only fair. Single-conversion IF circuitry results in mediocre image rejection. Signal-seek frequency scanning stops only on very strong signals. Power button activates 90-minute sleep delay; works as full-time "on" control only if held down for two seconds, a minor inconvenience. Takes an additional five seconds to fully turn on (or boot up). Small, cramped keys. *YB 550PE:* No AC adaptor included. *YB 550PE and PL-230:* Audio crispness on FM through earpieces not fully up to Grundig standard. Keypad has oddly placed zero key. Telescopic antenna placement on right side disallows tilting to left. Illumination dim. Snap-on elevation panel must be removed to replace batteries. Battery cover comes loose easily if elevation panel not attached. One of our two units displayed FM 50 Hz high, whereas world band frequencies on both samples were 1 kHz high.

☞ The Tecsun PL-230 is essentially identical to the YB 550PE except for color and the inclusion of rechargeable batteries and an AC adaptor/charger.

Verdict: Under-$100 radios used to look blah and often sounded that way, but no more. These stylish portables are straight-

For thrifty consumers who prefer Sangean products, the ATS 404 fits the bill. No barnburner, but it is sensible for trips.

forward to use and full of software conveniences. However, images and weak-signal sensitivity keep them from reaching their full potential.

✪✪⅜
Sangean ATS 404, Sangean ATS 404P

Price: *ATS 404:* $79.95 in the United States. CAD$99.99 in Canada. €67.00 in Germany. *ATS 404P:* €77.00 in Germany. *ADP-808 120V AC adaptor:* $12.95 in the United States.

Pro: Superior weak-signal sensitivity. Several handy tuning features. Stereo FM through earpieces, included. Dual-zone 24/12-hour clock displays seconds numerically. Alarm with sleep delay. Travel power lock. Illuminated LCD. Battery indicator. *ATS 404P:* Includes ANT 60 accessory antenna.

Con: Single-conversion IF circuitry results in poor image rejection. No tuning knob. Overloading, controllable by shortening telescopic antenna on world band and collapsing it on mediumwave AM band. Picks up some internal digital "buzz." Tunes only in 5 kHz increments. No signal-strength indicator. Frequency and time cannot be displayed simultaneously. Travel power lock does not disable LCD illumination. No handle or carrying strap. AC adaptor extra. Country of manufacture (China) not specified on radio or box. No batteries (four "AA" needed).

Verdict: Better values can be found elsewhere.

New for 2007
✪✪
Kchibo KK-C55, Sharper Image SN401

Price: $49.95 in the United States.

Pro: Helpful tuning features include up/down slewing, signal-seek frequency scanning, instant access to world band segments, keypad (*see* Con), 40 station presets (*see* Con) and "auto-store" that enters the first ten strongest stations of a segment into a memory bank. Good sensitivity for price class. Crisp audio (*see* Con) with superior intelligibility and loudness for small radio. Keys have good feel. Excellent timed LCD illumination. Above average FM performance. FM in stereo through earphones. Japanese FM. Telescopic antenna swivels and rotates. World Time clock (*see* Con). Two separate alarms include five-minute snooze and up to a 100-minute sleep delay. Travel power lock. Battery indicator. Cloth travel pouch (*see* Con), earbuds and clip-on wire antenna. Insertable elevation tab, attached to carrying strap, tilts radio to handy operating angle. External power jack (*see* Con).

Con: Excessive digital noise mixes with most world band signals and is amplified when radio is handheld or finger is placed near LCD. Single-conversion IF circuitry results in poor image rejection. Poor dynamic range; no circuit to help control resulting overloading. No tuning knob. Slew band-scanning limited by half-second muting. Nonstandard keypad format compromises ergonomics. World band coverage of 5.9 to 18 MHz misses 2, 3, 4, 5, 19, 21 and 25 MHz (120, 90, 75, 60, 15, 13 and 11 meter) segments and 5730–5895 kHz portion of 6 MHz (49 meter) segment. Only ten station presets for world band. World band tunes only in 5 kHz steps and displays in XX.XXx MHz format. Mediumwave AM useless in Western Hemisphere, as tuning step fixed at 9 kHz instead of appropriate 10 kHz; too, omits 1630–1705 kHz portion of expanded band. Other than frequency/clock, LCD characters tiny and hard to read. Bass control actually single-level high cut switch, not bass boost. Volatile memory. Clock shares display with frequency readout, so shows only when radio off or button pushed. No signal strength indicator. Battery cover not hinged. No AC adaptor. Required two "AAA" batteries not included; these require more frequent replacement than larger "AA" cells. Cloth travel pouch slightly malodorous.

Verdict: The affordable Kchibo KK-C55 offers just about every desirable tuning feature and is suitable for travel. Nevertheless, this Chinese offering misses important frequencies and is hopeless on mediumwave AM in the Americas. Its noisy microprocessor degrades reception, too.

Kchibo's KK-C55, also sold as the Sharper Image SN401, is okay for travel. Yet, it is limited by mediocre performance, peculiar ergonomics and AM tuning issues.   D. Zantow

Evaluation of New Model: Although there's no tuning knob, the Kchibo KK-C55 offers a variety of tuning options including a keypad with a truly offbeat layout. There are the usual up/down slewing controls, but they suffer from muting that weakens bandscanning.

Especially interesting is a novel tuning feature that stores the first ten received signals found when scanning a chosen band or world band segment. It sounds better on paper than in practice, as the scan starts at the bottom of a band/segment, then when ten signals have been found that's it. Push the button again and it stores the same ten channels.

World band coverage is reasonable, but misses the 2, 3, 4, 5, 19, 21 and 25 MHz segments and the 5730–5895 kHz portion of 6 MHz. Disruptive images abound, thanks to single-conversion IF circuitry.

However, world band sensitivity is good—so much so that it can overload the receiver with just its diminutive built-in telescopic antenna, much less the included clip-on antenna. There's no attenuator, but shortening the telescopic antenna helps tame overloading by reducing sensitivity. Alas, good sensitivity doesn't overcome digital noise from the radio's microprocessor. This often mixes in with the received world band signal, making it less pleasant.

Audio from the internal speaker is punchy and useful. Unsurprisingly, given the radio's small size, there's scarcely any bass response. There is a "bass" button, but it is merely a high-cut tone control rather than a bass boost.

Tuning Wrong for Americas

Incredibly for a radio marketed within North America, the mediumwave AM tuning step is fixed at 9 kHz; thus, it's not user-switchable to the 10 kHz channel spacing used in the Western Hemisphere. You can't even rely on the keypad to get around this, as any entered frequency defaults to the nearest 9 kHz channel. Depending on how close that channel is to the proper 10 kHz channel, reception can vary from normal to impossible, with many stations coming in distorted from being off-tuned.

FM performance, thankfully, is another story. It is above average, and stereo audio through the included earpieces is quite pleasant. Covers Japanese FM, too.

✪⅞
Grundig G2000A "Porsche Design"

Price: $79.95 in the United States. AUD$199.00 in Australia. *G2ACA 120V AC adaptor:* $12.95 in the United States. CAD$19.95 in Canada.

Grundig's G2000A looks great, but little else.

Pro: One of the most functionally attractive world band radios on the market. Generally superior ergonomics include a handy flip-open leather protective case that seconds as an elevation panel to tilt radio to handy operating angle. Leather case excellent at protecting front, top and rear of the receiver (*see* Con). Leather case affixed to receiver with snaps and magnetic catches, so nearly impossible to misplace. Superior adjacent-channel rejection—selectivity—for price and size class. Keypad (in proper telephone format), handy meter-band carousel control, signal-seek and up/down slew tuning. Twenty station presets, of which ten are for world band and the rest for FM and mediumwave AM stations. FM stereo through earpieces, included. World Time 24-hour clock. Timer/alarm with sleep delay. Illuminated display. Travel power lock. *North America:* Toll-free tech support.

Con: Pedestrian audio. Weak-signal sensitivity mediocre between 9400–26100 kHz, improving slightly between 2300–7400 kHz. Single-conversion IF circuitry results in poor image rejection. Does not tune such important world band ranges as 7405–7550 and 9350–9395 kHz. Tunes world band only in 5 kHz steps and displays in nonstandard XX.XX/XX.XX$_5$ MHz format. No tuning knob. Annoying one-second pause when tuning from one channel to the next. Old-technology SW1/SW2 switch complicates tuning. Protruding power button can get in the way of nearby slew-tuning and meter-carousel keys. Using 9/10 kHz mediumwave AM channel switch erases station presets and clock setting. Leather case makes it difficult to retrieve folded telescopic antenna. Leather case does not protect bottom or sides of radio. Magnetic catches weak on leather case. No carrying strap. Signal-strength indicator nigh useless. Clock not displayed separately from frequency. No batteries (three "AA" required).

☞ At present there are no plans to sell this model under the Etón name.

Verdict: This German-styled, Chinese-manufactured portable is awash in tasteful design, but performance is another story.

New for 2007

✪⅞ ⊘
Etón E1100, Grundig G1100

Price: $49.95 in the United States, CAD$69.95 in Canada.

Pro: Tunes by knob, not thumbwheel as did predecessor model (*see* Con). Slightly better world band coverage than predecessor model (*see* Con). Good world band and mediumwave AM sensitivity. Pleasant, vigorous audio (*see* Con). Easy-to-read LCD has large digits and good contrast. Clever, effective LCD illumination turns on and off by rotating tuning knob or pushing button. Travel power lock (*see* Con). Telescopic antenna swivels and rotates. Weak battery indicator. Elevation panel tilts radio to handy operating angle. World Time clock (*see* Con) with alarm, clock radio and snooze; may also be set to 12-hour format. Sleep delay up to two hours. FM in stereo through included earbuds; FM stereo indicator. Two "AA" batteries included. Superior carrying case. *North America:* Toll-free tech support.

Con: Single conversion IF circuitry results in poor image rejection, with signals repeating at reduced strength 910 kHz down. Selectivity only okay. Analog tuned with digital frequency counter, so tunes only by stiff knob; thus, it lacks such helpful tuning aids as station presets, keypad and scanning. Analog tuning uses string and pulley configuration to turn variable capacitors; this results in play and makes it harder than usual to zero in on stations. Lacks coverage of little-used 2 and 25 MHz (120 and 11 meter) world band segments; also misses relatively unimportant 3 MHz (90 meter) segment and 5.73–5.9 MHz portion of important 6 MHz (49 meter) segment. Unhandy bandswitch must be accessed often to tune mediumwave AM and within shortwave spectra. Placing hand on or near cabinet rear causes frequency drift of up to 5 kHz. Placing hand or finger on LCD generates buzzing on mediumwave AM and lower world band frequencies. Audio has limited bass. FM hampered by overloading from strong local signals. Frequency reads out only in 5 kHz increments in XX.XX/XX.XX₅ MHz format.

The G1100 is the latest upgrade to an established Grundig model.

No signal-strength indicator. Clock reads out only when radio off. Travel power lock does not disable LCD illumination. No AC adaptor (3V DC center-tip negative needed). Battery cover not hinged to prevent loss.

Verdict: A slight upgrade over its G1000A predecessor, the '1100 has more spit and polish, and better daytime frequency coverage, than most cheaper alternatives. It's also backed up by a solid warranty and, in North America, a free help line.

The E1100/G1100 occupies a spot between "throwaway" models that are passable performers and sometimes not sold outside China, and more highly rated models that cost more.

Evaluation of New Model: The new Etón E1100/Grundig G1100 replaces the G1000A and is improved by a skosh. For example, it uses a real tuning knob instead of a thumbwheel and the bandswitch is more solid—it doesn't cut out at all.

There's greater world band coverage, too, with exact coverage varying slightly from sample to sample: 3985 to 4445, 4680 to 5260, 5910 to 6615, 7015 to 7730, 9160 to 10135, 11595 to 12560, 13530 to 14285, 15050 to 16040, 17375 to 18290 and 21555 to 22140 kHz. Mediumwave AM is 521 to 1733 kHz, while FM tunes 86.3 to 108.5 MHz.

The addition of the tropical 5 MHz (60 meter) segment is a nice plus, even if the lesser

2, 3 and 25 MHz (120, 90 and 11 meter) segments remain uncovered. More significant is that the '1100 skips 5730–5905 kHz within the important 49 meter segment, as well as 11500–11590 kHz and 21450–21550 kHz in the major 25 and 13 meter segments. Also AWOL: 3900–3980 kHz in the 75 meter segment used outside the Americas and the relatively new 18900–19020 kHz (15 meter) segment.

The '1100, like its predecessor, is analog tuned with the frequency being read out digitally on an LCD. That LCD has large digits with superior contrast and effective illumination which extinguishes with a button push or the when the tuning knob stops rotating.

The '1100's black cabinet is attractive and finished with rubbery paint, like Etón's higher-end E1 and E5 models. Handy features include an elevation panel to angle the radio to a handy operating angle. It works well, and the telescopic antenna swivels and rotates.

Sensitivity is good for the radio's class, giving weaker signals a sporting chance of being heard. However, selectivity is only okay, as the lone bandwidth filter is broad enough that adjacent-channel interference is sometimes unnecessarily annoying. Too, single-conversion IF circuitry creates disruptive images 910 kHz down from fundamental signals.

A worthy radio should welcome human contact, not be harmed by it. Yet, resting part of a hand on the '1100's back panel tends to throw off the tuned frequency by up to 5 kHz. Moreover, touching the LCD can cause audible buzzing by amplifying digital hash from the clock/frequency-counter's IC.

Grundig almost always signifies superior world band audio, and the '1100 is no exception. For a set of this type the audio is pleasant, relatively powerful and doesn't break up even at high volume. This makes it unusually useful outdoors or in relatively noisy environments. Still, like most diminutive portables it lacks any real bass response.

The '1100 tunes with a knob, an ergonomic plus over the erstwhile G1000A's thumb-wheel. Yet, that knob is stiff and the tuning-string system creates play, so it can be a chore to zero in on a station.

FM is in stereo through headphones or earbuds, and there's a stereo indicator. However, that band overloads easily, making weak-signal reception relatively difficult except when you're listening far from nearby FM transmitters.

The clock displays in either 12 or 24 hour format. A sleep-delay timer comes on automatically when power is turned on, but if the power button is held down for an extra second the radio stays on normally. Otherwise, the sleep delay can be set to turn off the radio after 5, 10, 15, 30, 45, 60, 75, 90 or 120 minutes. There's also a clock radio or bird-chirping alarm to rouse you from your slumber. For slow risers there's also a ten-minute snooze control.

The Etón E1100/Grundig G1100 is a pleasant low-cost radio for travel and occasional use at home. It's one of the better "radios on the cheap" and is backed up in North America by a free customer-friendly help line.

New for 2007
✪⅞
Kchibo KK-C36

Price: *via stores.ebay.com/v-com-collections (see RP2000 review for vendor specifics):* $44.80 including air shipping from China to other countries. As of presstime, not available from vendors outside China.

Pro: Helpful tuning features include up/down slewing, signal-seek frequency scanning, instant access to world band segments, keypad (*see* Con) and two dozen station presets (*see* Con). Crisp audio (*see* Con) with superior intelligibility and loudness for small radio. Keys have good feel (*see* Con). Telescopic antenna swivels and rotates. Travel power lock (*see* Con). Small elevation panel tilts radio to handy operating angle. World Time clock (*see* Con). 100-minute sleep delay. FM in stereo through headphones. Cloth travel pouch (*see* Con), earbuds and clip-on wire antenna. External power jack (*see* Con).

Con: Not available outside China except via eBay and with no warranty and questionable shipment insurance. Excessive digital noise mixes with some world band signals and is amplified when radio is handheld or finger is placed near LCD; however, this is less noticeable than on kindred KK-C55 (*see*). Single-conversion IF circuitry results in poor image rejection. Poor dynamic range; no circuit to help control resulting overloading. No tuning knob. Slew band-scanning limited by half-second muting. Off-beat keypad format degrades ergonomics. World band coverage, in two "bands," of 2.3 to 7.3 and 9.5 to 26.1 MHz misses chunks of the 7 and 9 MHz (41 and 31 meter) segments. Changing world band frequencies can require extra step of choosing "band." Only six station presets per "band." World band tunes only in 5 kHz steps and displays in XX.XXx MHz format. Mediumwave AM omits 1630–1705 kHz portion of expanded band. Mediocre FM performance. Small buttons/keys. Other than frequency/clock, LCD characters tiny and hard to read. Volatile memory. LCD has modestly sized digits and dim illumination. Travel power lock does not disable LCD illumination. Clock shares display with frequency readout, so shows only when radio off or button pushed. No clock radio or alarm. No signal strength indicator. Battery cover not hinged. No AC adaptor. Required two "AAA" batteries not included; these require more frequent replacement than larger "AA" cells. Cloth travel pouch slightly malodorous.

Verdict: The budget-priced Kchibo KK-C36 is a simplified version of the sibling KK-C55 (*see*). Yet, in some ways it's better. For example, digital noise is less intrusive and there are selectable mediumwave AM tuning steps. Broader world band coverage, too, except for a significant gap between 7.3 and 9.5 MHz.

Nicely sized and priced for travel, but this Chinese model feels cheap, has mediocre FM and is ergonomically inferior.

Evaluation of New Model: Although it has no tuning knob, the Kchibo KK-C36 offers a variety of tuning options—including a keypad with a seriously offbeat layout. There

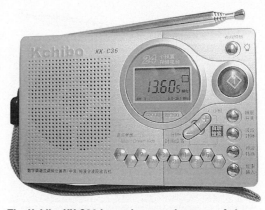

The Kchibo KK-C36 is one in a growing army of cheap portables for folks in China, where world band is valued for uncensored news.   D. Zantow.

are the usual up/down slewing controls, although with muting that compromises bandscanning. World band coverage is broad, but misses important frequencies found between 7.3 and 9.5 MHz.

Audio from the internal speaker is punchy and intelligible, but there's little bass response. Limited dynamic range can cause overloading at times with the built-in telescopic antenna, but it's not a significant problem. Single-conversion IF circuitry results in poor image rejection.

The radio's microprocessor emits some digital noise. This occasionally bothers world band, but it is audibly less of an issue than with the costlier KK-C55. Another real plus over the 'C55 is that mediumwave AM tuning steps are selectable (9 or 10 kHz).

In all, the Kchibo KK-C36 is no barnburner; yet, it cuts the mustard for travel even considering it lacks an alarm. And if it's lost or stolen, you won't have to file a claim with Lloyd's of London.

✪¾ ⊘
Grundig G1000A, Tecsun DR-910

Price: *Grundig:* $49.95 as available in the United States. CAD$69.95 in Canada.

Pro: Clock/timer with sleep delay (*see* Con). Illuminated LCD has bigger digits than most models of this size. Elevation panel tilts

The Grundig G1000A does what is expected for the price, but adds solid warranty and support.

radio to handy operating angle. FM in stereo with earbuds, included. Two "AA" batteries included. Superior carrying case. *North America:* Toll-free tech support.

Con: Analog tuned with digital frequency counter, so tunes only by thumbwheel, which is slightly touchy. Does not tune relatively unimportant 2, 3, 4, 5, 19 and 25 MHz (120, 90, 75, 60, 15 and 11 meter) segments; misses a small amount of expanded coverage of important 41 and 31 meter segments. Single-conversion IF circuitry results in poor image rejection. Audio lacks bass response. Frequency drift with changes in temperature. Clock in 12-hour format, displays only when radio off.

The Sangean PT-50 is priced higher than its performance warrants. Available in the United Kingdom as the Roberts Travelling Lite 2.

Displays in nonstandard XX.XX/XX.XX$_5$ MHz format. "Play" in bandswitch allows wiggling to slightly alter frequency readout. FM overloads in presence of strong signals, remediable by shorting antenna (which also reduces weak-signal sensitivity). On our units, FM frequency misread by 100 kHz (half a channel). If finger placed over LCD display, buzzing audible on mediumwave AM and lower world band frequencies. No AC adaptor.

Verdict: More spit and polish, and better daytime frequency coverage, than truly cheaper alternatives. It's also backed up by a solid warranty from a reputable company. The G1000A occupies a spot between "throwaway" models that are passable performers, and more highly rated models that cost more.

⭐¾

Sangean PT-50, Roberts Travelling Lite 2

Price: *Sangean:* $79.95 in the United States. CAD$99.00 in Canada. *Roberts:* under £50.00 in the United Kingdom.

Pro: Unusually attractive, sheathed in tan leather. Flip-open leather case excellent at protecting front, top and rear of the receiver (*see* Con). Leather case affixed to receiver with snaps and magnetic catches, so nearly impossible to misplace. Two clocks, with separate display windows for home time and World Time. Changing home time to summer (savings) setting does not alter World Time. Handy disc to select time in any of 24 world zones (*see* Con). 24 or 12 hour clock format (*see* Con). Illuminated display. Reasonably clean, pleasant speaker audio for size (*see* Con). Travel power lock (*see* Con). FM in stereo through earpieces (*see* Con). Generally good mediumwave AM performance (*see* Con). Low-battery indicator. Stereo indicator (*see* Con). Battery cover hinged to avoid loss. Keys "clicky," with excellent feel. Alarm/clock radio with sleep delay and snooze. Rubber feet on bottom to prevent slipping.

Con: Analog tuned with digital frequency counter, so tunes only by thumbwheel, which is slightly touchy. Bandswitch must be adjusted when going from one world band segment to another, complicating operation. World band coverage omits 5730–5795 kHz portion of 49 meters; 6890–6990 and 7535–7600 kHz portions of 41 meters; 9250–9305 kHz portion of 31 meters; and all of 120, 90, 75, 60, 15, 13 and 11 meters. Frequency display nonstandard, being in Megahertz and reading out only to the nearest 10 kHz; thus, 6155 kHz shows as 6.15 and/or 6.16 MHz. Single-conversion IF circuitry results in poor image rejection. World band sensitivity and selectivity only fair. No external antenna socket. Speaker audio weak in bass. Audio amplifier lacks punch; stations with weak audio hard to hear, or break into distortion. Frequency drift with changes in temperature. Time-format selection applies to World and home displays alike, so 24 hours can't be used for World Time and 12 hours for home. Small LCDs with thin characters for size of radio. FM performance ordinaire, with mediocre capture ratio; in strong-signal situations there can be overloading. FM stereo indicator worked at some test locations, but not all. Pedestrian spurious-signal rejection on mediumwave AM. No meaningful signal-strength indicator. Bandswitch designates world band segments as 1–7 rather than as MHz. No AC adaptor (needs 3-6V DC, center negative), batteries (two "AA" required) or earpieces. No audio line output for recording, home FM transmitters and outboard audio systems. Leather case: 1) collapses when used as elevation panel; 2) no perforations over speaker, so case has to be opened for listening; 3) does not protect receiver's sides or bottom; 4) when case closed, telescopic antenna can only be extended roughly horizontally, to the left; and 5) even when open, case blocks folded telescopic antenna and there is no cabinet detent for finger, so unfolding antenna is cumbersome (best is not to push antenna into the cabinet's snap-in antenna catch). Travel power lock does not deactivate LCD illumination key. Country of origin, China, not shown on radio, manual or box.

Verdict: Great clock, so-so radio. Unusually handy as a multi-zone timepiece and a class-act eyeful. Yet, by today's yardstick

the PT-50's radio performance and features are inferior to various other models priced comparably or lower.

New for 2007
✪¾ *ⓒ*
Tecsun R9702

Price: *via stores.ebay.com/v-com-collections (see RP2000 review for vendor specifics):* $31.80 including air shipping from China to other countries. As of presstime, not available from vendors outside China.

Pro: Dual conversion design provides worthy image rejection, exceptional at this price. Superior audio quality with decent bass and plenty of volume. Sensitive on world band. Large, easy-to-read LCD with good contrast and useful illumination. Mediumwave AM sensitivity above average for genre. FM in stereo through provided earbuds. Telescopic antenna rotates and swivels. Elevation panel tilts radio to handy operating angle. External power jack (3V DC, negative tip). Outboard wire antenna. Alarm (*see* Con) Superior travel case (*see* Con).

Con: Not available outside China except via eBay and with no warranty and questionable shipment insurance. Analog tuned with digital frequency counter, so tunes only by stiff knob; thus, it lacks such helpful tuning aids as station presets, keypad and scanning. Frequency displays only to the nearest

Tecsun's R9702, new for 2007, serves the burgeoning world band market in China. Elsewhere, try eBay.

10 kHz. World band coverage misses important 21 MHz (13 meter) segment and lesser 2, 3, 4, 5, 19 and 25 MHz (120, 90, 75, 60, 15 and 11 meter) segments. Shortwave spectrum divided into two "bands," complicating world band tuning. Selectivity only fair. Minor spurious signals. Clock, only in 12-hour format, doesn't display independent of frequency. No keyboard lock. No signal strength indicator. Mediumwave AM coverage omits 1645–1705 kHz. Battery cover not hinged. No clock radio; buzzer alarm unpleasant if volume turned up. No snooze or sleep timers. Required two "AA" batteries not included. Travel case has slight creosote odor that lessens with airing.

Verdict: Best of the truly cheap. With pleasant performance, display illumination, alarm and useful carrying case, this bargain is hard to beat for travel.

Evaluation of New Model: The Tecsun R9702 is not quite mini enough for a normal pocket, but comes with an unusually solid, if initially malodorous, travel case. Frequency readout is shared with the clock's integrated circuit, so it shows only to the nearest 10 kHz. The LCD is easy to read, has good contrast and its timed illumination works well.

World band is covered in two receiver "bands," which complicates tuning slightly: 5.30 to 10.35 MHz and 11.34 to 18.72 MHz, which omit the important 21 MHz (13 meter) segment and lesser 2, 3, 4, 5, 19 and 25 MHz (120, 90, 75, 60, 15 and 11 meter) segments.

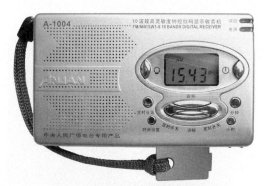

Like most radios for Chinese consumers, the Anjan A-1004 is cheap, with digital readout to help locate frequencies that are overcoming jamming.   D. Zantow

Tuning is only by knob, which although a bit stiff is smooth with little play. Still, the tuning setup is no bandscanner's delight.

What really makes the R9702 stand out among truly cheap radios is dual conversion. It works well at rejecting images, even if some other spurious signals appear here and there. Audio quality is superior, too—for its size and price the radio sounds quite pleasant, with a touch of bass and plenty of volume.

Sensitivity is commendable with the built-in telescopic antenna. However, dynamic range is limited, so adding the included wire antenna or a better external antenna tends to generate overloading. Selectivity is too broad for congested situations, but it's adequate for most world band listening.

Although 1645–1705 kHz is omitted, mediumwave AM has superior sensitivity and pleasant performance. FM, too.

This Tecsun model puts a whole new light on bargain-priced world band portables. There are many better radios available, but nothing else touches the R9702 for this kind of loose change.

✪⅝
Anjan A-1004

Price: *via stores.ebay.com/v-com-collections* (see *RP2000 review for vendor specifics*): $28.90 including air shipping from China to other countries. As of presstime, not available from vendors outside China.

Pro: Appears to be solidly made; includes a beefy aluminum front panel in lieu of the customary plastic. Almost totally free from the digital buzzing that plagues many other analog-tuned models with digital frequency readout. Reasonable sensitivity for price class. LCD illumination, unusually effective (*see* Con). Pleasant room-filling audio for such a small package (*see* Con). In some respects, tuning wheel superior for price class (*see* Con). Antenna swivels. Clock/alarm function (*see* Con). Insertable elevation tab, attached to carrying strap, tilts radio to handy operating angle. Build quality appears to be above average for class.

Con: Not available outside China except via eBay and with no warranty and questionable shipment insurance. Analog tuned with digital frequency counter, so tunes only by thumbwheel; this has some backlash and tends to be touchy. Single-conversion IF circuitry results in poor image rejection, particularly noticeable with a short outboard antenna. Audio lacks any trace of bass. World band coverage omits the 2, 3, 4, 5 and 25 MHz (120, 90, 75, 60 and 11 meter) world band segments. Always defaults to FM when first turned on. Frequency display nonstandard, being in Megahertz and reading out only to the nearest 10 kHz; thus, 6155 kHz shows as 6.15 and/or 6.16 MHz. Volume control touchy, especially on FM. Some batteries fit so tight as to be almost impossible to insert. Battery cover not hinged. Clock only in 12-hour format. Does not tune 1640–1710 kHz portion of the mediumwave AM band. Mediumwave AM sensitivity poor. FM sensitivity marginal. FM in mono only. No travel lock. Button must be kept depressed for LCD to be illuminated. Batteries (2 × "AA") and AC adaptor not included.

Verdict: The Anjan A-1004's metal front panel helps it stand apart from most portables. This classy touch appears to be characteristic of what seems to be above-average build quality within its price class. Audio, too, is okay, while overall performance is about as much as you'll find among cheap analog models with digital frequency readout.

Still, this is no breakthrough model. Image rejection and selectivity are lousy, there's overloading, tuning coverage isn't quite complete, frequency readout is imprecise and controls can be touchy. FM and mediumwave AM performance are both wanting, too.

New for 2007
✪½
Degen DE108

Price: *via stores.ebay.com/radio-and-component (see RP2000 review for vendor specifics):* $41.90 including worldwide air shipping from China. As of presstime, not available from vendors outside China.

The new Degen DE108 is a mediocre performer that's woefully lacking in tuning features. Other models offer more for about the same money.   D. Zantow

Pro: Reasonably good selectivity from single bandwidth. Good voice-audio quality, with ample volume, for a small speaker (*see* Con). Dual-zone 24-hour clock. Clicky keys have superior feel. Large, easy-to-read LCD (*see* Con) with good contrast and helpful silvery-green background. Clock radio. Weak-battery indicator. Battery cover hinged to avoid loss (*see* Con). Travel power lock. FM in stereo through earbuds, included (*see* Con). Hum-free 110V or 220V AC adaptor, depending on shipping destination. Cloth travel pouch.

Con: Not available outside China except via eBay and with no warranty. No helpful tuning features except up/down slewing, which has excessive muting; also, effective signal-seek/presets scanning and 30 station presets—but only ten for world band. Coverage of 5950–15600 kHz misses important 17 and 21 MHz (16 and 13 meter) world band segments, skips portions of major 6 and 15 MHz (49 and 19 meter) segments, and omits lesser 2, 3, 4, 5, 19 and 25 (120, 90, 75, 60, 15 and 11 meter) segments. Single-conversion IF circuitry results in poor image rejection. Poor dynamic range. Uninspiring sensitivity. Selectivity somewhat broad. Tunes world band only in 5 kHz steps and displays in nonstandard XX.XX/XX.XX$_5$ MHz format. No signal-strength indicator. FM exceptionally poor: distorts badly and tends to overload; appears to be a design issue possibly complicated by quality control. Clock doesn't display when frequency is shown. Except for time and frequency, LCD characters small. Woefully flimsy battery cover; ours broke almost immediately, yet another indication that Degen's build quality is on the decline. Volatile memory. Mediumwave AM tuning increments not user-switchable; comes with 9 kHz or 10 kHz steps, depending on shipping destination. Mediumwave AM coverage of American version omits 1625–1705 kHz portion of extended band. World band below roughly 10 MHz and mediumwave AM suffer slightly from LCD digital hash. Telescopic antenna does not rotate or swivel. Two "AA" batteries not included.

Verdict: The Degen DE108 is delightfully uncomplicated and inexpensive. Yet, sometimes less isn't more: The '108 is woefully lacking in helpful tuning features and several aspects of performance. Maybe build quality, too.

There are better lions in radio's jungle. Look elsewhere.

Evaluation of New Model: In a relatively short time Degen has become a major player in the design and manufacture of world band portables for itself and other firms. Their new DE108 sports a fashionably retro approach, with the look and feel of a no-nonsense 1960s specialty device. Think of yesteryear's MG-TD *vs.* today's Pontiac Solstice—both beloved, yet thoroughly different.

A major downside to this is that you quickly miss tuning features—keypad, knob and the like—found on less Zen-like models. That's because the '108 tunes only three ways: up/down slewing, station presets and signal-seek/presets scanning.

Scanning works well, but the remaining options leave much to be desired. Slewing chugs along at a snail's pace, and it's muted so everything is tomb quiet until it's stopped at a frequency. And although there are 30 station presets, only ten function on world band—even fewer if some are programmed to act as world band segment finders.

Performance is scarcely better. World band sensitivity with the built-in telescopic antenna is merely so-so, and adding even a modest length of wire to overcome this can result in overloading. Selectivity, although broad, is adequate for most major stations, but images proliferate 910 kHz below fundamental frequencies.

Digital buzzing appears on world band below around 10 MHz, especially when the radio is handheld. Fortunately, most signals are hefty enough to override this intrusion.

The frequency/clock display is very easy to read and has good contrast aided by a silvery-green background—thankfully, too, as the LCD isn't illuminated. Otherwise, information displayed on the LCD tends to be tiny even for 20-20 eyes.

The 1625–1705 kHz portion of the mediumwave AM isn't covered, so a number of stations may be missed at your location. Also, mediumwave AM sensitivity is inadequate for long-haul listening, and digital buzz sometimes intrudes. Tuning steps are fixed at 9 kHz or 10 kHz, depending on where the radio is being sent or sold.

Alas, FM fares even worse, with serious distortion across the entire tuned range—overloading, too. We've encountered these shortcomings in some other Degen models, but never to this degree. Degen's quality control, once well above average, appears to have become hit-or-miss over the past year, so these FM shortcomings may be less pronounced on other samples.

In that regard, the battery cover is ridiculously flimsy, and a hinge pin on ours broke almost immediately. Degen started out in 2003 by offering high performance and superior build quality at a value price. The DE108 adds to the perception that their products are increasingly becoming more cheap than value.

New for 2007
½
Tecsun R-333, Roadstar TRA-2415/N

Price: *via stores.ebay.com/v-com-collections (see RP2000 review for vendor specifics):*

$41.90 including air shipping from China to other countries.

Pro: Weak-signal sensitivity quite reasonable. Pleasant audio (*see* Con). Large, easy-to-read LCD with good contrast and timed illumination. Telescopic antenna swivels and rotates. Superior carrying handle. Clock radio (*see* Con). Batteries need changing less often than most (*see* Con).

Con: No warranty and questionable shipment insurance when purchased on eBay. Analog tuned with digital frequency counter, so tunes only by hit-and-miss thumbwheel that's only partially improved by fine-tuning control; also, can require extra step of choosing shortwave "band." Does not tune 2, 3, 19, 21 and 25 MHz (120, 90, 15, 13 and 11 meter) world band segments and 1650–1705 kHz portion of extended mediumwave AM band. Displays only to nearest 10 kHz (two world band channels) in nonstandard XX.XX MHz format. Poor selectivity. Single-conversion IF circuitry results in poor image rejection. Audio lacks bass response. FM mediocre and only in mono. Clock in 12-hour format, displays only when radio off. Clock radio has no snooze or sleep delay. No jack for AC adaptor, much less the adaptor itself. No travel power lock. Battery cover not hinged. Required three "D" batteries not included.

☞ The R-333 pushes the size envelope for a compact model—it's just over eight inches (21 cm) wide—yet, is not quite large enough to be thought of as a laptop.

Verdict: Cheap nominal clock radio from China with superior illuminated LCD and good audio. There's little else to commend it, not even certain customary clock-radio functions.

Evaluation of New Model: The R-333, like the identical Roadstar TRA-2415/N, is touted as clock radio but doesn't live up to its billing. There is a single on-only event—no surprise here—but there's no alarm buzzer selectable in place of radio audio. Worse, there are no sleep or snooze delays.

The no-frills Tecsun R-333 is analog tuned with digital frequency readout. Its LCD is

The Tecsun R-333 is supposed to be a nice clock radio. It doesn't even do that very well. D. Zantow

substantial, illuminated and easy-to-read, but it shows frequency in nonstandard XX.XX MHz format and to only the nearest 10 kHz.

Tuning is by a thumbwheel which has play; it often zips past a desired signal on the first pass. The fine-tuning control helps, but unearthing frequencies is still a pain. Interestingly, this control's range varies by frequency—the higher you tune, the greater the sweep: about plus or minus 3.5 kHz on low frequencies, rising to 20 kHz at the high end.

The shortwave spectrum is covered in two manually selected "bands": 3.64 to 10.40 MHz and 9.68 to 18.56 MHz, thus omitting the 2, 3, 19 and 21 MHz segments. The extended mediumwave AM band misses 1650–1705 kHz.

The speaker is relatively large and a treat to the ears even if bass response is limited. World band sensitivity is quite decent and is aided by a lack of digital buzz. Selectivity, however, is woefully inadequate and images abound.

Mediumwave AM performance is acceptable, but FM lacks both sensitivity and any vestige of selectivity.

The R-333 uses three "D" cells—not included— so battery changes are relatively infrequent. Thankfully, too, as there is not even a jack for an AC adaptor.

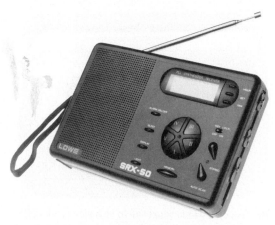

The SRX-50, years out of production, has resurfaced as "new old stock."

✪½
Lowe SRX-50

Price: £24.95 in the United Kingdom.

Pro: Five world band station presets, plus ten station presets for mediumwave AM and FM. Relatively simple to operate. Illuminated display. Alarm/snooze. FM stereo via earpieces, included. World Time clock. Longwave.

Con: Does not tune important 5800–5895, 15505–15695, 17500–17900 and 21750–21850 kHz portions of 49, 19, 16 and 13

The jWIN JX-M14 very nearly gets last place among world band radios. Nevertheless, it is dirt cheap for Christmas stockings, party favors and the like. D. Zantow

meters. No tuning knob; tunes only by presets and multi-speed up/down slewing/scanning in 5 kHz steps. Frequencies displayed in XX.XX/XX.XX$_5$ MHz format. Poor image rejection. Mediocre selectivity. Lacks bass response. Does not receive 1605–1705 kHz portion of mediumwave AM band. No signal-strength indicator. No travel power lock. Clock not displayed independent of frequency. Mediumwave AM tuning increment only 9 kHz, not switchable, which makes for inexact tuning in the Americas where 10 kHz is the norm. Power switch shows no "off," although "auto radio" power-switch position performs comparable role.

Verdict: Although thoroughly outclassed by newer low-cost models, this apparently "new old stock" sometimes surfaces at retail in the U.K., most recently at Waters & Stanton (wsplc.com). Now usually promoted simply as "SRX-50."

✪½
jWIN JX-M14

Price: $14.95 in the United States.

Pro: Handy small size for travel. Clock with timer/alarm (*see* Con). Elevation panel tilts radio to handy operating angle. Earbuds included (in separate bubble pack).

Con: Mediocre weak-signal sensitivity; helps considerably to clip a few yards of wire to the built-in antenna. Mediocre selectivity. Analog tuned with digital frequency counter, so tunes only by thumbwheel, which is stiff. Does not tune 120, 75, 90, 60, 15, 13 or 11 meter segments; misses a small amount of expanded coverage of 49 and 41 meter segments. Single-conversion IF circuitry results in poor image rejection. Audio lacks bass response. Frequency counter completely omits last digit so, say, 9575 kHz appears as either 9.57 or 9.58 MHz. Clock in 12-hour format only, displays only when radio off. Display not illuminated. If hand is placed on rear of cabinet, world band drifts up to 10 kHz. Frequency drift with changes in temperature. LCD buzzes on mediumwave AM; if finger placed over LCD, buzz also audible on lower world band frequencies. Mediumwave weak-signal sensitivity uninspiring. FM overloads in strong-signal environments, remediable by shorting antenna (which also reduces weak-signal sensitivity). When first turned on, radio always reverts to FM band. FM in mono only. Two "AA" batteries not included. Warranty in the United States only 90 days and requires $12 advance payment for "return shipping"; add to that the owner's cost to ship, and warranty is of dubious value; best purchased from dealer who will swap if DOA.

Verdict: At almost a throwaway price, the Chinese-made jWIN JX-M14 is a passable portable for casual use on trips or as a stocking stuffer, provided a hank of wire is clipped on to give world band signals a boost. Usually found in offbeat catalogs.

New for 2007

✪

Degen DE203

Price: *via stores.ebay.com/v-com-collections (see RP2000 review for vendor specifics):* $43.90 including air shipping from China to other countries. As of presstime, not available from vendors outside China.

Pro: Dual conversion. Resists overloading, aided if necessary by one-step attenuator. Large, easy-to-read LCD with good contrast and helpful silvery background; illuminated (*see* Con). World Time clock. Clock radio. External antenna jack for world band and FM. Elevation panel tilts radio to handy operating angle. Telescopic antenna swivels and rotates. More bass than most similarly sized models. Aluminum front panel. FM in stereo through provided earbuds. Cloth travel pouch. Indoor wire antenna.

Con: Not available outside China except via eBay and with no warranty and questionable shipment insurance. Spurious signals cause some world band signals to be significantly degraded by varying-pitch whistles. Analog tuned with digital frequency counter, so tunes only by stiff knob; thus, it lacks such helpful tuning aids as station presets, keypad and scanning. Frequency displays only to the nearest 10 kHz. Analog tuning uses string and pulley configuration

Degen's DE203, PASSPORT's Running Dog Radio for 2007. Its howls would be the envy of the late Wolfman Jack.

D. Zantow

to turn variable capacitors; this is poorly executed and results in considerable play, making it much harder than usual to zero in on stations. Omits important 21 MHz (13 meter) segment and lesser 2, 3, 4, 5, 19 and 25 MHz (120, 90, 75, 60, 15 and 11 meter) world band segments; also, 15655–15825 kHz portion of 19 meters and bits of other segments. Poor sensitivity aided only slightly by added wire or other accessory antenna. Selectivity only fair. Weak audio with audible distortion. Poor LCD illumination, from one side only. Omits 1625–1705 kHz portion of mediumwave AM band. Poor mediumwave AM sensitivity. Poor FM sensitivity. Batteries very tight in cavity, complicating insertion and removal; nevertheless, on our unit a battery spring didn't have enough contact pressure for the radio to operate until the spring was stretched. Battery cover not hinged. Required two "AA" batteries not included. No snooze or sleep timers.

Verdict: Limbo radio—how low can you go?

Evaluation of New Model: The new Degen DE203 is billed as being "stylish," with "99K electroplated" gold buttons and an aluminum front panel. All this plus double conversion for under $45, and it looks mighty tempting.

To keeps costs in check, the '203's frequency readout shares the clock's integrated circuit and shows only to the nearest 10 kHz. World band coverage is adequate, too, even

ICOM'S IC-R20 HANDHELD

The popularity and frequency coverage of handheld scanners keep marching on. Some even cover world band, where they've traditionally performed poorly.

At around US$500/£300 the 'R20 is costlier than nearly any dedicated world band portable; yet, it is comfortably within the norm for compact world band portables. Frequency coverage in the United States, where eavesdropping on cellular bands is *verboten*, is 150 kHz–822 MHz, 851–867 MHz and 896–3305 MHz. Elsewhere, or within the United States for government use, it's 150 kHz to 3305 MHz.

A neat tuning-related feature is "dual watch," which allows scanning aficionados to monitor two signals simultaneously. Alas, this multitasking goodie doesn't work with world band.

The large LCD is not easy to read except when illuminated. Keys have good feel; otherwise, ergonomics are only so-so because of limited "real estate" for controls. Tuning is by knob, keypad, up/down slewing and a thousand presets in increments of .01, .1, 5 , 6.25, 8.33, 9, 10, 12.5, 15, 20, 25, 30, 50 and 100 kHz.

The 'R20 has three bandwidths, each assigned by the received mode so none can be selected independent of mode. Unfortunately, the bandwidth for the AM mode, which includes world band, is a whopping 12 kHz. The single-sideband bandwidth, around 3 kHz, comes to the rescue by allowing for worthy ECSS reception of world band and medium-wave AM stations. It's a tiresome procedure but does the trick.

Alas, sensitivity disappoints—only powerful signals are suitably audible with the telescopic antenna. Another letdown is that the antenna tends to flop over when fully extended. The 'R20's dynamic range is significantly limited, too, so a serious outboard antenna tends to introduce overloading. Tweaking the RF gain control and single-step 30 dB attenuator can help, but not always. However, stability, as well as image and spurious-signal rejection, are commendable.

Speaker audio lacks punch, but otherwise is good considering the radio's size. There's also a built-in digital audio recorder. Its 65-minute "fine" setting is hardly high fidelity, but fares nicely for world band. There's a utility (homepage.ntlworld. com/tony.ling/radio/IC-R20/R20um23.htm, not tested) to convert the R20's .icw audio files to .wav. It's free, but takes some doing to install and make function, and requires Icom's CS-R20 software and cable package.

The Icom IC-R20 makes a tempting choice for scanning signals on VHF and above, and offers built-in recording. For certain niche applications, including low-profile field surveillance, these characteristics can come together to make it a best-of-breed choice.

For world band, though, the 'R20 is mainly an adjunct to scanning and for inboard recording.

Radios with broadband frequency coverage simplify engineering, production, shipment and inventory control—no wonder they keep cropping up. Alas, this tantalizing concept keeps falling short except with costly receivers, and the handheld Icom IC-R20 is no exception.

if restricted to seven segments: roughly 5.78 to 6.42, 6.88 to 7.52, 9.37 to 10.02, 11.48 to 12.12, 13.38 to 14.02, 15.00 to 15.65 and 17.50 to 18.15 MHz. This omits the 2, 3, 4, 5, 19, 21 and 25 MHz (120, 90, 75, 60, 15, 13 and 11 meter) segments; too, the extreme lower tip of 6 MHz (49 meters) and upper bits of 7 and 15 MHz (41 and 19 meters).

The LCD is easy to read by day, with good contrast and a helpful silvery background—even if at night the single-side illumination is ineffective. Alas, from here things go downhill.

For starters the tuning knob is stiff, with plenty of "rubber band" play that makes it difficult to land on a chosen frequency. Too, world band sensitivity is downright poor with the built-in telescopic antenna, while the included wire antenna and other external antennas help only marginally. Selectivity is little better, being too broad for proper world band reception.

The speaker is relatively large, offering a touch more bass than other small models. Unfortunately, there's audible distortion, and the audio, being weak, lacks punch.

Howls of Derision

Dual conversion is rare, indeed, on a radio at this price. Alas, there are powerful spurious signals that compromise double conversion's benefits by causing varying-pitch whistles. Only a minority of signals is impacted, but the resulting howls are worthy of Wolfman Jack.

Mediumwave AM coverage omits 1625–1705 kHz. Sensitivity is mediocre, as well—FM, too, which winds up being for powerful local stations.

Batteries are absurdly tight in their cavity, frustrating insertion and removal. Ironically, one negative contact spring didn't have enough pressure for the radio to operate until we stretched it. The battery cover isn't hinged, either.

Three years ago Degen was full of promise. Now, it's like a restaurant that's gotten good reviews then takes advantage of its reputation by serving swill. How the mighty fall!

LAP PORTABLES
Pleasant for Home, Acceptable for Travel

A lap portable is for use primarily around the home and yard, plus on occasional trips. They are large enough to perform well, usually sound better than compact models, yet are not too big to fit into a carry-on or briefcase. Most take 3–4 "D" (UM-1) or "C" (UM-2) cells, plus sometimes a couple of "AA" (UM-3) cells for memory backup.

These are typically just under a foot wide—that's 30 cm—and weigh in around 3–5 pounds, or 1.4–2.3 kg. For air travel, that's okay if you are a dedicated listener, but a bit much otherwise.

Retested for 2007
★★★★⅜ 📖 *Passport's Choice*
Etón E1

Price: *E1:* $499.95 in the United States. CAD$599.00 in Canada. £399.95 in the United Kingdom. €499.95 in Germany. *E1, refurbished:* $399.95 as available in the United States. *AudioVox CNP1000 XM antenna with cable:* $47.95 in the United States. *AudioVox CNP-EXT50 extension cord for XM antenna:* $17.95 in the United States. *KOK1-to-SO-239 aftermarket antenna jack adaptor:* $7.95 in the United States. *KOK1 aftermarket male connector (for raw antenna cable):* $4.95 in the United States. *Universal Radio Large Portable Stand:* $16.95 in the United States.

Pro: Includes virtually every tuning method available, including frequency/presets scanning, up/down slewing, keypad frequency selection, keypad selection of world band segments and a tuning knob. Tuning knob (*see* Con) features variable rate incremental tuning (VRIT); for many this makes band-scanning more convenient. 1,700 easy-to-use presets don't erase if batteries removed; 500 allow for user-written ID tags, while the remainder have factory-created country ID

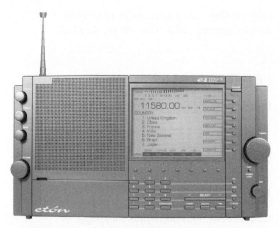

Nobody—including us—expected the Etón E1, after years of false starts and name changes, to be more than just another nice portable. How wrong we were.

tags. Keypad frequency may be entered in kHz or MHz. Pleasant audio quality, aided by separate bass and treble controls (*see* Con). Overall receiver distortion unusually low (*see* Con). Full three-Watt (nominal) audio amplifier with AC adaptor; when batteries in use, amplifier output is automatically reduced so battery drain can be cut by half. Agreeable ergonomics, including keys with superior feel. Passband tuning (PBT, a/k/a IF shift), a first for a portable; performance excellent. Synchronous selectable sideband holds lock unusually well; adjacent-channel interference reduction and tonal response aided by passband tuning adjustment. Synchronous double sideband overcomes selective fading distortion and enhances fidelity during twilight and darkness (mixed skywave/groundwave) reception of fringe mediumwave AM stations "in the clear." Wide (20 kHz signal spacing) dynamic range good, IP3 excellent with preamp off, to the point that resistance to overloading, even with Beverage antennas, comparable to that of excellent tabletop supersets; wide DR/IP3 still tests as good with preamp on (*see* Con). Blocking good. Phase noise good, although still intrudes beyond 80 dB down. Sensitivity/noise floor good-to-excellent with preamp off, excellent-to-superb with 10 dB preamp on. Three well-chosen voice/music bandwidths (2.5, 5 and 8 kHz) with skirt selectivity and ultimate rejection

that are excellent or better. Image rejection approaches professional caliber. Excellent first IF rejection. Tuning and display in 10 Hz steps, exceptionally precise for a portable; 100 Hz and 1 kHz tuning steps also selectable. On our current unit, frequency display came from factory absolutely accurate after lengthy warmup (*see* Con); frequency readout accuracy user-adjustable with a small flat-blade screwdriver through first vent slot just to right of "CE" sticker on back of cabinet. No chuffing or muting when tuning. Octave filters provide good front end selectivity by tabletop standards, which is exceptional for a portable. Single-sideband performance above average for a portable, aided by excellent frequency stability. Signal-strength indicator, with 21 bars, uncommonly accurate from S3 through 60 dB over S9 even by professional standards. Audio line output jack (stereo on FM/XM) with proper level to feed external amplifier/speaker system, recorder or FM/AM microtransmitter; also, external speaker jack and separate jack for headphones or earpieces. Audio line input jack allows radio to be used as amp/speaker for CD players and the like. Useful battery status indicator. User-selectable slow/fast AGC decay adjustment; a third AGC option, "Auto," aids band scanning by switching from slow to fast when radio tuned. Squelch. Telescopic antenna large and robust (*see* Con). Switches for internal/external antennas (if radio sounds "deaf," ensure these are in correct positions). Clock displays separately from frequency (*see* Con). Two-event timer with selectable on/off times. Snooze and sleep delay. FM above average with excellent sensitivity, aided by switchable FM preamp (17 dB). 0.1–30 MHz tuning range includes longwave broadcast band. Japanese FM. Three-level LCD illumination (*see* Con). Travel power lock. Elevation panel (*see* Con) helps tilt radio to handy operating angle. Well-written printed owner's manual; also on CD-ROM along with quick-start guide. *United States and Canada:* XM ready, easily implemented (*see* Con). Atomic-type clock automatically kept exceptionally accurate by signals on XM or world band WWV/ WWVH (but not longwave WWVB in Colorado on 0.06 MHz) (*see* Con). XM module easily removable for future uses or modes. One year parts and labor warranty. Excellent toll-free tech support. *Elsewhere, including EU:* New version under consideration would replace XM facility with one for DAB.

Con: No carrying handle or strap, nor is there any provision for one to be user-affixed—not even a pair of inconspicuous threaded screw holes. When 2.5 kHz bandwidth used with BFO (or certain PBT settings with wider bandwidths), audio suffers from harshness resulting from high-order distortion products. Muted-sounding audio comes off as somewhat lifeless; needs to be crisper to reach fidelity potential. Narrow (5 kHz signal spacing) dynamic range/IP3 poor, although IP3 improves to fair with preamp off. Preamp, used by default with the telescopic antenna, generates mixing products in stressful reception situations; ironically, a major external antenna without the preamp tends to remedy the problem. Unlike that on the sibling Satellit 800 portatop, the E1's tuning knob shaft lacks ball bearings; it feels slightly grizzly when rotated and some units also have a minor degree of wobble. No rubber grip around tuning knob's circumference; no finger dimple, either (remediable, see fingerdimple.com). Front-mounted battery access door difficult to open. Telescopic antenna flops over when moved from full upright position. Dot-matrix LCD has limited useful viewing angle and lacks contrast in bright rooms or with illumination off; best contrast is found at angle provided by aftermarket Universal Radio stand, although built-in elevation panel also helps some. Non-standard connector for world band external antennas, and no adaptor or plug included. Variable-rate incremental tuning (VRIT), which some users don't care for, cannot be disabled. Mediumwave AM lacks directional reception, as it relies on the telescopic antenna in lieu of a customary horizontal ferrite-rod antenna. Included AC adaptor produces minor hum at headphone output. Lacks certain features, such as tunable notch and noise blanker, found on tabletop receivers. No PC interface. No attenuator or RF gain control, although neither needed. No dedicated but-

tons for presets. Frequency readout drifts very slightly until full warmup; our latest unit's readout was off by 30 Hz at cold start before settling to full accuracy after two hours. Clock display lacks numeric seconds; local time option in 24-hour format only. Line input jack requires above-average audio level to perform properly. Elevation panel flimsy. Paint on knobs, buttons and cabinet could eventually wear through. Four "D" cells not included. Like essentially all other world band portables, not designed to receive DRM digital broadcasts, nor is there a 12 kHz IF output to feed a DRM-configured PC. *United States and Canada:* XM reception requires purchase of separate outboard antenna and payment of monthly fee. XM reception not possible when traveling outside United States and Canada. Significant current consumption when XM circuitry in use. *United States:* Does not provide digital reception of HD Radio broadcasts.

Verdict: The Etón E1 hasn't disappointed. It continues to offer a killer combination of features and performance never before found in a portable. The E1 now completely dominates the performance end of the world band portable market, and rightfully so.

Observations of New Sample: In January 2006 Etón recalled units from serial numbers 3067 to 5462, as a PC board defect allowed AC adaptor voltage to back up into the internal "D" batteries. This created the possibility that the cells could swell and even explode. The recall came off with textbook precision, allowing new boards to be immediately installed. Our current test unit, s/n 7164, is from later production.

With three minor exceptions—one minus, two plus—our mid-2006 receiver has performed identically to those tested in 2005. On one hand, unlike with 2005 units, the current receiver's tuning knob has a more obvious touch of wobble. On the other hand, with the AC adaptor in use the audio line output is finally free from hum. Too, single-sideband modes are now more readily selected when receiver in AM-sync mode.

There have been a number of credible reports detailing how the E1's frequency readout has sometimes been off by the better part of 100 Hz. Accordingly, we once again checked carefully for this. Too, in 2006 there were reports of display failures that Etón apparently has been working to correct.

At cold start the frequency display on our latest unit was indeed off by 30 Hz. However, after lengthy warmup it read out spot-on throughout the mediumwave AM and shortwave spectra. Whether this reflects luck of the draw or improved factory alignment, only time will tell. However, as a fallback there is an adjustment inside the radio so service personnel can tweak the reading.

As before, the receiver comes with no antenna adaptor, so it can't accept conventional world band antenna plugs. Last year the manufacturer stated a suitable adaptor would likely be included in later production, but this much-needed improvement appears to have fallen through the cracks. Although inexpensive adaptors are available at radio specialty firms, virtually none of Etón's many consumer electronics dealers offers them.

Portables almost invariably earn little more than a passing nod from world band DX cognoscenti scouring for tough radio catches. The ca. 1974 Barlow-Wadley XCR-30 Mk II

NUMBERS: TOP PORTABLES

	Etón E1	Sony ICF-SW77
Max. Sensitivity/Noise Floor	0.15 μV **S**/–132 dBm **E**[4]	0.16 μV **S**/–133 dBm **E**[1]
Blocking	123 dB **G**	121 dB **G**
Bandwidths *(Shape Factors)*	8.0 *(1:1.45* **S***)*, 5.0 *(1:1.6* **E***)*, 2.5 *(1.7* **E***)*	6.0 *(1:1.9* **E***)*, 3.3 *(1:2.0* **G***)* kHz
Ultimate Rejection	80 dB **E**[5]	70 dB **G**
Front-End Selectivity	**G**[6]	— [2]
Image Rejection	>90 dB **S**	80 dB **E**
First IF Rejection	75 dB **E**	80 dB **E**
Dynamic Range/IP3 (5 kHz)	55 dB **P**/–50 dBm **P**[7]	64 dB **P**/–37 dBm **P**
Dynamic Range/IP3 (20 kHz)	87 dB **G**/–2 dBm **G**[8]	82 dB **P**/–10 dBm **G**
Phase Noise	113 dBc **G**	122 dBc **E**
AGC Threshold	0.3 μV **G**[9]	2.0 μV **G**
Overall Distortion, sync	2.6% **G**[10]	2.3% **E**/3.3% **G**[3]

IBS Lab Ratings: **S** Superb   **E** Excellent   **G** Good   **F** Fair   **P** Poor

(1) Sensitivity varies considerably by frequency at 2 MHz and between 10–29.9 MHz; *viz.*, from 0.16 μV to1.40 μV **S** - **G**. Noise floor varies by frequency from –133 dBm to –117 dBm **E** - **G**. Neither measurement could be made at 5 MHz because of spurious responses, noise and leakage.

(2) Cannot be determined.

(3) Wide/narrow bandwidths.

(4) Preamp on; 0.28 μV **E**/–126 **G** with preamp off.

(5) Phase noise prevents accurate measurement beyond 80 dB.

(6) Octave filters, unusually good for a portable.

(7) Preamp on; 57 dB **P**/–39 dBm **F** with preamp off.

(8) Preamp on; 88 dB **G**/+7 dBm **E** with preamp off.

(9) Preamp on; 0.9 μV **S** with preamp off.

(10) Harmonic distortion includes several high-order products.

PORTABLES

and ca. 1985 Sony ICF-2010/2001D were partial exceptions because of benchmark technology. Yet, the E1 is the first portable ever to earn the respect of serious DXers to the point where it is regarded as competitive with pricey tabletop models.

📄 An *RDI WHITE PAPER* is available for this model.

✪✪✪¾
Sony ICF-SW77

Price: €499.00 in Germany.

Pro: A rich variety of tuning and other features, including sophisticated "page" tuning that some enjoy but others dislike; includes 162 station presets, two-speed tuning knob, signal-seek tuning (*see* Con), keypad tuning and meter-band access. Synchronous selectable sideband is exceptionally handy to operate; it significantly reduces selective-fading distortion and adjacent-channel interference on world band, longwave and mediumwave AM signals; although the sync chip part number was changed not long back, its performance is virtually unchanged (*see* Con). Two well-chosen bandwidths (6.0 kHz and 3.3 kHz) provide superior adjacent-channel rejection. Excellent image rejection and first-IF rejection, both 80 dB. Excellent-to-superb weak-signal sensitivity (noise floor –133 dBm, sensitivity 0.16 microvolts) in and around lower-middle portion of shortwave spectrum where most listening is done (*see* Con). Weak-signal sensitivity still excellent (noise floor –130 dBm, sensitivity 0.21 microvolts) within little-used 120 meter segment (*see* Con). Superb overall distortion, almost always under one percent. Dynamic range (82 dB) and third-order intercept point (–10 dBm) fairly good at 20 kHz signal spacing (*see* Con). Tunes in very precise 0.05 kHz increments; displays in 0.1 kHz increments; these and other factors make this model superior to any other portable for single-sideband reception, although portatop and tabletop models usually fare better yet. Continuous separate bass and treble tone controls, a rarity. Two illuminated multi-function liquid crystal displays. Dual-zone clock, displays separately from frequency. Station name

Sony's ICF-2010/ICF-2001D was once the *ne plus ultra* of portables, followed by the Sony ICF-SW77. Some 'SW77 units are still available.

appears on LCD when station presets used. 10-level signal-strength indicator (*see* Con). Excellent stability, less than 20 Hz drift after ten-second warmup. Flip-up chart for calculating time differences. VCR-type five-event timer controls radio and optional outboard recorder alike. Superior FM audio quality. Stereo FM through earpieces, included. Travel power lock. Japanese FM (most versions) and longwave. AC adaptor, hum-free. Outboard reel passive wire antenna accessory aids slightly with weak-signal reception. Antenna connector included. Rubber strip helps prevent sliding.

Con: No longer distributed by Sony outside Germany; given past practice, it may not be available even in Germany once present supplies are exhausted. "Page" tuning system relatively complex to operate; many find that station presets can't be accessed simply. World band and mediumwave AM audio slightly muffled even when wide bandwidth in use. Synthesizer chuffing degrades reception quality during bandscanning by knob. Dynamic range (64 dB) and third-order intercept point (–37 dBm) only fair at 5 kHz signal spacing. Weak-signal sensitivity varies from fair to superb, depending on where between 2 and 30 MHz receiver is being tuned. Synchronous selectable sideband holds lock reasonably. Synchronous selectable sideband tends to lose lock if batteries weak, or if NiCd cells are used. Synchronous selectable sideband alignment can vary with temperature, factory alignment and battery voltage, causing synchronous selectable sideband reception to be slightly more muffled in one sideband than the other. Signal-seek tuning skips over weaker signals. Flimsy 11-element telescopic antenna (the older version of the 'SW77 had nine elements). LCD characters small for size of receiver. Display illumination does not stay on with AC power. Unusual tuning knob design disliked by some. On mediumwave AM band, relatively insensitive, sometimes with spurious sounds during single-sideband reception; this doesn't apply to world band reception, however. Mundane reception of difficult FM signals. Signal-strength indicator grossly overreads, covering only a 20 dB range with maximum reading at only 3 microvolts. AGC threshold, 2 microvolts (good). Painted surfaces can wear off with heavy use. No batteries (four "C" required).

Verdict: The Japanese-made Sony ICF-SW77 has been a strong contender among portables since it was improved some time back. After the Sony ICF-2010 was discontinued a few years ago, the '77 became uncontested as the top portable.

The '77 has always been tops among portables for single-sideband reception, beating out even the legendary '2010. It's also one of the very few models with continuously tuned bass and treble controls. Ergonomics, however, are a mixed bag; so if you're interested consider trying it out first.

The RP2000 is the first receiver from Redsun, a new Chinese manufacturer. It performs surprisingly well, with delightful audio. A fancier model is in the works.

D. Zantow

The '77 is now available only in Germany, where thiecom.de and others export worldwide. Don't be surprised if it ceases to be offered there once existing supplies are sold, so if you want this venerable receiver now's the time to spring into action.

New for 2007
◑◑¾ ⊘ *Passport's Choice*
Redsun RP2000, Redsun RP2100, Roadstar TRA-2350P

Price: *RP2000 via stores.ebay.com/radio-and-component, including 117-to-230V AC converter for North America:* $94.90 including air shipping from China to the United States. $101.90 including air shipping elsewhere outside China.

Pro: Helpful tuning features include 50 station presets, of which 30 are for world band (*see* Con); two-speed (1/5 kHz) "mute free" knob tuning with speed dimple (*see* Con); up/down slewing; signal-seek frequency scanning that works well; and "Q.Tune" for instant access to world band segments (*see* Con). Worthy sensitivity to weak world band and mediumwave AM signals; comparable selectivity (adjacent-channel rejection), with two well-chosen bandwidths. Top-notch audio quality with separate and continuously variable bass and treble controls, beefy speaker magnet and superior audio electronics. Decent image rejection (*see* Con). Excellent FM performance, in stereo through headphones and line-output jack. Virtually no frequency drift. Travel power lock. Large LCD with good contrast; LCD and button illumination activated when any knob turned or button pushed (*see* Con). Five-bar signal strength indicator (*see* Con). One-step attenuator and RF gain control (*see* Con). User-selectable 9 kHz or 10 kHz mediumwave AM steps. Internal-external antenna switch for shortwave and FM. Separate mediumwave AM external antenna connection with spring-clip terminals (*see* Con). No inboard single sideband, but 455 kHz IF output jack for *i.a.* an outboard single-sideband module that vendor states will be available from Redsun before long. Stereo line output jacks for audio recording. "Roger beep" for pushbuttons; can be switched off. Batteries can be recharged internally. Robust telescopic antenna swivels and rotates. Excellent carrying handle folds into top of cabinet. Three-step battery indicator. Two clocks—World Time and local, 12 and 24 hour. Sleep delay, up to 90 minutes. Two clock-radio/alarm timers with handy snooze bar. Powered by shielded internal AC mains transformer (*see* Con) instead of customary outboard AC adaptor; nevertheless, may be powered instead by any external 9V DC source, including an approved AC adaptor (*see* second ☞). Chinese eBay vendors provide 117-to-230V AC converter transformers for North America (*see* Con). Also may be operated from—user's choice—four "D" or four "AA" batteries. Outboard passive reel accessory antenna aids slightly in weak-signal reception.

Con: No warranty when purchased on eBay (*see* second ☞). Not available except with single-voltage 220V inboard power supply that's not UL approved. 117-to-230V AC converter transformer provided by eBay vendors not UL or CE approved. No keypad, major omission on $100 model with synthesized tuning. Mediocre dynamic range not ameliorated by attenuator or RF gain control. Poor front-end selectivity, so local mediumwave AM stations can ghost into shortwave spectrum and disrupt some world band reception. Smattering of weak images appear 910 kHz down from the fundamental frequencies of powerful signals. LCD unevenly illuminated, thus partially dim; also, illumination shifts from "on" to timed-off when tuning knob turned. Shortwave spectrum divided into three "bands," complicating world band tuning and allowing only ten presets per "band." Carousel makes choosing presets a sequential chore. Volatile memory, including presets. "Q.Tune" for world band segments does not store last tuned frequency, although band selector switch does. Signal strength indicator overreads. Frequency display can be off by 1 kHz or so. Band-edge beep can't be turned off. Slightly annoying chuffing as tuning knob turned. Slight tuning-knob wobble. Up/down slewing mutes, hindering bandscanning. Volume control has minor

play. With stereo headphones, at lower volume the left ear is a bit louder than the right. Button-pressing usually requires that radio be held in place with other hand. No elevation panel or tail bail; also, no rubber or similar protection for table or desktop. Clocks don't display independent of frequency readout. Sensitivity drops off above around 23 MHz, not an issue with world band. Nonstandard antenna and IF output jacks. Internal mediumwave AM antenna doesn't disconnect when outboard antenna connected, degrading directionality of outboard antenna. Earpieces and required four "AA" or "D" batteries not included.

☞ The RP2100 (not tested) is the domestic version, with markings in Chinese. The RP2000 nominally for export, uses English, as does the TRA-2350P (not tested). According to the manufacturer they are otherwise identical.

☞ A sample was purchased via Chinese eBay seller Liypn at stores.ebay.com/v-com-collections, which we have used in the past. It has the largest selection of hard-to-find Chinese world band radio products. Our RP2000 included a 117-to-230V voltage converter transformer lacking UL or CE approval; also, helpful antenna and IF output plugs not normally provided by Redsun. However, the radio, like most others we ordered this time from Liypn, took weeks to arrive and was poorly packed.

Even with dubious packing, our past orders from Liypn have all arrived undamaged. However, this time the RP2000 arrived with a dented speaker grille. The vendor's disingenuous response was to instruct us to file a claim at our local post office, which is impossible because any nominal insurance would have been taken out in China. Over time perhaps this vendor can be successfully prodded to provide restitution in cases like this, but the slow response, poor packing and unhelpful reaction to damage were not encouraging.

We ordered for the first time from another Chinese eBay vendor, Tquchina, at stores.ebay.com/radio-and-component, with completely different results except for pricing and the included voltage converter. Unlike with Liypn, the shipment arrived promptly—in just over a week—with better packing and no damage. Tquchina's listed offerings are fewer than those of Liypn, but reportedly they can special order unlisted items upon request.

Although Tquchina performed better this time around than Liypn, any hardware ordered from China lacks warranty and repair support. Too, using both a radio and a voltage converter that haven't been UL or CE approved is a double-barreled risk that is disallowed in the European Community and a number of American localities. Better is to forget the free converter and bypass the inboard power supply completely by using a suitably approved outboard 120V AC-to-9V DC adaptor—500 mA, center pin negative—available domestically for around the equivalent of $20.

Verdict: Exceptional audio quality from a welcome new Chinese manufacturer.

The Redsun RP2000/RP2100 offers decent overall performance along with a superior speaker and continuously variable bass and treble controls. As a result its audio quality is about as good as it gets. For pleasant and affordable listening to world band news, music and entertainment it is hard to beat, which accounts for the Passport's Choice.

Nevertheless, it craves better front-end selectivity and dynamic range, along with synchronous selectable sideband, inboard single-sideband reception and especially a keypad. Certain of these omissions are promised to be remedied in Redsun's forthcoming and costlier RP3000.

Evaluation of New Model: Many new Chinese radio manufacturers have surfaced in recent years. The latest, Redsun, sounds like a Mao-era football team, but its debut offering fares surprisingly well.

The Redsun RP2000/2100 sports an attractive black cabinet with large LCD digits having good contrast. The speaker grille is metal, not plastic, and knobs are generously spaced for large hands. It uses PLL tuning circuitry, so there is virtually no frequency drift.

Its handle is long, tough, useful and folds flat across the cabinet top. The display and buttons illuminate for about ten seconds when any button or knob is used, although LCD illumination is uneven and thus partially dim.

Mediumwave AM tunes 520–1710 kHz in 9 or 10 kHz steps, while FM covers the usual 87–108 MHz. Shortwave is 1711 to 29999 kHz, but broken up into three "bands" that complicate world band tuning: SW1 1711–10010 kHz, SW2 9990–20010 kHz and SW3 19990–29999 kHz.

Of the 50 station presets, ten are for each of the three shortwave "bands," ten for mediumwave AM and ten for FM. The channel preset is displayed, 1 through 10, on the LCD, but presets selection is serial via a single-direction carousel button; to go from, say, 1 to 8 you have to press that button fully eight times. The memory circuitry is volatile, but it takes a good day or two after the LCD fades away before data disappears.

There is no keypad for direct frequency entry—disappointing for a receiver with synthesized tuning—but with the archaic three "band" shortwave scheme its utility would be diminished, anyway.

Buttons have good tactile feel along with a user-selectable "Roger beep." Yet, they are so stiff that you need to grip the cabinet with your other hand to keep the radio from sliding away, and there's no elevation panel or tilt bail to help avoid this. There is also slight hesitation before a button push "takes," and at times even a second push is needed (apparently a minor software flaw).

"Q.Tune" instantly tunes to the edge of any chosen world band segment within the range of the chosen shortwave "band." Signal-seek scanning works very well, locking onto strong stations but, like the related slewing circuit, it mutes as it scans. Thankfully, the tuning knob does not suffer from muting—just faint, unobtrusive chuffing.

Sensitivity is quite respectable, although it drops off above around 23 MHz—not a problem for most, as the practical world band upper limit is 22 MHz. It's quiet too, with none of the digital buzz or hiss that plague some other Chinese portables.

Two well-chosen bandwidths offer helpful fidelity-*vs.*-selectivity flexibility. When adjacent-channel interference isn't an issue, the wider filter in combination with the continuously tuned bass and treble controls makes for a real aural treat.

Dual conversion keeps images pretty much at bay, although a few appear 910 kHz below a powerful signal's fundamental frequency.

More significant is poor front-end selectivity, which allows beefy local mediumwave AM signals to "repeat" at within the shortwave spectrum. These occasionally bother world band segments.

Dynamic range comes up short, as well, allowing overloading to disrupt reception. This is especially noticeable at night around the 6 MHz world band segment even with nothing more than the built-in telescopic antenna. Although there's a one-step attenuator and an RF gain control, neither helps much.

There's no synchronous selectable sideband, hardly surprising at this price. More peculiar is that instead of built-in single-sideband demodulation there is a 455 kHz IF output that reportedly is to feed a forthcoming outboard single-sideband accessory. The last time this bits-and-pieces approach was being peddled was over half a century ago, when single sideband was new stuff.

A switch selects between the built-in shortwave/FM telescopic antenna and an external antenna. However, external-antenna and IF output jacks are nonstandard. There's also a pair of spring clips for an outboard mediumwave AM antenna, but because the internal loopstick antenna cannot be disabled the all-important directionality of any outboard antenna is seriously degraded.

FM performance is a delight. Sensitivity and selectivity are superior, and there's stereo output for headphones, as well as through the line output for recording and the like.

AC mains power is from a shielded inboard transformer— no hum, buzzes or any other nasty sounds here. Alas, it's only for 220V AC and isn't UL approved. The safest bet, then, for North Americans is to obtain a UL approved AC adaptor so the inboard power supply can be bypassed altogether.

Battery operation is by either four "D" or four "AA" batteries; this allows weight-conscious travelers to use lightweight "AA" cells. Too, if they are rechargeable they can be juiced inside the radio.

The Redsun RP2000/RP2100 is a surprisingly good first shot for a new manufacturer. Performance limitations keep it from being remotely like a "DX receiver," and some key features aren't present. Yet, for supremely pleasant listening to major world band stations it's right up there among the very best.

✪✪½

Roberts R827

Price: £159.95 or less in the United Kingdom.

Pro: Superior overall world band performance. Numerous tuning features, including 18 world band station presets. Two bandwidths for good fidelity/interference

The R827 is Roberts' most pleasant sounding model. It is related to the Sangean ATS-818CS.

tradeoff. Analog clarifier with center detent and stable circuitry allows single-sideband signals to be tuned with uncommon precision, thus allowing for superior audio phasing for a portable (see Con). Illuminated display. Signal-strength indicator. Dual-zone 24-hour clock, with one zone displayed separately from frequency. Alarm/timer with sleep delay. Travel power lock. FM stereo through earpieces. AC adaptor. Longwave.

Con: Tends to mute when tuning knob turned quickly, making bandscanning difficult. Keypad not in telephone format. Touchy variable control for single-sideband fine tuning. Does not come with tape-recorder jack. No batteries (four "D" and three "AA" needed). Country of manufacture, China (formerly Taiwan), not specified on radio or box.

Verdict: This is a decent, predictable radio—performance and features, alike—and reasonably priced.

✪✪⅜ *Ⓒ*
Etón S350DL, Tecsun BCL-3000

Price: *Etón S350DL:* $99.95 in the United States. CAD$149.99 or less in Canada. £69.95 in the United Kingdom. *Etón/Lextronix S350DL:* €139.00 in Germany. *PAL-to-F*

Etón's S350DL sounds great, but is limited by analog tuning. Solid distribution, warranty and customer support insulate it from the otherwise-superior Redsun RP2000.

adaptor for external FM antenna: $2.29 in the United States. *Franzus FR-22 120>220V AC transformer for BCL-3000:* $15–18 in the United States.

Pro: Speaker audio quality substantially above norm for world band portables. Separate bass and treble tone controls help shape audio frequency response. Reasonably powerful audio, helpful for where ambient noise is at least average. Two bandwidths, well-chosen, provide effective and flexible adjacent-channel rejection *vis-à-vis* audio fidelity. Sensitive to weak signals. No synthesizer, so exceptionally free from circuit noise ("hiss") and no chuffing while tuning. Relatively intuitive to operate, even for newcomers. World Time clock (see Con) with alarm, clock radio and sleep delay; may also be set to 12-hour format. Four-level (eight bar) signal-strength indicator. Battery-level indicator (see Con). Low battery consumption, combined with four "D" cells, greatly reduces need for battery replacement. Most comfortable carrying handle of any world band radio tested; also, seconds as a shoulder strap. Easy-to-read LCD has large numbers, high contrast, is visible from a variety of angles and is brightly illuminated. LCD illumination may be left on fulltime or timed to turn off; illumination also comes on when tuning knob turned. FM reception quality slightly above average. FM in stereo through headphones. Sturdy, flexible telescopic antenna. RCA phono sockets provide stereo line output for recording, home FM transmitters and outboard audio systems. Mediumwave AM reception better than most. Battery cavity allows for four "AA" cells in addition to, or in lieu of, the usual four "D" cells; user-switchable between "AA" and "D," for example to select "AA" should "D" cells die. Available in red or black. *Etón:* Supplied outboard AC adaptor can be left behind on trips, making it lighter than BCL-3000. Superior toll-free tech support. *Tecsun:* Built-in 220V AC power supply eliminates need for outboard AC adaptor.

Con: Analog tuned with digital frequency counter, so tunes only by pair of concentric (fast/slow) knobs; thus, it lacks such helpful tuning aids as station presets, keypad and scanning. Unhandy MW/SW1/SW2/SW3 switch must be accessed often to tune mediumwave AM and within shortwave spectra; switch can be touchy, affecting frequency readings. Analog tuning uses string-pulley-gear hardware to turn variable capacitors, which results in frequency drift typically under 2 kHz on the DL version, along with some play and backlash—drift much improved over units produced before mid-2005. Single-conversion IF circuitry results in poor image rejection. No single sideband. Power button activates 90-minute sleep delay; works as full-time "on" control only if held down three seconds (*see* third ☞, below). Some user-correctable night-time overloading in strong-signal parts of the world. Does not tune relatively unused 2 MHz (120 meter) tropical world band segment. Clock not displayed independent of frequency, but button allows time to replace frequency for three seconds. Clock tends to be off slightly over time. Nominal 30 MHz low-pass filter has such high apparent insertion loss as to be useless except as a *de facto* attenuator. Battery-level indicator gives little warning before radio becomes inoperative. Batteries (4 × "D") not included. AC adaptor less handy than built-in power supply. *North America:* Minor but audible hum from speaker, headphones and line output with supplied 120V AC adaptor.

☞ As of presstime a smattering of the original S350 units—reviewed in earlier editions of PASSPORT— were still available new in Germany, the United Kingdom and North America. The new, improved "DL" version is preferable.

Verdict: The Grundig/Etón S350DL—sold in China as the similar Tecsun BCL-3000—is full of welcome surprises as well as the other variety. The big plus is sound, which is unmistakably above average. Flaws, too, are obvious and real: images, no single-sideband demodulation, a paucity of tuning aids and residual frequency drift. So, this analog-tuned model is not for DXing and can't demodulate most utility and ham signals.

But for world band listening it sounds terrific, is value priced and has superior customer support within North America and Europe.

PORTATOPS
Superior for Home and the Road

Portatops aren't as small as travel portables nor as rugged as tabletop models. Yet, they offer performance and fidelity approaching that of good tabletops but without sticker shock. And, like all portables, they work anywhere off batteries.

❶❶❶❶⅜ 📖 ⓔ *Passport's Choice*
Grundig Satellit 800

Price: *S800 (repacked/reconditioned):* $419.95 including 120V AC adaptor and headphones in the United States. *S800 (new):* €849.00 including dual-voltage AC adaptor and headphones in Germany.

Pro: Superior, room-filling tonal quality with continuous bass and treble controls. Full-size padded headphones. Excellent synchronous selectable sideband, with 27 dB of unwanted-sideband rejection to reduce interference and selective-fading distortion with world band, longwave and mediumwave AM signals. Synchronous selectable sideband also boosts recoverable audio from faint signals and halves overall distortion to 2.4% in AM mode on audio frequencies from 100–3,000 Hz. Three voice/music bandwidths: 7 kHz, 5.8 kHz and 2.6 kHz. Bandwidths generally

The portatop Satellit 800 is probably the last of Grundig's big, beefy receivers. Dealers' stocks are expected to be depleted by late 2007.

have excellent shape factors and ultimate rejection; all are selectable independent of mode (or dependent, if user prefers), and function with synchronous selectable sideband. Slow/fast AGC decay (*see* Con). Numerous helpful tuning aids, including 70 tunable station presets that store many variables (*see* Con); also, presets may be scanned (*see* Con). Excellent ergonomics, including many dedicated, widely spaced controls; exceptionally smooth knob tuning aided by ball bearings (*see* Con); and foolproof frequency entry. Superb LCD with large, bold characters and high contrast clearly viewed from virtually any angle (*see* Con). Analog signal-strength indicator (*see* Con). Single-sideband reception above portable norm (*see* Con), with rock-solid frequency stability and 50 Hz tuning increments. High- and low-impedance inputs for 0.1–30 MHz external antennas. With built-in telescopic antenna, weak-signal shortwave sensitivity equal to or better than that of top-rated portables. Weak-signal shortwave sensitivity with external antenna can be boosted by setting switch to "whip" to add preamplification (sometimes generates overloading). Superior blocking performance aids consistency of weak-signal sensitivity. Generally superior dynamic range and third-order intercept point. Two-event on/off timer and two 24-hour clocks (*see* Con). Large, tough telescopic antenna includes spring-loaded detents for vertical, 45-degree and 90-degree swiveling; also rotates freely (*see* Con). Versatile display and signal strength meter illumination choices. FM—mono through built-in speaker, stereo through outboard speakers, headphones and line output—performs well, although capture ratio only average and nearby FM transmitters may cause overloading. Longwave. Built-in ferrite rod antenna for 0.1–1.8 MHz. Covers 118–137 MHz aeronautical band, but only in AM mode and without synchronous selectable sideband. Excellent long carrying handle. AC adaptor—120V AC or 220V AC, depending on country of sale; otherwise, alkaline batteries need changing every 35 hours or so. Battery-strength indicator (*see* Con). Rack-type handles protect front panel. *North America:* Superior repairs in and out of one-year warranty by R.L. Drake Company. Excellent toll-free tech support.

Con: Huge (20⅜ inches—517 mm—wide) and weighty (15 pounds or 6.8 kg with batteries). Cabinet and components of portable-radio quality. Rarely available new except from one German dealer (thiecom. de). Available elsewhere only as a factory refurb from one American dealer (universal-radio.com) Synthesizer phase noise, only fair, slightly impacts reception of weak-signals adjacent to powerful signals and in other circumstances. Lacks notch filter, noise blanker, passband tuning and digital signal processing (DSP) found on some tabletops. When ungrounded (e.g., AC adaptor not connected to a grounded AC socket) and powered by batteries, vigorous "hash" when tuning knob being turned within portions of mediumwave AM band. Each key push must each be done within three seconds, lest receiver wind up mis-tuned or in unwanted operating mode. No signal-seek frequency scanning. Signal-strength indicator greatly underreads. Outboard AC adaptor in lieu of inboard power supply. Single sideband's 50 Hz synthesizer increments allow tuning to be out of phase by up to 25 Hz, diminishing audio fidelity. Fast AGC decay setting handy for bandscanning, but sometimes causes distortion with powerful signals; remedied by using slow AGC when not bandscanning. Numerous modest birdies on longwave, mediumwave AM, shortwave and FM bands; few cause heterodyne interference to world band signals. Ergonomics, although excellent, not ideal; e.g., no rows and columns of dedicated buttons for station presets. Sharp bevel on tuning knob. Neither clock displays when frequency shown; instead, pushbutton replaces frequency with time for three seconds. Both clocks only in 24-hour format and neither displays seconds numerically. For faint-signal DXing, recoverable audio with an outboard antenna, although good, not fully equal to that of most tabletop models. Using built-in antenna, sensitivity to weak signals not of DX caliber in mediumwave AM band; remedied by using Terk AM Advantage or similar accessory. Some frontal (only) radiation of digital noise from LCD, rarely a problem in actual use. When receiver leaned backward, telescopic antenna, if angled, spins rearward. Battery-strength indicator doesn't come on until immediately before radio mutes from low battery voltage. Misleading location of battery spring clips makes it easy to insert half the batteries in wrong direction, albeit to no permanent ill effect. Battery cover may come loose if receiver bumped in a specific and unusual manner. Antenna switches located unhandily on rear panel. "USB" on LCD displays as "LISB." No schematic or repair manual available, making service difficult except at authorized repair facility. No batteries (6 "D" needed).

☞ Prior to 2003 there were a number of batches manufactured with an above-average defect rate. After that, production quality settled down.

☞ Refurbished units reportedly include gift and similar types of returns from department stores and other outlets where customers tend to be unfamiliar with world band radio. Refurbishing is done at R. L. Drake's facility in Ohio.

Verdict: Big Bertha. The beefy Grundig Satellit 800 offers near-tabletop performance at a near-portable price. Great audio quality and ergonomics, and it receives well with just its telescopic antenna.

With pricing down and quality up, this receiver commands unusual attention. Alas, it's no longer in production so get it while you can.

📃 An *RDI WHITE PAPER* is available for this model.

WORLD BAND CASSETTE RECORDERS

What happens if your favorite show comes on at an inconvenient time? Why, tape it, of course, with a world band cassette recorder—just like on your VCR.

Two models are offered, and there's no question which is better: the Sony. Smaller, too, so it is less likely to raise eyebrows among airport security personnel. But there's a whopping price difference over the Sangean, and the Sony is getting hard to find.

Another of Sony's vanishing glories is the ICF-SW1000T/TS. It was and is the ultimate in world band cassette recorders.

✪✪✪⅛ *Passport's Choice*
Sony ICF-SW1000T, Sony ICF-SW1000TS

Price: *ICF-SW1000T:* €439.00 in Germany. *AC-E30HG 120V AC adaptor:* $19.95. *ICF-SW1000TS:* ¥46,000 as available in Japan.

Pro: Built-in recorder in rear of cabinet, with two events of up to 90 minutes each, selectable in ten-minute increments. Relatively compact for travel, also helpful to avoid airport security hassles. High-tech synchronous selectable sideband; this generally performs well, reducing adjacent-channel interference and selective-fading distortion on world band, longwave and mediumwave AM signals while adding slightly to weak-signal sensitivity (*see* Con). Single bandwidth, especially when synchronous selectable sideband is used, exceptionally effective at adjacent-channel rejection. Numerous helpful tuning features, including keypad, two-speed up/down slew, 32 station presets and signal-seek frequency scanning. Thirty of the 32 station presets are within three easy-to-use "pages" so stations can be clustered. Weak-signal sensitivity above average up to about 16 MHz. Demodulates single-sideband signals (*see* Con). World Time 24-hour clock, easy to set (*see* Con). Sleep delay. Illuminated LCD readable from a wide variety of angles. Travel power lock, also useful to keep recorder from being inadvertently switched on while cabinet being grasped (*see* Con). Easy on batteries. Records on both sides of tape without having to flip cassette (provided FWD is selected along with the "turning-around arrow"). Auto record level (*see* Con). "ISS" switch helps radio avoid interference from recorder's bias circuitry. FM stereo through earphones; earbuds included. Japanese FM (most versions) and longwave. Outboard reel passive wire antenna accessory aids slightly with weak-signal reception. Dead-battery indicator. Lapel mic (*see* Con). *ICF-SW1000TS:* AC adaptor (100V AC only). AN-LP1 active antenna.

Con: Discontinued and thus hard to find, although some stocks remain. Pedestrian speaker audio quality. Synchronous selectable sideband tends to lose lock if batteries not fresh, or if NiCd cells are used. Synchronous selectable sideband alignment can vary with temperature, factory alignment and battery voltage, causing synchronous selectable sideband reception to be slightly more muffled in one sideband than the other. No tuning knob. Clock not readable when radio switched on except for ten seconds when key is pushed. No meaningful signal-strength indicator, which negates its otherwise obvious role for traveling technical monitors. No recording-level indicator or tape counter. Slow rewind. Fast forward and reverse use buttons that have to be held down. No built-in mic; outboard (lapel) mic is mono. Reception is interrupted for a good two seconds when recording first commenc-

es. No pause control. Single lock deactivates controls for radio and recorder alike; separate locks would have been preferable. Tuning resolution of 0.1 kHz allows single-sideband signals to be mis-tuned by up to 50 Hz. Frequency readout to 1 kHz, rather than 0.1 kHz tuning increment. Lacks flip-out elevation panel; instead, uses less handy plug-in tab to tilt radio to handy operating angle. FM sometimes overloads. Telescopic antenna exits from the side, which limits tilting choices for FM. Misleading location of battery springs makes it easy to insert one of the two "AA" radio batteries in the wrong direction, albeit to no ill effect. No batteries (three "AA" required, two for radio and one for recorder). *ICF-SW1000T:* 120V AC or other adaptor costs extra (avoid Sony multivoltage adaptors, as they don't provide enough torque for starting tape drive).

Verdict: Strictly speaking, Sony's pricey ICF-SW1000T/ICF-SW1000TS is the world's only true world band cassette recorder—past or present. Made in Japan, it is an innovative little package with surprisingly good battery life and build quality. The rub is that it was discontinued in 2004 and has become difficult to find (e.g., at exporter thiecom.de).

✪✪½ @
Sangean ATS-818ACS, Sangean ATS-818ACS "Deluxe"

Price: *ATS-818:* $219.95 in the United States. CAD$239.99 in Canada. €168.00 in Germany. *ATS-818 "Deluxe":* $249.95 in the United States.

Pro: Built-in cassette recorder. Price low relative to competition. Superior overall world band performance. Numerous tuning features, including 18 world band station presets. Two bandwidths for good fidelity/interference tradeoff. Analog clarifier with center detent and stable circuitry allows single-sideband signals to be tuned with uncommon precision, thus allowing for superior audio phasing for a portable (*see* Con). Illuminated display. Signal-strength indicator. Dual-zone 24-hour clock, with one zone displayed separately from frequency. Alarm/timer with sleep delay. Travel

The Sangean ATS-818ACS lacks recording bells and whistles, but gets the job done properly. Attractively priced and easily found.

power lock. Stereo through earpieces. Longwave. Built-in condenser mic. AC adaptor. *ATS818ACS "Deluxe," available only from C. Crane Company:* Eliminates muting between stations when bandscanning; also, RCA instead of mini jack for external antennas.

Con: Recorder has no multiple recording events, just one "on" time (quits when tape runs out). Tends to mute when tuning knob turned quickly, making bandscanning difficult (the C. Crane Company offers a $20.00/$29.95 modification to remedy this). Wide bandwidth a bit broad for world band reception without synchronous selectable sideband. Keypad not in telephone format. Touchy single-sideband clarifier. Recorder has no level indicator and no counter. Fast-

forward and rewind controls installed facing backwards. No batteries (four "D" and three "AA" needed). Country of manufacture, China (formerly Taiwan), not specified on radio or box.

Verdict: A great buy, although recording is only single-event with no timed "off."

The PASSPORT *portable-radio review team: Lawrence Magne and David Zantow; also, Tony Jones, with laboratory measurements performed independently by Rob Sherwood. Additional feedback from Guy Atkins, David Crystal, Toshimichi Ohtake, Craig Tyson, David Walcutt and George Zeller.*

COMING UP:

Chinese portable manufacturers aren't yet ready to take a breather from their tireless introduction of new models. In particular, keep an eye on the new firm of Redsun to see whether its promise is equaled by its expanding product line.

First DRM Portable

Major manufacturers plan to release the first genuine DRM portables in 2007—the Sangean DRM-40, for starters. The only prior attempt, by another Asian firm, was a technical flop and never went into regular production. However, this time around holds more promise, in part because Texas Instruments has partnered with RadioScape to create two special DRM-DAB chips that reduce the engineering required by radio manufacturers.

Icom IC-R9500: New Performance Threshold?

For those with exacting tastes and deep pockets, Icom is about to release the IC-R9500 professional-grade receiver with synchronous selectable sideband. This extremely wideband superset will probably go for around ten kilobucks or €8,400 before VAT, and for the American public it will also be available in a cellular-blocked version.

That price places it above nearly any professional model covered to date in PASSPORT REPORTS. But judging from the means by which it was engineered and the resulting exceptional circuitry—it is not based on any existing Icom products—it has the potential to establish a new threshold for receiver performance.

Coming Up: Sangean's DRM-40 (top) and Icom's IC-R9500 superset.

Passport to Preparedness

Radios for Emergencies

When civilization's facade is stripped away, trusted information is the coin of the realm. For this, world band delivers when others can't. It's invaluable in any crisis, but especially during warlike acts when domestic media may be unavailable or restrained.

World band is nature's radio, soaring direct without wires or gatekeepers. That's because it bounces off heavenly layers invulnerable to failure or manipulation—no satellites, no cables, no local towers.

Being prepared with world band is straightforward and runs from $40 to $100 for an emergency radio. Options include $10 for a wire antenna; also, a second, conventional, portable if you want optimal world band reception.

#1. Act in Advance

Already have a world band portable? Then spare batteries allow it to serve in a crisis, especially with a Sun Star solar battery charger from C. Crane, Universal Radio and others. But remember that during 9/11 batteries became scarce to nonexistent in Manhattan. Radio manufacturers took notice and have been creating self-powered alternatives.

A solar battery charger is ideal for many emergencies. Shown, the Sun Star "11 in One."

If you don't yet own a world band portable, consider getting one now—not after a crisis, when anything decent will have already flown off the shelf. Go through PASSPORT REPORTS' pages—the choice is vast.

Favor models that handle single-sideband signals, explained in "Worldly Words." These can eavesdrop on ham radio and various aeronautical and other utility communications; under the right conditions, also the low-powered American Forces Radio and Television Service. Also, avoid battery hogs and look for effectively illuminated LCDs, *de rigeur* for tuning in the dark—illuminated keypads help, too.

What to avoid? Cheap ordinary radios lacking digital frequency readout. Their imprecise dials make stations hard to find, they don't demodulate single-sideband signals and most are marginal performers. Windup radios can have powerful advantages in an emergency, but all are rudimentary radio performers with limited long-term reliability. Best is to treat them as complimentary to a well-rated regular portable.

Among windups only the Freeplay Summit and Kaito KA008 meet PASSPORT's minimum testing requirements. However, we've bent the rules to include one analog-tuned portable series because it outsells all others combined and has significant emergency features.

#2. Does It Work?

An emergency radio has to actually work during a crisis, so you've got to check it out.

Pick a nice day, then step outdoors and tune to foreign stations that are weak but intelligible. Head to your safe room and compare how those same frequencies come in. If reception is similar, you're ready for the day of reckoning. If it's not, put up a simple outdoor wire antenna, such as Radio Shack's "Outdoor Antenna Kit" (278-758). Cut it to a convenient length, then run the feedline into your room without damaging the insulation. Or, if yard space is an issue, check out the compact antennas reviewed in PASSPORT REPORTS.

Either way, keep PASSPORT nearby so you'll know what's on, when.

Favor models that receive "utility" communications and American Forces Radio.

#3. What's Available

For battery powered radios look over "Portables for 2007." Dozens of models are tested, analyzed and rated.

Self-powered emergency portables fall into two categories: radios and novelties. We pored over offerings worldwide and found more of the latter than the former, but winnowed out several that we can call radios without damaging a polygraph needle. Read on . . .

★¼
Freeplay Summit (International), Freeplay Summit (USA)

Price: *Summit (International):* CAD$129.99 in Canada. £59.99 in the United Kingdom. €99.95 in Germany. AUD$199.90 in Australia. *Summit (USA):* $99.95 or less in the United States.

Pro: Relatively technologically advanced for an emergency radio, including five world band presets and 25 more for other bands. Powered by rechargeable battery pack which, in turn, is juiced three ways: foolproof cranked alternator, solar energy and AC adaptor. NiMH battery pack replaceable, although nominally radio runs even if pack no longer takes a charge. Reasonably pleasant audio quality. Timed LCD illumination. Low-battery and crank-charge indicators. World Time 24-hour clock with alarm and sleep functions can also display in 12-hour format. Accessory reel antenna and AC adaptor. Travel power lock. Mediumwave AM tunes in 9/10 kHz steps. FM includes NTSC (North American) channel 6 TV audio. Longwave. More stylish than most. *Summit (International):* AC adaptor adjusts to line voltage (110–240V AC) anywhere in the world (*see* Con). Three types of power plugs for different countries; also, carrying pouch. *Summit (USA):* 120V AC adaptor, works well.

Con: Slow battery recharge; full replenishment requires 24 hours with AC adaptor, 40 hours using sunlight, or 40 minutes of carpal-crunch-ing cranking. Poor sensitivity on world band using built-in but undersized telescopic antenna; reel-in accessory antenna, included, helps slightly. Lacks non-radio emergency features found on some other windup radios. Poor selectivity. Poor image rejection. Shortwave coverage of 5.95–15.6 MHz omits 2, 3, 4, 5, 17, 19, 21 and 25 MHz (120, 90, 75, 60, 16, 15, 13 and 11 meter) world band segments, along with lower end of 6 MHz (49 meters) and upper end of 15 MHz (19 meters). Inconvenient to tune, with no keypad, no tuning knob and "signal-seek" scanning that stops only at very powerful stations; this essentially leaves only single-speed (slow) up/down slewing and five world band presets to navigate the airwaves. No volume knob or slider; level adjustable only through up/down slew controls. Mutes for a second whenever slew button pressed, an annoyance when bandscanning. Does not continuously display frequency—reverts back to clock after ten seconds. Tunes world band only in 5 kHz steps and displays in nonstandard XX.XX MHz/XX.XX$_5$ MHz format. LCD hard to read in low light without illumination, which fades away after only four seconds. FM overloads in strong-signal environments. One of the two units we purchased new was defective. No handle or carrying strap. *Summit (International):* Multivoltage AC adaptor disturbs reception with vigorous noise and hum; best is either to replace it with an aftermarket transformer or to keep it unplugged except to charge battery pack.

☞ "International" and "USA" are informal terms used to differentiate between two *defacto* versions. Freeplay products have changed North American and other distributors frequently in recent months, so check with dealers for current warranty information.

Verdict: Yes, world band performance is mediocre. And, yes, it is bereft of most tuning aids and non-radio emergency features. Still, the Chinese-made Freeplay Summit is the most acceptable emergency radio we have come across, and it performs reasonably on FM and mediumwave AM.

The Freeplay Summit lacks non-radio emergency aids, but is the best self-powered radio performer.

New for 2007

✪⅛

Kaito KA008

Price: $39.95 in the United States. CAD$38.97 in Canada.

Pro: Three ways to power the radio directly, as well as indirectly by charging a battery pack: 1) hand crank, 2) solar cells and 3) AC adaptor. Can also conventionally be powered by three ordinary "AA" batteries (*see* Con). Good world band sensitivity. Digital frequency readout (*see* Con). Generally wide coverage of shortwave spectrum for a radio of this type (*see* Con). Clock (*see* Con) with one-event alarm. Built in LED flashlight. LCD illuminated by LED (*see* Con). Loud, punchy audio (*see* Con). Telescopic antenna swivels and rotates. Unique LED battery status indicator. Includes 120V AC adaptor/charger, rechargeable battery pack, earbuds, short outboard wire antenna (*see* Con) and waterproof carrying bag.

Con: Extremely sloppy tuning. Poor image and ultimate rejection. Poor FM performance. Frequency display/clock illumination too dim to be of any real use, a significant drawback for an emergency radio. Quality control appears below par. Analog-tuned with digital frequency counter, so lacks such digital tuning aids as station presets and keypad. Frequency display reads out only to nearest 10 kHz in XX.XX MHz format. Audio distorts at high volume. Battery cover not hinged to prevent loss. World band coverage misses relatively unimportant 2 and 3 MHz segments. Included wire antenna virtually worthless. FM in mono only. Clock only in 12-hour format, no option for 24-hour World Time. Three "AA" batteries not included for dry cell operation.

☞ The Kaito KA009 (around $45, not tested) is nominally similar, but adds coverage of the American weather band and VHF-TV audio.

Verdict: A marginal improvement over needle-and-dial emergency radios, the Kaito KA008 is inexpensive and has unusually flexible power. Alas, performance is poor, tuning is extremely sloppy and quality

With poor performance, sloppy tuning and dim backlighting, the new Kaito KA008 doesn't measure up.

control appears to be wanting. Worse, LCD illumination is virtually useless, making tuning a shot in the dark when there's no electricity or sunlight.

Overall, it suffices for rudimentary emergency situations—nothing more.

Evaluation of New Model: The Kaito KA008, unlike most other emergency radios, offers digital frequency readout. That's nice, but it doesn't accomplish this by using digitally synthesized tuning. Rather, it uses analog tuning tied into a frequency counter shared with the clock's IC. That simplified approach helps keep down costs, but also results in frequencies being shown only to the nearest 10 kHz (XX.XX MHz), whereas world band uses 5 kHz channels. Too, analog tuning precludes the use of station presets, keypad tuning and other conveniences found on radios with digitally synthesized tuning.

Flexible Power

A crank powers the radio either directly or by recharging the internal battery pack. With a totally dead battery, two minutes of cranking provides more or less ten minutes of playing time—more if volume is low, less at the radio's considerable but distorted full loudness. Alternatively, three ordinary (e.g., alkaline) "AA" batteries can be used, although the battery cover is not hinged to prevent loss.

There's also a solar panel on the rear that, like the crank, powers the set directly or by charging the battery pack. Sounds like a splendid idea, but it takes a healthy dose of sunlight to operate the set directly, and even then the audio is weaker than usual. Best is to stick to using the solar panel to charge batteries, but it's good to know that if they conk out there is a fallback—important for any emergency device.

Like the crank and solar cells, the included adaptor (120V AC in North America, presumably 220V AC in most other parts of the world) can also operate the radio directly or to charge the battery pack. It works as it should, and spares you from wearisome cranking or having to make human sacrifices to the sun god.

A 24-page owner's manual does a good job of explaining how to operate the radio. The included zip-style tote bag acts as a sealed waterproof pouch—a neat idea for an emergency radio. However, there's no room for the AC adaptor.

There are two LEDs on the front panel to indicate battery status. When the battery pack is properly charged a green LED labeled "HI" lights up; when the cells are near total discharge the illumination switches over to a red "LO" LED. There's yet another LED for tuning and charge-crank indication.

Good Coverage, Poor Performance

World band is divided into four "bands," roughly SW1 4000–9200 kHz, SW2 8910–14300 kHz , SW3 13850–19400 kHz and SW4 18680–26500 kHz. This is good coverage, even though it excludes the relatively unimportant 2, 3 and 4 MHz (120, 90 and 75 meter) world band segments. Mediumwave AM coverage is complete, from 520 to 1770 kHz, while FM is 86.8 to 108.8 MHz. These parameters vary from sample to sample and with fluctuations in battery power.

World band sensitivity with the built-in telescopic antenna is quite good. However, the included short outboard wire antenna has a weird plug that fits into the earphone jack; it does next to nothing to improve world band reception, although it helps FM slightly. Better is use an alligator or claw clip to affix a short insulated wire to the collapsed telescopic antenna.

An earmark of low-cost design is image-prone single conversion circuitry. On the '880 the result is so awful that image signals 910 kHz down in frequency are nearly as strong as the source signal. Think of big aftershocks after an earthquake, and you'll get the idea.

Selectivity, although mediocre, is adequate for most world band signals. However, very strong mediumwave AM signals completely swamp a wide frequency range. Otherwise, mediumwave AM performance, although pedestrian, is adequate.

FM performance is another story—little sensitivity, so only the strongest stations are heard. Too, the capture ratio, like in some battles, is poor. Our unit also has intermittent FM reception because of a defective bandswitch or solder joint.

But the '008's biggest bugaboo is the tuning system. World band segments are nicely spread out for easy tuning, but the tuning knob has so much play that using it is like trying to climb a hill with roller skates.

The cabinet's left side has a white LED flashlight, albeit sans lens—this ought to be *de rigeur* with all emergency radios. However, the timed green LED that is supposed to illuminate the clock/frequency display is too dim to be of any real use. Given that in many emergencies there's no electricity, what's the point of digital frequency readout if it's not readily readable in bad light?

The Kaito KA008 works adequately for simple emergencies. Nevertheless, it falls flatter than yesterday's soufflé for regular world band listening and lacks important non-radio emergency features found on competing models.

The PASSPORT emergency radio review team: David Zantow and Lawrence Magne.

McRADIOS: MILLIONS SOLD

Grundig FR-200, Etón FR-250, Tecsun Green-88

Price: *Grundig FR-200:* $39.95 in the United States. CAD$49.99 in Canada. *Etón FR-200:* £24.95 in the United Kingdom. AUD$79.95 in Australia. *Etón/Lextronix FR-200:* €29.95 in Germany. *Etón FR-250:* $49.95 in the United States. CAD$60.00 in Canada. *Etón/Lextronix FR-250:* €59.00 in Germany. *AC adaptor (110–120V AC to 4.5V DC):* $12.95 in the United States. CAD$12.95 in Canada.

Standalone Dynamo

World band radios can be major sellers. For example, there have been millions of Grundig FR-200 and Etón FR-250 radios reportedly sold in North America in recent years, and it's growing. A Tecsun version is being offered in China and Etón recently opened a new sales facility in Europe.

These sibling and related models succeed thanks to ubiquitous advertising, widespread availability and bargain pricing. They are powered not by ordinary batteries, but by a replaceable NiMH battery pack charged by crank-driven dynamo. Even if the battery pack dies the dynamo can power the radio.

Cellphone Recharge

A key non-radio feature of the '250 is its cellphone recharger—imagine this at the World Trade Center on 9/11! It includes a short cable and adapter plugs for popular phones.

The front panel sports a bright flashlight to keep the boogie man at bay—in a blackout this could be as important as the radio. The '200 uses a bulb, while the '250 goes one better with long-life but none-too-bright LEDs that second as a flashing red light. For hiking, traveling or bouncing around car trunks there's a rugged canvas bag with magnetic catch. The '250 also includes a siren loud enough to make neighborhood dogs bark.

Rudimentary Radio

The '200 has two shortwave "bands" of 3.2–7.6 MHz and 9.2–22 MHz. These include nearly all world band segments, which in a national emergency could be the only source for credible news.

Alas, the frequency readout crams hundreds of world band stations into a wee couple of inches (five centimeters) of analog dial space, and the tuning knob has play. Global signals can be hunted down only by ear, and even then it's hard to tell whether you're hearing the station's real signal or its image 900 kHz or so down. However, there's a fine tuning control to make the process smoother.

Enter the FR-250. It has seven separate world band segments nicely spread out and augmented by a fine tuning knob. Coverage omits the 3, 4, 5, 19 and 21 MHz (90, 75, 60, 15 and 13 meter) segments included on the '200, but it's a good tradeoff. As on the '200, the tuning knob has play.

Etón's emergency Volksradio, the FR-250 charges cellphones.

Audio quality is pleasant with both models, but otherwise reception quality is elemental. Sensitivity to weak world band signals is marginal—so is selectivity and image rejection. As to single-sideband signals, forget it.

FM, in mono only, includes NTSC (North American) channel 6 TV audio. FM overloads in strong-signal environments, but otherwise both it and mediumwave AM perform reasonably well.

The FR-200 and FR-250 don't send radio hearts aflutter. But they are eminently affordable, suffice for emergencies, are widely available and provide a number of non-radio emergency aids. Both come with a one-year warranty and superior product support.

Etón FR-350, American Red Cross ARC-350

Price: *FR-350 and ARC-350:* $59.95 in the United States.

The new Etón FR-350—no relation to the Etón S350—is the water resistant version of the FR-250. However, it's in a different package and has an additional daytime world band segment: 21 MHz.

Cross Your Heart, Hope Not to Die

Perhaps more interestingly, like the rest of Etón's "FR" line it is also offered as part of the new ARC series. Except for appearance, these are identical except that a portion of their sales is donated to the American Red Cross.

The '350 tunes the important world band segments, skipping only 2, 3, 4 and 5 MHz used mainly by weak domestic stations in Latin America, Africa and Asia. The cabinet is slimmer than other FR models and includes a canvas carrying case and handy shoulder strap.

Rubber side panels and covered rear jacks help keep out water. To check this out we gave our '350 a vigorous shower, and its innards emerged drier than a good Martini. This is an obvious plus not only for marine settings, but also for hurricanes, floods, tornadoes and tsunamis.

The power scheme is like what's on the larger, lower-cost '250. It comes with a replaceable NiMH battery pack that is charged internally by, among other things, a hand-cranked dynamo; an important backup is that the dynamo can also power the radio directly if the batteries are worn or missing. Three standard "AA" batteries (not included) can be used instead—say, if the dynamo fails—although it takes some doing to open the battery cavity.

An AC adaptor/battery charger is included, a convenience over the '250 and '200. Although it reduces tiresome cranking and resulting dynamo wear, it also creates annoying hum at low volume.

Zero-Hour Aids

Like on the '250, the '350's dynamo can recharge cellphones. Anyone who has heard 9/11 recordings where conversations were cut short by dying cellphone batteries will appreciate that this can be a life-or-death feature. A short cable and adapter plugs are included for most major makes of phones.

The '350, like the '250, includes a flashlight with two white LEDs for a modest degree of illumination, along with a switchable flashing red LED for visual warning. LEDs generally have a much longer life than conventional filament bulbs, so the flashlight might outlast the radio. Flashlights use more juice than little radios, so having dynamo power means reliable lighting no matter how long an outage lasts. Claustrophobics trapped in dark places may appreciate this more than the radio itself.

There's also a LOUD siren, and it's no toy. As hurricane Katrina showed, when people are stranded in attics or trapped under rubble, an ear-blaster like this can make the difference between being overlooked and being rescued. So long as you can turn the crank occasionally the siren can keep wailing indefinitely.

No Digital Readout

The '350's frequency readout is analog, not digital, so finding a station is no stroll in the park: On our sample the dial is off by around 50 kHz, or fully ten world band channels. World band frequencies are spread out onto eight slide rule-type "bands," which allow for much easier fine tuning as opposed to the '200's "two 'bands' for everything."

On the '250 a concentric fine-tuning knob means you don't need safecracker's fingers to dial around. There is no such knob on the '350, although it is also is less needed because of the eight widely spread "bands." But the '350's string-and-pulley analog tuning configuration creates tuning knob play, and on our unit that knob also rubs against the cabinet.

Same Performance, Different Features

The '350's world band performance and build quality are rudimentary and very close to that of the '250 and '200. For starters, single-conversion circuitry results in dismal image rejection. Sensitivity is marginal, selectivity isn't much better, and there's no single-sideband reception to receive hams, utilities or American Forces Radio. Audio, on the other hand, is surprisingly powerful and pleasant.

World band is uniquely resistant to censorship at the border. Yet, any worthwhile emergency radio also needs to do yeoman's work with local and regional stations. Here, the '350 fares well. Its mediumwave AM band tunes to the Western Hemisphere/Pacific's upper frequency limit of 1705 kHz, while FM covers 87.5 to 108 MHz and outputs to earpieces in mono. Both bands pull in stations nicely in urban and rural environments alike.

The Etón FR-350 and ARC-350 are not radio's equivalent of a Lamborghini or even close. But they do what's important: provide you and your loved ones with valuable tools to pull through a catastrophe. They're affordable, widely distributed and have a number of meaningful non-radio emergency features. Both include a one-year warranty and superior product support.

With reception virtually identical across Etón's FR and ARC product line, which to purchase comes down to price and what features you want—be careful, though, as some other models in the FR/ARC series don't cover world band. All models tested offer adequate radio performance for emergency and other occasional use, but none provides radio performance equal to that of most Etón and other similarly priced but conventional world band portables (see "Portables for 2007").

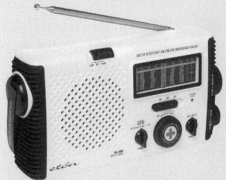

Yet, radio aside, nothing else quite equals the '350 for a full range of serious and effective emergency aids.

Sales of Etón's best emergency radio, the ARC FR-350, help the American Red Cross.

Tabletop Receivers for 2007

Tabletop receivers excel at flushing out faint stations swamped by competing signals. That's why they are prized by radio aficionados known as DXers—DX being telegraph shorthand for "long distance."

But tabletop models aren't for everybody, and it shows. Even in prosperous North America and Europe, tabletop unit sales have been under competitive pressure from such portable street rods as the Etón E1.

Most tabletop models cost much more than portables; yet, they're far less expensive than professional supersets. For the price of a tabletop you tend to get not only excellent performance, but also worthy construction and ruggedness. They are also relatively easy to service and are backed up by knowledgeable repair facilities.

What you rarely find in a tabletop is reception of the everyday 87.5–108 MHz FM band. For this, look to a portable.

When the Going Gets Tough . . .

Not only DXers prefer tabletop sets. Like professional models and the very best portables, tabletops are ideally suited for where signals suffer from interference or tend to be weak—western and midwestern North America, for example, or Australia and New Zealand.

Even elsewhere, signals weaken when they pass over or near the magnetic North Pole, which periodically erupts into geomagnetic fury. To check, place a string on a globe—a conventional map won't do—between your location and the station's transmitter as shown in the Blue Pages. If the string passes near or above latitude 60 degrees north, beware.

Find major updates to the 2007 PASSPORT REPORTS at www.passband.com.

Antennas Rarely Overload

One reason most tabletops do well is they accept outboard antennas without the side effects these can cause with everyday portables.

It's hard to overstate the benefit of a worthy accessory antenna properly placed outdoors or, in a pinch, on a balcony or window. Just as a sailboat zips along with a proper sail, so, too, a receiver benefits from an antenna that can grab more signals. Test results and ratings of a wide variety of antennas—small and large, indoor and out—are also in PASSPORT REPORTS.

Daytime Signals Enhanced

Some programs formerly aired during evening prime time are now heard, instead, by day. These tend to be weaker, especially as most aren't beamed your way. But they are also among the most interesting.

Thanks to the scattering properties of shortwave you can eavesdrop on many off-beam signals, but it's harder. This is where a superior receiver's longer reach comes in.

But not always. Let's say you have a portable with a modest outdoor antenna, but reception is being disrupted by electrical noise—nearby dimmers, digital devices and whatnot. Reception may not improve with a tabletop model, as its superior circuitry boosts noises just as much as signals.

However, even here there may be an out. An active loop antenna (see Compact Antennas for 2007) can potentially improve the signal-to-noise ratio because it can be aimed away from noise sources. So, you may profit from a good tabletop model even when there's local electrical noise—provided you have the right antenna, properly aimed.

Apartment Solutions

If your antenna is within a high-rise building, performance can disappoint—reinforced concrete soaks up signals. Too, in urban areas nearby broadcast, cellular and other transmitters can interfere.

In these environments a good bet for tough stations is a superior receiver using a suitable antenna. Experiment with something like a homebrew insulated-wire antenna along, or just outside, a window or balcony. Or try an everyday telescopic car antenna that angles out, like a wall flagpole, from a window or balcony ledge.

You can also amplify your homebrew antenna with a good active preselector. Even simpler are factory-made amplified (active) antennas with reception elements and amplifiers in separate modules. All are covered in PASSPORT REPORTS.

If you don't live in an apartment, consider a first-rate passive (unamplified) outdoor wire antenna, usually under $100. Performance findings and installation tips are detailed in the Radio Database International White Paper, *Popular Outdoor Antennas*, and are also summarized in "Wire Antennas for 2007."

DRM Digital Broadcasts

Some tabletop models come "DRM Ready" to receive digital world band broadcasts now being introduced by broadcasters and manufacturers.

However, DRM Ready isn't Plug and Play. Today's receivers can reproduce DRM transmissions only when connected to a PC with separately purchased DRM software. For this combo to perform properly, it's best to use an outboard antenna located for minimum pickup of digital noise from your computer hardware. Shielded cables help, too.

With a powerful DRM signal having a high bit rate and no interference, the result is virtually local-quality audio fidelity—to this extent, DRM lives up to its promise. However, shortcomings exist: inferior long-distance (multi-hop) performance; susceptibility to disruption by noise and interference, includ-ing jamming; and creation of wideband interference to analog stations on nearby frequencies.

Yet, DRM is a work in progress with powerful backers, so results are likely to improve over time. Bottom line, it makes sense to favor a receiver with at least the potential to reproduce DRM.

Shortwave's Hidden Offerings

Although virtually all shortwave listeners enjoy world band, some also seek out utility and ham signals nestled between world band segments. These have reception challenges and rewards of their own and, unlike world band, don't require much in the way of receiver audio quality. This allows some receivers to stand out even when their world band audio isn't inspiring. The Icom IC-R75 and Japan Radio NRD-545 are two popular examples.

Other highly rated tabletop models perform solidly with all kinds of signals.

2007: Icom's Modular Concept

Icom's new IC-R1500 is an intriguing new type of "tabletop" receiver. Actually, it's the Icom IC-PCR1500 black box receiver mated to a control module so it can be operated without a PC.

It's not a concept endearing to traditionalists, but it is creative and may be welcomed by others. It's flexible enough for mobile use, too.

Complete Findings Now Available

Our unabridged laboratory and hands-on test results for each receiver are too exhaustive to reproduce here. However, they are available for selected current and classic models as PASSPORT's Radio Database International White Papers—details are elsewhere in this PASSPORT.

Tips for Using this Section

Receivers are listed in order of suitability for listening to difficult-to-hear world band stations; important secondary consideration is given to audio fidelity, ergonomics and perceived build quality. Street selling prices are cited, including British and Australian VAT/GST where applicable. Prices vary, so take them as the general guide they are meant to be.

Unless otherwise stated, all tabletop models have the following characteristics. *See* Worldly Words for terms used.

- Digital frequency synthesis and display.
- Full coverage of at least the 155–29999 kHz longwave, mediumwave AM and shortwave spectra—including all world band frequencies—but no coverage of the FM broadcast band (87.5–108 MHz). Models designed for sale in certain countries have reduced shortwave tuning ranges.
- A wide variety of helpful tuning features.
- Synchronous selectable sideband via high-rejection IF filtering (not lower-rejection phase cancellation), which greatly reduces adjacent-channel interference and selective-fading distortion.

☞ ECSS: Many tabletop models can tune to the nearest 10 Hz or even 1 Hz, allowing the operator to use the receiver's single-sideband circuitry to manually phase its BFO (internally generated carrier) with the station's transmitted carrier. Called "ECSS" (exalted-carrier, selectable-sideband) tuning, this can be used in lieu of synchronous selectable sideband. However, in addition to the relative inconvenience of this technique, unlike synchronous selectable sideband, which re-phases continually and perfectly, ECSS is always slightly out of phase. This causes at least some degree of harmonic distortion to music and speech, while tuning to the nearest Hertz can generate slow-sweep fading (for this reason, mis-phasing by two or three Hertz may provide better results).

- Proper demodulation of modes used by non-world-band shortwave signals, except for models designed to be sold in certain countries. These modes include single sideband (LSB/USB) and CW ("Morse code"); also, with suitable ancillary devices, radioteletype (RTTY), frequency shift key (FSK) and radiofax (FAX).

- Meaningful signal-strength indication.
- Illuminated display.

What Passport's Rating Symbols Mean

Star ratings: ✪✪✪✪✪ is best. Stars reflect overall performance and meaningful features, plus to some extent ergonomics and perceived build quality. Price, appearance, country of manufacture and the like are not taken into account. With tabletop models there is a slightly greater emphasis on the ability to flush out tough, hard-to-hear signals, as this is one of the main reasons these sets are chosen. Nevertheless, to facilitate comparison the tabletop rating standards are very similar to those used for the professional and portable models reviewed elsewhere in this PASSPORT REPORTS.

Passport's Choice. La crème de la crème. Our test team's personal picks of the litter—models we would buy or have bought for our personal use. Unlike star ratings, these choices are unapologetically subjective.

✪: A relative bargain, with decidedly more performance than the price would suggest. However, none of these receivers is cheap.

✪✪✪✪✪ 📋 *Passport's Choice*

AOR AR7030 PLUS, AOR AR7030

Price ('7030 receivers): *AR7030 PLUS:* $1,499.95 in the United States. £949.00 or less in the United Kingdom. *AR7030:* £799.00 or less in the United Kingdom. €1,039.00 in Germany.

Price (options—all '7030 models): *Optional MuRata ceramic bandwidth filters:* $59.95–79.95 each plus installation in the United States. £29.99–39.99 each including installation in the United Kingdom. €49.00 each plus installation in Germany. *Optional Collins mechanical bandwidth filters:* $99.95 each plus installation in the United States. £74.00 each including installation in the United Kingdom. €95.00–99.95 each plus installation in Germany. *FL124 daughter board for up to three crystal filters:* US$59.95

Britain's **AOR AR7030 PLUS** is today's top-performing tabletop model. Attractive styling, too.

plus $25.00 installation in the United States. £24.99 including installation in the United Kingdom. €50.00 plus installation in Germany. *FL-624 Boger aftermarket daughter board for up to six crystal filters:* contact Boger-Funk in Germany for price. *XTL2.4 crystal filter, 2.4 kHz bandwidth:* £79.00 including installation in the United Kingdom; special-order part from AOR Japan, so requires waiting period. *Aftermarket (Icom, Kenwood, JRC, Inrad, Kiwa et al.) 455 kHz crystal bandwidth filters:* equivalent of $150–300 each plus installation worldwide, depending on filter and vendor. *SM7030 service kit:* $89.95 in the United States. £39.95 in the United Kingdom. €98.00 in Germany. *BP123 inboard rechargeable battery with inboard recharger (nominally results in minor performance drop-off):* £99.99 in the United Kingdom. €179.00 in Germany.

Price (options—AR7030 PLUS):
UPNB7030 notch filter: $339.95 plus $25.00 installation in the United States. £163.00 including installation in the United Kingdom. €280.70 plus installation in Germany.

Price (options—AR7030): *NB7030 noise blanker & notch filter:* £198.00 including installation in the United Kingdom. €298.00 plus installation in Germany.

Pro: In terms of overall performance for program listening, as good a receiver as we've ever tested. With one exception (*see* Con), exceptionally quiet circuitry enhances DXing and weak-signal listening, alike.

Superb world band and mediumwave AM audio quality when used with a first-rate outboard speaker or audio system. Synchronous selectable sideband performs exceptionally well at reducing distortion caused by selective fading, as well as at diminishing or eliminating adjacent-channel interference; also has synchronous double sideband. Superb dynamic range and third-order intercept point at both wide (+11 dBm at 20 kHz, approaching +20 dBm at 50 kHz) and narrow (–3 dBm at 5 kHz) signal spacing. Superb image rejection (102 dB). Superb first IF rejection (99 dB). Superb AGC threshold with preamp on. Four voice bandwidths (AR7030 2.3, 7.0, 8.2 and 10.3 kHz), using cascaded ceramic filters; optional filters can raise total to six bandwidths—ceramic, mechanical or crystal (crystal filters require optional daughter board) (*see* Con). Bandwidths using ceramic filters have excellent shape factors and superb ultimate rejection. Sensitivity to weak signals excellent (–131 dB noise floor, 0.2 &V sensitivity) with preamp on (*see* Con: *AR7030*). Advanced tuning and operating features aplenty, including passband tuning. Optional tunable audio (AF) notch filter and noise blanker; notch extremely effective, with little loss of audio fidelity. Automatically self-aligns and centers bandwidth filters—whether ceramic, mechanical or crystal—for optimum performance, then displays measured bandwidth of each. Remote keypad (*see* Con). Accepts two antennas. IF output. World Time 24-hour clock displays seconds, calendar and timer/sleep-delay. Outstanding performance with local, distant and multipath twilight-fringe mediumwave AM signals. Superior service at U.K. factory [AOR (UK)] and U.S. distributor (Universal Radio). Website (www.aoruk.com/7030bulletin.htm) provides technical updates and information. Owner's manual available online (www.aoruk.com/manuals.htm). *AR7030 PLUS:* 400 scannable presets, instead of 100, with 14-character alphanumeric readout for station names (*see* Con). Bandwidth choices (2.3, 4.6, 6.6 and 9.8 kHz) preferable to those of AR7030. Optical encoder for tuning inherently more reliable than mechanical encoder on AR7030 (*see* Con).

Con: Unusually convoluted ergonomics, including tree-logic operating scheme, especially in the PLUS version; once the initial glow of ownership has passed, some find this to be tiresome. No keypad on receiver; instead, keypad is part of an infrared wireless remote control which has to be aimed carefully at receiver's front or back. Although the remote can operate from across a room, LCD characters too small to be seen from such a distance. LCD omits certain useful information, such as signal strength, when radio in various status modes. Front end selectivity only fair. When four standard ceramic bandwidth filters are used with two optional mechanical filters, ultimate rejection, although superb with widest three bandwidths, cannot be measured beyond –80/–85 dB on narrowest three bandwidths because of phase noise; still, ultimate rejection is excellent or better with these configurations. Optional Collins filters measure as having poorer shape factors (1:1.8 to 1:2) than standard MuRata ceramic filters (1:1.5 to 1:1.7). LCD emits some digital electrical noise, a potential issue only if an amplified (active) antenna is used with its pickup element (e.g. telescopic rod) placed near receiver. 2.3 kHz bandwidth has some circuit noise (hiss) in single sideband or ECSS modes. Uses outboard AC adaptor instead of built-in power supply. *AR7030:* Unusual built-in preamplifier/attenuator design links both functions, so receiver noise rises slightly when preamplifier used in +10 dB position, or attenuator used at –10 dB setting. Lacks, and would profit from, a bandwidth of around 4 or 5 kHz; optional Collins mechanical bandwidth filter of 3.5 kHz (nominal at –3 dB, measures 4.17 kHz at –6 dB) thus worth considering. Only 100 presets and no alphanumeric readout. Mechanical tuning encoder occasionally skips frequency increments, especially if it has not been used for awhile. Not available from North American distributor. *AR7030 PLUS:* Tuning knob feel only fair.

Verdict: Engineered by John Thorpe and manufactured in England, the AR7030 is a smashing performer, with audio quality that can be a pleasure hour after hour. And it's even better and more robust in its PLUS incarnation.

But there is a catch. Like BMW's iDrive, many functions are shoehorned into a tree-logic control scheme. The resulting ergonomics are uniquely hostile—especially in the PLUS version—even if operation ultimately is not that difficult to master. *Best bet:* Before buying, either lay hands on a '7030 or study the free online owner's manuals (www.aoruk.com/pdf/7030m.pdf and www.aoruk.com/pdf/fpu.pdf).

Ergonomics aside, for serious DXing the '7030 is today's top performer on the scotch side of a professional receiver, but there's more. With a suitable outboard speaker it is also one of the best sounding receivers at any price for hearing world band and mediumwave AM shows under a wide range of reception conditions.

An *RDI WHITE PAPER* is available for this model.

✪✪✪✪½
Japan Radio NRD-545

Price: $1,799.95 in the United States. CAD$3,199.00 in Canada. £1,599.00 or less in the United Kingdom. €1,798.00 in Germany. AUD$3,589.00 in Australia. *NVA-319 external speaker:* $199.95 in the United States. £199.00 in the United Kingdom. €259.00 in Germany. *CHE-199 VHF-UHF converter:* $369.95 in the United States. €398.00 in Germany. *CGD-197 frequency stabilizer:* $99.95 in the United States. €149.00 in Germany.

Pro: Superior build quality, right down to the steel cabinet with machined screws. Easily upgraded by changing software ROMs. Fully 998 bandwidths provide unprecedented flexibility. Razor-sharp skirt selectivity, especially with voice bandwidths. Outstanding array of tuning aids, including 1,000 station presets (*see* Con). Wide array of reception aids, including passband offset, excellent manual/automatic tunable notch, and synchronous selectable sideband having good lock. Superb reception of single-sideband and other "utility" signals. Demodulates C-Quam AM stereo signals, which then need to be fed through an external audio amplifier, not provided (the headphone jack can't be used for this, as it is monaural). Highly adjustable AGC in all modes requiring BFO (*see* Con). Tunes in ultra-precise 1 Hz increments, although displays only in 10 Hz increments. Ergonomics, including the physical quality of tuning knob and other controls, among the very best. Some useful audio shaping. Computer interface with free NRDWIN software (*see* Con); among other things, is effective at processing RTTY signals. Virtually no spurious radiation of digital "buzz." Hiss-free audio-out port for

recording or feeding low-power FM transmitter to hear world band around the house. Internal AC power supply is quiet and generates little heat. Power cord detaches handily from receiver, like on a PC, making it easy to replace. Includes a "CARE package" of all needed metric plugs and connectors, along with a 12V DC power cord.

Con: Ultimate rejection only fair, although average ultimate rejection equivalent is 10–15 dB better; this unusual gap comes about from intermodulation (IMD) inside the digital signal processor, and results in

NUMBERS: TOP TABLETOPS

	AOR AR7030 PLUS	Japan Radio NRD-545
Max. WB Sensitivity/Noise Floor	0.2 μV ❸/–131 dBm ❸[1]	0.2 μV ❸/–130 dBm ❸[4]
Blocking	>125 dB ❸	>127 dB ❸
Shape Factors, voice BWs	1:1.5–1:1.7 ❸	1:1.1 ❺
Ultimate Rejection	90 dB ❺	65 dB ❻
Front-End Selectivity	❼	❸
Image Rejection	102 dB ❺	>75 dB ❸
First IF Rejection	99 dB ❺	>90 dB ❺
Dynamic Range/IP3 (5 kHz)	82 dB ❸/–3 dBm ❺	66 dB ❼/–31 dBm ❼[5]
Dynamic Range/IP3 (20 kHz)	91 dB ❸/+11 dBm ❺	NA[6,7]
Phase Noise	129 dBc ❸	118 dBc ❻
AGC Threshold	0.7 μV ❺[2]	2 μV ❻
Overall Distortion, sync	0.5–3% ❺-❻[3]	0.1–7% ❺-❼[3]
Stability	2 Hz ❺	20 Hz ❻
Notch filter depth	55 dB ❺	37 dB ❻[8]

IBS Lab Ratings: ❺ Superb   ❸ Excellent   ❻ Good   ❼ Fair   ❼ Poor

(1) Preamplifier on. With preamp off: 0.35 μV ❸/–126 dBm ❻.

(2) Preamplifier on. With preamp off: 2 μV ❻.

(3) Usually <1% ❺.

(4) NRD-545SE: 0.16 ❺/–133 dBm ❸.

(5) NRD-545SE: 73 dB ❻/–23 dBm ❻.

(6) Not measurable at 20 kHz separation. At 10 kHz: 80 dB ❼❻/–10 dBm ❼❻.

(7) NRD-545SE: 89 dB ❻/+1 dBm ❸.

(8) DSP notch tunes only 100–2,500 Hz.

audible "monkey chatter" under certain specific and uncommon reception conditions. Audio quality sometimes tough sledding in the unvarnished AM mode—using synchronous selectable sideband helps greatly. No AGC adjustment in AM mode or with synchronous selectable sideband, and lone AGC decay rate too fast. Dynamic range only fair. Synchronous selectable sideband sometimes slow to kick in. Notch filter won't attenuate heterodynes (whistles) any higher in pitch than 2,500 Hz AF. Noise reduction circuit only marginally useful. Signal-strength indicator overreads at higher levels. Frequency display misreads by up to 30 Hz, especially at higher tuned frequencies, and gets worse as the months pass by. Station presets don't store synchronous-AM settings. Audio amplifier lacks oomph with some poorly modulated signals. No IF output, nor can one be retrofitted. NRD Win software, at least the current v1.00, handles only uploads, not downloads, and works only on com port 1 that is usually already in use. World Time 24-hour clock doesn't show when frequency displayed. No tilt bail or feet. Anti-reflective paint on buttons and knobs becomes shiny with wear.

Verdict: In many ways Japan Radio's NRD-545 is a remarkable performer, especially for utility and world band DXing below 5.1 MHz. With its first-class ergonomics and the fine feel of superior construction, it is always a pleasure to operate.

Yet, more is needed to make this the ultimate receiver it could be. By now Japan Radio should have issued a ROM upgrade to remedy at least some of these long-standing issues, but contrary to urban legend *nada* as yet, and nothing appears to be in the offing.

Whether "monkey chatter" and other manifestations of DSP overload are an issue varies markedly from one listening situation to another—some hear it, others never do or feel it is insignificant. It depends on the specifics of the signal being received, what part of the world you are in and your own aural perceptions. Reader feedback suggests that most don't find it to be a significant drawback.

The Japan Radio NRD-545 offers DSP technology and rugged construction. As JRC is a maritime electronics manufacturer, musical audio reproduction isn't a priority.

★★★½
Japan Radio "NRD-545SE"

Price: *NRD-545SE:* $1,899.00 in the United States. *Retrofit to change an existing receiver to "SE":* $104.00 plus receiver shipping both ways.

Pro: Dynamic range, 5 kHz signal spacing, improves from 66 dB to 73 dB. Occasional enhancement of tough-signal reception.

Con: Not available outside North America. *With 8 kHz replacement filter:* Audio bandwidth reduced by 20 percent at the high end. *With 6 kHz replacement filter (not tested):* Audio bandwidth reduced by about 40 percent at the high end.

☞ For all except those who largely confine their listening to tough DX or utility catches, the 8 kHz filter is a preferable choice over the 6 kHz option.

Verdict: Sherwood Engineering, an American firm, replaces the stock DSP protection filter with one of two narrower filters of comparable quality. In principle, this should provide beaucoup decibels of audible improvement in the "monkey chatter" sometimes encountered on the '545 from adjacent-channel signals. Perhaps, but we couldn't hear the difference. What was noticed, instead, was an unwelcome reduction in audio crispness with world band signals—as well as, of course, with mediumwave AM reception.

The '545 is best suited to non-broadcast-listening applications, anyway, so for some DXers the Sherwood modification provides a modestly positive tradeoff. For these, the aural drawback of the Sherwood modification can be less important than its 7 dB improvement in dynamic range and occasional enhancement of tough-signal reception.

But if your main interest is in listening to world band programs, this modification is not the way to go.

✪✪✪✪½ ✪
Icom IC-R75 (Kiwa)

Price (Kiwa modifications): *Synchronous detector upgrade:* $45.00 in the United States. *Audio upgrade:* $35.00 in the United States. *Audio "Hi-Fi" upgrade:* $35.00 in the United States.

Pro: Synchronous detection performance improved slightly, with synchronous selectable sideband actually being somewhat functional with narrow bandwidth. Added high-end audio response marginally improves fidelity with wider IF bandwidth settings. Generally high-quality parts and installation. Prompt turnaround.

Con: When synchronous detector loses lock during deep fades, there is a heterodyne squeal or warble not evident before modification; slow AGC setting occasionally helps ameliorate this. Slight increase in audible

hiss with narrow bandwidth settings. Modifications not readily undone and may invalidate Icom's warranty, although in practice this may not be enforced.

☞ Kiwa's regular $35 audio upgrade extends the audio response of the audio amplifier, but doesn't impact the record (line) output. For yet another $35 the "hi-fi" upgrade provides even better audio—through the record (line) output, as well as speaker and headphones. The "hi-fi" upgrade normally results in a 4.3 kHz bandwidth, but 5.5 kHz is an available alternative; we chose this.

Verdict: Of the three tested Kiwa modifications for the popular Icom IC-R75, the audio "Hi-Fi" is the most useful. Runner up is the synchronous detector upgrade, which provides minor but useful improvement. All are reasonably priced but are best deferred until the factory warranty has expired.

✪✪✪✪⅜ ✪
Icom IC-R75

Price: *Receiver with UT-106 DSP accessory:* $569.95 in the United States. AUD$1,089.00 in Australia. *Receiver without UT-106 DSP accessory:* CAD$899.00 in Canada. €749.00 in Germany. AUD$965.00 in Australia. *UT-106 DSP accessory:* CAD$250.00 in Canada. €99.00 in Germany. *Icom Replacement Bandwidth Filters (e.g., FL-257 3.3 kHz):* $159.95 in the United States. CAD$340.00 in Canada. €169.00 in Germany. *SP-23 amplified audio-shaping speaker:* $169.95 in the United States. €129.00 in Germany. *Pyramid PS-3KX aftermarket 120V AC 13.8V DC regulated power supply:* $22.95 in the United States.

Pro: Dual passband offset acts as variable bandwidth and a form of IF shift (*see* Con). Reception of faint signals alongside powerful competing ones aided by excellent ultimate selectivity and good blocking. Excellent front-end selectivity, with seven filters for the shortwave range and more for elsewhere. Two levels of preamplification, 10 dB and 20 dB, can be switched off.

The Icom IC-R75 is popularly priced. It is a favorite for monitoring utility stations like Air Force One.

Excellent weak-signal sensitivity and good AGC threshold with +20 dB preamplification. Superior rejection of spurious signals, including images. Excellent stability, essential for unattended reception of RTTY and certain other types of utility transmissions. Excels in reception of utility and ham signals, as well as world band signals tuned via "ECSS" technique. Ten tuning steps. Can tune and display in exacting 1Hz increments (*see* Con). Adjustable UT-106 DSP audio accessory with automatic variable notch filter, normally an extra-cost option, helps to a degree in improving intelligibility, but not pleasantness, of some tough signals; also, it reduces heterodyne ("whistle") interference. Fairly good ergonomics, including smooth-turning weighted tuning knob; nice touch is spinning finger dimple, even if it doesn't spin very well. "Control Central" LCD easy to read and evenly illuminated by 24 LEDs with dimmer. Adjustable AGC—fast, slow, off. Tuning knob uses reliable optical encoder normally found only on professional receivers, rather than everyday mechanical variety. Low overall distortion. Pleasant and hiss-free audio with suitable outboard speaker; audio-shaping amplified Icom SP-23, although pricey, works well for a number of applications. 101 station presets. Two antenna inputs, switchable. Digital bar graph signal-strength indicator, although not as desirable as an analog meter, is unusually linear above S-9 and can be set to hold a peak reading briefly. Audio-out port for recording or feeding low-power FM transmitter to hear world band around the house. World Time 24-hour clock, timer and sleep delay (*see* Con). Tunes to 60 MHz, including 6 meter VHF ham band. Tilt bail (*see* Con).

Con: Synchronous detector virtually non-functional; operates reasonably only with modification by user or specialty firm, or by addition of a specialized auxiliary device. Dual passband offset usually has little impact on received world band signals and is inoperative when synchronous detection is in use. DSP's automatic variable notch tends not to work with AM-mode signals not received via "ECSS" technique (tuning AM-mode signals as though they were single sideband). Mediocre audio through internal speaker, and no tone control to offset slightly bassy reproduction that originates prior to the audio stage; audio improves to pleasant with an appropriate external speaker, especially one that offsets the receiver's slight bassiness. Suboptimal audio recovery with weak AM-mode signals having heavy fading; largely remediable by "ECSS" tuning and switching off AGC. Display misreads up to 20 Hz, somewhat negating the precise 1 Hz tuning. Keypad requires frequencies to be entered in MHz format with decimal or trailing zeroes, a pointless inconvenience. Some knobs small. Uses outboard AD-55 "floor brick" 120V AC adaptor in lieu of internal power supply; adaptor's emission field may be picked up by nearby indoor antennas or unshielded antenna lead-in wiring, which can cause minor hum on received signals (remediable by moving antenna or using shielded lead-in cable). AC adaptor puts out over 17.5V while the receiver is designed to run off 13.8V, so receiver runs hot and thus its voltage regulator's reliability suffers; dropping input voltage to 13–14V, such as with the Pyramid PS-3KX aftermarket regulated power supply, eliminates this shortcoming. Can read clock or presets IDs or frequency, but no more than one at the same time. RF/AGC control operates peculiarly. Tilt bail lacks rubber protection for furniture surface. Keyboard beep appears at audio line output. No schematic provided.

Verdict: The Japanese-made Icom IC-R75, formerly $800 in the United States, is now a tempting value. It is first-rate for unearthing tough utility and ham signals, as well as world band signals received via manual ECSS tuning (*see* "Weird Words")—the receiver's exacting frequency steps facilitate tuning world band signals as though they were single sideband. For these applications nothing else equals it on the sunny side of a kilobuck.

It is less of an unqualified success for world band broadcasts. Its hopeless synchronous detector performance is only very slightly improved by modifications from specialty firms like Kiwa (see preceding review).

Sherwood's SE-3 Mk III D accessory brings the 'R75's fidelity to life by entirely replacing the synchronous and audio circuits, but it costs almost as much as the receiver and complicates operation.

✪✪✪✪
Icom IC-R8500A

Price: *IC-R8500A-02 (U.S. version, cellular reception blocked):* discontinued. *ICF-8500A (unblocked):* $1,699.95 (government use or export only) in the United States. CAD$2,599.00 in Canada. €1,498.00 in Germany. AUD$3,220.00 in Australia. *CR-293 frequency stabilizer:* $279.95 in the United States. €109.00 in Germany. *External speakers:* Up to three Icom speakers available worldwide, with prices ranging from under $65 to $220 or equivalent. *Aftermarket Sherwood SE-3 Mk III D:* $569.00 in the United States. *Aftermarket BHT DSP noise canceller (www.radio.bhinstrumentation.co.uk/index. html):* under £90 in the United Kingdom.

Pro: Wide-spectrum multimode coverage from 0.1–2000 MHz includes longwave, mediumwave AM, shortwave and scanner frequencies. Physically very rugged, with professional-grade cast-aluminum chassis and impressive computer-type innards. Generally superior ergonomics, with generous-sized front panel having large and well-spaced controls, plus outstanding tuning knob with numerous tuning steps. 1,000 station presets and 100 auto-write presets have handy naming function. Superb weak-signal sensitivity. Pleasant, low-distortion audio aided by audio peak filter. Passband tuning ("IF shift"). Unusually readable LCD. Tunes and displays in precise 10 Hz increments. Three antenna connections. Clock-timer, combined with record output and recorder-activation jack, make for superior hands-off recording of favorite programs, as well as for feeding a low-power FM transmitter to hear world band around the house.

Con: No longer available to the public in the United States and certain other countries, although Canadian mail-order electronics firms have been known to ship the unblocked version to customers in the United States. No synchronous selectable sideband. Bandwidth choices for world band and other AM-mode signals leap from a very narrow 2.7 kHz to a broad 7.1 kHz with nothing between, where something is most needed; third bandwidth is 13.7 kHz, too wide for world band, and no provision is made for a fourth bandwidth filter. Only one single-sideband bandwidth. Unhandy carousel-style bandwidth selection with no permanent indication of which bandwidth is in use. Poor dynamic range, surprising at this price point. Passband tuning ("IF shift") does not work in the AM mode, used by world band and mediumwave AM-band stations. No tunable notch filter. Built-in speaker mediocre. Uses outboard AC adaptor instead of inboard power supply.

☞ Also tested with Sherwood SE-3 Mk III D aftermarket accessory, which proved to be outstanding at adding selectable synchronous sideband. This combo also provides passband tuning in the AM mode which is used by nearly all world band stations. Adding the SE-3 and replacing the widest bandwidth with a 4 to 5 kHz bandwidth filter dramatically improve performance on shortwave, mediumwave AM and longwave.

Verdict: The large Icom IC-R8500 is a scanner that happens to cover world band, rather than *vice versa*.

As a standalone world band radio, this Japanese-made wideband receiver makes little sense. Yet, it is well worth considering if you want an all-in-one scanner that also serves as a shortwave receiver.

Icom's broadband IC-R8500A is now outlawed in the United States, where certain listening is *verboten*.

✪✪✪✪
AOR AR5000A+3

Price: *AR5000A+3 (cellular-blocked version) receiver:* $2,499.95 in the United States. *AR5000A+3 (full-coverage version) receiver:* $2,599.95 (government use or export only) in the United States. CAD$3,599.00 in Canada. £1,999.00 in the United Kingdom. €1,979.00 in Germany. AUD$2,699.00 in Australia. *Collins 6 kHz mechanical filter (recommended):* $99.95 in the United States. £76.00 in the United Kingdom. *SDU-5600 spectrum display unit:* $1,449.95 in the United States. £1,099 in the United Kingdom. €1,310.00 in Germany.

A segmented-coverage AOR AR5000A+3 is sold in the United States. Elsewhere, it tunes 0.01–3,000 MHz.

Pro: Ultra-wide-spectrum multimode coverage from 0.01–3,000 MHz includes longwave, mediumwave AM, shortwave and scanner frequencies. Helpful tuning features include 2,000 station presets in 20 banks of 100 presets each. Narrow bandwidth filter and optional Collins wide filter both have superb skirt selectivity (standard wide filter's skirt selectivity unmeasurable because of limited ultimate rejection). Synchronous selectable and double sideband (*see* Con). Front-end selectivity, image rejection, IF rejection, weak-signal sensitivity, AGC threshold and frequency stability all superior. Exceptionally precise frequency readout to nearest Hertz. Most accurate displayed frequency measurement of any receiver tested to date. Superb circuit shielding results in virtually zero radiated digital "buzz." IF output (*see* Con). DRM modifiable;

see www.aoruk.com/drm.htm#ar5000_drm or www.drmrx.org/receiver_mods.html. Automatic Frequency Control (AFC) works on AM-mode, as well as FM, signals. Owner's manual, important because of operating system, unusually helpful.

Con: Synchronous detector loses lock easily, especially if selectable sideband feature in use, greatly detracting from the utility of this high-tech feature. Substandard rejection of unwanted sideband with selectable synchronous sideband. Overall distortion rises when synchronous detector used. Ultimate rejection of "narrow" 2.7 kHz bandwidth filter only 60 dB. Ultimate rejection mediocre (50 dB) with standard 7.6 kHz "wide" bandwidth filter, improves to an uninspiring 60 dB when replaced by optional 6 kHz "wide" Collins mechanical filter. Installation of optional Collins filter requires expertise, patience and special equipment. Poor dynamic range. Cumber-

COMING UP: AOR TO OFFER DSP?

AOR (UK) is seriously contemplating the engineering and eventual manufacture of a 0.x–30 MHz DSP tabletop receiver. Should it materialize, release is expected to be "some way off," according to the manufacturer—years, although at this embryonic juncture nobody seems to have a feel for specifics.

Assuming DRM becomes truly viable, the proposed receiver is scheduled to include a 12 kHz IF output to aid in deciphering DRM. Should the contemplated receiver get approved for development, the engineering team would likely consist of veteran John Thorpe working in concert with other engineers in the United Kingdom.

AOR states that the existing AR7030 series is scheduled to stay in production for some time—at least until the release of a possible new model, and maybe beyond.

some ergonomics. No passband offset. No tunable notch filter. Needs good external speaker for good audio quality. World Time 24-hour clock does not show when frequency displayed. IF output frequency 10.7 MHz instead of standard 455 kHz.

Verdict: Unbeatable in some respects, inferior in others—it comes down to what you want the radio for. The optional 6 kHz Collins filter is strongly recommended, but it should be installed by the dealer at the time of purchase. Although some AOR receivers are engineered and manufactured in the United Kingdom, this model is strictly Japanese.

✪✪✪✪
Palstar R30C/Sherwood, Palstar R30CC/Sherwood

Price: *Sherwood SE-3 Mk III D:* $569.00 in the United States. *Palstar R30C/CC:* See below.

Pro: SE-3 provides nearly flawless synchronous selectable sideband, reducing adjacent-channel interference while enhancing audio fidelity. Foolproof installation; plugs right into the Palstar's existing IF output.

Con: Buzz occasionally heard during weak-signal reception. SE-3 costs roughly as much as a regular Palstar receiver.

Verdict: If you're going to spend $569 to upgrade a $595–675 receiver, you may as well spring for another model.

✪✪✪⅞ ✐
Palstar R30C, Palstar R30CC

Price: *R30C:* $595.00 in the United States. £419.95 in the United Kingdom. *R30CC:* $675.00 in the United States. £469.00 in the United Kingdom. €663.70 in Germany. *SP30 speaker:* $59.95 in the United States. £34.95 in the United Kingdom.

☞ We've tested the CC, but not the C version. The C uses a MuRata filter in the wide position and a Collins mechanical filter in the narrow setting. That same narrow Collins filter is used in the CC version, but there's also a Collins filter in the wide position.

Pro: Generally good dynamic range. Overall distortion averages 0.5 percent, superb, in single-sideband mode (in AM mode, averages 2.9 percent, good, at 60% modulation

---

BUILD YOUR OWN

Most shortwave kits are novelties or regenerative radios. But there is one exception: Ten-Tec's small 1254 world band radio, $195. Parts quality for this superheterodyne appears to be excellent, while assembly runs at least 24 hours. It has 15 station presets, but lacks keypad, signal-strength indicator, synchronous selectable sideband, tilt bail, LSB/USB settings and adjustable AGC. Tuning increments are 500 Hz for single sideband and 5 kHz for AM-mode, plus there is an analog clarifier for tweaking between increments.

Phase noise, front-end selectivity, and longwave and mediumwave AM sensitivity are poor. Bandwidth is a respectable 5.6 kHz, and there is worthy ultimate rejection, image rejection, world band sensitivity, blocking, AGC threshold and frequency stability. Dynamic range and first IF rejection are fair, while overall distortion is good—with an external speaker, audio is pleasant.

The Ten-Tec 1254 is a fun weekend project, and the manufacturer's track record for hand-holding means that when you're through the radio should really work.

Heathkit may have faded into history, but there's still the Ten-Tec 1254 receiver kit.

and 4.4 percent, fair, at 95% modulation) (*see* Con, *R30CC*). Every other performance variable measures either good or excellent in PASSPORT's lab, and birdies are virtually absent. Excellent AGC performance with AM-mode and single-sideband signals. Robust physical construction of cabinet and related hardware. Microprocessor section well shielded to minimize radiation of digital "buzz." Features include selectable slow/fast AGC decay (*see* Con), 20–100 Hz/100–500 Hz VRIT (slow/fast variable-rate incremental tuning) knob, 0.5 MHz slew and 455 kHz IF output. One hundred non-volatile station presets, using a generally well-thought-out scheme (*see* Con); they store frequency, bandwidth, mode, AGC setting and attenuator setting; also, presets displayed by channel number or frequency. Excellent illuminated analog signal-strength meter reads in useful S1–9/+60 dB standard and is reasonably accurate (*see* Con). LCD and signal-strength indicator illumination can be switched off. Also operates from ten firmly secured "AA" internal batteries (*see* Con). Lightweight and small (*see* Con). Good AM-mode sensitivity within longwave and mediumwave AM bands. Audio line output has suitable level and is properly located on back panel. Self-resetting circuit breaker for outboard power (e.g., AC adaptor); fuse used with internal batteries and comes with spare fuses. Tilt bail quite useful (*see* Con). Optional AA30A and AM-30 active antennas, evaluated elsewhere in this PASSPORT REPORTS. *R30C:* Pleasant audio quality with wide (7.7 kHz) bandwidth (*see* Con). *R30CC:* Virtually superb skirt selectivity (1:1.4 wide and 1:1.5 narrow) and ultimate rejection (90 dB); bandwidths measure 6.3 kHz and 2.6 kHz, using Collins mechanical filters. Adjacent-channel 5 kHz heterodyne whistles largely absent with wide bandwidth (*see* Con, *R30CC*). Audio quality pleasant with wide bandwidth (*see* Con).

Con: No keypad for direct frequency entry, not even as an outboard mouse-type option; only some of the very cheapest of portables now don't come with or offer a keypad. No 5 kHz tuning step choice to aid in bandscanning. Lacks control to hop from one world band segment to another; instead, uses 0.5

Decades back, American tabletop receivers were simple, yet robust, out of necessity. Today, Ohio's Palstar keeps its receivers simple and robust by choice.
Universal Radio

MHz fast-slew increments. No synchronous selectable sideband without pricey Sherwood SE-3 Mk III D aftermarket accessory (see preceding review). ECSS tuning can be up to 10 Hz out of phase because of 20 Hz minimum tuning increment. Mechanical tuning encoder play gives tuning knob sloppy feel, making precise ECSS tuning difficult; an optical encoder might have helped avoided this while adding to reliability. Lightweight plastic tuning knob lacks mass to provide good tuning feel. Lacks features found in top-gun receivers, such as tunable notch filter, noise blanker, passband tuning and adjustable RF gain. Recovered audio fine with most signals, but with truly weak signals is not of the DX caliber found with top-gun receivers. No visual indication of which bandwidth is being used. No tone controls. Small identical front-panel buttons, including the MEM button which if accidentally pressed can erase a preset. Station presets not as intuitive or easy to select as with various other models; lacks frequency information on existing presets during memory storage. No AGC off. No RF gain control. Uses AC adaptor instead of built-in power supply. High battery consumption. Batteries frustratingly difficult to install, requiring partial disassembly of the receiver and care not to damage speaker connections or confuse polarities. Receiver's lightness and tilt bail's lack of rubber sheathing allow it to slide around, especially when tuning knob pushed to change VRIT increments; the added weight of batteries helps slightly. Unsheathed tilt bail digs into some surfaces. Mono headphone jack produces output in only one ear of stereo 'phones (remedied by user-purchased mono-to-stereo adaptor). Signal-strength meter illumination dims when volume turned high with AM-mode signals; LCD illumination unaffected. Three bulbs used for illumination are soldered into place, making replacement difficult, although they should last a very long time. *R30C:* Wide bandwidth slightly broad for a model lacking synchronous selectable sideband, often allowing adjacent-channel (5 kHz) heterodyne whistles to be heard; largely remedied by detuning 1–2 kHz, which unlike with some receivers doesn't significantly increase distortion. *R30CC:* Intermittent microphonics in AM mode when using narrow bandwidth and internal speaker. Audio frequency response with wide filter makes for slightly muffled audio as compared with R30C; largely remedied by detuning 1–2 kHz, which unlike with some receivers doesn't significantly increase distortion.

☞ Works best when grounded.

Verdict: Although Ohio-made Palstar R30C/CC receivers are conspicuously lacking in tuning and performance features, what they set out to do, they tend to do to a high standard. If you can abide the convoluted battery installation procedure and don't mind having to add an outboard antenna, either version can work as a field portable.

Nevertheless, these receivers lack a distinct identity. Although audio is fairly pleasant, especially in the original and now-discontinued basic version, there's no synchronous selectable sideband to make it a premium listening radio. Too, audio quality in the

current versions' narrow setting tends to be muffled.

The lack of operating features is especially disappointing—not even a keypad, something routinely found on portables costing a fraction as much. And the lack of signal-tweaking features, along with pedestrian weak-signal recovered audio, preclude serious DX use.

Yet, not everybody fits neatly into standard categories. One size doesn't fit all, and to that end the R30C/CC's straightforward concept and physical robustness make it a clear alternative.

★★★¾ ✪ 📄
Yaesu FRG-100 (as available)

Price: *FRG-100:* $599.95 in the United States. *TCXO-4 frequency stabilizer:* $99.95 in the United States. *Universal Radio SWL Remote and RCU-1400 remote control:* $89.90 in the United States.

Pro: Commendable performance in many respects. Includes three bandwidths, a noise blanker, selectable AGC, two attenuators, the ability to select 16 pre-programmed world band segments, two clocks, on-off timers, 52 tunable station presets that store frequency and mode data, a variety of scanning schemes and an all-mode squelch.

Con: Available only through less than a handful of vendors. No factory-provided keypad for direct frequency entry, although a two-part user-installable aftermarket infrared keypad system is available in most countries by post from an American source (Universal Radio); it also allows for remote control of a variety of receiver functions, although not volume. No synchronous selectable sideband. Lacks features found in "top-gun" receivers: passband tuning, notch filter, adjustable RF gain. Simple controls and display, combined with complex functions, can make certain operations confusing. Dynamic range only fair. Uses AC adaptor instead of built-in power supply.

Verdict: Every year we think the FRG-100 will cease to be available, yet year after year

The Yaesu FRG-100 is still available new, although it hasn't been manufactured for years.

it soldiers on. Why? It is a snail-slow seller. Given this, it could well continue to be available for another year or so.

In the tradition of the Yaesu FRG-7 that started it all, this minimalist model is sparse on factory-provided features. Yet, the FRG-100 succeeds in delivering worthy performance within an attractive price class. Although owners are scarce, they usually report being pleased.

An *RDI WHITE PAPER* is available for this model.

New for 2007
✪✪✪⅝
Icom IC-R1500

Price: *IC-R1500 with control head and "black box" receiver:* $699.95 in the United States. CAD$799.00 in Canada. £419.95 in the United Kingdom. TBA in Germany. AUD$785.00 in Australia. *UT-106 DSP unit:* $139.95 in the United States. CAD$250.00 in Canada. £84.99 in the United Kingdom. €99.00 in Germany. *OPC-1156 11½ foot (3.5 meter) controller extension cable:* $26.00 in the United States. £24.99 in the United Kingdom. €13.95 in Germany. *OPC-441 16½ foot (five-meter) speaker extension cable:* $33.00 in the United States. CAD29.00 as available in Canada. £24.99 in the United Kingdom. €29.95 in Germany. *CP-12L 12V DC cigarette lighter power cable:* $27.95 in the United States. CAD$60.00 in Canada. *OPC-254L 12V DC fused power cord:* $10.95

in the United States. CAD$25.00 in Canada. *Aftermarket RF Systems DPX-30 antenna splitter for separate shortwave and scanner antennas:* $99.95 in the United States. €76.20 in Germany.

Pro: Generally excellent wired control head so '1500 can also be used as a standalone tabletop or, to a degree with the optional CP-12L power cord, a mobile receiver (*see* Con)—as well as a PC-controlled model *à la* sibling PC-R1500 (*see* PC Controlled Receivers chapter). Wideband frequency coverage in three versions: *(blocked U.S. version)* 0.01–810, 851–867, 896–1811, 1852–1868, 1897–2305.9, 2357–2812, 2853–2869, 2898–3109.8, 3136–3154.8, 3181–3300 MHz; *(blocked French version)* 0.01–30, 50.2–51.2, 87.5–108, 144–146, 430–440 and 1240–1300 MHz; *(unblocked version)* 0.01–3300 MHz; with all versions, specifications not guaranteed 0.01–0.5 and 3000–3300 MHz; BFO operation (single sideband and CW) up to 1300 MHz. Very good shortwave sensitivity. Tunes and displays in unusually precise 1 Hz increments. Vast number of user-selectable tuning steps. Useful manual ECSS operation (*see* Con) aided by Gibraltar-class stability. Selectable fast/slow AGC decay (*see* Con). Three different user screens when PC controlled in lieu of control head. Excellent 'scope for up to a 1 MHz peek at radio spectrum in real time, 1–10 MHz in non-real time. Generally good IF shift (*see* Con). Operating software works well and can be flash-ROM updated online. Fully 2600 station presets clustered

The Icom IC-R1500 heralds a new breed—a "black box" PC receiver made into a tabletop by adding a control head (next page).

The Icom IC-R1500 control head allows the PC-only IC-PCR1500 to act as a tabletop model.

D. Zantow

into 26 pages of 100 channels each. Generally pleasant audio quality (*see* Con). Audio available not only through the set's internal speaker (*see* Con) or an external speaker, but also via USB through the PC's audio system (*see* Con). Can record audio in .wav format onto hard drive (*see* Con). One-step (20 dB) attenuator (*see* Con). Optional UT-106 AF-DSP unit (not tested).

Con: Poor dynamic range—no RF or IF gain control to help alleviate overloading, and attenuator has only one step. No synchronous selectable sideband; manual ECSS alternative sounds slightly out of phase even with 1 Hz tuning step. Control head provides most, but not all, operating functions available from PC control; for example, there's no keypad or spectrum 'scope, and presets simultaneously display only one frequency or alphanumeric tag. Control head has no stand or mounting bracket for desktop or mobile use, nor can it be attached to the body of the "black box." At one test location, some distortion encountered with single-sideband signals through the 3 kHz bandwidth. Slight hiss. Audio only fair through black box's built-in speaker. Audio a bit weak through computer's USB port. No AGC off. IF shift operates only in single-sideband and CW modes. Mediumwave sensitivity only fair. Poor longwave sensitivity. Marginal noise blanker. No on/off multi-event timing for audio recording. Telescopic antenna and cable virtually useless on shortwave and not much better elsewhere within tuned frequency ranges. Software installation not always easy and only via computer's USB port (no serial connection provided). No schematic or block diagrams.

Verdict: The wideband Icom IC-R1500 is the more-or-less standalone version of the IC-PCR1500 computer-controlled black box receiver. It consists of the same basic box used by the 'PCR1500, along with an external wired control head that allows it to act independently as a real, if decidedly unusual, tabletop or, to a degree, a mobile receiver. Thus, the 'R1500 can be operated by PC or, using the control head, by itself—but not both at the same time. The control head includes an illuminated LCD, tuning knob, volume, squelch and other controls. Nevertheless, operation is more flexible using a PC, as it includes keypad tuning and other pluses not found when using the control head.

Evaluation of New Model: *See* Receivers for PCs. Then, under Icom IC-R1500, *see* Verdict, followed by Evaluation of New Models.

New for 2007
Icom IC-R2500

The $1,000 Icom IC-R2500 (not tested) uses the same platform as the '1500, but adds diversity reception to help reduce fading effects (two widely spaced antennas—or, outside the shortwave spectrum, one horizontally and one vertically polarized—are required). Synchronous selectable sideband also reduces the effects of AM-mode fading, but is unavailable on the '2500.

Additional extras are multi-channel monitoring/display, P25 (public service digital) board, D-Star and other features oriented to VHF/UHF/SHF scanning.

✪✪✪ 🖉
Yaesu VR-5000

Price: *VR-5000 Receiver, including single-voltage AC adaptor:* $599.95 in the United States. CAD$899.00 or more in Canada. £499.95 in the United Kingdom. €598.00 in Germany. AUD$1,320.90 in Australia. *DSP-1 digital notch, bandpass and noise reduction unit:* $119.95 in the United States. CAD$199.00 in Canada. £94.95 in the United Kingdom. €85.00 in Germany. *DVS-4 16-second digital audio recorder:* $44.95 in the United States. CAD$80.00 in Canada. £29.95 in the United Kingdom. €28.50 in Germany. *FVS-1A voice synthesizer (as available):* $44.95 in the United States. CAD$75.00 in Canada. €37.00 in Germany. *Pyramid PS-3KX aftermarket 120V AC>13.8V DC regulated power supply:* $22.95 in the United States.

Pro: Unusually wide frequency coverage, 100 kHz through 2.6 GHz (U.S. version omits cellular frequencies 869–894 MHz). Two thousand alphanumeric-displayed station presets, which can be linked to any of up to 100 groupings of presets. Up to 50 programmable start/stop search ranges. Large and potentially useful "band scope" spectrum display (*see* Con). Bandwidths have superb skirt selectivity, with shape factors between 1:1.3 and 1:1.4. Wide AM bandwidth (17.2 kHz) allows local mediumwave AM stations to be received with superior fidelity (*see* Con). Flexible software settings provide a high degree of control over selected parameters. Sophisticated scanning choices, although they are of limited use because of false signals generated by receiver's inadequate dynamic range (*see* Con). Dual-receive function, with sub-receiver circuitry feeding "band scope" spectrum display; when display not in use, two signals may be monitored simultaneously, provided they are within 20 MHz of each other. Sensitivity to weak signals excellent-to-superb within shortwave spectrum, although combined with receiver's inadequate dynamic range this tends to cause overloading when a worthy antenna is used (*see* Con). Appears to be robustly constructed. External spectrum display, fed by receiver's 10.7 MHz IF output, can perform very well for narrow-parameter scans (*see* Con). Two 24-hour clocks, both of which are shown except when spectrum display mode is in use; one clock tied into an elementary map display and database of time in a wide choice of world cities. On-off timer allows for up to 48 automatic events. Sleep-delay/alarm timers. Lightweight and compact. Multi-level display dimmer. Optional DSP unit includes adjustable notch filtering, a bandpass feature and noise reduction (*see* Con). Tone control. Built-in "CAT" computer control interface (*see* Con). Control and memory backup/management software available from www.g4hfq.co.uk.

Con: Exceptionally poor dynamic range (49 dB at 5 kHz signal spacing, 64 dB at 20 kHz spacing) and IF/image rejection (as low as 30 dB) for a tabletop model; for listeners in such high-signal parts of the world as Europe, North Africa and eastern North America, this shortcoming all but cripples reception of shortwave signals unless a very modest antenna is used; the degree to which VHF-UHF is degraded depends *inter alia* upon the extent of powerful transmissions in the vicinity of the receiver. No synchronous selectable sideband, a major drawback for world band and mediumwave AM listening, but not for shortwave utility/ham, VHF or UHF reception. Has only one single-sideband bandwidth, a relatively broad 4.0 kHz. Wide AM bandwidth (17.2 kHz) of no use for shortwave reception. For world band listening, the middle (8.7 kHz) AM bandwidth lets through adjacent-channel 5 kHz heterodyne, while narrow band-

Yaesu's VR-5000 features wideband coverage at a rock-bottom price, but has poor dynamic range.

width (consistently 3.9 kHz, not the 4.0 kHz of the SSB bandwidth) produces muffled audio. Line output level low. Audio distorts at higher volume settings. Limited bass response. Audio hissy, especially noticeable with a good outboard speaker. DSP-1 option a mediocre overall performer and adds distortion. Phase noise measures 94 dBc, poor. AGC threshold measures 11 microvolts, poor. No adjustment of AGC decay. Single-sideband AGC decay too slow. Most recent sample's (firmware v1u.17) tuning encoder sometimes has rotational delay that requires three clicks instead of one to commence down-frequency tuning when reversing direction from clockwise to counterclockwise. Mediocre tuning-knob feel. Signal-strength indicator has only five levels and overreads; an alternative software-selectable signal-strength indicator—not easy to get in and out of—has no markings other than a single reference level. Built-in spectrum display's dynamic range only 20 dB (–80 to –100 dBm), with a very slow scan rate. Single-sideband frequency readout of latest sample more accurate, but after warmup LSB is still 70 Hz and USB 100 Hz off. Long learning curve: Thirty buttons (often densely spaced, lilliputian and multifunction)—along with carouseling mode/tune-step selection and a menu-driven command scheme—combine to produce ergonomics that are not intuitive. Only one low-impedance antenna connector, inadequate for a wideband device that calls for multiple antennas. Longwave sensitivity mediocre. Clocks don't display seconds numerically. Marginal display contrast. Although four LEDs used for backlighting, the result is unevenly distributed. Uses AC adaptor instead of built-in power supply; adaptor and receiver both tend to run warm. Repeated microprocessor lockups, sometimes displayed as *"ERROR* LOW VOLTAGE,"* even though the receiver now comes with a 7.2V NiCd battery pack to help prevent this; unplugging set for ten minutes resolves problem until it occurs again, but the only permanent solution appears to be replacing the receiver's AC adaptor with a properly bypassed and regulated non-switching AC adaptor/DC power supply of at least one ampere that produces no less than 13.5V DC—certainly no less than 13.2V DC—and no more than 13.8V DC (we use a lab power supply, but in North America the Pyramid 2.5 amp PS-3KX appears promising). Even with aforementioned battery, clock has to be reset if power fails. Squelch doesn't function through audio line output (for recording, etc.). Line output gain is somewhat low. Sub-receiver doesn't feed line output. Computer interface lacks viable command structure, limiting usefulness. Tilt feet have inadequate rise. Owner's manual (0104q-DY) doesn't cover all receiver functions, so user has to learn much by trial and error. *United States:* Based on our recent experiences, customer support appears to be indifferent.

Verdict: With existing technology, DC-to-daylight receivers that provide excellent shortwave performance are costly to produce. This is reflected in their steep prices.

The relatively affordable wideband Yaesu VR-5000 tries to overcome this. This Japanese-made model acts as a VHF/UHF scanner as well as a shortwave receiver, but falls woefully shy for world band reception in strong-signal parts of the world. Elsewhere, it fares better on shortwave, especially if a modest antenna is used. VHF/UHF performance depends on the number and strength of local transmitters.

SI-TEX NAV-FAX 200 is the only remaining version of this small receiver, once sold under various names.

✪✪✪ 🅔
SI-TEX NAV-FAX 200

Price: $399.00 in the United States from www.si-tex.com. *SI-TEX ACNF 120V AC* *adaptor:* $19.95 in the United States. *NASA PA30 antenna:* €45.50 in Germany.

Pro: Superior rejection of images. High third-order intercept point for superior strong-signal handling capability. Bandwidths have superb ultimate rejection. Comes with Mscan Meteo Pro Lite software (www.mscan.com) for WEFAX, RTTY and NAVTEX reception using a PC with Windows XP or older Windows OS. Comes with wire antenna and audio patch cable. Two-year warranty at repair facility in Florida.

Con: No keypad, and variable-rate tuning knob is difficult to control. Broad skirt selectivity. Single-sideband bandwidth relatively wide. Volume control fussy to adjust. Synthesizer tunes in relatively coarse 1 kHz increments, supplemented by an analog fine-tuning "clarifier" control. Only ten station presets. Single sideband requires both tuning controls to be adjusted. No synchronous selectable sideband, notch filter or passband tuning. Frequency readout off by 2 kHz in single-sideband mode. Uses AC adaptor instead of built-in power supply. No clock, timer or sleep-delay feature. Not widely available.

☞ Available until recently with variations as the AKD Target HF-3M, NASA HF-4 and NASA HF-4E/S.

Verdict: Pleasant world band performance at an affordable price, although numerous features are absent and operation is more frustrating than on many other models. Logical for yachting.

 ½

Realistic DX-394

Price (as available): £199.95 in the United Kingdom.

Pro: Low price where there are still units in stock. Advanced tuning features include 160 tunable presets (*see* Con). Tunes in precise 10 Hz increments. Modest size, light weight and built-in telescopic antenna provide some portable capability. Bandwidths have superior shape factors and ultimate rejection. Two 24-hour clocks, one of which

The Realistic DX-394 has been out of production for years, but one U.K. dealer still sells it new.

shows independent of frequency display. Five programmable timers. 30/60 minute snooze feature. Noise blanker.

Con: What appear to be four bandwidths turn out to be virtually one, and it is too wide for optimum reception of many signals. Bandwidths, such as they are, not selectable independent of mode. No synchronous selectable sideband. Presets cumbersome to use. Poor dynamic range for a tabletop, a potential problem in Europe and other strong-signal parts of the world if an external antenna is used. Overall distortion, although acceptable, higher than desirable.

Verdict: Discontinued five years ago, but as of presstime it is still being offered at www.haydon.info. Modest dimensions and equally modest performance.

The PASSPORT *tabletop-model review team consists of Lawrence Magne and David Zantow, with George Zeller; also, David Crystal, George Heidelman, Tony Jones, Chuck Rippel and David Walcutt, along with Craig Tyson. Laboratory measurements by J. Robert Sherwood.*

Professional Receivers for 2007

They Really Rock, but Sticker Shock.

Professional receivers usually operate in the shadows: low-profile intelligence surveillance, along with military and commercial communications. Although few are engineered for optimal performance on shortwave/HF, those that are can't be beat for flushing out tough world band signals. Unsurprisingly, they also eavesdrop with aplomb on military, civilian and espionage utility signals.

Three Types

There are three types of professional receivers: easy for human operation, complex for human operation and no direct human operation.

The first is for personnel with minimal radio training. After all, if an AWACS radioman is disabled, uncomplicated operation allows buddies to take over. But operational simplicity also means performance compromises, so these receivers aren't covered here.

The second and smaller category goes to the other extreme, with no-holds-barred features and performance. These rarities are for skilled operators and are evaluated here in PASSPORT REPORTS.

Simplest are "black box" professional receivers with virtually no on-unit controls. These operate remotely or from computers, often at official surveillance facilities. PASSPORT REPORTS doesn't test these as, aside from their stratospheric prices, some of the best are sold only to U.S. Federal agencies and NATO organizations. Indeed, some are so hush-hush that even manufacturers' names are aliases.

Nevertheless, there is a small but enthusiastic civilian market for con-sumer-grade black box receivers. These have been tested, evaluated and rated in "Receivers for PCs."

Two Models Available to Public

Professional receivers are physically and electrically robust, with resistance to hostile environments and rough handling. Additionally, components are consistent, so board swapping and other field repairs can be done easily and without compromising performance.

Professional receivers tested by PASSPORT continue to be officially classified as "NLR"—no license required—so they're not subject to U.S. Government export controls. Still, especially with Watkins-Johnson, there may be a wait. If you want one as a gift in lieu of another boring Rolex watch, check out availability well in advance.

> Find major updates to the 2007 PASSPORT REPORTS at www.passband.com.

DRM Reception

The tested model from Ten-Tec is engineered to receive DRM digital world band broadcasts. While the Watkins-Johnson equivalent isn't DRM ready, this appears to be only because no user has as yet tried creating what's needed.

DRM requires that the receiver interface with a PC using separately purchased DRM software (www.drmrx.org).

Superior Antenna Required

A top-rated, properly erected antenna is a must for any professional receiver. For test findings and installation tips, read the in-depth Radio Database International White Paper, *Evaluation of Popular Outdoor Antennas.* There are also antenna reviews in PASSPORT REPORTS.

Is reception being disrupted by nearby electrical noise, even with a good antenna? If so, a fancier receiver might be a waste of money. Before springing for a pricey new model, try eliminating the source of noise or reducing it by repositioning your antenna. If all else fails, obtain a Wellbrook loop antenna—*see* "Compact Antennas for 2007."

Protect Your Investment

Professional receivers are rugged and typically include MOV surge protection. Nevertheless, it helps to plug a serious radio into a serious non-MOV surge arrestor, such as Zero-Surge (www.zerosurge.com) and Brick Wall (www.brickwall.com). We've used probably a dozen ZeroSurges over the past two decades with nary a hiccup or need for replacement.

Any receiver's outdoor antenna should be fed through a static protector. This is especially so with the Watkins-Johnson WJ-8711A when it's not equipped with the 8711/PRE option. Even then, it's wise to disconnect all outdoor antennas whenever a thunderstorm threatens.

DSP Audio

Most professional and a few consumer-grade receivers use DSP (digital signal processing) audio. In principle, there is no reason DSP audio quality can't equal that of conventional models. But a multi-stage DSP receiver is complex, requiring gobs of processing power. Today's DSP receivers use microprocessors that fall a bit short, one result being that static crashes tend to sound harsher.

Helping offset this is recoverable audio, which with tough DX signals tends to be slightly better with DSP professional receivers. This is why these are not strangers to "DXpeditions," where the most stubborn of radio signals are flushed out.

For world band, the Sherwood SE-3 fidelity-enhancing accessory is exceptionally helpful with current and discontinued professional receivers. While it doesn't fundamentally resolve the DSP audio issue, it helps significantly. It also provides exceptional-quality synchronous selectable sideband, a major plus. Downsides are cost, operating complexity and a BFO not as stable as those on some professional receivers.

Tips for Using this Section

Professional receivers are listed in order of suitability for listening to difficult-to-hear world band stations. Important secondary consideration is given to audio fidelity, ergonomics and reception of utility signals. Build quality is superior unless otherwise indicated. Selling prices, street, are as of when we go to press, and include European VAT and Australian GST where applicable.

Unless otherwise stated, all professional models have the following characteristics. *See* Worldly Words to understand specialized terms.

- Digital signal processing, including digital frequency synthesis and display.
- Full coverage of at least the 5–29999 kHz VLF/LF/MF/HF portions of the radio spectrum, encompassing all the long-wave, mediumwave AM and shortwave portions—including all world band frequencies—but no coverage of the standard FM broadcast band (87.5–108 MHz).
- A wide variety of helpful tuning features, including tuning and frequency display in 1 Hz increments.
- Synchronous selectable sideband via high-rejection IF filtering (not lower-rejection phasing), which greatly reduces adjacent-channel interference and fading distortion. On some models this is referred to as "SAM" (synchronous AM).

☞ **ECSS:** Professional models tune to the nearest 1 Hz, allowing the user to use the receiver's single-sideband circuitry to manually phase its BFO (internally generated carrier) with the station's transmitted carrier. Called "ECSS" (exalted-carrier, selectable-sideband) tuning, this can be used with AM-mode signals in lieu of synchronous selectable sideband. However, in addition to the relative inconvenience of this technique, unlike synchronous detection, which rephases continually and essentially perfectly, ECSS is always slightly out of phase. This causes at least some degree of harmonic distortion to music and speech, while tuning to the nearest Hertz can generate slow-sweep fading (for this reason, high-pass audio filtering or mis-phasing by two or three Hertz may provide better results).

- Proper demodulation of modes used by non-world-band—utility and amateur—shortwave signals. These modes include single sideband (LSB/USB and sometimes ISB) and CW ("Morse code"); also, with suitable ancillary devices, radioteletype (RTTY), frequency shift key (FSK) and radiofax (FAX).
- Meaningful signal-strength indication.
- Illuminated display.
- Superior build quality, robustness and sample-to-sample consistency as compared to consumer-grade tabletop receivers.
- Audio output for recording or low-power FM retransmission to hear world band around your domicile.

What PASSPORT's Rating Symbols Mean

Star ratings: ✪✪✪✪✪ is best. Stars reflect overall performance and meaningful features, plus to some extent ergonomics and perceived build quality. Price, appearance, country of manufacture and the like are not taken into account. With professional models there is a strong emphasis on the ability to flush out tough, hard-to-hear signals, as this is usually the main reason these sets are chosen by world band enthusiasts. Nevertheless, to facilitate comparison professional receiver rating standards are very similar to those used for the tabletop and portable models reviewed elsewhere in this PASSPORT REPORTS.

Passport's Choice. La crème de la crème. Our test team's personal picks of the litter—models we would buy or have bought for our personal use. Unlike star ratings, these choices are unapologetically subjective.

✪✪✪✪✪ *Passport's Choice*
Watkins-Johnson WJ-8711A

Price (receiver, factory options; single-quantity prices change often): *WJ-8711A:* $5,500.00 plus shipping worldwide. *871Y/SEU DSP Speech Enhancement Unit:* $1,200.00. *8711/PRE Sub-Octave Preselector:* $1,100.00. *871Y/DSO1 Digital Signal Output Unit:* $1,150.00.

Price (aftermarket options): *Hammond RCBS1900517BK1 steel cabinet and 1421A mounting screws and cup washers:* $120–140 in the United States from manufacturer (www.hammondmfg.com/rackrcbs.htm) or Newark Electronics (www.newark.com). *Sherwood SE-3 MK III accessory:* $569.00 plus shipping worldwide.

Pro: Proven robust. BITE diagnostics and physical layout allows technically qualified users to make most repairs on-site. Users can upgrade receiver performance

Watkins-Johnson's WJ-8711A, when only the very best will do.

over time by EPROM replacement. Exceptional overall performance. Unsurpassed reception of feeble world band DX signals, especially when mated to Sherwood SE-3 synchronous selectable sideband device and WJ-871Y/SEU noise-reduction unit (*see* Con). Unusually effective "ECSS" reception, tuning AM-mode signals as though they were single sideband. Superb reception of non-AM mode "utility" stations. Generally superior audio quality when coupled to Sherwood SE-3 fidelity-enhancing accessory, the W-J speech enhancement unit and a worthy external speaker (*see* Con). Unparalleled bandwidth flexibility, with no less than 66 outstandingly high-quality bandwidths. Trimmer on back panel allows frequency readout to be user-aligned against a known frequency standard, such as WWV/WWVH or a laboratory device.

Extraordinary operational flexibility—virtually every receiver parameter is adjustable. One hundred station presets. Synchronous detection ("SAM," for synchronous AM) reduces selective-fading distortion with world band, mediumwave AM and longwave signals, and works even on very narrow voice bandwidths (*see* Con). Rock stable. Built-in preamplifier. Tunable notch filter. Effective noise blanking. Highly adjustable scanning of both frequency ranges and station presets. Easy-to-read displays. Large tuning knob. Unusually effective mediumwave AM performance. Can be fully and effectively computer and remote controlled. Passband shift (*see* Con). Numerous outputs for data collection from received signals, as well as ancillary hardware; includes 455 kHz IF output, which makes for instant installation of Sherwood

NUMBERS: PROFESSIONAL RECEIVERS

	Watkins-Johnson WJ-8711A	Ten-Tec RX-340
Max. WB Sensitivity/Noise Floor	0.13 μV **S**/−136 dBm **E**	0.17 μV **S**/−130 dBm **E**[1]
Blocking	123 dB **G**	109 dB **F**
Shape Factors, voice BWs	1:1.21–1:1.26 **S**	1:1.15–1:1.33 **S**
Ultimate Rejection	>80 dB **E**	70 dB **G**
Front-End Selectivity	**F**/**E**[2]	**E**
Image Rejection	80 dB **E**	>100 dB **S**
First IF Rejection	—[3]	>100 dB **S**
Dynamic Range/IP3 (5 kHz)	74 dB **G**/−18 dBm **E**	55 dB **P**/−39 dBm **F**
Dynamic Range/IP3 (20 kHz)	99 dB **S**/+20 dBm **S**	86 dB **G**/+7 dBm **E**
Phase Noise	115 dBc **G**	113 dBc **G**
AGC Threshold	0.1 μV **P**	0.3 μV **G**[4]
Overall Distortion, sync	8.2% **P**	2.6% **G**
Stability	5 Hz **S**	5 Hz **S**
Notch filter depth	58 dB **S**	58 dB **S**

IBS Lab Ratings: **S** Superb   **E** Excellent   **G** Good   **F** Fair   **P** Poor

(1) Preamp on. With preamp off, 0.55 μV **G**/−122 dBm **G**.

(2) **F** standard/**E** with optional preselector.

(3) Adequate, but could not measure precisely.

(4) Preamp on. With preamp off, 1.3 μV **G**.

SE-3 accessory and balanced line outputs (connect to balanced hookup to minimize radiation of digital "buzz"). Remote control and dial-up data collection; Windows control software available from manufacturer. Among the most likely of all world band receivers tested to be able to be retrofitted for eventual reception of digital world band broadcasts. Inboard AC power supply, which runs unusually cool, senses incoming current and automatically adjusts 90–264 VAC, 47–440 Hz—a plus during brownouts or with line voltage or frequency swings. Superior-quality factory service (see Con). Comprehensive and well-written operating manual, packed with technical information and schematic diagrams. Hammond aftermarket cabinet exceptionally robust.

Con: Static crashes and modulation-splash interference sound noticeably harsher than on analog receivers, although this has been improved in latest operating software. Synchronous detection not sideband-selectable, so it can't reduce adjacent-channel interference (remediable by Sherwood SE-3). Basic receiver has mediocre audio in straight AM mode; "ECSS" tuning or synchronous detection, especially with optional speech enhancement unit (W1 noise-reduction setting), alleviates this. Some clipping distortion in single-sideband mode. Complex to operate to full advantage. Circuitry puts out a high degree of digital buzz, relying for the most part on the panels for electrical shielding; one consequence is that various versions emanate digital buzz through the nonstandard rear-panel audio terminals, as well as through the signal-strength meter and front-panel headphone jack—this problem lessened when Sherwood SE-3 used. Antennas with shielded (e.g., coaxial) feedlines less likely to pick up receiver-generated digital "buzz." Passband shift operates only in CW mode. Jekyll-and-Hyde ergonomics: sometimes wonderful, sometimes awful. Front-panel rack "ears" protrude, with the right one getting in the way of the tuning knob; fortunately, ears are easily removed. Mediocre front-end selectivity, remediable by 8711/PRE option (with insignificant 1.2 dB insertion loss); e.g. for those living near mediumwave AM transmitters. 871Y/SEU

option reduces audio gain and is extremely difficult to install; best to have all options factory-installed. Signal-strength indicator's gradations in dBm only. No DC power input. Keypad lettering wears off with use; replacement keys available at around $8 each, but minimum parts order is $100. Each receiver is built on order (1-800/954-3577), so it can take up to four months for delivery. Factory service can take as much as two months. Cabinet extra, available only on aftermarket from Hammond. Plastic feet have no front elevation and allow receiver to slide around. Available only through U.S. manufacturer, DRS Technologies (www.drs.com); receiver and factory options have been subjected to a number of price increases since 2000.

Verdict: The American-made WJ-8711A is, by a skosh, the ultimate machine for down-and-dirty world band DXing when money is no object.

Had there not been digital "buzz," inexcusable at this price—and had there been better audio quality, a tone control, passband shift and synchronous selectable sideband—the '8711A would have been even better, especially for enjoying programs. Fortunately, the Sherwood SE-3 accessory remedies virtually all these problems and improves DX reception, to boot; W-J's optional 871Y/SEU complements, rather than competes with, the SE-3 for improving recovered audio.

Overall, the WJ-8711A DSP, properly configured, is as good as it gets. It is exceptionally well suited to demanding connoisseurs with the appropriate financial wherewithal—provided they seek an extreme degree of manual receiver control.

DRM Ready
✪✪✪✪✪ *Passport's Choice*
Ten-Tec RX-340

Price: $4,250.00 in the United States. £3,299.00 in the United Kingdom. $6,900AUD in Australia. *Hammond RCBS1900513GY2 or RCBS1900513BK1 13" deep cabinet (www.hammondmfg.com/rack-rcbs.htm): $99.95 in the United States. Ten-*

Tec #307G (gray) external speaker: $98.00 in the United States. *Ten-Tec #307B (black) external speaker:* £89.00 in the United Kingdom. *Sherwood SE-3 MK III accessory:* $569.00 plus shipping worldwide.

Pro: Appears to be robust (*see* Con). BITE diagnostics and physical layout allow technically qualified users to make most repairs on-site. Users can upgrade receiver performance over time by replacing one or another of three socketed EPROM chips (currently v1.10A). Superb overall performance, including unsurpassed readability of feeble world band DX signals, especially when mated to the Sherwood SE-3 device; in particular, superlative image and IF rejection, both >100 dB. Few birdies. Audio quality usually worthy when receiver coupled to Sherwood SE-3 accessory and a good external speaker. Average overall distortion in single-sideband mode a low 0.2 percent; in other modes, under 2.7 percent. Exceptional bandwidth flexibility, with no less than 57 outstandingly high-quality bandwidths having shape factors of 1:1.33 or better; bandwidth distribution exceptionally good for world band listening and DXing, along with other activities (*see* Con). Receives digital (DRM) world band broadcasts by connecting it to a PC using DRM software purchased separately. Tunes and displays accurately in ultra-precise 1 Hz increments. Extraordinary operational flexibility—virtually every receiver parameter is adjustable; e.g., the AGC's various time constants have 118 million possible combinations, plus pushbutton AGC "DUMP" to temporarily deactivate AGC (*see* Con). Worthy front-panel ergonomics, valuable given the exceptional degree of manual operation; includes easy-to-read displays (*see* Con). Also, large, properly weighted rubber-track tuning knob with fixed dimple and Oak Grigsby optical encoder provide superior tuning feel and reliability; tuning knob tension user-adjustable for personalized feel. Attractive front panel. Two hundred station presets, 201 including the scratchpad. Synchronous selectable sideband ("SAM," for synchronous AM), reduces selective-fading distortion, as well as diminishes or eliminates adjacent-channel interference,

with world band, mediumwave AM and longwave signals; with earlier software, the lock was easily lost, but from v1.10A lock now holds acceptably (*see* Con). Built-in half-octave preselector comes standard. Built-in preamplifier (*see* Con). Adjustable noise blanker, works well in most situations (*see* Con). Stable as Gibraltar. Tunable DSP notch filter with exceptional depth of 58 dB (*see* Con). Passband shift (passband tuning) works exceptionally well (*see* Con). Unusually effective ECSS reception by tuning AM-mode signals as though they were single sideband. Superb reception of "utility" (non-AM mode) stations using a wide variety of modes and including fast filters for delay-critical digital modes. Highly adjustable scanning of both frequency ranges and station presets. Can be fully and effectively computer and remotely controlled (*see* Con). Numerous outputs for data collection and ancillary hardware, including 455 kHz IF output for instant hookup of Sherwood SE-3 accessory. Remote control and dial-up data collection. Superb analog signal-strength indicator (*see* Con). Inboard AC power supply senses incoming current and automatically adjusts to anything from 90–264 VAC, 48–440 Hz—a plus during brownouts or with line voltage or frequency swings. Superior control over fluorescent display dimming (*see* Con). Repair service at the Tennessee factory, $60 an hour, is reasonably priced by professional standards; although nominal repair turnaround is two to five weeks, in practice it is usually closer to two weeks. Comprehensive and well-written operating manual, packed with technical information and schematic diagrams.

Con: DSP microprocessor limitations result in poor dynamic range and fair IP3 at 5 kHz signal spacing. Blocking, phase noise and ultimate rejection pretty good but not of professional caliber. Complex to operate to full advantage. Static crashes sound harsher than on analog receivers. Not all bandwidths available in all modes. Spurious signals noted around 6 MHz segment (49 meters) at night at one test location equipped with superior antennas. When 9–10 dB preamplifier turned on, AGC acts on noise unless IF gain reduced by 10 dB.

Ten-Tec's RX-340 costs thousands. Yet, for a professional model it is modestly priced.

Notch filter does not work in AM, synchronous selectable sideband or ISB modes. Synchronous selectable sideband, although improved over early production, loses lock easier than some other models; e.g., if listening to one sideband and there is a strong signal impacting the other sideband, lock can be momentarily lost; remediable by Sherwood SE-3 accessory. Passband shift tunes only plus or minus 2 kHz and does not work in ISB or synchronous selectable sideband modes; remediable with Sherwood SE-3. Audio quality not all it could be; profits from Sherwood SE-3 accessory and an outboard speaker with quality fidelity. Occasional "popping" sound, notably when synchronous selectable sideband or ISB in use—may be from DSP overload. No AGC off except by holding down DUMP button. Noise blanker not effective at some test locations; for example, various other receivers work better at reducing certain noises. Audio power, especially through headphones, could be greater. With stereo headphones, one channel of headphone audio cuts out near full volume; also, at one position at lower volume. On our unit, occasional minor buzz from internal speaker. Keypad not in telephone format; rather, uses computer numeric-keypad layout. Some ergonomic clumsiness when going back and forth between station presets and VFO tuning; too, "Aux Parameter" and "Memory Scan" knobs touchy to adjust. Signal-strength indicator illuminated less than display. Digital "buzz" from fluorescent display emits from front of receiver, although not elsewhere. Standard serial cable does not work for computer control; instead, connector DB-25 pins have to be custom wired. No DC power input. Cabinet extra, available only on aftermarket from Hammond.

Verdict: With an exceptional degree of manual control, the Ten-Tec RX-340, when coupled to fidelity-enhancing hardware, is a superb DSP receiver for serious users who want no-compromise performance for years to come.

It is technologically advanced and can interface with a PC to receive digital (DRM) world band broadcasts. The '340 is a sensible value, too—even with bells and whistles and a 2006 price increase, it costs considerably less than a fully equipped WJ-8711A.

> A professional receiver needs a superior external antenna and a decent receiving location.

The PASSPORT *professional-model review team consists of David Walcutt, David Zantow and George Zeller, with Tony Jones, Lawrence Magne and Chuck Rippel. Laboratory measurements by J. Robert Sherwood.*

Little Black Boxes: Receivers for PCs

It's great to have knobs and keys to dig out signals, but not always. A dedicated core of radio enthusiasts and professionals prefer PC-controlled boxes.

As with a good marriage, mating a receiver with a PC allows each to enhance the other. Yet, this synergy can be offset by drawbacks, such as hardware complications, software glitches and instability—radio in-

terference, too, from PC monitors, cables and so on. Professional receiving facilities are set up to overcome these challenges, but at home it's a lot tougher.

Official surveillance organizations have traditionally been the chief market for PC-controlled receivers. However, they favor commercial models priced beyond the means of ordinary mortals—Ten-Tec's forthcoming RX-400, at something under $6,000, being a relatively "affordable" example. So, PASSPORT REPORTS focuses on models selling for under the equivalent of $1,200.

Digital Broadcasts

DRM ready receivers can process Digital Radio Mondiale (DRM) world band and other broadcasts. These require separately purchased DRM software and, eventually, software updates.

Even better are models with *DRM reception*, where you can hear DRM with no additional software or hardware—just an everyday PC. Until now, such receivers didn't exist. But for 2007 the Italian firm of Elad offers the pioneering FDM77 with hassle-free DRM reception.

Mating receivers with PCs can allow for digital reception.

Operating System Decides Functionality

PASSPORT REPORTS' tests have taken place using Windows XP-Pro and XP-Home—there's a sporting chance tested receivers will work with Vista, as well. If you're using Mac or Linux, check manufacturers' websites for the growing roster of acceptable operating systems.

For long-term ownership, keep in mind that once a receiver becomes discontinued, it eventually may not work to full advantage with new or revised computer operating systems. This can be overcome by retaining the ability to use the legacy OS—for example, in a separate disk partition.

No matter how carefully a PC-controlled receiver is tested, its performance depends partly on your computer's configuration. To avoid an unwelcome surprise, it's best to purchase on a returnable basis.

Tips for Using this Section

Receivers are listed in order of suitability for listening to difficult-to-hear world band stations; important secondary consideration is given to audio fidelity, ergonomics and perceived build quality. Street selling prices are cited, including British and Australian VAT/GST where applicable. Prices vary, so take them as the general guide they are meant to be.

Unless otherwise stated, all PC-controlled models have the following characteristics. *See* Worldly Words for terms used.

- Digital frequency synthesis and display.
- Full coverage of at least the 155–29999 kHz longwave, mediumwave AM and shortwave spectra—including all world band frequencies—but no coverage of the FM broadcast band (87.5–108 MHz). Models designed for sale in certain countries have reduced shortwave tuning ranges.
- A wide variety of helpful tuning features.
- No synchronous selectable sideband.

☞ ECSS: PC-controlled models typically tune to the nearest 10 Hz or even 1 Hz, allowing the operator to use the receiver's single-sideband circuitry to manually phase its BFO (internally generated carrier) with the station's transmitted carrier. Called "ECSS" (exalted-carrier, selectable-sideband) tuning, this can be used in lieu of synchronous selectable sideband. However, in addition to the relative inconvenience of this technique, unlike synchronous selectable sideband, which re-phases continually and perfectly, ECSS is always slightly out of phase. This causes at least some degree of harmonic distortion to music and speech, while tuning to the nearest Hertz can generate slow-sweep fading (for this reason, misphasing by two or three Hertz may provide better results).

• Proper demodulation of modes used by non-world-band shortwave signals. These modes include single sideband (LSB/USB) and CW ("Morse code"); also, with suitable ancillary devices, radioteletype (RTTY), frequency shift key (FSK) and radiofax (FAX).
• Meaningful signal-strength indication.

PC receiver ratings in recent years have included a small but real degree of higher standing vis-à-vis tabletop, professional and portable models. This year's star ratings have thus been adjusted to better facilitate cross-genre comparisons.

What PASSPORT's Rating Symbols Mean

Star ratings: ✪✪✪✪✪ is best. Stars reflect overall performance and meaningful features, plus to some extent ergonomics and perceived build quality. Price, appearance, country of manufacture and the like are not taken into account. To facilitate comparison, rating standards are very similar to those used for tabletop, professional and portable models reviewed elsewhere in this PASSPORT REPORTS.

Passport's Choice. La crème de la crème. Our test team's personal picks of the litter—models we would buy or have bought for our personal use. Unlike star ratings, these choices are unapologetically subjective.

❷: A relative bargain, with decidedly more performance than the price would suggest. However, none of these receivers is cheap.

DRM Ready
✪✪✪✪¼ *Passport's Choice*
WiNRADiO G303i, WiNRADiO G303i-PD/P, WiNRADiO G303e, WiNRADiO G303e-PD/P

Price: *G303i:* $499.95 in the United States. CAD$699.00 in Canada. £329.95 in the United Kingdom. AUD$726.00 in Australia. *G303i-PD/P:* $599.95 in the United States. CAD$899.00 in Canada. £389.95 in the United Kingdom. €698.00 in Germany. *G303e (external, not tested):* $599.95 in the United States. £389.95 in the United Kingdom. AUD$871.20 in Australia. *G303e-PD/P (external, not tested):* $699.95 in the United States. £449.95 in the United Kingdom. €875.00 in Germany. *DRM software:* $49.95 worldwide or £29.95 in the United Kingdom from www.winradio.com/home/download-drm.htm.

Pro: Plug and play aids setup. Once receiver is installed, the included software loads without problem; software uses open-source code, which allows for development of third-party software. With optional software, receives digital (DRM) world band and other broadcasts; DRM software distributed by WiNRADiO, so odds are good for successful installation and performance. Superb stability. Tunes and displays in ultra-precise 1 Hz increments. A thousand station presets, which can be clustered into any of 16 groups (see Con—Other). Excellent shape factors (1:1.6, 1:1.8) for 5.0 kHz and 3.2 kHz bandwidths aid selectivity/adjacent-channel rejection; 1.8 kHz bandwidth measures with good shape factor (1:2.3); many additional bandwidths available in the PD/P version, and perform similarly. Excellent shortwave sensitivity (0.21 &V)/noise floor (–130 dBm), good mediumwave AM and longwave sensitivity (0.4 &V)/noise floor (–125 dBm). Potentially excellent audio quality (see below). Excellent dynamic range (90 dB) and third-order intercept point (+5 dBm) at 20 kHz signal spacing (*see* Con—AGC/AVC). Phase noise excellent (*see* Con—AGC/AVC). Image rejection excellent. Spurious signals essentially absent. Screen, and operation in general, unusually pleasant and intuitive. Single-sideband performance generally excellent with strong signals (*see* Con—AGC/AVC). AGC fast, medium, slow and off. Spectrum display shows real-time signal activity, performs commendably and in particular provides signal strength readings to within plus or minus 3 dB. Spectrum scope sweeps between two user-chosen frequencies, displays the output while receiver mutes, then a mouse click can select a desired "peak"; it works quickly and well, and when the step size is set to small (e.g., 1 kHz), resolution is excellent and quite useful, resolving signals having as little as 350 Hz separation. Large signal-strength indicator highly accurate, as good as we've ever tested; displays both as digitally and as a digitized "analog meter"; reads out in "S" units, dBm or microvolts. Two easy-to-read on-screen clocks for World Time and local time, display seconds numerically, as well as date. Superior, timely and free factory assistance via email, seemingly throughout the week. *G303i-PD/P (professional demodulation):* Continuously adjustable bandwidths from 1Hz to 15 kHz (single sideband/ECSS 1 Hz to 7.5 kHz), with bandwidth presets, aid greatly in providing optimum tradeoff between audio fidelity and adjacent-channel interference rejection. AVC settings, limited to "on-off" in standard version, allow for control over decay and attack times. Improved audio quality in some test configurations. Demodulates ISB signals used by a small proportion of utility stations. SINAD and THD distortion indicators. AF squelch for FM mode. Operating software can be updated online, albeit with minor complication under limited circumstances.

Pro/Con—Sound: Outstanding freedom from distortion aids in providing good audio quality with appropriate sound cards/chips and speakers; sound quality and level can run the gamut from excellent to awful, depending on the PC's sound card or chipset, which needs to be full duplex. Sound Blaster

Best is WiNRADiO's G303 series. It is fairly priced for all it does.

16 cards are recommended by manufacturer, but not all models work. During our tests the $130 Sound Blaster Audigy 2 performed with considerable distortion—it doesn't offer full duplex operation for the line input—whereas the $43 Sound Blaster PCI 512 worked splendidly. (ISA sound cards perform terribly; quite sensibly, these are not recommended by the manufacturer.) All input settings for the audio card need to be carefully set to match the settings within the receiver's software. If wrong, there may be no audio or it may be grossly distorted. Indeed, a sound card isn't always necessary, as some sound chipsets commonly found within PCs produce excellent audio with the G303i. Another reason the chipset may be preferable is that Sound Blaster manuals recommend that if there is an audio chipset on the motherboard, it first be disabled in the BIOS and all related software uninstalled—potentially a Maalox Moment. However, even with a suitable board or chipset installed, the user must carefully set the AGC and AVC (automatic volume control, termed "Audio AGC" on the G303i) for distortion-free audio. Powerful amplified speakers provide room-filling sound and allow the AVC to be kept off, thus reducing band noise that can be intrusive when it is on during weak-signal reception.

Con—AGC/AVC: Weak-signal reception can be compromised by the AGC, which "sees" 10–15 kHz of spectrum within the IF upon which to act. So, if an adjacent world band channel signal is 20 dB or more stronger than a desired weak signal, the AGC's action tends to cause the adjacent signal to mask the desired signal. Inadequate gain with the AVC ("Audio AGC") off, but the aggressive AVC adds listening strain with single-sideband signals, as it tends to increase band noise between words or other modulation peaks. Powerful outboard amplified speakers help reduce the need for the additional audio gain brought about by the AVC and thus are desirable, but be prepared for jumps in volume when you tune to strong stations. Reception sometimes further improves if the AGC is switched off and IF gain is manually decreased, but the operator then has to "ride" the volume control

to smooth out major fluctuations. Manual ECSS tuning frequently helps, too. During moments of transient overload, the AVC can contribute to the creation of leading-edge "pops" with powerful signals (slightly more noticeable in the PD/P version). Single-sideband performance, particularly within crowded amateur bands, can be even more audibly compromised by the aforementioned out-of-passband AGC action. Dynamic range/IP3 at 5 kHz signal spacing couldn't be measured with AGC on, as test signals trigger the AGC and keep the receiver from going into overload; measure-

NUMBERS: TOP PC RECEIVERS

	WiNRADiO G303i (G313i)	Ten-Tec RX-320D
Sensitivity, World Band	0.21 (0.3 μV Ⓔ)	0.31 to 0.7 μV Ⓔ-Ⓕ[1]
Noise Floor, World Band	–130 dBm Ⓔ (–126 dBm Ⓖ)	–126 to –119 dBm Ⓖ-Ⓕ[2]
Blocking	120 dB Ⓖ (116 dB Ⓖ)	>146 dB Ⓢ
Shape Factors, voice BWs	1:1.6 Ⓔ-1:2.4 Ⓖ (1:1.7 Ⓔ-1:2.4 Ⓖ)	n/a[3]
Ultimate Rejection	70 dB Ⓖ (75 dB Ⓔ)	60 dB Ⓖ
Front-End Selectivity	Ⓖ (Ⓕ)	Ⓕ
Image Rejection	85 dB Ⓔ (75 dB Ⓔ)	60 dB Ⓖ
First IF Rejection	52 dB Ⓕ (51 dB Ⓕ)	60 dB Ⓖ
Dynamic Range/IP3 (5 kHz)	45 dB Ⓟ/–62 dBm Ⓟ (43 dB, Ⓟ/–62 dBm Ⓟ)	n/a[3]
Dynamic Range/IP3 (20 kHz)	90 dB Ⓔ/+5 dBm Ⓔ (85 dB Ⓖ/+2 dBm Ⓔ)	n/a[3]
Phase Noise	124 dBc Ⓔ[4] (120 dBc Ⓔ)	106 dBc Ⓕ
AGC Threshold	2.7 to 8.0 μV Ⓖ-Ⓟ (18 μV Ⓟ[5])	4.0 μV Ⓕ
Overall Distortion, voice	<1.0% Ⓢ (<1.0% Ⓢ[6])	<1% Ⓢ
Stability	5 Hz, Ⓢ (10 Hz Ⓔ)	80 Hz, Ⓖ
Notch filter depth	n/a (30 dB Ⓖ)	n/a

IBS Lab Ratings: Ⓢ Superb   Ⓔ Excellent   Ⓖ Good   Ⓕ Fair   Ⓟ Poor

(1) Excellent 60 meters and up.
(2) Good 60 meters and up.
(3) Could not be measured accurately because of synthesizer noise and spurious signals, but appears to be very good.
(4) Worse at close-in measurement.
(5) 0.3 μV Ⓖ with AVC enabled at –3 dB.
(6) See writeup, Con: DSP audio.

ment with the AGC off resulted in exceptionally poor numbers (45 db/–62 dBm). Phase noise poor when measured close-in (5 kHz signal spacing) for the same reason.

Con—Other: No synchronous selectable sideband, and double-sideband "AMS" mode loses lock easily. First IF rejection only fair. Front-end selectivity, although adequate for most uses, could be better. Station presets ("memory channels") store only frequency and mode, not bandwidth, AGC or attenuation settings. No passband offset or tunable notch filter. Emits a "pop-screech" sound when first brought up or when switching from standard to professional demodulator. Uses only SMA antenna connection, typically found on handheld devices rather than tabletop receivers; an SMA-to-BNC adapter is included, but for the many shortwave antennas with neither type of plug a second adaptor or changed plug is needed. On our sample, country of manufacture not found on receiver, box or enclosed printed matter; however, website indicates manufacturing facility is in Melbourne, Australia. Erratum sheet suggests that a discone antenna be used; this is fine for reception above roughly 25 MHz; however, in our tests we confirmed that conventional shortwave antennas provide much broader frequency coverage with the G303i, just as they do with other shortwave receivers.

☞ Minimum of 1 GHz Pentium recommended by manufacturer, although in the process of checking this out we obtained acceptable results using vintage 400 MHz and 500 MHz Pentium II processors with Windows 2000. However, if your PC is multitasking, then 2 GHz or more helps keep the PC from bogging down. Primary testing was done using various desktop Pentium IV PCs at 1.5–2.4 GHz, 256–512 MHz RAM and Windows 2000, XP-Home and XP-Pro operating systems. WiNRADiO operating software used during tests were v1.07, v1.14, v1.25 and v1.26.

Verdict: The G303 is the best PC receiver tested, especially in the preferred Professional Demodulator version. It can also be configured for reception of DRM digital broadcast signals and is a pleasure to operate.

The G303 provides laboratory-quality spectrum displays and signal-strength indication. These spectrum-data functions are top drawer, regardless of price or type of receiver, and that's just the beginning of things done well. The few significant warts: AGC/AVC behavior, possible audio hassles during installation, and the absence of synchronous selectable sideband.

Nevertheless, WiNRADiO's G303 is an excellent value among tested PC-controlled receivers for shortwave. Although its costlier G313 sibling has certain advantages, for most the G303 is at least its equal for world band reception.

DRM Ready
✪✪✪✪
WiNRADiO G313i, WiNRADiO G313e

Price: *G313i:* $949.95 in the United States and worldwide. CAD$1,349.00 in Canada. £599.95 in the United Kingdom. €1,229 in Germany. AUD$1,452.00 in Australia. *G313e (external, not tested):* $1,149.95 in the United States and worldwide. CAD$1,499.00 in Canada. £699.95 in the United Kingdom. AUD$1,742.40 in Australia. *DRM software:* $49.95 worldwide or £29.95 in the United Kingdom from www.winradio.com/home/download-drm.htm. *Mini-Circuits BLP-30 BNC-to-BNC 30 MHz low-pass filter:* $32.95 in the United States.

The WiNRADiO G313 is unusually flexible, with unlimited DSP bandwidths. Many other features, too.

Pro: Unlimited bandwidths—DSP bandwidths continuously variable in one Hertz increments from 1 Hz through 15 kHz (LSB/USB through 7.5 kHz). Bandwidth "presets" enhance ergonomics. Spectrum display either wideband (*see* Con) or narrowband; narrow allows for first-rate test and measurement of audio-frequency response of AM or single-sideband mode signals, spectra of data transmissions, frequency accuracy, amplitude modulation depth, frequency deviation, THD (total harmonic distortion) and SINAD (signal plus noise plus distortion to noise plus distortion ratio). Unlimited station presets—one thousand per file, each of which can be clustered into any of 16 groups; number of files limited only by hard disk capacity, so virtually no limit to presets. Station presets store frequency, IF shift, bandwidth and mode (*see* Con). Four VFOs. Large signal-strength indicator as linear as any other tested to date. Signal-strength indicator displays both digitally and as a digitized "analog meter." Signal-strength indicator reads out in "S" units, dBm or microvolts. Manufacturer's website, unusually helpful, includes downloadable calibration utility for signal-strength indicator. Open source code allows for third-party development of software. Includes DSP electronics for audio, so sound card acts only as an optional audio amplifier (*see* Con) (*cf.* WiNRADiO G303), or 313's audio output can feed outboard audio system. Superb level of overall distortion (*see* Con: DSP audio). Notch filter, tunable 0–7500 Hz, has good (30 dB) rejection (*see* Con). Synchronous double sideband to help overcome selective fading distortion and enhance fidelity during twilight and darkness (mixed skywave/groundwave) reception of fringe mediumwave AM stations (*see* Con). Integrated audio recorder, a convenience for those without ReplayRadio or similar. Integrated IF recorder stores spectrum slice for subsequent analysis of received signals, and to "re-receive" the same swath of signals over and again experimenting with, for example, IF bandwidth, notch filter and noise blanker settings (*see* Con). Plug and play receiver software installed with no problems with XP Pro and XP Home. Does not overuse computer resources even while multitask-

ing. Excellent shape factors at wider voice bandwidths (*see* Con). Excellent ultimate rejection. Excellent image rejection. Excellent phase noise as measured in lab (*see* Con). Spurious signals essentially nil. Screen, and operation in general, unusually pleasant and intuitive (*see* Con). Automatic frequency control (AFC) with FM and AM mode signals. With optional software, receives digital (DRM) world band and other broadcasts; DRM software distributed by WiNRADiO, so odds are good for successful installation and performance. Demodulates ISB signals used by some utility stations. Single-step (18 dB) attenuator. Receiver incremental tuning (RIT) aids with transceiving. Two easy-to-read clocks displayed on screen for World Time; also, second clock for local time (*see* Con); both show seconds numerically, as well as day and date. FM mode squelch. FM broadcasts receivable with extra-cost option. Operating software can be updated online. Excellent owner's manual. Superior, timely and free factory assistance via email, seemingly throughout the week.

Con: DSP audio causes static crashes and local noise to sound unusually harsh, potentially increasing listening fatigue. Synchronous detector lacks meaningful selectable sideband, IF shift notwithstanding. Poor AGC threshold contributes to reduced audibility of weak signals; improved by enabling switchable AVC at a low level, although this also increases pumping with single-sideband signals. AGC gain determined by all signals within the 15 kHz first IF filter, so background noise and audio can change in concert with on/off (e.g., CW) activity from adjacent carriers within the 15 kHz filter window; this can be an issue with utility and ham monitoring, but only rarely disturbs world band signals. Mediocre front-end selectivity, largely remediable by adding a Mini-Circuits BLP-30 or other outboard ~30 MHz low-pass filter. Poor close-in (5 kHz signal spacing) dynamic range/IP3. Bandwidth shape factors slip from excellent at wider bandwidths (e.g., 6 kHz) to fair at narrower voice bandwidths (e.g., 1.9 kHz). Phase noise or a kind of local oscillator noise keeps CW bandwidths (e.g., 0.5 kHz) from being measurable at –60 dB; consequently,

CW shape factors also not measurable. Significant audible distortion if computer-screen volume turned up high; remediable if level not adjusted beyond "6"; sound card or outboard audio amplifier can provide additional volume if needed. Cyclical background sound, which doesn't vary with carrier-BFO phasing, in manual ECSS mode. Mixed ergonomics—some functions a pleasure, others not. Tuning-steps in 5 kHz increments (world band channel spacing) impractical with mouse scroll wheel, as three keys have to be held down simultaneously; instead, up/down screen slew arrows can be used. Some screen icons small for typical PC displays/video cards. Real-time (always active) spectrum analyzer coverage width limited to 20 kHz (+/– 10 kHz), a pity given the exceptional resolution and analytical capabilities. IF recorder bandwidth also limited to 20 kHz. Tunable notch filter includes adjustable notch breadth, a creative but marginal option that complicates notch use. Notch filter takes unusually long to adjust properly using keypad, and small indicators make it prone to operating errors with GUI. First IF rejection only fair. Wideband spectrum analyzer not in real time, has disappointing resolution and thus of minor utility. SMA antenna connection; SMA-to-BNC adapter included, but for the many shortwave antennas with neither type of plug a second adaptor or changed plug is needed. Station presets don't store AGC or attenuator values. Noise blanker only marginally effective. Local-time (secondary) clock displays only in 24-hour format—no AM/PM.

Verdict: With audio processing independent of the host PC—and heaps of additional goodies—the Australian WiNRADiO G313 is in many ways a solid improvement over the lower-cost WiNRADiO G303.

Alas, there's a hefty price to be paid for not using the PC sound card for audio processing: DSP harshness that aggravates static crashes and more. This limits its appeal, especially for tropical band and mediumwave AM DXing, but how much depends on your hearing and listening preferences.

The G313 is tempting for DRM, and it has excellent synchronous detection for allevi-

ating selective fading distortion—a serious issue with dusk-to-dawn fringe analog mediumwave AM reception. But its selectable sideband capability is effectively nonexistent, and the "IF shift" doesn't help. This is a huge drawback in a kilobuck receiver, given that effective synchronous selectable sideband can be found on a $150 portable.

So, the G313's price/performance ratio is uninspiring for listening to broadcasts or monitoring utility/ham signals. But it excels with signal analysis and storage, thanks to a high-resolution spectrum analyzer with excellent test, measurement and recording capabilities. Add to that a highly linear and adjustable signal-strength indicator, and you can see why this model is spot-on for certain professional/surveillance applications. This also explains the kilobuck price, dirt cheap by professional standards.

Better for most world band listeners is the sibling WiNRADiO G303. How it sounds is partly a function of the host PC's sound card, but its audio is usually less tiring than that of the G313—particularly with static.

And it costs half as much.

DRM Ready
✪✪✪⅛ Ⓒ *Passport's Choice*
Ten-Tec RX-320D

Price: *RX-320D:* $349.00 plus shipping worldwide. £248.00 in the United Kingdom. €359.00 in Germany. AUD$668.00 in Australia. *DRM software:* $49.95 worldwide from www.winradio.com/home/download-drm.htm. *Third-party control software:* Varies from free to $99 worldwide.

Pro: The "D" version's 12 kHz IF output allows the receiver to receive digital (DRM) world band and other broadcasts by using DRM software purchased separately. Superior dynamic range. Apparently superb bandwidth shape factors (*see* Con). In addition to the supplied factory control software, third-party software is available, often for free, and may improve operation. Up to 34 bandwidths with third-party software. Tunes in extremely precise 1 Hz increments (10

Ten-Tec's RX320D is the best buy among PC models. Priced less than some portables, this American receiver can also process digital DRM broadcasts.

the audio under certain reception conditions. Synthesizer phase noise measures only fair; among the consequences are that bandwidth shape factors cannot be measured exactly. Some tuning ergonomics only fair as compared with certain standalone receivers. No tunable notch filter. Passband offset doesn't function in AM mode. Signal-strength indicator, calibrated 0–80, too sensitive, reading 20 with no antenna connected and 30 with only band noise being received. Mediocre front-end selectivity can allow powerful mediumwave AM stations to "ghost" into the shortwave spectrum, thus degrading reception of world band stations. Uses AC adaptor instead of built-in power supply. Spectrum display does not function with some third-party software and is only a so-so performer. Mediumwave AM reception below 1 MHz suffers from reduced sensitivity, and longwave sensitivity is atrocious. No internal speaker on outboard receiver module. World Time clock tied into computer's clock, which may not be accurate without periodic adjustment. Almost no retail sources outside the United States.

Verdict: The American-made Ten-Tec RX-320D is attractively priced, even though it requires that the owner obtain aftermarket DRM software. It performs very nicely and is usually well-supported by the manufacturer.

Hz with tested factory software); displays to the nearest Hertz, and frequency readout is easily user-aligned. Large, easy-to-read digital frequency display and faux-analog frequency bar. For PCs with sound cards, outstanding freedom from distortion aids in providing good audio quality with most but not all cards and speakers. Fairly good audio, but with limited treble, also available through radio for PCs without sound cards. Superb blocking performance helps maintain consistently good world band sensitivity. Passband offset (*see* Con). Spectrum display with wide variety of useful sweep widths (*see* Con). World Time on-screen clock (*see* Con). Adjustable AGC decay. Thousands of station presets, with first-rate memory configuration, access and sorting—including by station name and frequency. Only PC-controlled model tested which returns to last tuned frequency when PC turned off. Operating software can be updated online. Superior owner's manual. Generally superior factory help and repair support.

Con: No synchronous selectable sideband, although George Privalov's Control Panel Program now automates retuning of drifty AM-mode signals received as "ECSS." Some characteristic "DSP roughness" in

New for 2007
Icom IC-PCR2500, Icom IC-R2500

The $850 (£475) Icom IC-PCR2500 and $1,000 (£530) Icom IC-R2500 (both not tested) use the same platform as the '1500 series evaluated below. However, they add diversity reception to help reduce fading effects (accomplished with two widely spaced antennas—or, outside the shortwave spectrum, one horizontally and one vertically polarized). Synchronous selectable sideband also reduces the effects of AM-mode fading, but is unavailable on the '2500.

Additional extras are multi-channel monitoring/display, P25 (public service digital) board, D-Star (but not Icom's digital audio standard for PMR446) and other features oriented to VHF/UHF/SHF scanning.

New for 2007

❍❍❍⅝
Icom IC-PCR1500, Icom IC-R1500

Price: *IC-PCR1500 "black box" receiver:* $579.95 in the United States. CAD$699.95 in Canada. £369.95 in the United Kingdom. TBA in Germany. AUD$899.00 in Australia. *IC-R1500 with control head and "black box" receiver:* $699.95 in the United States. CAD$799.00 in Canada. £419.95 in the United Kingdom. TBA in Germany. *UT-106 DSP unit:* $139.95 in the United States. CAD$250.00 in Canada. £84.99 in the United Kingdom. €99.00 in Germany. *OPC-1156 11½ foot (3.5 meter) controller extension cable:* $26.00 in the United States. £24.99 in the United Kingdom. €13.95 in Germany. *OPC-441 16½ foot (5 meter) speaker extension cable:* $24.95 in the United States. CAD$29.00 as available in Canada. £24.99 in the United Kingdom. €29.95 in Germany. *CP-12L 12V DC cigarette lighter power cable:* $27.95 in the United States. CAD$60.00 in Canada. *OPC-254L 12V DC fused power cord:* $10.95 in the United States. CAD$25.00 in Canada. *Aftermarket RF Systems DPX-30 antenna combiner (to 2000 MHz) for separate shortwave and scanner antennas:* $99.95 in the United States. €76.20 in Germany. *Aftermarket Diamond CX-210N two-position antenna switch (to 3000 MHz):* $69.95 in the United States. *Aftermarket Daiwa CS-201 GII two-position antenna switch (to 1300 MHz):* $37.95 in the United States. *Aftermarket Alpha Delta 4B/N four-position antenna switch (to 1300 MHz):* $94.95 in the United States.

Pro: Wideband frequency coverage in three versions: *(blocked U.S. version)* 0.01–810, 851–867, 896–1811, 1852–1868, 1897–2305.9, 2357–2812, 2853–2869, 2898–3109.8, 3136–3154.8, 3181–3300 MHz; *(blocked French version)* 0.01–30, 50.2–51.2, 87.5–108, 144–146, 430–440 and 1240–1300 MHz; *(unblocked version)* 0.01–3300 MHz; with all versions, specifications not guaranteed 0.01–0.5 and 3000–3300 MHz; BFO operation (single sideband and CW) up to 1300 MHz; includes FM broadcast reception. Fully 2600 station presets clustered into 26 pages of 100 channels each. Tunes

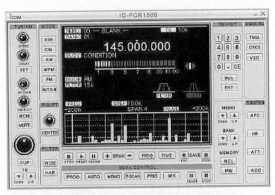

The IC-PCR1500 is Icom's value-priced offering. It shares a platform with the costlier IC-PCR2500, while both are available with a control head so they can second as quasi-tabletop receivers.

and displays in unusually precise 1 Hz increments. Vast number of user-selectable tuning steps. Useful manual ECSS operation (*see* Con) aided by Gibraltar-class stability. Very good shortwave sensitivity. Selectable fast/slow AGC decay (*see* Con). Generally good IF shift (*see* Con). Operating software and firmware work well and can be updated online at www.icom.co.jp/world/download/index.htm. Plenty of IF gain and AGC runs in the final bandwidth, which help provide single-sideband performance that's significantly above average among PC-controlled models (*see* Con). Generally pleasant audio quality (*see* Con). Audio available not only through the set's internal speaker (*see* Con) or an external speaker, but also via USB through the PC's audio system (*see* Con). Can record audio in .wav format onto hard drive (*see* Con). One-step (20 dB) attenuator (*see* Con). Optional UT-106 AF-DSP unit (not tested). *IC-PCR1500 and IC-R1500 via PC:* Three different PC user screens. Excellent 'scope for up to a 1 MHz peek at radio spectrum in real time, 1–10 MHz in non-real time (see *Con*). Keypad tuning. Up to 22 alphanumeric tags and frequencies for presets display simultaneously. *IC-R1500:* Generally excellent wired control head so '1500 can also be used as a standalone tabletop receiver or, to a degree with the optional CP-12L power cord, a mobile receiver (*see* Con), as well as a PC-controlled model *à la* the IC-PCR1500.

Con: Few bandwidth choices. Poor dynamic range at 5 and 20 kHz separation points, although this improves considerably at wider spacing. No RF or IF gain control to help alleviate overloading, and attenuator has only one step. No synchronous selectable sideband; manual ECSS alternative sounds slightly out of phase even with 1 Hz tuning step. With one PC configuration, but not others, some distortion encountered with single-sideband signals through 3 kHz bandwidth. Slight hiss. Audio only fair through black box's built-in speaker. Audio a bit weak through computer's USB port. No AGC off. IF shift operates only in single-sideband and CW modes. Mediumwave sensitivity only fair. Poor longwave sensitivity. Marginal noise blanker. No on/off multi-event timing for audio recording. Telescopic antenna and cable virtually useless on shortwave and not much better elsewhere within tuned frequency ranges. Software installation not always easy. No schematic or block diagrams.
IC-R1500: Control head provides most, but not all, operating functions available from PC control; for example, there's no keypad or spectrum 'scope, and presets simultaneously display only one frequency or alphanumeric tag. Control head has no stand or mounting bracket for desktop or mobile use, nor can it be attached to the body of the "black box."

Verdict: Icom's '1500 series is a worthy step ahead of the discontinued IC-PCR1000. For starters, audio can be fed into a computer through its USB port and even recorded to hard disk. The '1500 series also uses an internal speaker or can feed an external speaker, and there's less audio hiss.

Frequency coverage is vast, and performance is generally worthy by broadband standards. Even though the '1500 series suffers from poor dynamic range at 5 and 20 kHz separation points, this improves dramatically at wider separation. However, a paucity of bandwidth choices and the lack of synchronous selectable sideband are all significant drawbacks in this price class. The excellent recording facility would have profited from multi-event timing, as well.

Icom's '1500 series receivers are especially attractive for broadband use with PCs to enhance performance and operation. In keeping with Icom tradition, they are also dramatically better than most other PC models for single-sideband reception of utility and amateur signals. Ergonomics are top-drawer, too, reflecting user-friendly software that's about as good as it gets. Between these pluses and pleasant audio quality, the '1500 lends itself to being enjoyed for hours on end.

Evaluation of New Models: When replacing the earlier IC-PCR1000, Icom took an altogether new tack. First, it created a straightforward replacement, the IC-PCR1500 "black box" PC-controlled receiver. But the kicker is the separate control head they've engineered to combo with the black box. In so doing, they have created the novel standalone IC-R1500 tabletop model that, with some creativity and an optional power cord, can morph into a mobile receiver.

As both models use the same black-box guts, this evaluation refers to both except where otherwise indicated.

The 'R1500 can be operated from the control head or a PC, but not both at the same time. The head includes an illuminated LCD and buttons, along with a tuning knob, volume and squelch controls. It looks uncannily like the Icom IC-208 amateur transceiver's detachable front panel.

However, the 'R1500's control head doesn't include all the operating features available when a PC is used. For example, it has no keypad and can't display, among other goodies, the spectrum 'scope. The head, which knobs aside is only around an inch (25 mm) thick, can also slide around during use, and there's no mounting bracket to attach it to a table or even the black box. You either have to live with this or come up with a creative remedy.

¡Muy Robusto!

Like the earlier 'PCR1000, the '1500 appears to be robustly constructed inside and out. For example, the black-box housing is made of steel, not plastic, and its front panel includes an on/off rocker switch with green "on" LED. Four stick-on padded foam feet are included should you wish to affix them.

A BNC antenna input accepts an external antenna or the short window-mounted telescopic antenna/cable that's provided. This lone socket works for the receiver's entire frequency range, but antennas for one range rarely function properly for other ranges. Thus, broadband users have to manually connect and disconnect various antennas, like garden hoses. Fortunately, aftermarket antenna combiners and switches are widely available, although almost none are rated close to the '1500's upper frequency limit.

The '1500 receivers include generous coverage of the radio spectrum (*see* Pro, above). For aficionados who roam radio's vast prairies this is both convenient and relatively cost-effective. Yet, the downside is that performance tends to suffer in one or more respects.

From a consumers' perspective this often makes little sense. Most folks concentrate on a given chunk of the radio spectrum—either mediumwave AM/shortwave, on one hand, or scanner frequencies above 30 MHz, on the other—not vast electromagnetic swathes.

The primary reason for broadband thus is not driven by consumer demand. Rather, by reducing the number of required models— the '1500 is both a shortwave receiver and a scanner—it simplifies engineering, distribution and marketing. The 'R1500's modular approach carries this mindset one step further by making "one and a half" models work as two.

This also helps explain why there is only one antenna input. Icom knows that relatively few buyers will make regular use of the receiver's vast broadband potential, so they trim production costs accordingly.

Computer/Software Requirements

The '1500 receivers require more processing power than the erstwhile IC-PCR1000. The 'PCR1000 requirements are:

- Intel® 486DX4 or later CPU (Pentium® 100 MHz or faster recommended);

- Microsoft® Windows® 98, ME, 2000 or XP;
- minimum 10 MB of free hard drive space;
- minimum 16 MB of RAM; and
- floppy drive, RS-232 serial interface, and monitor with at least 640 × 480 resolution.

The new 'R1500 (when used with a PC) and 'PCR1500 requirements are:

- Intel® Pentium® III 450 MHz or faster (Pentium® 4 recommended);
- Microsoft® Windows® 98SE, ME, 2000 or XP;
- minimum 50 MB of free hard drive space, plus additional space for audio recording or storing of 'scope data;
- minimum 128 MB of RAM (256 MB or more recommended);
- CD-ROM, USB 2.0 or 1.1, monitor with at least 1024 × 768 resolution in high color, and scroll-wheel mouse and/or other pointing device.

Configurations used for these tests were Intel® Pentium® 4, 1.5 GHz or faster computers with 512 MB or greater RAM using XP Home/XP Professional.

Driver and Software Installation

The operating software and USB driver come on a CD packed with the receiver and can be updated online; these usually install without problem. Once this is done, connect the black box's AC adaptor, attach a good antenna (and control head with the 'R1500) and you're ready to rock.

That's if all goes well, but there can be potholes along the way.

First involves driver installation. The owner's manual states that the included USB driver is needed only if two receivers are connected to a PC at the same time. However, we couldn't get a singleton receiver to operate with a PC until the driver was installed.

This glitch notwithstanding, installation instructions need to be followed carefully. For example, the manual warns of something unexpected: The driver is actually installed twice.

Second comes software installation, which normally proceeds without hiccups except with one of the three audio choices.

The simplest audio alternative is to use the black box's built-in speaker. It doesn't sound great, but a related choice is to bypass it by plug in headphones or a worthy external speaker. Either way, software isn't involved so potential headaches are avoided.

But best for gamers and most others is to take advantage of the PC's existing audio card, speakers and .wav-recordable hard drive. Trouble is, setting this up wasn't problem-free with any of our XP test configurations.

Clicking a speaker icon brings up an "audio setting screen," but following the manual's instructions on page 90 it took two attempts before it finally worked. To succeed without this grief, select the PC's soundcard from Sounds and Audio Devices Properties>Audio>Sound Playback within XP's control panel, as otherwise the program defaults to USB audio which does not work. Too, once this erroneous USB selection had been corrected, we discovered through trial-and-error that it is necessary to exit and restart the program for the new settings to "take."

Once audio has been channeled through the computer's USB port, the .wav and volume settings in the XP sounds-and-audio box both need to be raised to maximum to even approach proper level. This works, but simultaneously makes most other of the PC's audio applications sound too loud. The end result may be that you decide against using computer audio, but this also means you won't be able to record to hard disk.

Even if the '1500's audio is configured through a PC, the receiver's internal speaker—or outboard speaker/headphones—can also be used. However, there is half a second or so of time lag between these and the PC audio, so it's best to use one or the other, but not both at the same time.

As always with Windows, there are so many configurations that our limited test setups only scratch the surface. So, keep your wits about you, and if possible run Ghost or some other disk clone immediately before attempting '1500 setup.

Three Windows, Small Icons

Three discrete windows are provided: multifunction, which is practical; simple (lite); and component, while looks like a rack mount and can select or deselect four different blocs of functions. Simple lacks such features as the 'scope, but because it chews up less resources it is useful for, say, sitting on a frequency while multitasking on the computer.

Many on-screen controls are adequately sized, but some icons are annoyingly small: volume, squelch, speed and delay. Ditto the on-screen keyboard. The PC's numeric keypad offers a solution, as it also can be used to enter frequencies, but the "CE" (clear entry) key is available only on-screen.

The mouse scroll wheel works nicely as a *de facto* tuning knob. If your mouse doesn't have a wheel, this is a dirt-cheap retrofit at any office supplies store.

Alas, frequencies entered on the numeric keypad or the screen's keyboard need to be entered in Megahertz, so don't forget to "dot your entry."

Spectrum 'Scope

Like the radio-spectrum 'scope on Yaesu's VR-5000, the 'scope on the '1500 resembles a bar-graph "cube." It's interactive, so a click of the mouse on any given bar provides instant reception of whatever signal is on that frequency. It's a really handy feature that works mighty well.

The 'scope appears on two of the three available PC windows, but not the simple window or the 'R1500's control head. The visible frequency range—"sweep"—depends on the selectable tuning step, so the choice is completely up to the user.

With the 'scope displaying in real time the maximum sweep is 1 MHz (plus or minus 500 kHz), while AM and FM modes operate freely and are not muted. On shortwave this sweep is usually more than enough and keeps the screen from being overcrowded with signal pips.

To display a broader 1–10 MHz sweep the 'scope no longer operates in real time. AM and FM modes are muted, too—instead, you hear the scanner zipping through the spectrum until it stops at a signal. It then provides a frozen-in-time spectrum "snapshot" until, after having resumed scanning, it stops at another signal and refreshes the screen.

Regardless of sweep width, single-sideband and CW modes are always muted when the 'scope is in use.

Commendable Sensitivity

Sensitivity and related noise floor lab measurements are excellent-to-superb within all world band segments. However, even using the same aftermarket outdoor antenna this is not enough for the '1500 to equal a top-rated tabletop in unearthing faint signals in the clear. If you use the included telescopic antenna, instead, results are far worse, with only the most powerful signals managing to punch through.

Mediumwave AM sensitivity is only fair, and longwave is downright poor; both fairly beg for an unusually high-gain loop antenna. FM broadcasts in the usual 87.5–108 MHz band come in well, even if not at audiophile standard, thanks to respectable sensitivity and a good capture ratio—but even here a proper antenna helps, too.

A digital 28-segment signal-strength indicator appears on two of the three PC screens, whereas the 'R1500's control head uses a simpler 14-segment indicator. Although both overread somewhat, they are decidedly above average and very useful.

Inferior Dynamic Range

Substandard dynamic range is the curse of affordable broadband receivers. Almost any dedicated world band tabletop—and even some better portables and portatops—do better.

So it is with the discontinued IC-PCR1000. Its dynamic range is poor, so the receiver tends to overload within virile world band segments.

Alas, the '1500 series also has poor dynamic range. Yet, in the pantheon of underachievement the '1500 is less poor than the '1000, so there's less overloading. To help make this a Maalox moment, there's no RF or IF gain control to help matters and the attenuator's lone 20 dB step is usually overkill.

Selectivity Only Okay

The '1500 series uses traditional IF circuitry rather than DSP. There are two advantages: 1) audio fidelity tends to be better, and 2) digital processing power isn't required.

The optional UT-106 module (not tested) uses DSP not for bandwidth filtering, but to add automatic notch filtering and noise reduction. Even without the UT-106, a noise blanker is included with the '1500, but it's ineffective against manmade interference and is not adjustable.

Ceramic IF bandwidth filters are used and vary as to which filter can be used with what mode (*see* table, Measured Bandwidth).

Trouble is, discrete bandwidth filters are costly, whereas with DSP filtering the cost is similar whether there are two bandwidths or two hundred. So, on the '1500 there are only two world band widths—3 kHz and 9 kHz—this makes for mighty slim pickings. Additional AM-mode bandwidths are needed: around a true 6 kHz and, if possible, 4 kHz.

Single sideband (LSB/USB) doesn't fare well, either, with 3 kHz being the only practical bandwidth. As for CW, which needs bandwidths under 1 kHz, it gets flipped off without so much as a single meaningful offering.

The '1500's paucity of bandwidths is especially regrettable, as the few which are provided have superb or almost-superb skirt selectivity. (We were unable to accurately measure ultimate selectivity because of receiver limitations, but it is good or better.)

The ~18 kHz bandwidth offers wideband fidelity with local mediumwave AM powerhouses. However, when a worthy antenna is used, powerful signals slop over around 60 kHz on either side. This implies that this filter's ultimate selectivity, although at least good, is not really up to the task.

MIA: Synchronous Selectable Sideband

With synchronous selectable sideband having been available for years even on affordable portables, it would seem that this neat feature would be *de rigueur* on relatively costly tabletop and PC-controlled world band receivers.

Not so the '1500 series. Thus, when adjacent-channel interference and/or selective fading arise the only way to obtain most of the benefits of sync is to rely on ECSS; that is, to carefully tune AM-mode signals using the receiver's single-sideband circuitry. Thanks in part to the '1500's superb stability and 1 Hz tuning, this works nicely. Still, you need the fingers of a safecracker and ears of a bat to closely phase the transmitted carrier with the receiver's synthesized carrier (BFO). Even then, there is always a scintilla of phase mismatch that becomes increasingly audible as the quality of the audio output improves, such as when the audio is fed through a PC with excellent speakers.

The displayed frequencies are accurate to within plus or minus 4 Hz, which helps when tuning ECSS. This accuracy is superb by any yardstick—better than many tabletop supersets.

The IF shift is handy, although it works only with single sideband and CW. The '1500's PC windows include a center "detent" button to restore the IF shift's setting to zero—a nice touch.

Oodles of Tuning Steps

Broadband multimodal coverage calls for more tuning steps than what's needed simply under 30 MHz. The '1500's vast rundown: 1 Hz, 10Hz, 20 Hz, 50 Hz, 100 Hz, 500 Hz, 1 kHz, 2.5 kHz, 5 kHz, 6.25 kHz, 8.33 kHz, 9 kHz, 10 kHz, 12.5 kHz, 15 kHz, 20 kHz, 25 kHz, 30 kHz, 50 kHz, 100 kHz, 125 kHz,150 kHz, 200 kHz, 500 kHz, 1 MHz, 10 MHz and one user-defined step. There are various factory defaults, but the user can override them at any time. Once a step is chosen for a given portion of the tuned radio spectrum, it becomes the new default unless and until the user changes it anew.

Audio Quality Generally Pleasant

Audio quality is generally quite pleasant, with low overall distortion and hiss—audible advantages over the discontinued '1000. This helps make the '1500 series relatively enjoyable for listening to world band news and music hour after hour.

One glitch in the single-sideband mode found with one PC configuration, but no others: At the 3 kHz bandwidth there is audible clipping distortion on audio peaks. This is irrespective of AGC setting or whether the audio is from the radio's speaker or the PC.

Presets Aplenty

In the spirit of never being too rich or having too many choices, the '1500 has a whop-

	MEASURED BANDWIDTH (NOMINAL)				
Mode	3.0 kHz (2.8 kHz)	9.0 kHz (6 kHz)	17.6 kHz (15 kHz)	69 kHz (50 kHz)	(230 kHz)
CW	■	■			
LSB/USB	■	■			
AM	■	■	■	■	
FM (narrow)		■	■	■	
FM (wide)				■	■

ping 2,600 station presets. Trying to find any one preset in this thicket could resemble an archeological dig, so they are split up into 26 manageable pages of 100 channels each.

Each page and preset can be assigned a 64-character alphanumeric tag, and up to 22 of these can be displayed simultaneously on a PC screen in addition to the frequency. These are ergonomic gems, being a cinch to enter and change in the "memory edit" screen. They also can be copied, moved or deleted with uncommon ease, and shortcut keys can be used. Kudos to Icom—this has been well thought out and works extremely well.

The 'R1500's control head displays only one tag at a time, relying on toggling to change the displayed preset. The head shows one tag or one frequency, but not both simultaneously—a user setting decides which.

Hard Driving Recorder

The '1500 records audio in .wav format to a PC hard drive. If "rec remote" is chosen, recording takes place only when squelch is broken—a choice mainly relevant to scanning above 30 MHz. There have been add-on recording programs like this over the years, but this one is built in and works nicely. There are no level settings to fiddle with; just choose the red "rec" button, click on the subsequent "red record" button and you're off. Each .wav file is automatically date stamped, and you can designate the target folder with ease.

Downside? Wav files take up more space than a sumo wrestler unless they are converted. To help out, there are three sampling rates: high quality at 44.1 kHz, okay quality at 22.05 kHz and telephone quality at 11.025 kHz. A one-hour recording devours 300 Megabytes of hard drive at 44.1 kHz, while at 22.05 kHz it needs only150 MB and at 11.025 kHz the file shrinks to a relatively svelte 75 MB.

This is yet another example of how Icom has done its ergonomic homework, as recording works very well and is delightfully easy to use. But there is one major omission: no event timing, so no turnkey recording. With multi-event on/off timing and MP3 output, the '1500 would have been ideal for creating archived audio for on-demand listening or podcast downloading.

IC-R1500: Standalone Operation

The 'R1500 comes with a wired control head so the "black box" can be operated without a computer. The head includes an LCD display, volume and squelch controls, but you can't use the head and a PC at the same time, and the head has no spectrum 'scope.

The cable between the control head and black box runs 11½ feet (3.5 meters), while the optional OPC-1156 extension doubles this. Speaker audio doesn't pass though that cable, so the optional OPC-441 speaker cable is also needed.

The head's illuminated buttons have good tactile response, and the indented tuning knob spins nicely, with no play. The LCD's excellent illumination is in any of three different colors: green, amber or yellow, with adjustable brightness and contrast.

There is no optional or standard mounting bracket to affix the lightweight head to a tabletop or other surface, or even the receiver's black box. If you want this, you'll have to devise a homebrew solution.

The head has no keypad, nor does Icom offer an optional mouse-type outboard keypad. To help compensate you can push the V/MHz button; between the tuning knob and this, the receiver can be tuned in big gulps. You get used to this novel approach, but it still amounts to a chore.

Warts and all, the fairly priced control head makes for an extremely useful addition to the plain black box.

Attractive for Broadband Coverage

The Icom IC-R1500 and the PC-only IC-PCR1500 are a noticeable improvement over the old IC-PCR1000. They're attractively priced for when broadband coverage is needed in one user-friendly package.

New for 2007
DRM Reception
✪✪✪½
ELAD FDM77

Price: *FDM77, including DRM software:* $599.99 in the United States. £399.95 in the United Kingdom. €639.00 in Germany.

Pro: Receives world band and other DRM transmissions immediately after connection to a PC. Commendable ergonomics (*see* Con), with superior graphic interface and large icons. Handy tuning features include numeric selection directly above each digit, using keyboard arrows; MHz or kHz keypad entry, using PC keyboard or on-screen virtual keypad; up/down slewing, using on-screen or keyboard arrows; knob tuning, using mouse wheel or on-screen virtual tuning knob; 200 station presets per page, with as many page files as PC's hard disk can hold; two VFOs; and auto band-scanning with real-time graphic spectrum display (*see* Con). 1 Hz frequency resolution (*see* Con) and tuning step. Large, accurate signal-strength indicator using screen graphics that make it look like an analog "S" meter. Nineteen DSP bandwidths with shape factors that improve from good (1:2.1) to superb (1:1.4) as bandwidth narrows. Two variable notch filters with superb (50 dB) heterodyne (whistle) rejection. IF shift to aid in adjacent-channel interference rejection. Very good audio that includes a six-band graphic equalizer that can be bypassed by "flat" selection. Good sensitivity (0.5 µV) and noise floor (–125 dBm) with preamplifier on (*see* Con). Good image rejection (74 dB) and paucity of other spurious signals. AGC threshold good (3 µV) with preamplifier on (*see* Con). Overall distortion excellent-to-superb (2.2% to 0.1%), especially in single-sideband mode. Front-end selectivity good, thanks to octave filtering. Superb first IF rejection (93 dB). Drift under 100 Hz from near-cold start. Graphically displays 20 kHz of radio-spectrum, audio spectrum and oscilloscope. Selectable 10 dB preamp. Two antenna connectors: SO-239 for significant antennas; and BNC with an additional 20 dB of preamplification for use with whip and other short antennas. 15 dB attenua-tor. WAV recorder, with single-event timer, stores onto hard drive. World Time and local clocks (*see* Con). Operating software and firmware can be updated online from manufacturer's sometimes-poky server. Convenient mute button.

Con: No synchronous selectable sideband. Ergonomics, although usually superior, are compromised because bandwidth selection requires unnecessary screen shifting and the main screen doesn't show which bandwidth is in use; also, installation sometimes unforgiving (e.g., high-pitched audio can mix with received output if directions on CD and in owner's manual not followed precisely). Graphic equalizer can degrade audio quality in certain situations, requiring that the flat setting be substituted. AGC controlled by 455 kHz intermediate bandwidth of 7.5 kHz that's usually much wider than the PC sound card's DSP bandwidth; so, for example, when listening to a weak single-sideband signal and there's a stronger signal 5 kHz or less away on the opposite sideband, the weak signal can made impossible to copy because the AGC is controlled by the undesired signal. Phase noise (98 dBc) poor; prevents accurate assessment of blocking performance, which because of this measures as poor—even though it may actually be much better. AGC threshold drops to poor (8 µV) with preamplifier off. Sensitivity drops to only fair with preamplifier off. Measured dynamic range of 63 dB consistent at 50, 20 and 5 kHz separation points (translates to fair at 5 kHz separation, poor at 20 kHz separation); nevertheless, resisted overloading effectively during hands-on testing. Radio spectrum display shows only narrow 20 kHz slice—i.e., plus or minus 10 kHz on either side of the received signal. No noise blanker. Most front-panel LEDs are blue and excessively bright. Station presets store only frequency and mode, not such other variables as bandwidth. No external speaker jack, so audio must run through computer's sound card. Frequency display on our unit misreads by around 45 Hz. Runs warm; plastic end caps affixed with double-stick tape that loses stickiness as cabinet heats up. SO-239 antenna connector very loose on our unit; nevertheless, Universal

Radio, Elad's North American Elad distributor and repair facility, indicates that to date there have no other FDM77 repair issues. Manual states USB 2.0 required; our tests underscore that this, as opposed to USB 1.0, is necessary to avoid jerky responses and locking up. Clock shows local time only in 24-hour format; although only 24-hour format shown, LCD inappropriately displays AM and PM Owner's manual, although recently improved, not all it could be.

☞ Tested with v1.06 firmware and v1.15 and v3.06 operating software; all comments refer to results with the latter software. The manufacturer advises that v4.0 software, in beta during our tests, is forthcoming.

Verdict: The Italian-made Elad FDM77 gets high marks for being the first to offer hassle-free DRM reception. It is also user friendly and performs nicely with conventional analog signals—even though it lacks synchronous selectable sideband.

Evaluation of New Model: The attractive Elad FDM77 is housed in a sturdy extruded aluminum cabinet with rubbery plastic end caps. It comes with operating software on a CD, plus there are free online upgrades after you register the radio and get a username and password. The '77 also includes an AC adaptor, an audio cable, a USB cable and a printed owner's manual. Full-spec coverage is from 100 kHz to 55 MHz, plus there's reduced performance from 10 to 100 kHz and 55 to 65 MHz.

On-screen there is an oscilloscope, an audio spectrum display and a 20 kHz-wide display of radio spectrum occupancy. This shows, in real time, everything happening 10 kHz on either side of the received signal—a narrow slice, indeed, but useful for some situations.

A built-in .wav recorder includes a handy single-event on/off timer programmable for day, month, year and so on—right down to the second—and stores onto the PC's hard disk. Use the PC to convert .wav to MP3, and you can take your analog or digital world band recordings anywhere, anytime without needing a permission slip from the recording industry.

From Italy comes the ELAD FDM77, the first PC receiver equipped for DRM reception.

Helpful tuning features abound. There are 200 station presets per page, with as many page files as the PC's hard disk can hold. Also, there's keyboard frequency selection directly above each frequency digit; keyboard or on-screen direct frequency entry; keyboard up/down slewing; a tuning knob that's virtual or uses the mouse wheel; and two VFOs. Alas, presets store only frequency and mode, not such other useful variables as bandwidth and AGC settings.

As with many other ancillary PC devices, the '77's power switch is on the rear panel with a power-on LED up front. There's also a USB activity LED and a seven-LED signal strength indicator to complement the excellent virtual "S" meter. The power and signal-strength LEDs, all blue, are annoyingly bright.

The '77's cabinet runs very warm. Its plastic end caps, held in place by double-sided tape, pull off easily once the cabinet heats up and the tape loses its stickiness. It's a small point, but it imparts a cheesy feel to an otherwise solid product. Snap-on caps or self-tapping screws would have been preferable.

Add PC, then Stir

Like most PC receivers, the Elad FDM77 is strictly for Windows. Nominal PC requirements are Windows 2000 or XP; Pentium 700 MHz, but Pentium IV 1.2 GHz or better recommended; 128 MB RAM, but 512 MB or better recommended; 50 MB or more of free hard disk space; 16-bit Sound Blaster compatible audio (line or mic) without AGC;

VGA 1024 × 768 with 16-bit color; and USB 2.0. Indeed, when we tried USB 1.0, instead, there were jerky responses and lock ups.

Overall, it appears that the minimum requirements are scarcely adequate, while the recommended specs are more like comfortable minima.

Operating software is on CD, although after the '77 has been registered you can check online to see if there's a later version available. It installs in three parts, potentially with no problems provided you first study the CD's installation instructions, as well as those in the owner's manual, and don't miss a beat along the way. Before installing, all power management in the BIOS and Windows should be disabled, along with all USB auto-power shutoffs and legacy support.

Underscoring this is that the software and, to an extent, the drivers do not uninstall successfully, as the registry doesn't get cleaned out properly. So, read the instructions completely beforehand, then follow them meticulously to ensure you get it right the first time.

First, install the main program, then bring up the software and ensure that "stand alone" and "USB" boxes are both checked in the setup screen. Then plug in the AC adaptor, USB cable and audio cable from the '77's 12 kHz output jack—this goes to the sound card's aux or mic jack.

The next step, USB driver installation, can get tricky, so carefully read the installation instructions on the CD. Assuming this goes well, use the included disk to install a second driver—that for the virtual cable.

Again, read the installation instructions all the way through, as sometimes information elsewhere pertains to what's given early on.

Among other things, this can lead to nasty high-pitched audio mixing in with signals (resolving this requires checking off and adjusting a different set of Windows audio options).

Finally, for proper DRM reception the 12 kHz output level needs to be optimized.

Pleasant Operation

The '77's screen interface is refreshingly user friendly, with large characters. It includes a sizable virtual "S" meter that gives accurate signal-strength readings and is easy to read. It used to be that the user could set the screen's background color to be blue, green or orange. Now, thanks to revised operating software, you can have any color you want so long as it is yellowy-orange.

To minimize pickup of electrical noise from the cojoined PC configuration, it helps greatly to use an outdoor antenna with a coaxial lead-in cable, especially as the '77 has no noise blanker. The SO-239 antenna connector is ideal for this, but there's also a BNC antenna connector for a whip antenna. This BNC input incorporates a 20 dB impedance-matching amplifier that, like Popeye's spinach, gives a mighty kick with other types of short antennas, too—provided the 10 dB main preamp is turned off to prevent overloading.

The '77 has front-end octave bandpass filtering that works well to, for example, keep mediumwave AM signals from ghosting onto world band frequencies. Overall spurious signal rejection is worthy and there's precious little frequency drift.

World band and single-sideband audio quality is quite pleasant, with low overall distortion. A six-band graphic equalizer helps make listening even more pleasant, but if it makes matter worse—for example, with DRM signals—use the "flat" setting.

Modes are AM, USB, LSB, CW and DRM. No, not "DRM ready"—this is the real thing, processing DRM world band signals from the get-go. There's no separate DRM software to scrounge around for, and no holding your breath to see if it works properly—just turn the radio on. This makes customer-oriented

DSP BANDWIDTH FILTERS (Hz)

250	1250	2250	4000	8000
500	1500	2500	5000	9000
750	1750	2750	6000	*10000
1000	2000	3000	7000	

* for DRM *et al.*

Elad something of a 21st century radio pioneer.

There's no synchronous selectable sideband, so manual ECSS is the only way to approximate sync's benefits. ECSS operation is thankfully simplified by 1 Hz tuning and frequency-display resolution.

DSP software controls the AGC and demodulation, along with the 19 bandwidths from 250 Hz to 10 kHz. These bandwidths perform well, especially at narrow settings, plus there's IF shift to help with adjacent-channel interference—particularly with ECSS.

Bandwidth selection calls for another screen to be brought up, and the main receiver display doesn't show the current bandwidth. These ergonomic speed bumps, along with occasionally unforgiving installation, are the only real exceptions to the '77's overall user friendliness.

Overall, performance with traditional analog world band signals comes off even better than our generally positive lab numbers might suggest. Weak-signal reception is commendable and overloading was not an issue during our tests. Audio quality and worthy interference rejection are pluses, too, even if synchronous selectable sideband is sorely missed.

DRM—The Eagle Has Landed

For some years, now, a coalition of broadcast electronics firms, international broadcasters and transmission organizations has been developing a unique form of digital transmission suitable for world band, as well as domestic, radio.

The resulting Digital Radio Mondiale (DRM) has real pros and real cons. Yet, until now all this was largely academic, as it was impossible to find a receiver that could process DRM without, at a minimum, the installation of aftermarket DRM software.

Elad's FDM77 ends all that. Granted, it is a PC receiver, not a standalone portable or tabletop. But once the '77 and PC are mated, DRM signals come tumbling in from around the globe. We found the 77's DRM painless to use and generally pleasant to hear.

Like all digital signals, when DRM works, it works; when it doesn't, it doesn't. One night a solid signal can provide excellent results, with clean audio and few dropouts. You're just about ready to shout, "Hallelujah," when the next night a middling signal sounds like Max Headroom with hiccups. Interference disrupts abnormally, too.

Comparable analog world band signals are significantly more consistent and forgiving. Of course, they also lack DRM's spicier, steadier audio when conditions are right.

How good is DRM? In theory, if a station is putting in a powerful one-hop signal on a clear channel, it should be able to use a fairly high bit rate to provide an FM-quality signal. Indeed, reliable listener reports indicate that this sometimes happens. But our firsthand listening suggests that real-world bit rates are lower, typically resulting in audio more like that of a lower-quality MP3 file.

That may not be FM quality, but it's darned good—when conditions are right. And therein lies the rub, for offsetting this shining potential is a Faustian tradeoff of dropouts and susceptibility to interference. Solid, clear analog broadcasts can sound pretty darned good, too, especially with synchronous detection, and they're robust and don't drop out.

Nevertheless, it's obvious that DRM has improved significantly over what we encountered just a few years back, and Elad's new FDM77 handles it with aplomb. Whether DRM will succeed over the long haul remains to be seen, but the ability to receive these digital broadcasts without fuss or bother is a major arrow in the '77's bulging quiver.

Presumably Elad's continuing software revisions will incorporate updates to DRM. This is no small point, as DRM, like any other worthwhile software, needs to improve over time and adapt to new operating systems.

DRM Ready
✪✪✪⅜
RFSPACE SDR-14

Price: *RFSPACE SDR-14:* $1,099.95 in the United States. *Comet HS-10 SMA-to-SO-239*

The RFSPACE SDR-14 is unusually specialized. It performs nicely with selected applications.

antenna adaptor cable: $17.99 in the United States. *DRM software:* $49.95 worldwide from www.winradio.com/home/download-drm.htm.

Pro: Excellent spectrum display shows, with audio ("demodulation"), up to a 150 kHz slice of radio spectrum; this can also be recorded to disk and played back in any mode or bandwidth (*see* Con). Worthy sensitivity. DSP bandwidth filtering feels razor sharp and performs beautifully. Relatively free from overloading. Stable. Tunes and displays down to 1 Hz increments. Passband tuning (*see* Con). Three-level attenuator, labeled as RF gain control. Adjustable AGC decay and hang times. Good quality, flexible USB cable. Receives 30–260 MHz minus front end filtering or amplification (*see* Con). Third-party software development supported. SpectraVue software nominally has Linux server support (not tested), in addition to Windows. With optional software, receives digital (DRM) world band and other broadcasts. World Time (UTC) clock shows date and day of the week. Operating software can be updated online from www.moetronix.com/spectravue.htm. Build quality appears solid. One year warranty. Fifteen day return privilege when ordered from the manufacturer. Helpful PDF operating manual (*see* Con).

Con: AC adaptor's switching circuitry emits noise that disrupts reception even with outdoor antenna and shielded lead-in. Initial installation not always successful, necessitating troubleshooting with or without the assistance of the manufacturer; however, manufacturer's phone number and street address aren't published. SMA antenna connector, with no adaptor included for non-

SMA antenna plugs; for most shortwave antennas an adaptor or new antenna plug is required. No synchronous selectable or double sideband, tunable notch filter, presets or scanning. Passband tuning operates only in LSB and USB modes and is complex to use. Noise blanker performs marginally, and no DSP noise reduction offered. Inadequate front end filtering, so mediumwave AM stations may bleed through slightly to impact world band listening. With demodulation, spectrum display limited to 150 kHz maximum bandwidth. Marginally useful 30–260 MHz reception, with an abundance of spurious signals that not even maximum attenuation can overcome. Requires a speedy computer with large disk capacity to use to full benefit; even then, heavy resource drain may impact multitasking. Harsh audio quality in AM mode. About a half-second lag when operating controls and when listening (demodulation, see story). No power switch, even though manufacturer recommends receiver be powered down when not in use. Operation manual, only on CD, not printed as a book.

☞ The included switching AC adaptor is appalling and should be substituted with a non-switching type. Requirements are 12V DC output, one ampere minimum rating, center (tip) positive.

☞ Tested: software .014, SpectraVue 1.30.

Verdict: The RFSPACE SDR-14 is a niche device that does one thing very well: recording a slice of spectrum for later playback and analysis. Here, its advantage over the WiNRADiO G313 is that the slice may be up to 150 kHz, rather than 20 kHz.

However, this broader coverage comes at a price. The SDR-14, unlike the G313, requires a speedy processor and substantial disk—especially in a multitasking environment. And it is nowhere as flexible outside its niche as the G313.

However appropriate the SDR-14 is for spectrum analysis, it is a dismal choice for world band listening or DXing.

Robert Sherwood and David Zantow, with Lawrence Magne.

WHERE TO FIND IT: INDEX TO TESTED RADIOS

PASSPORT REPORTS evaluates nearly every digitally tuned receiver on the market. Here is where each review is found, with those that are new, forthcoming, revised, rebranded or retested for 2007 in **bold**. Those that are also oriented to DRM reception are in *italics*.

Comprehensive Radio Database International White Papers® are available for a number of popular new and classic premium receivers. Each RDI White Paper®—$6.95 in North America, $9.95 airmail elsewhere, including shipping—contains virtually all our panel's findings and comments during hands-on testing, as well as laboratory measurements and what these mean to you. These unabridged reports are available from key world band dealers, or order 24/7 from www.passband.com, autovoice +1 215/598-9018 or fax +1 215/598 3794—or write PASSPORT RDI White Papers, Box 300, Penn's Park, PA 18943 USA.

▤ *Radio Database International White Paper*® available.

Wire Antennas for 2007

Simple portables work nicely off their built-in telescopic antennas, and there are excellent compact antennas for tabletop and premium-portable models. Yet, outdoor wire antennas are still the best and cheapest way to boost a worthy receiver's world band reception.

First, three truths:

• *Location.* If you can't put a wire antenna outdoors, consider a compact (see next article). Erect safely and for best performance.

• *Apples and oranges.* Simple antennas for simple portables, sophisticated antennas for fancy stuff.

• *Signal-to-noise:* Boosting signals isn't enough. Success requires that signals be enhanced relative to electrical and receiver noise. The result—more signal, less noise—improves the signal-to-noise ratio.

When Wire Antennas Help

No surprise—stations already booming in aren't going to do better with an improved antenna. Your receiver's signal-strength indicator may read higher, but its automatic-gain control (AGC) ensures that what you hear isn't going to sound much different than before. In fact, it might sound worse.

With all portables except premium models, forget sophisticated antennas—outdoor or in, passive or active. Make do with the radio's built-in telescopic antenna, or for more oomph use an inverted-L wire antenna (see below) or one of the simpler compact antennas.

At the other extreme, a first-rate outdoor antenna is essential to elite receivers, which is why these rarely have built-in antennas.

Volksantenna

Inverted-L antennas are simple, flexible and inexpensive. Inconspicuous, too, as they have no unsightly traps and, being end-fed, their feedlines are usually next to the house rather than dangling out in the open. For most radios they provide excellent results, and are even reasonable for omnidirectional mediumwave AM reception.

Rough-and-ready inverted-Ls are cheap and usually rate three stars, sometimes more. Among those available in the United States is Radio Shack's $10 Outdoor Antenna Kit (278-758) with wire, insulators and other bits. Add loose change for a claw/alligator clip or other connector.

World band and specialty outlets often stock inverted-L antennas, as well as such add-ons as baluns (see Worldly Words) and antenna tuners. These are made from superior materials and priced accordingly; for example, for Brits it's £26 for the Watson SWL-DX1 and £40 for the Moonraker Skywire. Other offerings are creative end-fed variants of the classic inverted-L.

At full length, a typical inverted-L antenna can be too long for many portables, causing overloading from hefty incoming signals. Experiment, but usually the cheaper the portable, the shorter the inverted-L antenna should be. Unlike other antenna types, the inverted-L can be readily shortened to avoid overloading or to fit into your yard.

> **Simple antennas for simple radios, fancy antennas for fancy receivers.**

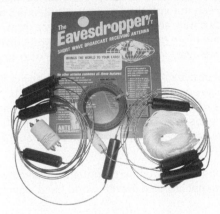

The Eavesdropper Model T, like its automobile namesake, features a straightforward design and comes ready to use.

Longwires Reduce Fading

Acres aplenty?

Lengthy inverted-L antennas, detailed in the RDI White Paper on outdoor antennas, can be over 200 feet, or 60 meters. These homebrew skyhooks are readily assembled from parts found at world band and amateur radio outlets and flea markets.

They qualify as genuine longwire antennas, thanks to their having one or more wavelengths (see "Weird Words"). This helps reduce fading—something shorter antennas can't do—while improving the all important signal-to-noise ratio.

Antenna Pitfalls

A good antenna static protector is essential during nearby thunderstorms, windy snowfalls and sandstorms. These generate electrical charges that can seriously damage your radio.

Some of the best are made by Alpha Delta Communications. It's also a good idea to have a surge arrestor or UPS on the power line, too—just like with a PC.

Most Americans don't encounter legal prohibitions on erecting world band antennas. However, covenants and deed restrictions, increasingly common in gated and other communities, can limit choices. Regardless, the Golden Rule of Aerials applies: Outdoor antennas should be neither unsightly nor particularly visible. If you want to annoy neighbors, put out pink plastic flamingos.

Most wire antennas are robustly constructed to withstand ice buildup during storms, but wire sometimes stretches. Bungee straps or pulley counterweights help prevent this.

Antennas Need Fresh Air

Digital devices create so much RF pollution—electrical noise—that proper antenna location is increasingly a must. Indoors is usually the worst place.

You don't bathe in dirty water, so don't put your antenna where it is electrically "dirty." Instead, place it away from your home, electrical lines, cables and other potential noise sources. Once your antenna is hanging free in the breeze, you're probably going to hear less noise bothering stations.

MUTT AND JEFF

Accessory antennas come in two flavors: unamplified or "passive" (usually outdoor), and amplified or "active" (indoor, outdoor or both). An unamplified antenna uses a wire or rod receiving element which carries radio signals straight to the receiver. The wire antennas in this article are all unamplified and fairly long.

Amplified or active antennas have receiving elements that are shorter but electronically boosted. A few sought-after models even outperform big outdoor antennas, at least with staticky signals below 5 MHz. As yards shrink and restrictive covenants grow, limited-space amplified antennas are becoming more popular. Even landed homeowners sometimes prefer them because most are relatively inconspicuous and are easy to erect.

But amplified antennas have potential drawbacks. First, their short receiving elements usually don't provide the signal-to-noise enhancement of lengthier elements. Second, antenna amplifiers can generate noise of their own. Third, these amplifiers can overload, with results like when a receiver overloads . . . a mighty mumbling mishmash up and down the dial. Indeed, if antenna amplification is excessive it can overload the receiver, too.

Finally, amplified compact antennas often have mediocre front-end selectivity. This can allow local mediumwave AM signals to get jumbled in with world band signals.

Safe Installation

Safety is Rule One during installation. Avoid falls or making contact with potentially lethal electrical utility and other lines. If you want to be fried, go to the beach.

There's much more to this than can be covered here, but it's detailed in the RADIO DATABASE INTERNATIONAL report, *Evaluation of Popular Outdoor Antennas*. Also, check out www.universal-radio.com/catalog/sw_ant/safeswl.html.

What's Best?

In that RDI White Paper are also test results for a number of popular outdoor wire antennas, three of which are summarized here. All are dipoles which rely on traps for frequency resonance, but a variety of mounting layouts are used:

- End-fed sloper, with the antenna about 30 degrees from horizontal.
- Center-fed tapered wing, with a tall (about 20 feet or 6 meters) mounting amidships, plus two lower mountings.
- Center-fed horizontal, hung between two points of comparable height.

PASSPORT's star ratings mean the same thing regardless of whether an antenna is active or passive, big or little, indoor or out. This helps when you're trying to compare one type of antenna with another in PASSPORT REPORTS.

Nevertheless, passive antennas are more tricky than actives to evaluate properly. That's because performance is more dependent on such imponderables as local soil, moisture and bedrock. So, don't hold back from "rolling your own" or buying something that, tests be damned, you think might do well at your location. There are countless designs on the market, and most wire antennas are frugal and forgiving.

✪✪✪¾ *Passport's Choice*
Alpha Delta DX-Ultra

Price: $129.95 in the United States. $179.00CAD in Canada. Coaxial cable extra.

Pro: Best overall performer of any antenna tested, passive or active. Little variation in performance from one world band segment to another. Rugged construction. Comes with built-in static protection. Wing design appropriate for certain yard layouts. Covers mediumwave AM band.

Con: Assembly a major undertaking, with stiff wire having to be bent and fed through spacer holes, then affixed. Unusually lengthy, 80 feet or 25 meters. Coaxial cable lead-in not included. Relatively heavy, adding to erection effort. Warranty only six months.

Verdict: The Alpha Delta DX-Ultra rewards sweat equity—it is really more of a kit than a finished product. First, you have to purchase the needed lead-in cable and other hard-

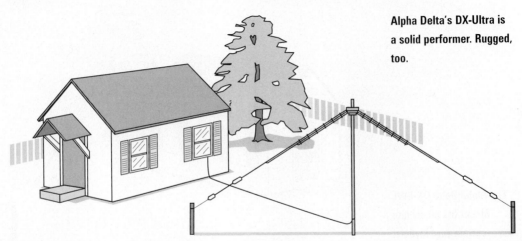

Alpha Delta's **DX-Ultra** is a solid performer. Rugged, too.

ware bits, then assemble, bend and stretch the many stiff wires, section by section.

Because the wire used should outlast the Pyramids, assembly is a trying and unforgiving exercise. Each wire needs to be rigorously and properly affixed, lest it slip loose and the erected antenna comes tumbling down, as it did at one of our test sites.

While all outdoor antennas require yard space, the Ultra is the longest manufactured antenna tested. It is also relatively heavy, making installation an even more tiresome chore than it already is. In ice-prone climates, be sure any trees or poles attached to the antenna are sturdy. And don't even think about using a chimney.

But if you have yard space and don't object to assembly and erection hurdles, you are rewarded with a mighty robust performer. It is outmatched only by hugely long inverted-L aerials and costly professional-grade antennas.

❂❂❂❂½ Passport's Choice
Alpha Delta DX-SWL Sloper

Price: $89.95 in the United States. $149.00CAD in Canada. Coaxial cable and static protector extra.

Pro: Rugged construction. Sloper design uses traps to keep the length down to 60 feet (18 meters), making it suitable for

certain yard layouts. Covers mediumwave AM band.

Con: Requires assembly, a significant exercise. Does not include static protection. Coaxial cable lead-in not included. Warranty only six months.

☞ A greatly shortened version of the Ultra, the 40-foot (12 meter) DX-SWL-S (not tested), is available for $69.95, with coaxial cable and static protector extra. Its nominal coverage is 3.2-22 MHz, omitting the little-used 2 MHz (120 meter) world band segment. Although both Sloper versions nominally don't cover the scarcely used 25 MHz (11 meter) world band segment, our measurements of the full-length Sloper show excellent results at 25650-26100 kHz.

Verdict: An excellent choice where space is limited, but it's a chore to assemble.

❂❂❂❂⅛ Passport's Choice
Eavesdropper Model T, Eavesdropper Model C

Price: *Model T:* $89.95, complete, in the United States. *Model C:* $89.95 in the United States. Coaxial cable extra.

Pro: Unusually compact at 43 feet or 13 meters, it fits into many yards. Comes with built-in static protection. One-year warranty, after which repairs made "at nominal cost." *Model T:* Easiest to install of any

The Alpha Delta DX-SWL Sloper fits nicely into certain yard layouts.

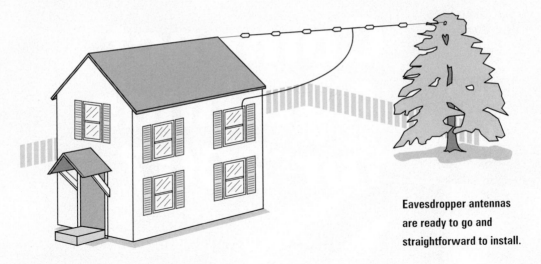

Eavesdropper antennas are ready to go and straightforward to install.

Passport's Choice antenna—unpack, and it's ready to hang. Comes with ribbon lead-in wire, which tends to have less signal loss than coaxial cable. *Model C:* Easier than most to install, with virtually everything included and assembled but the coaxial cable lead-in.

Con: Some performance drop within the 2 MHz (120 meter) and 3 MHz (90 meter) tropical world band segments. *Model C:* Coaxial cable lead-in not included.

☞ Eavesdropper also makes the $89.95 sloper antenna (not tested) similar to Alpha Delta's DX-SWL Sloper. It comes with a static arrestor, but no coaxial cable lead-in.

Verdict: If your teeth gnash when you see "Some Assembly Required," take heart. The Eavesdropper T, unlike Alpha Delta alternatives, comes ready to go and is straightforward to erect. At most, you might want to get a pair of bungee straps to provide flexibility at the ends.

The size is user-friendly, too—the result of a compromise. There's no getting around the rule that the longer the antenna, the more likely it is to do well at low frequencies. Eavesdropper's designer, the late Jim Meadow, once told PASSPORT that he found few folks tuning below 4.7 MHz, but many people with limited yard space. So, he shrunk the Eavesdropper by focusing on performance above 4.7 MHz, yet allowed it to function decently lower down.

Our tests confirm this. The Eavesdropper horizontal trap dipoles perform quite nicely above 4.7 MHz, with a notch less gain than Alpha-Delta models in the 2 MHz and 3 MHz tropical world band segments.

In practice the ribbon lead-in wire used by the T version works well, using phasing to help cancel out electrical noise. Too, it stands up to the elements and usually has less signal loss than coaxial cable used by its C sibling.

As a practical matter the decisive consideration may be your yard layout.

Prepared by Stephen Bohac, Jock Elliott, Tony Jones, Lawrence Magne, David Walcutt and George Zeller.

Compact Antennas for 2007

Do you seek out world band by day, when signals are weaker, or elusive stations anytime? If so, put an accessory antenna near the head of your wish list.

Best are outdoor wire antennas that are unamplified—*passive*. Trouble is, they are lengthy, a pain to erect (think "big trees") and require yard space. But if you lack acreage, face community restrictions or are allergic to high-wire gymnastics, consider a compact antenna.

Compacts have a loop, small rod or short wire receiving element to grab signals. But these are usually not big enough to have much oomph, so an amplifier is used to make up the difference. The antenna then becomes *active*. Today, nearly all compact antennas are active and nearly all active antennas are compact.

Most are ideal for townhouses, apartments and hotels—sometimes suitable for travel, too. But with detached houses now occupying more available lot size, even large homes may not have space for a passive wire antenna. Too, pretentious neighbors sometimes sniff that visible outdoor antennas look vulgarian, like clotheslines.

Greatly Improved

Early amplified antennas were noisy, overloaded easily, generated harmonic "false" signals and suffered if placed outdoors. They quickly earned a reputation for failing to deliver.

Now, you can choose from several solid performers. While these antennas still don't fully equal their outdoor wire cousins, the gap has narrowed considerably. Indeed, some occasionally outperform passive wire antennas on lower frequencies during high-static periods.

Proximate *vs.* Remote

Compact antennas are either proximate or remote. A proximate model has its receiving element on or near an amplifier box by the receiver. A remote antenna, whether active or passive, allows the receiving element to be mounted farther away—either indoors or, with some models, outdoors where reception tends to be superior.

Remote units are the way to go, as the receiving element can be put where electrical noise is weak but radio signals are strong. Proximate models give no such choice unless the receiver itself is placed where reception is best.

Some receivers emit electrical noise, usually from the front panel's digital display. So, if you must use a proximate antenna put it behind or alongside the radio.

New for 2007: the best active antenna ever.

Few need an antenna rotor except for mediumwave AM DX. For this the Yaesu G-5500 is ideal, as it slews on two axes.

Loops Reduce Noise

Loop antennas inherently tend to pick up signals with less static and related noise than do other designs. Too, they are relatively directional, so they can be pointed away from local electrical noise. All this improves the important signal-to-noise ratio—especially within lower frequency segments.

Wellbrook loops are especially effective because they can be outdoors and, unlike some other loops, are balanced. During high-static months their superior signal-to-noise ratios can make the difference between hearing only static and understanding what's being said.

Most active antennas are designed for table-top models, but not all. Degen's DE31, also sold under the Kaito and Thieking brands, is a low-cost option oriented to casual portable use.

No Juice Needed

Often the first thing to go in an emergency is electricity. Batteries sometimes fill in, but nothing beats not needing electricity in the first place.

The R.F. Systems GMDSS-1 is that most unusual of antennas: short, yet with no electronic amplification. And it is tough enough to withstand serious abuse without flinching.

Preselection *vs.* Broadband

Broadband electronic amplifiers can cause all sorts of mischief. Some add noise and spurious signals, especially from the mediumwave AM band. Yet others overload a receiver with too much gain.

A partial fix is tunable or switchable preselection. This helps keep unwanted signals at bay by limiting the band of frequencies which get full amplification. Problem is, they almost always have controls that need tweaking. A high-pass filter or band rejection filter (e.g., from Kiwa Electronics or Par Electronics) can also help keep powerful mediumwave AM stations from ghosting in to disturb world band reception.

How Much Oomph?

One way to judge an active antenna is simply by how much gain it provides. That's like judging a car only by its horsepower.

An active antenna should provide signal levels similar to those from a good passive wire antenna. With less gain, receiver circuit noise can become audible; too much gain and the receiver's circuitry—maybe the antenna's, too—can become dysfunctional. Like Smucker's, it needs to be just right.

When Your Antenna Arrives

Tips to help your antenna reach its potential:

Active antennas work best off batteries, which avoid hum and buzz caused by AC mains power. But if your antenna uses an AC adaptor, keep it and electrical cords away from the receiving element and feedline. If there's hum anyway, try substituting a higher-end AC adaptor from Radio Shack or other supplier.

Antenna performance is one part technology, another part geography and geology, and a third part installation. PASSPORT reports on the first and give tips on the third. Yet, much depends on the second—local conditions.

You can enhance those odds by placing the receiving element at various locations. Jerry-rig the antenna until you're satisfied the best spot has been found, then nail it down for good.

Finally, if your radio has multiple antenna inputs, try each to see which works best.

What PASSPORT's Ratings Mean

Star ratings: ✪✪✪✪✪ is best for any type of antenna, but in reality even the best of compact antennas don't yet merit more than four stars when compared against long passive antennas. To help in deciding, star ratings for compact antennas can be compared directly against those for "lasso" antennas found elsewhere in this PASSPORT REPORTS. Stars reflect overall world band performance and meaningful features, plus to some extent ergonomics and build quality. Price, appearance, country of manufacture and the like are not taken into account.

Passport's Choice. La crème de la crème. Our test team's personal picks of the litter—models we would buy or have bought for our personal use. Unlike star ratings, these choices are unapologetically subjective.

☮: A relative bargain, with decidedly more performance than the price would suggest. Active antennas are listed in descending order of merit. Unless otherwise indicated each has a one-year warranty.

Wellbrook's ALA 100 quasi-kit calls for a homemade loop, like this biggie at PASSPORT's Rocky Mountain site. The extra effort pays off in top-drawer performance, but the result can be visually unappealing. J.R. Sherwood

New for 2007
★★★★½ *Passport's Choice*
Wellbrook ALA 100

Head amp and control unit; requires large homemade outdoor loop. Active, remote, broadband, 0.05–30 MHz

Price: £139.00 plus £5.00 shipping in the United Kingdom and Eire. £139.00 plus £15.00 shipping elsewhere.

Pro: With large (40-foot, 12-meter) loop receiving element and relatively low-gain amplifier, has best signal-to-noise ratio, notably above 10 MHz, of any active model tested. Reduced pickup of thunderstorm static, especially below 8 MHz during local summer. Balanced loop design inherently helps reduce pickup of local electrical noise. Performance characteristics make it unusually complementary to passive outdoor wire antennas. Superior build quality. Supplied 117V AC adaptor (Stancor STA-300R) among best tested for not causing hum or buzzing. Although any large loop is inherently susceptible to inductive pickup of local thunderstorm static, during our tests the antenna's amplifier has not suffered static damage during storms; indeed, even nearby one kilowatt shortwave transmissions have not damaged it. Protected circuitry, using an easily replaced 315 mA fuse. Superior factory support. Easier to ship and less costly than other tested Wellbrook loops.

Con: Significant undertaking to install, as quasi-kit ALA100 requires construction of 26–59 foot (8–18 meter) homemade loop receiving element. As a practical matter receiving element should be mounted outdoors, another installation burden; too, if element's framework made from white PVC it can be an eyesore. Only moderate gain for reception within such modest-signal areas as Western Hemisphere, Asia and Australasia—a drawback only with receivers having relatively noisy circuitry. Impractical to rotate, thus inappropriate for nulling co-channel interference on mediumwave AM. BNC connector at the receiving element's base open to weather and thus needs to be user-sealed with Coax Seal, electrical putty or similar. Encapsulated amplifier makes repair impossible. Manufacturer cautions against allowing sunlight to damage head amplifier's plastic housing; yet, after three years of intense exposure at our high-UV main test site, Wellbrook's plastic seems no worse for the wear than any other outdoor antenna's plastic. No coaxial cable supplied. Available for purchase or export only two cumbersome ways: via Sterling cheque or International Money Order through the Welsh manufacturer (www. wellbrook.uk.com), or with credit card via an English dealer's unsecured email address (sales@shortwave.co.uk).

☞ Star rating is with relatively large pickup element of around 40-feet (12-meters) in length. Performance drops at smaller lengths, such as near 25 feet (7.6 meters).

Verdict: Size matters, and this quasi-kit active antenna can get seriously big by compact antenna standards. Indeed, it almost occupies a "neither" world somewhere between truly compact active antennas and long passive wire antennas.

No plug-and-play, the plus-size ALA100 is a major slog to construct and install. Yet, the payoff for your toil, sweat and tears is exceptional quietness—a *sine qua non* for faint-signal reception.

If its installation, size, appearance and purchase hurdles don't deter you, you won't find a better active model than the British-made Wellbrook ALA 100. If you already use a passive outdoor wire antenna, this model's unique receiving characteristics should be unusually complementary.

Evaluation of New Model: Wellbrook's new ALA100 is an interesting antenna—"antenna," really, as it has only three parts: 1) a weather-resistant amplifier for mounting at a loop receiving element, 2) an antenna interface box nestled indoors between the loop and the receiver, and 3) an AC adaptor.

Where's the all-important loop receiving element? In your mirror. You have to create, construct and erect it yourself—plus provide 50-ohm coax with BNC plugs at each end to connect the outdoor amplifier to the indoor antenna interface box.

Part of the secret to this antenna's good performance is its mating of a low-gain amplifier to a receiving element with exceptional capture length that more than makes up for the amp's reduced gain. This makes the '100 something of a hybrid between a passive outdoor wire antenna and a typical short-element active antenna. No surprise, then, that the '100 does almost as well and occasionally better than as a high-performance passive wire antenna. Too, the amplifier's limited gain helps keep overloading at bay within the mediumwave AM band.

Jumbo Loop

Wellbrook recommends that the loop be around 8–18 meters (26–59 feet) in length, so we constructed three: two delta (triangle) loops of 25 feet (7.6 meters) and a square loop of 40-feet (12 meters). Both deltas use #20 insulated wire with the flat part affixed to an upstairs wooden railing; in practice #20 appears to be too thin to withstand the wind and elements, as it tends to break at the connection with the amplifier. Yet, it's ideal for curling up and taking back and forth to, say, a vacation house for a week or two.

The first delta is not equilateral, as the horizontal leg is shorter than the legs going down in a V. It does nicely. The second delta has all three legs of equal length and works even better.

However, best by far has been the long square loop (photo) dangled from a 35-foot (11 meter) tree. It uses #14 wire and a rigid frame of half-inch schedule 40 PVC with elbow fittings. The 90-degree elbows turned out to be too sharp for fishing #14 wire, so it was tied onto the PVC frame. Alas, the antenna's sheer weight causes the bottom PVC to sag.

Lessons learned: Sixteen-gauge wire would perform just as well, yet be more flexible, weigh less and fit better into the amplifier's input holes. Lightweight RG-58A or RG-8X coax can also help keep down overall weight, and nonconductive bracing would maintain a more aesthetically pleasing square shape.

Yet, no matter how you slice it, with white PVC the loop looks like a plumber's nightmare. Most electrical PVC conduit and some schedule 80 plumbing PVC are gray, which in most settings is less visually offensive.

"Grass" Disappears

The square loop may be ugly, but it's a performance barnburner, even nudging out the sibling ALA 330S. A band 'scope confirms what the ears hear: that the 40-foot loop is remarkably quiet. You don't notice any background noise from the loop element's amp, and below 18 MHz the 'scope doesn't show the usual "grass" from the amplifier.

Mediumwave AM reception is predictably good with the 40-foot loop. Yet, a nearby transmitter almost causes overloading at our main test location, so we haven't attempted a longer loop. In any event a 40-foot loop peaks around 25 MHz, so a larger loop may be counterproductive. First,

it would increase mediumwave AM pickup, thus increasing the propensity to overload. Second, it would reduce pickup between 20 and 30 MHz (including 13 and 11 meter segments), shifting the peak to near 15 MHz (19 meters) where such gain is rarely needed.

But at any of the recommended lengths the sheer loop size makes it is impractical to rotate. So, co-channel mediumwave AM interference can't be nulled—a pity, as the Wellbrook's balanced design is otherwise ideal for providing deep nulls. Yet, sometime, someplace, somebody will set up a Jolly Green Giant configuration to rotate a full-bore ALA 100 loop for mediumwave AM nulling. The results should be most interesting.

INSTALLATION TIPS

When a remote compact antenna is installed properly it can perform very well. The bad news is that if you have room outdoors to mount it properly, you may also have room for a passive wire antenna that will perform better, yet. Probably cheaper, too.

Here are tips on placement of weather-resistant remote models, but creativity rules—experiment freely.

- Outdoors, put the receiving element in the clear, away from objects. Metal degrades performance, so especially keep it away from metal and, if possible, use a nonconductive mast or capped PVC pipe. Optimum height from ground is usually around 10–25 feet or 3–8 meters. Here, "ground" refers to the electrical ground—not only *terra firma*, but also reinforced concrete roofs and the like.

  Running a metal mast through a loop's receiving element can degrade performance. So, if you use a metal mast simply affix it to the mounting flange and stop there. In Wellbrook's case, its mounting flange is plenty tough, as evidenced by years of being exposed to blistery winds, ice and snow at our Rocky Mountain test cabin. The manufacturer states that the flange is good for winds up to 80 MPH (130 km/h), but our own experience suggests that it is even more robust.

  If a mast is impractical try a tree. Although sap is electrically conductive, this is a reasonable fallback, especially with hardwood deciduous varieties other than sugar maple. You may have to do some trimming to keep leaves away from the receiving element.

- When yard placement is impractical, place the receiving element outdoors as far as you dare. In a high-rise building consider using a balcony or just outside a window. For example, if the receiving element is a rod, point it away from the building 70 degrees or so, like a wall flagpole. If you reside on the top floor, the roof may also be a good bet.

  If outdoor placement is out of the question at your house, try the attic if the roof isn't metal. With Wellbrook models this beats having it hog an entire room.

- If all else fails affix the receiving element against the inside-center of a large window. Radio signals, like light, sail right through glass.

Go Forth and Create

The Wellbrook ALA100 is not just a first-rate assemblage of hardware. It allows you the opportunity to experiment to obtain the best possible results at your location. You can try different shapes, for example: round, oval, octagon, square, delta and so on. And besides schedule 40 PVC, there's schedule 80 and both come in various sizes. Even better, look into lightweight electrical PVC conduit with gentle elbows, as these facilitate fishing so the loop's wire can be mounted inboard.

★★★★ *Passport's Choice*
Wellbrook ALA 330S

Outdoor-indoor loop. Active, remote, broadband, 2.3–30 MHz

Price: *ALA 330S:* £189.00 plus £10.00 shipping in the United Kingdom and Eire. £189.00 plus £30.00 shipping elsewhere. *Upgrade kit '330 to '330S:* £80.00 plus £10.00 shipping in the United Kingdom and Eire. £80.00 plus £15.00 shipping elsewhere.

Pro: Among the best signal-to-noise ratios, including at times reduced pickup of thunderstorm static, on all shortwave frequencies, of any active model tested; low-noise/low-static pickup characteristics most noticeable below 8 MHz, especially during local summer, when it sometimes outperforms sophisticated outdoor wire antennas. Higher shortwave gain (above 3 MHz) than sibling '1530/'1530+, which helps get signals into a better AGC range on most receivers. Balanced loop design inherently helps reduce pickup of local electrical noise; additionally, aluminum loop receiving element can be affixed to a low-cost TV rotor to improve reception by directionally nulling local electrical noise and, to a lesser degree, static. Rotatability also can slightly reduce co-channel shortwave interference below 4 or 5 MHz and even occasionally on higher frequencies. Superior build quality, including rigorous weatherproofing (*see* Con). Supplied 117V AC adaptor (Stancor STA-300R) among best tested for not causing hum or buzzing (*see* Con). Although any large loop is inherently susceptible to inductive pickup of local thunderstorm static, during our tests of the prior and current versions the antenna's amplifier has never suffered static damage during storms; indeed, even nearby one kilowatt shortwave transmissions have not damaged it. Protected circuitry, using an easily replaced 315 mA fuse. Threaded flange on "S" version improves mounting of loop receiving element (*see* Con). Superior factory support.

Con: Only moderate gain for reception within such modest-signal areas as Western Hemisphere, Asia and Australasia—a drawback only with receivers having relatively noisy circuitry. Slightly less gain than ALA 1530 within little-used 2.3–2.5 MHz (120 meter) tropical world band segment, a drawback only with receivers having relatively noisy circuitry. Mediumwave AM gain significantly inferior to that of the '1530. Flange for loop receiving element has metric pipe threading; most U.S. users will need to re-thread. Loop receiving element, about one meter across, is large and cumbersome to ship, although loop is slightly smaller than in the prior version. Mounting mast and optional rotor add to cost and complexity. BNC connector at the receiving element's base is open to the weather and thus needs to be user-sealed with Coax Seal, electrical putty or similar. Encapsulated amplifier makes repair impossible. Manufacturer cautions against allowing high winds to stress mounting flange; however, one of our units survived 90+ mph Rocky Mountain winds until the locally procured pipe coupling to which we had attached the antenna snapped. Manufacturer cautions against allowing sunlight to damage head amplifier's plastic housing; yet, after three years of intense exposure at a high-UV PASSPORT test site, Wellbrook's plastic seems no worse for the wear than any other outdoor antenna's plastic. Adaptor supplied for 117V AC runs very warm after being plugged in for a few hours, while amplifier tends to run slightly warm; nonetheless, after three years of use at PASSPORT test facility, neither has acted up. No coaxial cable supplied. Available for purchase or export only two cumbersome ways: via Sterling cheque or International Money Order through the Welsh manufacturer (www.wellbrook.uk.com), or with credit card via an English dealer's unsecured email address (sales@shortwave.co.uk).

☞ The manufacturer offers a kit to convert the earlier ALA 330 to the improved "S" version. Recommended.

Verdict: This excellent active antenna shines when it comes to reducing the impact of static and noise on weak signals below 8 MHz.

For limited-space situations, and even to complement passive wire antennas on large properties, the '330S is hard to equal. However, if your receiver tends to sound "hissy" with weak signals, then it probably needs an antenna which gives even more gain than the '330S so it can overcome internal receiver noise. Of course, with top-rated tabletop models this is not an issue.

For best reception the antenna should be mounted outdoors, away from the house and atop a rotor. However, this is more important with the ALA 1530 model (*see below*) when used for longwave and mediumwave AM reception. In the real world of limited options, reasonable results on shortwave are sometimes obtained even indoors sans rotor or with manual rotation, provided the usual caveats are followed for placement of the reception element. But there's no getting around the laws of physics: The Wellbrook loop is an antenna, and all antennas work much better when not shielded by absorptive materials or placed near sources of electrical interference.

What's not to like? An ordering procedure that's inconvenient and démodé. There are no dealers outside the United Kingdom, and as there is still no secure way for those beyond U.K. borders to order by credit card on the Internet.

Overall, the '330S isn't in the same league as top-rated outdoor wire antennas. However, it can outperform even those antennas with some static-prone signals or when local electrical noise is a problem—provided it is erected properly.

Wellbrook's ALA 330S is engineered specifically for the shortwave spectrum. It's a logical choice for those living near mediumwave AM stations.   J.R. Sherwood

Premium Version for 2007
Regular Version Retested for 2007

✪✪✪⅞ *Passport's Choice*
Wellbrook ALA 1530, Wellbrook ALA 1530P

Outdoor-indoor loop. Active, remote, broadband, 0.15–30 MHz

Price: *ALA1530+:* £180.00 plus £10.00 shipping in the United Kingdom and Eire. £180.00 plus £30.00 shipping elsewhere. *ALA 1530:* £159.00 plus £10.00 shipping in the United Kingdom and Eire. £159.00 plus £30.00 shipping elsewhere. *ALA 1530P (not tested):* £159.00 plus £10.00 shipping in the United Kingdom and Eire. £159.95 plus £30.00 shipping elsewhere. *Yaesu G-5500/G-5500B twin-axis rotor:* $639.95 in the United States. CAD$1,060.00 in Canada. £559.00 in the United Kingdom. €659.00 in Germany.

For world band and distant mediumwave AM, the Wellbrook ALA 1530/1530P is hard to beat when mediumwave AM stations aren't nearby. J.R. Sherwood

Pro: Covers at comparable levels of performance not only shortwave, but also mediumwave AM and longwave (*see* Con). Mediumwave AM and longwave performance superb when coupled to a Yaesu G-5500/G-5500B rotor, which has twin-axis directionality; also, rotor also can slightly reduce co-channel shortwave interference below 4 or 5 MHz and even occasionally on higher frequencies. Very nearly the best signal-to-noise ratio among active models tested, including reduced pickup of thunderstorm static. Balanced loop design inherently helps reduce pickup of local electrical noise. Low-noise/low-static pickup characteristic most noticeable below 8 MHz during summer, when it sometimes outperforms sophisticated outdoor wire antennas. Slightly more gain than sibling ALA 330S within little-used 2.3–2.5 MHz (120 meter) tropical world band segment. Superior build quality, including rigorous weatherproofing (*see* Con). Supplied AC adaptor, properly bypassed and regulated, is among the best tested for not causing hum or buzzing (*see* Con). Although any large loop's amplifier is

inherently susceptible to inductive pickup of local thunderstorm static, during our tests the antenna's amp never suffered static damage during storms; indeed, even nearby one kilowatt shortwave transmissions did no damage to the antenna amplifier. Protected circuitry, using an easily replaced 315 mA fuse. Superior factory support. *ALA 1530+:* Nominal full-spec operating frequency range of 50 kHz to 100 MHz. Nominal mediumwave AM IP3 improvement, resulting from nominal faint drop in mediumwave AM gain; however, neither can be confirmed as they are too small to measure—or matter. *ALA 1530:* Nominal full-spec operating frequency range of 150 kHz (30 kHz with reduced sensitivity) to 30 MHz.

Con: Extended frequency range, as compared to the sibling '330S, can result in mediumwave AM signals surfacing within the shortwave spectrum, degrading reception—usually a more significant issue in urban and suburban North America than elsewhere (even an unsophisticated rotor can help by turning the antenna perpendicular to an offending mediumwave AM signal's axis); this tends to be less of a problem at night because of reduced local transmitting powers, and is less of a problem in our latest unit. Prone to overloading some receivers in locations rich with strong mediumwave AM signals; this also tends to be less of a problem at night because of reduced local transmitting powers. Only moderate gain, slightly less than sibling ALA 330S, for reception within such modest-signal areas as Western Hemisphere, Asia and Australasia. Balanced loop receiving element, about one meter across, not easy to mount and is large and cumbersome to ship. Mounting mast and optional rotor add to cost and complexity of erection. BNC connector at the receiving element's base is open to the weather and thus needs to be user-sealed with Coax Seal, electrical putty or similar. Encapsulated amplifier makes repair impossible. Manufacturer cautions against allowing high winds to stress mounting flange; however, after three years of wind and sun at one outdoor test location, nothing untoward has materialized. Manufacturer cautions against allowing sunlight to damage head amplifier's plastic housing; yet, after three years of intense exposure at a high-UV PASSPORT test site, Wellbrook's plastic seems no worse for the wear than any other outdoor antenna's plastic. Adaptor supplied for 117V AC runs warm after being plugged in for a few hours, while amplifier tends to run slightly warm; nonetheless, after three years of use at PASSPORT test facility, neither has acted up. No coaxial cable supplied. Available for purchase or export only two cumbersome ways: via Sterling cheque or International Money Order through the Welsh manufacturer (www.wellbrook.uk.com), or with credit card via an English dealer's unsecured email address (sales@shortwave.co.uk).

☞ An antenna tuner may improve signal level by as much as 6 dB.

☞ Mediumwave AM and longwave performance directionality may suffer if the '1530 is not mounted well away from other antennas.

☞ The '1530 is the sibling of the former ALA 330, not the newer ALA 330S.

☞ The "P" version, not tested, uses a semi-rigid plastic loop rather than aluminum and is for indoor use.

Verdict: Interested in distant broadcast goodies below the shortwave spectrum, as well as tuning world band? If so, the Wellbrook ALA 1530+ and ALA 1530 are hard to beat—so long as you don't live near local mediumwave AM transmission facilities. A rotor is *de rigeur* for nulling co-channel interference below 1.7 MHz, and also may help a skosh with tropical world band stations. As with all Wellbrook loop antennas the '1530+ and '1530 excel at rejecting noise and static, particularly below 8 MHz.

For multiband coverage, including mediumwave AM and longwave, the '1530+ and '1530 are both top-drawer choices. Both are comparably solid performers for world band, although not quite equal to siblings ALA 100 and ALA 330S.

Last year's unit or this year's, Plus or regular version, differences come down to how many angels can be put on the head of a pin. Wellbrook simply rules this segment of the antenna market.

Evaluation of "Plus" Version: The frequency specification for the Plus version has been stretched in both directions: from 50 kHz to 100 MHz in place of the regular version's 150 kHz to 30 MHz; as there is no frequency response specification for either loop, this could mean any number of things. Too, the Plus has a nominal peak response within the 87.5–108 MHz FM band, which should interest FM DXers who can't or prefer not to use large multi-element yagis.

The '1530+ nominally has slightly less mediumwave AM gain and marginally better resistance to overloading than the '1530,

STEALTH ANTENNAS

Listeners facing antenna restrictions have concocted a dog's breakfast of hidden and camouflaged outdoor wire antennas. Some look like a clothesline or part of a badminton net. Yet others are tucked underneath awnings or canopies.

Some folks play to urban apathy by hanging thin-wire antennas out in the open, then waiting to see what happens. One creative Australian even told a curious neighbor that his loop antenna was an "art sculpture"—it worked!

Trompe d'oeil antennas can perform surprisingly well when mated to the MFJ-1020C, around $90. Just remove its telescopic antenna and—*voilà*—it becomes a Grade A tunable active preselector.

Deep pockets? If you want something suitably James Bondish, the SGC Stealth Antenna Kit (not tested) from wsplc.com is £329.95 in the United Kingdom, $544.77 plus shipping overseas.

but the changes are too small to be statistically significant. In principle this variation may be of interest in marginal high-RF environments, but as a practical matter we found no perceptible difference even in a location with reasonable strong nearby mediumwave AM stations. As expected, within the shortwave spectrum the two versions fare identically.

Changes in Latest Regular Version: No meaningful changes were found. The latest sample of the regular ALA 1530 performs as did the last unit.

❂❂❂½ *Passport's Choice*

RF Systems DX-One Professional Mark II

Outdoor-indoor "eggbeater." Active, remote, broadband, 0.02–60 MHz.

Price: *DX-One Pro antenna:* $669.95 in the United States. £359.95 in the United Kingdom. €498.00 in Germany.

The pricey RF Systems DX-One Professional Mark II has outstanding dynamic range. J.R. Sherwood

Pro: Outstanding dynamic range. Very low noise. Outputs for two receivers. Comes standard with switchable band rejection filter to reduce the chances of mediumwave AM signals ghosting into the shortwave spectrum. Receiving element has outstanding build quality. Coaxial connector at head amplifier is completely shielded from the weather by a clever mechanical design. Superior low noise, high gain performance on mediumwave AM.

Con: Unbalanced design makes antenna susceptible to importing buzz at some locations; this is especially noticeable because of otherwise-excellent performance. AC power supply not bypassed as well as it could be, causing slight hum on some signals. More likely than most antennas to exacerbate fading, even though design nominally reduces fading effects. No coaxial cable supplied. Output position for 10 dB gain measures +6 dB. Warranty only six months.

Verdict: The pricey RF Systems DX-One Professional Mark II is a superior performer. As with any antenna having a small capture area and an unbalanced design, at some locations it is prone to picking up local electrical noise. Made in the Netherlands.

❂❂❂½

DX Engineering DXE-ARAH-1P

Outdoor-indoor dipole. Active, remote, broadband 0.06–30 MHz.

Price: *DXE-ARAH-1P:* $259.00 (about $300 with shipping) in the United States. *Aftermarket coaxial cable and plugs (required):* Usually $15–45 in the United States.

Pro: Unusual capture length helps produce superior signal-to-noise ratio. Unlike with some other compact antennas, feedline does not act as involuntary antenna. Worthy gain above about 9 MHz, rising to peak at 27 MHz. Excellent freedom from mediumwave AM "ghosting" when internal jumper configured to roll off below 3 MHz. Very good mediumwave AM and longwave performance when 1) internal jumper configured for flat response, and 2) antenna located in relatively rural setting with no nearby mediumwave AM stations. Excellent build quality. Circuit board not potted, facilitating repair.

Con: Uses two nine-foot (2.75 meter) CB whips for pickup element, so takes up much more space than usual for a compact antenna. Eighteen-foot (5.5 meter) wingspan limits mounting options if rotatability desired to null co-channel interference on mediumwave AM. If configured by jumper to receive mediumwave AM, overloading/intermodulation may occur at urban and suburban locations—especially with nearby stations below 1 MHz; according to the factory, single-whip version (DXE-ARAV-1P, $229 plus shipping) doesn't have this problem but requires grounding. Mediumwave AM and longwave gain drops sharply when jumper configured to avoid intermodulation within shortwave spectrum. Amplifier box not weatherproof without obtaining and applying sealant. No coaxial cables or printed owner's manual. Not widely available; when ordered from manufacturer, shipping charges not indicated until order nearly completed.

Verdict: A robustly constructed performer that is more active than compact. It acquits itself well from about 5 to 30 MHz, but similar performance can be had for less, while better performance isn't much costlier.

✪✪✪
Dressler ARA 100 HDX

Outdoor-indoor rod. Active, remote, broadband, 0.04–40 MHz.

Price: $549.95 in the United States.

Pro: Superior build quality, with fiberglass whip and foam-encapsulated head amplifier to resist the weather (*see* Con). Very good gain below 20 MHz (*see* Con). Superior signal-to-noise ratio. Handy detachable "N" connector on bottom. AC adaptor with properly bypassed and regulated DC output is better than most. Suitable for packing diagonally in wide suitcase.

Con: Even though it has an amplifier with superior dynamic range, tends to overload

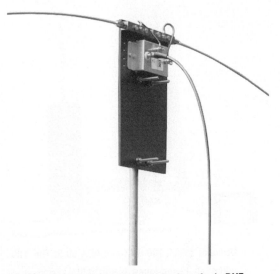

Like the Wellbrook ALA 100, DX Engineering's DXE-ARAH-1P is unusually large.   J.R. Sherwood

in urban/suburban environments awash in powerful mediumwave AM signals unless antenna element mounted close to the ground; this tends to be less of a problem at night because of reduced local transmitting powers. Encapsulated design makes most repairs impossible. Above 20 MHz gain begins to fall off slightly. Body of antenna runs slightly warm. "N" connector at the head amplifier/receiving element exposed to weather, needs to be sealed with Coax Seal, electrical putty or similar by user. Gain control cumbersome to adjust; fortunately, in practice it is rarely needed. Reader reports suggest that ordering direct from the factory can be a frustrating experience.

☞ Star rating applies only when used where there is not significant ambient mediumwave RF, as the Dressler ARA 100 HDX, unless mounted close to the ground, is prone to overloading at locations rich with strong mediumwave AM signals or low-band VHF-TV stations. At some locations, even mounting antenna on the ground does not eliminate overloading. Mediumwave AM overloading seems exacerbated by pickup from coaxial cable lead-in, as it is not properly decoupled from antenna (unlike Wellbrook and DX Engineering models, which can be mounted high with long cables).

Dressler's ARA 100 HDX and ARA 60 S. The '100, although discontinued, is still sold.   J. R. Sherwood

☞ Discontinued in 2006 and no longer stocked by most dealers. However, Universal Radio in the United States estimates that it has enough inventory to handle orders well into 2007. Also, check out the similar Dressler ARA 60 S, below.

Verdict: The robust Dressler ARA 100 HDX, made in Germany, is an excellent but costly low-noise antenna for locations not near one or more powerful mediumwave AM or low-band VHF-TV transmitters. Discontinued, but still available new.

❋❋❋ ✍ *Passport's Choice*
MFJ-1020C (with short wire element)

Outdoor-indoor wire. Active, remote, manual preselection, 0.3–40 MHz.

Price: *MFJ-1020C (without antenna wire or insulators):* $89.95 in the United States. CAD$119.95 in Canada. £89.95 in the United Kingdom. €89.00 in Germany. *MFJ-1312D 120V AC adaptor:* $15.95 in the United States. CAD$29.00 in Canada. *MFJ-1312DX 240V AC adaptor:* £15.95 in the United Kingdom. *Radio Shack 278-758 "Outdoor Antenna Kit":* $9.99 in the United States.

Pro: Superior dynamic range, so functions effectively with an outboard wire receiving element, preferably mounted outdoors, in lieu of built-in telescopic antenna element.

Sharp preselector peak unusually effective in preventing overloading. Works best off battery (*see* Con). Choice of PL-259 or RCA connections. Suitable for travel. 30-day money-back guarantee if purchased from manufacturer.

Con: Preselector complicates operation; tune control needs adjustment even with modest frequency changes, especially within the mediumwave AM band. Knobs small and touchy to adjust. High current draw (measures 30 mA), so battery runs down quickly. Removing sheet-metal screws often to change battery should eventually result in stripping unless great care is taken. AC adaptor, optional, causes significant hum on many received signals.

☞ The '1020C serves little or no useful purpose as a tunable preselector for reasonably long inverted-L antennas (anything above around 50–75 feet or 15–20 meters) or resonant outdoor wire antennas. Additionally, the amplifier circuit is always present, so the '1020C cannot be used as an unamplified preselector targeted to improve front-end selectivity with significant wire antennas. Simply reducing amplification gain to improve front-end selectivity may or may not help to a degree, but it won't improve the signal-to-noise ratio or dynamic range. The reason is that the amplifier's gain potentiometer is merely an output pad (measured range of 40 dB).

☞ Two manufacturing flaws found on one of our "B" version units tested in the past, but the latest "C" unit had no defects. The owner's manual warns of possible "taking off" if the gain is set too high, but during our tests using a variety of receivers we encountered oscillation with only one model.

Verdict: The '1020C has a little secret: It's only okay the way the manufacturer sells it as a proximate active antenna, but as a preselector with an outdoor random-length wire antenna it is a worthy low-cost performer—better, in fact, than MFJ's designated shortwave preselector. Simply collapse (or, better, remove) the built-in telescopic antenna, then connect an outboard wire antenna to the '1020C's external antenna input. For this, Radio Shack's "Outdoor

Antenna Kit" or equivalent works fine if the receiving element has been significantly shortened to a convenient length.

Alas, the optional AC adaptor introduces hum much of the time, battery drain is considerable, and changing the built-in battery is inconvenient and relies on wear-prone sheet-metal screws. Best bet, unless you're into experimenting with power supplies: Skip the adaptor and use a large outboard rechargeable battery.

Peso for peso, the MFJ-1020C fed by a remote wire receiving element is the best buy among active antennas. The rub is that the use of several yards or meters of wire, preferably outdoors, makes it something of a hybrid requiring more space than other active antennas. But for many row houses, townhouses, ground-floor and rooftop apartments with a patch of outdoor space it can be a godsend. If visibility is an issue, use ultra-thin wire for the receiving element.

The MFJ-1020C is pitched as a proximate active antenna. Yet, it is also MFJ's best for amplifying a homebrew wire receiving element. J.R. Sherwood

⭑⭑⭑
Dressler ARA 60 S

Outdoor-indoor rod. Active, remote, broadband, 0.04–60/100 MHz.

Price: $349.95 in the United States. £239.95 in the United Kingdom. €209.00 in Germany.

Pro: Superior build quality, with fiberglass whip and foam-encapsulated head amplifier to resist weather (*see* Con). Very good and consistent gain, even above 20 MHz. AC adaptor with properly bypassed and regulated DC output is better than most. Suitable for packing diagonally in wide suitcase.

Con: Encapsulated design makes most repairs impossible. RG-58 coaxial cable permanently attached on antenna end, making user replacement impossible. Gain control cumbersome to adjust; fortunately, in practice it is rarely needed. Reader reports suggest that ordering direct from the factory can be a frustrating experience.

☞ Star rating applies only when used where there is not significant ambient mediumwave RF, as the Dressler ARA 60 S, unless mounted close to the ground, appears

to be prone to overloading at locations rich with strong mediumwave AM signals or low-band VHF-TV stations. At some locations, even mounting antenna on the ground may not eliminate overloading. Mediumwave AM overloading seems exacerbated by pickup from coaxial cable lead-in, as it does not appear to be properly decoupled from antenna (unlike Wellbrook and DX Engineering models, which can be mounted high with long cables).

Verdict: The robust Dressler ARA 60 S, made in Germany, is an excellent low-noise antenna for locations not near one or more powerful mediumwave AM or low-band VHF-TV transmitters. It is very similar to the ARA 100 HDX—even its dynamic range and overloading performance are virtually identical. This makes the German-made ARA 60 S an excellent lower-cost alternative to the ARA 100 HDX.

⭑⭑⅞
RF Systems GMDSS-1

Outdoor vertical rod. Passive, remote, broadband, 0.1–25 MHz.

Price: *Antenna:* $219.95 in the United States. €150.00 in the Netherlands. *AK-1 mounting bracket kit:* $22.95 in the United States. *AK-2 mounting bracket kit:* $34.95 in the United States. €32.00 in the Netherlands.

Pro: Superior signal-to-noise ratio for a compact antenna except within 21 MHz segment. Superior rejection of local electrical noise. Passive (unamplified) design avoids hum, buzz and other shortcomings often inherent with active antennas (*see* Con). No amplification required; yet, from about 9 MHz through 12 MHz this short antenna (6.5 feet, two meters) produces signals almost comparable to those from a lengthy outdoor wire antenna (*see* Con). Passive design allows it to function in emergency situations where electricity is not assured. Vertical configuration unusually appropriate for certain locations; can be further camouflaged with non-metallic paint. Superior build quality, using stainless steel and heavy UV resistant PVC; also, internal helical receiving element is rigorously sealed (*see* Con). No radials required, unusual for a vertical antenna. Worthy mediumwave AM reception for a nondirectional antenna.

Con: Except for approximately 9 MHz through 12 MHz, weak-signal performance varies from fair to poor, depending on the tuned frequency. A mounting kit is required and is extra. The AK-1 mounting bracket kit, sold in North America, not stainless. Connecting cable between antenna and radio not included.

☞ A slightly less costly ($199.95) variant of the GMDSS-1 is the RF Systems MTA-1, which nominally operates to full specification from 0.5–30 MHz.

Verdict: Although unamplified and scarcely taller than most men, the RF Systems GMDSS-1 vertical performs surprisingly well. However, pedestrian signal oomph in many world band segments limits its attraction except with a high-sensitivity receiver or an active preselector. Some portables also benefit from the modest signal input.

Made in the Netherlands, it is constructed like a tank. Between this and its complete independence from electricity, it is unusually appropriate for emergencies, civil disorders and hostile climates.

RF Systems' GMDSS-1 uses no power. It's tough, but suboptimal for faint signals.   D. Zantow

New for 2007
✪✪⅞
AOR LA380

Indoor loop. Active, essentially proximate, manual preselection 3–40 MHz/ broadband 0.01–3 MHz & 40–500 MHz

Price: *LA380 antenna:* $369.95 in the United States. £189.00 in the United Kingdom. *BNC female-to-PL259 adaptor:* $4.95 in the United States.

Pro: Above-average gain. High-Q tunable preselector reduces the possibility of overload between 3 and 40 MHz (*see* Con). Rotatability nulls (reduces) local electrical noise and static below 10 MHz, to a lesser extent up to about 18 MHz. Rotatability can sometimes also slightly reduce co-channel shortwave interference; as is the norm with loop antennas, this modest nulling of co-channel skywave interference is best at frequencies below 5 MHz. Outstanding reception of time signals on 40 and 60 kHz, which have preset tuning. Very easy to rotate and tune, with large knobs. Loop receiving element can be remotely mounted up to 16 feet (five meters) away (*see* Con). Hum-free AC adaptor complemented by built-in voltage regulator in base unit. Knobs use set screws. Very solid metal lower box that has beefy non-stick-on rubber feet; uses machined, not self-tapping, cabinet/loop and BNC-connector screws. Three-foot male-to-male BNC cable. Small footprint. One-foot (30 cm) loop and small base module make antenna suitable for travel.

Con: Quasi-proximate model with preselector controls on receiving element; however, to be practical that element needs to be within user's grasp to adjust 3–40 MHz tunable preselector. High-"Q" preselection requires frequent tweaking when frequencies changed between 3–40 MHz. Tunable preselection, desirable, limited to 3–40 MHz; except for 40 and 60 kHz, which are specially peaked, other frequencies are broadband. Mediocre mediumwave AM performance. Male BNC connector on receiving element not snug, rocks slightly. Tuned by inexpensive plastic-cased tuning capacitor, underwhelming for price class. Receiving element in plastic box; cover merely snaps on. Lacks 16-foot (five meter) male BNC/BNC cable for nominal remote mounting of receiving element. Lacks BNC female-to-PL259 adaptor for connection to many models of tabletop receivers.

Verdict: The nicely sized AOR LA380 is a decent performer—free from spurious signals, overloading and hum. Yet, its tunable preselector is part of the receiving element and needs frequent tweaking, so remote mounting isn't practical.

Where local electrical noise doesn't intrude, the '380's superior gain, handy size and ease of rotation make it an effective choice for indoor use. Made in Japan, generally well constructed and priced accordingly.

Evaluation of New Model: The AOR LA380 consists of a base unit with amplifier, a 30 cm (one foot) loop with tunable preselection and "band" selection knobs—an AC adaptor, too. The '380 is a tuned, unbalanced loop, unlike Wellbrook's untuned, balanced loops. However, dividing the shortwave spectrum into two "bands" and peaking within those "bands" results in excellent gain and reduces the possibility of overload.

Unlike the predecessor LA350, which needed four interchangeable receiving elements, the '380 uses a single one-foot (30 cm) element—an ergonomic leap forward. It offers nominal coverage of 10 kHz to 500 MHz, but with rare exception best performance is where high-Q tunable preselection takes place: 3 to 40 MHz.

The LA380 has healthy gain within that preselection tuning range, improving somewhat as frequency rises. For example, it produces hefty signals in the important 15 MHz (19 meter) daytime world band segment.

Outside the preselector's frequency range, operation is broadband—handy, as no tuning is required. But there's also no peaking except for longwave time signals in Japan (40 kHz) and WWVB in Ft. Collins, CO (60 kHz). Interestingly, the diminutive LA380 picks up WWVB with as much aplomb as a 40-foot (12 meter) ALA 100 loop (*see*), and about 15 dB better than the excellent ALA 1530 loop (*see*).

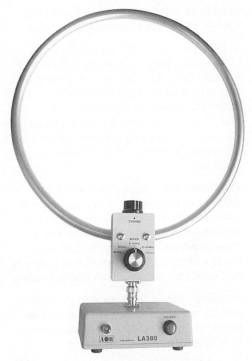

Loop antennas tend to be large, but not the small-footprint **AOR LA380**. It is tunable and fully rotatable.   D. Zantow

Mediumwave AM performance is another story. In the required "other" band setting, the LA380 is vastly inferior to the ALA 1530—even the ALA 330S, not designed for mediumwave AM, performs better. Loops have long been antennas of choice for mediumwave AM, but every rule has an exception and the '380 is it.

A loop characteristically shows a figure-of-eight reception pattern on longwave and mediumwave AM. But as this loop is unbalanced, this classic pattern is more like a lopsided-eight around the lower-middle part of the shortwave spectrum. For example, it has a hypercardioid pattern that's particularly noticeable within the 7 MHz (41 meter) world band segment.

Remote Placement Impractical

AOR recommends placing the loop pickup element near a window. However, it also points out that a coaxial cable extension of up to 16 feet (five meters) will allow for remote placement of the pickup element.

In principle, this should do wonders to enhance reception by improving the signal-to-noise ratio. Alas, this option is woefully impractical, as the loop needs to be retuned after each significant frequency change and all tuning controls are on the pickup element. The resulting bending and reaching is enough to wear down Jane Fonda on Gatorade.

The supplied AC adaptor works well on world band frequencies. AOR recommends using a better-regulated power supply for mediumwave AM reception to overcome noise generated by the supplied AC adaptor. However, the '350 performs so poorly in that band that the recommendation is moot.

Traveling? The AL380 is easy to assemble and fits reasonably into a suitcase. But be prepared for the inevitable furrowed brows from diligent airport inspectors.

✪✪¾ ✪ *Passport's Choice*
Sony AN-LP1

Indoor-portable loop. Active, remote, manual preselection, 3.9–4.3/4.7–25 MHz.

Sony's AN-LP1 has long been the best portable antenna. Alas, it's virtually impossible to obtain new, and used samples don't surface often.   J.R. Sherwood

Price: ¥8,800 as available in Japan.

Pro: Excellent for use with portables. Very good overall performance, including generally superior gain (*see* Con), especially within world band segments—yet surprisingly free from side effects. Battery operation, so no internally caused hum or noise (*see* Con). Clever compact folding design for airline and other travel; also handy for institutional use where antenna must be stashed periodically. Can be used even with portables that have no antenna input jack (*see* Con). Plug-in filter to reduce local electrical noise (*see* Con). Low battery consumption (*see* Con).

Con: Discontinued, so hard-to-impossible to find anymore. Indoors only—can't be mounted outdoors during inclement weather. Functions acceptably on shortwave only 3.9–4.3 MHz and 4.7–25 MHz, with no mediumwave AM or longwave coverage. Gain varies markedly throughout the shortwave spectrum, in large part because the preselector's step-tuned resonances lack variable peaking. Preselector bandswitching complicates operation slightly. Operates only from batteries (two "AA," not included)—no AC adaptor provided, not even a socket for one. Consumer-grade plastic construction with no shielding. When clipped onto a telescopic antenna instead of fed through an antenna jack, the lack of a ground connection reduces performance. Plug-in noise filter unit reduces signal strength by several decibels.

☞ Sony recommends that the AN-LP1 not be used with the discontinued Sony ICF-SW77 receiver. However, our tests indicate that so long as the control box and loop receiving element are kept as far as possible from the radio, the antenna performs well.

☞ The Sony ICF-SW07 compact portable comes with an AN-LP2 antenna. This is virtually identical in concept and performance to the AN-LP1, except that because it is designed solely for use with the 'SW07 it has automatic preselection to simplify operation. The AN-LP2 cannot be used with other radios, even those from Sony.

Verdict: This is the handiest model for travelers wanting superior world band reception on portables—and it is truly portable. It is often a worthy choice for portatop and table-top models, as well, provided you don't mind battery-only operation. This Japanese-made device has generally excellent gain, low noise and few side effects. Priced right, too.

There is limited frequency coverage—90/120 meter DXers should look else-where—and the loop receiving element cannot be mounted permanently outdoors. Too, the lack of variable preselector peaking causes gain to vary greatly by frequency. Otherwise, the Sony AN-LP1 has been nothing short of a bargain.

The AN-LP1 was discontinued in the first half of 2006, so it's almost impossible to find at retail. Other than going to a few Japanese outlets, who even then have to special-order it, the only hope is to try eBay.

The TPA proximate antenna. Ameco is one of the oldest surviving names in American electronics. J.R. Sherwood

✪✪½ 🅒
Ameco TPA

Indoor rod. Active, proximate, manual preselection, 0.22–30 MHz.

Price: $76.95 in the United States. CAD$119.95 in Canada.

Pro: Highest recovered signal with the longest supplied antenna of the four proximate models tested. Most pleasant unit to tune to proper frequency. Superior ergonomics, including easy-to- read front panel with good-sized metal knobs (*see* Con). Superior gain below 10 MHz. Suitable for travel.

Con: Proximate model, so receiving element has to be placed near receiver. Above 15 MHz gain slips to slightly below average. Overloads with external antenna; because gain potentiometer is in the first stage, decreasing gain may increase overloading as current drops through the FET. Preselector complicates operation, compromising otherwise-superior ergonomics. No rubber feet, slides around in use; user-remediable. No AC adaptor. Consumer-grade plastic construction with no shielding. Comes with no printed information on warranty; however, manufacturer states by telephone that it is the customary one year.

Verdict: Back in the heyday of Hammarlund, Hallicrafters and National, there also was Ameco with its CW learning kits and the like. While most other American radio firms were crushed by the advance of technology, Ameco stayed light on its feet and survived. Well, sort of. Since 2004 Ameco has been associated with a new firm, Milestone Technologies of Colorado.

Ameco's TPA active antenna remains one of the best proximate models tested for bringing in usable signals with a telescopic antenna, and signal recovery is excellent. However, when connected to an external antenna it overloads badly, and reducing gain doesn't help.

✪✪½
McKay Dymek DA100E, McKay Dymek DA100EM, Stoner Dymek DA100E, Stoner Dymek DA100EM

Indoor-outdoor-marine rod. Active, remote, broadband, 0.05–30 MHz.

Price: *DA100E:* $179.95 in the United States. *DA100EM (marine version, not tested):* $199.95 in the United States.

Pro: Respectable gain and noise. Generally good build quality, with worthy coaxial cable and an effectively sealed receiving element;

Although George McKay died in 2005, his DA100-series base and marine antennas continue to evolve.

J.R. Sherwood

marine version (not tested) appears to be even better yet for resisting weather. Jack for second antenna when turned off. Minor gain rolloff at higher shortwave frequencies. Marginally suitable for travel. *DA100EM (not tested):* Weather-resistant fiberglass whip and brass fittings help ensure continued optimum performance.

Con: Slightly higher noise floor compared to other models. Some controls may confuse initially. Dynamic range among the lowest of any model tested; for many applications in the Americas this is adequate, but for use near local transmitters, or in Europe and other strong-signal parts of the world, the antenna is best purchased on a returnable basis. *DA100E:* Telescopic antenna allows moisture and avian waste penetration between segments, and thus potential resistance and/or spurious signals; user should seal these gaps with Coax Seal, electrical putty or similar. Telescopic antenna could, in principle, be de-telescoped by birds, ice and the like, although we did not actually encounter this. Warranty only 30 days.

Verdict: The DA100E is a proven "out of the box" choice, with generally excellent weatherproofing and coaxial cable. Because its dynamic range is relatively modest, it is more prone than some other models to overload, especially in an urban environment or other high-signal-strength location. In principle the extra twenty bucks for the

marine version should be a good investment, provided its fiberglass whip is not too visible for your location.

✪✪¼
MFJ-1024

Indoor-outdoor rod. Active, remote, broadband, 0.05–30 MHz.

Price: $149.95 in the United States. £139.95 in the United Kingdom. €161 in Germany. *MFJ-1312D 120V AC adaptor:* $15.95 in the United States. CAD$29.00 in Canada. *MFJ-1312DX 240V AC adaptor:* £15.95 in the United Kingdom.

Pro: Overall good gain and low noise. A/B selector for quick connection to another receiver. "Aux" input for passive antenna. Marginally suitable for travel. 30-day money-back guarantee if purchased from manufacturer.

Con: Significant hum with supplied AC adaptor; remedied when we substituted a suitable aftermarket adaptor. Non-standard power socket complicates substitution of AC adaptor; also, adaptor's sub-mini plug can spark when inserted while the adaptor is plugged in; adaptor should be unplugged beforehand. Dynamic range among the lowest of any model tested; for many applications in the Americas it is adequate, but for use near local transmitters, or in Europe and other strong-signal parts of the world, antenna is best purchased on a returnable basis. Slightly increased noise floor compared to other models. Telescopic antenna allows moisture and avian waste penetration between segments, and thus potential resistance and/or spurious signals; user should seal these gaps with Coax Seal, electrical putty or similar. Telescopic antenna could, in principle, be de-telescoped by birds, ice and the like after installation, although we did not actually encounter this. Control box/amplifier has no external weather sealing to protect from moisture, although the printed circuit board nominally comes with a water-resistant coating. Coaxial cable to receiver not provided. Mediocre coaxial cable provided between control box and receiving element. On our unit, a coaxial connector came poorly soldered from the factory.

Verdict: The MFJ-1024, made in America, performs almost identically to the Stoner Dymek DA100E, but sells for $40 less. However, that gap lessens if you factor in the cost of a worthy AC adaptor—assuming you can find or alter one to fit the unusual power jack—and the quality of the 1024's coaxial cable is not in Dymek's league.

✪✪¼
MFJ-1020C

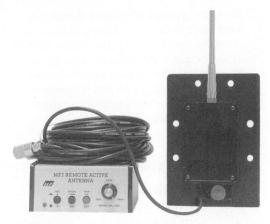

The MFJ 1024 succeeds because it is remote, yet straightforward to erect and operate.   J.R. Sherwood

Indoor rod. Active, proximate, manual preselection, 0.3–40 MHz.

Price: *MFJ-1020C:* $89.95 in the United States. CAD$119.95 in Canada. £89.95 in the United Kingdom. €89.00 in Germany. *MFJ-1312D 120V AC adaptor:* $15.95 in the United States. CAD$29.00 in Canada. *MFJ-1312DX 240V AC adaptor:* £15.95 in the United Kingdom.

Pro: Rating rises to three stars if converted from a proximate to a remote model by connecting a wire to the external antenna input; see separate review, above. Superior dynamic range, and sharp preselector peak unusually effective in preventing overloading. Works best off battery (*see* Con). Choice of PL-259 or RCA connections. Suitable for travel. 30-day money-back guarantee if purchased from manufacturer.

Con: Proximate model, so receiving element has to be placed near receiver (can be converted, *see* Pro). Preselector complicates operation; tune control needs adjustment even with modest frequency changes, especially within the mediumwave AM band. Knobs small and touchy to adjust. High current draw (measures 30 mA), so battery runs down quickly. Removing sheet-metal screws often to change battery should eventually result in stripping unless great care is taken. AC adaptor, optional, causes significant hum on many received signals.

☞ Two manufacturing flaws found on one of our "B" version units tested in the past,

but this year's "C" unit had no defects. The owner's manual warns of possible "taking off" if the gain is set too high, but during our tests using a variety of receivers we encountered oscillation with only one model.

Verdict: The MFJ-1020C, made in the United States, is okay as a proximate antenna with its own telescopic antenna. However, it works much better when coupled to a random-length wire in lieu of the built-in telescopic antenna; see the separate review earlier in this article.

The MFJ 1020C "twofer" works either as a proximate active antenna or as an amplifier for a remote antenna.

J.R. Sherwood

Alas, the optional AC adaptor introduces hum much of the time, battery drain is considerable, and changing the built-in battery is inconvenient and relies on wear-prone sheet-metal screws. Best bet, unless you're into experimenting with power supplies: Skip the adaptor and use a large outboard rechargeable battery.

★★ ◉
Degen DE31, Kaito KA31, Thieking DE31

Indoor-portable loop. Active, remote, manual preselection, 3.9–22 MHz

Price: *Kaito KA31:* $39.95 in the United States. *Thieking DE31:* €59.00 in Germany. *Thieking DE31A (not tested):* €72.50 in Germany.

Pro: Appropriate for use with portables. Meaningful gain, especially above 9 MHz. Very good dynamic range. Low noise and absence of spurious signals. Battery operation, so no internally caused hum or noise (*see* Con). Compact collapsible design for airline and other travel; also handy for institutional use where antenna must be stashed

With the demise of Sony's AN-LP1 portable antenna, the Kaito KA31 has taken up the slack. Also sold as the Degen DE31 and Thieking DE31.

periodically. Long cable (*see* Con) allows loop to be placed relatively far from radio. Adaptor sometimes allows for connection to a receiver lacking 1/8-inch antenna jack (*see* Con). Fairly low current draw (*see* Con).

Con: Indoors only—can't be mounted outdoors during inclement weather. Tunes only 3.9–22 MHz, so no mediumwave AM or longwave coverage. Touchy tuning control. Operates only from batteries (two "AAA," not included) and has no AC adaptor or socket. Battery consumption, although low, nearly twice manufacturer's specification, so replacement rises accordingly. Consumer-grade plastic construction with no shielding. When clipped onto radio's telescopic antenna instead of fed through an antenna jack, the lack of a ground connection on the radio greatly reduces performance. Rotation for local-noise reduction impeded by limp-rope design. Small suction cup fails if it and glass surface not exceptionally clean. Affixed suction cup not easy to remove. No carrying pouch to keep parts together. No reel to keep main cable from being tangled.

Verdict: Respectable performance, minimal investment.

★★
Vectronics AT-100

Indoor rod. Active, proximate, manual preselection, 0.3–30 MHz.

Price: $89.95 in the United States. CAD$109.00 in Canada. £69.95 in the United Kingdom.

Pro: Good—sometimes excellent—gain (*see* Con), especially in the mediumwave AM band. Good dynamic range. Most knobs are commendably large. Suitable for travel.

Con: Proximate model, so receiving element has to be placed near receiver. No AC power; although it accepts an AC adaptor, the lack of polarity markings complicates adaptor choice (it is center-pin positive). Preselector complicates operation, especially as it is stiff to tune and thus awkward to peak. Our unit oscillated badly with some receivers, limiting usable gain—although it was more stable with other receivers, and thus appears to be a function of the load presented by a given receiver.

Verdict: If ever there were a product that needs to be purchased on a returnable basis, this is it. W ith one receiver, this American-made model gives welcome gain and worthy performance; with another, it goes into oscillation nearly at the drop of a hat.

★¾
Palstar AA30/AA30A/AA30P

Indoor rod. Active, proximate, manual preselection, 0.3–30 MHz.

Price: *AA30/AA30A:* $99.95 in the United States. £69.95 in the United Kingdom.

Pro: Moderate-to-good gain. Tuning control easily peaked. Can be powered directly by the Palstar R30/R30C and Lowe HF-350 tabletop receivers, an internal battery or an AC adaptor. Suitable for travel.

Con: Spurious oscillation throughout 14–30 MHz range. Overloads with external antenna. Proximate model, so receiving element has to be placed near receiver. Preselector complicates operation. No AC adaptor.

☞ Although the AA30A's cabinets are silk screened simply as "AA30," the accompanying owner's manual refers to the "AA30A."

Verdict: Oscillation makes this a dubious choice except for reception below 14 MHz. Manufactured in the United States.

★¾ ✆
MFJ-1022

Indoor rod. Active, proximate, broadband, 0.3–200 MHz.

Price: *MFJ-1022:* $59.95 in the United States. £59.95 in the United Kingdom. €62.00 in Germany. *MFJ-1312D 120V AC adaptor:* $14.95 in the United States. CAD$29.00 in Canada. *MFJ-1312DX 240V AC adaptor:* £15.95 in the United Kingdom.

Pro: Unusually broadband coverage reaches well into VHF spectrum. Considerable gain, peaking at 22.5 MHz, audibly helps signals that do not suffer from intermodulation.

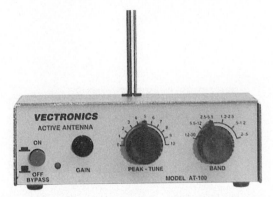

The Vectronics AT-100 outperforms the visually identical Palstar AA30, but this could be luck of the draw.

J.R. Sherwood

Idiot-proof to operate. Works best off battery (*see* Con). Suitable for travel. 30-day money-back guarantee if purchased from manufacturer.

Con: Proximate model, so receiving element has to be placed near receiver. Broadband design results in local mediumwave AM stations ghosting up to 2.7 MHz, and to a lesser degree up through the 3 MHz (90 meter) tropical world band segment at many locations; this often drops at night because of reduced local transmitting powers. Broadband design and high gain not infrequently results in intermodulation products/spurious signals and hiss between reasonable-level signals, and sometimes mixing with weaker signals. Within tropical world band segments, modest-level static from nearby thunderstorms, when coupled with overloading from local mediumwave AM signals,

The Palstar AA30 comes up short, as better performance can be found for less. J.R. Sherwood

The MFJ-1022 is no street rod. Yet, it is genuinely inexpensive, easy to operate and has a small footprint.

J.R. Sherwood

sometimes cause odd background sounds that are not heard with other antennas. High current draw (measures 35 mA), so battery runs down quickly. Removing sheet-metal screws often to change battery should eventually result in stripping unless great care is taken. AC adaptor, optional, causes significant hum on many received signals.

Verdict: Priced to move and offering broadband coverage, this compact antenna from MFJ couldn't be simpler to operate—one button, that's it. For helping to improve the listening quality of modest-strength international broadcasting signals, it works quite nicely. But don't expect to do much DXing, especially of the tropical world band segments unless you live well away from any mediumwave AM stations and maybe not even then. Forget the AC adaptor and stick to batteries.

_____

Prepared by Robert Sherwood and David Zantow, with Lawrence Magne; also, George Heidelman and Chuck Rippel.

WHERE TO FIND IT: INDEX TO TESTED ANTENNAS

PASSPORT REPORTS evaluates the most relevant indoor and outdoor antennas on the market. Here's where to find each review, with models that are new, revised or retested for 2007 shown in **bold**. Passive—unamplified—antennas are in *italics*.

A comprehensive Radio Database International White Paper®, PASSPORT® *Evaluation of Popular Outdoor Antennas*, is available for $6.95 in North America, $9.95 airmail elsewhere, including shipping. It encompasses virtually all our panel's findings and comments during testing of passive wire antennas. Also included are details for proper and safe installation, along with instructions for inverted-L construction. This unabridged report is available from key world band dealers, or order 24/7 from www.passband.com, autovoice +1 215/598-9018 or fax +1 215/598 3794—or write PASSPORT RDI White Papers, Box 300, Penn's Park, PA 18943 USA.

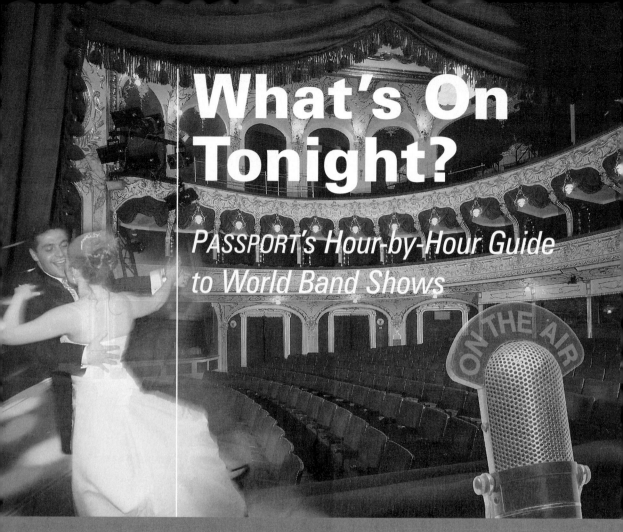

What's On Tonight?

PASSPORT's Hour-by-Hour Guide to World Band Shows

World band offers shows rarely found elsewhere. PASSPORT's "What's On" guide includes these, along with other English-language programs, with the best tagged:

■ Station superior, with several excellent shows

● Show worth hearing

Some stations provide schedules, others don't. Yet, even among those that do, data isn't always credible or complete. To resolve this, PASSPORT monitors stations around the world, firsthand, to detail schedule activity throughout the year. Additionally, to be as useful as possible, PASSPORT's schedules consist not just of observed activity, but also that which we have creatively opined will appear well into the year ahead. This predictive material is based on decades of experience, and is original from us. Although this is inherently less exact than real-time data, it has proven to be useful.

Primary frequencies are given for North America, western Europe, East Asia and Australasia, plus the Middle East, southern Africa and Southeast Asia. If you want secondary and seasonal channels, or frequencies for other parts of the world, check out "Worldwide Broadcasts in English" and the Blue Pages.

To eliminate confusion, World Time and World Day are used—both explained in "Getting Started" and "Worldly Words." Seasons are for the Northern Hemisphere (summer around July, winter around January).

00:00–05:59
North America—Evening Prime Time
Europe & Mideast—Early Morning
Australasia & East Asia—Midday and Afternoon

00:00

■**Radio Netherlands.** Tuesday through Saturday (weekday evenings in North America) there's ●*Newsline* (current events) followed by a 30-minute feature: ●*Research File* (Tuesday), ●*EuroQuest* (Wednesday), ●*Documentary* (Thursday), *Dutch Horizons* (Friday), and ●*A Good Life* (Saturday). Sunday's combo is a news feature and *Vox Humana*, replaced Monday by *Amsterdam Forum* and *Dutch Extra.* Fifty-seven minutes to eastern North America winter on 6165 kHz, and summer on 9845 kHz.

Radio Bulgaria. Winter only at this time. Tuesday through Saturday (weekday evenings in North America), *News* is followed by *Events and Developments*, replaced Sunday and Monday by *Views Behind the News.* The remaining time is taken up by regular programs such as *Keyword Bulgaria* and *Time Out for Music*, and weekly features like ●*Folk Studio* (Monday), *Sports* (Tuesday), *Magazine Economy* (Wednesday), *The Way We Live* (Thursday), *History Club* (Friday), *DX Programme* (Saturday) and *Answering Your Letters*, a listener-response show, on

Sunday. Sixty minutes to eastern North America and Central America on 7400 and 9400 kHz. One hour earlier in summer.

Radio Canada International. The start of a two-hour broadcast. Tuesday through Saturday (weekday evenings in North America), opens with *The World at Six* and continues with *As It Happens*, a combination of international stories, Canadian news and general human interest features. On the remaining days it's ●*The World This Weekend* and either Sunday's comedy show or Monday's *Maple Leaf Mailbag.* To eastern North America and the Caribbean on 9755 kHz. For a separate broadcast to Asia, see the next item.

Radio Canada International. Tuesday through Saturday, starts with *The World At Six*, replaced Sunday and Monday by ●*The World This Weekend*. The contents of the second half-hour vary seasonally. One hour to Southeast Asia winter on 9880 kHz, and summer on 11700 kHz.

Radio Japan. *News*, then Tuesday through Saturday (weekday evenings local American date) it's *A Song for Everyone* followed

00:00–00:30

Vladimir Zhamkin, director of the Voice of Russia World Service in English. VoR

by *Japan and the World 44 Minutes* (an in-depth look at current trends and events in Japan and elsewhere). This is replaced Sunday by *World Interactive*, and Monday by *Weekend Japanology* and *Japan Music Scene*. One hour to eastern North America on 6145 kHz via the powerful relay facilities of Radio Canada International in Sackville, New Brunswick. A separate 15-minute news bulletin for Southeast Asia is aired on 13650 and 17810 kHz.

Radio Exterior de España ("Spanish National Radio"). Tuesday through Saturday (local weekday evenings in the Americas), there's Spanish and international *news*, commentary, Spanish pop music, a review of the Spanish press, and a general interest feature. Weekends, it's all features, including rebroadcasts of some of the weekday programs. Sixty minutes to eastern North America winter on 6055 kHz, and summer on 15385 kHz. Popular with many listeners.

China Radio International. *News* and reports fill the first half-hour, and are followed by a daily feature: *Front Line* (Monday), *Biz China* (Tuesday), *China Horizons* (Wednesday), ●*Voices from Other Lands* (Thursday), *Life in China* (Friday), *Listeners' Garden*

(Saturday) and *In the Spotlight* (Sunday). To Europe winter on 7130 and 7345 kHz, and summer on 7130 and 9725 kHz; to North America year-round on 6020 and 9570 kHz; to East Asia winter on 5915 kHz, and summer on 13750 kHz; and to Southeast Asia winter on 11650 and 11885 kHz, and summer on 11885 and 15115 kHz. Note that these days are World Time; locally in North America it will be the previous evening.

Radio Ukraine International. Summer only at this time. Ample coverage of local issues, including news, sports, politics and culture. Worth hearing is ●*Music from Ukraine*, which fills most of the Monday (Sunday evening in the Americas) broadcast. Sixty minutes to eastern North America on 7440 (or 5810) kHz. One hour later in winter. Budget and technical limitations have reduced audibility of this station to only a fraction of what it used to be.

Voice of Greece. Monday and summer only at this time, and actually starts at 0005. Fifty-five minutes of music in *It's All Greek to Me*. To North America on 7475 and 9420 kHz; and to Australasia on 15650 kHz. One hour later in winter. Note that Monday World Time is Sunday evening in North America.

Radio Australia. Part of a 24-hour service to Asia and the Pacific. Begins with *World News*, the Monday through Friday it's *The Breakfast Club*, a mix of talk and music for listeners in the Pacific. Winter Saturdays, there's *Asia Review*, *Asia Pacific Business* and *Talking Point*; and Sunday's feature is *The Spirit of Things*. In summer, Saturday features are *In the Loop (Rewind)* and *Australian Express*, replaced Sunday by *Background Briefing* (investigative journalism) and *Perspective*. On 9660, 12080, 13630, 15240, 15415 (from 0030), 17715, 17750 (from 0030), 17775 and 17795 kHz. In North America (best during summer) try 17715 and 17795 kHz; and in East Asia tune to 13630 kHz. For Southeast Asia there's 15415, 17750 and 17775 kHz.

Radio Prague, Czech Republic. Summer only at this time. *News*, then Tuesday through Saturday (weekday evenings in the Americas) there's *Current Affairs* and one or more features: *One on One* (Tuesday); *Talking Point* (Wednesday); *Czechs in History*, *Czechs Today* or *Spotlight* (Thursday); *Panorama* and *Czech Science* (Friday); and *Business Briefs* and *The Arts* on Saturday. The Sunday lineup is *Magazine*, *ABC of Czech* and *One on One*; replaced Monday by *Mailbox* and *Letter from Prague* followed by *Encore* (classical music), *Magic Carpet* (Czech world music) or *Czech Books*. Thirty minutes to North America and the Caribbean on 7345 and 9440 kHz. One hour later in winter.

Radio Austria International. Winter only at this time. Tuesday through Saturday (weekday evenings in the Americas), the 15-minute *Report from Austria* is aired at 0013. Sunday and Monday, it's ●*Report from Austria–The Week in Review* at 0005. The remainder of the broadcast is in German and (Tuesday through Saturday) Spanish. To Central America on 7325 kHz. One hour later in summer.

Radio Thailand. *Newshour*. Thirty minutes to eastern and southern Africa, winter on 9680 kHz and summer on 9570 kHz.

All India Radio. The final 45 minutes of a much larger block of programming targeted at East and Southeast Asia, and heard well beyond. To East Asia on 9950, 11645 and 13605 kHz; and to Southeast Asia on 9705, 11620 and 13605 kHz.

Radio Cairo, Egypt. The final half-hour of a 90-minute broadcast to eastern North America. *Arabic by Radio* can be heard on the hour, and there's a daily *news* bulletin at 0015. See 2300 for more specifics. Winter on 11885 (or 11895) kHz, and summer on 11950 kHz.

Radio New Zealand International. A friendly package of *news* and features sometimes replaced by live sports commentary. Part of a 24-hour broadcast for the South Pacific, but also heard in parts of North America (especially during summer) on 15720 or 17675 kHz.

AFRTS Shortwave, USA. Network news, live sports, music and features in the upper-sideband mode from the Armed Forces Radio & Television Service. Transmitted from modestly powered U.S. Navy stations around the globe. Try 4319, 5446.5, 5765, 6350, 7811, 10320, 12133.5, 12579 and 13362 kHz.

00:30

Radio Vilnius, Lithuania. Thirty minutes of news and background reports, mainly about Lithuania. Of broader appeal is *Mailbag*, aired every other Sunday (Saturday evenings local American date). For some Lithuanian music, try the next evening, towards the end of the broadcast. To eastern North America winter on 9875 kHz and summer on 11690 kHz.

Radio Austria International. Winter only at this time. Tuesday through Saturday (weekday evenings in the Americas), there's 15 minutes of *Report from Austria* at 0043. Sunday and Monday, it's ●*Report from Austria–The Week in Review* at 0033. The remainder of the broadcast is in German and (Tuesday through Saturday) Spanish. To eastern North America on 7325 kHz. One hour later in summer.

00:30–01:00

Radio Thailand. *Newshour*. Thirty minutes to central and eastern North America on 5890 kHz, via a relay in Greenville, North Carolina.

01:00

Radio Canada International. The second of two hours to eastern North America and the Caribbean. Tuesday through Saturday (weekday evenings in North America), continues with *As It Happens*. On the remaining days, there's Sunday's ●*Global Village* (world music) and Monday's *Writers and Company*. On 9755 kHz. For a separate broadcast to western North America, see the next item.

Radio Canada International. Summer only. Tuesday through Saturday (weekday evenings in North America), opens with *The World at Six* and continues with news and background reports in *As It Happens*. On the remaining days it's ●*The World This Weekend* and either Sunday's comedy show or Monday's *Maple Leaf Mailbag*. To central and western North America on 13710 kHz. There is no equivalent winter broadcast.

■Radio Netherlands. Repeat of the 0000 broadcast; see there for specifics. Fifty-seven minutes to central North America on 6165 kHz winter, and 9845 kHz summer.

Radio Austria International. Summer only at this time. Tuesday through Saturday (weekday evenings in the Americas), there's *Report from Austria* at 0113. Sunday and Monday, it's ●*Report from Austria–The Week in Review* at 0105. The remainder of the broadcast is in German and (Tuesday through Saturday) Spanish. To Central America on 9870 kHz. One hour earlier in winter.

Radio Budapest, Hungary. Summer only at this time. *News* and features, most of which are broadcast on a non-regular basis. Thirty minutes to North America on 9590 kHz. One hour later in winter.

Radio Prague, Czech Republic. *News*, then Tuesday through Saturday (weekday eve-nings in the Americas) there's the in-depth *Current Affairs* and a feature or two: *One on One* (Tuesday), *Talking Point* (Wednesday), *Czechs in History*, *Czechs Today* or *Spotlight* (Thursday), *Panorama* and *Czech Science* (Friday), and *Business Briefs* and *The Arts* on Saturday. The Sunday news is followed by *Magazine*, *ABC of Czech* and a repeat of Wednesday's *One on One*; and Monday's lineup is *Mailbox* and *Letter from Prague* followed by *Encore* (classical music), *Magic Carpet* (Czech world music) or *Czech Books*. Thirty minutes to eastern and central North America and the Caribbean on 6200 and 7345 kHz.

RAI International—Radio Roma, Italy. Actually starts at 0055. *News* and Italian music make up this 20-minute broadcast to North America on 11800 kHz.

Radio Japan. *News*, then Tuesday through Saturday it's *A Song for Everyone* and *Japan and the World 44 Minutes* (an in-depth look at trends and events in Japan and beyond). This is replaced Sunday by *J-Melo* and *Pop Joins the World*, and Monday by *World Inter-active*. One hour to East Asia on 17845 kHz; to South Asia on 15325 kHz; to Southeast Asia on 11860 and 17810 kHz; to Austral-asia on 17685 kHz; to South America on 11935 kHz; to western North America and Central America on 17825 kHz; and to the Mideast on 5960 (summer), 6030 (winter) and 17560 kHz. The broadcast on 17685 kHz has different programming after 0115.

China Radio International. Repeat of the 0000 broadcast, but with news updates. One hour winter to North America on 6005 and 9580 kHz; and summer on 9580 and 9790 kHz, via CRI's Cuban and Canadian relays. Also to Europe winter on 7130 and 7345 kHz, and summer on 9410 and 9725 kHz. For a separate broadcast to North America, see the next item.

China Radio International. Weekdays, *News* is followed by *China Drive*, an upbeat "drive-time" show. This is replaced Sat-urday by *CRI Roundup* and ●*China Roots* (ethnic music), and Sunday by *Reports from Developing Countries* and *China Beat*

A World of Listening from Sangean and Universal!

SANGEAN

ATS-909

The **ATS-909** is the flagship of the Sangean line. It packs features and performance into a very compact and stylish package. Coverage includes all long wave, medium wave and shortwave frequencies. FM and FM stereo to the headphone jack is also available. Shortwave performance is enhanced with a wide-narrow bandwidth switch and excellent single side band performance. Five tuning methods are featured: keypad, auto scan, manual up-down, memory recall or tuning knob. The alphanumeric memory lets you store 306 presets. The three event clock-timer displays even when the radio is tuning and has 42 world city zones. The large backlit LCD also features a signal strength and battery bar graph. The ATS-909 will display RDS on PL, PS and CT for station name and clock time in areas where this service is available. Also features a record jack and tone switch. Includes AC adapter, carry case, stereo ear buds and Sangean ANT-60 roll-up antenna. 8" x 5" x 1". Requires four AA cells (not supplied). #1909

DRM-40

The **Sangean DRM-40** is the radio many shortwave listeners have been waiting for. Finally, a receiver that tunes longwave, medium wave and shortwave with built-in support of DAB, RDS and DRM. Yes, DRM! DAB is form of digital broadcast widely employed in Europe, but not currently in use North America. RDS (Radio Data System) provides information such as station name, song titles and traffic information. DRM (Digital Radio Mondiale) provides FM quality sound via shortwave. The Sangean DRM-40 will also include a Secure Data slot for MP3 audio playback from SD cards. This radio also has a clock radio function with selectable radio or buzzer alarm and sleep mode. Other refinements include: USB port, external antenna jack, line and earphone outputs. Operates from 120 VAC 60 Hz or four D cells. #0040

ATS-818ACS

Have you been waiting for a quality digital world band radio with a built-in cassette recorder? Now you have it in the exciting **Sangean ATS-818ACS**. This no-compromise receiver has full dual-conversion shortwave coverage (1.6 - 30 MHz) plus long wave, AM and FM (stereo to headphone jack). A BFO control is included for smooth SSB/CW reception. A big LCD display with dial lamp shows: frequency (1 kHz on SW), 24 hour time, battery indicator and signal strength. The receiver features an RF gain, tone control, wide-narrow selectivity, keypad entry, external antenna jack, manual tuning knob, plus 54 memories (18 for shortwave). The monaural recorder has a built-in mic and auto-shutoff. Includes AC power adapter. Requires 4 D cells and 3 AA cells (not supplied). 11" x 7" x 2". #1069

ATS-505P

The **Sangean ATS-505P** covers LW, AM, FM and all shortwave frequencies. The backlit display shows frequency or 12/24 time. Tune via the tuning knob, Up-Down buttons, auto tune, keypad or from the 45 memories. Other features include: SSB clarify knob, 9/10 kHz AM step, dial lock, stereo-mono switch, alarm by radio or buzzer, sleep-timer, tune LED, external antenna input and 6 VDC jack. With: AC adapter, ANT-60 wind-up antenna, case and earphones. Requires four AA cells. 8.5" x 5.3" x 1.6". #3505

PT-80

The Sangean PT-80 Pro-Travel is a compact digital radio with LW, AM, FM and continuous shortwave coverage. This dual conversion receiver features: 45 memories, single side-band, backlit LCD, dial lock plus dual world time clock with alarm, snooze and sleep. Tune by: keypad, autoscan, memory recall or rotary knob. Switches are provided for: Local-DX, dial lock and stereomono. With external antenna jack. Includes: AC adapter, earphones, wind-up antenna and butter-soft leather pouch. Requires 4 AA cells (not supplied). #1080

Sangean makes more than world class shortwave radios! Please visit the Universal Radio website to learn about Sangean specialty receivers including their exciting new HD - High Definition models.

(Chinese popular music). One hour to North America on 6020 and 9570 kHz via CRI's Albanian relay. Note that these days are World Time; locally in North America it will be the previous evening.

Voice of Vietnam. A relay via the facilities of Radio Canada International. Begins with *news*, then there's *Commentary* or *Weekly Review*, followed by short features and some pleasant Vietnamese music (especially at weekends). A listener-response segment airs at 0115 Thursday (Wednesday evening local American date). Thirty minutes to eastern North America, with reception better to the south. On 6175 kHz. Repeated at 0230 and 0330 on the same channel.

Voice of Russia World Service. Summer only at this hour, and the start of a four-hour block of programming for North America. *News*, then Tuesday through Saturday (weekday evenings in North America), there's more news programming. This is replaced Sunday and Monday by *Moscow Mailbag*. The second half-hour contains some interesting fare, with just about everyone's favorite being Tuesday's ●*Folk Box*. Other shows include *Moscow Calling* (Friday), *Our Homeland* (Sunday), *Timelines* (Monday), Wednesday's ●*Jazz Show*, and Saturday's evocative ●*Christian Message from Moscow*. Best for eastern North America are 7250 and 9665 kHz (replaced by 7180 kHz in autumn). Farther west, use 15555 and (if in use) 15595 kHz.

Radio Habana Cuba. The start of a two-hour cyclical broadcast to North America. Tuesday through Sunday (Monday through Saturday evenings in North America), the first half-hour consists of international and Cuban *news* followed by *RHC's Viewpoint*. The next 30 minutes consist of a *news* bulletin and the sports-oriented *Time Out* (five minutes each) plus a feature: *Caribbean Outlook* (Tuesday and Friday), *DXers Unlimited* (Wednesday and Sunday), the *Mailbag Show* (Thursday) and *Weekly Review* (Saturday). Monday, the hour is split between *Weekly Review* and *Mailbag Show*. To eastern and central North America on 6000 and 9820 kHz.

Voice of Greece. Monday and winter only at this time. Actually starts at 0105. Fifty-five minutes of music in *It's All Greek to Me*. To North America on 5865 (or 9420) and 7475 kHz; and to Australasia on 12105 kHz. One hour earlier in summer. Note that Monday World Time is Sunday evening in North America.

Voice of Korea, North Korea. The dinosaur of world band and the last of the old-style communist stations. One hour to East Asia on 3560, 7140, 9345 and 9730 kHz; and to Central America on 11735, 13760 and 15180 kHz.

Radio Taiwan International. Ten minutes of *News*, followed by features: *The Undiscovered Country, Asia Review* and *Let's Learn Chinese* (Monday); *Made in Taiwan* and *We've Got Mail* (Tuesday); *Strait Talk, Speak Out* and ●*Jade Bells and Bamboo Pipes* (Wednesday); *Trends, People* and *Instant Noodles* (Thursday); *Ilha Formosa, Generation Why* and *Musical Chairs* (Friday); *Taiwan Inc.* and *Groove Zone* (Saturday); and *News Talk, Taipei Magazine* and *Stage, Screen and Studio* (Sunday). One hour to East Asia on 15465 kHz, and to the Philippines on 11875 kHz. The latter frequency is also heard in parts of Australia.

Radio Australia. Part of a 24-hour service to Asia and the Pacific, but which can also be heard at this time in parts of North America (better to the west). Begins with *World News*, then Monday through Friday it's the final hour of *The Breakfast Club*. Winter weekends, there's live sport in *Grandstand*. In summer, this is replaced by Saturday's *Pacific Review* and *Asia Pacific Business*, and Sunday's *The Spirit of Things*. On 9660, 12080, 13630, 15240, 15415, 17715, 17750, 17775 (till 0130) and 17795 kHz. In North America (best during summer) try 17715 and 17795 kHz; in East Asia tune to 13630 kHz; and best for Southeast Asia are 15415, 17750 and 17775 kHz.

Radio Ukraine International. Winter only at this time; see 0000 for specifics. Sixty minutes of informative programming targeted at eastern North America. On 5880 (or 5910) kHz. One hour earlier in summer.

Radio Romania International. Starts with *Radio Newsreel*, a combination of news, commentary and press review. Features on Romania complete the broadcast. Regular spots include Tuesday's *Pro Memoria* (Romanian history), *Romanian Hits* and *Pages of Romanian Literature*; Wednesday's *Business Club*; Thursday's *Society Today* and *Romanian Musicians*; and Friday's *Traveller's Guide*, *Listeners Letterbox* and ●*The Skylark* (Romanian folk music). Saturday fare includes *Terra the 21st Century*, ●*The Folk Music Box* and *Over Coffee with Artists*; and Sunday there's *World of Culture*, *RRI Encyclopedia* and *Radio Pictures*. Monday's broadcast includes *Sunday Studio* and *Letter from Bucharest*. Fifty-five minutes to eastern North America winter on 6150 and 9515 kHz; and summer on 9690 and 11825 kHz. Note that these days are World Time; locally in North America it will be the previous evening.

Radio New Zealand International. Continues with *news* and features sometimes replaced by live sports commentary. Continuous to the South Pacific, and also heard in parts of North America (especially during summer). On 15720 or 17675 kHz.

AFRTS Shortwave, USA. Network news, live sports, music and features in the upper-sideband mode from the Armed Forces Radio & Television Service. Transmitted from modestly powered U.S. Navy stations around the globe. Try 4319, 5446.5, 5765, 6350, 7811, 10320, 12133.5, 12579 and 13362 kHz.

01:30

Radio Sweden. Tuesday through Saturday (weekday evenings in North America), it's a smorgasbord of *news* and features about Sweden: *Culture* (Tuesday), *Discover* (Wednesday), *Real Life* (Thursday), *Lifestyle* (Friday), and *Inside Sweden* on Saturday. Sunday features rotate on a weekly basis: *Sweden Today*, *HeadSet*, *A J&J Lifestyle* and *Studio 49*; and Monday it's *Network Europe*. Thirty minutes to South Asia winter on 11550 kHz, and summer on 9435 kHz. Also

to North America, summer only, on 6010 kHz. The broadcast to North America is one hour later during winter.

Radio Austria International. Summer only at this time. Tuesday through Saturday (weekday evenings in the Americas), there's 15 minutes of *Report from Austria* at 0143. Sunday and Monday, it's ●*Report from Austria–The Week in Review* at 0135. The remainder of the broadcast is in German and (Tuesday through Saturday) Spanish. To eastern North America on 9870 kHz. One hour earlier in winter.

Radio Vilnius, Lithuania. Winter only at this time. Thirty minutes of mostly *news* and background reports about events in Lithuania. A listener-response program, *Mailbag*, is aired every other Sunday. For a little Lithuanian music, try the second half of Monday's broadcast. To eastern North America on 7325 kHz. One hour earlier in summer.

Voice of the Islamic Republic of Iran. Unlike the broadcasts to other parts of the world, the programs at this time are from the separate "Voice of Justice" service. One hour to North America winter on 6120 and 9665 kHz, and summer on 7235 and 9495 kHz.

01:45

Radio Tirana, Albania. Tuesday through Sunday (Monday through Saturday evenings in North America) and summer only at this time. Approximately 15 minutes of *news* and commentary from this small Balkan country. To North America on 6115 and 7450 kHz. One hour later in winter.

02:00

Radio Cairo, Egypt. The first hour of a 90-minute broadcast to North America. A ten-minute *news* bulletin is aired at 0215, with the remaining time taken up by short features on Egypt, the Middle East and Islam. For the intellectual listener there's *Literary Readings* at 0245 Monday, and *Mod-*

02:00–02:00

Taipei is home to Radio Taiwan International, as well as foreign stations that send audio for retransmission by RTI's world band transmitters.   M. Guha

ern *Arabic Poetry* at the same time Friday. More general fare is available in *Listener's Mail* at 0225 Thursday and Saturday. To North America on 7270 kHz.

Voice of Greece. Sunday and summer only at this time. Sixty minutes of *Greeks Everywhere* (also known as *Hellenes Around the World*). To North America on 7475 and 9420 kHz; and to Australasia on 17520 kHz. One hour later in winter. Note that Sunday World Time is Saturday evening in North America.

Radio Argentina al Exterior—RAE Tuesday through Saturday only (local weekday evenings in the Americas). A freewheeling presentation of news, press review, short features and local Argentinian music. Not the easiest station to tune, but popular with many of those who can hear it. Fifty-five minutes nominally to North America on 11710 kHz, but tends to be best heard in the southern U.S. and the Caribbean. Sometimes pre-empted by live soccer commentary in Spanish.

Radio Budapest, Hungary. Winter only at this time. *News* and features, most of which are broadcast on a non-regular basis. Thirty minutes to North America on 6110 kHz. One hour earlier in summer.

Radio Bulgaria. Summer only at this time. Starts with *News*, then Tuesday through Saturday (weekday evenings in North America) there's *Events and Developments*, replaced Sunday and Monday by *Views Behind the News*. The remaining time is split between regular programs like *Keyword Bulgaria* and *Time Out for Music*, and weekly features like ●*Folk Studio* (Monday), *Sports* (Tuesday), *Magazine Economy* (Wednesday), *The Way We Live* (Thursday), *History Club* (Friday), *DX Programme* (for radio enthusiasts, Saturday) and *Answering Your Letters*, a listener-response show, on Sunday. Sixty minutes to eastern North America and Central America on 9700 and 11700 kHz. One hour later in winter.

Voice of Croatia. Summer only at this time. Nominally 15 minutes of news, reports and interviews, but actual length varies. To North and South America on 9925 kHz. One hour later in winter.

Radio Prague, Czech Republic. Winter only at this time. *News*, then Tuesday through Saturday (weekday evenings in the Americas) it's a combination of *Current Affairs* and one or more features: *One on One* (Tuesday), *Talking Point* (Wednesday), *Czechs in History*, *Czechs Today* or *Spotlight* (Thursday), *Panorama* and *Czech Science* (Friday), and *Business Briefs* and *The Arts* on Saturday. The Sunday lineup is *Magazine*, *ABC of Czech* and *One on One*; replaced Monday by *Mailbox* and *Letter from Prague* followed by *Encore* (classical music), *Magic Carpet* (Czech world music) or *Czech Books*. A half-hour to North America on 6200 and 7345 kHz. One hour earlier in summer.

Radio Taiwan International. Ten minutes of *News*, followed by features. Monday (Sunday evening in North America) there's *The Undiscovered Country*, *Asia Review* and *Let's Learn Chinese*. These are replaced on successive days by *Made in Taiwan* and

We've Got Mail (Tuesday); *Strait Talk, Speak Out* and ●*Jade Bells and Bamboo Pipes* (Wednesday); *Trends, People* and *Instant Noodles* (Thursday); *Ilha Formosa, Generation Why* and *Musical Chairs* (Friday); *Taiwan Inc.* and *Groove Zone* (Saturday); and *News Talk, Taipei Magazine* and *Stage, Screen and Studio* (Sunday). One hour to eastern and central North America on 5950 and 9680 kHz.

Voice of Russia World Service. Winter, the start of a four-hour block of programming to North America; summer, it's the beginning of the second hour. *News,* features and music to suit all tastes. Winter fare includes *Update* (0211 Tuesday through Saturday), replaced Sunday and Monday by *Moscow Mailbag*. The second half-hour includes ●*Folk Box* (Tuesday), ●*Jazz Show* (Wednesday), *Moscow Calling* (Friday), ●*Christian Message from Moscow* (Saturday), *Our Homeland* (Sunday) and *Timelines* (Monday). In summer, *News and Views* replaces *Update* and Sunday's *Moscow Mailbag,* with *Sunday Panorama* filling the Monday slot. There's a news summary on the half-hour, then *The VOR Treasure Store* (Saturday), ●*Songs from Russia* (Sunday), *Russian by Radio* (Monday and Friday), *Kaleidoscope* (Tuesday), *Musical Tales* and *Russia: People and Events* (Wednesday) and *Our Homeland* (Thursday). Note that these days are World Time; locally in North America it will be the previous evening. For eastern North America winter, tune to 7180 and 7250 kHz; summer, it's 9665 and 9860 kHz. Listeners in western states should go for 15475 and 15595 kHz in winter; and 15555 and 15595 kHz in summer.

Radio Habana Cuba. The second half of a two-hour broadcast to eastern and central North America. Tuesday through Sunday (Monday through Saturday evenings in North America), opens with 10 minutes of international *news.* Next comes *Spotlight on the Americas* (Tuesday through Saturday) or Sunday's *The World of Stamps.* The final 30 minutes consists of news-oriented programming. The Monday slots are *From Havana* and ●*The Jazz Place* or *Breakthrough* (science). On 6000 and 9820 kHz.

Radio Thailand. *News Magazine.* Thirty minutes to western North America on 5890 kHz, via a relay in Delano, California.

Radio Belarus. Monday, Tuesday, Wednesday, Friday and Saturday, summer only at this time. See 0300 for details. Thirty minutes to Europe on 5970, 6170 and 7210 kHz. One hour later in winter. Sometimes audible in eastern North America.

Radio Australia. Continuous programming to Asia and the Pacific, but well heard in parts of North America (especially to the west). Begins with *World News,* then Monday through Friday it's *The World Today* (comprehensive coverage of world events). Weekends, it's all sport in *Grandstand* and (summer Saturdays) *Total Rugby* and *The Sports Factor.* On 9660, 12080, 13630, 15240, 15415, 15515, 17750 and 21725 kHz. Best heard in North America (especially during summer) on 15515 kHz; in East Asia on 13630 and 21725 kHz; and in Southeast Asia on 15415 and 17750 kHz.

KBS World Radio, South Korea. Opens with 10 minutes of *news,* then Tuesday through Saturday (weekday evenings in the Americas), a commentary. This is followed by 30 minutes of *Seoul Calling* and a 15-minute feature: *Shaping Korea, Business Watch, Korea Spotlight, Korea Today and Tomorrow* and *Seoul Report,* respectively. Sunday, the news is followed by *Worldwide Friendship* (a listener-response program), and Monday by *Korean Pop Interactive.* Sixty minutes to North America on 9560 and 15575 kHz, and to South America (and often heard in Japan) on 11810 kHz.

Voice of Korea, North Korea. Repeat of the 0100 broadcast. One hour to South East Asia on 13650 and 15100 kHz. Also audible in parts of East Asia on 4405 kHz.

AFRTS Shortwave, USA. Network news, live sports, music and features in the upper-sideband mode from the Armed Forces Radio & Television Service. Transmitted from modestly powered U.S. Navy stations around the globe. Try 4319, 5446.5, 5765, 6350, 7811, 10320, 12133.5, 12579 and 13362 kHz.

02:30–03:00

02:30

Radio Sweden. Tuesday through Saturday (weekday evenings in North America), *News* is followed by features about Sweden: *Culture* (Tuesday), *Discover* (Wednesday), *Real Life* (Thursday), *Lifestyle* (Friday), and *Inside Sweden* on Saturday. Sunday features rotate on a weekly basis: *Sweden Today, HeadSet, A J&J Lifestyle* and *Studio 49*; and Monday it's *Network Europe*.

Thirty minutes to North America winter on 6010 kHz.

Radio Tirana, Albania. Tuesday through Sunday (Monday through Saturday evenings in North America) and summer only at this time. Thirty minutes of Balkan news and music to North America on 6115 and 7450 kHz. One hour later during winter.

Radio Budapest, Hungary. Summer only at this time. *News* and features, only a few of which are broadcast on a regular basis. Thirty minutes to North America on 9795 kHz. One hour later in winter.

Radio Belarus. Summer Sundays only at this time. Thirty minutes of local *news* and interviews, plus some Belarusian music. To Europe on 5970, 6170 and 7210 kHz. One hour later in winter. Sometimes audible in eastern North America.

Voice of Vietnam. Repeat of the 0100 broadcast; see there for specifics. A relay to eastern North America via the facilities of Radio Canada International on 6175 kHz. Reception is better to the south.

02:45

Radio Tirana, Albania. Tuesday through Sunday (Monday through Saturday local American date) and winter only at this time. Approximately 15 minutes of *news* and commentary from one of Europe's least known countries. To North America on 6115 and 7450 kHz. One hour earlier in summer.

Vatican Radio. Actually starts at 0250. Concentrates heavily, but not exclusively, on issues affecting Catholics around the world. Thirty minutes to eastern North America on 7305 and 9610 kHz.

03:00

Radio Taiwan International. Repeat of the 0200 broadcast; see there for specifics. One hour to western North America on 5950 kHz, to South America on 15215 kHz, and to Southeast Asia on 15320 kHz.

China Radio International. *News* and reports fill the first half-hour, and are followed by a daily feature: *Front Line* (Monday), *Biz China* (Tuesday), *China Horizons* (Wednesday), ●*Voices from Other Lands* (Thursday), *Life in China* (Friday), *Listeners' Garden* (Saturday) and *In the Spotlight* (Sunday). One hour to North America on 9690 and 9790 kHz. Also available to East Asia winter on 9460, 13620 and 15120 kHz; and summer on 13750, 15120 and 15785 kHz. Note that these days are World Time; locally in North America it will be the previous evening.

Radio Ukraine International. Summer only at this time, and a repeat of the 0000 broadcast; see there for specifics. Sixty minutes to eastern North America on 7540 (or 5810) kHz. One hour later in winter.

Voice of Russia World Service. Continuous programming to North America at this hour. *News*, then winter it's *News and Views*—except Monday (Sunday evening in North America) when *Sunday Panorama* is aired instead. Features during the second half-hour include *The VOR Treasure Store* (Saturday), ●*Songs from Russia* and *Russia: People and Events* (Sunday), *Russian by Radio* (Monday and Friday), *Kaleidoscope* (Tuesday), *Musical Tales* and *Russia: People and Events* (Wednesday) and *Our Homeland* (Thursday). In summer, the news is followed by a feature: *This is Russia* (Monday), *Musical Tales* (Tuesday), *Moscow Mailbag* (Wednesday and Saturday), *Science Plus* (Thursday) and *Newmarket* (business) on Friday. More features follow a brief news summary on the half-hour and include Monday's *Moscow Calling*, Wednesday's

Guest Speaker and *Life as it is*, and Friday's ●*Russia–1,000 Years of Music*. Pride of place at this hour goes to Sunday's 45-minute ●*Music and Musicians*. In eastern North America, choose between 7180, 7250 and 7350 kHz in winter, and 9665, 9860 and 9880 kHz in summer. For western North America, there's 15425, 15475 and 15595 kHz in winter; and 15455, 15555 and 15595 kHz in summer.

Voice of Greece. Sunday and winter only at this time. Sixty minutes of *Greeks Everywhere* (also known as *Hellenes Around the World*). To North America on 5865 (or 9420) and 7475 kHz; and to Australasia on 12105 kHz. One hour earlier in summer. Note that Sunday World Time is Saturday evening in North America.

Radio Belarus. Monday, Tuesday, Wednesday, Friday and Saturday, winter only at this time. Thirty minutes of local *news* and interviews, plus a little Belarusian music.

All transmissions at this hour are repeats of broadcasts originally aired earlier. To Europe on 5970, 6155 and 7210 kHz, and one hour earlier in summer. Sometimes heard in eastern North America.

Radio Australia. *World News*, then Monday through Friday there's *Regional Sport*. For Asia there's a 15-minute feature: *In Conversation* (Monday), ●*Ockham's Razor* (Tuesday), *Lingua Franca* (Wednesday), *The Ark* (Thursday) and *Talking Point* on Friday. Except for Friday's *Sports Factor*, the second half-hour features a series of reports: *Health* (Monday), *Law* (Tuesday), *Religion* (Wednesday) and *Media* (Thursday). The Pacific gets the first 45 minutes of *In the Loop*. Weekends, for all areas, there's live sports coverage in *Grandstand*. Continuous to Asia and the Pacific on 9660, 12080, 13630, 15240, 15415, 15515, 17750 and 21725 kHz. Also heard in North America (best in summer) on 15515 kHz. In East Asia, tune to 13630

03:00–04:00

Japan Short Wave Club attendees. Seated (dark T-shirt) Yuji Ozaki, assistant to K. Ozaki; Kazuo Ozaki, HCJB Japanese program host; Dennis Adams, HCJB Asia/Pacific Director; and Mr. Chiyoda. Standing (bananas) is Mr. Tanno; PASSPORT's Toshimichi Ohtake; Mrs. Y. Ozaki, HCJB assistant; Mr. Arai; Mr. Yokoyama; and Mr. Harada.

T. Ohtake

and 21725 kHz; for Southeast Asia, there's 15415 and 17750 kHz.

Radio Habana Cuba. Repeat of the 0100 broadcast. To eastern and central North America on 6000 and 9820 kHz.

Voice of Croatia. Winter only at this time. Nominally 15 minutes of news, reports and interviews, but actual length varies. To North and South America on 7285 kHz. One hour earlier in summer.

Radio Prague, Czech Republic. Summer only at this hour; see 0400 for program specifics. A half-hour to North America on 7345 and 9870 kHz. This is by far the best opportunity for listeners in western states. One hour later in winter.

Radio Cairo, Egypt. The final half-hour of a 90-minute broadcast to North America on 7270 kHz.

Radio Bulgaria. Winter only at this time, and a repeat of the 0000 broadcast; see there for specifics. A distinctly Bulgarian potpourri of news, commentary, features and music. Not to be missed is Monday's ●*Folk Studio* (Sunday evening local American date). Sixty minutes to eastern North America and Central America on 7400 and 9400 kHz. One hour earlier in summer.

Radio Japan. *News*, then weekdays it's *A Song for Everyone* and *Asian Top News*. These are followed by a 35-minute feature: *Japan Music Archives* (Monday), Japanese language lessons (Tuesday and Thursday), *Japan Music Travelogue* (Wednesday), and *Count Down Japan* (Japanese popular music) on Friday. *Weekend Japanology* and *Japan Music Scene* fill the Saturday slots, and *World Interactive* is aired Sunday. Sixty minutes to Australasia on 21610 kHz.

Radio New Zealand International. Continues with *news* and features targeted at a regional audience. Part of a 24-hour transmission for the South Pacific, but also heard in parts of North America (especially during summer). On 15720 or 17675 kHz. Often carries commentaries of local sporting events. Popular with many listeners.

Voice of Korea, North Korea. Abysmal programs from the last of the old-style communist stations. Worth a listen just to hear how bad they are. One hour to East Asia on 3560, 7140, 9345 and 9730 kHz.

Voice of Turkey. Summer only at this time. *News*, followed by *Review of the Turkish Press* and features (some of them exotic and unusual). Selections of Turkish popular and classical music complete the program. Fifty minutes to Europe and North America on 5975 kHz, and to the Mideast on 7270 kHz. One hour later during winter.

Voice of America. The start of four hours of continuous programming to Africa. Monday through Friday, *Daybreak Africa* fills the first half-hour, and is followed by *World News Now*. Weekends, 30 minutes of news are followed by Saturday's *Press Conference USA* or Sunday's *Issues in the News*. On 4930, 6035 (winter), 6080, 7340 (till 0330), 9885 and (summer) 12080 and 15580 kHz. Best for southern Africa are 4930 and 9885 kHz.

AFRTS Shortwave, USA. Network news, live sports, music and features in the upper-sideband mode from the Armed Forces Radio & Television Service. Transmitted from modestly powered U.S. Navy stations around the globe. Try 4319, 5446.5, 5765, 6350, 7811, 10320, 12133.5, 12579 and 13362 kHz.

03:30

Radio Sweden. Tuesday through Saturday (weekday evenings in North America), it's a smorgasbord of *news* and features about Sweden: *Culture* (Tuesday), *Discover* (Wednesday), *Real Life* (Thursday), *Lifestyle* (Friday), and *Inside Sweden* on Saturday. Sunday features rotate on a weekly basis: *Sweden Today, HeadSet, A J&J Lifestyle* and *Studio 49*; and Monday there's *Network Europe*. Thirty minutes to western North America on 6010 kHz, and one hour earlier in summer.

Radio Prague, Czech Republic. Summer only at this time. See the 0400 winter broadcast for North America for program specifics. Thirty minutes to the Mideast and South Asia on 9445 and 11600 kHz. One hour later in winter.

Kol Israel. Summer only at this time. *News* for 15 minutes from Israel Radio's domestic network. To Europe and eastern North America on 11590 and 13720 kHz, and to Australasia on 17600 kHz. One hour later in winter.

Radio Budapest, Hungary. This time winter only. *News* and features, most of which are broadcast on a non-regular basis. Thirty minutes to North America on 9855 kHz. One hour earlier in summer.

Radio Belarus. Winter Sundays only at this time. Thirty minutes of local *news*, reports and interviews, plus some Belarusian music. To Europe on 5970, 6155 and 7210 kHz. One hour earlier in summer. Sometimes audible in eastern North America.

Voice of Vietnam. A relay via the facilities of Radio Canada International. Begins with *news*, then there's *Commentary* or *Weekly Review*, followed by short features and some pleasant Vietnamese music (particularly at weekends). A half-hour to eastern North America on 6175 kHz.

Radio Tirana, Albania. Tuesday through Monday (Monday through Saturday evenings local American date) and winter only at this time. *News*, features and Albanian music (especially Sunday). Thirty minutes to North America on 6115 and 7450 kHz. One hour earlier in summer.

04:00

■**Radio Netherlands.** Summer only at this time; see 0500 for specifics. Fifty-seven minutes to western North America on 6165 and 9590 kHz, and one hour later in winter.

Radio Habana Cuba. Repeat of the 0200 broadcast. To eastern and central North America on 6000 and 9820 kHz.

Radio Prague, Czech Republic. Winter only at this time. *News*, then Tuesday through Saturday (weekday evenings in the Americas) there's the in-depth *Current Affairs* and a feature or two: *One on One* (Tuesday), *Talking Point* (Wednesday), *Czechs in History, Czechs Today* or *Spotlight* (Thursday), *Panorama* and *Czech Science* (Friday), and *Business Briefs* and *The Arts* on Saturday. The Sunday news is followed by *Magazine, ABC of Czech* and a repeat of Wednesday's *One on One*; and Monday's lineup is *Mailbox* and *Letter from Prague* followed by *Encore* (classical music), *Magic Carpet* (Czech world music) or *Czech Books*. Thirty minutes to North America on 6200 and 7345 kHz. By far the best opportunity for western states. One hour earlier in summer.

■**Radio France Internationale.** Weekdays only at this time. Starts with a bulletin of African *news* and an international news-flash. Next, there's a review of the French dailies, an in-depth look at events in Africa, the main news event of the day in France, and sports. Thirty information-packed minutes to East Africa on 7315 (winter), 9805 and (summer) 11700 kHz. Heard well beyond the intended target area.

Radio Ukraine International. Winter only at this time, and a repeat of the 0100 broadcast. Ample coverage of local issues, including news, sports, politics and culture. Well worth a listen is ●*Music from Ukraine*, which fills most of the Monday (Sunday evening in the Americas) broadcast. Sixty minutes to eastern North America on 5880 (or 5910) kHz. One hour earlier in summer.

Radio Australia. *World News*, then Monday through Friday, it's the final hour of *In the Loop* for listeners in the Pacific. Asia gets one or more features: *National Interest* (Monday), *Counterpoint* (Tuesday), *Rear Vision* and *Innovations* (Wednesday), *Background Briefing* (investigative journalism, Thursday), and ●*The Science Show* on Friday. Weekends, it's live sport in *Grandstand*. Continuous to Asia and the Pacific on 9660, 12080, 13630, 15240, 15415 (from 0430), 15515, 17750 and 21725 kHz. Should also be audible in parts of North America (best during summer) on 15515 kHz. In East Asia, go for 13630 and 21725 kHz; for Southeast Asia, there's 15415 and 17750 kHz.

■**Deutsche Welle,** Germany. *News*, followed Tuesday through Saturday by the well produced ●*NewsLink*—commentary, interviews, background reports and analysis. On the half-hour there's *Insight* and *Business German* (Tuesday), *World in Progress* (Wednesday), ●*Money Talks* (Thursday), *Living Planet* (Friday) and *Spectrum* (Saturday). The Sunday feature is ●*Inside Europe*, replaced Monday by *African Focus* and *Dialogue*. Sixty minutes to Africa winter on 5905, 6180, 7225, 9565 and 15445 kHz; and summer on 7225, 9630, 12045 and 15445 kHz. Audible in southern Africa midyear on 12045 kHz.

Radio Romania International. Starts with *Radio Newsreel*, a combination of news, commentary and press review. Features on Romania complete the broadcast. Regular spots include Tuesday's *Pro Memoria* (Romanian history), *Romanian Hits* and *Pages of Romanian Literature*; Wednesday's *Business Club*; Thursday's *Society Today* and *Romanian Musicians*; and Friday's *Traveller's Guide*, *Listeners Letterbox* and ●*The Skylark* (Romanian folk music). Saturday fare includes *Terra the 21st Century*, ●*The Folk Music Box* and *Over Coffee with Artists*; and Sunday there's *World of Culture*, *RRI Encyclopedia* and *Radio Pictures*. Monday's broadcast includes *Sunday Studio* and *Letter from Bucharest*. Fifty-five minutes to western North America winter on 6115 and 9515 kHz, and summer on 9780 and 11795 kHz; and to South Asia winter on 9690 and 11895 kHz, and summer on 15110 and 17870 kHz. Note that these days are World Time; locally in western North America it will be the previous evening.

Voice of Turkey. Winter only at this time. See 0300 for specifics. Fifty minutes to Europe and North America on 6020 kHz, and to the Mideast on 7240 kHz. One hour earlier in summer.

China Radio International. Repeat of the 0300 broadcast (see there for specifics); one hour to North America winter on 6190 kHz, and summer on 6020 and 6080 kHz. Also to East Asia winter on 9460, 13620 and 15120 kHz; and summer on 13750, 15120 and 15785 kHz.

Radio New Zealand International. Continuous programming for the South Pacific. Part of a much longer broadcast, which is also heard in parts of North America (especially during summer). On 13730 or 15720 kHz. Sometimes carries commentaries of local sports events.

04:00–04:30

RFI reports from beyond Georges Haussmann's traditional Paris. Today's city includes the commercial Défense district, with its more-modern-than-thou Grande Arche holding 30,000 office workers. Some see La Défense as an architectural leap—others view it as a Jacques Tati satire sprung to life.

Shutterstock/Alexander Mul

Voice of Russia World Service. Continues to North America at this hour. Opens with *News*, then a feature. Winter, there's *This is Russia* (Monday), *Musical Tales* (Tuesday), *Moscow Mailbag* (Wednesday and Saturday), *Science Plus* (Thursday) and *Newmarket* (business) on Friday. More features follow a brief news summary on the half-hour, including *Moscow Calling* (Monday), *Guest Speaker* and *Life as it is* (Wednesday) and ●*Russia–1,000 Years of Music* on Friday. Not to be missed at this hour is Sunday's 45-minute ●*Music and Musicians*. The summer schedule has plenty of variety, and includes *Musical Tales* and *The VOR Treasure Store* (Monday), *Moscow Mailbag*, ●*Music Around Us* and ●*Music at Your Request* (Tuesday), *Science Plus* and *Our Homeland* (Wednesday), the business-oriented *Newmarket* and ●*Folk Box* (Thursday), *Moscow Mailbag* and *The VOR Treasure Store* (Friday), *This is Russia* and *Timelines* (Saturday), and *Musical Tales* and *Kaleidoscope* (Sunday). Note that these days are World Time; locally in North America it will be the previous evening. In eastern North America, choose from 7150, 7180 and 7350 kHz in winter, and 9665, 9860 and 9880 kHz in summer. Best winter bets for the West Coast are 9840, 12010, 15425 and 15475 kHz; and summer there's 15455, 15555 and 15595 kHz.

Voice of America. Continuous programming to Africa. Monday through Friday, *Daybreak Africa* fills the first half-hour, and is followed by *World News Now*. Weekends, 30 minutes of news are followed by *On the Line*. On 4930, 4960, 6080, 9575 and (till 0430) 9885 kHz; also winter on 9775 kHz, and summer on 11835, 12080 and 15580 kHz. Best for southern Africa is 4930 kHz; and heard in North America on 9575 kHz.

AFRTS Shortwave, USA. Network news, live sports, music and features in the upper-sideband mode from the Armed Forces Radio & Television Service. Transmitted from modestly powered U.S. Navy stations around the globe. Try 4319, 5446.5, 5765, 6350, 7811, 10320, 12133.5, 12579 and 13362 kHz.

04:30

Radio Prague, Czech Republic. Winter only at this time. See the 0400 broadcast to North America for program specifics. Thirty minutes to the Mideast and South Asia on 9885 and 11600 kHz. One hour earlier in summer.

Kol Israel. Winter only at this time. *News* for 15 minutes from Israel Radio's domestic network. To Europe and eastern North America on 6280 (or 9345) and 7545 kHz, and to Australasia on 15640 or 17600 kHz. One hour earlier in summer.

04:45–05:30

Cathedral Square, Havana. Radio Habana Cuba rarely reports on Cubans' religious activities.

Shutterstock/Grigory Kubatyan

04:45

RAI International—Radio Roma, Italy. *News* and Italian music make up this 15-minute broadcast to southern Europe and North Africa. Winter on 5965 and 7170 kHz; and summer on 6145 and 7235 kHz.

05:00

■**Radio Netherlands.** Winter only at this time. Tuesday through Saturday (weekday evenings in North America) there's ●*Newsline* (current events) followed by a 30-minute feature: ●*Research File* (Tuesday), ●*EuroQuest* (Wednesday), ●*Documentary* (Thursday), *Dutch Horizons* (Friday), and ●*A Good Life* (Saturday). Sunday's combo is a news feature and *Vox Humana*, replaced Monday by *Amsterdam Forum* and *Dutch Extra*. Fifty-seven minutes to eastern North America on 6165 kHz, and one hour earlier in summer. Also available to Australasia on 11710 kHz (two hours later midyear).

■**Deutsche Welle,** Germany. *News*, then Tuesday through Saturday it's ●*NewsLink*—commentary, interviews, background reports and analysis. This is replaced Sunday by *Mailbag*, and Monday by *African Focus*. Thirty minutes to Africa, winter on 6180, 7285, 9755, 12045 and 15410 kHz; and summer on 9630, 9700, 15410 and 17800 kHz. Best for southern Africa are

12035 kHz in winter (summer in the Southern Hemisphere) and 9630 and 9700 kHz midyear.

■**Radio France Internationale.** Monday through Friday only at this time. Similar to the 0400 broadcast, but without the international newsflash. Thirty minutes to East Africa (and heard well beyond) on any two channels from 9805 11995, 13680 and 15160 kHz.

Vatican Radio. Summer only at this time. Twenty minutes of programming oriented to Catholics. To Europe on 4005, 5885 and 7250 kHz. One hour later in winter.

Radio Japan. *News*, then Monday through Friday there's *Japan and the World 44 Minutes* (an in-depth look at current trends and events). This is replaced Saturday by *World Interactive* and Sunday by *J-Melo* and *Pop Joins the World*. One hour to Europe on 5975 and 7230 kHz; to East Asia on 15195 kHz; to Southeast Asia on 17810 kHz; to Australasia on 21755 kHz; and to western North America on 6110 kHz.

China Radio International. *News* and reports fill the first half-hour, and are followed by a daily feature: *Front Line* (Monday), *Biz China* (Tuesday), *China Horizons* (Wednesday), ●*Voices from Other Lands* (Thursday), *Life in China* (Friday), *Listeners' Garden* (Saturday) and *In the Spotlight* (Sunday). One hour to central and western North America on 5960 (winter), 6020 (summer) and 6190 kHz via CRI's Canadian relay. Also available to the Mideast on 7220 (winter), 11710 (summer), 15285 (winter) and 17505 kHz. Note that these days are World Time; locally in North America it will be the previous evening.

Radio Habana Cuba. The start of a two-hour broadcast for North America and Central America. Tuesday through Sunday (Monday through Saturday evenings in North America), the first half-hour consists of international and Cuban news followed by *RHC's Viewpoint*. The next 30 minutes consist of a news bulletin and the sports-oriented *Time Out* (five minutes each) plus a feature: *Caribbean Outlook* (Tuesday and

Friday), *DXers Unlimited* (Wednesday and Sunday), the *Mailbag Show* (Thursday) and *Weekly Review* (Saturday). Monday, the hour is split between *Weekly Review* and *Mailbag Show*. On 6000, 6060, 9550 and 11760 kHz.

Radio Austria International. Summer Sundays only, and actually starts at 0505. See 0600 for more details. To the Mideast on 17870 kHz, and one hour later in winter.

Radio New Zealand International. Continues with regional programming for the South Pacific. Part of a 24-hour broadcast, which is also heard in parts of North America (especially during summer). On 9615 or 15720 kHz.

Radio Australia. *World News*, then Monday through Friday, continues with current events: *The World Today* for Asia, and *Pacific Beat* (including *On the Mat* and a sports bulletin) for listeners in the Pacific. Weekends, it's live sport in *Grandstand*. Continuous to Asia and the Pacific on 9660, 12080, 13630, 15160, 15240, 15415 (from 0530), 15515 and 17750 kHz. In North America (best during summer) try 15160 and 15515 kHz. Best for East Asia is 13630 kHz; in Southeast Asia use 15415 or 17750 kHz.

Voice of Russia World Service. Winter, the final 60 minutes of a four-hour block of programming to North America; summer, the first of four hours to Australasia. Opens with *News*, followed winter by features: *Musical Tales* and *The VOR Treasure Store* (Monday), *Moscow Mailbag*, ●*Music Around Us* and ●*Music at Your Request* (Tuesday), *Science Plus* and *Our Homeland* (Wednesday), the business-oriented *Newmarket* and ●*Folk Box* (Thursday), *Moscow Mailbag* and *The VOR Treasure Store* (Friday), *This is Russia* and *Timelines* (Saturday), and *Musical Tales* and *Kaleidoscope* (Sunday). Note that these days are World Time; locally in North America it will be the previous evening. Tuesday through Saturday summer, there's *Focus on Asia and the Pacific*, replaced Sunday by *This is Russia* and Monday by *Moscow Mailbag*. On the half-hour, look for ●*Music Around Us* and ●*Music at Your Request* (Friday), *The VOR Treasure*

Store (Sunday), *Our Homeland* (Thursday), ●*Christian Message from Moscow* (Saturday), *Russian by Radio* (Monday and Wednesday) and *Kaleidoscope* on Tuesday. Winter only to eastern North America on 7150, 7180 and 7350 kHz, and to western parts on 9840, 12010 and 15425 kHz. Summer (winter in the Southern Hemisphere) to Australasia on 17635 and 21790 kHz.

AFRTS Shortwave, USA. Network news, live sports, music and features in the upper-sideband mode from the Armed Forces Radio & Television Service. Transmitted from modestly powered U.S. Navy stations around the globe. Try 4319, 5446.5, 5765, 6350, 7811, 10320, 12133.5, 12579 and 13362 kHz.

05:30

Radio Thailand. Thirty minutes of *news* and short features relayed from one of the station's domestic services. To Europe winter on 13770 kHz, and summer on 17655 kHz.

06:00–11:59
Australasia & East Asia—Evening Prime Time
Western North America—Late Evening
Europe & Mideast—Morning and Midday

06:00

■**Deutsche Welle,** Germany. *News,* then Tuesday through Saturday it's ●*News-Link*—commentary, interviews, background reports and analysis. This is followed by *Insight* and *Business German* (Tuesday), *World in Progress* (Wednesday), ●*Money Talks* (Thursday), *Living Planet* (Friday), and *Spectrum* (Saturday). Sunday fare is *Mailbag,* replaced Monday by *African Focus* and *Dialogue.* Sixty minutes to Europe on 6140 kHz. The first half-hour is also available to West Africa winter on 7240, 7285, 9565 and 12045 kHz; and summer on 7170, 15275 and 17860 kHz.

Radio Habana Cuba. The second half of a two-hour broadcast. Tuesday through Sunday (Monday through Saturday evenings in North America), opens with 10 minutes of international news. Next comes *Spotlight on the Americas* (Tuesday through Saturday) or Sunday's *The World of Stamps.* The final 30 minutes consists of news-oriented programming. The Monday slots are *From Havana* and ●*The Jazz Place* or *Breakthrough* (science). To North and Central America on 6000, 6060, 9550 and 11760 kHz.

China Radio International. Winter only at this time, and a repeat of the 0500 broadcast (see there for specifics). One hour to western North America on 6115 kHz.

Radio Japan. *News,* then weekdays it's *A Song for Everyone* and *Asian Top News.* This is followed by a 35-minute feature: *Japan Music Archives* (Monday), Japanese language lessons (Tuesday and Thursday), *Japan Music Travelogue* (Wednesday), and *Count Down Japan* (Japanese popular music) on Friday. On the remaining days, *J-Melo* and *Pop Joins the World* fill the Saturday slots and *Weekend Japanology* and *Japan Music*

Scene are aired on Sunday. One hour to Europe on 7230 kHz; to East Asia on 11715, 11760 and 15195 kHz; to Southeast Asia on 11740 kHz; to Australasia on 21755 kHz; and to Hawaii on 17870 kHz (this channel has different programming after 0615). Also to western North America winter on 11690 kHz, and summer on 13630 kHz.

Radio Austria International. Winter Sundays only. The 25-minute ●*Report from Austria–The Week in Review* is aired at 0605, and then repeated at 0635. The remainder of the one-hour broadcast is in German. To the Mideast on 17870 kHz, and one hour earlier in summer.

■**Radio France Internationale.** Weekdays only at this time. Similar to the 0400 broadcast (see there for specifics), but includes a report on the day's main international story. Thirty minutes to East and West Africa winter on 9865, 11995 and 13680 kHz; and summer on 9570, 15160 and 17800 kHz. Heard well beyond the intended target area.

Radio Australia. Begins with *World News,* then Monday through Friday there's *Regional Sports* and *Talking Point* (replaced Friday by *Asia Pacific Business*). Listeners in the Pacific then get a relay of Radio New Zealand International's *Dateline Pacific.* For Asia there's *Health Report* (Monday), *Law Report* (Tuesday), *Religion Report* (Wednesday), *Media Report* (Thursday), and *The Sports Factor* on Friday. These are replaced weekends by live sports coverage in *Grandstand.* Continuous to Asia and the Pacific on 9660, 12080, 13630, 15160, 15240, 15415, 15515 and 17750 kHz. Listeners in North America should try 15160 and 15515 kHz. In East Asia, tune to 13630 kHz; for Southeast Asia, use 15415 or 17750 kHz.

Radio New Zealand International. Continues with regional programming for the

South Pacific, which is also heard in parts of North America (especially during summer). On 9615 or 15720 kHz.

Voice of Russia World Service. *News*, then winter it's *Focus on Asia and the Pacific* (Tuesday through Saturday), *This is Russia* (Sunday) and *Moscow Mailbag* (Monday). On the half-hour, look for ●*Music Around Us* and ●*Music at Your Request* (Friday), *The VOR Treasure Store* (Sunday), *Our Homeland* (Thursday), ●*Christian Message from Moscow* (Saturday), *Russian by Radio* (Monday and Wednesday) and *Kaleidoscope* on Tuesday. In summer, the news is followed by *Science Plus* (Monday), *This is Russia* (Tuesday and Friday), the business-oriented *Newmarket* (Wednesday), *Musical Tales* (Saturday) and *Moscow Mailbag* on the remaining days. The second half-hour offers plenty of variety: *Kaleidoscope* (Monday), *Russian by Radio* (Tuesday), ●*Jazz Show* (Wednesday), *The VOR Treasure Store* (Thursday), *Moscow Calling* (Friday), ●*Folk Box* (Saturday) and *Timelines* on Sunday. Continuous programming to Australasia winter on 17665 and 17805 kHz, and summer on 17635 and 21790 kHz.

Vatican Radio. Winter only at this time. Twenty minutes with a heavy Catholic slant. To Europe on 4005, 5885 and 7250 kHz. One hour earlier in summer.

Voice of Malaysia. *News*, followed Monday, Wednesday, Friday and Sunday by a two-minute Malayan language lesson (replaced by a local pop hit on Tuesday). The next 33 minutes are given over to *Hits All the Way*. Saturday, it's the 35-minute *Mailbag*. The hour is rounded off with a feature: *New Horizon* (Monday), *ASEAN Focus* (Tuesday), *Malaysia in Perspective* (Wednesday), *Personality* (Thursday), *News and Views* (Friday), and *Weekly Roundup* and *Current Affairs* on the weekend. The first hour of a 150-minute broadcast to Southeast Asia and Australasia on 6175, 9750 and 15295 kHz.

AFRTS Shortwave, USA. Network news, live sports, music and features in the upper-sideband mode from the Armed Forces Radio & Television Service. Transmitted from modestly powered U.S. Navy stations around the globe. Try 4319, 5446.5, 5765, 6350, 7811, 10320, 12133.5, 12579 and 13362 kHz.

06:30

Radio Bulgaria. Summer only at this time. *News*, followed by *Answering Your Letters* (Monday), ●*Folk Studio* (Tuesday) and *DX Programme* (Sunday). Most of the remaining airtime is taken up by *Time Out for Music*. Thirty minutes to Europe on 9500 and 11500 kHz. One hour later in winter.

Radio Romania International. *News* and commentary followed by short features on Romania. Twenty-five minutes to western Europe winter on 7180 and 9690 kHz, and summer on 9655 and 11830 kHz. Also available to Australasia winter (summer in the Southern Hemisphere) on 15135 and 17780 kHz, and midyear on 15440 and 17770 kHz.

07:00

■**Radio Netherlands.** Summer only at this time. Monday through Friday it's ●*Newsline*, then a feature: ●*Research File* (Monday), ●*EuroQuest* (Tuesday), ●*Documentary* (Wednesday), *Dutch Horizons* (Thursday) and ●*A Good Life* (Friday). Saturday, there's a news feature followed by *Vox Humana*, replaced Sunday by *Amsterdam Forum* and *Dutch Extra*. Fifty-seven minutes to Australasia on 9700 kHz, and two hours earlier in winter.

■**Deutsche Welle, Germany.** *News*, followed weekdays by the excellent ●*NewsLink*—commentary, interviews, background reports and analysis. The second half-hour features *Spectrum* (Monday), ●*A World of Music* (Tuesday), ●*Arts on the Air* (Wednesday), *Living in Germany* and *Treasures of the World* (Thursday) and *Cool* (a youth show, Friday). Weekend fare consists of Saturday's ●*Inside Europe* and Sunday's ●*Concert Hour*. Sixty minutes to Europe on 6140 kHz.

07:00–08:00

The Voice of Malaysia offers insight into activities in and around Kuala Lumpur—"KL" as it's known locally. The station is popular throughout Asia and Australasia, where it provides good signals.

Shutterstock/TAOLMOR

Radio Prague, Czech Republic. Summer only at this time. See 0800 for specifics. Thirty minutes to Europe on 9880 and 11600 kHz. One hour later in winter.

China Radio International. *News* and reports fill the first half-hour, and are followed by a daily feature: *Front Line* (Monday), *Biz China* (Tuesday), *China Horizons* (Wednesday), ●*Voices from Other Lands* (Thursday), *Life in China* (Friday), *Listeners' Garden* (Saturday) and *In the Spotlight* (Sunday). One hour to Europe winter on 11785 and 17490 kHz.

Radio Australia. *World News*, then Monday through Friday, listeners in the Pacific get a repeat of *Pacific Beat*. For Asia there's *Life Matters* (Monday through Thursday) and *PM* (current events) on Friday. Winter weekends, there's a roundup of the latest sports action in *Grandstand Wrap*, then Saturday's *Rural Reporter* or Sunday's *Innovations*. These are replaced summer by the final hour of *Grandstand* (live sport). Continuous to Asia and the Pacific on 9660, 12080, 13630, 15160, 15240, 15415 and 17750 kHz. Listeners in North America can try 13630 (West Coast) and 15160 kHz (best during summer), while East Asia is served by 13630 kHz. For Southeast Asia, there's 15415 and 17750 kHz.

Voice of Malaysia. Starts weekdays with 45 minutes of *Fascinating Malaysia*, replaced Saturday by *Malaysia Rama* and *Malaysia in Perspective*, and Sunday by *ASEAN Melody* and *Destination Malaysia*. Not much doubt about where the broadcast originates! The hour ends with a 15-minute feature. Continuous to Southeast Asia and Australasia on 6175, 9750 and 15295 kHz.

Voice of Russia World Service. Continuous programming to Australasia. Winter, opens with *News*, then features: *Science Plus* (Monday), *This is Russia* (Tuesday and Friday), *Newmarket* (Wednesday), *Musical Tales* (Saturday) and *Moscow Mailbag*, on the remaining days. For the second half-hour there's *Kaleidoscope* (Monday), *Russian by Radio* (Tuesday), *Jazz Show* (Wednesday), *The VOR Treasure Store* (Thursday), *Moscow Calling* (Friday), ●*Folk Box* (Saturday) and *Timelines* on Sunday. Summer, the news is followed by the informative *Update* on Tuesday, Thursday and Saturday. Other offerings include *This is Russia* (Wednesday), *Moscow Mailbag* (Friday) and *Newmarket* (Sunday). Class act of the week is Monday's masterpiece, ●*Music and Musicians*. On the half-hour there's a summary of the latest news, then more features: ●*Folk Box* (Tuesday), *Our Homeland* (Wednesday and Friday), ●*Jazz Show* (Thursday), *Kaleidoscope* (Saturday) and ●*Songs from Russia* and *Russia: People and Events* on Sunday. Winter (local summer) there's 17665 and 17805 kHz; and midyear, 17495, 17635 and 21790 kHz.

Radio New Zealand International. Continues with regional programming for the South Pacific, which is also heard in parts of North America (especially during summer). On 7145, 9885 or 15720 kHz.

Radio Taiwan International. Ten minutes of *News*, followed by features. Monday (Sunday evening in North America) there's *The Undiscovered Country, Asia Review* and *Let's Learn Chinese.* These are replaced on other days by *Made in Taiwan* and *We've Got Mail* (Tuesday); *Strait Talk, Speak Out* and ●*Jade Bells and Bamboo Pipes* (Wednesday); *Trends, People* and *Instant Noodles* (Thursday); *Ilha Formosa, Generation Why* and *Musical Chairs* (Friday); *Taiwan Inc.* and *Groove Zone* (Saturday); and *News Talk, Taipei Magazine* and *Stage, Screen and Studio* (Sunday). One hour to western North America on 5950 kHz.

AFRTS Shortwave, USA. Network news, live sports, music and features in the upper-sideband mode from the Armed Forces Radio & Television Service. Transmitted from modestly powered U.S. Navy stations around the globe. Try 4319, 5446.5, 5765, 6350, 7811, 10320, 12133.5, 12579 and 13362 kHz.

07:30

Radio Bulgaria. This time winter only. *News,* followed by *Answering Your Letters* (Monday), ●*Folk Studio* (Tuesday) and *DX Programme* (Sunday). Most of the remaining airtime is taken up by *Time Out for Music.* Thirty minutes to Europe on 9500 and 11500 kHz, and hour earlier in summer.

08:00

■**Deutsche Welle,** Germany. *News,* then Monday through Friday there's commentary, interviews, background reports and analysis in ●*NewsLink.* On the half-hour,

look for ●*Focus on Folk* (Monday), *Insight* and *Business German* (Tuesday), *World in Progress* (Wednesday), ●*Money Talks* (Thursday) and *Living Planet* (Friday). Saturday's pairing is ●*Network Europe* and *Dialogue,* replaced Sunday by *Mailbag.* Sixty minutes to Europe on 6140 kHz.

Voice of Malaysia. *News* and commentary, then *Golden Oldies.* The final half-hour of a much longer transmission targeted at Southeast Asia and Australasia on 6175, 9750 and 15295 kHz.

Radio Prague, Czech Republic. Winter only at this time. *News,* then Monday through Friday it's the in-depth *Current Affairs* and one or more features: *One on One* (Monday), *Talking Point* (Tuesday), *Czechs in History, Czechs Today* or *Spotlight* (Wednesday), *Panorama* and *Czech Science* (Thursday), and *Business Briefs* and *The Arts* (Friday). Weekends, the news is followed by Saturday's *Insight Central Europe* or Sunday's *Mailbox* and *Letter from Prague* followed by *Encore* (classical music), *Magic Carpet* (Czech world music) or *Czech Books.* Thirty minutes to Europe on 7345 and 9860 kHz. One hour earlier in summer.

Radio Australia. Part of a 24-hour service to Asia and the Pacific, but which can also be heard at this time throughout much of North America. Begins with a bulletin of *World News,* then Monday through Friday there's an in-depth look at current events in *PM.* Winter weekends, there's *Asia Pacific Review* and *Jazz Notes* (Saturday), and *Correspondents' Report* and *Rear Vision* (Sunday). These are replaced summer by Saturday's *Total Rugby* and *In the Loop (Rewind),* and Sunday's *Grandstand Wrap* and *Innovations.* On 5995, 9580, 9590, 9710, 12080, 13630, 15240, 15415 (the first half-hour is weekends only) and 17750 kHz. Audible in parts of North America on 9580, 9590 and 13630 kHz. Best for East Asia is 15240 kHz, with 15415 and 17750 kHz the channels for Southeast Asia.

Voice of Russia World Service. Continuous programming to Australasia. Winter, *News* is followed by the informative *Update*

08:00–10:00

on Tuesday, Thursday and Saturday. Other offerings include *This is Russia* (Wednesday), *Moscow Mailbag* (Friday) and *Newmarket* (Sunday). Highlight of the week is Monday's ●*Music and Musicians*. On the half-hour there's a summary of the latest news, then more features: ●*Folk Box* (Tuesday), *Our Homeland* (Wednesday and Friday), ●*Jazz Show* (Thursday), *Kaleidoscope* (Saturday) and ●*Songs from Russia* and *Russia: People and Events* on Sunday. In summer, the news is followed Tuesday through Sunday by *News and Views*, and Monday by *This is Russia*. On the half-hour there's a summary of the latest news and a feature: *Our Homeland* (Monday), *Kaleidoscope* (Tuesday), *The VOR Treasure Store* (Wednesday), ●*Folk Box* (Thursday), ●*Jazz Show* (Friday), ●*Christian Message from Moscow* (Saturday) and *Timelines* on Sunday. Winter (local summer) there's 17665, 17805 and 17495 kHz; and midyear, 17495, 17635 and 21790 kHz.

Radio Taiwan International. Ten minutes of *News*, followed by features: *The Undiscovered Country*, *Asia Review* and *Let's Learn Chinese* (Monday); *Made in Taiwan* and *We've Got Mail* (Tuesday); *Strait Talk*, *Speak Out* and ●*Jade Bells and Bamboo Pipes* (Wednesday); *Trends*, *People* and *Instant Noodles* (Thursday); *Ilha Formosa*, *Generation Why* and *Musical Chairs* (Friday); *Taiwan Inc.* and *Groove Zone* (Saturday); and *News Talk*, *Taipei Magazine* and *Stage, Screen and Studio* (Sunday). One hour to Australasia and Southeast Asia on 9610 kHz.

Radio New Zealand International. Continues with regional programming for the South Pacific. Part of a 24-hour broadcast which is also heard in parts of North America (especially during summer). On 7145 or 9885 kHz.

China Radio International. Repeat of the 0700 broadcast, but with news updates. One hour to Europe on 11785 and 17490 kHz; and to East Asia winter on 9415 kHz, and summer on 11620 kHz.

KBS World Radio, South Korea. Opens with 10 minutes of *news*, then Monday

through Friday, a commentary. This is followed by 30 minutes of *Seoul Calling* and a 15-minute feature: *Shaping Korea*, *Business Watch*, *Korea Spotlight*, *Korea Today and Tomorrow* and *Seoul Report*, respectively. Saturday's news is followed by *Worldwide Friendship* (a listener-response show), and Sunday by *Korean Pop Interactive*. Sixty minutes to Europe on 9640 kHz, and to Southeast Asia on 9570 kHz.

AFRTS Shortwave, USA. Network news, live sports, music and features in the upper-sideband mode from the Armed Forces Radio & Television Service. Transmitted from modestly powered U.S. Navy stations around the globe. Try 4319, 5446.5, 5765, 6350, 7811, 10320, 12133.5, 12579 and 13362 kHz.

08:30

Radio Vilnius, Lithuania. Summer only at this time. Thirty minutes of mostly *news* and background reports about events in Lithuania. Of broader appeal is *Mailbag*, aired every other Sunday. For a little Lithuanian music, try the second half of Monday's broadcast. To western Europe on 9710 kHz. One hour later in winter.

09:00

■**Deutsche Welle,** Germany. *News*, then Monday through Friday it's the excellent ●*NewsLink*—commentary, interviews, background reports and analysis. The second half-hour features *Spectrum* (Monday), ●*A World of Music* (Tuesday), ●*Arts on the Air* (Wednesday), *Living in Germany* and *Treasures of the World* (Thursday) and *Cool* (a well produced youth show, Friday). Weekend features are Saturday's ●*Inside Europe*, and Sunday's ●*Network Europe* and *Hits in Germany*. Sixty minutes to Europe on 6140 kHz.

China Radio International. *News* and reports fill the first half-hour, and are followed by a daily feature: *Front Line* (Monday), *Biz China* (Tuesday), *China Horizons* (Wednesday), ●*Voices from Other Lands* (Thursday),

Life in China (Friday), *Listeners' Garden* (Saturday) and *In the Spotlight* (Sunday). One hour to Europe on 17490 kHz; to East Asia winter on 9415 kHz, and summer on 11620 kHz; and to Australasia on 15210 and 17690 kHz.

Voice of Greece. Sunday and summer only at this time, and actually starts at 0905. Fifty-five minutes of music in *It's All Greek to Me*. To Europe on 9420, 12120 and 15630 kHz. Two hours later in winter.

Radio New Zealand International. Continuous programming for the islands of the South Pacific on 7145 or 9885 kHz. Audible in much of North America, especially in summer.

Voice of Russia World Service. Winter only at this time, and the last of four hours for Australasia. Tuesday through Sunday, *News* is followed by *News and Views*, replaced Monday by *This is Russia*. On the half-hour there's a news summary and a feature: *Our Homeland* (Monday), *Kaleidoscope* (Tuesday), *The VOR Treasure Store* (Wednesday), ●*Folk Box* (Thursday), ●*Jazz Show* (Friday), ●*Christian Message from Moscow* (Saturday) and *Timelines* on Sunday. On 17495 and 17665 kHz.

Radio Prague, Czech Republic. Summer only at this time. See 1000 for specifics. Thirty minutes to Europe on 9880 kHz; and to South Asia and West Africa on 21745 kHz. One hour later in winter.

Radio Australia. *World News*, then Monday through Friday it's *Australia Talks Back* (a call-in show). Winter Saturdays there's *Margaret Throsby*, replaced summer by *Asia Review* and *Jazz Notes*. Sunday, it's *The Music Show Part I*. Continuous to Asia and the Pacific on 9580, 9590, 11880, 15240 and 15415 kHz; and heard in North America on 9580 and 9590 kHz. Best for East Asia is 15240 kHz; and for Southeast Asia, 11880 and 15415 kHz.

AFRTS Shortwave, USA. Network news, live sports, music and features in the upper-sideband mode from the Armed Forces Radio & Television Service. Transmitted

A central mission of Radio Taiwan International is to provide a free flow of news to Chinese compatriots throughout the world, as well as to foreign audiences.
M. Guha

from modestly powered U.S. Navy stations around the globe. Try 4319, 5446.5, 5765, 6350, 7811, 10320, 12133.5, 12579 and 13362 kHz.

09:30

Radio Vilnius, Lithuania. Winter only at this time. Thirty minutes of mostly *news* and background reports about events in Lithuania. A listener-response program, *Mailbag*, is aired every other Sunday. For a little Lithuanian music, try the second half of Monday's broadcast. To western Europe on 9710 kHz. One hour earlier in summer.

Kol Israel. Summer only at this time. *News* for 15 minutes from Israel Radio's domestic network. To Europe and eastern North America on 13680 and 15760 kHz. One hour later in winter.

10:00

■**Radio Netherlands.** Monday through Friday it's ●*Newsline*, then a feature: ●*Research File* (Monday), ●*EuroQuest*

10:00–10:30

Elisabeth Cummings, world band listener from London, dines with Frederica Dochinoiu of Radio Romania International at the 1984 EDXC conference in Rebild, Denmark.   F. Dochinoiu

(Tuesday), ●*Documentary* (Wednesday), *Dutch Horizons* (Thursday) and ●*A Good Life* (Friday). Saturday, there's a news feature followed by *Vox Humana*, replaced Sunday by *Amsterdam Forum* and *Dutch Extra*. Fifty-seven minutes to East and Southeast Asia winter on 6040, 9795 and 12065 kHz; and summer on 12065, 13710 and 13820 kHz. Also widely heard in Australia.

Radio Australia. Monday through Friday, there's *World News*, *Asia Pacific* (regional current events) and a feature: *Health Report* (Monday), *Law Report* (Tuesday), *Religious Report* (Wednesday), *Media Report* (Thursday) and *Sports Factor* (Friday). The Saturday slots are taken by *Asia Pacific Business*, *Talking Point* and *Verbatim*; Sunday, it's the second part of *The Music Show*. Continuous to Asia and the Pacific on 9580, 9590, 11880, 15240 and 15415 kHz; and heard in North America on 9580 and 9590 kHz. Listeners in East Asia should tune to 15240 kHz; and Southeast Asia has 11880 and 15415 kHz.

Radio Prague, Czech Republic. Winter only at this time. *News*, then Monday through Friday there's *Current Affairs* and a feature or two: *One on One* (Monday), *Talking Point* (Tuesday), *Czechs in History*, *Czechs Today* or *Spotlight* (Wednesday), *Panorama* and *Czech*

Science (Thursday), and *Business Briefs* and *The Arts* (Friday). On Saturday the news is followed by *Magazine*, *ABC of Czech* and a repeat of Tuesday's *One on One*. Sunday's lineup is *Mailbox* and *Letter from Prague* followed by *Encore* (classical music), *Magic Carpet* (Czech world music) or *Czech Books*. Thirty minutes to South Asia and West Africa on 21745 kHz, but audible well beyond. One hour earlier in summer.

Radio Japan. *News*, then Monday through Friday it's *A Song for Everyone* and *Japan and the World 44 Minutes* (an in-depth look at current trends and events). This is replaced Saturday by *World Interactive*, and Sunday by *Weekend Japanology* and *Japan Music Scene*. One hour to East Asia on 11730 kHz, to Southeast Asia on 9695 kHz, to Europe on 17585 kHz, to the Mideast on 17720 kHz, to eastern North America on 6120 kHz, and to Australasia on 21755 kHz.

Voice of Mongolia. Original programming is aired on Monday, Wednesday and Friday, and is repeated on the following day. Starts with *News*, and then it's either a listener-response program (Monday) or reports and interviews. The entire Sunday broadcast is devoted to exotic Mongolian music. Thirty minutes to Southeast Asia and Australasia on 12085 (or 12015) kHz. Often well heard in parts of the United States during March and September.

China Radio International. Weekdays, *News* is followed by *China Drive*, an upbeat "drive-time" show. This is replaced Saturday by *CRI Roundup* and ●*China Roots* (ethnic music), and Sunday by *Reports from Developing Countries* and *China Beat* (Chinese popular music). One hour to Europe on 17490 kHz; to East Asia winter on 5955, 7135 and 7215 kHz; and summer on 11610, 11635 and 13620 kHz; and to Australasia on 15210 and 17690 kHz.

All India Radio. *News*, then a composite program of commentary, press review and features, interspersed with exotic Indian music. Look for a listener-response segment, *Faithfully Yours*, at 1030 Monday. One hour to East Asia on 15020, 15235 (or 15410)

and 17800 kHz, and to Australasia on 13710 (or 13695), 17510 and 17895 kHz. Also beamed to Sri Lanka on 15260 kHz.

Voice of Korea, North Korea. Mind-numbing programs on themes such as the application of socialist thinking to steel production are basic fare for this world band curiosity. Worth the occasional listen just to hear how bad it is. One hour to Central America on 6285 (or 15180) and 9335 (or 11710) kHz; and to Southeast Asia on 6185 (or 11735) and 9850 (or 13650) kHz. Also audible in parts of East Asia on 3560 kHz.

Voice of Vietnam. Begins with *news*, then there's *Commentary* or *Weekly Review* followed by short features and pleasant Vietnamese music (especially at weekends). A half-hour to Southeast Asia on 9840 and 12020 kHz.

AFRTS Shortwave, USA. Network news, live sports, music and features in the upper-sideband mode from the Armed Forces Radio & Television Service. Transmitted from modestly powered U.S. Navy stations around the globe. Try 4319, 5446.5, 5765, 6350, 7811, 10320, 12133.5, 12579 and 13362 kHz.

10:30

Radio Prague, Czech Republic. This time summer only. Repeat of the 0700 broadcast but with different programming on Saturday: *Magazine, ABC of Czech* and *One on One* replace *Insight Central Europe*. Thirty minutes to northern Europe on 9880 and 11665 kHz. One hour later during winter.

Kol Israel. Winter only at this time. *News* for 15 minutes from Israel Radio's domestic network. To Europe and eastern North America on 9345, 15640 and 17535 kHz. One hour earlier in summer.

Voice of the Islamic Republic of Iran. News, commentary and features, and a little Iranian music. Strongly reflects an Islamic point of view. One hour to South Asia, and widely heard elsewhere. Winter on 15460 and 15480 kHz, and summer on 15600 and 17660 kHz.

11:00–11:30

11:00

■**BBC World Service for the Caribbean.**
The first 60 minutes of a two-hour broadcast. Weekdays, opens with *news*, then *Caribbean Report*, *Sport Caribbean*, *Caribbean Magazine*, *World Briefing*, *Analysis* and *Sports Roundup*. These are replaced weekends by *World Briefing* and Saturday's *Politics UK* (sometimes replaced by a documentary) or Sunday's ●*Heart and Soul*. Winter on 5875 and 6130 kHz, and summer on 6130 and 9660 kHz.

■**Radio Netherlands.** Summer only at this time; see 1200 for specifics. Fifty-seven minutes to eastern North America on 11675 kHz, and one hour later in winter.

China Radio International. Weekdays, *News* is followed by *China Drive*, an upbeat "drive-time" show. This is replaced Saturday by *CRI Roundup* and ●*China Roots* (ethnic music), and Sunday by *Reports from Developing Countries* and *China Beat* (Chinese popular music). One hour to Europe on 13650 (summer), 13665 (winter) and 17490 kHz; and to eastern North America winter on 5960 kHz, and summer on 6040 kHz.

Radio Taiwan International. Ten minutes of *News*, followed by features: *Made in Taiwan*, *Asia Review* and *Let's Learn Chinese* (Monday); *Strait Talk* and *We've Got Mail* (Tuesday); *Trends*, *Speak Out* and ●*Jade Bells and Bamboo Pipes* (Wednesday); *Ilha Formosa*, *People* and *Instant Noodles* (Thursday); *Taiwan Inc.*, *Generation Why* and *Musical Chairs* (Friday); *News Talk* and *Groove Zone* (Saturday); and *The Undiscovered Country*, *Taipei Magazine* and *Stage, Screen and Studio* (Sunday). Sixty minutes to Southeast Asia on 7445 kHz.

Radio Australia. *World News*, followed Monday through Friday by a bulletin of the latest sports news and *PM* (current events). Weekends, there's Saturday's *Asia Review* and *All in the Mind*, replaced Sunday by *Sunday Profile* and *Speaking Out*. Continuous to East Asia and the Pacific on 5995, 6020, 9475, 9560, 9580, 9590, 11880,

12080 and (till 1130) 15240 kHz; and heard in much of North America on 6020, 9580 and 9590 kHz. Listeners in Southeast Asia should tune to 9475 and 11880 kHz. For East Asia there's 9560 and (till 1130) 15240 kHz.

Radio Ukraine International. Summer only at this time. An hour's ample coverage of just about all things Ukrainian, including news, sports, politics and culture. A popular feature is ●*Music from Ukraine*, which fills most of the Sunday broadcast. Sixty minutes to western Europe on 15675 (or 9950) kHz. One hour later in winter.

Voice of Greece. Sunday and winter only at this time, and actually starts at 1105. Fifty-five minutes of music in *It's All Greek to Me*. To Europe on 12105 and 15630 kHz. Two hours earlier in summer.

Voice of Vietnam. Repeat of the 1000 broadcast; see there for specifics. A half-hour to Southeast Asia on 7285 kHz.

Radio Japan. *News*, then weekdays it's *A Song for Everyone* and *Asian Top News*. These are followed by a 35-minute feature: *Japan Music Archives* (Monday), Japanese language lessons (Tuesday and Thursday), *Japan Music Travelogue* (Wednesday), and *Count Down Japan* (Japanese popular music) on Friday. *World Interactive* fills the Saturday slot, and is replaced Sunday by *J-Melo* and *Pop Joins the World*. One hour to eastern North America on 6120 kHz; to East Asia on 11730 kHz; and to Southeast Asia on 9695 kHz.

Radio Singapore International. A three-hour package for Southeast Asia, and widely heard in Australasia. Starts with ten minutes of *news* (five at weekends), then Monday through Friday there's *Business and Market Report*, replaced Saturday by *Business Ideas*, and Sunday by *Connections*. These are followed by several mini-features, including a daily news and weather bulletin on the half-hour. Monday's lineup is *Undertones*, *Discovering Singapore*, *The Write Stuff* and *E-Z Beat*; and is replaced Tuesday by *A World of Our Own*, *Young Expressions*, *The Business Feature*, *Assignment*

11:00–11:30

Family Radio's Steve Budensiek checks WYFR audio files by accessing the station's Dalet audio system. WYFR, Curtis Jarvis

and a shorter edition of *E-Z Beat*; Wednesday offers *Perspective*, *Traveller's Tales*, *Eco-Watch*, *The Business Feature* and *Classic Gold*; Thursday has *Frontiers*, *Eco-Watch*, *The Business Feature*, *Potluck* and *Love Songs*; and Friday brings *Asian Journal*, *Arts Arena*, *The Business Feature*, *Indonesian Media Watch* and *Classic Gold*. Saturday's list includes *Regional Press Review* and *Frontiers* and Sunday there's *Comment*, *Discovering Singapore* and *Science and Technology*. On 6080 and 6150 kHz.

AFRTS Shortwave, USA. Network news, live sports, music and features in the upper-sideband mode from the Armed Forces Radio & Television Service. Transmitted from modestly powered U.S. Navy stations around the globe. Try 4319, 5446.5, 5765, 6350, 7811, 10320, 12133.5, 12579 and 13362 kHz.

11:30

Radio Bulgaria. Summer only at this time. *News*, followed by *DX Programme* (for radio enthusiasts, Sunday), *Answering Your Letters* (a listener-response show, Monday), and ●*Folk Studio* (Bulgarian folk music, Tuesday). Most of the remaining airtime is

taken up by *Time Out for Music*. Thirty minutes to Europe on 11700 and 15700 kHz, and one hour later in winter.

Radio Prague, Czech Republic. Winter only at this time. *News*, then Monday through Friday it's *Current Affairs* plus one or more features: *One on One* (Monday), *Talking Point* (Tuesday), *Czechs in History*, *Czechs Today* or *Spotlight* (Wednesday), *Panorama* and *Czech Science* (Thursday), and *Business Briefs* and *The Arts* on Friday. The Saturday news is followed by *Magazine*, *ABC of Czech* and a repeat of Tuesday's *One on One*. Sunday's lineup is *Mailbox* and *Letter from Prague* followed by *Encore* (classical music), *Magic Carpet* (Czech world music) or *Czech Books*. Thirty minutes to northern Europe on 11640 kHz, and to East Africa on 21745 kHz. The latter channel is also audible in parts of the Mideast. The European broadcast is one hour earlier in summer, but there is no corresponding transmission for East Africa.

Voice of Vietnam. *News*, then *Commentary* or *Weekly Review* followed by short features and pleasant Vietnamese music (especially at weekends). A listener-response segment airs at 1145 Wednesday. To East Asia on 9840 and 12020 kHz.

12:00–17:59
Western Australia & East Asia—Evening Prime Time
North America—Morning and Lunchtime
Europe & Mideast—Afternoon and Early Evening

12:00

■**BBC World Service for the Caribbean.** The final 60 minutes of a two-hour broadcast. Weekdays, opens with *news*, then *Caribbean Business, Caribbean Report*, and *Caribbean Magazine*. The second half-hour features *Outlook* or news programming. These are replaced weekends by *Newshour*. On 9660 and 9750 kHz.

Radio Canada International. *News*, then *Writers and Company* (Monday), *Ideas* (Tuesday through Saturday) and ●*Quirks and Quarks* (a science show) on Sunday. One hour to East and Southeast Asia winter on 7105 and 9665 kHz, and summer on 9660 and 15170 kHz.

■**Radio Netherlands.** Winter only at this time. Monday through Friday, opens with ●*Newsline* (current events) and closes with a feature: ●*Research File* (science, Monday), ●*EuroQuest* (Tuesday), ●*Documentary* (Wednesday), *Dutch Horizons* (Thursday) and ●*A Good Life* on Friday. Saturday, there's a news feature followed by *Vox Humana*, replaced Sunday by *Amsterdam Forum* and *Dutch Extra* Fifty-seven minutes to eastern North America on 9890 kHz, and one hour earlier in summer.

China Radio International. *News* and reports fill the first half-hour, and are followed by a daily feature: *Front Line* (Monday), *Biz China* (Tuesday), *China Horizons* (Wednesday), ●*Voices from Other Lands* (Thursday), *Life in China* (Friday), *Listeners' Garden* (Saturday) and *In the Spotlight* (Sunday). One hour to Europe on 13650 (summer), 13665 (winter), 13790 and 17490 kHz; to eastern North America winter only on 9560 kHz; to East Asia on 5955 kHz; to Southeast Asia on 9730 and 11980 kHz, and to Australasia on 9760 and 11760 kHz.

KBS World Radio, South Korea. Opens with 10 minutes of *news*, then Monday through Friday, a commentary. This is followed by 30 minutes of *Seoul Calling* and a 15-minute feature: *Shaping Korea, Business Watch, Korea Spotlight, Korea Today and Tomorrow* and *Seoul Report*, respectively. Saturday's news is followed by *Worldwide Friendship* (a listener-response show), and Sunday by *Korean Pop Interactive*. Sixty minutes to eastern North America on 9650 kHz via their Canadian relay.

■**Radio France Internationale.** Opens with a *news* bulletin, then there's a 25-minute feature— *French Lesson, Crossroads, Voices, Rendez-Vous, World Tracks, Weekend* or *Club 9516* (a listener-response program). Thirty minutes to West Africa winter on 15275 kHz, and summer on 17815 kHz, and to East Africa on 21620 (or 17800) kHz.

Radio Polonia, Poland. This time summer only. Sixty minutes of news, commentary, features and music—all with a Polish accent. Weekdays, starts with *News from Poland*—a potpourri of news, reports, interviews and press review. This is followed Monday by *Focus* (an arts program) and *Chart Show* (a look at Polish pop music); Tuesday by *A Day in the Life* (interviews) and *Request Show*; Wednesday by *Around Poland* and *Bookworm*; Thursday by *Letter from Poland* and *Multimedia Show*; and Friday by *Business Week* and *Discovering Chopin* (or an alternative classical music feature). The Saturday broadcast begins with *From the Weeklies*, and is followed by *Insight Central Europe* (a joint-production with other stations of the region) and *Soundcheck* (new Polish music releases). The Sunday lineup includes *Europe East* (correspondents' reports) and *In Touch*, a listener-response program. To western Europe on 9525 and 11850 kHz. One hour later in winter.

Radio Austria International. Summer only at this time. Weekdays, there's the 15-minute *Report from Austria* at 1205. Saturday and Sunday, ●*Report from Austria–The Week in Review* airs at 1205 and 1235. The remainder of the one-hour broadcast is in German. To Europe on 6155 and 13730 kHz, and to Asia and Australasia on 17715 kHz. One hour later in winter.

Radio Australia. *World News*, then Monday through Thursday it's *Late Night Live* (round-table discussion). On the remaining days there's *Best of Late Night Live* (Friday), ●*Saturday Night Country*, and *Sunday Night*. Continuous to Asia and the Pacific on 5995, 6020, 9475, 9560, 9580, 9590 and 11880 kHz; and well heard in much of North America on 6020, 9580 and 9590 kHz. Listeners in East Asia can tune to 9460 kHz; and in Southeast Asia to 9475 and 11880 kHz.

Radio Ukraine International. Winter only at this time. See 1100 for specifics. Sixty

minutes to Europe on 9925 kHz. One hour earlier in summer.

Radio Singapore International. The second of three hours of continuous programming to Southeast Asia and beyond. Starts with five minutes of *news*, followed weekdays by *Newsline*. Most of the remaining time is devoted to short features. There's a weekday *Business and Market Report* on the half-hour, replaced weekends by a *news* bulletin. Monday's lineup includes *Perspective, Indonesian Media Watch, Frontiers, Eco-Watch* and *Young Expressions*; Tuesday, there's *Asian Journal, Undertones, Discovering Singapore* and *Film Talk*; replaced Wednesday by *Call from America, The Write Stuff, Snapshots* and *A World of Our Own*; Thursday offers, among others, *Connections, Comment, Assignment* and *Arts Arena*; and Friday has *Regional Press Review, Business Ideas* and *Limelight*. Saturday's *Connections, Perspective, Indonesian Media*

12:00–13:00

Around-the-clock shifts of studio engineers control audio functions at Radio Taiwan International's Danshui facility.   M. Guha

Watch, Young Expressions and *Comment* are replaced Sunday by *Regional Press Review, Business Ideas, Call from America, Undertones* and *Potluck*. On 6080 and 6150 kHz.

Radio Taiwan International. Repeat of the 1100 broadcast; see there for specifics. One hour to East Asia on 7130 kHz.

Voice of America. *East Asia News Now.* Weekends, the second half-hour consists of Saturday's *Press Conference USA,* and Sunday's *Issues in the News.* The first of four hours of continuous programming to East and Southeast Asia; winter on 9645, 9760, 11705 and 13625 kHz; and summer on 6160, 9645, 9760, 11750 and 13625 kHz. For Australasia there's 9645 kHz.

AFRTS Shortwave, USA. Network news, live sports, music and features in the upper-sideband mode from the Armed Forces Radio & Television Service. Transmitted from modestly powered U.S. Navy stations around the globe. Try 4319, 5446.5, 5765, 6350, 7811, 10320, 12133.5, 12579 and 13362 kHz.

12:15

Radio Cairo, Egypt. The start of a 75-minute package of news, religion, culture and entertainment, much of it devoted to Arab and Islamic themes. The initial quarter hour consists of virtually anything, from quizzes to Islamic religious talks, then there's *news* and commentary, followed by political and cultural items. To South and Southeast Asia on 17835 kHz.

12:30

Radio Bulgaria. Winter only at this time. *News,* then *DX Programme* (for radio enthusiasts, Sunday), *Answering Your Letters* (a listener-response show, Monday), and ●*Folk Studio* (Bulgarian folk music, Tuesday). Most of the remaining airtime is taken up by *Time Out for Music.* Thirty minutes to Europe on 11700 and 15700 kHz and one hour earlier in summer.

Bangladesh Betar. *News,* followed by Islamic and general interest features and pleasant Bengali music. Thirty minutes to Southeast Asia, also heard in Europe, on 7185 kHz.

Voice of Vietnam. Repeat of the 1100 transmission; see there for specifics. A half-hour to Southeast Asia on 9840 and 12020 kHz. Frequencies may vary slightly.

Radio Thailand. Thirty minutes of *news* and short features to Southeast Asia and Australasia, winter on 9810 kHz and summer on 9835 kHz.

Voice of Turkey. This time summer only. Fifty-five minutes of *news,* features and Turkish music. To Europe on 15450 kHz, and to Southeast Asia and Australasia on 15535 kHz. One hour later in winter.

Radio Sweden. Summer only at this time. Monday through Friday, *News* is followed by features about Sweden: *Culture* (Monday), *Discover* (Tuesday), *Real Life* (Wednesday), *Lifestyle* (Thursday), and *Inside Sweden* on Friday. Saturday features rotate on a weekly basis: *Sweden Today, HeadSet, A J&J Lifestyle* and *Studio 49;* and Sunday there's *Network Europe.* Thirty minutes to North America on 15240 kHz; and to Asia and Australasia on 13580 and 15735 kHz. One hour later in winter.

13:00

Radio Canada International. Summer only at this time, and a relay of programs from the Canadian Broadcasting Corporation. Monday through Friday, it's *The Current*, replaced Saturday by *The House* and Sunday by the first hour of *The Sunday Edition* To eastern North America and the Caribbean on 9515, 13655 and 17800 kHz.

China Radio International. Repeat of the 1200 broadcast; see there for specifics. One hour to Europe on 13610 and 13790 kHz; to North America winter on 9570 and 15230 kHz, and summer on 9570, 9650 and 15260 kHz; to East Asia on 5955 kHz; to Southeast Asia on 9730, 9870 and 11980 kHz; and to Australasia on 9760 and 11760 kHz.

■**Deutsche Welle,** Germany. *News*, then weekdays it's ●*NewsLink*—commentary, interviews, background reports and analysis. Next, on the half-hour, there's *Spectrum* (Monday), *Insight* and *Business German* (Tuesday), *World in Progress* (Wednesday), ●*Money Talks* (Thursday) and *Living Planet* (Friday). Saturday's feature is the 55-minute ●*Concert Hour*, replaced Sunday by *Mailbag*. Sixty minutes to Europe on 6140 kHz.

Radio Polonia, Poland. This time winter only. *News*, commentary, music and a variety of features. See 1200 for specifics. Sixty minutes to Europe on 9525 and 11850 kHz. One hour earlier in summer.

Radio Prague, Czech Republic. Summer only at this hour. *News*, then Monday through Friday it's *Current Affairs* plus one or more features: *One on One* (Monday), *Talking Point* (Tuesday), *Czechs in History*, *Czechs Today* or *Spotlight* (Wednesday), *Panorama* and *Czech Science* (Thursday), and *Business Briefs* and *The Arts* on Friday. The Saturday news is followed by *Insight Central Europe*, and Sunday's lineup is *Mailbox* and *Letter from Prague* followed by *Encore* (classical music), *Magic Carpet* (Czech world music) or *Czech Books*. Thirty minutes to northern Europe on 13580 kHz, and to East Africa on 17540 kHz.

Radio Romania International. Starts with *Radio Newsreel*, a combination of news, commentary and press review. Features on Romania complete the broadcast. Regular spots include *Pro Memoria* (Romanian history), *Romanian Hits* and *Pages of Romanian Literature* (Monday); *Business Club* (Tuesday); *Society Today* and *Romanian*

RRI's English Department. Standing: Eugenia Chira (jeans), cultural programs; Ioana Masariu, chief; Frederica Dochinoiu, retired chief; Michaela Ignatescu, "Science Magazine"; Anamaria Palcu, "Sunday Studio." Sitting: Diana Vajeu, "Letterbox"; Daniel Mangu, now in the U.K.; Iulian Muresan, "Living in Romania." F. Dochinoiu

13:00–14:00

Musicians (Wednesday); *Traveller's Guide, Listeners Letterbox* and ●*The Skylark* (Romanian folk music) on Thursday; and *Terra the 21st Century*, ●*The Folk Music Box* and *Over Coffee with Artists* on Friday. Saturday, there's *World of Culture, RRI Encyclopedia* and *Radio Pictures*; and Sunday's broadcast includes *Sunday Studio* and *Letter from Bucharest*. Fifty-five minutes to Europe winter on 15105 and 17745 kHz; and summer on 11845 and 15105 kHz.

Radio Jordan. Summer only at this time. The first hour of a partial relay of the station's domestic broadcasts, beamed to Europe on 11690 kHz. Continuous till 1630 (1730 in winter).

KBS World Radio, South Korea. Opens with 10 minutes of *news*, then Monday through Friday, a commentary. This is followed by 30 minutes of *Seoul Calling* and a 15-minute feature: *Shaping Korea, Business Watch, Korea Spotlight, Korea Today and Tomorrow* and *Seoul Report*, respectively. Saturday's news is followed by *Worldwide Friendship* (a listener-response show), and Sunday by *Korean Pop Interactive*. Sixty minutes to Southeast Asia on 9570 and 9770 kHz.

Radio Austria International. Winter only at this time. Weekdays, there's 15 minutes of *Report from Austria* at 1205. Saturday and Sunday, ●*Report from Austria–The Week in Review* airs at 1205 and 1235. The remainder of the one-hour broadcast is in German. To Europe on 6155 and 13730 kHz, and to Asia and Australasia on 17855 kHz. One hour earlier in summer.

Radio Cairo, Egypt. The final half-hour of the 1215 broadcast, consisting of listener participation programs, Arabic language lessons and a summary of the latest news. To South and Southeast Asia on 17835 kHz.

Radio Australia. Monday through Friday, *News* is followed by *Asia Pacific* and a feature: *Innovations* (Monday), *Australian Express* (Tuesday), *Rural Reporter* (Wednesday), *Rear Vision* (Thursday) and *All in the Mind* (Friday). Weekends, it's the second hour of ●*Saturday Night Country* and *Sunday Night*. Continuous programming to Asia and the Pacific on 5995, 6020, 9560, 9580 and 9590 kHz; and easily audible in much of North America on 6020 (West Coast), 9580 and 9590 kHz. In East Asia, try 9560 kHz.

Radio Singapore International. The third and final hour of a daily broadcast to Southeast Asia and beyond. Starts with a five-minute bulletin of the latest *news*, then most days it's music: *Singapop* (local talent, Monday and Thursday); *Rhythm in the Sun* (Latin sounds, Tuesday and Sunday); *Spin the Globe* (world music, Wednesday and Saturday); and *Hot Trax* (new releases, Friday). There's another news bulletin on the half-hour, then a short feature. Monday's offering is *Traveller's Tales*, replaced Tuesday by *The Write Stuff*. Wednesday's feature is *Potluck*; Thursday has *Call from America*; and Friday it's *Snapshots*. These are followed by the 15-minute *Newsline*. Weekend fare is made up of Saturday's *Assignment, Film Talk* and *Arts Arena*; and Sunday's *A World of Our Own* and *Limelight*. The broadcast ends with yet another five-minute news update. On 6080 and 6150 kHz.

Voice of Korea, North Korea. Abysmal programs from the last of the old-time communist stations. Socialist thinking coexists with choral tributes to the Great Leader. One hour to Europe on 7570 (or 13760) and 12015 (or 15245) kHz; and to North America on 9335 and 11710 kHz. Also heard in parts of East Asia on 4405 kHz.

Voice of America. Continuous programming to East and Southeast Asia. The weekday *East Asia News Now* is replaced weekends by *Jazz America*. On 9645, 9760, 11705 (winter) and 13625 kHz. Heard in Australasia on 9645 kHz. Continuous programming to East and Southeast Asia winter on 6110, 9645, 9760 and 11705 kHz; and summer on 9645 kHz. In Australasia tune to 9645 kHz.

AFRTS Shortwave, USA. Network news, live sports, music and features in the upper-sideband mode from the Armed Forces Radio & Television Service. Transmitted from modestly powered U.S. Navy stations

13:00–14:00

Vienna's Belvedere Palace, constructed in 1721–22 for Prince Eugene of Savoy, who never got to live there. Today it is home to 19th and 20th century art masterworks.

Shutterstock/Roman Milert

around the globe. Try 4319, 5446.5, 5765, 6350, 7811, 10320, 12133.5, 12579 and 13362 kHz.

13:30

Voice of Turkey. This time winter only. *News,* then *Review of the Turkish Press* and some unusual features with a strong local flavor. Selections of Turkish popular and classical music complete the program. Fifty-five minutes to Europe on 12035 kHz, and to South and Southeast Asia and Australasia on 11735 kHz. One hour earlier in summer.

Radio Sweden. See 1230 for program details. Thirty minutes to North America on 15240 kHz; and to Asia and Australasia winter on 7420 and 11550 kHz, and summer on 15735 kHz.

Voice of Vietnam. *News,* then *Commentary* or *Weekly Review* followed by short features and pleasant Vietnamese music (especially at weekends). A listener-response segment airs at 1345 Wednesday. To East Asia on 9840 and 12020 kHz.

All India Radio. The first half-hour of a 90-minute block of regional and international *news,* commentary, exotic Indian music, and a variety of talks and features of gen-

eral interest. To Southeast Asia and beyond on 9690, 11620 and 13710 kHz.

14:00

Radio Japan. *News,* then Monday through Friday it's *Japan and the World 44 Minutes* (an in-depth look at current trends and events). On the remaining days there's Saturday's *Weekend Japanology* and *Japan Music Scene,* and Sunday's *Pop Joins the World.* One hour to Southeast Asia on 7200 kHz; to Australasia on 11840 kHz; and to South Asia winter on 9875 kHz, and summer on 11730 kHz.

■Radio France Internationale. Weekdays, opens with international and Asian *news,* then in-depth reports, a look at the main news event of the day in France, and sports. *Asia-Pacific,* replaces the international report on Saturday, and Sunday fare includes a weekly report on cultural events in France and a phone-in feature. These are followed on the half-hour by a 25-minute feature— *French Lesson, Crossroads, Voices, Rendez-Vous, World Tracks, Weekend* or *Club 9516* (a listener-response program). An hour of interesting and well-produced programming to South Asia winter on 5920 kHz, and summer on 7220 kHz. Sometimes audible in western parts of Australia.

14:00–15:00

■**Deutsche Welle,** Germany. *News*, then Monday through Friday there's ●*NewsLink*. This is followed on the half-hour by ●*Focus on Folk* (Monday), ●*A World of Music* (Tuesday), ●*Arts on the Air* (Wednesday), *Living in Germany* and *Treasures of the World* (Thursday) and the youth-oriented *Cool* (Friday). Weekends, the Saturday news is followed by ●*Inside Europe*; and Sunday by ●*Network Europe* and *Dialogue*. Sixty minutes to Europe on 6140 kHz.

Voice of Greece. Saturday and summer only at this time. Sixty minutes of *Greeks Everywhere* (also known as *Hellenes Around the World*). To Europe on 9420 and 15630 kHz, and one hour later in winter. Often pre-empted by live sports commentary in Greek.

Voice of Russia World Service. Summer only at this time. Eleven minutes of *News*, followed Monday through Saturday by much of the same in *News and Views*. Completing the lineup is *Sunday Panorama*. The second half-hour includes some of the station's better entertainment features: ●*Folk Box* (Monday), ●*Music Around Us* and ●*Music at Your Request* (Tuesday and Thursday), ●*Jazz Show* (Wednesday), *Our Homeland* (Friday), *Timelines* (Saturday) and *Kaleidoscope* on Sunday. To Southeast Asia on 7165, 12055, 15605 and 17645 kHz. One hour later in winter.

■**Radio Netherlands.** The first 60 minutes of an approximately two-hour block of programming for South Asia. Monday through Friday, opens with ●*Newsline* (current events), then a feature: ●*Research File* (Monday), ●*EuroQuest* (Tuesday), ●*Documentary* (Wednesday), *Dutch Horizons* (Thursday) and ●*A Good Life* (Friday). The weekend opens with Saturday's news feature and *Vox Humana*, which are repeated on Sunday. Winter on 9345, 12080 and 15595 kHz; and summer on 9345, 9890 and 11835 kHz. Heard well beyond the target area.

Radio Australia. Weekdays, *World News* is followed by one or two features: *Big Ideas* (Monday), *Awaye* (Tuesday), *All in the Mind* and *Philosopher's Stone* (Wednesday), *Hindsight* (Thursday), and *Movietime* and *Arts on RA* on Friday. Weekends, it's the third hour of ●*Saturday Night Country* and *Sunday Night*. Continuous to Asia and the Pacific on 5995, 6080, 7240, 9475 (from 1430), 9590 and (from 1430) 11660 kHz (5995, 7240 and 9590 kHz are audible in North America, especially to the west). In Southeast Asia, use 6080, 9475 and 11660 kHz.

Radio Prague, Czech Republic. Winter only at this time. *News*, then Monday through Friday it's *Current Affairs* plus one or more features: *One on One* (Monday), *Talking Point* (Tuesday), *Czechs in History, Czechs Today* or *Spotlight* (Wednesday), *Panorama* and *Czech Science* (Thursday), and *Business Briefs* and *The Arts* on Friday. The Saturday news is followed by *Insight Central Europe*, and Sunday's lineup is *Mailbox* and *Letter from Prague* followed by *Encore* (classical music), *Magic Carpet* (Czech world music) or *Czech Books*. A friendly half-hour to eastern North America on 21745 kHz, and to South Asia on 11600 kHz.

Radio Taiwan International. Ten minutes of *News*, followed by features: *Made in Taiwan, Asia Review* and *Let's Learn Chinese* (Monday); *Strait Talk* and *We've Got Mail* (Tuesday); *Trends, Speak Out* and ●*Jade Bells and Bamboo Pipes* (Wednesday); *Ilha Formosa, People* and *Instant Noodles* (Thursday); *Taiwan Inc., Generation Why* and *Musical Chairs* (Friday); *News Talk* and *Groove Zone* (Saturday); and *The Undiscovered Country, Taipei Magazine* and *Stage, Screen and Studio* (Sunday). Sixty minutes to Southeast Asia on 15265 kHz.

China Radio International. *News* and reports fill the first half-hour, and are followed by a daily feature: *Front Line* (Monday), *Biz China* (Tuesday), *China Horizons* (Wednesday), ●*Voices from Other Lands* (Thursday), *Life in China* (Friday), *Listeners' Garden* (Saturday) and *In the Spotlight* (Sunday). One hour to Europe winter on 9795, 11765 and 13610 kHz; and summer on 13610, 13710 and 13790 kHz; to North America on 13740 and (winter) 15230 kHz; to East Asia on 5955 kHz; to Southeast Asia on 9560 (winter) and 9870 kHz; and to eastern and southern Africa on 13685 and 17630 kHz.

Voice of Africa, Libya. The first 60 minutes of a two-hour broadcast. Includes some lively African music. Look for a bulletin of *news* on the half-hour. To Central and East Africa on 17725 and 21695 (or 17850) kHz. Sometimes heard in North America, especially to the south.

All India Radio. The final hour of a 90-minute composite program of commentary, press review, features and exotic Indian music. To Southeast Asia and beyond on 9690, 11620 and 13710 kHz.

Radio Canada International. Winter weekdays, it's *The Current*; and summer, *Sounds Like Canada*. Winter Saturdays, there's a look at Canadian politics in *The House*; and summer it's the entertaining ●*Vinyl Café*. On Sunday there's 60 minutes of the three-hour show, *The Sunday Edition*. To eastern North America and the Caribbean winter on 9515, 13655 and 17820 kHz; and summer on 9515, 13655 and 17800 kHz.

Radio Jordan. Winter, starts at this time; summer, it's the second hour of a partial relay of the station's domestic broadcasts, and continuous till 1630 (1730 in winter). Aimed at European listeners but also audible in parts of eastern North America, especially during winter. On 11690 kHz.

Voice of America. Continuous programming to East and Southeast Asia. The weekday *Talk to America* is replaced weekends by 30 minutes of news fare, Saturday's *On the Line*, Sunday's *Encounter* and an editorial. Winter on 9760 and 11705 kHz, and summer on 7125, 9760 and 15185 kHz.

Radio Thailand. Thirty minutes of tourist features for Southeast Asia and Australasia. Winter on 9725 kHz, and summer on 9830 kHz.

AFRTS Shortwave, USA. Network news, live sports, music and features in the upper-sideband mode from the Armed Forces Radio & Television Service. Transmitted from modestly powered U.S. Navy stations around the globe. Try 4319, 5446.5, 5765, 6350, 7811, 10320, 12133.5, 12579 and 13362 kHz.

14:30

Radio Sweden. Winter only at this time. Monday through Friday, *News* is followed by features about Sweden: *Culture* (Monday), *Discover* (Tuesday), *Real Life* (Wednesday), *Lifestyle* (Thursday), and *Inside Sweden* on Friday. Saturday features rotate on a weekly basis: *Sweden Today, HeadSet, A J&J Lifestyle* and *Studio 49*; and Sunday there's *Network Europe*. Thirty minutes to North America on 15240 kHz, and to Asia and Australasia on 11550 kHz. One hour earlier in summer.

15:00

China Radio International. See 1400 for program details. One hour to Europe winter on 9435 and 9525 kHz, and summer on 11965 and 13640 kHz; to western North America on 13740 kHz; to East Asia on 5955 kHz; to Southeast Asia on 7325 and 9870 kHz; and to eastern and southern Africa on 6100, 13685 and 17630 kHz.

Radio Austria International. Summer only at this time. Monday, the 15-minute *Report from Austria* airs at 1505 and 1545; Tuesday through Friday, the times are 1515 and 1545. Saturday and Sunday, there's ●*News from Austria–The Week in Review* at 1505 and 1535. The remainder of the broadcast is in German. To western North America on 13775 kHz, and one hour later in winter.

■**Radio Netherlands.** The final 57 minutes of an approximately two-hour broadcast targeted at South Asia. Monday through Friday, starts with a feature and ends with ●*Newsline* (current events). The features are repeats of programs aired during the previous six days, and are all worthy of a second hearing: ●*EuroQuest* (Monday), ●*A Good Life* (Tuesday), *Dutch Horizons* (Wednesday) ●*Research File* (science, Thursday) and ●*Documentary* (winner of several prestigious awards) on Friday.

15:00–15:30

Much of KBS' radio output in Seoul is automated. Outgoing programming is monitored and routed using sophisticated consoles, such as these in the master control room.

M. Guha

Weekend fare consists of Saturday's *Dutch Horizons* and a news feature; and Sunday's *Amsterdam Forum* and *Dutch Extra.* Winter on 9345, 12080 and 15595 kHz; and summer on 9345, 9890 and 11835 kHz. Heard well beyond the target area.

Voice of Greece. Saturday and winter only at this time. Sixty minutes of *Greeks Everywhere* (also known as *Hellenes Around the World*). To Europe on 9420 and 15630 kHz, and one hour earlier in summer. Often pre-empted by live sports commentary in Greek.

Radio Australia. *World News,* then weekdays there's *Asia Pacific* and a feature on the half-hour: *Health Report* (Monday), *Law Report* (Tuesday), *Religion Report* (Wednesday), *Media Report* (Thursday) and *The Sports Factor* on Friday. These are replaced weekends by the final hour of ●*Saturday Night Country* and *Sunday Night.* Continuous programming to the Pacific (and well heard in western North America) on 5995, 7240 and 9590 kHz. Additionally available to Southeast Asia on 6080, 9475 and 11660 kHz.

■**Deutsche Welle,** Germany. *News,* then weekdays it's ●*NewsLink*—commentary, interviews, background reports and analysis. Next, on the half-hour, there's *Spectrum*

(Monday), *Insight* and *Business German* (Tuesday), *World in Progress* (Wednesday), ●*Money Talks* (Thursday) and *Living Planet* (Friday). Saturday's features are ●*Network Europe, Treasures of the World* and *German by Radio;* and the 55-minute ●*Concert Hour* fills the Sunday slot. Sixty minutes to Europe on 6140 kHz.

Voice of Africa, Libya. The final 60 minutes of a two-hour broadcast. Look for a bulletin of *news* on the half-hour. To Central and East Africa on 17725 and 21695 (or 17850) kHz. Sometimes heard in North America, especially to the south.

Voice of America. Continuous programming for East and Southeast Asia. The weekday lineup is five minutes of *news* followed by 55 minutes of music in *Border Crossings.* Weekends, there's a half-hour of news fare followed by Saturday's *Our World* or Sunday's *On the Line,* and an editorial. Winter on 13735 and 15460 kHz; and summer on 7125 and 15185 kHz. For Australasia, there's 15460 kHz in winter, and 15185 kHz midyear.

Radio Canada International. Weekdays, it's *Sounds Like Canada,* from the Canadian Broadcasting Corporation. Winter Saturdays, there's ●*Quirks and Quarks* (a science show with a difference) and summer it's the entertaining ●*Vinyl Café*. On Sunday there's 60 minutes of the three-hour show, *The Sunday Edition*. To North America and the Caribbean, winter on 9515, 13655 and 17820 kHz; and summer on 9515, 13655 and 17800 kHz. For a separate broadcast to South Asia, see the next item.

Radio Canada International. *News*, then Monday through Friday it's *Canada Today*, replaced Saturday by *Business Sense* and Sunday by *Maple Leaf Mailbag* (a listener-response show). On the half-hour there's *Spotlight* (Wednesday and Sunday), *Media Zone* (Monday), *The Maple Leaf Mailbag* (re-peat, Tuesday), *Business Sense* (Thursday) and *Sci-Tech File* on Friday and Saturday. Sixty minutes to South Asia winter on 9635, 11870 and 11975 kHz; and summer on 11675, 15360 and 17720 kHz. Heard well beyond the intended target area, especially to the west.

Radio Japan. *News*, then weekdays it's *A Song for Everyone* and *Asian Top News*. A 35-minute feature completes the broadcast: *Japan Music Archives* (Monday), Japanese language lessons (Tuesday and Thursday), *Japan Music Travelogue* (Wednesday), and *Count Down Japan* (Japanese popular music) on Friday. Weekends, there's Saturday's *J-Melo* and *Pop Joins the World*, and Sunday's *World Interactive*. One hour to East Asia on 6190 kHz; to South Asia winter on 9875 kHz, and summer on 11730 kHz; to South-east Asia on 7200 kHz; and to western North America and Central America on 9505 kHz.

Voice of Russia World Service. Winter, *News* is followed Monday through Saturday by *News and Views*, and Sunday by *Sunday Panorama*. The second half-hour is all fea-tures: ●*Folk Box* (Monday), ●*Music Around Us* and ●*Music at Your Request* (Tuesday and Thursday), ●*Jazz Show* (Wednesday), *Our Homeland* (Friday), *Timelines* (Satur-day) and *Kaleidoscope* on Sunday. Summer weekdays, the news is followed by more of the same in *Focus on Asia and the Pacific*, replaced Saturday by *This is Russia* and Sunday by *Moscow Mailbag*. The features that follow include some of the station's

best: ●*Jazz Show* (Monday), *Our Home-land* (Tuesday), *The VOR Treasure Store* (Wednesday), ●*Folk Box* (Thursday), ●*Songs from Russia* and *Russia: People and Events* (Friday), ●*Christian Message from Moscow* (Saturday) and *Russian by Radio* on Sunday. To Southeast Asia winter on 6205, 7415 and 9660 kHz; and summer on 9660 kHz. Also available summer to Europe on 7370, 12040 (or 9810) and 15455 (or 11980) kHz; and to the Mideast on 11985 kHz.

Voice of Mongolia. Original programming is aired on Monday, Wednesday and Friday, and is repeated on the following day. Starts with *News*, and then it's either a listener-response program (Monday) or reports and interviews. The entire Sunday broadcast is devoted to exotic Mongolian music. Thirty minutes to West and Central Asia on 12015 kHz, and sometimes heard in Europe.

Radio Jordan. A partial relay of the station's domestic broadcasts, beamed to Europe on 11690 kHz. Continuous till 1630 (1730 in winter). Audible in parts of eastern North America, especially during winter.

Voice of Korea, North Korea. Repeat of the 1300 broadcast. One hour to Europe on 7570 (or 13760) and 12015 (or 15245) kHz; and to North America on 9335 and 11710 kHz. Also heard in parts of East Asia on 4405 kHz.

Voice of Vietnam. Repeat of the 1100 transmission; see there for specifics. A half-hour to Southeast Asia on 7285, 9840 and 12020 kHz. Frequencies may vary slightly.

AFRTS Shortwave, USA. Network news, live sports, music and features in the up-per-sideband mode from the Armed Forces Radio & Television Service. Transmitted from modestly powered U.S. Navy stations around the globe. Try 4319, 5446.5, 5765, 6350, 7811, 10320, 12133.5, 12579 and 13362 kHz.

15:30

Voice of the Islamic Republic of Iran. News, commentary and features, strongly

15:30–16:00

reflecting an Islamic point of view. One hour to South and Southeast Asia (also heard in parts of Australasia), winter on 7330 and 9940 kHz, and summer on 7370 and 9635 kHz.

16:00

■**Radio France Internationale.** The first half-hour includes *news* and reports from across Africa, international newsflashes and news about France. Next is a 25-minute feature— *French Lesson*, *Crossroads*, *Voices*, *Rendez-Vous*, *World Tracks*, *Weekend* or *Club 9516* (a listener-response program). A fast-moving hour to Africa winter on 9730, 11615 (or 15605) and 15160 kHz; and summer on 7170, 15160 and 17605 kHz. Best for southern Africa are 9730 and 7170 kHz.

Radio Austria International. Winter only at this time. Monday, the 15-minute *Report from Austria* airs at 1605 and 1645; Tuesday through Friday, the times are 1615 and 1645. Saturday and Sunday, there's ●*News from Austria–The Week in Review* at 1605 and 1635. The remainder of the broadcast is in German To western North America on 13675 kHz, and one hour earlier in summer.

■**Deutsche Welle,** Germany. *News*, then the daily ●*NewsLink*—commentary, interviews, background reports and analysis. The final 30 minutes consist of *Insight* and *Treasures of the World* (Monday), *World in Progress* (Tuesday), ●*Money Talks* (Wednesday), *Living Planet* (Thursday), *Dialogue* (Friday), the youth-oriented *Cool* (Saturday), and *Mailbag* (Sunday). Sixty minutes to South Asia winter on 6170, 9795 and 11695 kHz; and summer on 6170, 9485 and 15705 kHz. The winter frequency of 11695 kHz is well heard in parts of Australia.

KBS World Radio, South Korea. Opens with 10 minutes of *news*, then Monday through Friday, a commentary. This is followed by 30 minutes of *Seoul Calling* and a 15-minute feature: *Shaping Korea*, *Business Watch*, *Korea Spotlight*, *Korea Today and Tomorrow* and *Seoul Report*, respectively. Saturday's news is followed by *Worldwide*

Friendship (a listener-response show), and Sunday by *Korean Pop Interactive*. One hour to East Asia on 5975 kHz.

Radio Taiwan International. Ten minutes of *News*, followed by features: *Made in Taiwan*, *Asia Review* and *Let's Learn Chinese* (Monday); *Strait Talk* and *We've Got Mail* (Tuesday); *Trends*, *Speak Out* and ●*Jade Bells and Bamboo Pipes* (Wednesday); *Ilha Formosa*, *People* and *Instant Noodles* (Thursday); *Taiwan Inc.*, *Generation Why* and *Musical Chairs* (Friday); *News Talk* and *Groove Zone* (Saturday); and *The Undiscovered Country*, *Taipei Magazine* and *Stage, Screen and Studio* on Sunday. Sixty minutes to South Asia and southern China on 11550 kHz, and heard well beyond.

Voice of Korea, North Korea. Not quite the old-time communist station it was, but the "Beloved Leader" and "Unrivaled Great Man" continue to feature prominently, as does socialist thinking. One hour to the Mideast and Africa on 9975 (or 9990) and 11535 (or 11545) kHz. Also audible in parts of East Asia on 3560 kHz.

Radio Prague, Czech Republic. Summer only at this time. *News*, then Monday through Friday it's *Current Affairs* plus one or more features: *One on One* (Monday), *Talking Point* (Tuesday), *Czechs in History*, *Czechs Today* or *Spotlight* (Wednesday), *Panorama* and *Czech Science* (Thursday), and *Business Briefs* and *The Arts* on Friday. The Saturday news is followed by *Magazine*, *ABC of Czech* and a repeat of Tuesday's *One on One*. Sunday's lineup is *Mailbox* and *Letter from Prague* followed by *Encore* (classical music), *Magic Carpet* (Czech world music) or *Czech Books*. A half-hour to Europe on 5930 kHz, and to East Africa on 17485 kHz. The transmission for Europe is one hour later in winter, but there is no corresponding broadcast for East Africa.

Voice of Vietnam. *News*, then *Commentary* or *Weekly Review* followed by short features and pleasant Vietnamese music (especially at weekends). A listener-response segment airs at 1615 Wednesday. A half-hour to Europe on 7280 and 9730 kHz. Also available to West and Central Africa on 7220 and 9550 kHz.

Radio Australia. Continuous programming to Asia and the Pacific. Monday through Friday, *World News* is followed by *Australia Talks Back*, and weekends by *Margaret Throsby* (Saturday) and ●*The Science Show* (Sunday). Beamed to the Pacific on 5995, 7240 and 9710 kHz; and to Southeast Asia on 6080, 9475 and 11660 kHz. Also well heard in western North America on 5995 and 7240 kHz.

Radio Ethiopia. An hour-long broadcast divided into two parts by the 1630 *news* bulletin. Regular weekday features include *Kaleidoscope* and *Women's Forum* (Monday), *Press Review* and *Africa in Focus* (Tuesday), *Guest of the Week* and *Ethiopia Today* (Wednesday), *Ethiopian Music* and *Spotlight* (Thursday) and *Press Review* and *Introducing Ethiopia* on Friday. For weekend listening, there's *Contact* and *Ethiopia This Week* (Saturday), or Sunday's *Listeners' Choice* and *Commentary*. Best heard in parts of Africa and the Mideast, but sometimes audible in Europe. On 7165, 9560 and 11800 kHz.

Radio Jordan. A partial relay of the station's domestic broadcasts, beamed to Europe on 11690 kHz. The final half-hour in summer, but a full 60 minutes in winter. Sometimes audible in parts of eastern North America, especially during winter.

Voice of Russia World Service. Continuous programming to Europe and beyond. *News*, then very much a mixed bag, depending on the day and season. Winter weekdays, there's *Focus on Asia and the Pacific*, with Saturday's *This is Russia* and Sunday's *Moscow Mailbag* making up the week. On the half-hour, choose from: ●*Jazz Show* (Monday), *Our Homeland* (Tuesday), *The VOR Treasure Store* (Wednesday), ●*Folk Box* (Thursday), ●*Songs from Russia* and *Russia: People and Events* (Friday), ●*Christian Message from Moscow* (Saturday) and *Russian by Radio* (Sunday). Summer, the news is followed by *Science Plus* (Monday and Wednesday), *Moscow Mailbag* (Tuesday and Friday), the business-oriented *Newmarket* (Thursday), *Musical Tales* (Saturday) and *This is Russia* on Sunday. More features follow a news summary on the half-hour, including *Guest Speaker* and *Life as it is* (Tuesday), ●*Russia–1,000 Years of Music* (Thursday), *Moscow Calling* (Saturday) and *Timelines* on Sunday. To Europe winter on 6130 and 7320 kHz, and summer on 7370 kHz; and to the Mideast winter on 9470 kHz, and summer on 11985 kHz.

Radio Canada International. Winter only at this hour. Weekdays, there's *Sounds Like Canada*, replaced Saturday by ●*Quirks and Quarks* (science), and Sunday by the final hour of *The Sunday Edition*. To eastern North America and the Caribbean on 9515, 13655 and 17820 kHz.

China Radio International. *News* and reports fill the first half-hour, and are followed by a daily feature: *Front Line* (Monday), *Biz China* (Tuesday), *China Horizons* (Wednesday), ●*Voices from Other Lands* (Thursday), *Life in China* (Friday), *Listeners' Garden* (Saturday) and *In the Spotlight* (Sunday). One hour to Europe winter on 7255, 9435 and 9525 kHz; and summer on 11940, 11965 and 13760 kHz. Also to southern Africa on 6100, 9570 and 11900 kHz.

Radio Cairo, Egypt. The first 60 minutes of a two-hour broadcast of Arab music and features on Egyptian and Islamic themes, with *news*, commentary, quizzes, mailbag shows, and answers to listeners' questions. To southern Africa winter on 11785 kHz, and midyear on 11740 kHz.

Voice of America. Continuous programming for Africa. Monday through Friday, it's *Africa News Tonight* and *Sonny Side of Sports*, replaced weekends by *Nightline Africa*. Winter on 4930, 15240, 17715 and 17895 kHz; and summer on 4930, 6080, 15410 and 15580 kHz. Best for southern Africa is 4930 kHz.

AFRTS Shortwave, USA. Network news, live sports, music and features in the upper-sideband mode from the Armed Forces Radio & Television Service. Transmitted from modestly powered U.S. Navy stations

16:00–17:00

around the globe. Try 4319, 5446.5, 5765, 6350, 7811, 10320, 12133.5, 12579 and 13362 kHz.

16:30

Xizang [Tibet] People's Broadcasting Station, China. *Holy Tibet*, a 30-minute package of information and local (mostly popular) music. Sometimes acknowledges listeners' reception reports during the program. Well heard in East Asia, and sometimes provides fair reception in Europe. On 4905, 4920, 5240, 6110, 6130, 6200 and 7385 kHz.

17:00

Radio Prague, Czech Republic. See 1800 for program specifics. Thirty minutes winter to West Africa on 15710 kHz, and summer to Central Africa on 17485 kHz. Also year round to Europe on 5930 kHz.

Radio Australia. Continuous programming to Asia and the Pacific. Starts with *World News*, then a feature: *Innovations* (Monday),

Radio Polonia presents "Discovering Chopin." Poland's musical legend is also honored at this monument in Warsaw which was destroyed in World War II, but reconstructed in 1958.   Shutterstock/Martin Pietak

Australian Express (Tuesday), *Rural Reporter* (Wednesday), *Rear Vision* (Thursday), and *Big Ideas* on Friday. Monday through Thursday, *In the Loop (Rewind)* completes the hour. *Classic Late Night Live* fills the Saturday slot, and Sunday there's *In the Loop (Rewind)* and winter's *The Sports Factor* or summer's *Total Rugby*. Beamed to the Pacific on 5995, 9580, 9710 and 11880 kHz; and to Southeast Asia on 6080 and 9475 kHz. Also audible in parts of western North America on 5995 and 11880 kHz.

Radio Polonia, Poland. This time summer only. Monday through Friday, opens with *News from Poland*—a compendium of news, reports and interviews. A couple of features complete the broadcast. Monday's combo is *Around Poland* and *Bookworm*; Tuesday, it's *Letter from Poland* and *Multimedia Show*; Wednesday, *A Day in the Life* (interviews) and *Discovering Chopin* (or an alternative classical music program); Thursday, *Focus* (the arts in Poland) and *Soundcheck* (new Polish music releases); and Friday, *Business Week* and *In Touch*, a listener-response show. The Saturday broadcast begins with *Europe East* (correspondents' reports), and is followed by *From The Weeklies* and *Chart Show*. Sundays, it's five minutes of news followed by *Insight Central Europe* (a joint-production with other stations of the region) and *Request Show*. Sixty minutes to western Europe on 7220 and 7265 kHz. One hour later in winter.

Radio Jordan. Winter only at this time. The final 30 minutes of a partial relay of the station's domestic broadcasts. To Europe on 11690 kHz.

Voice of Russia World Service. Continuous programming to Europe and beyond. Winter, *News* is followed by *Science Plus* (Monday and Wednesday), *Moscow Mailbag* (Tuesday and Friday), the business-oriented *Newmarket* (Thursday), *Musical Tales* (Saturday) and *This is Russia* on Sunday. More features follow a news summary on the half-hour and include *Guest Speaker* and *Life as it is* (Tuesday), ●*Russia–1,000 Years of Music* (Thursday), *Moscow Calling* (Saturday) and *Timelines* on Sunday. In summer,

16:00–17:00

Once the main railroad junction in downtown Beijing, this elegant edifice is now a movie house, an Internet café and a fast food restaurant that peddles fake Kentucky Fried Chicken.
M. Guha

the news is followed by *Moscow Mailbag* (Monday and Thursday), *Newmarket* (Tuesday), and *This is Russia* (Wednesday and Friday). Weekends, it's the excellent ●*Music and Musicians*. On the half-hour, the lineup includes *Kaleidoscope* (Monday), ●*Music Around Us* and ●*Music at Your Request* (Tuesday), *Our Homeland* (Wednesday), *Musical Tales* and *Russia: People and Events* (Thursday) and ●*Folk Box* on Friday. To Europe winter on 7320 kHz, and summer on 7379, 9890 and (weekends) 9820 and 11675 kHz. For the Mideast, tune to 7360 and 9470 kHz in winter, and 11985 kHz in summer. In Southern Africa, try 11510 kHz midyear.

Radio Japan. *News*, then weekdays it's *A Song for Everyone* and *Japan and the World 44 Minutes* (in-depth reporting). Saturday's feature is *World Interactive*, replaced Sunday by *J-Melo* and *Pop Joins the World*. One hour to Europe on 11970 kHz; to southern Africa on 15355 kHz; and to western North America and Central America on 9535 kHz.

Radio Taiwan International. Ten minutes of *News*, followed by features: *Made in Taiwan*, *Asia Review* and *Let's Learn Chinese* (Monday); *Strait Talk* and *We've Got Mail*

(Tuesday); *Trends*, *Speak Out* and ●*Jade Bells and Bamboo Pipes* (Wednesday); *Ilha Formosa*, *People* and *Instant Noodles* (Thursday); *Taiwan Inc.*, *Generation Why* and *Musical Chairs* (Friday); *News Talk* and *Groove Zone* (Saturday); and *The Undiscovered Country*, *Taipei Magazine* and *Stage, Screen and Studio* on Sunday. Sixty minutes to central and southern Africa winter on 11850 kHz, and summer on 15690 kHz.

China Radio International. Weekdays, *News* is followed by *China Drive*, an upbeat "drive-time" show. This is replaced Saturday by *CRI Roundup* and ●*China Roots* (ethnic music), and Sunday by *Reports from Developing Countries* and *China Beat* (Chinese popular music). One hour to Europe winter on 6100 and 7255 kHz, and summer on 9695, 11940 and 13760 kHz; and to eastern and southern Africa on 6100, 9570 and 11900 kHz.

Voice of Vietnam. Summer only at this time. Thirty minutes to western Europe via an Austrian relay on 9725 kHz. See 1800 for specifics. One hour later in winter.

Voice of America. Continues with programs for Africa. Monday through Fri-

17:00–18:00

Radio Netherlands harks back to the earliest days of global radio, which helps account for its consistently superior programs.   Shutterstock/Rebecca Picard

day, it's *World News Now*, then a feature: *Inquiry* (Monday), *Housecall* (a call-in health program, Tuesday), *Reporters' Roundtable* (Thursday) and *Sonny Side of Sports* (Friday). Wednesday, there's a full hour of *World News Now*. Weekends, 30 minutes of news are followed by Saturday's *Press Conference USA* or Sunday's *Encounter*. Audible well beyond where it is targeted. Winter on 13710, 15240 and 15445 kHz; and summer on 6080, 15410 and 15580 kHz. In southern Africa, tune to 15240 kHz in winter, and 15410 kHz midyear.

■**Radio France Internationale.** An additional half-hour (see 1600) of predominantly African fare. Monday through Friday, focuses on *news* from the eastern part of Africa. Weekends, there's *Spotlight on Africa*, health issues, features on French culture, sports, media in Africa, and a phone-in feature, *On-Line*. To East Africa winter on 11615 (or 15605) kHz, and summer on 17605 kHz.

Radio Cairo, Egypt. See 1600 for specifics. Continues with a broadcast to southern Africa, winter on 11785 kHz, and summer on 11740 kHz.

AFRTS Shortwave, USA. Network news, live sports, music and features in the upper-sideband mode from the Armed Forces Radio & Television Service. Transmitted from modestly powered U.S. Navy stations around the globe. Try 4319, 5446.5, 5765, 6350, 7811, 10320, 12133.5, 12579 and 13362 kHz.

17:30

Radio Bulgaria. Summer only at this time. *News*, followed weekdays by *Events and Developments*, and Saturday and Sunday by *Views Behind the News*. Thirty minutes to Europe on 9500 and 11500 kHz, and one hour later in winter.

Kol Israel. Summer only at this time. *News* for 15 minutes from Israel Radio's domestic network. To Europe and eastern North America on 9345, 11590 and 13675 kHz. One hour later in winter.

Radio Sweden. Summer only at this hour; see 1830 for program details. Thirty minutes of news and features for Europe and the Mideast on 6065 kHz. One hour later in winter.

17:45

All India Radio. The first 15 minutes of a two-hour broadcast to Europe, Africa and the Mideast, consisting of regional and international *news*, commentary, a variety of talks and features, press review and exotic Indian music. Continuous till 1945. To Europe on 7410, 9950 and 11620 kHz; to West Africa on 9445, 13605 and 15155 kHz; and to East Africa on 11935, 15075 and 17670 kHz.

Bangladesh Betar. *Voice of Islam*, a 30-minute broadcast focusing on Islamic themes. To Europe on 7185 kHz.

18:00–23:59
Europe & Mideast—Evening Prime Time
East Asia—Early Morning
Australasia—Morning
Eastern North America—Afternoon and Suppertime
Western North America—Midday

18:00

■**Radio Netherlands.** The first 60 minutes of an approximately three-hour broadcast targeted at Africa, and heard well beyond. Monday through Friday, the initial 27 minutes are taken up by ●*Newsline* (current events), with a feature occupying the next half-hour: ●*Research File* (Monday), ●*Euro-Quest* (Tuesday), ●*Documentary* (Wednesday), *Dutch Horizons* (Thursday) and ●*A Good Life* on Friday. A news feature and *Vox Humana* fill the Saturday slots, and are replaced Sunday by *Amsterdam Forum* and *Dutch Extra*. On 6020, 7120 (summer), 9895 (winter) and 11655 kHz. Best for southern Africa is 6020 kHz.

Voice of Vietnam. Begins with *news*, which is followed by *Commentary* or *Weekly Review*, short features and some pleasant Vietnamese music (especially at weekends). A half-hour to Europe on 5955 kHz. Via an Austrian relay, and should provide good reception. One hour earlier in summer.

All India Radio. Continuation of the transmission to Europe, Africa and the Mideast (see 1745). *News* and commentary, followed by programming of a more general nature. Look for a listener-response segment, *Faithfully Yours*, at 1830 Monday. To Europe on 7410, 9950 and 11620 kHz; to West Africa on 9445, 13605 and 15155 kHz; and to East Africa on 11935, 15075 and 17670 kHz.

Radio Prague, Czech Republic. Winter only at this time. *News*, then Monday through Friday there's *Current Affairs* and one or more features: *One on One* (Monday), *Talking Point* (Tuesday), *Czechs in History*, *Czechs Today* or *Spotlight* (Wednesday), *Panorama* and *Czech Science* (Thursday), and *Business Briefs* and *The Arts* (Friday).

On Saturday the news is followed by *Insight Central Europe*, and Sunday fare is *Mailbox* and *Letter from Prague* followed by *Encore* (classical music), *Magic Carpet* (Czech world music) or *Czech Books*. Thirty minutes to Europe on 5930 kHz, and to Australasia on 9400 kHz. Europe's broadcast is one hour earlier in summer, but for Australasia it's two hours later.

Radio Romania International. Starts with *Radio Newsreel*, a combination of news, commentary and press review. Features on Romania complete the broadcast. Regular spots include *Pro Memoria* (Romanian history), *Romanian Hits* and *Pages of Romanian Literature* (Monday); *Business Club* (Tuesday); *Society Today* and *Romanian Musicians* (Wednesday); *Traveller's Guide*, *Listeners Letterbox* and ●*The Skylark* (Romanian folk music) on Thursday; and *Terra the 21st Century*, ●*The Folk Music Box* and *Over Coffee with Artists* on Friday. Saturday, there's *World of Culture*, *RRI Encyclopedia* and *Radio Pictures*; and Sunday's broadcast includes *Sunday Studio* and *Letter from Bucharest*. Fifty-five minutes to Europe winter on 7120 and 9640 kHz, and summer on 9635 and 11730 kHz.

Radio Australia. Sunday through Thursday, *World News* is followed by *Pacific Beat* (news and current events). The Friday slots are *Pacific Review* and *Australian Express*. Winter Saturdays there's *Correspondents' Report* and the first half-hour of *Australia All Over*, replaced summer by *In the Loop (Rewind)* and ●*Australian Country Style*. Part of a continuous 24-hour service, and at this hour beamed to the Pacific on 6080, 7240, 9580, 9710 and 11880 kHz; to East Asia on 6080 kHz; and to Southeast Asia on 9475 kHz. In western North America, try 11880 kHz.

18:00–19:00

Tatyana Shvetsova prepares her program at the Voice of Russia's English service. Its shows are now as good as they've ever been.   VoR

Radio Polonia, Poland. This time winter only. See 1700 for program specifics. *News*, features and music reflecting Polish life and culture. Sixty minutes to Europe on 7220 and 7265 kHz. One hour earlier in summer.

Voice of Russia World Service. Continuous programming to Europe and beyond. Predominantly news-related fare during the initial half-hour in summer, but the winter schedule offers a more varied diet. Winter, *News* is followed by *Moscow Mailbag* (Monday and Thursday), *Newmarket* (Tuesday) and *This is Russia* on Wednesday and Friday. Weekends, it's the excellent ●*Music and Musicians*. On the half-hour, the lineup includes *Kaleidoscope* (Monday), ●*Music Around Us* and ●*Music at Your Request* (Tuesday), *Our Homeland* (Wednesday), *Musical Tales* and *Russia: People and Events* (Thursday) and ●*Folk Box* on Friday. Summer weekdays, the first half-hour consists of *news* followed by *Update*. The Saturday slot is filled by *Newmarket*, replaced Sunday by *Musical Tales*. More features complete the hour, and include *Guest Speaker* and *Life as it is* (Tuesday), ●*Russia–1,000 Years of Music* (Thursday), *Kaleidoscope* (Saturday) and ●*Christian Message from Moscow* on Sunday. To Europe winter on 7290, 7320 and (weekends) 5950 and 6175 kHz; and summer on 7370, 9820, 9890 and 11630 (or 9480) kHz. Also available winter only

to the Mideast on 7360 kHz. In southern Africa, tune to 11510 and (midyear) 9745 kHz.

Radio Argentina al Exterior—R.A.E. Monday through Friday only. *News*, press review and short features on Argentina, plus folk music and tangos. Fifty-five minutes to Europe on 9690 and 15345 kHz.

Voice of America. Continues with programs for Africa. Monday through Friday, there's *Africa News Tonight* and *Sonny Side of Sports* (except Wednesday, when there's *Straight Talk Africa*). These are replaced weekends by *Nightline Africa*. Winter on 4930 (from 1830 weekdays), 6035, 11975, 13710, 15240 and 17895 kHz; and summer on 4930 (from 1830 weekdays), 6080, 15410, 15580 and 17895 kHz. Best for southern Africa is 4930 kHz.

China Radio International. *News* and reports fill the first half-hour, and are followed by a daily feature: *Front Line* (Monday), *Biz China* (Tuesday), *China Horizons* (Wednesday), ●*Voices from Other Lands* (Thursday), *Life in China* (Friday), *Listeners' Garden* (Saturday) and *In the Spotlight* (Sunday). To Europe winter on 6100 kHz; and summer on 9600, 11940 and 13760 kHz.

Radio Taiwan International. Ten minutes of *News*, followed by features: *Made in Taiwan*, *Asia Review* and *Let's Learn Chinese* (Monday); *Strait Talk* and *We've Got Mail* (Tuesday); *Trends*, *Speak Out* and ●*Jade Bells and Bamboo Pipes* (Wednesday); *Ilha Formosa*, *People* and *Instant Noodles* (Thursday); *Taiwan Inc.*, *Generation Why* and *Musical Chairs* (Friday); *News Talk* and *Groove Zone* (Saturday); and *The Undiscovered Country*, *Taipei Magazine* and *Stage, Screen and Studio* (Sunday). One hour to western Europe on 3965 kHz.

Radio Canada International. *News*, then Monday through Friday it's *Canada Today*, replaced Saturday by *Business Sense* and Sunday by *Maple Leaf Mailbag* (a listener-response show). On the half-hour there's *Spotlight* (Wednesday and Sunday), *Media Zone* (Monday), *The Maple Leaf Mailbag* (repeat, Tuesday), *Business Sense* (Thursday)

18:00–19:00

and *Sci-Tech File* on Friday and Saturday. One hour to Africa winter on 7185, 11875, 15365 and 17740 kHz, and summer on 9530, 11765, 13730 and 15255 kHz. Best for southern Africa is 17740 kHz in winter (summer in the Southern Hemisphere), and 13730 kHz midyear. Heard well beyond the African continent.

AFRTS Shortwave, USA. Network news, live sports, music and features in the upper-sideband mode from the Armed Forces Radio & Television Service. Transmitted from modestly powered U.S. Navy stations around the globe. Try 4319, 5446.5, 5765, 6350, 7811, 10320, 12133.5, 12579 and 13362 kHz.

18:15

Bangladesh Betar. *News*, followed by Islamic and general interest features; some nice Bengali music, too. Thirty minutes to Europe on 7185 kHz.

18:30

Radio Bulgaria. This time winter only. *News*, then *Events and Developments* (week-days) or *Views Behind the News* (Saturday and Sunday). Thirty minutes to Europe on 5800 and 7500 kHz, and one hour earlier in summer.

Voice of Turkey. This time summer only. *News*, then *Review of the Turkish Press* followed by features on Turkish history, culture and international relations. Some enjoyable Turkish music, too. Fifty minutes to western Europe on 9785 kHz. One hour later in winter.

Kol Israel. Winter only at this time. *News* for 15 minutes from Israel Radio's domestic network. To Europe and eastern North America on 7545, 9345 and 11590 kHz. One hour earlier in summer.

Radio Sweden. Winter only at this time. Monday through Friday, *News* is followed by features about Sweden: *Culture* (Monday), *Discover* (Tuesday), *Real Life* (Wednesday), *Lifestyle* (Thursday), and *Inside Sweden*

on Friday. Saturday features rotate on a weekly basis: *Sweden Today, HeadSet, A J&J Lifestyle* and *Studio 49*; and Sunday there's *Network Europe*. Thirty minutes to Europe and the Mideast on 6065 kHz. One hour earlier in summer.

18:45

Radio Tirana, Albania. Monday through Saturday, and summer only at this time. Approximately 15 minutes of *news* and commentary from this small Balkan country. To Europe on 7465 and 9920 kHz. One hour later in winter.

19:00

■**Radio Netherlands.** The second hour of an approximately three-hour block of programming for Africa. Monday through Friday, starts with a feature and ends with ●*Newsline* (current events). The features are repeats of programs aired during the previous six days, and are well worth a second hearing: ●*EuroQuest* (Monday), ●*A Good Life* (Tuesday), *Dutch Horizons* (Wednesday) ●*Research File* (science, Thursday) and the award-winning ●*Documentary* on Friday. Weekends, Saturday's *Dutch Horizons* and Sunday's *Vox Humana* are followed by a news feature. On 5905 (summer), 7120 (best for southern Africa), 9895 (winter), 11655 and 17810 kHz. In southern Africa, tune to 7120 kHz. The weekend broadcasts are also available to North America, winter on 15315, 15525 and 17725 kHz; and summer on 15315, 17660 and 17735 kHz. On other days, listeners in the United States should try 17810 kHz, which is via a relay in the Netherlands Antilles.

Radio Australia. Begins with *World News*, then Sunday through Thursday it's the second hour of *Pacific Beat* (in-depth reporting on the region). Friday's slots go to *Asia Review* and *Rural Reporter*. Winter Saturdays, it's a continuation of *Australia All Over*; in summer, there's *Correspondents' Report* and the first half-hour of *Australia All*

19:00–20:00

Over. Continuous to Asia and the Pacific on 6080, 7240, 9500, 9580, 9710 and 11880 kHz. Listeners in western North America should try 11880 kHz, and best for East Asia is 6080 kHz. For Southeast Asia there's 9500 kHz.

Kol Israel. Summer only at this time. Twenty-five minutes of even-handed and comprehensive news reporting from and about Israel. To Europe and eastern North America on 9400 and 11590 kHz; and to southern Africa on 15640 kHz. One hour later in winter.

All India Radio. The final 45 minutes of a two-hour broadcast to Europe, Africa and the Mideast (see 1745). Starts off with *news*, then continues with a mixed bag of features and Indian music. To Europe on 7410, 9950 and 11620 kHz; to West Africa on 9445, 13605 and 15155 kHz; and to East Africa on 11935, 15075 and 17670 kHz.

Radio Budapest, Hungary. Summer only at this time. *News* and features, few of which are broadcast on a regular basis. Thirty minutes to Europe on 3975 and 6025 kHz. One hour later in winter.

■**Deutsche Welle,** Germany. *News*, then the daily ●*NewsLink*—commentary, interviews, background reports and analysis. Thirty minutes to Central, East and southern Africa winter on 7210, 9735, 11865, 12025 and 15275 kHz; and summer on 13780 and 15620 kHz. Best for southern Africa is 12025 kHz in winter, and 15620 kHz in summer.

Voice of Russia World Service. Continuous programming to Europe at this hour. Winter, *News* is followed weekdays by more of the same in *Update*, replaced Saturday by *Newmarket*, and Sunday by *Musical Tales*. A series of features complete the hour, and include *Guest Speaker* and *Life as it is* (Tuesday), ●*Russia–1,000 Years of Music* (Thursday), *Kaleidoscope* (Saturday) and ●*Christian Message from Moscow* (Sunday). Monday through Saturday summer, it's *News and Views*, replaced Sunday by *Sunday Panorama*. On the half-hour, a news summary is followed by features: *Our Homeland*

(Sunday and Monday), *Russian by Radio* (Tuesday), ●*Jazz Show* (Wednesday), *VOR Treasure Store* (Thursday), *Moscow Calling* (Friday) and ●*Christian Message from Moscow* on Saturday. On 6175 and 7290 kHz in winter; and 7195, 7310, 9890 and 12070 kHz in summer.

China Radio International. *News* and reports fill the first half-hour, and are followed by a daily feature: *Front Line* (Monday), *Biz China* (Tuesday), *China Horizons* (Wednesday), ●*Voices from Other Lands* (Thursday), *Life in China* (Friday), *Listeners' Garden* (Saturday) and *In the Spotlight* (Sunday). One hour to the Mideast and North Africa on 7295 and 9435 (or 9440) kHz. Also available summer only to Europe on 11940 kHz.

Radio Thailand. A 60-minute package of *news*, features and (if you're lucky) enjoyable Thai music. To Northern Europe winter on 9805 kHz, and summer on 7155 kHz.

Voice of Korea, North Korea. For now, of curiosity value only. An hour of old-style communist programming to Europe on 7570 (or 13760) and 12015 (or 15245) kHz. Also heard in parts of East Asia on 4405 kHz.

Voice of Vietnam. Repeat of the 1800 transmission (see there for specifics). A half-hour to Europe on 7280 and 9730 kHz.

Voice of America. Continuous programming for Africa. Opens with 30 minutes of news, with programs in Special (slow speed) English completing the hour. Winter on 4930, 4940, 6035, 11975, 13710, 15240, 15580 and 17895 kHz; and summer on 4930, 4940, 6080, 15410, 15445, 15580 and 17895 kHz. Best for southern Africa is 4930 kHz. In North America, try 15580 kHz in winter, and 15445 kHz in summer.

KBS World Radio, South Korea. Opens with 10 minutes of *news*, then Monday through Friday, a commentary. This is followed by 30 minutes of *Seoul Calling* and a 15-minute feature: *Shaping Korea, Business Watch, Korea Spotlight, Korea Today and Tomorrow* and *Seoul Report*, respectively. Saturday's news is followed by *Worldwide Friendship* (a listener-response show), and

Sunday by *Korean Pop Interactive*. Sixty minutes to East Asia on 5975 kHz, and to Europe on 7275 kHz.

Voice of Korea, North Korea. Repeat of the 1800 broadcast. The last of the old-time communist stations. One hour to the Mideast on 9975 kHz; and to southern Africa on 7100 and 11710 (or 11910) kHz. Also heard in parts of East Asia on 4405 kHz.

AFRTS Shortwave, USA. Network news, live sports, music and features in the upper-sideband mode from the Armed Forces Radio & Television Service. Transmitted from modestly powered U.S. Navy stations around the globe. Try 4319, 5446.5, 5765, 6350, 7811, 10320, 12133.5, 12579 and 13362 kHz.

19:30

Voice of Turkey. Winter only at this time. See 1830 for program details. Some unusual programs and friendly presentation make for entertaining listening. Fifty minutes to western Europe on 6055 kHz. One hour earlier in summer.

Voice of the Islamic Republic of Iran. A one-hour broadcast of news, commentary and features reflecting Islamic values. To Europe winter on 6010 and 7320 kHz, and summer on 6205 (or 7540) and 7205 kHz. Also available to southern Africa winter on 9855 and 11695 kHz, and midyear on 9800 and 9925 kHz.

Radio Sweden. Summer only at this time, and a repeat of the 1730 broadcast. See 1830 for program details. Thirty minutes to Europe and the Mideast on 6065 kHz, and one hour later in winter.

RAI International—Radio Roma, Italy. Actually starts at 1935. Approximately 12 minutes of *news*, then some Italian music. Twenty minutes to western Europe winter on 6035 and 9760 kHz, and summer on 5960 and 9845 kHz.

Radio Belarus. Monday, Tuesday, Thursday and Friday, summer only at this time. See 2030 for specifics. Thirty minutes to

Europe on 7105, 7280 and 7290 kHz. One hour later in winter.

19:45

Radio Tirana, Albania. Monday through Saturday, and winter only at this time. Approximately 15 minutes of *news* and commentary from this small Balkan country. To Europe on 7465 and 7530 kHz. One hour earlier in summer.

Vatican Radio. Summer only at this time, and actually starts at 1950. Twenty minutes of programming oriented to Catholics. To Europe on 4005, 5885 and 7250 kHz. One hour later in winter.

20:00

■**Deutsche Welle,** Germany. *News*, then Monday through Friday there's the in-depth ●*NewsLink*. The second half-hour consists of features: *Insight* and *Business German* (Monday), *World in Progress* (Tuesday), ●*Money Talks* (Wednesday), *Living Planet* (Thursday) and *Spectrum* (Friday). The weekend *Sports Report* is followed by *Inspired Minds* (Saturday) and *Mailbag* (Sunday). One hour to East, Central and southern Africa, winter on 6145, 9735, 12025 and 15725 kHz; and summer on 7130, 11795, 13780 and 15205 kHz. Best for southern Africa is 12025 kHz in winter, and 7130 kHz midyear.

Radio Canada International. Summer only at this time. *News*, then Monday through Friday it's *Canada Today*, replaced Saturday by *Business Sense* and Sunday by *Maple Leaf Mailbag* (a listener-response show). On the half-hour there's *Spotlight* (Wednesday and Sunday), *Media Zone* (Monday), *The Maple Leaf Mailbag* (repeat, Tuesday), *Business Sense* (Thursday) and *Sci-Tech File* on Friday and Saturday. Sixty minutes to Europe, North Africa and the Mideast on 5850, 7235, 11765 and 15325 kHz. One hour later during winter.

■**Radio Netherlands.** The final 57 minutes of an approximately three-hour broadcast

20:00–20:00

targeted at Africa. Monday through Friday, opens with a feature: ●*Research File* (Monday), ●*EuroQuest* (Tuesday), ●*Documentary* (Wednesday), *Dutch Horizons* (Thursday) and ●*A Good Life* (Friday). ●*Newsline* (current events) completes the broadcast. Weekend fare consists of Saturday's *Vox Humana* and news feature, and Sunday's *Amsterdam Forum* and *Dutch Extra*. On 5905 (summer), 7120 (best for southern Africa), 9895 (winter), 11655 and 17810 kHz. The weekend broadcasts are also available to North America, winter on 15315, 15525 and 17725 kHz; and summer on 15315, 17660 and 17735 kHz. On other days, listeners in the United States can try 17810 kHz, which is via a relay in the Netherlands Antilles.

Radio Damascus, Syria. Actually starts at 2005. *News*, a daily press review, and different features for each day of the week. These can be heard at approximately 2030 and 2045, and include a mix of political commentary, Islamic philosophy and Arab and Syrian culture. Most of the transmission, however, is given over to Syrian and some western popular music. One hour to Europe, occasionally audible in eastern North America, on 12085 and 9330 kHz. Low audio level is often a problem.

Radio Australia. Starts with *World News*, then Sunday through Thursday it's the final hour of *Pacific Beat* (in-depth reporting). Winter, the Friday slots are *Correspondents' Notebook, Saturday AM* and *Saturday Extra*; and summer, *Pacific Review* and ●*Australian Country Style*. Saturday, it's a continuation of *Australia All Over* (a popular show from the domestic ABC Local Radio network). Continuous programming to the Pacific on 6080 and 7240 (Friday and Saturday only), 9580, 11650, 11660, 11880 and 12080 kHz; and to Southeast Asia on 9500 kHz. In western North America, try 11650, 11660 and 11880 kHz.

Voice of Russia World Service. Continuous programming to Europe at this hour. Monday through Saturday winter, there's *News and Views*, replaced Sunday by *Sunday Panorama*. On the half-hour, a news summary is followed by features: *Our Homeland* (Sunday and Monday), *Russian by Radio* (Tuesday), ●*Jazz Show* (Wednesday), *VOR Treasure Store* (Thursday), *Moscow Calling* (Friday) and ●*Christian Message from Moscow* (Saturday). Monday through Saturday summer, *News* is followed by features: *Science Plus* (Monday), *Moscow Mailbag* (Tuesday and Friday), *Newmarket* (Wednesday and Saturday) and *This is Russia* on Thursday. Pick of the features during the second half-hour are: ●*Songs from Russia* (Monday), ●*Music Around Us* (Tuesday), *Musical Tales* (Wednesday), ●*Folk Box* (Thursday) and ●*Jazz Show* on Friday. Highlight of the week is ●*Music and Musicians* which follows the news on Sunday. Winter on 6145, 7290 and 7330 kHz; and summer on 7370, 9890, 12070 and 15455 kHz. Some channels are audible in eastern North America.

Radio Exterior de España ("Spanish National Radio"). Weekdays only at this time. Spanish and international *news*, commentary, Spanish pop music, a review of the Spanish press, and a general interest feature. Sixty minutes to Europe winter on 9690 kHz, and summer on 15290 kHz; and to North and West Africa winter on 9595 kHz, and summer on 9570 kHz.

Radio Budapest, Hungary. Winter only at this time. *News* and features, most of which are broadcast on a non-regular basis. Thirty minutes to Europe on 3975 and 6025 kHz. One hour earlier in summer.

China Radio International. *News* and reports fill the first half-hour, and are followed by a daily feature: *Front Line* (Monday), *Biz China* (Tuesday), *China Horizons* (Wednesday), ●*Voices from Other Lands* (Thursday), *Life in China* (Friday), *Listeners' Garden* (Saturday) and *In the Spotlight* (Sunday). One hour to Europe on 5960, 7190, 7285, 9490 (winter), 9600 and (summer) 9800 kHz; to the Mideast and North Africa on 7295 and 9440 kHz; and to eastern and southern Africa on 11640 and 13630 kHz.

Radio Tirana, Albania. Monday through Saturday, summer only at this time. *News*, short features and some lively Albanian music (especially Saturday). Thirty minutes

20:00–20:00

Whether reporting on
Parliament or presenting
cultural affairs, Radio
Budapest remains a
trusted warhorse of world
band radio.

Shutterstock/Antoine Beyeler

to Europe on 7465 kHz. One hour later in winter

Kol Israel. Winter only at this time. Twenty-five minutes of *news* and in-depth reporting from and about Israel. To Europe and eastern North America on 6280 (or 11590) and 7545 kHz; and to southern Africa on 15640 kHz. One hour earlier in summer.

Voice of Vietnam. *News*, then it's either *Commentary* or *Weekly Review*, which in turn is followed by short features. Look for some pleasant Vietnamese music towards the end of the broadcast (more at weekends). A half-hour to Europe on 7280 and 9730 kHz.

Voice of Mongolia. Original programming is aired on Monday, Wednesday and Friday, and is repeated on the following day. Starts with *News*, and then it's either a listener-response program (Monday) or reports and interviews. The entire Sunday broadcast is devoted to exotic Mongolian music. Thirty minutes to West and Central Asia on 12015 kHz, and occasionally heard in Europe.

Radio Prague, Czech Republic. Summer only at this time. *News*, then Monday through Friday it's *Current Affairs* plus one or more features: *One on One* (Monday), *Talking Point* (Tuesday), *Czechs in History*,

Czechs Today or *Spotlight* (Wednesday), *Panorama* and *Czech Science* (Thursday) and *Business Briefs* and *The Arts* on Friday. The Saturday news is followed by *Magazine*, *ABC of Czech* and a repeat of Tuesday's *One on One*. Sunday's lineup is *Mailbox* and *Letter from Prague* followed by *Encore* (classical music), *Magic Carpet* (Czech world music) or *Czech Books*. Thirty minutes to western Europe on 5930 kHz, and to Southeast Asia and Australasia on 11600 kHz. One hour later in winter.

Voice of America. Continuous programming for Africa. Monday through Friday, it's *Africa Beat* (modern African music, guest DJ spots, interviews), replaced weekends by ●*Music Time in Africa*. Winter on 4930, 4940, 6035, 11975, 15240 and 15580 kHz; and summer on 4930, 4940, 15445 and 15580 kHz. Best for southern Africa is 4930 kHz. In North America, try 15580 kHz in winter, and 15445 kHz in summer.

AFRTS Shortwave, USA. Network news, live sports, music and features in the upper-sideband mode from the Armed Forces Radio & Television Service. Transmitted from modestly powered U.S. Navy stations around the globe. Try 4319, 5446.5, 5765, 6350, 7811, 10320, 12133.5, 12579 and 13362 kHz.

20:30–21:00

20:30

Radio Sweden. Winter only at this time. Monday through Friday, *News* is followed by features about Sweden: *Culture* (Monday), *Discover* (Tuesday), *Real Life* (Wednesday), *Lifestyle* (Thursday), and *Inside Sweden* on Friday. Saturday features rotate on a weekly basis: *Sweden Today*, *HeadSet*, *A J&J Lifestyle* and *Studio 49*; and Sunday there's *Network Europe*. Thirty minutes to Europe and the Mideast (one hour earlier in summer) on 6065 kHz, and to Asia and Australasia (one hour later in summer) on 7420 kHz.

Radio Thailand. Fifteen minutes of *news* targeted at Europe. Winter on 9535 kHz, and summer on 9680 kHz.

Voice of Turkey. This time summer only. *News*, followed by *Review of the Turkish Press* and features with a strong local flavor. Selections of Turkish popular and classical music complete the program. Fifty minutes

The Voice of Turkey reports on the country's pivotal East-West role. Istanbul's Ortaköy Camii mosque represents Islam, yet it lies within a district of free-spirited artists and students.   Shutterstock/Fuat Kose

to Southeast Asia and Australasia on 7170 kHz. One hour later during winter.

Radio Belarus. Monday, Tuesday, Thursday and Friday, winter only at this time. Monday and Thursday, there's news, background reports and commentary in *Belarus Today*. This is replaced Tuesday by *Events* (political and economic analysis) and Friday by *Cultural Variety* (science, art, music and replies to listeners' letters). Thirty minutes to Europe on 7125, 7340 and 7440 kHz. Occasionally heard in eastern North America.

Radio Habana Cuba. The first half of a 60-minute broadcast. Monday through Saturday, there's international and Cuban news followed by *RHC's Viewpoint*. This is replaced Sunday by *Weekly Review*. To the Caribbean on 9505 kHz, and to eastern North America on 11760 kHz.

Voice of Vietnam. *News*, then it's either *Commentary* or *Weekly Review*, which in turn is followed by short features. Look for some pleasant Vietnamese music, especially at weekends. A half-hour to West and Central Africa on 7220 and 9550 kHz, and heard far beyond.

RAI International—Radio Roma, Italy. Actually starts at 2025. Twenty minutes of *news* and Italian music to the Mideast. Winter on 5985 kHz; and summer on 5970 (irregular) and 11875 kHz.

20:45

All India Radio. The first 15 minutes of a much longer broadcast, consisting of a press review, Indian music, regional and international *news*, commentary, and a variety of talks and features of general interest. Continuous till 2230. To Western Europe on 7410, 9445, 9950 and 11620 kHz; and to Australasia on 9910, 11620 and 11715 kHz. Early risers in Southeast Asia can try the channels for Australasia.

Vatican Radio. Winter only at this time, and actually starts at 2050. Twenty minutes of predominantly Catholic fare. To Europe on 4005, 5885 and 7250 kHz. One hour earlier in summer.

21:00

■**BBC World Service for the Caribbean.**
The first 60 minutes of a two-hour broadcast. Weekdays, opens with *news*, then there's *Sports Roundup*, *Caribbean Report*, *Business Daily* and another edition of *Sports Roundup*. Weekend fare consists of *World Briefing*, *Sports Roundup* and either Saturday's *Discovery* (science) or Sunday's ●*The Instant Guide* and *Over To You*. On 9660 (winter), 11675 and (summer) 13765 kHz.

Radio Exterior de España ("Spanish National Radio"). Summer weekends only at this time. Features, including rebroadcasts of programs aired earlier in the week. One hour to Europe on 9840 kHz, and to North and West Africa on 9570 kHz. Sometimes pre-empted by live sports in Spanish, and may start around 2135, or not at all. One hour later in winter.

Radio Ukraine International. Summer only at this time. *News*, commentary, reports and interviews, providing ample coverage of Ukrainian life. A listener-response program is aired Saturday, and most of Sunday's broadcast is a showpiece for Ukrainian music. Sixty minutes to western Europe on 7490 (or 5830) kHz. One hour later in winter. Should be easily heard despite the station's technical limitations.

Radio Canada International. Winter only at this time. See 2000 for program specifics. Sixty minutes to western Europe and North Africa on 5850 and 9770 kHz. One hour earlier in summer.

Radio Prague, Czech Republic. Winter only at this time. See 2000 for program details. *News* and features on Czech life and culture. A half-hour to western Europe (and easily audible in parts of eastern North America) on 5930 kHz, and to Southeast Asia and Australasia on 9430 kHz. One hour earlier in summer.

Radio Bulgaria. This time summer only. Starts with *News*, then Monday through Friday there's *Events and Developments*, replaced weekends by *Views Behind the News*. The remaining time is taken up by

Radio Bulgaria features "Time Out for Music" and "Folk Studio," both devoted to Bulgaria's little-known musical traditions that include the bagpipe.

Shuttershock/Anton Gavrailov

regular programs such as *Keyword Bulgaria* and *Time Out for Music*, and weekly features like *Sports* (Monday), *Magazine Economy* (Tuesday), *The Way We Live* (Wednesday), *History Club* (Thursday), *DX Programme* (for radio enthusiasts, Friday) and *Answering Your Letters* (a listener-response show, Saturday). The week's highlight is Sunday's ●*Folk Studio* (Bulgarian folk music). Sixty minutes to Europe on 5800 and 7500 kHz. One hour later during winter.

China Radio International. Repeat of the 2000 transmission; see there for specifics. One hour to Europe on 5960, 7190, 7285, 9490 (winter), 9600 and (summer) kHz. A 30-minute reduced version is also available for eastern and southern Africa on 11640 and 13630 kHz.

Voice of Russia World Service. Winter only at this time. *News*, then *Science Plus* (Monday), *Moscow Mailbag* (Tuesday and Friday), the business-oriented *Newmarket* (Wednesday and Saturday), *This is Russia* (Thursday) and the excellent ●*Music and Musicians* on Sunday. Pick of the features during the second half-hour are: ●*Songs from Russia* (Monday), ●*Music Around Us* (Tuesday), *Musical Tales* (Wednesday), ●*Folk Box* (Thursday) and ●*Jazz Show* on Friday. One hour earlier in summer. To Europe on

7330 and 7390 kHz. Some channels are audible in eastern North America.

Radio Budapest, Hungary. Summer only at this time. *News* and features, few of which are broadcast on a regular basis. Thirty minutes to Europe on 6025 kHz, and to southern Africa on 9525 kHz. One hour later in winter.

Radio Belarus. Summer Sundays only at this time. *Legacy*, focusing on history, preservation and cultural heritage. Thirty minutes to Europe on 7105, 7280 and 7290 kHz. One hour later in winter.

Radio Japan. *News*, then Monday through Friday (Tuesday through Saturday local date in Australasia) it's *A Song for Everyone* and *Asian Top News*. A 35-minute feature completes the hour: *Japan Music Archives* (Monday), Japanese language lessons (Tuesday and Thursday), *Japan Music Travelogue* (Wednesday), and *Count Down Japan* (Japanese popular music) on Friday. *Weekend Japanology* and *Japan Music Scene* fill the Saturday slots, and *J-Melo* and *Pop Joins the World* are aired Sunday. Sixty minutes to Europe on 6055 (summer), 6090 (winter) and 6180 kHz; to Australasia on 6035 kHz; to western North America on 17825 kHz; to Hawaii on 21670 kHz; and to Central Africa on 11855 kHz. The broadcast on 17825 kHz has different programming after 2115.

Voice of America. The final 60 minutes of seven hours of continuous programming for Africa. Opens with *news*, then it's music: *American Gold* (Monday), *Roots and Branches* (Tuesday), *Classic Rock* (Wednesday), *Top Twenty* (Thursday), *Hip Hop Connection* (Friday and Saturday), and *Fusion* (jazz) on Sunday. Winter on 11975, 13710, 15240 and 15580 kHz; and summer on 6080 and 15580 kHz.

Radio Australia. *World News*, then Sunday through Thursday there's a look at current events in *AM*, followed by a relay of Radio New Zealand International's *Dateline Pacific*. Winter Fridays, it's the final hour of *Saturday Extra*; summer, there's *Saturday AM* and the first half-hour of *Saturday Extra*. On the remaining day, it's Saturday's

Australia All Over. Continuous to the Pacific on 9660, 11650, 11660, 12080, 13630 and 15515 kHz; and to Southeast Asia on 9500 and 11695 kHz. Listeners in western North America should try 11650 and 11660 kHz.

■**Deutsche Welle,** Germany. *News*, and then the daily ●*NewsLink*—commentary, interviews, background reports and analysis. On the half-hour the weekday lineup is ●*A World of Music* (Monday), ●*Arts on the Air* (Tuesday), *Living in Germany* and *Treasures of the World* (Wednesday), the youth-oriented *Cool* (Thursday) and *Hits in Germany* (Friday). Weekends, *Sports Report* is followed by *German by Radio* (Saturday) and *Inspired Minds* (Sunday). One hour to West Africa, and audible in much of eastern and southern North America and the Caribbean. Winter on 7280, 9615 and 11690 kHz; and summer on 9440, 11865 and 15205 kHz. In North America, try 9615 and 11690 kHz in winter, and 11865 and 15205 kHz in summer.

KBS World Radio, South Korea. Summer only at this time. Opens with 10 minutes of *news*, then Monday through Friday, a commentary. This is followed by a 15-minute feature: *Shaping Korea, Business Watch, Korea Spotlight, Korea Today and Tomorrow* and *Seoul Report*, respectively. Saturday's news is followed by *Worldwide Friendship* (a listener-response show), and Sunday by *Korean Pop Interactive*. Thirty minutes to Europe on 3955 kHz.

Radio Tirana, Albania. Monday through Saturday, winter only at this time. Thirty minutes of news, short features and Albanian music. To Europe on 7465 kHz. One hour earlier in summer

Voice of Korea, North Korea. Repeat of the 1800 broadcast. The last of the old-time communist stations. One hour to Europe on 7570 (or 13760) and 12015 (or 15245) kHz. Also heard in parts of East Asia on 4405 kHz.

Radio Habana Cuba. The final 30 minutes of a one-hour broadcast. Monday through Saturday, there's a *news* bulletin and the sports-oriented *Time Out* (five minutes each), then a feature: *Caribbean Outlook* (Monday and Thursday), *DXers Unlimited*

(Tuesday and Saturday), the *Mailbag Show* (Wednesday) and *Weekly Review* (Friday). These are replaced Sunday by a longer edition of *Mailbag Show*. To the Caribbean on 9505 kHz, and to eastern North America on 11760 kHz.

All India Radio. Continues to Western Europe on 7410, 9445, 9950 and 11620 kHz; and to Australasia on 9910, 11620 and 11715 kHz. Look for a listener-response segment, *Faithfully Yours*, at 2120 Monday. The European frequencies are audible in parts of eastern North America, while those for Australasia are also heard in Southeast Asia.

21:15

Radio Damascus, Syria. Actually starts at 2110. *News*, a daily press review, and different features for each day of the week. These include a mix of political commentary, Islamic themes and Arab and Syrian culture. The transmission also contains Syrian and some western popular music. Sixty minutes to North America and Australasia on 12085 and 9330 kHz. Audio level is often very low.

Radio Cairo, Egypt. The start of a 90-minute broadcast focusing on Arab and Egyptian themes. The initial quarter-hour of general programming is followed by *news*, commentary and political items. This in turn is followed by a cultural program until 2215, when the station again reverts to more general fare. A big signal to Europe on 9990 kHz.

AFRTS Shortwave, USA. Network news, live sports, music and features in the upper-sideband mode from the Armed Forces Radio & Television Service. Transmitted from modestly powered U.S. Navy stations around the globe. Try 4319, 5446.5, 5765, 6350, 7811, 10320, 12133.5, 12579 and 13362 kHz.

21:30

Radio Romania International. *News* and commentary followed by short features on

Radio Habana Cuba has slowly morphed from such tendentious fare as the anthem, "¡Cuba sí, yanquis no!" This widely heard voice is still 99 44/100 percent Fidelista, but it now favors persuasion, entertainment and even the occasional report from the domed Capitolio. Shutterstock/Jose Miguel Hernandez Leon

Romania. Twenty-five minutes to Europe winter on 6055 and 7145 kHz, and summer on 7210 and 9535 kHz; and to eastern North America winter on 9755 and 11940 kHz, and summer on 11940 and 15465 kHz.

Radio Prague, Czech Republic. Summer only at this time; see 2230 for program specifics. Thirty minutes to North America on 11600 kHz, and to West Africa on 9410 kHz. The broadcast for North America is one hour later in winter, but there is no corresponding broadcast for West Africa.

Voice of Turkey. This time winter only. *News*, followed by *Review of the Turkish Press* and features, some of them unusual. Exotic Turkish music, too. Fifty minutes to

Southeast Asia and Australasia on 9525 kHz. One hour earlier in summer.

Radio Sweden. Summer only at this time; see 2230 for specifics. Thirty minutes of news and features about Sweden to Europe and the Mideast on 6065 kHz, and to Australasia on 7420 kHz.

22:00

Radio Canada International. Summer only at this time; see 2300 for specifics. Sixty minutes to eastern North America on 6100 kHz, and one hour later in winter.

■**BBC World Service for the Caribbean.** The final 60 minutes of a two-hour broadcast. Starts with *news*, then weekdays there's *World Briefing*, *World Business Report* and a feature: *Health Check* (Monday), *Digital Planet* (Tuesday), *Discovery* (science, Wednesday), ●*One Planet* (Thursday) and *Science in Action* (Friday). These are replaced Saturday by *From Our Own Correspondent* and ●*World Business Review*, and Sunday by a documentary and ●*Heart and Soul*. Winter on 5975 and 9660 kHz, and summer on 5975 and 13765 kHz.

Radio Bulgaria. This time winter only. See 2100 for specifics. News and features from the Balkans—don't miss Sunday's ●*Folk Studio* (Bulgarian folk music). Sixty minutes to Europe, also heard in parts of eastern North America, on 5800 and 7500 kHz. One hour earlier in summer.

Radio Cairo, Egypt. The second half of a 90-minute broadcast to Europe on 9990 kHz; see 2115 for program details.

Radio Exterior de España ("Spanish National Radio"). Winter weekends only at this time. Features, including repeats of programs aired earlier in the week. One hour to Europe on 9680 kHz, and to North and West Africa on 9595 kHz. Sometimes pre-empted by live sports in Spanish, and may start around 2235, or not at all. One hour earlier in summer.

China Radio International. Weekdays, *News* is followed by *China Drive*, an upbeat "drive-time" show. This is replaced Saturday by *CRI Roundup* and ●*China Roots* (ethnic music), and Sunday by *Reports from Developing Countries* and *China Beat* (Chinese popular music). One hour to Europe winter on 7175 kHz, and summer on 7170 kHz, via CRI's Moscow relay.

Voice of America. The first of two hours to East and Southeast Asia and the Pacific. Predominantly news fare at this hour. To East and Southeast Asia winter on 15185, 15305, 15290 and 17740 kHz; and summer on 7215, 11725, 15185 and 15290 kHz. For Australasia there's 15185 and 17740 kHz in winter, and 11725 kHz midyear.

RAI International—Radio Roma, Italy. Actually starts at 2205. Twenty-five minutes of *news* and Italian music to East Asia winter on 6000 (or 6090) kHz, and summer on 11895 kHz.

Radio Australia. *News*, followed Sunday through Thursday by *AM* (current events) and, from 2240, *Breakfast Club*. Winter Fridays, there's *In the Loop (Rewind)* and *Talking Point*, replaced summer by the final hour of *Saturday Extra*. Saturday, winter's *Correspondents' Report* and *Innovations* are replaced summer by the final segment of *Australia All Over*. Continuous programming to the Pacific on 13630, 15230, 15515 and 17785 kHz; to East Asia on 15240 kHz; and to Southeast Asia on 13620 kHz. In North America, try 17785 kHz, especially during summer.

Radio Taiwan International. Ten minutes of *News*, followed by features: *Made in Taiwan*, *Asia Review* and *Let's Learn Chinese* (Monday); *Strait Talk* and *We've Got Mail* (Tuesday); *Trends*, *Speak Out* and ●*Jade Bells and Bamboo Pipes* (Wednesday); *Ilha Formosa*, *People* and *Instant Noodles* (Thursday); *Taiwan Inc.*, *Generation Why* and *Musical Chairs* (Friday); *News Talk* and *Groove Zone* (Saturday); and *The Undiscovered Country*, *Taipei Magazine* and *Stage, Screen and Studio* on Sunday. One hour to Europe via RTI's North American relay, winter on 9355 kHz, and summer on 15600 kHz.

Radio Belarus. Winter Sundays only at this time. *Legacy*, focusing on history, preservation and cultural heritage. Thirty minutes to Europe on 7125, 7280 and 7290 kHz. One hour earlier in summer. Sometimes audible in eastern North America.

Radio Budapest, Hungary. Winter only at this time. *News* and features, most of which are broadcast on a non-regular basis. Thirty minutes to Europe on 6025 kHz, and to southern Africa on 9535 (or 9795) kHz. One hour earlier in summer.

Voice of Turkey. Summer only at this time. *News*, then *Review of the Turkish Press* and features on Turkish history and culture. Selections of Turkish popular and classical music complete the program. Fifty minutes to western Europe and eastern North America on 9830 kHz. One hour later during winter.

Radio Ukraine International. Winter only at this time. A potpourri of things Ukrainian, with the Sunday broadcast often featuring some excellent music. Sixty minutes to Europe and beyond on 5840 kHz. One hour earlier in summer.

All India Radio. The final half-hour of a transmission to Western Europe and Australasia, consisting mainly of news-related fare. To Western Europe on 7410, 9445, 9950 and 11620 kHz; and to Australasia on 9910, 11620 and 11715 kHz. Frequencies for Europe are audible in parts of eastern North America, while those for Australasia are also heard in Southeast Asia.

AFRTS Shortwave, USA. Network news, live sports, music and features in the upper-sideband mode from the Armed Forces Radio & Television Service. Transmitted from modestly powered U.S. Navy stations around the globe. Try 4319, 5446.5, 5765, 6350, 7811, 10320, 12133.5, 12579 and 13362 kHz.

22:15

Voice of Croatia. Summer only at this time. Nominally 15 minutes of news, reports and interviews, but actual length varies. To eastern North America and South America on 9925 kHz. One hour later in winter.

22:30

Radio Sweden. Winter only at this time. Monday through Friday, it's a smorgasbord of *news* and features about Sweden: *Culture* (Tuesday), *Discover* (Wednesday), *Real Life* (Thursday), *Lifestyle* (Friday), and *Inside Sweden* on Saturday. Sunday features rotate on a weekly basis: *Sweden Today*, *HeadSet*, *A J&J Lifestyle* and *Studio 49*; and Monday it's *Network Europe*. Thirty minutes to Europe and the Mideast on 6065 kHz, and one hour earlier in summer.

Radio Prague, Czech Republic. *News*, then Monday through Friday there's *Current Affairs* followed by a feature or two. Monday's *One on One* is replaced Tuesday by *Talking Point* (interviews); Wednesday's slot is *Czechs in History*; *Czechs Today* or *Spotlight*; Thursday's features are *Panorama* and *Czech Science*; and Friday brings *Business Briefs* and *The Arts*. Saturday's *Insight Central Europe* is replaced Sunday by *Mailbox* and *Letter from Prague* followed by *Encore* (classical music), *Magic Carpet* (Czech world music) or *Czech Books*. A half-hour to North America winter on 5930 and 9435 kHz, and summer on 7345 and 9415 kHz.

22:45

All India Radio. The first 15 minutes of a much longer broadcast, consisting of Indian music, regional and international *news*, commentary, and a variety of talks and features of general interest. Continuous till 0045. To East Asia on 9950, 11645 and 13605 kHz; and to Southeast Asia on 9705, 11620 and 13605 kHz.

23:00

Radio Canada International. Winter only at this time. Monday through Friday, opens with *The World at Six* and continues with *As It Happens* (Canadian and international news and reports). On the remaining days it's ●*The World This Weekend* and either Sunday's comedy show or Monday's *Maple Leaf Mailbag*. To eastern North America on 6100 and 6195 kHz. One hour earlier in summer.

23:00–23:30

Bulgarian street festivals sound as good on radio as they look in print.

Shutterstock/Penka Todorova Vitkova

Voice of Turkey. Winter only at this hour; see 2200 for specifics. Fifty minutes to western Europe and eastern North America on 5960 kHz. One hour earlier in summer.

Radio Habana Cuba. Monday through Saturday, there's international and Cuban news followed by *RHC's Viewpoint*. On the half-hour there's a *news* bulletin and the sports-oriented *Time Out* (five minutes each), then a feature: *Caribbean Outlook* (Monday and Thursday), *DXers Unlimited* (Tuesday and Saturday), the *Mailbag Show* (Wednesday) and *Weekly Review* (Friday). Sunday fare includes *Weekly Review* and a longer edition of *Mailbag Show*. One hour to the Caribbean on 9550 kHz.

Radio Australia. *World News*, followed Sunday through Thursday by *Connect Asia* (news, commentary and analysis), and Friday by *Asia Review* and *Australian Express*. Winter Saturdays, there's *Background Briefing* and *Perspective*, replaced summer by *Correspondents' Report* and *Innovations*. Continuous to the Pacific on 9660, 12080, 13630, 15230, 17785 and 17795 kHz; to East Asia on 13630 and (till 2330) 15240 kHz; and to Southeast Asia on 13620 and (from 2330) 15415 and 17750 kHz. Listeners in North America should try 17785 and 17795 kHz, especially during summer.

China Radio International. *News* and reports fill the first half-hour, and are followed by a daily feature: *Front Line* (Sunday), *Biz China* (Monday), *China Horizons* (Tuesday), ●*Voices from Other Lands* (Wednesday), *Life in China* (Thursday), *Listeners' Garden* (Friday) and *In the Spotlight* (Saturday). One hour to the United States and Caribbean via CRI's Cuban and Canadian relays, winter on 5990, 6040 and 11970 kHz; and summer on 5990, 6145 and 13680 kHz. Also available to East Asia winter on 5915 kHz, and summer on 11685 kHz.

Radio Cairo, Egypt. The first hour of a 90-minute broadcast to eastern North America. A ten-minute *news* bulletin is aired at 2315, with the remaining time taken up by short features on Egypt, the Middle East and Islam. For the intellectual listener there's *Literary Readings* at 2345 Monday, and *Modern Arabic Poetry* at the same time Friday. More general fare is available in *Listener's Mail* at 2325 Thursday and Saturday. Winter on 11885 (or 11895) kHz, and summer on 11950 kHz.

Radio Romania International. Starts with *Radio Newsreel*, a combination of news, commentary and press review. Features on Romania complete the broadcast. Regular spots include *Pro Memoria* (Romanian history), *Romanian Hits* and *Pages of Romanian Literature* (Monday); *Business Club* (Tuesday); *Society Today* and *Romanian Musicians* (Wednesday); *Traveller's Guide, Listeners Letterbox* and ●*The Skylark* (Romanian folk music) on Thursday; and *Terra the 21st Century,* ●*The Folk Music Box* and *Over Coffee with Artists* on Friday. Saturday, there's *World of Culture, RRI Encyclopedia* and *Radio Pictures*; and Sunday's broadcast includes *Sunday Studio* and *Letter from Bucharest.* Fifty-five minutes to western Europe winter on 6015 and 7105 kHz, and summer on 6140 and 7265 kHz. Also to eastern North America winter on 6115 and 9610 kHz; and summer on 9645 and 11940 kHz.

Radio Bulgaria. Summer only at this time. Starts with *News,* then Monday through Friday there's *Events and Developments,* replaced weekends by *Views Behind the News.* The remaining time is taken up by regular programs such as *Keyword Bulgaria* and *Time Out for Music,* and weekly features like *Sports* (Monday), *Magazine Economy* (Tuesday), *The Way We Live* (Wednesday), *History Club* (Thursday), *DX Programme* (for radio enthusiasts, Friday) and *Answering Your Letters* (a listener-response show, Saturday). The week's highlight is Sunday's ●*Folk Studio* (Bulgarian folk music). Sixty minutes to eastern North America on 9700 and 11700 kHz. One hour later during winter.

All India Radio. Continuous programming to East and Southeast Asia. A potpourri of *news,* commentary, features and exotic Indian music. To East Asia on 9950, 11645 and 13605 kHz; and to Southeast Asia on 9705, 11620 and 13605 kHz.

Voice of America. The second and final hour of news-oriented programming to East and Southeast Asia and the Pacific. To East and Southeast Asia winter on 15185, 15305, 15290 and 17740 kHz; and summer on 7215, 11725, 15185 and 15290 kHz. For Australasia there's 15185 and 17740 kHz in winter, and 11725 kHz midyear.

AFRTS Shortwave, USA. Network news, live sports, music and features in the upper-sideband mode from the Armed Forces Radio & Television Service. Transmitted from modestly powered U.S. Navy stations around the globe. Try 4319, 5446.5, 5765, 6350, 7811, 10320, 12133.5, 12579 and 13362 kHz.

23:15

Voice of Croatia. Winter only at this time. Nominally 15 minutes of news, reports and interviews, but actual length varies. To eastern North America and South America on 7285 kHz. One hour earlier in summer.

23:30

Radio Prague, Czech Republic. Winter only at this time. *News,* then Monday through Friday there's *Current Affairs* and one or more features: *One on One* (Monday), *Talking Point* (Tuesday), *Czechs in History, Czechs Today* or *Spotlight* (Wednesday), *Panorama* and *Czech Science* (Thursday), and *Business Briefs* and *The Arts* (Friday). On Saturday the news is followed by *Insight Central Europe,* and Sunday's lineup is *Mailbox* and *Letter from Prague* followed by *Encore* (classical music), *Magic Carpet* (Czech world music) or *Czech Books.* Thirty minutes to eastern North America on 5930 and 7345 kHz, and one hour earlier in summer.

Radio Vilnius, Lithuania. Thirty minutes of mostly *news* and background reports about events in Lithuania. Of broader appeal is *Mailbag,* aired every other Saturday. For some Lithuanian music, try the second half of Sunday's broadcast. To eastern North America winter on 7325 kHz, and summer on 9875 kHz.

Voice of Vietnam. *News,* then *Commentary* or *Weekly Review.* These are followed by short features and some pleasant Vietnamese music (especially at the weekend). A half-hour to Southeast Asia on 9840 and 12020 kHz. Frequencies may vary slightly.

Prepared by Tony Jones and the staff of Passport to World Band Radio.

WHERE IN THE WORLD ARE PLAYS AND COMEDIES?

World band radio is the cat's meow for information and analysis. There's news from nearly everywhere and every perspective.

But drama? The BBC World Service used to pride itself on radio theater, but except for "BBC World Drama" it's gone bye-bye. Comedy? Zero, aside from such CBC offerings as "Madly Off in All Directions" aired by Radio Canada International.

Heyday Radio

But all is not lost. Before there was television and even after, the best talent from Broadway, Hollywood and the U.K. churned out innumerable radio shows. Virtually all were aired over mediumwave AM, while some were also on world band for the domestic hinterland and troops overseas. Script, direction and acting quality varied enormously, but most were pretty good and some were excellent. After all, back then radio was king and jobs were few, so it attracted serious talent.

Something like eighty percent of old radio shows have been lost forever. Yet, thousands remain and are finding renewed life over such outlets as WNAR-AM in Lansdale, Pennsylvania. Station owner David McCrork uses a micro-power transmitter on 1620 kHz to serve locals, but it's the free simulcast at www.wnar-am.com that pulls in listeners worldwide.

Orson Welles, the first "Shadow."

WNAR stands out because its shows are regularly scheduled 24/7. So, for example, at 8:30 PM local time weeknights there's the Lone Ranger, followed by Superman, whereas on Saturdays at that time it's Groucho Marx. Sundays at 11:30 PM is Sherlock Holmes, preceded by The Shadow at ten, then Gangbusters.

Screen Guild Theater, Sealtest Playhouse, Edgar Bergen, Dragnet, Gunsmoke, Dr. Who, Dimension X, Ozzie and Harriet, Duffy's Tavern, Columbia Workshop, Radio City Playhouse—in all, something like 100 different shows are on at specific times, just as they were when first aired during the thirty-odd years preceding the mid-1960s.

There are other such outlets on satellite radio and the web, but few have regular schedules and most charge a subscription fee. One excellent exception is "The Big Broadcast," aired Sunday evenings over WAMU-FM in Washington and simulcast at www.wamu.org/audio/wamu.asx or on-demand anytime at www.wamu.org/programs/bb. Radio historian Ed Walker provides insight into the shows and ensures they meet modern standards of audio quality—thanks in part to a relationship with Audio Classics Archives.

Fireside Theater

Most folks are narrowly focused when they're at a computer. Listening to music at the same time is one thing, but keeping mentally attuned to a play or comedy skit stretches multitasking. To get around this, you can go remote by using household WiFi and a laptop, but audio quality is likely to suffer unless you add good speakers.

You can also use a dedicated WiFi Internet radio, such as the new Acoustic Energy (www.acousticenergy.com), $299.95 from C. Crane (www.ccrane.com). In the past this approach has been a sales dud, but this may be changing now.

Even handier if you're not into channel surfing is to connect an FM micro-transmitter to a PC's sound card output. It's easy and, in North America, legal if you choose an approved model and don't modify it or lengthen its antenna. By the time you read this these should be legal throughout the EU, as well.

Some micro-transmitters come as kits that typically aren't approved for transmission or fire safety. Yet other models don't cover all frequencies or are complicated to tune. C. Crane's $69.95 FMT suffers from neither of these drawbacks. It also appears to be the most popular choice within North America.

NetPlay Radio's transmitter (www.netplayradio.com), $189.95, is robust and easily tunes all frequencies, but high audio frequencies tend to trail off. Too, its order webpage hasn't worked for years so you have to call in.

Decade (www.decade.ca) offers a wide range of professional-grade FM low-power and micro-transmitters for use in Canada and sometimes also the United States, EU and beyond. More practically, they sell the $49.95 (CAD$65) ST-27 consumer-grade model that's legal in many countries. Decade has a solid record of providing excellent service with quick turnaround.

AM micro-transmitters are another story. Kits can be illegal and even pose a potential fire hazard, but legal pre-constructed offerings are scarce. The ready-to-use ActRadio (around $300, www.actradio.com) works nicely enough but its motorized preselector is prone to acting up—fortunately, service is dependable. WNAR's Hamilton micro-transmitter (www.am1000rangemaster.com) appears to be about as good as it gets, but runs around a kilobuck before haggling.

Lazy Man's Radio

ReplayRadio ($39.95, www.replay-radio.com) makes receiving and recording Internet radio a sophisticated turnkey operation. If your PC is always on, ReplayRadio can be set to tune hundreds of different web stations automatically throughout each day of the week and record whichever shows you specify. This first-rate software is stable and easy to set up and use.

Over the Air

In North America you can also dial around the AM band Sundays around and after sunset. World band choices are few, but try Tennessee's WWCR at various times on weekdays. Also, Maine's WBCQ offers Ed Bolton's recreations of lost "Amos 'n' Andy" shows.

—Janette Porcelet, with Tony Jones, Marie Lamb and Lawrence Magne.

Addresses PLUS—2007

Station Postal and Email Addresses . . . PLUS Webcasts, Websites, Who's Who, Phones, Faxes, Bureaus, Future Plans, Items for Sale, Giveaways . . . PLUS Summer and Winter Times in Each Country!

PASSPORT mainly shows how stations reach out to you, but Addresses PLUS also explains how you can reach out to stations. It details—country by country—how broadcasters go beyond world band radio to keep in touch, inform and entertain.

Making Contact

When broadcasting was in its infancy, listeners sent in "applause" cards to let stations how well they were being received. To say "thanks," stations would reply with a letter or illustrated card verifying ("QSLing" in Morse code) that the station the listener heard was, in fact, theirs. While they were at it, some stations threw in a free souvenir—station calendar, pennant or sticker.

The tradition continues, although obtaining QSLs is tougher than it used to be. You can learn how to provide station feedback by looking under "Verification" in PASSPORT's "Worldly Words." Some stations also sell stuff—radios, CDs, DVDs, publications, clothing, tote bags, caps, watches, clocks, pens, knives, letter openers, lighters, refrigerator magnets and keyrings.

Postal Reimbursement

Most stations reply to listener correspondence—even email—through the postal system. That way, they can send out printed schedules, verification cards and other "hands-on" souvenirs. Major stations usually do this for free, but less prosperous operations often seek reimbursement for postage.

Most effective, especially for Latin American and Indonesian stations, is to enclose some unused (mint) stamps from the station's country. These are available from Plum's Airmail Postage, 12 Glenn Road, Flemington NJ 08822 USA, plumdx@msn.com, phone +1 (908) 788-1020, fax +1 (908) 782 2612. One way to help ensure your return-postage stamps are properly used is to stick them onto a pre-addressed return airmail envelope—self-addressed stamped envelope, or SASE.

You can also prompt reluctant stations by donating one U.S. dollar, preferably hidden from prying eyes by a piece of foil-covered carbon paper or the like. Registration often helps, as cash tends to get stolen. In some countries, though, registered mail is a prime target for would-be thieves, especially in parts of Latin America. International Reply Coupons (IRCs), which recipients may exchange locally for air or surface stamps, are available at a number of post offices worldwide, particularly in large cities. Thing is, they're increasingly hard to find, relatively costly, not fully effective, and aren't accepted by postal authorities in some countries.

Stamp Out Crime

Mail theft is still a problem in some countries, although the overall situation is improving. We identify problem areas and offer proven countermeasures, but start by using common sense. For example, some postal employees are stamp collectors and steal mail with unusual stamps, so use everyday stamps. A postal meter, PC-generated postage or an aerogram are other options.

> Stations sometimes complement world band by simulcasting on the Internet.

London, home-away-from-home for international news agencies, is also headquarters for the legendary BBC World Service.

Shutterstock/Andrew Chambers

¿Que Hora Es?

World Time, explained in "Setting Your World Time Clock," is essential if you want to find out when your favorite station is on. But if you want to know what time it is in any given country, World Time and "Addresses PLUS" come together to provide the answer.

Here's how. So that you don't have to wrestle with seasonal changes in your own time, "Addresses PLUS" gives local times for each country in terms of hours' difference from World Time (it stays constant year-round). For example, if you look below under "Albania," you'll see that country is World Time +1; that is, one hour ahead of World Time. So, if World Time is 12:00, the local time in Albania is 13:00 (1:00 PM). On the other hand, México City is World Time –6; that is, six hours behind World Time. If World Time is 12:00, in México City it's 6:00 AM.

Local times shown in parentheses are for the middle of the year—roughly April–October; specific dates of seasonal-time changeovers for individual countries can be obtained at www.timeanddate.com/world-clock.

Spotted Something New?

Has something changed since we went to press? A missing detail? Please let us know! Your update information, especially copies of material received from stations, is highly valued. Contact the IBS Editorial Office, Box 300, Penn's Park, PA 18943 USA, fax +1 (215) 598 3794, addresses@passband.com.

Muchas gracias to the kindly folks and helpful organizations mentioned at the end of this chapter for their tireless cooperation in the preparation of this section. Without you, none of this would have been possible.

Using Passport's Addresses PLUS Section

Stations included: All stations are listed if known to reply, however erratically. Also, new stations which possibly may reply to correspondence from listeners.

Leased-time programs: Private organizations/NGOs that lease program time, but which possess no world band transmitters of their own, are usually not listed. However, they can usually be reached at the stations over which they are heard.

Postal addresses are given. These sometimes differ from transmitter locations in the Blue Pages.

Phone and fax numbers. To help avoid confusion, telephone numbers have hyphens, fax numbers don't. All are configured for international dialing once you add your country's International access code (011 in the United States and Canada, 010 in the United Kingdom, and so on). For domestic dialing within countries outside the United States, Canada and the Caribbean, replace the country code (1-3 digits preceded by a "+") by a zero.

Giveaways. If you want freebies, say so politely in your correspondence. These are usually available until supplies run out.

Webcasting. World band stations which use streaming audio to simulcast and/or provide archived programming over the Internet are indicated by ▣.

Unless otherwise indicated, stations:

- Reply regularly within six months or so to most listeners' correspondence in English.
- Provide, upon request, free station schedules and verification ("QSL") postcards or letters (*see* Verification in "Worldly Words"). When other items are available for free or for purchase, it is specified.
- Do not require compensation for postage costs incurred in replying to you. Where compensation is appropriate, details are provided.

Local times. These are given in difference from World Time. For example, "World Time -5" means that if you subtract five hours from World Time, you'll get the local time in that country. So, if it were 11:00 World Time, it would be 06:00 local time in that country. Times in (parentheses) are for the middle of the year—roughly April-October. For exact changeover dates, see the above explanatory paragraph under "¿Que Hora Es?"

AFGHANISTAN   World Time +4:30

Radio Afghanistan (when operating), Afghan Radio & TV, P.O. Box 544, Ansari Wat, Kabul, Afghanistan. Contact: Foreign Relations Department.

ALBANIA   World Time +1 (+2 midyear)

Radio Tirana, External Service, Rruga Ismail Qemali Nr. 11, Tirana, Albania. Phone/Fax: +355 (4) 223-650. Fax: (technical directorate) +355 (4) 226 203. Email: (reception reports) dcico@abcom-al.com. Contact: Astrit Ibro, Director of External Services; Adriana Bislea, English Department; Clara Ruci, Journalist/Translator/Broadcaster; Marjeta Thoma; Pandi Skaka, Producer; Diana Koci; (technical directorate) Arben Mehilli, Technical Director ARTV; (frequency management) Mrs. Drita Cico, Head of RTV Monitoring Center. May send free stickers and postcards. Email reports welcome.

ALGERIA   World Time +1

☞**Radio Algérienne (ENRS)**, 21 Boulevard des Martyrs, Algiers, Algeria. Phone: (Direction Générale) +213 (2) 148-3790. Fax: (Direction Générale) +213 (2) 123 0823. Email: (Direction Générale) dg@algerian-radio.dz; (International Relations) relex@algerian-radio.dz; (Direction Technique) technique@algerian-radio.dz. Web: (includes on-demand and streaming audio) www.algerian-radio.dz. Replies iregularly. French or Arabic preferred, but English accepted. Return postage helpful. Formerly transmitted direct from Algeria, but currently broadcasts via transmitters in the United Kingdom.

ANGOLA   World Time +1

☞**Rádio Nacional de Angola**, Caixa Postal 1329, Luanda, Angola. Fax: +244 (2) 391 234. Email: (general, including reception reports) diop@rna.ao; (Magalhães) josela30@hotmail.com; (technical) rochapinto@rna.ao; (reception reports only) departamento133@hotmail.com. Web: (includes streaming audio) www.rna.ao; if the audio link doesn't work, try www.netangola.com/p/default.htm. Contact: Dr. Júlio Mendonça, Director do Departamento de Intercâmbio e Opinião Pública; [Ms.] Josefa Canzuela Magalhães, Departamento de Intercâmbio e Opinião Pública; Dr. Manuel Rabelais, Director Geral; (technical) Cândido Rocha Pinto, Director dos Serviços Técnicos. Replies irregularly. Best is to correspond in Portuguese and include $1, return postage or 2 IRCs.

ANTARCTICA   World Time –3 Base Antárctica Esperanza

Radio Nacional Arcángel San Gabriel—LRA36, Base Esperanza, V9411XAD Antártida Argentina, Argentina. Phone/Fax: +54 (2964) 421 519. Email: lra36@infovia.com.ar. Return postage required. Replies to correspondence in Spanish, and sometimes to correspondence in English or French, depending on who is at the station (the staff changes each year, usually around February). If no reply, try sending your correspondence (but don't write the station's name on the envelope) and 2 IRCs via the helpful Gabriel Iván Barrera, Casilla 2868, C1000WBC Buenos Aires, Argentina.

Much has been destroyed in Afghanistan's wars, including a world band service that was once widely heard and even relayed by the USSR. Recently, India donated a new transmitter to revive Radio Afghanistan.

Shutterstock/Shamsul bin Fitri

ANGUILLA   World Time –4

Caribbean Beacon, Box 690, Anguilla, British West Indies. Phone: +1 (264) 497- 4340. Fax: +1 (264) 497 4311. Email: beacon@anguillanet.com. Contact: Monsell Hazell, Chief Engineer; Doris Lussington. $2 or return postage helpful. Relays University Network—*see* USA.

ARGENTINA   World Time –3

Radio Baluarte (when operating), Casilla de Correo 45, 3370 Puerto Iguazú, Provincia de Misiones, Argentina. Phone: +54 (3737) 422-557. Email: icnfuturo@hotmail.com. Contact: Hugo Eidinger, Director. Free tourist literature. Return postage helpful. The same programs are aired on 100.7 MHz, and both outlets are believed to be unlicensed. However, given the current radio licensing situation in the country, this is not unusual.

Radiodifusión Argentina al Exterior—RAE, Casilla de Correos 555, C1000WBC Buenos Aires, Argentina. Phone/Fax: +54 (11) 4325-6368; (technical) +54 (11) 4325-5270. Email: (general) rae@radionacional.gov.ar; (technical) operativa@radionacional.gov.ar; (Marcela Campos) camposrae@fibertel.com.ar (this address is to be phased out); (German Section) raedeutsch@yahoo.com.ar. Web: www.radionacional.gov.ar/rae/rae.asp. Contact: (general) John Anthony Middleton, Head of English Team; María Dolores López, Spanish Team; (administration) Marcela G. R. Campos, Directora; (technical) Gabriel Iván Barrera, DX Editor. Return postage (3 IRCs) appreciated. The station asks listeners not to send currency notes, as it's a breach of local postal regulations. Reports covering at least 20-30 minutes of reception are appreciated.

☞**Radio Nacional Buenos Aires**, Maipú 555, C1006ACE Buenos Aires, Argentina. Phone: +54 (11) 4325-9100. Fax: (management—Gerencia General) +54 (11) 4325 9433; (Director) +54 (11) 4325-4590, +54 (11) 4322-4313; (technical—Gerencia Operativa) +54 (11) 4325-5270. Email: (general) info@radionacional.gov.ar, or buenosaires@radionacional.gov.ar; (Director) direccion@radionacional.gov.ar, or mariogiorgi@uol.com.ar; (technical) operativa@radionacional.gov.ar. Web: (includes streaming audio) www.radionacional.gov.ar. Contact: (general) Mario Giorgi, Director; (technical) Alberto Enríquez. Return postage (3 IRCs) helpful. Prefers correspondence in Spanish, and usually replies via RAE (see, above). If no reply, try sending your correspondence (but don't write the station's name on your envelope) and 3 IRCs via the helpful Gabriel Iván Barrera, Casilla 2868, C1000WBC Buenos Aires, Argentina.

ASCENSION   World Time exactly

BBC World Service—Atlantic Relay Station, English Bay, Ascension (South Atlantic Ocean). Fax: +247 6117. Contact: (technical) Jeff Cant, Staff Manager; M.R. Watkins, Assistant Resident Engineer; Mrs. Nicola Nicholls, Transmitter Engineer. Nontechnical correspondence should be sent to the BBC World Service in London (see).

AUSTRALIA   World Time +11 (+10 midyear) Victoria (VIC), New South Wales (NSW), Australian Capital Territory (ACT) and Tasmania (TAS); +10:30 (+9:30 midyear) South Australia (SA); +10 Queensland (QLD); +9:30 Northern Territory (NT); +8 Western Australia (WA)

Australian Broadcasting Corporation Northern Territory HF Service—ABC Radio 8DDD Darwin, Administrative Center for the Northern Territory Shortwave Service, ABC, Box 9994, GPO Darwin NT 0801, Australia; (street address) 1 Cavenagh Street, Darwin NT 0800, Australia. Phone: +61 (8) 8943-3222; (engineering) +61 (8) 8943-3209. Fax: +61 (8) 8943 3235, +61 (8) 8943 3208. Contact: (general) Tony Bowden, Branch Manager; (administration) Barbra Lilliebridge, Administration Officer; (technical) Peter Camilleri; Yvonne Corby. Free stickers and postcards. "Traveller's Guide to ABC Radio" for $1. T-shirts US$20. Three IRCs or return postage helpful.

BBC World Service via Radio Australia—For verification direct from the Australian transmitters, contact John Westland, Director of English Programs at Radio Australia (see). Nontechnical correspondence should be sent to the BBC World Service in London (see).

Christian Vision Communications (CVC), P.O. Box 6361, Maroochydore, QLD 4558, Australia. Phone: +61-7-5477-1555. Fax: +61-7-5477-1727. Email: (technical and nontechnical) enquiry@cvc.tv; (reception reports) dxer@cvc.tv, dxer@voice.com.au; ("Mailbag" program) mailbag@cvc.tv. Web: (includes on-demand and streaming audio) www.cvc.tv. Contact: (general) Mike Edmiston, Director; Raymond Moti, Station Manager; Richard Daniel, Corporate Relations Manager. May send T-shirt, baseball cap, key ring or other small gifts. Formerly Voice International Limited, and before that, Christian Voice International Australia.

HONG KONG ADDRESS (CHINESE SERVICE): Liu Sheng, Flat 1b, 67 Ha Heung Road, Kowloon, Hong Kong, China.

INDIA ADDRESS (HINDI SERVICE): CVC, P.O. Box 1, Kangra, Pin Code 176001, Himachal, India. Email: mail@thevoiceasia.com.

INDONESIA ADDRESS (INDONESIAN SERVICE): CVC, P.O. Box 2634, Jakarta Pusat, 10026 Indonesia. Phone: +62 (21) 390-0039.

INTERNATIONAL TOLL-FREE NUMBERS: (Indonesia only) 001-803-61-555; (India only) 000-800-610-1019.

TRANSMITTER SITE: CVC, PMB 5777, Darwin NT 0801, Australia. Phone: (general) +61 (8) 8981-6591, (operations manager)

+61 (8) 8981-8822. Fax: +61 (8) 8981 2846. Contact: Mrs. Lorna Manning, Site Administrator; Robert Egoroff, Operations Manager.

Community Development Radio Service—CDRS, ARDS, Box 1671, Nhulunbuy NT 0881, Australia; (street address) 19 Pera Circuit, Nhulunbuy NT 0880, Australia. Phone: +61 (8) 8987-3910. Fax: +61 (8) 8987 3912. Email: (general) nhulun@ards.com.au, mediaservices@ards.com.au; (technical) dale@ards.com.au. Web: (includes on-demand audio) http://www.ards.com.au/broadcast.htm. Contact: Dale Chesson, Radio Service Manager.

CVC—see Christian Vision Communications.

EDXP News Report, 404 Mont Albert Road, Mont Albert, Victoria 3127, Australia. Phone/Fax: +61 (3) 9898-2906. Email: info@edxp.org. Web: http://edxp.org. Contact: Bob Padula. " EDXP News Report" is compiled by the "Electronic DX Press" and airs over several world band stations. Focuses on shortwave broadcasters beaming to, or located in Asia and the Pacific. Currently heard on Adventist World Radio, HCJB-Australia, WINB, WWCR, and World Harvest Radio. Verifies postal reports with full-detail "EDXP" QSL cards showing Australian fauna, flora, and scenery. Return postage required; four 50c stamps within Australia, and one IRC or US dollar elsewhere. Email reports welcome, and are confirmed with animated Web-delivered QSLs. Does not verify reports on Internet broadcasts.

HCJB Australia, P.O. Box 291, Kilsyth VIC 3137, Australia. Phone: +61 (3) 9761-4844. Fax: +61 (3) 9761 4061. Email: office@hcjb.org.au. Contact: Derek Kickbush, Director of Broadcasting; Dennis Adams; David Yetman, Frequency Manager.

VERIFICATION OF RECEPTION REPORTS: Voice of the Great Southland, GPO Box 691, Melbourne VIC 3001, Australia. Email: english@hcjb.org.au; (Yetman) dyetman@hcjb.org.au. One IRC required for postal reply. Listeners to the Japanese broadcasts can send their reception reports to: HCJB Section, Yodobashi Church, Hyakunincho 1-17-8, Shinjuku-ku, Tokyo 169-0073, Japan. Return postage (169 yen stamp) required within Japan.

NEW DELHI OFFICE: Radio GMTA, P.O. Box 4960, New Delhi 110 029 India.

Radio Australia, GPO Box 428G, Melbourne VIC 3001, Australia. Phone: ("Openline" voice mail for listeners' messages and requests) +61 (3) 9626-1825; (switchboard) +61 (3) 9626-1800; (English programs) +61 (3) 9626-1922; (marketing manager) +61 (3) 9626 1723. Fax: (general) +61 (3) 9626 1899. Email: (general) english@ra.abc.net.au; (marketing manager) marketing@radioaustralia.net.au. (Web: (includes on-demand and streaming audio) www.radioaustralia.net.au. Contact: (general) Brendon Telfer, Head of English Language Programming; Tony Hastings, Director of Programs; Mark Hemetsberger, Marketing & Communications Manager; Jean-Gabriel Manguy, Head; (technical) Nigel Holmes, Chief Engineer, Transmission Management Unit. All reception reports received by Radio Australia are forwarded to the Australian Radio DX Club for assessment and checking. ARDXC will forward completed QSLs to Radio Australia for mailing. For further information, contact Brendon Telfer, Director of English Programs at Radio Australia (Email: telfer.brendon@abc.net.au).

SAN FRANCISCO OFFICE, SCHEDULES: 2654 17th Avenue, San Francisco CA 94116 USA. Phone: +1 (415) 564-9968. Email: GPoppin@aol.com. Contact: George Poppin. This address, a volunteer office, only provides Radio Australia schedules to listeners (return postage not required). All other correspondence should be sent directly to the main office in Melbourne.

AUSTRIA   World Time +1 (+2 midyear)

📻**Radio Austria International**, Listener Service, Argentinierstrasse 30a, A-1040 Vienna, Austria. Phone: +43 (1) 50101-16060. Fax: +43 (1) 50101 16066. Email: (frequency schedules, comments, reception reports) roi.service@orf.at. Web: (includes online reception report form) http://oe1.orf.at/service/international_en; (on-demand and streaming audio from ÖE1, which makes up most of Radio Austria International's European service) http://oe1.orf.at. Contact: (general) Vera Bock, Listener Service; (English Department) David Ward.
FREQUENCY MANAGEMENT: ORF Sendetechnik, Attn. Ernst Vranka, Würzburggasse 30, A-1136 Vienna, Austria. Phone: +43 (1) 87878-12629. Fax: +43 (1) 87878 12773. Email: ernst.vranka@orf.at. Contact: Ing. Ernst Vranka, Frequency Manager.
Trans World Radio—*see* USA.

AZERBAIJAN   World Time +4 (+5 midyear)

Voice of Azerbaijan, Medhi Hüseyin küçäsi 1, 370011 Baku, Azerbaijan. Free postcards, and occasionally, books. $1 or return postage helpful. Replies irregularly to correspondence in English.

BAHRAIN   World Time +3

Coalition Maritime Forces (CMF) Radio One—*see* International Waters.
Radio Bahrain (when operating), Broadcasting and Television, Ministry of Information, P.O. Box 194, Al Manāmah, Bahrain. Phone: (Arabic Service) +973 781-888; (English Service) +973 629-085. Fax: (Arabic Service) +973 681 544; (English Service) +973 780 911. Web: www.gna.gov.bh/brtc/radio.html. Contact: A. Suliman (for Director of Broadcasting). $1 or IRC required. Replies irregularly.

BANGLADESH   World Time +6

📻**Bangladesh Betar**
NONTECHNICAL: External Services, Bangladesh Betar, Shah Bagh Post Box No. 2204, Dhaka 1000, Bangladesh; (street address) Betar Bhaban Sher-e-Bangla Nagar, Agargaon Road, Dhaka 1207, Bangladesh. Phone: (director general) +880 (2) 8615-294; (Rahman Khan) +880 (2) 8613-949; (external services) +880 (2) 8618-119. Fax:(director general) +880 (2) 8612 021. Email: (director general) dgbetar@bd.drik.net; dgbetar@bttb.net.bd; (external services) ts- betar@bdonline.com. Web: (includes on-demand audio) www.betar.org.bd. Contact: Setub Uddin Ahmed, Director - External Services; Ashfaque-ur Rahman Khan, Director - Programmes.
TECHNICAL: Research and Receiving Centre, National Broadcasting Authority, 121 Kazi Nazrul Islam Avenue, Shah Bagh, Dhaka-1000, Bangladesh. Phone: +880 (2) 8625-904. Fax: +880 (2) 8612 021. Email: rrc@dhaka.net. Contact: Md. Kamal Uddin; Md. Motiar Rahman, Senior Engineer; Ahmed Quamruzzaman, Station Engineer. Sometimes verifies reception reports.

BELARUS   World Time +2 (+3 midyear)

Belarusian Radio—*see* Radio Station Belarus for details.
Radio Grodno—*see* Radio Hrodna.
Radio Hrodna, ul. Horhaha 85, Hrodna 230015, Belarus. Correspondence should be addressed to the attention of Mr.

Alexander Bakurskiy. Verifies reception reports in Russian, Belarusian or English.
Radio Mahiliou, Mahiliou, Belarus. Email: radiomogilev@tut.by. Contact: Yury Kurpatin. Verifies reception reports in Russian or Belarusian. May also respond to reports in English or German. Return postage helpful.
Radio Moghilev—*see* Radio Mahiliou.
📻**Radio Station Belarus**, 4 Krasnaya St., Minsk 220807, Belarus. Phone: (external service, director) +375 (17) 284-4277; (English and German departments) +375 (17) 293-5875. Fax: (foreign language services) +375 (17) 293 5810. Email: (domestic Belarusian Radio) tvr@tvr.by; (external services) radio-minsk@tvr.by. Web: (includes on-demand and streaming audio) www.radiobelarus.tvr.by. Contact: Naum Galperovich, Director External Service; Viacheslav Laktjushin, Head of Foreign Language Services (also Head of English Service); Elena Khoroshevich, Head of German Service; Larisa Suarez. Free Belarusian stamps.

BELGIUM   World Time +1 (+2 midyear)

📻**RTBF-International**, Bd. Auguste Reyers 52, B-1044 Brussels, Belgium. Phone: +32 (2) 737-4014. Fax: +32 (2) 737 3032. Email: prc@rtbf.be, rtbfi@rtbf.be. Web: (includes on-demand and streaming audio) www.rtbf.be. Contact: Jean-Pol Hecq, Directeur des Relations Internationales (or "Head, International Service" if writing in English). Broadcasts are essentially a relay of programs from the domestic services "La Première" and "Vivacité" of RTBF (Radio-Télévision Belge de la Communauté Française) via a transmitter in Wavre. Return postage not required. Accepts email reception reports.
Radio Traumland, P.O. Box 15, B-4730 Raeren, Belgium. Phone: +31 87 301-722. Email: radiotraumland@skynet.be. Email reports can only be confirmed with electronic QSLs; for a postal reply include 1 IRC, $1, 1 Euro or mint Belgian/German stamps. Transmits via T-Systems International facilities in Germany (see).
📻**Radio Vlaanderen Internationaal (RVI)**, B-1043 Brussels, Belgium. Phone: +32 (2) 741-5611, +32 (2) 741-3806/7, +32 (2) 741-3802. Fax: +32 (2) 741-4689. Email: info@rvi.be. Web: (includes on-demand and streaming audio) www.rvi.be. Contact: (station manager) Wim Jansen; (listener mail) Tine De Bruycker; Rita Penne.
Transmitter Documentation Project (TDP), P.O. Box 1, B-2310 Rijkevorsel, Belgium. Phone: +32 (3) 314-7800. Fax: +32 (3) 314 1212. Email: info@transmitter.org. Web: www.broadcast.be; (shortwave schedule) www.airtime.be/schedule.html. Contact: Ludo Maes, Managing Director. A free online publication by Belgian Dxer Ludo Maes. TDP lists current and past shortwave transmitters used worldwide in country order with station name, transmitter site & geographical coordinates, transmitter type, power and year of installation etc. Also brokers leased airtime over world band transmitters.

BENIN   World Time +1

📻**Office de Radiodiffusion et Télévision du Benin** (when operating), Boite Postale 366, Cotonou, Benin. Phone/Fax: +229 302-184. Contact: Fidèle Ayikoue, Directeur Generale; (technical) Anastase Adjoko, Chef du Service Technique. Return postage, $1 or IRC required. Replies irregularly and slowly to correspondence in French.
PARAKOU REGIONAL STATION: ORTB-Parakou, Boite Postale 128, Parakou, Benin. Phone: +229 610-773, +229 611-096,

+229 611080. Fax: +229 610 881. Contact: (general) J. de Matha, Le Chef de la Station; (technical) Léon Donou, Chef des Services Techniques. Return postage required. Replies tend to be extremely irregular, and a safer option is to send correspondence to the Cotonou address.

BHUTAN   World Time +6

🖥Bhutan Broadcasting Service

STATION: Department of Information and Broadcasting, Ministry of Communications, P.O. Box 101, Thimphu, Bhutan. Phone: +975 (2) 323-071/72. Fax: +975 (2) 323 073. Email: (general) webmaster@bbs.com.bt; (News and Current Affairs) news@bbs.com.bt; (Thinley Tobgay Dorji) thinley@bbs.com.bt; (Sonam Tobgay) toby@bbs.com.bt. Web: (includes on-demand and streaming audio) www.bbs.com.bt. Contact: (general) Thinley Tobgay Dorji, News Coordinator; Ms. Sherpem Sherpa, Web Editor & Presenter "Bhutan this Week" & "Internet on the Radio"; Kinga Singye, Executive Director; (technical) Dorji Wangchuk, Station Engineer. Three IRCs, return postage or $2 required. Replies irregularly; correspondence to the U.N. Mission (see following) may be more fruitful.
UNITED NATIONS MISSION: Permanent Mission of the Kingdom of Bhutan to the United Nations, Two United Nations Plaza, 27th Floor, New York NY 10017 USA. Fax: +1 (212) 826 2998. Contact: Mrs. Kunzang C. Namgyel, Third Secretary; Mrs. Sonam Yangchen, Attaché; Ms. Leki Wangmo, Second Secretary; Hari K. Chhetri, Second Secretary. Free newspapers and booklet on the history of Bhutan.

BOLIVIA   World Time −4

NOTE ON STATION IDENTIFICATIONS: Many Bolivian stations listed as "Radio . . ." may also announce as "Radio Emisora . . ." or "Radiodifusora . . ."
Paititi Radiodifusión—see Radio Paitití, below.
Radio Camargo—see Radio Emisoras Camargo, below.
Radio Centenario "La Nueva"
MAIN OFFICE: Casilla 818, Santa Cruz de la Sierra, Bolivia. Phone: +591 (3) 352-9265. Fax: +591 (3) 352 4747. Email: mision.eplabol@scbbs-bo.com. Contact: Napoleón Ardaya B., Director. May send a calendar. Free stickers. Return postage or $1 required. Audio cassettes of contemporary Christian music and Bolivian folk music $10, including postage; CDs of Christian folk music $15, including postage. Replies to correspondence in English or Spanish.
U.S. BRANCH OFFICE: LATCOM, 1218 Croton Avenue, New Castle PA 16101 USA. Phone: +1 (412) 652-0101. Fax: +1 (412) 652 4654. Contact: Hope Cummins.
Radio Chicha, Tocla, Provincia Nor-Chichas, Departamento de Potosí, Bolivia.
Radio Eco
MAIN ADDRESS: Correo Central, Reyes, Ballivián, Beni, Bolivia. Contact: Gonzalo Espinoza Cortés, Director. Free station literature. $1 or return postage required. Replies to correspondence in Spanish.
ALTERNATIVE ADDRESS: Rolmán Medina Méndez, Correo Central, Reyes, Ballivián, Bolivia.
Radio Emisoras Ballivián (when operating), Correo Central, San Borja, Beni, Bolivia. Replies to correspondence in Spanish, and sometimes sends pennant.
Radio Emisoras Camargo, Casilla Postal 9, Camargo, Provincia Nor-Cinti, Chuquisaca, Bolivia. Email: jlgarpas@hotmail.com. Contact: Pablo García B., Gerente Propietario; José Luís

García. Return postage or $1 required. Replies slowly to correspondence in Spanish.
Radio Emisoras Minería—see Radiodifusoras Minería.
Radio Estacion Frontera, Casilla de Correo 179, Cobija, Departamento de Pando, Bolivia.
Radio Estambul, Avenida Primero de Mayo esq. Loreto, Guayaramerín, Beni, Bolivia. Phone: +591 (3) 855-4145. Email: ninafelima@hotmail.com Contact: Sra. Felima Bruno de Yamal, Propietaria, who welcomes postcards, pennants or small flags from foreign listeners.
🖥Radio Fides, Casilla 9143, La Paz, Bolivia. Fax: +591 (2) 237 9030. Email: rafides@fidesbolivia.com (if that fails, try: sistemas@radiofides.com). Web: (includes on-demand and streaming audio) http://fidesbolivia.com. Contact: R.P. Eduardo Pérez Iribarne, S.J., Director. Replies occasionally to correspondence in Spanish.
Radio Guanay (when operating), calle Boston de Guanay 123, Guanay, La Paz, Bolivia; or Casilla de Correo 15012, La Paz, Bolivia. Replies irregularly to correspondence in Spanish.
🖥Radio Illimani, Av. Camacho 1485, Edificio La Urbana - 6to Piso, La Paz, Bolivia. Phone: +591 (2) 220-0473, +591 (2) 220-0390, +591 (2) 220-0282. Email: illimani@comunica.gov.bo. Web: (includes streaming audio) www.comunica.gov.bo (click on "Radio Illimani"). Contact: Arturo Cruz, Director. $1 required, and registered mail recommended. Replies irregularly to friendly correspondence in Spanish.
Radio Juan XXIII [Veintitrés] (when operating), Avenida Santa Cruz al frente de la plaza principal, San Ignacio de Velasco, Santa Cruz, Bolivia. Phone: +591 (3962) 2087. Phone/Fax: +591 (3962) 2188. Contact: Pbro. Elías Cortezón, Director; María Elffy Gutiérrez Méndez, Encargada de la Discoteca. Return postage or $1 required. Replies occasionally to correspondence in Spanish.
Radio La Cruz del Sur (when operating), Casilla 1408, La Paz, Bolivia. Phone: +591 (2) 222-0541. Fax: +591 (2) 224 3337. Email: cruzdelsur@zuper.net. Contact: Carlos Montesinos, Director. $1 or return postage required. Replies slowly to correspondence in Spanish.
Radio La Voz del Campesino, Sipe Sipe, Provincia de Quillacollo, Departamento de Cochabamba, Bolivia. No known replies, but try using the good offices of DXer Rogildo Fontenelle Aragão: rogfara@yahoo.com.br, rogfara@bolivia.com (correspond in Spanish or Portuguese).
Radio Mallku, Casilla No. 16, Uyuni, Provincia Antonio Quijarro, Departamento de Potosí, Bolivia. Phone: +591 (2693) 2145. Email: (FRUTCAS parent organization) frutcas@hotmail.es. Contact: Freddy Juárez Huarachi, Director; Erwin Freddy Mamani Machaca, Jefe de Prensa y Programación. Spanish preferred. Return postage in the form of two U.S. dollars appreciated, as the station depends on donations for its existence. Station owned by La Federación Unica de Trabajadores Campesinos del Altiplano Sud (FRUTCAS) and formerly known as Radio A.N.D.E.S.
Radio Minería—see Radiodifusoras Minería.
Radio Mosoj Chaski, Casilla 4493, Cochabamba, Bolivia; (street address) Calle Abaroa 254, Cochabamba, Bolivia. Phone: +591 (4) 422-0641, +591 (4) 422-0644. Fax: +591 (44) 251 041. Email: chaski@bo.net. Contact: Paul G. Pittman, Administrator; Ann Matthews, Director. Replies to correspondence in Spanish or English. Return postage helpful.
NORTH AMERICAN OFFICE: Quechuan Radio, c/o SIM USA, P.O. Box 7900, Charlotte NC 28241 USA.
Radio Norteña, Caranavi, Departamento de La Paz, Bolivia.
Radio Nacional de Huanuni, Casilla 681, Oruro, Bolivia. Con-

tact: Rafael Linneo Morales, Director General; Alfredo Murillo, Director. Return postage or $1 required. Replies irregularly to correspondence in Spanish.

Radio Nueva Esperanza (when operating), Raúl Salmón 92 entre calles 4 y 5, Zona 12 de Octubre, El Alto, La Paz, Bolivia.

Radio Paitití, Casilla 172, Guayaramerín, Beni, Bolivia. Contact: Armando Mollinedo Bacarreza, Director; Luis Carlos Santa Cruz Cuéllar, Director Gerente; Ancir Vaca Cuéllar, Gerente-Propietario. Free pennants. Return postage or $3 required. Replies irregularly to correspondence in Spanish.

Radio Panamericana, Casilla 5263, La Paz, Bolivia; (street address) Av. 16 de Julio, Edif. 16 de Julio, Of. 902, El Prado, La Paz, Bolivia. Phone: +591 (2) 231-2644, +591 (2) 231-1383, +591 (2) 231-3980. Fax: +591 (2) 233-4271. Email: pana@panamericanabolivia.com. Web: (includes streaming audio) www.panamericanabolivia.com. Contact: Daniel Sánchez Rocha, Director. Replies irregularly, with correspondence in Spanish preferred. $1 or 2 IRCs helpful.

Radio Perla del Acre (when operating), Casilla 7, Cobija, Departamento de Pando, Bolivia. Return postage or $1 required. Replies irregularly to correspondence in Spanish.

Radio Pío XII [Doce], Casilla 434, Oruro, Bolivia. Phone: +591 (258) 20-250. Fax: +591 (258) 20 544. Email: rpiodoce@entelnet. bo. Web: www.radiopio12.org. Contact: Pbro. Roberto Durette, OMI, Director General; José Blanco Villanueva. Return postage necessary.

Radio San Gabriel, Casilla 4792, La Paz, Bolivia. Phone: +591 (2) 241-4371. Phone/Fax: +591 (2) 241-1174. Email:

TIPS FOR WINNING CORRESPONDENCE

Golden Rule: Write unto others as you would have them write unto you. The milk of human kindness is mighty skim these days, so a considerate message stands out.

Be interesting and helpful from the recipient's point of view, yet friendly without being chummy. Comments on specific programs are almost always appreciated, even if you are sending what is basically a technical report.

Incorporate language courtesies. Using the broadcaster's tongue is always best—Addresses PLUS indicates when it is a requirement—but English is usually the next-best bet. When writing in any language to Spanish-speaking countries, remember that what gringos think of as the "last name" is actually written as the penultimate name. Thus, Juan Antonio Vargas García, which can also be written as Juan Antonio Vargas G., refers to Sr. Vargas; so your salutation should read, *Estimado Sr. Vargas*.

What's that "García" doing there, then? That's *mamita's* father's family name. Latinos more or less solved the problem of gender fairness in names long before Anglos.

But, wait—what about Portuguese, used by all those stations in Brazil? Same concept, but in reverse. *Mamá's* father's family name is penultimate, and the "real" last name is where English-speakers are used to it, at the end.

In Chinese, the "last" name comes first. However, when writing in English, Chinese names are often reversed for the benefit of *weiguoren*—foreigners. For example, "Li" is a common Chinese last name, so if you see "Li Dan," it's "Mr. Li." But if it's "Dan Li"—and certainly if it's been Westernized into "Dan Lee"—he's already a step or two ahead of you, and it's still "Mr. Li" (or Lee). Less widely known is that the same can also occur in Hungarian. For example, "Bartók Béla" for Béla Bartók.

If in doubt, fall back on the ever-safe "Dear Sir" or "Dear Madam"—"Hi" is still not appropriate with most letters—or use email, where salutations are not expected but "Hi" is increasingly but not universally accepted. Avoid first names, too, especially for recipients outside the United States. However, if you know the recipient is an amateur radio operator ("ham"), it is safe to use the first name if you include ham call letters in the address; e.g. Norman Gorman, WA3CRN, Station Engineer.

Be patient, as replies by post take weeks, sometimes months. Slow responders, those that tend to take many months to reply, are cited in Addresses PLUS. Erratic repliers, too.

rsg@fundayni.rds.org.bo; (technical, including reception reports) remoc@entelnet.bo. Contact: (general) Hno. [Brother] José Canut Saurat, Director General; Sra. Martha Portugal, Dpto. de Publicidad; (technical) Rómulo Copaja Alcón, Director Técnico. $1 or return postage helpful. Free book on station, Aymara calendars and *La Voz del Pueblo Aymara* magazine. Replies fairly regularly to correspondence in Spanish. Station of the Hermanos de la Salle Catholic religious order.

Radio San Miguel, Casilla 102, Riberalta, Beni, Bolivia. Phone: +591 (385) 8268, +591 (385) 8363. Fax: +591 (385) 8268. Free stickers and pennants; has a different pennant each year. Return postage or $1 required. Replies irregularly to correspondence in Spanish.

Radio Santa Ana, Calle Sucre No. 250, Santa Ana de Yacuma, Beni, Bolivia. Contact: Mario Roberto Suárez, Director; Mariano Verdugo. Return postage or $1 required. Replies irregularly to correspondence in Spanish.

Radio Santa Cruz, Emisora del Instituto Radiofónico Fé y Alegría (IRFA), Casilla 672, Santa Cruz, Bolivia; (street address) Calle Mario Flores esq. Guendá N° 20, Santa Cruz de la Sierra, Bolivia. Phone: +591 (3) 353-1817. Fax: +591 (3) 353 2257. Email: irfacruz@entelnet.bo. Contact: José Velasco, Director; Srta. María Yolanda Marcó Escobar, Secretaria de Dirección. Free pamphlets, stickers and pennants. Welcomes correspondence in English, French and Spanish, but return postage required for a reply.

Radio Tacana, Tumupasa, Provincia Iturralde, Departamento de La Paz, Bolivia.

Radio Uncia (if reactivated), Plaza 6 de Agosto y calle Villazón, Uncia, Departamento de Potosí, Bolivia.

Radio Virgen de los Remedios, Casilla 198, Tupiza, Departamento de Potosí, Bolivia; (street address) Parroquia Nuestra Señora de la Candelaria, Tupiza, Departamento de Potosí, Bolivia. Phone: +591 (269) 44-662. Email: radiovirgenderemedios@hotmail.com. Contact: Padre Estanislao Odroniec.

Radio Yura (La Voz de los Ayllus), Casilla 326, Yura, Provincia Quijarro, Departamento de Potosí, Bolivia. Phone: +591 (281) 36-216. Email: radioyura@hotmail.com. Contact: Omar Flores. Free pennant and stickers. Replies slowly to correspondence in Spanish.

Radiodifusoras Minería (when operating), Casilla de Correo 247, Oruro, Bolivia. Phone: +591 (252) 77-736. Contact: Dr. José Carlos Gómez Espinoza, Gerente Propietario; Srta. Costa Colque Flores, Responsable del programa "Minería Cultural." Free pennants. Replies to correspondence in Spanish.

Radiodifusoras Trópico, Casilla 60, Trinidad, Beni, Bolivia. Contact: Eduardo Avila Alberdi, Director. Replies slowly to correspondence in Spanish. Return postage required for reply.

BOTSWANA   World Time +2

IBB Botswana Transmitting Station

TRANSMITTER SITE: International Broadcasting Bureau, Botswana Relay Station, Moepeng Hill, Selebi-Phikwe, Botswana; (postal address) International Broadcasting Bureau, Botswana Transmitting Station, Private Bag 0038, Selebi-Phikwe, Botswana. Phone: +267 810-932. Fax: +267 261 0185. Email: manager_botswana@bot.ibb.gov. Contact: Station Manager or Transmitting Plant Supervisor. This address for specialized technical correspondence only, although reception reports may occasionally be verified. All other correspondence should be directed to the regular VOA or IBB addresses (*see* USA).

Radio Botswana, (when operating) Private Bag 0060, Gaborone, Botswana. Phone: +267 352-541, +267 352-861. Fax:

+267 357 138. Contact: (general) Ted Makgekgenene, Director; (technical) Kingsley Reetsang, Principal Broadcasting Engineer. Free stickers, pennants and pins. Return postage, $1 or 2 IRCs required. Replies slowly and irregularly.

BRAZIL   World Time −1 (−2 midyear) Atlantic Islands; −2 (−3 midyear) Eastern, including Brasília and Rio de Janeiro; −3 (−4 midyear) Western; −4 Northwestern; −5 Acre. There are often slight variations from one year to the next. Information regarding Daylight Saving Time can be found at http://pcdsh01.on.br.

NOTE: Postal authorities recommend that, because of the level of theft in the Brazilian postal system, correspondence to Brazil be sent only via registered mail.

CBN Anhanguera—*see* Rádio Anhanguera (Goiânia).

Rádio 8 de Setembro (when operating), Rua José Bonifacio 765, Centro, 13690-970 Descalvado SP, Brazil. Email: (Scapin) rscapin@gmail.com. Contact: Rafael Scapin. Replies to correspondence in Portuguese or English.

Rádio Alvorada (Londrina), Rua Dom Bosco 145, Bairro Iguaçu, 86060-340 Londrina PR, Brazil. Phone: +55 (43) 3347-0606. Fax: +55 (43) 3347 0303. Email: alvorada@radioalvorada.am.br. Contact: Padre Silvio Andrei, Diretor. Web: www.radioalvorada.am.br. $1 or return postage. Replies to correspondence in Portuguese.

Rádio Alvorada (Parintins), Rua Governador Leopoldo Neves 516, 69151-460 Parintins AM, Brazil. Phone: +55 (92) 3533-2002, +55 (92) 3533-3097. Fax: +55 (92) 3533 2004. Email: alvorada@redewsp.com.br, radio-alvorada@uol.com.br. Contact: Raimunda Ribeiro da Silva, Diretora. Return postage required. Replies occasionally to correspondence in Portuguese.

Rádio Alvorada (Rio Branco), Avenida Ceará 2150, Jardim Nazle, 69900-460 Rio Branco AC, Brazil. Phone: +55 (68) 3226-2301. Email: seve@jornalatribuna.com.br. Contact: José Severiano, Diretor. Occasionally replies to correspondence in Portuguese.

Rádio Araguaia—FM sister-station to Rádio Anhanguera (*see* next entry) and sometimes relayed via the latter's shortwave outlet. Usually identifies as "Araguaia FM."

Rádio Anhanguera (Araguaína), BR-157 Km. 1103, Zona Rural, 77804-970 Araguaína TO, Brazil. Return postage required. Occasionally replies to correspondence in Portuguese. Sometimes airs programming from sister-station Rádio Araguaia, 97.1 FM (*see* previous item).

🕭 **Rádio Anhanguera (Goiânia)**, Rua Thomas Edison, Quadra 7, Setor Serrinha, 74835-130 Goiânia GO, Brazil; or Caixa Postal 13, 74823-000 Goiânia GO, Brazil. Email: anhanguera@radioexecutiva.com.br. Web: (streaming audio only) http://goiasnet.globo.com/tv_radio. Contact: Fábio de Campos Roriz, Diretor; Eng. Domingo Vicente Tinoco. Return postage required. Replies to correspondence in Portuguese, often slowly. Although—like its namesake in Araguaína (*see*, above)—a member of the Sistema de Rádio da Organização Jaime Câmara, this station is also an affiliate of the CBN network and often identifies as "CBN Anhanguera," especially when airing news programming.

Rádio Aparecida, Avenida Getúlio Vargas 185, Centro, 12570-000 Aparecida SP, Brazil; or Caixa Postal 2, 12570-970 Aparecida SP, Brazil. Phone/Fax: +55 (12) 3104-4400. Fax: +55 (12) 3104-4427. Email: (nontechnical) radioaparecida@radio-aparecida.com.br; (Macedo) cassianomac@yahoo.com. Web: www.radioaparecida.com.br. Contact: Padre Inácio Medeiros,

Diretor; Savio Trevisan, Departamento Técnico; José Moura; Cassiano Alves Macedo, Producer, "Encontro DX" (aired 2200 Saturday; one hour earlier when Brazil on DST). Return postage or $1 required. Replies to correspondence in Portuguese.

Rádio Bandeirantes, Rua Radiantes 13, Bairro Morumbi, 05699-900 São Paulo SP, Brazil. Phone: +55 (11) 3745-7552; (listener feedback) +55 (11) 3743-8040. Fax: +55 (11) 3745 8065. Email: (general) rbradio@band.com.br, rbnoar@band.com.br; (Huertas) ahuertas@band.com.br. Web: (includes streaming audio) www.radiobandeirantes.com.br. Contact: Augusto Huertas, Técnico Rádios. Free stickers, pennants and canceled Brazilian stamps. $1 or return postage required.

Rádio Baré, Av. Tefé 3025, Japiim, 69078-000 Manaus AM, Brazil. Phone: +55 (92) 2101-5500. Web: www.radiobare.com.br. Contact: Sidiclei Santos. Replies to correspondence in Portuguese.

Rádio Boa Vontade, Av. São Paulo 722 - 3° andar, Bairro São Geraldo, 90230-160 Porto Alegre RS, Brazil. Phone: +55 (51) 3325-7019, +55 (51) 3374-0203. Email: rbv1300@yahoo.com.br, rbv1300am@hotmail.com. Web: (includes streaming audio) www.redeboavontade.com.br. Contact: José Joaquim Martins Rodrigues, Gerente da Rádio. Replies to correspondence in Portuguese.

Rádio Brasil, Av. Benjamin Constant, 1214, 5° andar, 13010-141 Campinas SP, Brazil. Email: radio@brasilcampinas.com. Web: www.brasilcampinas.com. Contact: Adilson Gasparini, Diretor Comercial e Artístico. Email reports accepted. Free stickers. Replies to correspondence in Portuguese.

Rádio Brasil Central, Caixa Postal 330, 74001-970 Goiânia GO, Brazil; (street address) Rua SC-1 No. 299, Parque Santa Cruz, 74860-270 Goiânia GO, Brazil. Phone: +55 (62) 201-7600. Email: rbc@agecom.go.gov.br. Web: www.agecom.go.gov.br/AM. Contact: Sílvio José da Silva, Gerente Executivo; Oscar Simões da Costa, Gerente Administrativo. Free stickers. $1 or return postage required. Replies to correspondence in Portuguese, and sometimes to correspondence in English.

Rádio Cacique (when operating), Rua Saldanha da Gama 168, Centro, 18010-060, Sorocaba SP, Brazil. Phone: +55 (15) 3234-3444, +55 (15) 231-3712. Email: radioc@radioc.com.br. Web: www.radiocacique.com.br. Contact: Edir Correa.

Rádio Caiari, Rua das Crianças 4646, Bairro Areal da Floresta, 78912-210 Porto Velho RO, Brazil. Phone: (studio) +55 (69) 3227-2277, +55 (69) 3216-0707; Phone/Fax: (Commercial Dept.) +55 (69) 3210-3621. Email: comercialcaiari@gmail.com, or online form. Web: www.radiocaiari.com.br. Contact: José Maria Gonzáles, Diretor; Alisângela Lima, Gerente Operacional. Free stickers. Return postage helpful. Replies irregularly to correspondence in Portuguese.

Rádio Canção Nova, Caixa Postal 57, 12630-000 Cachoeira Paulista SP, Brazil; (street address) Rua João Paulo II s/n, Alto da Bela Vista, 12630-000 Cachoeira Paulista SP, Brazil. Phone: (studio) +55 (12) 3186-2046. Fax: (general) +55 (12) 3186 2022 Email: (general) online form (radio@cancaonova.com.br may also work); (reception reports) dx@cancaonova.com. Web: (includes streaming audio) www.cancaonova.com/portal/canais/radio. Free stickers, pennants and station brochure sometimes sent on request. May send magazines. $1 helpful.

Rádio Capixaba, Caixa Postal 509, 29000-000 Vitória ES, Brazil; (street address) Av. Santo Antônio 366, 29025-000 Vitória ES, Brazil. Email: radiocap@terra.com.br. Contact: Jairo Gouvea Maia, Diretor; Sr. Sardinha, Técnico. Replies occasionally to correspondence in Portuguese.

Rádio Clube de Marília, Caixa Postal 326, 17500-970, Marília SP, Brazil. Replies to correspondence in Portuguese. Phone:

+55 (14) 3422-3006. Email: (general) online form; (Beato) beato@radioitaipu.com.br. Web: www.radioitaipu.com.br/radioclube.php. Contact: José Marques Beato, Diretor Geral

Rádio Clube de Varginha (when operating), Caixa Postal 102, 37000-000 Varginha MG, Brazil. Email: sistemaclube@varginha.com.br. Contact: Mariela Silva Gómez. Return postage required. Replies to correspondence in Spanish and Portuguese.

Rádio Clube do Pará, Av. Almirante Barroso 2190 - 3° andar, Marco, 66095-020 Belém PA, Brazil. Phone/Fax: +55 (91) 3084-0137. Email: timaocampeao@expert.com.br. Web: (includes streaming audio) www.radioclubedopara.com.br. Contact: Guilherme Guerreiro, Diretor. Replies to correspondence in Portuguese or English, and verifies reception reports. Free stickers, postcards and occasional T-shirt.

Radio Clube Paranaense, Rua Rockefeller 1311, Prado Velho, 80230-130 Curitiba PR, Brazil. Phone: +55 (41) 332-2772. Fax: +55 (41) 332-2398. Email: (commercial department.) clubcoml@rla13.pucpr.br. Web: (includes streaming audio) www.clubeb2.com.br. Contact: Toni Casagrande, Diretor; Vicente Mickosz, Superintendente; Marisa Ap. Zanon, Gerente Administrativa.

Rádio Congonhas, Praça da Basílica 130, 36404-000 Congonhas MG, Brazil. Replies to correspondence in Portuguese.

Rádio Cultura Araraquara, Avenida Bento de Abreu 789, Bairro Fonte Luminosa, 14802-396 Araraquara SP, Brazil. Phone: +55 (16) 3303-7799. Fax: +55 (16) 3303 7792. Email: (administration) cultura@radiocultura.net; (listener feedback) ouvintes@radiocultura.net; (Wagner Luiz) wagner@radiocultura.net. Web: (includes streaming audio) www.radiocultura.net. Contact: Wagner Luiz, Diretor Artístico. Return postage required. Replies slowly to correspondence in Portuguese.

Rádio Cultura Filadélfia, Avenida Brasil 531, Sala 74, 85851-000 Foz do Iguaçu PR, Brazil. Phone: +55 (45) 523-2930. Replies irregularly to correspondence in Portuguese.

Rádio Cultura Ondas Tropicais, Rua Barcelos s/n, Praça 14 de Janeiro, 69020-200 Manaus AM, Brazil. Phone: +55 (92) 2101-4967, +55 (92) 2101-4953. Fax: +55 (92) 2101 4950. Email: radiocultura@hotmail.com. Contact: Maria Jerusalem dos Santos (also known as Jerusa Santos), Diretora. Replies to correspondence in Portuguese. Return postage appreciated. Station is part of the FUNTEC (Fundação Televisão e Rádio Cultura do Amazonas) network.

Rádio Cultura São Paulo, Rua Vladimir Herzog 75, Água Branca, 05036-900 São Paulo SP, Brazil; or Caixa Postal 11544, 05049-970 São Paulo SP, Brazil. Phone: (general) +55 (11) 3874-3122; (Cultura AM) +55 (11) 3874-3081; (Cultura FM) +55 (11) 3874-3092. Fax: +55 (11) 3611 2014. Email: (Cultura AM, relayed on 9615 and 17815 kHz) falecom@radiocultura.am.br; (Cultura FM, relayed on 6170 kHz) falecom@radioculturasp.fm.br. Web: (includes streaming audio) www.tvcultura.com.br. Contact: Eduardo Weber, Coordenador de Produção Cultura AM. $1 or return postage required. Replies slowly to postal correspondence in Portuguese.

Rádio Difusora Acreana, Rua Benjamin Constant 1232, Centro, 69900-161 Rio Branco AC, Brazil. Phone: +55 (68) 3223-9696. Fax: +55 (68) 3223 8610. Email: radiodifusoraac@contilnet.com.br. Web: (streaming audio) www.ac.gov.br. Contact: Antônio Washington de Aquino Sobrinho, Gerente Geral. Replies irregularly to correspondence in Portuguese.

Rádio Difusora Cáceres, Caixa Postal 297, 78200-000 Cáceres MT, Brazil; (street address) Rua Tiradentes 979, Centro, 78200-000 Cáceres MT, Brazil. Phone: +55 (65) 223-3830. Fax: +55 (65) 223-5986. Contact: Sra. Maridalva Amaral Vignard. $1 or return postage required. Replies occasionally to correspondence in Portuguese.

Rádio Difusora de Londrina, Caixa Postal 916, 86000-000 Londrina PR, Brazil; (street address) Rua Sergipe, 843 – Sala 05, 86010-360 Londrina PR, Brazil. Phone: +55 (43) 3322-1105; Phone/fax: +55 (43) 3324-7369. Email: radiodifusora690@aol.com. Web: www.radiodifusoradelondrina.com.br. Contact: Oscar Simões, Diretor. Free tourist brochure, which sometimes seconds as a verification. $1 or return postage helpful. Replies irregularly to correspondence in Portuguese.

Rádio Difusora de Macapá, Rua Cândido Mendes 525, Centro, 68900-100 Macapá AP, Brazil. Phone: +55 (96) 3212-1120. Fax: +55 (96) 3212 1116. Email:difusoramcp@yahoo.com.br. Contact: Carlos Luiz Pereira Marques. $1 or return postage required. Replies irregularly to correspondence in Portuguese or English. Sometimes sends stickers, key rings and—on rare occasions—T-shirts.

Rádio Difusora de Poços de Caldas, Rua Rio Grande do Sul 631- 1º andar, Centro, 37701-001 Poços de Caldas MG, Brazil. Phone/Fax: +55 (35) 3722-1530. Email: difusora@difusorapocos.com.br. Web: www.difusorapocos.com.br. Contact: (general) Orlando Cioffi, Diretor Geral; (technical) Ronaldo Cioffi, Diretor Técnico. $1 or return postage required. Replies to correspondence in Portuguese.

☏Rádio Difusora do Amazonas, Av. Eduardo Ribeiro 639 - 20º andar, Centro, 69010-001 Manaus AM, Brazil. Phone: +55 (92) 3633-1009. Fax: +55 (92) 3234 3750. Email: difusora@internext.com.br; (Fesinha de Souza Anzoatégui) fesinha@uol.com.br; (Commercial Dept.) sac@difusoramanaus.com.br; (Josué Filho) josuefilhocomunicando@bol.com.br. Web: (includes streaming audio) www.difusoramanaus.com.br. Contact: Josué Filho. Replies to correspondence in Portuguese. $1 or return postage helpful.

☏Rádio Difusora Roraima, Avenida Capitão Ene Garcez 860, São Francisco, 69301-160 Boa Vista RR, Brazil. Phone/Fax: +55 (95) 623-2259. Email: radiorr@hotmail.com. Web: (includes streaming audio) www.radiororaima.com.br. Contact: Francisco Geraldo de França. Return postage required. Replies occasionally to correspondence in Portuguese.

Rádio Difusora Taubaté (if reactivated), Rua Dr. Sousa Alves 960, 12020-030 Taubaté SP, Brazil. Contact: Emilio Amadei Beringhs Neto, Diretor Superintendente. May send free stickers, pens, keychains and T-shirts. Return postage or $1 helpful.

Rádio Educação Rural (Campo Grande), Avenida Mato Grosso 530, Centro, 79002-906 Campo Grande MS, Brazil. Phone: +55 (67) 384-3164, +55 (67) 382-2238, +55 (67) 384-3345. Contact: Ângelo Jayme Venturelli, Diretor. $1 or return postage required. Replies to correspondence in Portuguese.

Rádio Educação Rural (Coari), Praça São Sebastião 228, 69460-000 Coari AM, Brazil. Phone: +55 (97) 3561-2474. Fax: +55 (97) 3561 2633. Email: radiocoari@hotmail.com. Contact: Cícero Marques. $1 or return postage helpful. Replies irregularly to correspondence in Portuguese.

Rádio Educação Rural de Tefé, Caixa Postal 21, 69470-000 Tefé AM, Brazil. Phone: +55 (97) 3343-3017. Fax: +55 (97) 3343-2663. Email: rert@osite.com.br, fjoaquim@mandic.com.br. Contact: Thomas Schwamborn, Diretor Administrativo. Verifies reception reports.

Rádio Educadora 6 de Agosto, Rua Coronel Brandão s/n, Bairro Aeroporto, 69930-000 Xapuri AC, Brazil. Phone: +55 (68) 3542-3063. Fax: +55 (68) 3452 2367 (mark to the attention of the station, for forwarding, as this number belongs to the local town council). Email: raimari.cardoso@hotmail.com.br. Contact: Raimari Sombra Cardoso, Coordenador. Replies to correspondence in Portuguese.

Rádio Educativa 6 de Agosto—*see* Rádio Educadora 6 de Agosto, above.

Rádio Educadora (Bragança), Praça das Bandeiras s/n, 68600-000 Bragança PA, Brazil. Phone: +55 (91) 3425-1295. Fax: +55 (91) 3425 1702. Email: fundacaoeducadora@uol.com.br. Contact: Padre Maurício de Souza, Presidente. $1 or return postage required. Replies to correspondence in Portuguese.

Rádio Educadora (Guajará Mirim), Praça Mário Corrêa No.90, 78957-000 Guajará Mirim RO, Brazil. Phone: +55 (69) 3541-2274. Fax: +55 (69) 3541 6333. Email: radioeducadora@uol.com.br. Web: www.brasilcatolico.com.br/cursos/radiohome2.htm. Contact: José Hélio, Diretor. Return postage helpful. Replies to correspondence in Portuguese.

☏Rádio Educadora (Limeira), Caixa Postal 105, 13480-970 Limeira SP, Brazil; (street address) Rua Prof. Maria Aparecida Martinelli Faveri 988, Jardim Elisa Fumagalli, 13485-316 Limeira SP, Brazil. Email: (Bortolan) bab@zaz.com.br. Web: (streaming audio only) www.educadoraam.com.br. Contact: Bruno Arcaro Bortolan, Gerente; Rosemary Ap. Giratto, Secretária Administrativa. Free stickers.

☏Rádio Gaúcha, Avenida Ipiranga 1075 - 3º andar, Bairro Azenha, 90160-093 Porto Alegre RS, Brazil. Phone: +55 (51) 3218-6600. Fax: +55 (51) 3218 6680. Email: (listener feedback) reportagem@rdgaucha.com.br; (technical) caio.klein@rdgaucha.com.br. Web: (includes on-demand and streaming audio) www.rdgaucha.com.br. Contact: Caio Klein, Gerente Técnico. Replies to correspondence, preferably in Portuguese. Reception reports should be sent to the attention of "Eng. Caio Klein" at the station address above.

Rádio Gazeta, Avenida Paulista 900, Cerqueira César, 01310-940 São Paulo SP, Brazil. Phone: +55 (11) 3170-5757. Fax: +55 (11) 3170 5630. Email: (Fundação Cásper Líbero parent organization) fcl@fcl.com.br. Web: (Fundação Cásper Líbero parent organization) www.fcl.com.br. Contact: Shakespeare Ettinger, Supervisor Geral de Operação; Bernardo Leite da Costa; José Roberto Mignone Cheibub, Gerente Geral; Ing. Aníbal Horta Figueiredo. Free stickers. $1 or return postage necessary. Replies to correspondence in Portuguese.

☏Rádio Globo (Rio de Janeiro), Rua do Russel 434, Glória, 22210-210 Rio de Janeiro RJ, Brazil. Phone: +55 (21) 2555-8282. Fax: +55 (21) 2558 6385. Email: (administration) gerenciaamrio@radioglobo.com.br; (technical, Küssler) gilberto.kussler@sgr.com.br. Web: (includes streaming audio) http://radioclick.globo.com/globobrasil. Contact: Gilberto Küssler, Gerente Técnico. Rarely replies to correspondence, but try sending reception reports, in Portuguese, to Gilberto Küssler. Return postage helpful.

☏Rádio Globo (São Paulo), Rua das Palmeiras 315, Santa Cecilia, 01226-901 São Paulo SP, Brazil. Phone: +55 (11) 3824-3217. Fax: +55 (11) 3824 3210. Web: (includes streaming audio) http://radioclick.globo.com/globobrasil. Contact: (nontechnical) Paulo Novis, Diretor Geral; (technical) Roberto Cidade, Gerente Técnico. Replies occasionally to correspondence in Portuguese.

☏Rádio Guaíba, Rua Caldas Júnior 219 - 2º Andar, 90019-900 Porto Alegre RS, Brazil. Phone: +55 (51) 3215-6222. Email: (administration) diretor@radioguaiba.com.br; (technical) centraltecnica@radioguaiba.com.br. Web: (includes streaming audio) www.radioguaiba.com.br. Contact: Ademar J. Dallanora, Gerente Administrativo. Return postage helpful. Free stickers.

Rádio Guarujá (Florianópolis), Caixa Postal 45, 88000-000 Florianópolis SC, Brazil. Email: guaruja@radioguaruja.com.br. Web: www.radioguaruja.com.br. Contact: Mario Silva, Diretor; Joana Sempre Bom Braz, Assessora de Marketing e Comunicação; Rosa Michels de Souza. Return postage required. Replies irregularly to correspondence in Portuguese.

NEW YORK OFFICE: 45 West 46 Street, 5th Floor, Manhattan, NY 10036 USA.

📻Rádio Guarujá (Guarujá SP), Rua José Vaz Porto 175, Vila Santa Rosa, 11431-190 Guarujá SP, Brazil. Phone: +55 (13) 3386-6092; (listener feedback) +55 (13) 3386-6965. Email: (general) atendimento@radioguarujaam.com.br; (technical) radioguarujaam@radioguarujaam.com.br; (Rampazo) rampazo@radioguarujaam.com.br, rampazo@superig.com.br. Web: (includes streaming audio) www.radioguarujaam.com.br. Contact: Orivaldo Rampazo, Diretor. Replies to correspondence in Portuguese and verifies reception reports. Free stickers and station brochure.

Rádio Guarujá Paulista—*see* Rádio Guarujá (Guarujá SP), above.

📻Rádio Inconfidência, Avenida Raja Gabáglia 1666, Luxemburgo, 30350-540 Belo Horizonte MG, Brazil. Phone: +55 (31) 3297-7344, +55 (31) 3297-5803; (transmitter site) +55 (31) 3394-1388. Fax: +55 (31) 3297 7348. Phone/Fax: (Commercial Dept.) +55 (31) 3297-7343. Email: inconfidencia@inconfidencia.com.br. Web: (includes streaming audio) www.inconfidencia.com.br. Contact: Isaias Lansky, Diretor; Manuel Emilio de Lima Torres, Diretor Superintendente; Jairo Antolio Lima, Diretor Artístico; Eugenio Silva. Free stickers and postcards. May send CD of Brazilian music. $1 or return postage helpful.

Rádio Integração (if reactivated), Rua de Alagoas 270, Colégio, 69980-000 Cruzeiro do Sul AC, Brazil. Phone: +55 (68) 3322-4637. Fax: +55 (68) 3322 6511. Email: rtvi@omegasul.com.br. Contact: Albelia Bezerra da Cunha, Diretora. Return postage helpful.

📻Rádio Itatiaia, Rua Itatiaia 117, 31210-170 Belo Horizonte MG, Brazil. Fax: +55 (31) 446 2900. Email: itatiaia@itatiaia.com.br. Web: (includes on-demand and streaming audio) www.itatiaia.com.br/am/index.html. Contact: Lúcia Araújo Bessa, Assistente da Diretória; Claudio Carneiro.

Rádio Jornal "A Crítica" (when operating), Av. André Araujo 1024A, Aleixo, 69060-001 Manaus AM, Brazil. Phone/Fax: +55 (92) 2123-1000. Email: walteryallas@acritica.com.br. Contact: Walter Yallas.

Rádio Marumby (Curitiba)—*see* Rádio Novas de Paz.

📻Rádio Marumby (Florianópolis), Caixa Postal 296, 88010-970 Florianópolis SC, Brazil; (street address) Rua Angelo Laporta 841, 88020-600 Florianópolis SC, Brazil. Email: dafaie@pop.com.br. Web: (includes streaming audio) www.marumby.cjb.net; (includes on-demand audio) www.gmuh.com.br/radio/radio.htm. Contact: Davi Campos, Diretor Artístico; Dr. Cesino Bernardino, Presidente, GMUH; Jair Albano, Diretor. $1 or return postage required. Free diploma and stickers. Replies to correspondence in Portuguese.

GMUH MISSIONARY PARENT ORGANIZATION: Gideões Missionários da Última Hora—GMUH, Rua Joaquim Nunes 244, 88340-000 Camboriú SC, Brazil; (postal address) Caixa Postal 2004, 88340-000 Camboriú SC, Brazil. Phone: +55 (47) 261-3232. Email: gmuh@gmuh.com.br. Web: www.gmuh.com.br.

📻Rádio Meteorologia Paulista, Rua Capitão João Marques 89, Jardim Centenário, 14940-000 Ibitinga, São Paulo SP, Brazil; or Caixa Postal 91, 14940-000 Ibitinga SP, Brazil. Phone: +55 (16) 242-6378/79/80. Fax: +55 (16) 242 5056. Email: radioibitinga@radioibitinga.com.br. Web: (includes streaming audio from Ternura FM, relayed several hours each day by Rádio Meteorologia Paulista) www.radioibitinga.com.br/meteorologia. Contact: Roque de Rosa, Diretor. Replies to correspondence in Portuguese. $1 or return postage required.

Rádio Missões da Amazônia, Travessa Dr. Lauro Sodré 299, 68250-000 Óbidos PA, Brazil. Phone/Fax: +55 (93) 3547-1699.

Web: www.kaleb.hpg.ig.com.br. Contact: Ronald Santos, Diretor. Return postage required. Replies occasionally to correspondence in Portuguese.

📻Rádio Mundial, Av. Paulista 2198-Térreo, Cerqueira César, 01310-300 São Paulo SP, Brazil. Phone: +55 (11) 3016 5999. Email: (general) radiomundial@radiomundial.com; (administration) administrativo@radiomundial.com.br. Web: (includes streaming audio) www.radiomundial.com.br. Contact: (non-technical) Luci Rothschild de Abreu, Diretora Presidente.

REDE CBS PARENT ORGANIZATION: Rede CBS, Av. Paulista, 2200 - 14° andar, Cerqueira César, 01310-300 São Paulo SP, Brazil. Phone: +55 (11) 3016 5999. Fax: +55 (11) 3016 5980. Email: comercial@redecbs.com.br. Web: www.redecbs.com.br.

Rádio Municipal, Avenida Álvaro Maia s/n, 69750-000 São Gabriel da Cachoeira AM, Brazil. Phone/Fax: +55 (97) 3471-1768. Email: rmunicipalsgc@yahoo.com.br. Contact: Rosane da Conceição Rodrigues Neto, Diretora. Return postage necessary. Replies to correspondence in Portuguese. Formerly Rádio Nacional de São Gabriel da Cachoeira, prior to the station's transfer from Radiobrás to the local municipality.

📻Rádio Nacional da Amazônia, Caixa Postal 258, 70359-970 Brasília-DF, Brazil; or SCRN 702/703 - Edif. Radiobrás - Subsolo, 70710-750 Brasília-DF, Brazil. Phone: +55 (61) 327-1981. Email: nacionaloc@radiobras.gov.br. Web: (includes streaming audio) www.radiobras.gov.br (click on "Rádio Nacional"). Contact: (technical) Taís Ladeira de Madeiros, Chefe da Divisão de Ondas Curtas da Radiobrás. Free stickers. Will occasionally verify reception reports if a prepared card is included.

Rádio Novas de Paz, Avenida Paraná 1896, 82510-000 Curitiba PR, Brazil; or Caixa Postal 22, 80000-000 Curitiba PR, Brazil. Phone: +55 (41) 257-4109. Contact: João Falavinha Ienzen, Gerente. $1 or return postage required. Replies irregularly to correspondence in Portuguese.

Rádio Novo Tempo, Caixa Postal 146, 79002-970 Campo Grande MS, Brazil; (street address) Rua Amando de Oliveira 135, Bairro Amambaí, 79005-370 Campo Grande MS, Brazil. Email: novotempo.ms@usb.org.br; (Ramos) ellen.ramos@usb.org.br. Web: www.asm.org.br (click on "Rádio Novo Tempo"). Contact: Ellen Ramos, Locutora; Pastor Paulo Melo. Return postage required. Replies to correspondence in Portuguese. A station of the Seventh Day Adventists.

Rádio Oito de Setembro—see Rádio 8 de Setembro.

Rádio Pioneira de Teresina, Rua 24 de Janeiro 150 sul, 64001-230 Teresina PI, Brazil. Phone: +55 (86) 3221-8121. Fax: +55 (86) 3221 8122. Email: (general) pioneira@radiopioneira.am.br; (management) gerencia@radiopioneira.am.br; (comments on programs) programacao@radiopioneira.am.br; (director) rosemiro@radiopioneira.am.br. Web: www.radiopioneira.am.br. Contact: Rosemiro Robinson da Costa. $1 or return postage required. Replies slowly to correspondence in Portuguese.

◨Rádio Record, Caixa Postal 7920, 04084-002 São Paulo SP, Brazil. Email: radiorecord@rederecord.com.br. Web: (includes streaming audio) www.rederecord.com.br/radiorecord. Contact: Mário Luíz Catto, Diretor Geral; Antonio Carlos Miranda. Free stickers. Return postage or $1 required. Replies occasionally to correspondence in Portuguese.

Rádio Relógio, Rua Paramopama 131, Ribeira, Ilha do Governador, 21930-110 Rio de Janeiro RJ, Brazil. Phone: +55 (21) 2467-0201. Fax: +55 (21) 2467 4656. Email: radiorelogio@ig.com.br. Contact: Olindo Coutinho, Diretor Geral; Renato Castro. Replies occasionally to correspondence in Portuguese.

Rádio Rio Mar, Rua José Clemente 500, Centro, 69010-070 Manaus AM, Brazil. Phone: +55 (92) 3633-2295. Fax: +55 (92) 3232 5020. Email: decom@click21.com.br. Contact: Martin James Lauman, Superintendente. Replies to correspondence in Portuguese. $1 or return postage helpful.

Rádio Roraima—see Rádio Difusora Roraima.

Rádio Rural (Petrolina), Caixa Postal 8, 56300-000 Petrolina PE, Brazil. Phone: +55 (87) 3861-2874, +55 (87) 3862-1522. Email: emissorarural@silcons.com.br. Contact: Padre Bianchi, Gerente; Maria Letecia de Andrade Nunes. Return postage necessary. Replies to correspondence in Portuguese.

Rádio Rural (Santarém), Avenida São Sebastião 622 - Bloco A, 68005-090 Santarém PA, Brazil. Phone: +55 (93) 3523-1006. Fax: +55 (93) 3523 2685. Email: radiorural@vsp.com.br, edilrural@gmail.com.br. Contact: Padre Edilberto Moura Sena, Coordenador. Replies slowly to correspondence in Portuguese. Free stickers. Return postage or $1 required.

◨Rádio Senado, Caixa Postal 070-747, 70359-970 Brasília DF, Brazil; (physical address) Praça dos Três Poderes, Anexo II - Bloco B - Térreo, 70165-900 Brasília DF, Brazil. Phone: (general) +55 (61) 311-4691, +55 (61) 311-1257; (technical) +55 (61) 311-1285; (shortwave department) +55 (61) 311-1238. Fax: (general) +55 (61) 311 4238. Email: radio@senado.gov.br; (Fabiano) max@senado.gov.br. Web: www.senado.gov.br/radio/ondascurtas.asp; (streaming audio from FM Service, partly relayed on shortwave) mms://bombadil.senado.gov.br/wmtencoder/radio.wmv. Contact: Max Fabiano, Diretor; (technical) José Carlos Sigmaringa, Coordenador do Núcleo de Ondas Curtas.

◨Rádio Trans Mundial, Caixa Postal 18300, 04626-970 São Paulo SP, Brazil; (street address) Rua Épiro 110, 04635-030 São Paulo SP, Brazil. Phone/Fax: +55 (11) 5031-3533. Email: (general) rtm@transmundial.com.br; (technical) tecnica@transmundial.com.br; ("Amigos do Rádio" DX-program) amigosdoradio@transmundial.com.br. Web: (includes streaming audio) www.transmundial.com.br. Contact: José Carlos de Santos, Diretor; Rudolf Grimm, programa "Amigos do Rádio." Free stickers, postcards, bookmarkers or other small gifts. Sells religious books and CDs of religious music (from hymns to bossa nova). Prices, in local currency, can be found at the Website (click on "Publicações"). Programming comes from São Paulo, but transmitter site is located in Santa Maria, Rio Grande do Sul.

Rádio Tupi, Rua João Negrão 595, Centro, 80010-200, Curitiba PR, Brazil. Phone: +55 (41) 323-1353. Contact: (technical) Eng. Latuf Aurani (who is based in São Paulo). Relays "Voz de Libertação" (see). Rarely replies, and only to correspondence in Portuguese.

Rádio Vale do Xingu, Rua Primeira de Janeiro 1359, Catedral, 68371-020 Altamira PA, Brazil. Phone/Fax: +55 (93) 3515-1182, +55 (93) 3515-4899, +55 (93) 3515-4411. Email: radioetv@valedoxingu.com.br. Contact: Ana Claudia Barros, Diretora.

Rádio Verdes Florestas, Fundação Verdes Florestas, Rua Mário Lobão 81, 69980-000 Cruzeiro do Sul AC, Brazil; (transmitter location) Estrado do Aeroporto, km 02, Bairro Nossa Senhora das Graças, Cruzeiro do Sul AC, Brazil. Phone/Fax: +55 (68) 3322-3309, +55 (68) 3322-2634. Email: verdesflorestas@yahoo.com.br. Contact: José Graci Soares Rezende. Return postage required. Replies occasionally to correspondence in Portuguese.

◨Rádio Voz do Coração Imaculado (when operating), Caixa Postal 354, 75001-970 Anápolis GO, Brazil; (street address) Rua Barão de Cotegipe s/n, Centro, 75001-970 Anápolis GO, Brazil. Email: radioimaculada@immacolata.com. Web: (includes streaming audio) www.immacolata.com/radiovoz. Contact: Padre Domingos M. Esposito. Operation tends to be irregular, as the station is funded entirely from religious donations.

Super Rádio Alvorada —see Rádio Alvorada (Rio Branco).

◨Voz de Libertação. Ubiquitous programming originating from the "Deus é Amor" Pentecostal church's Rádio Universo (1300 kHz) in São Bernardo do Campo, São Paulo, and aired over several shortwave stations, especially Rádio Tupi, Curitiba (see). Streaming audio is available at the "Deus é Amor" Website, www.ipda.org.br.

Voz do Coração Imaculado—see Rádio Voz do Coração Imaculado.

BRITISH INDIAN OCEAN TERRITORY   World Time +6

AFRTS-American Forces Radio and Television Service (Shortwave), Naval Media Center, PSC 466 Box 14, FPO AP 96595-0014 USA. Phone: +246 370-3680. Fax: +246 370 3681. Replies irregularly.

BULGARIA   World Time +2 (+3 midyear)

◨Radio Bulgaria

NONTECHNICAL AND TECHNICAL: P.O. Box 900, 1000 Sofia, Bulgaria; or (street address) 4 Dragan Tsankov Blvd., 1040 Sofia, Bulgaria. Phone: (general) +359 (2) 985-241; (Managing Director) +359 (2) 854-604. Fax: (general, usually weekdays only) +359 (2) 871 060, +359 (2) 871 061, +359 (2) 650 560; (Managing Director) +359 (2) 946 1576; +359 (2) 988 5103;

(Frequency Manager) +359 (2) 963 4464. Email: (English program and schedule information) english@bnr.bg (same format for other languages, e.g. french@ . . .; spanish@ . . .). Web: (includes on-demand audio, plus streaming audio from domestice services not aired on shortwave) www.bnr.bg. Contact: (general) Mrs. Iva Delcheva, English Section; Svilen Stoicheff, Head of English Section; Ludmila Petra, Spanish Section; (administration and technical) Anguel H. Nedyalkov, Managing Director; (technical) Atanas Tzenov, Director. Replies regularly, but sometimes slowly. Return postage helpful. Verifies email reports with QSL cards. For concerns about frequency usage, contact BTC, below, with copies to Messrs. Nedyalkov and Tzenov of Radio Bulgaria.

FREQUENCY MANAGEMENT AND TRANSMISSION OPERATIONS: Bulgarian Telecommunications Company (BTC), Ltd., 8 Totleben Blvd., 1606 Sofia, Bulgaria. Phone: +359 (2) 88-00-75. Fax: +359 (2) 87 58 85, +359 (2) 80 25 80. Contact: Roumen Petkov, Frequency Manager; Mrs. Margarita Krasteva, Radio Regulatory Department.

Radio Varna, 22 Primorski blvd, 9000 Varna, Bulgaria. Phone: +359 (52) 602-802. Fax: +359 (52) 664 411. Email: bnr@radiovarna.com. Web: (includes streaming audio from the domestic service, not aired on shortwave) www.radiovarna.com. Contact: (technical) Kostadin Kovachev, Chief Engineer.

BURKINA FASO   World Time exactly

Radiodiffusion-Télévision Burkina, B.P. 7029, Ouagadougou, Burkina Faso. Phone: +226 310-441. Contact: Tahéré Ouedraogo, Le Chef des Programmes. Replies irregularly to correspondence in French. IRC or return postage helpful.

BURMA—see MYANMAR.

BURUNDI   World Time +2

La Voix de la Révolution, B.P. 1900, Bujumbura, Burundi. Phone: +257 22-37-42. Fax: +257 22 65 47, +257 22 66 13. Email: rtnb@cbinf.com. $1 required.

CANADA   World Time –3:30 (–2:30 midyear) Newfoundland; –4 (–3 midyear) Atlantic; –5 (–4 midyear) Eastern, including Québec and Ontario; –6 (–5 midyear) Central; except Saskatchewan; –6 Saskatchewan; –7 (–6 midyear) Mountain; –8 (–7 midyear) Pacific, including Yukon.

Canadian Broadcasting Corporation (CBC)—English Programs, P.O. Box 500, Station A, Toronto, Ontario, M5W 1E6, Canada. Phone: (toll-free, Canada only) +1 (866) 306-4636; (Audience Relations) +1 (416) 205-3700. Email: cbcinput@toronto.cbc.ca. Web: (includes on-demand and streaming audio) www.radio.cbc.ca. CBC prepares some of the programs heard over Radio Canada International (*see*).

LONDON NEWS BUREAU: CBC, 43-51 Great Titchfield Street, London W1P 8DD, United Kingdom. Phone: +44 (20) 7412-9200. Fax: +44 (20) 7631 3095.

PARIS NEWS BUREAU: CBC, 17 avenue Matignon, F-75008 Paris, France. Phone: +33 (1) 4421-1515. Fax: +33 (1) 4421 1514.

WASHINGTON NEWS BUREAU: CBC, National Press Building, Suite 500, 529 14th Street NW, Washington DC 20045 USA. Phone: +1 (202) 383-2900.

Canadian Broadcasting Corporation (CBC)—French Programs, Société Radio-Canada, C.P. 6000, succ. centre-ville, Montréal, Québec, H3C 3A8, Canada. Phone: (Audience Relations) +1 (514) 597-6000. Web: (includes on-demand and streaming audio) www.radio-canada.ca. Welcomes correspondence, but may not reply due to shortage of staff. CBC prepares some of the programs heard over Radio Canada International (*see*).

CBC Northern Québec Shortwave Service—*see* Radio Canada International, below.

CFRX-CFRB

MAIN ADDRESS: 2 St. Clair Avenue West, Toronto, Ontario, M4V 1L6, Canada. Phone:(main switchboard) +1 (416) 924-5711; (talk shows switchboard) +1 (416) 872-1010; (news centre) +1 (416) 924-6717. Fax: (main fax line) +1 (416) 872 8683; (CFRB news fax line) +1 (416) 323 6816. Email: (comments on programs) cfrbcomments@cfrb.com; (News Director) news@cfrb.com; (general, nontechnical) info@cfrb.com; opsmngr@cfrb.com. Web: (includes on-demand and streaming audio) www.cfrb.com. Contact: (nontechnical) Carlo Massaro, Information Officer; Steve Kowch, Operations Manager. Reception reports should be sent to the verification address, below.

VERIFICATION ADDRESS: Ontario DX Association, 155 Main St. N., Apt. 313, Newmarket, Ontario, L3Y 8C2, Canada. Email: odxa@rogers.com. Web: www.odxa.on.ca. Contact: Steve Canney, VA3SC.

CFVP-CKMX, AM 1060, Standard Broadcasting, P.O. Box 2750, Station 'M', Calgary, Alberta, T2P 4P8, Canada. Phone: (general) +1 (403) 240-5800; (news) +1 (403) 240-5844; (technical) +1 (403) 240-5867. Fax: (general and technical) +1 (403) 240 5801; (news) +1 (403) 246 7099. Contact: (general) Gary Russell, General Manager; Beverley Van Tighem, Executive Assistant; (technical) Ken Pasolli, Technical Director.

CHU. Radio Station CHU, National Research Council of Canada, 1200 Montreal Road, Bldg M-36, Ottawa, Ontario, K1A 0R6, Canada. Phone: +1 (613) 993-5186. Fax: +1 (613) 952 1394. Email: radio.chu@nrc.ca. Web: http://inms-ienm.nrc-cnrc.gc.ca/time_services/shortwave_broadcasts_e.html. Contact: Dr. Rob Douglas; Dr. Jean-Simon Boulanger, Group Leader; Ray Pelletier, Technical Officer. Official standard frequency and World Time station for Canada on 3330, 7335 and 14670 kHz. Brochure available upon request. Those with a personal computer, Bell 103 compatible modem and appropriate software can get the exact time, from CHU's cesium clock, via the telephone; details available upon request, or direct from the Website. Verifies reception reports with a QSL card.

CKZN, CBC Newfoundland and Labrador, P.O. Box 12010, Station 'A', St. John's, Newfoundland, A1B 3T8, Canada. Phone: +1 (709) 576-5155. Fax: +1 (709) 576 5099. Email: (administration) radiomgt@stjohns.cbc.ca; (engineer) keith_durnford@cbc.ca. Web: (includes on-demand audio) www.stjohns.cbc.ca; (streaming audio) www.cbc.ca/listen/index.html# (click on "St. John's"). Contact: (general) Heather Elliott, Communications Officer; (technical) Shawn R. Williams, Manager, Transmission and Distribution; Keith Durnford, Supervisor, Transmission Operations; Terry Brett, Transmitter Department; Rosemary Sampson. Free CBC sticker and verification card with the history of Newfoundland included. Don't enclose money, stamps or IRCs with correspondence, as they will only have to be returned. Relays CBN (St. John's, 640 kHz) except at 1000-1330 World Time (one hour earlier in summer) when programming comes from CFGB Goose Bay.

CFGB ADDRESS: CBC Radio, Box 1029 Station C, Happy Valley, Goose Bay, Labrador, Newfoundland A0P 1C0, Canada. Email: (program relayed via CKZN) labmorns@cbc.ca.

🔲**CKZU-CBU**, CBC, P.O. Box 4600, Vancouver, British Columbia, V6B 4A2, Canada—for verification of reception reports, mark the envelope, "Attention: Engineering." Phone: (general) +1 (604) 662-6000; (toll-free, U.S. and Canada only) 1-800-961-6161; (engineering) +1 (604) 662-6060. Fax: +1 (604) 662 6350. Email: (general) webmaster@vancouver.cbc. ca; (Newbury) newburyd@vancouver.cbc.ca. Web: (includes on-demand audio) www.vancouver.cbc.ca; (streaming audio) www.cbc.ca/listen/index.html# (click on "Vancouver"). Contact: (general) Public Relations; (technical) Dave Newbury, Transmission Engineer.

Église du Christ, C.P. 2026, Jonquière, Québec, G7X 7XC, Canada. Phone: +1 (514) 387-6163. Fax: +1 (514) 387-1153. E-mail: egliseduchrist@videotron.ca. Web: www3.sympatico. ca/micdan. Contact: Jean Grenier. Broadcasts via a transmitter in the United Kingdom.

High Adventure Gospel Communication Ministries—*see* Bible Voice Broadcasting, United Kingdom.

🔲**Radio Canada International**

NOTE: (CBC Northern Québec Service) The following P. O Box 6000 postal address and street address are also valid for the Northern Québec Service, provided that you mention the name of the service and "17th Floor" on the envelope. RCI does not issue technical verifications for Northern Québec Service transmissions.

MAIN OFFICE: P.O. Box 6000, Montréal, Québec, H3C 3A8, Canada; or (street address) 1400 boulevard René-Lévesque Est, Montréal, Québec, H2L 2M2, Canada. Phone: (general) +1 (514) 597-7500; (Audience Relations, Bill Westenhaver) +1 (514) 597-5899; (Listener Response phone number, English/French) +1 (514) 528-8821 (collect calls not accepted). Fax: (Audience Relations) +1 (514) 597 7760. Email: info@rcinet.ca. Web: (includes online reception report form and on-demand and streaming audio) www.rcinet.ca. Contact: (general and technical verifications) Bill Westenhaver, Audience Relations; Stéphane Parent, Producer/Host "Le courrier mondial"; Ian Jones, Producer/Host "The Maple Leaf Mailbag"; (administration) Jean Larin, Director. Free stickers, antenna booklet and lapel pins on request. May send other small gifts.

TRANSMISSION OFFICE, INTERNATIONAL SERVICES, CBC TRANSMISSION: Room B52-70, 1400 boulevard René-Lévesque Est, Montréal, Québec, H2L 2M2, Canada. Phone: +1 (514) 597-7618/19. Fax: +1 (514) 284 2052. Email: master_control@moncton.radio-canada.ca; (Théorêt) gerald_theoret@radio-canada.ca; (Bouliane) jacques_bouliane@radio-canada.ca. Contact: (general) Gérald Théorêt, Frequency Manager, CBC Transmission Management; Ms. Nicole Vincent, Frequency Management; (administration) Jacques Bouliane, Senior Manager, International Services. This office only for informing about transmitter-related problems (interference, modulation quality, etc.), especially by fax or email. Verifications are not given out at this office; requests for verification should be sent to the main office, above.

TRANSMITTER SITE: CBC, P.O. Box 6131, Sackville New Brunswick, E4L 1G6, Canada. Phone: +1 (506) 536-2690/1. Fax: +1 (506) 536 2342. Contact: Raymond Bristol, Sackville Plant Manager, CBC Transmission. All correspondence not concerned with transmitting equipment should be directed to the appropriate address in Montréal, above. Free tours given during normal working hours.

MONITORING STATION: P.O. Box 460, Station Main Stittsville, Ontario, K2S 1A6, Canada. Phone: +1 (613) 831-4802. Fax: +1 (613) 831 0343. Email: derek.williams@cbc.ca. Contact: Derek Williams, Manager of Monitoring.

Shortwave Classroom, R. Tait McKenzie Public School, 175 Paterson Street, Almonte, Ontario, K0A 1A0, Canada. Phone: +1 (613) 256-8248. Fax: +1 (613) 256 4791. Email: neil.carletonn@ucdsb.on.ca. Contact: Neil Carleton, VE3NCE, Editor & Publisher. *The Shortwave Classroom* newsletter was published three times per year as a nonprofit volunteer project for teachers around the world that use shortwave listening in the classroom, or as a club activity, to teach about global perspectives, media studies, world geography, languages, social studies and other subjects. Although no longer published, a set of back issues with articles and classroom tips from teachers around the globe is available for $10.

CENTRAL AFRICAN REPUBLIC   World Time +1

Radio Centrafrique (when operating), Radiodiffusion-Télévision Centrafricaine, B.P. 940, Bangui, Central African Republic. Contact: (technical) Directeur des Services Techniques. Replies on rare occasions to correspondence in French. Return postage required.

🔲**Radio Ndeke Luka** (when operating), PNUD, B.P. 872, Bangui, Central African Republic. Email: (including reception reports) ndekeluka@hotmail.com. Contact: Cédrine Beney, Chargée de projet. Replies to correspondence in French, and may reply in French to correspondence in English. The station is managed by the Fondation Hirondelle, based in Switzerland, and operates under the aegis of the United Nations, in partnership with the UNDP (United Nations Development Programme). The main studio is located in Bangui. Broadcasts domestically on FM, and produces a program aired irregularly via shortwave facilities in the United Kingdom or the United Arab Emirates.
FONDATION HIRONDELLE: 3 Rue Traversière, CH 1018-Lausanne, Switzerland. Phone: +41 (21) 647-2805. Fax: +41 (21) 647 4469. Email info@hirondelle.org. Web: (includes on-demand news bulletins from Radio Ndeke Luka) www.hirondelle.org. Verifies reception reports.

CHAD   World Time +1

Radiodiffusion Nationale Tchadienne—N'djamena, B.P. 892, N'Djamena, Chad. Contact: Djimadoum Ngoka Kilamian; Ousmane Mahamat. Two IRCs or return postage required. Replies slowly to correspondence in French.

CHILE   World Time –3 (–4 midyear)

🔲**CVC—La Voz** (formerly Radio Voz Cristiana)
TRANSMISSION FACILITIES: Casilla 395, Talagante, Santiago, Chile. Phone: (engineering) +56 (2) 855-7046. Fax: +56 (2) 855 7053. Email: (chief engineer) antonio@cvclavoz.cl; (operations manager) gisela@cvclavoz.cl. Web: www.cvclavoz.com. Contact: Antonio Reyes B., Chief Engineer; Gisela Vergara, Operations Manager. Free program and frequency schedules. Sometimes verifies reception reports.
PROGRAM PRODUCTION: P.O. Box 2889, Miami FL 33144 USA; (street address) 15485 Eagle Nest Lane, Suite 220, Miami Lakes FL 33014 USA. Phone: +1 (305) 231-7704; (Portuguese Service) +1 (305) 231-7742. Email: (Gallardo) info@vozcristiana.com; (listener feedback) comentarios@vozcristiana.com. Web: (includes streaming audio) www.vozcristiana.com. Contact: (administration) Juan Mark Gallardo, Gerente de Programación.
ENGINEERING DEPARTMENT: Ryder Street, West Bromwich, West Midlands B70 0EJ, United Kingdom. Phone: +44 (121) 522-6087. Fax: +44 (121) 522 6083. Email: andrewflynn@christianvision.com. Contact: Andrew Flynn, Head of Engineering.

Ian McFarland worked for a time at Radio Japan. He enjoys a friendly visit with a colleague from China Radio International at the annual Kulpsville Winterfest (swlfest.com).

J. Brinker

Radio Esperanza

OFFICE: Casilla 830, Temuco, Chile. Phone: +56 (45) 213-790. Phone/Fax: +56 (45) 367-070. Email: esperanza@telsur.cl. Contact: (general) Juanita Cárcamo, Departmento de Programación; Eleazar Jara, Dpto. de Programación; Ramón P. Woerner K., Publicidad; Alberto Higueras Martínez, Locutor; (verifications) Rodolfo Campos, Director; (technical) Juan Luis Puentes, Dpto. Técnico. Free pennants, stickers, bookmarks and tourist information. Two IRCs, $1 or 2 U.S. stamps appreciated. Replies, often slowly, to correspondence in Spanish or English.

STUDIO: Calle Luis Durand 03057, Temuco, Chile. Phone/Fax: +56 (45) 240-161.

Radio Parinacota, Casilla 82, Arica, Chile. Phone: +56 (58) 245-889. Phone/Fax: +56 (58) 245 986. Email: rparinacota@latinmail.com. Contact: Tomislav Simunovich Gran, Director.

CHINA World Time +8; still nominally +6 ("Urümqi Time") in the Xinjiang Uighur Autonomous Region, but in practice +8 is observed there, as well.

NOTE: If a Chinese regional station does not respond to your correspondence within four months, send your reception reports to China Radio International (*see*) which will verify them. CRI apparently no longer forwards correspondence to regional stations, as it sometimes did in the past.

📻Central People's Broadcasting Station (CPBS)—China National Radio (Zhongyang Renmin Guangbo Diantai), P.O. Box 4501, Beijing 100866, China. Phone: +86 (10) 6851-2435, +86 (10) 6851-5522. Fax: +86 (10) 6851 6630. Email: cn@cnradio.com; (services for Taiwan) cnrtw@cnrtw.com. Web: (includes on-demand and streaming audio) www.cnradio.com; (services for Taiwan) www.nihaotw.com. Contact: Wang Changquan, Audience Department, China National Radio. Tape recordings of music and news $5 plus postage. CPBS T-shirts $10 plus postage; also sells ties and other items with CPBS logo. No credit cards. Free stickers, pennants and other small souvenirs. Return postage helpful. Responds regularly to correspondence in English or Standard Chinese (Mandarin). Although in recent years this station has officially been called "China National

Radio" in English-language documents, all on-air identifications in Standard Chinese continue to be "Zhongyang Renmin Guangbo Dientai" (Central People's Broadcasting Station). To quote from the Website of China's State Administration of Radio, Film and TV: "The station moved to Beijing on March 25, 1949. It was renamed the Central People's Broadcasting Station (it [sic] English name was changed to China National Radio later on) . . ."

China Business Radio. The Second Program of Central People's Broadcasting Station—China National Radio (*see*).

China Huayi Broadcasting Company—*see* China Huayi Broadcasting Corporation, below.

📻China Huayi Broadcasting Corporation, P.O. Box 251, Fuzhou, Fujian 350001, China. Email: (station) hanyu@chbcnews.com; (Yuan Jia) chrisyuanjia@sohu.com; Web: (includes streaming audio) www.chbcnews.com. Contact: Lin Hai Chun, Announcer; Yuan Jia, Program Manager. Replies to correspondence in English or Chinese. Although the station refers to itself in English as China Huayi Broadcasting Company, the correct translation of the Chinese name is China Huayi Broadcasting Corporation.

VERIFICATION OF RECEPTION REPORTS: Although verifications are sometimes received direct from the station, reception reports are best sent to the QSL Manager: Qiao Xiaoli, Fen Jin Xing Cun 3-4-304, Changshu, Jiangsu 215500, China. Recordings accepted, and return postage (IRC, $1US or 1 euro) required for a QSL card. Email: 2883752@163.com.

China National Radio—*see* Central People's Broadcasting Station (CPBS), above.

📻China Radio International

MAIN OFFICE, NON-CHINESE LANGUAGES SERVICE: 16A Shijingshan Street, Beijing 100040, China; (English Service) P.O. Box 4216, CRI-2, Beijing 100040 China (other language sections also use this address, but with a different CRI number; for example, it's CRI-39 for the Portuguese Service). Phone: (Director's office) +86 (10) 6889-1625; (Audience Relations.) +86 (10) 6889-1617, +86 (10) 6889-1652; (English newsroom/current affairs) +86 (10) 6889-1619; (Technical Director) +86 (10) 6609-2577. Fax: (Director's office) +86 (10) 6889 1582;

(English Service) +86 (10) 6889 1378, +86 (10) 6889 1379; (audience relations) +86 (10) 6889 3175; (administration) +86 (10) 6851 3174; (German Service) +86 (10) 6889 2053; (Spanish Service) +86 (10) 6889 1909. Email: (English) crieng@cri.com.cn, yinglian@cri.com.cn, garden@cri.com.cn; (Listener's Liason) gaohuiying@crifm.com; (English, technical, including reception reports) crieng@crifm.com; (Chinese) chn@cri.com.cn; (French) crifra@cri.com.cn; (German) ger@cri.com.cn (see also the entry for the Berlin Bureau, below); (Japanese) jap@cri.com.cn; (Portuguese) cripor@cri.com.cn; (Spanish) spa@cri.com.cn. Web: (includes on-demand and streaming audio) www.chinabroadcast.cn; (English, official) http://en.chinabroadcast.cn; (English, unofficial, but regularly updated) http://pw2.netcom.com/~jleq/cri1.htm. Contact: Yang Lei, Director, English Service; Peichun Li, Deputy Director, English Service; Ms. Wang Anjing, Director of Audience Relations, English Service; Ying Lian, English Service; Gao Huiying, Editor, Listener's Liason; Shang Chunyan, "Listener's Garden"; Yu Meng, Editor; (administration) Li Dan, President, China Radio International; Xia Jixuan, Vice President; Wang Gengnian Director General; Xia Jixuan, Chen Minyi, Chao Tieqi and Wang Dongmei, Deputy Directors, China Radio International; Xin Liancai, Director International Relations, China Radio International. Free bi-monthly *Messenger* newsletter for loyal listeners, pennants, stickers, desk calendars, pins and handmade papercuts. Every year, China Radio International holds contests and quizzes, with the overall winner getting a free trip to China. T-shirts for $8. Two-volume, 820-page set of *Day-to-Day Chinese* language-lesson books $15, including postage worldwide; a 155-page book, *Learn to Speak Chinese: Sentence by Sentence*, plus two cassettes for $15. Two Chinese music tapes for $15. Various other books (on arts, medicine, Chinese idioms etc.) in English available from Audience Relations Department, English Service, China Radio International, 100040 Beijing, China. Payment by postal money order to Mr. Li Yi. Every year, the Audience Relations Department will renew the mailing list of the *Messenger* newsletter. CRI is also relayed via shortwave transmitters in Canada, Cuba, France, French Guiana, Mali, Russia and Spain.

ARLINGTON NEWS BUREAU: 2000 South Eads Street APT#712, Arlington VA 22202 USA. Phone: +1 (703) 521-8689. Contact: Mr. Yongjing Li.

BERLIN BUREAU: Berliner Büro, Gürtelstr. 32 B, D-10247 Berlin, Germany. Phone: +49 (30) 2966-8998. Fax: +49 (30) 2966 8997. Email: deyubu@hotmail.com. Correspondence to CRI's German Service can be sent to this office.

CHINA (HONG KONG) NEWS BUREAU: 387 Queen's Road East, Room 1503, Hong Kong, China. Phone: +852 2834-0384. Contact: Ms. He Jincao.

JERUSALEM NEWS BUREAU: Flat 16, Hagdud Ha'ivri 12, Jerusalem 92345, Israel. Phone: +972 (2) 566-6084. Contact: Ms. Liu Suyun.

LONDON NEWS BUREAU: 13B Clifton Gardens, Golders Green, London NW11 7ER, United Kingdom. Phone: +44 (20) 8458-6943. Contact: Ms. Wu Manling.

NEW YORK NEWS BUREAU: 630 First Avenue #35K, New York NY 10016 USA. Fax: +1 (212) 889 2076. Contact: Mr Qian Jun.

SYDNEY NEWS BUREAU: Unit 53, Block A15 Herbert Street, St. Leonards NSW 2065, Australia. Phone: +61 (2) 9436-1493. Contact: Mr. Yang Binyuan.

WASHINGTON BUREAU: 1600 South Eads Street, # 1005N, Arlington VA 22202 USA. Phone: +1 (703) 486-0330. Fax: +1 (703) 521 8689. Email: crius@comcast.net. Contact: Qinduo Xu, Chief Correspondent.

SAN FRANCISCO OFFICE, SCHEDULES: 2654 17th Avenue, San Francisco CA 94116 USA. Phone: +1 (415) 564-9968. Email: GPoppin@aol.com. Contact: George Poppin. This address, a volunteer office, only provides CRI schedules to listeners (return postage not required). All other correspondence should be sent directly to the main office in Beijing.

FREQUENCY PLANNING DIVISION: Radio and Television of People's Republic of China, 2 Fuxingmenwai Street, Beijing 100866, China; or P.O. Box 2144, Beijing 100866, China. Phone: (Yang Minmin) +86 (10) 8609-2064; (Zheng Shuguang & Pang Junhua) +86 (10) 8069-2120. Fax: +86 (10) 6609 2176. Contact: Ms. Yang Minmin, Manager, Frequency Coordination; Mr. Zheng Shuguang, Frequency Manager; Mrs. Ling Li Wen, Frequency Manager; Ms. Pang Junhua, Frequency Manager.

MAIN OFFICE, CHINESE LANGUAGES SERVICE: China Radio International, Beijing 100040, China. Prefers correspondence in Chinese (Mandarin).

MONITORING CENTER: 2 Fuxingmenwai Street, Beijing 100866, China or P.O Box 4502 Beijing 100866, China. Phone: +86 (10) 8609-1745/6. Fax: +86 (10) 8609 2176, +86 (10) 8609 3269. Email: mc@chinasarft.gov.cn, jczhxjch@public.fhnet.cn.net. Contact: Ms. Zhang Wei, Chief Engineer, Monitoring Department; Zhao Chengping, Monitoring Manager; Ms. Xu Tao, Deputy Director of Monitoring Department.

Fujian People's Broadcasting Station, 2 Gutian Lu, Fuzhou, Fujian 350001, China. $1 or IRC helpful. Web: (includes on-demand audio) www.66163.com/fjbs. Contact: Audience Relations Section. Replies irregularly and usually slowly. Prefers correspondence in Chinese.

Gannan People's Broadcasting Station, 49 Renmin Xijie, Hezuo Zhen, Xiahe, Gian Su 747000, China. Verifies reception reports written in Chinese or English. Return postage not required.

Guangxi Foreign Broadcasting Station, 12 Min Zu Avenue, Nanning, Guangxi 530022, China. Phone: +86 (771) 585-4403, +86 (771) 587-4745. Email: gxfbs2003@yahoo.com.cn. Web: www.gxradio.com/index/dwgbjj.htm; (streaming audio) www.gxradio.com. Free stickers and handmade papercuts. IRC helpful. Replies irregularly. Broadcasts in Vietnamese and Cantonese to listeners in Vietnam.

Hulunbuir People's Broadcasting Station, 11 Shengli Dajie, Hailar, Hulun Buir, Nei Menggu 021008, China. Phone: +86 (825) 6100-2065. Fax: +86 (825) 6100 2054. Replies in Chinese to correspondence in Chinese or English, and verifies reception reports.

Heilongjiang People's Broadcasting Station, 181 Zhongshan Lu, Harbin, Heilongjiang 150001, China. Phone: +86 (451) 8289-3443; (Korean Service) +86 (451) 8289-8873. Fax: +86 (451) 8289 3539. Email: am621@sina.com; (Korean Service) 873k@873k.com. Web: (includes on-demand audio) www.am621.com.cn; (Korean Service) www.873k.com. Rarely replies.

Hunan People's Broadcasting Station, 167 Yuhua Lu, Changsha, Hunan 410007, China. Phone: +86 (731) 554-7202. Fax: +86 (731) 554 7220. Email: hnradio@163.com; (news channel, relayed on shortwave) hnradio@public.cs.hn.cn. Web: (includes on-demand and streaming audio) www.hnradio.com; (news channel, relayed on shortwave) www.hnradio.com/hnradio/weixing/weixing.htm; (streaming audio page) www.hnradio.com/ssst/index.htm. Rarely replies.

Nei Menggu (Inner Mongolia) People's Broadcasting Station, 19 Xinhua Dajie, Hohhot, Nei Menggu 010058, China. Email: nmrb@nmrb.com.cn; imbs@163.net. Web: www.nmrb.cn. Replies irregularly, mainly to correspondence in Chinese.

▣**Qinghai People's Broadcasting Station**, 96 Kunlun Lu, Xining, Qinghai 810001, China. Email: qhradio@sina.com. Web: (includes streaming audio) www.qhradio.com. Contact: Technical Department. Verifies reception reports in Chinese or English. $1 helpful.

Radio Television Hong Kong, C.P.O Box 70200, Kowloon, Hong Kong, China. Provides weather reports for the South China Sea Yacht Race (*see* www.rhkyc.org.hk./chinacoastrace-week.htm) on 3940 kHz.
CAPE D'AGUILAR HF STATION: P.O. Box 9896, GPO Hong Kong, China. Phone:
+852 2888-1128; (station manager) +852 2888-1122; (assistant engineer) +852 2888-1130. Fax: +852 2809 2434. Contact: K.C. Liu, Station Manager; (technical) Lam Chi Keung, Assistant Engineer. Provides transmission facilities for weather reports to the South China Sea Yacht Race (*see*, above).

Shaanxi People's Broadcasting Station, 336 Chang'an Nanlu, Xi'an, Shaanxi 710061, China. Web: www.sxradio.com.cn. Replies irregularly to correspondence in Chinese.

Sichuan People's Broadcasting Station, 119-1 Hongxing Zhonglu, Chengdu, Sichuan 610017, China. Replies occasionally.

Voice of China (Zhonghua zhi Sheng). The First Program of Central People's Broadcasting Station—China National Radio (*see*).

▣**Voice of Jinling** (Jinling zhi Sheng), P.O. Box 268, Nanjing, Jiangsu 210002, China. Fax: +86 (25) 413 235. Email: vojl@163.net. Web: (streaming audio, and on-demand until the next transmission) mms://vod.jsgd.com.cn/audio0. Contact: [Ms.] Ruoyi Liu, Announcer/Reporter. Free stickers and calendars, plus Chinese-language color station brochure. Replies to correspondence in Chinese or English. Voice of Jinling is the Taiwan Service of Jiangsu People's Broadcasting Station.

Voice of Pujiang (Pujiang zhi Sheng), P.O. Box 3064, Shanghai 200002, China. Phone: +86 (21) 6208-2797. Fax: +86 (21) 6208 2850. Replies irregularly to correspondence in Chinese or English.

▣**Voice of the Strait** (Haixia zhi Sheng), P.O. Box 187, Fuzhou, Fujian 350012, China. Email: (English) vos@am666.net. Web: (includes streaming audio) www.vos.com.cn. Replies irregularly to correspondence in Chinese or English.
"FOCUS ON CHINA" ENGLISH PROGRAM: Box 308, Hong Kong, China. Email: (host "Jacqueline") hua_diao@hotmail.com.

▣**Xinjiang People's Broadcasting Station**, 84 Tuanjie Lu, Urümqi, Xinjiang 830044, China. Phone: +86 (991) 256-0089. Email: mw738@21cn.com. Web: (includes on-demand and streaming audio) www.xjbs.com.cn. Contact: Ms. Zhao Donglan, Editorial Office. Free tourist booklet, postcards and used Chinese stamps. Replies in Chinese to correspondence in Chinese or English. Verifies reception reports. $1 or 1 IRC helpful.

Xizang People's Broadcasting Station, 180 Beijing Zhonglu, Lhasa, Xizang 850000, China. Phone: (director) +86 (891) 681-9516; (technical division) +86 (891) 681-9521; (technical manager) +86 (891) 681-9525; (chief engineer) +86 (891) 681-9529. Phone/Fax: (general) +86 (891) 682-7910. Email: xzzbs2003@yahoo.com.cn. Web: www.tibetradio.cn. Contact: Mo Shu-ji, Director; (technical) Tuo Bao-shen, Technical Manager; Wang Yong (Chief Engineer). Chinese or Tibetan preferred, since correspondence in English is processed by freelance translators hired only when accumulated mail reaches a critical mass. Return postage required. Sometimes announces itself in English as "China Tibet Broadcasting Company" or "Tibet China Broadcasting Station."

"HOLY TIBET" ENGLISH PROGRAM: Foreign Affairs Office, China Tibet People's Broadcasting Company, 41 Beijing Middle Road, Lhasa, Xizang 850000, China. Phone: +86 (891) 681-9541. Contact: Ms.Tse Ring Dekye, Producer/Announcer. Two IRCs requested. Verifies reception reports.

Yunnan Broadcasting Station, 73 Renmin Xilu, Kunming, Yunnan 650031, China. Broadcasts in Chinese and Vietnamese to Vietnam.

▣**Yunnan People's Broadcasting Station**, 73 Renmin Xilu, Central Building of Broadcasting and TV, Kunming, 650031 Yunnan, China. Phone: +86 (871) 531-0270. Fax: +86 (871) 531 0360. Email: zxl@ynbit.com. Web: (includes streaming audio from music channel, not available on shortwave) www.ynradio.com.cn. Contact: Sheng Hongpeng or F.K. Fan. Free Chinese-language brochure on Yunnan Province, but no QSL cards. $1 or return postage helpful. Replies irregularly to correspondence in Chinese, and sometimes English.

CHINA (TAIWAN)   World Time +8

China Radio, 53 Min Chuan West Road 9th Floor, Taipei 10418, Taiwan, Republic of China. Phone: +886 (2) 2598-1009. Fax: +886 (2) 2598 8348. Email: (Adams) readams@usa.net. Contact: Richard E. Adams, Station Director. Verifies reception reports. A religious broadcaster, sometimes referred to as "True Light Station," transmitting via leased facilities in Petropavlovsk-Kamchatskiy, Russia.

▣**Fu Hsing Broadcasting Station**, 5 Lane 280, Section 5, Chungshan North Road, Taipei 111, Taiwan, Republic of China. Email: fushinge@ms63.hinet.net. Web: (includes streaming audio) www.fhbs.com.tw. Contact: Xieyi Zhao, Station Manager. Free key rings and other small souvenirs. Replies to correspondence in Chinese or English and verifies reception reports. Return postage not required.

▣**Radio Taiwan International (RTI)**, P.O. Box 24-38 (or P.O. Box 24-777), Taipei 10651, Taiwan, Republic of China; (street address) 55 Pei-An Road, Taipei 104, Taiwan, Republic of China. Phone: +886 (2) 2885-6168, X-752 or 753; (English) X-385 or 387; (French) X-386; (German) X-382; (Japanese) X-328; (Spanish) X-384. Fax: +886 (2) 2885 0023; (European languages) +886 (2) 2886 7088; (Japanese) +886 (2) 2885 2254. Email: (general) rti@rti.org.tw; (English) prog@rti.org.tw; (French) fren@rti.org.tw; (German) deutsch@rti.org.tw; (Japanese) jpn@rti.org.tw. Web: (includes on-demand and streaming audio) www.rti.org.tw. Contact: (general) Wayne Wang Tao-Fang, Chief of International Affairs Section; (administration) Lin Feng-Jeng, Chairman; (technical) Peter Lee, Manager, Engineering Department. Free stickers. May send publications and an occasional surprise gift. Broadcasts to the Americas are relayed via WYFR's Okeechobee site in the USA. Also uses relay facilities in France, Germany and the United Kingdom.
BANGKOK OFFICE: P.O. Box 44 PorNorFor Trairat Bangkhen Bangkok 10223 Thailand.
BERLIN OFFICE: Postfach 30 92 43, D-10760 Berlin, Germany.
DAKAR OFFICE: B.P. 6867, Dakar, Senegal.
HANOI OFFICE: G.P.O. Box 104 Hanoi, Vietnam.
MOSCOW OFFICE: 24/2Tverskaya St., Korpus 1, gate 4, 3rd Fl, 103050 Moscow, Russia. Contact: Chang Yu-tang.
NEW DELHI OFFICE: P.O. Box 4914, Safdarjung Enclave, New Delhi, 110 029 India.
SURABAYA OFFICE: P.O. Box 1024, Surabaya, 60008 Indonesia.

▣**Trans World Broadcasting Ministry**, 467 Chih Sien 1st Road 7/F, Kaohsiung 800, Taiwan, Republic of China. Phone: +886 (7) 235-9223/4. Fax: +886 (7) 235 9220. Email: youth@twbm.com. Web: (includes on-demand audio) www.twbm.com. Contact: Naishang Kuo, Manager; Daosheng Yao, Recording Engineer. Broadcasts via facilities of Radio Taiwan International (*see*). *NORTH AMERICAN OFFICE:* 1 Spruce Street, Millbrae CA 94030 USA. Phone: +1 (925) 283-0210; (toll-free outside San Francisco Bay area) 1-866-235-224. Fax: +1 (415) 337 1846. Email: contact@twbm.

▣**Voice of Han**, B Building 5F, 3 Hsin-Yi Road, Sec.1, Taipei, Taiwan, Republic of China. Phone: +886 (2) 2321-5053. Fax: +886 (2) 2393 0970. Email: tony257@ms55.hinet.net. Web: (includes streaming audio) www.voh.com.tw. Contact: Tony Tu.

Voice of Kuanghua—the Mainland Service of Voice of Han (*see*).

CLANDESTINE

Clandestine broadcasts are often subject to abrupt change or termination. Being operated by anti-establishment political and/or military organizations, these groups tend to be suspicious of outsiders' motives. Thus, they are more likely to reply to contacts from those who communicate in the station's native tongue, and who are perceived to be at least somewhat favorably disposed to their cause. Most will provide, upon request, printed matter on their cause, though not necessarily in English. For detailed information on clandestine stations, refer to one of the following Internet sites:

ClandestineRadio.com (www.ClandestineRadio.com) specializes in background information on these stations and is organized by region and target country.

Clandestine Radio Watch (www.schoechi.de) contains clandestine radio information plus a twice monthly report on the latest news and developments affecting the study of clandestine radio.

"Al Mustaqbal"—*see* USA.

"Coalition Maritime Forces (CMF) Radio One"—*see* International Waters.

"Degar Radio," Montagnard Foundation, Inc., P.O. Box 171114, Spartanburg SC 29301 USA. Phone: +1 (864) 576-0698. Fax: +1 (864) 595 1940. Email: degar@montagnard-foundation.org; (Kok Sor) kksor@montagnard-foundation.org, ksorpo@yahoo.com. Web: (Montagnard Foundation parent organization) www.montagnard-foundation.org. Contact: Kok Sor, President, Montagnard Foundation. Mint stamps or $1 helpful.

▣**"Dejen Radio,"** Liberty Bell Communications, Inc., P.O. Box 792, Indianapolis IN 46206-0792 USA. Email: dejen@ethiopiancommentator.com. Web: (on-demand audio) www.ethiopiancommentator.com/dejenradio. Contact: Hailemariam Adebe, President, Liberty Bell Communications, Inc. Replies irregularly.

▣**"Democratic Voice of Burma"** ("Democratic Myanmar a-Than"), P.O. Box 6720, St. Olavs Plass, N-0130 Oslo, Norway. Phone: (Director/Chief Editor) +47 (22) 868-486; (Aministration) +47 (22) 868-472. Email: (general) comment@dvb.no; (Director) director@dvb.no; (technical problems) comments@dvb.no. Web: (includes on-demand audio) www.dvb.no. Contact: (general) Dr. Anng Kin, Listener Liaison; Aye Chan Naing, Daily Editor; (administration) Harn Yawnghwe, Director; Daw Khin Pyone, Manager; (technical) Saw Neslon Ku, Studio Technician; Petter Bernsten; or Technical Dept. Norwegian kroner requested for a reply, but presumably Norwegian mint stamps would also suffice. Programs produced by Burmese democratic

movements, as well as professional and independent radio journalists, to provide informational and educational services for the democracy movement inside and outside Burma. Opposes the current Myanmar government. Transmitted originally via facilities in Norway, but more recently has broadcast from sites in Germany, Madagascar and Central Asia.

"Freedom Broadcast for North Korea"—*see* Radio Free North Korea.

▣**"Hmong Lao Radio,"** P.O. Box 6426, St. Paul MN 55106 USA. Phone: +1 (651) 292-0774. Fax: +1 (651) 292 0795. Email: (Vang) vangcy@charter.net. Web: (includes on-demand audio) www.h-lr.com. Contact: Cha Vang. Verifies reception reports. Transmits via facilities in Taiwan, and also carried by World Harvest Radio (*see* USA).

"Information Radio" (when operating), 193rd Special Operations Wing, 81 Constellation Court, Middletown PA 17057 USA. Email: (Public Affairs Officer) pa.193sow@paharr.ang.af.mil. Web: (193rd Special Operation Wing parent organization) www.paharr.ang.af.mil. Contact: Public Affairs Officer. Psy-ops station operated by the 193rd Special Operations Wing of the Pennsylvania Air National Guard.

▣**"Minghui Radio."** Web: (includes on-demand audio) www.mhradio.org. Via leased facilities in Taiwan, and supports the Falun Dafa organization.

▣**"Minivan Radio,"** 64 Milford Street, Salisbury SP1 2BP, United Kingdom. Email: minivanradio@gmail.com. Web: (on-demand audio) http://radio.minivannews.com. Contact: Monica Michie. Return postage helpful. Promotes human rights in the Maldives and is opposed to the present government. Via facilities of Germany's T-Systems International (*see*).

"Moj Them Radio," P.O. Box 75666, Saint Paul MN 55175-0666 USA. Email: info@mojthem.com. Web: (includes on-demand audio) www.mojthem.com.

"National Radio of the Democratic Saharan Arab Republic"—*see* Radio Nacional de la República Arabe Saharaui Democrática, Western Sahara.

"Quê H_ng Radio"—*see* USA.

"Open Radio for North Korea," ("Yollin Pukhan Pang-song"), 3901 Fair Ridge Drive, Fairfax VA 22033 USA. Email: nkradio@nkradio.com. Web: www.nkradio.com. *OFFICE IN SOUTH KOREA:* Phone: +82 (2) 737-4880. Fax: +82 (2) 737 6715.

▣**"Radio Anternacional,"** BM Box 1499, London WC1N 3XX, United Kingdom. Phone: +44 (20) 8962-2707. Fax: +44 (20) 8346 2203. Email: radio7520@yahoo.com; (Majedi) azarmajedi@yahoo.com. Web: (includes on-demand audio) www.radio-international.org. Contact: Ms. Azar Majedi. Broadcasts via a transmitter in Moldova. Has ties to the Worker-Communist Party of Iran.

"Radio Free Afghanistan"—*see* USA.

"Radio Free North Korea" ("Jayu Pukhan Pangsong"), Room 502, Sinjeong Building, Sinjeong 7 dong 210-16, Yengcheong-gu, Seoul, Republic of Korea. Phone: +82 (2) 2652-8350. Fax: +82 (2) 2652 8349. Web: www.freenk.net.

▣**"Radio Free Southern Cameroons."** Email: rfscboard@fdrsoutherncameroons.info, radiofreesoutherncameroons@yahoo.com. Web: (includes on-demand audio) www.fdrsoutherncameroons.info. Broadcasts via a transmitter in western Russia.

"Radio Freedom, Voice of the Ogadeni People"—*see* "Radio Xoriyo"

▣**"Radio Horyaal,"** P.O. Box 51045, Scarborough, Ontario, Canada. Email: radio@horyaal.net. Web: (includes on-demand audio) www.horyaal.net. Broadcasts via a transmitter in western Russia.

📻**"Radio Insurgente."** Web: (includes on-demand audio) www.radioinsurgente.org. Station of the Mexican "Ejército Zapatista de Liberación National."

"Radio International"—see "Radio Anternacional."

"Radio Nacional de la República Arabe Saharaui Democrática"—see Western Sahara.

📻**"Radio Payam-e Dost"** (Bahá'í Radio International), P.O. Box 765, Great Falls VA 22066 USA. Phone: +1 (703) 671-8888. Fax: +1 (301) 292 6947. Email: payam@bahairadio.org. Web: (includes on-demand audio) www.bahairadio.org. Does not verify reception reports.

📻**"Radio República,"** P.O. Box 110235, Hialeah FL 33011 USA. Email: info@radiorepublica.org. Web: (includes streaming audio) www.radiorepublica.org. Broadcasts are produced by the Florida-based "Directorio Democrático Cubano," and are partly funded by the U.S. government. Via WRMI (see USA) and transmitters in Germany and the United Kingdom.

"Radio Seda-ye Iran"—see KRSI, USA.

"Radio Nile"—see Netherlands.

"Radio Voice of ENUF," c/o Ethiopian National United Front (ENUF), P. O. Box 2206, Washington DC 20013-2206 USA. Opposed to the current Ethiopian government.

ENUF PARENT ORGANIZATION: Phone: +1 (214) 594-2102. Fax: +1 (909) 985 7741. Email: info@enufforethiopia.org. Web: www.enufforethiopia.org.

📻**"Radio Voice of Oromo Liberation"** ("Raadiyoo Sagalee Qabsoo Bilisummaa Oromoo"). Email: rsqbo@yahoo.com. Web: (includes on-demand audio) http://www.oromia.org/rsqbo/rsqbo.htm. Broadcasts via a transmitter in western Russia.

"Radio Voice of the People"—see Zimbabwe

"Radio VOP"—see Zimbabwe.

📻**"Radio Xoriyo,"** ("Halkani wa Radio Xoriyo, Codkii Ummadda Odageniya"). Email: radioxoriyo@ogaden.com; ogaden@yahoo.com (some verifications received from these addresses). If these fail, try webmaster@ogaden.com. Web: (archived audio of most recent broadcast; click on "Radio Xoriyo") www.ogaden.com. Broadcasts are supportive of the Ogadenia National Liberation Front, and hostile to the Ethiopian government. Via facilities of Germany's T-Systems International (see).

"Radio Waaberi," 5529 Walnut Blossom Dr. #5, San Jose CA 95123 USA. Email: info@radiowaaberi.org. Web: (includes on-demand audio) www.radiowaaberi.org. Contact: Ali Gulaid, President. A Somali broadcast to East Africa via Germany's T-Systems International (see).

"Shiokaze"—see Japan.

"Sudan Radio Service"—see USA.

📻**"SW Radio Africa"** (when operating), P.O. Box 243, Borehamwood, Herts., WD6 4WA, United Kingdom. Phone: +44 (20) 8387-1441. Email: (general) views@swradioafrica.com; mail@swradioafrica.com; (technical) tech@swradioafrica.com; (Jackson) gerry@swradioafrica.com. Web: (includes on-demand and streaming audio) www.swradioafrica.com. Contact: [Ms.] Gerry Jackson, Station Manager; (technical) Keith Farquharson, Technical Manager. Return postage helpful. Run by exiled Zimbabweans in the United Kingdom, and opposes the Mugabe government.

📻**"Tensae Ethiopia Voice of Unity,"** P.O.Box 2945, Washington DC 20013 USA. Phone: +1 (202) 276 1645, +1 678 437 5597. Email: ethiopia44@yahoo.com. Web: (includes on-demand audio) www.tensae.net. Broadcasts via a transmitter in western Russia.

EUROPEAN OFFICE (GERMANY): Phone: +49 (69) 6640-3923. Fax: +49 (69) 6636 6672, +49 (69) 3399 8632, +49 (69) 6636 6674. Email: tensae.ethiopia@gmail.com. Some reception reports to this address have been verified by email.

📻**"Voice of Biafra International,"** 733 15th Street NW, Suite 700, Washington DC 20005 USA. Phone: +1 (202) 347-2983. Email: biafrafoundation@yahoo.com; (Nkwocha) oguchi@pacbell.net; oguchi@mbay.net. Web: (includes on-demand audio) www.biafraland.com/vobi.htm. Contact: Oguchi Nkwocha, M.D.; Chima Osondu. A project of the Biafra Foundation and the Biafra Actualization Forum.

"Voice of China" ("Zhongguo zhi Yin"), P.O. Box 273538, Concord CA 94527 USA; or (street address) 2261 Morello Avenue - Suite A, Pleasant Hill, California 94523 USA. Web: www.china21century.org/default.asp?menu=xu (click on "VOC"). Financial support from the Foundation for China in the 21st Century. Transmits via facilities in Taiwan.

SPONSORING ORGANIZATION: Foundation for China in the 21st Century, P.O. Box 11696, Berkeley CA 94701 USA. Email: info@china21century.org.

📻**"Voice of China Reborn."** Email: china@vocr.org. Web: (includes on-demand audio) www.vocr.org.

"Voice of Delina" ("Dimtsi Delina"), Tesfa Delina Foundation, Inc., 17326 Edwards Road, Suite A-230, Cerritos CA 90703 USA. Email: tesfa@delina.org, info@delina.org. Web: (Tesfa Delina Foundation parent organization) www.delina.org. Opposed to the current Eritrean government.

📻**"Voice of Democratic Eritrea International"** ("Sawt Eritrea al-Dimuqratiya-Sawtu Jabhat al-Tahrir al-Eritrea"), Postfach 1946, D-65409 Rüsselsheim, Germany. Phone: +49 (228) 356-181. Email: (ELF-RC parent organization) elfrc@nharnet.com. Web: (includes on-demand audio) www.nharnet.com/Radio/radiopage.htm. Contact: Seyoum O. Michael, Member of Executive Committee, ELF-RC; Neguse Tseggon. Station of the Eritrean Liberation Front-Revolutionary Council, hostile to the government of Eritrea. Via facilities of T-Systems International (see), in Germany.

📻**Voice of Eritrea."** Email: epm_voe@yahoo.com. Web: (includes on-demand audio) www.maihabar.org. Broadcast of the Eritrean People's Movement.

📻**"Voice of Ethiopian People"** (when operating), P.O. Box 28152, San Jose CA 95159 USA. Web: (includes on-demand audio) www.voep.net. Opposes the current government in Ethiopia. Via a transmitter in western Russia.

"Voice of Ethiopian Unity"—see "Voice of the Democratic Path of Ethiopian Unity.

"Voice of Iranian Kurdistan" ("Seda-ye Kordestan-e Iran"). Fax: +1 (270) 682 4654. Email: info@rdki.com; rdk_iran@yahoo.com. Web: (includes on-demand audio) www.rdki.com. For further contact, try one of the PDKI (Democratic Party of Iranian Kurdistan parent organization) offices, below.

PDKI INTERNATIONAL BUREAU: AFK, Boite Postale 102, F-75623 Paris Cedex 13, France. Phone: +33 (1) 4585-6431. Fax: +33 (1) 4585 2093. Email: pdkiran@club-internet.fr. Web: www.pdk-iran.org. Contact: Khosrow Abdollahi. Replies to correspondence in English.

PDKI CANADA BUREAU: P.O. Box 29010, London, Ontario N6K 4L9, Canada. Phone/Fax: +1 (519) 680-7784. Email: pdkicanada@pdki.org. Web: www.pdki.org.

"Voice of Iraqi Kurdistan"—see Iraq.

"Voice of Jammu Kashmir Freedom" ("Sadai Hurriyati Jammu Kashmir"), P.O. Box 102, Muzaffarabad, Azad Kashmir, via Pakistan. Contact: Programme Manager. Pro-Moslem and favors Azad Kashmiri independence from India. Believed to transmit via facilities of Radio Pakistan. Return postage not required, and replies to correspondence in English.

📻**"Voice of Komala"** (when operating), c/o Representation of Komala Abroad, Postfach 800272, D-51002 Köln, Germany;

Phone/Fax: (North America) +1 (561) 760 5814. Email: komala_radio@hotmail.com. Web: (includes on-demand audio) http://radio.komala.org. Replies to correspondence in English.

📻**"Voice of Liberty"** ("Dimtsi Harnet Ertra"). Email: vol@selfi-democracy.com. Web: (includes on-demand audio) http://selfi-democracy.com. Supports the opposition-in-exile Eritrean Democratic Party. Broadcasts via a transmitter in western Russia.

ERITREAN DEMOCRATIC PARTY PARENT ORGANIZATION: P.O. Box 93982, Atlanta GA 30377-0982 USA. Email: northamerica@selfi-democracy.com; (European office) europe@selfi-democracy.com.

"Voice of Mesopotamia" ("Dengê Mezopotamya")
Phone: +32 (53) 648-827/29. Fax: +32 (53) 680 779. Email: info@denge-mezopotamya.com. Web: www.denge-mezopotamya.com. Contact: Ahmed Dicle, Director.

KURDISTAN WORKERS PARTY (PKK, also known as Kongra-Gel, KGK) SPONSORING ORGANIZATION: Email: info@kongra-gel.com. Web: www.kongra-gel.com.

"Voice of Oromia Independence." Email: ganamo@hotmail.com, or online form. Web: (includes on-demand audio) www.awofio.com. Broadcast of the Front for Independence of Oromia (Adda Walabummaa Oromiyaa) via a transmitter in western Russia.

📻**"Voice of Oromo Liberation"** ("Sagalee Bilisummaa Oromoo"), Postfach 510610, D-13366 Berlin, Germany; or SBO, Prinzenallee 81, D-13357 Berlin, Germany. Phone/Fax: +49 (30) 494 3372. Email: sbo13366@aol.com. Web: (includes on-demand audio) www.oromoliberationfront.org/sbo.html. Contact: Taye Teferah, European Coordinator. Occasionally replies to correspondence in English or German. Return postage required. Station of the Oromo Liberation Front of Ethiopia, an Oromo nationalist organization. Via Germany's T-Systems International (see).

OROMO LIBERATION FRONT USA OFFICE: P.O. Box 73247, Washington DC 20056 USA. Phone: +1 (202) 462-5477. Fax: +1 (202) 332 7011.

"Voice of the Communist Party of Iran" ("Seda-ye Hezb-e Komunist-e Iran")
COMMUNIST PARTY OF IRAN SPONSORING ORGANIZATION: C.D.C.R.I., Box 704 45, S-107 25 Stockholm, Sweden. Phone/Fax: +46 (8) 786-8054. Email: cpi@cpiran.org. Web: www.cpiran.org.

"Voice of the Democratic Alliance"
Web: (Democratic Alliance parent organization) http://www.erit-alliance.org. Airs via the facilities of Radio Ethiopia, and is opposed to the Eritrean government.

📻**"Voice of the Democratic Path of Ethiopian Unity,"** Finote Democracy, P.O. Box 88675, Los Angeles CA 90009 USA. Email: efdpu@finote.org. Web: (includes on-demand audio) www.finote.org. Via Germany's T-Systems International (see).

EUROPEAN ADDRESS: Finote Democracy, Postbus 10573, 1001 EN, Amsterdam, Netherlands.

"Voice of the Kurdistan People"—see Iraq.

"Voice of the Iranian Revolution"—same contact details as "Voice of the Communist Party of Iran" (see).

"Voice of the Worker" ("Seda-ye Kargar") (when operating)
WORKER-COMMUNIST PARTY OF IRAN (WPI) PARENT ORGANIZATION: Email: wpi@wpiran.org. Web: www.wpiran.org.

WPI INTERNATIONAL OFFICE: WPI, Office of International Relations, Suite 730, 28 Old Brompton Road, South Kensington, London SW7 3SS, United Kingdom. Phone: +44 (77) 7989-8968. Fax: +44 (87) 0136 2182. Email: wpi.international.office@ukonline.co.uk, markazi@ukonline.co.uk.

📻**"Voice of Tibet"**
ADMINISTRATIVE OFFICE: Voice of Tibet Foundation, St. Olavsgate 24, N-0166 Oslo, Norway. Phone: (administration) +47 2211-2700. Fax: +47 2211 5474. Email: voti@online.no; (Norbu) votibet@online.no. Web: (includes on-demand audio) www.vot.org. Contact: Øystein Alme, Project Manager [sometimes referred to as "Director"]; Chophel Norbu, Project Coordinator.

MAIN EDITORIAL OFFICE: Voice of Tibet, Narthang Building, Gangchen Kyishong, Dharamsala-176 215 H.P., India. Phone: +91 (1892) 228-179/222, +91 (1892) 222 384. Fax: +91 (1892) 224 957. Email: (general) vot1@gov.tibet.net; (editor-in-chief) voteditor@gov.tibet.net. Contact: Karma Yeshi Nazee, Editor-in-Chief; Tenzin Peldon, Assistant Editor. A joint venture of the Norwegian Human Rights House, Norwegian Tibet Committee and World-View International. Programs focus on Tibetan culture, education, human rights and news from Tibet. Opposed to Chinese control of Tibet. A colorful QSL card is issued from the office in Dharamsala. Return postage helpful. Broadcasts via transmitters in Madagascar and Tajikistan.

"Voices from the Diaspora" (if reactivated)—a broadcast produced by Save the Gambia Democracy Project, and aired via the facilities of T-Systems International (see) in Germany.

SAVE THE GAMBIA DEMOCRACY PROJECT PARENT ORGANIZATION: Email: stgdp@sunugambia.com. Web: www.sunugambia.com.

VERIFICATIONS: If no reply is received direct from the STGDP, send your report to Jeff White at WRMI (see USA) who brokers the transmissions, or to Walter Brodowsky at Germany's T-Systems International (see).

"Voz de la Resistencia"
Email: (FARC-EP parent organization) elbarcino@laneta.apc.org (updated transmission schedules and QSLs available from this address, but correspond in Spanish). Contact: Olga Lucía Marín, Comisión Internacional de las FARC-EP. Station of the Fuerzas Armadas Revolucionarias de Colombia - Ejercito del Pueblo.

COLOMBIA   World Time –5

NOTE: Colombia, the country, is always spelled with two o's. It should never be written as "Columbia."

Alcaravan Radio—see La Voz de Tu Conciencia.

Caracol Villavicencio—see La Voz de los Centauros.

Ecos del Atrato (if reactivated), Apartado Aéreo 196, Quibdó, Chocó, Colombia. Phone: +57 (49) 711-450. Contact: Absalón Palacios Agualimpia, Administrador. Free pennants. Replies to correspondence in Spanish.

La Voz de Tu Conciencia, Calle 44 No. 13-67, Santafé de Bogotá, D.C., Colombia. Phone: +57 (1) 338-4716. Email: contacto@fuerzadepaz.com, libreria@fuerzadepaz.com; (Stendal, specialized technical correspondence only) martinstendal@etb.net.co. Web: www.fuerzadepaz.com/emisoras.asp. Contact: Russel Martin Stendal, Administrador. Station is actually located in Puerto Lleras, in the guerrilla "combat zone." Sometimes carries programming from sister stations Alcaravan Radio (1530 kHz) or Marfil Estéreo (88.8 MHz). Replies to correspondence in English or Spanish. Return postage helpful. Free stickers.

La Voz de los Centauros (Caracol Villavicencio) (when operating), Cra. 31 No. 37-71 Of. 1001, Villavicencio, Meta, Colombia. Phone: +57 (986) 214-995; (technical) +57 (986) 662-3666. Fax: +57 (986) 623 954. Contact: Carlos Torres Leyva, Gerencia; or Olga Arenas, Administradora. Replies to correspondence in Spanish.

La Voz del Guaviare, Carrera 22 con Calle 9, San José del Guaviare, Colombia. Phone: +57 (986) 840-153/4. Fax: +57 (986) 840 102. Email: mercorio@col3.telecom.com.co. Contact: Luis Fernando Román Robayo, Director General. Replies slowly to correspondence in Spanish.

La Voz del Llano (when operating), Calle 41B No. 30-11, Barrio La Grama, Villavicencio, Meta, Colombia; or (postal address in Bogotá) Apartado Aéreo 67751, Santafé de Bogotá, Colombia. Phone: +57 (986) 624-102. Fax: +57 (986) 625 045. Contact: Luis F. Rivero, Director. Replies occasionally to correspondence in Spanish. $1 or return postage necessary.

Marfil Estéreo—*see* La Voz de Tu Conciencia.

Ondas del Orteguaza (when operating), Calle 16, No. 12-48, piso 2, Florencia, Caquetá, Colombia. Phone: +57 (88) 352-558. Contact: Sandra Liliana Vásquez, Secretaria; Señora Elisa Viuda de Santos; Henry Valencia Vásquez. Free stickers. IRC, return postage or $1 required. Replies occasionally to correspondence in Spanish.

Radio Líder (when operating), Apartado Aéreo 19823, Santafé de Bogotá, Colombia; (street address) Calle 45 No. 13-70, Santafé de Bogotá, Colombia. Phone: +57 (1) 323-1500. Fax: +57 (1) 288 4020. Email: radiolider@cadenamelodia.com. Web: www.cadenamelodia.com. Rarely replies. A station of the Cadena Melodía network.

CONGO (DEMOCRATIC REPUBLIC)   World Time

+1 Western, including Kinshasa; +2 Eastern

Radio Bukavu (when operating), B.P. 475, Bukavu, Democratic Republic of the Congo. $1 or return postage required. Replies slowly. Correspondence in French preferred.

Radio CANDIP, B.P. 373, Bunia, Democratic Republic of Congo. Letters should preferably be sent via registered mail. $1 or return postage required. Correspondence in French preferred.

Radio Kahuzi, c/o AIMServe, Box 53435 (BUKAVU), Nairobi, Kenya. Email: radiokahuzi@kivu-online.com, or besi@alltel. net. Web: www.besi.org. Contact: Richard & Kathy McDonald. Verifies reception reports by email.

HOME OFFICE: Believers Express Service, Inc. (BESI), P.O. Box 189, Eastanollee, GA 30538 USA. Phone: +1 (706) 282-0495. Fax: +1 (706) 886 0658. Email: besi@besi.org. Contact: Barbara Smith, Home Office Secretary. Verifies reception reports.

Radio Lubumbashi (when operating), B.P. 7296, Lubumbashi, Democratic Republic of the Congo. Letters should be sent via registered mail. $1 or 3 IRCs helpful. Correspondence in French preferred.

🖃**Radio Okapi**, 12 Av. des Aviateurs, Kinshasa, Gombe, Democratic Republic of the Congo. Email: online form. Web: (includes on-demand and streaming audio) www.radiookapi. net. A joint project involving the United Nations Mission in the Democratic Republic of the Congo (MONUC) and the Swiss-based Fondation Hirondelle.

MONUC:

(USA) P.O. Box 4653, Grand Central Station, New York NY 10163-4653 USA. Phone: +1 (212) 963-0103. Fax: +1 (212) 963 0205. Email: info@monuc.org. Web: www.monuc.org. Verifies reception reports.

(Congo) 12 Av. des Aviateurs, Kinshasa, Gombe, Democratic Republic of the Congo; or B.P. 8811, Kinshasa 1, Democratic Republic of the Congo. Phone: +243 81- 890-6000. Fax: +243 890 56208. Contact: Georges Schleger, VE2EK, Communications Officer & Head of Technical Services.

FONDATION HIRONDELLE: 3 Rue Traversière, CH 1018-Lausanne, Switzerland. Phone: +41 (21) 647-2805. Fax: +41 (21) 647 4469. Email: info@hirondelle.org. Web: www.hirondelle. org. Verifies reception reports.

Radio-Télévision Nationale Congolaise (if reactivated), B.P. 3171, Kinshasa-Gombe, Democratic Republic of the Congo. Letters should be sent via registered mail. $1 or 3 IRCs helpful. Correspondence in French preferred.

CONGO (REPUBLIC)   World Time +1

Radiodiffusion Nationale Congolaise (also announces as "Radio Nationale" or "Radio Congo"), Tèlèdiffusion du Congo, B.P. 2912, Brazzaville, Congo. Email: (technical) actu_rtnc@hotmail.com. Contact: Félix Lossombo, Le Directeur Administratif et Financier; Gaspard Bemba, Le Directeur de l'Inspection Technique des Réseaux et de la Qualité des Services; Jean Médard Bokatola. Return postage required, but smallest denomination currency notes (e.g. $1US or 1 euro) reportedly cannot be changed into local currency. Replies irregularly to letters in French (and sometimes, English) sent via registered mail.

COSTA RICA   World Time -6

🖃**Faro del Caribe**—**TIFC** (when operating), Apartado 2710, 1000 San José, Costa Rica. Phone: +506 226-4358, +506 227-5048, +506 286-1755. Fax: +506 227-1725. Email: radio@farodelcaribe.org, 1080@farodelcaribe.org; (technical) tecnico@farodelcaribe.org. Web: (includes streaming audio) www.farodelcaribe.org. Contact: Lic. Ronald Ortiz R., Administrador; (technical) Salvador López, Ingeniero. Free stickers, pennants, books and bibles. $1 or IRCs helpful. Verifies reception reports in Spanish or English.

U.S. OFFICE, NONTECHNICAL: Misión Latinoamericana, P.O. Box 620485, Orlando FL 32862 USA.

Radio Exterior de España—**Cariari Relay Station**, Cariari de Pococí, Costa Rica. Phone: +506 767-7308, +506 767-7311. Fax: +506 225 2938.

Radio Universidad de Costa Rica (when operating), Apartado 1-06, 2060 Universidad de Costa Rica, San Pedro de Montes de Oca, San José, Costa Rica. Phone: (general) +506 207-4727; (studio) +506 225-3936. Fax: +506 207 5459. Email: radioucr@cariari.ucr.ac.cr. Web: http://cariari.ucr.ac.cr/~radioucr/radioucr. Contact: Marco González Muñoz; Henry Jones, Locutor de Planta; Nora Garita B., Directora. Marco González is a radio amateur, call-sign TI3AGM. Free postcards, station brochure and stickers. Replies slowly to correspondence in Spanish or English. $1 or return postage required.

University Network—*see* USA.

CROATIA   World Time +1 (+2 midyear)

🖃**Croatian Radio-Television (Hrvatska Radio-Televizija, HRT)**

MAIN OFFICE: Hrvatska Radio-Televizija (HRT), Prisavlje 3, HR-10000 Zagreb, Croatia. Phone: (operator) +385 (1) 634-2634. Fax: +385 (1) 634 3712. Web: (includes on-demand and streaming audio) www.hrt.hr.

Hrvatski Radio (Croatian Radio), address as above. Phone: +385 (1) 634-2634. Fax: +385 (1) 634 3877. Contact: Ivanka Lucev, Managing Director; Domagoj Versic, Programme Director.

🖃**Glas Hrvatske (Voice of Croatia)**, Phone: +385 (1) 634-2601; (Editor-in-Chief) +385 (1) 634-2602. Email: (general) voiceofcroatia@hrt.hr; (Zlatko Kuretic) zlatko.kuretic@hrt.hr.

Web: (includes streaming audio) www.hrt.hr/hr/glashrvatske/index.htm. Contact: Zlatko Kuretic, Editor-in-Chief.
TRANSMISSION COMPANY: Odasiljaci i Veze d.o.o (Transmitters & Communications Ltd)., Ulica grada Vukovara 269d, HR-10000 Zagreb, Croatia. Phone: +385 (1) 6186-000. Fax: +385 (1) 6186 100. Email: nikola.percin@oiv.hr. Web: www.oiv.hr. Contact: Nikola Percin, Managing Director. This independent state-owned company replaces the former Transmitters and Communications Department of HRT.
SHORTWAVE COORDINATION: Email: kresimir.ruscic@oiv.hr. Contact: Kresimir Ruscic.
TRANSMITTING STATION DEANOVEC: P.O. Box 3, HR-10313 Graberje Ivanicko, Croatia. Phone: +385 (1) 2830-533. Fax: +385 (1) 2830 534. Email: dane.palic@oiv.hr. Contact: Dane Pavlic, Head of Station. Croatian Radio operates two services on world band: the domestic (first) national radio program, transmitted via HRT's Deanovec shortwave station for listeners in Europe; and an external service "Glas Hrvatske" (Voice of Croatia) in Croatian, with news segments in English and Spanish for Croatian expatriates, which airs via T-Systems International (see) in Julich, Germany.

CUBA   World Time –4

🔊 **Radio Habana Cuba**, Apartado Postal 6240, 10600 La Habana, Cuba. Phone: (general) +53 (7) 878-4954; (English Department) +53 (7) 877-6628. Fax: +53 (7) 870 5810. Email: radiohc@enet.cu; (Arnie Coro) arnie@rhc.cu, coro@enet.cu. Web: (includes on-demand and streaming audio) www.radiohc.cu; (streaming audio) http://multimedia-radio.cubasi.cu. Contact: (general) Lourdes López, Head of Correspondence Department; Isabel García, Director of English Department; (administration) Luis López López, General Director; (technical) Arnaldo Coro Antich, ("Arnie Coro"), Producer, "DXers Unlimited"; Arturo González, Head of Technical Department. Free pennants, stickers, keychains, pins and other small souvenirs. DX Listeners' Club. Free sample Granma International newspaper. Contests with various prizes, including trips to Cuba.
🔊 **Radio Rebelde**, Departamento de Relaciones Públicas, Apartado Postal 6277, 10600 La Habana 6, Cuba; (street address) Calle 23 n° 258 entre L y M, El Vedado, 10600 La Habana, Cuba. For technical correspondence (including reception reports), substitute "Servicio de Onda Corta" in place of "Departamento de Relaciones Públicas." Reception reports can also be emailed to Radio Habana Cuba's Arnie Coro (arnie@radiohc.cu) for forwarding to Radio Rebelde. Phone: +53 (7) 831-3514. Fax: +53 (7) 334 270. Email: (technical and nontechnical): relapubli@rebelde.icrt.cu. Web (includes on-demand and streaming audio): www.radiorebelde.com.cu; (streaming audio) http://multimedia-radio.cubasi.cu. Contact: Jorge Luis Martín Cuevas, Jefe de Relaciones Públicas. Replies slowly, with correspondence in Spanish preferred.

CYPRUS   World Time +2 (+3 midyear)

🔊 **Bayrak Radio International** (when operating), BRTK Campus, Dr. Fazil Küçük Boulevard, P.O. Box 417, Lefkosa - T.R.N.C., via Mersin 10, Turkey. Phone: +90 (392) 225-5555. Fax: (general) +90 (392) 225 4581. Email: (general) brt@cc.emu.edu.tr; (technical, including reception reports) tosun@cc.emu.edu.tr. Web: (includes streaming audio) www.brt.gov.nc.tr. Contact: Mustafa Tosun, Head of Transmission Department; Halil Balbaz, Transmitter Manager; Ülfet Kortmaz, Head of Bayrak International; Bertil Wedin, Producer of "Magazine North."

BBC World Service—East Mediterranean Relay Station, P.O. Box 209, Limassol, Cyprus. Contact: Steve Welch. This address for technical matters only. Other correspondence should be sent to the BBC World Service in London (see).
🔊 **Cyprus Broadcasting Corporation**, Broadcasting House, P.O. Box 4824, Nicosia 1397, Cyprus; (street address) RIK Street, Athalassa, Nicosia 2120, Cyprus. Phone: +357 (2) 286-2000. Fax: +357 (2) 231 4050. Email: rik@cybc.com.cy. Web: (includes streaming audio from domestic services not on shortwave) www.cybc.com.cy. Contact: (general) Pavlos Soteriades, Director General; Evangella Gregoriou, Head of Public and International Relations; (technical) Andreas Michaelides, Director of Technical Services. Free stickers. Replies irregularly, sometimes slowly. IRC or $1 helpful.

CZECH REPUBLIC   World Time +1 (+2 midyear)

🔊 **Radio Prague**, Czech Radio, Vinohradská 12, 12099 Prague 2, Czech Republic. Phone: +420 (2) 2155-2900; (Czech Department) +420 (2) 2155-2922; (English Department) +420 (2) 2155-2930; (German Department) +420 (2) 2155-2941; (French Department) +420 (2) 2155-2911; (Spanish Department) +420 (2) 2155-2950; (Russian Department) +420 (2) 2155-2964. Phone/Fax: (Oldrich Čip, technical) +420 (2) 2271-5005. Fax: (all languages) +420 (2) 2155 2903. Email: (general) cr@radio.cz; (Director) Miroslav.Krupicka@radio.cz; (English Department) english@radio.cz; (German Department) deutsch@radio.cz; (French Department) francais@radio.cz; (Spanish Department) espanol@radio.cz; (Russian Department) rusky@radio.cz; (Program Director) Gerald.Schubert@radio.cz; (Internet Department) cr@radio.cz; (free news texts) robot@radio.cz, writing "Subscribe English" (or other desired language) within the subject line; (technical, chief engineer) cip@radio.cz. Web: (includes on-demand and streaming audio) www.radio.cz. Contact: (general) Marie Pittnerova; Gerald Schubert, Editor-in-Chief; (administration) Miroslav Krupička, Director; (technical) Oldrich Čip, Chief Engineer. Free stickers; also key chains, pens, bookmarks, mouse pads and other souvenirs when available.
RFE-RL—see USA.

DENMARK   World Time +1 (+2 midyear)

World Music Radio (when operating), P. O. Box 112, DK-8900 Randers, Denmark. Phone: (Monday through Friday, 0800-1400 World Time) +45 70 222 222. Fax: +45 70 222 888. E-mail: wmr@wmr.dk. URL: www.wmr.dk. Contact: Stig Hartvig Nielsen. Return postage required.

DIEGO GARCIA—see BRITISH INDIAN OCEAN TERRITORY

DJIBOUTI   World Time +3

🔊 **Radio Télévision de Djibouti**, Boite Postale 97, Djibouti, Djibouti; (street address) Avenue Saint Laurent du Var, Djibouti, Djibouti. Phone: +253 352-294. Fax: +253 356 502. Email: (general) rtd@intnet.dj; (information) rtd-information@intnet.dj; (technical) rtdtech@intnet.dj. Web: (includes on-demand audio) www.rtd.dj. Contact: (general) Abdi Atteyeh Abdi, Directeur Général; (technical) Yahya Moussed, Chef du Service Technique. Verifies reception reports. Transmission facilities are located at Dorale, about 10 km west of Djibouti City.

DOMINICAN REPUBLIC   World Time –4

⏱**Radio Amanecer Internacional**, Apartado Postal 1500, Santo Domingo, Dominican Republic; (street address) Juan Sánchez Ramírez #40, Santo Domingo, Dominican Republic. Phone: +1 (809) 688-5600, +1 (809) 688-5609. Fax: +1 (809) 227 1869. Email: cabina@radioamanecer.org, or online form. Web: (includes streaming audio) www.radioamanecer.org. Contact: (general) Lic. Germán Lorenzo, Director; (technical) Ing. Sócrates Domínguez. $1 or return postage required. Replies slowly to correspondence in Spanish.

Radio Barahona (when operating), Apartado 201, Barahona, Dominican Republic; or (street address) Gustavo Mejía Ricart No. 293, Apto. 2-B, Ensanche Quisqueya, Santo Domingo, Dominican Republic. Phone: +1 (809) 524-4040. Fax: +1 (809) 524 5461. Contact: (general) Rodolfo Z. Lama Jaar, Administrador; (technical) Ing. Roberto Lama Sajour, Administrador General. Free stickers. Letters should be sent via registered mail. $1 or return postage helpful. Replies to correspondence in Spanish.

EMPRESAS RADIOFÓNICAS PARENT ORGANIZATION: Empresas Radiofónicas S.A., Apartado Postal 20339, Santo Domingo, Dominican Republic. Phone: +1 (809) 567-9698. Fax: +1 (809) 472-3313. Web: www.suprafm.com.

Radio Cima Cien (when operating), Apartado 804, Santo Domingo, Dominican Republic. Fax: +1 (809) 541 1088. Contact: Roberto Vargas, Director. Free pennants, postcards, coins and taped music. Roberto likes collecting stamps and coins.

Radio Cristal Internacional (when operating), Apartado Postal 894, Santo Domingo, Dominican Republic; or (street address) Calle Pepillo Salcedo No. 18, Altos, Santo Domingo, Dominican Republic. Phone: +1 (809) 565-1460, +1 (809) 566-5411. Fax: +1 (809) 567 9107. Contact: (general) Fernando Hermón Gross, Director de Programas; Margarita Reyes, Secretaria; (administration) Darío Badía, Director General; or Héctor Badía, Director de Administración. Seeks reception reports. Return postage of $2 appreciated.

ECUADOR   World Time –5 (–4 sometimes, in times of drought); –6 Galapagos

NOTE: IRCs are exchangeable only in the cities of Quito and Guayaquil, so enclosing $2 for return postage may be helpful when writing to stations in other locations.

Escuelas Radiofónicas Populares del Ecuador (if reactivated), Juan de Velasco 4755 y Guayaquil, Casilla Postal 06-01-341, Riobamba, Chimborazo, Ecuador. Phone: +593 (3) 961-608, +593 (3) 960-247. Fax: +593 (3) 961 625. Email: admin@esrapoec.ecuanex.net.ec. Web: www.ded.org.ec/essapa01.htm. Contact: Juan Pérez Sarmiento, Director Ejecutivo; María Ercilia López, Secretaria. Free pennants and key rings. "Chimborazo" cassette of Ecuadorian music for 10,000 sucres plus postage; T-shirts for 12,000 sucres plus postage; and caps with station logo for 8,000 sucres plus postage. Return postage helpful. Replies to correspondence in Spanish.

⏱**HCJB World Radio, The Voice of the Andes**
STATION: Casilla 17-17-691, Quito, Ecuador. Phone: (general) +593 (2) 226-6808 (X-4441, 1300-2200 World Time Monday through Friday, for the English Dept.); (frequency management) +593 (2) 226-6808 (X-4627); (*DX Partyline* English program, toll-free, U.S. only, for reception reports, loggings and other correspondence) +1 866 343-0791. Fax: (general) +593 (2) 226 7263; (frequency manager) +593 (2) 226 4765. Email: (Graham) agraham@hcjb.org.ec; (frequency management) irops@hcjb.

org.ec; (language sections) format is language@hcjb.org.ec; so to reach, say, the Spanish Department, it would be spanish@hcjb.org.ec. Web: (English, includes on-demand audio and online reception report form) www.hcjb.org; (Spanish, includes on-demand and streaming audio) www.vozandes.org. Contact: (general) English [or other language] Department; (administration) Jim Estes, HCJB Regional Director; Doug Weber, Radio Director; Allen Graham, Frequency Manager. Free religious brochures, calendars, stickers and pennants. IRC or $1 required.

INTERNATIONAL HEADQUARTERS: HCJB World Radio, P.O. Box 39800, Colorado Springs CO 80949-9800 USA; (street address) 1065 Garden of the Gods Rd., Colorado Springs CO 80907 USA. Phone: +1 (719) 590-9800. Fax: +1 (719) 590 9801. Email: info@hcjb.org; (Hirst) jhirst@hcjb.org. Contact: Jon Hirst, Communications Director; Andrew Braio, Public Information; (administration) Richard D. Jacquin, Director, International Operations. Various items sold via U.S. address—catalog available. This address is not a mail drop, so listeners' correspondence, except those concerned with purchasing HCJB items, should be directed to the usual Quito address.

ENGINEERING CENTER: HCJB World Engineering Center, 2830 South 17th Street, Elkhart IN 46517 USA. Phone: +1 (574) 970 4252. Fax: +1 (574) 293 9910. Email: info@hcjbeng.org. Web: www.hcjbeng.org. Contact: Dave Pasechnik, Project Manager; Bob Moore, Engineering. This address only for those professionally concerned with the design and manufacture of transmitter and antenna equipment. Listeners' correspondence should be directed to the usual Quito address.

REGIONAL OFFICES: Although HCJB has over 20 regional offices throughout the world, the station wishes that all listener correspondence be directed to the station in Quito, as the regional offices do not serve as mail drops for the station.

HD2IOA, Instituto Oceanográfico de la Armada (INOCAR), Avenida de la Marina, Vía Puerto Marítimo, Código Postal 5940, Guayaquil, Ecuador. HD2IOA is a time signal station operated by Ecuador's Naval Oceanographic Institute. Replies to correspondence in Spanish and verifies reception reports.

INSTITUTO OCEANOGRÁFICO DE LA ARMADA PARENT ORGANIZATION:
Phone: +593 (4) 248-1300. Fax: +593 (4) 248 5166. Email: inocar@inocar.mil.ec. Web: www.inocar.mil.ec.

La Voz de Saquisilí—Radio Libertador (when operating), Calle 24 de Mayo, Saquisilí, Cotopaxi, Ecuador. Phone: +593 (3) 721-035. Contact: Arturo Mena Herrera, Gerente-Propietario. Reception reports actively solicited. Return postage, in the form of $2 or mint Ecuadorian stamps, appreciated; IRCs difficult to exchange. Spanish strongly preferred.

La Voz del Napo, Misión Josefina, Juan Montalvo s/n, Tena, Napo, Ecuador. Phone: +593 (6) 886-356. Email: coljav20@yahoo.es, lavozdelnapo@yahoo.es. Contact: Padre Humberto Dorigatti, Director. Free pennants and stickers. $2 or return postage required. Replies irregularly to correspondence in Spanish or Italian.

La Voz del Upano
STATION: Vicariato Apostólico de Méndez, Misión Salesiana, 10 de Agosto s/n, Macas, Provincia de Morona Santiago, Ecuador. Phone: +593 (7) 505-247. Email: radioupano@easynet.net.ec. Contact: Sra. Leonor Guzmán, Directora. Free pennants and calendars. On one occasion, not necessarily to be repeated, sent tape of Ecuadorian folk music for $2. Otherwise, $2 required. Replies to correspondence in Spanish.
QUITO OFFICE: Procura Salesiana, Equinoccio 623 y Queseras del Medio, Quito, Ecuador. Phone: +593 (2) 255-1012.

Radio Buen Pastor—*see* Radio El Buen Pastor.

Radio Centinela del Sur (C.D.S. Internacional), Casilla 11-01-106, Loja, Ecuador; (studios) Olmedo 11-56 y Mercadillo, Loja, Ecuador. Phone: +593 (7) 561-166, +593 (7) 570-211. Fax: +593 (7) 562 270. Contact: (general) Marcos G. Coronel V., Director de Programas; José A. Coronel V., Director del programa "Ovación"; (technical) José A. Coronel Illescas, Gerente General. Return postage required. Replies occasionally to correspondence in Spanish.

Radio Centro, Casilla 18-01-574, Ambato, Ecuador. Phone: +593 (3) 822-240, +593 (3) 841-126. Fax: +593 (3) 829 824. Contact: Luis Alberto Gamboa Tello, Director Gerente; Lic. María Elena de López. Free stickers. Return postage appreciated. Replies to correspondence in Spanish.

Radio Chaskis, Jirón Roldos Aguilera y Panamericana Norte, Otavalo, Imbabura, Ecuador; (offices) Calle Bolívar 805 y Juan Montalvo, Otavalo, Imbabura, Ecuador. Phone: +593 (62) 920-922, +593 (62) 920-256. Email: radiochaskis@hotmail.com. Contact: Luis Enrique Cachiguango Cotacachi, Propietario. Welcomes correspondence in Spanish, but replies are irregular because of limited resources.

Radiodifusora Cultural Católica La Voz del Upano—*see* La Voz del Upano, above.

Radiodifusora Cultural, La Voz del Napo—*see* La Voz del Napo, above.

Radio El Buen Pastor, Asociación Cristiana de Indígenas Saraguros (ACIS), Reino de Quito y Azuay, Correo Central, Saraguro, Loja, Ecuador. Phone: +593 (2) 00-146. Contact: (general) Dean Pablo Davis, Sub-director; Segundo Poma, Director; Mark Vogan, OMS Missionary; Mike Schrode, OMS Ecuador Field Director; Juana Guamán, Secretaria; Zoila Vacacela, Secretaria; (technical) Miguel Kelly. $2 or return postage in the form of mint Ecuadorian stamps required, as IRCs are difficult to exchange in Ecuador. Station is keen to receive reception reports; may respond to English, but correspondence in Spanish preferred. $10 required for QSL card and pennant.

Radio Federación Shuar, Casilla 17-01-1422, Quito, Ecuador. Phone/Fax: +593 (2) 250-4264. Contact: Manuel Jesús Vinza Chacucuy, Director; Yurank Tsapak Rubén Gerardo, Director; Prof. Albino M. Utitiaj P., Director de Medios. Return postage or $2 required. Replies irregularly to correspondence in Spanish.

Radio María, Baquerizo Moreno 281 y Leonidas Plaza, Quito, Ecuador. Phone: +593 (2) 256-4714. Web: (includes streaming audio) www.radiomariaecuador.org. A Catholic radio network currently leasing airtime over La Voz del Napo (*see*), but which is looking into the possiblity of setting up its own shortwave station.

Radio Oriental, Casilla 260, Tena, Napo, Ecuador. Phone: +593 (6) 886-033, +593 (6) 886-388. Contact: Luis Enrique Espín Espinosa, Gerente General. $2 or return postage helpful. Reception reports welcome.

Radio Quito, Casilla 17-21-1971, Quito, Ecuador. Phone/Fax: +593 (2) 250 8301. Email: radioquito@ecuadoradio.com. Web: (includes streaming audio) www.elcomercio.com/secciones.asp?seid=329. Contact: Xavier Almeida, Gerente General; José Almeida, Subgerente. Free stickers. Return postage normally required, but occasionally verifies email reports. Replies slowly, but regularly.

EGYPT   World Time +2 (+3 midyear)

WARNING: MAIL THEFT. Feedback from PASSPORT readership indicates that money is sometimes stolen from envelopes sent to Radio Cairo.

Egyptian Radio, P.O. Box 1186, 11511 Cairo, Egypt. Email: ertu@ertu.gov.eg. Web: (under constuction) www.ertu.gov.eg; (streaming audio) http://live.sis.gov.eg/live. For additional details, *see* Radio Cairo, below.

Radio Cairo

NONTECHNICAL: P.O. Box 566, Cairo 11511, Egypt. Phone: +20 (2) 677-8945. Fax: +20 (2) 575 9553. Email: (English Service) egyptianoverseas_english@hotmail.com; (Spanish Service) radioelcairoespa@yahoo.com; (Brazilian Service) brazilian_prog@egyptradio.tv. Web: www.freewebs.com/overseas-radio. Contact: Mrs. Amal Badr, Head of English Programme; Mrs. Sahar Kalil, Director of English Service to North America and Producer, "Questions and Answers"; Marwan Khattab; Mrs. Magda Hamman, Secretary. Free stickers, postcards, stamps, maps, papyrus souvenirs, calendars and *External Services of Radio Cairo* book. Free booklet and individually tutored Arabic-language lessons with loaned textbooks from Kamila Abdullah, Director General, Arabic by Radio, Radio Cairo, P.O. Box 325, Cairo, Egypt. Arabic-language religious, cultural and language-learning audio and video tapes from the Egyptian Radio and Television Union sold via Sono Cairo Audio-Video, P.O. Box 2017, Cairo, Egypt; when ordering video tapes, inquire to ensure they function on the television standard (NTSC, PAL or SECAM) in your country. Once replied regularly, if slowly, but recently replies have been increasingly scarce. Comments welcomed about audio quality—*see* TECHNICAL, below. Avoid enclosing money (*see* WARNING, above).

TECHNICAL: Broadcast Engineering Department, Maspero TV Building, Egyptian Radio and Television Union, P.O. Box 1186, 11511 Cairo, Egypt. Phone/Fax: +20 (2) 574-6840. Email: (general) freqmeg@yahoo.com; (Lawrence) niveenl@hotmail.com. Contact: Hamdy Emara, Chairman of Engineering Sector; Mrs. Rokaya M. Kamel, Head of Engineering & Training; Mrs.Laila Hamdalla, Director of Monitoring & Frequency Management; Mrs. Niveen W. Lawrence, Director of Shortwave Department. Comments and suggestions on audio quality and level especially welcomed. One PASSPORT reader reported that his letter to this address was returned by the Egyptian postal authorities, but we have not received any other reports of returned mail.

EL SALVADOR   World Time –6

Radio Imperial (when operating), Apartado 56, Sonsonante, El Salvador. Fax: +503 450-0189. Contact: (general) Nubia Ericka García, Directora; Pastor Pedro Mendoza López; (technical) Moisés B. Cruz G., Ingeniero. Replies to correspondence in English or Spanish, and verifies reception reports by fax, if number provided. $1 helpful.

ENGLAND—*see* UNITED KINGDOM.

EQUATORIAL GUINEA   World Time +1

Radio Africa, P.O. Box 851, Malabo, Equatorial Guinea. Email: radioafrica@myway.com.

U.S. ADDRESS FOR CORRESPONDENCE AND VERIFICATIONS: Pan American Broadcasting, 2021 The Alameda, Suite 240, San Jose CA 95126-1145 USA. Phone: +1 (408) 996-2033; (toll-free, U.S. only) 1-800-726-2620. Fax: +1 (408) 252 6855. Email: info@panambc.com; (Bernald) gbernald@panambc.com; (Jung) cjung@panambc.com. Web: www.panambc.com. Contact: (listener correspondence) Terry Kraemer; (general) Carmen Jung, Office and Sales Administrator; Gene Bernald, President. $1, mint U.S. stamps or 2 IRCs required for reply.

Radio East Africa—same details as "Radio Africa," above.
Radio Nacional de Guinea Ecuatorial—Bata ("Radio Bata"), Apartado 749, Bata, Río Muni, Equatorial Guinea. Phone: +240 (8) 2592. Fax: +240 (8) 2093. Contact: José Mba Obama, Director. Not known to reply to correspondence.
Radio Nacional de Guinea Ecuatorial—Malabo ("Radio Malabo"), Apartado 195, Malabo, Isla Bioko, Equatorial Guinea. Phone: +240 (9) 2260. Fax: (general) +240 (9) 2097; (technical) +240 (9) 3122. Contact: (general) Román Manuel Mané-Abaga, Jefe de Programación; Ciprano Somon Suakin; Manuel Sobede, Inspector de Servicios de Radio y TV; (technical) Hermenegildo Moliko Chele, Jefe Servicios Técnicos de Radio y Televisión. $1 or return postage required. Replies irregularly to correspondence in Spanish.

ERITREA   World Time +3

Radio UNMEE—*see* United Nations.
Voice of the Broad Masses of Eritrea (Dimtsi Hafash), Ministry of Information, Radio Division, P.O. Box 872, Asmara, Eritrea; or Ministry of Information, Technical Branch, P.O. Box 242, Asmara, Eritrea. Phone: +291 (1) 116-084, +291 (1) 120-497. Fax: +291 (1) 126 747. Email: nesredin@tse.com.er. Web: (includes on-demand audio) www.shabait.com (click on "Dimtsi Hafash"). Contact: Ghebreab Ghebremedhin; Berhane Gerzgiher, Director, Engineering Division. Return postage or $1 helpful. Free information on history of the station and about Eritrea.

ETHIOPIA   World Time +3

Radio Ethiopia: (external service) P.O. Box 654; (domestic service) P.O. Box 1020—both in Addis Ababa, Ethiopia (address your correspondence to "Audience Relations"). Phone: (main office) +251 (1) 116-427, +251 (1) 551-011; (engineering) +251 (1) 200-948. Fax: +251 (1) 552 263. Web: www.angelfire.com/biz/radioethiopia. Contact: (external service, general) Kahsai Tewoldemedhin, Program Director; Ms. Woinshet Woldeyes, Secretary, Audience Relations; Ms. Ellene Mocria, Head of Audience Relations; Yohaness Ruphael, Producer, "Contact"; (administration) Kasa Miliko, Head of Station; (technical) Terefe Ghebre Medhin; Zegeye Solomon. Free stickers and tourist brochures. Poor replier.
Radio Fana (Radio Torch), P.O. Box 30702, Addis Ababa, Ethiopia. Phone: +251 (1) 516-777. Fax: +251 (1) 515 039. Email: rfana@telecom.net.et. Web: (includes on-demand audio) www.radiofana.com. Contact: Woldu Yemessel, General Manager; Mesfin Alemayehu, Head, External Relations; Girma Lema, Head, Planning and Research Department. Station is autonomous and receives its income from non-governmental educational sponsorship.
Voice of the Tigray Revolution, P.O. Box 450, Mek'ele, Tigray, Ethiopia. Contact: Fre Tesfamichael, Director. $1 helpful.

FINLAND   World Time +2 (+3 midyear)

Scandinavian Weekend Radio (international service), P.O. Box 99, FIN-34801, Virrat, Finland. Phone: (live when on air and SMS service) +358 (400) 995-559. Fax: (when on air) +358 (3) 475 5776. Email: (general) info@swradio.net; (technical) esa.saunamaki@swradio.net; (reception reports) online report form. Web: www.swradio.net. Contact: Alpo Heinonen; Esa Saunamäki, Chief Editor; Teemu Lehtimäki, QSL Manager. Two IRCs, $2 or 2 euros required for verification via mail. Web reports verified via the internet.

Calvi, Corsica, one of the 26 *régions* of France reported on by RFI.   L. Ryden

FRANCE   World Time +1 (+2 midyear)

Le Héraut de la Christian Science, B.P. 80014, F-95601 Eaubonne Cedex, France.
Email: (Flamand) jflamand@club-internet.fr. Web: www.cs2paris.org/radios.html. Contact: Josette Flamand. Broadcasts via facilities of Germany's T-Systems International (*see*).
SCHEDULES AND RELIGIOUS PUBLICATIONS: Le Héraut, P.O. Box 1524, Boston MA 02117-1524 USA. Email: heraut@csps.com. Web: www.tfccs.com/gv/csps/herald/french/radio.jhtml.
Radio France Internationale (RFI)
MAIN OFFICE: B.P. 9516, F-75016 Paris Cedex 16, France; (street address) 116, avenue du président Kennedy, F-75016 Paris, France. Phone: (general) +33 (1) 5640-1212; (International Affairs and Program Placement) +33 (1) 4430-8932, +33 (1) 4430-8949; (Service de la communication) +33 (1) 4230-2951; (Audience Relations) +33 (1) 4430-8969/70/71; (Media Relations) +33 (1) 4230-2985; (Développement et de la communication) +33 (1) 4430-8921; *(Fréquence Monde)* +33 (1) 4230-1086; (English Service) +33 (1) 5640-3062; (Spanish Department) +33 (1) 4230-3048. Fax: (general) +33 (1) 5640 4759; (International Affairs and Program Placement) +33 (1) 4430 8920; (Audience Relations) +33 (1) 4430 8999; (other nontechnical) +33 (1) 4230 4481; (English Service) +33 (1) 5640 2674; (Spanish Department) +33 (1) 4230 4669. Email: (Audience Relations) courrier.auditeurs@rfi.fr; (English Service) english.service@rfi.fr; (Maguire) john.maguire@rfi.fr; (Spanish Service) america.latina@rfi.fr. Web: (includes on-demand and streaming audio) www.rfi.fr. Contact: John Maguire, Editor, English Language Service; J.P. Charbonnier, Producer, "Lettres des Auditeurs"; Joël Amar, International Affairs/Program Placement Department; Arnaud Littardi, Directeur du développement et de la communication; Nicolas Levkov, Rédactions en Langues Etrangères; Daniel Franco, Rédaction en français; Mme. Anne Toulouse, Rédacteur en chef du Service Mondiale en français; Christine Berbudeau, Rédacteur en chef, *Fréquence* **Monde**; Marc Verney, Attaché de Presse; (administration) Jean-Paul Cluzel, Président-Directeur Général; (technical) M. Raymond Pincon, Producer, "Le Courrier Technique." Free *Fréquence* **Monde** bi-monthly magazine in French upon request. Free souvenir keychains, pins, lighters, pencils, T-shirts and stickers have been received by some—especially when visiting the

headquarters at 116 avenue du Président Kennedy, in the 16th Arrondissement. Can provide supplementary materials for "Dites-moi tout" French-language course; write to the attention of Mme. Chantal de Grandpre, "Dites-moi tout." "Le Club des Auditeurs" French-language listener's club ("Club 9516" for English-language listeners); applicants must provide name, address and two passport-type photos, whereupon they will receive a membership card and the club bulletin. RFI exists primarily to defend and promote Francophone culture, but also provides meaningful information and cultural perspectives in non-French languages.

TRANSMISSION OFFICE, TECHNICAL: TéléDiffusion de France, Direction de la Production et des Méthodes, Service ondes courtes, 10 rue d'Oradour sur Glane, 75732 Paris Cedex 15, France. Phone: (Gruson) +33 (1) 5595-1553; (Meunier) +33 (1) 5595-1161. Fax: +33 (1) 5595 2137. Email: (Gruson) jacques.gruson@tdf.fr; (Penneroux) michel.penneroux@tdf.fr. Contact: Jacques Gruson; Alain Meunier; Michel Penneroux, Business Development Manager AM-HF; Mme Annick Daronian or Mme Sylvie Greuillet (short wave service). This office is for informing about transmitter-related problems (interference, modulation quality), and also for reception reports and verifications.

UNITED STATES PROMOTIONAL, SCHOOL LIAISON, PROGRAM PLACEMENT AND CULTURAL EXCHANGE OFFICES:

NEW ORLEANS: Services Culturels, Suite 2105, Ambassade de France, 300 Poydras Street, New Orleans LA 70130 USA. Phone: +1 (504) 523-5394. Phone/Fax: +1 (504) 529-7502. Contact: Adam-Anthony Steg, Attaché Audiovisuel. This office promotes RFI, especially to language teachers and others in the educational community within the southern United States, and arranges for bi-national cultural exchanges. It also sets up RFI feeds to local radio stations within the southern United States.

NEW YORK: Audiovisual Bureau, Radio France Internationale, 972 Fifth Avenue, New York NY 10021 USA. Phone: +1 (212) 439-1452. Fax: +1 (212) 439 1455. Contact: Gérard Blondel or Julien Vin. This office promotes RFI, especially to language teachers and others within the educational community outside the southern United States, and arranges for bi-national cultural exchanges. It also sets up RFI feeds to local radio stations within much of the United States.

NEW YORK NEWS BUREAU: 1290 Avenue of the Americas, New York NY 10019 USA. Phone: +1 (212) 581-1771. Fax: +1 (212) 541 4309. Contact: Ms. Auberi Edler, Reporter; Bruno Albin, Reporter.

WASHINGTON NEWS BUREAU: 529 14th Street NW, Suite 1126, Washington DC 20045 USA. Phone: +1 (202) 879-6706. Contact: Pierre J. Cayrol.

SAN FRANCISCO OFFICE, SCHEDULES: 2654 17th Avenue, San Francisco CA 94116 USA. Phone: +1 (415) 564-9968. Email: GPoppin@aol.com. Contact: George Poppin. This address, a volunteer office, only provides RFI schedules to listeners (return postage not required). All other correspondence should be sent directly to the main office in Paris.

📻Radio Monte Carlo-Middle East

MAIN OFFICE: Radio Monte Carlo-Moyen Orient, 116 avenue du président Kennedy, F-75116 Paris, France; or B.P. 371, Paris 16, France. Email: contact@rmc-mo.com. Web: (includes on-demand and streaming audio) www.rmc-mo.com. A station of the RFI group whose programs are produced in Paris and aired via a mediumwave AM transmitter in Cyprus; also via FM in France and parts of the Middle East. Provides programs for RFI's Arabic service. A daily Arabic program is also broadcast on shortwave to North America via Radio Canada International's Sackville facilitities.

CYPRUS ADDRESS: P.O. Box 2026, Nicosia, Cyprus. Contact: M. Pavlides, Chef de Station. Reception reports have sometimes been verified via this address.

Voice of Orthodoxy—see Voix de l'Orthodoxie, below.

Voix de l'Orthodoxie, B.P. 416-08, F-75366 Paris Cedex 08, France. Phone: +33 (1) 4977-0366. Fax: +33 (1) 4353 4066. Email: voix.orthodoxie@wanadoo.fr. Web: www.russie.net/orthodoxie/vo. Contact: Michel Solovieff, General Secretary. Broadcasts religious programming to Russia via a shortwave transmitter in Kazakstan. Verifies reception reports, including those written in English.

ADDRESS IN RUSSIA: Golos Pravoslavia, 39 Nab. Leyt. Schmidta, 199034 St. Petersburg, Russia. Phone/Fax: +7 (812) 323-2867.

FRENCH GUIANA   World Time –3

Radio France Internationale Guyane Relay Station, Télédiffusion de France S.A., Délégation Territoriale de Guyane, B.P. 7024, 97307 Cayenne Cedex, French Guiana. Phone: Tel: +594 350-550. Fax: +594 350 555. Contact: (technical) Le Responsable pour Groupe Maintenance. All correspondence concerning nontechnical matters should be sent directly to the main addresses (see) for Radio France Internationale in France. Can consider replies only to technical correspondence in French. Sometimes verifies reception reports.

GABON   World Time +1

Afrique Numéro Un, B.P. 1, Libreville, Gabon. Fax: +241 742 133. Email: online form. Web: (includes streaming audio) www.africa1.com. Contact: (general) Gaston Didace Singangoye; Jean Félix Ngawin Ndong; (technical) Mme. Marguerite Bayimbi, Le Directeur [sic] Technique. Free calendars and bumper stickers. $1, 2 IRCs or return postage helpful. Replies very slowly.

RTV Gabonaise, B.P. 10150, Libreville, Gabon. Contact: André Ranaud-Renombo, Le Directeur Technique, Adjoint Radio. Free stickers. $1 required. Replies occasionally, but slowly, to correspondence in French.

GEORGIA   World Time +4

📻**Georgian Radio** (if reactivated), TV-Radio Tbilisi, ul. M. Kostava 68, Tbilisi 380071, Republic of Georgia. Phone: (external service) +995 (32) 360-063. Fax: +995 (32) 955 137. Email: foraf@geotvr.ge. Web: (includes streaming audio from domestic service not on shortwave) www.geotvr.ge. Contact: Ms. Tamar Kintsurashvili, General Director. Replies erratically and slowly, in part due to financial restrictions. Return postage or $1 helpful.

Radio Hara, Rustaveli Ave. 52, II Floor, Apt. 211-212, Tbilisi, Georgia. Email: league@geoconst.org.ge. Contact: Nino Berdznishvili, Program Manager; Zourab Shengelia. Programs are produced by the Georgian-Abkhazian Relations Institute.

Republic of Abkhazia Radio, Abkhaz State Radio and TV Co., Aidgylara Street 34, Sukhum 384900, Republic of Abkhazia; or Zvanba Street 8, Sukhum 384900, Republic of Abkhazia. However, given the problems in getting mail to Abkhazia, the station requests that reception reports be sent to the following address: National Library of Abkhazia, Krasnodar District, P.O. Box 964, 354000 Sochi, Russia. Phone: +995 (881) 24-867, +995 (881) 25-321. Fax: +995 (881) 21 144. Contact: Zurab Argun, Director.

GERMANY   World Time +1 (+2 midyear)

Christliche Wissenschaft (Christian Science), Radiosendungen, E. Bethmann, Postfach 7330, D-22832 Norderstedt, Germany; or CS-Radiosendungen, Alexanderplatz 2, D-20099 Hamburg, Germany. Contact: Erich Bethmann. Replies to correspondence in German and verifies reception reports. Return postage helpful. Via facilities of T-Systems International (see).

T-Systems International. See "Shortwave Radio Station Jülich—T-Systems International AG."

◻Deutsche Welle

MAIN OFFICE: Kurt-Schumacher-Str. 3, D-53113 Bonn, Germany; or (postal address) Deutsche Welle, D-53110 Bonn, Germany. Phone: (English Service) +49 (228) 429-4144. Fax: +1 (228) 429 3000; (English Service) +49 (228) 429 2860. Email: online@dw-world.de; (English Service) feedback. english@dw-world.de. To reach specific individuals by email at Deutsche Welle the format is: firstname.lastname@dw-world. de. For language courses: feedback.radio@dw-world.de. Web: (includes on-demand and streaming audio) www.dw-world. de. Contact: Erik Bettermann, Director General; Marco Vollmar, Head of English and German Services. Broadcasts via transmitters in Germany, Canada, Madagascar, Kazakhstan, Netherlands Antilles, Portugal, Russia, Rwanda, Singapore, Sri Lanka and Taiwan.

CUSTOMER SERVICE: Phone: +49 (228) 429-4000. Fax: +49 (228) 429 154000. Email: info@dw-world.de. All technical mail and QSL-reports should be sent to the Customer Service.

◻Deutschlandfunk, Raderberggürtel 40, D-50968 Köln, Germany. Phone: +49 (221) 345-0. Fax: +49 (221) 345 4802. Email: (program information) deutschlandfunk@dradio.de. Web: (includes on-demand and streaming audio) www.dradio.de/dlf. Verifies reception reports in German or English.

◻DeutschlandRadio-Berlin, Hans-Rosenthal-Platz, D-10825 Berlin Schönberg, Germany. Phone: +49 (30) 8503-0. Fax: +49 (30) 8503 6168. Email: (program information) dkultur@dradio. de Web: (includes on-demand and streaming audio) www.dradio.de/dkultur. Contact: Dr. Karl-Heinz Stamm; Ulrich Reuter. Verifies reception reports in German or English. Sometimes sends stickers, pens, magazines and other souvenirs.

Evangeliums-Radio-Hamburg, Postfach 920741, D-21137 Hamburg, Germany. Phone: +49 (40) 702-7025. Email: evangeliums-radio-hamburg@t-online.de. Web: www.evr-hamburg. de. Verifies reception reports in German or English. On world band via T-Systems International (see), and locally on FM and cable.

◻Freie Volksmission Krefeld.(Free People's Mission Krefeld), Postfach 100707, D-47707 Krefeld, Germany; (street address) Freie Volksmission, Am Herbertzhof 15, D-47809 Krefeld, Germany; (English correspondence) Mission Center, P.O. Box 100707, D-47707 Krefeld, Germany. Phone: +49 (2151) 545-151. Email: postmaster@freie-volksmission.de. Web: (includes on-demand and streaming audio) www.freie-volksmission.de. Replies to correspondence in English or German. Via T-Systems International (see).

Hamburger Lokalradio

STUDIO ADDRESS: Kulturzentrum Lola, Lohbrügger, Landstrasse 8, D-21031 Hamburg, Germany. Phone: +49 (40) 7269-2422. Fax: +49 (40) 7269 2423. Web: www.hamburger-lokalradio. de, www.hhlr.de.

EDITORIAL ADDRESS: Michael Kittner, Hamburger Lokalradio, Max-Eichholz-Ring 18, D-21031 Hamburg, Germany. Phone/Fax: +49 (40) 738-2417. Email: m.kittner@freenet.de. Contact: Michael Kittner.

Broadcasts regularly on FM and cable, and intermittently on world band via T-Systems International (see) and a Latvian transmitter. Replies to correspondence in German or English. Return postage required for postal reply.

Missionswerk Friedensstimme, Postfach 100638, D-51606 Gummersbach, Germany; (street address) Gimborner Str. 20, D-51709 Marienheide, Germany. Phone: +49 (2261) 24717. Fax: +49 (2261) 60170. Contact: N. Berg. Replies to correspondence and verifies reception reports in German or Russian. Broadcasts to Russia via T-Systems International (see).

◻Missionswerk Werner Heukelbach, D-51700 Bergneustadt 2, Germany. Email: info@missionswerk-heukelbach.de. Web: (includes on-demand audio) www.missionswerk-heukelbach. de. Contact: Manfred Paul. Religious broadcaster heard via the Voice of Russia, and formerly via T-Systems International (see). Replies to correspondence in German or English and verifies reception reports.

MV Baltic Radio, R&R Medienservice, Roland Rohde, Seestrasse 17, D-19089 Göhren, Germany. Phone: +49 (3861) 301-380, +49 (178) 895-3872. Fax: +49 (3861) 302 9720. Email: info@rrms.de, info@mvbalticradio.de. Web: www.mvbalticradio.de. Contact: Roland Rohde. Replies to correspondence in German or English, and verifies reception reports. IRC or $1 required for postal reply. A monthly broadcast produced in Göhren (Mecklenburg-Vorpommern) and aired via facilities of T-Systems International (see).

◻Radio Multikulti, Rundfunk Berlin-Brandenburg, D-14046 Berlin, Germany; (street address) Rundfunk Berlin-Brandenburg, Masurenallee 8-14, D-14057 Berlin, Germany. Phone: +49 (30) 3031-1655. Email: multikulti@rbb-online. de. Web: (includes on-demand and streaming audio) www. multikulti.de. Provides programming for the Romany transmissions of Deutsche Welle (see) and verifies reception reports on these broadcasts. Accepts email reports, which are verified with QSL cards.

◻Radio Santec, Marienstrasse 1, D-97070 Würzburg, Germany. Phone: (0800-1600 Central European Time, Monday through Friday) +49 (931) 3903-264. Fax: +49 (931) 3903 195. Email: info@radio-santec.de. Web: (includes on-demand and streaming audio) www.radio-santec.com. Reception reports verified with QSL cards only if requested. Radio Santec is the radio branch of Universelles Leben (Universal Life).

Shortwave Radio Station Jülich—T-Systems Business Services GmbH, Media & Broadcast, Rundfunksendestelle Jülich, Merscher Höehe D-52428 Jülich, Germany. Phone: (head of station) +49 (2461) 697-310; (technical engineer) +49 (2461) 697-330. Email: (Hirte) guenter.hirte@t-systems. com; (Goslawski) roman.goslawski@t-systems.com. Contact: Günter Hirte, Head of Shortwave Radio Station Jülich; Roman Goslawski, Deputy Head of Shortwave Radio Station Jülich.

SALES OFFICE SHORTWAVE, T-SYSTEMS BUSINESS SERVICES GMBH, MEDIA & BROADCAST: Bastionstrasse 11-19, D-52438 Jülich, Germany. Phone: (Brodowsky, Sales & Marketing) +49 (2461) 937-164; (Horst Tobias, Frequency Manager) +49 (2461) 340-451. Fax: (sales office) +49 (2461) 937 165; (frequency management office) +49 (2461) 340 452. Email: walter. brodowsky@t-systems.com. Contact: Walter Brodowsky, Sales & Marketing Manager for Shortwave Broadcasts; Horst Tobias, Frequency Manager. Reception reports accepted by mail or fax, and should be clearly marked to the attention of Walter Brodowsky. T-Systems International operates transmitters on German soil used by Deutsche Welle, as well as those leased to various international world band stations.

NOTE: In March 2006, the Jülich transmitting station was sold to CVC (see Australia), media arm of the United Kingdom's

Christian Vision. Under the terms of the sale, T-Systems International will continue to service its clients at Jülich until the end of 2007, at which time Christian Vision will take full operational control.

Stimme des Evangeliums, Evangelische Missions-Gemeinden, Jahnstrasse 9, D-89182 Bernstadt, Germany. Phone: +49 (7348) 948-026. Fax: +49 (7348) 948-027. Contact: Pastor Albert Giessler. Verifies reception reports in German or English. A broadcast of the Evangelical Missions Congregations in Germany, and aired via T-Systems International (see) in Jülich.

T-Systems International—see Shortwave Radio Station Jülich—T-Systems International.

GHANA   World Time exactly

WARNING—CONFIDENCE ARTISTS: Attempted correspondence with Radio Ghana may result in requests, perhaps resulting from mail theft, from skilled confidence artists for money, free electronic or other products, publications or immigration sponsorship. To help avoid this, correspondence to Radio Ghana should be sent via registered mail.

Ghana Broadcasting Corporation, P.O. Box 1633, Accra, Ghana; (street address) Broadcasting House, Ring Road Central, Kanda, Accra, Ghana. Phone/Fax: +233 (21) 768-975, +233 (21) 221- 161, +233 (21) 786-561. Email: online form. Web: www.gbcghana.com. Contact: (general) Director of Corporate Affairs; (administration) Director of Radio; (technical) Director of Engineering, or Propagation Department. Replies tend to be erratic, and reception reports are best sent to the attention of the Propagation Engineer, GBC Monitoring Station. Enclosing an IRC, return postage or $1 and registering your letter should improve the chances of a reply.

GREECE   World Time +2 (+3 midyear)

🔲**Foni tis Helladas** (Voice of Greece)
NONTECHNICAL: ERA-5, The Voice of Greece, 432 Mesogion, Aghia Paraskevi, 15342 Athens, Greece. Phone: +30 210-606-6895/96, +30 210-606-6297/98, +30 210-606-6398. Fax: +30 210 606 6309. Email: (including reception reports) era5@ert.gr. Web: (includes streaming audio) www.voiceofgreece.gr. Contact: Angeliki Barka, Head of Programmes; Gina Vogiatzoglou, Managing Director. Free tourist literature.
TECHNICAL: ERA-5, General Technical Directorate, Mesogion 432, 15342 Athens, Greece. Phone: (Charalambopoulos) +30 210-606-5585. Fax: +30 210 606 6264. Email: (reception reports) era5@ert.gr; apodimos_era5@ert.gr; (technical information, schedules, Charalambopoulos) bcharalabopoulos@ert.gr. Contact: Babis Charalambopoulos, Planning Engineer. Technical reception reports may be sent via mail, fax or email.

🔲**Radiophonikos Stathmos Makedonias**, Angelaki 14, 54636 Thessaloniki, Greece. Phone: +30 2310-299-400. Fax: +30 2310 299 550. Email: eupro@ert3.gr. Web: (includes streaming audio) www.ert3.gr. Contact: (general) Mrs. Tatiana Tsioli, Program Director; Lefty Kongalides, Head of International Relations; (technical) Dimitrios Keramidas, Engineer. Free booklets, stickers and other small souvenirs.

GREENLAND   World Time exactly Northeast; –1 (World Time midyear) Eastern; –3 (–2 midyear) Central; –4 Western

Kalaalit Nunaata Radioa (KNR), Postbok 1007, DK-3900 Nuuk, Greenland; (street address) Vandsøvej 15, DK-3900 Nuuk, Greenland. Phone: +299 361-500. Fax: +299 361 502. Email: info@knr.gl, (Pedersen) isp@knr.gl. Web: www.knr.gl.

Contact: Ms. Ivalu Søvndahl Pedersen, Communication Assistant. Does not operate on shortwave, but relays part of its programming to fishermen on 3815 kHz via a 100-watt USB transmitter of the Ammassalik Radio coastal station in Tasiilaq (see, below). Replies to correspondence in English, and verifies reception reports.

OZL Ammassalik Radio, Silasiorpimmut B920, DK-3913 Tasiilaq, Greenland. Email: ozl@tele.gl. Replies to correspondence in English, and verifies reception reports.

GUAM   World Time +10

Adventist World Radio—KSDA
OPERATIONS AND ENGINEERING: P.O. Box 8990, Agat, GU 96928 USA. Phone: +1 (671) 565-2289. Fax: +1 (671) 565 2983. Email: brook@awr.org. Contact: Brook Powers. This address for specialized technical correspondence only. For further information, see AWR listing under USA.

Trans World Radio—KTWR
MAIN OFFICE, ENGINEERING INQUIRIES & FREQUENCY COORDINATION ONLY: P.O. Box 8780, Agat, GU 96928 USA. Phone: +1 (671) 828-8637. Fax: +1 (671) 828 8636. Email: (White) cwhite@guam.twr.org; (Ross) ktwrfcd@guam.twr.org. Contact: Chuck White, Chief Engineer/Station Manager; George Ross, Frequency Coordination Manager. This office will also verify email reports with a QSL card. Requests reports covering 15-30 minutes of programming. All English listener mail of a nontechnical nature should be sent to the Australian office (see next entry). Addresses for listener mail in other languages are given in the broadcasts. Also, see Trans World Radio, USA.
ENGLISH LISTENER MAIL, NONTECHNICAL: Trans World Radio, P.O. Box 390, Box Hill, Victoria 3128, Australia. Phone: +61 (3) 9899 3800. Fax: +61 (3) 9899 3900. Email: infoaus@twr.org. Web: http://twraustralia.org. Contact: John Reeder, National Director.

GUATEMALA   World Time –6 (–7 midyear)

Radio Amistad (if reactivated), Iglesia Bautista Getsemani, San Pedro La Laguna, Solola, Guatemala.
ADDRESS FOR RECEPTION REPORTS: David Daniell, Asesor de Comunicaciones, Apartado Postal 25, Bulevares MX, 53140 Mexico. Phone/Fax: +52 (55) 5572-9633. Email: dpdaniell@aol.com. Replies to correspondence in English or Spanish.

Radio Buenas Nuevas, 13020 San Sebastián, Huehuetenango, Guatemala. Contact: Israel G. Rodas Mérida, Gerente. $1 or return postage helpful. Free religious and station information in Spanish. Sometimes includes a small pennant. Replies to correspondence in Spanish.

Radio Coatán—see Radio Cultural Coatán.

🔲**Radio Cultural—TGNA** (when operating), Apartado 601, 01901 Guatemala City, Guatemala; (studios) 4Av. 30-09 Zona 3, Guatemala City, Guatemala. Phone: +502 2472-1745, +502 2471-4378, +502 2440-0260. Fax: +502 2440-0260. Email: tgn@radiocultural.com; tgna@guate.net. Web: (includes streaming audio) www.radiocultural.com. Contact: Wayne Berger, Chief Engineer; Heidy Chávez; [Ms.] Yojhana Ajsivinac, Secretary. Free religious printed matter, tourist information and pennant (when available). Return postage or $1 appreciated.

Radio Cultural Coatán—TGCT, San Sebastián Coátan 13035, Huehuetenango, Guatemala. Phone: +502 7758-3491, +502 7758-5494. Contact: Diego Sebastián Miguel, Locutor. $1 or return postage required. Often announces as just "Radio Coatán."

Radio K'ekchi—TGVC (when operating), 3ra Calle 7-15, Zona 1, 16015 Fray Bartolomé de las Casas, Alta Verapaz, Guatemala; (Media Consultant) David Daniell, Asesor de Comunicaciones, Apartado Postal 25, Bulevares MX, 53140 Mexico. Phone: (station) +502 7950-0299; (Daniell, Phone/Fax) +52 (55) 5572-9633. Fax: (station) +502 7950 0398. Email: dpdaniell@aol.com. Contact: (general) Gilberto Sun Xicol, Gerente; Ancelmo Cuc Chub, Director; Mateo Botzoc, Director de Programas; (technical) Larry Baysinger, Ingeniero Jefe. Free paper pennant. $1 or return postage required. Replies to correspondence in Spanish.

Radio Maya de Barillas—TGBA (if reactivated), 13026 Villa de Barillas, Huehuetenango, Guatemala. Contact: José Castañeda, Pastor Evangélico y Gerente. Free pennants and pins. Station is very interested in receiving reception reports. $1 or return postage required. Replies occasionally to correspondence in Spanish.

Radio Verdad, Apartado Postal 5, Chiquimula, Guatemala. Email: radioverdad@intelnett.com. Web: www.radioverdad. org. Contact: Dr. Édgar Amilcar Madrid Morales, Gerente. May send free pennants & calendars. Replies to correspondence in Spanish or English. Return postage appreciated. An evangelical and educational station.

GUINEA   World Time exactly

Radiodiffusion-Télévision Guinéenne, B.P. 391, Conakry, Guinea. If no reply is forthcoming from this address, try sending your letter to: D.G.R./P.T.T., B.P. 3322, Conakry, Guinea. Phone/Fax: +224 451-408. Email: (Issa Conde, Directeur) issaconde@yahoo.fr. Contact: (general) Yaoussou Diaby, Journaliste Sportif; Boubacar Yacine Diallo, Directeur Général/ORTG; Issa Conde, Directeur; Seny Camara; (administration) Momo Toure, Chef Services Administratifs; (technical, studio) Mbaye Gagne, Chef de Studio; (technical, overall) Direction des Services Techniques. Return postage or $1 required. Replies very irregularly to correspondence in French.

GUYANA   World Time –3

🎙**Voice of Guyana**, Homestretch Avenue, Georgetown, Guyana. Phone: +592 223- 5162. Fax: +592 223 5163. Email: vog560am@homeviewguyana.com. Web: (includes streaming audio) www.homeviewguyana.com. Contact: (general) Mrs. Jasminee Sahoye, Programme Manager; (technical) Roy Marshall, Senior Technician; Shiroxley Goodman, Chief Engineer. $1 or IRC helpful. Sending a spare sticker from another station helps assure a reply. Note that when the station's mediumwave AM transmitter is down because of a component fault, parts of the shortwave unit are sometimes 'borrowed' until spares become available. As a result, the station is sometimes off shortwave for several weeks at a time.

HOLLAND—see NETHERLANDS

HONDURAS   World Time –6

🎙**La Voz Evangélica—HRVC**
MAIN OFFICE: Apartado Postal 3252, Tegucigalpa, M.D.C., Honduras. Phone: +504 234-3468/69/70. Fax: +504 233 3933. Email: programas@hrvc.org. Web: (includes streaming audio): www.hrvc.org. Contact: (general) Srta. Orfa Esther Durón Mendoza, Secretaria; Tereso Ramos, Director de Programación;

Alan Maradiaga; Modesto Palma, Jefe, Depto. Tráfico; (technical) Carlos Paguada, Director del Dpto. Técnico; (administration) Venancio Mejía, Gerente; Nelson Perdomo, Director. Free calendars. Three IRCs or $1 required. Replies to correspondence in English, Spanish, Portuguese or German.
REGIONAL OFFICE, SAN PEDRO SULA: Apartado 2336, San Pedro Sula, Honduras. Phone: +504 557-5030. Contact: Hernán Miranda, Director.
REGIONAL OFFICE, LA CEIBA: Apartado 164, La Ceiba, Honduras. Phone: +504 443-2390. Contact: José Banegas, Director.
Radio HRMI, Radio Misiones Internacionales
STATION: Apartado Postal 20583, Comayagüela, M.D.C., Honduras. Phone: +504 233-9029, +504 238-4933. Contact: Wayne Downs, Director. $1 or return postage helpful.
U.S. OFFICE: IMF World Missions, P.O. Box 6321, San Bernardino CA 92412, USA. Phone +1 (909) 466-5793. Fax: +1 (909) 370 4862. Email: jkpimf@msn.com. Contact: Dr. James K. Planck, President; Gustavo Roa, Coordinator.
Radio Luz y Vida—HRPC, Apartado 303, San Pedro Sula, Honduras; (reception reports in English) HRPC Radio, P. O. Box 303, San Pedro Sula, Honduras. Phone: +504 654-1221. Fax: +504 557 0394. Email: efmhonduras@globalnet.hn. Contact: Donald R. Moore, Station Director; or, to have your letter read over the air, "English Friendship Program." Return postage or $1 appreciated.

HUNGARY   World Time +1 (+2 midyear)

🎙**Kossuth Rádió**, Bródy Sándor utca 5-7, H-1800 Budapest, Hungary. Phone: +36 (1) 328-7945. Web: (includes on-demand and streaming audio) www.radio.hu/index.php?rovat_id=76; (English) www.english.radio.hu/rovat/1056.
🎙**Radio Budapest**, Bródy Sándor utca 5-7, H-1800 Budapest, Hungary. Phone: (general) +36 (1) 328-7224, +36 (1) 328-8328, +36 (1) 328-7357 +36 (1) 328-8588, +36 (1) 328-7710, +36 (1) 328-7723; (voice mail, English) +36 (1) 328-8320; (voice mail, German) +36 (1) 328-7325; (administration) +36 (1) 328-7503, +36 (1) 328-8415; (technical) +36 (1) 328-7226, +36 (1) 328-8923. Fax: (general) +36 (1) 328 8517; (administration) +36 (1) 328 8838; (technical) +36 (1) 328 7105. Email: (English) english@kaf.radio.hu; (German) nemet1@kaf. radio.hu; (Spanish) espanol@kaf.radio.hu; (technical) (Füszfás) fuszfasla@muszak.radio.hu. Web: www.english.radio.hu/index. php?rovat_id=1059; (on-demand audio) http://real1.radio. hu/nemzeti.htm. Contact: (English Language Service) Ágnes Kevi, Correspondence; Mrs. Ilona Kolipka; Louis Horváth, DX Editor; Sándor Laczkó, Editor; (administration) László Krassó, Director, Foreign Broadcasting; Dr. Zsuzsa Mészáros, Vice-Director, Foreign Broadcasting; (technical) László Füszfás, Deputy Technical Director, Magyar Rádió. Free pennant when available. Replies irregularly, due to limited resources.
TRANSMISSION AUTHORITY: Ministry of Transport, Communications and Water Management, P.O. Box 87, H-1400 Budapest, Hungary. Phone: +36 (1) 461-3390. Fax: +36 (1) 461 3392. Email: (Horváth) horvathf@cms.khvm.hu. Contact: Ferenc Horváth, Frequency Manager, Radio Communications Engineering Services.

ICELAND   World Time exactly

🎙**Ríkisútvarpid**, International Relations Department, Efstaleiti 1, IS-150 Reykjavík, Iceland. Phone: +354 515-3000. Fax: +354 515 3010. Email: isradio@ruv.is. Web: (includes streaming audio) www.ruv.is. Contact: Dóra Ingvadóttir, Head of International Relations; Markús Öern Antonsson, Director.

Once found only in portions of Italy, pizza is now a staple nearly everywhere. Here, colleagues enjoy a large veggie takeout at All India Radio's Khampur facility in greater Delhi.   Alokesh Gupta

INDIA   World Time +5:30

WARNING—MAIL THEFT: PASSPORT readers report that letters to India containing IRCs and other valuables have disappeared en route when not registered. Best is either to register your letter or to send correspondence in an unsealed envelope, and without enclosures.

VERIFICATION OF REGIONAL STATIONS: All Indian regional stations can be verified via New Delhi (*see* All India Radio—External Services Division for contact details), but some listeners prefer contacting each station individually, in the hope of receiving a direct QSL. Well-known Indian DXer Jose Jacob makes the following suggestions: address your report to the station engineer of the respective station; specify the time of reception in both World Time (UTC) and Indian Standard Time (IST); instead of using the SINPO code, write a brief summary of reception quality; and if possible, report on local programs rather than relays of national programming from New Delhi. Jose adds that reports should be written in English, and return postage is not required. Enclosing currency notes is against the law.

Akashvani—All India Radio

ADMINISTRATION/ENGINEERING: Directorate General of All India Radio, Akashvani Bhawan, 1 Sansad Marg, New Delhi-110 001, India. Phone: +91 (11) 2342-1006, +91 (11) 2371-5413; (Director General) +91 (11) 2371-0300 Ext. 102; (Engineer-in-Chief) +91 (11) 2342-1058; (Phone/Fax) +91 (11) 2342-1459; (Director, Spectrum Management) +91 (11) 2342-1062, +91 (11) 2342-1145. Fax: +91 (11) 2371 11956; (Director General) +91 (11) 2342 1956. Email: airlive@air.org.in; (Director General) dgair@air.org.in; (Engineer-in-Chief) einc@air.org.in; (Director, Spectrum Management) faair@nda.vsnl.net.in. Web: (includes streaming audio) www.allindiaradio.gov.in. Contact: (technical) K.M. Paul, Engineer-in-Chief; Y.K. Sharma, Director, Spectrum Management; Devendra Singh, Deputy Director, Spectrum Management.

AUDIENCE RESEARCH: Audience Research Unit, All India Radio, Press Trust of India Building, 2nd floor, Sansad Marg, New Delhi-110 001, India. Phone: (general) +91 (11) 2371-0033, +91 (11) 2371-9215; (Director) +91 (11) 2338-6506. Contact: Ramesh Chandra, Director.

CENTRAL MONITORING STATION: All India Radio, Ayanagar, New Delhi-110 047, India. Phone: +91 (11) 2650-2955, +91 (11) 2650 1763. Contact: Y.K. Sharma, Director.

COMMERCIAL SERVICE: Vividh Bharati Service, AIR, P.O. Box 11497, 101 M.K. Road, Mumbai-400 020, India. Phone: +91 (22) 2203-7193.

INTERNATIONAL MONITORING STATION—MAIN OFFICE: International Monitoring Station, All India Radio, Dr. K.S. Krishnan Road, Todapur, New Delhi-110 097, India. Phone: +91 (11) 2584-2939. Contact: B.L. Kasturiya, Deputy Director; D.P. Chhabra or R.K. Malviya, Assistant Research Engineers—Frequency Planning.

NATIONAL CHANNEL: AIR, Gate 22, Jawaharlal Nehru Stadium, Lodhi Road, New Delhi-110 003. Phone: +91 (11) 2584-3825; (station engineer) +91 (11) 2584-3207. Contact: J.K. Das, Director; V.D. Sharma, Station Engineer.

NEWS SERVICES DIVISION: News Services Division, Broadcasting House, 1 Sansad Marg, New Delhi-110 001, India. Phone: (newsroom) +91 (11) 2342-1006, +91 (11) 2371-5413; (Special Director General—News) +91 (11) 2371-0084, +91 (11) 2373-1510; (News on phone in English) +91 (11) 2332-4343; (News on phone in Hindi) +91 (11) 2332-4242. Fax: +91 (11) 2371 1196. Email: nsdair@giasdl01.vsnl.net.in. Contact: B.I. Saini, Special Director General—News.

PROGRAMMING: Broadcasting House, 1 Sansad Marg, New Delhi-110 001 India. Phone: (general) +91 (11) 2371-5411.

RESEARCH AND DEVELOPMENT: Office of the Chief Engineer R&D, All India Radio, 14-B Ring Road, Indraprastha Estate, New Delhi-110 002, India. Phone: (general) +91 (11) 2337-8211/12; (Chief Engineer) +91 (11) 2337 9255, +91 (11) 2337-9329. Fax: +91 (11) 2331 8329, +91 (11) 2331 6674. Email: rdair@nda.vsnl.net.in. Web: www.air.kode.net. Contact: B.L. Mathur, Chief Engineer.

TRANSCRIPTION AND PROGRAM EXCHANGE SERVICES: Akashvani Bhawan, 1 Sansad Marg, New Delhi-110 001, India. Phone: (Director, Transcription & Program Exchange Services; V.A. Magazine) +91 (11) 2342-1927. Contact: D.P. Jadav, Director.

All India Radio—Aizawl, Radio Tila, Tuikhuahtlang, Aizawl-796 001, Mizoram, India. Phone: (engineering) +91 (389) 2322-415. Fax: +91 (389) 2322 114. Email: aizawl@air.org.in. Contact: (technical) S. Nellai Nayagam, Station Engineer.

All India Radio—Aligarh, Anoopshahar Road, Aligarh-202 001, Uttar Pradesh, India. Phone: (engineering) +91 (571) 2700-972. Email: aligarh@air.org.in. Contact: S.K. Agarwal, Station Engineer.

All India Radio—Bangalore Shortwave Transmitting Centre

HEADQUARTERS: see All India Radio—External Services Division.

AIR OFFICE NEAR TRANSMITTERS: Superintending Engineer, Super Power Transmitters, All India Radio, Yelahanka New Town, Bangalore-560 065, Karnataka, India. Phone: +91 (80) 2226-1243. Email: bangalore.spt@air.org.in. Contact: (technical) L.M. Ambhast, Superintending Engineer; T. Rajendran, Station Engineer.

All India Radio—Bhopal, Akashvani Bhawan, Shyamla Hills, Bhopal-462 002, Madhya Pradesh, India. Phone: (engineering) +91 (755) 2661-241. Email: bhopal@air.org.in. Contact: (technical) Sudhir Sodhia, Station Engineer.

All India Radio—Chennai

EXTERNAL SERVICES: see All India Radio—External Services Division.

DOMESTIC SERVICE: Avadi, Chennai-600 002, Tamil Nadu, India. Phone: (engineering) +91 (44) 2638-3204. Email: chennai.avadi@air.org.in.

📻All India Radio—External Services Division

MAIN ADDRESS: Broadcasting House, 1 Sansad Marg, P.O. Box 500, Parliament Street, New Delhi-110 001, India. Phone: (engineering) +91 (11) 2371-5411. Contact: (general) P.P. Setia, Director of External Services; S.C. Panda, Audience Relations Officer; "Faithfully Yours" program. Email (Research Dept.): rdair@giasdl01.vsnl.net.in. Web: (includes on-demand audio and online reception report form) www.allindiaradio.gov.in. Contact: (DX Program, Tamil External Service) Thanka Jaisakthivel, Producer & Presenter. QSL cards for this DX program are available from: Vanoli Ulagam (Radio World), Thiraikadal Adaivaram Thamiizh Naatham, All India Radio, Kamarajar Salai, Chennai-600004, Tamil Nadu, India. Replies can be somewhat erratic from External Services Division.

VERIFICATION ADDRESS: Spectrum Management, All India Radio, Room 204, Akashani Bhavan, New Delhi-110 001, India; or P.O. Box 500, New Delhi-110 001, India. Fax: +91 (11) 2342 1062, +91 (11) 2342 1145. Email: spectrum-manager@air.org. in, or online form (www.allindiaradio.gov.in/recepfdk.html). Contact: Y. K. Sharma, Director, Spectrum Management & Synergy. Audio files accepted.

All India Radio—Gangtok, Old M.L.A. Hostel, Gangtok-737 101, Sikkim, India. Phone: (engineering) +91 (3592) 202-636. Email: gangtok@air.org.in. Contact: (general) Y.P. Yolmo, Station Director; (technical) A.K. Sarkar, Assistant Engineer.

All India Radio—Gorakhpur

NEPALESE EXTERNAL SERVICE: see All India Radio—External Services Division.

DOMESTIC SERVICE: Town Hall, Post Bag 26, Gorakhpur-273 001, Uttar Pradesh, India. Phone/Fax: (engineering) +91 (551) 2337-401. Email: gorakhpur@air.org.in. Contact: (technical) Dr. S.M. Pradhan, Superintending Engineer; P.P. Shukle, Station Engineer.

All India Radio—Guwahati

EXTERNAL SERVICES: see All India Radio—External Services Division.

DOMESTIC SERVICE: P.O. Box 28, Chandmari, Guwahati-781 003, Assam, India. Phone: (engineering) +91 (361) 2660-235. Email: guwahati@air.org.in. Contact: (technical) P.C. Sanghi, Superintending Engineer; H.S. Dhillon, Station Engineer.

All India Radio—Hyderabad, Rocklands, Saifabad, Hyderabad-500 004, Andhra Pradesh, India. Phone: (engineering) +91 (40) 2323-4904. Fax: +91 (40) 2323 2239, +91 (40) 2323 4282. Email: hyderabad@air.org.in. Contact: (technical) S.S. Reddy, Superintending Engineer; P.S. Nagabhushanam, Station Engineer.

All India Radio—Imphal, Palau Road, Imphal-795 001, Manipur, India. Phone: (engineering) +91 (385) 220-534. Email: imphal@air.org.in. Contact: (technical) M. Jayaraman, Superintending Engineer.

All India Radio—Itanagar, Naharlagun, Itanagar-791 111, Arunachal Pradesh, India. Phone: (engineering) +91 (360) 2212-881. Fax: +91 (360) 2213 008, +91 (360) 2212 933. Email: itanagar@air.org.in. Contact: J.T. Jirdoh, Station Director; P.K. Bez Baruah, Assistant Station Engineer; P. Sanghi, Superintending Engineer. Verifications direct from station are difficult, as engineering is done by staff visiting from the Regional Engineering Headquarters at AIR—Guwahati (see); that address might be worth contacting if all else fails.

All India Radio—Jaipur, 5 Park House, Mirza Ismail Road, Jaipur-302 001, Rajasthan, India. Phone: (engineering) +91 (141) 2366-263. Fax: +91 (141) 2363 196. Email: jaipur@air.org.in. Contact: (technical) S.C. Sharma, Station Engineer; C.L. Goel, Assistant Station Engineer.

All India Radio—Jammu—see Radio Kashmir—Jammu.

All India Radio—Jeypore, Jeypore-764 005, Orissa, India. Phone: (engineering) +91 (6854) 232-524. Email: jeypore@air. org.in. Contact: K. Naryan Das, Assistant Station Engineer.

All India Radio—Kohima, P.O. Box 42, Kohima-797 001, Nagaland, India. Phone: (engineering) +91 (370) 2245-556. Email: kohima@air.org.in. Contact: (technical) M. Tyagi, Superintending Engineer; K.K Jose, Assistant Engineer; K. Morang, Assistant Station Engineer. Return postage, $1 or IRC helpful.

All India Radio—Kolkata, G.P.O. Box 696, Kolkata—700 001, West Bengal, India. Phone: (engineering) +91 (33) 2248-1705. Email: kolkata@air.org.in. Contact: (technical) S.K. Pal, Superintending Engineer.

All India Radio—Kurseong, Mehta Club Building, Kurseong-734 203, Darjeeling District, West Bengal, India. Phone: (engineering) +91 (354) 2344-350. Email: kurseong@air.org. in. Contact: (general) George Kuruvilla, Assistant Director; (technical) R.K. Sinha, Chief Engineer; B.K. Behara, Station Engineer.

All India Radio—Lucknow, 18 Vidhan Sabha Marg, Lucknow-226 001, Uttar Pradesh, India. Phone: (engineering) +91 (522) 2237-601. Email: lucknow@air.org.in. Contact: Dr. S.M. Pradhan, Superintending Engineer. This station now appears to be replying via the External Services Division, New Delhi.

All India Radio—Mumbai

EXTERNAL SERVICES: see All India Radio—External Services Division.

COMMERCIAL SERVICE (VIVIDH BHARATI): All India Radio, P.O. Box 19705, 101 M K Road, Mumbai-400 091, Maharashtra, India. Phone: (director) +91 (22) 2869-2698; (engineering) +91 (22) 2868-7351. Email: vbs@vsnl.com. Contact: Vijayalakshmi Sinha, Director; (technical) Superintending Engineer.

DOMESTIC SERVICE: Broadcasting House, Backbay Reclamation, Mumbai-400 020, Maharashtra, India. Phone: (engineering) +91 (22) 2202-9853. Email: mumbai.malad@air.org.in.

All India Radio—New Delhi, Broadcasting House, New Delhi-110 011, India. Phone: (engineering) +91 (11) 2371 0113. Email: delhi.bh@air.org.in. Contact: (technical) V. Chaudhry, Superintending Engineer.

HIGH POWER TRANSMITTERS (250 kW), KHAMPUR: New Delhi-110036, India. Phone: +91 (11) 2720-2158. Email: delhi. khampur@air.org.in.

HIGH POWER TRANSMITTERS (50 & 100 kW), KINGSWAY: New Delhi-110009, India. Phone: +91 (11) 2743-6661. Email: hptkingsway@yahoo.com.

All India Radio—Panaji Shortwave Transmitting Centre

HEADQUARTERS: see All India Radio—External Services Division, above.

HIGH POWER TRANSMITTERS, AIR: Goa University PO, Goa-403206, India. Phone: (engineering) +91 (832) 2230-696. Email: panaji.spt@air.org.in; airtrgoa@sancharnet.in. Contact: (technical) S. Jayaraman, Superintending Engineer.

All India Radio—Port Blair, Haddo Post, Dilanipur, Port Blair-744 102, South Andaman, Andaman and Nicobar Islands, Union Territory, India. Phone: (engineering) +91 (3192) 230-682. Fax: +91 (3192) 230 260. Email: portblair@air.org.in. Contact: V.M. Ratnaprasad, Station Engineer. Registering letters appears to be useful.

All India Radio—Ranchi, 6 Ratu Road, Ranchi-834 001, Jharkhand, India. Phone: (engineering) +91 (651) 2283-310. Email: ranchi@air.org.in. Contact: (technical) H.K. Sinha, Superintending Engineer.

All India Radio—Shillong, P.O. Box 14, Shillong-793 001, Meghalaya, India. Phone: (engineering) +91 (364) 2222-272.

Email: shillong.nes@air.org.in. Contact: (general) C. Lalsaronga, Director NEIS; (technical) R. Venugopal, Superintending Engineer; H. Diengdoh, Station Engineer. Free booklet on station's history. Replies tend to be rare, due to a shortage of staff.

All India Radio—Shimla, Choura Maidan, Shimla-171 004, Himachal Pradesh, India. Phone: (engineering) +91 (177) 2811-355. Email: shimla@air.org.in. Contact: (technical) V.K. Upadhayay, Superintending Engineer; Krishna Murari, Assistant Engineer. Return postage helpful.

All India Radio—Srinagar—*see* Radio Kashmir—Srinagar.

All India Radio—Thiruvananthapuram, P.O. Box 403, Bhakti Vilas, Vazuthacaud, Thiruvananthapuram-695 014, Kerala, India. Phone: (engineering) +91 (471) 2325-009. Fax: +91 (471) 2324 406, +91 (471) 2324 982. Email: thiruvananthapuram@air.org.in. Contact: KV. Ramachandran, Station Engineer.

Radio Kashmir—Jammu, Palace Road, Jammu-188 001, Jammu and Kashmir, India. Phone: (engineering) +91 (191) 2544-411. Email: jammu@air.org.in.

Radio Kashmir—Leh, Leh-194 101, Ladakh District, Jammu and Kashmir, India. Phone: (engineering) +91 (1982) 252-080. Email: leh@air.org.in. Contact: (technical) L.K. Gandotar, Station Engineer; T.S. Sreekumar, Assistant Station Engineer.

Radio Kashmir—Srinagar, Sherwani Road, Srinagar-190 001, Jammu and Kashmir, India. Phone: (engineering) +91 (194) 2452-100/177. Email: srinagar@air.org.in. Contact: G.H. Zia, Station Director; V.P. Singh, Superintending Engineer.

📻**Trans World Radio—India**, L-15 Green Park, New Delhi - 110 016, India. Phone: +91 (11) 2651-5790. Email: info@twr.in; (Devadoss) ddevadoss@in.twrsa.org. Web: (includes on-demand and streaming audio) www.radiovv.org, www.radio882.com. Verifies reception reports by email. Contact: E. Daniel Devadoss; Shakti Verma, Technical Director

INDONESIA   World Time +7 Western: Waktu Indonesia Bagian Barat (Jawa, Sumatera); +8 Central: Waktu Indonesia Bagian Tengal (Bali, Kalimantan, Sulawesi, Nusa Tenggara); +9 Eastern: Waktu Indonesia Bagian Timur (Papua, Maluku)

NOTE: Except where otherwise indicated, Indonesian stations, especially those of the Radio Republik Indonesia (RRI) network, will reply to at least some correspondence in English. However, correspondence in Indonesian is more likely to ensure a reply.

Kang Guru Radio English, Indonesia Australia Language Foundation, P.O. Box 3095, Denpasar 80030, Bali, Indonesia. Phone: +62 (361) 225-243. Fax: +62 (361) 263 509. Email: kangguru@ialf.edu; (Pearson) rpearson@ialf.edu. Web: www.kangguru.org. Contact: Kevin Dalton, Kang Guru Project Manager; Rachel Pearson, ELT Media and Training Specialist; Ms. Ogi Yutarini, Project Coordinating Officer. Free "Kang Guru" magazine. This program is aired over various RRI outlets, including Jakarta and Sorong.

Radio Pemerintah Daerah Kabupaten TK II—RPDK Manggarai, Ruteng, Flores, Nusa Tenggara Timur, Indonesia. Contact: Simon Saleh, B.A. Return postage required.

Radio Pemerintah Daerah Kabupaten Daerah TK II—RSPK Ngada, Jalan Soekarno-Hatta, Bjawa, Flores, Nusa Tenggara Tengah, Indonesia. Phone: +62 (384) 21-142. Contact: Drs. Petrus Tena, Kepala Studio.

Radio Republik Indonesia—RRI Ambon (when operating), Jalan Jendral Akhmad Yani 1, Ambon 97124, Maluku, Indonesia. Phone: +62 (911) 52-740, +62 (911) 53-261, +62 (911) 53-263. Fax: +62 (911) 53 262. Contact: Drs. H. Ali Amran; Pirla C. Noija, Kepala Seksi Siaran. A very poor replier to correspondence in recent years. Correspondence in Indonesian and return postage essential.

Radio Republik Indonesia—RRI Banda Aceh (when operating), Kotak Pos 112, Banda Aceh 23243, Aceh, Indonesia. Phone: +62 (651) 22-116/156. Contact: Parmono Prawira, Technical Director; Ahmad Prambahan, Head; S.H. Rosa Kim. Return postage helpful.

Radio Republik Indonesia—Bandar Lampung, *see* RRI Tanjung Karang listing below.

Radio Republik Indonesia—RRI Bandung (when operating), Stasiun Regional 1, Kotak Pos 1055, Bandung 40122, Jawa Barat, Indonesia. Email: rribandung@yahoo.com. Web: www.kangguru.org/rristationprofiles.htm. Contact: Drs. Idrus Alkaf, Kepala Stasiun; Mrs. Ati Kusmiati; Eem Suhaemi, Kepala Seksi Siaran. Return postage or IRC helpful.

Radio Republik Indonesia—RRI Banjarmasin (when operating), Stasiun Nusantara 111, Kotak Pos 117, Banjarmasin 70234, Kalimantan Selatan, Indonesia. Phone: +62 (511) 268-601, +62 (511) 261-562. Fax: +62 (511) 252 238. Contact: Jul Chaidir, Stasiun Kepala; Harmyn Husein. Free stickers. Return postage or IRCs helpful.

Radio Republik Indonesia—RRI Bengkulu, Stasiun Regional 1, Kotak Pos 13 Kawat, Kotamadya Bengkulu 38227, Indonesia. Phone: +62 (736) 350-811. Fax: +62 (736) 350 927. Contact: Drs. Drs. Jasran Abubakar, Kepala Stasiun. Free picture postcards, decals and tourist literature. Return postage or 2 IRCs helpful.

Radio Republik Indonesia—RRI Biak (when operating), Kotak Pos 505, Biak 98117, Papua, Indonesia. Phone: +62 (981) 21-211, +62 (981) 21-197. Fax: +62 (981) 21 905. Contact: Butje Latuperissa, Kepala Seksi Siaran; Drs. D.A. Siahainenia, Kepala Stasiun. Correspondence in Indonesian preferred.

Radio Republik Indonesia—RRI Bukittinggi (when operating), Stasiun Regional 1 Bukittinggi, Jalan Prof. Muhammad Yamin 199, Aurkuning, Bukittinggi 26131, Propinsi Sumatera Barat, Indonesia. Phone: +62 (752) 21-319, +62 (752) 21-320. Fax: +62 (752) 367 132. Contact: Mr. Effendi, Sekretaris; Zul Arifin Mukhtar, SH; Samirwan Sarjana Hukum, Producer, "Phone in Program." Replies to correspondence in Indonesian or English. Return postage helpful.

Radio Republik Indonesia—RRI Denpasar (when operating), Kotak Pos 3031, Denpasar 80233, Bali, Indonesia. Phone: +62 (361) 222-161, +62 (361) 223-087. Fax: +62 (361) 227 312. Contact: I Gusti Ngurah Oka, Kepala Stasiun. Replies slowly to correspondence in Indonesian. Return postage or IRCs helpful.

Radio Republik Indonesia—RRI Dili (when operating), Stasiun Regional 1 Dili, Jalan Kaikoli, Kotak Pos 103, Dili 88000, Timor-Timur, Indonesia. Contact: Harry A. Silalahi, Kepala Stasiun; Arnoldus Klau; Paul J. Amalo, BA. Return postage or $1 helpful. Replies occasionally to correspondence in Indonesian.

Radio Republik Indonesia—RRI Fak Fak, Jalan Kapten P. Tendean, Kotak Pos 54, Fak-Fak 98612, Papua, Indonesia. Phone: +62 (956) 22-519, +62 (956) 22-521. Contact: Bahrun Siregar, Kepala Stasiun; Aloys Ngotra, Kepala Seksi Siaran; Drs. Tukiran Erlantoko; Richart Tan, Kepala Sub Seksi Siaran Kata. Station plans to upgrade its transmitting facilities with the help of the Japanese government. Return postage required. Replies occasionally.

Radio Republik Indonesia—RRI Gorontalo, Jalan Jendral Sudirman 30, Gorontalo 96115, Sulawesi Utara, Indonesia. Fax: +62 (435) 821 590/91. Contact: Drs. Bagus Edi Asmoro; Drs. Muhammad. Assad, Kepala Stasiun; Saleh S. Thalib, Technical

Manager. Return postage helpful. Replies occasionally, preferably to correspondence in Indonesian.

⧉Radio Republik Indonesia—RRI Jakarta

STATION: Stasiun Nasional Jakarta, Kotak Pos 356, Jakarta 10110, Daerah Khusus Jakarta Raya, Indonesia; or (street address) Jalan Medan Merdeka Barat 4-5, Jakarta 10110, Indonesia. Phone: +62 (21) 345-9091, +62 (21) 384-6817. Fax: +62 (21) 345 7132, +62 (21) 345 7134. Email: rri@rri-online. com. Web: (includes on-demand audio) www.rri-online.com. Contact: Drs. Beni Koesbani, Kepala Stasiun; Drs. Nuryudi, MM. Return postage helpful. Replies irregularly.

"DATELINE" ENGLISH PROGRAM: see Kang Guru Radio English.

TRANSMITTERS DIVISION: Jalan Merdeka Barat 4-5, Jakarta 10110 Indonesia. Phone/Fax: +62 (21) 385-7831. Email: sruslan@yahoo.com, sruslan@msn.com. Contact: Sunarya Ruslan, Head of Transmitters Division.

Radio Republik Indonesia—RRI Jambi (when operating), Jalan Jendral A. Yani 5, Telanaipura, Jambi 36122, Propinsi Jambi, Indonesia. Contact: Kepala Siaran; H. Asmuni Lubis, BA. Return postage helpful.

Radio Republik Indonesia—RRI Jayapura, Kotak Pos 1077, Jayapura 99200, Papua, Indonesia. Phone: +62 (967) 33-339. Fax: +62 (967) 33 439. Contact: Harry Liborang, Direktorat Radio; Hartono, Bidang Teknik; Dr. David Alex Siahainenia, Kepala. Return postage of $1 helpful. Replies to correspondence in Indonesian or English.

Radio Republik Indonesia—RRI Kendari, Kotak Pos 7, Kendari 93111, Sulawesi Tenggara, Indonesia. Phone: +62 (401) 21-464. Fax: +62 (401) 21 730. Contact: Drs. M. Hazir Kasrah, Manajer Seksi Siaran. Return postage required. Replies slowly to correspondence in Indonesian.

Radio Republik Indonesia—RRI Kupang (Regional I) (when operating), Jalan Tompello 8, Kupang 85225, Timor, Indonesia. Phone: +62 (380) 821-437, +62 (380) 825-444. Fax: +62 (380) 833 149. Contact: Drs. P.M. Tisera, Kepala Stasiun; Qustigap Bagang, Kepala Seksi Siaran; Said Rasyid, Kepala Studio. Return postage helpful. Correspondence in Indonesian preferred. Replies occasionally.

Radio Republik Indonesia—RRI Madiun (when operating), Jalan Mayjend Panjaitan 10, Madiun 63133, Jawa Timur, Indonesia. Phone: +62 (351) 464-419, +62 (351) 459-198, +62 (351) 462-726, +62 (351) 459-495. Fax: +62 (351) 464 964. Web: www.kangguru.org/rristationprofiles.htm. Contact: Sri Lestari, SS; Imam Soeprapto, Kepala Seksi Siaran. Replies to correspondence in Indonesian or English. Return postage helpful.

Radio Republik Indonesia—RRI Makassar, Jalan Riburane 3, Makassar, 90111, Sulawesi Selatan, Indonesia. Phone: +62 (411) 321-853. Contact: H. La Sirama, S. Sos., Senior Manager of Broadcasting Division. Replies irregularly to correspondence in Indonesian or English. Return postage, $1 or IRCs helpful.

Radio Republik Indonesia—RRI Malang (when operating), Kotak Pos 78, Malang 65140, Jawa Timur, Indonesia; or (street address) Jalan Candi Panggung No. 58, Mojolangu, Malang 65142, Indonesia. Email: makobu@mlg.globalxtrem. net. Contact: Drs.Tjutju Tjuar Na Adikorya, Kepala Stasiun; Ml. Mawahib, Kepala Seksi Siaran; Dra Hartati Soekemi, Mengetahui. Return postage required. Free history and other booklets. Replies irregularly to correspondence in Indonesian.

Radio Republik Indonesia—RRI Manado (when operating), Kotak Pos 1110, Manado 95124 Propinsi Sulawesi Utara, Indonesia. Phone: +62 (431) 863-392. Fax: +62 (431) 863 492. Contact: Costher H. Gulton, Kepala Stasiun; Untung Santoso, Kepala Seksi Teknik. Free stickers and postcards. Return post-

age or $1 required. Replies occasionally to correspondence in Indonesian.

Radio Republik Indonesia—RRI Manokwari (when operating), Regional II, Jalan Merdeka 68, Manokwari 98311, Papua, Indonesia. Phone: +62 (962) 21-343. Contact: Eddy Kusbandi, Manager; Nurdin Mokogintu. Return postage helpful.

Radio Republik Indonesia—RRI Mataram (when operating), Stasiun Regional I Mataram, Jalan Langko 83 Ampenan, Mataram 83114, Nusa Tenggara Barat, Indonesia. Phone: +62 (370) 23-713, +62 (370) 21-355. Contact: Drs. Hamid Djasman, Kepala; Bochri Rachman, Ketua Dewan Pimpinan Harian. Free stickers. Return postage required. With sufficient return postage or small token gift, sometimes sends tourist information and Batik print. Replies to correspondence in Indonesian.

Radio Republik Indonesia—RRI Medan (when operating), Jalan Letkol Martinus Lubis 5, Medan 20232, Sumatera, Indonesia. Phone: +62 (61) 324-222/441. Fax: +62 (61) 512 161. Contact: Kepala Stasiun, Ujamalul Abidin Ass; Drs. S. Parlin Tobing, SH, Produsennya, "Kontak Pendengar"; Drs. H. Suryanta Saleh. Free stickers. Return postage required. Replies to correspondence in Indonesian.

Radio Republik Indonesia—RRI Merauke, Stasiun Regional 1, Kotak Pos 11, Merauke 99611, Papua, Indonesia. Phone: +62 (971) 21-396, +62 (971) 21-376. Contact: (general) Drs. Buang Akhir, Direktor; Achmad Ruskaya B.A., Kepala Stasiun, Drs.Tuanakotta Semuel, Kepala Seksi Siaran; John Manuputty, Kepala Subseksi Pemancar; (technical) Daf'an Kubangun, Kepala Seksi Tehnik. Return postage helpful.

Radio Republik Indonesia—RRI Nabire (when operating), Kotak Pos 110, Jalan Merdeka 74 Nabire 98811, Papua, Indonesia. Phone: +62 (984) 21-013. Contact: Muchtar Yushaputra, Kepala Stasiun. Free stickers and occasional free picture postcards. Return postage or IRCs helpful.

Radio Republik Indonesia—RRI Padang, Kotak Pos 77, Padang 25111, Sumatera Barat, Indonesia. Phone: +61 (751) 28-363, +62 (751) 21-030, +62 (751) 27-482. Contact: H. Hutabarat, Kepala Stasiun; Amir Hasan, Kepala Seksi Siaran. Return postage helpful.

Radio Republik Indonesia—RRI Palangkaraya (when operating), Jalan M. Husni Thamrin 1, Palangkaraya 73111, Kalimantan Tengah, Indonesia. Phone: +62 (536) 21-779. Fax: +62 (536) 21 778. Contact: Andy Sunandar; Drs.Amiruddin; S. Polin; A.F. Herry Purwanto; Meyiwati SH; Supardal Djojosubrojo, Sarjana Hukum; Dr. S. Parlin Tobing, Station Manager; Murniaty Oesin, Transmission Department Engineer; Gumer Kamis; Ricky D. Wader, Kepala Stasiun. Return postage helpful. Will respond to correspondence in Indonesian or English.

Radio Republik Indonesia—RRI Palembang (when operating), Jalan Radio 2, Km. 4, Palembang 30128, Sumatera Selatan, Indonesia. Phone: +62 (711) 350-811, +62 (711) 309-977, +62 (711) 350-927. Contact: Drs. H. Mursjid Noor, Kepala Stasiun; H.Ahmad Syukri Ahkab, Kepala Seksi Siaran; H.Iskandar Suradilaga. Return postage helpful. Replies slowly and occasionally.

Radio Republik Indonesia—RRI Palu, Jalan R.A. Kartini 39, Palu 94112, Sulawesi Tengah, Indonesia. Phone: +62 (451) 21-621, +62 (451) 94-112. Contact: Akson Boole; Nyonyah Netty Ch. Soriton, Kepala Seksi Siaran; Gugun Santoso; Untung Santoso, Kepala Seksi Teknik; M. Hasjim, Head of Programming. Return postage required. Replies slowly to correspondence in Indonesian.

Radio Republik Indonesia—RRI Pekanbaru (when operating), Kotak Pos 51, Pekanbaru 28113, Kepulauan Riau, Indonesia. Phone: +62 (761) 22-081, +62 (761) 23-606, +62 (761)

Susilo Bambang Yudhoyono, former general and president of Indonesia, reviews his guard at the Presidential Merdeka Palace.

Shutterstock/Shamshahrin Shamsudin

25-111. Fax: +62 (761) 23 605. Contact: (general) Hendri Yunis, ST, Kepala Stasiun, Ketua DPH; Arisun Agus, Kepala Seksi Siaran; Drs. H. Syamsidi, Kepala Supag Tata Usaha; Zainal Abbas. Return postage helpful.

Radio Republik Indonesia—RRI Pontianak, Kotak Pos 1005, Pontianak 78117, Kalimantan Barat, Indonesia. Phone: +62 (561) 734-987. Fax: +62 (561) 734 659. Contact: Ruddy Banding, Kepala Seksi Siaran; Achmad Ruskaya, BA; Drs. Effendi Afati, Producer, "Dalam Acara Kantong Surat"; Subagio, Kepala Sub Bagian Tata Usaha; Augustwus Campek; Rahayu Widati; Suryadharma, Kepala Sub Seksi Programa; Muchlis Marzuki B.A. Return postage or $1 helpful. Replies some of the time to correspondence in Indonesian (preferred) or English.

Radio Republik Indonesia—RRI Samarinda, Kotak Pos 45, Samarinda, Kalimantan Timur 75110, Indonesia. Phone: +62 (541) 743-495. Fax: +62 (541) 741 693. Contact: Siti Thomah, Kepala Seksi Siaran; Tyranus Lenjau, English Announcer; S. Yati; Marthin Tapparan; Sunendra, Kepala Stasiun. May send tourist brochures and maps. Return postage helpful. Replies to correspondence in Indonesian.

Radio Republik Indonesia—RRI Semarang (when operating), Kotak Pos 1073, Semarang 50241, Jawa Tengah, Indonesia. Phone: +62 (24) 831-6686, +62 (24) 831-6661, +62 (24) 831-6330. (Phone/Fax, marketing) +62 (24) 831-6330. Web: www.kangguru.org/rristationprofiles.htm. Contact: Djarwanto, SH; Drs. Sabeni, Doktorandus; Drs. Purwadi, Program Director; Dra. Endang Widiastuti, Kepala Sub Seksi Periklanan Jasa dan Hak Cipta; H. Sutakno, Kepala Stasiun; Mardanon, Kepala Teknik. Return postage helpful.

Radio Republik Indonesia—RRI Serui, Jalan Pattimura Kotak Pos 19, Serui 98213, Papua, Indonesia. Phone: +62 (983) 31-150, +62 (983) 31-121. Contact: M. Yawandare, Manager Siaran. Replies occasionally to correspondence in Indonesian, although Mr. Yawandare also understands English. IRC or return postage helpful.

Radio Republik Indonesia—RRI Sibolga (when operating), Jalan Ade Irma Suryani, Nasution No. 11, Sibolga 22513, Sumatera Utara, Indonesia. Phone: +61 (631) 21-183, +62 (631) 22-506, +62 (631) 22-947. Contact: Mrs. Laiya; Mrs. S. Sitoupul; B.A. Tanjung. Return postage required. Replies occasionally to correspondence in Indonesian.

Radio Republik Indonesia—RRI Sorong
STATION: Kotak Pos 146, Sorong 98414, Papua, Indonesia. Phone: +62 (951) 21-003, +62 (951) 22-111, +62 (951) 22-611. Contact: Drs. Sallomo Hamid; Tetty Rumbay S., Kasubsi Siaran Kata; Mrs. Tien Widarsanto, Resa Kasi Siaran; Ressa Molle; Mughpar Yushaputra, Kepala Stasiun; Umar Solle, Station Manager; Linda Rumbay. Return postage helpful. Replies to correspondence in English.
"DATELINE" ENGLISH PROGRAM: See Kang Guru Radio English.

Radio Republik Indonesia—RRI Sumenep (when operating), Jalan Urip Sumoharjo 26, Sumenep 69411, Madura, Jawa Timur, Indonesia. Phone: +62 (328) 62-317, +62 (328) 21-811, +62 (328) 21-317, +62 (328) 66-768. Contact: Dian Irianto, Kepala Stasiun. Return postage helpful.

Radio Republik Indonesia—RRI Surabaya, (when operating) Stasiun Regional 1, Kotak Pos 239, Surabaya 60271, Jawa Timur, Indonesia. Phone: +62 (31) 534-1327, +62 (31) 534-2327, +62 (31) 534-1327, +62 (31) 534-5474, +62 (31) 534-0478, +62 (31) 547-3610. Fax: +62 (31) 534 2351. Contact: Zainal Abbas, Kepala Stasiun; Usmany Johozua, Kepala Seksi Siaran; Drs. E. Agus Widjaja, MM, Kasi Siaran; Pardjingat, Kepala Seksi Teknik; Ny Koen Tarjadi. Return postage or IRCs helpful.

Radio Republik Indonesia—RRI Surakarta (when operating), Kotak Pos 40, Surakarta 57133, Jawa Tengah, Indonesia. Phone: +62 (271) 634-004/05, +62 (271) 638-145, +62 (271) 654-399, +62 (271) 641-178. Fax: +62 (271) 642 208. Contact: H. Tomo, B.A., Head of Broadcasting; Titiek Sudartik, S.H., Kepala. Return postage helpful.

Radio Republik Indonesia—RRI Tanjungkarang, Kotak Pos 24, Bandar Lampung 35213, Indonesia. Phone: +62 (721) 555-2280, +62 (721) 569-720. Fax: +62 (721) 562 767. Contact: M. Nasir Agun, Kepala Stasiun; Hi Hanafie Umar; Djarot Nursinggih, Tech. Transmission; Drs. Doewadji, Kepala Seksi Siaran; Drs. Zulhaqqi Hafiz, Kepala Sub Seksi Periklanan; Asmara Haidar Manaf. Return postage helpful. Also identifies as RRI Bandar Lampung. Replies in Indonesian to correspondence in Indonesian or English.

Radio Republik Indonesia—RRI Tanjungpinang, Stasiun RRI Regional II Tanjungpinang, Kotak Pos 8, Tanjungpinang 29123, Kepulauan Riau, Indonesia. Phone: +62 (771) 21-278, +62 (771) 21-540, +62 (771) 21-916, +62 (771) 29-123. Contact: M. Yazid, Kepala Stasiun; Wan Suhardi, Produsennya, "Siaran Bahasa Melayu"; Rosakim, Sarjana Hukum. Return postage helpful. Replies occasionally to correspondence in Indonesian or English.

Radio Republik Indonesia—RRI Ternate (when operating), Jalan Sultan Khairun, Kedaton, Ternate 97720 (Ternate), Maluku Utara, Indonesia. Phone: +62 (921) 21-582, +62 (921) 21-762, +62 (921) 25-525. Contact: (general) Abd. Latief Kamarudin, Kepala Stasiun; (technical) Rusdy Bachmid, Head of Engineering; Abubakar Alhadar. Return postage helpful.

Radio Republik Indonesia Tual (when operating), Watden, Pulau Kai, Tual 97661 Maluku, Indonesia.

Radio Republik Indonesia—RRI Wamena (when operating), RRI Regional II, Kotak Pos 10, Wamena, Papua 99511, Indonesia. Phone: +62 (969) 31-380. Fax: +62 (969) 31 299. Contact: Yoswa Kumurawak, Penjab Subseksi Pemancar. Return postage helpful.

Radio Republik Indonesia—RRI Yogyakarta (when operating), Jalan Amat Jazuli 4, Kotak Pos 18, Yogyakarta 55224, Jawa Tengah, Indonesia. Fax: +62 (274) 2784. Phone: +62 (274) 512-783/85, +62 (274) 580-333. Email: rri-yk@yogya.wasantara.

net.id. Contact: Phoenix Sudomo Sudaryo; Tris Mulyanti, Seksi Programa Siaran; Martono, ub. Kabid Penyelenggaraan Siaran; Mr. Kadis, Technical Department; Drs. H. Hamdan Sjahbeni, Kepala Stasiun. IRC, return postage or $1 helpful. Replies occasionally to correspondence in Indonesian or English.

Radio Siaran Pemerintah Daerah TK II—RSPD Halmahera Tengah, Soasio, Jalan A. Malawat, Soasio, Maluku Tengah 97812, Indonesia. Contact: Drs. S. Chalid A. Latif, Kepala Badan Pengelola.

Voice of Indonesia, Kotak Pos 1157, Jakarta 10001, Daerah Khusus Jakarta Raya, Indonesia; (street address) Jalan Medan Merdeka Barat No. 4-5, Jakarta 10110 Indonesia. Phone: +62 (21) 345-6811. Fax: +62 (21) 350 0990. Email: voi@rri-online.com. Web: www.rri-online.com. Contact: Anastasia Yasmine, Head of Foreign Affairs Section; Amy Aisha, Presenter, "Listeners Mailbag." Free stickers and calendars. Correspondence is best addressed to the individual language sections. Be careful when addressing your letters to the station as mail sent to the Voice of Indonesia, Japanese Section, has sometimes been incorrectly delivered to NHK's Jakarta Bureau. Very slow in replying but enclosing 4 IRCs may help speed things up.

INTERNATIONAL WATERS

Coalition Maritime Forces (CMF) Radio One, MARLO Bahrain, PSC 451 Box 330, FPO AE 09834-2800, USA. Email: (including reception reports) marlo.bahrain@marlobahrain.org. Web: (MARLO Bahrain parent organization) www.marlobahrain.org. Station of the Maritime Liaison Office (MARLO) of the United States Navy. Broadcasts via low power transmitters on ships in the Persian Gulf and nearby waters. Verifies reception reports.

IRAN   World Time +3:30

NOTE: Although Iran previously used Daylight Saving Time in summer for more than a decade, the Iranian goverment decided in March 2006 to keep the clocks on Iranian Standard Time the whole year.

◙Voice of the Islamic Republic of Iran

MAIN OFFICE: IRIB External Services, P.O. Box 19395-6767, Tehran, Iran. Phone: +98 (21) 204-2808; (English Service) +98 (21) 201-3720, +98 (21) 216-2895, +98 (21) 216-2734. Fax: +98 (21) 205 1635, +98 (21) 204 1097, + 98 (21) 291 095; (English Service) +98 (21) 201 3770; (technical) +98 (21) 654 841. Email: (all technical matters other than reception reports) sw@irib.ir, tech@irib.ir; (English Service) englishradio@irib.ir (same format for German and Spanish, e.g. spanishradio@irib.ir); (French Service) radio_fr@irib.ir. Web: (includes streaming audio) www.irib.ir/worldservice. Contact: Mohammad B. Khoshnevisan, IRIB English Radio. Free books on Islam, magazines, calendars, bookmarkers, tourist literature and postcards. Verifications require a minimum of two days' reception data on two or more separate broadcasts, plus return postage. Is currently asking listeners to send their telephone numbers so that they can be called by the station. You can send your phone number to the postal address above, or fax it to: + 98 (21) 1635.

SIRJAN TRANSMITTING STATION: P.O. Box 369, Sirjan, Iran. Contact: Aliasghar Shakoori Moghaddam, Head of Sirjan Station.

Mashhad Regional Radio, P.O. Box 555, Mashhad Center, Jomhoriye Eslame, Iran. Contact: J. Ghanbari, General Director.

IRAQ   World Time +3 (+4 midyear)

◙Voice of Iraqi Kurdistan ("Aira dangi Kurdestana Iraqiyah"). Web: (includes streaming audio) http://kdp.nu (click on "KDP's Media," then on "KDP info"). Station of the Kurdistan Democratic Party-Iraq (KDP), led by Masoud Barzani. Broadcasts from its own transmitting facilities, located in the Kurdish section of Iraq. To contact the station or to obtain verification of reception reports, try going via one of the following KDP offices:

KDP INTERNATIONAL RELATIONS BUREAU (U.K.): Phone: +44 (207) 498-2664. Fax: +44 (207) 498 2531. Email: kdpinternational@yahoo.com.

KDP REPRESENTATION IN WASHINGTON: 17115 Leesburg Pike #110, Falls Church VA 22043 USA. Phone: +1 (703) 533-5882. Fax: +1 (703) 599 5886. Email: pdk7usa@aol.com.

KDP-SWEDEN OFFICE: Email: party@kdp.se. Web: (includes streaming audio) www.kdp.se. Contact: Alex Atroushi. Reception reports to this address have sometimes been verified by email.

ISRAEL   World Time +2 (+3 midyear)

Bezeq—Israel Telecommunication Corp. Ltd., Engineering and Planning Division, Radio and T.V. Broadcasting Section, P.O. Box 62081, Tel-Aviv 61620, Israel. Phone: +972 (3) 626-4562, +972 (3) 626-4500. Fax: +972 (3) 626 4559. Email: (Oren) mosheor@bezeq.com; or rms2@bezeqint.net. Web: www.bezeq.co.il. Contact: Moshe Oren, Frequency Manager. Bezeq is responsible for transmitting the programs of the Israel Broadcasting Authority (IBA), which *inter alia* parents Kol Israel. This address only for pointing out transmitter-related problems (interference, modulation quality, network mixups, etc.), especially by fax, of transmitters based in Israel. Does not verify reception reports.

◙Galei Zahal (Israel Defence Forces Radio), Zahal, Military Mail No. 01005, Israel. Phone: +972 (3) 512-6666. Fax: +972 (3) 512 6760. Email: glz@galatz.co.il. Web: (includes on-demand and streaming audio) www.glz.msn.co.il.

◙Kol Israel (Israel Radio International), P.O. Box 1082, Jerusalem 91010, Israel. Phone: (general) +972 (2) 530-2222; (Engineering Dept.) +972 (2) 501-3453; (Hebrew voice mail for Reshet Bet program "The Israel Connection") +972 (3) 765-1929. Fax: (English Service) +972 (2) 530 2424. Email: (general) ask@israel-info.gov.il; (English Service) englishradio@iba.org.il; (correspondence relating to reception problems, only) engineering@israelradio.org; (Reshet Bet program for Israelis abroad) kesherisraeli@yahoo.com. Web: (includes on-demand and streaming audio) www.israelradio.org; (on-demand and streaming audio) www.iba.org.il. Contact: Edmond Sehayeq, Head of Programming, Arabic, Persian and Yemenite broadcasts; Yishai Eldar, Reporter, English News Department; Steve Linde, Head of English News Department; Sara Gabbai, Head of Western Broadcasting Department; (administration) Yonni Ben-Menachem, Director of External Broadcasting; (technical, frequency management) Raphael Kochanowski, Director of Liaison and Coordination, Engineering Dept. No verifications or freebies, due to limited budget.

SAN FRANCISCO OFFICE, SCHEDULES: 2654 17th Avenue, San Francisco CA 94116 USA. Phone: +1 (415) 564-9968. Email: GPoppin@aol.com. Contact: George Poppin. This address, a volunteer office, only provides Kol Israel schedules to listeners (return postage not required). All other correspondence should be sent directly to the main office in Jerusalem.

ITALY   World Time +1 (+2 midyear)

▣**Italian Radio Relay Service**, IRRS-Shortwave, Nexus-IBA, P.O. Box 11028, 20110 Milano, Italy; (reception reports) P.O. Box 10980, 20110 Milano, Italy. Phone: +39 (02) 266-6971. Fax: +39 (02) 7063 8151. Email: (general) info@nexus.org; (reception reports) reports@nexus.org; (Cotroneo) alfredo@nexus.org; (Norton) ron@nexus.org. Web: www.nexus.org/radio.htm; (streaming audio) http://mp3.nexus.org; (International Public Access Radio) www.nexus.org/IPAR; (European Gospel Radio) www.egradio.org. Contact: (general) Vanessa Dickinson; Anna S. Boschetti, President; Alfredo E. Cotroneo, CEO; (technical) Ron Norton, Verification Manager. Correspondence and reception reports by email are answered promptly and at no charge, but for budget reasons the station may be unable to reply to all postal correspondence. Two IRCs or $1 helpful.

▣**Radio Roma-RAI International** (external service)
MAIN OFFICE: (street address) External Service, Centro RAI, Saxa Rubra, 00188 Rome, Italy; (postal address, including reception reports) P.O. Box 320, Correspondence Sector, 00100 Rome, Italy. Phone: +39 (06) 33-17-2360. Fax: +39 (06) 33 17 18 95, +39 (06) 322 6070. Email: ondacorta@rai.it, raiinternational@rai.it, or online form. Web: (includes online reception report form and on-demand and streaming audio) www.raiinternational.rai.it/radio. Contact: (general) Rosaria Vassallo, Correspondence Sector; Augusto Milana, Editor-in-Chief, Shortwave Programs in Foreign Languages; Esther Casas, Servicio Español; (administration) Angela Buttiglione, Managing Director; Gabriella Tambroni, Assistant Director. Free stickers, banners, calendars and *RAI Calling from Rome* magazine. Can provide supplementary materials, including on VHS and CD-ROM, for Italian-language video course, "Viva l' italiano," with an audio equivalent soon to be offered, as well. Is constructing "a new, more powerful and sophisticated shortwave transmitting center" in Tuscany; when this is activated, RAI International plans to expand news, cultural items and music in Italian and various other language services—including Spanish & Portuguese, plus new services in Chinese and Japanese. Responses can be very slow. Pictures of RAI's Shortwave Center at Prato Smeraldo can be found at www.mediasuk.org/archive.
SHORTWAVE FREQUENCY MONITORING OFFICE: RaiWay Monitoring Centre, Centro di Controllo, Via Mirabellino 1, 20052 Monza (MI), Italy. Phone: +39 (039) 388-389. Fax: +39 (02) 3199 6245, +39 (039) 386-222. Email: raiway.hfmonitoring@rai.it,

cqmonza@rai.it. Contact: Mrs. Lucia Luisa La Franceschina; Mario Ballabio.
ENGINEERING OFFICE, ROME: Via Teulada 66, 00195 Rome, Italy. Phone: +39 (06) 331-70721. Fax: +39 (06) 331 75142, +39 (06) 372 3376. Email: isola@rai.it. Contact: Clara Isola.
ENGINEERING OFFICE, TURIN: Via Cernaia 33, 10121 Turin, Italy. Phone: +39 (011) 810-2293. Fax: +39 (011) 575 9610. Email: allamano@rai.it. Contact: Giuseppe Allamano, HF Frequency Planning.
NEW YORK OFFICE, NONTECHNICAL: 1350 Avenue of the Americas—21st floor, New York NY 10019 USA. Phone: +1 (212) 468-2500. Fax: +1 (212) 765 1956. Contact: Umberto Bonetti, Deputy Director of Radio Division. RAI caps, aprons and tote bags for sale at Boutique RAI, c/o the aforementioned New York address.
SAN FRANCISCO OFFICE, SCHEDULES: 2654 17th Avenue, San Francisco CA 94116 USA. Phone: +1 (415) 564-9968. Email: GPoppin@aol.com. Contact: George Poppin. This address, a volunteer office, only provides RAI schedules to listeners (return postage not required). All other correspondence should be sent directly to the main office in Rome.
RTV Italiana-RAI (domestic service), Centro RAI, Saxa Rubra, 00188 Rome, Italy. Fax: +39 (06) 322 6070. Email: grr@rai.it. Web: www.rai.it.

JAPAN   World Time +9

▣**Radio Japan/NHK World**
MAIN OFFICE: NHK World, Nippon Hoso Kyokai, Tokyo 150-8001, Japan. Phone: +81 (3) 3465-1111. Fax: (general) +81 (3) 3481 1350; (" from Tokyo" and Production Center) +81 (3) 3465 0966. Email: (general) nhkworld@nhk.jp; ("World Interactive" program) interactive@nhk.jp; (Spanish Section) rj-espa@intl.nhk.or.jp. Web: (English, includes on-demand and streaming audio) www.nhk.or.jp/english; (Japanese, includes on-demand and streaming audio) www.nhk.or.jp/nhkworld. Contact: (administration) Saburo Eguchi, Deputy Director General; Shuichiro Sunohara, Deputy Director International Planning & Programming; Tadao Sakomizu, Director, English Service; Ms. Kyoko Hirotani, Planning & Programming Division.
ENGINEERING ADMINISTRATION DEPARTMENT: Nippon Hoso Kyokai, Tokyo 150-8001, Japan. Phone: +81 (3) 5455-5395, +81 (3) 5455-5384, +81 (3) 5455-5376, +81 (3) 5455-2288. Fax: +81 (3) 3485 0952, + 81 (3) 3481 4985. Email: (general) rj-freq@eng.nhk.or.jp; yoshimi@eng.nhk.or.jp, kurasima@eng.nhk.or.jp. Contact: Fujimoto Hiroki, Frequency Manager; Akira Mizuguchi, Transmissions Manager; Tetsuya Itsuk; Toshiki Kurashima.
MONITORING DIVISION: NHK World/Radio Japan. Fax: +81 (3) 3481 1877. Email: info@intl.nhk.or.jp.
HONG KONG BUREAU: Phone: +852 2509-0238.
EUROPEAN (LONDON) BUREAU: Phone: +44 (20) 7393-8100.
LOS ANGELES OFFICE: Phone: +1 (310) 586-1600.
USA (NEW YORK) BUREAU: Phone: +1 (212) 704-9898.
▣**Radio Nikkei**, Nikkei Radio Broadcasting Corporation, 9-15 Akasaka 1-chome, Minato-ku, Tokyo 107-8373, Japan. Fax: +81 (3) 3583 9062. Web: (includes on-demand and streaming audio) www.radionikkei.jp. Contact: H. Nagao, Public Relations; M. Teshima; Ms. Terumi Onoda; H. Ono. Sending a reception report may help with a reply. Free stickers and Japanese stamps. $1 or 2 IRCs helpful.
Shiokaze (Sea Breeze), 3-8-401 Koraku 2-chome, Bunkyo-ku, Tokyo 112-0004, Japan. Email: chosakai@circus.ocn.ne.jp. Web: www.chosa-kai.jp. Broadcast of the Investigation Com-

Boy Scouts continue to be held in high esteem in South Korea, where scouting norms dovetail with Korean cultural values. M. Guha

mission on Missing Japanese Probably Related to North Korea (COMJAM). Via Taiwan. Verifies reception reports, including those sent by email.

JORDAN World Time +2 (+3 midyear)

📻Radio Jordan, P.O. Box 909, Amman, Jordan; or P.O. Box 1041, Amman, Jordan. Phone: (general) +962 (6) 477-4111; (International Relations) +962 (6) 477-8578; (English Service) +962 (6) 475-7410, +962 (6) 477-3111; (Arabic Service) +962 (6) 463-6454; (Saleh) +962 (6) 474-8048; (Al-Arini) +962 (6) 474-9161. Fax: (general) +962 (6) 478 8115; (English Service) +962 (6) 420 7862; (Al-Arini) +962 (6) 474 9190. Email: (general) general@jrtv.gov.jo, or online form; (programs) rj@jrtv.gov.jo; (schedule) feedback@jrtv.gov.jo; (technical) eng@jrtv.gov.jo; (Director of Radio TV Engineering) arini@jrtv.gov.jo. Web: (includes streaming audio) www.jrtv.jo/rj. Contact: (general) Jawad Zada, Director of Foreign Service; Mrs. Firyal Zamakhshari, Director of Arabic Programs; Qasral Mushatta; (administrative) Abdul Hamid Al Majali, Director of Radio; Mrs. Fatima Massri, Director of International Relations; Muwaffaq al-Rahayifah, Director of Shortwave Services; (technical) Youssef Al-Arini, Director of Radio TV Engineering. Free stickers. Replies irregularly and slowly. Enclosing $1 helps.

KENYA World Time

Kenya Broadcasting Corporation, P.O. Box 30456, Harry Thuku Road, 00100 Nairobi, Kenya. Phone: +254 (20) 334-567. Fax: +254 (20) 220 675. Email: (general) kbc@swiftkenya.com; (management) mdkbc@swiftkenya.com; (technical services) kbctechnical@swiftkenya.com. Web: www.kbc.co.ke. Contact: (general) Henry Makokha, Liaison Office; (administration) Joe Matano Khamisi, Managing Director; (technical) Nathan Lamu, Senior Principal Technical Officer; Augustine Kenyanjier Gochui; Lawrence Holnati, Engineering Division; Daniel Githua, Assistant Manager Technical Services (Radio). IRC required. Replies irregularly. If all you want is verfication of your reception report(s), you may have better luck sending your letter to: Engineer in Charge, Maralal Radio Station, P.O. Box 38, Maralal, Kenya.

KOREA (DPR) World Time +9

Korean Central Broadcasting Station, Chongsung-dong, Moranbong District, Pyongyang, Democratic People's Republic of Korea. If you don't speak Korean, try sending your correspondence via the Voice of Korea (see).

Regional KCBS stations—Not known to reply, but a long-shot possibility is to try corresponding in Korean to the Pyongyang address, above.

Pyongyang Broadcasting Station—Correspondence should be sent to the Voice of Korea (see next item), which sometimes verifies reception reports on PBS broadcasts.

Voice of Korea, External Service, Radio-Television Broadcasting Committee of the DPRK, Pyongyang, Democratic People's Republic of Korea (not "North Korea"). Phone: +850 (2) 381-6035. Fax: +850 (2) 381 4416. Phone and fax numbers valid only in those countries with direct telephone service to North Korea. Free publications, pennants, calendars, newspapers, artistic prints and pins. Do not include dutiable items in your envelope. Replies are irregular, as mail from countries not having diplomatic relations with North Korea is sent via circuitous routes and apparently does not always arrive. One way around the problem is to add "VIA BEIJING, CHINA" to the address, but replies via this route tend to be slow in coming. An alternative route is to send your letters via the English Section of China Radio International. Place your correspondence in a separate envelope addressed to the Voice of Korea, and ask CRI to forward your letter to Pyongyang. Explain the mail situation to the folks in Beijing and you may have success. Another gambit is to send your correspondence to an associate in a country—such as China, Ukraine or India—having reasonable relations with North Korea, and ask that it be forwarded. Send correspondence in a sealed envelope without any address on the back. That should be sent inside another envelope. Include 3 IRCs to cover the cost of forwarding.

KOREA (REPUBLIC) World Time +9

📻KBS World Radio

MAIN OFFICE, INTERNATIONAL BROADCASTING DEPARTMENT: KBS World Radio, Global Center, Korean Broadcasting

System, Yoido-dong 18, Youngdeungpo-gu, Seoul, Republic of Korea 150-790. Phone: (general) +82 (2) 781-3650/60/70; (English Section) +82 (2) 781-3674/5/6; (Korean Section) +82 (2) 781-3669/71/72/73; (German Section) +82 (2) 781-3682/3/9; (Japanese Section) +82 (2) 781-3654/5/6 (Spanish Section) +82 (2) 781-3679/81/97. Fax: (general) +82 (2) 781 3694/5/6. Email: (English) english@kbs.co.kr; (German) german@kbs.co.kr; (Japanese) japanese@kbs.co.kr; (Spanish) spanish@kbs.co.kr; (other language sections use the same format, except for Vietnamese: vietnam@kbs.co.kr); (Executive Director) hheejoo@kbs.co.kr. Web: (includes streaming audio) http://world.kbs.co.kr. Contact: Ms. Hee Joo Han, Executive Director, KBS World-External Radio & TV; Park Young-seok, Chief; (administration) Sang Myung Kim; (English Section) Chae Hong-Pyo, Manager; Ms. Seung Joo ("Sophia") Hong, Producer; Mr. Chun Hye-Jin, DX Editor, *Seoul Calling*; (Korean Section) Hae Ok Lee, Producer; (Japanese Section) Ms. Hye Young Kim, Producer; (Spanish Section) Ms. Sujin Cho, Producer; (German Section) Chung Soon Wan, Manager; Lee Bum Suk, Producer; Sabastian Ratzer, Journalist. Free stickers, calendars, *Let's Learn Korean* book and a wide variety of other small souvenirs. *History of Korea* is available on CD-ROM (upon request) and via the station's Website.

ADDRESS IN ARGENTINA: KBS World Radio, Casilla de Correo 950, S2000WAJ Rosario, Argentina.

ENGINEERING DEPARTMENT: IBC, Center, Korean Broadcasting System, Yoido-dong 18, Youngdeungpo-Gu, Seoul, Republic of Korea 150-790. Phone: (general) +82 (2) 781-5141/5137; (Radio Transmission Division) +82 (2) 781-5663. Fax: +82 (2) 781 5159. Email: (Radio Transmission Division) poeto@hanmail. net; (Frequency Manager) kdhy@kbs.co.kr; (Planning Engineer) pulo5@kbs.co.kr. Contact: Mr. Oh Daesik, Radio Transmission Division; Mr. Dae-hyun Kim, Frequency Manager; Mr. Chun-soo Lee, Planning Engineer.

📻**Korean Broadcasting System (KBS)**, 18 Yoido-dong, Youngdeungpo-gu, Seoul, Republic of Korea 150-790. Phone: +82 (2) 781-1000; (duty officer) +82 (2) 781-1711/1792; (news desk) +82 (2) 781-4444; (overseas assistance) +82 (2) 781-1473/1497. Fax: +82 (2) 781 1698, +82 (2) 781 2399. Email: pr@kbs.co.kr. Web: (includes streaming audio) http://kbs. co.kr.

KUWAIT   World Time +3

IBB Kuwait Transmitting Station, c/o American Embassy-Bayan, P.O.Box 77, Safat, 13001 Kuwait, Kuwait. Contact: Transmitter Plant Supervisor. This address for specialized technical correspondence only, although reception reports may occasionally be verified. All other correspondence should be directed to the regular VOA or IBB addresses (*see* USA).

📻**Radio Kuwait**, P.O. Box 397, 13004 Safat, Kuwait; (technical) Department of Frequency Management, P.O. Box 967, 13010 Safat, Kuwait. Phone: (general) +965 242-3774; (technical) +965 241-5301. Fax: (general) +965 245 6660; (technical) +965 241 5946. Email: info@media.gov.kw. Web: (streaming audio) www.media.gov.kw. Contact: (general) Manager, External Service; (technical) Wessam Najaf. Sometimes gives away stickers, desk calendars, pens or key chains.

TRANSMISSION AND FREQUENCY MANAGEMENT OFFICE: Ministry of Information, P.O. Box 967 13010 Safat, Kuwait. Phone: +965 241-3590, +965 243-6193. Fax: +965 241 7830. Email: kwtfreq@media.gov.kw, kwtfreq@yahoo.com. Contact: Ahmed J. Alawdhi, Head of Frequency Section.

KYRGYZSTAN   World Time +6

📻**Kyrgyz Radio**, Kyrgyz TV and Radio Center, 59 Jash Gvardiya Boulevard, 720010 Bishkek, Kyrgyzstan. Phone: (general) +996 (312) 253-404, +996 (312) 255-741; (Director) +996 (312) 255-700, +996 (312) 255-709; (Assemov) +996 (312) 650-7341, +996 (312) 255-703; (technical) +996 (312) 257-771. Fax: +996 (312) 257 952. Email: snbckr@hotmail.kg, ntrk@ktr.kg, rkaktr@elcat.kg. Web: (includes streaming audio) www.ktr.kg/ tv/en. Contact: (administration) Myrsakul Mambetaliev, Director; (general) Talant Assemov, Editor - Kyrgyz/Russian/German news; Gulnara Abdulaeva, Announcer - Kyrgyz/Russian/German news; (technical) Mirbek Uursabekov, Technical Director. Kyrgyz and Russian preferred, but correspondence in English or German can also be processed. For quick processing of reception reports, use email in German to Talant Assemov.

TRANSMISSION FACILITIES: Ministry of Transport and Communications, 42 Issanova Street, 720000 Bishkek, Kyrgyzstan. Phone: +996 (312) 216-672. Fax: +996 (312) 213 667. Contact: Jantoro Satybaldiyev, Minister. The shortwave transmitting station is located at Krasnaya-Rechka (Red River), a military encampment in the Issk-Ata region, about 40 km south of Bishkek.

Radio Maranatha, Kulatov Street 8/1, Room 411, Bishkek, Kyrgyzstan. Phone: +996 (312) 273-845.

Hit Shortwave—music programming aired over Radio Maranatha (*see*, above).

LAO PEOPLE'S DEMOCRATIC REPUBLIC
World Time +7

NOTE: Although universally known as Laos, the official name of the country is "Lao People's Democratic Republic." English has now replaced French as the preferred foreign language.

Houa Phanh Provincial Radio Station, Sam Neua, Houa Phanh Province, Lao P.D.R. Phone: +856 (64) 312-008. Fax: +856 (21) 312 017. Contact: Mr. Veeyang, Hmong Announcer, and the only person who speaks English at the station; Ms. Nouan Thong, Lao Announcer; Mr. Vilaphone Bounsouvanh, Director; Mr. Khong Kam, Engineer.

📻**Lao National Radio**

PROGRAM OFFICE AND NATIONAL STUDIOS: Lao National Radio, Phaynam Road, Vientiane, Lao P.D.R; (postal address) P.O. Box 310, Vientiane, Lao P.D.R. Phone: +856 (21) 212-097/428/429/431/432; (Head of English service & External Relations) +856 (21) 252-863. Fax: +856 (21) 212 430. Email: (Head of English Service) laonatradio@lnr.org.la. Web: (includes on-demand audio in Lao and English) www.lnr.org.la. Contact: Mr. Bounthan Inthaxay, Director General; Mr. Inpanh Satchaphansy, Head of English Service & External relations; Mr. Vorasak Pravongviengkham, Head of French Service; Ms. Mativarn Simanithone, Deputy Head, English Section; Ms Chanthery Vichitsavanh, Announcer, English Section. Sometimes includes a program schedule and Laotian stamps when replying.

HF TRANSMITTER SITE: Transmitting Station KM6, Phone Tong Road, Ban Chommany Neuk, Vientiane Province, Lao P.D.R. Phone: +856 (21) 710-181. Contact: Mr. Sysamone Phommaxay, Station Engineer.

TECHNICAL OFFICE: Mass Media Department, Ministry of Information & Culture, 01000 Thanon Setthathirath, Vientiane, Lao P.D.R; or P.O. Box 122, Vientiane, Lao P.D.R. Phone/Fax: +856 (21) 212-424. Email: dy_sisombath@yahoo.com. Contact: Mr. Dy Sisombath, Deputy Director General & Manager, Technical Network Expansion Planning.

LEBANON   World Time +2 (+3 midyear)

📻**Radio Voice of Charity**, Rue Fouad Chéhab, Jounieh, Lebanon; or B.P. 850, Jounieh, Lebanon. Phone: +961 (9) 918-090, +961 (9) 917-917, +961 (9) 636-344. Fax: +961 (9) 930 272. Email: mahaba@radiocharity.org.lb. Web: (includes streaming audio from domestic service) www.radiocharity.org. Contact: Father Fadi Tabet, General Director. Operates domestically on FM, and airs a 30-minute daily Arabic broadcast via the shortwave facilities of Vatican Radio. Replies to correspondence in English, French or Arabic, and verifies reception reports. Return postage helpful.

LESOTHO   World Time +2

📻**Radio Lesotho** (if reactivated), P.O. Box 552, Maseru 100, Lesotho. Phone/Fax: +266 323-371. Email: online form. Web: (includes streaming audio) www.radioles.co.ls. Contact: (administration) Ms. Mpine Tente, Principal Secretary, Ministry of Information and Broadcasting; (technical) Motlatsi Monyane, Chief Engineer. Return postage necessary, but do not include currency notes—local currency exchange laws are very strict.

LIBERIA   World Time exactly

Radio ELWA, Box 192, Monrovia, Liberia. Phone: +231 (6) 515-511. Email: radio.staff@radioelwa.org; (Nyantee) moses.nyantee@radioelwa.org. Web: www.elwaministries.org/radio.htm. Contact: Moses T. Nyantee, Station Manager.

Radio Veritas, P.O. Box 3569, Monrovia, Liberia. Phone: +231 221-658. Email: radioveritas@hotmail.com. Contact: Ledgerhood Rennie, Station Manager.

Star Radio, P.O. Box 3081, 1000 Monrovia 10, Liberia; (street address) Old CID Road, Mamba Point, Monrovia, Liberia. Phone: +231 (6) 518-572. Email: starradio_liberia@yahoo.com. Web: www.starradio.org.lr. Contact: James Morlu, Station Manager. An independent station supported by the Swiss-based Fondation Hirondelle. Transmits round the clock on 104 FM in Monrovia, and airs morning and evening broadcasts on world band via a leased transmitter on Ascension Island.
FONDATION HIRONDELLE: 3 Rue Traversière, CH 1018-Lausanne, Switzerland. Phone: +41 (21) 647-2805. Fax: +41 (21) 647 4469. Email info@hirondelle.org. Web: www.hirondelle.org. Contact: Darcy Christen, Star Radio Program Officer. Verifies reception reports.

LIBYA   World Time +2

📻**Libyan Jamahiriyah Broadcasting Corporation**, P.O. Box 9333, Tripoli, Libya. Phone: +218 (21) 361-4508. Fax: +218 (21) 489 4240. Email: info@ljbc.net. Web: (includes streaming audio) www.ljbc.net. Contact: Youssef Aimoujrab.

Voice of Africa, P.O. Box 4677, Soug al Jama, Tripoli, Libya. Phone: +218 (21) 444-0112, +218 (21) 444-9106. Fax: +218 (21) 444 9875. Email: (Arabic) info@ljbc.net; (English) info@en.ljbc.net; (French) info@fr.ljbc.net. Web: (under construction) www.voiceofafrica.com.ly. The external service of the Libyan Jamahiriyah Broadcasting Corporation. Replies slowly and irregularly.

LITHUANIA   World Time +2 (+3 midyear)

📻**Radio Vilnius**, Lietuvos Radijas, Konarskio 49, LT-2600 Vilnius, Lithuania. Phone: +370 (5) 236-3079. Email: radiovilnius@lrt.lt. Web: (includes on-demand audio) www.lrt.lt (click on "English"). Contact: Ms. Ilona Rukiene, Head of English Department. Free stickers, pennants, Lithuanian stamps and other souvenirs.

MADAGASCAR   World Time +3

Radio Feon'ny Filazantsara. A broadcast produced by the Lutheran Church of Madagascar (Fiangonana Loterana Malagasy) and aired via the Madagascar relay of Radio Nederland (*see*). *LUTHERAN CHURCH OF MADAGASCAR:* Fiangonana Loterana Malagasy. P.O. Box 741, 101 Antananarivo, Madagascar. Phone: +261 321-2107, +261 2022-21001. Fax: +261 2022 33767. Email: flm@wanadoo.mg.

Radio Madagasikara, B.P. 442 - Anosy, 101 Antananarivo, Madagascar. Phone: +261 2022-21745. Fax: +261 2022 32715. Email: (Director's Office) mmdir@dts.mg; (Editorial Dept.) mminfo@dts.mg; (Program Dept.) mmprog@dts.mg; (Webmaster) radmad@dts.mg. Web: http://takelaka.dts.mg/radmad. Contact: Mlle. Rakotonirina Soa Herimanitia, Secrétaire de Direction, a young lady who collects stamps; Mamy Rafenomanantsoa, Directeur; J.J. Rakotonirina, who has been known to request hi-fi catalogs. $1 required, and enclosing used stamps from various countries may help. Tape recordings accepted. Replies slowly and somewhat irregularly, usually to correspondence in French.

Radio Nederland Wereldomroep—Madagascar Relay, B.P. 404, Antananarivo, Madagascar. Contact: (technical) Rahamefy Eddy, Technische Dienst; J.A. Ratobimiarana, Chief Engineer. Nontechnical correspondence should be sent to Radio Nederland Wereldomreop in the Netherlands (*see*).

MALAWI   World Time +2

Malawi Broadcasting Corporation (when operating), P.O. Box 30133, Chichiri, Blantyre 3, Malawi. Phone: (general) +265 671-222; (transmitting station) +265 694-208. Fax: +265 671 257, +265 671 353. Email: dgmbc@malawi.net. Contact: (general) Wilson Bankuku, Director General; J.O. Mndeke; T.J. Sineta; (technical) Abraham E. Nsapato, Controller of Transmitters; Phillip Chinseu, Engineering Consultant; Joseph Chikagwa, Director of Engineering. Tends to be irregular due to lack of transmitter spares. Return postage or $1 helpful, as the station is underfunded.

MALAYSIA   World Time +8

Asia-Pacific Broadcasting Union (ABU), P.O. Box 1164, 59700 Kuala Lumpur, Malaysia; (street address) 2nd Floor, Bangunan IPTAR, Angkasapuri, 50614 Kuala Lumpur, Malaysia. Phone: (general) +60 (3) 2282-3592; (Programme Department)+60 (3) 2282-2480; (Technical Department) +60 (3) 2282-3108. Fax: +60 (3) 2282 5292. Email: (Office of Secretary-General) sg@abu.org.my; (Programme Department) prog@abu.org.my; (Technical Department) tech@abu.org.my. Web: www.abu.org.my. Contact: (administration) David Astley, Secretary-General; (technical) Sharad Sadhu and Rukmin Wijemanne, Senior Engineers, Technical Department.

📻**Radio Malaysia, Kuala Lumpur**
MAIN OFFICE: RTM, Angkasapuri, Bukit Putra, 50614 Kuala Lumpur, Malaysia; (postal address) RTM, P.O. Box 11272, 50740 Kuala Lumpur, Malaysia. Phone: +60 (3) 2282-5333, +60 (3) 2282-4976. Email: (programs) programradio@rtm.net.my; (technical) teknikalradio@rtm.net.my. Web: (includes

streaming audio) www.rtm.net.my. Contact: (general) Madzhi Johari, Director of Radio; (technical) Ms. Aminah Din, Deputy Director Engineering (Radio); Abdullah Bin Shahadan, Engineer, Transmission and Monitoring; Ong Poh, Chief Engineer. May sell T-shirts and key chains. Return postage required.

ENGINEERING DIVISION: 3rd Floor, Angkasapum, 50616 Kuala Lumpur, Malaysia. Phone: +60 (3) 2285-7544. Fax: +60 (3) 2283 2446. Email: zulrahim@rtm.net.my. Contact: Zulkifli Ab Rahim.

TRANSMISSION OFFICE: Controller of Engineering, Department of Broadcasting (RTM), 43000 Kajang, Selangor Darul Ehsan, Malaysia. Phone: +60 (3) 8736-1530, +60 (3) 8736-1530/1863. Fax: +60 (3) 8736 1226/7. Email: rtmkjg@rtm.net.my. Contact: Jeffrey Looi; Ab Wahid Bin Hamid, Supervisor, Transmission Engineering.

Radio Malaysia Sarawak (Kuching), RTM Sarawak, Jalan Satok, 93614 Kuching, Sarawak, Malaysia. Phone: +60 (82) 248-422. Fax: +60 (82) 241 914. Email: rtmkuc@rtm.net.my. Contact: (general) Yusof Ally, Director of Broadcasting; Mohd. Hulman Abdollah; Wilson Eddie Gaong, Head of Secretariat for Director of Broadcasting; (technical, but also nontechnical) Colin A. Minoi, Technical Correspondence; (technical) Kho Kwang Khoon, Deputy Director of Engineering. Return postage helpful.

Radio Malaysia Sarawak (Miri), RTM Miri, Bangunan Penyiaran, 98000 Miri, Sarawak, Malaysia. Phone: +60 (85) 423-645. Fax: +60 (85) 411 430. Email: rtmmiri@rtm.net.my. $1 or return postage helpful.

Radio Malaysia Sarawak (Sibu), RTM Sibu, Bangunan Penyiaran, 96009 Sibu, Sarawak, Malaysia. Phone: +60 (84) 323-566. Fax: +60 (84) 321 717. Email: rtmsibu@rtm.net.my. $1 or return postage required. Replies irregularly and slowly.

Voice of Islam—Program of the Voice of Malaysia (*see*, below).

◾**Voice of Malaysia**, Suara Malaysia, Wisma Radio Angkasapuri, P.O. Box 11272, 50740 Kuala Lumpur, Malaysia. Phone: (general) +60 (3) 2288-7824; (English Service) +60 (3) 2282-7826. Fax: +60 (3) 2284 7594. Email: vom@rtm.net.my; (technical, Kajang transmitter site) rtmkjg@po.jaring.my. Web: http://202.190.233.9/vom/utama.htm; (streaming audio) www.rtm.net.my. Contact: (general) Mrs. Mahani bte Ujang, Supervisor, English Service; Hajjah Wan Chuk Othman, English Service; (administration) Santokh Singh Gill, Director; Mrs. Adilan bte Omar, Assistant Director; (technical) Lin Chew, Director of Engineering; (Kajang transmitter site) Kok Yoon Yeen, Technical Assistant. Free calendars, stickers or other small souvenirs. Two IRCs or return postage helpful. Replies slowly and irregularly.

MALI   World Time exactly

Office de Radiodiffusion Télévision du Mali, B.P. 171, Bamako, Mali. Phone: +223 212-019, +223 212-474. Fax: +223 214 205. Email: (general) ortm@ortm.net; (Traore) cotraore@sotelma.ml. Web: www.ortm.net. Contact: Karamoko Issiaka Daman, Directeur des Programmes; (administration) Abdoulaye Sidibe, Directeur General; (Technical) Nouhoum Traore. $1 or IRC helpful. Replies slowly and irregularly to correspondence in French (preferred) or English.

MAURITANIA   World Time exactly

Radio Mauritanie, B.P. 200, Nouakchott, Mauritania. Phone: +222 525-2101. Fax: +222 525 1264. Email: rm@mauritania.

mr. Contact: Madame Amir Feu; Lemrabott Boukhary; Madame Fatimetou Fall Dite Ami, Secretaire de Direction; Mr. El Hadj Diagne; Mr. Hane Abou. Return postage or $1 required. Rarely replies.

MEXICO   World Time −6 (−5 midyear) Central, South and Eastern, including D.F.; −7 (−6 midyear) Mountain; −7 Sonora; −8 (−7 midyear) Pacific

Candela FM—*see* RASA Onda Corta.

◾**Radio Educación Onda Corta**—**XEPPM**, Apartado Postal 21-465, 04021 - México, D.F., Mexico; (street address) Angel Urraza No. 622, 03100 - Col. del Valle, México D.F., Mexico. Phone: (switchboard) +52 (55) 1500-1050; (director's office) +52 (55) 1500-1051; (transmission plant) +52 (55) 5745-7282. Email: (general) informes@radioeducacion.edu.mx; (Lidia Camacho) direccion@radioeducacion.edu.mx; (Nicolás Hernández) nhem@radioeducacion.edu.mx. Web:(includes on-demand and streaming audio) www.radioeducacion.edu.mx. Contact: (general) Lic. María Del Carmen Limón Celorio, Directora de Producción y Planeación; (administration) Lic. Lidia Camacho Camacho, Directora General; (technical) Ing. Jesús Aguilera Jiménez, Subdirector de Desarrollo Técnico; Nicolás Hernández Menchaca, Jefe del Departamento de Planta Transmisora. Free stickers, calendars and station photo. Return postage or $1 required. Replies, sometimes slowly, to correspondence in English, Spanish, Italian or French.

Radio Huayacocotla—**XEJN**, Apartado Postal 13, 92601 - Huayacocotla, VER, Mexico; (street address) "Radio Huaya," Gutiérrez Najera s/n, 92600 - Huayacocotla, VER, Mexico. Phone: +52 (774) 758-0067. Contact: Pedro Ruperto Albino, Coordinador. Return postage or $1 helpful. Replies irregularly to correspondence in Spanish.

Radio Mil Onda Corta—**XEOI**, Prol. Paseo de la Reforma No. 115, Col. Paseo de las Lomas, 01330 - México, D.F., Mexico; or Apartado Postal 21-1000, 04021-México, D.F., Mexico (this address for reception reports and listeners' correspondence on the station's shortwave broadcasts, and mark the envelope to the attention of Dr. Julián Santiago Díez de Bonilla). Phone: (studios) +52 (55) 5258-1351; (NRM Comunicaciones parent organization) +52 (55) 5258-1200. Email: radiomil@nrm.com.mx; (reception reports) ingenieria@nrm.com.mx. Web: www.nrm.com.mx/estaciones/radiomil. Contact: (administration) Lic. Gustavo Alvite Martínez, Director de Radio Mil; Edilberto Huesca P., Vicepresidente Ejecutivo de NRM Comunicaciones; (technical) Juan Iturria, Ingeniero Jefe; (shortwave service) Dr. Julián Santiago Díez de Bonilla. Free stickers. $1 or return postage required.

◾**Radio Transcontinental**—**XERTA**, Plaza San Juan N° 5, 1er piso - Despacho 2, Centro Histórico, 06050 - México D.F., Mexico. Phone: +52 (55) 5518-4938. Email: charlaxerta@yahoo.com.mx; (Castañeda) rubencastaneda@hotmail.com. Web: (includes streaming audio) www.misionradio.com. Contact: Verónica Coria Miranda, Representante Ejecutiva; Lic. Rubén Castañeda Espíndola, Director General.

◾**Radio UNAM [Universidad Nacional Autónoma de México]**—**XEYU** (when operating), Adolfo Prieto 133, Colonia del Valle, 03100 - México D.F., Mexico. Phone: +52 (55) 5623-3250, +52 (55) 5623-3251, +52 (55) 5687-3989; (listener feedback) +52 (55) 5536-8989; (toll-free within Mexico) 01-800-505-2688. Fax: +52 (55) 5543 6852. Email: radiounam@www.unam.mx; (Trujillo) armandot@servidor.unam.mx. Web: (includes on-demand and streaming audio) www.unam.mx/radiounam. Contact: Mtro. Fernando Alvarez del Castillo A., Director General; (technical) Eusebio Mejía, Encargado Técnico; Ing. Armando Trujillo Pantoja, Subdirector de Operación e Innovación Tecnológica. Free tourist literature and stickers. $1 or return postage required. Replies irregularly to correspondence in Spanish.

Radio Universidad—XEXQ Onda Corta, Apartado Postal 456, 78001 - San Luis Potosí, SLP, Mexico; (street address) Gral. Mariano Arista 245, Centro Histórico, 78000 - San Luis Potosí, SLP, Mexico. Phone: +52 (444) 826-1345; (studio) +52 (444) 826-1347. Fax: +52 (444) 826 1388. Contact: Lic. Leticia Zavala Pérez, Coordinadora; Lizbeth Deyanira Tapia Hernández, Radio Operadora.

MOLDOVA   World Time +2 (+3 midyear)

Radio DMR, Rose Luxembourg Street 10, Tiraspol 3300, Republic of Moldova. Email: radiopmr@inbox.ru. Web: www.president-pmr.org. Contact: Arkady D Shablienko, Director; Ms. Antonina N. Voronkova, Editor-in-Chief; Ernest A. Vardanean, Editor and Translator; Vadim A. Rudomiotov, Announcer; Vlad Butuk, Technician Engineer. Replies to correspondence in Russian or English. Return postage helpful. Broadcasts from the separatist, pro-Russian, "Dniester Moldavian Republic" (also known as "Trans-Dniester Moldavian Republic").

MONGOLIA   World Time +8 (+9 midyear)

Mongolian Radio—same postal and email addresses as Voice of Mongolia, below). Phone: (administration) +976 (11) 323-520, +976 (11) 328-978; (editorial) +976 (11) 329-766; (MRTV parent organization) +976 (11) 326-663. Fax: +976 (11) 327 234. Email: mr@mongol.net. Contact: A. Buidakhmet, Director.

Voice of Mongolia, C.P.O. Box 365, Ulaanbaatar 13, Mongolia. Phone: +976 (1) 321-624; (English Section) +976 (11) 327-900. Fax: +976 (11) 323 096; (English Section) +976 (11) 327 234. Email: mr@mongol.net; (Densmaa) densmaa9@yahoo.com. Contact: (general) Mrs. Narantuya, Chief of Foreign Service; Z. Densmaa, Mail Editor; Mrs. Oyunchimeg Alagsai, Head of English Department; Ms. Tsegmid Burmaa, Japanese Department; (administration) Ch. Surenjav, Director; (technical) Ing. Ganhuu, Chief of Technical Department. Correpondence should be directed to the relevant language section and 2 IRCs or 1$ appreciated. Sometimes very slow in replying. Accepts taped reception reports, preferably containing five-minute excerpts of the broadcast(s) reported, but cassettes cannot be returned. Free pennants, postcards, newspapers, Mongolian stamps, and occasionally, CDs of Mongolian music.
TECHNICAL DEPARTMENT: C.P.O Box 1126, Ulaanbaatar Mongolia. Phone: +976 (11) 363-584. Fax: +976 (11) 327 900. Email: aem@mongol.net. Contact: Mr. Tumurbaatar Gantumur, Director of Technical Department; Ms. Buyanbaatar Unur, Engineer, Technical Center of Transmission System.

MOROCCO   World Time exactly

IBB Morocco Transmitting Station, Briech. Phone: (office) +212 (9) 93-24-81. Fax: +212 (9) 93 55 71. Contact: Station Manager. These numbers for urgent technical matters only. Otherwise, does not welcome direct correspondence; *see* USA for acceptable VOA and IBB Washington addresses and related information.

⬛Radio Medi Un
MAIN OFFICE: B.P. 2055, Tanger, Morocco; (street address) 3, rue Emsallah, 90000 Tanger, Morocco. Phone: +212 3993-

6363. Fax: +212 3993 5755. Email: (general) medi1@medi1.com; (technical) technique@medi1.com; or multi-contact online form. Web: (includes on-demand and streaming audio) www.medi1.com (or www.medi1.co.ma). Contact: J. Dryk, Responsable Haute Fréquence. Two IRCs helpful. Free stickers. Correspondence in French preferred.
PARIS BUREAU, NONTECHNICAL: 78 Avenue Raymond Poincaré, F-75016 Paris, France. Phone: +33 (1) 45-01-53-30. Correspondence in French preferred.
Radio Mediterranée Internationale—*see* Radio Medi Un.
Radiodiffusion-Télévision Marocaine, 1 rue El Brihi, Rabat, Morocco. Phone: +212 (7) 766-881/83/85, +212 (7) 701-740, +212 (7) 201-404. Fax: +212 (7) 722 047, +212 (7) 703 208. Email: rtm@rtm.gov.ma; (technical) hammouda@rtm.gov.ma.Contact: (nontechnical and technical) Ms. Naaman Khadija, Ingénieur d'Etat en Télécommunication; Abed Bendalh; Rahal Sabir; (technical) Tanone Mohammed Jamaledine, Technical Director; Hammouda Mohammed, Engineer. Correspondence welcomed in English, French, Arabic or Berber, but rarely replies.

MYANMAR (BURMA)   World Time +6:30

Defense Forces Broadcasting Unit, Taunggi, Shan State, Myanmar. Email: sny@mandalay.net.mm. Occasionally replies to correspondence in English.
⬛Myanma Radio, GPO Box 1432, Yangon-11181, Myanmar; or (street address) 426, Pyay Road, Yangon-11041, Myanmar. Phone: +95 (1) 531-850. Fax: +95 (1) 525 428. Email: mrtv@mptmail.net.mm. Web: (includes streaming audio) www.myanmar.com/RADIO_TV.HTM. Contact: Ko Ko Htway, Director (Broadcasting).

NAGORNO-KARABAGH   World Time +4 (+5 midyear)

Voice of Justice, Tigranmetz Street 23a, Stepanakert, Nagorno-Karabagh. Contact: Mikael Hajyan, Station Manager. Replies to correspondence in Armenian, Azeri, Russian or German.

NAMIBIA   World Time +2 (+1 midyear)

Radio Namibia/Namibian Broadcasting Corporation, P.O. Box 321, Windhoek 9000, Namibia. Phone: (general) +264 (61) 291-3111; (National Radio—English Service) +264 (61)

Announcer at Namibian Broadcasting Corporation's studio in Windhoek.   NBC

291-2440; (German Service) +264 (61) 291-2330; (Schachtsch-neider) +264 (61) 291-2188. Fax: (general) +264 (61) 217 760; (German Service) +264 (61) 291 2291; (Duwe, technical) +264 (61) 231 881. Email: (general) webmaster@nbc.com.na; (German Service) gssecretary@nbc.com.na. To contact individuals, the format is initiallastname@nbc.com.na; so to reach, say, Peter Schachtschneider, it would be pschachtschneider@nbc.com.na. Web: www.nbc.com.na. Contact: (general) Corry Tjaveondja, Manager, National Radio; (technical) Peter Schachtschneider, Manager, Transmitter Maintenance; Joe Duwe, Chief Technician. Free stickers.

NEPAL   World Time +5:45

☞**Radio Nepal**, G.P.O. Box 634, Singha Durbar, Kathmandu, Nepal. Phone: (general) +977 (1) 424-3569, +977 (1) 423-1803/4; (executive director) +977 (1) 422-3910; (programme section) +977 (1) 424-2569; (engineering) +977 (1) 424-1923; (chief engineer) +977 (1) 425-5467. Fax: (executive director) +977 (1) 422 1952; (news division) +977 (1) 422 8652. Email: (director) radio@rne.wlink.com.np; (technical) radio@engg.wlink.com.np. Web: (includes on-demand audio) www.radionepal.org. Contact: (general) Tapanath Shukla, Executive Director; Ram Sharan Karki, Deputy Executive Director; P. Shivakoti, Director; Pandav Sunuwar, Chief of Programme Section; (technical) Ramesh Jung Kharkee, Chief Engineer - Transmission; Bishnu Prasad Shivakoti, Chief Engineer - Studios and Planning. 3 IRCs necessary, but station urges that neither mint stamps nor cash be enclosed, as this invites theft by Nepalese postal employees. Replies irregularly.
KHUMALTAR SHORTWAVE STATION: Phone: +977 1 552-1221, +977 (1) 554-3480. Fax: +977 1 554 3481. Email: radio@txs.wlink.com.np. Contact: Padma Jyoti Dhakhwa, Chief Technical Officer; Madhu Sudan Thapa, Deputy Chief Technical Officer.

NETHERLANDS   World Time +1 (+2 midyear)

☞**Radio Nederland Wereldomroep (Radio Netherlands)**
MAIN OFFICE: P.O. Box 222, 1200 JG Hilversum, The Netherlands. Phone: (general) +31 (35) 672-4211; (English Language Service) +31 (35) 672-4242; (24-hour listener Answerline) +31 (35) 672-4222. Fax: (general) +31 (35) 672 4207, but indicate destination department on fax cover sheet; (English Language Service) +31 (35) 672 4239. Email: (English Service) letters@rnw.nl; (Spanish Service): cartas@rnw.nl; ("Media Network") media@rnw.nl. Web: (includes on-demand and streaming audio) www.radionetherlands.nl. Contact: (management) Jan Hoek, Director-General; Joop Dalmeijer, Editor-in-Chief; Mike Shaw, Head of English Language Service. The Radio Netherlands Music Department produces concerts heard on many NPR stations in North America, as well as a line of CDs, mainly of classical, jazz, world music and the Euro Hit 40. Most of the productions are only for rebroadcasting on other stations, but recordings on the NM Classics label are for sale. More details available at www.rnmusic.nl. Visitors welcome, but must call in advance.
PROGRAMME DISTRIBUTION, NETWORK AND FREQUENCY PLANNING: P.O. Box 222, 1200 JG Hilversum, The Netherlands. Phone: +31 (35) 672-4422. Fax: +31 (35) 672 4429. Contact: Leo van der Woude, Frequency Manager; Jan Willem Drexhage, Head of Programme Distribution.
☞**Radio Nile**, Plot No. 15, Komi Crescent, Lusira, 338829 Kampala, Uganda. Phone: +256 (41) 220-334. Return postage requested. Programs produced by the New Sudan Council of Churches (NSCC) at studios in the Netherlands and Uganda. Transmits via the Radio Nederland relay station in Madagascar, and is a project sponsored by the Dutch public broadcaster NCRV and supported by Pax Christi and the Interchurch Organization for Development Corporation.
ADDRESS IN THE NETHERLANDS: P.O. Box 19318, 3501 DH Utrecht, Netherlands.

NETHERLANDS ANTILLES   World Time −4

Radio Nederland Wereldomroep—Bonaire Relay, P.O. Box 45, Kralendijk, Netherlands Antilles. This address for specialized technical correspondence only. All other correspondence should be sent to Radio Nederland Wereldomroep in the Netherlands (*see*).

NEW ZEALAND   World Time +13 (+12 midyear)

☞**Radio New Zealand International (Te Reo Irirangi O Aotearoa, O Te Moana-nui-a-kiwa)**, P.O. Box 123, Wellington, New Zealand. Phone: +64 (4) 474-1437. Fax: +64 (4) 474 1433, +64 (4) 474 1886. Email: info@rnzi.com. Web: (includes on-demand and streaming audio and online reception report form) www.rnzi.com. Contact: Florence de Ruiter, Listener Mail; Myra Oh, Producer, "Mailbox"; (administration) Ms. Linden Clark, Manager; (technical) Adrian Sainsbury, Technical Manager. Free stickers, schedule/flyer about station, map of New Zealand and tourist literature available. English/Maori T-shirts for US$20; sweatshirts $40; interesting variety of CDs, as well as music cassettes and spoken programs, in Domestic "Replay Radio" catalog (VISA/MC). Two IRCs or $2 for QSL card, one IRC for schedule/catalog. Email reports verified by email only.
Radio Reading Service—ZLXA, P.O. Box 360, Levin 5500, New Zealand. Phone: (general) +64 (6) 368-2229; (engineering) +64 (25) 985-360. Fax: +64 (6) 368 7290. Email: (general, including reception reports) info@radioreading.org; (Bell) abell@radioreading.org; (Stokoe) bstokoe@radioreading.org. Web: www.radioreading.org. Contact: (general) Ash Bell, Manager/Station Director; (technical, including reception reports) Brian Stokoe. Operated by volunteers 24 hours a day, seven days a week. Station is owned by the "New Zealand Radio for the Print Disabled Inc." Free brochure, postcards and stickers. $1, return postage or 3 IRCs appreciated.

NICARAGUA   World Time −6 (−7 midyear)

Radio Miskut (when operating), Barrio Pancasan, Puerto Cabezas, R.A.A.N., Nicaragua. Phone: +505 (282) 2443. Fax: +505 (267) 3032. Contact: Lic. Evaristo Mercado Pérez, Director de Operación y de Programas; Abigail Zúñiga Fagoth. Replies slowly and irregularly to correspondence in English or Spanish. $2 helpful, as is registering your letter.

NIGER   World Time +1

☞**La Voix du Sahel**, O.R.T.N., B.P. 361, Niamey, Niger. Phone: (director) +227 722-208, +227 979-241; (technical director) +227 722-747, +227 928-014. Fax: +227 723 5 48. Email: (director) maigaric@yahoo.fr; (technical director) maraka_laouali@yahoo.fr. Web: (includes on-demand audio) www.ortn-niger.com. Contact: (administration) Mahaman Chamsou Maïgari, Directeur; (technical) Laouali Maraka, Directeur technique ORTN. $1 helpful. Correspondence in French preferred.

NIGERIA   World Time +1

WARNING—MAIL THEFT: For the time being, correspondence from abroad to Nigerian addresses has a relatively high probability of being stolen.

WARNING—CONFIDENCE ARTISTS: For years, now, correspondence with Nigerian stations has sometimes resulted in letters from highly skilled "pen pal" confidence artists. These typically offer to send you large sums of money, if you will provide details of your bank account or similar information (after which they clean out your account). Other scams are disguised as tempting business proposals; or requests for money, free electronic or other products, publications or immigration sponsorship. Persons thus approached should contact their country's diplomatic offices. For example, Americans should contact the Diplomatic Security Section of the Department of State [phone +1 (202) 647-4000], or an American embassy or consulate.

Radio Nigeria—Abuja, Broadcasting House, P.M.B. 71, Gark1, Abuja, Federal Capital Territory, Nigeria. Phone: +234 (9) 882-1065. Fax: +234 (9) 882 1341. Contact: Ben Obeta. Two IRCs, return postage or $1 required. Replies slowly.

Radio Nigeria—Enugu (if reactivated), P.M.B. 1051, Enugu, Enugu State, Nigeria. Phone: +234 (42) 254-400. Fax: +234 (42) 254 173. Two IRCs, return postage or $1 required. Replies slowly.

Radio Nigeria—Ibadan (when operating), Broadcasting House, P.M.B. 5003, Ibadan, Oyo State, Nigeria. Phone: +234 (22) 241-4093, +234 (22) 241-4106. Fax: +234 (22) 241 3930. $1 or return postage required. Replies slowly.

Radio Nigeria—Kaduna, P.O. Box 250, Kaduna (Kaduna), Nigeria. Contact: Shehu Muhammad, Chief Technical Officer. $1 or return postage required. Replies slowly.

Radio Nigeria—Lagos (if reactivated), Broadcasting House, P.M.B. 12504, Ikoyi, Lagos, Nigeria. Phone: +234 (1) 269-0301. Fax: +234 (1) 269 0073. Two IRCs or return postage helpful. Replies slowly and irregularly.

Voice of Nigeria
ABUJA OFFICE: 6th Floor, Radio House Herbert Macaulay, Garki, Abuja, Federal Capital Territory, Nigeria. Phone: +234 (9) 234-6973, +234 (9) 234-4017. Fax: +234 (9) 234 6970. Email: (general) vonabuja@rosecom.net; (English Service) englishvon@yahoo.com; (Idowu) tidowu@yahoo.com. Web: www.voiceofnigeria.org. Contact: Ayodele Suleiman, Director of Programming; Tope Idowu, Editor *"Voice Of Nigeria Airwaves"* program magazine & Special Assistant to the Director General; Frank Iloye, Station Manager; (technical) Timothy Gyang, Deputy Director, Engineering.
LAGOS OFFICE: P.M.B. 40003, Falomo, Lagos, Nigeria. Phone: +234 (1) 269-3075, +234 (1) 269-3078. Fax: +234 (1) 269 3078, +234 (9) 269 1944. Email: vonlagos@nigol.net.ng.
Replies from the station tend to be erratic, but continue to generate unsolicited correspondence from supposed "pen pals" (*see WARNING—CONFIDENCE ARTISTS*, above); faxes, which are much less likely to be intercepted, may be more fruitful. Two IRCs or return postage helpful.

NORTHERN MARIANA ISLANDS   World Time +10

Far East Broadcasting Company—Radio Station KFBS, P.O. Box 500209, Saipan, Mariana Islands MP 96950 USA. Phone: +1 (670) 322-3841. Fax: +1 (670) 322 3060. Email: saipan@febc.org. Web: www.febi.org. Contact: Robert Springer, Director; Irene Gabbie, QSL Secretary. Replies sometimes take months. Also, *see* FEBC Radio International, USA.

NORWAY   World Time +1 (+2 midyear).

UKEsenderen,d Elgesetergate 1, N-7030 Trondheim, Norway. Email: uka@uka.no. Web: www.uka.no. A student station which operates on 7215 kHz for approximately three weeks (mid-October to early November) in odd-numbered years.

OMAN   World Time +4

BBC World Service—A'Seela Relay Station
Resident Engineer, VT Communications, BBC Relay Station, P.O. Box 40, Al Ashkarah, Post Code 422, Oman. Email: rebers@omantel.net.com. Contact: Dave Battey, Resident Engineer; Afrah Al Orimi. Nontechnical correspondence should be sent to the BBC World Service in London (*see*).

Radio Sultanate of Oman, Ministry of Information, P.O. Box 600, Muscat, Post Code 113, Sultanate of Oman. Phone: +968 2460-2127, +968 2460-4577, +968 2460-3222, +968 2460-3888; (frequency managment) +968 2460-2494; (engineering) +968 2460-1538. Fax: (general) +968 2469 3770; (frequency management) +968 2460 4629, +968 2460 7239. Email: (general) feedback_rd@oman_radio.gov.om; (frequency management) moifreqs@omantel.net.om, abulukman@hotmail.com. Web: (includes streaming audio) www.oman-radio.gov.om. Contact: (Directorate General of Technical Affairs) Mohamed Al Marhoubi, Director General of Engineering; Salim Al-Nomani, Director of Frequency Management. Verifies reception reports. $1, mint stamps or 3 IRCs helpful.

PAKISTAN   World Time +5 (+6 midyear)

Pakistan Broadcasting Corporation—same address, fax and contact details as Radio Pakistan, below. Web: (includes on-demand and streaming audio) www.radio.gov.pk.

Radio Pakistan, P.O. Box 1393, Islamabad 44000, Pakistan; (street address) Broadcasting House, Constitution Avenue, Islamabad 44000, Pakistan. Phone: +92 (51) 921-6942, +92 (51) 921-7321. Fax: +92 (51) 920 1861, +92 (51) 920 1118, +92 (51) 922 3877. Email: (general) cnoradio@isb.comsats.net.pk, info@radio.gov.pk; (technical) cfmpbchq@isb.comsats.net.pk (reception reports to this address have been verified with QSL cards). Web: www.radio.gov.pk/ext_svc.htm. Contact: (technical) Ahmed Nawaz, Senior Broadcast Engineer, Room No. 324, Frequency Management Cell; Muhammad Ayub, Engineering Manager; Iftikhar Malik, Senior Broadcast Engineer & Frequency Manager, Frequency Management Cell; Ajmal Kokhar, Controller, Frequency Management; Syed Asmat Ali Shah, Senior Broadcasting Engineer; Zulfiqar Ahmad, Director of Engineering; Nasirahmad Bajwa, Frequency Management. Free stickers, pennants and *Pakistan Calling* magazine. May also send pocket calendar. Replies irregularly to postal correspondence; better is to use email if you can. Plans to replace two 50 kW transmitters with 500 kW units if and when funding is forthcoming.

PALAU   World Time +9

Radio Station T8BZ (formerly KHBN and name still used), P.O. Box 66, Koror, Palau PW 96940. Phone: +680 488-2162, +680 544-1050. Fax: (main office) +680 488 2163; (engineering) +680 544 1008. Email:(general) hamadmin@palaunet.com, highadventure@fastmail.fm; (technical) cacciatore@lineone.net. Contact: (technical) Ben Chen, Engineering Manager. IRC requested.

PAPUA NEW GUINEA   World Time +10

NOTE: Regional stations are sometimes off the air due to financial or technical problems which can take weeks or months to resolve. IRCs are reportedly not exchangeable in the country, and some provincial stations prefer mint stamps to US currency notes.

Catholic Radio Network, P.O. Box 7671, Boroko, NCD, Papua New Guinea. Email: news@rtapng.com.pg. Web: www.catholicpng.org.pg. Contact: Fr. Zdzislaw Mlak, Station Manager. Replies irregularly.

RECEPTION REPORTS: Email: wwilson@tepng.com. Contact: Wayne Wilson, Construction Manager, TE(PNG).

National Broadcasting Corporation of Papua New Guinea, P.O. Box 1359, Boroko 111, NCD, Papua New Guinea. Phone: +675 325-5233, + 675 325-5949, +675 325-6779. Fax: +675 323 0404, +675 325 0796, +675 325 6296. Email: pom@nbc.com.pg. Web: (under construction) www.nbc.com.pg. Contact: (general) Joseph Ealedona, Managing Director; Ephraim Tammy, Director, Radio Services; (technical) Bob Kabewa, Sr. Technical Officer; F. Maredey, Chief Engineer. Return postage helpful. Replies irregularly.

Radio Bougainville, P.O. Box 35, Buka, NSP, Papua New Guinea. Contact: Ivo Tsika, Station Manager; Aloysius Rumina, Provincial Programme Manager; Ms. Christine Talei, Assistant Provincial Manager; Aloysius Laukai, Senior Programme Officer. Replies irregularly.

Radio Central (when operating), P.O. Box 1359, Boroko, NCD, Papua New Guinea. Contact: Steven Gamini, Station Manager; Lahui Lovai, Provincial Programme Manager; Amos Langit, Technician. Return postage (mint stamps) helpful. Replies irregularly.

Radio Eastern Highlands (when operating), P.O. Box 311, Goroka, EHP, Papua New Guinea. Phone: +675 732-1533, +675 732-1733. Contact: Tony Mill, Station Manager; Tonko Nonao, Program Manager; Ignas Yanam, Technical Officer; Kiri Nige, Engineering Division. $1 or return postage required. Replies irregularly.

Radio East New Britain (when operating), P.O. Box 393, Rabaul, ENBP, Papua New Guinea. Contact: Esekia Mael, Station Manager; Oemas Kumaina, Provincial Program Manager. Return postage required. Replies slowly.

Radio East Sepik, P.O. Box 65, Wewak, ESP, Papua New Guinea. Contact: Elias Albert, Assistant Provincial Program Manager; Luke Umbo, Station Manager.

Radio Enga (when operating), P.O. Box 300, Wabag, Enga Province, Papua New Guinea. Phone: +675 547-1213. Contact: (general) John Lyein Kur, Station Manager; Robert Papuvo, (technical) Gabriel Paiao, Station Technician.

Radio Gulf (when operating), P.O. Box 36, Kerema, Gulf, Papua New Guinea. Contact: Tmothy Akia, Station Manager; Timothy Akia, Provincial Program Manager.

Radio Madang, P.O. Box 2138, Madang, Papua New Guinea. Phone: +675 852-2415. Fax: +675 852 2360. Email: (Gedabing) geo@daltron.com.pg. Contact: Geo Gedabing, Provincial Programme Manager. Return postage helpful.

Radio Manus, P.O. Box 505, Lorengau, Manus, Papua New Guinea. Phone: +675 470-9029. Fax: +675 470 9079. Contact: (technical and nontechnical) John P. Mandrakamu, Provincial Program Manager. Station is seeking the help of DXers and broadcasting professionals in obtaining a second hand, but still usable broadcasting quality CD player that could be donated to Radio Manus. Replies regularly. Return postage appreciated.

Radio Milne Bay (when operating), P.O. Box 111, Alotau, Milne Bay, Papua New Guinea. Contact: (general) Trevor Webumo,

Assistant Manager; Simon Muraga, Station Manager; Raka Petuely, Program Officer; (technical) Philip Maik, Technician. Return postage in the form of mint stamps helpful.

Radio Morobe (when operating), P.O. Box 1262, Lae, Morobe, Papua New Guinea. Fax: +675 472 6423. Contact: Henry Tamarus, Provincial Director; Ken L. Tropu, Assistant Program Manager; Peter W. Manua, Program Manager; Aloysius R. Nase, Station Manager.

Radio New Ireland (when operating), P.O. Box 140, Kavieng, New Ireland, Papua New Guinea. Contact: Tonko Nanao, Provincial Director; Otto A. Malatana, Station Manager; Ruben Bale, Provincial Program Manager. Currently off air due to a shortage of transmitter spares. Return postage or $1 helpful.

Radio Northern (when operating), Voice of Oro, P.O. Box 137, Popondetta, Oro, Papua New Guinea. Contact: Roma Tererembo, Assistant Provincial Programme Manager; Misael Pendaia, Station Manager. Return postage required.

Radio Sandaun, P.O. Box 37, Vanimo, Sandaun Province, Papua New Guinea. Contact: (nontechnical) Gabriel Deckwalen, Station Manager; Celina Korei, Station Journalist; Elias Rathley, Provincial Programme Manager; Mrs. Maria Nauot, Secretary; (technical) Paia Ottawa, Technician. $1 helpful.

Radio Simbu, P.O. Box 228, Kundiawa, Chimbu, Papua New Guinea. Phone: +675 735-1038, +675 735-1082. Fax: +675 735 1012. Contact: (general) Jack Wera, Manager; Tony Mill Waine, Provincial Programme Manager; Felix Tsiki; Thomas Ghiyandiule, Producer, "Pasikam Long ol Pipel." Cassette recordings $5. Free two-Kina banknotes.

Radio Southern Highlands (when operating), P.O. Box 104, Mendi, SHP, Papua New Guinea. Contact: (general) Andrew Meles, Director Provincial Radio; Miriam Piapo, Programme Officer; Benard Kagaro, Programme Officer; Lucy Aluy, Programme Officer; Jacob Mambi, Shift Officer; Nicholas Sambu, Producer, "Questions and Answers"; (technical) Ronald Helori, Station Technician. $1 or return postage helpful; or donate a wall poster of a rock band, singer or American landscape.

Radio Western, P.O. Box 23, Daru, Western Province, Papua New Guinea. Contact: Robin Wainetti, Manager; (technical) Samson Tobel, Technician. $1 or return postage required. Replies irregularly.

Radio Western Highlands (when operating), P.O. Box 311, Mount Hagen, WHP, Papua New Guinea. Contact: (general) Anna Pundia, Station Manager; (technical) Esau Okole, Technician. $1 or return postage helpful. Replies occasionally. Often off the air because of theft, armed robbery or inadequate security for the station's staff.

Radio West New Britain, P.O. Box 412, Kimbe, WNBP, Papua New Guinea. Fax: +675 983 5600. Contact: Valuka Lowa, Provincial Station Manager; Darius Gilime, Provincial Program Manager; Lemeck Kuam, Producer, "Questions and Answers"; Esekial Mael. Return postage required.

Wantok Radio Light, P.O. Box 1273, Port Moresby, NCD, Papua New Guinea. Fax: +675 321 4465. Email: online form; (Olson, technical) david@heart-to-serve.com. Web: www.wantokradio.net. Contact: (general) Sarah Good; (technical) David Olson, Chief Engineer. Return postage required for postal reply. Verifies reception reports. Wantok Radio Light is the shortwave station of the PNG Christian Broadcasting Network, and is a joint project involving Life Radio Ministries, HCJB World Radio and others.

PARAGUAY   World Time –3 (–4 midyear)

Radio Nacional del Paraguay (when operating), Blas Garay 241 entre Yegros e Iturbe, Asunción, Paraguay. Phone: +595

(21) 390-375. Fax: +595 (21) 390 376. Email: info@rnpy.com. Web: www.rnpy.com. Contact: Carlos María Franco, Director. Free tourist brochure. $1 or return postage required. Replies, sometimes slowly, to correspondence in Spanish.

PERU World Time –5

NOTE: Obtaining replies from Peruvian stations calls for creativity, tact, patience—and the proper use of Spanish, not form letters and the like.

Frecuencia Líder (Radio Bambamarca), Jirón Jorge Chávez 416, Bambamarca, Hualgayoc, Cajamarca, Peru. Phone: (office) +51 (74) 713-260; (studio) +51 (74) 713-249. Contact: (general) Valentín Peralta Díaz, Gerente; Irma Peralta Rojas; Carlos Antonio Peralta Rojas; (technical) Oscar Lino Peralta Rojas. Free station photos. *La Historia de Bambamarca* book for 5 Soles; cassettes of Peruvian and Latin American folk music for 4 Soles each; T-shirts for 10 Soles each (sending US$1 per Sol should suffice and cover foreign postage costs, as well). Replies occasionally to correspondence in Spanish. Considering replacing their transmitter to improve reception.

Frecuencia San Ignacio, Jirón Villanueva Pinillos 330, San Ignacio, Cajamarca, Peru. Contact: Franklin R. Hoyos Cóndor, Director Gerente; Ignacio Gómez Torres, Técnico de Sonido. Replies to correspondence in Spanish. $1 or return postage necessary.

Frecuencia VH—*see* Radio Frecuencia VH.

La Voz de la Selva—*see* Radio La Voz de la Selva.

La Voz del Campesino—*see* Radio La Voz del Campesino.

Ondas del Suroriente—*see* Radio Ondas del Suroriente.

Radio Altura, Casilla de Correo 140, Cerro de Pasco, Pasco, Peru. Phone: +51 (63) 721-875, +51 (63) 722-398. Contact: Oswaldo de la Cruz Vásquez, Gerente General. Replies to correspondence in Spanish.

Radio Ancash, Casilla de Correo 221, Huaraz, Peru. Phone: +51 (43) 421-359, +51 (43) 426-807. Contact: Armando Moreno Romero, Gerente General. Replies to correspondence in Spanish.

Radio Andahuaylas (when operating), Jr. Ayacucho No. 248, Andahuaylas, Apurímac, Peru. Contact: Sr. Daniel Andréu C., Gerente. $1 required. Replies irregularly to correspondence in Spanish.

Radio Andina, Real 175, Huancayo, Junín, Peru. Phone: +51 (64) 231-123. Replies infrequently to correspondence in Spanish.

Radio Atlántida (when operating)

STATION: Jirón Arica 441, Iquitos, Loreto, Peru. Phone: +51 (94) 234-452, +51 (94) 234-962. Contact: Pablo Rojas Bardales.

LISTENER CORRESPONDENCE: Sra. Carmela López Paredes, Directora del prgrama "Trocha Turística," Jirón Arica 1083, Iquitos, Loreto, Peru. Free pennants and tourist information. $1 or return postage required. Replies to most correspondence in Spanish, the preferred language, and some correspondence in English.

Radio Bambamarca—*see* Frecuencia Líder, above.

Radio Bethel—*see* Radio Bethel Arequipa, below.

🖥**Radio Bethel Arequipa** (when operating), Avenida Unión 215 - 3ᵉʳ piso, Distrito Miraflores, Arequipa, Peru. Contact: Josué Ascarruz Pacheco. Usually announces as "Radio Bethel" and belongs to the "Movimiento Misionero Mundial" evengelistic organization.

RADIO BETHEL PARENT STATION IN LIMA: Avenida 28 de Julio 1781, La Victoria, Lima, Peru. Phone: +51 (1) 613-1717, +51 (1) 613-1725. Fax: +51 (1) 613 1726. Email: webmaster@bethelradio.com.pe. Web: (includes on-demand and streaming audio) www.bethelradio.com.pe. Provides some of the programming for its namesake in Arequipa.

Radio Cajamarca, Jirón La Mar 675, Cajamarca, Peru. Phone: +51 (44) 921-014. Contact: Porfirio Cruz Potosí.

Radio Chincheros, Jirón Apurímac s/n, Chincheros, Departamento de Apurímac, Peru.

Radio Chota, Jirón Anaximandro Vega 690, Apartado Postal 3, Chota, Cajamarca, Peru. Phone: +51 (76) 351-240. Contact: Aladino Gavidia Huamán, Administrador. $1 or return postage required. Replies slowly to correspondence in Spanish.

🖥**Radio Cultural Amauta**, Apartado Postal 24, Huanta, Ayacucho, Peru; (street address) Jr. Cahuide 278, Huanta, Ayacucho, Peru. Phone/Fax: +51 (64) 832-153. Email: arca@terra.com.pe. Web: (includes streaming audio) www.rca.es.vg. Contact: Pelagio Ñaupa Gálvez, Administrador; Miriam Gavilán, locutora.

Radio Cusco, Apartado Postal 251, Cusco, Peru. Phone: (general)+51 (84) 225-851; (management) +51 (84) 232-457. Fax: +51 (84) 223 308. Contact: Sra. Juana Huamán Yépez, Administradora; Raúl Siú Almonte, Gerente General; (technical) Benjamín Yábar Alvarez. Free pennants, postcards and key rings. Audio cassettes of Peruvian music $10 plus postage. $1 or return postage required. Replies irregularly to correspondence in Spanish or English. Station is looking for folk music recordings from around the world to use in their programs.

Radio del Pacífico, Apartado Postal 4236, Lima 1, Peru. Phone: +51 (1) 433-3275. Fax: +51 (1) 433 3276. Contact: J. Petronio

Allauca, Secretario, Departamento de Relaciones Públicas; Julio Villarreal. $1 or return postage required. Replies occasionally to correspondence in Spanish.

Radio El Sol de los Andes, Jirón 2 de Mayo 257, Juliaca, Peru. Phone: +51 (54) 321-115. Fax: +51 (54) 322 981. Contact: Armando Alarcón Velarde.

Radio Espacial, Jirón Bolívar Nº 130, Otuzco, Peru. Phone: +51 (44) 436-236.

Radio Frecuencia VH ("La Voz de Celendín"; "RVC"), Jirón José Gálvez 1030, Celendín, Cajamarca, Peru. Contact: Fernando Vásquez Castro, Propietario.

Radio Frecuencia San Ignacio—*see* Frecuencia San Ignacio.

Radio Horizonte, Apartado Postal 69 (or Santo Domingo 639), Chachapoyas, Amazonas, Peru. Phone: +51 (41) 477-793. Contact: Sra. Rocío García Rubio, Ing. Electrónico, Directora; Percy Chuquizuta Alvarado, Locutor; María Montaldo Echaiz, Locutora; Marcelo Mozambite Chavarry, Locutor; Ing. María Dolores Gutiérrez Atienza, Administradora; Juan Nancy Ruíz de Valdez, Secretaria; Yoel Toro Morales, Técnico de Transmisión; María Soledad Sánchez Castro, Administradora. Replies to correspondence in English, French, German and Spanish. $1 required.

Radio Huanta 2000, Jirón Gervacio Santillana 455, Huanta, Peru. Phone: +51 (64) 932-105. Fax: +51 (64) 832 105. Contact: Ronaldo Sapaico Maravi, Departmento Técnico; or Sra. Lucila Orellana de Paz, Administradora. Free photo of staff. Return postage or $1 appreciated. Replies to correspondence in Spanish.

Radio Huarmaca (when operating), Av. Grau 454 (detrás de Inversiones La Loretana), Distrito de Huarmaca, Provincia de Huancabamba, Región Grau, Peru. Contact: Simón Zavaleta Pérez. Return postage helpful.

Radio Ilucán, Jirón Lima 290, Cutervo, Región Nororiental del Marañón, Peru. Phone: +51 (44) 737-010, +51 (44) 737-231. Email: radioilucan@hotmail.com. Contact: José Gálvez Salazar, Gerente Administrativo. $1 required. Replies occasionally to correspondence in Spanish.

Radio La Hora, Av. Garcilaso 180, Cusco, Peru. Phone: +51 (84) 225-615, +51 (84) 231-371. Contact: (general) Edmundo Montesinos Gallo, Gerente General; (reception reports) Carlos Gamarra Moscoso, who is also a DXer. Free stickers, pins, pennants and postcards of Cusco. Return postage required. Replies to correspondence in Spanish. Reception reports are best sent direct to Carlos Gamarra's home address: Av. Garcilaso 411, Wanchaq, Cusco, Peru.

Radio La Voz, Andahuaylas, Apurímac, Peru. Contact: Lucio Fuentes, Director Gerente.

Radio La Voz de Bolívar, Jirón Cáceres s/n, Bolivar, Provincia de Bolívar, Departamento de La Libertad, Peru. Phone: +51 4423-0277 Contact: Julio Dávila Echevarría, Gerente. May send free pennant. Return postage helpful.

Radio La Voz de Chiriaco (when operating), Jirón Ricardo Palma s/n, Chiriaco, Distrito de Imaza, Provincia de Bagua, Departamento de Amazonas, Peru. Contact: Hildebrando López Pintado, Director; Santos Castañeda Cubas, Director Gerente; Fidel Huamuro Curinambe, Técnico de Mantenimiento. $1 or return postage helpful.

Radio La Voz de la Selva, Jirón Abtao 255, Casilla de Correo 207, Iquitos, Loreto, Peru. Phone: +51 (94) 265-245. Fax: +51 (94) 264 531. Email: lvsradio@terra.com.pe. Contact: Julia Jáuregui Rengifo, Directora; Marcelino Esteban Benito, Director; Pedro Sandoval Guzmán, Announcer; Mery Blas Rojas. Replies to correspondence in Spanish.

Radio La Voz de las Huarinjas, Barrio El Altillo s/n, Huancabamba, Piura, Peru. Phone: +51 (74) 473-126, +51 (74) 473-259. Contact: Alfonso García Silva, Gerente Director (also the owner of the station); Bill Yeltsin, Administrador. Replies to correspondence in Spanish.

Radio La Voz del Campesino, Av. Ramón Castilla s/n en la salida a Chiclayo, Huarmaca, Provincia de Huancabamba, Piura, Peru. Contact: Fermín Santos. Replies slowly and irregularly to correspondence in Spanish.

Radio Libertad de Junín, Cerro de Pasco 528, Apartado Postal 2, Junín, Peru. Phone: +51 (64) 344-026. Contact: Mauro Chaccha G., Director Gerente. Replies slowly to correspondence in Spanish. Return postage necessary.

Radio Luz y Sonido, Apartado Postal 280, Huánuco, Peru; or (street address) Jirón Dos de Mayo 1286, Oficina 205, Huánuco, Peru. Phone: +51 (62) 512-394, +51 (62) 518-500. Fax: +51 (62) 511 985. Contact: (technical) Jorge Benavides Moreno; (nontechnical) Pedro Martínez Tineo, Director Ejecutivo; Lic. Orlando Bravo Jesús; Seydel Saavedra Cabrera, Operador/Locutor. Return postage or $2 required. Replies to correspondence in Spanish, Italian and Portuguese. Sells video cassettes of local folk dances and religious and tourist themes.

Radio Macedonia (when operating), Seminario Bautista Macedonia, Casilla 1677, Arequipa, Peru. Phone/Fax: +51 (54) 444-376. Email: (W.A. Gardner) gardner@world-evangelism.com. Contact: W. Austin Gardner; Chris Gardner. Replies to correspondence in Spanish or English.
U.S. PARENT ORGANIZATION: Macedonia World Baptist Missions Inc., P.O. Box 519, Braselton GA 30517 USA. Phone: +1 (706) 654-2818. Fax: +1 (706) 654 2816. Email: mwbm@mwbm.org. Web: http://mwbm.org.

Radio Madre de Dios, Apartado Postal 37, Puerto Maldonado, Madre de Dios, Peru; (street address) Daniel Alcides Carrión 385, Puerto Maldonado, Madre de Dios, Peru. Phone: +51 (82) 571-050. Fax: +51 (82) 571 018, +51 (82) 573 542. Contact: (administration) Padre Rufino Lobo Alonso, Director; (general) Alcides Arguedas Márquez, Director del programa "Un Festival de Música Internacional," heard Mondays 0100 to 0200 World Time. Sr. Arguedas is interested in feedback for this letterbox program. Replies to correspondence in Spanish. $1 or return postage appreciated.

Radio Marañón, Apartado Postal 50, Jaén, Cajamarca, Peru; or (street address) Francisco de Orellana 343, Jaén, Cajamarca, Peru. Phone: +51 (44) 731-147, +51 (44) 732-168. Fax: +51 (44) 732 580. Email: (general) correo@radiomaranon.org.pe; (director) pmaguiro@radiomaranon.org.pe. Web: www.radiomaranon.org.pe. Contact: Francisco Muguiro Ibarra S.J., Director. Return postage necessary. May send free pennant. Replies slowly to correspondence in Spanish and (sometimes) English.

Radio Melodía, San Camilo 501-A, Cercado, Arequipa, Peru. Phone: +51 (54) 205-811, +51 (54) 223-661. Fax: +51 (54) 204 420. Contact: Elba Alvarez Delgado, Gerente. Replies to correspondence in Spanish.

Radio Municipal, Jirón Tacna 385, Panao, Pachitea, Huánuco, Peru. Email: dalsmop1@hotmail.com. Contact: Pablo Alfredo Albornoz Rojas, Gerente Técnico, who collects station stickers and pennants. Replies to correspondence in Spanish.

Radio Naylamp (if reactivated), Avenida Andrés Avelino Cáceres 800, Lambayeque, Peru. Phone: +51 (74) 283-353. Contact: Dr. Juan José Grández Vargas, Director Gerente; Delicia Coronel Muñoz, who is interested in receiving postcards and the like. Free stickers, pennants and calendars. Return postage necessary.

Radio Ondas del Huallaga, Jirón Leoncio Prado 723, Apartado Postal 343, Huánuco, Peru. Phone: +51 (62) 511-525, +51 (62) 512-428. Contact: Flaviano Llanos Malpartida, Representante Legal. $1 or return postage required. Replies to correspondence in Spanish.

Radio Ondas del Suroriente, Jirón Ricardo Palma 510, Quillabamba, La Convención, Cusco, Peru.

◫**Radio Oriente**, Vicariato Apostólico, Calle Progreso 112-114, Yurimaguas, Alta Amazonas, Loreto, Peru. Phone: +51 (65) 352-156, +51 (65) 351-611. Fax: +51 (94) 352 128. Email: (general) info@radiooriente.org; (director) rovay@qnet.co.pe, geovanni@radiooriente.org. Web: (includes streaming audio) www.radiooriente.org. Contact: (general) Sra. Elisa Cancino Hidalgo; Juan Antonio López-Manzanares M., Director; (technical) Pedro Capo Moragues, Gerente Técnico. $1 or return postage required. Replies occasionally to correspondence in English, French, Spanish and Catalan.

Radio Paucartambo, Plaza de Armas 124, Paucartambo, Departamento de Cusco, Peru.

Radio Quillabamba, Jirón Ricardo Palma 442, Apartado Postal 76, Quillabamba, La Convención, Cusco, Peru. Phone: +51 (84) 281-002. Fax: +51 (84) 281 771. Contact: Padre Francisco Javier Panera, Director. Replies very irregularly to correspondence in Spanish.

Radio Reina de la Selva, Jirón Ayacucho 944, Plaza de Armas, Chachapoyas, Región Nor Oriental del Marañón, Peru. Phone: +51 (74) 757-203. Contact: José David Reina Noriega, Gerente General; Jorge Oscar Reina Noriega, Director General. Replies irregularly to correspondence in Spanish. Return postage necessary.

Radio San Andrés, La Municipalidad, Distrito de San Andrés, Provincia de Cutervo, Departamento de Cajamarca, Peru. Email: (Meza) leoncio_meza@hotmail.com. Contact: Leoncio Samane Meza.

Radio San Antonio (Callalli), Parroquia San Antonio de Padua, Plaza Principal s/n, Callalli, Departamento de Arequipa, Peru. Contact: Hermano [Brother] Rolando.

Radio San Antonio (Villa Atalaya), Jirón Iquitos s/n, Villa Atalaya, Departamento de Ucayali, Peru. Email: (Zerdin) zerdin@terra.com.pe. Contact: Gerardo Zerdin.

Radio San Miguel, Av. Huayna Cápac 146, Huánchac, Cusco, Peru. Contact: Sra. Catalina Pérez de Alencastre, Gerente General; Margarita Mercado. Replies to correspondence in Spanish.

Radio San Miguel de El Faique (if reactivated), Distrito de El Faique, Provincia de Huancabamba, Departamento de Piura, Peru.

Radio San Nicolás, Jirón Amazonas 114, Rodríguez de Mendoza, Peru. Contact: Juan José Grández Santillán, Gerente; Violeta Grández Vargas, Administradora. Return postage necessary.

Radio Santa Ana, Av. San Martín 636, Santa Ana, Provincia La Convención, Cusco, Peru.

Radio Santa Mónica (when operating), Urbanización Marcavalle P-20, Cusco, Peru. Phone:+ 51 (84) 225-357. Contact: Nicolás Córdoba Orozco, Gerente General. Replies irregularly to correspondence in Spanish. Return postage or $1 required.

Radio Santa Rosa, Jirón Camaná 170, Casilla 4451, Lima 01, Peru. Phone: +51 (1) 427-7488. Fax: +51 (1) 426 9219. Email: radiosantarosa@terra.com.pe. Web: http://barrioperu.terra.com.pe/radiosantarosa. Contact: Padre Juan Sokolich Alvarado, Director; Lucy Palma Barreda. Free stickers and pennants. $1 or return postage necessary. Replies to correspondence in Spanish or English.

Radio Sicuani, Jirón 2 de Mayo 212, Sicuani, Canchis, Cusco, Peru; or Apartado Postal 45, Sicuani, Peru. Phone: +51 (84) 351-136, +51 (84) 351-698. Fax: +51 (84) 351 697. Email: cecosda@mail.cosapidata.com.pe. Contact: Mario Ochoa Vargas, Director.

Radio Tacna, Aniceto Ibarra 436, Casilla de Correo 370, Tacna, Peru. Phone: +51 (52) 714-871. Fax: +51 (52) 723 745. Email: scaceres@viabcp.com. Contact: (nontechnical and technical) Ing. Alfonso Cáceres Contreras, Gerente de Operaciones; (administration) Yolanda Vda. de Cáceres C., Directora Gerente. Free stickers and samples of *Correo* local newspaper. $1 or return postage helpful. Audio cassettes of Peruvian and other music $2 plus postage. Replies irregularly to correspondence in Spanish or English.

Radio Tawantinsuyo, Av. Sol N° 806, Cusco, Peru. Phone: +51 (84) 226-955, +51 (84) 228-411. Contact: Iván Montesinos, Gerente. Has a very attractive QSL card, but only replies occasionally to correspondence, which should be in Spanish.

Radio Tarma, Jirón Molino del Amo 167, Apartado Postal 167, Tarma, Peru. Phone/Fax: +51 (64) 321-167, +51 (64) 321-510. Contact: Mario Monteverde Pomareda, Gerente General. Sometimes sends 100 Inti banknote in return when $1 enclosed. Free stickers. $1 or return postage required. Replies irregularly to correspondence in Spanish.

◫**Radio Unión**, Av. José Pardo 138, Miraflores, Lima 27, Peru. Phone: +51 (1) 712-0145. Email: admin@unionlaradio.com. Web: (includes streaming audio) www.unionlaradio.com. Contact: Raúl Rubbeck Jiménez, Director Gerente; Juan Zubiaga Santiváñez, Gerente; Natividad Albizuri Salinas, Secretaria; Juan Carlos Sologuren, Dpto. de Administración, who collects stamps. Free satin pennants and stickers. IRC required, and enclosing used or new stamps from various countries is especially appreciated. Replies irregularly to correspondence and tape recordings, with Spanish preferred.

◫**Radio Universal**, Jr. José Santos Chocano G-11, Urbanización Santa Mónica, Cusco, Peru. Phone: +51 (84) 226-765, +51 (84) 238-822. Fax: +51 (84) 234 494. Email: webmaster@radiounivesalcusco.com. Web: (includes streaming audio) www.radiouniversalcusco.com. Contact: Luis Villasante Colpaer, Gerente.

◫**Radio Victoria**, Jr.Reynel 320, Mirones Bajo, Lima 1, Peru. Phone: +51 (1) 336-5448. Fax: +51 (1) 427 1195. Email: (Ramos) silvioramos777@hotmail.com. Web: (streaming audio) ipda.com.pe. Contact: Henrique Silvio Ramos, Administrador. Replies to correspondence in Spanish. Free stickers. Station owned by the Brazilian-run Pentecostal Church "Dios Es Amor," with local headquarters at Av. Arica 248, Lima; Phone: +51 (1) 330-8023. Their program "La Voz de la Liberación" is produced locally and aired over numerous Peruvian shortwave stations.

◫**Radio Virgen del Carmen ("RVC")**, Plaza Bolognesi N° 142, Cercado, Huancavelica, Peru. Fax: +51 (67) 451-257. Email: (López Alvarado) jlopez_alvarado@hotmail.com. Web: (includes sreaming audio) www.radiovirgendelcarmen.com. Contact: José Santos López Alvarado, Director General. Replies irregularly to correspondence in Spanish. Return postage helpful.

Radio Visión, Jr. Juan Fanning, Urbanización San Juan, Chiclayo, Departamento de Lambayeque, Peru. Email: consultas@iplacosecha.org; (Pastor Córdova) iplacosecha13@yahoo.es. Contact: Jorge Tessen; Pastor Francisco Córdova Rodríguez. Replies to correspondence in Spanish. Return postage helpful for postal reply. Station owned by Iglesia Pentecostal "La Cosecha."

Radiodifusoras Huancabamba, Calle Unión 409, Huancabamba, Piura, Peru. Phone: +51 (74) 473-233. Contact: Federico Ibáñez Maticorena, Director.

PHILIPPINES   World Time +8

Far East Broadcasting Company—FEBC Radio International (External Service)
MAIN OFFICE: P.O. Box 1, Valenzuela, Metro Manila, Philippines 0560. Phone: (general) +63 (2) 292-5603, +63 (2) 292-9403, +63 (2) 292-5790; (International Broadcast Manager) +63 (2) 292-5603 ext. 158. Fax: +63 (2) 292 9430, +63 (2) 292-5603, +63 (2) 291 4982; (International Broadcast Manager) +63 (2) 292 9724, but lacks funds to provide faxed replies. Email: febcomphil@febc.org.ph; info@febc.org.ph (reception reports to this address are sometimes verified with a QSL card); (Peter McIntyre) pm@febc.jfm.org.ph; (Larry Podmore) lpodmore@febc.jmf.org.ph; (Chris Cooper) ccooper@febc.org.ph. Web: www.febi.org. Contact: (general) Peter McIntyre, Manager, International Operations Division; (administration) Carlos Peña, Managing Director; Chris Cooper, International Broadcast Manager; (engineering) Ing. Renato Valentin, Frequency Manager; Larry Podmore, IBG Chief Engineer. Free stickers and calendar cards. Three IRCs appreciated for airmail reply. Plans to add a new 100 kW shortwave transmitter.
INTERNATIONAL SCHEDULING OFFICE: FEBC, 20 Ayer Rajah Crescent, Technopreneur Center, #09-22, Singapore 139964, Singapore. Phone: +65 6773-9017. Fax: +65 6773 9018. Email: freqmgr@febi.org. Contact: Chris Cooper, Information Systems Manager.
NEW DELHI BUREAU, NONTECHNICAL: c/o FEBC, Box 6, New Delhi-110 001, India.

IBB Philippines Transmitting Station
MAIN ADDRESS: International Broadcasting Bureau, Philippines Transmitting Station, c/o US Embassy, 1201 Roxas Boulevard, Ermita 1000, Manila, Philippines.
ALTERNATIVE ADDRESS: IBB/PTS, PSC 500 Box 28, FPO AP 96515-1000.
These addresses for specialized technical correspondence only, although reception reports may occasionally be verified. All other correspondence should be directed to the regular VOA or IBB addresses (*see* USA).

⬛Philippine Broadcasting Service—DUR2 (when operating), Bureau of Broadcasting Services, Media Center, Bohol Avenue, Quezon City, Philippines. Relays DZRB Radio ng Bayan and DZRM Radio Manila. Web: (Radio ng Bayan streaming audio) www.pbs.gov.ph.

Radyo Pilipinas, the Voice of Democracy, Philippine Broadcasting Service, 4th Floor, PIA Building, Visayas Avenue, Quezon City 1100, Metro Manila, Philippines. Phone: (general) +63 (2) 924-2620, +63 (2) 920-3963, +63 (2) 924-2548; (engineering, Phone/Fax) +63 (2) 924-2268. Email: (general) radyo_pilipinas_overseas@yahoo.com (if this fails, try: pbs.pao@pbs.gov.ph); (Mike Pangilinan, technical) mpangilinan@pbs.ops.gov.ph. Web: www.pbs.gov.ph/DZRP_page.htm. Contact: (nontechnical) Evelyn Salvador Agato, Officer-in-Charge; Tanny V. Rodriguez, Station Manager; Joy Montero; (technical) Danilo Alberto, Supervisor; Miguelito ("Mike") Pangilinan, Chief Engineer. Free postcards and stickers. Verifies reception reports.

⬛Radio Veritas Asia
STUDIOS AND ADMINISTRATIVE HEADQUARTERS: P.O. Box 2642, Quezon City, 1166 Philippines. Phone: +63 (2) 939-0011 to 14, +63 (2) 939-4692; (technical director) +63 (2) 938-1940. Fax: (general) +63 (2) 938 1940; (frequency manager) +63 (2) 939 7556. Email: (general) rveritas-asia@rveritas-asia.org, or online form; (program department) rvaprogram@rveritas-asia.org; (audience research) rva-ars@rveritas-asia.org; (technical) technical@rveritas-asia.org. Web: (includes on-demand and streaming audio) www.rveritas-asia.org. Contact: (administration) Ms. Erlinda G. So, Manager; (general) Ms. Cleofe R. Labindao, Audience Relations Officer; Ms. Shiela Hermida, Audience Relations Section; Mrs. Regie de Juan Galindez; Msgr. Pietro Nguyen Van Tai, Program Director; (technical) Honorio L. Llavore, Technical Director; Alex M. Movilla, Assistant Technical Director; Alfonso L. Macaranas, Frequency and Monitoring. Free caps, T-shirts, stickers, pennants, rulers, pens, postcards and calendars. Free bi-monthly newsletter *UPLINK*. Return postage appreciated.
TRANSMITTER SITE: Radio Veritas Asia, Palauig, Zambales, Philippines. Contact: Fr. Hugo Delbaere, CICM, Technical Consultant.
BRUSSELS BUREAUS AND MAIL DROPS: Catholic Radio and Television Network, 32-34 Rue de l' Association, B-1000 Brussels, Belgium; or UNDA, 12 Rue de l'Orme, B-1040 Brussels, Belgium.

PIRATE

Pirate radio stations are usually one-person operations airing home-brew entertainment and/or iconoclastic viewpoints. In order to avoid detection by the authorities, they tend to appear irregularly, with little concern for the niceties of conventional program scheduling. Most are found in Europe chiefly on weekends and holidays, often just above 6200 and 7375 kHz; and in North America mainly during evenings, just below 7000 kHz (usually 6925 plus or minus 10 kHz). These *sub rosa* stations and their addresses are subject to unusually abrupt change or termination, sometimes as a result of forays by radio authorities.

A popular Internet source of information is the Free Radio Network (www.frn.net). For Europirate DX news, try:
Swedish Report Service: SRS, Ostra Porten 29, SE-442 54 Ytterby, Sweden. Web: www.srs.pp.se.
Free Radio Service Holland: FRSH, P.O. Box 2727, NL-6049 ZG Herten, Netherlands. Email: freak55@gironet.nl, or peter.verbruggen@tip.nl. Web: www.gironet.nl/home/freak55/nl.htm. Publishes the quarterly "FRS Newsletter."
FRC-Finland, P.O. Box 82, FIN-40101 Jyvaskyla, Finland.
A good list of pirate links can be found at: www.alfalima.net/links-links.htm.
For up-to-date listener discussions and other pirate-radio information on the Internet, the usenet URLs are: alt.radio.pirate and rec.radio.pirate.

POLAND   World Time +1 (+2 midyear)

⬛Bible Christian Association (BCA). Email (English and Polish) kontakt@radio.zapraszamy.pl. Web: (includes on-demand audio) www.radio.zapraszamy.pl. Rarely replies. Reception reports are best sent to Walter Brodowsky at Germany's T-Systems International (*see*) from where the broadcasts are transmitted.

⬛Radio Polonia, P.O. Box 46, PL-00-977 Warsaw, Poland; (street address) al. Niepodległości 77/85, 00-977 Warsaw, Poland. Phone: (general) +48 (22) 645-9305; (English Section) +48 (22) 645-9262; (German Section) +48 (22) 645-9333; (placement liaison) +48 (2) 645-9002. Fax: (general and administration) +48 (22) 645 5917. Email: (general): radio.polonia@radio.com.pl; (Polish Section) polonia@radio.com.pl; (English Section) english.section@radio.com.pl; (German Section) deutsche.redaktion@radio.com.pl; (Esperanto Section) esperanto.redakcio@radio.com.pl. Web: (includes on-demand

English department
of Radio Romania
International: (front)
Eugen Nasta, Justina
Irimia, Eugenia Chira,
Iulian Muresan; (rear)
Cristina Tiberian, Daniel
Bilt, Diana Vajeu, Mihaela
Ignatescu, Cristina
Mateescu. RRI

and streaming audio) www.polskieradio.pl/polonia. Contact: (general) Rafał Kiepuszewski, Editor, English Service; (administration) Jerzy M. Nowakowski, Managing Director; Wanda Samborska, Managing Director; Bogumiła Berdychowska, Deputy Managing Director; Maciej Lętowski, Executive Manager. On-air Polish language course with free printed material. Free stickers, pens, key rings, stamps and sometimes T-shirts, depending on resources.

PORTUGAL World Time exactly (+1 midyear); Azores World Time –1 (World Time midyear)

Deutsche Welle—Relay Station Sines, Pro-Funk GmbH, Monte Mudo, P-7520-065 Sines, Portugal. Phone: +351 (269) 870-280. Fax: +351 (269) 870 290. Email: profunk@mail.telepac.pt. This address for specialised technical correspondence only. All other correspondence (including reception reports) should be directed to the main offices in Bonn, Germany (see). Also used by RDP Internacional (see next entry).

📻RDP Internacional—Rádio Portugal, Av. Marechal Gomes da Costa nº 37, 1849-030 Lisboa, Portugal. Phone: (general) +351 (21) 382-0000. Fax: (general) +351 (21) 382 0165. Email: (general) rdpinternacional@rdp.pt; (reception reports and listener correspondence) isabelsaraiva@rdp.pt. Web: (includes streaming audio and bilingual English-Portuguese online reception report form) http://programas.rtp.pt/EPG/radio. Contact: Isabel Saraiva, Listeners' Service Department. Verifies reception reports. Return postage not required. Free stickers and other small gifts. May also send literature from the Portuguese National Tourist Office.

DIRECÇÃO TÉCNICA-GRUPO REDES DE EMISSORES: Av. Marechal Gomes da Costa, 37, Bloco B-2º 1849-030 Lisbon Portugal. Phone: +351 (21) 382-0228. Fax: +351 (21) 382 0098. Email: teresaabreu@rdp.pt, paulacarvalho@rdp.pt. Contact: Mrs. Teresa Beatriz Abreu, Frequency Manager; or Ms. Paula Carvalho.

ROMANIA World Time +2 (+3 midyear)

📻Radio România International, 60-62 Berthelot St., RO-70747 Bucharest, Romania; or P.O. Box 111, RO-70756 Bucharest, Romania. Phone: (general) +40 (21) 222-2556, +40 (21) 303-1172, +40 (21) 303-1488, +40 (21) 312-3645; (English Department) +40 (21) 303-1357, +40 (21) 303-1465; (engineering) +40 (21) 303-1193. Fax: (English Service) +40 (21) 319 0562; (Engineering Services) +40 (21) 312 1056/7, +40 (21) 615 6992. Email: (general) rri@rri.ro; (English Service) engl@rri.ro. Web: (includes streaming audio) www.rri.ro; (on-demand audio) www.wrn.org/listeners/stations/station.php?StationID=106. Contact: Ioana Masariu, Head of the English Service; Daniel Biltz, Editor "DX Mailbag." Replies slowly. Concerns about frequency management should be directed to the PTT (see, below), with copies to the Romanian Autonomous Company (see farther below) and to a suitable official at RRI.

TRANSMISSION AND FREQUENCY MANAGEMENT, PTT: General Directorate of Regulations, Ministry of Communications, 14a Al. Libertatii, R-70060 Bucharest, Romania. Phone: +40 (21) 400-1312, +40 (21) 400-177. Fax: +40 (21) 400 1230. Email: marian@snr.ro. Contact: Mrs. Elena Danila, Head of Frequency Management Department.

TRANSMISSION AND FREQUENCY MANAGEMENT, AUTONOMOUS COMPANY: Romanian Autonomous Company for Radio Communications, 14a Al. Libertatii, R-70060 Bucharest, Romania. Phone: +40 (21) 400-1072. Fax: +40 (21) 400 1228, +40 (1) 335 5965. Email: marian@snr.ro. Contact: Mr. Marian Ionitá, Executive Director of Operations.

RUSSIA (Times given for republics, oblasts and krays):

• World Time +2 (+3 midyear) Kaliningradskaya;
• World Time +3 (+4 midyear) Adygeya, Arkhangelskaya, Astrakhanskaya, Belgorodskaya, Bryanskaya, Chechnya, Chuvashiya, Dagestan, Ingushetiya, Kabardino-Balkariya, Kalmykiya, Kaluzhskaya, Karachayevo-Cherkesiya, Ivanovskaya, Karelia, Kirovskaya, Komi, Kostromskaya, Krasnodarskiy, Kurskaya, Leningradskaya (including St. Petersburg), Lipetskaya, Mariy-El, Mordoviya, Moskovskaya (including the capital, Moscow), Murmanskaya, Nenetskiy, Nizhegorodskaya, Novgorodskaya, Severnaya Osetiya, Orlovskaya, Penzenskaya, Pskovskaya, Rostovskaya, Ryazanskaya, Saratovskaya, Smolenskaya, Stavropolskiy, Tambovskaya, Tatarstan, Tulskaya, Tverskaya, Ulyanovskaya, Vladimirskaya, Volgogradskaya, Vologodskaya, Voronezhskaya, Yaroslavskaya;
• World Time +4 (+5 midyear) Samarskaya, Udmurtiya;
• World Time +5 (+6 midyear) Bashkortostan, Chelyabinskaya, Khanty-Mansiyskiy, Komi-Permyatskiy, Kurganskaya, Orenburgskaya, Permskaya, Sverdlovskaya, Tyumenskaya, Yamalo-Nenetskiy;

- World Time +6 (+7 midyear) Altayskiy, Novosibirskaya, Omskaya, Tomskaya;
- World Time +7 (+8 midyear) Evenkiyskiy, Kemerovskaya, Khakasiya, Krasnoyarskiy, Taymyrskiy, Tyva;
- World Time +8 (+9 midyear) Buryatiya, Irkutskaya, Ust-Ordynskiy;
- World Time +9 (+10 midyear) Aginskiy-Buryatskiy, Amurskaya, Chitinskaya, Sakha;
- World Time +10 (+11 midyear) Khabarovskiy, Primorskiy, Yevreyskaya;
- World Time +11 (+12 midyear) Magadanskaya, Sakhalinskaya;
- World Time +12 (+13 midyear) Chukotskiy, Kamchatskaya, Koryakskiy.

C.I.S. FREQUENCY MANAGEMENT ENGINEERING OFFICE: General Radio Frequency Center, 25 Pyatnitskaya Str., 113326 Moscow, Russia. Phone: +7 (095) 950-6022; Phone/Fax: +7 (095) 789-3587. Email: (Titov) a_titov@vor.ru. Web: (General Radio Frequency Center parent organization) www.grfc.ru. Contact: (general) Mrs. Nina Bykova, Monitoring Coordinator; (administration) Anatoliy T. Titov, Chief of Division for SW and MW Frequency Broadcasting Schedules. This office is responsible for the operation of radio broadcasting in the Russian Federation, as well as for frequency usage of transmitters throughout much of the C.I.S. Correspondence should be concerned only with significant technical observations or engineering suggestions concerning frequency management improvement—not regular requests for verifications. Correspondence in Russian preferred, but English accepted.

Adygey Radio—*see* Maykop Radio.

Amur Radio—*see* Blagoveschensk Radio.

Arkhangel'sk Radio, GTRK "Pomorye," ul. Popova 2, 163061 Arkhangel'sk, Arkhangel'skaya Oblast, Russia; or U1PR, Valentin G. Kalasnikov, ul. Suvorov 2, kv. 16, Arkhangel'sk, Arkhangel'skaya Oblast, Russia. Replies irregularly to correspondence in Russian.

Blagoveschensk Radio, GTRK "Amur," per Svyatitelya Innokentiya 15, 675000 Blagoveschensk, Russia. Contact: V.I. Kal'chenko, Chief Engineer.

Buryat Radio—*see* Ulan-Ude Radio.

Kabardino-Balkar Radio—*see* Nalchik Radio.

Kamchatka Rybatskaya—a special service for fishermen off the coasts of China, Japan and western North America; *see* Petropavlovsk-Kamchatskiy Radio for contact details.

Khanty-Mansiysk Radio, GTRK "Yugoriya," ul. Mira 7, 626200 Khanty-Mansiysk, Russia. Contact: (technical) Vladimir Sokolov, Engineer.

Krasnoyarsk Radio, Krasnoyarskaya GTRK, "Tsentr Rossii," ul. Mechnikova 44A, 660028 Krasnoyarsk, Krasnoyarskiy Kray, Russia. Email: postmaster@telegid.krasnoyarsk.su. Contact: Valeriy Korotchenko; Anatoliy A. Potehin, RA0AKE. Free local information booklets in English/Russian. Replies in Russian to correspondence in Russian or English. Return postage helpful.

Kyzyl Radio, GTRK "Tyva," ul. Gornaya 31, 667003 Kyzyl, Respublika Tyva, Russia. Email: tv@tuva.ru. Replies to correspondence in Russian.

Magadan Radio, GTRK "Magadan," ul. Kommuny 8/12, 685024 Magadan, Magadanskaya Oblast, Russia. Phone: +7 (41322) 22-935. Fax: +7 (41322) 24 977. Email: center@magtrk.ru. Web: www.magtrk.ru. Contact: Viktor Loktionov, V.G. Kuznetsov. Return postage helpful. Occasionally replies to correspondence in Russian.

Mariy Radio—*see* Yoshkar-Ola Radio.

Mayak—*see* Radiostantsiya Mayak.

Maykop Radio, GTRK "Adygeya," ul. Zhukovskogo 24, 385000 Maykop, Republic of Adygeya, Russia. Contact: A.T. Kerashev, Chairman. English accepted but Russian preferred. Return postage helpful.

Murmansk Radio, GTRK "Murman," per. Rusanova 7, 183032 Murmansk, Murmanskaya Oblast, Russia. Phone: +7 (8152) 472-327. Email: radio@tvmurman.com. Web: http://sampo.ru/~tvmurman/index_ie.html. Contact: D. Perederi (chairman).

Nalchik Radio, GTRK "Kabbalk Teleradio," pr. Lenina 3, 360000 Nalchik, Republic of Kabardino-Balkariya, Russia. Contact: Kamal Makitov, Vice-Chairman. Replies to correspondence in Russian.

Perm Radio, Permskaya GTRK "T-7," ul. Tekhnicheskaya 7, 614070 Perm, Permskaya Oblast, Russia. Contact: M. Levin, Senior Editor; A. Losev, Acting Chief Editor.

Petropavlovsk-Kamchatskiy Radio, GTRK "Kamchatka," ul. Sovetskaya 62, 683000 Petropavlovsk-Kamchatskiy, Kamchatskaya Oblast, Russia. Contact: A.F. Borodin, Head of GTRK "Kamchatka." Email: gtrkbuh@mail.iks.ru. $1 required for postal reply. Replies in Russian to correspondence in Russian or English. Currently inactive on shortwave, apart from a special program for fishermen—*see* Kamchatka Rybatskaya.

Radio Gardarika (when operating), Radio Studio Dom Radio, Ligovsky Prospekt 174, 197002 St. Petersburg, Russia. Email: studiosw@metroclub.ru. Contact: Suvorov Alexey, Shortwave Project Manager. Replies to correspondence in Russian or English. Return postage helpful.

Radio Nalchik—*see* Nalchik Radio, above.

Radio Radonezh—*see* Radiostantsiya Radonezh

⊠**Radio Rossii** (Russia's Radio), GRK "Radio Rossii," Yamskogo Polya 5-YA ul. 19/21, 125040 Moscow, Russia. Phone: +7 (495) 213-1054, +7 (495) 250-0511, +7 (495) 251-4050. Fax: +7 (495) 250 0105, +7 (495) 233 6449, +7 (495) 214 4767. Email: mail@radiorus.ru; direction@radiorus.ru Web: (includes on-demand and streaming audio) www.radiorus.ru. Contact: Sergei Yerofeyev, Director of International Operations [sic]; Sergei Davidov, Director. Free English-language information sheet.

Radio Studio—*see* Radio Gardarika.

⊠**Radiostantsiya Radonezh**, ul. Pyatnitskaya 25, Moscow 115326, Russia. Phone/Fax: +7 (495) 950-6356. Email: radonezh@radonezh.ru. Web: (includes on-demand and streaming audio) www.radonezh.ru/radio. Replies to correspondence in Russian or English.

⊠**Radiostantsiya Tikhiy Okean** ("Radio Station Pacific Ocean"), GTRK "Vladivostok," ul. Uborevicha 20-A, 690950 Vladivostok, Primorskiy Kray, Russia. Phone: +7 (4232) 223-454. Email: ptr@ptr-vlad.ru. Web: (includes streaming audio) www.ptr-vlad.ru/tv&radio; (unofficial, includes schedule) http://oceandx.narod.ru. Contact: (technical) Alexey Giryuk, Engineer, Technical Department. $2 return postage helpful. Replies to correspondence in Russian or English, and verifies reception reports. A program for mariners produced by Primorye Radio and aired on 810 kHz mediumwave AM and shortwave.

Russian International Radio (Russkoye Mezhdunarodnoye Radio)—a service of the Voice of Russia (*see*) in cooperation with the domestic Russkoye Radio. Email: rir@vor.ru.

Sakhalin Radio, GTRK "Sakhalin," ul. Komsomolskaya 209, 693000 Yuzhno-Sakhalinsk, Sakhalinskaya Oblast, Russia. Phone: (Director of Radio) +7 (42422) 729-349. Phone/Fax: (GTRK parent company) +7 (42422) 35286. Email:

Michail Chernykh, Elena Golovkina and Nikolai Zakharov enjoy afternoon coffee at the Voice of Russia in Moscow. Broadcasts from here were vital to Russia's resistance, especially once Hitler's troops reached Moscow.   VoR

gtrk@sakhalin.ru; (Romanov) romanov@gtrk.sakhalin.su. Web: www.gtrk.ru/Company/o_radio.html. Contact: S. Romanov, Director of Radio.

⌨Special Radio (Spezialnoye Radio), Office 417, Efremova st. 10, 113092 Moscow, Russia. Phone/Fax: +7 (495) 775-4821. Email: admin@specialradio.ru; (Anikeeva) anikmay@specialradio.ru. Web: (includes streaming audio) www.specialradio.ru Contact: Maria Anikeeva, Press Secretary/PR Manager. An Internet broadcaster which describes itself as "an international corporate Internet project of musicians and contemporary art activists." The shortwave broadcast, "Actual music from Russia," is via a hired transmitter.

Tatarstan Wave ("Tatarstan Dulkynda"), GTRK "Tatarstan," ul. Gor'kogo 15, 420015 Kazan, Tatarstan, Russia. Phone: (general) +7 (8432) 384-846; (editorial) +7 (8432) 367-493. Fax: +7 (8432) 361 283. Email: root@gtrkrt.kazan.su; postmaster@stvcrt.kazan.su. Contact: Hania Hazipovna Galinova. Formerly known as Voice of Tatarstan.
ADDRESS FOR RECEPTION REPORTS: QSL Manager, P.O. Box 134, 420136 Kazan, Tatarstan, Russia. Contact: Ildus Ibatullin, QSL Manager. Offers an honorary diploma in return for 12 correct reports in a given year. The diploma costs 2 IRCs for Russia and 4 IRCs elsewhere. Accepts reports in Russian or English. Return postage helpful.

Ulan-Ude Radio, Buryatskaya GTRK, ul. Erbanova 7, 670000 Ulan-Ude, Republic of Buryatia, Russia. Contact: Z.A. Telin; Mrs. M.V. Urbaeva, 1st Vice-Chairman; L.S. Shikhanova.

⌨Voice of Russia, FGU RGRK "Golos Rossii," ul. Pyatnitskaya 25, 115326 Moscow, Russia. Phone: (Chairman) +7 (495) 950-6331; (International Relations Department) +7 (495) 950-6440; (Technical Department) +7 (495) 950-6115. Fax: (Chairman) +7 (495) 230 2828; (Letters Department, World Service in English) +7 (495) 951 9552. Email: (Letters Department, World Service in English) world@vor.ru; (for all language services) letters@vor.ru; (Spanish) cartas@vor.ru; (German) post-de@vor.ru. Web: (includes on-demand and streaming audio) www.vor.ru. Contact: (Letters Department, World Service in English) Elena Osipova or Elena Frolovskaya; (Chairman) Armen Oganesyan; (International Relations Department) Victor Kopytin, Director; (Technical Department) Mrs. Rachel Staviskaya, Director; (World Service in English) Vladimir Zhamkin, Director. For language services other than English contact the International Relations Department.
SAN FRANCISCO OFFICE, SCHEDULES: 2654 17th Avenue, San Francisco CA 94116 USA. Phone: +1 (415) 564-9968. Email: GPoppin@aol.com. Contact: George Poppin. This address, a volunteer office, only provides Voice of Russia schedules to listeners (return postage not required). All other correspondence should be sent directly to the Voice of Russia in Moscow.

Yakutsk Radio, NVK "Sakha," ul. Ordzhonikidze 48, 677007 Yakutsk, Respublika Sakha, Russia. Contact: (general) Alexandra Borisova; Lia Sharoborina, Advertising Editor; Albina Danilova, Producer, "Your Letters"; (technical) Sergei Bobnev, Technical Director. Russian books $15; audio cassettes $10. Free station stickers and original Yakutian souvenirs. Replies to correspondence in English.

RWANDA   World Time +2

Deutsche Welle—Relay Station Kigali. Correspondence should be directed to the main offices in Bonn, Germany (see).

Radio Rwanda, B.P. 83, Kigali, Rwanda. Phone: +250 76180. Fax: +250 76185. Email: radiorwanda@yahoo.com. Contact: Marcel Singirankabo. $1 required. Occasionally replies, with correspondence in French preferred.

ST. HELENA   World Time exactly

Radio St. Helena (when operating once each year), Broadway House, Main Street, Jamestown, St. Helena, South Atlantic Ocean. Phone: +290 4669. Fax: +290 4542. Email: radio.sthelena@helanta.sh. Contact: Station Manager. Verifies reception reports if 3 IRCs included. Does not verify email reports. Is on the air on world band only once each year—usually late October or early November.

SAO TOME E PRINCIPE   World Time exactly

Voice of America/IBB—São Tomé Relay Station, P.O. Box 522, São Tomé, São Tomé e Príncipe. Contact: Charles L. Lewis, Transmitting Station Manager. This address for specialized technical correspondence only. All other correspondence, including reception reports, should be sent to the usual VOA or IBB addresses in Washington (*see* USA).

SAUDI ARABIA   World Time +3

🖳**Broadcasting Service of the Kingdom of Saudi Arabia**, P.O. Box 61718, Riyadh-11575, Saudi Arabia. Phone: (general) +966 (1) 404-2795; (administration) +966 (1) 442-5493; (engineering) +966 (1) 442-5170; (frequency management) +966 (1) 442-5127. Fax: (general) +966 (1) 402 8177; (engineering and frequency management) +966 (1) 404 1692. Email: (frequency management) freq.mgt@saudinform.org; (Al-Samnan) alsamnan@yahoo.com. Web: (streaming audio) www.saudi-radio.net. Contact: (general) Mutlaq A. Albegami; (technical) Suleiman Al-Samnan, Director of Engineering; Youssef Dhim, Frequency Management. Free travel information and book on Saudi history.

SENEGAL   World Time exactly

🖳**West Africa Democracy Radio (WADR)**, P.O. Box 16650, Dakar-Fann, Senegal; (street address) Sacré-Coeur 1, Villa N 8408, Dakar, Senegal. Phone: +221 869-1569. Fax: +221 864 7009. Email: wadr@wadr.org; (Abdou Lô) abdoulo@wadr.org, abdoulo@hotmail.fr. Web: (includes on-demand audio) www.wadr.org. Contact: Abdou Lô, Bilingual Researcher. Verifies reception reports. Correspondence in French preferred. One IRC or $1 requested for postal reply. Broadcasts via leased facilities in the United Kingdom.

SERBIA   World Time +1 (+2 midyear)

🖳**International Radio Serbia** (when operating), Hilendarska 2, P.O. Box 200, 11000 Beograd, Serbia. Phone: +381 (11) 324-4455. Fax: +381 (11) 323 2014. Email: radioyu@bitsyu.net. Web: (includes on-demand audio) www.radioyu.org. Replies irregularly. $1 helpful.
Radio Beograd—a service of Radio-Televizija Srbije (*see*, below).
🖳**Radio-Televizija Srbije** (when operating), Takovska 10, 11000 Beograd, Serbia. Phone: +381 (11) 321-2000. Email: rtstv@rts.co.yu. Web: (includes streaming audio) www.rts.co.yu. Broadcasts irregularly via the transmitters of International Radio Serbia (*see*).

SEYCHELLES   World Time +4

BBC World Service—Indian Ocean Relay Station, P.O. Box 448, Victoria, Mahé, Seychelles. Phone: +248 78-496. Fax: +248 78 500. Contact: (technical) Albert Quatre, Senior Engineer. Nontechnical correspondence should be sent to the BBC World Service in London (*see*).

SIERRA LEONE   World Time exactly

Radio UNAMSIL (when operating), Mammy Yoko Hotel, P.O. Box 5, Freetown, Sierra Leone. Email: info@unamsil.org; patrickcoker@unamsil.org. Web: (UNAMSIL parent organiza-

tion) www.unamsil.org. Contact: Patrick Coker; Sheila Dallas, Station Manager & Executive Producer. Station of the United Nations Mission in Sierra Leone.
Sierra Leone Broadcasting Service (if reactivated), New England, Freetown, Sierra Leone. Phone: +232 (22) 240-123; +232 (22) 240-173; +232 (22) 240-497, 232 (22) 241-919. Fax: +232 (22) 240 922. Contact: Cyril Juxon-Smith, Officer in Charge; Henry Goodaig Hjax, Assistant Engineer.

SINGAPORE   World Time +8

BBC World Service—Far Eastern Relay Station, VT Communications, 51 Turut Track, Singapore 718930, Singapore. Phone: + 65 6793-7511/3. Fax: +65 6793 7834. Email: (Wui Pin Yong) wuipin@singnet.com.sg. Contact: (technical) Mr. Wui Pin Yong, Operations Manager; or Far East Resident Engineer. Nontechnical correspondence should be sent to the BBC World Service in London (*see*).
🖳**MediaCorp Radio**, Farrer Road, P.O. Box 968, Singapore 912899, Singapore; (street address) Caldecott Broadcast Centre, Caldecott Hill, Andrew Road, Singapore 299939, Singapore. Phone: (general) +65 6333-3888; (transmitting station) +65 6793-7651. Fax: +65 6251 5628. Web: (includes streaming audio) www.mediacorpradio.com.sg. Free regular and Post-It stickers, pens, umbrellas, mugs, towels, wallets and lapel pins. Do not include currency in envelope. Successor to the former Radio Corporation of Singapore.
🖳**Radio Singapore International**, Farrer Road, P.O. Box 5300, Singapore 912899, Singapore; (street address) Caldecott Broadcast Centre, Annex Building Level 1, Andrew Road, Singapore 299939, Singapore. Phone: (general) + 65 6359-7663; (English Service) + 65 6359-7671. Fax: (general) +65 6259 1357. Email: info@rsi.sg; (English Service) english@rsi.sg (if these don't work, try the online email form). Web: (includes on-demand audio) www.rsi.sg. Contact: (general) Sakuntala Gupta, Programme Director, English Service; Augustine Anthuvan, Assistant Programme Director, English Service; (technical) Lim Wing Kee, RSI Engineering. Free souvenir T-shirts and key chains to selected listeners. Do not include currency in envelope.

SOLOMON ISLANDS   World Time +11

Solomon Islands Broadcasting Corporation (Radio Happy Isles), P.O. Box 654, Honiara, Solomon Islands. Phone: +677 20051. Fax: +677 23159, +677 25652. Email: sibcnews@solomon.com.sb. Web: www.sibconline.com.sb. Contact: (general) David Palapu, Manager Broadcast Operations; Julian Maka'a, Producer, "Listeners From Far Away"; Walter Nalangu, News & Current Affairs; Rachel Rahi'i, Commercial/Advertising; Bart Basi, Programmes; (administration) Grace Ngatulu; (technical) Cornelius Rathamana, Chief Engineer. IRC or $1 helpful. Problems with the domestic mail system may cause delays.

SOMALIA   World Time +3

Radio Galkayo (when operating), 2 Griffith Avenue, Roseville NSW 2069, Australia. Phone/Fax: +61 (2) 9417-1066. Email: svoron@hotmail.com. Contact: Sam Voron, VK2BVS, 6O0A, Australian Director. Replies to email correspondence at no charge, but $5, AUS$5 or 5 IRCs required for postal replies. A community radio station in the Mudug region, Puntland State, northern Somalia and supported by local and overseas volunteers. Seeks volunteers, donations of radio equipment and airline tickets, and is setting up a Radio Galkayo Amateur Radio Club station.

Radio Hargeysa—*see* SOMALILAND.

📻**Radio Shabelle**, Global Building, 3rd Floor, Mogadishu, Somalia. Phone: +252 (1) 659-699, +252 (1) 227-733, +252 (5) 933-111. Fax: +252 (1) 659 699. Email: radio@shabelle.net; info@shabelle.net; (Malik) maalik@shabelle.net. Web: (includes on-demand audio) www.shabelle.net. Contact:Abdi Malik Yusuf Mohamud, Chairman.

SOMALILAND   World Time +3

NOTE: "Somaliland," claimed as an independent nation, is diplomatically recognized only as part of Somalia.

📻**Radio Hargeysa** (when operating), P.O. Box 14, Hargeysa, Somaliland, Somalia. Email: radiohargeysa@yahoo.com. Web: (on-demand audio) www.radiosomaliland.com/radiohargeisa. html. Contact: Muhammad Said Muhummad, Manager.

ADDRESS IN GERMANY: c/o Konsularische Vertretung Somaliland, Baldur Drobnica, Zedernweg 6, D-50127 Bergheim, Germany. Contact: Baldur Drobnica. Verifies reception reports (including those in English). Return postage required ($1 for Europe, $3 elsewhere). Baldur Drobnica is a radio amateur, call-sign DJ6SI.

SOUTH AFRICA   World Time +2

BBC World Service via South Africa—For verification direct from the South African transmitters, contact Sentech (*see*, below). Nontechnical correspondence should be sent to the BBC World Service in London (*see*).

📻**Channel Africa**, P.O. Box 91313, Auckland Park 2006, South Africa. Phone: (executive editor) +27 (11) 714-2255; (technical) +27 (11) 714-2537. Fax: (executive editor) + 27 (11) 714 2537; (technical) +27 (11) 714 2072. Email: (general) africancan@channelafrica.org; (Ntenteni) ntentenit@sabc. co.za; (Moloto) molotod@sabc.co.za; (Mate, technical) matemm@channelafrica.org. Web: (includes on-demand and streaming audio) www.channelafrica.org. Contact: (general) Thami Ntenteni, Executive Editor; David Moloto, Content Senior Manager; (technical) Maurice M. Mate, Web & Technical Senior Manager. Reception reports are best directed to Sentech (*see*), which operates the transmission facilities.

📻**Radiosondergrense (Radio Without Boundaries)**, Posbus 91312, Auckland Park 2006, South Africa. Phone: +27 (11) 714-2702. Fax: +27 (11) 714 3472. Email: info@rsg.co.za. Web: (includes streaming audio) www.rsg.co.za. Reception reports are best directed to Sentech (*see*, below), which operates the shortwave transmission facilities. A domestic service of the South African Broadcasting Corporation, and formerly known as Afrikaans Stereo. The shortwave operation is scheduled to be eventually replaced by a satellite and FM network.

Sentech Ltd., Transmission Planning, Private Bag X06, Honeydew 2040, South Africa. Phone: (general) +27 (11) 471-4400, +27 (11) 691-7000; (shortwave) +27 (11) 471-4658. Fax: (shortwave) +27 (11) 471 4754. Email: (Kathy Otto) ottok@sentech.co.za. Web: (schedules & frequencies) www. sentech.co.za. Contact: Kathy Otto, HF Coverage Planner. Sentech verifies reception reports on transmissions from the Meyerton shortwave facilities.

📻**South African Radio League—Amateur Radio Mirror International**, P.O. Box 90438, Garsfontein 0042, South Africa. Email: armi@sarl.org.za. Web: www.sarl.org.za/public/ARMI/

Radio Exterior de España's English service offers a wealth of news, followed by educational and entertainment features.   REE

ARMI.asp; (on-demand audio) www.amsatsa.org.za. Accepts email reception reports. Amateur Radio Mirror International is a weekly broadcast aired via Sentech's Meyerton facilities.

Trans World Radio Africa

NONTECHNICAL CORRESPONDENCE: Trans World Radio Africa, P.O. Box 4232, Kempton Park 1620, South Africa. Phone: +27 (11) 974-2886. Fax: +27 (11) 974 9960. Email: online form. Web: www.twrafrica.org.

TECHNICAL CORRESPONDENCE: Reception reports and other technical correspondence are best directed to Sentech (*see*, above) or to TWR's Swaziland office (*see*). Also, *see* USA.

SPAIN   World Time +1 (+2 midyear)

📻**Radio Exterior de España (Spanish National Radio, World Service)**

MAIN OFFICE: Apartado de Correos 156.202, E-28080 Madrid, Spain. Phone: (general) +34 (91) 346-1081/1083; (Audience Relations) +34 (91) 346-1149. Fax: +34 (91) 346 1815. Email: (Director) dir_ree.rne@rtve.es; (Spanish programming, listener feedback) audiencia_ree.rne@rtve.es, radioexterior. espana@rtve.es. Web: (includes on-demand and streaming audio) www.ree.rne.es. Contact: (Audience Relations) Pilar Salvador M.; (Assistant Director) Pedro Fernández Céspedes; (Director) Francisco Fernández Oria. Free stickers and tourist information. Verification of reception reports is temporarily suspended due to "staffing and budget constraints." Listeners are requested not to send cash or IRCs, since the limited services which still exist are free. An alternative, for those who understand Spanish, is to send a reception report on the program "Españoles en la Mar" which is produced in the Canary Islands by Mary Cortés. Times and frequencies can be found at the REE Website. Reports should be sent to: Programa "Españoles en la Mar," Apartado Postal 1233, Santa Cruz de Tenerife, Islas Canarias, Spain. Magazines and small souvenirs are sometimes included with verifications from this address. Correspondence in Spanish preferred, but English also accepted.

TRANSCRIPTION SERVICE: Radio Nacional de España, Servicio de Transcripciones, Apartado 156.200, Casa de la Radio (Prado del Rey), E-28223 Madrid, Spain.

HF FREQUENCY PLANNING OFFICE: Prado del Rey. Pozuelo de Alarcom, E-28223 Madrid, Spain. Phone: (Huerta) +34 (91) 346-1276; (Arlanzón) +34 (91) 346-1639; (Almarza) +34 (91) 346-

1978. Fax: (Huerta & Almarza) +34 (91) 346 1402; (Alanzón) +34 (91) 346 1275. Email: (Almarza) planif_red2.rne@rtve.es; (Huerta & Arlanzón) plan_red.rne@rtve.es. Contact: Fernando Almarza, Frequency Planning; Salvador Arlanzón, HF Frequency Manager; José Maria Huerta, Technical Director.

NOBLEJAS TRANSMITTER SITE: Centro Emisor de RNE en Onda Corta, Ctra. Dos Barrios s/n, E-45350 Noblejas-Toledo, Spain.

COSTA RICA RELAY FACILITY—see Costa Rica.

SRI LANKA   World Time +5:30

Deutsche Welle—Relay Station Sri Lanka, 92/1 D.S. Sena-nayake Mawatha, Colombo 08, Sri Lanka. Phone: +94 (11) 2464-483. Fax: +94 (11) 2699 450. Contact: R. Groschkus, Resident Engineer. This address for specialized technical correspondence only. All other correspondence should be sent to Deutsche Welle in Germany (*see*).

Radio Japan/NHK—All correspondence should be sent to the Radio Japan address in Tokyo (*see* Japan).

▣Sri Lanka Broadcasting Corporation (also announces as "Radio Sri Lanka" in the external service), P.O. Box 574, Independence Square, Colombo 7, Sri Lanka. Phone: +94 (11) 2697-491. Fax: (general) +94 (11) 2691 568; (Director General) +94 (11) 2695 488. Email: slbc@sri.lanka.net, slbcddge@sri.lanka.net. Web: (includes streaming audio) www.slbc.lk.

Voice of America/IBB—Iranawila Relay Station.
ADDRESS: Station Manager, IBB Sri Lanka Transmitting Station, c/o U.S. Embassy, 210 Galle Road, Colombo 3, Sri Lanka. Contact: Walter Patterson, Station Manager. This address for specialized technical correspondence only, although some reception reports may be verified, depending on who is at the site. All other correspondence should be directed to the regular VOA or IBB addresses (*see* USA).

SUDAN   World Time +3

Radio Peace
ADDRESS FOR RECEPTION REPORTS: pete@edmedia.org. Contact: Peter Stover, who requests that audio attachments not be sent with reception reports.

▣Sudan Radio and TV Corporation (SRTC), P.O. Box 572, Omdurman, Sudan. Phone: +249 (11) 555-684. Phone/Fax: (technical) +249 (15) 550-492. Email: (technical) salihb@maktoob.com. Web: www.srtc.gov.sd; (streaming audio) www.sudanradio.info. Contact: (general) Mohammed Elfatih El Sumoal; (technical) Bachir Saleh, Deputy Director of Engineering. Replies irregularly. Return postage necessary.

SURINAME   World Time –3

▣Radio Apintie, Postbus 595, Paramaribo, Suriname; (street address) verl. Gemenelandsweg 37, Paramaribo, Suriname. Phone: (studio) +597 400-500, (office) +597 400-450. Fax: +597 400 684. Email: apintie@sr.net. Web: (includes streaming audio) www.apintie.sr. Contact: Charles E. Vervuurt, Director. Free pennant. Return postage or $1 required. Email reception reports preferred, since local mail service is unreliable.

SWAZILAND   World Time +2

Trans World Radio, P.O. Box 64, Manzini, Swaziland. Phone: +268 505-2781/2/3. Fax: +268 505 5333. Email: (Chief Engineer) sstavrop@twr.org; (Mrs. Stavropoulos) lstavrop@twr.org; (Greg Shaw) gshaw@twr.org. Web: (transmission schedule)

www.twrafrica.org/programmes/index.asp. Contact: (general) Greg Shaw, Follow-up Department; G.J. Alary, Station Director; Joseph Ndzinisa, Program Manager; (technical) Mrs. L. Stavropoulos, DX Secretary. Free stickers, postcards and calendars. A free Bible Study course is available. May swap canceled stamps. $1, return postage or 3 IRCs required. Also, *see* USA.

SWEDEN   World Time +1 (+2 midyear)

IBRA Radio, SE-141 99 Stockholm, Sweden. Phone: +46 (8) 608-9680. Fax: +46 (8) 608 9650. Email: ibra@ibra.se. Web: (Swedish) www.ibra.se; (English) www.ibra.org. Contact: Mikael Stjernberg, Public Relations Manager; Helene Hasslof. Free pennants and stickers. IBRA Radio's programs are aired over various world band stations, including Trans World Radio and FEBA Radio; and also broadcast independently via transmitters in Germany and Russia. Accepts email reception reports.

▣Radio Sweden, SE-105 10 Stockholm, Sweden. Phone: (general) +46 (8) 784-7288 or +46 (8) 784-7207; (listener voice mail) +46 (8) 784-7238; (technical department) +46 (8) 784-7282/6. Fax: (general) +46 (8) 667 6283; (listener service) +46 8 660 2990. Email: (general) radiosweden@sr.se; (English Service) mark.cummins@sr.se; george.wood@sr.se; (PR & Information) victoria.padin@sr.se, frida.sjolander@sr.se; (technical) anders.backlin@sr.se. Web: (includes on-demand and streaming audio) www.sr.se/rs or (shortcut to the English web page) www.radiosweden.org. Contact: (administration) Anne Sseruwagi, Director General, SR International; Gundula Adolfsson, Head of Radio Sweden; (English Service) Mark Cummins, Head of English Service; Gabby Katz, Producer; Bill Schiller, Producer; George Wood, Webmaster; (public relations and information) Victoria Padin, or Frida Sjolander; (technical department) Anders Backlin.

TRANSMISSION AUTHORITY: TERACOM, Svensk Rundradio AB, P.O. Box 17666, SE-118 92 Stockholm, Sweden. Phone: (general) +46 (8) 555-420-00; (Wiberg) +46 (8) 555-420-66. Fax: (general) +46 (8) 555 420 01; (Wiberg) +46 (8) 555 20 60. Email: (general) info@teracom.se; (Wiberg) magnus.wiberg@teracom.se. Web: www.teracom.se. Contact: (Frequency Planning Dept.—Head Office): Magnus Wiberg; (Engineering) Hakan Widenstedt, Chief Engineer. Free stickers; sometimes free T-shirts to those monitoring during special test transmissions. Seeks monitoring feedback for new frequency usages.

SWITZERLAND   World Time +1 (+2 midyear)

European Broadcasting Union, 17A Ancienne Route, CH-1218 Grand-Saconnex, Geneva, Switzerland; or Case Postal 67, CH-1218 Grand-Saconnex, Geneva, Switzerland. Phone: +41 (22) 717-2111. Fax: +41 (22) 747 2010. Email: ebu@ebu.ch. Web: www.ebu.ch. Contact: Mr. Jean Réveillon, Secretary-General. Umbrella organization for broadcasters in 49 European and Mediterranean countries.

International Telecommunication Union, Place des Nations, CH-1211 Geneva 20, Switzerland. Phone: (switchboard) +41 (22) 730-5111; (Broadcasting Services Division) +41 (22) 730-5933, +41 (22) 730-6136; (Terrestrial Services Department) +41 (22) 730-5514. Fax: (general) +41 (22) 733 7256; (Broadcasting Services Division) +41 (22) 730 5785. Email: (general) itumail@itu.int; (schedules and reference tables) brmail@itu.int. The ITU is the world's official regulatory body for all telecommunication activities, including world band radio. Offers a wide range of official multilingual telecommunication publications in print and/or digital formats.

■**Radio Réveil**, Paroles, Les Chapons 4, CH-2022 Bevaix, Switzerland. Phone: +41 (32) 846-1655. Fax: +41 (32) 846 2547. Email: contact@paroles.ch. Web (includes on-demand audio): www.paroles.ch. An evangelical radio ministry, part of the larger Radio Réveil Paroles de Vie organization, which apart from broadcasting to much of Europe on longwave, mediumwave AM and FM, also targets an African audience via the shortwave facilities of Germany's T-Systems International (*see*). Replies to correspondence in French or English, and verifies reception reports.

Stimme des Trostes, Missionswerk Arche, CH-9642 Ebnat-Kappel, Switzerland. Contact: Herbert Skutzik, Secretary. Replies to correspondence in German or English, and verifies reception reports. Return postage helpful. Via Germany's T-Systems International (*see*).

SYRIA   World Time +2 (+3 midyear)

■**Radio Damascus**, Syrian Radio and Television, P.O. Box 4702, Damascus, Syria. Phone: +963 (11) 221-7653. Fax: +963 (11) 222 2692. Email: radio@rtv.gov.sy; mostafab@scs-net.org; mmhrez@shuf.com; (Riad Sharaf Al-Din) riadsharafaldin@yahoo.com; (Marian Galindo, comments and reception reports in Spanish) radiodamasco@yahoo.com. Web: (includes on-demand audio) www.rtv.gov.sy. Contact: Adnan Salhab; Farid Shalash; Mohamed Hamida; (Spanish Section) Riad Sharaf Al-Din, Supervisor de Programas; Marian Galindo, Locutora; (technical) Mazen Al-Achhab, Head of Frequency Department. Free stickers, pennants and occasionally books and newspapers. Replies can be highly erratic, and sometimes slow. Members of the Spanish Section have suggested listeners use email, because of letters going astray.

TAIWAN—see CHINA (TAIWAN)

TAJIKISTAN   World Time +5

Radio Tajikistan, Chapaev Street 31, 734025 Dushanbe, Tajikistan; or English Service, International Service, Radio Tajikistan, P.O. Box 108, 734025 Dushanbe, Tajikistan. Phone: (Director) +992 (372) 210-877, +992 (372) 277-417; (English Department) +992 (372) 277-417; (Ramazonov) +992 (372) 277-667, +992 (372) 277-347. Fax: +992 (372) 211 198. Email: treng@td.silk.org. Web: http://radio.tojikiston.com. Contact: (administration) Abduqodir Talbakov, Director - Tajik Radio; Nasrullo Ramazonov, Foreign Relations Department. Correspondence in Russian or Tajik preferred. There is no official policy for verification of listeners' reports, so try sending reception reports and correspondence in English to the attention of Mr. Ramazonov, who is currently the sole English speaker at the station. Caution should be exercised when contacting him via email, as it is his personal account and he is charged for both incoming and outgoing mail. In addition, all email is routinely monitored and censored. Return postage (IRCs) helpful.

Tajik Radio, ul. Chapaeva 31, 734025 Dushanbe, Tajikistan. Contact information as for Radio Tajikistan, above.

TANZANIA   World Time +3

Radio Tanzania, Nyerere Road, P.O. Box 9191, Dar es Salaam, Tanzania. Phone: +255 (51) 860-760. Fax: +255 (51) 865 577. Email: radiotanzania@raha.com; (reception reports) nyamwocha@yahoo.com. Contact: (general) Abdul Ngarawa, Director of Broadcasting; Mrs. Edda Sanga, Controller of Programs; Ndaro Nyamwocha; Ms. Penzi Nyamungumi, Head of English Service and International Relations Unit; (technical) Taha Usi, Chief Engineer; Emmanuel Mangula, Deputy Chief Engineer. Replies to correspondence in English. Reports should go directly to Mr. Nyamwocha listed above. $1 return postage helpful.

Voice of Tanzania—Zanzibar, Department of Broadcasting, Radio Tanzania Zanzibar, P.O. Box 1178, Zanzibar, Tanzania—if this address brings no reply, try P.O. Box 2503. Phone: +255 (54) 231-088. Fax: + 255 (54) 257 207. Contact: Yusuf Omar Sunda, Director-General. $1 return postage helpful.

THAILAND   World Time +7

BBC World Service—Asia Relay Station, P.O. Box 20, Muang, Nakhon Sawan 60000, Thailand; (physical address) Mu 1, Tambon Ban Kaeng, Muang District, Nakhon Sawan 6000, Thailand. Phone: +66 5622-7275/6. Fax: +66 (56) 227 277. Contact: Ms. Jaruwan Meesaurtong, Executive Secretary; Ms. Sukontha Saisaengthong, Senior Engineer. Nontechnical correspondence should be sent to the BBC World Service in London (*see* UK).

IBB Thailand Transmitting Station, P.O. Box 99, Ampur Muang, Udon Thani 41000, Thailand. Email: thai@voa.gov. This address for specialized technical correspondence only, although some reception reports may be verified. All other correspondence should be directed to the regular VOA or IBB addresses (*see* USA).

Radio Thailand World Service, 236 Vibhavadi Rangsit Road, Huai Khwang, Bangkok 10320, Thailand. Phone: + 66 (2) 277-4022. Fax: +66 (2) 274 9298/9, +66 (2) 277 1840. Email: (general) radiothailandbkk@yahoo.com. Web: www.hsk9.com. Contact: Mrs. Chantima Choeysanguan, Executive Director; Ms. Porntip Utogapach, Director; Ms. Suweraya Lohavicharn, Producer; (technical) Mr. Boontharm Ratanasang, Director; Mr. Weerasac Cherngchow, Assistant Director. Free pennants. Replies irregularly, especially to those who persist.

TRANSMITTER SITE: Rang-sit, Tumbol Klong haa, Amphur Klong laung, Pathumthani Province 12120, Thailand. Phone: +62 (30) 27-523. Contact: Mano Tamkal, Technician.

TOGO   World Time exactly

■**Radio Lomé** (when operating), B.P. 434, Lomé, Togo. Phone: +228 221-2492/3. Fax: +228 221 3673. E-mail: radiolome@radiolome.tg. Web: (includes streaming audio) www.radiolome.tg. Return postage, $1 or 2 IRCs helpful. French preferred, but English accepted.

TUNISIA   World Time +1 (+2 midyear)

Arab States Broadcasting Union, 6, rue des Enterpreneurs, Z.I. Ariana Cedex, TN-1080 Tunis, Tunisia. Phone: +216 (71) 703-855. Fax: +216 (71) 704 203. Email: a.suleiman@asbu.intl.tn. Contact: Abdelrahim Suleiman, Director, Technical Department; Bassil Ahmad Zoubi, Head of Transmission Department.

■**Radiodiffusion Télévision Tunisienne**, 71 Avenue de la Liberté, TN-1070 Tunis, Tunisia. Phone: +216 (1) 801-177. Fax: +216 (1) 781 927. Email: info@radiotunis.com. Web: (includes on-demand and streaming audio) www.radiotunis.com/news.html. Contact: Mongai Caffai, Director General; Mohamed Abdelkafi, Director; Kamel Cherif, Directeur; Masmoudi Mahmoud; Mr. Bechir Betteib, Director of Operations; Smaoui Sadok, Le

Sous-Directeur Technique. Replies irregularly and slowly to correspondence in French or Arabic. $1 helpful. For reception reports try: Le Chef de Service du Controle de la Récepcion de l'Office National de la Télediffusion, O.N.T, Cité Ennassim I, Bourjel, B.P. 399, TN-1080 Tunis, Tunisia. Phone: +216 (1) 801-177. Fax: +216 (1) 781 927. Email: ont.@ati.tn. Contact: Abdesselem Slim.

TURKEY   World Time +2 (+3 midyear)

📻Voice of Turkey (Turkish Radio-Television Corporation External Service)

MAIN OFFICE, NONTECHNICAL: TRT External Services Department, TRT Sitesi, Turan Güne_ Blv., Or-An Çankaya, 06450 Ankara, Turkey; or P.K. 333, Yeni_ehir, 06443 Ankara, Turkey. Phone: (general) +90 (312) 490-9800/9801; (English desk) +90 (312) 490-9842. Fax: (English desk) +90 (312) 490 9846. Email: (English desk) englishdesk@trt.net.tr; (French Service) francais@trt,net,tr; (German Service) deutsch@trt.net.tr; (Spanish Service) espanol@trt.net.tr. Web: (includes streaming audio) www.trt.net.tr; (transmission schedule) www.trt.net.tr/ww-wtrt/frekanstsr.aspx. Contact: (English and non-technical) Mr. Osman Erkan, Chief, English desk; Michael Daventry, English Announcer. Technical correspondence, such as on reception quality should be directed to: Ms. Sedef Somaltin *(see* next entry below). On-air language courses offered in Arabic and German, but no printed course material. Free stickers, pennants, and tourist literature.

MAIN OFFICE, TECHNICAL (FOR EMIRLER AND ÇAKIRLAR TRANSMITTER SITES AND FOR FREQUENCY MANAGEMENT): TRT Teknik Yardimcilik, TRT Sitesi, Kat: 5/C, 06109 ORAN, Ankara, Turkey. Phone: +90 (312) 490-1732. Fax: +90 (312) 490 1733. Email: sedef.somaltin@trt.net.tr, kiymet.erdal@trt.net.tr. Contact: Mr. Haluk Buran, TRT Deputy Director General (Head of Engineering); Ms. Sedef Somaltin, Engineer & Frequency Manager; Ms. Kiymet Erdal, Engineer & Frequency Manager. The HFBC seasonal schedules can be reached directly from: www.trt.net.tr/duyurufiles/vot.htm.

SAN FRANCISCO OFFICE, SCHEDULES: 2654 17th Avenue, San Francisco CA 94116 USA. Phone: +1 (415) 564-9968. Email: GPoppin@aol.com. Contact: George Poppin. This address, a volunteer office, only provides TRT schedules to listeners (return postage not required). All other correspondence should be sent directly to Ankara.

TURKMENISTAN   World Time +5

Radio Turkmenistan, National TV and Radio Broadcasting Company, Mollanepes St. 3, 744000 Ashgabat, Turkmenistan. Phone: +993 (12) 251-515. Fax: +993 (12) 251 421. Contact: (administration) Yu M. Pashaev, Deputy Chairman of State Television and Radio Company; (technical) G. Khanmamedov; Kakali Karayev, Chief of Technical Department; A.A Armanklichev, Deputy Chief, Technical Department. This country is currently under strict censorship and media people are closely watched. A lot of foreign mail addressed to a particular person may attract the attention of the security services. Best is not to address your mail to particular individuals but to the station itself.

UGANDA   World Time +3

Radio Uganda (Uganda Broadcasting Corporation)
GENERAL OFFICE: P.O. Box 7142, Kampala, Uganda. Phone: +256 (41) 257-256. Fax: +256 (41) 257 252. Email:

ugabro@infocom.co.ug. Contact: (general) Charles Byekwaso, Controller of Programmes; Machel Rachel Makibuuka; Mrs. Florence Sewanyana, Head of Public Relations. $1 or return postage required. Replies infrequently and slowly. Correspondence to this address has sometimes been returned with the annotation "storage period overdue"—presumably because the mail is not collected on a regular basis.

ENGINEERING DIVISION: P.O. Box 2038, Kampala, Uganda. Phone: +256 (41) 256-647. Contact: Leopold B. Lubega, Principal Broadcasting Engineer; Rachel Nakibuuka, Secretary. Four IRCs or $2 required. Enclosing a self addressed envelope may also help to get a reply.

UKRAINE   World Time +2 (+3 midyear)

Radio Ukraine International, Kreshchatyk Str. 26, 01001 Kyiv, Ukraine. Phone: (Ukrainian Service) +380 (44) 279-1757; (English Service) + 380 (44) 279-5484; (German Service) +380 (44) 279-3134. Fax: (Ukrainian Service) +380 (44) 279 7894; (English Service) +380 (44) 279 7356; (Technical Department) +380 (44) 239 6029. Email: (Ukrainian Service) marinenko@nrcu.gov.ua; (English Service) vsru@nrcu.gov.ua; (German Service) rui@nrcu.gov.ua; (technical, including reception reports) egorov@nrcu.gov.ua. Web: (includes streaming audio) www.nrcu.gov.ua. Contact: Olexander Dykyi, Director; Inna Chichinadze, Deputy-Director; Mykola Marynenko, Editor-in-Chief, Ukrainian Section; Volodymyr Perpadia, Editor-in-Chief, German Section; Zhanna Mescherska, Editor-in-Chief, English Section; (technical) Alexander Egorov, Head of Technical Department. Free stickers, calendars and Ukrainian stamps.

UNITED KINGDOM   World Time exactly (+1 midyear)

BBC Monitoring, Caversham Park, Reading, Berkshire RG4 8TZ, United Kingdom. Phone: (Marketing Unit) +44 (118) 948-6289. Fax: (Marketing Unit) +44 (118) 946 3823. Email: marketing@mon.bbc.co.uk. Media information is a vital tool for broadcast news organisations, modern governments, analysts and journalists alike. BBC Monitoring focuses on providing hard news including international affairs, major domestic and regional developments, political and military conflict, disasters and crime. As well as reporting news from the media, BBC Monitoring has a specialist department, Media Services, which reports news about the media in individual countries and trends in the media industry, regionally and globally.

Mediafile is a service available by subscription relating to the media industry around the world which includes items based on their own research as well as reports monitored from the mass media. Reports can be delivered by email or retrieved from their database.

Please contact the Marketing Department for subscription prices and information on their other products.

📻**BBC World Service**

MAIN OFFICE, NONTECHNICAL: Bush House, Strand, London WC2B 4PH, United Kingdom. Phone: (general) +44 (20) 7240-3456; (Press Office) +44 (20) 7557-2947/1; (International Marketing) +44 (20) 7557-1143. Fax: (Audience Relations) +44 (20) 7557 1258; ("Write On" listeners' letters program) +44 (20) 7436 2800; (Audience and Market Research) +44 (20) 7557 1254; (International Marketing) +44 (20) 7557 1254. Email: (general listener correspondence) worldservice@bbc.co.uk; ("Write On") writeon@bbc.co.uk. Web: (includes on-demand and streaming audio) www.bbc.co.uk/worldservice. Also, *see*

Ascension, Oman, Seychelles, Singapore and Thailand. Does not verify reception reports due to budget limitations.
SAN FRANCISCO OFFICE, SCHEDULES: 2654 17th Avenue, San Francisco CA 94116 USA. Phone: +1 (415) 564-9968. Email: GPoppin@aol.com. Contact: George Poppin. This address, a volunteer office, only provides BBC World Service schedules to listeners (return postage not required). All other correspondence should be sent directly to the main office in London.
TECHNICAL: See VT Communications.

BFBS—British Forces Broadcasting Service (when operating), Services Sound and Vision, Chalfont Grove, Narcot Lane, Chalfont St. Peter, Gerrards Cross, Buckinghamshire SL9 8TN, United Kingdom; or BFBS Worldwide, P.O. Box 903, Gerrards Cross, Buckinghamshire SL9 8TN, United Kingdom. Email: (general) adminofficer@bfbs.com. Web: (includes on-demand and streaming audio) www.ssvc.com/bfbs. Normally only on satellite and FM, but hires additional shortwave facilities when British troops are fighting overseas.

Bible Voice Broadcasting
EUROPEAN OFFICE: P. O. Box 220, Leeds LS26 0WW, United Kingdom. Phone: +44 (1900) 827-355. Email: mail@biblevoice.org; (schedules) reception@biblevoice.org. Web: www.biblevoice.org. Contact: Martin and Liz Thompson.
NORTH AMERICAN OFFICE: High Adventure Gospel Communication Ministries, P.O. Box 425, Station E, Toronto, ON M6H 4E3, Canada. Phone: +1 (905) 898-5447; (toll-free, U.S. and Canada only) 1-800-550-4670. Email: highadventure@sympatico.ca. Contact: Mrs. Marty McLaughlin.
Bible Voice Broadcasting is a partnership between Bible Voice (U.K.) and High Adventure Gospel Communication Ministries (Canada).

Commonwealth Broadcasting Association, CBA Secretariat, 17 Fleet Street, London EC4Y 1AA, United Kingdom. Phone: +44 (20) 7583-5550. Fax: +44 (20) 7583 5549. Email: cba@cba.org.uk. Web: www.cba.org.uk. Publishes the annual *Commonwealth Broadcaster Directory* and the quarterly *Commonwealth Broadcaster* (online subscription form available).

FEBA Radio, Ivy Arch Road, Worthing, West Sussex BN14 8BX, United Kingdom. Phone: +44 (1903) 237-281. Fax: +44 (1903) 205 294. Email: (general) info@feba.org.uk; (Whittington) rwhittington@feba.org.uk. Web: www.feba.org.uk. Contact: (nontechnical) Angela Brooke, Supporter Relations; (technical) Richard Whittington, Schedule Engineer. Does not verify reception reports. Try sending reports to individual program producers (addresses are usually given over the air).

IBC-Tamil, 3 College Fields, Prince George's Road, Colliers Wood, London SW19 2PT, United Kingdom. Phone: +44 (20) 8100-0012. Fax: +44 (20) 8100 0003. Email: radio@ibctamil.co.uk. Web: (includes on-demand and streaming audio) www.ibctamil.co.uk. Contact: A.C. Tarcisius, Managing Director; S. Shivaranjith, Manager; K. Pillai; or Public Relations Officer. Replies irregularly.

VT Communications, 20 Lincoln's Inn Fields, London WC2A 3ED, United Kingdom. Phone: +44 (20) 7969-0000. Fax: +44 (20) 7396 6223. Email: marketing@merlincommunications.com. Web: www.vtplc.com/communications. Contact: Fiona Lowry, Chief Executive; Rory Maclachlan, Director of International Communications & Digital Services; Ciaran Fitzgerald, Head of Engineering & Operations; Richard Hurd, Head of Transmission Sales; Laura Jelf, Marketing Manager; Kirsty Love, Marketing Coordinator. Formerly known as Merlin Communications International. Does not verify reception reports.

WRN (formerly World Radio Network), P.O. Box 1212, London SW8 2ZF, United Kingdom. Phone: +44 (20) 7896-9010. Fax: +

44 (20) 7896 9007. Email: (general) email@wrn.org; (Ayris) tim.ayris@wrn.org. Web: (includes on-demand and streaming audio) www.wrn.org. Contact: Tim Ayris, Broadcast Sales Manager for WRN's networks. Provides Webcasts and program placements for international broadcasters.

UNITED NATIONS   World Time –5 (–4 midyear)

Radio UNMEE
Web: (includes on-demand audio) www.un.org/Depts/dpko/unmee/radio.htm.
NEW YORK OFFICE: Same contact details as United Nations Radio, below.
ERITREA OFFICE: P.O. Box 5805, Asmara, Eritrea. Phone: +291 (1) 151-908. Email: kellyb@un.org.
ETHIOPIA OFFICE: ECA Building, P.O. Box 3001, Addis Ababa, Ethiopia. Phone: +251 (1) 443-396. Email: walkera@un.org.
Radio service of the United Nations Mission in Eritrea and Ethiopia (UNMEE). Aired via facilities in the United Arab Emirates, and also relayed over Eritrea's national radio, Voice of the Broad Masses of Eritrea.

United Nations Radio, Secretariat Building, Room S-850A, United Nations, New York NY 10017 USA; or write to the station over which UN Radio was heard. Phone: +1 (917) 367-5007. Fax: +1 (212) 963 6869. Email: (general) unradio@un.org; (comments on programs) audio-visual@un.org; (reception reports) smithd@un.org; (Villanueva) villanueva1@un.org. Web: (includes on-demand audio) www.un.org/radio; (on-demand audio) www.wrn.org/ondemand/unitednations.html. Contact: (general) Sylvester E. Rowe, Chief, Radio and Video Service; Ayman El-Amir, Chief, Radio Section, Department of Public Information; (reception reports) David Smith; Trixie Villanueva; (technical and nontechnical) Sandra Guy, Secretary. Free stamps and *UN Frequency* publication. Reception reports (including those sent by email) are verified with a QSL card.
GENEVA OFFICE: Room G209, Palais des Nations, CH-1211 Geneva 10, Switzerland. Phone: +41 (22) 917-4222. Fax: +41 (22) 917 0123.

URUGUAY   World Time –3 (sometimes –2, to save electricity)

Banda Oriental—*see* Radio Sarandí del Yí.

Emisora Ciudad de Montevideo (when operating), Canelones 2061, 11200 Montevideo, Uruguay. Phone: +598 (2) 402-0142, +598 (2) 402-4242. Fax: +598 (2) 402 0700. Email: online form. Web: (includes streaming audio) www.emisoraciudaddemontevideo.com.uy. Contact: Aramazd Yizmeyian, Director General. Free stickers. Return postage helpful.

Radiodifusion Nacional—*see* S.O.D.R.E.

Radio Oriental (if reactivated on shortwave), Cerrito 475, 11000 Montevideo, Uruguay. Phone/Fax: +598 (2) 916-1130. Email: (Management) director@oriental.com.uy; (general) info@oriental.com.uy, secretaria@oriental.com.uy. Web: (includes streaming audio) www.oriental.com.uy. Contact: Presbítero Jorge Techera, Director; (technical) José A. Porro, Technician. Correspondence in Spanish preferred.

Radio Sarandí del Yí (if reactivated), Sarandí 328, 97100 Sarandí del Yí, Uruguay. Phone/Fax: +598 (367) 9155. Email: (owner) norasan@adinet.com.uy. Contact: Nora San Martín de Porro, Propietaria.

Radio Universo (when activated), Ferrer 1265, 27000 Castillos, Dpto. de Rocha, Uruguay. Email: am1480@adinet.com.uy. Contact: Juan Héber Brañas, Propietario. Currently only on

1480 kHz mediumwave AM, but has been granted a license to operate on shortwave.

S.O.D.R.E. (when operating), Radiodifusión Nacional, Casilla 1412, 11000 Montevideo, Uruguay. Phone: +598 (2) 916-1933; (technical) +598 (2) 915-7865. Email: dirradio@sodre.gub. uy. Web: www.sodre.gub.uy. Contact: (management) Sergio Sacomani, Director de Radiodifusión Nacional; (technical) José Cuello, División Técnica Radio.

USA
World Time –4 Atlantic, including Puerto Rico and Virgin Islands; –5 (–4 midyear) Eastern, –6 (–5 midyear) Central, including northwest and southwest Indiana; –7 (–6 midyear) Mountain, except Arizona; –7 Arizona; –8 (–7 midyear) Pacific; –9 (–8 midyear) Alaska, except Aleutian Islands; –10 (–9 midyear) Aleutian Islands; –10 Hawaii; –11 Samoa

Adventist World Radio
HEADQUARTERS: 12501 Old Columbia Pike, Silver Spring MD 20904 USA. Phone: +1 (301) 680-6304; (toll-free, U.S. only) l-800-337-4297. Fax: +1 (301) 680 6303. Email: info@awr.org. Web: (includes on-demand audio) www.awr.org.
NONTECHNICAL LISTENER CORRESPONDENCE: E-mail: letters@awr.org.
RECEPTION REPORTS:
LISTENERS IN AFRICA, AMERICAS AND EUROPE: P.O. Box 29235, Indianapolis IN 46229 USA. Phone/Fax: +1 (317) 891-8540. Email: adrian@awr.org. Contact: Dr. Adrian M. Peterson. Provides technical information and processes reception reports and issues QSL cards.
LISTENERS IN ASIA AND THE PACIFIC: Adventist World Radio—Asia/Pacific, 798 Thompson Road, Singapore 298186, Singapore. Email: aproffice@awr.org, aspaclistener@awr.org. Contact: Akinori Kaibe.
OPERATIONS AND ENGINEERING: See Guam.
AWR EUROPE FREQUENCY MANAGEMENT OFFICE: Postfach 100252, D-64202 Darmstadt, Germany. Phone: (Dedio) +49 (6151) 953-151; (Crillo) +49 (6151) 953-153. Fax: +61 (6151) 953 152. Email: (Dedio) dedio@awr.org; (Cirillo) pino@awr.org. Contact: Claudius Dedio, Frequency Coordinator; Giuseppe Cirillo, Monitoring Engineer.
Al Mustaqbal (when operating), EDC, 1000 Potomac Street NW - Suite 350, Washington DC 20007 USA. Phone: +1 (202) 572-3700. Fax: +1 (202) 223-4059. Email: (Houssein) ahoussein@edc.org. Web: http://main.edc.org/international/region.asp?region=Africa&country=ETHIOPIA. Contact: Abdoulkhader Houssein. A project of Education Development Center, Inc., funded by the U.S. Agency for International Development (USAID), and targeted at Somali-speaking children in Ethiopia. Broadcast via a transmitter in the United Arab Emirates. Off the air during school vacations.

AFRTS-American Forces Radio and Television Service (Shortwave), Naval Media Center, NDW Anacostia Annex, 2713 Mitscher Road SW, Washington DC 20373-5819 USA. Web:http://myafn.dodmedia.osd.mil/radio/shortwave; (AFRTS parent organization) www.afrts.osd.mil; (2-minute on-demand audio news clips): www.defenselink.mil/news/radio; (Naval Media Center) www.mediacen.navy.mil. The Naval Media Center is responsible for all AFRTS broadcasts aired on shortwave.
VERIFICATION OF RECEPTION REPORTS: Department of Defense, Naval Media Center Detachment, AFRTS-DMC, 23755 Z Street, Bldg. 2730, Riverside CA 92518-2017 USA (mark the envelope, "Attn: Officer in Charge"). Email: qsl@dodmedia.osd. mil. Replies irregularly.

FLORIDA ADDRESS: NCTS-Jacksonville-Detachment Key West, Building A 1004, Naval Air Station Boca Chica, Key West, FL 33040 USA.
Also, *see* British Indian Ocean Territory.

Aurora Communications (under construction), Mile 129, Sterling Highway, Ninilchik, Alaska, USA. Plans to commence broadcasts to Russia when circumstances allow.

Broadcasting Board of Governors (BBG), 330 Independence Avenue SW, Room 3360, Washington DC 20237 USA. Phone: +1 (202) 619-2538. Fax: +1 (202) 619 1241. Email: pubaff@ibb. gov. Web: www.bbg.gov. Contact: Kathleen Harrington, Public Relations. The BBG, created in 1994 and headed by nine members nominated by the President, is the overseeing agency for all official non-military United States international broadcasting operations, including the VOA, RFE-RL, Radio Martí and Radio Free Asia.

Eternal Good News, International Radio Broadcasts, Wilshire Church of Christ, Oklahoma City OK USA; or P.O.Box 5333, Edmond OK 73083, USA. Phone: +1 (405) 359-1235, +1 (405) 340-0877. Email: eternalgoodnews@sbcglobal.net. Web: (includes on-demand audio) www.oldpaths.net/Works/Radio/Wilshire/index.html. Contact: Germaine Charles Lockwood, Evangelist; Sandra Lockwood, Secretary. Programs are aired via world band transmitters in Germany, Russia and United Arab Emirates, as well as U.S. station World Harvest Radio.

Family Radio Worldwide
NONTECHNICAL: Family Stations, Inc., 290 Hegenberger Road, Oakland CA 94621-1436 USA. Phone: (general) +1 (510) 568-6200; (toll-free, U.S. only) 1-800-543-1495; (engineering) +1 (510) 568-6200 ext. 242. Fax: (main office) +1 (510) 568 6200. Email: (general) famradio@familyradio.com; (international department, shortwave program schedules) internatio nal@familyradio.com. Web: (includes streaming audio) www.familyradio.com. Contact: (general) Harold Camping, General Manager; David Hoff, Manager of International Department. Free gospel tracts (50 languages), books, booklets, quarterly *Family Radio News* magazine and frequency schedule. Free CD containing domestic and international program schedules plus audio lessons in MP 3 format and bible study materials. 2 IRCs helpful.
TECHNICAL: WYFR—Family Radio, 10400 NW 240th Street, Okeechobee FL 34972 USA. Phone: +1 (863) 763-0281. Fax: +1 (863) 763 8867. Email: (technical) fsiyfr@okeechobee. com; (frequency schedule) wyfr@okeechobee.com. Contact: Dan Elyea, Engineering Manager; Edward F. Dearborn, Chief Operator; (frequency schedule) Evelyn Marcy.

FEBC Radio International
INTERNATIONAL HEADQUARTERS: Far East Broadcasting Company, Inc., P.O. Box 1, La Mirada CA 90637 USA. Phone: +1 (310) 947-4651. Fax: +1 (310) 943 0160. Email: febc@febc. org. Web: www.febi.org. Operates world band stations in the Philippines and Northern Mariana Islands (see). Does not verify reception reports from this address.

Federal Communications Commission, 445 12th Street SW, Washington DC 20554 USA. Phone: +1 (202) 418-0190; (toll-free, U.S. only) 1-888-225-5322. Fax: +1 (202) 418 0232. Email: tpolzin@fcc.gov. Web: (general) www.fcc.gov; (high frequency operating schedules) http://ftp.fcc.gov/ib/sand/neg/hf_web/seasons.html. Contact: (International Bureau, technical) Thomas E. Polzin.

Fundamental Broadcasting Network, Grace Missionary Baptist Church, 520 Roberts Road, Newport NC 28570 USA. Phone: +1 (252) 223-6088; (toll-free, U.S. only) 1-800-245-9685; (Robinson) +1 (252) 223-4600. Email: (general) fbn@clis.

com; (technical, David Robinson) davidwr@clis.com. Web: (includes streaming audio) www.fbnradio.com. Contact: Pastor Clyde Eborn; (technical) David Robinson, Chief Engineer. Verifies reception reports if an IRC or (within the USA) an SASE is included. Accepts email reports. Free stickers. A religious and educational non-commercial broadcasting network which operates sister stations WBOH and WTJC.

Gospel for Asia, 1800 Golden Trail Court, Carrollton TX 75010 USA. Phone: +1 (972) 300-7777; (toll-free, U.S. only) 1-800-946-2742. Email: info@gfa.org. Web: www.gfa.org. Transmits via facilities in Germany and U.A.E.

CALIFORNIA OFFICE: P.O. Box 1210 Somis, California 93066 USA. Email: gfaradio@mygfa.org. Contact: Rhonda Penland, Coordinator.

CANADIAN OFFICE: 245 King Street E., Stoney Creek, ON L8G 1L9, Canada. Phone: +1 (905) 662-2101. Email: infocanada@gfa.org.

UNITED KINGDOM OFFICE: P.O. Box 166, York YO10 5WA, United Kingdom. Phone: +44 (1904) 643-233. Email: infouk@gfa.org.

International Broadcasting Bureau (IBB)—Reports to the Broadcasting Board of Governors (*see*), and includes, among others, the Voice of America, RFE-RL, Radio Martí and Radio Free Asia. IBB Engineering (Office of Engineering and Technical Operations) provides broadcast services for these stations. Contact: (administration) Brian Conniff, Director; Joseph O'Connell, Director of External Affairs. Web: www.ibb.gov/ibbpage.html.

FREQUENCY AND MONITORING OFFICE, TECHNICAL: IBB/EOF: Spectrum Management Division, International Broadcasting Bureau (IBB), Room 4611 Cohen Bldg., 330 Independence Avenue SW, Washington DC 20237 USA. Phone: +1 (202) 619-1669. Fax: +1 (202) 619 1680. Email: (scheduling) dferguson@ibb.gov; (monitoring) bw@his.com. Web: (general) http://monitor.ibb.gov; (email reception report form) http://monitor.ibb.gov/now_you_try_it.html. Contact: Bill Whitacre (bw@his.com).

KAIJ

ADMINISTRATION OFFICE: Two-if-by-Sea Broadcasting Co., 22720 SE 410th St., Enumclaw WA 89022 USA. Phone/Fax: (Mike Parker, California) +1 (818) 606-1254; (Washington State office, if and when operating) +1 (206) 825 4517. Email: (Parker) mparker@kaij.org. Web: www.kaij.org. Contact: Mike Parker (mark envelope, "please forward"). Replies occasionally.

TRANSMITTER SITE: RR#3 Box 120, Frisco TX 75034 USA; or Highway 380 West, Prosper TX 75078 USA (physical location: Highway 380, 3.6 miles west of State Rt. 289, near Denton TX; transmitters and antennas located on Belt Line Road along the lake in Coppell TX). Phone: +1 (972) 346-2758. Contact: Walt Green or Fred Bithell. Station encourages mail to be sent to the administration office, which seldom replies.

KJES—King Jesus Eternal Savior

STATION: The Lord's Ranch, 230 High Valley Road, Vado NM 88072-7221 USA. Phone: +1 (505) 233-2090. Fax: +1 (505) 233 3019. Email: kjes@family.net. Contact: Michael Reuter, Manager. $1 or return postage appreciated.

SPONSORING ORGANIZATION: Our Lady's Youth Center, P.O. Box 1422, El Paso TX 79948 USA. Phone: +1 (915) 533-9122.

⊠KNLS—New Life Station

OPERATIONS CENTER: World Christian Broadcasting, 605 Bradley Ct., Franklin TN 37067 USA (letters sent to the Alaska transmitter site are usually forwarded to Franklin). Phone: +1 (615) 371-8707 ext.140. Fax: +1 (615) 371 8791. Email:

Dan Elyea, shown in 1983, has been WYFR station manager since its transmitter site was moved from Scituate, Mass. to Okeechobee, Florida in 1978.

Curtis Jarvis, WYFR

knls@aol.com. Web: (includes on-demand audio of sample programs) www.knls.org. Contact: (general) Dale R. Ward, Executive Producer; L. Wesley Jones, Director of Follow-Up Teaching; Rob Scobey, Senior Producer, English Language Service; (technical) F.M. Perry, Frequency Coordinator. Free *Alaska Calling!* newsletter and station pennants. Free spiritual literature and bibles in Russian, Mandarin or English. Free Alaska books, tapes, postcards and cloth patches. Two free DX books for beginners. Special, individually numbered, limited edition, verification cards issued for each new transmission period to the first 200 listeners providing confirmed reception reports. Stamp and postcard exchange. Return postage appreciated.

TRANSMITTER SITE: P.O. Box 473, Anchor Point AK 99556 USA. Phone: +1 (907) 235-8262. Fax: +1 (907) 235 2326. Contact: (technical) Kevin Chambers, Chief Engineer.

⊠KRSI—Radio Sedaye Iran (when operating), Suite 207, 9744 Wilshire Boulevard, Beverly Hills CA 90212-1812 USA. Phone: +1 (310) 888-2818. Fax: +1 (310) 859 8444. Web: (includes streaming audio and online email form) www.krsi.net. Operates via a closed broadcasting system and the Internet. Transmits irregularly on shortwave, and via different countries.

⊠KTBN—Trinity Broadcasting Network:

GENERAL CORRESPONDENCE: P.O. Box A, Santa Ana CA 92711 USA. Phone: +1 (714) 832-2950. Fax: +1 (714) 730 0661. Email: comments@tbn.org. Web: (Trinity Broadcasting Network, includes streaming audio) www.tbn.org; (shortwave) www.tbn.org/index.php/2/21.html. Contact: Dr. Paul F. Crouch, Managing Director. Monthly TBN newsletter. Free booklets, stickers and small souvenirs sometimes available.

TECHNICAL CORRESPONDENCE: Engineering/QSL Department, 2442 Michelle Drive, Tustin CA 92780-7015 USA. Phone: +1 (714) 665-2145. Fax: +1 (714) 730 0661. Email: (Gilroy) cgilroy@tbn.org. Contact: Cheryl Gilroy, QSL Manager; Ben Miller, Vice President, Engineering. Responds to reception reports; write to: Trinity Broadcasting Network, Attention: Superpower KTBN Radio QSL Manager Cheryl Gilroy, 2442 Michelle Drive, Tustin CA 92780 USA. Return postage (IRC or SASE) appreciated. Although a California operation, KTBN's shortwave transmitter is located at Salt Lake City, Utah.

KTMI—Transformation Media International (under construction), 240 2nd Avenue SW, Albany OR 97321 USA. Phone:

+1 (541) 259-5900. Fax: +1 (541) 812 7611. Email: (Brosnan) mbrosnan03@yahoo.com; (Lund) bob@lund.com. Contact: Ms. Michele Brosnan, Director of Operations; Robert Lund, Chief Engineer.

🔊**KVOH—La Voz de Restauración**, 4409 W. Adams Blvd., Los Angeles CA 90016 USA. Phone: +1 (323) 766-2454. Fax: +1 (323) 766-2458. Email: comentarios@kvoh.org. Web: (includes streaming audio) www.restauracion.com/radio.html.

🔊**KWHR-World Harvest Radio:**

ADMINISTRATION OFFICE: See World Harvest Radio.

TRANSMITTER: Although located 6 1/2 miles southwest of Naalehu, 8 miles north of South Cape, and 2000 feet west of South Point (Ka La) Road (the antennas are easily visible from this road) on Big Island, Hawaii, the operators of this rural transmitter site maintain no post office box in or near Naalehu, and their telephone number is unlisted, Best bet is to contact them via their administration office (see World Harvest Radio), or to drive in unannounced (it's just off South Point Road) the next time you vacation on Big Island.

🔊 **Leading The Way**, P.O. Box 20100, Atlanta GA 30325 USA. Phone: +1 (404) 841-0100. Email: (Wattenbarger) adam@leadingtheway.org; (reception reports) qsl@leadingtheway.org. Web: www.leadingtheway.org; (includes on-demand audio) www.oneplace.com/ministries/leading_the_way. Contact: Adam Wattenbarger, Senior Producer for Radio. Airs via U.K. facilities of VT Merlin Communications (see) and various world band religious broadcasters.

Leinwoll (Stanley)—Telecommunication Consultant, 305 E. 86th Street, Suite 21S-W, New York NY 10028 USA. Phone: +1 (212) 987-0456. Fax: +1 (212) 987 3532. Email: stanL00011@aol.com. Contact: Stanley Leinwoll, President. This firm provides frequency management and other engineering services for some private U.S. world band stations, but does not correspond with the general public.

🔊**Little Saigon Radio**, 15781 Brookhurst St. - Suite 101, Westminster CA 92683 USA. Phone: +1 (714) 918-4444. Web: (includes streaming audio from domestic service) www. littlesaigonradio.com. Contact: Joe Dinh, Technical Director. A Californian mediumwave AM station which airs a special broadcast for Vietnam via leased facilities in Taiwan.

National Association of Shortwave Broadcasters, 10400 NW 240th Street, Okeechobee, FL 34972 USA; P.O. Box 8700, Cary NC 27512 USA. Phone: +1 (863) 763-0281. Fax: +1 (863) 763 8867. Email: nasbmem@rocketmail.com. Web: www.shortwave.org. Contact: Dan Elyea, Secretary-Treasurer. Association of most private U.S. world band stations, as well as a group of other international broadcasters, equipment manufacturers and organizations related to shortwave broadcasting. Includes committees on various subjects, such as digital shortwave radio. Interfaces with the Federal Communications Commission's International Bureau and other broadcasting-related organizations to advance the interests of its members. Publishes NASB Newsletter for members and associates and is available for free via their website. Annual one-day convention held in Washington DC early each spring; non-members wishing to attend should contact the Secretary-Treasurer in advance; convention fee typically $50 per person.

🔊**Overcomer Ministry** ("Voice of the Last Day Prophet of God"), P.O. Box 691, Walterboro SC 29488 USA. Phone: (0900-1700 local time, Sunday through Friday) +1 (803) 538-3892. Fax: +1 (843) 628 4131. Email: brotherstair@overcomerministry.org. Web: (includes on-demand and streaming audio) www.overcomerministry.org. Contact: Brother R.G. Stair. Sample "Overcomer" newsletter and various pamphlets free upon request. Via Germany's T-Systems International (see) and various U.S. stations.

Pan American Broadcasting, 2021 The Alameda, Suite 240, San Jose CA 95126-1145 USA. Phone: +1 (408) 996-2033; (toll-free, U.S. only) 1-800-726-2620. Fax: +1 (408) 252 6855. Email: info@panambc.com; (Bernald) gbernald@panambc.com; (Jung) cjung@panambc.com. Web: www.panambc.com. Contact: (listener correspondence) Terry Kraemer; (general) Carmen Jung, Office and Sales Administrator; Gene Bernald, President. $1, mint U.S. stamps or 2 IRCs required for reply. Operates transmitters in Equatorial Guinea (see) and hires airtime over a number of world band stations, plus T-Systems International facilities in Germany.

🔊**Quê Huong Radio**, 2670 South White Road, Suite 165, San Jose CA 95148 USA. Phone: +1 (408) 223-3130. Fax: +1 (408) 223 3131. Email: qhradio@aol.com. Web: (includes on-demand audio) www.quehuongmedia.com. Contact: Nguyen Khoi, Manager. A Californian Vietnamese station operating on mediumwave AM, and which broadcasts to Vietnam via transmitters in Russia or Central Asia.

🔊**Radio Farda**—a joint venture between Radio Free Europe-Radio Liberty (see) and the Voice of America (see). Email: radiofarda@rferl.com. Web: (includes on-demand and streaming audio) www.radiofarda.com. Broadcasts a mix of news, information and popular Iranian and western music to younger audiences in Iran.

🔊**Radio Free Afghanistan**—the Afghan service of Radio Free Europe-Radio Liberty (see). Web: (includes on-demand and streaming audio) www.azadiradio.org.

🔊**Radio Free Asia**, Suite 300, 2025 M Street NW, Washington DC 20036 USA (for reports on reception, add "Reception Reports" before "Radio Free Asia"). You can also submit reception reports at: www.techweb.rfa.org (click on the QSL REPORTS link) or send them via email to: QSL@rfa.org. Phone: (general) +1 (202) 530-4900; (president) +1 (202) 457-4901;(vice president of editorial) +1 (202) 530-4907; (vice-president of administration) +1 (202) 530-4902); (chief technology officer) +1 (202) 530-4958; (director of production support) +1 (202) 530-4943. Fax: +1 (202) 530 7794, +1 (202) 721 7468. Email: (individuals) the format is lastnameinitial@rfa.org; so to reach, say the CTO, David Baden, it would be badend@rfa.org; (language sections) the format is language@rfa.org; so to contact, say, the Vietnamese section, address your message to vietnamese@rfa.org; (general) communications@rfa.org; (reception reports) qsl@rfa.org. Web: (includes on-demand audio) www.rfa.org; (automated reception report system) www.techweb.rfa.org. Contact: (administration) Libby Liu, President; Daniel Southerland, Vice President of Editorial; (technical) David M. Baden, Chief Technology Officer; A. J. Janitschek, Manager of Production Support; Sam Stevens, Director of Technical Support. RFA, originally created in 1996 as the Asia Pacific Network, is funded as a private nonprofit U.S. corporation by a grant from the US Congress to the Broadcasting Board of Governors (see).

HONG KONG OFFICE: Room 904, Mass Mutal Tower, 38 Gloucester Road, Wanchai, Hong Kong, China.

THAILAND OFFICE: Maxim House, 112 Witthayu Road, Pathomwan, Bangkok 10330, Thailand.

🔊**Radio Free Europe-Radio Liberty/RFE-RL**

PRAGUE HEADQUARTERS: Vinohradská 1, 110 00 Prague 1, Czech Republic. Phone: +420 (2) 2112-1111; (outreach coordinator) +420 (2) 2112-2407; (president) +420 (2) 2112-3000; (news desk) +420 (2) 2112-3629; (public relations) +420 (2) 2112-3012; (technical operations) +420 (2) 2112-3700;

Church of Our Lady Before Tyn in Old City, Prague, home to RFE-RL.
Shutterstock/Natalia Bratslavsky

(broadcast operations) +420 (2) 2112-3550; (affiliate relations). +420 (2) 2112-2539. Fax: +420 (2) 2112 3013; (president) +420 (2) 2112 3002; (news desk) +420 (2) 2112 3613; (public relations) +420 (2) 2112 2995; (technical operations) +420 (2) 2112 3702; (broadcast operations) +420 (2) 2112 3540; (affiliate operations) +420 (2) 2112 4563. Email: the format is lastnameinitial@rferl.org; so to reach, say, Luke Springer, it would be springerl@rferl.org; (reception reports) lukaso@rferl.org. Web: (includes on-demand and streaming audio) www.rferl.org. Contact: Kestutis Girnius, Managing Editor, News and Current Affairs; Luke Springer, Deputy Director, Technology; Jana Horakova, Public Relations Coordinator; Uldis Grava, Marketing Director; Christopher Carzoli, Broadcast Operations Director; Ondrej Lukas, Outreach Coordinator.

WASHINGTON OFFICE: 1201 Connecticut Avenue NW, Washington DC 20036 USA. Phone: +1 (202) 457-6900; (Director of Communications) +1 202) 457-6947; (newsdesk) +1 (202) 457-6950; (technical) +1 (202) 457-6963. Fax: +1 (202) 457 6992; (news desk) +1 (202) 457 6997; (technical) +1 (202) 457 6913. Email and Web: *see,* above. Contact: Don Jensen, Director of Communications. A private non-profit corporation funded by a grant from the Broadcasting Board of Governors, RFE/RL broadcasts in 21 languages (but not English) from transmission facilities now part of the International Broadcasting Bureau (IBB), *see.*

⬛Radio Martí, Office of Cuba Broadcasting, 4201 N.W. 77th Avenue, Miami FL 33166 USA. Phone: +1 (305) 437-7000; (Director) +1 (305) 437-7117; (Technical Operations) +1 (305) 437-7051. Fax: +1 (305) 437 7016. Email: infomarti@ocb.ibb.gov. Web: (includes on-demand and streaming audio) www.martinoticias.com/radio.asp. Contact: (technical) Michael Pallone, Director, Engineering and Technical Operations; Tom Warden, Chief of Radio Operations.

Smyrna Radio International (projected), c/o Smyrna Baptist Church, 7000 Pensacola Blvd., Pensacola FL 32505 USA. Phone: +1 (850) 477-0998.

⬛Sound of Hope Radio Network, 2520 Wyandotte Street - Suite A, Mountain View CA 94043 USA. Phone: +1 (866) 432-7764. Fax: +1 (415) 276 5861. Email: (general) englishfe

edback@soundofhope.org, contact@soundofhope.org; (reception reports) 9ping@soundofhope.org. Web: (includes on-demand audio) www.soundofhope.org. Transmits via facilities in Taiwan.

Southern Sudan Interactive Radio Instruction (sSIRI) (when operating)—a project of the Education Development Center (*see* Sudan Radio Service, below, for contact information). Broadcasts are via a transmitter in western Russia, brokered by VT Communications (*see* United Kingdom). Is off the air during school holidays in southern Sudan.

PRODUCTION STUDIOS, KENYA: 28 Mugumo Road, P.O. Box 25010, 00603 Lavington, Nairobi, Kenya.

⬛Sudan Radio Service, Education Development Center, 1000 Potomac Street NW, Suite 350, Washington DC 20007 USA. Phone: +1 (202) 572-3700. Fax: +1 (202) 223 4059. Email: srs@edc.org; (Groce) jgroce@edc.org, jgroce@sudanradio.org. (Laflin) mlaflin@edc.org. Web: (includes on-demand audio) www.sudanradio.org; (EDC parent organization) www.edc.org. Contact: Jeremy Groce, Radio Programming Advisor, EDC; Mike Laflin, Director, EDC.

PRODUCTION STUDIOS, KENYA: c/o EDC, P.O. Box 4392, 00100 Nairobi, Kenya. Phone: +254 (20) 570-906, +254 (20) 572-269. Fax: +254 (20) 576 520. Email: srs@sudanradio.org; (Renzi) mtamburo@sudanradio.org. Contact: Tamburo Michael Renzi, SRS Marketing Coordinator.

⬛Trans World Radio

INTERNATIONAL HEADQUARTERS: P.O. Box 8700, Cary NC 27512-8700 USA. Phone: +1 (919) 460-3700; (toll-free, U.S. only) 1-800-456-7897. Fax: +1 (919) 460 3702. Email: info2@twr.org. Web: (includes on-demand audio) www.gospelcom.net/twr. Contact: (general) Jon Vaught, Public Relations; Richard Greene, Director, Public Relations; Joe Fort, Director, Broadcaster Relations; Bill Danick; (technical) Glenn W. Sink, Assistant Vice President, International Operations. Free "Towers to Eternity" publication for those living in the U.S. This address for nontechnical correspondence only.

TRANS WORLD RADIO EUROPE (TECHNICAL): Trans World Radio, Postfach 141, A-1235 Vienna, Austria. Phone: +43 (1) 863-12-0. Fax: +43 (1) 863 1220, +43 (1) 862 1257. Email:

eurofreq@twr-europe.at. Contact: Bernhard Schraut, Deputy Technical Director; Kalman Dobos, Frequency Coordinator. Verifies reception reports.

TRANS WORLD RADIO EUROPE (NONTECHNICAL): Trans World Radio Europe, Communications Department, P.O. Box 12, 820 02 Bratislava 22, Slovakia. Fax: +421 (2) 4329 3729. Web: www.twreurope.org.

Also, *see* Guam, India, South Africa and Swaziland.

Truth for the World, P.O. Box 5048, Duluth GA 30096-0065 USA. Email: tftworld@aol.com; (Grubb) jmgrubb@tftw.org. Web: www.tftw.org. Contact: Don Blackwell, Director of Broadcasting; John M. Grubb, Chinese Missions. Airs Chinese programming via a transmitter in Taiwan, and English programs via world band stations in Equatorial Guinea, Sri Lanka, U.S.A. and elsewhere.

◨**University Network**, P.O. Box 1, Los Angeles CA 90053 USA. Phone: +1 (818) 240-8151; (toll-free, U.S. and Canada only) 1-800-338-3030. Web: (includes streaming audio) www.drgenescott.com. Transmits over KAIJ and WWCR (USA); Caribbean Beacon (Anguilla, West Indies) and the former AWR facilities in Cahuita, Costa Rica. Does not verify reception reports.

◨**Voice of America—All Transmitter Locations**
(Main Office) 330 Independence Avenue SW, Washington DC 20237 USA; (listener feedback) Voice of America, Audience Mail, Room 4409, 330 Independence Ave SW, Washington DC 20237 USA. If contacting the VOA directly is impractical, write c/o the American Embassy in your country. Phone: (Office of Public Affairs) +1 (202) 401-7000; (Audience Mail Division) +1 (202) 619-2770; (Africa Division) +1 (202) 619-1666, +1 (202) 619-2879; (Office of Research) +1 (202) 619-4965; (administration) +1 (202) 619-1088. Fax: (Office of Public Affairs) +1 (202) 619 1241; (Africa Division) +1 (202) 619 1664; (Audience Mail Division and Office of Research) +1 (202) 619 0211. Email: (general business) publicaffairs@voa.gov; (reception reports and schedule requests) letters@voa.gov; (listener feedback) letters@voanews.com; (VOA Special English) special@voanews.com. Web: (includes on-demand and streaming audio) www.voa.gov. Contact: Mrs. Betty Lacy Thompson, Chief, Audience Mail Division, B/K. G759A Cohen; Larry James, Director, English Programs Division; Joe O'Connell, Director, Office of Public Affairs; Leo Sarkisian; Rita Rochelle, Africa Division; George Mackenzie, Audience Research Officer; (reception reports) Mrs. Irene Greene, QSL Desk, Audience Mail Division, Room G-759-C. May send free stickers, fridge magnets pens and calendars. Also, *see* Botswana, Greece, Morocco, Philippines, São Tomé e Príncipe, Sri Lanka and Thailand.

VOA ASIA NEWS CENTER: 17ᵗʰ Floor Asia Orient Tower, 33 Lockhart Road, Wanchai, Hong Kong, China. Phone: +852 2526-9809. Fax: +852 2877 8805. Email: jenjano@voanews.com. Contact: Jennifer A. Janin, Director.

Voice of America/IBB—Delano Relay Station, Rt. 1, Box 1350, Delano CA 93215 USA; (physical address) 11015 Melcher Road, Delano CA 93215 USA. Phone: +1 (805) 725-0150. Fax: +1 (805) 725 6511. Email: (Vodenik) jvodenik@del.ibb.gov, k9hsp@juno.com. Contact: (technical) John Vodenik, Engineer. Photos of this facility can be seen at the following Website: www. hawkins.pair.com/voadelano.shtml. Nontechnical correspondence should be sent to the VOA address in Washington.

Voice of America/IBB—Greenville Relay Station, P.O. Box 1826, Greenville NC 27834 USA. Phone: (site A) +1 (252) 752-7115 or (site B) +1 (252) 752-7181. Fax: (site A) +1 (252) 758 8742 or (site B) +1 (252) 752 5959. Contact: (technical) Bruce Hunter, Manager; Glenn Ruckleson. Nontechnical correspondence should be sent to the VOA address in Washington.

Voice of Joy, Box 610411, Dallas, TX 75261 USA. Email: voiceofjoy@comcast.net. Web: www.voiceofjoy.net. Contact: Dean Phillips. Broadcasts irregularly via transmitters in various countries. Verifies reception reports.

◨**WBCQ—"The Planet,"** 274 Britton Road, Monticello ME 04760 3110 USA. Phone: +1 (207) 985-7547; (transmitter site, urgent technical matters only) +1 (207) 538-9180. Email: wbcq@gwi.net. Web: (includes on-demand audio) http://the-planet.wbcq.net. Contact: Allan H. Weiner, Owner; Elayne Star, Assistant Manager. Verifies reception reports if 1 IRC or (within USA) an SASE is included. Does not verify email reports.

WBOH—*see* Fundamental Broadcasting Network.

◨**WEWN—EWTN Global Catholic Radio**, 5817 Old Leeds Rd., Birmingham AL 35210 USA. Phone: +1 (205) 271-2900. Fax: +1 (205) 271 2926. Email: (general) wewn@ewtn.com; (technical) radio@ewtn.com; (Spanish) rcm@ewtn.com. To contact individuals, the format is initiallastname@ewtn.com; so to reach, say, Thom Price, it would be tprice@ewtn.com. Web: (includes on-demand and streaming audio and online reception report form) www.ewtn.com/radio. Contact: (general) Thom Price, Director of English Programming; Doug Archer, Director of Spanish Programming; (marketing) John Pepe, Radio Marketing Manager; (administration) Michael Warsaw, President; Doug Keck, Sr. Vice-President, Programming & Production; Scott Hults, Vice President, Communications; Frank Leurck, Station Manager; (technical) Terry Borders, Vice President Engineering; Glen Tapley, Frequency Manager. Listener correspondence welcome. IRC or return postage appreciated for correspondence. Although a Catholic entity, WEWN is not an official station of the Vatican, which operates its own Vatican Radio (*see*).

◨**WHRA-World Harvest Radio:**
ADMINISTRATION OFFICE: See World Harvest Radio.
TRANSMITTERS: Located in Greenbush, Maine. Technical and other correspondence should be sent to the main office of World Harvest Radio (*see*).

◨**WHRI-World Harvest Radio:**
ADMINISTRATION OFFICE: See World Harvest Radio.
TRANSMITTERS: Located in Cypress Creek, South Carolina. Technical and other correspondence should be sent to the main office of World Harvest Radio (*see*).

WINB—World International Broadcasters, 2900 Windsor Road, P.O. Box 88, Red Lion PA 17356 USA. Phone: (all departments) +1 (717) 244-5360. Fax: +1 (717) 246 0363. Email: (general) info@winb.com; (reception reports) winb40th@yahoo.com. Web: www.winb.com. Contact: (general) Mrs. Sally Spyker, Manager; (Sales & Frequency Manager) Hans Johnson; (technical) Fred W. Wise, Technical Director; John H. Norris, Owner. Return postage helpful outside United States. No giveaways or items for sale.

◨**WJIE Shortwave** (when operating), P.O. Box 197309, Louisville KY 40259 USA. Phone: +1 (502) 968-1220. Fax: +1 (502) 964 3304. Email: wjiesw@hotmail.com; (Rumsey) doug@wjie.org (put "WJIE International Shortwave" in the Subject line); (Freeman, technical) morgan@wjie.org. Web: (includes streaming audio) www.wjiesw.com. Contact: Morgan Freeman; Doug Rumsey.

◨**WMLK—Assemblies of Yahweh**, 190 Frantz Road, P.O. Box C, Bethel PA 19507 USA. Phone: +1 (717) 933-4518, +1 (717) 933-4880; (toll-free, U.S. only) 1-800-523-3827. Email: (general) aoy@wmlkradio.net; (technical) technician@wmlkradio. net; (Elder Meyer) jacobmeyer@wmlkradio.net; (McAvin) garymcavin@wmlkradio.net. Web: (includes streaming audio) www.wmlkradio.net. Contact: (general) Elder Jacob O. Meyer, Manager and Producer of "The Open Door to the Living World"; (technical) Gary McAvin, Operating Engineer. Free stickers,

The Sacred Name Broadcaster monthly magazine, and other religious material. Bibles, audio and video (VHS) tapes and religious paperback books offered. Enclosing return postage ($1 or IRCs) helps speed things up.

World Harvest Radio, LeSEA Broadcasting, 61300 Ironwood Road, South Bend IN 46614 USA; or P.O. Box 12, South Bend IN 46624 USA. Phone: +1 (219) 291-8200. Fax: +1 (219) 291 9043. Email: (general) whr@lesea.com; (Sarkisian) lsarkisian@lesea.com. Web: (includes streaming audio and online reception report form) www.whr.org; (LeSEA Broadcasting parent organization, includes streaming audio) www.lesea.com. Contact: (technical) Lori Sarkisian. World Harvest Radio T-shirts available. Return postage appreciated.
ENGINEERING DEPARTMENT: P.O. Box 50450, Indianapolis, IN 46250 USA.

WRMI—Radio Miami International, 175 Fontainebleau Blvd., Suite 1N4, Miami FL 33172 USA. Phone: +1 (305) 559-9764. Fax: +1 (305) 559 8186. Email: info@wrmi.net. Web: (includes streaming audio) www.wrmi.net. Contact: (technical and nontechnical) Jeff White, General Manager/Sales Manager. Free station stickers and tourist brochures. Sells "public access" airtime to nearly anyone to say virtually anything for $1 per minute.

WRNO WORLDWIDE (if reactivated), c/o Good News World Outreach, P.O. Box 895, Fort Worth TX 76101 USA. Phone: +1 (817) 850-9990. Fax: +1 (817) 850 9994. Email: wrno@mailup.net. Web:www.wrnoworldwide.org. Contact: Dr. Robert Mawire; Janet Mawire.
TRANSMITTER SITE: 4539 I-10 Service Road North, Metairie LA 70006 USA.

WTJC—*see* Fundamental Broadcasting Network.

WWBS (if reactivated), P.O. Box 18174. Macon GA 31209 USA. Phone: +1 (912) 477-3433. Email: wwbsradio@aol.com. Contact: Joanne Josey. Return postage required for postal reply.

WWCR—World Wide Christian Radio, F.W. Robbert Broadcasting Co., 1300 WWCR Avenue, Nashville TN 37218 USA. Phone: (general) +1 (615) 255-1300. Fax: +1 (615) 255 1311. Email: wwcr@wwcr.com. Web: (includes streaming audio) www.wwcr.com. Contact: (nontechnical) Cathy Soares, Program Director; (technical) Zach Harper, Operations Manager. Free program guides, updated monthly. Return postage helpful. For items sold on the air and tapes of programs, contact the producers of the programs, and *not* WWCR. Replies as time permits. Carries programs from various political organizations, which may be contacted directly.

WWRB—World Wide Religious Broadcasters, c/o Airline Transport Communications, Box 7, Manchester TN 37349-0007 USA. Phone/Fax: +1 (931) 841-0492. Email: (general) online form; (Dave Frantz) dfrantz@tennessee.com. Web: www.wwrb.org. Contact: Dave Frantz, Chief Engineer; Angela Frantz. Verifies reception reports with a large certificate and automatic membership of the WWRB Shortwave Listener's Club. Does not accept email reports.

WWV/WWVB (official time and frequency stations): NIST Radio Station WWV, 2000 East County Road #58, Ft. Collins CO 80524 USA. Phone: +1 (303) 497-3914. Fax: +1 (303) 497 4063. Email: (general) nist.radio@boulder.nist.gov; (Deutch) deutch@boulder.nist.gov. Web: http://tf.nist.gov/timefreq/stations/wwv.html. Contact: Matthew J. ("Matt") Deutch, Engineer-in-Charge. Along with branch sister station WWVH in Hawaii (*see*, below), WWV and WWVB are the official time and frequency stations of the United States, operating over longwave (WWVB) on 60 kHz, and over shortwave (WWV) on 2500, 5000, 10000, 15000 and 20000 kHz.

PARENT ORGANIZATION: National Institute of Standards and Technology, Time and Frequency Division, 325 Broadway, Boulder CO 80305-3328 USA. Phone: +1 (303) 497-5453. Fax: +1 303-497-6461. Email: (Lowe) lowe@boulder.nist.gov. Contact: John P. Lowe, Group Leader.

WWVH (official time and frequency station): NIST Radio Station WWVH, P.O. Box 417, Kekaha, Kauai HI 96752 USA. Phone: +1 (808) 335-4361; (streaming audio) +1 (808) 335-4363; (Automated Computer Time Service) +1 (808) 335 4721. Fax: +1 (808) 335 4747. Email: (general) wwvh@boulder.nist.gov; (Okayama) okayama@boulder.nist.gov. Web: http://tf.nist.gov/stations/wwvh.htm. Contact: Dean T. Okayama, Engineer-in-Charge. Along with sister stations WWV and WWVB (*see* preceding), WWVH is the official time and frequency station of the United States, operating on 2500, 5000, 10000 and 15000 kHz.

WYFR—Family Radio—*see* Family Radio Worldwide.

VANUATU   World Time +11

Radio Vanuatu, Information and Public Relations, Private Mail Bag 049, Port Vila, Vanuatu. Phone: +678 22999, +678 23026. Fax: +678 22026. Contact: Maxwell E. Maltok, General Manager; Ambong Thompson, Head of Programmes; Allan Kalfabun, Sales and Marketing Consultant, who is interested in exchanging letters and souvenirs from other countries; (technical) Warren Robert, Acting Technical Manager; K.J. Page, Principal Engineer; Willie Daniel, Technician.

VATICAN CITY STATE   World Time +1 (+2 midyear)

Radio Vaticana (Vatican Radio)
MAIN AND PROMOTION OFFICES: 00120 Città del Vaticano, Vatican City State. Phone: (general) +39 (06) 6988-3551; (Director General) +39 (06) 6988-3945; (Programme Director) +39 (06) 6988-3996; (Publicity and Promotion Department) +39 (06) 6988-3045; (technical, general) +39 (06) 6988-4897; (frequency management) +39 (06) 6988-5258. Fax: (general) +39 (06) 6988 4565; (frequency management) +39 (06) 6988 5062. Email: sedoc@vatiradio.va; (Director General) dirgen@vatiradio.va; (frequency management) mc6790@mclink.it; gestfreq@vatiradio.va; (technical direction, general) sectec@vatiradio.va; (Programme Director) dirpro@vatiradio.va; (Publicity and Promotion Department) promo@vatiradio.va; (English Section) englishpr@vatiradio.va; (French Section) magfra@vatiradio.va; (German Section) deutsch@vatiradio.va. Web: (includes on-demand and streaming audio) www.vatican.va/news_services/radio; (includes on-demand and streaming audio) www.vaticanradio.org. Contact: (general) Elisabetta Vitalini Sacconi, Promotion Office and schedules; Carol Ganbardella, Secretary, English Service; Eileen O'Neill, Head of Program Development, English Service; Fr. Lech Rynkiewicz S.J., Head of Promotion Office; Fr. Andrzej Koprowski S.J., Program Director; Dr. Giacomo Ghisani, Head of International Relations; Sean Patrick Lovett, Head of English Service; Veronica Scarisbrick, Producer, "On the Air;" (administration) Fr. Federico Lombardi S.J., Director General; (technical) Sergio Salvatori, Assistant Frequency Manager, Direzione Tecnica; Dr. Alberto Gasbarri, Technical Director; Giovanni Serra, Frequency Management Department. Correspondence sought on religious and programming matters, rather than the technical minutiae of radio. Free station stickers and paper pennants.
INDIA OFFICE: Loyola College, P.B. No 3301, Chennai-600 03, India. Fax: +91 (44) 2825 7340. Email: (Tamil) tamil@vatiradio.va; (Hindi) hindi@vatiradio.va; (English) india@vatiradio.va.

Broadcasters' Forum at the 1994 Monitoring Times convention in Atlanta. Monitoring Times held memorable conventions for several years.

Frederica Dochinoiu, RRI

REGIONAL OFFICE, INDIA: Pastoral Orientation Centre, P.B. No 2251, Palarivattom, India. Fax: +91 (484) 2336 227. Email: (Malayalam) malayalam@vatiradio.va.

JAPAN OFFICE: 2-10-10 Shiomi, Koto-ku, Tokyo 135, Japan. Fax: +81 (3) 5632 4457.

VENEZUELA   World Time –4

Ecos del Torbes (if reactivated), Apartado 152, San Cristóbal 5001-A, Táchira, Venezuela. Phone: (general) +58 (276) 341-4189. Contact: (general) Lic. Dinorah González Zerpa, Gerente; Simón Zaidman Krenter; (technical) Ing. Iván Escobar S., Jefe Técnico.

Observatorio Cagigal—YVTO (when operating), Apartado 6745, Armada 84-DHN, Caracas 103, Venezuela. Phone: +58 (212) 481-2266. Email: armdhn@ven.net, shlv@dhn.mil.ve. Contact: Luis Ojeda Pérez, Director; Jesús Alberto Escalona, Director Técnico. $1 or return postage helpful.

Radio Amazonas (when operating), Av. Simón Bolívar 4, Puerto Ayacucho 7101, Amazonas, Venezuela. Contact: Angel María Pérez, Propietario.

ADDRESS FOR RECEPTION REPORTS: Sr. Jorge García Rangel, Radio Amazonas QSL Manager, Calle Roma, Qta: Costa Rica No. A-16, Urbanización Alto Barinas, Barinas 5201, Venezuela. Two IRC's or $2 required.

Radio Nacional de Venezuela - Antena Internacional, Final Calle Las Marías, El Pedregal de Chapellín, 1050 Caracas, Venezuela. Phone: +58 (212) 730-6022, +58 (212) 730-6666. Fax: +58 (212) 731 1457 Email: ondacortavenezuela@hotmail. com. Web: (includes streaming audio from domestic services not on shortwave) www.rnv.gov.ve. Contact: Ali Méndez Martínez, periodista y representativo de onda corta; José Luis Noguera, Director. Currently broadcasts via the transmission facilities of Radio Habana Cuba. "Antena Internacional" is also aired at 0600-0700 World Time on mediumwave AM via Radio Nacional's domestic "Canal Informativo," available in streaming audio at the RNV Website.

Radio Táchira (if reactivated), Apartado 152, San Cristóbal 5001-A, Táchira, Venezuela. Phone: +58 (276) 356-7444, +58

(276) 355-0560. Contact: Desirée González Zerpa, Directora; Sra. Albertina, Secretaria; Eleázar Silva Malavé, Gerente.

Radio Valera (if reactivated), Av. 10 No. 9-31, Valera 3102, Trujillo, Venezuela. Phone: +58 (271) 225-3978. Contact: Gladys Barroeta; Mariela Leal. Replies to correspondence in Spanish. Return postage required.

VIETNAM   World Time +7

NOTE: Reception reports on Vietnamese regional stations should be sent to the Voice of Vietnam Overseas Service (see).

Voice of Vietnam—Domestic Service (Đài Tiếng Nói Viêt Nam, TNVN)—Addresses and contact numbers as for all sections of Voice of Vietnam—Overseas Service, below. Contact: Phan Quang, Director General.

Voice of Vietnam—Overseas Service

TRANSMISSION FACILITY (MAIN ADDRESS FOR NONTECHNI-CAL CORRESPONDENCE AND GENERAL VERIFICATIONS): 58 Quán Sú, Hànôi, Vietnam. Phone: +84 (4) 934-4231. Fax: +84 (4) 934 4230. Email: qhqt.vov@hn.vnn.vn; rtc.vov@hn.vnn.vn; ktpt@hn.vnn.vn; (English) english@vovnews.vn. Web: (includes on-demand and streaming audio) www.vov.org.vn. Contact: Ms. Hoang Minh Nguyet, Director of International Relations. STUDIOS (NONTECHNICAL CORRESPONDENCE AND GEN-ERAL VERIFICATIONS): 45 Ba Trieu Street, Hànôi, Vietnam. Phone: (director) +84 (4) 825-7870; (English service) +84 (4) 934-2456, +84 (4) 825-4482; (newsroom) +84 (4) 825-5761, +84 (4) 825-5862. Fax: (English service) +84 (4) 826 6707. Email: btdn.vov@hn.vnn.vn; (Spanish Service contact) tieng-noi_vietnam2004@yahoo.es. Contact: Ms. Nguyen Thi Hue, Director, Overseas Service. Voice of Vietnam Overseas Service broadcasts in 11 foreign languages, namely English, French, Japanese, Russian, Spanish, Mandarin, Cantonese, Indonesian, Lao, Thai, Khmer and Vietnamese for overseas Vietnamese. TECHNICAL CORRESPONDENCE: Office of Radio Reception Quality, Central Department of Radio and Television Broad-cast Engineering, Vietnam General Corporation of Posts and Telecommunications, Hànôi, Vietnam.

WESTERN SAHARA   World Time exactly

☞ **Radio Nacional de la República Arabe Saharaui Democrática** (when operating), c/o Directeur d'Information, Frente Polisario, B.P. 10, El-Mouradia, 16000 Algiers, Algeria. Email: rasdradio@yahoo.es. Web: (streaming audio) http://web.jet.es/rasd/radionacional.htm. Email correspondence recommended, as postal service is unreliable. Pro-Polisario Front, and supported by the Algerian government. Operates from Rabuni, near Tindouf, on the Algerian side of the border with Western Sahara.

YEMEN   World Time +3

☞ **Republic of Yemen Radio**, Ministry of Information, P.O. Box 2182, Sana'a-al Hasbah, Yemen; (alternative address, technical) Technical Department, P. O. Box 2371, Sana'a, Yemen. Phone: (general) +967 (1) 282-005; (Technical Department) +967 (1) 282-060/1. Fax: (general) +967 (1) 230 761; (Technical Department) +967 (1) 282 053. Email: yradio@y.net.ye, hussein3itu@y.net.ye; (Tashi, technical) ali_tashy@yahoo.com. Web: (includes on-demand audio): www.yradio.gov.ye. Contact: (general) English Service; (administration) Mohammed Dahwan, General Director of Sana'a Radio; (technical) Eng. Ali Ahmed Tashi, Technical Department Director.

ZAMBIA   World Time +2

☞ **The Voice - Africa**
STATION: Private Bag E606, Lusaka, Zambia. Phone: +260 (1) 274-251. Fax: +260 (1) 274 526. Email: cvoice@zamnet.zm. Web: (includes streaming audio) www.voiceafrica.net. Contact: Philip Haggar, Station Manager; Lenganji Nanyangwe, Assistant to Station Manager; Beatrice Phiri. Free calendars and stickers; pens, as available. Free religious books and items under selected circumstances. Sells T-shirts and sundry other items. $1 or 2 IRCs appreciated for reply. Verifies reception reports. Broadcasts Christian teachings and music, as well as news and programs on farming, sport, education, health, business and children's affairs. Formerly known as Radio Christian Voice.
U. K. OFFICE: The Voice, P.O. Box 3040, West Bromwich, West Midlands, B70 0EJ, United Kingdom. Phone:+44 (121) 224-1614. Fax: +44 (121) 224 1613. Email: feedback@voiceafrica.net; (Joynes) sandra@voiceafrica.net. Contact: Sandra Joynes, Office Administrator.
Radio Zambia, Mass Media Complex, Alick Nkhata Road, P.O. Box 50015, Lusaka 10101, Zambia. Phone: (general) +260 (1) 254-989, +260 (1) 253-301, +260 (1) 252-005; (Public Relations) +260 (1) 254-989, X-216; (engineering) +260 (1) 250-380. Fax: +260 (1) 254 317, +260 (1) 254 013. Email: (general, including reception reports) znbc@microlink.zm. Web: www.znbc.co.zm; (streaming audio) www.coppernet.zm/home.html. Contact: (general) Keith M. Nalumango, Director of Programmes; Lawson Chishimba, Public Relations Manager; (administration) Duncan H. Mbazima, Director-General; (technical) James M. Phiri, Director of Engineering. Free *Zamwaves* newsletter. Sometimes gives away stickers, postcards and small publications. $1 required, and postal correspondence should be sent via registered mail. Tours given of the station Tuesdays to Fridays between 9:00 AM and noon local time; inquire in advance. Used to reply slowly and irregularly, but seems to be better now.

ZIMBABWE   World Time +2

Radio Voice of the People, P.O. Box 5750, Harare, Zimbabwe. Phone: +263 (4) 707-123, +263 (91) 913-560. Email: voxpopzim@yahoo.co.uk, voxpop@ecoweb.co.zw. Web: www.vopradio.co.zw. Contact: John Masuku, Executive Director. Airs via Radio Nederland facilities in Madagascar.
Radio VOP—*see* Radio Voice of the People, above.
☞ **Zimbabwe Broadcasting Corporation**, Broadcasting Center, Pockets Hill, P.O. Box HG444, Highlands, Harare, Zimbabwe. Phone: +263 (4) 498-610, +263 (4) 498-630; (Guinea Fowl Shortwave Transmitting Station) +263 (54) 22-104. Fax: +263 (4) 498 613. Email: zbc@zbc.co.zw; (general enquiries) pr@zbc.co.zw; (engineering) hbt@zbc.co.zw. Web: (includes streaming audio) www.zbc.co.zw. Contact: (general) Rugare Sangomoyo; Lydia Muzenda; (administration) Alum Mpofu, Chief Executive Officer; (news details) Munyaradzi Hwengwere; (Broadcasting Technology, Engineering) Craig Matambo. $1 helpful.

Prepared by Craig Tyson (Australia), editor, with Tony Jones (Paraguay). Special thanks to George Allegado II (USA), Gabriel Iván Barrera (Argentina), Dino Bloise (USA), Héctor García Bojorge (Mexico), David Crystal (Israel), Graeme Dixon (New Zealand), Jose Jacob (India), Marie Lamb (USA), Grant Murray (Canada), Gary Neal (USA), Fotios Padazopulos (USA), George Poppin (USA), Célio Romais (Brazil) and Paulo Roberto e Souza (Brazil); also, the following organizations for their support and cooperation: Conexión Digital *and* RUS-DX/Anatoly Klepov (Russia).

Worldwide Broadcasts in English— 2007

Country-by-Country Guide to Best-Heard Stations

Dozens of countries reach out in English, and this is where you'll find their times and frequencies. For what shows are on, hour-by-hour, check out "What's On Tonight."

•**Top Times:** "Best Times and Frequencies," earlier in PASSPORT, pinpoints where each world band segment is found and offers helpful tuning tips. Focus on late afternoon and evening, when most programs are beamed your way—although around dawn and early afternoon can be productive, as well.

☞ Dusk and evening, tune segments between 5730 and 10000 kHz in winter, 5730 and 15800 kHz in summer. Daytime it's 9250-21850 kHz winter, 11500-21850 kHz summer. Around dawn explore 5730-17900 kHz year-round for fewer but intriguing catches.

Times and days of the week are in World Time (UTC), explained in "Setting Your World Time Clock" and "Worldly Words"; for local times in each country see "Addresses PLUS." Midyear, typically April through October, some stations are an hour earlier (◧) or later (◨) because of Daylight Saving/Summer Time. Stations may also extend their hours for holidays, emergencies or sports events.

Frequencies used only seasonally are labeled ◨ for summer (midyear) and ◧ for winter.

• **Strongest frequencies:** Frequencies in *italics* tend to be best, as they are from relay transmitters that may be near you. Some signals not beamed your way may also be heard, especially when targeted to nearby parts of the world. Frequencies with no target zones are typically for domestic coverage, so they're unlikely to be heard unless you're in or near that country.

Indigenous Music

Programs not in English? Turn to "Voices from Home" or the Blue Pages. Stations for diaspora sometimes carry delightful native music that's enjoyable listening, regardless of language.

Schedules for Entire Year

To be as useful as possible over the months to come, PASSPORT's schedules consist not just of observed activity, but also that which we have creatively opined will take place during the forthcoming year. This predictive material is based on decades of experience and is original from us. Although inherently not as exact as real-time data, over the years it's been of tangible value to PASSPORT readers.

> **Relay frequencies should be strong, but even those beamed elsewhere may be audible.**

The Millennium Capsule offers a spectacular panorama of London, home to the BBC World Service and countless broadcasting bureaus.

Shutterstock/Zsolt Nyulaszi

ALBANIA

RADIO TIRANA
0245-0300 &	
0330-0400 ⬛	Tu-Su 6115 & Tu-Su 7450 (E North Am)
1845-1900	⬛ M-Sa 7465 (Europe), ⬛ M-Sa 9920 (W Europe)
1945-2000	⬛ M-Sa 7465 & ⬛ M-Sa 7530/5910 (W Europe)
2100-2130 ⬛	M-Sa 7465 (Europe)

ARGENTINA

RADIO ARGENTINA AL EXTERIOR-RAE
0200-0300	Tu-Sa 11710 (Americas)
1800-1900	M-F 9690 (Europe & N Africa), M-F 15345 (Europe)

AUSTRALIA

CVC
0100-0300	*7355* (S Asia)
0300-0600	*13685* (S Asia)
0500-0600	*9430* (W Africa & C Africa)
0515-1545	*9555* (C Africa & S Africa)
0600-0700	⬛ *11720* & ⬛ *15640* (W Africa & C Africa)
0600-0900	15335 (S Asia & SE Asia)
0700-0900	*15640* (W Africa & C Africa)
0900-1100	11955 (SE Asia)
1100-1800	13635 (S Asia & SE Asia)
1200-1400	⬛ *15565/15715* & ⬛ *17860* (Mideast)
1200-1500	*13830* (E Europe)
1400-1700	⬛ *11830* & ⬛ *15795* (Mideast)
1500-1700	⬛ *9655/11705* & ⬛ *13800* (E Europe)
1500-1800	⬛ *15680* & ⬛ *15715* (W Africa & C Africa)
1800-2000	⬛ *9765* (W Africa & C Africa)
1800-2100	⬛ *13820* (W Africa & C Africa)
2000-2100	⬛ *7285* (W Africa & C Africa)

RADIO AUSTRALIA
0000-0130	17775 (SE Asia)
0000-0200	17715 (Pacific & N America), 17795 (Pacific & W North Am)
0000-0800	9660 (Pacific), 13630 (Pacific & E Asia), 15240 (Pacific)
0000-0900	12080 (S Pacific), 17750 (SE Asia)
0030-0400	15415 (SE Asia)
0200-0500	21725 (E Asia)
0200-0700	15515 (Pacific & N America)
0430-0500	15415 (SE Asia)
0500-0800	15160 (Pacific & N America)
0530-0800	15415 (SE Asia)
0700-0900	13630 (Pacific & W North Am)
0800-0900	5995 & 9710 (Pacific)
0800-1130	*15240* (E Asia)
0800-1400	9580 (Pacific & N America)
0800-1600	9590 (Pacific & W North Am)
0830-0900	15415 (SE Asia)
0900-0930	Sa/Su 15415 (SE Asia)
0900-1300	11880 (SE Asia)
0930-1100	15415 (SE Asia)
1100-1200	12080 (S Pacific)
1100-1300	9475 (SE Asia)
1100-1400	5995 (Pacific), 6020 (Pacific & W North Am), 9560 (E Asia & Pacific)
1400-1700	7240 (Pacific & W North Am)
1400-1800	5995 (Pacific & W North Am), 6080 (SE Asia)
1430-1700	11660 (SE Asia)
1430-1900	9475 (SE Asia)
1600-2000	9710 (Pacific)
1700-2100	9580 (Pacific), 11880 (Pacific & W North Am)
1800-2000	6080 (Pacific & E Asia), 7240 (Pacific)
1900-2200	9500 (SE Asia)
2000-2100	F/Sa 6080 & F/Sa 7240 (Pacific)
2000-2200	11650 & 11660 (Pacific & W North Am), 12080 (S Pacific)
2100-2200	9660 (Pacific), 11695 (SE Asia)
2100-2300	13630 & 15515 (Pacific)
2200-2330	*15240* (E Asia)
2200-2400	13620 (SE Asia), 15230 (Pacific), 17785/21740 (Pacific & N America)

The Musikverein concert hall, Vienna, reflects Austria's love affair with classical music. When Radio Austria International went global 45 years back, it initially played nothing but Strauss waltzes.

Shutterstock/Bob Cheung

| 2300-2400 | 9660 (Pacific), 12080 (S Pacific), 13630 (Pacific & E Asia), 17795 (Pacific & W North Am) |
| 2330-2400 | 15415 & 17750 (SE Asia) |

AUSTRIA

RADIO AUSTRIA INTERNATIONAL

0005-0015	⚏ Su/M 7325 (C America)
0015-0030	⚏ 7325 (C America)
0035-0045	⚏ Su/M 7325 (E North Am)
0045-0100	⚏ 7325 (E North Am)
0105-0115	⚏ Su/M 9870 (C America)
0115-0130	⚏ 9870 (C America)
0135-0145	⚏ Su/M 9870 (E North Am)
0145-0200	⚏ 9870 (E North Am)
0605-0630 & 0635-0700 ⬅	Su 17870 (Mideast)
1205-1220	⚏ M 17715 (SE Asia & Australasia)
1205-1230	⚏ Sa/Su 17715 (SE Asia & Australasia)
1215-1230	⚏ Tu-F 17715 (SE Asia & Australasia)
1235-1300	⚏ Sa/Su 17715 (SE Asia & Australasia)
1245-1300	⚏ M-F 17715 (SE Asia & Australasia)
1305-1320 ⬅	M 6155 & M 13730 (Europe)
1305-1320	⚏ M 17855 (SE Asia & Australasia)
1305-1330 ⬅	Sa/Su 6155 & Sa/Su 13730 (Europe)
1315-1330	⚏ Tu-F 17855 (SE Asia & Australasia)
1335-1345	⚏ Sa/Su 17855 (SE Asia & Australasia)
1335-1400 ⬅	Sa/Su 6155 & Sa/Su 13730 (Europe)
1345-1400 ⬅	Tu-F 6155 & Tu-F 13730 (Europe)
1345-1400	⚏ 17855 (SE Asia & Australasia)
1505-1520	⚏ M 13775 (W North Am)
1505-1530	⚏ Sa/Su 13775 (W North Am)
1515-1530	⚏ Tu-F 13775 (W North Am)
1535-1600	⚏ Sa/Su 13775 (W North Am)
1545-1600	⚏ M-F 13775 (W North Am)
1605-1620	⚏ M 13675 (W North Am)
1605-1630	⚏ Sa/Su 13675 (W North Am)
1615-1630	⚏ Tu-F 13675 (W North Am)
1635-1700	⚏ Sa/Su 13675 (W North Am)
1645-1700	⚏ M-F 13675 (W North Am)
2335-2345 ➡	Sa/Su 9870 (S America)
2345-2400	9870 (S America)

BANGLADESH
BANGLADESH BETAR
1230-1300	7185 (SE Asia)
1745-1815 &	
1815-1900	7185 (Europe)

BELARUS
RADIO BELARUS—(W Europe)
0200-0230	⒮ M-W/F/Sa 6170
0230-0300	⒮ Su 6170
0300-0330 ▨	M-W/F/Sa 5970 & M-W/F/Sa 7210
0300-0330	⒲ M-W/F/Sa 6155
0330-0400 ▨	Su 5970 & Su 7210
0330-0400	⒲ Su 6155
1930-2000	⒮ M/Tu/Th/F 7280 & ⒮ M/Tu/Th/F 7290
2030-2100 ▨	M/Tu/Th/F 7105
2030-2100	⒲ M/Tu/Th/F 7340 & ⒲ M/Tu/Th/F 7440
2100-2130	⒮ Su 7280 & ⒮ Su 7290
2200-2230 ▨	Su 7105
2200-2230	⒲ Su 7340 & ⒲ Su 7440

BULGARIA
RADIO BULGARIA
0000-0100 ▨	9700 (E North Am)
0000-0100	⒲ 7400 (E North Am)
0200-0300	⒮ 11700 (E North Am)
0300-0400 ▨	9700 (E North Am)
0300-0400	⒲ 7400 (E North Am)
0730-0800 ▨	11500 (W Europe)
0730-0800	⒲ 9500 (W Europe)
1230-1300 ▨	11700 & 15700 (W Europe)
1730-1800	⒮ 9500 & ⒮ 11500 (W Europe)
1830-1900	⒲ 5800 & ⒲ 7500 (W Europe)
2200-2300 ▨	5800 & 7500 (W Europe)
2300-2400	⒮ 11700 (E North Am)

CANADA
CANADIAN BROADCASTING CORP—(E North Am)
0000-0300 ▨	Su 9625
0200-0300 ▨	Tu-Sa 9625
0300-0310 &	
0330-0609 ▨	M 9625
0400-0609 ▨	Su 9625
0500-0609 ▨	Tu-Sa 9625
1200-1255 ▨	M-F 9625
1200-1505 ▨	Sa 9625
1200-1700 ▨	Su 9625
1600-1615 &	
1700-1805 ▨	Sa 9625
1800-2400 ▨	Su 9625
1945-2015,	
2200-2225 &	
2240-2330 ▨	M-F 9625

CFRX-CFRB—(E North Am)
24 Hr	6070

CFVP-CKMX—(W North Am)
24 Hr	6030

CKZN—(E North Am)
24 Hr	6160

CKZU-CBU—(W North Am)
24 Hr	6160

RADIO CANADA INTERNATIONAL
0000-0100	⒲ 9880 & ⒮ 11700 (SE Asia)
0000-0200	9755 (N America & C America)
0100-0200	⒲ 5840 & ⒲ 5970 (S Asia), ⒮ 13710 (W North Am)
1200-1300	⒲ 7105 & ⒮ 9660 (E Asia), ⒲ 9665 (SE Asia), ⒮ 15170 (E Asia & SE Asia)
1300-1600	⒮ 17800 (C America)
1400-1700 ▨	9515 & 13655 (E North Am & C America)
1400-1700	⒲ 17820 (C America)
1500-1600	⒲ 9635, ⒮ 11675, ⒲ 11870, ⒲ 11975, ⒮ 15360 & ⒮ 17720 (S Asia)
1800-1900	⒲ 7185, ⒲ 9530 & ⒮ 11765 (E Africa), ⒲ 11875 (C Africa & E Africa), ⒮ 13730 (C Africa & S Africa), ⒮ 15255 (W Africa), ⒲ 15365 & ⒲ 17740 (W Africa & C Africa)
1900-2000	⒲ 9770 (E Africa), ⒮ 13730 (C Africa & E Africa)
2000-2100	⒮ 7235 (W Europe & N Africa), ⒮ 11765 (Europe & Mideast), ⒮ 15325 (W Europe)
2000-2200	⒮ 17765 (C America)
2100-2200 ▨	5850 (W Europe)
2100-2200	⒲ 9770 (W Europe)
2100-2300	⒲ 15180 (C America)

2300-2400 ◀ 6100 (E North Am)
2300-2400 🆆 6195 (N America)

CHINA

CHINA RADIO INTERNATIONAL

0000-0100 🆆 5915 (E Asia), 6075 (S Asia), 7130 (Europe), 7180 (S Asia), 11885 (SE Asia), 🆆 11900 & 🆂 13750 (E Asia)

0000-0200 *6020* (N America), 🆆 7345 (Europe), *9570* (N America), 🆂 9725 (Europe), 🆆 11650 & 🆂 15115 (SE Asia)

0100-0200 🆆 *6005* (N America), 🆆 6075 (S Asia), 🆆 7130 (Europe), 🆆 7180 (S Asia), 🆂 9410 (Europe), 🆂 9535 (S Asia), *9580* (E North Am), 🆂 *9790* (W North Am), 🆂 11870 (S Asia), 🆆 11885 & 🆂 15785 (SE Asia)

0200-0300 13640 (S Asia)

0200-0400 11770 (S Asia)

0300-0400 *9690* (N America & C America), *9790* (W North Am), 15110 (S Asia)

0300-0500 🆆 9460, 🆆 13620 & 🆂 13750 (E Asia), 15120 (C Asia & E Asia), 🆂 15785 (E Asia)

0400-0500 🆂 *6080* (N America), 🆆 *6190* (W North Am)

0400-0600 🆂 *6020* (W North Am), 17725 & 17855 (C Asia)

0500-0600 🆆 *5960* (N America), *6190* (W North Am), 🆆 *7220* (N Africa)

0500-0700 🆂 *11710* (N Africa), 17505 (N Africa & W Africa)

0500-0900 11880, 15465 & 17540 (S Asia)

0500-1100 15350 (S Asia)

0600-0700 🆆 *6115* (W North Am), 🆆 *11750* (N Africa), 🆆 11770, 🆂 11870 & 15140 (Mideast)

0600-0800 🆆 13645, 🆂 13660 & 17710 (SE Asia)

0700-0900 🆆 *11785* & 🆂 *13710* (W Europe)

0700-1300 17490 (Europe)

0800-1000 🆆 9415 & 🆂 11620 (E Asia)

0900-1000 17750 (S Asia)

0900-1100 15210 & 17690 (Australasia)

1000-1100 🆆 5955 (E Asia), 🆆 7135, 🆆 7215, 🆂 11610 & 🆂 11635 (C Asia & E Asia), 🆂 13620 (E Asia), 15190 (S Asia)

1000-1200 🆂 *6040* (E North Am), 13590 & 13720 (SE Asia)

1100-1200 🆆 *5960* (E North Am), 🆂 *11750* (W North Am), 11795 & 13645 (S Asia)

1100-1300 11650 (S Asia), 🆂 *13650* & 🆆 *13665* (W Europe)

1100-1500 5955 (E Asia), 🆂 11660 (S Asia)

1200-1300 🆆 7250 & 9460 (S Asia), 🆆 9590 (E Europe), 9760 (Australasia), 11690 (C Asia), 🆆 12080 & 🆂 13645 (S Asia)

1200-1400 9730 (SE Asia), 11760 (Australasia), 11980 (SE Asia), 🆂 13610 (S Asia), 13790 (Europe)

1300-1400 🆆 7300 (S Asia), *9570* (E North Am), 🆂 *9650* (E North Am & C America), 9760/11900 (Australasia), 🆆 *11885* (W North Am), 🆂 13755 (S Asia), 🆂 *15260* (W North Am), 🆆 *15540* & 🆂 *17625* (S America)

1300-1500 9765 (SE Asia), 13610 (Europe), 🆆 *15230* (E North Am & C America)

1300-1600 9870 (SE Asia)

1400-1500 9560 & 🆂 9560 (S Asia), 🆆 9700 & 🆆 9795 (Europe), 11675 & 11765 (S Asia), 🆂 13710 & 🆂 13790 (Europe)

1400-1600 11775 (S Asia), 🆆 *13675* (W North Am), *13685* (E Africa), *13740* (W North Am), *17630* (C Africa)

1500-1600 5955 (E Asia), 7160 (S Asia), 7325 (SE Asia), 9785 (S Asia), 🆂 13640 (Europe)

1500-1700 🆆 9435, 🆆 9525 & 🆂 11965 (Europe)

1500-1800 *6100* (S Africa)

Paris' legendary Opéra has been superceded by L'Opéra de la Bastille, an ultramodern edifice for avant garde productions. Shutterstock/Nicholas Peter Gavin Davies

1600-1800	▥ 7255 (Europe), 9570 (E Africa & S Africa), 11900 (S Africa)
1600-1900	⬛ 13760 (Europe)
1600-2000	⬛ 11940 (Europe)
1700-1800	▥ 6100 & ⬛ 9695 (Europe)
1800-1900	▥ 6100 (E Europe & W Asia), ⬛ 9600 (Europe)
1900-2000	9440/9435 (Mideast, W Africa & C Africa)
1900-2100	7295 (Mideast & N Africa)
2000-2100	9440 (Mideast, W Africa & C Africa)
2000-2130	*11640* (E Africa & S Africa), *13630* (E Africa)
2000-2200	*5960* (W Europe), 7190 (Europe), *7285* & ▥ 9490 (W Europe), 9600 (Europe), ⬛ 9800 (W Europe)
2200-2300	▥ 5915 (E Asia), ▥ *7170* & ⬛ *7175* (N Europe), ⬛ 9590 (E Asia)

2300-2400	5915 & ▥ 5975 (S Asia), *5990* (C America), ▥ *6040* (E North Am), ▥ 6145 (E Asia), ⬛ *6145* (E North Am), 7180 (S Asia), ⬛ 11685 (E Asia), ▥ *11970* & ⬛ *13680* (W North Am)

CHINA (TAIWAN)

RADIO TAIWAN INTERNATIONAL

0200-0300	*5950* (E North Am), *9680* (N America), 11875 (SE Asia), 15465 (E Asia)
0300-0400	*5950* (W North Am), *15215* (S America), 15320 (SE Asia)
0700-0800	*5950* (W North Am)
0800-0900	9610 (SE Asia & Australasia)
1100-1200	7445 (SE Asia)
1200-1300	7130 (E Asia)
1400-1500	15265 (SE Asia)
1600-1700	11550 (E Asia & S Asia)
1700-1800	▥ *11850* (C Africa), ⬛ *15690* (C Africa & S Africa)
1800-1900	*3965* (W Europe)
2200-2300	▥ *9355* & ⬛ *15600* (Europe)

CROATIA

CROATIAN RADIO—(Europe)

1905-1915 ▭	6165

VOICE OF CROATIA

0200-0215	⬛ *9925* (N America & S America)
0300-0315	▥ *7285* (N America & S America)
2215-2230	⬛ *9925* (S America)
2315-2330	▥ *7285* (S America)

CUBA

RADIO HABANA CUBA

0100-0500	6000 (E North Am), 9820 (N America)
0500-0700	6000 (W North Am), 6060 (E North Am), 9550 (W North Am), 11760 (Americas)
2030-2130	9505 (C America), 11760 (N America)
2300-2400	9550 (C America)

CZECH REPUBLIC

RADIO PRAGUE

0000-0030	[S] 7345 (E North Am & C America), [S] 9440 (N America & C America)
0100-0130	6200 & 7345 (N America & C America)
0200-0230	[W] 6200 & [W] 7345 (N America & C America)
0300-0330	[S] 7345 (N America & C America), [S] 9870 (W North Am & C America)
0330-0400	[S] 9445 (Mideast & E Africa), [S] 11600 (Mideast & S Asia)
0400-0430	[W] *6100* (W North Am), [W] 6200 (W North Am & C America), [W] 7345 (N America & C America)
0430-0500	[W] 9885 (Mideast), [W] 11600 (Mideast & S Asia)
0700-0730	[S] 9880 & [S] 11600 (W Europe)
0800-0830	[W] 7345 & [W] 9860 (W Europe)
0900-0930	[S] 21745 (S Asia & W Africa)
1000-1030	[W] 21745 (S Asia & W Africa)
1030-1100	[S] 9880 & [S] 11615 (N Europe)
1130-1200	[W] 11640 (N Europe), [W] 21745 (E Africa & Mideast)
1300-1330	[S] 13580 (N Europe), [S] 21745 (E Africa)
1400-1430	[W] 11600 (S Asia), [W] 21745 (N America)
1600-1630	[S] 17485 (E Africa)
1700-1730 ⬅	5930 (W Europe)
1700-1730	[W] 15710 (W Africa & C Africa), [S] 17485 (C Africa)
1800-1830 ⬅	5930 (W Europe)
1800-1830	[W] 9400 (Asia & Australasia)
2000-2030	[S] 11600 (SE Asia & Australasia)
2100-2130 ⬅	5930 (W Europe)
2100-2130	[W] 9430 (SE Asia & Australasia)
2130-2200	[S] 9800 (W Africa & C Africa), [S] 11600 (N America)
2230-2300	[W] 5930 (N America), [S] 7345 (E North Am & C America), [S] 9415 (N America), [W] 9435 (W Africa & C Africa)
2330-2400	[W] 5930 (N America), [W] 7345 (E North Am & C America)

EGYPT

RADIO CAIRO

0000-0030	11885/11950 (E North Am)
0200-0330	7270 (N America)
1215-1330	17835 (S Asia & SE Asia)
1630-1830	[W] 11785 & [S] 11880 (S Africa)
2030-2200	15375 (W Africa)
2115-2245	9990 (Europe)
2300-2400	11885 (E North Am)

FRANCE

RADIO FRANCE INTERNATIONALE

0400-0430	[W] M-F 7315 & [W] M-F 9805 (E Africa)
0500-0530	[W] M-F 9805/13680, [W] M-F 11995 & [S] M-F 13680 (E Africa)
0600-0630	[W] M-F 7315 (W Africa & C Africa), [S] M-F *9570* & [W] M-F *9865* (W Africa), [W] M-F 11995/15160, [W] M-F 13680, [S] M-F 15160 & [S] M-F 17800 (E Africa)
0700-0800	[W] 11725 (W Africa & C Africa), 15605 (W Africa)
1200-1230	[W] *15275* (W Africa), [S] 17800/21620 (E Africa), [S] *17815* (W Africa), [W] 21620 (E Africa)
1400-1500	[W] *5920* & [S] *7220* (S Asia)
1600-1700	[S] *7170* & [W] *9730* (E Africa & S Africa), [W] 11615/15605 (C Africa & E Africa), *15160* (W Africa & C Africa), [S] 17605 (E Africa)

GERMANY

DEUTSCHE WELLE

0000-0100	*7265* (SE Asia), [W] *9900* & [W] *15320* (E Asia)

0300-0400	*7330* & *9480* (S Asia), *9795* (SE Asia)
0400-0500	[W] 5905 (W Africa), [W] *6180* & [S] *7225* (C Africa & E Africa), [S] *7225* (W Africa), [W] 9565 (C Africa), [S] *9630* (C Africa & E Africa), [S] 12045 (E Africa), *15445* (C Africa & E Africa)
0500-0530	[W] *6180* (C Africa & E Africa), [W] *7285* (W Africa), [S] *9630* (C Africa & S Africa), [W] *9755* (W Africa), [W] *12045* (S Africa), [S] *15410* (C Africa & E Africa), [W] *15410* (E Africa, C Africa & S Africa), [S] *17800* (E Africa & S Africa)
0500-0600	[S] *9700* (C Africa & S Africa)
0600-0630	[W] *7170* (W Africa), [W] *7240* (W Africa & C Africa), [W] *7285* (W Africa), [W] *9565* (C Africa), [W] *12045* (W Africa & C Africa), [S] 15275 (W Africa)
0600-0700	[S] *17860* (W Africa & C Africa)
0600-1000	*6140* (W Europe)
0900-1000	*17700* & *21780* (E Asia & SE Asia)
1200-1400	[S] *11900* (E North Am & C America)
1300-1600	*6140* (W Europe)
1600-1700	*6170*, [S] *9485* & [W] *9795* (S Asia), [W] 11695 (S Asia, SE Asia & Australasia), [S] 15705 (S Asia)
1900-1930	[W] *7245*, [W] 9735 & [W] *11690* (C Africa & E Africa), [W] *12025* (C Africa, E Africa & S Africa), [W] *15275* & [S] 15620 (C Africa & E Africa)
2000-2100	[W] *6145* (C Africa & E Africa), [S] *7130* (S Africa), [W] 9735 (C Africa & E Africa), [W] *9830* (W Africa & C Africa), [S] 11795 (C Africa), [W] *12025* (C Africa & S Africa), [S] 13780 (C Africa & E Africa), [S] 15205 (C Africa & S Africa), [W] *15275* (C Africa & E Africa)
2100-2200	[W] 7280 & [S] 9440 (W Africa), [W] *9615* (W Africa & C Africa), [W] *11690*, [S] *11865* & [S] *15205* (W Africa)

GREECE

FONI TIS HELLADAS

0000-0100	[S] M 9420 (Europe & Americas)
0100-0200 ⇦	M 7475 (Europe & Americas)
0100-0200	[W] M 5865/9420 (Europe & N America)
0200-0300	[S] Su 9420 (Europe & Americas)
0300-0400 ⇦	Su 7475 (Europe & Americas)
0300-0400	[W] Su 5865/9420 (Europe & N America)
1500-1600 ⇦	Sa 9420 (Europe), Sa 15630 (W Europe & Atlantic)

HUNGARY

RADIO BUDAPEST

0100-0130	[S] 9590 (N America)
0200-0230	[W] 6110 (N America)
0230-0300	[S] 9795 (N America)
0330-0400	[W] 6035 (N America)
1500-1530	[S] Su 9690 (N Europe)
1600-1630 ⇦	Su 6025 (Europe)
1600-1630	[W] Su 9565 (N Europe)
2000-2030 ⇦	3975 (Europe), 6025 (W Europe)
2100-2130	[S] 9525 (S Africa)
2200-2230 ⇦	6025 (Europe)
2200-2230	[W] 9535 (S Africa)

INDIA

ALL INDIA RADIO

0000-0045	9705 (E Asia & SE Asia), 9950 (E Asia), 11620 (SE Asia), 11645 (E Asia), 13605 (E Asia & SE Asia)
1000-1100	13695/13710 (E Asia & Australasia), 15020 (E

All India Radio transmitter engineer gingerly adjusts a high-voltage transformer. Over the years more than one person attempting at this has wound up as Crispy the Cadaver.

M. Guha

	Asia), 15260 (S Asia), 15410/15135 (E Asia), 17510 (Australasia), 17800 (E Asia), 17895 (Australasia)
1330-1500	9690, 11620 & 13710 (SE Asia)
1745-1945	7410 (Europe), 9445 (W Africa), 9950 & 11620 (Europe), 11935 (E Africa), 13605 (W Africa), 15075 (E Africa), 15155 (W Africa), 17670 (E Africa)
2045-2230	7410 & 9445 (Europe), 9910 (Australasia), 9950 (Europe), 11620 & 11715 (Australasia)
2245-2400	9705 (E Asia & SE Asia), 9950 (E Asia), 11620 (SE Asia), 11645 (E Asia), 13605 (E Asia & SE Asia)

INDONESIA

VOICE OF INDONESIA

0200-0300	11785 (Irr) & 15150/9525 (E Asia, SE Asia & Pacific)
0800-0900	11785/9525 (Australasia)
2000-2100	9525/15150 & 11785 (Irr) (Europe)

IRAN

VOICE OF THE ISLAMIC REPUBLIC

0130-0230	☰ 6120, ☰ 7160, ☰ 7235 & ☰ 9495 (N America)
1030-1130	☰ 15460, ☰ 15480, ☰ 15600 & ☰ 17660 (S Asia)
1530-1630	☰ 6160, ☰ 7330, ☰ 7370 & ☰ 9635 (S Asia & SE Asia)
1930-2030	☰ 6010, ☰ 6205, ☰ 7205 & ☰ 7320 (Europe), ☰ 9800, ☰ 9855, ☰ 9925 & ☰ 11695 (S Africa)

ISRAEL

KOL ISRAEL

0330-0345	☰ 11590/9345 & ☰ 13720/7530 (W Europe & E North Am), ☰ 17600 (Australasia)
0430-0445	☰ 6280/9345 & ☰ 7545 (W Europe & E North Am), ☰ 15640 (Australasia)
0930-0945	☰ 13680 (W Europe), ☰ 15760 (W Europe & E North Am)
1030-1045	☰ 15640 (W Europe & E North Am), ☰ 17535 (W Europe & N America)

Seoul food. This unpretentious cafeteria serves nothing but fresh homemade dishes.
M. Guha

1730-1745	**S** 9345 (W Europe), **S** 13675 (W Europe & E North Am)
1830-1845 ◀	11590 (W Europe & E North Am)
1830-1845	**W** 7545 (W Europe), **W** 9345 (W Europe & E North Am)
1900-1925	**S** 9400 (W Europe), **S** 11590 (W Europe & E North Am)
2000-2025 ◀	15640 (S Africa)
2000-2025	**W** 6280/11590, **W** 7545 & **W** 9435 (W Europe & E North Am)

ITALY

RAI INTERNATIONAL

0055-0115	11800 (N America)
0445-0500	**W** 5965 (S Europe & N Africa), **S** 6110 & **W** 6120 (N Africa), **W** 7170, **S** 7235 & **S** 9800 (S Europe & N Africa)
1935-1955	**S** 5960, **W** 6035, **W** 9760 & **S** 9845 (W Europe)
2025-2045	**S** 6020, **W** 6020 & **S** 6050 (Mideast)
2205-2230	**W** 6000/6090 & **S** 11895 (E Asia)

RAI-RADIOTELEVISIONE ITALIANA—
(Europe, Mideast & N Africa)

0003-0012,	
0103-0112,	
0203-0212,	
0303-0312 &	
0403-0412 ◀	6060

JAPAN

RADIO JAPAN

0000-0015	13650 & 17810 (SE Asia)
0000-0100	*6145* (E North Am)
0100-0200	**S** *5960* & **W** *6030* (Mideast), *11860* (SE Asia), *11935* (S America), 15325 (S Asia), 17560 (Mideast), 17685 (Australasia), 17810 (SE Asia), 17825 (W North Am & C America), 17845 (E Asia)
0300-0400	21610 (Australasia)
0500-0600	*5975* (W Europe), *6110* (W North Am), 17810 (SE Asia)
0500-0700	*7230* (Europe), 15195 (E Asia), 21755 (Australasia)
0600-0700	**W** 11690 (W North Am & C America), 11715 (E Asia), *11740* (SE Asia), 11760 (E Asia), **S** 13630 (W North Am & C America), 17870 (Pacific)
1000-1100	*17585* (Europe), *17720* (Mideast), 21755 (Australasia)
1000-1200	*6120* (E North Am), 9695 (SE Asia), 11730 (E Asia)
1400-1500	*11840* (Australasia)
1400-1600	7200 (SE Asia), **W** 9875 & **S** 11730 (S Asia)

1500-1600	6190 (E Asia), 9505 (W North Am & C America)
1700-1800	9535 (W North Am & C America), 11970 (Europe), *15355* (S Africa)
2100-2200	*6035* (Australasia), 🅂 *6055* & 🅦 *6090* (W Europe), *6180* (N Europe), *11855* (C Africa), 17825 (W North Am & C America), 21670 (Pacific)

JORDAN

RADIO JORDAN—(W Europe & E North Am)

| 1400-1730 ▣ | 11690 |

KOREA (DPR)

VOICE OF KOREA

0100-0200	3560, 7140, 9345 & 9730 (E Asia), 11735, 13760 & 15180 (C America)
0200-0300	4405 (E Asia), 13650 & 15100 (SE Asia)
0300-0400	3560, 7140, 9345 & 9730 (E Asia)
1000-1100	3560 (E Asia), 🅦 6185 (SE Asia), 🅦 6285 & 🅦 9335 (C America), 🅦 9850 (SE Asia), 🅂 11710 (C America), 🅂 11735 & 🅂 13650 (SE Asia), 🅂 15180 (C America)
1300-1400 & 1500-1600	4405 (E Asia), 🅦 7570 (W Europe), 9335 & 11710 (N America), 🅦 12015, 🅂 13760 & 🅂 15245 (W Europe)
1600-1700	3560 (E Asia), 9975/9990 & 11535/11545 (Mideast & N Africa)
1800-1900	4405 (E Asia), 🅦 7570, 🅦 12015, 🅂 13760 & 🅂 15245 (W Europe)
1900-2000	3560 (E Asia), 7100 (S Africa), 9975 (Mideast & N Africa), 11710/11910 (S Africa)
2100-2200	4405 (E Asia), 🅦 7570, 🅦 12015, 🅂 13760 & 🅂 15245 (W Europe)

KOREA (REPUBLIC)

KBS WORLD RADIO

0200-0300	*9560* (W North Am), 11810 (S America), 15575 (N America)
0800-0900	9570 (SE Asia), 9640 (Europe)
1200-1300	*9650* (N America)
1300-1400	9570 & 9770 (SE Asia)
1600-1700	5975 (E Asia)
1900-2000	5975 (E Asia), 7275 (Europe)
2100-2130	*3955* (W Europe)

LIBYA

RADIO JAMAHIRIYA

| 1400-1600 | 🅂 17725/21695 (E Africa), 🅦 17725 & 🅂 17850 (C Africa), 🅦 21695 (E Africa) |

LITHUANIA

RADIO VILNIUS

0030-0100 ▣	9875 (E North Am)
0030-0100	🅂 11690 (E North Am)
0130-0200	🅦 7325 (E North Am)
0930-1000 ▣	9710 (W Europe)
2330-2400	🅦 7325 (E North Am)

MOLDOVA

RADIO DMR—(Europe)

| 1700-1720 ▣ | M-F 6205 |
| 1720-1740 ▣ | F 6205 |

MONGOLIA

VOICE OF MONGOLIA

1000-1030	12085/12015 (E Asia, SE Asia & Australasia)
1500-1530	9720 (C Asia)
2 000-2030	9720 (E Europe & W Asia)

NETHERLANDS

RADIO NETHERLANDS

0000-0100	🅦 *6165* & 🅂 *9845* (E North Am)
0100-0200	🅦 *6165* & 🅂 *9845* (N America)
0400-0500	🅂 *6165* (N America)

0500-0600   ☐ *6165* (W North Am),
             ☐ *11710* (Australasia)
0700-0800   ☐ *9700* (Australasia)
1000-1100   ☐ *6040* (E Asia), ☐ *9790*
             (Australasia), ☐ *9795* (E
             Asia & SE Asia), ☐ *12065*
             (E Asia), ☐ *12065* (E Asia,
             SE Asia & Australasia),
             ☐ *13710* & ☐ *13820* (E Asia
             & SE Asia)
1100-1200   ☐ *11675* (E North Am)
1200-1300   ☐ *9890/11675* (E North
             Am)
1400-1600   *9345*, ☐ *9890*, ☐ *11835*,
             ☐ *12080* & ☐ *15595* (S
             Asia)
1800-1900   *6020* (S Africa)
1800-2000   ☐ 9895 & ☐ 11655 (E
             Africa)
1800-2100   ☐ *9895* (W Africa, C Africa
             & E Africa), ☐ *11655* (W
             Africa & C Africa)
1900-2100   *7120* (C Africa & S Africa),
             Sa/Su *15315* (N America),
             ☐ Sa/Su *15525* (E North
             Am), ☐ Sa/Su *17660* & ☐
             Sa/Su *17725* (W North Am),
             ☐ Sa/Su *17735* (E North
             Am), *17810* (W Africa)
2000-2100   ☐ 9895 & ☐ 11655 (W
             Africa)

NEW ZEALAND

RADIO NEW ZEALAND
INTERNATIONAL—(Pacific)
0000-0400   17675/15720
0000-0500   15720
0500-0700   9615/15720
0700-1100   7145/9885
1100-1300   9870/13840
1300-1750   ☐ 7145/6095 &
             ☐ 9870/9815
1750-1850   ☐ 6095 & ☐ 9845/9630
1850-2050   9630/11725/15720
2051-2400   15720/17675

OMAN

RADIO SULTANATE OF OMAN
0300-0400   15355 (Irr) (E Africa)
1400-1500   15140 (Irr) (Europe &
             Mideast)

PHILIPPINES

RADYO PILIPINAS—(S Asia & Mideast)
0200-0330   ☐ 11885, ☐ 12025,
             ☐ 15115, ☐ 15230,
             ☐ 15270 & ☐ 15510

POLAND

RADIO POLONIA
1300-1400 ☐   9525 & 11850 (W Europe)
1800-1900 ☐   7220 (W Europe), 7265 (N
              Europe)

ROMANIA

RADIO ROMANIA INTERNATIONAL
0100-0200   ☐ 6150, ☐ 9515, ☐ 9690 &
             ☐ 11825 (E North Am)
0400-0500   ☐ 6115 & ☐ 9515 (W North
             Am), ☐ 9690 (S Asia),
             ☐ 9780 & ☐ 11795 (W
             North Am), ☐ 11895,
             ☐ 15110 & ☐ 17870 (S Asia)
0630-0700   ☐ 7180, ☐ 9655, ☐ 9690 &
             ☐ 11830 (W Europe),
             ☐ 15135, ☐ 15440,
             ☐ 17770 & ☐ 17780
             (Australasia)
1300-1400   ☐ 11845, 15105 & ☐
             17745 (W Europe)
1800-1900   ☐ 7120, ☐ 9635, ☐ 9640 &
             ☐ 11730 (W Europe)
2130-2200   ☐ 6055 (W Europe),
             ☐ 6115 (E North Am),
             ☐ 7145, ☐ 7210 & ☐ 9535
             (W Europe), ☐ 9755, 11940
             & ☐ 15465 (E North Am)
2300-2400   ☐ 6015 (W Europe),
             ☐ 6115 (E North Am),
             ☐ 6140, ☐ 7105 & ☐ 7265
             (W Europe), ☐ 9610,
             ☐ 9645 & ☐ 11940 (E
             North Am)

RUSSIA

VOICE OF RUSSIA
0100-0500   ☐ *9665/7180* (E North Am),
             ☐ 15555 (W North Am)
0200-0300 ☐   *7250* (E North Am)
0200-0500   ☐ *9860* (E North Am),
             ☐ 15475 & ☐ 15595 (W
             North Am)

0200-0600   **W** *7180* (E North Am),
       W 15425 & **S** 15595 (W
       North Am)

0300-0500   **S** 9880 (E North Am),
       S 15425 & **S** 15455 (W
       North Am)

0300-0600   **W** *7350* (E North Am)

0400-0600   **W** 7150 (E North Am),
       W 9840 & **W** 12010 (W
       North Am)

0500-0900   **S** 17635 & **S** 21790
       (Australasia)

0600-0900   **W** 17805 & 21790
       (Australasia)

0600-1000   **W** 17665 (Australasia)

0800-1000 ◀ *17495* (SE Asia &
       Australasia)

1400-1500   **S** 7165 (E Asia & SE Asia),
       S 9745 & **S** *11755* (S Asia),
       S 12055 (SE Asia),
       S 15605 (S Asia), **S** 17645
       (S Asia & SE Asia)

1400-1600   **S** 7390 (E Asia & SE Asia)

1400-1900   **S** *7370* (Europe)

1500-1600 ◀ 6205 (SE Asia)

1500-1600   **W** 7350 (S Asia), *9660* (SE
       Asia), **S** 11985 (Mideast &
       E Africa), **S** 12040 &
       S 15455/11980 (Europe)

1500-1700   **W** 7260 (E Asia & SE Asia)

1500-1900   **W** 7415 (E Asia & SE Asia)

1600-1700 ◀ *4965 & 4975* (W Asia & S
       Asia)

1600-1700   **S** 6070 (S Asia), **W** 6130
       (Europe), **W** 7305 (S Asia),
       S 12055 (W Asia & S Asia),
       S *12115* (S Asia), **S** 15540
       (Mideast)

1600-1800   **S** 9405 (S Asia), **W** 9470 &
       11985 (Mideast & E Africa)

1600-1900   **W** 7320 (Europe)

1700-1800   **S** Sa/Su 9820 & **S** Sa/Su
       11675/7320 (N Europe)

1700-1900   **W** 5910 (S Asia), **W** 7360
       (Mideast)

1700-2100   **W** 9890 (Europe)

1800-1900   **W** Sa/Su 5950 & **W** Sa/Su
       6175 (N Europe), **S** 9745 (E
       Africa), **S** 9820 (N Europe),
       S 11630/9480 (Europe)

1800-2000 ◀ *11510* (E Africa & S Africa)

1800-2100   **W** 7290 (N Europe)

Kim Shippey, formerly of the Christian Science Monitor, interviews RRI's Frederica Dochinoiu.   RRI

1900-2000   **W** 6175 (N Europe),
       S 7310 (Europe), **W** 7335
       (E Africa & S Africa),
       W 7390 (Europe)

1900-2100   **S** 12070/7195 (Europe)

2000-2100   **W** 6145 & **S** 15455/11980
       (Europe)

2000-2200   **W** 7330 (Europe)

SINGAPORE

MEDIACORP RADIO

1400-1600 &
2300-1100   6150

RADIO SINGAPORE INTERNATIONAL—
(SE Asia)

1100-1400   6080 & 6150

SOUTH AFRICA

CHANNEL AFRICA

0300-0355   **S** 5960 & **W** 7390 (E
       Africa)

0300-0500   3345 (S Africa)

0500-0555   9685 (C Africa)

0500-0700	☒ 7390 (S Africa)
0500-0800	☒ 7240 (S Africa)
0600-0655	☒ 15255 (W Africa & C Africa)
0700-0800	☒ 9620 (S Africa)
1000-1200 &	
1400-1600	9620 (S Africa)
1500-1555	17770 (E Africa)
1700-1755	☒ 15235 & ☒ 15285 (W Africa & C Africa)
2000-2200	3345 (S Africa)

SPAIN

RADIO EXTERIOR DE ESPAÑA

0000-0100	☒ 6055 (N America), ☒ 15385 (N America & C America)
2000-2100	☒ M-F 9570 & ☒ M-F 9595 (N Africa & W Africa), ☒ M-F 9680 & ☒ M-F 15290 (Europe)
2100-2200	☒ Sa/Su 9570 (N Africa & W Africa), ☒ Sa/Su 9840 (Europe)
2200-2300	☒ Sa/Su 9595 (N Africa & W Africa), ☒ Sa/Su 9680 (Europe)

SWEDEN

RADIO SWEDEN

0130-0200	☒ 6010 (E North Am), ☒ 9435 & ☒ 11550 (S Asia)
0230-0300	6010 (N America)
0330-0400	☒ 6010 (W North Am)
1230-1300	☒ 13580 (E Asia & Australasia), ☒ 15735 (Asia & Australasia)
1300-1315 ▱	15240 (E North Am)
1330-1400 ▱	15240 (N America)
1330-1400	☒ 7420 (E Asia & Australasia), ☒ 11550 & ☒ 15735 (SE Asia & Australasia)
1430-1500 ▱	15240 (N America)
1430-1500	☒ 11550 (Asia & Australasia)
1830-1900 &	
2030-2100 ▱	6065 (Europe)
2030-2100 ➡	7420 (SE Asia & Australasia)
2230-2300 ▱	6065 (Europe)

SYRIA

RADIO DAMASCUS

2005-2105	9330 (Europe), 12085 (W Europe)
2110-2210	9330 (Australasia), 12085 (N America)

THAILAND

RADIO THAILAND

0000-0030	☒ 9570 & ☒ 9680 (E Africa & S Africa)
0030-0100	5890 (E North Am)
0200-0230	5890 (W North Am)
0530-0600	☒ 13770 & ☒ 17655 (Europe)
1230-1300	☒ 9810 & ☒ 9835 (SE Asia & Australasia)
1400-1430	☒ 9725 & ☒ 9830 (SE Asia & Australasia)
1900-2000	☒ 7155 & ☒ 9805 (N Europe)
2030-2045	☒ 9535 & ☒ 9680 (Europe)

TURKEY

VOICE OF TURKEY

0300-0350	☒ 5975 (Europe & N America), ☒ 7270 (Mideast)
0400-0450	☒ 6020 (Europe & N America), ☒ 7240 (Mideast)
1230-1325	☒ 15450 (W Europe), ☒ 15535 (S Asia, SE Asia & Australasia)
1330-1425	☒ 11735 (S Asia, SE Asia & Australasia), ☒ 12035 (W Europe)
1830-1920	☒ 9785 (W Europe)
1930-2020	☒ 6055 (W Europe)
2030-2120	☒ 7170 (S Asia, SE Asia & Australasia)
2130-2220	☒ 9525 (S Asia, SE Asia & Australasia)
2200-2250	☒ 9830 (W Europe & E North Am)
2300-2350	☒ 5960 (W Europe & E North Am)

UKRAINE

RADIO UKRAINE INTERNATIONAL

0000-0100	☒ 7440 (E North Am)
0100-0200	☒ 5910 (E North Am)

Pulteney Bridge, Bath, England, constructed 1769–1773. After having been grossly altered and damaged over the years, in the 20th century it was restored to an approximation of its original glory.

Shutterstock/Stephen Inglis

0300-0400	🄂 7440 (E North Am)
0400-0500	🅆 5910 (E North Am)
1100-1200	🄂 15675 (W Europe)
1200-1300	🅆 9925 (W Europe)
2100-2200	🄂 7420/7490 (W Europe)
2200-2300	🅆 5840 (W Europe)

UNITED KINGDOM

BBC WORLD SERVICE

0000-0030	*3915* (SE Asia), *11945* (E Asia)
0000-0100	5970 (S Asia), 9740 (SE Asia), 11955 (S Asia), 17615 & 🄂 *17655* (E Asia)
0000-0200	*6195* (SE Asia), *9410* (W Asia)
0000-0300	*15310* (S Asia), *15360* (SE Asia), *17790* (S Asia)
0000-0530	*15280/15285* (E Asia)
0030-0100	🄂 *9580* (S Asia)
0100-0300	*11955* (S Asia)
0200-0300	*9750* (E Africa), *9825* & *12095* (S America)
0200-0400	🅆 *6195* (W Asia)
0200-0500	🄂 *11760* (Mideast & W Asia)
0300-0400	6005 (S Africa), 🄂 *9410* (Europe), 9750 (E Africa), 🅆 *11760* (Mideast & W Asia), 12035 (E Africa)
0300-0500	*3255* (S Africa), 🄂 *7120* & 🅆 *11765* (W Africa & C Africa), *15360* (SE Asia), *17760* (E Asia)
0300-0600	🄂 6195 (Europe), *7160* (W Africa & C Africa), *15310* (S Asia)
0300-0700	*17790* (S Asia)
0300-1030	*21660* (E Asia)
0300-2200	6190 (S Africa)
0330-0600	*15420* (E Africa)
0400-0500	🅆 *7130* (Europe), *12035* (E Africa)
0400-0600 ✉	15575 (Mideast & W Asia)
0400-0600	🅆 *11760* (Mideast & W Asia), 🄂 12095 (E Europe)
0400-0700	🅆 6195 (Europe & Mideast)
0400-0720	*6005* (W Africa)
0500-0600	🄂 *11760* (Mideast & W Asia), 🅆 *11940* (S Africa), 🅆 *12095* (E Europe), 🄂 *15575* (W Asia)
0500-0700 ✉	9410 (Europe & Mideast)
0500-0700	*11765* (W Africa & C Africa), *17640* (E Africa)
0500-0800	*11955* (SE Asia), *15360* (E Asia, SE Asia & Australasia)
0500-1000	*17760* (E Asia & SE Asia)
0530-0600	M-F *17885* (E Africa)

0600-0700	7160 (W Europe), 12095 (E Europe)
0600-0730	*15575 (W Asia)*
0600-0800 ◨	*15565 (E Europe)*
0600-0800	Sa/Su *17885 (E Africa)*
0600-1600	*11940 (S Africa)*
0600-1800	*15310 (S Asia)*
0630-0700	15400 (W Africa & C Africa)
0700-0800 ◨	9410 (W Europe & N Africa)
0700-0800	**W** 6195 (W Europe & N Africa), *11765 (W Africa)*, **W** 12095 (E Europe), 17830 (N Africa)
0700-1000	*15400 (W Africa)*
0700-1400	*11760 (Mideast)*
0700-1500	17640 (E Europe & Mideast)
0700-1600	*17790 (S Asia)*
0700-1700	15485 (W Europe & N Africa)
0730-0900	Sa/Su *15575 (W Asia)*
0800-0900	**W** 6195 (SE Asia), **W** *9740* (SE Asia & Australasia), **S** *11955 (SE Asia)*, **S** *15360* (E Asia, SE Asia & Australasia)
0800-1000	*17830 (W Africa & C Africa)*
0800-1030	**W** *15280 (E Asia)*
0800-1300	*21470 (S Africa)*
0800-1400	*17885 (E Africa)*
0900-1030	**S** *15360 (E Asia)*
0900-1100	6195 (SE Asia), *9605 (E Asia)*
0900-1500	*15575 (W Asia)*
0900-1600	*9740 (SE Asia & Australasia)*
1000-1030	**W** *11945 (E Asia)*
1000-1100	6195 (C America & W North Am), Sa/Su *17830* (W Africa & C Africa)
1000-1130	Sa/Su *15400 (W Africa)*
1000-1400	**S** *17760 (E Asia)*
1030-1100	**W** *11750, 11945, 15285*, **W** *15545* & **S** *21660* (E Asia)
1100-1200	**W** *5875, 6130* & **S** *9660* (C America)
1100-1300	**W** *11855* & **S** *11865* (C America)
1100-1700	*6195 (SE Asia)*
1100-2100	*17830 (W Africa & C Africa)*
1200-1300	*9660 & 9750 (C America)*
1300-1400	**S** 12095 (Mideast), *15420 (E Africa)*, **S** 15565 (E Europe), **S** 17640 (E Europe & W Asia)
1300-1900	*21470 (S Africa)*
1400-1600	**W** *5970* & **S** *11750* (E Asia), 17640 (E Europe & W Asia)
1400-1700	15565 (E Europe), *21660* (E Africa)
1400-1800	12095 (Mideast)
1500-1530	**S** *9695*, **S** *11690*, **W** *11860*, *15420*, 21490 & **W** *21490* (E Africa)
1500-1600	5975 (S Asia)
1500-2300	15400 (W Africa)
1600-1700	**W** *11940* (S Africa), **S** 17790 (W Asia), **W** 17820 (N Africa)
1600-1800	3915 (S Asia & SE Asia), 7160 (SE Asia), **S** 15105 (W Europe & N Africa)
1600-1830	5975, **S** *9510* & **W** *9740* (S Asia)
1600-1900	**W** 12095 (E Europe)
1615-1700	**S** Sa/Su *9695*, **S** Sa/Su *11690*, **W** Sa/Su *11860*, Sa/Su *15420* & **W** Sa/Su *21490* (E Africa)
1700-1745	6005 & 9630 (E Africa)
1700-1800	**S** 15565 (E Europe), **W** 17820 (N Africa)
1700-1900	**W** 9410 (E Europe & W Asia), **S** *11945* (E Africa), **W** *15420* (C Africa & E Africa)
1700-2100	6195 (Europe)
1700-2200 ◨	*9410 (Europe)*
1700-2200	3255 (S Africa)
1800-1900	**S** 12095 (Mideast)
1800-2000	**W** 13700 (N Africa), **S** 17795 (W Europe & N Africa)
1830-2000	**W** *5975*, **W** *9740* & **S** *12045* (S Asia)
1830-2100	6005 & 9630 (E Africa)
1900-2100	*12095 (S Africa)*
2100-2200	3915 (S Asia & SE Asia), 6005 (S Africa), **W** *6110* (E Asia), 6195 (SE Asia), **W** *6195* (W Europe), *11675* (C America), **S** *11945* (E Asia)

2100-2300	▣ 9605 (W Africa), ▣ 9660 (C America), ⬛ 9860 (W Africa), ⬛ 13765 (C America)
2100-2400	5965 (E Asia)
2200-2300	▣ 5955 (E Asia & SE Asia), 5975 (C America), ⬛ 5990 (E Asia & SE Asia), 7105 & 9660 (SE Asia), 12080 (S Pacific)
2200-2400	6195 & 9740 (SE Asia)
2300-2400	3915 (SE Asia), ▣ 9605 & 11945 (E Asia), 11955 (SE Asia), ⬛ 15280 (E Asia)

USA

AFRTS-AMERICAN FORCES RADIO & TV SERVICE

24 Hr	4319/12579 USB (S Asia), 5447 USB (C America), 5765/13362 USB & 6350/10320 USB (Pacific), 7811 USB & 12134 USB (Americas)

FAMILY RADIO

0000-0045	⬛ 17805 (S America)
0000-0100	⬛ 6065 & ▣ 6085 (E North Am), ▣ 11720 (S America), ⬛ 11835 (W North Am)
0000-0445	9505 (N America)
0100-0200	15195 (S Asia)
0100-0445	6065 (E North Am)
0200-0245	⬛ 11835 (W North Am)
0200-0300	5985 (C America), ▣ 9525 (W North Am), 11855 (C America)
0300-0400	▣ 9985 (S America), 11740 (C America), ⬛ 15255 (S America)
0400-0500	7780 (Europe), 9715 (W North Am)
0400-0600	6855 (E North Am)
0500-0600	▣ 7520 & ⬛ 9355 (Europe)
0600-0700	⬛ 5810 & ▣ 6000 (C America), 9680 (N America), ⬛ 11530 (C Africa & S Africa), ▣ 11530 & ⬛ 11580 (Europe), ▣ 11580 (C Africa & S Africa)
0600-0745	7780 (Europe)
0700-0800	▣ 9495 & ⬛ 9505 (C America), 9715 (W North Am)
0700-0845	⬛ 9930 & ▣ 9985 (W Africa)
0700-1045	▣ 7455 (N America)
0700-1100	6855 (E North Am)
0700-1245	⬛ 5985 (N America)
0800-0845	5950 (W North Am)
0845-1145	▣ 5950 (W North Am)
0900-1100	9450 (E Asia)
0900-1145	⬛ 9755 (W North Am)
1000-1245	⬛ 5950 & ▣ 6890 (E North Am)
1100-1145	▣ 6000 & ⬛ 9550 (S America)
1100-1200	⬛ 7355 (C America), ⬛ 9625 (S America), ▣ 11725 (C America), ▣ 11830 (S America)
1100-1345	▣ 7780 (N America)
1200-1300	▣ 11530 & ⬛ 17505 (S America)
1200-1345	▣ 11970 (W North Am)
1200-1645	⬛ 17750 (W North Am)
1300-1400	11830 & ⬛ 11865 (N America)
1300-1500	9415 & 11560 (S Asia)
1300-1600	▣ 11855 & ⬛ 11910 (E North Am)
1400-1500	11520 (SE Asia), 13695 (E North Am)
1400-1645	▣ 11565 & ⬛ 11830 (N America), ▣ 17760 (W North Am)
1500-1545	▣ 15210 & ⬛ 15770 (S America)
1500-1600	6280 & 15520 (S Asia)
1600-1645	▣ 11830 & ⬛ 11865 (N America)
1600-1700	6085 (C America), ▣ 12010 & ⬛ 15520 (S Asia), ▣ 17690 (C Africa), ⬛ 21525 (C Africa & S Africa)
1600-1800	21455 (Europe)
1600-1945	13695 (E North Am), 18980 (Europe)
1700-1800 ➡	3955 (W Europe)
1700-1800	21680 (E Africa)
1700-2145	▣ 17555 & ⬛ 17795 (W North Am)
1800-1845	⬛ 17535 (W Africa)

Ray Jarvis uses advanced software to check and log transmitter frequencies for WYFR and Radio Taiwan International. Signals from Family Radio's Okeechobee facility span the globe, sometimes being heard better than Washington's official VOA.

Curtis Jarvis, WYFR

1800-1900	W *7240* (Mideast & W Asia), S *13780* (Mideast)
1800-2100	W 15115 (W Africa)
1800-2145	S 13800 & W 17535 (N America)
1900-1945	6085 (C America), W 15565 (Europe)
1900-2000	S 18930 (Europe)
1900-2100	*3230* (S Africa), *6020* (E Africa & S Africa)
1900-2200	S 17845 (W Africa)
1945-2000	S 13695 (E North Am)
1945-2145	S 18980 (Europe)
2000-2045	S 17750 (Europe)
2000-2200	W 5745 & W 6855 (Europe), W 7360 (W Europe), *15195* (E Africa), W 17575 & S 17725 (S America)
2100-2200	S 11565 (Europe), W *11655* (S Africa), W 15565 (W Africa)
2115-2315	W *11875* (W Africa)
2200-2245	S 15770 & W 21525 (C Africa & S Africa)
2200-2300	W 9690 (S America)
2200-2345	11740 (N America)
2300-2400	W 15170, S 15255, W 15400 & S 17750 (S America)

KAIJ—(N America)

0000-0200	5755/13815
0200-0800	5755
1400-2400	13815

KJES

0200-0300 ←	7555 (W North Am)
0300-0330 ←	7555 (N America)
1400-1500 ←	11715 (E North Am)
1500-1600 ←	11715 (W North Am)
1900-2000 ←	15385 (Australasia)

KNLS-NEW LIFE STATION—(E Asia)

0800-0900	W 9615 & S 11870
1000-1100	W 6150 & S 9795
1200-1300	W 6150, W 6915, S 9615 & S 9780
1400-1500	W 6150 & S 9795

KTBN—(E North Am)

0000-0100	W 7505 & S 15590
0100-1500	7505
1500-1600	W 7505 & S 15590
1600-2400	15590

TRANS WORLD RADIO

0430-0500	S M-F *3200*, M-F *4775* & W M-F *6120* (S Africa)
0500-0630	S *4775* & *6120* (S Africa)
0500-0900	W *7205* (S Africa), *9500* (S Africa & E Africa)
0600-0635	M-Sa *11640* (W Africa)
0630-0900	S *6120* (S Africa)
0730-0740	Sa/Su *15225* (SE Asia)
0740-0900	*15225* (SE Asia)
0745-0755 ←	Sa/Su *9870* & Sa/Su *11865* (W Europe)
0755-0850 ←	*9870* & *11865* (W Europe)
0800-0815	M-F *11840* (Australasia & S Pacific)

0815-0930	*11840* (Australasia & S Pacific)
0850-0920 ⇦	Su-F *9870* & Su-F *11865* (W Europe)
1315-1330	[W] Sa *7560* (S Asia)
1330-1400	*9585* (SE Asia)
1400-1500	*9975* (E Asia)
1630-1715	*6130* (S Africa)
1710-1725 ⇦	*5855* (W Asia & C Asia)
1715-2045	*3200* (S Africa)
1730-1900	*9500* (E Africa)

UNIVERSITY NETWORK

0000-0200	*13750* (C America)
0000-1200	*5030* (C America), *6150* (C America & S America), *7375* (S America)
24 Hr	*9725* (N America)
1200-2400	*11870* (S America)
2000-2400	*13750* (C America)

VOA-VOICE OF AMERICA

0000-0030	[S] *7555* (W Asia & S Asia)
0030-0100	[W] *7130*, [W] *9620*, [S] *9715* & [S] *9780* (SE Asia), [W] *11695* (S Asia & SE Asia), *11725* (E Asia), 11805 (SE Asia), [W] *12005* (E Asia), *15185* (SE Asia & S Pacific), 15205 (SE Asia), [S] 15290 (E Asia), [S] *15560* (SE Asia), [S] *17820* (E Asia)
0100-0200	[W] *7200*, 11705, [S] *11725*, [W] *11820* & [W] *12005* (S Asia)
0130-0200	[W] Tu-Sa 5960 & Tu-Sa 7405 (C America), [S] Tu-Sa 13740 (C America & S America)
0300-0330	[S] *7340* (E Africa & S Africa)
0300-0430	*9885* (C Africa)
0300-0500	[W] *15580* (W Africa & C Africa)
0300-0600	*4930* (S Africa), *6080* (C Africa & S Africa)
0300-0700	[S] *12080* (C Africa & E Africa), [S] *15580* (C Africa)
0400-0430	[S] *11835* (C Africa)
0400-0500	*4960* & [S] 9575 (W Africa & C Africa)
0430-0500	[S] *11835* (C Africa)
0430-0700	[W] *9885* (W Africa & C Africa)
0500-0630	[W] *6105* (W Africa & C Africa)
0500-0700	[S] *6180* (W Africa), [W] *15580* (C Africa & E Africa)
0530-0630	[S] M-F *13710* (Africa)
0600-0700	*6080* (W Africa), [W] *11835* (C Africa & S Africa)
1200-1300	[S] *6160* (SE Asia), [W] *11730* (S Asia & SE Asia), [S] *11750* (SE Asia), [W] *15190* (E Asia)
1200-1400	*9645* (SE Asia & Australasia), [W] *11705* (E Asia)
1200-1500	*9760* (E Asia, S Asia & SE Asia)
1400-1500	[W] *9695* & [W] *11655* (S Asia), [W] *11885* (SE Asia & S Pacific), [W] *12150* (S Asia), [S] *13795* (C Africa), [S] *15185* (SE Asia & S Pacific), [S] *15490* (S Asia), [S] *17685* (C Africa & S Africa), [S] *17730* (C Africa & E Africa), [W] *17895* (C Africa)
1400-1530	[W] *6080* (C Africa & S Africa)
1400-1600	*7125* (S Asia), [W] *15205* (S Asia & C Asia), [W] *15580* & *17715* (C Africa & E Africa)
1400-2100	[S] *15580* (C Africa)
1400-2200	[S] *6080* (C Africa & S Africa)
1500-1600	[W] *6110* & [S] *6160* (S Asia & SE Asia), [W] *7175* (E Asia), [S] *9590* (S Asia & SE Asia), [W] *9645* (S Asia), [S] *9760* (S Asia & SE Asia), [W] *9760* (E Asia, S Asia & SE Asia), [W] *11890* (S Asia), [S] *12040* (E Asia), [W] *12150* & *13735* (E Asia & SE Asia), [S] *13795* (C Africa & E Africa), [W] *13865* (E Africa), [S] *15105* & [S] *15195* (S Asia), [S] *15445* (W Asia & S Asia), [W] *15460* & [S] *15550* (SE Asia & Australasia), *17895* (C Africa)
1530-1800	[W] *6080* (C Africa)
1600-1700	[S] *12080* (C Africa), [S] *13600* (SE Asia & Australasia), [W] *13600* (C Africa & S Africa), [W] *15445*

(C Africa & E Africa), 🅦
17640 (E Africa), 🅦 *17715*
(C Africa & E Africa), 🅂
17895 (C Africa & S Africa),
🅦 *17895* (C Africa)

1600-1730	*4930* (S Africa)
1600-2100	🅦 *15580* (Africa)
1700-1730	🅦 M-F *11815*, 🅦 M-F *13755* & M-F *17730* (S Africa)
1700-1800	🅦 *15445* (C Africa & E Africa)
1700-2000	🅦 *13710* (E Africa & S Africa)
1700-2200	🅂 *15410* (Africa)
1730-1830	Sa/Su *4930* (S Africa)
1800-1830	17730 (S Africa)
1800-2000	🅦 11975 (W Africa & C Africa), 🅂 *17895* (C Africa & S Africa), 🅦 *17895* (C Africa)
1800-2200	🅦 *6080* (W Africa)
1830-2100	*4930* (S Africa)
1900-2000	🅂 *7395*, 🅂 *9670*, 🅦 *9785* & 🅦 *12015* (Mideast)
1900-2030	*4940* (W Africa & C Africa)
1900-2100	🅦 *15240* & 🅂 *15445* (W Africa & C Africa)
2000-2100	🅦 *11975* & 🅦 *13710* (C Africa)
2030-2100	Sa/Su *4940* (W Africa & C Africa)
2030-2130	🅦 *7595* (W Asia & S Asia)
2030-2400	🅂 *7555* (W Asia & S Asia)
2100-2200	🅦 *15580* (W Africa & C Africa), 🅂 *15580* (C Africa, E Africa & S Africa)
2130-2400	🅦 *7405* (W Asia & S Asia)
2200-2400	🅦 *7120* & 🅂 *7215* (SE Asia), *11725* (E Asia & S Pacific), *15185* (SE Asia & S Pacific), *15290* (E Asia)
2230-2300	🅦 *7230*, 🅦 *9780* & *13755* (E Asia)
2230-2400	🅂 *9570* & 🅂 *15145* (E Asia)
2300-2400	🅦 *6180*, 🅦 *7205*, 🅂 *13755* & 🅦 *15150* (E Asia)
2330-2400	🅂 *7260* (SE Asia), 🅦 *11655* (E Asia), 🅦 *13640* & 🅂 *13725* (SE Asia)

WBCQ-"THE PLANET"—(N America)

0000-0100 📧	5105
0000-0230 📧	9330/13610 LSB
0000-0530 📧	7415
0100-0500 📧	M/Sa 5105
0230-0500 📧	Tu-Su 9330/13610 LSB
0530-0600 📧	Su/M 7415
0600-0800 📧	Su 7415
1700-2030 📧	M-F 17495/18910
1945-2100 📧	M-F 7415 & M-F 9330/13610 LSB
2030-2200 📧	M-Sa 17495/18910
2100-2200 📧	M-Sa 7415
2100-2400 📧	M-F 5105 & 9330/13610 LSB
2200-2400 📧	7415 & M-F 17495/18910

WBOH—(C America)

0200-1105 &	
1200-0100 📧	5920

WEWN

0000-0500	5810 (N America)
0500-1300	5850 (N America)
0600-0900 📧	7570 (Europe)
1300-1400	🅂 5850 & 🅦 9955 (N America)
1400-1600	9955 (N America)
1600-2000	🅦 15785 (Europe)
1600-2200	🅦 9450 & 🅂 13615 (N America)
1700-2000	🅂 15220 (Europe)
2000-2200	🅂 15220 & 🅦 17595 (W Africa)
2200-2400	🅦 7560 (Europe), 9975 (N America), 🅂 15745 (W Africa)

WRMI-RADIO MIAMI INTERNATIONAL

0000-0500 📧	Tu-Sa 7385 (N America)
0500-1000 📧	7385 (N America)
1000-1045 📧	Su-F 9955 (C America)
1045-1100 📧	9955 (C America)
1100-1200 📧	Su 9955 (C America)
1200-1230 📧	Sa 9955 (C America)
1230-1300 📧	Sa/Su 9955 (C America)
1300-1400 📧	9955 (C America)
1400-1700 &	
2100-2300 📧	7385 (N America)
2300-2400 📧	M-F 7385 (N America)

WTJC—(E North Am)

0400-0300 📧	9370

WWCR

0000-0100	🅂 3210/7465 & 🅦 3210 (E North Am)
0000-0200	5935/13845 & 🅦 7465 (E North Am)

0000-1200	5070 (E North Am)
0100-0300	5765/7465 (E North Am)
0100-0900	3210 (E North Am)
0200-1200	5935 (E North Am)
0300-1100	5765 (E North Am)
0900-1000	3210/9985 (E North Am)
1000-1100	▣ 9985 & ▣ Su-F 15825 (E North Am)
1100-1130	▣ Sa/Su 15825 (E North Am)
1100-1200	▣ Su-F 15825 (E North Am)
1100-1400	5765/7465 (E North Am)
1130-1200	▣ 15825 (E North Am)
1200-1230	▣ 15825 & ▣ Sa/Su 15825 (E North Am)
1200-1300	▣ 5070 (E North Am)
1200-1400	5935/13845 (E North Am)
1230-2100	15825 (E North Am)
1400-1600	7465/9985 (E North Am), 12160 (Irr) (E North Am & Europe)
1400-2400	13845 (E North Am)
1600-1800	9985 (E North Am)
1600-2200	12160 (E North Am & Europe)
1800-1900	▣ 9975 & ▣ 9985 (E North Am)
1900-2200	9975 (E North Am)
2100-2145	▣ Sa/Su 15825 (E North Am)
2100-2200	▣ 15825/7465 (Irr) (E North Am)
2145-2200	▣ 15825 (E North Am)
2200-2245	▣ Sa/Su 9985 (E North Am)
2200-2400	5070/12160 (E North Am & Europe), ▣ 7465 (E North Am)
2300-2400	▣ 3210/9985 (E North Am)

VATICAN STATE
VATICAN RADIO

0250-0310	7305 (E North Am), 9610 (E North Am & C America)
0600-0620 ✉	4005 (Europe), 5885 (W Europe)
0620-0700 ✉	5885 (W Europe)
0730-0745 ✉	M-Sa 4005 (Europe), M-Sa 5885 (W Europe), M-Sa 7250 (Europe), M-Sa 11740 (W Europe & N Africa)
1715-1730 ✉	4005 (Europe), 5885 & 9645 (W Europe)
2050-2110 ✉	4005 & 5885 (Europe)

VIETNAM
VOICE OF VIETNAM

0100-0130, 0230-0300 & 0330-0400	*6175* (E North Am & C America)
1000-1030	9840 & 12020 (SE Asia)
1100-1130	7285 (SE Asia)
1130-1200	9840 & 12020 (E Asia)
1230-1300	9840 & 12020 (SE Asia)
1330-1400	9840 & 12020 (E Asia)
1500-1530	7285, 9840 & 12020 (SE Asia)
1600-1630	7220 (W Africa & C Africa), 7280 (Europe), 9550 (W Africa & C Africa), 9730 (Europe)
1700-1730	▣ *9725* (W Europe)
1800-1830	▣ *5955* (W Europe)
1900-1930	7280 & 9730 (Europe)
2030-2100	7220 (W Africa & C Africa), 7280 (Europe), 9550 (W Africa & C Africa), 9730 (Europe)
2330-2400	9840 & 12020 (SE Asia)

YEMEN
REPUBLIC OF YEMEN RADIO—(Mideast)

1800-1900	9780

A new pope has generated renewed interest in Vatican Radio, easily audible in English throughout Europe and the Americas. Shutterstock/Marco van Belleghem

Voices from Home—2007

Country-by-Country Guide to Native Broadcasts

For some, English offerings are merely icing on the cake. Their real interest is in eavesdropping on broadcasts for *nativos*—the home folks. These can be enjoyable regardless of language, especially when they offer traditional music.

Some you'll hear, many you won't, sometimes because they've gone for political or economic reasons. Keep in mind that most native-language broadcasts are weaker than those in English, so you'll need patience, an electrically quiet location and superior hardware. PASSPORT REPORTS shows which radios and antennas work best.

When to Listen

Some broadcasts come in daytime between 9300 and 21850 kHz. However, signals from Latin America and sub-Saharan Africa peek through near twilight or during darkness, especially from 4700 to 5100 kHz. See "Best Times and Frequencies" for specifics.

Times and days of the week are in World Time (UTC), explained in "Setting Your World Time Clock" and "Worldly Words"; for local times in each country see "Addresses PLUS." Midyear, typically April through October, some stations are an hour earlier (◨) or later (◧) because of Daylight Saving/Summer Time. Stations may also extend their hours for holidays, emergencies or sports events.

Frequencies used only seasonally are labeled ◲ for summer (midyear) and ◱ for winter. Frequencies in *italics* may be best, as they come from relay transmitters that may be near you. Signals not aimed your way may also be heard, especially when beamed to nearby regions. Frequencies with no target zones are usually for domestic coverage, so they're unlikely to be heard unless you're in or near that country.

> Expats often enjoy a mix of world band, TV and the Internet.

Schedules for Entire Year

To be as useful as possible over the months to come, PASSPORT's schedules consist not just of observed activity, but also that which we have creatively opined will take place during the forthcoming year. This predictive material is based on decades of experience and is original from us. Although inherently not as exact as real-time data, over the years it's been of tangible value to PASSPORT readers.

Safari in Tarangire National Park, Tanzania. In the African bush, world band is essential to keep in touch.

Shutterstock/Jessica Bethke

ALBANIA—Albanian

RADIO TIRANA

0000-0130 ←	7450 (E North Am)
0730-1000 ←	7105 (Europe)
2030-2200	[S] 5910 (Europe)
2130-2300	[W] 6110 (Europe)

ARGENTINA—Spanish

RADIO ARGENTINA AL EXTERIOR-RAE

1200-1400	M-F 11710 (S America)
2200-2400	M-F 6060 (C America & S America), M-F 11710 (Europe & N Africa), M-F 15345 (Europe)

RADIO NACIONAL

0000-0100	M 11710 (S America)
0000-0230	Su/M 6060 (C America & S America), Su/M 15345 (Americas)
0230-0300	M 6060 (C America & S America), M 15345 (Americas)
0900-1200	6060 (S America)
1800-2000	Su 6060 & Su 11710 (S America), Su 15345 (Europe)
2000-2200	Sa/Su 11710 (S America)
2000-2400	Sa/Su 6060 (S America), Sa/Su 15345 (Europe)
2200-2400	Su 11710 (S America)

AUSTRIA—German

RADIO AUSTRIA INTERNATIONAL

0005-0015	[W] Tu-Sa 7325 (C America)
0035-0045	[W] Tu-Sa 7325 (E North Am)
0105-0115	[S] Tu-Sa 9870 (C America)
0135-0145	[S] Tu-Sa 9870 (E North Am)
0500-1305 ←	6155 & 13730 (Europe)
0600-0700 ←	M-Sa 17870 (Mideast)
1200-1215	[S] Tu-F 17715 (SE Asia & Australasia)
1220-1300	[S] M 17715 (SE Asia & Australasia)
1230-1245	[S] M-F 17715 (SE Asia & Australasia)
1300-1315	[W] Tu-F 17855 (SE Asia & Australasia)
1305-1345 ←	Tu-F 6155 & Tu-F 13730 (Europe)
1320-1400 ←	M 6155 & M 13730 (Europe)
1320-1400	[W] M 17855 (SE Asia & Australasia)
1330-1345	[W] M-F 17855 (SE Asia & Australasia)
1400-1830 ←	13730 (Europe)
1400-2308 ←	6155 (Europe)
1500-1515	[S] Tu-F *13775* (W North Am)
1520-1530	[S] M *13775* (W North Am)
1530-1545	[S] M-F *13775* (W North Am)
1600-1615	[W] Tu-F *13675* (W North Am)
1620-1630	[W] M *13675* (W North Am)
1630-1645	[W] M-F *13675* (W North Am)
1830-2308 ←	5945 (Europe, N Africa & Mideast)
2335-2345 →	M-F 9870 (S America)

BANGLADESH—Bangla

BANGLADESH BETAR

1630-1730	7185 (Mideast)
1915-2000	7185 (Europe)

BRAZIL—Portuguese

RADIO BANDEIRANTES

24 Hr	6090, 9645, 11925

RADIO BRASIL CENTRAL

0000-0330 →	4985, 11815
0330-0600 →	4985 (Irr), 11815 (Irr)
0600-2400 →	4985, 11815

RADIO CULTURA

0000-0200 →	6170, 9615, 17815
0700-2400 →	9615, 17815
0800-0900 & 0900-2400 →	6170

RADIO GUAIBA

0700-0300 →	6000, 11785

RADIO NACIONAL DA AMAZONIA

0000-0050	6185
0000-0230 →	11780
0230-0650 →	Su 11780
0650-2400 →	11780
0655-0750	[W] 6185
0750-1850 & 2055-2400	6185

BULGARIA—Bulgarian

RADIO BULGARIA

0000-0100	[S] 11500 (S America), [S] 11700 (E North Am)

Manaus, Brazil, and its Teatro Amazonas. Brazilians abroad have many choices on world band, but reception can be a challenge.

Shutterstock/Alvaro Pantoja

0100-0200 ⇦	9500 (S America), 9700 (E North Am)
0100-0200	[W] 7400 (E North Am), [W] 7500 (S America)
0400-0430	[S] Sa/Su 7200 (S Europe), [S] Sa/Su 9400 (E Europe)
0430-0500	[S] 7200 (S Europe), [S] 9400 (E Europe)
0500-0530 ⇦	Sa/Su 7500 (E Europe), Sa/Su 9500 & Sa/Su 11500 (W Europe)
0500-0530	[W] Sa/Su 5800 (E Europe), [W] Sa/Su 5900 (S Europe)
0530-0600 ⇦	7500 (E Europe), 9500 & 11500 (W Europe)
0530-0600	[W] 5800 (E Europe), [W] 5900 (S Europe)
1100-1130 ⇦	7200 (S Europe), 11600 (E Europe), 11700 (W Europe), 13600 (E Europe), 15700 (W Europe)
1300-1500 ⇦	11700 & 15700 (W Europe)
1500-1600	[S] 7200 (S Europe), [S] 9400 (E Europe), [S] 11500 (Mideast)
1600-1700 ⇦	7500 (E Europe), 17500 (S Africa)
1600-1700	[W] 5800 (E Europe), [W] 5900 (S Europe), [W] 9400 (Mideast)
1800-2000	[S] 9700 (W Europe)
1900-2000 ⇦	5900 (S Europe)
1900-2100 ⇦	7400 (Mideast)
1900-2100	[W] 9400 (W Europe)

RADIO VARNA—(Europe & Mideast)

0000-0300	[S] M 9300
0000-0400	[W] M 7600
2100-2400	[S] Su 9300
2200-2400	[W] Su 7600

CANADA—French

CANADIAN BROADCASTING CORP—(E North Am)

0100-0300 ⇦	M 9625
0300-0400 ⇦	Su 9625 & Tu-Sa 9625
1300-1310 & 1500-1555 ⇦	M-F 9625
1700-1715 ⇦	Su 9625
1900-1945 ⇦	M-F 9625
1900-2310 ⇦	Sa 9625

RADIO CANADA INTERNATIONAL

0000-0100 ⇦	6100 (E North Am)
0300-0400	[S] 6040 (E North Am)
0400-0500	[W] 6080 (E North Am)
1100-1300	[S] 9515 (E North Am & C America)
1200-1400	[W] 6120 (E North Am & C America)
1430-1500	[W] *9780* & [S] *15295* (E Asia)
1600-2000	[S] 17765 (C America)
1700-2100	[W] 17835 (C America)
1800-1900	[W] 13650 (N Africa & W Africa)
1900-2000	[S] *7235* (W Europe & N Africa), [W] *9670* (C Africa), [S] *11765* (E Africa), [W] *11845* & [W] 13650 (N Africa & W Africa),

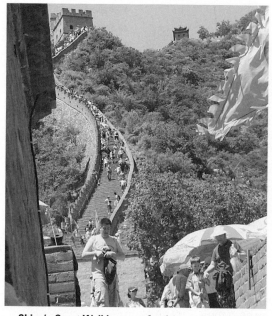

China's Great Wall kept out foreigners. Today, China's "Firedrake" jammers try to keep out foreign ideas.

M. Guha

	S 15235 &
	S *15255* (W Africa),
	S 15325 (W Europe),
	W 15365 & **W** 17740 (W Africa & C Africa)
2000-2100 **◀**	*5850* (W Europe)
2100-2200	**W** *7235*, **S** *9690*, **W** *9805*, **S** *11810*, **W** 11845 & **S** 15325 (N Africa)
2200-2300	**S** 15180 (C America)
2300-2330	**W** *6160* & **W** *7195* (E Asia), **S** *9525* & **W** *12045* (E Asia & SE Asia), **S** *13660* (E Asia)
2300-2400	**W** 15180 (C America)

CHINA

CENTRAL PEOPLE'S BROADCASTING STATION
Chinese

0000-0003	5925, 7620, 9665
0000-0030	**W** 7130, **W** 7305, 7335, **W** 7375, 9820/11845, 11710, **S** 11750, **S** 11800, **S** 11835
0000-0100	**W** 6125, **W** 6165, **W** 7150, **W** 7275, **W** 7315, 9480,

	W 9775, **S** 9810, **W** 9830, 9845, **S** 11660, **W** 11740, **W** 11860, 11925, **S** 15270, **S** 15380, **S** 15480, **S** 15540, **S** 17565, **S** 17595
0000-0104	6165, 9170
0000-0130	**W** 7290, **S** 17890
0000-0200	**W** 6155, 9755, 9890, **S** 15500
0000-0300	**W** 4800, 7140, 9570, **S** 9590, 9630
0000-0400	9530, 11685
0000-0600	4750, 6030, 7230, 9500, 9620, 9645, 9675, 11610, 11670, 11720, 11760, 11960, 13610, 15300, 15550, 17625
0030-0600	11750, 11800, 11835, 11845, 11915
0055-0613	9685/15710, 11620, 11935
0100-0400	15570
0100-0600	9720, 9810, 11660, 15270, 15370, 15380, 15480, 15540, 17550, 17565, 17595
0130-0600	17605, 17890
0200-0500	11630, 12055, 15390
0200-0600	12080, 13700, 15500
0300-0600	17580
0355-0900	11905
0355-1100	15880
0500-0600	9530, 11685, 15570
0600-0730	W-M 17565
0600-0800	Th-Tu 9530, Th-Tu 11685, W-M 11750, Th-Tu 11845, W-M 15550, Th-Tu 15570
0600-0830	W-M 9645
0600-0850	W-M 4750, W-M 6030, W-M 7230, W-M 9500, W-M 9675, W-M 11720, W-M 11760, W-M 11960, W-M 13610, W-M 13700, W-M 15300, W-M 15370, W-M 15380, W-M 15480, W-M 17550, W-M 17580, W-M 17595, W-M 17605, W-M 17890
0600-0855	Th-Tu 9620, Th-Tu 9720, Th-Tu 9810, Th-Tu 11610, Th-M 11660, Th-Tu 11670,

	Th-Tu 11800, Th-Tu 11915, Th-Tu 12080, Th-Tu 15270, Th-Tu 15500, Th-Tu 15540, Th-Tu 17625
0600-0900	Th-Tu 11835
0700-0850	W-M 11630, W-M 12055, W-M 15390
0730-0850	[W] W-M 9830, [S] W-M 17565
0800-0850	W-M 7305/11750, [W] W-M 7345, [S] W-M 15550
0800-0855	Th-Tu 9820/11845
0800-1000	9570
0800-1100	[W] 4800, [S] 9590
0800-1200	[W] 9630
0800-1300	[W] 3985, [S] 7140
0800-1500	[S] 6165
0830-0850	[W] W-M 4460, [S] W-M 9645
0850-0900	11630, 11960, 12055, [S] 15390
0850-1000	9675, 15480, 17580, 17595, 17605
0850-1030	17550
0850-1100	11720, 13700, 15370, 15380
0850-1130	7305/11750
0850-1200	11760, 15300, 17890
0850-1230	[W] 7345, [S] 15550
0850-1300	[W] 4460, [S] 9645, [W] 9830, 13610, [S] 17565
0850-1733	4750, 6030, 7230, 9500
0855-1000	9720, 9820/11845, 11915, 12080, 15500
0855-1030	11800
0855-1100	[S] 11660, 15540
0855-1200	11670, [S] 15270, 17625
0855-1230	9810
0855-1300	11610
0855-1601	9620
0900-1030	9530
0900-1100	[W] 7315
0900-1130	[W] 6175, [S] 11960
0900-1200	[W] 6165, [W] 9775, [S] 11905
0900-1300	[W] 7350, [W] 9480, [S] 11685, [S] 15570
0955-2200	9410
0955-2400	5925, 7620
1000-1100	11630, 12055, [S] 15390
1000-1200	[W] 5030, [W] 6090, [W] 6125, [W] 7335, [S] 9570, [S] 9675, [W] 11710, [S] 11915, [W] 11925, [S] 17580, [S] 17595, [S] 17605
1000-1300	[W] 11860, [S] 12080, [S] 15480
1000-1400	[W] 6155, [S] 15500
1000-1601	9820
1030-1130	[W] 9845, [S] 17550
1030-1200	[W] 6010, [S] 9530
1030-1400	[W] 7375, [S] 11800
1100-1230	[S] 7275, [W] 15380
1100-1300	[W] 9710, [W] 9890, [S] 11720, [W] 11740, [S] 13700, [S] 15540
1100-1601	7315
1100-1733	4800
1100-1804	9170
1130-1733	6175, 7305, 9845
1200-1300	6010
1200-1400	[W] 9860, 11630, [S] 15300
1200-1500	[W] 6080
1200-1601	6065, 6090, 7335, 9515, 9775
1200-1730	11925
1200-1733	5030, 6125, 7110, 7290, 11710
1200-1804	6165
1230-1601	7150
1230-1733	7275, 7345
1300-1601	3985, 7130, 7140, 9755, 11740
1300-1733	4460, 9710, 9810, 9830, 9890, 11860
1400-1600	7350
1400-1601	6010, 6155, 7375, 9730/9480
1400-1733	9860
1500-1733	6080
2000-2200	6175, 9810
2000-2230	7275, 9900
2000-2300	5030, 7345, 9830, 11860
2000-2330	4460, 7305, 9710
2000-2400	4750, 4800, 6030, 6125, 6950, 7230, 7290, 9455, 9500, 9630, 9655, 9845, 9890, 11630, 11710, 11925
2055-2400	6165, 9170
2100-2300	6010, 6090, 6155, 6190, 7130, 7140, 7315, 7360, 9480
2100-2330	6065
2100-2400	7150, 7335, [W] 7375, 9515, 9620, 9755, 9775, 9820, 11740, [S] 11800

Radio Taiwan
International produces
good signals worldwide.
Its Danshui transmission
facility is but part of a
global network that brings
this about.   M. Guha

2200-2400	⬜ 6175, 9665, ⬛ 11960, 13610
2230-2400	⬜ 7275, 15300, ⬛ 15380
2300-2400	⬜ 6155, ⬜ 6165, ⬜ 7130, 7140, ⬜ 7315, ⬜ 7345, 9570, 9675, ⬜ 9830, 11610, ⬛ 11660, ⬛ 11835, ⬜ 11860, ⬛ 15480, ⬛ 15500, ⬛ 15550, ⬛ 17565
2330-2400	⬜ 7305, 9645, 11670, 11720, ⬛ 11750

CHINA RADIO INTERNATIONAL
Chinese

0000-0100	⬛ *5960* (E North Am), ⬜ *6005* (N America), ⬜ *6040* (E North Am), 11780 (E Asia), ⬜ 11845 (SE Asia), ⬛ 11900 (E Asia), ⬛ *11930* (W North Am), ⬛ *12035* & 13580 (SE Asia)
0000-0300	13655 (E Asia)
0100-0200	⬜ 7250, ⬜ 7300 & ⬛ 11650 (S Asia)
0100-0400	15160 (E Asia)
0200-0300	⬜ 7330 (Mideast & N Africa), *9580* (E North Am), *9690* (N America & C America), ⬛ *9815* (S America)
0200-0400	*6020* & *9570* (N America)
0300-0400	⬜ 9450 (S Asia), ⬜ 9590 (Europe), ⬜ 13655 (E Asia),

	⬛ 13690 (Europe), ⬛ 15230 (E Asia), 17540 (S Asia)
0300-0600	15130 (E Asia)
0400-0500	13640 & 15170 (S Asia)
0500-0700	⬜ 13620 & ⬜ 13655 (E Asia), 15120 (C Asia & E Asia), 15170, ⬛ 15230 & ⬛ 15785 (E Asia)
0600-0800	⬜ 13750, ⬛ 17615 & 17740 (SE Asia)
0600-0900	17650 (Europe)
0700-0900	⬛ *11775* & ⬜ *11855* (W Europe)
0800-0900	11640, ⬜ 13610 & ⬛ 15230 (E Asia)
0800-1000	15565 & 17560 (W Asia & C Asia)
0800-1100	9880 (E Asia)
0900-1000	7190, ⬜ 9440 & ⬛ 13620 (E Asia), ⬜ 13850 (SE Asia), 15440 (Australasia), ⬛ 17540 (SE Asia), 17670 (Australasia)
0900-1100	11980, 15250 & ⬜ 15340 (SE Asia), 15525 & 17500 (S Asia), ⬛ 17530 (SE Asia)
1000-1100	⬜ 7255 & ⬛ 9890 (C Asia & E Asia), 13850 (SE Asia), ⬛ 17540 (C Asia & E Asia)
1000-1200	17650 (Europe)
1100-1200	7160 (E Asia), ⬜ 11620

	(Australasia), [W] 11680 (S Asia), [S] 11750 (E Asia), [S] 15460 (Australasia)
1100-1300	[S] 13755 (S Asia)
1200-1300	[W] 7180 (E Asia), [W] 7205 (S Asia), *9570* (E North Am), 15110 (Mideast), [S] 15150 (Europe), [W] *15540* & [S] *17625* (S America)
1200-1400	7160 & 9855 (SE Asia)
1300-1400	7205 (E Asia), 13650 (Mideast)
1400-1500	7210 (E Asia)
1400-1600	[S] *15220* (W North Am)
1500-1600	[W] 7150 (E Asia), 7265 & [S] 9560 (S Asia), [W] 9700, [W] 9740, [S] 13680 & [S] 13710 (Europe)
1600-1700	[W] *17735* (W North Am)
1730-1800	7160 (Mideast)
1730-1830	[W] 6150 (Europe), [W] 7120 (S Asia), [W] 7315 (Mideast), 9645 (W Africa), [S] 9685 (Europe), [W] 9695/9745 & [S] 9745 (Mideast), [S] 11660 (Europe)
1800-1900	*6100* (S Africa)
2000-2100	7120 (Europe), 7245 (Mideast & N Africa), 7335 (Europe), 9865 (Mideast)
2200-2300	[S] 5915 (S Europe & N Africa), 5975 (Mideast), 6140 (SE Asia), 7190 (E Asia), 7220/7215 (SE Asia), 7265 (Mideast & W Asia), [W] 7305 (E Asia), 7325, 9460 & [S] 9470 (SE Asia), [S] 9675 (E Asia)
2230-2300	*15505* (W Africa, C Africa & E Africa)
2230-2400	*11975* (N Africa)
2300-2400	*7170* (W Africa), 11900 (E Asia)

Cantonese

0000-0100	11820 & 17495 (SE Asia)
0400-0500	*9790* (W North Am), [W] 13655, 15160 & [S] 15230 (E Asia)
0700-0800	11640, [W] 13610 & [S] 15230 (E Asia)
1000-1100	15440 & 17670 (Australasia)

1100-1200	9540 (Australasia), 9590 & 9645 (SE Asia), 13580 (Australasia)
1200-1300	[W] *9560* & [S] *11855* (E North Am & C America)
1700-1800	[W] 7220 (E Africa & S Africa), [S] 9435 (E Africa)
1900-2000	[S] 7120 & [W] 7215 (Mideast), [W] 9770 & [S] 11895 (Europe)
2300-2400	6140, [S] 7325, [W] 9425, 9460, 11945/11935 & [S] 15100 (SE Asia)

CHINA (TAIWAN)

RADIO TAIWAN INTERNATIONAL
Amoy

0000-0100	11875 (SE Asia), *15440* (W North Am)
0500-0600	15580 (SE Asia)
1000-1100	11605 (E Asia)
1200-1300	11715 (SE Asia)
1300-1400	11635 & 15465 (SE Asia)
2100-2200	[W] *5950* & [S] *13695* (E North Am)

Chinese

0000-0300	9660 (E Asia)
0000-0400	15245 (E Asia)
0000-0500	11640 & 11885 (E Asia)
0100-0200	[W] *11825, 15215* & [S] *17845* (S America)
0200-0500	15290 (SE Asia)
0400-0500	*5950* (W North Am), *9680* (N America), 15320 (SE Asia)
0400-0600	15270 (SE Asia)
0500-0600	[W] *9495* & [S] *9505* (C America)
0600-1000	11795 (E Asia)
0900-1000	11520 (SE Asia), 11605 (E Asia), 11635 (SE Asia), 11715 (Australasia), 15525 (SE Asia)
0900-1100	9415 (E Asia)
0900-1400	6150 (E Asia)
0900-1500	6085 (E Asia)
0900-1600	11665 (E Asia)
0900-1800	7185 (E Asia)
1000-1400	9780 (E Asia)
1100-1200	11715 (Australasia)
1100-1500	11780 (E Asia)

1100-1800	9680 (E Asia)
1200-1300	11605 (E Asia), 15465 (SE Asia)
1300-1400	15265 (SE Asia)
1300-1500	7445 (SE Asia)
1400-1800	6145 & 7130 (E Asia)
1600-1800	7365 (E Asia)
1900-2000	9955, [S] *17750* & [W] *17760* (Europe)
2200-2300	*3965* (W Europe)
2200-2400	*5950* (E North Am), 6105 & 6150 (E Asia), 11635 (SE Asia), 11710 & 11885 (E Asia), *15440* (W North Am)
2300-2400	9660 & 15245 (E Asia)

Cantonese

0100-0200	*5950* (E North Am), 15290 (SE Asia), *15440* (W North Am)
0200-0300	15610 (SE Asia)
0500-0600	*5950* (W North Am), *9680* (N America), 15320 (SE Asia)
1000-1100	11635 (SE Asia), 11715 (Australasia), 15270 & 15525 (SE Asia)
1200-1300	6105 (E Asia), 11915 (SE Asia)
2200-2300	[W] *5745* & [S] *11565* (Europe)

VOICE OF HAN—(E Asia)

Chinese

24 Hr	9745

CROATIA—Croatian

CROATIAN RADIO

0400-1000	[S] 13830 (Europe)
0500-1800 ⇦	9830 (Europe)
0500-1905 ⇦	6165 (Europe)
1000-2200	13830 (Europe & Mideast)
1915-2400 ⇦	6165 (Europe)
2200-2300	[S] 13830 (Europe)

VOICE OF CROATIA

0000-0100	[S] *9925* (E North Am & S America)
0000-0200	[W] *7285* (E North Am & S America)
0100-0200	[S] *9925* (N America & S America)
0200-0300	[W] *7285* (N America & S America)
0215-0230 &	
0250-0300	[S] *9925* (N America & S America)
0300-0500	[S] *9925* (W North Am)
0315-0330 &	
0350-0400	[W] *7285* (N America & S America)
0400-0600	[W] *7285* (W North Am)
0500-0800 ⇦	*9470* (Australasia)
0600-1000	[S] *13820/11610* & [W] *13820/11690* (Australasia)
2200-2215 &	
2250-2300	[S] *9925* (S America)
2300-2315	[W] *7285* (S America)
2300-2400	[S] *9925* (E North Am & S America)
2350-2400	[W] *7285* (S America)

CUBA—Spanish

RADIO HABANA CUBA

0000-0100	6000 (E North Am), 9820 (N America)
0000-0500	5965 (C America), 6060 (E North Am), 6140 (C America), 9600 (S America), 11760 (Americas), 11875 & 15230 (S America)
0200-0500	9550 (C America)
1100-1400	6000 (C America)
1100-1500	9550 (C America), 11805 (S America), 12000 (E North Am), 15230 (S America)
2100-2300	9550 & 11800 (C America), 15230 (S America)
2300-2400	M-F 6000 (E North Am), M-F 11875 (S America)

RADIO REBELDE

24 Hr	5025
0300-0400	6120 (C America)
1000-1300	9505 & 11655 (C America)
1100-1300	9600 (C America)
1600-1800	11655 & 15570 (C America)

CZECH REPUBLIC—Czech

RADIO PRAGUE

0030-0100	[W] 5930 (S America), [W] 7345 (N America & C America)

0130-0200 [S] 6200 (N America & C America), [S] 7345 (S America)

0230-0300 [W] 6200 & [S] 7345 (N America & C America), [W] 7345 (S America), [S] 9870 (W North Am & C America)

0330-0400 [W] 6200 (W North Am & C America), [W] 7345 (N America & C America)

0830-0900 [S] 15710 (E Africa & Mideast)

0930-1000 [◄►] 11600 (W Europe & N Africa)

0930-1000 [S] 21745 (S Asia & W Africa), [W] 21745 (E Africa & Mideast)

1030-1100 [W] 21745 (S Asia & W Africa)

1100-1130 [S] 11615 (N Europe), [S] 15710 (S Asia)

1200-1230 [W] 11640 (N Europe), [W] 21745 (S Asia, SE Asia & Australasia)

1330-1400 [◄►] 6055 (Europe), 7345 (W Europe)

1330-1400 [S] 13580 (N Europe), [S] 21745 (E Africa)

1430-1500 [W] 11600 (S Asia), [W] 21745 (N America)

1530-1600 [S] 17485 (E Africa)

1630-1700 [◄►] 5930 (W Europe)

1630-1700 [W] 15710 (W Africa & C Africa)

1730-1800 [S] 5930 (E Europe, Asia & Australasia), [S] 17485 (C Africa)

1830-1900 [W] 5930 (W Europe), [W] 9400 (Asia & Australasia)

1930-2000 [S] 11600 (SE Asia & Australasia)

2030-2100 [◄►] 5930 (W Europe)

2030-2100 [W] 9430 (SE Asia & Australasia)

2100-2130 [S] 9800 (W Africa & C Africa), [S] 11600 (W Europe & N Africa)

2200-2230 [W] 5930 (W Europe), [W] 9435 (W Europe & S America)

2330-2400 [S] 7345 (S America), [S] 9440 (N America & C America)

One of the many marinas on the island of Hvar, Croatia. Croatia offers not one, but two world band services for mariners and countrymen abroad.

Shutterstock/Gordana Sermek

EGYPT—Arabic

EGYPTIAN RADIO

0000-0030 [◄►] 11665 (E Africa)

0000-0400 [◄►] 12050 (Europe & E North Am)

0700-1100 [◄►] 15115 (W Africa)

1200-2400 [◄►] 12050 (Europe & E North Am)

1900-2400 [◄►] 11665 (E Africa)

RADIO CAIRO

0000-0045 9735 & 11755 (S America)

0030-0430 11885/11950 (E North Am)

1015-1215 17775 (Mideast)

1300-1600 15365 (C Africa)

2000-2200 7270 (Australasia)

2330-2400 9735 & 11755 (S America)

FRANCE—French

RADIO FRANCE INTERNATIONALE

0000-0100 *15110* (SE Asia)

0300-0400 *5925* (C Africa & E Africa)

0400-0430 [W] Sa/Su 9805 (E Africa)

0400-0500 [W] 5925, 7135 & [S] *7150* (C Africa), [W] *7270* (S Africa)

0400-0600 *15210* (E Africa)

0500-0530 [W] Sa/Su 9805/13680, [W] Sa/Su 11995 & [S] Sa/Su 13680 (E Africa)

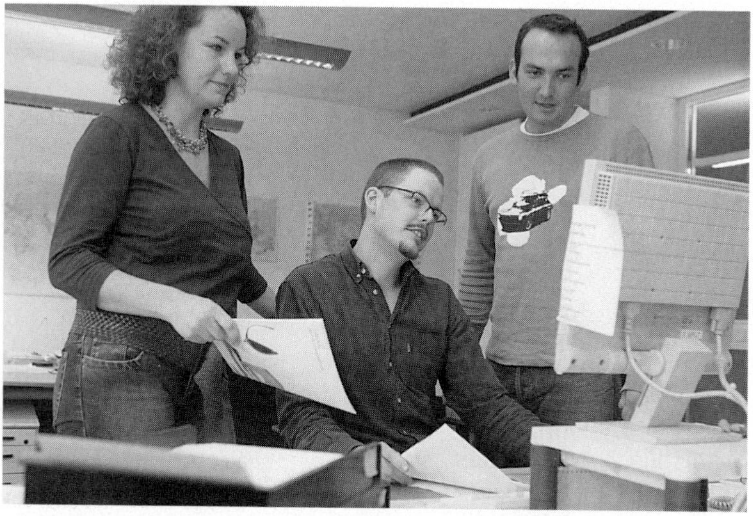

Deutsche Welle's "Arts on the Air" reporters Anja Küppers, James Fletcher and Sam Edmonds huddle to finalize a script. DW

0500-0600 [W] 5925 (N Africa & W Africa), [W] 7135 & [S] 9790 (W Africa), [W] 9790 (C Africa), [S] 11700/7135 (N Africa & W Africa), [S] 15300 (C Africa & S Africa)

0500-0700 [W] 7135 (N Africa & W Africa)

0600-0630 [S] Sa/Su *9570* & [W] Sa/Su *9865* (W Africa), [W] Sa/Su 11995/15160, [W] Sa/Su 13680, [S] Sa/Su 15160 & [S] Sa/Su 17800 (E Africa)

0600-0700 [W] 5925 (W Africa), 9790 & [S] 11700 (N Africa & W Africa), [W] 11700 (C Africa & S Africa), 13695 (C Africa), [S] 13695/7135 (N Africa & W Africa), [S] 15300 (C Africa & S Africa), *17770* (C Africa)

0630-0700 [S] *9570* & [W] *9865* (W Africa)

0700-0800 [W] 9790, 11700 & 13695 (N Africa & W Africa), [W] 13695 & *15170* (C Africa), 15300 (W Africa, C Africa & S Africa)

0700-1000 17850 (C Africa & S Africa)

0800-0900 [S] 15300 (C Africa & S Africa)

0800-1000 13675 & 17620 (W Africa)

0800-1600 15300 (N Africa & W Africa)

0900-1700 [W] 21580 (C Africa & S Africa)

1000-1200 [W] 17620 (W Africa)

1000-1600 [S] 13675 (W Africa)

1100-1200 *17525* (C Africa)

1130-1200 6175 (W Europe & Atlantic), *13640* & [W] 17610 (C America)

1200-1400 *15160* (C Africa), 17620 (W Africa), [S] 17850 (C Africa & S Africa)

1200-1500 [W] 21685 (W Africa)

1230-1300 *17525* (C Africa), [W] 21620 (E Africa)

1330-1400 *15515* (C America)

1400-1600 [W] 17620 (W Africa)

1600-1700 [W] 11995, 13675 & [S] 15300 (W Africa), [W] 15300 (Africa), 17620 (W Africa)

1600-1800 [S] 17850 (C Africa & S Africa)

1700-1800 [W] 11705/15300 (C Africa & S Africa), [S] 13695 (N Africa & W Africa), [W] 13695 (Africa)

1700-1900 [S] 15300 (Africa)

1700-2100 11995 (W Africa)

1800-1900 [W] 9790 & 13695 (N Africa & W Africa)

1800-2000 11705 (C Africa & S Africa)

1900-2000 [W] 6175 (N Africa & W Africa), [S] *7160* (C Africa), [W] 7315 (W Africa), 9790

(Africa), [S] 15300 (W Africa)

1900-2100 [S] 13695 (N Africa & W Africa)

2000-2100 9790 (W Africa)

2000-2200 [W] 6175 (N Africa), 7160 (C Africa), 7315 (N Africa & W Africa)

2100-2200 [W] 7135 (N Africa & W Africa), [S] 9790 (W Africa)

2300-2400 [W] 12075, 15110/15350 & [S] 15595 (SE Asia)

GABON—French

AFRIQUE NUMERO UN

0500-2315 9580 (C Africa)

0700-0800 17630 (Irr) (W Africa)

0800-1600 17630 (W Africa)

1600-1900 15475 (W Africa & E North Am)

GERMANY—German

DEUTSCHE WELLE

0000-0200 [W] 7120 (W Asia), [W] 9440 (C Asia), 9545 & [W] 9655 (C America), [W] 11690 (S America), [S] 12040 (C America)

24 Hr 6075 (Europe)

0200-0400 [W] 6075 (Mideast), [S] 9825 (E Europe & W Asia), [S] 15640 (Mideast)

0400-0600 [S] 9620 (S Africa), [W] 9735, [S] 12025 & [W] 13780 (C Africa & E Africa), [S] 17575 (C Africa), [W] 17800 (E Africa & S Africa)

0600-0700 [W] 15410 (W Africa & C Africa)

0600-0800 [W] 7210 & [S] 9480 (N Europe), [W] 9545 (S Europe & Mideast), [W] 12025 (E Europe & W Asia), [S] 13780 (Mideast), [W] 13780 (W Africa & C Africa), [S] 15325 (W Africa), [S] 15545 (C Africa & S Africa)

0600-2000 9545 (S Europe & Atlantic)

0700-0800 [W] 12045 (W Africa)

0800-1000 [W] 7175 (N Europe), [S] 9480 (W Europe), [W] 9545 (S Europe & N Africa), [S] 9855 & 13780 (Australasia), [S] 15325 (N Africa & Atlantic), [S] 15680 & [W] 17525 (SE Asia & Australasia)

0800-1200 / 1000-1200 13780 (Mideast), [S] 5905 (C America), [W] 5910 (E Asia), [W] 6040 (E North Am & C America), [W] 7265 & [S] 7350 (E Asia), [W] 11510 (SE Asia & Australasia), [W] 15110 (Australasia), [S] 15595 (S America), [S] 17635 (E Asia & SE Asia), [W] 17770 (S America), [S] 17845 (E Asia & SE Asia), [W] 21840 (SE Asia & Australasia), [S] 21840 (S America)

1000-1400 [S] 9900 (SE Asia & Australasia)

1200-1400 [S] 9565 (C Asia), [W] 13780 (Mideast), [W] 15610 (C Asia), [W] 17630 & [S] 17845 (S Asia & SE Asia)

1200-1800 [S] 13780 (Mideast)

1400-1600 [S] 9655 (Mideast), [W] 13780 (Mideast & N Africa), [S] 15275 (Mideast), [W] 15275 (W Asia & C Asia), [W] 15335 (Mideast & W Asia)

1600-1800 [W] 7255 (E Africa), [W] 11685 (C Africa & S Africa), [W] 12055 (C Africa & E Africa), [W] 13780 (W Africa & C Africa), [S] 15275 & [S] 15680 (C Africa & E Africa)

1600-2000 / 1800-2000 [S] 6150 (C Africa & E Africa), [S] 9735 & [W] 11725 (W Africa), [S] 11795 (N Africa & C Africa), [W] 11945 (C Africa), [S] 15275 (N Africa & W Africa)

1800-2200 / 2000-2100 / 2000-2200 [S] 9545 (Europe), [W] 11935 (Australasia), [S] 7330 (Australasia), 9545 (Atlantic & S America), [S] 9875 (Australasia)

2100-2200 [W] 11935 (Australasia)

2200-2400 [W] 5900 (E Asia), [W] 7395 (E Asia & SE Asia), [S] 7420 (E

Asia), 9545 (S America),
S *9775* (C America & S
America), **W** *11690 & 11865*
(S America), **S** *11935 &*
S *11965* (SE Asia), **S** *15640*
(E Asia)

DEUTSCHLANDRADIO—(Europe)
24 Hr   6005

GREECE—Greek

FONΙ TIS HELLADAS

0000-0100 ▣	7475 (Europe & Americas)
0000-0100	**W** 5865/9420 (Europe & N America), **S** Tu-Su 9420 (Europe & Americas)
0100-0200 ▣	Tu-Su 7475 (Europe & Americas)
0100-0200	**W** Tu-Su 5865/9420 (Europe & N America), **S** 9420 (Europe & Americas)
0200-0300 ▣	7475 (Europe & Americas)
0200-0300	**W** 5865/9420 (Europe & N America), **S** M-Sa 9420 (Europe & Americas)
0300-0400 ▣	M-Sa 7475 (Europe & Americas)
0300-0400	**W** M-Sa 5865/9420 (Europe & N America)
0300-0600	**S** 9420 (Europe & Americas)
0400-0600	**S** 15630 (W Europe & Atlantic)
0400-0650 ▣	7475 (Europe & Americas)
0400-0700	**W** 5865/9420 (Europe & N America)
0600-0650	15630 (W Europe & Atlantic)
0600-1000	9420 (Europe)
0650-0700	**W** 15630 (W Europe & Atlantic)
0700-0800	**S** W-M 15630 & **W** 15630 (W Europe & Atlantic)
0800-0830	W-M 15630 (W Europe & Atlantic)
0830-0900	**W** W-M 15630 (W Europe & Atlantic)
0900-0930	W-M 15630 (W Europe & Atlantic)
0930-1000	**S** W-M 15630 (W Europe & Atlantic)
1100-1200	**W** W-M 15630 (W Europe & Atlantic)
1200-1300	**W** 15630 (W Europe & Atlantic)
1300-1600	15630 (W Europe & Atlantic)
1300-2400	9420 (Europe)
1600-1700	**S** Su-F 15630 & **W** 15630 (W Europe & Atlantic)
1600-2000	**W** 7475 (Europe)
1700-1800	**S** 15630 & **W** Su-F 15630 (W Europe & Atlantic)
1800-1850	**W** 15630 (W Europe & Atlantic)
2000-2400 ▣	7475 (Europe)
2300-2400	**W** 5865/9420 (Europe), **S** 9420 (Europe & Americas)

**RADIOFONIKOS STATHMOS
MAKEDONIAS**—(Europe)

1100-1655	9935
1700-2255	7450

HUNGARY—Hungarian

RADIO BUDAPEST

0000-0100 ▣	M 12030 (S America)
0000-0100	**W** M 9580 (S America), **S** 9770 (N America)
0100-0200	**W** 6110 (N America)
0130-0230	**S** 6040 (N America)
0230-0330	**W** 5980 & **W** 9855 (N America)
0330-0400	**W** 9775 (N America)
1100-1200	**S** 21590 (Australasia)
1200-1300	**W** 17670 (Australasia)
1400-1500 ▣	Su 6025 (Europe)
1700-1800	**S** 15335 (S Africa)
1800-1900	**S** 11840 (Australasia)
1900-2000 ▣	3975 & 6025 (Europe)
1900-2000	**W** 11760 (Australasia)
2000-2100	**W** 9620 (S Africa), **S** 11695 (E North Am)
2100-2200	3975 (Europe)
2200-2300	**W** 6140 (N America), **S** 9850 (S America)
2300-2400 ▣	6025 (Europe), 12030 (S America)
2300-2400	**W** 9580 & **S** Su 9850 (S America)

RADIO KOSSUTH—(Europe)

0500-1300 ▣	6025
1300-1700 ▣	M-Sa 6025

INDIA—Hindi

ALL INDIA RADIO

0315-0415	11840 & 13695 (Mideast & W Asia), 15075 (Mideast & E Africa), 15185 & 17715 (E Africa)
0430-0530	15075, 15185 & 17715 (E Africa)
1615-1730	7410 (Mideast & W Asia), 9950 (E Africa), 12025 & 13770 (Mideast & W Asia), 15075 & 17670 (E Africa)
1945-2045	7410, 9950 & 11620 (Europe)
2300-2400	9910, 11740 & 13795 (SE Asia)

ISRAEL

GALEI ZAHAL—(Europe)

Hebrew

24 Hr	6973/15785

KOL ISRAEL

Hebrew

0000-0330	[S] 11590/9345 (W Europe & E North Am)
0000-0430	[W] 7545 (W Europe & E North Am)
0400-0500	[S] 11590/9345 (W Europe & E North Am)
0500-0600	[W] 7545 (W Europe & E North Am)
0600-0800 ←	15760 (W Europe & E North Am)
0700-0930	[S] 15760 (W Europe & E North Am)
0800-1030 & 1130-1455	[W] 17535 (W Europe & N America)
1800-1900	[S] 13675 (W Europe & E North Am)
1900-1945	[W] 7545 (W Europe)
2000-2300	[S] 9400/11585 (W Europe & E North Am)
2100-2215 ←	15640/15615 (S America)
2100-2400	[W] 7545 (W Europe & E North Am)
2300-2400	[S] 11590/9345 (W Europe & E North Am)

Yiddish

1600-1625	[S] 9345 (W Europe)
1700-1725 ←	11590 (Europe), 15760 (W Europe & E North Am)
1700-1725	[W] 9345 (Europe)

ITALY—Italian

RAI INTERNATIONAL

0000-0055	9840 (S America), 11800 (N America)
0130-0230	[S] *6110* (S America), *11765* (C America)
0130-0315	9840 (S America), 11800 (N America)
0435-0445	[W] 5965 (S Europe & N Africa), [S] 6110 & [W] 6120 (N Africa), [W] 7170, [S] 7235 & [S] 9800 (S Europe & N Africa)
0455-0530	[S] 11900 & [W] 11985 (E Africa)
0630-0800	[W] 6100 & [S] 6195 (E Europe)
0800-1300	6195 (E Europe)
1000-1100	*11920* (Australasia)
1250-1620	[S] Su 11915 (N Africa & Mideast), [S] Su 15515 (C Africa & S Africa), [S] Su 17780 (N America), [S] Su 21515 (S America)
1350-1720 ←	Su 9670 (W Europe), Su 21710 (C Africa & S Africa)
1350-1720	[W] Su 21520 (N America), [W] Su 21550 (S America)
1400-1425	[S] 15280 & M-Sa 17780 (N America)
1400-1430	M-Sa 21520 (N America)
1500-1525	[S] M-Sa 9670 & M-Sa 9675 (S Europe & N Africa), [S] M-Sa 11720 & [W] M-Sa 11800 (N Africa & Mideast), [W] M-Sa 11815 & [S] M-Sa 11915 (S Europe & N Africa)
1555-1625	[S] M-Sa 9670, [W] M-Sa 9780, [S] M-Sa 11855 & [W] M-Sa 11860 (W Europe)
1700-1730	[W] M-Sa 5965 (Mideast), [W] M-Sa 6125 & [W] M-Sa 9845 (S Europe & N Africa), [W] M-Sa 11875 (E Africa), [W] M-Sa 15250 (C Africa), [S] M-Sa 15385 (C Africa & S Africa)
1700-1800	[S] 5985 (S Europe & N Africa), [S] 7175 (N Africa),

	[S] 9675 (S Europe & N Africa), [S] 11970 (E Africa), *15320* (C Africa & S Africa)
1730-1800	[W] 5965 (Mideast), [W] 6125 & [W] 9845 (S Europe & N Africa), [W] 11875 (E Africa), [W] 15250 (C Africa), [S] 15385 (C Africa & S Africa)
1830-1905	[W] 11800, [W] 15250, [S] 15380 & [S] 17780 (N America)
2240-2400	9840 (S America), 11800 (N America)

RAI-RADIOTELEVISIONE ITALIANA—(Europe, Mideast & N Africa)

0000-0003, 0012-0103, 0112-0203, 0212-0303, 0312-0403, 0412-0500 & 2300-2400 ⇦	6060

JAPAN—Japanese

RADIO JAPAN

0200-0300	*11860* (SE Asia), *11935* (S America), 17845 (E Asia)
0200-0500	*5960* (E North Am), 15195 (E Asia), 15325 (S Asia), 17810 (SE Asia)
0300-0400	*9660* (S America)
0300-0500	17560 (Mideast), 17685 (Australasia), 17825 (W North Am & C America)
0700-0800	6145, 6165 & 15195 (E Asia), 17870 (Pacific)
0700-0900	17860 (SE Asia)
0700-1000	*11740* (SE Asia), *11920* & 21755 (Australasia)
0800-1000	*9530* (S America), 9540 (W North Am & C America), 9825 (Pacific & S America), *11710* (N Europe), 15590 (S Asia), *17650* (W Africa), *17720* (Mideast)
0800-1700	9750 (E Asia)
0900-1600	11815 (SE Asia)
1300-1500	*11705* (E North Am)
1500-1700	9535 (W North Am & C America), *12045* (S Asia), *21630* (C Africa)
1600-1900	6035 (E Asia), 7200 (SE Asia)
1700-1800	*9750* (N Europe), [S] *11865* & [W] *12045* (S Asia), *21600* (S America)
1700-1900	*6175* (W Europe), 7140 (Australasia), [W] *9575* (Mideast & N Africa), 9835 (Pacific & S America), [S] *13740* (Mideast & N Africa)
1800-1900	*15355* (S Africa)
1900-2100	*6035* (Australasia)
2000-2100	6165 (E Asia), 11970 (Europe)
2000-2200	[W] 7225 & 11665 (SE Asia)
2000-2400	11910 (E Asia), [S] 13680 (SE Asia)
2100-2200	9560 (E Asia)
2200-2300	*6115* (W Europe), [W] *7115* & [S] *9650* (Mideast), *11770* (Australasia), *11895* (C America), *15220* (S America), 17825 (W North Am & C America)
2200-2400	[W] 11665 (SE Asia)
2300-2400	*17605* (S America)

RADIO NIKKEI

0000-0800	3925, Sa/Su 3945, Sa/Su 6115, Sa/Su 9760
0000-1400	6055, 9595
0800-1400 & 2030-2300	3925
2030-2400	6055, 9595
2300-2400	3925, F/Sa 3945, F/Sa 6115, F/Sa 9760

JORDAN—Arabic

RADIO JORDAN

0500-0810 ⇦	11810 (Mideast, S Asia & Australasia)
0600-0815 ⇦	11960 (E Europe)
1130-1300 ⇦	15290 (N Africa & C America)
1200-1600 ⇦	11810 (Mideast, S Asia & Australasia)
1745-2200	[S] 11810 (Mideast, S Asia & Australasia)
1845-2100 ⇦	9830 (W Europe)
1845-2300	[W] 6105 (Mideast, S Asia & Australasia)
2100-2300 ⇦	15435 (S America)

KOREA (DPR)—Korean

KOREAN CENTRAL BROADCASTING STATION

0000-0630	6100
0000-0930	9665
0000-1800	2850, 11680
0900-0950	4405, 7140 & 9345 (E Asia)
1200-1250	3560 (E Asia), 🆆 6185 (SE Asia), 🆆 6285 & 🆆 9335 (C America), 🆆 9850 (SE Asia), 🆂 11710 (C America), 🆂 11735, 🆂 13650 & 🆂 15180 (SE Asia)
1400-1450	3560 (E Asia), 🆆 6185, 🆆 9850, 🆂 11735 & 🆂 13650 (SE Asia)
1500-1800	6100
1700-1750	4405 (E Asia), 🆆 7570 (W Europe), 9335 & 11710 (N America), 🆆 12015, 🆂 13760 & 🆂 15245 (W Europe)
2000-2050	3560 (E Asia), 🆆 6285 (Europe), 7100 (S Africa), 9325 (Europe), 9975 & 11535 (Mideast & N Africa), 11710/11910 (S Africa), 🆂 12015 (Europe)
2000-2400	2850, 6100, 9665, 11680
2300-2350	3560, 4405 & 7140/7180 (E Asia), 🆆 7570 (W Europe), 9345, 9975 & 11535 (E Asia), 🆆 12015, 🆂 13760 & 🆂 15245 (W Europe)

PYONGYANG BROADCASTING STATION

0000-0050	3560, 7140 & 9345 (E Asia)
0000-0100	9730 (E Asia)
0000-0925	6248 (E Asia)
0000-1800	6398 (E Asia)
0000-1900	3320 (E Asia)
0200-0630	3250 (E Asia)
0700-0750	4405, 7140 & 9345 (E Asia)
0900-0950	3560, 9975 & 11735 (E Asia), 13760 & 15245 (E Europe)
1000-1050 & 1200-1250	4405, 7140 & 9345 (E Asia)
1300-1350	🆆 6285, 9325 & 🆂 12015 (Europe)
1500-1900	6248 (E Asia)
1500-2030	3250 (E Asia)
2100-2400	3320, 6248 & 6398 (E Asia)

KOREA (REPUBLIC)—Korean

KBS WORLD RADIO

0100-0200	15575 (N America)
0300-0400	11810 (S America)
0700-0800	9535 (Europe)
0900-1000	15210 (Europe)
0900-1100	5975 & 7275 (E Asia), 9570 (SE Asia), 9640 (Europe)
1000-1100	🆂 9650 (E North Am)
1200-1300	7275 (E Asia)
1400-1500	🆆 9650 (N America)
1600-1800	7275 (Europe), 15575 (Mideast & Africa)
1700-1900	5975 (E Asia), 7150 (Mideast), 9515 (Europe)
2100-2300	5975 (E Asia)

Korean electronics retailing is intensely competitive, yet world band radios are surprisingly scarce.   M. Guha

KUWAIT—Arabic

RADIO KUWAIT

0200-0500	6055 (Mideast & W Asia)
0200-0530	11675 (W North Am)
0200-1305	15495 (N Africa)
0400-0740	15505 (E Europe & W Asia)
0800-0925	15110 (S Asia & SE Asia)
0900-1305	6055 (Mideast & W Asia)
1015-1740	15505 (W Africa & C Africa)
1200-1505	17885 (E Asia & Australasia)
1300-1605	13620/11990 (Europe & E North Am)
1315-1600	15110 (S Asia)
1615-1800	11990 (Europe & E North Am)
1730-2100	9880 (N Africa)
1745-2130	15505 (Europe & E North Am)
1800-2400	15495 (W Africa & C Africa)
1815-2400	9855 (Europe & E North Am)

LIBYA—Arabic

RADIO JAMAHIRIYA—(W Africa & C Africa)

1700-1900	🅦 *7215*, 🅦 *9590* & 🆂 *11615*
1900-2200	🅦 *7205* & 🆂 *9590*
2200-2400	*7320*

LITHUANIA—Lithuanian

RADIO VILNIUS

0000-0030 ▣	9875 (E North Am)
0000-0030	🆂 11690 (E North Am)
0100-0130	🅦 7325 (E North Am)
0900-0930 ▣	9710 (W Europe)
2300-2330	🅦 7325 (E North Am)

MEXICO—Spanish

RADIO EDUCACION

0000-1200 ▣	6185

MOROCCO

RADIO MEDI UN—(Europe & N Africa)
Arabic & French

0500-0400	9575

RADIODIFFUSION TÉLÉVISION MAROCAINE
Arabic

0000-0500	🅦 5980 & 🆂 11920 (N Africa & Mideast)
0900-2200	15345/15340 (N Africa & Mideast)
1100-1500	15335 (Europe)
2200-2400	7135 (Europe)

NETHERLANDS—Dutch

RADIO NEDERLAND

0300-0400	🅦 *6190* (W North Am)
0400-0500	*5975* (C America), 🅦 *6165* (N America)
0500-0600	🆂 *6165* (W North Am), 🆂 *7125* (Europe)
0500-0700	🆂 *6015* (S Europe)
0600-0700 ▣	*5955* (Europe)
0600-0700	🅦 *6165* (W North Am), *9625* (Australasia), 🆂 *11655* (N Europe)
0600-0900 ▣	9895 (S Europe)
0700-0800	🅦 *6015* (W Europe), 🅦 *7125* (Europe), 🆂 *9610* (N Europe), *9625* (Australasia)
0700-0900	🅦 6035 (S Europe)
0700-1600 ▣	5955 (W Europe)
0800-0900 ▣	11935 (S Europe)
0900-1100	🅦 *6035* (Europe)
0900-1600 ▣	Sa/Su 9895 & Sa/Su 13700 (S Europe)
0930-1015	M-Sa *6020* (C America)
1100-1200	🅦 *21560* (SE Asia)
1200-1300	🅦 *17745* (E Asia), 🅦 *21480* (SE Asia)
1300-1400	*5910*, 🅦 *9655* & 🅦 *9900* (E Asia & SE Asia), 🆂 *12065* (S Asia & SE Asia), 🆂 *13735* (SE Asia), 🅦 *17580* & 🆂 *17585* (S Asia & SE Asia), 🅦 *17815* (SE Asia)
1500-1700	🆂 *13700* (S Europe & N Africa)
1600-1700 ▣	9895 (S Europe)
1600-1700	🅦 6035 & 🆂 9895 (S Europe), 🅦 *11655* (E Africa), *13840* (Mideast), 🆂 *15335* (Europe, Mideast & N Africa)
1600-1800 ▣	5955 (W Europe)

1700-1800   ▥ 6010 (S Europe), *6020* (S Africa), ▤ 9895 (C Africa), ▥ 9895 (E Africa & Europe), ▤ *11655* (E Africa), ▥ *11655* (E Africa & N Africa)

2100-2200   ▥ *7120* (C Africa), ▥ *15315* (S America), *17810* (W Africa), *17895* (S America)

2100-2300   ▤ *6015* & ▥ *6040* (Europe), ▥ 9895 (N Africa & C Africa)

2200-2300   ▥ *11730* (N Africa & W Africa), *15315* & ▤ *15540* (S America)

2300-2400   ▥ *6165* (E North Am), *9525* (C America & S America), ▤ *11970* (E North Am)

OMAN—Arabic

RADIO SULTANATE OF OMAN

0000-0200	9760 (Europe & Mideast)
0200-0300	15355 (E Africa)
0200-0400	▤ 6085/6000 & ▥ 6085/7175 (Mideast)
0400-0600	9515 (Mideast), 17590 (E Africa)
0600-0800	17630/17660 (Europe & Mideast)
0600-1400	13640 (Mideast)
0800-1000	17630 (Europe & Mideast)
1400-1800	15375 (E Africa)
1500-2200	15140 (Europe & Mideast)
1800-2000	6190 & 15355 (E Africa)
2000-2200	6085 (E Africa), 13640 (Europe & Mideast)
2200-2400	15355 (Europe & Mideast)
2300-2400	9760 (Europe & Mideast)

PHILIPPINES—Tagalog

RADYO PILIPINAS—(Mideast)

1730-1930   ▤ 11720, ▥ 11730, ▥ 11890, 15190 & ▤ 17720

POLAND—Polish

RADIO POLONIA

1130-1200 ◀	5965 (Europe), 7285 (E Europe)
1630-1730 ◀	6050 (W Europe)
2200-2300 ◀	6050 (E Europe), 7265 (W Europe)

PORTUGAL—Portuguese

RDP INTERNATIONAL

0000-0200	▤ Tu-Sa 15295 (S America)
0000-0300 ◀	Tu-Sa 9715 (E North Am), Tu-Sa 13700 (C America)
0000-0300	▥ Tu-Sa 11980 (S America)
0500-0800	▤ M-F 7240 (Europe)
0600-1300	▥ M-F 9815 (Europe)
0645-0800	▤ M-F 11850 (Europe)
0700-0800	▤ Sa/Su 12020 (Europe)
0700-1000	▤ Sa/Su 12000 (W Africa & S America), ▤ Sa/Su 15160 (E Africa & S Africa)
0745-0900	▥ M-F 11660 (Europe)
0800-1055	▥ Sa/Su 17710 (W Africa & S America)
0800-1100	▥ Sa/Su 21830 (E Africa & S Africa)
0800-1200	▤ 12020 (Europe)
0800-1455	▥ Sa/Su 11875 (Europe)
0830-1000	▤ Sa/Su 11955 (Europe)
0930-1100	▥ Sa/Su 9815 (Europe)
1000-1200	▤ M-F 15575 (W Africa & S America)
1100-1300 ◀	21830 (E Africa & S Africa)
1100-1300	▥ M-F 21655 (W Africa & S America)
1100-1700 ◀	Sa/Su 21655 (W Africa & S America)
1200-1300	▤ M-F 15560 (Irr) (E North Am)
1200-1355	▤ Sa/Su 12020 (Europe)
1200-2000	▤ Sa/Su/Holidays 15560 (E North Am)
1300-1500	▤ M-F 15770 (Mideast & S Asia)
1300-1655 ◀	Sa/Su 21830 (E Africa & S Africa)
1300-1700	▥ Sa/Su/Holidays 15575 (E North Am)
1400-1600	▤ Sa/Su 15555 (Europe), ▥ M-F 15690 (Mideast & S Asia)
1500-1800	▥ Sa/Su 11960 (Europe)
1600-1900	▤ 15555 (Europe)
1700-1900	▥ Sa/Su/Holidays 17825 & ▥ M-F 17825 (Irr) (E North Am)
1700-2000 ◀	M-F 17680 (E Africa & S Africa), 21655 (W Africa & S America)

From Moscow the Voice of Russia reaches the nation's diaspora in North America, Europe, Israel and the former Soviet republics. Shutterstock/

Troshkin Aleksei Aleksandrovich

1700-2000	M-F 11630 (Europe), Sa/Su 17680 (E Africa & S Africa)
1800-2100	W Sa/Su 11630 (Europe)
1900-2000	S Sa/Su 15555 (Europe)
1900-2100	W Sa/Su 15540 & W M-F 15540 (Irr) (E North Am)
1900-2300	S 9820 (Irr) (Europe), S 11945 (Irr) (S Africa)
2000-2100 ▄	Sa/Su 21655 (W Africa & S America)
2000-2100	W Sa/Su 17680 (E Africa & S Africa)
2000-2300	S M-F 15295 (Irr) (S America), S Sa/Su/ Holidays 15560 (Irr) (E North Am)
2000-2400	W 9460 (Irr) (Europe), W 11825 (Irr) (E Africa & S Africa), W 15555 (Irr) (W Africa & S America)
2100-2400	W 15540 (Irr) (E North Am)
2300-2400	S M-F 15295 (S America)

ROMANIA—Romanian

RADIO ROMANIA

0800-0900	W Su 11730 & S Su 11970 (Mideast), S Su 15270 (W Asia & S Asia), Su 15370 (Mideast), W Su 15430, W Su 17775 & S Su 17805 (W Asia & S Asia)

0900-1000	S Su 11875 (N Africa & Mideast), S Su 11945 (Mideast), W Su 15380 (N Africa & Mideast), Su 15430 (Mideast), S Su 15450 & W Su 17745 (N Africa & Mideast), W Su 17775 (Mideast)
1000-1100	S Su 11830 (W Europe), S Su 11990 (N Africa), S Su 15250 & W Su 15260 (W Europe), Su 15380 & W Su 17735 (N Africa), W Su 17825 (W Europe)

RADIO ROMANIA INTERNATIONAL

0100-0200	W 6040 & W 9640 (E North Am)
0100-0300	S 9525 (E North Am)
0200-0300	W 6040, W 9640 & S 11970 (E North Am)
1200-1300	S 7155, S 11920 & S 15195 (W Europe)
1300-1400	W 11795 & W 15170 (W Europe)
1400-1500	S 9760 & S 11965 (W Europe)
1500-1600	W 9595 & W 11970 (W Europe)
1600-1700	S 7195 & S 9690 (Mideast)
1700-1800	W 6110 & W 7220 (Mideast), S 9625 & S 11865 (W Europe)

1800-1900	🅢 9625 & 🅢 11765 (W Europe)
1900-2000	🅦 7125 (W Europe)
2000-2100	🅢 9630 & 🅢 11810 (W Europe)

RUSSIA—Russian
VOICE OF RUSSIA

0100-0200	🅢 *9860* (E North Am)
0100-0300	🅢 5900/6180 (S America), 🅢 9725 & 🅢 9880/5900 (E North Am), 🅢 12070/7260 (C America & S America), 🅢 15425 & 🅢 15455 (W North Am)
0200-0300	🅦 6195 (S America), 🅦 *7350* (E North Am)
0200-0400	🅦 7150 (E North Am), 🅦 7240 (N America), 🅦 7260 (C America & S America), 🅦 12010 & 🅦 13665 (W North Am)
0300-0400 ⬅	7330 (S America)
1200-1400	🅢 9745 (S Asia), 🅢 11670 (SE Asia & Australasia)
1200-1500	🅢 9555 (C Asia & S Asia), 🅢 9875 (C Asia)
1300-1400	🅦 5920 & 🅦 6145 (E Asia), 🅢 15540 (Mideast), 🅢 17645 (S Asia & SE Asia)
1300-1500	🅦 7260 (E Asia & SE Asia), 🅦 9495 (Australasia), 🅦 9770 (SE Asia & Australasia), 🅦 *9885* (S Asia), 🅦 15460/17570 (S Asia & SE Asia)
1300-1600	🅦 7365 (C Asia)
1300-1700	🅦 6185 (C Asia)
1300-1900	🅢 7370 (Europe)
1400-1500	🅦 5940 (E Asia), 🅦 5945 (C Asia & W Asia), 🅦 6205 (SE Asia), 🅦 7220 (E Asia), 🅦 7315 (W Asia & S Asia), 🅦 12055 (S Asia & SE Asia), 🅢 *15430* (Mideast)
1400-1700	🅢 11830 (Mideast)
1400-1800	🅢 9800 (C Asia)
1400-1900	🅢 9480/7285 (Europe)
1500-1600	🅦 *9555* (Mideast), 🅢 12055 (W Asia & S Asia), 🅢 13650/7130 (Mideast & W Asia)

1500-1700	🅢 9865 (C Asia)
1500-1900	🅦 5995 (C Asia)
1500-2000	🅦 5940 (Europe)
1500-2200	🅦 7445 (Mideast & W Asia)
1600-1700	🅦 6005 (Mideast), 🅦 7315 (W Asia & S Asia), 🅦 *9885* (S Asia)
1700-1800	🅦 5905 & 🅢 11630/9480 (Europe), 🅢 13855 & 🅢 15540 (Mideast)
1700-2100	🅢 12055/7165 (Mideast & W Asia)
1800-1900	🅦 5985 (Mideast & W Asia), 🅦 7390 (Europe)
1900-2000	🅢 11630/9480 (Europe)
2000-2100	🅦 *6170* (S Europe, N Africa & Mideast), 🅦 7230 (Europe & N Africa), 🅦 7390 (Europe)

SAUDI ARABIA—Arabic
BROADCASTING SERVICE OF THE KINGDOM

0300-0600	9580 (Mideast & E Africa), 15170 (E Europe & W Asia)
0300-0800	17895 (C Asia & E Asia)
0300-0900	9675 (Mideast)
0600-0900	15380 (Mideast), 17730 (N Africa), 17740 (W Europe)
0600-1700	11855 (Mideast & E Africa)
0900-1200	11935 (Mideast), 17615 (S Asia & SE Asia), 17805 (N Africa), 21495 (E Asia & SE Asia), 21705 (W Europe)
0900-1600	9675 (Mideast)
1200-1400	15380 (Mideast), 21600 (SE Asia)
1200-1500	17895 & 21505 (N Africa), 21640 (W Europe)
1300-1600	21460 (E Africa)
1500-1800	13710 & 15315 (N Africa), 15435 (W Europe)
1600-1800	15205 (W Europe), 17560 (C Africa & W Africa)
1700-2200	9580 (Mideast & E Africa)
1800-2300	9555 (N Africa), 9870 (W Europe), 11740 (C Africa & W Africa), 11820 (W Europe), 11915 (N Africa)

SINGAPORE—Chinese

MEDIACORP RADIO

1400-1600 &	
2300-1100	6000

RADIO SINGAPORE INTERNATIONAL—
(SE Asia)

1100-1400	6000 & 6185

SPAIN

RADIO EXTERIOR DE ESPAÑA
Galician, Catalan & Basque

1240-1255	[S] M-F *9765* (C America), [S] M-F *11815* (C America & S America), [S] M-F 13720 (W Europe), [S] M-F *15170* (W North Am), [S] M-F 15585 (Europe), [S] M-F 21540 (C Africa & S Africa), [S] M-F 21570 (S America), [S] M-F 21610 (Mideast), [S] M-F 21700 (N America & C America)
1340-1355	[W] M-F *5970* (C America), [W] M-F *15170* (W North Am), [W] M-F 15585 (Europe), [W] M-F 17595 (N America), [W] M-F 21540 (C Africa & S Africa), [W] M-F 21570 (S America), [W] M-F 21610 (Mideast)

Spanish

0000-0200	[S] 11680 & [W] 11945 (S America)
0000-0400	[S] *6020* & [W] *11815* (C America & S America)
0000-0500	[S] 9535 & [W] 9540 (N America & C America), 9620 (S America), 15160 (C America & S America)
0100-0600	6055 (N America)
0200-0600	[S] *3350* & [W] *6040* (C America), [S] *6125* & [W] *11880* (N America)
0500-0600	[S] 12035 (Europe)
0500-0700	11890 (Mideast)
0600-0700	[W] 13720 (W Europe)
0600-0800	[W] Sa/Su 5985 (W Europe), [W] Sa/Su 9710 (Europe)
0600-0900	12035 (Europe)
0700-0900	17770 & Sa/Su 21610 (Australasia)
0700-1240	13720 (W Europe)
0800-1000	M-F 21570 (S America)
0900-1240	15585 (Europe), 21540 (C Africa & S Africa), 21610 (Mideast)
1000-1200	*9660* (E Asia), M-F *11815* (C America & S America)
1000-1240	21570 (S America), [S] M-F 21700 (N America & C America)
1000-1300	[W] M-F 17595 (N America & C America)
1100-1200	[W] M-F *5970* (C America)
1100-1240	[S] M-F *9765* (C America), M-F *15170* (W North Am)
1200-1240	[S] M-F *11815* (C America & S America)
1200-1300	[W] M-Sa *5970* (C America)
1200-1400	[S] Su *9765* (C America), *11910* (SE Asia)
1200-1500	Su *15170* (W North Am & C America), Sa/Su 21700 (C America & S America)
1200-1600	[S] Su *11815* & [W] Su *15125* (C America & S America)
1240-1255	[W] 13720 (W Europe), [W] M-F *15170* (W North Am), [S] Sa/Su 15585 & [W] 15585 (Europe), [S] Sa/Su 21540 & [W] 21540 (C Africa & S Africa), [S] Sa/Su 21570 & [W] 21570 (S America), [S] Sa/Su 21610 & [W] 21610 (Mideast)
1240-1300	[S] Sa/Su 13720 (W Europe)
1255-1340	M-F *15170* (W North Am), 15585 (Europe), 21540 (C Africa & S Africa), 21570 (S America), 21610 (Mideast)
1255-1400	[S] M-F *9765* (C America)
1300-1340	[W] M-F *5970* (C America), [W] M-F 17595 (N America)
1300-1400	Sa/Su 13720 (W Europe)
1300-1500	[W] Su *5970* (C America), [S] 17595 (N America)
1340-1355	[S] M-F *15170* (W North Am), [S] 15585 & [W] Sa/Su 15585 (Europe), [S] 21540 & [W] Sa/Su 21540 (C Africa & S Africa), [S] 21570 & [W] Sa/Su 21570 (S America), [S] 21610 & [W] Sa/Su 21610 (Mideast)

1355-1500	M-F 17595 (N America), 21610 (Mideast)
1355-1700	15585 (Europe), 21570 (S America)
1400-1500	[S] Sa 15385 (W Africa & C Africa), [S] 17755 & [W] 21540 (C Africa & S Africa)
1500-1600	Su *9765* (C America), Su *17850* (W North Am)
1500-1700	M-Sa 15385 (W Africa & C Africa), 21610 (Mideast)
1500-1800	21700 (C America & S America)
1500-1900	17755 (C Africa & S Africa)
1600-1800	Sa/Su *9765* (C America), [S] Sa/Su *11815* & [W] Sa/Su *15125* (C America & S America), Sa/Su *17850* (W North Am)
1700-1900	17715 (S America)
1700-2000	Sa/Su 9665 (Europe)
1700-2300	7275 (Europe)
1800-2000	*9765* (C America), [S] *11815* & [W] *15125* (C America & S America), *17850* (W North Am)
1800-2100	Sa/Su 21700 (C America & S America)
1800-2230	M-F 21700 (Irr) (C America & S America)
1900-2100	Su 17755 (C Africa & S Africa)
1900-2300	15110 (N America & C America)
2000-2100	[S] Sa 9665 & [W] Sa/Su 9665 (Europe)
2000-2230	M-F *9765* (Irr) (C America), [S] M-F *11815* (Irr) & [W] M-F *15125* (Irr) (C America & S America), M-F *17850* (Irr) (W North Am)
2000-2300	Sa/Su *9765* (C America), [S] Sa/Su *11815* & [W] Sa/Su *15125* (C America & S America), Sa/Su *17850* (W North Am)
2100-2200	[W] Sa 9665 (Europe), [W] M-F 11625 (C Africa)
2100-2300	[W] Sa/Su 21700 (C America & S America)
2200-2300	7270 (N Africa & W Africa), [W] Sa 11625 (C Africa)
2300-2400	[S] 9535 & [W] 9540 (N America & C America), 9620, [S] 11680 & [W] 11945 (S America), [W] Su *15125* (Irr) & 15160 (C America & S America), Su *17850* (Irr) (W North Am)

SWEDEN—Swedish

RADIO SWEDEN

0000-0030	*9490* (S America)
0100-0130	[S] *6010* (E North Am), [W] *9490* (S America), [W] *11550* (S Asia)
0200-0230	*6010* (N America), [S] *9435* (S Asia)
0300-0330	[W] *6010* (W North Am), [S] *9490* (S America)
0330-0400	[S] M-F 11650 (Mideast & E Africa)
0400-0500	[S] M-F 11640 (Mideast & E Africa)
0430-0530	[W] M-F *13580* (Mideast & E Africa)
0500-0600	[S] M-F 9490 (W Europe & W Africa)
0500-0700 ⮜	M-F 6065 (Europe & N Africa)
0530-0700	[W] M-F 9490 (Mideast & E Africa)
0600-0800	[S] Sa 9490 (Europe & N Africa), [S] Sa 13580 (Mideast)
0700-0800	[W] M-F 9490 (E Europe & Mideast)
0700-0900 ⮜	Sa 6065 (Europe & N Africa)
0700-0900	[S] Su 9490 (Europe & N Africa), [S] Su 13580 (Mideast)
0800-1000 ⮜	Su 6065 (Europe & N Africa)
0800-1000	[W] Su 9490 (Europe & N Africa)
1000-1010	[S] 15735 (E Asia & Australasia)
1010-1030	[S] Sa/Su 15735 (E Asia & Australasia)
1030-1040	[S] 15735 (Asia & Australasia)
1040-1100	[S] Sa/Su 15735 (Asia & Australasia)

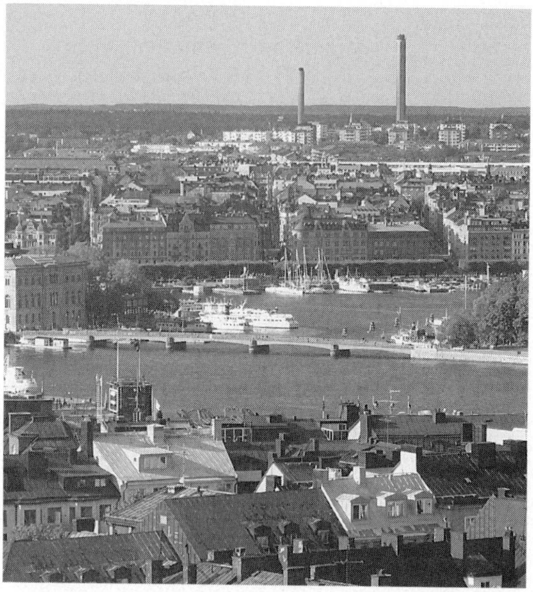

Although today's Swedes are disinclined to forsake their homeland, they routinely scour the globe by air and by sea. Radio Sweden reaches out to them wherever they are. Shutterstock/Aleksandar-Pal Sakala

1100-1110 ⇦ 9490 (Europe & N Africa)
1100-1110 [W] 7420 (E Asia & Australasia), [S] 15240 (E North Am)
1110-1130 ⇦ Sa/Su 9490 (Europe & N Africa)
1110-1130 [W] Sa/Su 7420 (E Asia & Australasia), [S] Sa/Su 15240 (E North Am)
1130-1140 ⇦ 21810 (Africa)
1130-1140 [W] *9490* (C America & Australasia), [W] 11610 (Asia & Australasia)
1130-1200 [S] *9490* (E North Am & C America)
1140-1200 ⇦ Sa/Su 21810 (Africa)
1140-1200 [W] Sa/Su *9490* (C America & Australasia), [W] Sa/Su 11610 (Asia & Australasia)
1200-1210 [W] *9490* (E North Am & C America)
1200-1215 [S] 15735 (Asia & Australasia)
1210-1230 [W] Sa/Su *9490* (E North Am & C America)
1215-1230 [S] M-F 15735 (E Asia & Australasia), [S] Sa/Su 15735 (Asia & Australasia)
1300-1315 [W] 7420 & [S] 15735 (E Asia & Australasia)
1315-1330 ⇦ M-F 15240 (N America), Sa/Su 15240 (E North Am)
1315-1330 [W] Sa/Su 7420 (E Asia & Australasia), [W] M-F 11550 & [S] M-F 15735 (SE Asia & Australasia), [S] Sa/Su 15735 (E Asia & Australasia)
1400-1415 [W] 11550 (SE Asia & Australasia)
1400-1430 ⇦ *15240* (N America)
1400-1430 [S] 15735 (SE Asia & Australasia)
1415-1430 [W] M-F 7420 (E Asia & Australasia), [W] Sa/Su 11550 (SE Asia & Australasia)
1500-1530 ⇦ 15240 (N America)
1500-1530 [S] 7475 (E Europe & W Asia), [W] 11550 (Asia & Australasia)
1545-1600 ⇦ 15240 (N America)
1545-1600 [S] 13580 (Mideast & W Africa), [S] 15735 (W Europe & W Africa)
1545-1700 ⇦ 6065 (Europe)
1600-1615 [S] M-F 13580 (Mideast & W Africa), [S] M-F 15735 (W Europe & W Africa)
1600-1630 [W] 5850 (E Europe & Mideast)
1645-1700 [W] 7420 (Mideast), [W] 11605 (W Europe & W Africa)
1700-1715 [W] M-F 7420 (Mideast), [W] M-F 11605 (W Europe & W Africa)
1700-1730 ⇦ M-Sa 6065 (Europe)
1715-1730 [W] M-F 7420 (Mideast)
1730-1800 ⇦ 6065 (Europe)
1800-1830 ⇦ Su 6065 (Europe)
1800-1830 [S] 11560 (Mideast), [S] 13710 (Mideast & W Africa)
1900-1930 ⇦ 6065 (Europe)
1900-1930 [W] 5820 (Mideast), [W] 7465 (W Europe & W Africa), [S] 11605 (Africa)

2000-2030 ➡ *7420* (SE Asia & Australasia)
2100-2200 W 5840 (W Europe & W Africa)
2100-2230 ◧ 6065 (Europe)

SYRIA—Arabic

RADIO DAMASCUS—(S America)
2330-0030   9330 & 12085

SYRIAN BROADCASTING SERVICE
1100-1400 ◧ 12085

THAILAND—Thai

RADIO THAILAND
0100-0200   *5890* (E North Am)
0230-0330   *5890* (W North Am)
1000-1100 W 7285 & S 11870 (SE Asia & Australasia)
1330-1400 W 7160 & S 11685 (E Asia)
1800-1900 S 9680 & W 11855 (Mideast)
2045-2115 W 9535 & S 9680 (Europe)

TUNISIA—Arabic

RTV TUNISIENNE
0200-0500 ◧ 9720 & 12005 (N Africa & Mideast)
0400-0630 ◧ 7275 (W Europe)
0400-0800 ◧ 7190 (N Africa)
1600-1900 ◧ 12005 (N Africa & Mideast)
1600-2100 ◧ 9720 (N Africa & Mideast)
1700-2110 ◧ 7225 (W Europe)
1700-2310 ◧ 7190 (N Africa)

TURKEY—Turkish

VOICE OF TURKEY
0000-0200 W 7300 (W Europe & N America)
0200-0400 W 7180 (W Asia & C Asia)
0400-0700 S 15225 (C Asia)
0400-0900 S 11750 (Mideast)
0700-1400 S 15350/9460 (Europe)
0800-1000 W 11925 (Mideast)
0800-1100 S 21730 (Australasia)
0800-1400 ◧ 11955 (N Africa & Mideast)
0800-1400 W 15350 (Europe)
1000-1400 W 17650 (Australasia)
1400-2200 W 5980 & S 9460 (Europe)
1600-2200 S 5960 (Mideast)

1630-2200 W 6080 (Mideast)
1700-2200 W 6120 (N Africa & Mideast), S 7215 (N Africa & W Africa)
2300-2400 W 7300 (W Europe & N America)

UKRAINE—Ukrainian

RADIO UKRAINE
0000-0100 W 5910 (E North Am)
0000-0500 S 7485 (W Asia)
0100-0300 S 7440 (E North Am)
0100-0600 W 5830 (W Asia)
0200-0400 W 5910 (E North Am)
0500-0800 S 9945 (W Europe)
0600-0900 W 7420 (W Europe)
0800-1100 S 15675 (W Europe)
0900-1200 W 9925 (W Europe)
1200-1300 S 15675 (W Europe)
1300-1400 W 9925 (W Europe)
1300-1700 S 7530 (W Asia)
1400-1800 W 5830 (W Asia)
1800-2000 S 7490 (W Europe)
1900-2100 W 5840 (W Europe)
2200-2300 S 7420/7490 (W Europe)
2300-2400 W 5840 (W Europe), S 7440 (E North Am)

VIETNAM—Vietnamese

VOICE OF VIETNAM
0000-0100   7285 (SE Asia)
0130-0230 & *6175* (E North Am & C America)
0430-0530   *6175* (N America & C America)
1500-1600   7220 & 9550 (W Africa & C Africa)
1700-1800   7280 & 9730 (Europe)
1730-1830 S *9725* (W Europe)
1830-1930 W *5955* (W Europe)
1930-2030 S *9725* (S Europe)
2030-2130 W *5970* (S Europe)

YEMEN—Arabic

REPUBLIC OF YEMEN RADIO—(Mideast)
0300-0650   9780
0300-1500   5950 & 6135
1700-1800 &
1900-2208   9780

Worldly Words

PASSPORT's Definitive Glossary of World Band Terms and Abbreviations

A variety of terms and abbreviations are used in world band parlance. Many are specialized and benefit from explanation; some are foreign words that need translation; while others are simply adaptations of everyday usage.

Here, then, is PASSPORT's A–Z guide to world band words and what they mean to your listening. For a thorough understanding of the specialized terms and lab tests used in evaluating world band radios, read the Radio Database International White Paper, *How to Interpret Receiver Lab Tests and Measurements*.

A. Summer schedule season for world band stations. *See* ☐. *See* HFCC. *Cf.* B.

Absorption. Reduction in signal strength during bounces (refraction) off the earth's ionosphere (*see* Propagation) or the earth itself.

AC. Alternating ("household" or "mains") Current, 120V throughout North America, 100V in Japan and usually 220-240V elsewhere in the world.

Active Antenna. An antenna that electronically amplifies signals. Active, or amplified, antennas are typically mounted indoors, but some weatherproofed models can also be erected outdoors. Active antennas take up relatively little space, but their amplification circuits may introduce certain problems that can result in unwanted sounds being heard (*see Dynamic Range*). *Cf.* Passive Antenna. *See* Feedline.

Adjacent-Channel Interference. *See* Interference.

Adjacent-Channel Rejection. *See* Selectivity.

AGC. *See* Automatic Gain Control.

AGC Threshold. The threshold at which the automatic gain control (AGC, *see*) chooses to act relates to both listening pleasure and audible sensitivity. If the threshold is too low, the AGC will tend to act on internal receiver noise and minor static, desensitizing the receiver. However, if the threshold is too high, variations in loudness will be uncomfortable to the ear, forcing the listener to manually twiddle with the volume control to do, in effect, what the AGC should be doing automatically. Measured in &V (microvolts).

Alt. Freq. Alternative frequency or channel. Frequency or channel which may be used in place of that which is regularly scheduled.

Amateur Radio. *See* Hams.

AM Band. The 520-1705 kHz radio broadcast band that lies within the 0.3-3.0 MHz (300-3,000 kHz) mediumwave (MW) or Medium Frequency (MF) portion of the radio spectrum. Outside North America it is usually called the mediumwave (MW) band. However, in parts of Latin America it is sometimes called, by the general public and a few stations, *onda larga*—longwave band (*see*)—strictly speaking, a misnomer. In the United States, travelers information stations (TIS) and other public information services are sometimes also found on 1710 kHz, making 1715 kHz the *de facto* upper limit of the American AM band.

AM Equivalent (AME). *See* Single Sideband (third paragraph).

AM Mode. *See* Mode.

Amplified Antenna. *See* Active Antenna.

Analog Frequency Readout. This type of received-frequency indication is used on radios having needle-and-dial or "slide-rule" tuning. This is much less accurate and handy than digital frequency readout. *See* Synthesizer. *Cf.* Digital Frequency Display.

Antenna. *See* Active Antenna, Feedline, Passive Antenna.

Antennae. The accepted spelling for feelers protruding from insects. In electronics, the preferred plural for "antenna" is "antennas."

Antenna Polarization. *See* Polarization.

Arrestor. *See* MOV.

Attenuator. A circuit, typically switched with one or more levels, to desensitize a receiver by reducing the strength of incoming signals. *See* RF Gain.

Audio Quality. At PASSPORT, audio quality refers to what in computer testing is called "benchmark" quality. This means, primarily, the freedom from distortion of a signal fed through a receiver's entire circuitry—*not* just the audio stage—from the antenna input through to the speaker terminals. A lesser characteristic of audio quality is the audio bandwidth needed for pleasant world band reception of music. Also, *see* Enhanced Fidelity.

Automatic Gain Control (AGC). Smooths out fluctuations in signal strength brought about by fading (*see*), a regular occurrence with world band signals, so a receiver's audio level tends to stay relatively constant. This is accomplished by AGC attack, then AGC hang, and finally AGC decay. Each of these three actions involved in smoothing a fade has a micro-time preset at the factory for optimum performance. Top-end receivers often provide for user control of at least the decay timing—a few rarified models also allow for user control over one or both of the other two actions. *See* AGC Threshold.

AV. A Voz—Portuguese for "The Voice." In PASSPORT, this term is also used to represent "The Voice of."

B. Winter schedule season for world band stations, typically valid from the last Sunday in October until the last Sunday in March. *See* ☐. *See* HFCC. *Cf.* A.

Balun. BALanced-to-UNbalanced device to match the two. Typically, a balun is placed between an unbalanced antenna feedline and a balanced antenna input, or *vice versa*.

Bands, Shortwave Broadcasting. *See* World Band Segments.

Bandwidth. A key variable that determines selectivity (*see*), bandwidth is the amount of radio signal, at –6 dB (–3 dB with *i.a.* professional gear), a radio's circuitry will let pass, and thus be heard. With world band channel spacing standardized at 5 kHz, the best single bandwidths are usually in the vicinity of 3 to 6 kHz. Better radios offer two or more selectable bandwidths: at least one of 5 to 9 kHz or so for when a station is in the clear, and one or more others between 2 to 6 kHz for when a station is hemmed in by other signals next to it; with synchronous selectable sideband (*see* Synchronous Detector), these bandwidths can safely be at the upper ends of these ranges to provide enhanced fidelity. Proper selectivity is a key determinant of the aural quality of what you hear, and some newer models of tabletop receivers have dozens of bandwidths.

Bandscanning. Hunting around for stations by continuously tuning up and/or down a given world band segment (*see*), such as in concert with PASSPORT's Blue Pages.

Baud. Measurement of the speed by which radioteletype (*see*), radiofax (*see*) and other digital data are transmitted. Baud is properly written entirely in lower case, and thus is abbreviated as b (baud), kb (kilobaud) or Mb (Megabaud). Baud rate standards are usually set by the international CCITT regulatory body.

BC. Broadcaster, Broadcasters, Broadcasting, Broadcasting Company, Broadcasting Corporation.

BCB (Broadcast Band). *See* AM Band.

BFO (beat-frequency oscillator). Carrier generated within a receiver. *Inter alia*, this replaces a received signal's full or vestigial transmitted carrier when a receiver is in the single-sideband mode (*see*) or synchronous selectable mode (*see*).

Birdie. A silent spurious signal, similar to a station's open carrier, created by circuit interaction within a receiver. The fewer and weaker the birdies within a receiver's tuning range, the better, although in reality birdies rarely degrade reception.

Blocking. The ability of a receiver to avoid being desensitized by powerful adjacent signals or signals from other nearby frequencies. Measured in dB (decibels) at 100 kHz signal spacing.

Boat Anchor. Radio argot for a classic or vintage tube-type communications receiver. These large, heavy biceps builders—

VOA reporter Dan Robinson schmoozes with China Radio International colleagues at the annual Kulpsville, Pennsylvania, international broadcasting Festival (swlfest.com).   J. Brinker

Jackie Gleason called them "real radios"—were manufactured mainly from before World War II through the mid-1970s, although a few continued to be available up to a decade later. The definitive reference for collectors of elder receivers is *Shortwave Receivers Past & Present* by Universal Radio.

BPL. Broadband over Power Lines. Emerging technology to allow Internet and other digital communication via AC (mains) power grids. Thus far it has seen only limited use, offering throughput faster than that of dial-up but slower than that of broadband. A major side effect is noise *(see)* radiation, which seriously disrupts traditional and DRM *(see)* world band radio reception. From the perspective of enhanced government oversight this is a positive tradeoff, as it blots out relatively unfettered world band information and replaces it with controllable Internet links.

Broadcast. A radio or television transmission meant for the general public. *Cf.* Utility Stations, Hams.

BS. Broadcasting Station, Broadcasting Service.

Buzz. Noise typically generated by digital electronic circuitry. *See* Noise.

Carrier. *See* Mode.

Cd. Ciudad—Spanish for "City."

Cellular Telephone Bands. In the United States, the cellular telephone bands are 824-849 and 869-894 MHz. Years ago, when analog cell transmissions were the norm, a powerful senator was overheard engaged in an awkward conversation. Shortly thereafter, receivers which could tune cellular frequencies were made illegal in the United States. As a practical matter, eavesdropping on these bands yields nothing intelligible because of the encrypted nature of digital cellular transmissions that by now have all but replaced analog. Receivers tuning these "forbidden" ranges are readily acquired in Canada and nearly every other part of the world except North Korea.

Channel. An everyday term to indicate where a station is supposed to be located on the dial. World band channels are standardized at 5 kHz spacing. Stations operating outside this norm are "off-channel" (for these, PASSPORT provides resolution to better than 1 kHz to aid in station identification).

Chuffing, Chugging. The sound made by some synthesized tuning systems when the tuning knob is turned. Called "chugging" or "chuffing," as it is suggestive of the rhythmic "chuf, chuf" sound of steam locomotives or "chugalug" gulping of beverages.

Cl. Club, Clube.

Co-Channel Interference. *See* Interference.

Coordinated Universal Time. *See* UTC, World Time.

Cult. Cultura, Cultural.

Curtain Antennas. Often used for long-distance world band transmitting, these consist of horizontal dipole arrays interconnected and typically strung between a pair of masts or towers that are usually fixed, but which sometimes can be rotated. Curtains produce excellent forward gain, reasonable directivity and a low takeoff angle that is desirable for successful long-distance broadcasts. *See* Polarization.

CW. Continuous wave, or telegraph-type ("Morse code," etc.) communication by telegraph key that opens and closes an unmodulated signal to create variations of long and short bursts that on a radio with a BFO *(see)* sound like dih-dah "beeps." Used mainly by hams *(see)*, occasionally by utility stations *(see)*.

DAB. Digital audio broadcasting. *See* Digital Radio Mondiale.

DC. Direct current, such as emanates from batteries. *Cf.* AC.

DC-to-Daylight. Hyperbolic slang for an exceptionally wide frequency tuning range. For example, some wideband receivers will tune from under 10 kHz to over 3 GHz *(see)*. However, in the United States it is illegal to sell new radios to the public that tune the cellular telephone bands *(see)*.

Default. The setting at which a control of a digitally operated electronic device, including many world band radios, normally operates, and to which it will eventually return (e.g., when the radio is next switched on).

Digital Frequency Display, Digital Frequency Readout. Indicates that a receiver displays the tuned frequency digitally, usually in kilohertz *(see)*. Because this is so much handier than an analog frequency readout, all models included in PASSPORT REPORTS have digital frequency readout. Most models with digital frequency display are synthesizer *(see)* tuned, but some low-cost models are analog tuned.

Digital Radio Mondiale (DRM). International organization (www.drm.org) seeking to convert world band and other transmissions from traditional analog mode to DRM digital mode, which is moving from its test phase to limited regular use. DRM transmissions—unlike the conventional analog variety—are easily jammed. *See* Mode, Interference.

Digital Signal Processing (DSP). Where digital circuitry and software are used to perform radio circuit functions traditionally done using analog circuits. Used on certain world band receivers; also, available as an add-on accessory for audio processing only.

Dipole Antenna. *See* Passive Antenna.

Distortion. *See* Overall Distortion.

Domestic Service. *See* DS.

Double Conversion a/k/a **Dual Conversion.** *See* IF.

DRM. *See* Digital Radio Mondiale.

DS. Domestic Service—Broadcasting intended primarily for audiences in the broadcaster's home country. However, some domestic programs are beamed on world band to expatriates and other kinfolk abroad, as well as interested foreigners. *Cf.* ES.

DSP. *See* Digital Signal Processing.

Dual Conversion a/k/a **Double Conversion.** *See* IF.

DX, DXers, DXing. From an old telegraph abbreviation for distance (D) unknown (X); thus, to DX is to communicate over a great distance. DXers are those who specialize in finding distant or exotic stations that are considered to be rare catches. Few world band listeners are considered to be regular DXers, but many others seek out DX stations every now and then—usually by bandscanning, which is facilitated by PASSPORT's Blue Pages.

DXpedition. Typically, a gathering of DXers who camp out in a remote location favorable to catching the toughest of stations. These DX bases are usually far away from electrically noisy AC power and cable TV lines.

Dynamic Range. The ability of, *i.a.*, a receiver or active antenna *(see)* to handle weak signals in the presence of strong competing signals within or near the same world band segment *(see* World Band Spectrum). Devices with inferior dynamic range sometimes "overload," especially with external antennas, causing a mishmash of false signals up and down—and even beyond—the segment being received. Dynamic range is closely related to the third-order intercept point, or IP3. Where possible, PASSPORT measures dynamic range and IP3 at the traditional 20 kHz and more challenging 5 kHz signal-separation, or signal spacing, points.

Earliest Heard (or Latest Heard). See key at the bottom of each Blue Page. If the PASSPORT monitoring team cannot establish the definite sign-on (or sign-off) time of a station, the earliest (or latest) time that the station could be traced is indicated by a left-facing or right-facing "arrowhead flag." This means that the station almost certainly operates beyond the time shown by that "flag." It also means that, unless you live relatively close to the station, you're unlikely to be able to hear it beyond that "flagged" time.

EBS. Economic Broadcasting Station, a type of broadcast operation in China.

ECSS (Exalted-Carrier Selectable Sideband). Manual tuning of a conventional AM-mode signal, using a receiver's single-sideband circuitry to zero-beat *(see)* the receiver's BFO with the transmitted signal's carrier. The better-sounding of the signal's sidebands is then selected by the listener. As ECSS is manual, there is a degree, however slight, of phase mismatch between the fade-prone transmitted carrier and the stable synthetic replacement carrier generated within the receiver. *Cf.* Synchronous Selectable Sideband, Synchronous Detector.

Ed, Educ. Educational, Educação, Educadora.

Electrical Noise. *See* Noise.

Elevation Panel, Elevation Rod. Plastic panel or metal rod which flips out from a radio's back or bottom panel to place the radio at a comfortable operating angle.

Elevation Tab. Plastic tab, typically affixed to a portable radio's carrying strap, which when inserted into the radio's back panel places the radio at a comfortable operating angle.

Em. Emissora, Emisora, Emissor, Emetteur—in effect, "station" in various languages.

Enhanced Fidelity. Radios with good audio performance and certain types of high-tech circuitry can improve the fidelity of world band signals. Among the newer fidelity-enhancing techniques is synchronous detection *(see* Synchronous Detector), especially when coupled with selectable sideband. Another technological means to improve fidelity is digital world band transmission, which is currently being implemented *(see* Digital Radio Mondiale).

EP. Emissor Provincial—Portuguese for "Provincial Station."

ER. Emissor Regional—Portuguese for "Regional Station."

Ergonomics. How handy and comfortable—intuitive—a set is to operate, especially hour after hour.

ES. External Service—Broadcasting intended primarily for audiences abroad. *Cf.* DS.

Exalted-Carrier Selectable Sideband. *See* ECSS.

External Service. *See* ES.

F. Friday.

Fading. Signals which scatter off the ionosphere *(see* Propagation) are subject to some degree of phase mismatch

as the scattered bits of signal arrive at a receiver at minutely varying times. This causes fading, where signal strength varies anywhere from a few times per minute to many times per second, the latter being known as "flutter fading" and often caused by disruption of the earth's geomagnetic field *(see* Great Circle Path). "Selective fading" is a special type that is audible on shortwave and mediumwave AM when a fade momentarily sweeps across a signal's three components (lower sideband, carrier, upper sideband), attenuating the carrier more than the sidebands; with the carrier thus attenuated, the result is "selective-fading distortion." *See* Automatic Gain Control, Propagation, Synchronous Detection.

Fax. *See* Radiofax.

Feeder, Shortwave. A utility *(see)* shortwave transmission from the broadcaster's home country to a shortwave or other relay site or local placement facility *(see)* some distance away. Although these specialized transmissions carry world band programs, they are not intended to be received by the general public. Many world band radios can process these quasi-broadcasts anyway. Shortwave feeders operate in lower sideband (LSB), upper sideband (USB) or independent sideband (termed ISL if heard on the lower side, ISU if heard on the upper side) modes. Feeders are now via satellites and Internet audio, but a few stations keep shortwave feeders in reserve should their satellite/Internet feeders fail. *See* Single Sideband, Utility Stations, NBFM.

Feedline. The wire or cable that runs between an antenna's receiving element(s) and a receiver. For sophisticated antennas, twin-lead ribbon feedlines are unusually efficient, and can reject much nearby electrical noise via phasing. However, coaxial cable feedlines are generally superior in high-local-electrical-noise environments. *See* Balun.

First IF Rejection. A relatively uncommon source of false signals occurs when powerful transmitters operate on the same frequency as a receiver's first intermediate frequency (IF). The ability of receiving circuitry to avoid such transmitters' causing reception problems is called "IF rejection."

Flutter Fading. *See* Fading.

FM. The FM broadcast band is now standardized at 87.5-108 MHz worldwide except in Japan (76-90 MHz) and parts of Eastern Europe (66-74 MHz). Also, for communications there is a special FM mode *(see* NBFM).

Frequency. The standard term to indicate where a station is located within the radio spectrum—regardless of whether it is "on-channel" or "off-channel" *(see* Channel). Below 30 MHz this is customarily expressed in kilohertz (kHz, *see*), but some receivers display in Megahertz (MHz, *see*). These differ only in the placement of a decimal; e.g., 5970 kHz is the same as 5.97 MHz. Either measurement is equally valid, but to minimize confusion PASSPORT and most stations designate frequencies only in kHz. *Cf.* Meters.

Frequency Synthesizer. *See* Synthesizer, Frequency.

Front-End Selectivity. The ability of the initial stage of receiving circuitry to admit only limited frequency ranges into succeeding stages of circuitry. Good front-end selectivity keeps signals from other, powerful bands or segments from being superimposed upon the frequency range you're tuning. For example, a receiver with good front-end selectivity will receive only shortwave signals within the range 3200-3400 kHz. However, a receiver with mediocre front-end selectivity might allow powerful local mediumwave AM stations from 520-1700 kHz to be heard "ghosting in" between 3200 and 3400 kHz, along with the desired shortwave signals. Obviously, mediumwave AM signals don't belong on shortwave. Receivers with inadequate front-end selectivity can benefit from the addition of a preselector *(see)* or a high-pass filter *(see)*.

GHz. Gigahertz, equivalent to 1,000 MHz *(see)*.

GMT. Greenwich Mean Time. *See* World Time.

Great Circle Path. The shortest route a signal takes to arrive at a receiving location, following the circumference of the earth. Normal printed maps are too distorted for this purpose, but an ideal solution is to take a globe and run a string from a station's transmitter site *(see PASSPORT's* Blue Pages) to your location. Among other things, the closer a signal's path is to the geomagnetic North Pole, the greater the chance of its being disrupted by flutter fading *(see* Fading) during geomagnetic propagational disturbances *(see* Propagation). An Internet search can turn up several software programs to generate great circle maps centered at your location, but for most a globe and string are more visually intuitive.

GUI. Graphical user interface for operating PCs and related hardware.

Hams. Government-licensed amateur radio hobbyists who *transmit* to each other by radio, often by voice using single sideband *(see)*, within special amateur bands. Many of these bands are within the shortwave spectrum *(see)*. This spectrum is also used by world band radio, but world band radio and ham radio, which laymen sometimes confuse with each other, are two very separate entities. The easiest way is to think of hams as making something like phone calls, whereas world band stations are like long-distance versions of ordinary mediumwave AM stations.

Harmonic, Harmonic Radiation, Harmonic Signal. Usually, an unwanted weak spurious repeat of a signal in multiple(s) of the fundamental, or "real," frequency. Thus, the third harmonic of a mediumwave AM station on 1120 kHz might be heard faintly on 4480 kHz within the world band spectrum. Stations almost always try to minimize harmonic radiation, as it wastes energy and spectrum space. However, in rare cases stations have been known to amplify a harmonic signal so they can operate inexpensively on a second frequency. Also, *see* Subharmonic.

Hash. Electrical buzzing noise. *See* Noise.

Hertz. *See* Hz.

Heterodyne. A whistle equal in pitch to the separation between two carriers. Thus, two world band stations 5 kHz apart will generate a 5000 Hz whistle unless receiver circuitry (e.g., *see* Notch Filter) keeps this from being audible.

High Fidelity. *See* Enhanced Fidelity.

High-Pass Filter. A filter which lets frequencies pass unattenuated only if they are above a designated frequency. For world band receivers and antennas, 2 MHz or thereabouts is the norm for high-pass filters, as this keeps out mediumwave AM and longwave signals.

HF (High Frequency). Shortwave. *See* Shortwave Spectrum.

HFCC (High Frequency Co-ordination Conference). Founded in 1990 and headquartered in Prague, the HFCC (www.hfcc.org) helps coordinate frequency usage by dozens of broadcasting organizations from numerous countries. These represent a solid majority of the global output for international shortwave broadcasting. Coordination meetings take place twice yearly: once for the "A" (summer) schedule season from the last Sunday in March until the last Sunday in October, another for "B" (winter), and these gatherings have been a great help in preventing frequency conflicts.

Hz. Hertz, a unit of frequency measurement formerly known as cycles per second (c/s). A thousand Hertz is equivalent to 1 kHz *(see)*. Also, *see* Frequency, Meters, MHz.

IBS. International Broadcasting Services, Ltd., publishers of PASSPORT TO WORLD BAND RADIO.

IF (Intermediate Frequency). Virtually all world band receivers use the "superheterodyne" principle, where tuned radio frequencies are converted to a single intermediate frequency to facilitate reception, then amplified and detected to produce audio. In virtually all world band portables and most tabletop models, this frequency is either 455 kHz or 450 kHz. If this is not complemented by a second and higher intermediate frequency (double conversion), "images" readily occur at twice the IF; i.e., 910 kHz or 900 kHz. *See* Image.

IF Shift. *See* Passband Offset.

Image. A common type of spurious signal found on low-cost "single conversion" (single IF) radios where a strong signal appears at reduced strength, usually on a frequency 910 kHz or 900 kHz lower down. For example, the BBC on 5875 kHz might repeat on 4965 kHz, its "image frequency." Double-conversion (two IF) receivers have little problem with images, but the additional IF circuitry adds to manufacturing cost. *See* IF, Spurious-Signal Rejection.

Impedance. Opposition, expressed in ohms, to the flow of alternating current. Components work best when impedance is comparable from one to another; so, for example, a receiver with a 75-ohm antenna socket will work best with antennas having a similar feedline impedance. Antenna tuning units can resolve this, albeit at the cost of added operational complexity.

Independent Sideband. *See* Single Sideband.

Interference. Sounds from other signals, notably on the same frequency ("co-channel interference"), or on an adjacent or other nearby channel(s) ("adjacent-channel interference"), that disturb the station you are trying to hear; DRM *(see)* signals cause interference over a wider frequency range than do conventional analog signals. Worthy radios reduce interference by having good selectivity *(see)* and synchronous selectable sideband *(see* Synchronous Detector). Nearby television sets and cable television wiring may also generate a special type of radio interference called TVI, a "growl," typically from a television horizontal oscillator, heard every 15 kHz or so. Sometimes referred to as QRM, a term based on Morse-code shorthand.

Intermediate Frequency. *See* IF.

International Reply Coupon (IRC). Sold by selected post offices in most parts of the world, IRCs amount to official international "scrip" that may be exchanged for postage in most countries of the world. Because they amount to an international form of postage repayment, over many decades they have been handy for listeners trying to encourage foreign stations to write them back. However, IRCs are very costly for the amount in stamps that is provided in return. Too, an increasing number of countries are not forthcoming about "cashing in" IRCs, which are fading from general use. Specifics on this and related matters are provided in the Addresses PLUS section of this PASSPORT.

International Telecommunication Union (ITU). The regulatory body, headquartered in Geneva, for all international telecommunications, including world band radio. Sometimes incorrectly referred to as the "International Telecommunications Union." In recent years, the ITU has become increasingly ineffective as a regulatory body for world band radio, with much of its former role having been taken up by the HFCC *(see)*.

Internet Radio. *See* Web radio.

Inverted-L Antenna. *See* Passive Antenna.

Ionosphere. *See* Propagation.

IP3. Third-order intercept point. *See* Dynamic Range.

IRC. *See* International Reply Coupon.

Irr. Irregular operation or hours of operation; i.e., schedule tends to be unpredictable.

ISB. Independent sideband. *See* Single Sideband.

ISL. Independent sideband, lower. *See* Feeder.

ISU. Independent sideband, upper. *See* Feeder.

ITU. *See* International Telecommunication Union.

Jamming. Deliberate interference to a transmission with the intent of discouraging listening. However, analog shortwave broadcasts, when properly transmitted, are uniquely resistant to jamming. This ability to avoid "gatekeeping" is a major reason why traditional shortwave continues to be the workhorse for international broadcasting. Jamming is practiced now much less than it was during the Cold War. The main exception is China, where superpower transmitters and rotatable curtain antennas from France are increasingly being used to disrupt world band broadcasts.

Keypad. On a world band radio, like a cell phone, a keypad can be used to control many variables. Radio keypads are used primarily so you can enter a station's frequency for reception, and the best keypads have real keys (not a membrane) in the standard telephone format of 3x4 with "zero" under the "8" key. Many keypads are also used for presets, but this means you have to remember code numbers for stations (e.g., BBC 5975 kHz is "07"); handier radios have separate keys for presets, while some others use LCD-displayed "pages" to access presets.

kHz. Kilohertz, the most common unit of frequency for measuring where a station is located on the world band dial if it is below 30,000 kHz. Formerly known as "kilocycles per second," or kc/s. 1,000 kilohertz equals one Megahertz. *See* Frequency. *Cf.* MHz, Meters.

kilohertz. *See* kHz. The "k" in "kilo" is not properly capitalized, although the computer modem industry got it wrong years back and most modem firms have as yet to correct the error.

kilowatt. *See* kW.

kW. A kilowatt(s), the most common unit of measurement for transmitter power (*see* Power).

LCD. Liquid-crystal display. LCDs, if properly designed, are fairly easily seen in bright light, but require illumination under darker conditions. LCDs—typically monochrome and gray on gray—also tend to have mediocre contrast, and sometimes can be read from only a certain angle or angles, but they consume nearly no battery power.

LED. Light-emitting diode. LEDs have a long life and are very easily read in the dark or in normal room light, but consume more battery power than LCDs and are hard to read in bright ambient light.

Lightning Arrestor. *See* MOV.

Line Output. Fixed-level audio output typically used to feed a recorder or outboard audio amplifier-speaker system.

Location. Physical location. In the case of a radio station, the transmitter location, which is what is cited in PASSPORT's Blue Pages, may be different from that of the studio location. Transmitter location is useful as a guide to reception quality. For example, if you're in eastern North America and wish to listen to the Voice of Russia, a transmitter located in St. Petersburg will almost certainly provide better reception than, say, one located in Siberia.

Longwave (LW) Band. The 148.5–283.5 kHz portion of the low-frequency (LF) radio spectrum used for domestic broadcasting in Europe, the Near East, North Africa, Russia and Mongolia. As a practical matter, these longwave signals, which have nothing to do with world band or other shortwave signals, are not readily audible in other parts of the world.

Longwire Antenna. *See* Passive Antenna.

Loop Antenna. Round (like a hula hoop) or square-ish antenna often used for reception of longwave, mediumwave AM and even shortwave signals. These can be highly directive below around 2 MHz, and can even show some directivity up to 5 MHz or 6 MHz. For this reason, most such antennas can be rotated and even tilted manually—or by an antenna rotor. "Barefoot" loops tend to have low gain, and thus need electrical amplification in order to reach their potential. When properly mounted, top-caliber amplified loops can produce superior signal-to-noise ratios that help with weak-signal (DX) reception.

☞ Strictly speaking, ferrite-rod antennas, found inside nearly every mediumwave AM radio as well as some specialty outboard antennas, are not loops. However, in everyday parlance these tiny antennas are often referred to as "loops" or "loopsticks."

Low-Pass Filter. A filter which lets frequencies pass unattenuated only if they are below a designated frequency. For world band receivers and antennas, 30 MHz or thereabouts is the norm for low-pass filters, as this keeps out VHF/UHF signals.

LSB. Lower Sideband. *See* Mode, Single Sideband, Feeder.

LV. La Voix, La Voz—French and Spanish for "The Voice." In PASSPORT, this term is also used to represent "The Voice of."

LW. *See* Longwave (LW) Band.

M. Monday.

Mains. *See* AC.

Manual Selectable Sideband. *See* ECSS.

Mediumwave Band, Mediumwave AM Band, Mediumwave Spectrum. *See* AM Band.

Megahertz. *See* MHz.

Memory, Memories. *See* Preset.

Meters (Wavelength). An elder unit of measurement used *i.a.* for individual world band segments of the shortwave spectrum. The frequency range covered by a given meters designation—also known as "wavelength"—can be gleaned from the following formula: *frequency (kHz) = 299,792 ÷ meters.* Thus, 49 meters comes out to a frequency of 6118 kHz—well within the range of frequencies included in that segment (*see* World Band Spectrum). Inversely, wavelength in meters can be derived from the following: *wavelength (meters) = 299,792 ÷ frequency (kHz).*

☞ The figure 299,792 is based on the speed of light (299,792,458 m/s) as agreed upon by the International Committee on Weights and Measurements in 1983. However, in practice this fumbling figure is rounded to 300,000 for computational purposes. Thus, in everyday practice the two formulas are: *frequency (kHz) = 300,000 ÷ meters; wavelength (meters) = 300,000 ÷ frequency (kHz).*

MHz. Megahertz, a common unit of frequency (*see*) to measure where a station is located on the dial, especially above 30 MHz, although in the purest sense all measurements above 3 MHz are supposed to be in MHz. In earlier days of radio this was known as "Megacycles per second," or Mc/s. One Megahertz equals 1,000 kilohertz. *See* Frequency. *Cf.* kHz, Meters.

Mode. Method of transmission of radio signals. World band radio broadcasts are almost always in the analog AM (amplitude modulation) mode, the same mode used in the mediumwave AM band (*see*). The AM mode consists of three components: two "sidebands," plus one "carrier" that resides between the two sidebands. Each sideband contains the same programming as the other, and the carrier carries no programming, so a few stations have experimented with the single-sideband (SSB, *see*) mode. SSB contains only one sideband, either the lower sideband (LSB) or upper sideband (USB), and a reduced carrier. It requires special radio circuitry to be demodulated, or made intelligible, which is the main reason SSB is unlikely to be widely adopted as a world band mode. However, major efforts are currently underway to implement digital-mode world band transmissions (*see* Digital Radio Mondiale).

☞ There are yet other modes used on shortwave, but not for world band. These include CW (Morse-type code, *see*), radiofax *(see)* and RTTY (radioteletype, *see*) used by utility *(see)* and ham *(see)* stations. A variant FM mode, narrow-band FM (NBFM, *see*), is also used by utility and ham operations; however, it is not for music or within the FM broadcast bands (*see* FM).

Modulation. The sounds contained within a radio signal.

MOV. Often used in power-line and antenna surge arrestors (a/k/a lightning arrestors) to shunt static and line-power surges to ground. MOVs perform well and are inexpensive, but tend to lose effectiveness with use; costlier alternatives are thus sometimes worth considering. On rare occasion they also appear to have been implicated in starting fires, so a UL or other recognized certification is helpful. For both these reasons MOV-based arrestors should be replaced at least once every decade that they are in service. *See* Surge Arrestor.

MW. Mediumwave AM band; *see* AM Band. Also, Megawatt, which equals 1,000 kW; *cf.* kilowatt; *see* Power.

N. New, Nueva, Nuevo, Nouvelle, Nacional, National, Nationale.

Nac. Nacional. Spanish and Portuguese for "National."

Narrow-band FM. *See* NBFM, Mode.

Nat, Natl, Nat'l. National, Nationale.

NB. *See* Noise Blanker.

NBFM. Narrow-band FM, used within the shortwave spectrum by some "utility" stations, including (between 25-30 MHz) point-to-point broadcast station remote links. *See* Mode.

Noise. Static, buzzes, pops and the like caused by the earth's atmosphere (typically lightning), and to a lesser extent by galactic noise. Also, electrical noise emanating from such man-made sources as electric blankets, fish-tank heaters, heating pads, electrical and gasoline motors, light dimmers, flickering light bulbs, non-incandescent lights, computers and computer peripherals, office machines, electric fences, electric utility wiring—especially with BPL *(see)*—and related components. Sometimes referred to as QRN, a term based on Morse-code shorthand.

Noise Blanker. Receiver circuit, often found on costly tabletop and profession models, that reduces the impact of pulse-type electrical noises (nearby light dimmers, etc.) or certain unusual types of pulse transmissions. In practice, these circuits use long-established designs which act only on pulses which are greater in strength than the received signal, although designs without this limitation exist on paper.

Noise Floor. *See* Sensitivity.

Notch Filter, Tunable. A feature found on some tabletop and professional receivers for reducing or rejecting annoying heterodyne *(see)* interference—the whistles, howls and squeals for which shortwave has traditionally been notorious. Some notch filters operate within the IF *(see)* stage, whereas others operate as audio filters. IF notch filters tend to respond exceptionally well where there is fading, whereas audio filters usually have more capacity to attack higher-pitched heterodynes.

Other. Programs are in a language other than one of the world's primary languages.

Overall Distortion. Nothing makes listening quite so tiring as distortion. PASSPORT has devised techniques to measure overall cumulative distortion from signal input through audio output—not just distortion within the audio stage. This level of distortion is thus equal to what is heard by the ear.

Overloading. *See* Dynamic Range.

Passband Offset. Continuously variable control that can be user-adjusted such that only the best-sounding portion of a given sideband is heard when the receiver is in either the single-sideband mode *(see)* or the synchronous selectable sideband mode *(see)*. This allows for a finer degree of control over adjacent-channel interference and tonal response than does a simple LSB or USB switch associated with a fixed BFO *(see)*. Also known as Passband Tuning, Passband Shift and IF Shift. The same nomenclature is sometimes used to describe variable-bandwidth circuitry.

Passband Shift. *See* Passband Offset.

Passband Tuning. *See* Passband Offset.

Passive Antenna. Not electronically amplified. Typically, such antennas are mounted outdoors, although the "tape-measure" type that comes as an accessory with some portables is usually strung indoors. For world band reception, virtually all outboard models for consumers are made from wire, rather than rods or tubular elements. The two most common designs are the inverted-L (so-called "longwire") and trapped dipole (mounted either horizontally or as a "sloper"). These antennas are usually preferable to active antennas (*cf.*), and are reviewed at length, along with construction and erection instructions, in the Radio Database International White Paper, *PASSPORT Evaluation of Popular Outdoor Antennas (Unamplified)*. *See* Feedline.

PBS. In China, People's Broadcasting Station.

Phase Cancellation. In synchronous selectable sideband *(see)*, two identical wave patterns (lower and upper sidebands) are brought together 180 degrees out of phase so as to cancel out the unwanted sideband. This is a less costly way of sideband attenuation than through the use of discrete IF filtering.

Phase Noise. Synthesizers and other circuits can create a "rushing" noise that is usually noticed only when the receiver is tuned alongside the edge of a powerful broadcast or other carrier. In effect, the signal becomes "modulated" by the noise. Phase noise is a useful measurement if you tune weak signals alongside powerful signals. Measured in dBc (decibels below carrier).

Pirate. Illegal radio station operated by enthusiast(s) with little if any political purpose other than to defy radio laws. Programs typically consist of music, satire or comments relevant to pirate colleagues.

Placement Facility. Typically a local FM or mediumwave AM station which leases airtime for one or more programs or program segments from an international broadcaster. These programs are usually supplied by satellite feed, although some placement facilities pick up programs via regular world band radio.

PLL (Phase-Locked Loop). With world band receivers, a PLL circuit means that the radio can be tuned digitally, often using a number of handy tuning techniques, such as a keypad *(see)* and presets *(see)*.

Polarization. Radio and other over-the-air signals tend to be either horizontally or vertically polarized. Unsurprisingly, stations which transmit using vertical antennas produce vertically polarized signals, and so on. Long-haul world band transmissions are almost always horizontally polarized (*see* Curtain Antennas), so most outdoor receiving antennas are also horizontal. However, the scattering effects of the ionosphere turn the single horizontal transmitted signal, like a bread slicer, into numerous bits (*see* Fading). Some continue on as horizontal while others morph into vertical, but most fall somewhere in between. As a result, the angle of receiving antenna elements tends to be noncritical for reception of long-distance shortwave signals.

Power. Transmitter power *before* antenna gain, expressed in kilowatts (kW). The present range of world band powers is virtually always 0.01 to 1,000 kW.

Power Lock. *See* Travel Power Lock.

PR. People's Republic.

Preamplifier. An inboard or outboard broadband amplifier to increase the strength of signals fed into a receiver's circuitry. Active antennas *(see)* incorporate a preamplifier or an amplified preselector *(see)*.

Preselector. A circuit—outboard as an accessory, or inboard as part of the receiver—that effectively limits the range of frequencies which can enter a receiver's circuitry or the circuitry of an active antenna *(see)*; that is, which improves front-end selectivity *(see)*. For example, a preselector may let in the range 15000-16000 kHz, thus helping ensure that your receiver or active antenna will not encounter problems within that range caused by signals from, say, 5730-6250 kHz or local mediumwave AM signals (520-1705 kHz). This range usually can be varied, manually or automatically, according to the frequency to which the receiver is being tuned. A preselector may be passive (unamplified) or active (amplified).

Preset. Allows you to select a station pre-stored in a radio's memory. The handiest presets require only one push of a button, as on a car radio.

Propagation. World band signals travel, like a basketball, up and down from the station to your radio. The "floor" below is the earth's surface, whereas the "player's hand" on high is the *ionosphere*, a gaseous layer that envelops the planet. While the earth's surface remains pretty much the same from day to day, the ionosphere—nature's own passive "satellite"—varies in how it propagates radio signals, depending on how much sunlight hits the "bounce points."

Thus, some world band segments do well mainly by day, whereas others are best by night. During winter there's less sunlight, so the "night bands" become unusually active, whereas the "day bands" become correspondingly less useful *(see* World Band Spectrum). Day-to-day changes in the sun's weather also cause short-term changes in world band radio reception; this explains why some days you can hear rare signals.

Additionally, the 11-year sunspot cycle has a long term effect on propagation, with sunspot maximum greatly enhancing reception on higher world band segments. The last maximum was in late 2000, while the next minimum is occurring around now.

These bounce, or refraction, points are not absolutely efficient. Some loss comes about from absorption *(see)*, and signal scattering brings about fading *(see)*.

Propagation, like the weather, varies considerably, which adds to the intrigue of world band radio. The accepted standard for propagation prediction is WWV (and sometimes WWVH) on 2500, 5000, 10000, 15000 and 20000 kHz. An explanation of prediction measurements is at www.boulder. nist.gov/timefreq/stations/iform.html#geo. Also, view www. sunspotcycle.com.

PS. Provincial Station, Pangsong.

Pto. Puerto, Porto.

QRM. *See* Interference.

QRN. *See* Noise.

QSL. *See* Verification.

R. Radio, Radiodiffusion, Radiodifusora, Radiodifusão, Radiophonikos, Radiostantsiya, Radyo, Radyosu, and so forth.

Radiofax, Radio Facsimile. Like ordinary telefax (facsimile by telephone lines), but by radio.

Radioteletype (RTTY). Characters, but not illustrations, transmitted by radio. *See* Baud.

RDI. Radio Database International®, a registered trademark of International Broadcasting Services, Ltd.

Receiver. Synonym for "radio," but sometimes—especially when called a "communications receiver"—implying a radio with superior tough-signal or utility-signal performance.

Reception Report. *See* Verification.

Reduced Carrier. *See* Single Sideband.

Reg. Regional.

Relay. A retransmission facility, often highlighted in "Worldwide Broadcasts in English" and "Voices from Home" in PASSPORT's WorldScan® section. Relay facilities are generally considered to be located outside the broadcaster's country. Being closer to the target audience, they usually provide superior reception. *See* Feeder.

Rep. Republic, République, República.

RF Gain. A variable control to reduce the gain of a receiver's earliest amplification, in the RF stage. However, modern receivers often function better without an RF stage, in which case an RF gain control usually acts simply as a variable attenuator *(see)*.

RN. *See* R and N.

RS. Radio Station, Radiostantsiya, Radiostudiya, Radiophonikos Stathmos.

RT, RTV. Radiodiffusion Télévision, Radio Télévision, and so forth.

RTTY. *See* Radioteletype.

◨ Transmission aired summer (midyear) only, typically from the last Sunday in March until the last Sunday in October; *see* "HFCC." *Cf.* ◧

S. San, Santa, Santo, São, Saint, Sainte. Also, South.

Sa. Saturday.

SASE. Self-addressed, stamped envelope. *See* introduction to Addresses PLUS in this PASSPORT.

Scan, Scanning. Circuitry within a radio that allows it to bandscan or memory scan automatically.

Season, Schedule Season. *See* HFCC.

Segments. *See* Shortwave Spectrum.

Selectivity. The ability of a radio to reject interference *(see)* from signals on adjacent channels. Thus, also known as adjacent-channel rejection, a key variable in radio quality. *See* Bandwidth. *See* Shape Factor. *See* Ultimate Rejection. *See* Synchronous Detector.

Sensitivity. The ability of a radio to receive weak signals; thus, also known as weak-signal sensitivity. Of special importance if you are listening during the day or tuning domestic tropical band broadcasts—or if you are located in such parts of the world as Western North America, Hawaii or Australasia, where signals tend to be relatively weak. The best measurement of sensitivity is the noise floor.

Shape Factor. Skirt selectivity helps reduce interference and increase audio fidelity. It is important if you will be tuning stations that are weaker than adjacent-channel signals. Skirt selectivity is measured by the shape factor, the ratio between the bandwidth at –6 dB (adjacent signal at about the same strength as the received station) and –60 dB (adjacent signal relatively much stronger), although with some professional receivers and in certain labs –3 dB is used in lieu of –6 dB. A

Shutterstock/Paul-André Belle-Isle

good shape factor provides the best defense against adjacent powerful signals' muscling their way in to disturb reception of the desired signal.

SHF. Super high frequency, 3-30 GHz.

Shortwave Spectrum. The shortwave spectrum—also known as the High Frequency (HF) spectrum—is that portion of the radio spectrum from 3 MHz through 30 MHz (3,000-30,000 kHz). The shortwave spectrum is occupied not only by world band radio (see World Band Segments), but also hams (see) and utility stations (see).

Sideband. See Mode.

Signal Polarization. See Polarization.

Signal Separation, Signal Separation Points. See Dynamic Range.

Signal Spacing. See Dynamic Range.

Signal-to-Noise Ratio. A common form of noise comes from a radio's (and/or active antenna's) electronic circuitry and usually sounds like "hiss." Depending upon its antenna's location, a receiver may also pick up and reproduce noise (see) from nearby electrical and electronic sources, such as power and cable TV lines, light dimmers and digital electronic products. A third type of noise, galactic, is rarely a problem, and even then can be heard only above 20 MHz. Thus, a key part of enjoyable radio reception is to have a worthy signal-to-noise ratio; that is, where the received radio signal is strong enough relative to the various noises that it drowns out those noises.

SINAD. Signal plus noise plus distortion to noise plus distortion ratio.

Single Sideband, Independent Sideband. Spectrum- and power-conserving modes of transmission commonly used by utility stations (see) and hams (see). Single-sideband transmitted signals usually consist of one full sideband (lower sideband, LSB; or, more typically, upper sideband, USB) and a reduced or suppressed carrier, but no second sideband. Very few broadcasters (e.g., the popular American AFRTS) use, or are expected ever to use, the single-sideband mode. Many world band radios are already capable of demodulating single-sideband transmissions, and some can even process independent-sideband signals.

Independent-sideband (ISB) signals are like single-sideband signals, but with both sidebands. Content is usually different in the two sidebands—for stereo, as in the original Kahn AM-stereo system where the left channel can be LSB, right channel USB. More typically, entirely different programming may be carried by each sideband, such as in a shortwave feed to a relay facility that retransmits two entirely different programs. See Feeder, Mode.

Certain world band broadcasters and time-standard stations emit single-sideband transmissions which have virtually no carrier reduction, or a minimum of reduction; say, 3 or 6 dB. These "AM equivalent" (AME) signals can be listened to, with slightly added distortion, on ordinary radios not equipped to demodulate pure single sideband signals. Properly designed synchronous detectors (see) help reduce distortion with AME transmissions. A variety of AME signals, called "compatible AM," include a minor FM component to help improve reception fidelity. This concept was experimented with decades ago by inventor Leonard Kahn and the VOA, but was not found to offer any meaningful improvement over ordinary AME transmission.

Site. See Location.

Skirt Selectivity. See Shape Factor.

Slew Controls. Up/down controls, usually buttons, to tune a radio. On many radios with synthesized tuning, slewing is used in lieu of tuning by knob. Better is when slew controls are complemented by a genuine tuning knob, which is more versatile for bandscanning.

Sloper Antenna. See Passive Antenna.

Solar Cycle. Synonym for "sunspot cycle." See Propagation.

SPR. Spurious (false) extra signal from a transmitter actually operating on another frequency. One such type is harmonic (see).

Spur. See SPR.

Spurious Signal. See SPR.

Spurious-Signal Rejection. The ability of a radio receiver to avoid producing false signals, such as images (see) and birdies (see), that might otherwise interfere with the clarity of the station you're trying to hear.

Squelch. A circuit which mutes a receiver until the received signal's strength exceeds a specified threshold, which is usually user-adjustable.

SSB. See Single Sideband.

St, Sta, Sto. Abbreviations for words that mean "Saint."

Stability. The ability of a receiver to rest exactly the tuned frequency without drifting.

Static. See Noise.

Static Arrestor. See Surge Arrestor.

Su. Sunday.

Subharmonic. A harmonic heard at 1.5 or 0.5 times the operating frequency. This anomaly is caused by the way signals are generated within vintage-model transmitters, and thus cannot take place with modern transmitters. For example, the subharmonic of a station on 3360 kHz might be heard faintly on 5040 or 1680 kHz. Also, see Harmonic.

Sunspot Cycle. See Propagation.

Superheterodyne. See IF.

Surge Arrestor. Protective device to eliminate the harmful impact of voltage spikes, which enter electronic equipment via AC (mains) power lines, telephone lines and radio/TV antennas. See MOV, although some premium arrestors (e.g., ZeroSurge) use non-MOV technologies.

SW. See Shortwave Spectrum.

SWL. Shortwave listener. The overwhelming preponderance of shortwave listening is to world band stations, but some radio enthusiasts also enjoy eavesdropping on utility stations (see) and hams (see).

Synchronous Detector, Synchronous Detection. Some world band radios are equipped with this high-tech circuit that greatly reduces fading distortion; unlike ECSS *(see)* it automatically steers clear of received *vs.* internally generated carrier phase mismatch. Better synchronous detectors also allow for synchronous selectable sideband *(see);* that is, the ability to select the less-interfered of the two sidebands of a world band or other AM-mode signal. *See* Mode, Phase Cancellation.

Synchronous Selectable Sideband. Derived from synchronous detection *(see)* circuitry, this function greatly reduces the impact of adjacent-channel interference *(see)* on listening.

Synthesizer, Frequency. Better world band receivers utilize a digital frequency synthesizer to tune signals. Among other things, such synthesizers allow for pushbutton tuning and presets, and display the exact frequency digitally—pluses that make tuning to the world considerably easier. Virtually a "must" feature. *See* Analog Frequency Readout, Digital Frequency Display.

Target. The part of the world where a transmission is beamed, a/k/a target zone.

Th. Thursday.

THD. Total harmonic distortion.

Third Order Intercept Point. *See* Dynamic Range.

Travel Power Lock. Control which disables the on/off switch to prevent a radio from switching on accidentally.

Transmitter Power. *See* Power.

Trap Dipole Antenna, Trapped Dipole Antenna. Dipole antenna with several coil "traps" that allow for optimum reception on several world band or other segments or bands. *See* Passive Antenna.

Tropical Band Segments. *See* World Band Segments.

Tu. Tuesday.

UHF. Ultra High Frequency, 300 MHz through 3 GHz.

Ultimate Rejection, Ultimate Selectivity. The point at which a receiver is no longer able to reject adjacent-channel interference. Ultimate rejection is important if you listen to signals that are markedly weaker than are adjacent signals. *See* Selectivity.

Universal Day. *See* World Time.

Universal Time. *See* World Time.

URL. Universal Resource Locator; i.e., the Internet address for a given webpage.

USB. Upper Sideband. *See* Mode, Single Sideband, Feeder.

UTC. Coordinated Universal Time. The occasional variation "Universal Time Coordinated" is not correct, although for everyday use it's okay to refer simply to "Universal Time." *See* World Time.

Utility Stations. Most signals within the shortwave spectrum are not world band stations. Rather, they are utility stations—radio telephones, ships at sea, aircraft, ionospheric sounders, over-the-horizon radar and the like—that transmit strange sounds (growls, gurgles, dih-dah sounds, etc.). Although these can be picked up on many receivers, they are rarely intended to be utilized by the general public. *Cf.* Broadcast, Feeders, Hams and Mode.

v. Variable frequency; i.e., one that is unstable or drifting because of a transmitter malfunction or, less often, to avoid jamming or other interference.

Variable-Rate Incremental Slewing (VRIS). Slewing button or other on/off bandscanning control where the tuning rate increases the longer the control is held down or otherwise kept on.

Variable-Rate Incremental Tuning (VRIT). Tuning knob or similar bandscanning control where the tuning rate increases the faster the control is turned. So, the faster the control is turned, the faster the *rate* in which frequencies zip by.

Verification. A "QSL" card or letter from a station verifying that a listener indeed heard that particular station. In order to stand a chance of qualifying for a verification card or letter, you should respond with a reception report shortly after having heard the transmission. You need to provide the station heard with, at a minimum, the following information in a three-number "SIO" code, in which "SIO 555" is best and "SIO 111" is worst:

- **S**ignal strength, with 5 being of excellent quality, comparable to that of a local mediumwave AM station, and 1 being inaudible or at least so weak as to be virtually unintelligible, 2 (faint, but somewhat intelligible), 3 (moderate strength) and 4 (good strength) represent the signal-strength levels usually encountered with world band stations.
- **I**nterference from other stations, with 5 indicating no interference whatsoever, and 1 indicating such extreme interference that the desired signal is virtually drowned out. Ratings of 2 (heavy interference), 3 (moderate interference) and 4 (slight interference) represent the differing degrees of interference more typically encountered with world band signals. If possible, indicate the names of the interfering station(s) and the channel(s) they are on. Otherwise, at least describe what the interference sounds like.
- **O**verall quality of the signal, with 5 being best, 1 worst.
- In addition to providing SIO findings, you should indicate which programs you've heard, as well as comments on how you liked or disliked those programs. Refer to the Addresses PLUS section of this edition for information on where and to whom your report should be sent, and whether return postage should be included.
- Expanded versions of the SIO reporting code are the SINPO and SINFO codes, where "N" refers to atmospheric noise, "F" to fading and "P" to propagation conditions on the same 1-5 scale. As atmospheric noise is rarely audible below 20 MHz and propagation conditions are highly subjective, SIO tends to provide more accurate feedback. Fading, however, is not hard for an experienced monitor to rate, but the SIFO code has never caught on.
- Few stations wish to receive unsolicited recordings of their transmissions. However, a few stations' websites actively seek MP3, RealAudio or other Internet-sent files or mailed CD recordings of certain transmissions.

VHF. Very high frequency spectrum, 30-300 MHz, which starts just above the shortwave spectrum *(see)* and ends at the UHF spectrum. *See* FM, which operates within the VHF spectrum. Somewhat confusingly, in German VHF is known as UKW (Ultra Short Wave), which is different from UHF (Ultra High Frequency).

Vo. Voice of.

VRIS. *See* Variable-Rate Incremental Slewing.

VRIT. *See* Variable-Rate Incremental Tuning.

◪ Transmission aired winter only, typically from the last Sunday in October until the last Sunday in March; *see* HFCC. *Cf.* ◪

W. Wednesday.

Wavelength. *See* Meters.

Weak-Signal Sensitivity. *See* Sensitivity.

Webcasting. *See* Web Radio.

Web Radio, Webcasts. Broadcasts aired over the Internet. These thousands of stations worldwide include simulcast FM, mediumwave AM and world band stations, as well as Internet-only stations. Although webcasting was originally unfettered, it has increasingly been subjected to official gatekeeping (censorship), as well as uniquely steep copyright and union royalties and rules that have hobbled web simulcasting by

AM/FM stations in the United States. This PASSPORT lists URL information for all world band stations which webcast live or on-demand.

World Band Radio. Broadcasts (news, music, sports and the like) transmitted within and just below the shortwave spectrum *(see)*. Virtually all are found within 14 discrete world band segments *(see)*. These broadcasting stations are similar to regular mediumwave AM band and FM band broadcasters, except that world band stations can be heard over enormous distances. As a result, they often carry programs created especially for audiences abroad. Traditional analog world band transmissions—with properly located, configured and operated facilities—are also uniquely difficult to "jam" *(see* Jamming), making world band the most effective vehicle for outflanking official censorship. Some world band stations have regular audiences in the tens of millions, and even over 100 million, including many who listen for extended periods. Although world band lacks the glamour of new broadcasting technologies, making it an easy target for tech-hungry officials, around 600 million people worldwide continue to listen.

World Band Segments. Fourteen slices within the shortwave spectrum *(see)* and upper reaches of the mediumwave spectrum *(see* AM Band) that are used almost exclusively for world band broadcasts. Those below 5.1 MHz are called "Tropical Band Segments." *See* "Best Times and Frequencies" sidebar elsewhere within this PASSPORT.

World Band Spectrum. *See* World Band Segments.

World Day. *See* World Time.

World Time. Also known as Coordinated Universal Time (UTC), Greenwich Mean Time (GMT), Zulu time (Z) and "military time." With over 150 countries on world band radio, if each announced its own local time you would need a calculator to figure it all out. To get around this, a single international time—World Time—is used. The differences between World Time and local time are detailed in the Addresses PLUS and Setting Your World Time Clock sections of this edition. World Time can also be determined simply by listening to time announcements given on the hour by world band stations—or minute by minute by WWV in the United States on 2500, 5000, 10000, 15000 and 20000 kHz; WWVH in Hawaii on 2500, 5000, 10000 and 15000 kHz; and CHU in Canada on 3330, 7335 and 14670 kHz. A 24-hour clock format is used, so "1800 World Time" means 6:00 PM World Time. If you're in, say, North America, Eastern Time is five hours behind World Time winters and four hours behind World Time summers, so 1800 World Time would be 1:00 PM EST or 2:00 PM EDT. The easiest solution is to use a 24-hour digital clock set to World Time. Many radios already have these built in, and World Time clocks are also available as accessories. World Time also applies to the days of the week. So if it's 9:00 PM (21:00) Wednesday in New York during the winter, it's 0200 *Thursday* World Time.

WS. World Service.

X-Band. The mediumwave AM band segment from 1605-1705 kHz in the Western Hemisphere, Australia and ultimately beyond. In the United States, travelers information stations (TIS) and other public information services are sometimes also found on 1710 kHz.

Zero beat. When tuning a world band or other AM-mode signal in the single-sideband mode, there is a whistle, or "beat," whose pitch is the result of the difference in frequency between the receiver's internally generated carrier (BFO, or beat-frequency oscillator) and the station's transmitted carrier. By tuning carefully, the listener can reduce the difference between these two carriers to the point where the whistle is deeper and deeper, to the point where it no longer audible. This silent sweet spot is known as "zero beat." *See* ECSS.

Zulu Time. *See* World Time.

Printed in Canada

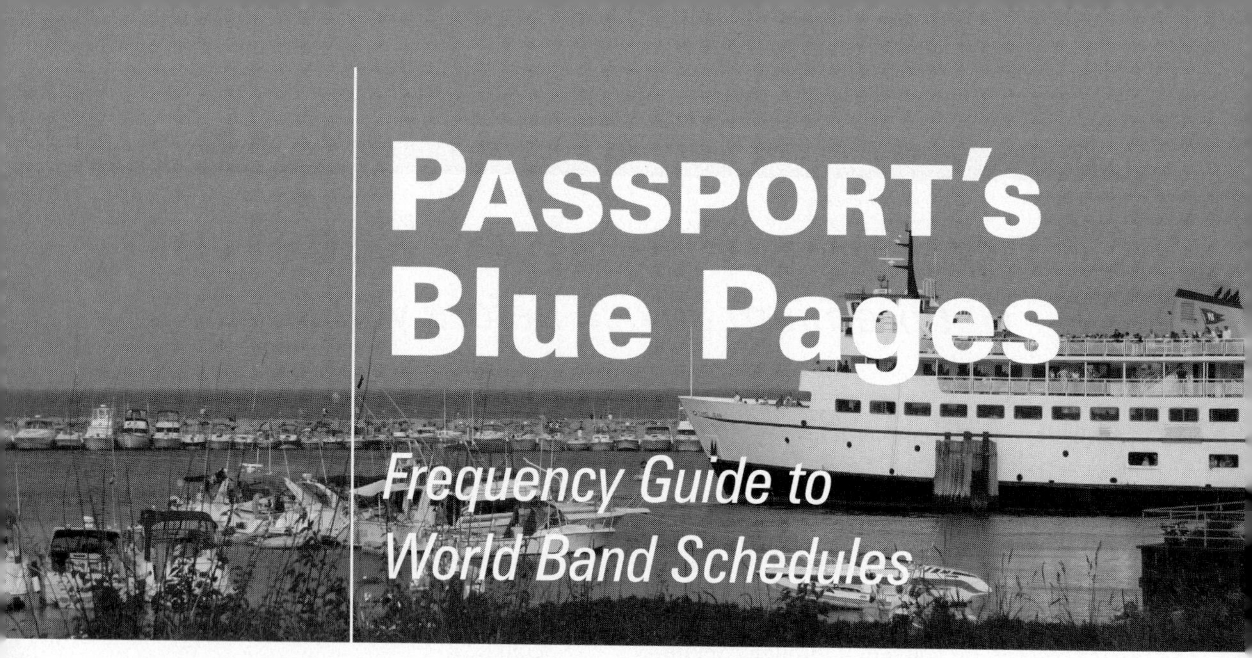

PASSPORT's Blue Pages

Frequency Guide to World Band Schedules

If you scan the world band airwaves, you'll find much more than what's aimed your way. That's because shortwave signals are scattered by the heavens, allowing stations not targeted to your area to be heard.

Blue Pages Identify Stations

But bandscanning can be frustrating if you don't have a "map"—PASSPORT's Blue Pages. Let's say you've stumbled across something Asian-sounding on 7410 kHz at 2035 World Time. The Blue Pages show All India Radio beamed to Western Europe, with 250 kW of power from Delhi. These suggest this is probably what you're hearing, even if you're not in Europe. You can also see that English from India will begin on that same channel in about ten minutes.

Signals targeted your way usually come in best, but those aimed elsewhere may also be heard—especially when they're beamed to nearby regions.

Schedules for Entire Year

Times and days of the week are in World Time, explained in "Setting Your World Time Clock" and "Worldly Words"; for local times in each country, see "Addresses PLUS." Midyear, some stations are an hour earlier (⬅) or later (➡) because of Daylight Saving/Summer Time. Frequencies used only seasonally are labeled [S] for summer (midyear) and [W] for winter. Stations may also extend hours of transmission, or air special programs, for national holidays, emergencies or sports events.

To be as useful as possible over the months to come, PASSPORT's schedules consist not just of observed activity, but also that which we have creatively opined will take place during the forthcoming year. This predictive material is based on decades of experience and is original from us. Although inherently not as exact as real-time data, over the years it has been of tangible value to PASSPORT readers.

Guide to Blue Pages Format

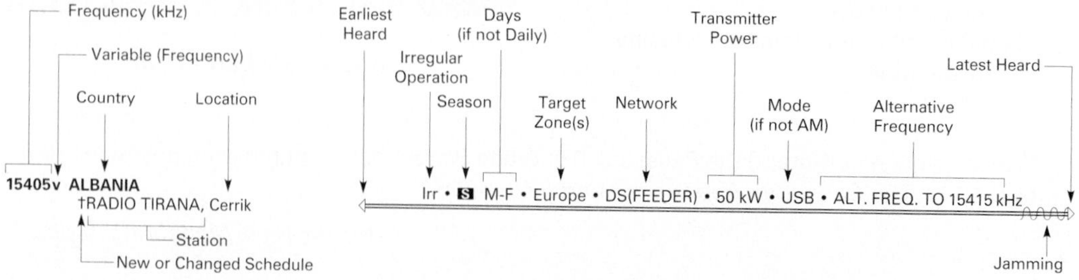

Frequency (kHz)
Variable (Frequency)
Country
Location
15405v ALBANIA
†RADIO TIRANA, Cerrik
Station
New or Changed Schedule
Earliest Heard
Days (if not Daily)
Irregular Operation
Season
Target Zone(s)
Network
Transmitter Power
Mode (if not AM)
Alternative Frequency
Latest Heard
Irr • [S] M-F • Europe • DS(FEEDER) • 50 kW • USB • ALT. FREQ. TO 15415 kHz
Jamming

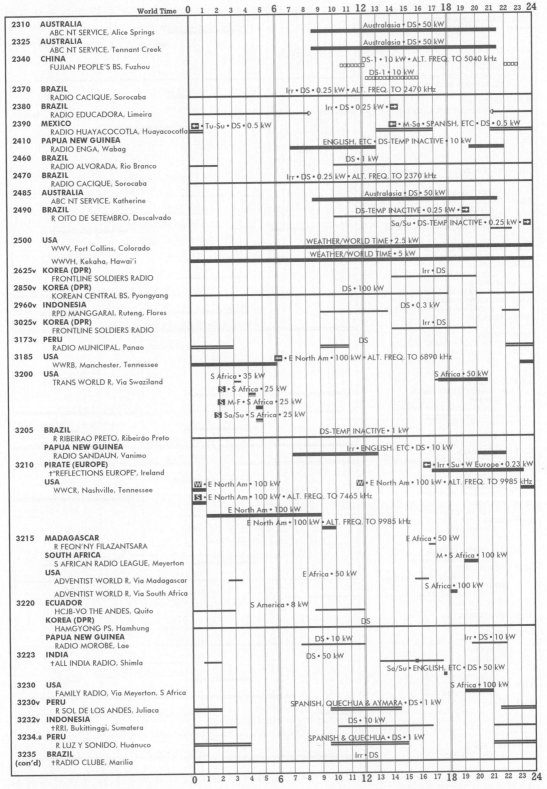

Freq	Country / Station	Details
2310	**AUSTRALIA** ABC NT SERVICE, Alice Springs	Australasia • DS • 50 kW
2325	**AUSTRALIA** ABC NT SERVICE, Tennant Creek	Australasia • DS • 50 kW
2340	**CHINA** FUJIAN PEOPLE'S BS, Fuzhou	DS-1 • 10 kW • ALT. FREQ. TO 5040 kHz DS-1 • 10 kW
2370	**BRAZIL** RADIO CACIQUE, Sorocaba	Irr • DS • 0.25 kW • ALT. FREQ. TO 2470 kHz
2380	**BRAZIL** RADIO EDUCADORA, Limeira	Irr • DS • 0.25 kW • ⮕
2390	**MEXICO** RADIO HUAYACOCOTLA, Huayacocotla	⮕ • Tu-Su • DS • 0.5 kW ⮕ • M-Sa • SPANISH, ETC • DS • 0.5 kW
2410	**PAPUA NEW GUINEA** RADIO ENGA, Wabag	ENGLISH, ETC • DS-TEMP INACTIVE • 10 kW
2460	**BRAZIL** RADIO ALVORADA, Rio Branco	DS • 1 kW
2470	**BRAZIL** RADIO CACIQUE, Sorocaba	Irr • DS • 0.25 kW • ALT. FREQ. TO 2370 kHz
2485	**AUSTRALIA** ABC NT SERVICE, Katherine	Australasia • DS • 50 kW
2490	**BRAZIL** R OITO DE SETEMBRO, Descalvado	DS-TEMP INACTIVE • 0.25 kW • ⮕ Sa/Su • DS-TEMP INACTIVE • 0.25 kW • ⮕
2500	**USA** WWV, Fort Collins, Colorado	WEATHER/WORLD TIME • 2.5 kW
	WWVH, Kekaha, Hawai'i	WEATHER/WORLD TIME • 5 kW
2625v	**KOREA (DPR)** FRONTLINE SOLDIERS RADIO	Irr • DS
2850v	**KOREA (DPR)** KOREAN CENTRAL BS, Pyongyang	DS • 100 kW
2960v	**INDONESIA** RPD MANGGARAI, Ruteng, Flores	DS • 0.3 kW
3025v	**KOREA (DPR)** FRONTLINE SOLDIERS RADIO	Irr • DS
3173v	**PERU** RADIO MUNICIPAL, Panao	DS
3185	**USA** WWRB, Manchester, Tennessee	⮕ • E North Am • 100 kW • ALT. FREQ. TO 6890 kHz
3200	**USA** TRANS WORLD R, Via Swaziland	S Africa • 35 kW S Africa • 50 kW S • S Africa • 25 kW S • M-F • S Africa • 25 kW S • Sa/Su • S Africa • 25 kW
3205	**BRAZIL** R RIBEIRAO PRETO, Ribeirão Preto	DS-TEMP INACTIVE • 1 kW
	PAPUA NEW GUINEA RADIO SANDAUN, Vanimo	Irr • ENGLISH, ETC • DS • 10 kW
3210	**PIRATE (EUROPE)** †"REFLECTIONS EUROPE", Ireland	⮕ • Irr • Su • W Europe • 0.23 kW
	USA WWCR, Nashville, Tennessee	W • E North Am • 100 kW W • E North Am • 100 kW • ALT. FREQ. TO 9985 kHz S • E North Am • 100 kW • ALT. FREQ. TO 7465 kHz E North Am • 100 kW E North Am • 100 kW • ALT. FREQ. TO 9985 kHz
3215	**MADAGASCAR** R FEON'NY FILAZANTSARA	E Africa • 50 kW
	SOUTH AFRICA S AFRICAN RADIO LEAGUE, Meyerton	M • S Africa • 100 kW
	USA ADVENTIST WORLD R, Via Madagascar	E Africa • 50 kW
	ADVENTIST WORLD R, Via South Africa	S Africa • 100 kW
3220	**ECUADOR** HCJB-VO THE ANDES, Quito	S America • 8 kW
	KOREA (DPR) HAMGYONG PS, Hamhung	DS
	PAPUA NEW GUINEA RADIO MOROBE, Lae	DS • 10 kW Irr • DS • 10 kW
3223	**INDIA** †ALL INDIA RADIO, Shimla	DS • 50 kW Sa/Su • ENGLISH, ETC • DS • 50 kW
3230	**USA** FAMILY RADIO, Via Meyerton, S Africa	S Africa • 100 kW
3230v	**PERU** R SOL DE LOS ANDES, Juliaca	SPANISH, QUECHUA & AYMARA • DS • 1 kW
3232v	**INDONESIA** †RRI, Bukittinggi, Sumatera	DS • 10 kW
3234.8	**PERU** R LUZ Y SONIDO, Huánuco	SPANISH & QUECHUA • DS • 1 kW
3235 (con'd)	**BRAZIL** †RADIO CLUBE, Marilia	Irr • DS

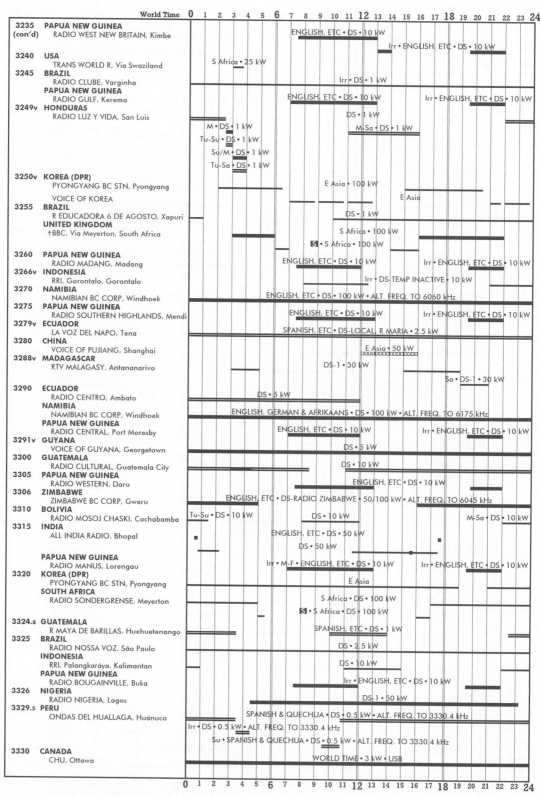

World Time 0 1 2 3 4 5 6 7 8 9 10 11 12 13 14 15 16 17 18 19 20 21 22 23 24

3235 **PAPUA NEW GUINEA**
(con'd)   RADIO WEST NEW BRITAIN, Kimbe — ENGLISH, ETC • DS • 10 kW — Irr • ENGLISH, ETC • DS • 10 kW

3240 **USA**
   TRANS WORLD R, Via Swaziland — S Africa • 25 kW

3245 **BRAZIL**
   RADIO CLUBE, Varginha — Irr • DS • 1 kW
   PAPUA NEW GUINEA
   RADIO GULF, Kerema — ENGLISH, ETC • DS • 10 kW — Irr • ENGLISH, ETC • DS • 10 kW

3249v **HONDURAS**
   RADIO LUZ Y VIDA, San Luis — DS • 1 kW
   M • DS • 1 kW
   M-Sa • DS • 1 kW
   Tu-Su • DS • 1 kW
   Su/M • DS • 1 kW
   Tu-Sa • DS • 1 kW

3250v **KOREA (DPR)**
   PYONGYANG BC STN, Pyongyang — E Asia • 100 kW
   VOICE OF KOREA — E Asia

3255 **BRAZIL**
   R EDUCADORA 6 DE AGOSTO, Xapuri — DS • 1 kW
   UNITED KINGDOM
   †BBC, Via Meyerton, South Africa — S Africa • 100 kW
   S • S Africa • 100 kW

3260 **PAPUA NEW GUINEA**
   RADIO MADANG, Madang — ENGLISH, ETC • DS • 10 kW — Irr • ENGLISH, ETC • DS • 10 kW

3266v **INDONESIA**
   RRI, Gorontalo, Gorontalo — Irr • DS • TEMP INACTIVE • 10 kW

3270 **NAMIBIA**
   NAMIBIAN BC CORP, Windhoek — ENGLISH, ETC • DS • 100 kW • ALT. FREQ. TO 6060 kHz

3275 **PAPUA NEW GUINEA**
   RADIO SOUTHERN HIGHLANDS, Mendi — ENGLISH, ETC • DS • 10 kW — Irr • ENGLISH, ETC • DS • 10 kW

3279v **ECUADOR**
   LA VOZ DEL NAPO, Tena — SPANISH, ETC • DS-LOCAL, R MARIA • 2.5 kW

3280 **CHINA**
   VOICE OF PUJIANG, Shanghai — E Asia • 50 kW

3288v **MADAGASCAR**
   RTV MALAGASY, Antananarivo — DS-1 • 30 kW — Sa • DS-1 • 30 kW

3290 **ECUADOR**
   RADIO CENTRO, Ambato — DS • 5 kW
   NAMIBIA
   NAMIBIAN BC CORP, Windhoek — ENGLISH, GERMAN & AFRIKAANS • DS • 100 kW • ALT. FREQ. TO 6175 kHz
   PAPUA NEW GUINEA
   RADIO CENTRAL, Port Moresby — ENGLISH, ETC • DS • 10 kW — Irr • ENGLISH, ETC • DS • 10 kW

3291v **GUYANA**
   VOICE OF GUYANA, Georgetown — DS • 5 kW

3300 **GUATEMALA**
   RADIO CULTURAL, Guatemala City — DS • 10 kW

3305 **PAPUA NEW GUINEA**
   RADIO WESTERN, Daru — ENGLISH, ETC • DS • 10 kW

3306 **ZIMBABWE**
   ZIMBABWE BC CORP, Gweru — ENGLISH, ETC • DS-RADIO ZIMBABWE • 50/100 kW • ALT. FREQ. TO 6045 kHz

3310 **BOLIVIA**
   RADIO MOSOJ CHASKI, Cochabamba — Tu-Su • DS • 10 kW — DS • 10 kW — M-Sa • DS • 10 kW

3315 **INDIA**
   ALL INDIA RADIO, Bhopal — ENGLISH, ETC • DS • 50 kW
   DS • 50 kW
   PAPUA NEW GUINEA
   RADIO MANUS, Lorengau — Irr • M-F • ENGLISH, ETC • DS • 10 kW — Irr • ENGLISH, ETC • DS • 10 kW

3320 **KOREA (DPR)**
   PYONGYANG BC STN, Pyongyang — E Asia
   SOUTH AFRICA
   RADIO SONDERGRENSE, Meyerton — S Africa • DS • 100 kW
   S • S Africa • DS • 100 kW

3324.8 **GUATEMALA**
   R MAYA DE BARILLAS, Huehuetenango — SPANISH, ETC • DS • 1 kW

3325 **BRAZIL**
   RADIO NOSSA VOZ, São Paulo — DS • 2.5 kW
   INDONESIA
   RRI, Palangkaráya, Kalimantan — DS • 10 kW
   PAPUA NEW GUINEA
   RADIO BOUGAINVILLE, Buka — Irr • ENGLISH, ETC • DS • 10 kW

3326 **NIGERIA**
   RADIO NIGERIA, Lagos — DS-1 • 50 kW

3329.5 **PERU**
   ONDAS DEL HUALLAGA, Huánuco — SPANISH & QUECHUA • DS • 0.5 kW • ALT. FREQ. TO 3330.4 kHz
   Irr • DS • 0.5 kW • ALT. FREQ. TO 3330.4 kHz
   Su • SPANISH & QUECHUA • DS • 0.5 kW • ALT. FREQ. TO 3330.4 kHz

3330 **CANADA**
   CHU, Ottawa — WORLD TIME • 3 kW • USB

0 1 2 3 4 5 6 7 8 9 10 11 12 13 14 15 16 17 18 19 20 21 22 23 24

ENGLISH ▬   ARABIC ⁙   CHINESE ▭▭   FRENCH ▬▬   GERMAN ▬▬   RUSSIAN ══   SPANISH ▬▬   OTHER ▬

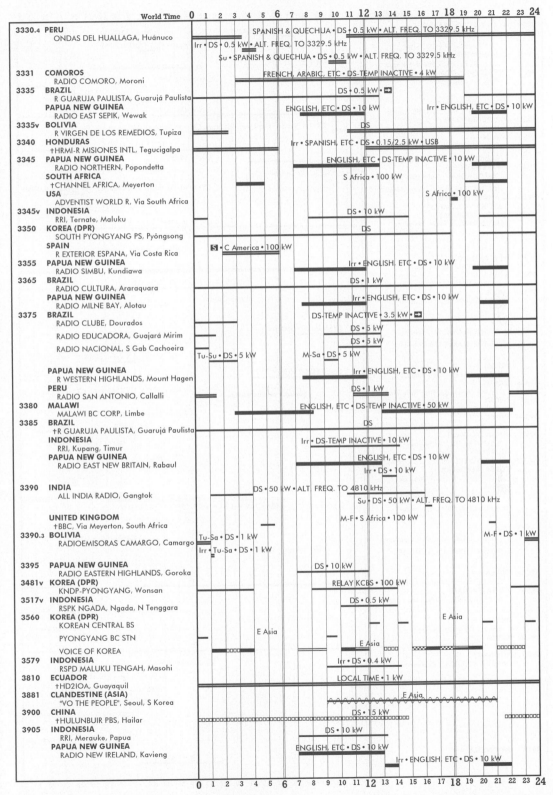

3330.4	**PERU**	
	ONDAS DEL HUALLAGA, Huánuco	SPANISH & QUECHUA • DS • 0.5 kW • ALT. FREQ. TO 3329.5 kHz
		Irr • DS • 0.5 kW • ALT. FREQ. TO 3329.5 kHz
		Su • SPANISH & QUECHUA • DS • 0.5 kW • ALT. FREQ. TO 3329.5 kHz
3331	**COMOROS**	
	RADIO COMORO, Moroni	FRENCH, ARABIC, ETC • DS-TEMP INACTIVE • 4 kW
3335	**BRAZIL**	
	R GUARUJA PAULISTA, Guarujá Paulista	DS • 0.5 kW • ⮕
	PAPUA NEW GUINEA	
	RADIO EAST SEPIK, Wewak	ENGLISH, ETC • DS • 10 kW Irr • ENGLISH, ETC • DS • 10 kW
3335v	**BOLIVIA**	
	R VIRGEN DE LOS REMEDIOS, Tupiza	DS
3340	**HONDURAS**	
	†HRMI-R MISIONES INTL, Tegucigalpa	Irr • SPANISH, ETC • DS • 0.15/2.5 kW • USB
3345	**PAPUA NEW GUINEA**	
	RADIO NORTHERN, Popondetta	ENGLISH, ETC • DS-TEMP INACTIVE • 10 kW
	SOUTH AFRICA	
	†CHANNEL AFRICA, Meyerton	S Africa • 100 kW
	USA	
	ADVENTIST WORLD R, Via South Africa	S Africa • 100 kW
3345v	**INDONESIA**	
	RRI, Ternate, Maluku	DS • 10 kW
3350	**KOREA (DPR)**	
	SOUTH PYONGYANG PS, Pyŏngsong	DS
	SPAIN	
	R EXTERIOR ESPANA, Via Costa Rica	🅂 • C America • 100 kW
3355	**PAPUA NEW GUINEA**	
	RADIO SIMBU, Kundiawa	Irr • ENGLISH, ETC • DS • 10 kW
3365	**BRAZIL**	
	RADIO CULTURA, Araraquara	DS • 1 kW
	PAPUA NEW GUINEA	
	RADIO MILNE BAY, Alotau	Irr • ENGLISH, ETC • DS • 10 kW
3375	**BRAZIL**	
	RADIO CLUBE, Dourados	DS-TEMP INACTIVE • 3.5 kW • ⮕
	RADIO EDUCADORA, Guajará Mirim	DS • 5 kW
	RADIO NACIONAL, S Gab Cachoeira	Tu-Su • DS • 5 kW M-Sa • DS • 5 kW
	PAPUA NEW GUINEA	
	R WESTERN HIGHLANDS, Mount Hagen	Irr • ENGLISH, ETC • DS • 10 kW
	PERU	
	RADIO SAN ANTONIO, Callalli	DS • 1 kW
3380	**MALAWI**	
	MALAWI BC CORP, Limbe	ENGLISH, ETC • DS-TEMP INACTIVE • 50 kW
3385	**BRAZIL**	
	†R GUARUJA PAULISTA, Guarujá Paulista	DS
	INDONESIA	
	RRI, Kupang, Timur	Irr • DS-TEMP INACTIVE • 10 kW
	PAPUA NEW GUINEA	
	RADIO EAST NEW BRITAIN, Rabaul	ENGLISH, ETC • DS • 10 kW
		Irr • DS • 10 kW
3390	**INDIA**	
	ALL INDIA RADIO, Gangtok	DS • 50 kW • ALT. FREQ. TO 4810 kHz
		Su • DS • 50 kW • ALT. FREQ. TO 4810 kHz
	UNITED KINGDOM	
	†BBC, Via Meyerton, South Africa	M-F • S Africa • 100 kW
3390.3	**BOLIVIA**	
	RADIOEMISORAS CAMARGO, Camargo	Tu-Sa • DS • 1 kW M-F • DS • 1 kW
		Irr • Tu-Sa • DS • 1 kW
3395	**PAPUA NEW GUINEA**	
	RADIO EASTERN HIGHLANDS, Goroka	DS • 10 kW
3481v	**KOREA (DPR)**	
	KNDP-PYONGYANG, Wonsan	RELAY KCBS • 100 kW
3517v	**INDONESIA**	
	RSPK NGADA, Ngada, N Tenggara	DS • 0.5 kW
3560	**KOREA (DPR)**	
	KOREAN CENTRAL BS	E Asia
	PYONGYANG BC STN	E Asia
	VOICE OF KOREA	E Asia
3579	**INDONESIA**	
	RSPD MALUKU TENGAH, Masohi	Irr • DS • 0.4 kW
3810	**ECUADOR**	
	†HD2IOA, Guayaquil	LOCAL TIME • 1 kW
3881	**CLANDESTINE (ASIA)**	
	"VO THE PEOPLE", Seoul, S Korea	E Asia
3900	**CHINA**	
	†HULUNBUIR PBS, Hailar	DS • 15 kW
3905	**INDONESIA**	
	RRI, Merauke, Papua	DS • 10 kW
	PAPUA NEW GUINEA	
	RADIO NEW IRELAND, Kavieng	ENGLISH, ETC • DS • 10 kW Irr • ENGLISH, ETC • DS • 10 kW

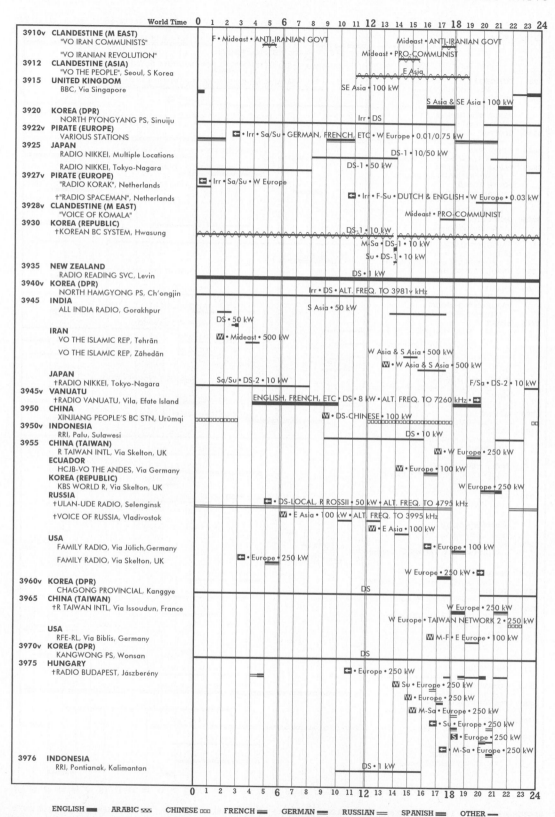

World Time 0 1 2 3 4 5 6 7 8 9 10 11 12 13 14 15 16 17 18 19 20 21 22 23 24

Freq	Station	
3910v	CLANDESTINE (M EAST)	
	"VO IRAN COMMUNISTS"	F • Mideast • ANTI-IRANIAN GOVT Mideast • ANTI-IRANIAN GOVT
	"VO IRANIAN REVOLUTION"	Mideast • PRO-COMMUNIST
3912	CLANDESTINE (ASIA)	
	"VO THE PEOPLE", Seoul, S Korea	E Asia
3915	UNITED KINGDOM	
	BBC, Via Singapore	SE Asia • 100 kW S Asia & SE Asia • 100 kW
3920	KOREA (DPR)	
	NORTH PYONGYANG PS, Sinuiju	Irr • DS
3922v	PIRATE (EUROPE)	
	VARIOUS STATIONS	• Irr • Sa/Su • GERMAN, FRENCH, ETC • W Europe • 0.01/0.75 kW
3925	JAPAN	
	RADIO NIKKEI, Multiple Locations	DS-1 • 10/50 kW
	RADIO NIKKEI, Tokyo-Nagara	DS-1 • 50 kW
3927v	PIRATE (EUROPE)	
	"RADIO KORAK", Netherlands	Irr • Sa/Su • W Europe
	†"RADIO SPACEMAN", Netherlands	• Irr • F-Su • DUTCH & ENGLISH • W Europe • 0.03 kW
3928v	CLANDESTINE (M EAST)	
	"VOICE OF KOMALA"	Mideast • PRO-COMMUNIST
3930	KOREA (REPUBLIC)	
	†KOREAN BC SYSTEM, Hwasung	DS-1 • 10 kW
		M-Sa • DS-1 • 10 kW
		Su • DS-1 • 10 kW
3935	NEW ZEALAND	
	RADIO READING SVC, Levin	DS • 1 kW
3940v	KOREA (DPR)	
	NORTH HAMGYONG PS, Ch'ongjin	Irr • DS • ALT. FREQ. TO 3981v kHz
3945	INDIA	
	ALL INDIA RADIO, Gorakhpur	S Asia • 50 kW DS • 50 kW
	IRAN	
	VO THE ISLAMIC REP, Tehrān	W • Mideast • 500 kW
	VO THE ISLAMIC REP, Zāhedān	W Asia & S Asia • 500 kW W • W Asia & S Asia • 500 kW
	JAPAN	
	†RADIO NIKKEI, Tokyo-Nagara	Sa/Su • DS-2 • 10 kW F/Sa • DS-2 • 10 kW
3945v	VANUATU	
	†RADIO VANUATU, Vila, Efate Island	ENGLISH, FRENCH, ETC • DS • 8 kW • ALT. FREQ. TO 7260 kHz •
3950	CHINA	
	XINJIANG PEOPLE'S BC STN, Urümqi	W • DS-CHINESE • 100 kW
3950v	INDONESIA	
	RRI, Palu, Sulawesi	DS • 10 kW
3955	CHINA (TAIWAN)	
	R TAIWAN INTL, Via Skelton, UK	W • W Europe • 250 kW
	ECUADOR	
	HCJB-VO THE ANDES, Via Germany	W • Europe • 100 kW
	KOREA (REPUBLIC)	
	KBS WORLD R, Via Skelton, UK	W Europe • 250 kW
	RUSSIA	
	†ULAN-UDE RADIO, Selenginsk	• DS-LOCAL, R ROSSII • 50 kW • ALT. FREQ. TO 4795 kHz
	†VOICE OF RUSSIA, Vladivostok	W • E Asia • 100 kW • ALT. FREQ. TO 3995 kHz W • E Asia • 100 kW
	USA	
	FAMILY RADIO, Via Jülich, Germany	• Europe • 100 kW
	FAMILY RADIO, Via Skelton, UK	• Europe • 250 kW W Europe • 250 kW •
3960v	KOREA (DPR)	
	CHAGONG PROVINCIAL, Kanggye	DS
3965	CHINA (TAIWAN)	
	†R TAIWAN INTL, Via Issoudun, France	W Europe • 250 kW W Europe • TAIWAN NETWORK 2 • 250 kW
	USA	
	RFE-RL, Via Biblis, Germany	W M-F • E Europe • 100 kW
3970v	KOREA (DPR)	
	KANGWONG PS, Wonsan	DS
3975	HUNGARY	
	†RADIO BUDAPEST, Jászberény	• Europe • 250 kW
		W Su • Europe • 250 kW
		W • Europe • 250 kW
		W M-Sa • Europe • 250 kW
		• Su • Europe • 250 kW
		S • Europe • 250 kW
		• M-Sa • Europe • 250 kW
3976	INDONESIA	
	RRI, Pontianak, Kalimantan	DS • 1 kW

0 1 2 3 4 5 6 7 8 9 10 11 12 13 14 15 16 17 18 19 20 21 22 23 24

ENGLISH ▬   ARABIC ▨   CHINESE ▢▢▢   FRENCH ▭   GERMAN ▬   RUSSIAN ═   SPANISH ▬   OTHER ▬

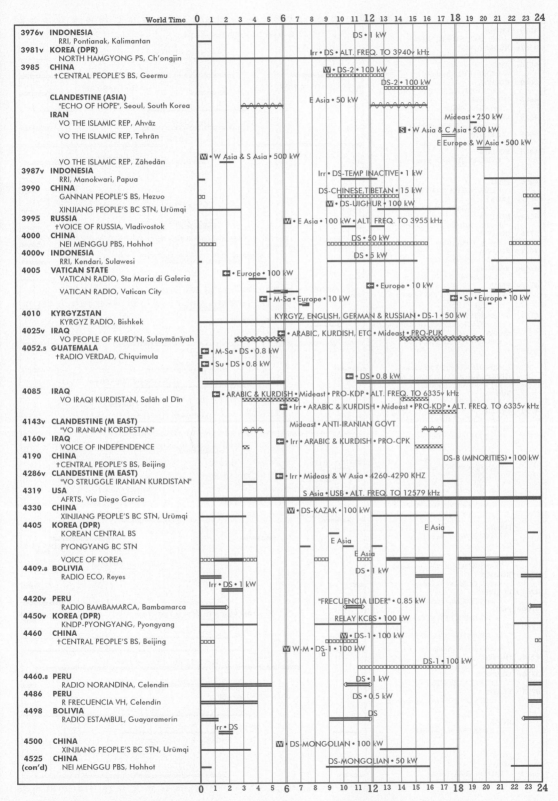

World Time

Freq	Country / Station	
3976v	**INDONESIA** — RRI, Pontianak, Kalimantan	DS • 1 kW
3981v	**KOREA (DPR)** — NORTH HAMGYONG PS, Ch'ongjin	Irr • DS • ALT. FREQ. TO 3940v kHz
3985	**CHINA** — †CENTRAL PEOPLE'S BS, Geermu	W • DS-2 • 100 kW / DS-2 • 100 kW
	CLANDESTINE (ASIA) — "ECHO OF HOPE", Seoul, South Korea	E Asia • 50 kW
	IRAN — VO THE ISLAMIC REP, Ahvāz	Mideast • 250 kW
	VO THE ISLAMIC REP, Tehrān	S • W Asia & C Asia • 500 kW / E Europe & W Asia • 500 kW
	VO THE ISLAMIC REP, Zāhedān	W • W Asia & S Asia • 500 kW
3987v	**INDONESIA** — RRI, Manokwari, Papua	Irr • DS-TEMP INACTIVE • 1 kW
3990	**CHINA** — GANNAN PEOPLE'S BS, Hezuo	DS-CHINESE,TIBETAN • 15 kW
	XINJIANG PEOPLE'S BC STN, Urümqi	W • DS-UIGHUR • 100 kW
3995	**RUSSIA** — †VOICE OF RUSSIA, Vladivostok	W • E Asia • 100 kW • ALT. FREQ. TO 3955 kHz
4000	**CHINA** — NEI MENGGU PBS, Hohhot	DS • 50 kW
4000v	**INDONESIA** — RRI, Kendari, Sulawesi	DS • 5 kW
4005	**VATICAN STATE** — VATICAN RADIO, Sta Maria di Galeria	← • Europe • 100 kW / ← • Europe • 10 kW
	VATICAN RADIO, Vatican City	← • M-Sa • Europe • 10 kW / ← • Su • Europe • 10 kW
4010	**KYRGYZSTAN** — KYRGYZ RADIO, Bishkek	KYRGYZ, ENGLISH, GERMAN & RUSSIAN • DS-1 • 50 kW
4025v	**IRAQ** — VO PEOPLE OF KURD'N, Sulaymānīyah	← • ARABIC, KURDISH, ETC • Mideast • PRO-PUK
4052.5	**GUATEMALA** — †RADIO VERDAD, Chiquimula	← • M-Sa • DS • 0.8 kW / ← • Su • DS • 0.8 kW / ← • DS • 0.8 kW
4085	**IRAQ** — VO IRAQI KURDISTAN, Salāh al Dīn	← • ARABIC & KURDISH • Mideast • PRO-KDP • ALT. FREQ. TO 6335v kHz / ← • Irr • ARABIC & KURDISH • Mideast • PRO-KDP • ALT. FREQ. TO 6335v kHz
4143v	**CLANDESTINE (M EAST)** — "VO IRANIAN KORDESTAN"	Mideast • ANTI-IRANIAN GOVT
4160v	**IRAQ** — VOICE OF INDEPENDENCE	← • Irr • ARABIC & KURDISH • PRO-CPK
4190	**CHINA** — †CENTRAL PEOPLE'S BS, Beijing	DS-8 (MINORITIES) • 100 kW
4286v	**CLANDESTINE (M EAST)** — "VO STRUGGLE IRANIAN KURDISTAN"	← • Irr • Mideast & W Asia • 4260-4290 KHZ
4319	**USA** — AFRTS, Via Diego Garcia	S Asia • USB • ALT. FREQ. TO 12579 kHz
4330	**CHINA** — XINJIANG PEOPLE'S BC STN, Urümqi	W • DS-KAZAK • 100 kW
4405	**KOREA (DPR)** — KOREAN CENTRAL BS	E Asia
	PYONGYANG BC STN	E Asia
	VOICE OF KOREA	E Asia
4409.8	**BOLIVIA** — RADIO ECO, Reyes	DS • 1 kW / Irr • DS • 1 kW
4420v	**PERU** — RADIO BAMBAMARCA, Bambamarca	"FRECUENCIA LIDER" • 0.85 kW
4450v	**KOREA (DPR)** — KNDP-PYONGYANG, Pyongyang	RELAY KCBS • 100 kW
4460	**CHINA** — †CENTRAL PEOPLE'S BS, Beijing	W • DS-1 • 100 kW / W • W-M • DS-1 • 100 kW / DS-1 • 100 kW
4460.8	**PERU** — RADIO NORANDINA, Celendin	DS • 1 kW
4486	**PERU** — R FRECUENCIA VH, Celendin	DS • 0.5 kW
4498	**BOLIVIA** — RADIO ESTAMBUL, Guayaramerín	DS / Irr • DS
4500	**CHINA** — XINJIANG PEOPLE'S BC STN, Urümqi	W • DS-MONGOLIAN • 100 kW
4525 (con'd)	**CHINA** — NEI MENGGU PBS, Hohhot	DS-MONGOLIAN • 50 kW

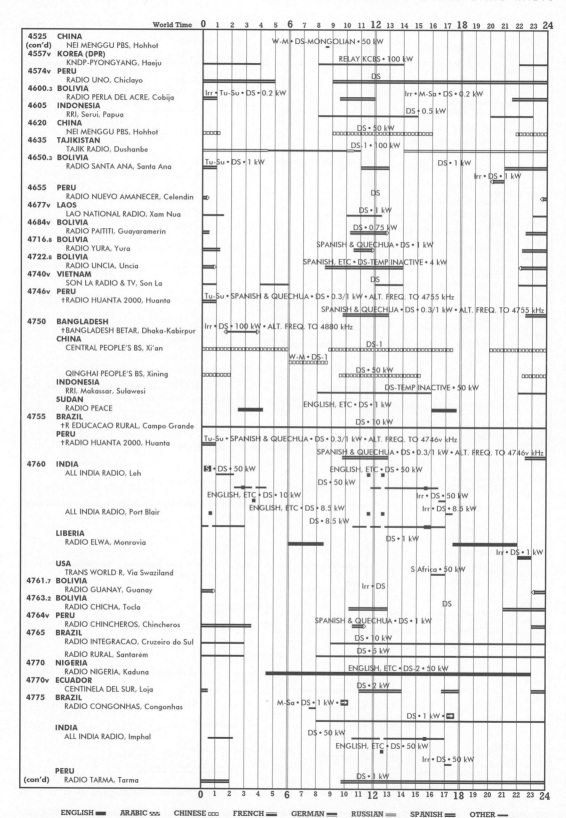

World Time 0 1 2 3 4 5 6 7 8 9 10 11 12 13 14 15 16 17 18 19 20 21 22 23 24

Freq	Country / Station	Notes
4525 (con'd)	CHINA — NEI MENGGU PBS, Hohhot	W-M • DS-MONGOLIAN • 50 kW
4557v	KOREA (DPR) — KNDP-PYONGYANG, Haeju	RELAY KCBS • 100 kW
4574v	PERU — RADIO UNO, Chiclayo	DS
4600.3	BOLIVIA — RADIO PERLA DEL ACRE, Cobija	Irr • Tu-Su • DS • 0.2 kW Irr • M-Sa • DS • 0.2 kW
4605	INDONESIA — RRI, Serui, Papua	DS • 0.5 kW
4620	CHINA — NEI MENGGU PBS, Hohhot	DS • 50 kW
4635	TAJIKISTAN — TAJIK RADIO, Dushanbe	DS-1 • 100 kW
4650.3	BOLIVIA — RADIO SANTA ANA, Santa Ana	Tu-Su • DS • 1 kW DS • 1 kW Irr • DS • 1 kW
4655	PERU — RADIO NUEVO AMANECER, Celendin	DS
4677v	LAOS — LAO NATIONAL RADIO, Xam Nua	DS • 1 kW
4684v	BOLIVIA — RADIO PAITITI, Guayaramerin	DS • 0.75 kW
4716.8	BOLIVIA — RADIO YURA, Yura	SPANISH & QUECHUA • DS • 1 kW
4722.8	BOLIVIA — RADIO UNCIA, Uncia	SPANISH, ETC • DS-TEMP INACTIVE • 4 kW
4740v	VIETNAM — SON LA RADIO & TV, Son La	DS
4746v	PERU — †RADIO HUANTA 2000, Huanta	Tu-Su • SPANISH & QUECHUA • DS • 0.3/1 kW • ALT. FREQ. TO 4755 kHz SPANISH & QUECHUA • DS • 0.3/1 kW • ALT. FREQ. TO 4755 kHz
4750	BANGLADESH — †BANGLADESH BETAR, Dhaka-Kabirpur	Irr • DS • 100 kW • ALT. FREQ. TO 4880 kHz
	CHINA — CENTRAL PEOPLE'S BS, Xi'an	DS-1 W-M • DS-1
	QINGHAI PEOPLE'S BS, Xining	DS • 50 kW
	INDONESIA — RRI, Makassar, Sulawesi	DS-TEMP INACTIVE • 50 kW
	SUDAN — RADIO PEACE	ENGLISH, ETC • DS • 1 kW
4755	BRAZIL — †R EDUCACAO RURAL, Campo Grande	DS • 10 kW
	PERU — †RADIO HUANTA 2000, Huanta	Tu-Su • SPANISH & QUECHUA • DS • 0.3/1 kW • ALT. FREQ. TO 4746v kHz SPANISH & QUECHUA • DS • 0.3/1 kW • ALT. FREQ. TO 4746v kHz
4760	INDIA — ALL INDIA RADIO, Leh	S • DS • 50 kW ENGLISH, ETC • DS • 50 kW DS • 50 kW
	ALL INDIA RADIO, Port Blair	ENGLISH, ETC • DS • 10 kW Irr • DS • 50 kW ENGLISH, ETC • DS • 8.5 kW Irr • DS • 8.5 kW DS • 8.5 kW
	LIBERIA — RADIO ELWA, Monrovia	DS • 1 kW Irr • DS • 1 kW
	USA — TRANS WORLD R, Via Swaziland	S Africa • 50 kW
4761.7	BOLIVIA — RADIO GUANAY, Guanay	Irr • DS
4763.2	BOLIVIA — RADIO CHICHA, Tocla	DS
4764v	PERU — RADIO CHINCHEROS, Chincheros	SPANISH & QUECHUA • DS • 1 kW
4765	BRAZIL — RADIO INTEGRACAO, Cruzeiro do Sul	DS • 10 kW
	RADIO RURAL, Santarém	DS • 5 kW
4770	NIGERIA — RADIO NIGERIA, Kaduna	ENGLISH, ETC • DS-2 • 50 kW
4770v	ECUADOR — CENTINELA DEL SUR, Loja	DS • 2 kW
4775	BRAZIL — RADIO CONGONHAS, Congonhas	M-Sa • DS • 1 kW • DS • 1 kW •
	INDIA — ALL INDIA RADIO, Imphal	DS • 50 kW ENGLISH, ETC • DS • 50 kW Irr • DS • 50 kW
(con'd)	PERU — RADIO TARMA, Tarma	DS • 1 kW

World Time 0 1 2 3 4 5 6 7 8 9 10 11 12 13 14 15 16 17 18 19 20 21 22 23 24

ENGLISH ▬   ARABIC ▨   CHINESE ▫▫▫   FRENCH ▬▬   GERMAN ▬▬   RUSSIAN ═══   SPANISH ▬▬   OTHER ▬

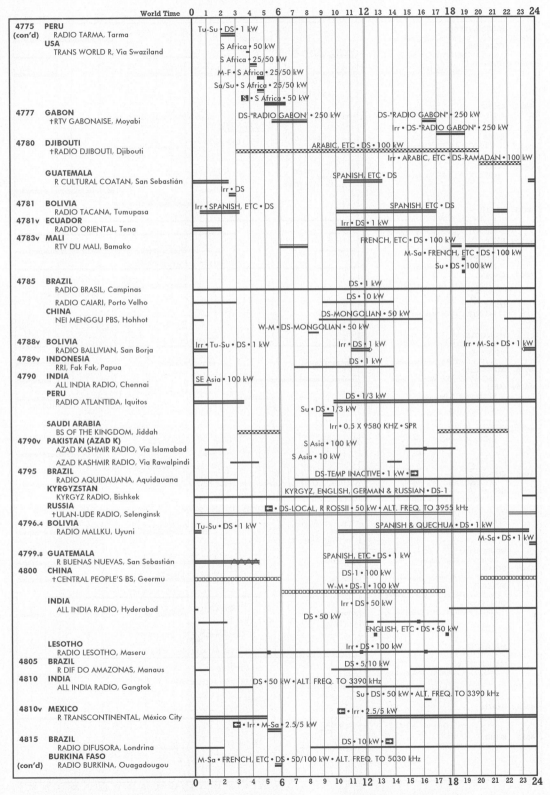

World Time		0 1 2 3 4 5 6 7 8 9 10 11 12 13 14 15 16 17 18 19 20 21 22 23 24
4775	**PERU**	
(con'd)	RADIO TARMA, Tarma	Tu-Su • DS • 1 kW
	USA	
	TRANS WORLD R, Via Swaziland	S Africa • 50 kW
		S Africa • 25/50 kW
		M-F • S Africa • 25/50 kW
		Sa/Su • S Africa • 25/50 kW
		S • S Africa • 50 kW
4777	**GABON**	
	†RTV GABONAISE, Moyabi	DS-"RADIO GABON" • 250 kW DS-"RADIO GABON" • 250 kW
		Irr • DS-"RADIO GABON" • 250 kW
4780	**DJIBOUTI**	
	†RADIO DJIBOUTI, Djibouti	ARABIC, ETC • DS • 100 kW
		Irr • ARABIC, ETC • DS-RAMADAN • 100 kW
	GUATEMALA	
	R CULTURAL COATAN, San Sebastián	SPANISH, ETC • DS
		Irr • DS
4781	**BOLIVIA**	
	RADIO TACANA, Tumupasa	Irr • SPANISH, ETC • DS SPANISH, ETC • DS
4781v	**ECUADOR**	
	RADIO ORIENTAL, Tena	Irr • DS • 1 kW
4783v	**MALI**	
	RTV DU MALI, Bamako	FRENCH, ETC • DS • 100 kW
		M-Sa • FRENCH, ETC • DS • 100 kW
		Su • DS • 100 kW
4785	**BRAZIL**	
	RADIO BRASIL, Campinas	DS • 1 kW
	RADIO CAIARI, Porto Velho	DS • 10 kW
	CHINA	
	NEI MENGGU PBS, Hohhot	DS-MONGOLIAN • 50 kW
		W-M • DS-MONGOLIAN • 50 kW
4788v	**BOLIVIA**	
	RADIO BALLIVIAN, San Borja	Irr • Tu-Su • DS • 1 kW Irr • DS • 1 kW Irr • M-Sa • DS • 1 kW
4789v	**INDONESIA**	
	RRI, Fak Fak, Papua	DS • 1 kW
4790	**INDIA**	
	ALL INDIA RADIO, Chennai	SE Asia • 100 kW
	PERU	
	RADIO ATLANTIDA, Iquitos	DS • 1/3 kW
		Su • DS • 1/3 kW
	SAUDI ARABIA	
	BS OF THE KINGDOM, Jiddah	Irr • 0.5 X 9580 KHZ • SPR
4790v	**PAKISTAN (AZAD K)**	
	AZAD KASHMIR RADIO, Via Islamabad	S Asia • 100 kW
	AZAD KASHMIR RADIO, Via Rawalpindi	S Asia • 10 kW
4795	**BRAZIL**	
	RADIO AQUIDAUANA, Aquidauana	DS-TEMP INACTIVE • 1 kW • ➡
	KYRGYZSTAN	
	KYRGYZ RADIO, Bishkek	KYRGYZ, ENGLISH, GERMAN & RUSSIAN • DS-1
	RUSSIA	
	†ULAN-UDE RADIO, Selenginsk	⬅ • DS-LOCAL, R ROSSII • 50 kW • ALT. FREQ. TO 3955 kHz
4796.4	**BOLIVIA**	
	RADIO MALLKU, Uyuni	Tu-Su • DS • 1 kW SPANISH & QUECHUA • DS • 1 kW
		M-Sa • DS • 1 kW
4799.8	**GUATEMALA**	
	R BUENAS NUEVAS, San Sebastián	SPANISH, ETC • DS • 1 kW
4800	**CHINA**	
	†CENTRAL PEOPLE'S BS, Geermu	DS-1 • 100 kW
		W-M • DS-1 • 100 kW
	INDIA	
	ALL INDIA RADIO, Hyderabad	Irr • DS • 50 kW
		DS • 50 kW
		ENGLISH, ETC • DS • 50 kW
	LESOTHO	
	RADIO LESOTHO, Maseru	Irr • DS • 100 kW
4805	**BRAZIL**	
	R DIF DO AMAZONAS, Manaus	DS • 5/10 kW
4810	**INDIA**	
	ALL INDIA RADIO, Gangtok	DS • 50 kW • ALT. FREQ. TO 3390 kHz
		Su • DS • 50 kW • ALT. FREQ. TO 3390 kHz
4810v	**MEXICO**	
	R TRANSCONTINENTAL, México City	⬅ • Irr • 2.5/5 kW
		⬅ • Irr • M-Sa • 2.5/5 kW
4815	**BRAZIL**	
	RADIO DIFUSORA, Londrina	DS • 10 kW • ➡
	BURKINA FASO	
(con'd)	RADIO BURKINA, Ouagadougou	M-Sa • FRENCH, ETC • DS • 50/100 kW • ALT. FREQ. TO 5030 kHz

0 1 2 3 4 5 6 7 8 9 10 11 12 13 14 15 16 17 18 19 20 21 22 23 24

SEASONAL S OR W   1-HR TIMESHIFT MIDYEAR ⬅ OR ➡   JAMMING / OR ∧   EARLIEST HEARD ◁   LATEST HEARD ▷   NEW FOR 2007 †

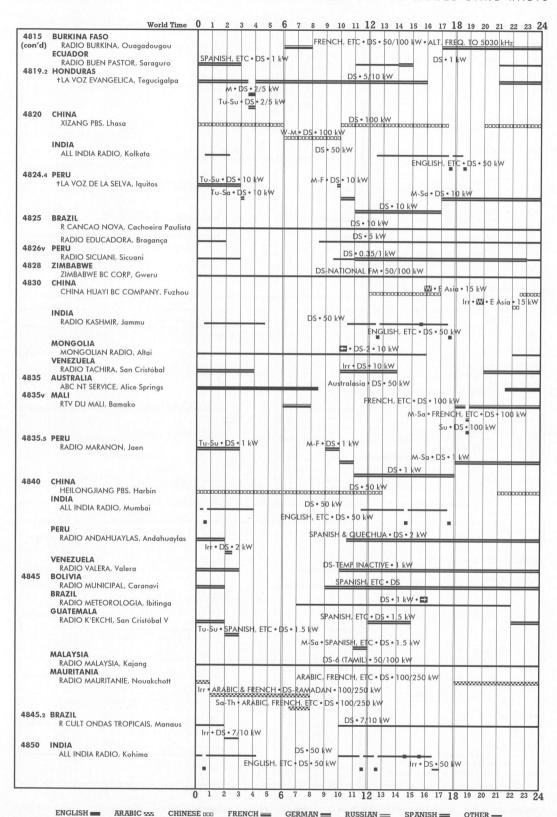

World Time 0 1 2 3 4 5 6 7 8 9 10 11 12 13 14 15 16 17 18 19 20 21 22 23 24

4815 **BURKINA FASO**
(con'd)   RADIO BURKINA, Ouagadougou — FRENCH, ETC • DS • 50/100 kW • ALT. FREQ. TO 5030 kHz
ECUADOR
    RADIO BUEN PASTOR, Saraguro — SPANISH, ETC • DS • 1 kW / DS • 1 kW
4819.2 **HONDURAS**
    †LA VOZ EVANGELICA, Tegucigalpa — DS • 5/10 kW
    M • DS • 2/5 kW
    Tu-Su • DS • 2/5 kW

4820 **CHINA**
    XIZANG PBS, Lhasa — DS • 100 kW
    W-M • DS • 100 kW

INDIA
    ALL INDIA RADIO, Kolkata — DS • 50 kW
    ENGLISH, ETC • DS • 50 kW

4824.4 **PERU**
    †LA VOZ DE LA SELVA, Iquitos — Tu-Su • DS • 10 kW / M-F • DS • 10 kW
    Tu-Sa • DS • 10 kW
    M-Sa • DS • 10 kW
    DS • 10 kW

4825 **BRAZIL**
    R CANCAO NOVA, Cachoeira Paulista — DS • 10 kW
    RADIO EDUCADORA, Bragança — DS • 5 kW
4826v **PERU**
    RADIO SICUANI, Sicuani — DS • 0.35/1 kW
4828 **ZIMBABWE**
    ZIMBABWE BC CORP, Gweru — DS-NATIONAL FM • 50/100 kW
4830 **CHINA**
    CHINA HUAYI BC COMPANY, Fuzhou — W • E Asia • 15 kW
    Irr • W • E Asia • 15 kW

INDIA
    RADIO KASHMIR, Jammu — DS • 50 kW
    ENGLISH, ETC • DS • 50 kW

MONGOLIA
    MONGOLIAN RADIO, Altai — DS-2 • 10 kW
VENEZUELA
    RADIO TACHIRA, San Cristóbal — Irr • DS • 10 kW
4835 **AUSTRALIA**
    ABC NT SERVICE, Alice Springs — Australasia • DS • 50 kW
4835v **MALI**
    RTV DU MALI, Bamako — FRENCH, ETC • DS • 100 kW
    M-Sa • FRENCH, ETC • DS • 100 kW
    Su • DS • 100 kW

4835.5 **PERU**
    RADIO MARANON, Jaen — Tu-Su • DS • 1 kW / M-F • DS • 1 kW
    M-Sa • DS • 1 kW
    DS • 1 kW

4840 **CHINA**
    HEILONGJIANG PBS, Harbin — DS • 50 kW
INDIA
    ALL INDIA RADIO, Mumbai — DS • 50 kW
    ENGLISH, ETC • DS • 50 kW

PERU
    RADIO ANDAHUAYLAS, Andahuaylas — SPANISH & QUECHUA • DS • 2 kW
    Irr • DS • 2 kW

VENEZUELA
    RADIO VALERA, Valera — DS-TEMP INACTIVE • 1 kW
4845 **BOLIVIA**
    RADIO MUNICIPAL, Caranavi — SPANISH, ETC • DS
BRAZIL
    RADIO METEOROLOGIA, Ibitinga — DS • 1 kW
GUATEMALA
    RADIO K'EKCHI, San Cristóbal V — SPANISH, ETC • DS • 1.5 kW
    Tu-Su • SPANISH, ETC • DS • 1.5 kW
    M-Sa • SPANISH, ETC • DS • 1.5 kW

MALAYSIA
    RADIO MALAYSIA, Kajang — DS-6 (TAMIL) • 50/100 kW
MAURITANIA
    RADIO MAURITANIE, Nouakchott — ARABIC, FRENCH, ETC • DS • 100/250 kW
    Irr • ARABIC & FRENCH • DS-RAMADAN • 100/250 kW
    Sa-Th • ARABIC, FRENCH, ETC • DS • 100/250 kW

4845.2 **BRAZIL**
    R CULT ONDAS TROPICAIS, Manaus — DS • 7/10 kW
    Irr • DS • 7/10 kW

4850 **INDIA**
    ALL INDIA RADIO, Kohima — DS • 50 kW
    ENGLISH, ETC • DS • 50 kW
    Irr • DS • 50 kW

0 1 2 3 4 5 6 7 8 9 10 11 12 13 14 15 16 17 18 19 20 21 22 23 24

ENGLISH ▬ ARABIC ⋙ CHINESE ▭▭ FRENCH ▬ GERMAN ▬ RUSSIAN ═ SPANISH ▬ OTHER ▬

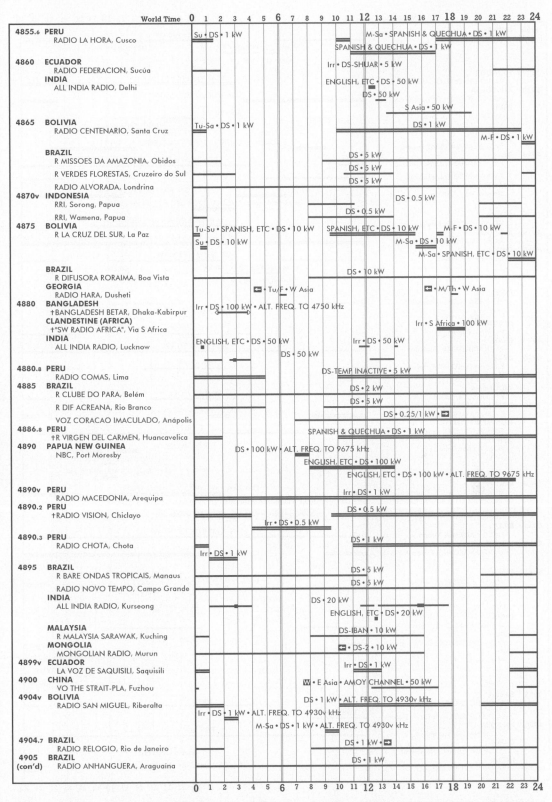

World Time   0 1 2 3 4 5 6 7 8 9 10 11 12 13 14 15 16 17 18 19 20 21 22 23 24

4855.6 PERU
RADIO LA HORA, Cusco — Su • DS • 1 kW — M-Sa • SPANISH & QUECHUA • DS • 1 kW
SPANISH & QUECHUA • DS • 1 kW

4860 ECUADOR
RADIO FEDERACION, Sucúa — Irr • DS-SHUAR • 5 kW
INDIA
ALL INDIA RADIO, Delhi — ENGLISH, ETC • DS • 50 kW
DS • 50 kW
S Asia • 50 kW

4865 BOLIVIA
RADIO CENTENARIO, Santa Cruz — Tu-Sa • DS • 1 kW — DS • 1 kW — M-F • DS • 1 kW

BRAZIL
R MISSOES DA AMAZONIA, Obidos — DS • 5 kW
R VERDES FLORESTAS, Cruzeiro do Sul — DS • 5 kW
RADIO ALVORADA, Londrina — DS • 5 kW

4870v INDONESIA
RRI, Sorong, Papua — DS • 0.5 kW
RRI, Wamena, Papua — DS • 0.5 kW

4875 BOLIVIA
R LA CRUZ DEL SUR, La Paz — Tu-Su • SPANISH, ETC • DS • 10 kW — SPANISH, ETC • DS • 10 kW — M-F • DS • 10 kW
Su • DS • 10 kW — M-Sa • DS • 10 kW
M-Sa • SPANISH, ETC • DS • 10 kW

BRAZIL
R DIFUSORA RORAIMA, Boa Vista — DS • 10 kW
GEORGIA
RADIO HARA, Dusheti — Tu/F • W Asia — M/Th • W Asia

4880 BANGLADESH
†BANGLADESH BETAR, Dhaka-Kabirpur — Irr • DS • 100 kW • ALT. FREQ. TO 4750 kHz
CLANDESTINE (AFRICA)
†"SW RADIO AFRICA", Via S Africa — Irr • S Africa • 100 kW
INDIA
ALL INDIA RADIO, Lucknow — ENGLISH, ETC • DS • 50 kW — Irr • DS • 50 kW
DS • 50 kW

4880.8 PERU
RADIO COMAS, Lima — DS-TEMP INACTIVE • 5 kW

4885 BRAZIL
R CLUBE DO PARA, Belém — DS • 2 kW
R DIF ACREANA, Rio Branco — DS • 5 kW
VOZ CORACAO IMACULADO, Anápolis — DS • 0.25/1 kW

4886.8 PERU
†R VIRGEN DEL CARMEN, Huancavelica — SPANISH & QUECHUA • DS • 1 kW

4890 PAPUA NEW GUINEA
NBC, Port Moresby — DS • 100 kW • ALT. FREQ. TO 9675 kHz
ENGLISH, ETC • DS • 100 kW
ENGLISH, ETC • DS • 100 kW • ALT. FREQ. TO 9675 kHz

4890v PERU
RADIO MACEDONIA, Arequipa — Irr • DS • 1 kW

4890.2 PERU
†RADIO VISION, Chiclayo — DS • 0.5 kW
Irr • DS • 0.5 kW

4890.3 PERU
RADIO CHOTA, Chota — DS • 1 kW
Irr • DS • 1 kW

4895 BRAZIL
R BARE ONDAS TROPICAIS, Manaus — DS • 5 kW
RADIO NOVO TEMPO, Campo Grande — DS • 5 kW
INDIA
ALL INDIA RADIO, Kurseong — DS • 20 kW
ENGLISH, ETC • DS • 20 kW
MALAYSIA
R MALAYSIA SARAWAK, Kuching — DS-IBAN • 10 kW
MONGOLIA
MONGOLIAN RADIO, Murun — DS-2 • 10 kW

4899v ECUADOR
LA VOZ DE SAQUISILI, Saquisili — Irr • DS • 1 kW

4900 CHINA
VO THE STRAIT-PLA, Fuzhou — W • E Asia • AMOY CHANNEL • 50 kW

4904v BOLIVIA
RADIO SAN MIGUEL, Riberalta — DS • 1 kW • ALT. FREQ. TO 4930v kHz
Irr • DS • 1 kW • ALT. FREQ. TO 4930v kHz
M-Sa • DS • 1 kW • ALT. FREQ. TO 4930v kHz

4904.7 BRAZIL
RADIO RELOGIO, Rio de Janeiro — DS • 1 kW

4905 BRAZIL
(con'd) RADIO ANHANGUERA, Araguaina — DS • 1 kW

0 1 2 3 4 5 6 7 8 9 10 11 12 13 14 15 16 17 18 19 20 21 22 23 24

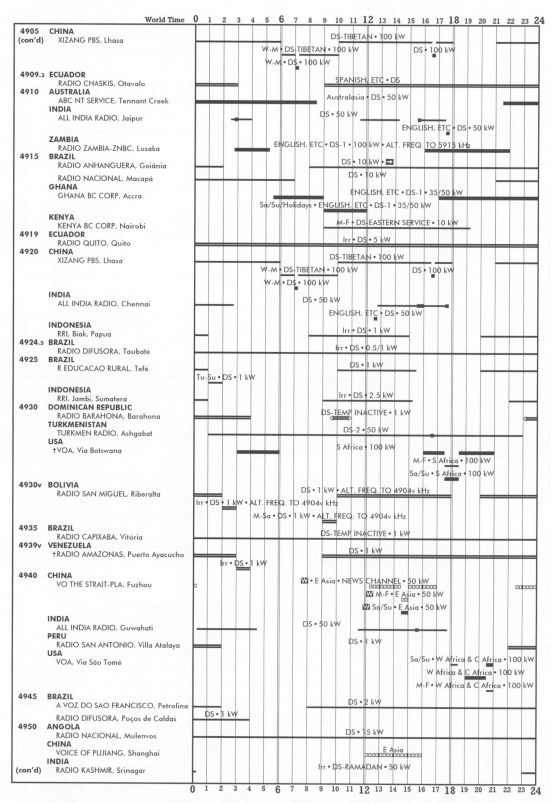

| World Time | 0 | 1 | 2 | 3 | 4 | 5 | 6 | 7 | 8 | 9 | 10 | 11 | 12 | 13 | 14 | 15 | 16 | 17 | 18 | 19 | 20 | 21 | 22 | 23 | 24 |

4905 CHINA
(con'd)   XIZANG PBS, Lhasa
- DS-TIBETAN • 100 kW
- W-M • DS-TIBETAN • 100 kW   DS • 100 kW
- W-M • DS • 100 kW

4909.3 ECUADOR
    RADIO CHASKIS, Otavalo
- SPANISH, ETC • DS

4910 AUSTRALIA
    ABC NT SERVICE, Tennant Creek
- Australasia • DS • 50 kW

    INDIA
    ALL INDIA RADIO, Jaipur
- DS • 50 kW
- ENGLISH, ETC • DS • 50 kW

    ZAMBIA
    RADIO ZAMBIA-ZNBC, Lusaka
- ENGLISH, ETC • DS-1 • 100 kW • ALT. FREQ. TO 5915 kHz

4915 BRAZIL
    RADIO ANHANGUERA, Goiânia
- DS • 10 kW ➡

    RADIO NACIONAL, Macapá
- DS • 10 kW

    GHANA
    GHANA BC CORP, Accra
- ENGLISH, ETC • DS-1 • 35/50 kW
- Sa/Su/Holidays • ENGLISH, ETC • DS-1 • 35/50 kW

    KENYA
    KENYA BC CORP, Nairobi
- M-F • DS-EASTERN SERVICE • 10 kW

4919 ECUADOR
    RADIO QUITO, Quito
- Irr • DS • 5 kW

4920 CHINA
    XIZANG PBS, Lhasa
- DS-TIBETAN • 100 kW
- W-M • DS-TIBETAN • 100 kW   DS • 100 kW
- W-M • DS • 100 kW

    INDIA
    ALL INDIA RADIO, Chennai
- DS • 50 kW
- ENGLISH, ETC • DS • 50 kW

    INDONESIA
    RRI, Biak, Papua
- Irr • DS • 1 kW

4924.5 BRAZIL
    RADIO DIFUSORA, Taubaté
- Irr • DS • 0.5/1 kW

4925 BRAZIL
    R EDUCACAO RURAL, Tefé
- DS • 1 kW
- Tu-Su • DS • 1 kW

    INDONESIA
    RRI, Jambi, Sumatera
- Irr • DS • 2.5 kW

4930 DOMINICAN REPUBLIC
    RADIO BARAHONA, Barahona
- DS-TEMP INACTIVE • 1 kW

    TURKMENISTAN
    TURKMEN RADIO, Ashgabat
- DS-2 • 50 kW

    USA
    †VOA, Via Botswana
- S Africa • 100 kW
- M-F • S Africa • 100 kW
- Sa/Su • S Africa • 100 kW

4930v BOLIVIA
    RADIO SAN MIGUEL, Riberalta
- DS • 1 kW • ALT. FREQ. TO 4904v kHz
- Irr • DS • 1 kW • ALT. FREQ. TO 4904v kHz
- M-Sa • DS • 1 kW • ALT. FREQ. TO 4904v kHz

4935 BRAZIL
    RADIO CAPIXABA, Vitória
- DS-TEMP INACTIVE • 1 kW

4939v VENEZUELA
    †RADIO AMAZONAS, Puerto Ayacucho
- DS • 1 kW
- Irr • DS • 1 kW

4940 CHINA
    VO THE STRAIT-PLA, Fuzhou
- W • E Asia • NEWS CHANNEL • 50 kW
- W M-F • E Asia • 50 kW
- W Sa/Su • E Asia • 50 kW

    INDIA
    ALL INDIA RADIO, Guwahati
- DS • 50 kW

    PERU
    RADIO SAN ANTONIO, Villa Atalaya
- DS • 1 kW

    USA
    VOA, Via São Tomé
- Sa/Su • W Africa & C Africa • 100 kW
- W Africa & C Africa • 100 kW
- M-F • W Africa & C Africa • 100 kW

4945 BRAZIL
    A VOZ DO SAO FRANCISCO, Petrolina
- DS • 2 kW

    RADIO DIFUSORA, Poços de Caldas
- DS • 1 kW

4950 ANGOLA
    RADIO NACIONAL, Mulenvos
- DS • 15 kW

    CHINA
    VOICE OF PUJIANG, Shanghai
- E Asia

    INDIA
(con'd)   RADIO KASHMIR, Srinagar
- Irr • DS-RAMADAN • 50 kW

| | 0 | 1 | 2 | 3 | 4 | 5 | 6 | 7 | 8 | 9 | 10 | 11 | 12 | 13 | 14 | 15 | 16 | 17 | 18 | 19 | 20 | 21 | 22 | 23 | 24 |

ENGLISH ▬   ARABIC ∾∾∾   CHINESE ▫▫▫   FRENCH ▬   GERMAN ▬   RUSSIAN ═   SPANISH ▬   OTHER ▬

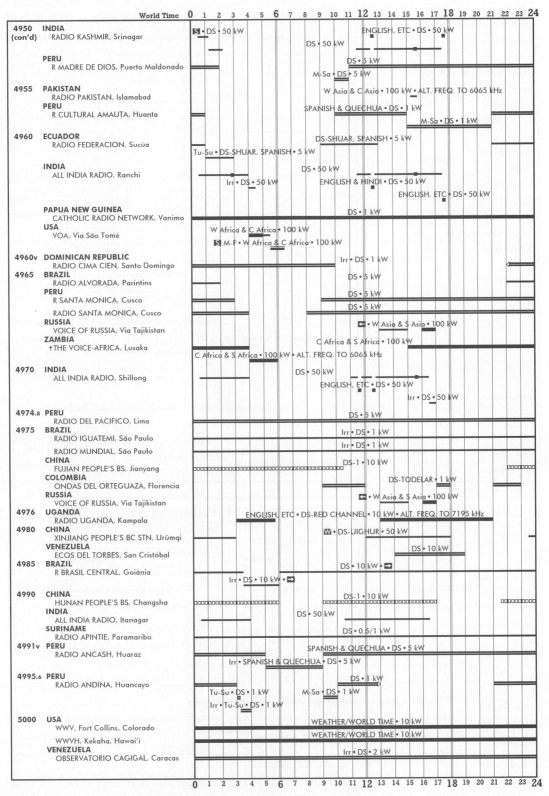

World Time 0 1 2 3 4 5 6 7 8 9 10 11 12 13 14 15 16 17 18 19 20 21 22 23 24

4950 **INDIA**
(con'd) RADIO KASHMIR, Srinagar
S • DS • 50 kW
ENGLISH, ETC • DS • 50 kW
DS • 50 kW

PERU
R MADRE DE DIOS, Puerto Maldonado
DS • 5 kW
M-Sa • DS • 5 kW

4955 **PAKISTAN**
RADIO PAKISTAN, Islamabad
W Asia & C Asia • 100 kW • ALT. FREQ. TO 6065 kHz
PERU
R CULTURAL AMAUTA, Huanta
SPANISH & QUECHUA • DS • 1 kW
M-Sa • DS • 1 kW

4960 **ECUADOR**
RADIO FEDERACION, Sucúa
DS-SHUAR, SPANISH • 5 kW
Tu-Su • DS-SHUAR, SPANISH • 5 kW

INDIA
ALL INDIA RADIO, Ranchi
DS • 50 kW
Irr • DS • 50 kW
ENGLISH & HINDI • DS • 50 kW
ENGLISH, ETC • DS • 50 kW

PAPUA NEW GUINEA
CATHOLIC RADIO NETWORK, Vanimo
DS • 1 kW
USA
VOA, Via São Tomé
W Africa & C Africa • 100 kW
S M-F • W Africa & C Africa • 100 kW

4960v **DOMINICAN REPUBLIC**
RADIO CIMA CIEN, Santo Domingo
Irr • DS • 1 kW
4965 **BRAZIL**
RADIO ALVORADA, Parintins
DS • 5 kW
PERU
R SANTA MONICA, Cusco
DS • 5 kW
RADIO SANTA MONICA, Cusco
DS • 5 kW
RUSSIA
VOICE OF RUSSIA, Via Tajikistan
• W Asia & S Asia • 100 kW
ZAMBIA
†THE VOICE-AFRICA, Lusaka
C Africa & S Africa • 100 kW
C Africa & S Africa • 100 kW • ALT. FREQ. TO 6065 kHz

4970 **INDIA**
ALL INDIA RADIO, Shillong
DS • 50 kW
ENGLISH, ETC • DS • 50 kW
Irr • DS • 50 kW

4974.8 **PERU**
RADIO DEL PACIFICO, Lima
DS • 5 kW
4975 **BRAZIL**
RADIO IGUATEMI, São Paulo
Irr • DS • 1 kW
RADIO MUNDIAL, São Paulo
Irr • DS • 1 kW
CHINA
FUJIAN PEOPLE'S BS, Jianyang
DS-1 • 10 kW
COLOMBIA
ONDAS DEL ORTEGUAZA, Florencia
DS-TODELAR • 1 kW
RUSSIA
VOICE OF RUSSIA, Via Tajikistan
• W Asia & S Asia • 100 kW
4976 **UGANDA**
RADIO UGANDA, Kampala
ENGLISH, ETC • DS-RED CHANNEL • 10 kW • ALT. FREQ. TO 7195 kHz
4980 **CHINA**
XINJIANG PEOPLE'S BC STN, Urümqi
W • DS-UIGHUR • 50 kW
VENEZUELA
ECOS DEL TORBES, San Cristóbal
DS • 10 kW
4985 **BRAZIL**
R BRASIL CENTRAL, Goiânia
DS • 10 kW •
Irr • DS • 10 kW •

4990 **CHINA**
HUNAN PEOPLE'S BS, Changsha
DS-1 • 10 kW
INDIA
ALL INDIA RADIO, Itanagar
DS • 50 kW
SURINAME
RADIO APINTIE, Paramaribo
DS • 0.5/1 kW
4991v **PERU**
RADIO ANCASH, Huaraz
SPANISH & QUECHUA • DS • 5 kW
Irr • SPANISH & QUECHUA • DS • 5 kW

4995.6 **PERU**
RADIO ANDINA, Huancayo
DS • 1 kW
Tu-Su • DS • 1 kW
M-Sa • DS • 1 kW
Irr • Tu-Su • DS • 1 kW

5000 **USA**
WWV, Fort Collins, Colorado
WEATHER/WORLD TIME • 10 kW
WWVH, Kekaha, Hawai'i
WEATHER/WORLD TIME • 10 kW
VENEZUELA
OBSERVATORIO CAGIGAL, Caracas
Irr • DS • 2 kW

0 1 2 3 4 5 6 7 8 9 10 11 12 13 14 15 16 17 18 19 20 21 22 23 24

SEASONAL S OR W   1-HR TIMESHIFT MIDYEAR ⬅ OR ➡   JAMMING / OR /\   EARLIEST HEARD ◁   LATEST HEARD ▷   NEW FOR 2007 †

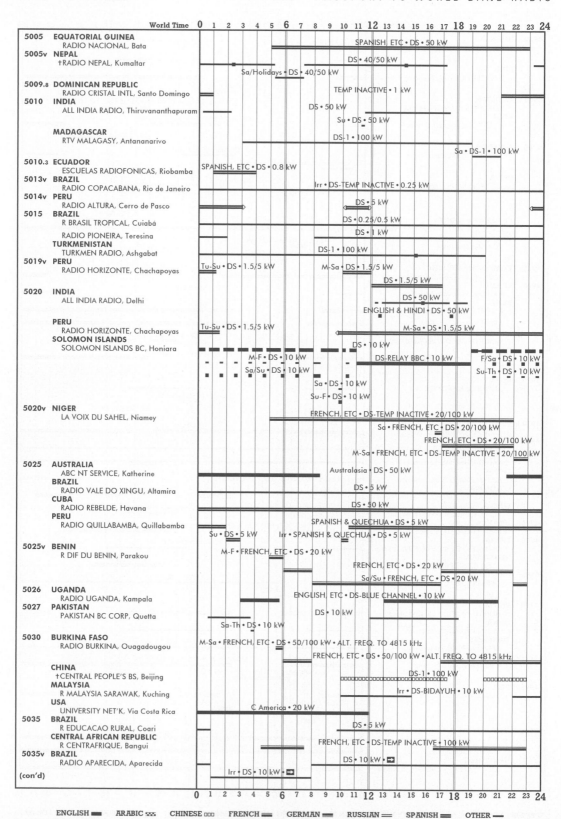

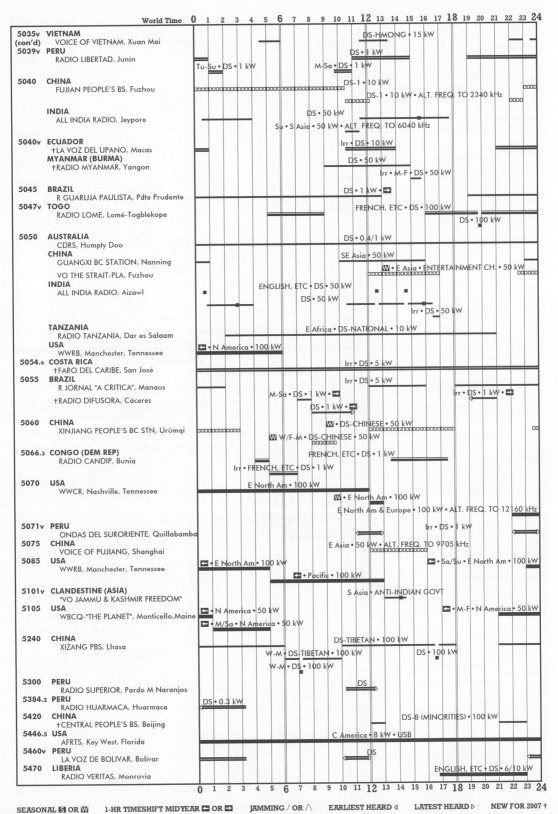

| World Time | 0 1 2 3 4 5 6 7 8 9 10 11 12 13 14 15 16 17 18 19 20 21 22 23 24 |

5035v VIETNAM
(con'd) VOICE OF VIETNAM, Xuan Mai — DS-HMONG • 15 kW

5039v PERU
RADIO LIBERTAD, Junín — DS • 1 kW; Tu-Su • DS • 1 kW; M-Sa • DS • 1 kW

5040 CHINA
FUJIAN PEOPLE'S BS, Fuzhou — DS-1 • 10 kW; DS-1 • 10 kW • ALT. FREQ. TO 2340 kHz

INDIA
ALL INDIA RADIO, Jeypore — DS • 50 kW; Su • S Asia • 50 kW • ALT. FREQ. TO 6040 kHz

5040v ECUADOR
†LA VOZ DEL UPANO, Macas — Irr • DS • 10 kW

MYANMAR (BURMA)
†RADIO MYANMAR, Yangon — DS • 50 kW; Irr • M-F • DS • 50 kW

5045 BRAZIL
R GUARUJA PAULISTA, Pdte Prudente — DS • 1 kW •

5047v TOGO
RADIO LOME, Lomé-Togblekope — FRENCH, ETC • DS • 100 kW; DS • 100 kW

5050 AUSTRALIA
CDRS, Humpty Doo — DS • 0.4/1 kW

CHINA
GUANGXI BC STATION, Nanning — SE Asia • 50 kW; W • E Asia • ENTERTAINMENT CH. • 50 kW

VO THE STRAIT-PLA, Fuzhou

INDIA
ALL INDIA RADIO, Aizawl — ENGLISH, ETC • DS • 50 kW; DS • 50 kW; Irr • DS • 50 kW

TANZANIA
RADIO TANZANIA, Dar es Salaam — E Africa • DS-NATIONAL • 10 kW

USA
WWRB, Manchester, Tennessee — N America • 100 kW

5054.6 COSTA RICA
†FARO DEL CARIBE, San José — Irr • DS • 5 kW

5055 BRAZIL
R JORNAL "A CRITICA", Manaus — Irr • DS • 5 kW; M-Sa • DS • 1 kW •; Irr • DS • 1 kW •

†RADIO DIFUSORA, Cáceres — DS • 1 kW •

5060 CHINA
XINJIANG PEOPLE'S BC STN, Urümqi — W • DS-CHINESE • 50 kW; W W/F-M • DS-CHINESE • 50 kW

5066.3 CONGO (DEM REP)
RADIO CANDIP, Bunia — FRENCH, ETC • DS • 1 kW; Irr • FRENCH, ETC • DS • 1 kW

5070 USA
WWCR, Nashville, Tennessee — E North Am • 100 kW; W • E North Am • 100 kW; E North Am & Europe • 100 kW • ALT. FREQ. TO 12160 kHz

5071v PERU
ONDAS DEL SURORIENTE, Quillabamba — Irr • DS • 1 kW

5075 CHINA
VOICE OF PUJIANG, Shanghai — E Asia • 50 kW • ALT. FREQ. TO 9705 kHz

5085 USA
WWRB, Manchester, Tennessee — E North Am • 100 kW; Sa/Su • E North Am • 100 kW; Pacific • 100 kW

5101v CLANDESTINE (ASIA)
"VO JAMMU & KASHMIR FREEDOM" — S Asia • ANTI-INDIAN GOVT

5105 USA
WBCQ-"THE PLANET", Monticello, Maine — N America • 50 kW; M-F • N America • 50 kW; M/Sa • N America • 50 kW

5240 CHINA
XIZANG PBS, Lhasa — DS-TIBETAN • 100 kW; W-M • DS-TIBETAN • 100 kW; DS • 100 kW; W-M • DS • 100 kW

5300 PERU
RADIO SUPERIOR, Pardo M Naranjos — DS

5384.2 PERU
RADIO HUARMACA, Huarmaca — DS • 0.3 kW

5420 CHINA
†CENTRAL PEOPLE'S BS, Beijing — DS-8 (MINORITIES) • 100 kW

5446.5 USA
AFRTS, Key West, Florida — C America • 8 kW • USB

5460v PERU
LA VOZ DE BOLIVAR, Bolivar — DS

5470 LIBERIA
RADIO VERITAS, Monrovia — ENGLISH, ETC • DS • 6/10 kW

| | 0 1 2 3 4 5 6 7 8 9 10 11 12 13 14 15 16 17 18 19 20 21 22 23 24 |

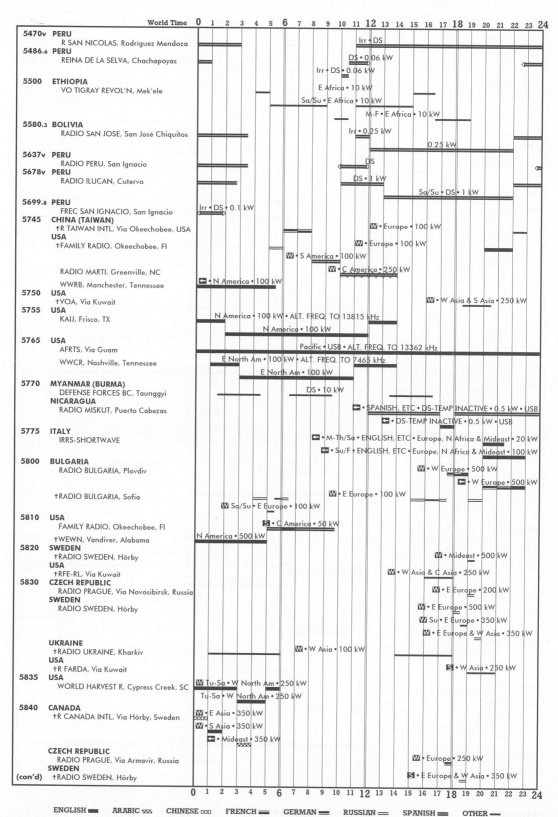

| | World Time | 0 | 1 | 2 | 3 | 4 | 5 | 6 | 7 | 8 | 9 | 10 | 11 | 12 | 13 | 14 | 15 | 16 | 17 | 18 | 19 | 20 | 21 | 22 | 23 | 24 |

5470v PERU
R SAN NICOLAS, Rodriguez Mendoza — Irr • DS

5486.6 PERU
REINA DE LA SELVA, Chachapoyas — DS • 0.06 kW
Irr • DS • 0.06 kW

5500 ETHIOPIA
VO TIGRAY REVOL'N, Mek'ele — E Africa • 10 kW
Sa/Su • E Africa • 10 kW
M–F • E Africa • 10 kW

5580.3 BOLIVIA
RADIO SAN JOSE, San José Chiquitos — Irr • 0.25 kW
0.25 kW

5637v PERU
RADIO PERU, San Ignacio — DS

5678v PERU
RADIO ILUCAN, Cutervo — DS • 1 kW
Sa/Su • DS • 1 kW

5699.8 PERU
FREC SAN IGNACIO, San Ignacio — Irr • DS • 0.1 kW

5745 CHINA (TAIWAN)
†R TAIWAN INTL, Via Okeechobee, USA — W • Europe • 100 kW

USA
†FAMILY RADIO, Okeechobee, Fl — W • Europe • 100 kW
W • S America • 100 kW
W • C America • 250 kW

RADIO MARTI, Greenville, NC

WWRB, Manchester, Tennessee — N America • 100 kW

5750 USA
†VOA, Via Kuwait — W • W Asia & S Asia • 250 kW

5755 USA
KAIJ, Frisco, TX — N America • 100 kW • ALT. FREQ. TO 13815 kHz
N America • 100 kW

5765 USA
AFRTS, Via Guam — Pacific • USB • ALT. FREQ. TO 13362 kHz

WWCR, Nashville, Tennessee — E North Am • 100 kW • ALT. FREQ. TO 7465 kHz
E North Am • 100 kW

5770 MYANMAR (BURMA)
DEFENSE FORCES BC, Taunggyi — DS • 10 kW

NICARAGUA
RADIO MISKUT, Puerto Cabezas — SPANISH, ETC • DS–TEMP INACTIVE • 0.5 kW • USB
DS–TEMP INACTIVE • 0.5 kW • USB

5775 ITALY
IRRS-SHORTWAVE — M–Th/Sa • ENGLISH, ETC • Europe, N Africa & Mideast • 20 kW
Su/F • ENGLISH, ETC • Europe, N Africa & Mideast • 100 kW

5800 BULGARIA
RADIO BULGARIA, Plovdiv — W • W Europe • 500 kW
W • W Europe • 500 kW

†RADIO BULGARIA, Sofia — W • E Europe • 100 kW
W Sa/Su • E Europe • 100 kW

5810 USA
FAMILY RADIO, Okeechobee, Fl — S • C America • 50 kW

†WEWN, Vandiver, Alabama — N America • 500 kW

5820 SWEDEN
†RADIO SWEDEN, Hörby — W • Mideast • 500 kW

USA
†RFE-RL, Via Kuwait — W • W Asia & C Asia • 250 kW

5830 CZECH REPUBLIC
RADIO PRAGUE, Via Novosibirsk, Russia — W • E Europe • 200 kW

SWEDEN
RADIO SWEDEN, Hörby — W • E Europe • 500 kW
W Su • E Europe • 350 kW
W • E Europe & W Asia • 350 kW

UKRAINE
†RADIO UKRAINE, Kharkiv — W • W Asia • 100 kW

USA
†R FARDA, Via Kuwait — S • W Asia • 250 kW

5835 USA
WORLD HARVEST R, Cypress Creek, SC — W Tu–Sa • W North Am • 250 kW
Tu–Sa • W North Am • 250 kW

5840 CANADA
†R CANADA INTL, Via Hörby, Sweden — W • E Asia • 350 kW
W • S Asia • 350 kW
• Mideast • 350 kW

CZECH REPUBLIC
RADIO PRAGUE, Via Armavir, Russia — W • Europe • 250 kW

SWEDEN
(con'd) †RADIO SWEDEN, Hörby — S • E Europe & W Asia • 350 kW

| | 0 | 1 | 2 | 3 | 4 | 5 | 6 | 7 | 8 | 9 | 10 | 11 | 12 | 13 | 14 | 15 | 16 | 17 | 18 | 19 | 20 | 21 | 22 | 23 | 24 |

ENGLISH ▬   ARABIC ﹏   CHINESE □□□   FRENCH ═   GERMAN ▬   RUSSIAN ═   SPANISH ▬   OTHER ▬

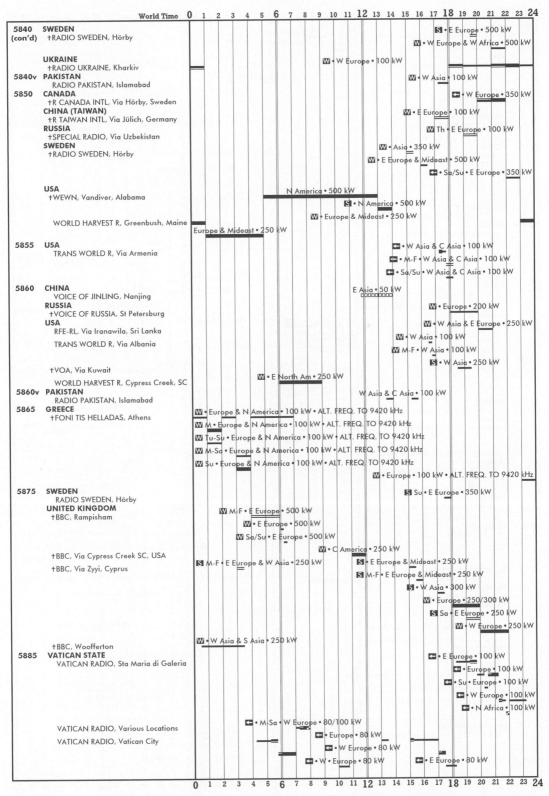

World Time 0 1 2 3 4 5 6 7 8 9 10 11 12 13 14 15 16 17 18 19 20 21 22 23 24

5840 (con'd) SWEDEN
†RADIO SWEDEN, Hörby
- [S] • E Europe • 500 kW
- [W] • W Europe & W Africa • 500 kW

UKRAINE
†RADIO UKRAINE, Kharkiv
- [W] • W Europe • 100 kW

5840v PAKISTAN
RADIO PAKISTAN, Islamabad
- [W] • W Asia • 100 kW

5850 CANADA
†R CANADA INTL, Via Hörby, Sweden
- ⬅ • W Europe • 350 kW

CHINA (TAIWAN)
†R TAIWAN INTL, Via Jülich, Germany
- [W] • E Europe • 100 kW

RUSSIA
†SPECIAL RADIO, Via Uzbekistan
- [W] Th • E Europe • 100 kW

SWEDEN
†RADIO SWEDEN, Hörby
- [W] • Asia • 350 kW
- [W] • E Europe & Mideast • 500 kW
- ⬅ • Sa/Su • E Europe • 350 kW

USA
†WEWN, Vandiver, Alabama
- N America • 500 kW
- [S] • N America • 500 kW

WORLD HARVEST R, Greenbush, Maine
- [W] • Europe & Mideast • 250 kW
- Europe & Mideast • 250 kW

5855 USA
TRANS WORLD R, Via Armenia
- ⬅ • W Asia & C Asia • 100 kW
- ⬅ • M-F • W Asia & C Asia • 100 kW
- ⬅ • Sa/Su • W Asia & C Asia • 100 kW

5860 CHINA
VOICE OF JINLING, Nanjing
- E Asia • 50 kW

RUSSIA
†VOICE OF RUSSIA, St Petersburg
- [W] • Europe • 200 kW

USA
RFE-RL, Via Iranawila, Sri Lanka
- [W] • W Asia & E Europe • 250 kW

TRANS WORLD R, Via Albania
- [W] • W Asia • 100 kW
- [W] M-F • W Asia • 100 kW

†VOA, Via Kuwait
- [S] • W Asia • 250 kW

WORLD HARVEST R, Cypress Creek, SC
- [W] • E North Am • 250 kW

5860v PAKISTAN
RADIO PAKISTAN, Islamabad
- W Asia & C Asia • 100 kW

5865 GREECE
†FONI TIS HELLADAS, Athens
- [W] • Europe & N America • 100 kW • ALT. FREQ. TO 9420 kHz
- [W] M • Europe & N America • 100 kW • ALT. FREQ. TO 9420 kHz
- [W] Tu-Su • Europe & N America • 100 kW • ALT. FREQ. TO 9420 kHz
- [W] M-Sa • Europe & N America • 100 kW • ALT. FREQ. TO 9420 kHz
- [W] Su • Europe & N America • 100 kW • ALT. FREQ. TO 9420 kHz
- [W] • Europe • 100 kW • ALT. FREQ. TO 9420 kHz

5875 SWEDEN
RADIO SWEDEN, Hörby
- [S] Su • E Europe • 350 kW

UNITED KINGDOM
†BBC, Rampisham
- [W] M-F • E Europe • 500 kW
- [W] • E Europe • 500 kW
- [W] Sa/Su • E Europe • 500 kW

†BBC, Via Cypress Creek SC, USA
- [W] • C America • 250 kW

†BBC, Via Zyyi, Cyprus
- [S] M-F • E Europe & W Asia • 250 kW
- [S] • E Europe & Mideast • 250 kW
- [S] M-F • E Europe & Mideast • 250 kW
- [S] • W Asia • 300 kW
- [W] • Europe • 250/300 kW
- [S] Sa • E Europe • 250 kW
- [W] • W Europe • 250 kW

†BBC, Woofferton
- [W] • W Asia & S Asia • 250 kW

5885 VATICAN STATE
VATICAN RADIO, Sta Maria di Galeria
- ⬅ • E Europe • 100 kW
- ⬅ • Europe • 100 kW
- ⬅ • Su • Europe • 100 kW
- ⬅ • W Europe • 100 kW
- ⬅ • N Africa • 100 kW

VATICAN RADIO, Various Locations
- ⬅ • M-Sa • W Europe • 80/100 kW

VATICAN RADIO, Vatican City
- ⬅ • Europe • 80 kW
- ⬅ • W Europe • 80 kW
- ⬅ • W • Europe • 80 kW
- ⬅ • E Europe • 80 kW

0 1 2 3 4 5 6 7 8 9 10 11 12 13 14 15 16 17 18 19 20 21 22 23 24

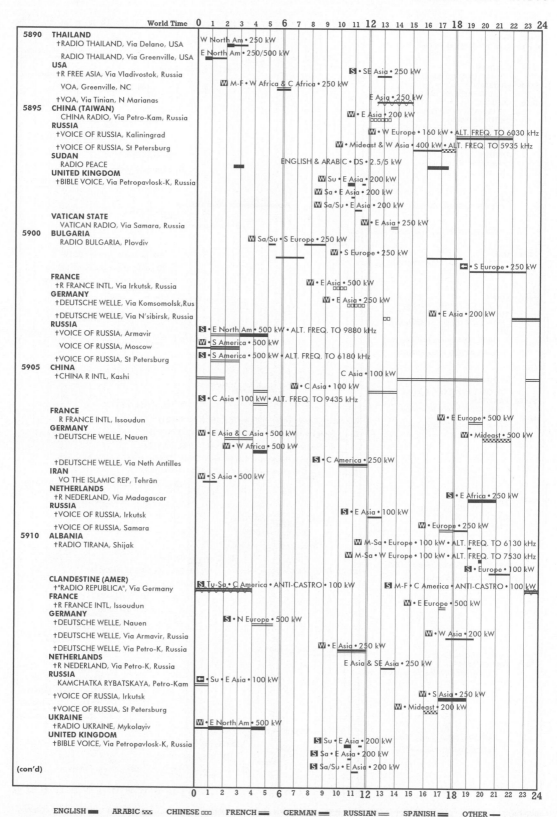

5890 THAILAND	
†RADIO THAILAND, Via Delano, USA	W North Am • 250 kW
RADIO THAILAND, Via Greenville, USA	E North Am • 250/500 kW
USA	
†R FREE ASIA, Via Vladivostok, Russia	S • SE Asia • 250 kW
VOA, Greenville, NC	W • M-F • W Africa & C Africa • 250 kW
†VOA, Via Tinian, N Marianas	E Asia • 250 kW
5895 CHINA (TAIWAN)	
CHINA RADIO, Via Petro-Kam, Russia	W • E Asia • 200 kW
RUSSIA	
†VOICE OF RUSSIA, Kaliningrad	W • W Europe • 160 kW • ALT. FREQ. TO 6030 kHz
†VOICE OF RUSSIA, St Petersburg	W • Mideast & W Asia • 400 kW • ALT. FREQ. TO 5935 kHz
SUDAN	
RADIO PEACE	ENGLISH & ARABIC • DS • 2.5/5 kW
UNITED KINGDOM	
†BIBLE VOICE, Via Petropavlosk-K, Russia	W Su • E Asia • 200 kW
	W Sa • E Asia • 200 kW
	W Sa/Su • E Asia • 200 kW
VATICAN STATE	
VATICAN RADIO, Via Samara, Russia	W • E Asia • 250 kW
5900 BULGARIA	
RADIO BULGARIA, Plovdiv	W Sa/Su • S Europe • 250 kW
	W • S Europe • 250 kW
	← • S Europe • 250 kW
FRANCE	
†R FRANCE INTL, Via Irkutsk, Russia	W • E Asia • 500 kW
GERMANY	
†DEUTSCHE WELLE, Via Komsomolsk, Rus	W • E Asia • 250 kW
†DEUTSCHE WELLE, Via N'sibirsk, Russia	W • E Asia • 200 kW
RUSSIA	
†VOICE OF RUSSIA, Armavir	S • E North Am • 500 kW • ALT. FREQ. TO 9880 kHz
VOICE OF RUSSIA, Moscow	W • S America • 500 kW
†VOICE OF RUSSIA, St Petersburg	S • S America • 500 kW • ALT. FREQ. TO 6180 kHz
5905 CHINA	
†CHINA R INTL, Kashi	C Asia • 100 kW
	W • C Asia • 100 kW
	S • C Asia • 100 kW • ALT. FREQ. TO 9435 kHz
FRANCE	
R FRANCE INTL, Issoudun	W • E Europe • 500 kW
GERMANY	
†DEUTSCHE WELLE, Nauen	W • E Asia & C Asia • 500 kW
	W • Mideast • 500 kW
	W • W Africa • 500 kW
†DEUTSCHE WELLE, Via Neth Antilles	S • C America • 250 kW
IRAN	
VO THE ISLAMIC REP, Tehrān	W • S Asia • 500 kW
NETHERLANDS	
†R NEDERLAND, Via Madagascar	S • E Africa • 250 kW
RUSSIA	
†VOICE OF RUSSIA, Irkutsk	S • E Asia • 100 kW
†VOICE OF RUSSIA, Samara	W • Europe • 250 kW
5910 ALBANIA	
†RADIO TIRANA, Shijak	W M-Sa • Europe • 100 kW • ALT. FREQ. TO 6130 kHz
	W M-Sa • W Europe • 100 kW • ALT. FREQ. TO 7530 kHz
	S • Europe • 100 kW
CLANDESTINE (AMER)	
†"RADIO REPUBLICA", Via Germany	S Tu-Sa • C America • ANTI-CASTRO • 100 kW S M-F • C America • ANTI-CASTRO • 100 kW
FRANCE	
†R FRANCE INTL, Issoudun	W • E Europe • 500 kW
GERMANY	
†DEUTSCHE WELLE, Nauen	S • N Europe • 500 kW
†DEUTSCHE WELLE, Via Armavir, Russia	W • W Asia • 200 kW
†DEUTSCHE WELLE, Via Petro-K, Russia	W • E Asia • 250 kW
NETHERLANDS	
†R NEDERLAND, Via Petro-K, Russia	E Asia & SE Asia • 250 kW
RUSSIA	
KAMCHATKA RYBATSKAYA, Petro-Kam	← • Su • E Asia • 100 kW
†VOICE OF RUSSIA, Irkutsk	W • S Asia • 250 kW
†VOICE OF RUSSIA, St Petersburg	W • Mideast • 200 kW
UKRAINE	
†RADIO UKRAINE, Mykolayiv	W • E North Am • 500 kW
UNITED KINGDOM	
†BIBLE VOICE, Via Petropavlosk-K, Russia	S Su • E Asia • 200 kW
	S Sa • E Asia • 200 kW
	S Sa/Su • E Asia • 200 kW
(con'd)	

ENGLISH ▬   ARABIC ⋙   CHINESE ⸬   FRENCH ═   GERMAN ▬   RUSSIAN ═   SPANISH ═   OTHER ▬

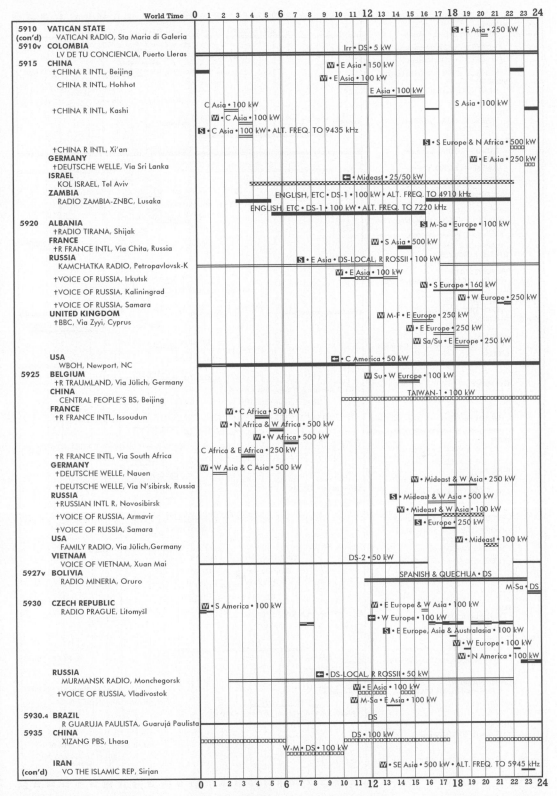

World Time 0 1 2 3 4 5 6 7 8 9 10 11 12 13 14 15 16 17 18 19 20 21 22 23 24

Freq	Country / Station	
5910 (con'd)	**VATICAN STATE** VATICAN RADIO, Sta Maria di Galeria	S • E Asia • 250 kW
5910v	**COLOMBIA** LV DE TU CONCIENCIA, Puerto Lleras	Irr • DS • 5 kW
5915	**CHINA** †CHINA R INTL, Beijing	W • E Asia • 150 kW
	CHINA R INTL, Hohhot	W • E Asia • 100 kW / E Asia • 100 kW
	†CHINA R INTL, Kashi	C Asia • 100 kW / W • C Asia • 100 kW / S • C Asia • 100 kW • ALT. FREQ. TO 9435 kHz / S Asia • 100 kW
	†CHINA R INTL, Xi'an	S • S Europe & N Africa • 500 kW
	GERMANY †DEUTSCHE WELLE, Via Sri Lanka	W • E Asia • 250 kW
	ISRAEL KOL ISRAEL, Tel Aviv	◄ • Mideast • 25/50 kW
	ZAMBIA RADIO ZAMBIA-ZNBC, Lusaka	ENGLISH, ETC • DS-1 • 100 kW • ALT. FREQ. TO 4910 kHz / ENGLISH, ETC • DS-1 • 100 kW • ALT. FREQ. TO 7220 kHz
5920	**ALBANIA** †RADIO TIRANA, Shijak	S • M-Sa • Europe • 100 kW
	FRANCE †R FRANCE INTL, Via Chita, Russia	W • S Asia • 500 kW
	RUSSIA KAMCHATKA RADIO, Petropavlovsk-K	S • E Asia • DS-LOCAL, R ROSSII • 100 kW
	†VOICE OF RUSSIA, Irkutsk	W • E Asia • 100 kW
	†VOICE OF RUSSIA, Kaliningrad	W • S Europe • 160 kW
	†VOICE OF RUSSIA, Samara	W • W Europe • 250 kW
	UNITED KINGDOM †BBC, Via Zyyi, Cyprus	W • M-F • E Europe • 250 kW / W • E Europe • 250 kW / W • Sa/Su • E Europe • 250 kW
	USA WBOH, Newport, NC	◄ • C America • 50 kW
5925	**BELGIUM** †R TRAUMLAND, Via Jülich, Germany	W • Su • W Europe • 100 kW
	CHINA CENTRAL PEOPLE'S BS, Beijing	TAIWAN-1 • 100 kW
	FRANCE †R FRANCE INTL, Issoudun	W • C Africa • 500 kW / W • N Africa & W Africa • 500 kW / W • W Africa • 500 kW
	†R FRANCE INTL, Via South Africa	C Africa & E Africa • 250 kW
	GERMANY †DEUTSCHE WELLE, Nauen	W • W Asia & C Asia • 500 kW
	†DEUTSCHE WELLE, Via N'sibirsk, Russia	W • Mideast & W Asia • 250 kW
	RUSSIA †RUSSIAN INTL R, Novosibirsk	S • Mideast & W Asia • 500 kW
	†VOICE OF RUSSIA, Armavir	W • Mideast & W Asia • 100 kW
	†VOICE OF RUSSIA, Samara	S • Europe • 250 kW
	USA FAMILY RADIO, Via Jülich, Germany	W • Mideast • 100 kW
	VIETNAM VOICE OF VIETNAM, Xuan Mai	DS-2 • 50 kW
5927v	**BOLIVIA** RADIO MINERIA, Oruro	SPANISH & QUECHUA • DS / M-Sa • DS
5930	**CZECH REPUBLIC** RADIO PRAGUE, Litomyšl	W • S America • 100 kW / W • E Europe & W Asia • 100 kW / ◄ • W Europe • 100 kW / S • E Europe, Asia & Australasia • 100 kW / W • W Europe • 100 kW / W • N America • 100 kW
	RUSSIA MURMANSK RADIO, Monchegorsk	◄ • DS-LOCAL, R ROSSII • 50 kW
	†VOICE OF RUSSIA, Vladivostok	W • E Asia • 100 kW / W • M-Sa • E Asia • 100 kW
5930.4	**BRAZIL** R GUARUJA PAULISTA, Guarujá Paulista	DS
5935	**CHINA** XIZANG PBS, Lhasa	DS • 100 kW / W-M • DS • 100 kW
(con'd)	**IRAN** VO THE ISLAMIC REP, Sirjan	W • SE Asia • 500 kW • ALT. FREQ. TO 5945 kHz

0 1 2 3 4 5 6 7 8 9 10 11 12 13 14 15 16 17 18 19 20 21 22 23 24

SEASONAL S OR W   1-HR TIMESHIFT MIDYEAR ◄ OR ►   JAMMING / OR /\   EARLIEST HEARD ◄   LATEST HEARD ►   NEW FOR 2007 †

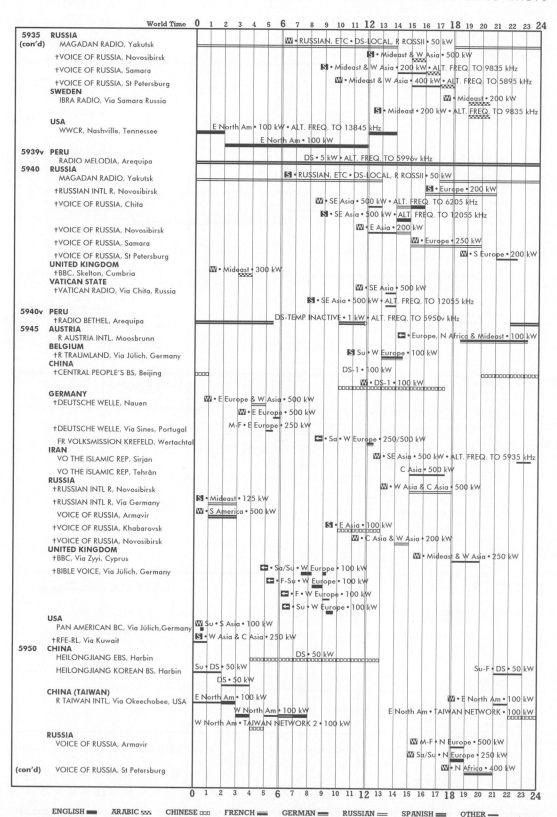

World Time		
5935 (con'd) **RUSSIA**		
MAGADAN RADIO, Yakutsk	W • RUSSIAN, ETC • DS-LOCAL, R ROSSII • 50 kW	
†VOICE OF RUSSIA, Novosibirsk	S • Mideast & W Asia • 500 kW	
†VOICE OF RUSSIA, Samara	S • Mideast & W Asia • 200 kW • ALT. FREQ. TO 9835 kHz	
†VOICE OF RUSSIA, St Petersburg	W • Mideast & W Asia • 400 kW • ALT. FREQ. TO 5895 kHz	
SWEDEN IBRA RADIO, Via Samara Russia	W • Mideast • 200 kW	
	S • Mideast • 200 kW • ALT. FREQ. TO 9835 kHz	
USA WWCR, Nashville, Tennessee	E North Am • 100 kW • ALT. FREQ. TO 13845 kHz	
	E North Am • 100 kW	
5939v PERU RADIO MELODIA, Arequipa	DS • 5 kW • ALT. FREQ. TO 5996v kHz	
5940 RUSSIA MAGADAN RADIO, Yakutsk	S • RUSSIAN, ETC • DS-LOCAL, R ROSSII • 50 kW	
†RUSSIAN INTL R, Novosibirsk	S • Europe • 200 kW	
†VOICE OF RUSSIA, Chita	W • SE Asia • 500 kW • ALT. FREQ. TO 6205 kHz	
	S • SE Asia • 500 kW • ALT FREQ. TO 12055 kHz	
†VOICE OF RUSSIA, Novosibirsk	W • E Asia • 200 kW	
†VOICE OF RUSSIA, Samara	W • Europe • 250 kW	
†VOICE OF RUSSIA, St Petersburg	W • S Europe • 200 kW	
UNITED KINGDOM †BBC, Skelton, Cumbria	W • Mideast • 300 kW	
VATICAN STATE †VATICAN RADIO, Via Chita, Russia	W • SE Asia • 500 kW	
	S • SE Asia • 500 kW • ALT. FREQ. TO 12055 kHz	
5940v PERU †RADIO BETHEL, Arequipa	DS-TEMP INACTIVE • 1 kW • ALT. FREQ. TO 5950v kHz	
5945 AUSTRIA R AUSTRIA INTL, Moosbrunn	⮕ • Europe, N Africa & Mideast • 100 kW	
BELGIUM †R TRAUMLAND, Via Jülich, Germany	S • W Europe • 100 kW	
CHINA †CENTRAL PEOPLE'S BS, Beijing	DS-1 • 100 kW	
	W • DS-1 • 100 kW	
GERMANY †DEUTSCHE WELLE, Nauen	W • E Europe & W Asia • 500 kW	
	W • E Europe • 500 kW	
	M-F • E Europe • 250 kW	
†DEUTSCHE WELLE, Via Sines, Portugal	⮕ • Sa • W Europe • 250/500 kW	
FR VOLKSMISSION KREFELD, Wertachtal		
IRAN VO THE ISLAMIC REP, Sirjan	W • SE Asia • 500 kW • ALT. FREQ. TO 5935 kHz	
VO THE ISLAMIC REP, Tehrān	C Asia • 500 kW	
RUSSIA †RUSSIAN INTL R, Novosibirsk	W • W Asia & C Asia • 500 kW	
†RUSSIAN INTL R, Via Germany	S • Mideast • 125 kW	
VOICE OF RUSSIA, Armavir	W • S America • 500 kW	
†VOICE OF RUSSIA, Khabarovsk	S • E Asia • 100 kW	
†VOICE OF RUSSIA, Novosibirsk	W • C Asia & W Asia • 200 kW	
UNITED KINGDOM †BBC, Via Zyyi, Cyprus	W • Mideast & W Asia • 250 kW	
†BIBLE VOICE, Via Jülich, Germany	⮕ • Sa/Su • W Europe • 100 kW	
	⮕ • F-Su • W Europe • 100 kW	
	⮕ • F • W Europe • 100 kW	
	⮕ • Su • W Europe • 100 kW	
USA PAN AMERICAN BC, Via Jülich, Germany	W Su • S Asia • 100 kW	
†RFE-RL, Via Kuwait	S • W Asia & C Asia • 250 kW	
5950 CHINA HEILONGJIANG EBS, Harbin	DS • 50 kW	
	Su • DS • 50 kW	Su-F • DS • 50 kW
HEILONGJIANG KOREAN BS, Harbin	DS • 50 kW	
CHINA (TAIWAN) R TAIWAN INTL, Via Okeechobee, USA	E North Am • 100 kW	W • E North Am • 100 kW
	W North Am • 100 kW	E North Am • TAIWAN NETWORK • 100 kW
	W North Am • TAIWAN NETWORK 2 • 100 kW	
RUSSIA VOICE OF RUSSIA, Armavir	W M-F • N Europe • 500 kW	
	W Sa/Su • N Europe • 250 kW	
(con'd) VOICE OF RUSSIA, St Petersburg	W • N Africa • 400 kW	

ENGLISH ▬   ARABIC ⸭⸭⸭   CHINESE ⸬⸬⸬   FRENCH ▬▬   GERMAN ▬▬   RUSSIAN ══   SPANISH ▬▬   OTHER ▬

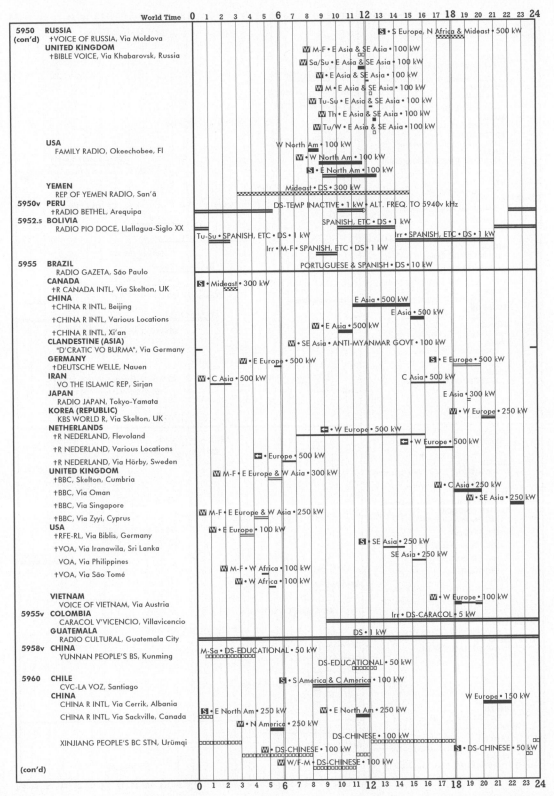

World Time

5950 RUSSIA
(con'd) †VOICE OF RUSSIA, Via Moldova — S · S Europe, N Africa & Mideast · 500 kW
UNITED KINGDOM
†BIBLE VOICE, Via Khabarovsk, Russia — W · M-F · E Asia & SE Asia · 100 kW
W · Sa/Su · E Asia & SE Asia · 100 kW
W · E Asia & SE Asia · 100 kW
W · M · E Asia & SE Asia · 100 kW
W · Tu-Su · E Asia & SE Asia · 100 kW
W · Th · E Asia & SE Asia · 100 kW
W · Tu/W · E Asia & SE Asia · 100 kW

USA
FAMILY RADIO, Okeechobee, Fl — W North Am · 100 kW
W · W North Am · 100 kW
S · E North Am · 100 kW

YEMEN
REP OF YEMEN RADIO, San'ā — Mideast · DS · 300 kW
5950v PERU
†RADIO BETHEL, Arequipa — DS-TEMP INACTIVE · 1 kW · ALT. FREQ. TO 5940v kHz
5952.5 BOLIVIA
RADIO PIO DOCE, Llallagua-Siglo XX — SPANISH, ETC · DS · 1 kW
Tu-Su · SPANISH, ETC · DS · 1 kW   Irr · SPANISH, ETC · DS · 1 kW
Irr · M-F · SPANISH, ETC · DS · 1 kW

5955 BRAZIL
RADIO GAZETA, São Paulo — PORTUGUESE & SPANISH · DS · 10 kW
CANADA
†R CANADA INTL, Via Skelton, UK — S · Mideast · 300 kW
CHINA
†CHINA R INTL, Beijing — E Asia · 500 kW
†CHINA R INTL, Various Locations — E Asia · 500 kW
†CHINA R INTL, Xi'an — W · E Asia · 500 kW
CLANDESTINE (ASIA)
"D'CRATIC VO BURMA", Via Germany — W · SE Asia · ANTI-MYANMAR GOVT · 100 kW
GERMANY
†DEUTSCHE WELLE, Nauen — W · E Europe · 500 kW   S · E Europe · 500 kW
IRAN
VO THE ISLAMIC REP, Sirjan — W · C Asia · 500 kW   C Asia · 500 kW
JAPAN
RADIO JAPAN, Tokyo-Yamata — E Asia · 300 kW
KOREA (REPUBLIC)
KBS WORLD R, Via Skelton, UK — W · W Europe · 250 kW
NETHERLANDS
†R NEDERLAND, Flevoland — ⇐ · W Europe · 500 kW
†R NEDERLAND, Various Locations — ⇐ · W Europe · 500 kW
†R NEDERLAND, Via Hörby, Sweden — ⇐ · Europe · 500 kW
UNITED KINGDOM
†BBC, Skelton, Cumbria — W · M-F · E Europe & W Asia · 300 kW
†BBC, Via Oman — W · C Asia · 250 kW
†BBC, Via Singapore — W · SE Asia · 250 kW
†BBC, Via Zyyi, Cyprus — W · M-F · E Europe & W Asia · 250 kW
USA
†RFE-RL, Via Biblis, Germany — W · E Europe · 100 kW
†VOA, Via Iranawila, Sri Lanka — S · SE Asia · 250 kW
VOA, Via Philippines — SE Asia · 250 kW
†VOA, Via São Tomé — W · M-F · W Africa · 100 kW
W · W Africa · 100 kW

VIETNAM
VOICE OF VIETNAM, Via Austria — W · W Europe · 100 kW
5955v COLOMBIA
CARACOL V'VICENCIO, Villavicencio — Irr · DS-CARACOL · 5 kW
GUATEMALA
RADIO CULTURAL, Guatemala City — DS · 1 kW
5958v CHINA
YUNNAN PEOPLE'S BS, Kunming — M-Sa · DS-EDUCATIONAL · 50 kW
DS-EDUCATIONAL · 50 kW

5960 CHILE
CVC-LA VOZ, Santiago — S · S America & C America · 100 kW
CHINA
CHINA R INTL, Via Cerrik, Albania — W Europe · 150 kW
CHINA R INTL, Via Sackville, Canada — S · E North Am · 250 kW   W · E North Am · 250 kW
W · N America · 250 kW

XINJIANG PEOPLE'S BC STN, Urümqi — DS-CHINESE · 100 kW   S · DS-CHINESE · 50 kW
W · DS-CHINESE · 100 kW
W/F-M · DS-CHINESE · 100 kW

(con'd)

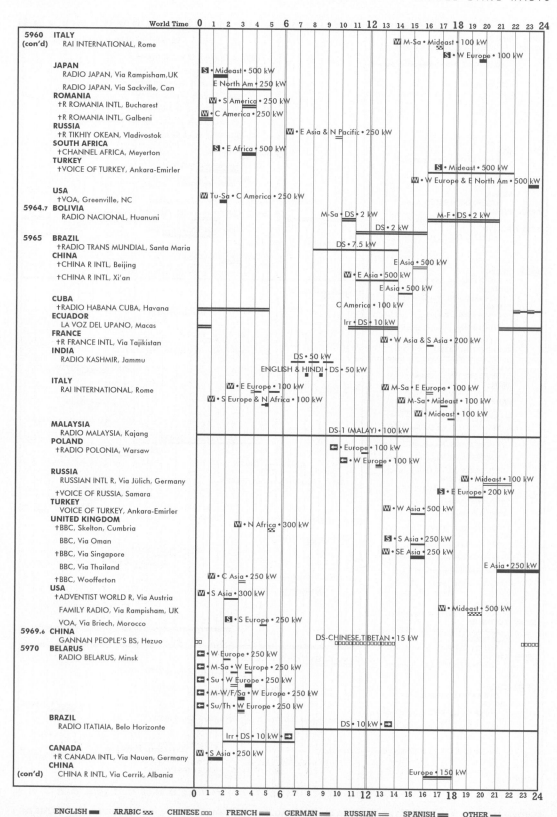

	World Time	0 1 2 3 4 5 6 7 8 9 10 11 12 13 14 15 16 17 18 19 20 21 22 23 24

5960 ITALY
(con'd) RAI INTERNATIONAL, Rome — W•M-Sa•Mideast•100 kW / S•W Europe•100 kW

JAPAN
RADIO JAPAN, Via Rampisham, UK — S•Mideast•500 kW
RADIO JAPAN, Via Sackville, Can — E North Am•250 kW
ROMANIA
†R ROMANIA INTL, Bucharest — W•S America•250 kW
†R ROMANIA INTL, Galbeni — W•C America•250 kW
RUSSIA
†R TIKHIY OKEAN, Vladivostok — W•E Asia & N Pacific•250 kW
SOUTH AFRICA
†CHANNEL AFRICA, Meyerton — S•E Africa•500 kW
TURKEY
†VOICE OF TURKEY, Ankara-Emirler — S•Mideast•500 kW / W•W Europe & E North Am•500 kW

USA
†VOA, Greenville, NC — W Tu-Sa•C America•250 kW
5964.7 BOLIVIA
RADIO NACIONAL, Huanuni — M-Sa•DS•2 kW / M-F•DS•2 kW / DS•2 kW

5965 BRAZIL
†RADIO TRANS MUNDIAL, Santa Maria — DS•7.5 kW
CHINA
†CHINA R INTL, Beijing — E Asia•500 kW
†CHINA R INTL, Xi'an — W•E Asia•500 kW / E Asia•500 kW

CUBA
†RADIO HABANA CUBA, Havana — C America•100 kW
ECUADOR
LA VOZ DEL UPANO, Macas — Irr•DS•10 kW
FRANCE
†R FRANCE INTL, Via Tajikistan — W•W Asia & S Asia•200 kW
INDIA
RADIO KASHMIR, Jammu — DS•50 kW / ENGLISH & HINDI•DS•50 kW

ITALY
RAI INTERNATIONAL, Rome — W•E Europe•100 kW / W M-Sa•E Europe•100 kW / W•S Europe & N Africa•100 kW / W M-Sa•Mideast•100 kW / W•Mideast•100 kW

MALAYSIA
RADIO MALAYSIA, Kajang — DS-1 (MALAY)•100 kW
POLAND
†RADIO POLONIA, Warsaw — Europe•100 kW / W Europe•100 kW

RUSSIA
RUSSIAN INTL R, Via Jülich, Germany — W•Mideast•100 kW
†VOICE OF RUSSIA, Samara — S•E Europe•200 kW
TURKEY
VOICE OF TURKEY, Ankara-Emirler — W•W Asia•500 kW
UNITED KINGDOM
†BBC, Skelton, Cumbria — W•N Africa•300 kW
BBC, Via Oman — S•S Asia•250 kW
†BBC, Via Singapore — W•SE Asia•250 kW
BBC, Via Thailand — E Asia•250 kW
†BBC, Woofferton — W•C Asia•250 kW
USA
†ADVENTIST WORLD R, Via Austria — W•S Asia•300 kW
FAMILY RADIO, Via Rampisham, UK — W•Mideast•500 kW
VOA, Via Briech, Morocco — S•S Europe•250 kW
5969.6 CHINA
GANNAN PEOPLE'S BS, Hezuo — DS-CHINESE, TIBETAN•15 kW
5970 BELARUS
RADIO BELARUS, Minsk — W Europe•250 kW / M-Sa•W Europe•250 kW / Su•W Europe•250 kW / M-W/F/Sa•W Europe•250 kW / Su/Th•W Europe•250 kW

BRAZIL
RADIO ITATIAIA, Belo Horizonte — DS•10 kW / Irr•DS•10 kW

CANADA
†R CANADA INTL, Via Nauen, Germany — W•S Asia•250 kW
CHINA
(con'd) CHINA R INTL, Via Cerrik, Albania — Europe•150 kW

	0 1 2 3 4 5 6 7 8 9 10 11 12 13 14 15 16 17 18 19 20 21 22 23 24

ENGLISH ▬ ARABIC ▨ CHINESE □□□ FRENCH ▬ GERMAN ═ RUSSIAN ═ SPANISH ═ OTHER —

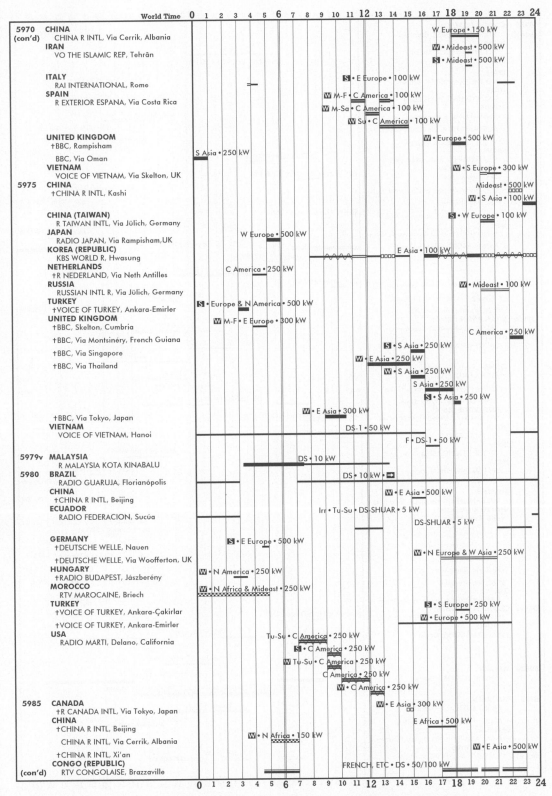

World Time	Station	Details
5970 (con'd)	**CHINA** CHINA R INTL, Via Cerrik, Albania	W Europe • 150 kW
	IRAN VO THE ISLAMIC REP, Tehrān	W • Mideast • 500 kW / S • Mideast • 500 kW
	ITALY RAI INTERNATIONAL, Rome	S • E Europe • 100 kW
	SPAIN R EXTERIOR ESPANA, Via Costa Rica	W M-F • C America • 100 kW / W M-Sa • C America • 100 kW / W Su • C America • 100 kW
	UNITED KINGDOM †BBC, Rampisham	W • Europe • 500 kW
	BBC, Via Oman	S Asia • 250 kW
	VIETNAM VOICE OF VIETNAM, Via Skelton, UK	W • S Europe • 300 kW
5975	**CHINA** †CHINA R INTL, Kashi	Mideast • 500 kW / W • S Asia • 100 kW
	CHINA (TAIWAN) R TAIWAN INTL, Via Jülich, Germany	S • W Europe • 100 kW
	JAPAN RADIO JAPAN, Via Rampisham, UK	W Europe • 500 kW
	KOREA (REPUBLIC) KBS WORLD R, Hwasung	E Asia • 100 kW
	NETHERLANDS †R NEDERLAND, Via Neth Antilles	C America • 250 kW
	RUSSIA RUSSIAN INTL R, Via Jülich, Germany	W • Mideast • 100 kW
	TURKEY †VOICE OF TURKEY, Ankara-Emirler	S • Europe & N America • 500 kW
	UNITED KINGDOM †BBC, Skelton, Cumbria	W M-F • E Europe • 300 kW
	†BBC, Via Montsinéry, French Guiana	C America • 250 kW
	†BBC, Via Singapore	S • S Asia • 250 kW
	†BBC, Via Thailand	W • E Asia • 250 kW / W • S Asia • 250 kW / S Asia • 250 kW / S • S Asia • 250 kW
	†BBC, Via Tokyo, Japan	W • E Asia • 300 kW
	VIETNAM VOICE OF VIETNAM, Hanoi	DS-1 • 50 kW / F • DS-1 • 50 kW
5979v	**MALAYSIA** R MALAYSIA KOTA KINABALU	DS • 10 kW
5980	**BRAZIL** RADIO GUARUJA, Florianópolis	DS • 10 kW
	CHINA †CHINA R INTL, Beijing	W • E Asia • 500 kW
	ECUADOR RADIO FEDERACION, Sucúa	Irr • Tu-Su • DS-SHUAR • 5 kW / DS-SHUAR • 5 kW
	GERMANY †DEUTSCHE WELLE, Nauen	S • E Europe • 500 kW
	†DEUTSCHE WELLE, Via Woofferton, UK	W • N Europe & W Asia • 250 kW
	HUNGARY †RADIO BUDAPEST, Jászberény	W • N America • 250 kW
	MOROCCO RTV MAROCAINE, Briech	W • N Africa & Mideast • 250 kW
	TURKEY †VOICE OF TURKEY, Ankara-Çakirlar	S • S Europe • 250 kW
	†VOICE OF TURKEY, Ankara-Emirler	W • Europe • 500 kW
	USA RADIO MARTI, Delano, California	Tu-Su • C America • 250 kW / S • C America • 250 kW / W Tu-Su • C America • 250 kW / C America • 250 kW / W • C America • 250 kW
5985	**CANADA** †R CANADA INTL, Via Tokyo, Japan	W • E Asia • 300 kW
	CHINA †CHINA R INTL, Beijing	E Africa • 500 kW
	CHINA R INTL, Via Cerrik, Albania	W • N Africa • 150 kW
	†CHINA R INTL, Xi'an	W • E Asia • 500 kW
	CONGO (REPUBLIC) (con'd) RTV CONGOLAISE, Brazzaville	FRENCH, ETC • DS • 50/100 kW

SEASONAL S OR W   1-HR TIMESHIFT MIDYEAR ⇐ OR ⇒   JAMMING / OR /\   EARLIEST HEARD ◁   LATEST HEARD ▷   NEW FOR 2007 †

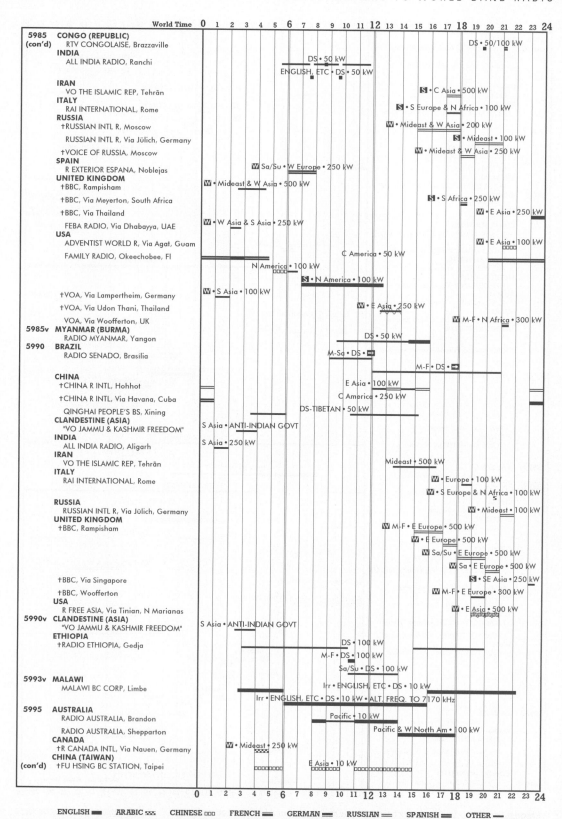

World Time 0 1 2 3 4 5 6 7 8 9 10 11 12 13 14 15 16 17 18 19 20 21 22 23 24

5985 **CONGO (REPUBLIC)**
(con'd) RTV CONGOLAISE, Brazzaville — D$ • 50/100 kW
INDIA
ALL INDIA RADIO, Ranchi — D$ • 50 kW / ENGLISH, ETC • DS • 50 kW
IRAN
VO THE ISLAMIC REP, Tehrān — S • C Asia • 500 kW
ITALY
RAI INTERNATIONAL, Rome — S • S Europe & N Africa • 100 kW
RUSSIA
†RUSSIAN INTL R, Moscow — W • Mideast & W Asia • 200 kW
RUSSIAN INTL R, Via Jülich, Germany — S • Mideast • 100 kW
†VOICE OF RUSSIA, Moscow — W • Mideast & W Asia • 250 kW
SPAIN
R EXTERIOR ESPANA, Noblejas — W • Sa/Su • W Europe • 250 kW
UNITED KINGDOM
†BBC, Rampisham — W • Mideast & W Asia • 500 kW
†BBC, Via Meyerton, South Africa — S • S Africa • 250 kW
†BBC, Via Thailand — W • E Asia • 250 kW
FEBA RADIO, Via Dhabayya, UAE — W • W Asia & S Asia • 250 kW
USA
ADVENTIST WORLD R, Via Agat, Guam — W • E Asia • 100 kW
FAMILY RADIO, Okeechobee, Fl — C America • 50 kW / N America • 100 kW / S • N America • 100 kW
†VOA, Via Lampertheim, Germany — W • S Asia • 100 kW
†VOA, Via Udon Thani, Thailand — W • E Asia • 250 kW
VOA, Via Woofferton, UK — W • M-F • N Africa • 300 kW

5985v **MYANMAR (BURMA)**
RADIO MYANMAR, Yangon — D$ • 50 kW

5990 **BRAZIL**
RADIO SENADO, Brasilia — M-Sa • DS • / M-F • DS •
CHINA
†CHINA R INTL, Hohhot — E Asia • 100 kW
†CHINA R INTL, Via Havana, Cuba — C America • 250 kW
QINGHAI PEOPLE'S BS, Xining — DS-TIBETAN • 50 kW
CLANDESTINE (ASIA)
"VO JAMMU & KASHMIR FREEDOM" — S Asia • ANTI-INDIAN GOVT
INDIA
ALL INDIA RADIO, Aligarh — S Asia • 250 kW
IRAN
VO THE ISLAMIC REP, Tehrān — Mideast • 500 kW
ITALY
RAI INTERNATIONAL, Rome — W • Europe • 100 kW / W • S Europe & N Africa • 100 kW
RUSSIA
RUSSIAN INTL R, Via Jülich, Germany — W • Mideast • 100 kW
UNITED KINGDOM
†BBC, Rampisham — W • M-F • E Europe • 500 kW / W • E Europe • 500 kW / W • Sa/Su • E Europe • 500 kW / W • Sa • E Europe • 500 kW
†BBC, Via Singapore — S • SE Asia • 250 kW
†BBC, Woofferton — W • M-F • E Europe • 300 kW
USA
R FREE ASIA, Via Tinian, N Marianas — W • E Asia • 500 kW

5990v **CLANDESTINE (ASIA)**
"VO JAMMU & KASHMIR FREEDOM" — S Asia • ANTI-INDIAN GOVT
ETHIOPIA
†RADIO ETHIOPIA, Gedja — DS • 100 kW / M-F • DS • 100 kW / Sa/Su • DS • 100 kW

5993v **MALAWI**
MALAWI BC CORP, Limbe — Irr • ENGLISH, ETC • DS • 10 kW / Irr • ENGLISH, ETC • DS • 10 kW • ALT. FREQ. TO 7170 kHz

5995 **AUSTRALIA**
RADIO AUSTRALIA, Brandon — Pacific • 10 kW
RADIO AUSTRALIA, Shepparton — Pacific & W North Am • 100 kW
CANADA
†R CANADA INTL, Via Nauen, Germany — W • Mideast • 250 kW
CHINA (TAIWAN)
(con'd) †FU HSING BC STATION, Taipei — E Asia • 10 kW

0 1 2 3 4 5 6 7 8 9 10 11 12 13 14 15 16 17 18 19 20 21 22 23 24

ENGLISH ▬ ARABIC ⋙ CHINESE ▱▱▱ FRENCH ▬ GERMAN ▬ RUSSIAN ═ SPANISH ▬ OTHER ▬

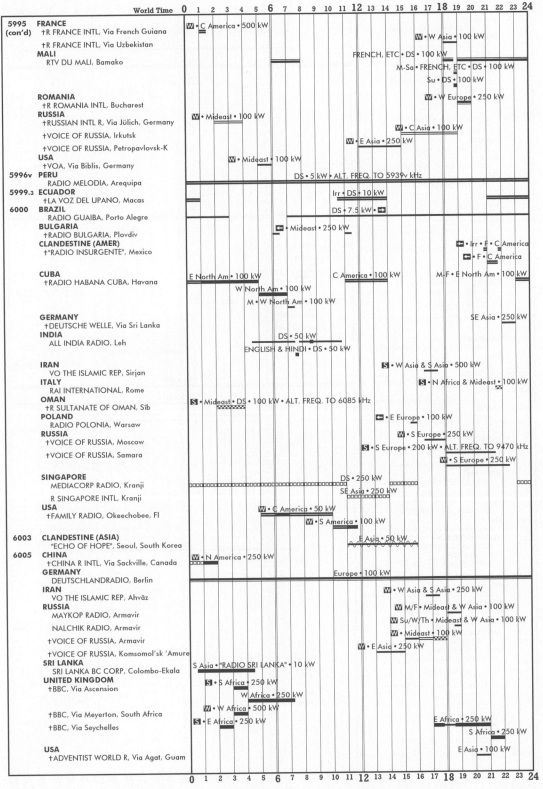

World Time 0 1 2 3 4 5 6 7 8 9 10 11 12 13 14 15 16 17 18 19 20 21 22 23 24

5995
(con'd) FRANCE
  †R FRANCE INTL, Via French Guiana — W • C America • 500 kW / W • W Asia • 100 kW
  †R FRANCE INTL, Via Uzbekistan
MALI
  RTV DU MALI, Bamako — FRENCH, ETC • DS • 100 kW / M-Sa • FRENCH, ETC • DS • 100 kW / Su • DS • 100 kW
ROMANIA
  †R ROMANIA INTL, Bucharest — W • W Europe • 250 kW
RUSSIA
  †RUSSIAN INTL R, Via Jülich, Germany — W • Mideast • 100 kW
  †VOICE OF RUSSIA, Irkutsk — W • C Asia • 100 kW
  †VOICE OF RUSSIA, Petropavlovsk-K — W • E Asia • 250 kW
USA
  †VOA, Via Biblis, Germany — W • Mideast • 100 kW
5996v PERU
  RADIO MELODIA, Arequipa — DS • 5 kW • ALT. FREQ. TO 5939v kHz
5999.3 ECUADOR
  †LA VOZ DEL UPANO, Macas — Irr • DS • 10 kW
6000 BRAZIL
  RADIO GUAIBA, Porto Alegre — DS • 7.5 kW • →
BULGARIA
  †RADIO BULGARIA, Plovdiv — → • Mideast • 250 kW
CLANDESTINE (AMER)
  †"RADIO INSURGENTE", Mexico — → • Irr • F • C America / → • F • C America
CUBA
  †RADIO HABANA CUBA, Havana — E North Am • 100 kW / C America • 100 kW / M-F • E North Am • 100 kW / W North Am • 100 kW / M • W North Am • 100 kW
GERMANY
  †DEUTSCHE WELLE, Via Sri Lanka — SE Asia • 250 kW
INDIA
  ALL INDIA RADIO, Leh — DS • 50 kW / ENGLISH & HINDI • DS • 50 kW
IRAN
  VO THE ISLAMIC REP, Sirjan — S • W Asia & S Asia • 500 kW
ITALY
  RAI INTERNATIONAL, Rome — S • N Africa & Mideast • 100 kW
OMAN
  †R SULTANATE OF OMAN, Sīb — S • Mideast • DS • 100 kW • ALT. FREQ. TO 6085 kHz
POLAND
  RADIO POLONIA, Warsaw — → • E Europe • 100 kW
RUSSIA
  †VOICE OF RUSSIA, Moscow — W • S Europe • 250 kW / S • S Europe • 200 kW • ALT. FREQ. TO 9470 kHz
  †VOICE OF RUSSIA, Samara — W • S Europe • 250 kW
SINGAPORE
  MEDIACORP RADIO, Kranji — DS • 250 kW
  R SINGAPORE INTL, Kranji — SE Asia • 250 kW
USA
  †FAMILY RADIO, Okeechobee, Fl — W • C America • 50 kW / W • S America • 100 kW
6003 CLANDESTINE (ASIA)
  "ECHO OF HOPE", Seoul, South Korea — E Asia • 50 kW
6005 CHINA
  †CHINA R INTL, Via Sackville, Canada — W • N America • 250 kW
GERMANY
  DEUTSCHLANDRADIO, Berlin — Europe • 100 kW
IRAN
  VO THE ISLAMIC REP, Ahvāz — W • W Asia & S Asia • 250 kW
RUSSIA
  MAYKOP RADIO, Armavir — W M/F • Mideast & W Asia • 100 kW
  NALCHIK RADIO, Armavir — W Su/W/Th • Mideast & W Asia • 100 kW
  †VOICE OF RUSSIA, Armavir — W • Mideast • 100 kW
  †VOICE OF RUSSIA, Komsomol'sk 'Amure — W • E Asia • 250 kW
SRI LANKA
  SRI LANKA BC CORP, Colombo-Ekala — S Asia • "RADIO SRI LANKA" • 10 kW
UNITED KINGDOM
  †BBC, Via Ascension — S • S Africa • 250 kW / W Africa • 250 kW
  †BBC, Via Meyerton, South Africa — W • W Africa • 500 kW
  †BBC, Via Seychelles — S • E Africa • 250 kW / E Africa • 250 kW / S Africa • 250 kW
USA
  †ADVENTIST WORLD R, Via Agat, Guam — E Asia • 100 kW

0 1 2 3 4 5 6 7 8 9 10 11 12 13 14 15 16 17 18 19 20 21 22 23 24

SEASONAL S OR W   1-HR TIMESHIFT MIDYEAR → OR →   JAMMING / OR ∧   EARLIEST HEARD ◁   LATEST HEARD ▷   NEW FOR 2007 †

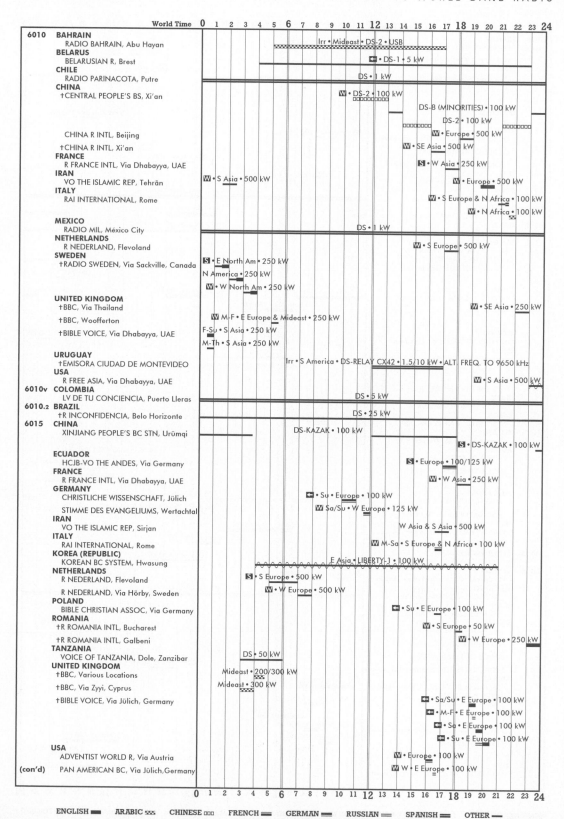

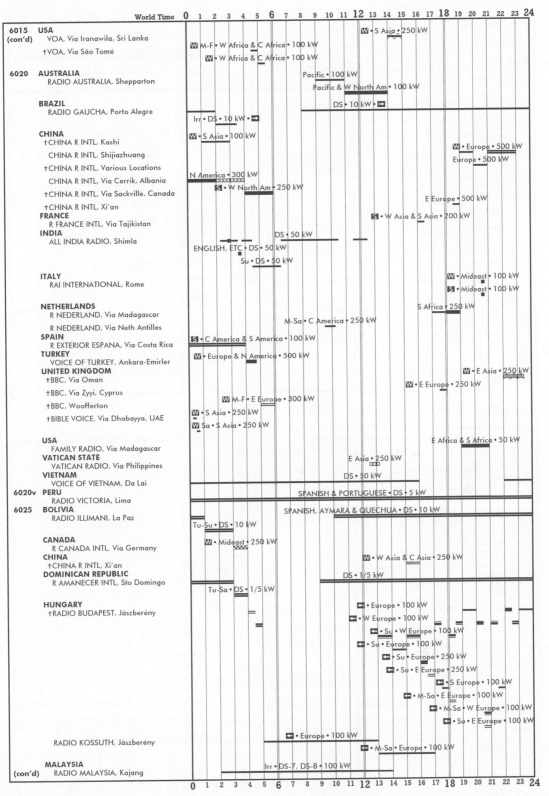

	World Time	0 1 2 3 4 5 6 7 8 9 10 11 12 13 14 15 16 17 18 19 20 21 22 23 24

6015 USA
(con'd)   VOA, Via Iranawila, Sri Lanka   — W • S Asia • 250 kW
    †VOA, Via São Tomé   — W • M-F • W Africa & C Africa • 100 kW
    W • W Africa & C Africa • 100 kW

6020 AUSTRALIA
    RADIO AUSTRALIA, Shepparton   Pacific • 100 kW
    Pacific & W North Am • 100 kW

BRAZIL
    RADIO GAUCHA, Porto Alegre   DS • 10 kW • →
    Irr • DS • 10 kW • →

CHINA
    †CHINA R INTL, Kashi   W • S Asia • 100 kW
    CHINA R INTL, Shijiazhuang   W • Europe • 500 kW
    †CHINA R INTL, Various Locations   Europe • 500 kW
    †CHINA R INTL, Via Cerrik, Albania   N America • 300 kW
    †CHINA R INTL, Via Sackville, Canada   S • W North Am • 250 kW
    †CHINA R INTL, Xi'an   E Europe • 500 kW
FRANCE
    R FRANCE INTL, Via Tajikistan   S • W Asia & S Asia • 200 kW
INDIA
    ALL INDIA RADIO, Shimla   DS • 50 kW
    ENGLISH, ETC • DS • 50 kW
    Su • DS • 50 kW

ITALY
    RAI INTERNATIONAL, Rome   W • Mideast • 100 kW
    S • Mideast • 100 kW

NETHERLANDS
    R NEDERLAND, Via Madagascar   S Africa • 250 kW
    R NEDERLAND, Via Neth Antilles   M-Sa • C America • 250 kW
SPAIN
    R EXTERIOR ESPANA, Via Costa Rica   S • C America & S America • 100 kW
TURKEY
    VOICE OF TURKEY, Ankara-Emirler   W • Europe & N America • 500 kW
UNITED KINGDOM
    †BBC, Via Oman   W • E Asia • 250 kW
    †BBC, Via Zyyi, Cyprus   W • E Europe • 250 kW
    †BBC, Woofferton   W • M-F • E Europe • 300 kW
    †BIBLE VOICE, Via Dhabayya, UAE   W • S Asia • 250 kW
    W • Sa • S Asia • 250 kW

USA
    FAMILY RADIO, Via Madagascar   E Africa & S Africa • 50 kW
VATICAN STATE
    VATICAN RADIO, Via Philippines   E Asia • 250 kW
VIETNAM
    VOICE OF VIETNAM, Da Lai   DS • 50 kW
6020v PERU
    RADIO VICTORIA, Lima   SPANISH & PORTUGUESE • DS • 5 kW
6025 BOLIVIA
    RADIO ILLIMANI, La Paz   SPANISH, AYMARA & QUECHUA • DS • 10 kW
    Tu-Su • DS • 10 kW

CANADA
    R CANADA INTL, Via Germany   W • Mideast • 250 kW
CHINA
    †CHINA R INTL, Xi'an   W • W Asia & C Asia • 250 kW
DOMINICAN REPUBLIC
    R AMANECER INTL, Sto Domingo   DS • 1/5 kW
    Tu-Sa • DS • 1/5 kW

HUNGARY
    †RADIO BUDAPEST, Jászberény   ← • Europe • 100 kW
    ← • W Europe • 100 kW
    ← • Su • W Europe • 100 kW
    ← • Su • Europe • 100 kW
    ← • Su • Europe • 250 kW
    ← • Su • E Europe • 250 kW
    ← • S Europe • 100 kW
    ← • M-Sa • E Europe • 100 kW
    ← • M-Sa • W Europe • 100 kW
    ← • Su • E Europe • 100 kW

    RADIO KOSSUTH, Jászberény   ← • Europe • 100 kW
    ← • M-Sa • Europe • 100 kW

MALAYSIA
(con'd)   RADIO MALAYSIA, Kajang   Irr • DS-7, DS-8 • 100 kW

	0 1 2 3 4 5 6 7 8 9 10 11 12 13 14 15 16 17 18 19 20 21 22 23 24

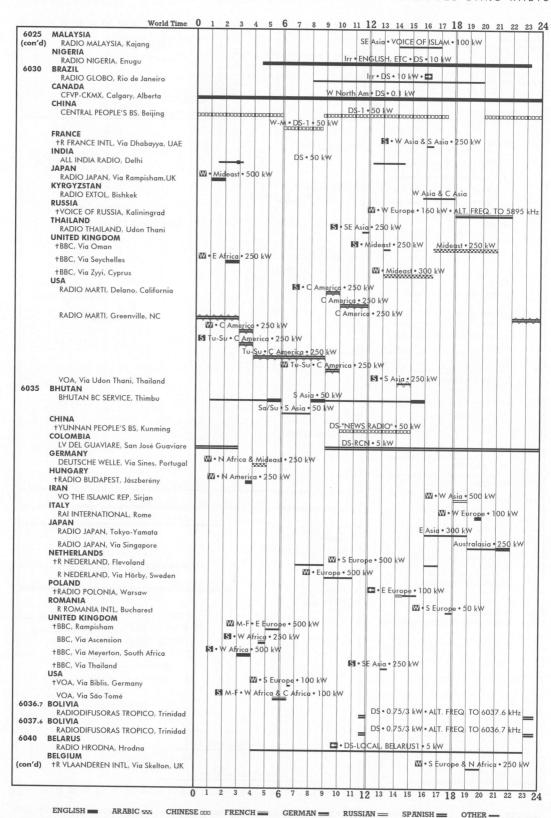

6025	**MALAYSIA**	
(con'd)	RADIO MALAYSIA, Kajang	SE Asia • VOICE OF ISLAM • 100 kW
	NIGERIA	
	RADIO NIGERIA, Enugu	Irr • ENGLISH, ETC • DS • 10 kW
6030	**BRAZIL**	
	RADIO GLOBO, Rio de Janeiro	Irr • DS • 10 kW
	CANADA	
	CFVP-CKMX, Calgary, Alberta	W North Am • DS • 0.1 kW
	CHINA	
	CENTRAL PEOPLE'S BS, Beijing	DS-1 • 50 kW / W-M • DS-1 • 50 kW
	FRANCE	
	†R FRANCE INTL, Via Dhabayya, UAE	W Asia & S Asia • 250 kW
	INDIA	
	ALL INDIA RADIO, Delhi	DS • 50 kW
	JAPAN	
	RADIO JAPAN, Via Rampisham, UK	W • Mideast • 500 kW
	KYRGYZSTAN	
	RADIO EXTOL, Bishkek	W Asia & C Asia
	RUSSIA	
	†VOICE OF RUSSIA, Kaliningrad	W • W Europe • 160 kW • ALT. FREQ. TO 5895 kHz
	THAILAND	
	RADIO THAILAND, Udon Thani	S • SE Asia • 250 kW
	UNITED KINGDOM	
	†BBC, Via Oman	S • Mideast • 250 kW / Mideast • 250 kW
	†BBC, Via Seychelles	W • E Africa • 250 kW
	†BBC, Via Zyyi, Cyprus	W • Mideast • 300 kW
	USA	
	RADIO MARTI, Delano, California	S • C America • 250 kW / C America • 250 kW / C America • 250 kW
	RADIO MARTI, Greenville, NC	W • C America • 250 kW / S Tu-Su • C America • 250 kW / Tu-Su • C America • 250 kW / W Tu-Su • C America • 250 kW / S • S Asia • 250 kW
	VOA, Via Udon Thani, Thailand	
6035	**BHUTAN**	
	BHUTAN BC SERVICE, Thimbu	S Asia • 50 kW / Sa/Su • S Asia • 50 kW
	CHINA	
	†YUNNAN PEOPLE'S BS, Kunming	DS-"NEWS RADIO" • 50 kW
	COLOMBIA	
	LV DEL GUAVIARE, San José Guaviare	DS-RCN • 5 kW
	GERMANY	
	DEUTSCHE WELLE, Via Sines, Portugal	W • N Africa & Mideast • 250 kW
	HUNGARY	
	†RADIO BUDAPEST, Jászberény	W • N America • 250 kW
	IRAN	
	VO THE ISLAMIC REP, Sirjan	W • W Asia • 500 kW
	ITALY	
	RAI INTERNATIONAL, Rome	W • W Europe • 100 kW
	JAPAN	
	RADIO JAPAN, Tokyo-Yamata	E Asia • 300 kW
	RADIO JAPAN, Via Singapore	Australasia • 250 kW
	NETHERLANDS	
	†R NEDERLAND, Flevoland	W • S Europe • 500 kW
	R NEDERLAND, Via Hörby, Sweden	W • Europe • 500 kW
	POLAND	
	†RADIO POLONIA, Warsaw	E Europe • 100 kW
	ROMANIA	
	R ROMANIA INTL, Bucharest	W • S Europe • 50 kW
	UNITED KINGDOM	
	†BBC, Rampisham	W M-F • E Europe • 500 kW
	BBC, Via Ascension	S • W Africa • 250 kW
	†BBC, Via Meyerton, South Africa	S • W Africa • 500 kW
	†BBC, Via Thailand	S • SE Asia • 250 kW
	USA	
	†VOA, Via Biblis, Germany	W • S Europe • 100 kW
	VOA, Via São Tomé	S M-F • W Africa & C Africa • 100 kW
6036.7	**BOLIVIA**	
	RADIODIFUSORAS TROPICO, Trinidad	DS • 0.75/3 kW • ALT. FREQ. TO 6037.6 kHz
6037.6	**BOLIVIA**	
	RADIODIFUSORAS TROPICO, Trinidad	DS • 0.75/3 kW • ALT. FREQ. TO 6036.7 kHz
6040	**BELARUS**	
	RADIO HRODNA, Hrodna	DS-LOCAL, BELARUS1 • 5 kW
	BELGIUM	
(con'd)	†R VLAANDEREN INTL, Via Skelton, UK	W • S Europe & N Africa • 250 kW

ENGLISH ▬   ARABIC ⌇⌇   CHINESE □□□   FRENCH ▭▭   GERMAN ▬   RUSSIAN ═   SPANISH ▬   OTHER ▬

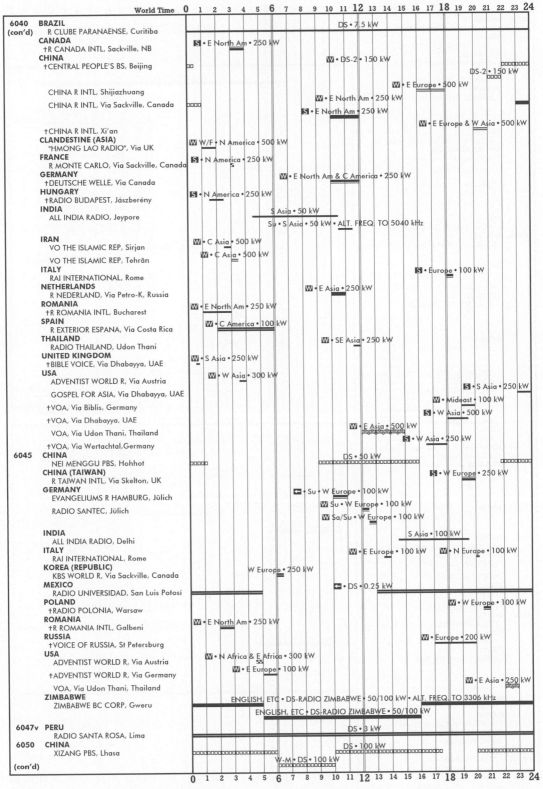

World Time 0 1 2 3 4 5 6 7 8 9 10 11 12 13 14 15 16 17 18 19 20 21 22 23 24

6040
(con'd) **BRAZIL**
  R CLUBE PARANAENSE, Curitiba — DS • 7.5 kW
  CANADA
  †R CANADA INTL, Sackville, NB — S • E North Am • 250 kW
  CHINA
  †CENTRAL PEOPLE'S BS, Beijing — W • DS-2 • 150 kW / DS-2 • 150 kW
  CHINA R INTL, Shijiazhuang — W • E Europe • 500 kW
  CHINA R INTL, Shijiazhuang — W • E North Am • 250 kW
  CHINA R INTL, Via Sackville, Canada — S • E North Am • 250 kW
  †CHINA R INTL, Xi'an — W • E Europe & W Asia • 500 kW
  CLANDESTINE (ASIA)
  "HMONG LAO RADIO", Via UK — W • W/F • N America • 500 kW
  FRANCE
  R MONTE CARLO, Via Sackville, Canada — S • N America • 250 kW
  GERMANY
  †DEUTSCHE WELLE, Via Canada — W • E North Am & C America • 250 kW
  HUNGARY
  †RADIO BUDAPEST, Jászberény — S • N America • 250 kW
  INDIA
  ALL INDIA RADIO, Jeypore — S Asia • 50 kW / Su • S Asia • 50 kW • ALT. FREQ. TO 5040 kHz
  IRAN
  VO THE ISLAMIC REP, Sirjan — W • C Asia • 500 kW
  VO THE ISLAMIC REP, Tehrān — W • C Asia • 500 kW
  ITALY
  RAI INTERNATIONAL, Rome — S • Europe • 100 kW
  NETHERLANDS
  R NEDERLAND, Via Petro-K, Russia — W • E Asia • 250 kW
  ROMANIA
  †R ROMANIA INTL, Bucharest — W • E North Am • 250 kW
  SPAIN
  R EXTERIOR ESPANA, Via Costa Rica — W • C America • 100 kW
  THAILAND
  RADIO THAILAND, Udon Thani — W • SE Asia • 250 kW
  UNITED KINGDOM
  †BIBLE VOICE, Via Dhabayya, UAE — W • S Asia • 250 kW
  USA
  ADVENTIST WORLD R, Via Austria — W • W Asia • 300 kW
  GOSPEL FOR ASIA, Via Dhabayya, UAE — S • S Asia • 250 kW
  †VOA, Via Biblis, Germany — W • Mideast • 100 kW
  †VOA, Via Dhabayya, UAE — S • W Asia • 500 kW
  VOA, Via Udon Thani, Thailand — W • E Asia • 500 kW
  †VOA, Via Wertachtal, Germany — S • W Asia • 250 kW

6045 **CHINA**
  NEI MENGGU PBS, Hohhot — DS • 50 kW
  CHINA (TAIWAN)
  R TAIWAN INTL, Via Skelton, UK — S • W Europe • 250 kW
  GERMANY
  EVANGELIUMS R HAMBURG, Jülich — Su • W Europe • 100 kW
  RADIO SANTEC, Jülich — W Su • W Europe • 100 kW
  RADIO SANTEC, Jülich — W Sa/Su • W Europe • 100 kW
  INDIA
  ALL INDIA RADIO, Delhi — S Asia • 100 kW
  ITALY
  RAI INTERNATIONAL, Rome — W • E Europe • 100 kW / W • N Eurape • 100 kW
  KOREA (REPUBLIC)
  KBS WORLD R, Via Sackville, Canada — W Europe • 250 kW
  MEXICO
  RADIO UNIVERSIDAD, San Luis Potosí — DS • 0.25 kW
  POLAND
  †RADIO POLONIA, Warsaw — W • W Europe • 100 kW
  ROMANIA
  †R ROMANIA INTL, Galbeni — W • E North Am • 250 kW
  RUSSIA
  †VOICE OF RUSSIA, St Petersburg — W • Europe • 200 kW
  USA
  ADVENTIST WORLD R, Via Austria — W • N Africa & E Africa • 300 kW
  †ADVENTIST WORLD R, Via Germany — W • E Europe • 100 kW
  VOA, Via Udon Thani, Thailand — W • E Asia • 250 kW
  ZIMBABWE
  ZIMBABWE BC CORP, Gweru — ENGLISH, ETC • DS-RADIO ZIMBABWE • 50/100 kW • ALT. FREQ. TO 3306 kHz
  ZIMBABWE BC CORP, Gweru — ENGLISH, ETC • DS-RADIO ZIMBABWE • 50/100 kW

6047v **PERU**
  RADIO SANTA ROSA, Lima — DS • 3 kW
6050 **CHINA**
  XIZANG PBS, Lhasa — DS • 100 kW / W-M • DS • 100 kW

(con'd)

0 1 2 3 4 5 6 7 8 9 10 11 12 13 14 15 16 17 18 19 20 21 22 23 24

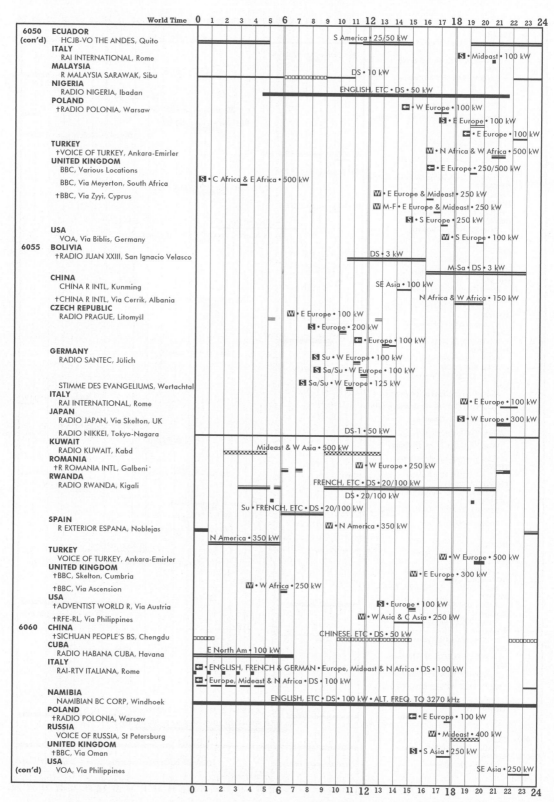

		World Time	0 1 2 3 4 5 6 7 8 9 10 11 12 13 14 15 16 17 18 19 20 21 22 23 24

6050 ECUADOR
(con'd)   HCJB-VO THE ANDES, Quito — S America • 25/50 kW

ITALY
RAI INTERNATIONAL, Rome — S • Mideast • 100 kW

MALAYSIA
R MALAYSIA SARAWAK, Sibu — DS • 10 kW

NIGERIA
RADIO NIGERIA, Ibadan — ENGLISH, ETC • DS • 50 kW

POLAND
†RADIO POLONIA, Warsaw — ← • W Europe • 100 kW
S • E Europe • 100 kW
← • E Europe • 100 kW

TURKEY
†VOICE OF TURKEY, Ankara-Emirler — W • N Africa & W Africa • 500 kW

UNITED KINGDOM
BBC, Various Locations — ← • E Europe • 250/500 kW

BBC, Via Meyerton, South Africa — S • C Africa & E Africa • 500 kW

†BBC, Via Zyyi, Cyprus — W • E Europe & Mideast • 250 kW
W M-F • E Europe & Mideast • 250 kW
S • S Europe • 250 kW

USA
VOA, Via Biblis, Germany — W • S Europe • 100 kW

6055 BOLIVIA
†RADIO JUAN XXIII, San Ignacio Velasco — DS • 3 kW
M-Sa • DS • 3 kW

CHINA
CHINA R INTL, Kunming — SE Asia • 100 kW

†CHINA R INTL, Via Cerrik, Albania — N Africa & W Africa • 150 kW

CZECH REPUBLIC
RADIO PRAGUE, Litomyšl — W • E Europe • 100 kW
S • Europe • 200 kW
← • Europe • 100 kW

GERMANY
RADIO SANTEC, Jülich — S Su • W Europe • 100 kW

STIMME DES EVANGELIUMS, Wertachtal — S Sa/Su • W Europe • 100 kW
S Sa/Su • W Europe • 125 kW

ITALY
RAI INTERNATIONAL, Rome — W • E Europe • 100 kW

JAPAN
RADIO JAPAN, Via Skelton, UK — S • W Europe • 300 kW

RADIO NIKKEI, Tokyo-Nagara — DS-1 • 50 kW

KUWAIT
RADIO KUWAIT, Kabd — Mideast & W Asia • 500 kW

ROMANIA
†R ROMANIA INTL, Galbeni — ← • W Europe • 250 kW

RWANDA
RADIO RWANDA, Kigali — FRENCH, ETC • DS • 20/100 kW
DS • 20/100 kW
Su • FRENCH, ETC • DS • 20/100 kW

SPAIN
R EXTERIOR ESPANA, Noblejas — W • N America • 350 kW
N America • 350 kW

TURKEY
VOICE OF TURKEY, Ankara-Emirler — W • W Europe • 500 kW

UNITED KINGDOM
†BBC, Skelton, Cumbria — W • E Europe • 300 kW

†BBC, Via Ascension — W • W Africa • 250 kW

USA
†ADVENTIST WORLD R, Via Austria — S • Europe • 100 kW

†RFE-RL, Via Philippines — W • W Asia & C Asia • 250 kW

6060 CHINA
†SICHUAN PEOPLE'S BS, Chengdu — CHINESE, ETC • DS • 50 kW

CUBA
RADIO HABANA CUBA, Havana — E North Am • 100 kW

ITALY
RAI-RTV ITALIANA, Rome — ← • ENGLISH, FRENCH & GERMAN • Europe, Mideast & N Africa • DS • 100 kW
← • Europe, Mideast & N Africa • DS • 100 kW

NAMIBIA
NAMIBIAN BC CORP, Windhoek — ENGLISH, ETC • DS • 100 kW • ALT. FREQ. TO 3270 kHz

POLAND
†RADIO POLONIA, Warsaw — ← • E Europe • 100 kW

RUSSIA
VOICE OF RUSSIA, St Petersburg — W • Mideast • 400 kW

UNITED KINGDOM
†BBC, Via Oman — S • S Asia • 250 kW

USA
(con'd)   VOA, Via Philippines — SE Asia • 250 kW

			0 1 2 3 4 5 6 7 8 9 10 11 12 13 14 15 16 17 18 19 20 21 22 23 24

ENGLISH ▬   ARABIC ⬚⬚⬚   CHINESE ▫▫▫   FRENCH ▭▭▭   GERMAN ▬▬   RUSSIAN ═══   SPANISH ▬▬   OTHER ▬

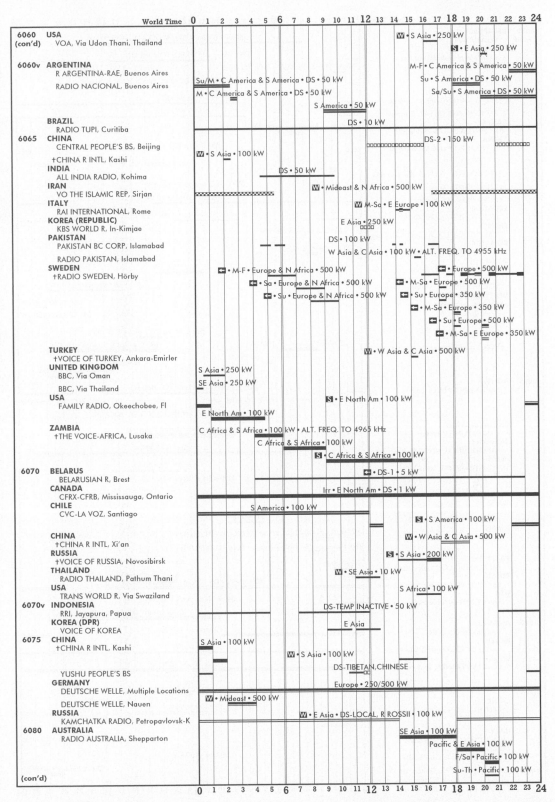

		World Time	0 1 2 3 4 5 6 7 8 9 10 11 12 13 14 15 16 17 18 19 20 21 22 23 24
6060 (con'd)	USA	VOA, Via Udon Thani, Thailand	W • S Asia • 250 kW / S • E Asia • 250 kW
6060v	ARGENTINA	R ARGENTINA-RAE, Buenos Aires	M-F • C America & S America • 50 kW / Su • S America • DS • 50 kW
		RADIO NACIONAL, Buenos Aires	Su/M • C America & S America • DS • 50 kW / M • C America & S America • DS • 50 kW / Sa/Su • S America • DS • 50 kW / S America • 50 kW
	BRAZIL	RADIO TUPI, Curitiba	DS • 10 kW
6065	CHINA	CENTRAL PEOPLE'S BS, Beijing	DS-2 • 150 kW / W • S Asia • 100 kW
		†CHINA R INTL, Kashi	
	INDIA	ALL INDIA RADIO, Kohima	DS • 50 kW
	IRAN	VO THE ISLAMIC REP, Sirjan	W • Mideast & N Africa • 500 kW
	ITALY	RAI INTERNATIONAL, Rome	W M-Sa • E Europe • 100 kW
	KOREA (REPUBLIC)	KBS WORLD R, In-Kimjae	E Asia • 250 kW
	PAKISTAN	PAKISTAN BC CORP, Islamabad	DS • 100 kW / W Asia & C Asia • 100 kW • ALT. FREQ. TO 4955 kHz
		RADIO PAKISTAN, Islamabad	
	SWEDEN	†RADIO SWEDEN, Hörby	⇦ • M-F • Europe & N Africa • 500 kW / ⇦ • Europe • 500 kW / ⇦ • Sa • Europe & N Africa • 500 kW / ⇦ • M-Sa • Europe • 500 kW / ⇦ • Su • Europe & N Africa • 500 kW / ⇦ • Su • Europe • 350 kW / ⇦ • M-Sa • Europe • 350 kW / ⇦ • Su • Europe • 500 kW / ⇦ • M-Sa • E Europe • 350 kW
	TURKEY	†VOICE OF TURKEY, Ankara-Emirler	W • W Asia & C Asia • 500 kW
	UNITED KINGDOM	BBC, Via Oman	S Asia • 250 kW
		BBC, Via Thailand	SE Asia • 250 kW
	USA	FAMILY RADIO, Okeechobee, Fl	S • E North Am • 100 kW / E North Am • 100 kW
	ZAMBIA	†THE VOICE-AFRICA, Lusaka	C Africa & S Africa • 100 kW • ALT. FREQ. TO 4965 kHz / C Africa & S Africa • 100 kW / S • C Africa & S Africa • 100 kW
6070	BELARUS	BELARUSIAN R, Brest	⇦ • DS-1 • 5 kW
	CANADA	CFRX-CFRB, Mississauga, Ontario	Irr • E North Am • DS • 1 kW
	CHILE	CVC-LA VOZ, Santiago	S America • 100 kW / S • S America • 100 kW
	CHINA	†CHINA R INTL, Xi'an	W • W Asia & C Asia • 500 kW
	RUSSIA	†VOICE OF RUSSIA, Novosibirsk	S • S Asia • 200 kW
	THAILAND	RADIO THAILAND, Pathum Thani	W • SE Asia • 10 kW
	USA	TRANS WORLD R, Via Swaziland	S Africa • 100 kW
6070v	INDONESIA	RRI, Jayapura, Papua	DS-TEMP INACTIVE • 50 kW
	KOREA (DPR)	VOICE OF KOREA	E Asia
6075	CHINA	†CHINA R INTL, Kashi	S Asia • 100 kW / W • S Asia • 100 kW
		YUSHU PEOPLE'S BS	DS-TIBETAN,CHINESE
	GERMANY	DEUTSCHE WELLE, Multiple Locations	Europe • 250/500 kW
		DEUTSCHE WELLE, Nauen	W • Mideast • 500 kW
	RUSSIA	KAMCHATKA RADIO, Petropavlovsk-K	W • E Asia • DS-LOCAL, R ROSSII • 100 kW
6080	AUSTRALIA	RADIO AUSTRALIA, Shepparton	SE Asia • 100 kW / Pacific & E Asia • 100 kW / F/Sa • Pacific • 100 kW / Su-Th • Pacific • 100 kW

(con'd)

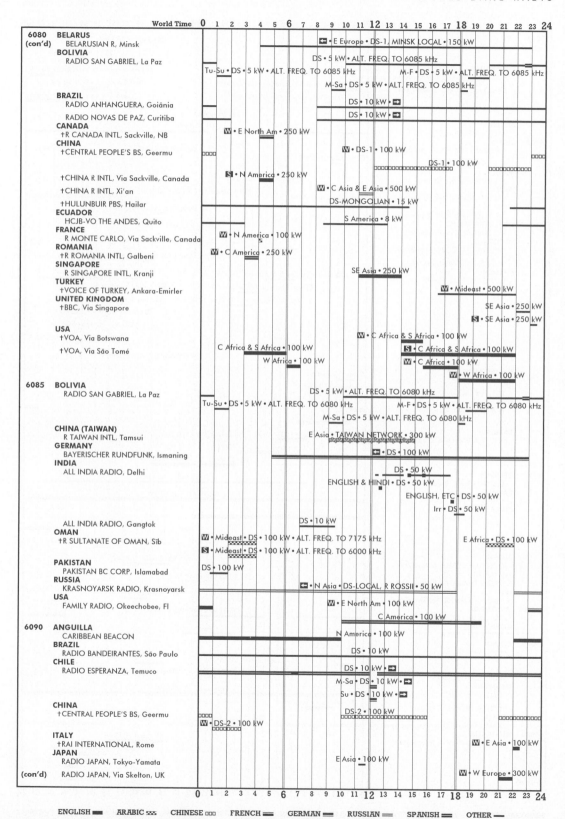

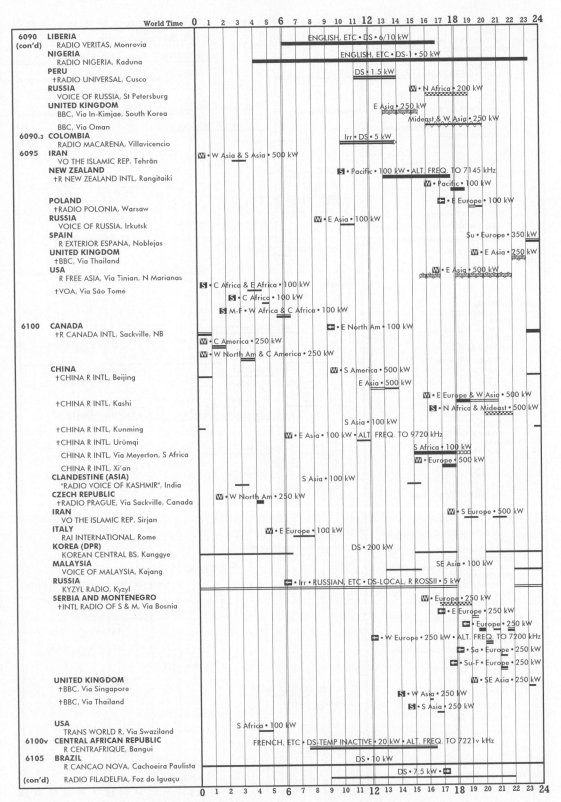

Freq	Country / Station	Schedule
6090 (con'd)	**LIBERIA** — RADIO VERITAS, Monrovia	ENGLISH, ETC • DS • 6/10 kW
	NIGERIA — RADIO NIGERIA, Kaduna	ENGLISH, ETC • DS-1 • 50 kW
	PERU — †RADIO UNIVERSAL, Cusco	DS • 1.5 kW
	RUSSIA — VOICE OF RUSSIA, St Petersburg	W • N Africa • 200 kW
	UNITED KINGDOM — BBC, Via In-Kimjae, South Korea	E Asia • 250 kW
	BBC, Via Oman	Mideast & W Asia • 250 kW
6090.3	**COLOMBIA** — RADIO MACARENA, Villavicencio	Irr • DS • 5 kW
6095	**IRAN** — VO THE ISLAMIC REP, Tehrän	W • W Asia & S Asia • 500 kW
	NEW ZEALAND — †R NEW ZEALAND INTL, Rangitaiki	S • Pacific • 100 kW • ALT. FREQ. TO 7145 kHz / W • Pacific • 100 kW
	POLAND — †RADIO POLONIA, Warsaw	• E Europe • 100 kW
	RUSSIA — VOICE OF RUSSIA, Irkutsk	W • E Asia • 100 kW
	SPAIN — R EXTERIOR ESPANA, Noblejas	Su • Europe • 350 kW
	UNITED KINGDOM — †BBC, Via Thailand	W • E Asia • 250 kW
	USA — R FREE ASIA, Via Tinian, N Marianas	W • E Asia • 500 kW
	†VOA, Via São Tomé	S • C Africa & E Africa • 100 kW / S • C Africa • 100 kW / S M-F • W Africa & C Africa • 100 kW
6100	**CANADA** — †R CANADA INTL, Sackville, NB	• E North Am • 100 kW / W • C America • 250 kW / W • W North Am & C America • 250 kW
	CHINA — †CHINA R INTL, Beijing	W • S America • 500 kW / E Asia • 500 kW / W • E Europe & W Asia • 500 kW
	†CHINA R INTL, Kashi	S • N Africa & Mideast • 500 kW
	†CHINA R INTL, Kunming	S Asia • 100 kW
	†CHINA R INTL, Urümqi	W • E Asia • 100 kW • ALT. FREQ. TO 9720 kHz
	CHINA R INTL, Via Meyerton, S Africa	S Africa • 100 kW
	CHINA R INTL, Xi'an	W • Europe • 500 kW
	CLANDESTINE (ASIA) — "RADIO VOICE OF KASHMIR", India	S Asia • 100 kW
	CZECH REPUBLIC — †RADIO PRAGUE, Via Sackville, Canada	W • W North Am • 250 kW
	IRAN — VO THE ISLAMIC REP, Sirjan	W • S Europe • 500 kW
	ITALY — RAI INTERNATIONAL, Rome	W • E Europe • 100 kW
	KOREA (DPR) — KOREAN CENTRAL BS, Kanggye	DS • 200 kW
	MALAYSIA — VOICE OF MALAYSIA, Kajang	SE Asia • 100 kW
	RUSSIA — KYZYL RADIO, Kyzyl	• Irr • RUSSIAN, ETC • DS-LOCAL, R ROSSII • 5 kW
	SERBIA AND MONTENEGRO — †INTL RADIO OF S & M, Via Bosnia	W • Europe • 250 kW / • E Europe • 250 kW / • Europe • 250 kW / • W Europe • 250 kW • ALT. FREQ. TO 7200 kHz / • Sa • Europe • 250 kW / • Su-F • Europe • 250 kW
	UNITED KINGDOM — †BBC, Via Singapore	W • SE Asia • 250 kW / S • W Asia • 250 kW
	†BBC, Via Thailand	S • S Asia • 250 kW
	USA — TRANS WORLD R, Via Swaziland	S Africa • 100 kW
6100v	**CENTRAL AFRICAN REPUBLIC** — R CENTRAFRIQUE, Bangui	FRENCH, ETC • DS-TEMP INACTIVE • 20 kW • ALT. FREQ. TO 7221v kHz
6105	**BRAZIL** — R CANCAO NOVA, Cachoeira Paulista	DS • 10 kW
(con'd)	RADIO FILADELFIA, Foz do Iguaçu	DS • 7.5 kW •

SEASONAL **S** OR **W**　　1-HR TIMESHIFT MIDYEAR ⇦ OR ⇨　　JAMMING / OR ∧　　EARLIEST HEARD ◁　　LATEST HEARD ▷　　NEW FOR 2007 †

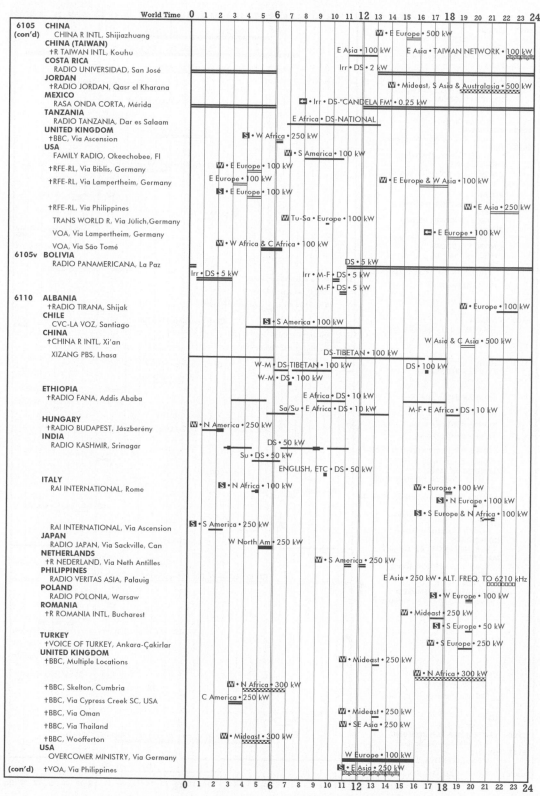

World Time 0 1 2 3 4 5 6 7 8 9 10 11 12 13 14 15 16 17 18 19 20 21 22 23 24

6105 CHINA
(con'd)   CHINA R INTL, Shijiazhuang — ☒ • E Europe • 500 kW
CHINA (TAIWAN)
   †R TAIWAN INTL, Kouhu — E Asia • 100 kW   E Asia • TAIWAN NETWORK • 100 kW
COSTA RICA
   RADIO UNIVERSIDAD, San José — Irr • DS • 2 kW
JORDAN
   †RADIO JORDAN, Qasr el Kharana — ☒ • Mideast, S Asia & Australasia • 500 kW
MEXICO
   RASA ONDA CORTA, Mérida — ⬜ • Irr • DS-"CANDELA FM" • 0.25 kW
TANZANIA
   RADIO TANZANIA, Dar es Salaam — E Africa • DS-NATIONAL
UNITED KINGDOM
   †BBC, Via Ascension — ☒ • W Africa • 250 kW
USA
   FAMILY RADIO, Okeechobee, Fl — ☒ • S America • 100 kW

   †RFE-RL, Via Biblis, Germany — ☒ • E Europe • 100 kW
   †RFE-RL, Via Lampertheim, Germany — E Europe • 100 kW   ☒ • E Europe & W Asia • 100 kW
                                        ☒ • E Europe • 100 kW

   †RFE-RL, Via Philippines — ☒ • E Asia • 250 kW
   TRANS WORLD R, Via Jülich, Germany — ☒ Tu-Sa • Europe • 100 kW
   VOA, Via Lampertheim, Germany — ⬜ • E Europe • 100 kW

   VOA, Via São Tomé — ☒ • W Africa & C Africa • 100 kW
6105v BOLIVIA
   RADIO PANAMERICANA, La Paz — ▬   DS • 5 kW
   Irr • DS • 5 kW   Irr • M-F • DS • 5 kW
                     M-F • DS • 5 kW

6110 ALBANIA
   †RADIO TIRANA, Shijak — ☒ • Europe • 100 kW
CHILE
   CVC-LA VOZ, Santiago — ☒ • S America • 100 kW
CHINA
   †CHINA R INTL, Xi'an — W Asia & C Asia • 500 kW

   XIZANG PBS, Lhasa — DS-TIBETAN • 100 kW
                       W-M • DS-TIBETAN • 100 kW   DS • 100 kW
                       W-M • DS • 100 kW

ETHIOPIA
   †RADIO FANA, Addis Ababa — E Africa • DS • 10 kW
                              Sa/Su • E Africa • DS • 10 kW   M-F • E Africa • DS • 10 kW
HUNGARY
   †RADIO BUDAPEST, Jászberény — ☒ • N America • 250 kW
INDIA
   RADIO KASHMIR, Srinagar — DS • 50 kW
                             Su • DS • 50 kW
                             ENGLISH, ETC • DS • 50 kW

ITALY
   RAI INTERNATIONAL, Rome — ☒ • N Africa • 100 kW   ☒ • Europe • 100 kW
                                                      ☒ • N Europe • 100 kW
                                                      ☒ • S Europe & N Africa • 100 kW

   RAI INTERNATIONAL, Via Ascension — ☒ • S America • 250 kW
JAPAN
   RADIO JAPAN, Via Sackville, Can — W North Am • 250 kW
NETHERLANDS
   †R NEDERLAND, Via Neth Antilles — ☒ • S America • 250 kW
PHILIPPINES
   RADIO VERITAS ASIA, Palauig — E Asia • 250 kW • ALT. FREQ. TO 6210 kHz
POLAND
   RADIO POLONIA, Warsaw — ☒ • W Europe • 100 kW
ROMANIA
   †R ROMANIA INTL, Bucharest — ☒ • Mideast • 250 kW
                                ☒ • S Europe • 50 kW
TURKEY
   †VOICE OF TURKEY, Ankara-Çakirlar — ☒ • S Europe • 250 kW
UNITED KINGDOM
   †BBC, Multiple Locations — ☒ • Mideast • 250 kW
                              ☒ • N Africa • 300 kW

   †BBC, Skelton, Cumbria — ☒ • N Africa • 300 kW
   †BBC, Via Cypress Creek SC, USA — C America • 250 kW
   †BBC, Via Oman — ☒ • Mideast • 250 kW
   †BBC, Via Thailand — ☒ • SE Asia • 250 kW
   †BBC, Woofferton — ☒ • Mideast • 300 kW
USA
   OVERCOMER MINISTRY, Via Germany — W Europe • 100 kW
(con'd)   †VOA, Via Philippines — ☒ • E Asia • 250 kW

0 1 2 3 4 5 6 7 8 9 10 11 12 13 14 15 16 17 18 19 20 21 22 23 24

ENGLISH ▬   ARABIC ⋙   CHINESE ☐☐☐   FRENCH ▬   GERMAN ▬   RUSSIAN ═   SPANISH ▭   OTHER ▬

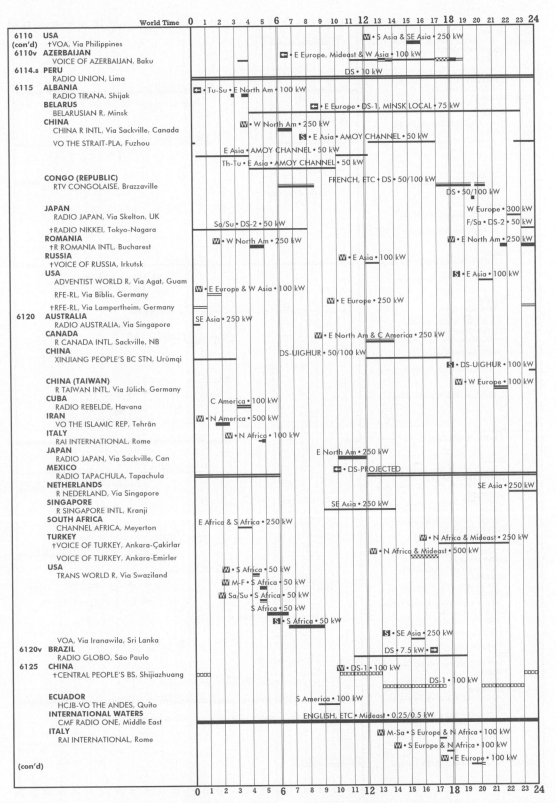

World Time 0 1 2 3 4 5 6 7 8 9 10 11 12 13 14 15 16 17 18 19 20 21 22 23 24

6110   **USA**
(con'd)   †VOA, Via Philippines   W • S Asia & SE Asia • 250 kW
6110v AZERBAIJAN
   VOICE OF AZERBAIJAN, Baku   • E Europe, Mideast & W Asia • 100 kW
6114.8 PERU
   RADIO UNION, Lima   DS • 10 kW
6115   **ALBANIA**
   RADIO TIRANA, Shijak   • Tu-Su • E North Am • 100 kW
   BELARUS
   BELARUSIAN R, Minsk   • E Europe • DS-1, MINSK LOCAL • 75 kW
   CHINA
   CHINA R INTL, Via Sackville, Canada   W • W North Am • 250 kW
   VO THE STRAIT-PLA, Fuzhou   S • E Asia • AMOY CHANNEL • 50 kW
   E Asia • AMOY CHANNEL • 50 kW
   Th-Tu • E Asia • AMOY CHANNEL • 50 kW
   CONGO (REPUBLIC)
   RTV CONGOLAISE, Brazzaville   FRENCH, ETC • DS • 50/100 kW
   DS • 50/100 kW
   JAPAN
   RADIO JAPAN, Via Skelton, UK   W Europe • 300 kW
   †RADIO NIKKEI, Tokyo-Nagara   Sa/Su • DS-2 • 50 kW   F/Sa • DS-2 • 50 kW
   ROMANIA
   †R ROMANIA INTL, Bucharest   W • W North Am • 250 kW   W • E North Am • 250 kW
   RUSSIA
   †VOICE OF RUSSIA, Irkutsk   W • E Asia • 100 kW
   USA
   ADVENTIST WORLD R, Via Agat, Guam   S • E Asia • 100 kW
   RFE-RL, Via Biblis, Germany   W • E Europe & W Asia • 100 kW
   †RFE-RL, Via Lampertheim, Germany   W • E Europe • 250 kW
6120   **AUSTRALIA**
   RADIO AUSTRALIA, Via Singapore   SE Asia • 250 kW
   CANADA
   R CANADA INTL, Sackville, NB   W • E North Am & C America • 250 kW
   CHINA
   XINJIANG PEOPLE'S BC STN, Urümqi   DS-UIGHUR • 50/100 kW
   S • DS-UIGHUR • 100 kW
   CHINA (TAIWAN)
   R TAIWAN INTL, Via Jülich, Germany   W • W Europe • 100 kW
   CUBA
   RADIO REBELDE, Havana   C America • 100 kW
   IRAN
   VO THE ISLAMIC REP, Tehrān   W • N America • 500 kW
   ITALY
   RAI INTERNATIONAL, Rome   W • N Africa • 100 kW
   JAPAN
   RADIO JAPAN, Via Sackville, Can   E North Am • 250 kW
   MEXICO
   RADIO TAPACHULA, Tapachula   • DS-PROJECTED
   NETHERLANDS
   R NEDERLAND, Via Singapore   SE Asia • 250 kW
   SINGAPORE
   R SINGAPORE INTL, Kranji   SE Asia • 250 kW
   SOUTH AFRICA
   CHANNEL AFRICA, Meyerton   E Africa & S Africa • 250 kW
   TURKEY
   †VOICE OF TURKEY, Ankara-Çakirlar   W • N Africa & Mideast • 250 kW
   VOICE OF TURKEY, Ankara-Emirler   W • N Africa & Mideast • 500 kW
   USA
   TRANS WORLD R, Via Swaziland   W • S Africa • 50 kW
   W M-F • S Africa • 50 kW
   W Sa/Su • S Africa • 50 kW
   S Africa • 50 kW
   S • S Africa • 50 kW
   VOA, Via Iranawila, Sri Lanka   S • SE Asia • 250 kW
6120v BRAZIL
   RADIO GLOBO, São Paulo   DS • 7.5 kW •
6125   **CHINA**
   †CENTRAL PEOPLE'S BS, Shijiazhuang   W • DS-1 • 100 kW
   DS-1 • 100 kW
   ECUADOR
   HCJB-VO THE ANDES, Quito   S America • 100 kW
   INTERNATIONAL WATERS
   CMF RADIO ONE, Middle East   ENGLISH, ETC • Mideast • 0.25/0.5 kW
   ITALY
   RAI INTERNATIONAL, Rome   W M-Sa • S Europe & N Africa • 100 kW
   W • S Europe & N Africa • 100 kW
   W • E Europe • 100 kW

(con'd)

0 1 2 3 4 5 6 7 8 9 10 11 12 13 14 15 16 17 18 19 20 21 22 23 24

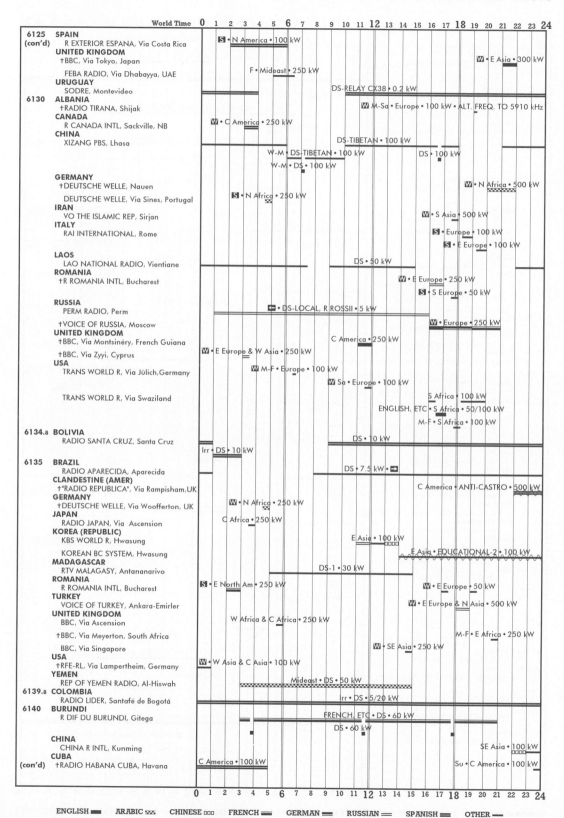

	World Time		
6125	**SPAIN**		
(con'd)	R EXTERIOR ESPANA, Via Costa Rica		S • N America • 100 kW
	UNITED KINGDOM		
	†BBC, Via Tokyo, Japan		W • E Asia • 300 kW
	FEBA RADIO, Via Dhabayya, UAE		F • Mideast • 250 kW
	URUGUAY		
	SODRE, Montevideo		DS-RELAY CX38 • 0.2 kW
6130	**ALBANIA**		
	†RADIO TIRANA, Shijak		W M-Sa • Europe • 100 kW • ALT. FREQ. TO 5910 kHz
	CANADA		
	R CANADA INTL, Sackville, NB		W • C America • 250 kW
	CHINA		
	XIZANG PBS, Lhasa		DS-TIBETAN • 100 kW
			W-M • DS-TIBETAN • 100 kW DS • 100 kW
			W-M • DS • 100 kW
	GERMANY		
	†DEUTSCHE WELLE, Nauen		W • N Africa • 500 kW
	DEUTSCHE WELLE, Via Sines, Portugal		S • N Africa • 250 kW
	IRAN		
	VO THE ISLAMIC REP, Sirjan		W • S Asia • 500 kW
	ITALY		
	RAI INTERNATIONAL, Rome		S • Europe • 100 kW
			S • E Europe • 100 kW
	LAOS		
	LAO NATIONAL RADIO, Vientiane		DS • 50 kW
	ROMANIA		
	†R ROMANIA INTL, Bucharest		W • E Europe • 250 kW
			S • S Europe • 50 kW
	RUSSIA		
	PERM RADIO, Perm		DS-LOCAL, R ROSSII • 5 kW
	†VOICE OF RUSSIA, Moscow		W • Europe • 250 kW
	UNITED KINGDOM		
	†BBC, Via Montsinéry, French Guiana		C America • 250 kW
	†BBC, Via Zyyi, Cyprus		W • E Europe & W Asia • 250 kW
	USA		
	TRANS WORLD R, Via Jülich, Germany		W M-F • Europe • 100 kW
			W Sa • Europe • 100 kW
	TRANS WORLD R, Via Swaziland		S Africa • 100 kW
			ENGLISH, ETC • S Africa • 50/100 kW
			M-F • S Africa • 100 kW
6134.8	**BOLIVIA**		
	RADIO SANTA CRUZ, Santa Cruz		DS • 10 kW
			Irr • DS • 10 kW
6135	**BRAZIL**		
	RADIO APARECIDA, Aparecida		DS • 7.5 kW • →
	CLANDESTINE (AMER)		
	†"RADIO REPUBLICA", Via Rampisham, UK		C America • ANTI-CASTRO • 500 kW
	GERMANY		
	†DEUTSCHE WELLE, Via Woofferton, UK		W • N Africa • 250 kW
	JAPAN		
	RADIO JAPAN, Via Ascension		C Africa • 250 kW
	KOREA (REPUBLIC)		
	KBS WORLD R, Hwasung		E Asia • 100 kW
	KOREAN BC SYSTEM, Hwasung		E Asia • EDUCATIONAL-2 • 100 kW
	MADAGASCAR		
	RTV MALAGASY, Antananarivo		DS-1 • 30 kW
	ROMANIA		
	R ROMANIA INTL, Bucharest		S • E North Am • 250 kW W • E Europe • 50 kW
	TURKEY		
	VOICE OF TURKEY, Ankara-Emirler		W • E Europe & N Asia • 500 kW
	UNITED KINGDOM		
	BBC, Via Ascension		W Africa & C Africa • 250 kW
	†BBC, Via Meyerton, South Africa		M-F • E Africa • 250 kW
	BBC, Via Singapore		W • SE Asia • 250 kW
	USA		
	†RFE-RL, Via Lampertheim, Germany		W • W Asia & C Asia • 100 kW
	YEMEN		
	REP OF YEMEN RADIO, Al-Hiswah		Mideast • DS • 50 kW
6139.8	**COLOMBIA**		
	RADIO LIDER, Santafé de Bogotá		Irr • DS • 5/20 kW
6140	**BURUNDI**		
	R DIF DU BURUNDI, Gitega		FRENCH, ETC • DS • 60 kW
			DS • 60 kW
	CHINA		
	CHINA R INTL, Kunming		SE Asia • 100 kW
	CUBA		
(con'd)	†RADIO HABANA CUBA, Havana		C America • 100 kW Su • C America • 100 kW

ENGLISH ▬   ARABIC ░░░   CHINESE □□□   FRENCH ▬   GERMAN ▬   RUSSIAN ═   SPANISH ▬   OTHER ▬

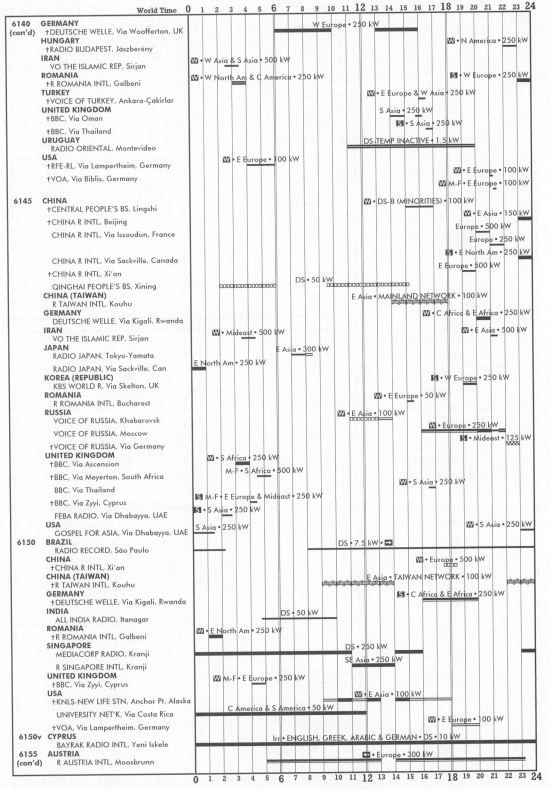

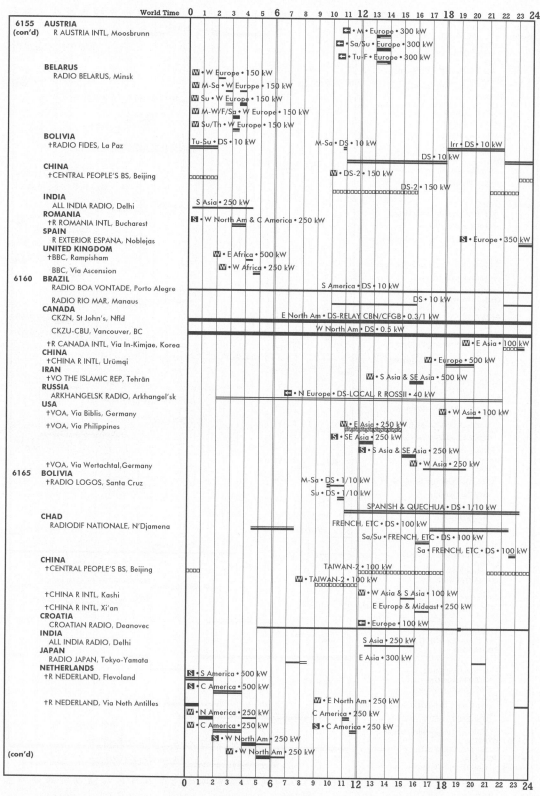

World Time 0 1 2 3 4 5 6 7 8 9 10 11 12 13 14 15 16 17 18 19 20 21 22 23 24

6155 AUSTRIA
(con'd)   R AUSTRIA INTL, Moosbrunn
  ◀ • M • Europe • 300 kW
  ◀ • Sa/Su • Europe • 300 kW
  ◀ • Tu-F • Europe • 300 kW

     BELARUS
        RADIO BELARUS, Minsk
  W • W Europe • 150 kW
  W • M-Sa • W Europe • 150 kW
  W • Su • W Europe • 150 kW
  W • M-W/F/Sa • W Europe • 150 kW
  W • Su/Th • W Europe • 150 kW

     BOLIVIA
        †RADIO FIDES, La Paz
  Tu-Su • DS • 10 kW   M-Sa • DS • 10 kW   Irr • DS • 10 kW
  DS • 10 kW

     CHINA
        †CENTRAL PEOPLE'S BS, Beijing
  W • DS-2 • 150 kW
  DS-2 • 150 kW

     INDIA
        ALL INDIA RADIO, Delhi
  S Asia • 250 kW
     ROMANIA
        †R ROMANIA INTL, Bucharest
  S • W North Am & C America • 250 kW
     SPAIN
        R EXTERIOR ESPANA, Noblejas
  S • Europe • 350 kW
     UNITED KINGDOM
        †BBC, Rampisham
  W • E Africa • 500 kW
        BBC, Via Ascension
  W • W Africa • 250 kW

6160 BRAZIL
        RADIO BOA VONTADE, Porto Alegre
  S America • DS • 10 kW
        RADIO RIO MAR, Manaus
  DS • 10 kW
     CANADA
        CKZN, St John's, Nfld
  E North Am • DS-RELAY CBN/CFGB • 0.3/1 kW
        CKZU-CBU, Vancouver, BC
  W North Am • DS • 0.5 kW

        †R CANADA INTL, Via In-Kimjae, Korea
  W • E Asia • 100 kW
     CHINA
        †CHINA R INTL, Urümqi
  W • Europe • 500 kW
     IRAN
        †VO THE ISLAMIC REP, Tehrän
  W • S Asia & SE Asia • 500 kW
     RUSSIA
        ARKHANGELSK RADIO, Arkhangel'sk
  ◀ • N Europe • DS-LOCAL, R ROSSII • 40 kW
     USA
        †VOA, Via Biblis, Germany
  W • W Asia • 100 kW

        †VOA, Via Philippines
  W • E Asia • 250 kW
  S • SE Asia • 250 kW
  S • S Asia & SE Asia • 250 kW
  W • W Asia • 250 kW

        †VOA, Via Wertachtal, Germany
6165 BOLIVIA
        †RADIO LOGOS, Santa Cruz
  M-Sa • DS • 1/10 kW
  Su • DS • 1/10 kW
  SPANISH & QUECHUA • DS • 1/10 kW

     CHAD
        RADIODIF NATIONALE, N'Djamena
  FRENCH, ETC • DS • 100 kW
  Sa/Su • FRENCH, ETC • DS • 100 kW
  Sa • FRENCH, ETC • DS • 100 kW

     CHINA
        †CENTRAL PEOPLE'S BS, Beijing
  TAIWAN-2 • 100 kW
  W • TAIWAN-2 • 100 kW

        †CHINA R INTL, Kashi
  W • W Asia & S Asia • 100 kW
        †CHINA R INTL, Xi'an
  E Europe & Mideast • 250 kW
     CROATIA
        CROATIAN RADIO, Deanovec
  ◀ • Europe • 100 kW
     INDIA
        ALL INDIA RADIO, Delhi
  S Asia • 250 kW
     JAPAN
        RADIO JAPAN, Tokyo-Yamata
  E Asia • 300 kW
     NETHERLANDS
        †R NEDERLAND, Flevoland
  S • S America • 500 kW
  S • C America • 500 kW

        †R NEDERLAND, Via Neth Antilles
  W • E North Am • 250 kW
  W • N America • 250 kW   C America • 250 kW
  W • C America • 250 kW   S • C America • 250 kW
  S • W North Am • 250 kW
(con'd)
  W • W North Am • 250 kW

  0 1 2 3 4 5 6 7 8 9 10 11 12 13 14 15 16 17 18 19 20 21 22 23 24

ENGLISH ▬   ARABIC ⠿   CHINESE ▦   FRENCH ▬   GERMAN ▬   RUSSIAN ═   SPANISH ▬   OTHER ▬

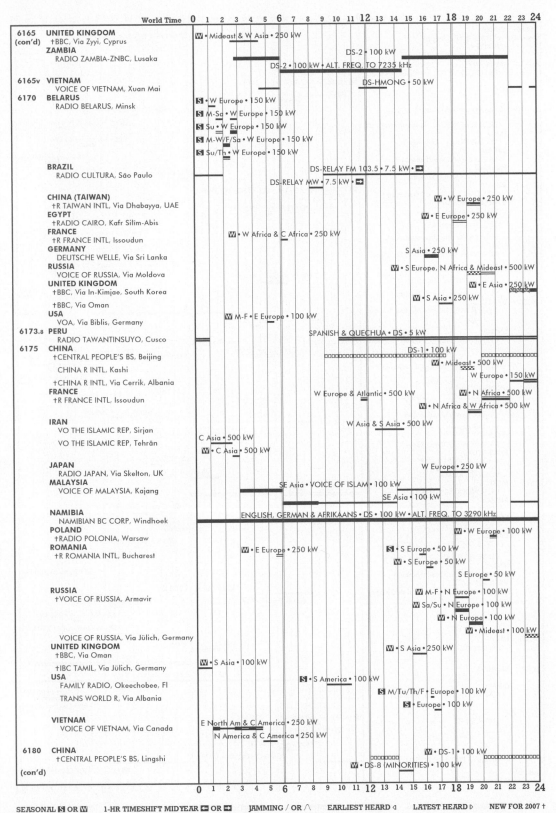

World Time	0 1 2 3 4 5 6 7 8 9 10 11 12 13 14 15 16 17 18 19 20 21 22 23 24
6165 (con'd) †BBC, Via Zyyi, Cyprus	W • Mideast & W Asia • 250 kW
UNITED KINGDOM	
ZAMBIA RADIO ZAMBIA-ZNBC, Lusaka	DS-2 • 100 kW / DS-2 • 100 kW • ALT. FREQ. TO 7235 kHz
6165v VIETNAM VOICE OF VIETNAM, Xuan Mai	DS-HMONG • 50 kW
6170 BELARUS RADIO BELARUS, Minsk	S • W Europe • 150 kW / S • M-Sa • W Europe • 150 kW / S • Su • W Europe • 150 kW / S • M-W/F/Sa • W Europe • 150 kW / S • Su/Th • W Europe • 150 kW
BRAZIL RADIO CULTURA, São Paulo	DS-RELAY FM 103.5 • 7.5 kW • ➡ / DS-RELAY MW • 7.5 kW • ➡
CHINA (TAIWAN) †R TAIWAN INTL, Via Dhabayya, UAE	W • W Europe • 250 kW
EGYPT †RADIO CAIRO, Kafr Silim-Abis	W • E Europe • 250 kW
FRANCE †R FRANCE INTL, Issoudun	W • W Africa & C Africa • 250 kW
GERMANY DEUTSCHE WELLE, Via Sri Lanka	S Asia • 250 kW
RUSSIA VOICE OF RUSSIA, Via Moldova	W • S Europe, N Africa & Mideast • 500 kW
UNITED KINGDOM †BBC, Via In-Kimjae, South Korea	W • E Asia • 250 kW
†BBC, Via Oman	W • S Asia • 250 kW
USA VOA, Via Biblis, Germany	W • M-F • E Europe • 100 kW
6173.8 PERU RADIO TAWANTINSUYO, Cusco	SPANISH & QUECHUA • DS • 5 kW
6175 CHINA †CENTRAL PEOPLE'S BS, Beijing	DS-1 • 100 kW
CHINA R INTL, Kashi	W • Mideast • 500 kW / W Europe • 150 kW
†CHINA R INTL, Via Cerrik, Albania	W Europe & Atlantic • 500 kW
FRANCE †R FRANCE INTL, Issoudun	W • N Africa • 500 kW / W • N Africa & W Africa • 500 kW
IRAN VO THE ISLAMIC REP, Sirjan	W Asia & S Asia • 500 kW
VO THE ISLAMIC REP, Tehrān	C Asia • 500 kW / W • C Asia • 500 kW
JAPAN RADIO JAPAN, Via Skelton, UK	W Europe • 250 kW
MALAYSIA VOICE OF MALAYSIA, Kajang	SE Asia • VOICE OF ISLAM • 100 kW / SE Asia • 100 kW
NAMIBIA NAMIBIAN BC CORP, Windhoek	ENGLISH, GERMAN & AFRIKAANS • DS • 100 kW • ALT. FREQ. TO 3290 kHz
POLAND †RADIO POLONIA, Warsaw	W • W Europe • 100 kW
ROMANIA †R ROMANIA INTL, Bucharest	W • E Europe • 250 kW / S • S Europe • 50 kW / W • S Europe • 50 kW / S Europe • 50 kW
RUSSIA †VOICE OF RUSSIA, Armavir	W • M-F • N Europe • 100 kW / W • Sa/Su • N Europe • 100 kW / W • N Europe • 100 kW / W • Mideast • 100 kW
VOICE OF RUSSIA, Via Jülich, Germany	
UNITED KINGDOM †BBC, Via Oman	W • S Asia • 250 kW / W • S Asia • 100 kW
†IBC TAMIL, Via Jülich, Germany	
USA FAMILY RADIO, Okeechobee, Fl	S • S America • 100 kW
TRANS WORLD R, Via Albania	S • M/Tu/Th/F • Europe • 100 kW / S • Europe • 100 kW
VIETNAM VOICE OF VIETNAM, Via Canada	E North Am & C America • 250 kW / N America & C America • 250 kW
6180 CHINA †CENTRAL PEOPLE'S BS, Lingshi (con'd)	W • DS-1 • 100 kW / W • DS-8 (MINORITIES) • 100 kW

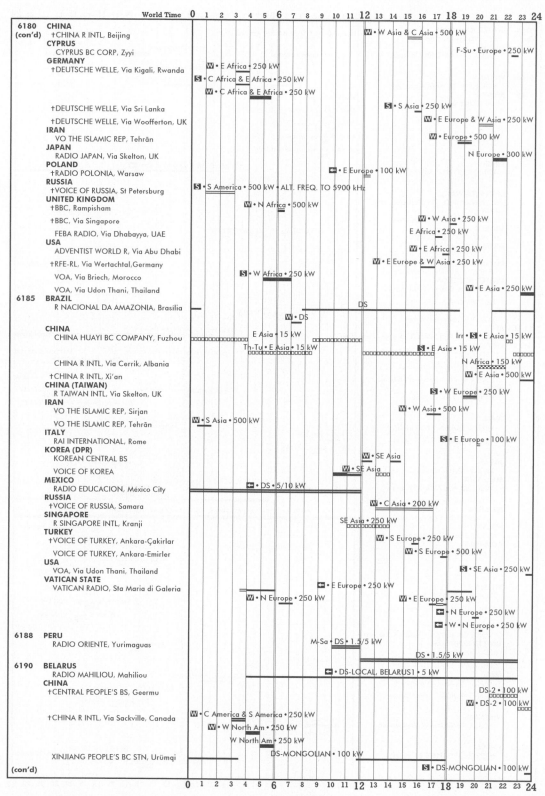

World Time 0 1 2 3 4 5 6 7 8 9 10 11 12 13 14 15 16 17 18 19 20 21 22 23 24

6180
(con'd) CHINA
†CHINA R INTL, Beijing — W • W Asia & C Asia • 500 kW
CYPRUS
CYPRUS BC CORP, Zyyi — F-Su • Europe • 250 kW
GERMANY
†DEUTSCHE WELLE, Via Kigali, Rwanda — W • E Africa • 250 kW
S • C Africa & E Africa • 250 kW
W • C Africa & E Africa • 250 kW
†DEUTSCHE WELLE, Via Sri Lanka — S • S Asia • 250 kW
†DEUTSCHE WELLE, Via Woofferton, UK — W • E Europe & W Asia • 250 kW
IRAN
VO THE ISLAMIC REP, Tehrān — W • Europe • 500 kW
JAPAN
RADIO JAPAN, Via Skelton, UK — N Europe • 300 kW
POLAND
†RADIO POLONIA, Warsaw — • E Europe • 100 kW
RUSSIA
†VOICE OF RUSSIA, St Petersburg — S • S America • 500 kW • ALT. FREQ. TO 5900 kHz
UNITED KINGDOM
†BBC, Rampisham — W • N Africa • 500 kW
†BBC, Via Singapore — W • W Asia • 250 kW
FEBA RADIO, Via Dhabayya, UAE — E Africa • 250 kW
USA
ADVENTIST WORLD R, Via Abu Dhabi — W • E Africa • 250 kW
†RFE-RL, Via Wertachtal, Germany — W • E Europe & W Asia • 250 kW
VOA, Via Briech, Morocco — S • W Africa • 250 kW
VOA, Via Udon Thani, Thailand — W • E Asia • 250 kW

6185 BRAZIL
R NACIONAL DA AMAZONIA, Brasilia — DS
CHINA
CHINA HUAYI BC COMPANY, Fuzhou — W • DS
E Asia • 15 kW   Irr • S • E Asia • 15 kW
Th-Tu • E Asia • 15 kW   S • E Asia • 15 kW
CHINA R INTL, Via Cerrik, Albania — N Africa • 150 kW
†CHINA R INTL, Xi'an — W • E Asia • 500 kW
CHINA (TAIWAN)
R TAIWAN INTL, Via Skelton, UK — S • W Europe • 250 kW
IRAN
VO THE ISLAMIC REP, Sirjan — W • W Asia • 500 kW
VO THE ISLAMIC REP, Tehrān — W • S Asia • 500 kW
ITALY
RAI INTERNATIONAL, Rome — S • E Europe • 100 kW
KOREA (DPR)
KOREAN CENTRAL BS — W • SE Asia
VOICE OF KOREA — W • SE Asia
MEXICO
RADIO EDUCACION, México City — • DS • 5/10 kW
RUSSIA
†VOICE OF RUSSIA, Samara — W • C Asia • 200 kW
SINGAPORE
R SINGAPORE INTL, Kranji — SE Asia • 250 kW
TURKEY
†VOICE OF TURKEY, Ankara-Çakirlar — W • S Europe • 250 kW
VOICE OF TURKEY, Ankara-Emirler — W • S Europe • 500 kW
USA
VOA, Via Udon Thani, Thailand — S • SE Asia • 250 kW
VATICAN STATE
VATICAN RADIO, Sta Maria di Galeria — • E Europe • 250 kW
W • N Europe • 250 kW   W • E Europe • 250 kW
• N Europe • 250 kW
• W • N Europe • 250 kW

6188 PERU
RADIO ORIENTE, Yurimaguas — M-Sa • DS • 1.5/5 kW
DS • 1.5/5 kW

6190 BELARUS
RADIO MAHILIOU, Mahiliou — • DS-LOCAL, BELARUS1 • 5 kW
CHINA
†CENTRAL PEOPLE'S BS, Geermu — DS-2 • 100 kW
W • DS-2 • 100 kW
†CHINA R INTL, Via Sackville, Canada — W • C America & S America • 250 kW
W • W North Am • 250 kW
W North Am • 250 kW
XINJIANG PEOPLE'S BC STN, Urümqi — DS-MONGOLIAN • 100 kW
(con'd) — S • DS-MONGOLIAN • 100 kW

0 1 2 3 4 5 6 7 8 9 10 11 12 13 14 15 16 17 18 19 20 21 22 23 24

ENGLISH ▬   ARABIC ⌇⌇⌇   CHINESE □□□   FRENCH ▭▭   GERMAN ▬▬   RUSSIAN ═══   SPANISH ▬▬   OTHER ▬

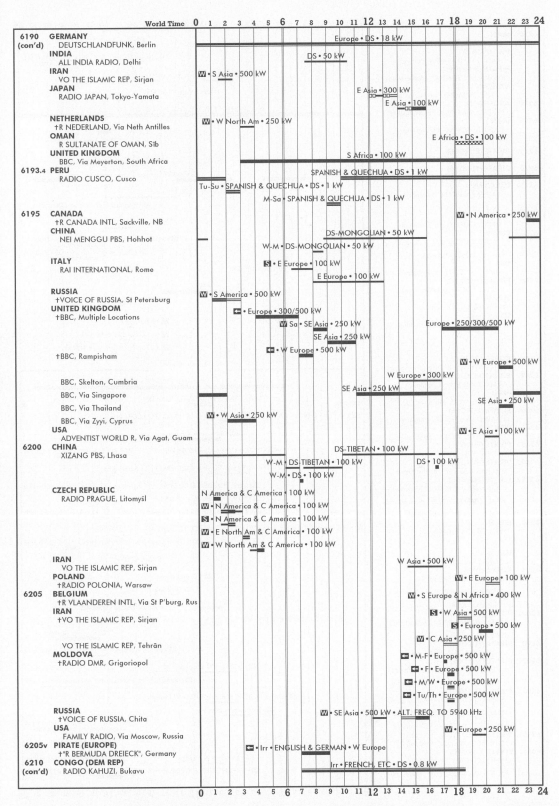

| | World Time | 0 | 1 | 2 | 3 | 4 | 5 | 6 | 7 | 8 | 9 | 10 | 11 | 12 | 13 | 14 | 15 | 16 | 17 | 18 | 19 | 20 | 21 | 22 | 23 | 24 |

6190 (con'd) GERMANY
DEUTSCHLANDFUNK, Berlin — Europe • DS • 18 kW

INDIA
ALL INDIA RADIO, Delhi — DS • 50 kW

IRAN
VO THE ISLAMIC REP, Sirjan — W • S Asia • 500 kW

JAPAN
RADIO JAPAN, Tokyo-Yamata — E Asia • 300 kW / E Asia • 100 kW

NETHERLANDS
†R NEDERLAND, Via Neth Antilles — W • W North Am • 250 kW

OMAN
R SULTANATE OF OMAN, Sīb — E Africa • DS • 100 kW

UNITED KINGDOM
BBC, Via Meyerton, South Africa — S Africa • 100 kW

6193.4 PERU
RADIO CUSCO, Cusco — SPANISH & QUECHUA • DS • 1 kW
Tu-Su • SPANISH & QUECHUA • DS • 1 kW
M-Sa • SPANISH & QUECHUA • DS • 1 kW

6195 CANADA
†R CANADA INTL, Sackville, NB — W • N America • 250 kW

CHINA
NEI MENGGU PBS, Hohhot — DS-MONGOLIAN • 50 kW
W-M • DS-MONGOLIAN • 50 kW

ITALY
RAI INTERNATIONAL, Rome — S • E Europe • 100 kW
E Europe • 100 kW

RUSSIA
†VOICE OF RUSSIA, St Petersburg — W • S America • 500 kW

UNITED KINGDOM
†BBC, Multiple Locations — Europe • 300/500 kW
W Sa • SE Asia • 250 kW
SE Asia • 250 kW
Europe • 250/300/500 kW

†BBC, Rampisham — W Europe • 500 kW
W • W Europe • 500 kW

BBC, Skelton, Cumbria — W Europe • 300 kW

BBC, Via Singapore — SE Asia • 250 kW

BBC, Via Thailand — SE Asia • 250 kW

BBC, Via Zyyi, Cyprus — W • W Asia • 250 kW

USA
ADVENTIST WORLD R, Via Agat, Guam — W • E Asia • 100 kW

6200 CHINA
XIZANG PBS, Lhasa — DS-TIBETAN • 100 kW
W-M • DS-TIBETAN • 100 kW
DS • 100 kW
W-M • DS • 100 kW

CZECH REPUBLIC
RADIO PRAGUE, Litomyšl — N America & C America • 100 kW
W • N America & C America • 100 kW
S • N America & C America • 100 kW
W • E North Am & C America • 100 kW
W • W North Am & C America • 100 kW

IRAN
VO THE ISLAMIC REP, Sirjan — W Asia • 500 kW

POLAND
†RADIO POLONIA, Warsaw — W • E Europe • 100 kW

6205 BELGIUM
†R VLAANDEREN INTL, Via St P'burg, Rus — W • S Europe & N Africa • 400 kW

IRAN
†VO THE ISLAMIC REP, Sirjan — S • W Asia • 500 kW
S • Europe • 500 kW
W • C Asia • 250 kW

VO THE ISLAMIC REP, Tehrān

MOLDOVA
†RADIO DMR, Grigoriopol — M-F • Europe • 500 kW
F • Europe • 500 kW
M/W • Europe • 500 kW
Tu/Th • Europe • 500 kW

RUSSIA
†VOICE OF RUSSIA, Chita — W • SE Asia • 500 kW • ALT. FREQ. TO 5940 kHz

USA
FAMILY RADIO, Via Moscow, Russia — W • Europe • 250 kW

6205v PIRATE (EUROPE)
†"R BERMUDA DREIECK", Germany — Irr • ENGLISH & GERMAN • W Europe

6210 (con'd) CONGO (DEM REP)
RADIO KAHUZI, Bukavu — Irr • FRENCH, ETC • DS • 0.8 kW

| | | 0 | 1 | 2 | 3 | 4 | 5 | 6 | 7 | 8 | 9 | 10 | 11 | 12 | 13 | 14 | 15 | 16 | 17 | 18 | 19 | 20 | 21 | 22 | 23 | 24 |

SEASONAL S OR W   1-HR TIMESHIFT MIDYEAR ⇐ OR ⇒   JAMMING / OR /\   EARLIEST HEARD ◁   LATEST HEARD ▷   NEW FOR 2007 †

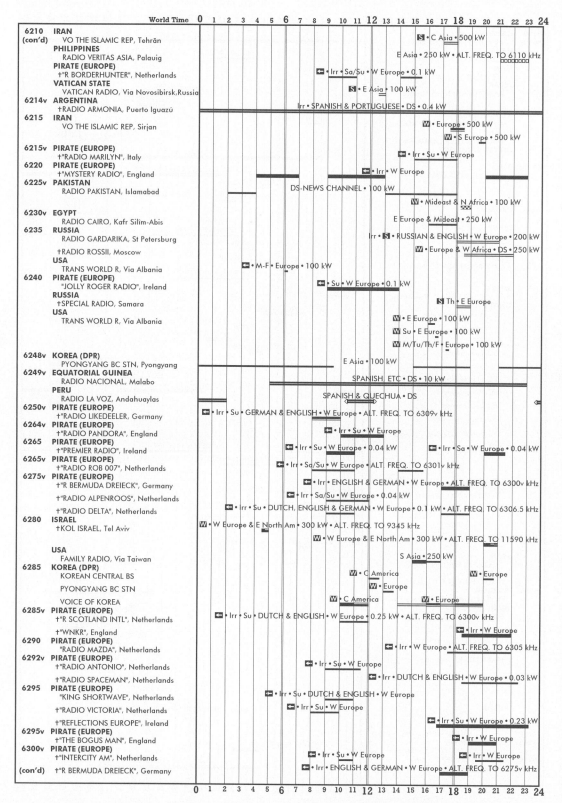

World Time 0 1 2 3 4 5 6 7 8 9 10 11 12 13 14 15 16 17 18 19 20 21 22 23 24

6210 (con'd)	IRAN
	VO THE ISLAMIC REP, Tehrān — S • C Asia • 500 kW
	PHILIPPINES
	RADIO VERITAS ASIA, Palauig — E Asia • 250 kW • ALT. FREQ. TO 6110 kHz
	PIRATE (EUROPE)
	†"R BORDERHUNTER", Netherlands — Irr • Sa/Su • W Europe • 0.1 kW
	VATICAN STATE
	VATICAN RADIO, Via Novosibirsk, Russia — S • E Asia • 100 kW
6214v	ARGENTINA
	†RADIO ARMONIA, Puerto Iguazú — Irr • SPANISH & PORTUGUESE • DS • 0.4 kW
6215	IRAN
	VO THE ISLAMIC REP, Sirjan — W • Europe • 500 kW / W • S Europe • 500 kW
6215v	PIRATE (EUROPE)
	†"RADIO MARILYN", Italy — Irr • Su • W Europe
6220	PIRATE (EUROPE)
	†"MYSTERY RADIO", England — Irr • W Europe
6225v	PAKISTAN
	RADIO PAKISTAN, Islamabad — DS-NEWS CHANNEL • 100 kW / W • Mideast & N Africa • 100 kW
6230v	EGYPT
	RADIO CAIRO, Kafr Silim-Abis — E Europe & Mideast • 250 kW
6235	RUSSIA
	RADIO GARDARIKA, St Petersburg — Irr • S • RUSSIAN & ENGLISH • W Europe • 200 kW
	†RADIO ROSSII, Moscow — W • Europe & W Africa • DS • 250 kW
	USA
	TRANS WORLD R, Via Albania — M-F • Europe • 100 kW
6240	PIRATE (EUROPE)
	"JOLLY ROGER RADIO", Ireland — Su • W Europe • 0.1 kW
	RUSSIA
	†SPECIAL RADIO, Samara — S • Th • E Europe
	USA
	TRANS WORLD R, Via Albania — W • E Europe • 100 kW / W • Su • E Europe • 100 kW / W • M/Tu/Th/F • Europe • 100 kW
6248v	KOREA (DPR)
	PYONGYANG BC STN, Pyongyang — E Asia • 100 kW
6249v	EQUATORIAL GUINEA
	RADIO NACIONAL, Malabo — SPANISH ETC • DS • 10 kW
	PERU
	RADIO LA VOZ, Andahuaylas — SPANISH & QUECHUA • DS
6250v	PIRATE (EUROPE)
	†"RADIO LIKEDEELER", Germany — Irr • Su • GERMAN & ENGLISH • W Europe • ALT. FREQ. TO 6309v kHz
6264v	PIRATE (EUROPE)
	†"RADIO PANDORA", England — Irr • Su • W Europe
6265	PIRATE (EUROPE)
	†"PREMIER RADIO", Ireland — Irr • Su • W Europe • 0.04 kW / Irr • Sa • W Europe • 0.04 kW
6265v	PIRATE (EUROPE)
	†"RADIO ROB 007", Netherlands — Irr • Sa/Su • W Europe • ALT. FREQ. TO 6301v kHz
6275v	PIRATE (EUROPE)
	†"R BERMUDA DREIECK", Germany — Irr • ENGLISH & GERMAN • W Europe • ALT. FREQ. TO 6300v kHz
	†"RADIO ALPENROOS", Netherlands — Irr • Sa/Su • W Europe • 0.04 kW
	†"RADIO DELTA", Netherlands — Irr • Su • DUTCH, ENGLISH & GERMAN • W Europe • 0.1 kW • ALT. FREQ. TO 6306.5 kHz
6280	ISRAEL
	†KOL ISRAEL, Tel Aviv — W • W Europe & E North Am • 300 kW • ALT. FREQ. TO 9345 kHz / W • W Europe & E North Am • 300 kW • ALT. FREQ. TO 11590 kHz
	USA
	FAMILY RADIO, Via Taiwan — S Asia • 250 kW
6285	KOREA (DPR)
	KOREAN CENTRAL BS — W • C America / W • Europe
	PYONGYANG BC STN — W • Europe
	VOICE OF KOREA — W • C America / W • Europe
6285v	PIRATE (EUROPE)
	†"R SCOTLAND INTL", Netherlands — Irr • Su • DUTCH & ENGLISH • W Europe • 0.25 kW • ALT. FREQ. TO 6300v kHz
	†"WNKR", England — Irr • W Europe
6290	PIRATE (EUROPE)
	"RADIO MAZDA", Netherlands — Irr • W Europe • ALT. FREQ. TO 6305 kHz
6292v	PIRATE (EUROPE)
	†"RADIO ANTONIO", Netherlands — Irr • Su • W Europe
	†"RADIO SPACEMAN", Netherlands — Irr • DUTCH & ENGLISH • W Europe • 0.03 kW
6295	PIRATE (EUROPE)
	"KING SHORTWAVE", Netherlands — Irr • Su • DUTCH & ENGLISH • W Europe
	†"RADIO VICTORIA", Netherlands — Irr • Su • W Europe
	†"REFLECTIONS EUROPE", Ireland — Irr • Su • W Europe • 0.23 kW
6295v	PIRATE (EUROPE)
	†"THE BOGUS MAN", England — Irr • W Europe
6300v	PIRATE (EUROPE)
	†"INTERCITY AM", Netherlands — Irr • Su • W Europe / Irr • W Europe
(con'd)	†"R BERMUDA DREIECK", Germany — Irr • ENGLISH & GERMAN • W Europe • ALT. FREQ. TO 6275v kHz

0 1 2 3 4 5 6 7 8 9 10 11 12 13 14 15 16 17 18 19 20 21 22 23 24

ENGLISH ▬ ARABIC ▨ CHINESE ▢▢▢ FRENCH ▬ GERMAN ▬ RUSSIAN ▭ SPANISH ▬ OTHER ▬

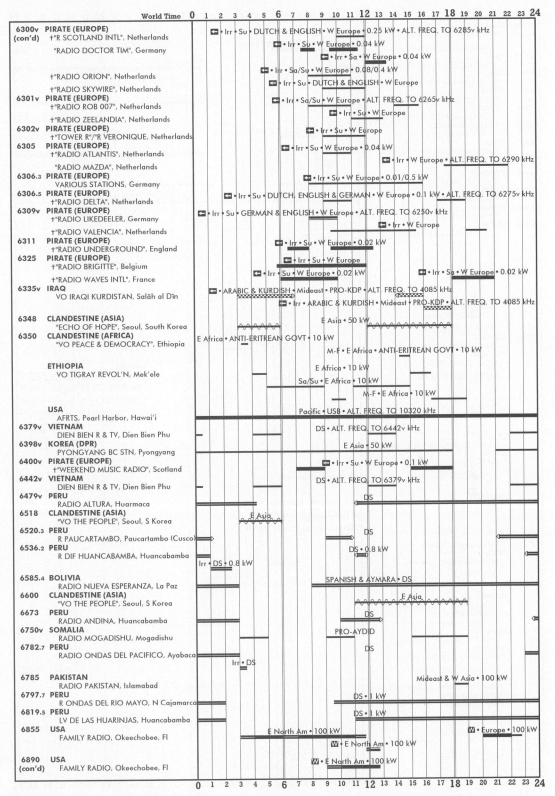

World Time 0 1 2 3 4 5 6 7 8 9 10 11 12 13 14 15 16 17 18 19 20 21 22 23 24

Freq	Station	
6300v (con'd)	PIRATE (EUROPE)	
	†"R SCOTLAND INTL", Netherlands	Irr • Su • DUTCH & ENGLISH • W Europe • 0.25 kW • ALT. FREQ. TO 6285v kHz
	"RADIO DOCTOR TIM", Germany	Irr • Su • W Europe • 0.04 kW
		Irr • Sa • W Europe • 0.04 kW
	†"RADIO ORION", Netherlands	Irr • Sa/Su • W Europe • 0.08/0.4 kW
	†"RADIO SKYWIRE", Netherlands	Irr • Su • DUTCH & ENGLISH • W Europe
6301v	PIRATE (EUROPE)	
	†"RADIO ROB 007", Netherlands	Irr • Sa/Su • W Europe • ALT. FREQ. TO 6265v kHz
	†"RADIO ZEELANDIA", Netherlands	Irr • Su • W Europe
6302v	PIRATE (EUROPE)	
	†"TOWER R"/"R VERONIQUE, Netherlands	Irr • Su • W Europe
6305	PIRATE (EUROPE)	
	†"RADIO ATLANTIS", Netherlands	Irr • Su • W Europe • 0.04 kW
	"RADIO MAZDA", Netherlands	Irr • W Europe • ALT. FREQ. TO 6290 kHz
6306.3	PIRATE (EUROPE)	
	VARIOUS STATIONS, Germany	Irr • Su • W Europe • 0.01/0.5 kW
6306.5	PIRATE (EUROPE)	
	†"RADIO DELTA", Netherlands	Irr • Su • DUTCH, ENGLISH & GERMAN • W Europe • 0.1 kW • ALT. FREQ. TO 6275v kHz
6309v	PIRATE (EUROPE)	
	†"RADIO LIKEDEELER, Germany	Irr • Su • GERMAN & ENGLISH • W Europe • ALT. FREQ. TO 6250v kHz
	†"RADIO VALENCIA", Netherlands	Irr • W Europe
6311	PIRATE (EUROPE)	
	†"RADIO UNDERGROUND", England	Irr • Su • W Europe • 0.02 kW
6325	PIRATE (EUROPE)	
	†"RADIO BRIGITTE", Belgium	Irr • Su • W Europe
	"RADIO WAVES INTL", France	Irr • Su • W Europe • 0.02 kW Irr • Sa • W Europe • 0.02 kW
6335v	IRAQ	
	VO IRAQI KURDISTAN, Salāh al Dīn	ARABIC & KURDISH • Mideast • PRO-KDP • ALT. FREQ. TO 4085 kHz
		Irr • ARABIC & KURDISH • Mideast • PRO-KDP • ALT. FREQ. TO 4085 kHz
6348	CLANDESTINE (ASIA)	
	"ECHO OF HOPE", Seoul, South Korea	E Asia • 50 kW
6350	CLANDESTINE (AFRICA)	
	"VO PEACE & DEMOCRACY", Ethiopia	E Africa • ANTI-ERITREAN GOVT • 10 kW
		M-F • E Africa • ANTI-ERITREAN GOVT • 10 kW
	ETHIOPIA	
	VO TIGRAY REVOL'N, Mek'ele	E Africa • 10 kW
		Sa/Su • E Africa • 10 kW
		M-F • E Africa • 10 kW
	USA	
	AFRTS, Pearl Harbor, Hawai'i	Pacific • USB • ALT. FREQ. TO 10320 kHz
6379v	VIETNAM	
	DIEN BIEN R & TV, Dien Bien Phu	DS • ALT. FREQ. TO 6442v kHz
6398v	KOREA (DPR)	
	PYONGYANG BC STN, Pyongyang	E Asia • 50 kW
6400v	PIRATE (EUROPE)	
	†"WEEKEND MUSIC RADIO", Scotland	Irr • Su • W Europe • 0.1 kW
6442v	VIETNAM	
	DIEN BIEN R & TV, Dien Bien Phu	DS • ALT. FREQ. TO 6379v kHz
6479v	PERU	
	RADIO ALTURA, Huarmaca	DS
6518	CLANDESTINE (ASIA)	
	"VO THE PEOPLE", Seoul, S Korea	E Asia
6520.3	PERU	
	R PAUCARTAMBO, Paucartambo (Cusco)	DS
6536.2	PERU	
	R DIF HUANCABAMBA, Huancabamba	DS • 0.8 kW
		Irr • DS • 0.8 kW
6585.4	BOLIVIA	
	RADIO NUEVA ESPERANZA, La Paz	SPANISH & AYMARA • DS
6600	CLANDESTINE (ASIA)	
	"VO THE PEOPLE", Seoul, S Korea	E Asia
6673	PERU	
	RADIO ANDINA, Huancabamba	DS
6750v	SOMALIA	
	RADIO MOGADISHU, Mogadishu	PRO-AYDID
6782.7	PERU	
	RADIO ONDAS DEL PACIFICO, Ayabaca	DS
		Irr • DS
6785	PAKISTAN	
	RADIO PAKISTAN, Islamabad	Mideast & W Asia • 100 kW
6797.7	PERU	
	R ONDAS DEL RIO MAYO, N Cajamarca	DS • 1 kW
6819.5	PERU	
	LV DE LAS HUARINJAS, Huancabamba	DS • 1 kW
6855	USA	
	FAMILY RADIO, Okeechobee, Fl	E North Am • 100 kW W • Europe • 100 kW
		W • E North Am • 100 kW
6890 (con'd)	USA	
	FAMILY RADIO, Okeechobee, Fl	W • E North Am • 100 kW

0 1 2 3 4 5 6 7 8 9 10 11 12 13 14 15 16 17 18 19 20 21 22 23 24

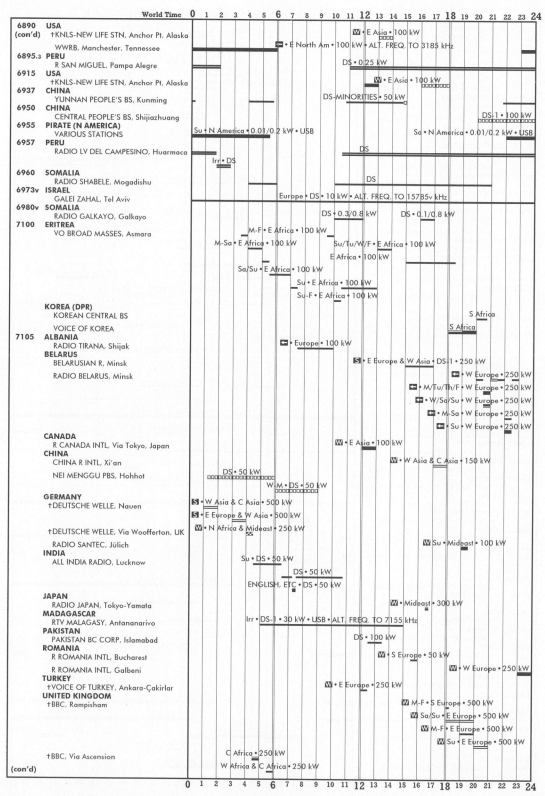

World Time 0 1 2 3 4 5 6 7 8 9 10 11 12 13 14 15 16 17 18 19 20 21 22 23 24

6890 (con'd)	USA	†KNLS-NEW LIFE STN, Anchor Pt, Alaska
		WWRB, Manchester, Tennessee
6895.3	PERU	R SAN MIGUEL, Pampa Alegre
6915	USA	†KNLS-NEW LIFE STN, Anchor Pt, Alaska
6937	CHINA	YUNNAN PEOPLE'S BS, Kunming
6950	CHINA	CENTRAL PEOPLE'S BS, Shijiazhuang
6955	PIRATE (N AMERICA)	VARIOUS STATIONS
6957	PERU	RADIO LV DEL CAMPESINO, Huarmaca
6960	SOMALIA	RADIO SHABELE, Mogadishu
6973v	ISRAEL	GALEI ZAHAL, Tel Aviv
6980v	SOMALIA	RADIO GALKAYO, Galkayo
7100	ERITREA	VO BROAD MASSES, Asmara

KOREA (DPR)
KOREAN CENTRAL BS
VOICE OF KOREA
7105 ALBANIA
RADIO TIRANA, Shijak
BELARUS
BELARUSIAN R, Minsk
RADIO BELARUS, Minsk

CANADA
R CANADA INTL, Via Tokyo, Japan
CHINA
CHINA R INTL, Xi'an
NEI MENGGU PBS, Hohhot
GERMANY
†DEUTSCHE WELLE, Nauen
†DEUTSCHE WELLE, Via Woofferton, UK
RADIO SANTEC, Jülich
INDIA
ALL INDIA RADIO, Lucknow
JAPAN
RADIO JAPAN, Tokyo-Yamata
MADAGASCAR
RTV MALAGASY, Antananarivo
PAKISTAN
PAKISTAN BC CORP, Islamabad
ROMANIA
R ROMANIA INTL, Bucharest
R ROMANIA INTL, Galbeni
TURKEY
†VOICE OF TURKEY, Ankara-Çakirlar
UNITED KINGDOM
†BBC, Rampisham
†BBC, Via Ascension
(con'd)

W • E Asia • 100 kW
E North Am • 100 kW • ALT. FREQ. TO 3185 kHz
DS • 0.25 kW
W • E Asia • 100 kW
DS-MINORITIES • 50 kW
DS-1 • 100 kW
Su • N America • 0.01/0.2 kW • USB   Sa • N America • 0.01/0.2 kW • USB
DS
Irr • DS
DS
Europe • DS • 10 kW • ALT. FREQ. TO 15785v kHz
DS • 0.3/0.8 kW   DS • 0.1/0.8 kW
M-F • E Africa • 100 kW
M-Sa • E Africa • 100 kW   Su/Tu/W/F • E Africa • 100 kW
E Africa • 100 kW
Sa/Su • E Africa • 100 kW
Su • E Africa • 100 kW
Su-F • E Africa • 100 kW
S Africa
S Africa
◄ • Europe • 100 kW
S • E Europe & W Asia • DS-1 • 250 kW
◄ • W Europe • 250 kW
◄ • M/Tu/Th/F • W Europe • 250 kW
◄ • W/Sa/Su • W Europe • 250 kW
◄ • M-Sa • W Europe • 250 kW
◄ • Su • W Europe • 250 kW
W • E Asia • 100 kW
W • W Asia & C Asia • 150 kW
DS • 50 kW
W • M • DS • 50 kW
S • W Asia & C Asia • 500 kW
S • E Europe & W Asia • 500 kW
W • N Africa & Mideast • 250 kW
W Su • Mideast • 100 kW
Su • DS • 50 kW
DS • 50 kW
ENGLISH, ETC • DS • 50 kW
W • Mideast • 300 kW
Irr • DS-1 • 30 kW • USB • ALT. FREQ. TO 7155 kHz
DS • 100 kW
W • S Europe • 50 kW
W • W Europe • 250 kW
W • E Europe • 250 kW
W M-F • S Europe • 500 kW
W Sa/Su • E Europe • 500 kW
W M-F • E Europe • 500 kW
W Su • E Europe • 500 kW
C Africa • 250 kW
W Africa & C Africa • 250 kW

0 1 2 3 4 5 6 7 8 9 10 11 12 13 14 15 16 17 18 19 20 21 22 23 24

ENGLISH ▬ ARABIC ▨ CHINESE ▫▫▫ FRENCH ▬ GERMAN ▬ RUSSIAN ═ SPANISH ▬ OTHER ▬

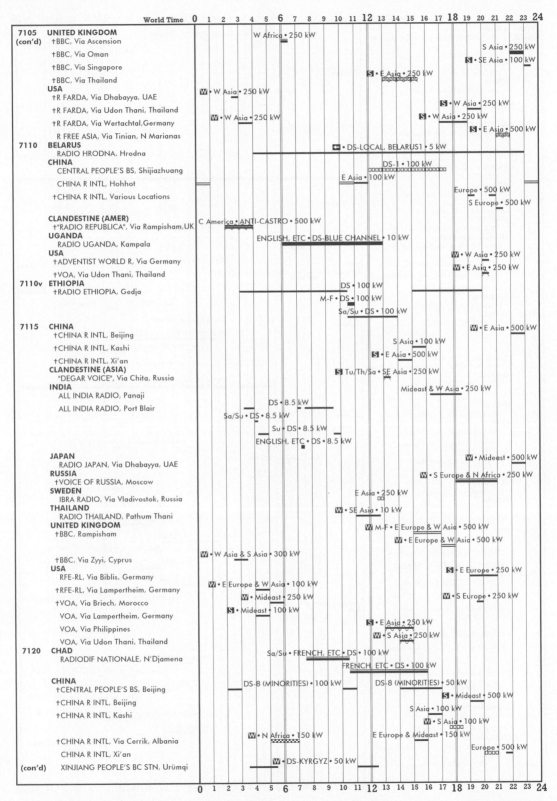

		World Time	0 1 2 3 4 5 6 7 8 9 10 11 12 13 14 15 16 17 18 19 20 21 22 23 24

7105 UNITED KINGDOM (con'd)
- †BBC, Via Ascension — W Africa • 250 kW
- †BBC, Via Oman — S Asia • 250 kW
- †BBC, Via Singapore — S • SE Asia • 100 kW
- †BBC, Via Thailand — S • E Asia • 250 kW

USA
- †R FARDA, Via Dhabayya, UAE — W • W Asia • 250 kW
- †R FARDA, Via Udon Thani, Thailand — S • W Asia • 250 kW
- †R FARDA, Via Wertachtal, Germany — W • W Asia • 250 kW — S • W Asia • 250 kW
- R FREE ASIA, Via Tinian, N Marianas — S • E Asia • 500 kW

7110 BELARUS
- RADIO HRODNA, Hrodna — ⇦ • DS-LOCAL, BELARUS1 • 5 kW

CHINA
- CENTRAL PEOPLE'S BS, Shijiazhuang — DS-1 • 100 kW
- CHINA R INTL, Hohhot — E Asia • 100 kW
- †CHINA R INTL, Various Locations — Europe • 500 kW / S Europe • 500 kW

CLANDESTINE (AMER)
- †"RADIO REPUBLICA", Via Rampisham, UK — C America • ANTI-CASTRO • 500 kW

UGANDA
- RADIO UGANDA, Kampala — ENGLISH, ETC • DS-BLUE CHANNEL • 10 kW

USA
- †ADVENTIST WORLD R, Via Germany — W • W Asia • 250 kW
- †VOA, Via Udon Thani, Thailand — W • E Asia • 250 kW

7110v ETHIOPIA
- †RADIO ETHIOPIA, Gedja — DS • 100 kW / M-F • DS • 100 kW / Sa/Su • DS • 100 kW

7115 CHINA
- †CHINA R INTL, Beijing — W • E Asia • 500 kW
- †CHINA R INTL, Kashi — S Asia • 100 kW
- †CHINA R INTL, Xi'an — S • E Asia • 500 kW

CLANDESTINE (ASIA)
- "DEGAR VOICE", Via Chita, Russia — S Tu/Th/Sa • SE Asia • 250 kW

INDIA
- ALL INDIA RADIO, Panaji — Mideast & W Asia • 250 kW
- ALL INDIA RADIO, Port Blair — DS • 8.5 kW / Sa/Su • DS • 8.5 kW / Su • DS • 8.5 kW / ENGLISH, ETC • DS • 8.5 kW

JAPAN
- RADIO JAPAN, Via Dhabayya, UAE — W • Mideast • 500 kW

RUSSIA
- †VOICE OF RUSSIA, Moscow — W • S Europe & N Africa • 250 kW

SWEDEN
- IBRA RADIO, Via Vladivostok, Russia — E Asia • 250 kW

THAILAND
- RADIO THAILAND, Pathum Thani — W • SE Asia • 10 kW

UNITED KINGDOM
- †BBC, Rampisham — W • M-F • E Europe & W Asia • 500 kW / W • E Europe & W Asia • 500 kW
- †BBC, Via Zyyi, Cyprus — W • W Asia & S Asia • 300 kW

USA
- RFE-RL, Via Biblis, Germany — S • E Europe • 250 kW
- †RFE-RL, Via Lampertheim, Germany — W • E Europe & W Asia • 100 kW
- †VOA, Via Briech, Morocco — W • Mideast • 250 kW — W • S Europe • 250 kW
- VOA, Via Lampertheim, Germany — S • Mideast • 100 kW
- VOA, Via Philippines — S • E Asia • 250 kW
- VOA, Via Udon Thani, Thailand — W • S Asia • 250 kW

7120 CHAD
- RADIODIF NATIONALE, N'Djamena — Sa/Su • FRENCH, ETC • DS • 100 kW / FRENCH, ETC • DS • 100 kW

CHINA
- †CENTRAL PEOPLE'S BS, Beijing — DS-8 (MINORITIES) • 100 kW / DS-8 (MINORITIES) • 50 kW
- †CHINA R INTL, Beijing — S • Mideast • 500 kW
- †CHINA R INTL, Kashi — S Asia • 100 kW / W • S Asia • 100 kW
- †CHINA R INTL, Via Cerrik, Albania — W • N Africa • 150 kW / E Europe & Mideast • 150 kW
- CHINA R INTL, Xi'an — Europe • 500 kW
- **(con'd)** XINJIANG PEOPLE'S BC STN, Urümqi — W • DS-KYRGYZ • 50 kW

			0 1 2 3 4 5 6 7 8 9 10 11 12 13 14 15 16 17 18 19 20 21 22 23 24

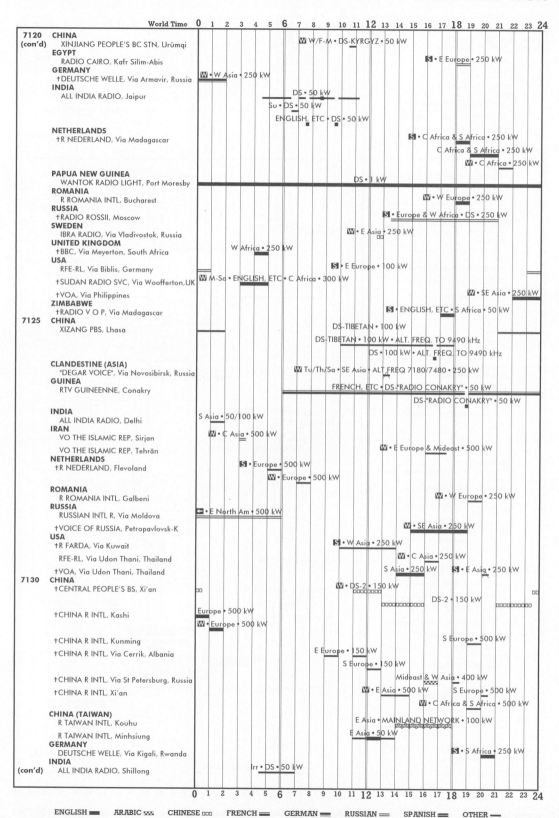

World Time	0 1 2 3 4 5 6 7 8 9 10 11 12 13 14 15 16 17 18 19 20 21 22 23 24

7120
(con'd) CHINA
   XINJIANG PEOPLE'S BC STN, Urümqi — W• W/F-M • DS-KYRGYZ • 50 kW
EGYPT
   RADIO CAIRO, Kafr Silim-Abis — S • E Europe • 250 kW
GERMANY
   †DEUTSCHE WELLE, Via Armavir, Russia — W • W Asia • 250 kW
INDIA
   ALL INDIA RADIO, Jaipur — DS • 50 kW / Su • DS • 50 kW / ENGLISH, ETC • DS • 50 kW
NETHERLANDS
   †R NEDERLAND, Via Madagascar — S • C Africa & S Africa • 250 kW / C Africa & S Africa • 250 kW / W • C Africa • 250 kW

PAPUA NEW GUINEA
   WANTOK RADIO LIGHT, Port Moresby — DS • 1 kW
ROMANIA
   R ROMANIA INTL, Bucharest — W • W Europe • 250 kW
RUSSIA
   †RADIO ROSSII, Moscow — S • Europe & W Africa • DS • 250 kW
SWEDEN
   IBRA RADIO, Via Vladivostok, Russia — W • E Asia • 250 kW
UNITED KINGDOM
   †BBC, Via Meyerton, South Africa — W Africa • 250 kW
USA
   RFE-RL, Via Biblis, Germany — S • E Europe • 100 kW
   †SUDAN RADIO SVC, Via Woofferton, UK — W • M-Sa • ENGLISH, ETC • C Africa • 300 kW
   †VOA, Via Philippines — W • SE Asia • 250 kW
ZIMBABWE
   †RADIO V O P, Via Madagascar — S • ENGLISH, ETC • S Africa • 50 kW
7125 CHINA
   XIZANG PBS, Lhasa — DS-TIBETAN • 100 kW / DS-TIBETAN • 100 kW • ALT. FREQ. TO 9490 kHz / DS • 100 kW • ALT. FREQ. TO 9490 kHz
CLANDESTINE (ASIA)
   "DEGAR VOICE", Via Novosibirsk, Russia — W • Tu/Th/Sa • SE Asia • ALT FREQ 7180/7480 • 250 kW
GUINEA
   RTV GUINEENNE, Conakry — FRENCH, ETC • DS-"RADIO CONAKRY" • 50 kW / DS-"RADIO CONAKRY" • 50 kW

INDIA
   ALL INDIA RADIO, Delhi — S Asia • 50/100 kW
IRAN
   VO THE ISLAMIC REP, Sirjan — W • C Asia • 500 kW
   VO THE ISLAMIC REP, Tehrān — W • E Europe & Mideast • 500 kW
NETHERLANDS
   †R NEDERLAND, Flevoland — S • Europe • 500 kW / W • Europe • 500 kW

ROMANIA
   R ROMANIA INTL, Galbeni — W • W Europe • 250 kW
RUSSIA
   RUSSIAN INTL R, Via Moldova — • E North Am • 500 kW
   †VOICE OF RUSSIA, Petropavlovsk-K — W • SE Asia • 250 kW
USA
   †R FARDA, Via Kuwait — S • W Asia • 250 kW
   RFE-RL, Via Udon Thani, Thailand — W • C Asia • 250 kW
   †VOA, Via Udon Thani, Thailand — S Asia • 250 kW / S • E Asia • 250 kW
7130 CHINA
   †CENTRAL PEOPLE'S BS, Xi'an — W • DS-2 • 150 kW / DS-2 • 150 kW
   †CHINA R INTL, Kashi — Europe • 500 kW / W • Europe • 500 kW
   †CHINA R INTL, Kunming — S Europe • 500 kW
   †CHINA R INTL, Via Cerrik, Albania — E Europe • 150 kW / S Europe • 150 kW
   †CHINA R INTL, Via St Petersburg, Russia — Mideast & W Asia • 400 kW
   †CHINA R INTL, Xi'an — W • E Asia • 500 kW / S Europe • 500 kW / W • C Africa & S Africa • 500 kW
CHINA (TAIWAN)
   R TAIWAN INTL, Kouhu — E Asia • MAINLAND NETWORK • 100 kW
   R TAIWAN INTL, Minhsiung — E Asia • 50 kW
GERMANY
   DEUTSCHE WELLE, Via Kigali, Rwanda — S • S Africa • 250 kW
INDIA
(con'd) ALL INDIA RADIO, Shillong — Irr • DS • 50 kW

	0 1 2 3 4 5 6 7 8 9 10 11 12 13 14 15 16 17 18 19 20 21 22 23 24

ENGLISH ▬ ARABIC ⌇⌇ CHINESE ▢▢▢ FRENCH ▬▬ GERMAN ▬ RUSSIAN ═ SPANISH ▬▬ OTHER ▬

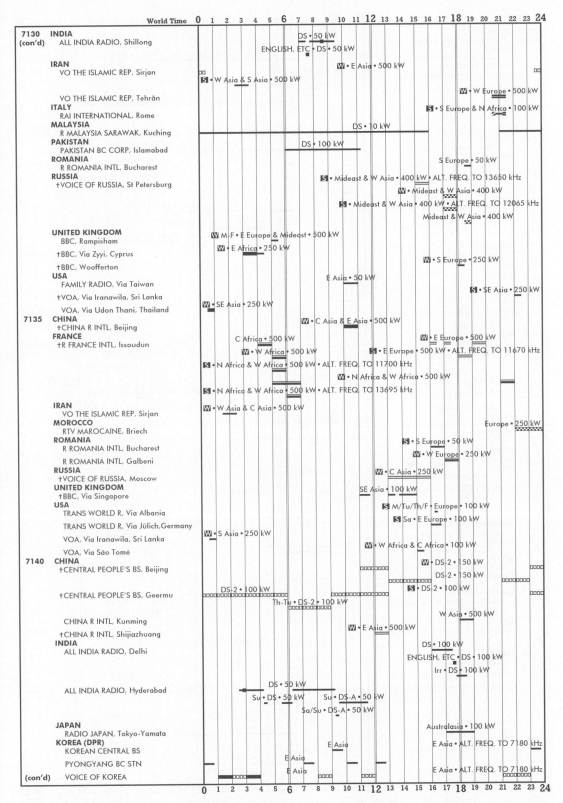

World Time   0 1 2 3 4 5 6 7 8 9 10 11 12 13 14 15 16 17 18 19 20 21 22 23 24

7130 INDIA
(con'd)   ALL INDIA RADIO, Shillong — DS • 50 kW / ENGLISH, ETC • DS • 50 kW

IRAN
VO THE ISLAMIC REP, Sirjan — W • E Asia • 500 kW / S • W Asia & S Asia • 500 kW / W • W Europe • 500 kW

VO THE ISLAMIC REP, Tehrān
ITALY
RAI INTERNATIONAL, Rome — S • S Europe & N Africa • 100 kW

MALAYSIA
R MALAYSIA SARAWAK, Kuching — DS • 10 kW

PAKISTAN
PAKISTAN BC CORP, Islamabad — DS • 100 kW

ROMANIA
R ROMANIA INTL, Bucharest — S Europe • 50 kW

RUSSIA
†VOICE OF RUSSIA, St Petersburg — S • Mideast & W Asia • 400 kW • ALT. FREQ. TO 13650 kHz / W • Mideast & W Asia • 400 kW / S • Mideast & W Asia • 400 kW • ALT. FREQ. TO 12065 kHz / Mideast & W Asia • 400 kW

UNITED KINGDOM
BBC, Rampisham — W • M-F • E Europe & Mideast • 500 kW
†BBC, Via Zyyi, Cyprus — W • E Africa • 250 kW
†BBC, Woofferton — W • S Europe • 250 kW

USA
FAMILY RADIO, Via Taiwan — E Asia • 50 kW
†VOA, Via Iranawila, Sri Lanka — S • SE Asia • 250 kW
VOA, Via Udon Thani, Thailand — W • SE Asia • 250 kW

7135 CHINA
†CHINA R INTL, Beijing — W • C Asia & E Asia • 500 kW

FRANCE
†R FRANCE INTL, Issoudun — C Africa • 500 kW / W • E Europe • 500 kW / W • W Africa • 500 kW / S • E Europe • 500 kW • ALT. FREQ. TO 11670 kHz / S • N Africa & W Africa • 500 kW • ALT. FREQ. TO 11700 kHz / W • N Africa & W Africa • 500 kW / S • N Africa & W Africa • 500 kW • ALT. FREQ. TO 13695 kHz

IRAN
VO THE ISLAMIC REP, Sirjan — W • W Asia & C Asia • 500 kW

MOROCCO
RTV MAROCAINE, Briech — Europe • 250 kW

ROMANIA
R ROMANIA INTL, Bucharest — S • S Europe • 50 kW
R ROMANIA INTL, Galbeni — W • W Europe • 250 kW

RUSSIA
†VOICE OF RUSSIA, Moscow — W • C Asia • 250 kW

UNITED KINGDOM
†BBC, Via Singapore — SE Asia • 100 kW

USA
TRANS WORLD R, Via Albania — S • M/Tu/Th/F • Europe • 100 kW
TRANS WORLD R, Via Jülich, Germany — S • Sa • E Europe • 100 kW
VOA, Via Iranawila, Sri Lanka — W • S Asia • 250 kW
VOA, Via São Tomé — W • W Africa & C Africa • 100 kW

7140 CHINA
†CENTRAL PEOPLE'S BS, Beijing — W • DS-2 • 150 kW / DS-2 • 150 kW / S • DS-2 • 100 kW
†CENTRAL PEOPLE'S BS, Geermu — DS-2 • 100 kW / Th-Tu • DS-2 • 100 kW
CHINA R INTL, Kunming — W Asia • 500 kW
†CHINA R INTL, Shijiazhuang — W • E Asia • 500 kW

INDIA
ALL INDIA RADIO, Delhi — DS • 100 kW / ENGLISH, ETC • DS • 100 kW / Irr • DS • 100 kW
ALL INDIA RADIO, Hyderabad — DS • 50 kW / Su • DS • 50 kW / Su • DS-A • 50 kW / Sa/Su • DS-A • 50 kW

JAPAN
RADIO JAPAN, Tokyo-Yamata — Australasia • 100 kW

KOREA (DPR)
KOREAN CENTRAL BS — E Asia / E Asia • ALT. FREQ. TO 7180 kHz
PYONGYANG BC STN — E Asia / E Asia • ALT. FREQ. TO 7180 kHz
(con'd)   VOICE OF KOREA

0 1 2 3 4 5 6 7 8 9 10 11 12 13 14 15 16 17 18 19 20 21 22 23 24

SEASONAL S OR W   1-HR TIMESHIFT MIDYEAR ⇐ OR ⇒   JAMMING / OR ∧   EARLIEST HEARD ◁   LATEST HEARD ▷   NEW FOR 2007 †

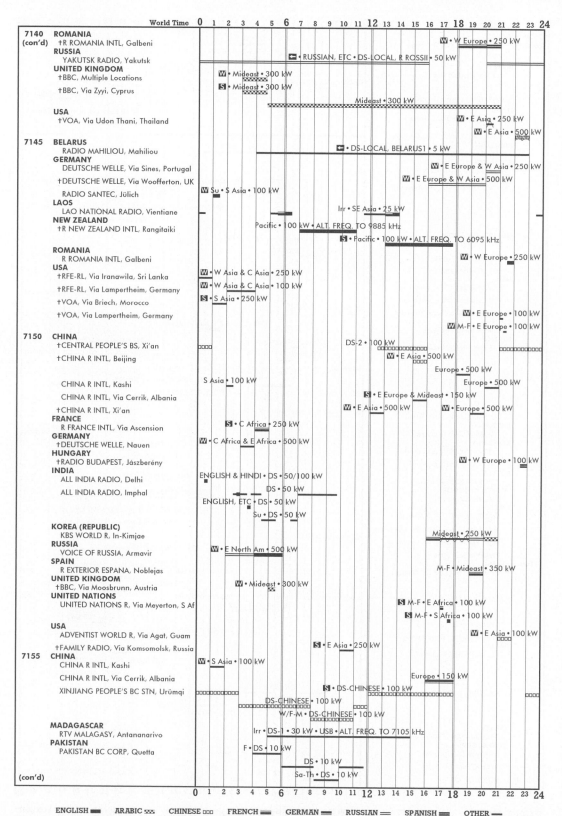

World Time 0 1 2 3 4 5 6 7 8 9 10 11 12 13 14 15 16 17 18 19 20 21 22 23 24

7140
(con'd)   **ROMANIA**
          †R ROMANIA INTL, Galbeni — W • W Europe • 250 kW
          RUSSIA
          YAKUTSK RADIO, Yakutsk — RUSSIAN, ETC • DS-LOCAL, R ROSSII • 50 kW
          UNITED KINGDOM
          †BBC, Multiple Locations — W • Mideast • 300 kW
          †BBC, Via Zyyi, Cyprus — S • Mideast • 300 kW
          Mideast • 300 kW
          USA
          †VOA, Via Udon Thani, Thailand — W • E Asia • 250 kW / W • E Asia • 500 kW

7145 **BELARUS**
          RADIO MAHILIOU, Mahiliou — DS-LOCAL, BELARUS1 • 5 kW
          GERMANY
          DEUTSCHE WELLE, Via Sines, Portugal — W • E Europe & W Asia • 250 kW
          †DEUTSCHE WELLE, Via Woofferton, UK — W • E Europe & W Asia • 500 kW
          RADIO SANTEC, Jülich — W Su • S Asia • 100 kW
          LAOS
          LAO NATIONAL RADIO, Vientiane — Irr • SE Asia • 25 kW
          NEW ZEALAND
          †R NEW ZEALAND INTL, Rangitaiki — Pacific • 100 kW • ALT. FREQ. TO 9885 kHz
          S • Pacific • 100 kW • ALT. FREQ. TO 6095 kHz
          ROMANIA
          R ROMANIA INTL, Galbeni — W • W Europe • 250 kW
          USA
          †RFE-RL, Via Iranawila, Sri Lanka — W • W Asia & C Asia • 250 kW
          †RFE-RL, Via Lampertheim, Germany — W • W Asia & C Asia • 100 kW
          †VOA, Via Briech, Morocco — S • S Asia • 250 kW
          †VOA, Via Lampertheim, Germany — W • E Europe • 100 kW / W M-F • E Europe • 100 kW

7150 **CHINA**
          †CENTRAL PEOPLE'S BS, Xi'an — DS-2 • 100 kW
          †CHINA R INTL, Beijing — W • E Asia • 500 kW / Europe • 500 kW
          CHINA R INTL, Kashi — S Asia • 100 kW / Europe • 500 kW
          CHINA R INTL, Via Cerrik, Albania — S • E Europe & Mideast • 150 kW
          †CHINA R INTL, Xi'an — W • E Asia • 500 kW / W • Europe • 500 kW
          FRANCE
          R FRANCE INTL, Via Ascension — S • C Africa • 250 kW
          GERMANY
          †DEUTSCHE WELLE, Nauen — W • C Africa & E Africa • 500 kW
          HUNGARY
          †RADIO BUDAPEST, Jászberény — W • W Europe • 100 kW
          INDIA
          ALL INDIA RADIO, Delhi — ENGLISH & HINDI • DS • 50/100 kW
          ALL INDIA RADIO, Imphal — DS • 50 kW
          ENGLISH, ETC • DS • 50 kW
          Su • DS • 50 kW
          KOREA (REPUBLIC)
          KBS WORLD R, In-Kimjae — Mideast • 250 kW
          RUSSIA
          VOICE OF RUSSIA, Armavir — W • E North Am • 500 kW
          SPAIN
          R EXTERIOR ESPANA, Noblejas — M-F • Mideast • 350 kW
          UNITED KINGDOM
          †BBC, Via Moosbrunn, Austria — W • Mideast • 300 kW
          UNITED NATIONS
          UNITED NATIONS R, Via Meyerton, S Af — S M-F • E Africa • 100 kW / S M-F • S Africa • 100 kW
          USA
          ADVENTIST WORLD R, Via Agat, Guam — W • E Asia • 100 kW
          †FAMILY RADIO, Via Komsomolsk, Russia — S • E Asia • 250 kW

7155 **CHINA**
          CHINA R INTL, Kashi — W • S Asia • 100 kW
          CHINA R INTL, Via Cerrik, Albania — Europe • 150 kW
          XINJIANG PEOPLE'S BC STN, Urümqi — S • DS-CHINESE • 100 kW / DS-CHINESE • 100 kW / W/F-M • DS-CHINESE • 100 kW
          MADAGASCAR
          RTV MALAGASY, Antananarivo — Irr • DS-1 • 30 kW • USB • ALT. FREQ. TO 7105 kHz
          PAKISTAN
          PAKISTAN BC CORP, Quetta — F • DS • 10 kW / DS • 10 kW / Sa-Th • DS • 10 kW

(con'd)

  0 1 2 3 4 5 6 7 8 9 10 11 12 13 14 15 16 17 18 19 20 21 22 23 24

ENGLISH ▪▪   ARABIC ░░   CHINESE ▫▫▫   FRENCH ▬▬   GERMAN ▬▬   RUSSIAN ══   SPANISH ▬▬   OTHER ──

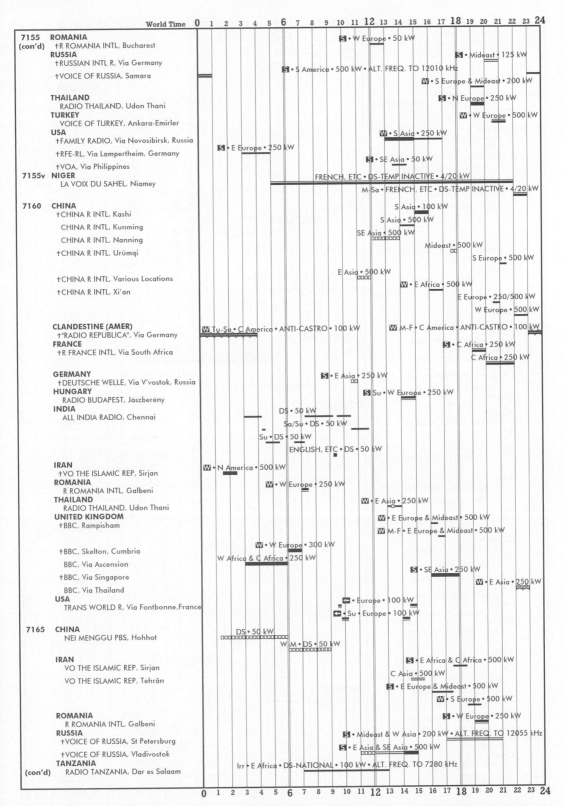

World Time 0 1 2 3 4 5 6 7 8 9 10 11 12 13 14 15 16 17 18 19 20 21 22 23 24

7155	ROMANIA
(con'd)	†R ROMANIA INTL, Bucharest
	RUSSIA
	†RUSSIAN INTL R, Via Germany
	†VOICE OF RUSSIA, Samara
	THAILAND
	RADIO THAILAND, Udon Thani
	TURKEY
	VOICE OF TURKEY, Ankara-Emirler
	USA
	†FAMILY RADIO, Via Novosibirsk, Russia
	†RFE-RL, Via Lampertheim, Germany
	†VOA, Via Philippines
7155v	NIGER
	LA VOIX DU SAHEL, Niamey
7160	CHINA
	†CHINA R INTL, Kashi
	CHINA R INTL, Kunming
	CHINA R INTL, Nanning
	†CHINA R INTL, Urümqi
	†CHINA R INTL, Various Locations
	†CHINA R INTL, Xi'an
	CLANDESTINE (AMER)
	†"RADIO REPUBLICA", Via Germany
	FRANCE
	†R FRANCE INTL, Via South Africa
	GERMANY
	†DEUTSCHE WELLE, Via V'vostok, Russia
	HUNGARY
	RADIO BUDAPEST, Jászberény
	INDIA
	ALL INDIA RADIO, Chennai
	IRAN
	†VO THE ISLAMIC REP, Sirjan
	ROMANIA
	R ROMANIA INTL, Galbeni
	THAILAND
	RADIO THAILAND, Udon Thani
	UNITED KINGDOM
	†BBC, Rampisham
	†BBC, Skelton, Cumbria
	BBC, Via Ascension
	†BBC, Via Singapore
	BBC, Via Thailand
	USA
	TRANS WORLD R, Via Fontbonne, France
7165	CHINA
	NEI MENGGU PBS, Hohhot
	IRAN
	VO THE ISLAMIC REP, Sirjan
	VO THE ISLAMIC REP, Tehrān
	ROMANIA
	R ROMANIA INTL, Galbeni
	RUSSIA
	†VOICE OF RUSSIA, St Petersburg
	†VOICE OF RUSSIA, Vladivostok
	TANZANIA
(con'd)	RADIO TANZANIA, Dar es Salaam

S • W Europe • 50 kW
S • Mideast • 125 kW
S • S America • 500 kW • ALT. FREQ. TO 12010 kHz
W • S Europe & Mideast • 200 kW
S • N Europe • 250 kW
W • W Europe • 500 kW
W • S Asia • 250 kW
S • E Europe • 250 kW
S • SE Asia • 50 kW
FRENCH, ETC • DS-TEMP INACTIVE • 4/20 kW
M-Sa • FRENCH, ETC • DS-TEMP INACTIVE • 4/20 kW
S Asia • 100 kW
S Asia • 500 kW
SE Asia • 500 kW
Mideast • 500 kW
S Europe • 500 kW
E Asia • 500 kW
W • E Africa • 500 kW
E Europe • 250/500 kW
W Europe • 500 kW
W Tu-Sa • C America • ANTI-CASTRO • 100 kW   W M-F • C America • ANTI-CASTRO • 100 kW
S • C Africa • 250 kW
C Africa • 250 kW
S • E Asia • 250 kW
S Su • W Europe • 250 kW
DS • 50 kW
Sa/Su • DS • 50 kW
Su • DS • 50 kW
ENGLISH, ETC • DS • 50 kW
W • N America • 500 kW
W • W Europe • 250 kW
W • E Asia • 250 kW
W • E Europe & Mideast • 500 kW
W M-F • E Europe & Mideast • 500 kW
W • W Europe • 300 kW
W Africa & C Africa • 250 kW
S • SE Asia • 250 kW
W • E Asia • 250 kW
• Europe • 100 kW
• Su • Europe • 100 kW
DS • 50 kW
W M • DS • 50 kW
S • E Africa & C Africa • 500 kW
C Asia • 500 kW
S • E Europe & Mideast • 500 kW
W • S Europe • 500 kW
S • W Europe • 250 kW
S • Mideast & W Asia • 200 kW • ALT. FREQ. TO 12055 kHz
S • E Asia & SE Asia • 500 kW
Irr • E Africa • DS-NATIONAL • 100 kW • ALT. FREQ. TO 7280 kHz

0 1 2 3 4 5 6 7 8 9 10 11 12 13 14 15 16 17 18 19 20 21 22 23 24

SEASONAL ⑤ OR ⑥   1-HR TIMESHIFT MIDYEAR ⬅ OR ➡   JAMMING / OR ∧   EARLIEST HEARD ◁   LATEST HEARD ▷   NEW FOR 2007 †

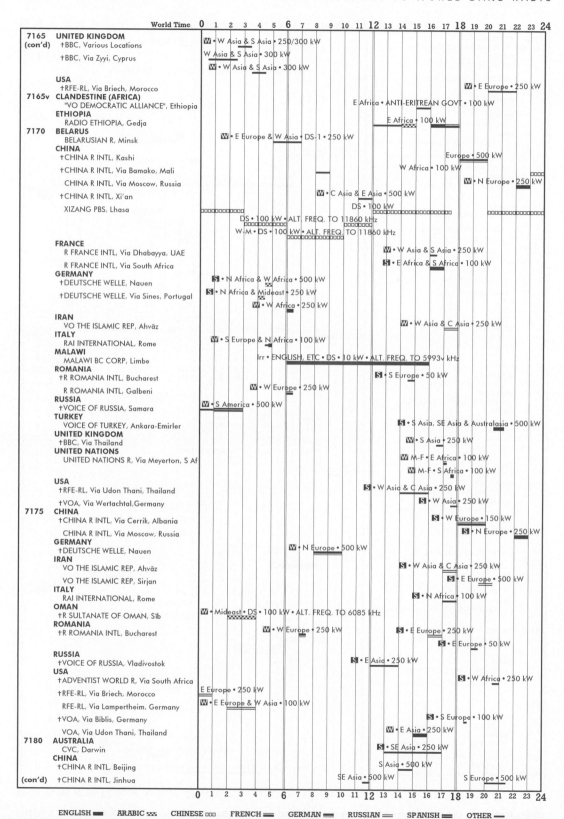

	World Time	0 1 2 3 4 5 6 7 8 9 10 11 12 13 14 15 16 17 18 19 20 21 22 23 24
7165	**UNITED KINGDOM**	
(con'd)	†BBC, Various Locations	W • W Asia & S Asia • 250/300 kW
	†BBC, Via Zyyi, Cyprus	W Asia & S Asia • 300 kW
		W • W Asia & S Asia • 300 kW
	USA	
	†RFE-RL, Via Briech, Morocco	W • E Europe • 250 kW
7165v	**CLANDESTINE (AFRICA)**	
	"VO DEMOCRATIC ALLIANCE", Ethiopia	E Africa • ANTI-ERITREAN GOVT • 100 kW
	ETHIOPIA	
	RADIO ETHIOPIA, Gedja	E Africa • 100 kW
7170	**BELARUS**	
	BELARUSIAN R, Minsk	W • E Europe & W Asia • DS-1 • 250 kW
	CHINA	
	†CHINA R INTL, Kashi	Europe • 500 kW
	†CHINA R INTL, Via Bamako, Mali	W Africa • 100 kW
	CHINA R INTL, Via Moscow, Russia	W • N Europe • 250 kW
	†CHINA R INTL, Xi'an	W • C Asia & E Asia • 500 kW
	XIZANG PBS, Lhasa	DS • 100 kW
		DS • 100 kW • ALT. FREQ. TO 11860 kHz
		W•M•DS • 100 kW • ALT. FREQ. TO 11860 kHz
	FRANCE	
	R FRANCE INTL, Via Dhabayya, UAE	W • W Asia & S Asia • 250 kW
	R FRANCE INTL, Via South Africa	S • E Africa & S Africa • 100 kW
	GERMANY	
	†DEUTSCHE WELLE, Nauen	S • N Africa & W Africa • 500 kW
	†DEUTSCHE WELLE, Via Sines, Portugal	S • N Africa & Mideast • 250 kW
		W • W Africa • 250 kW
	IRAN	
	VO THE ISLAMIC REP, Ahvāz	W • W Asia & C Asia • 250 kW
	ITALY	
	RAI INTERNATIONAL, Rome	W • S Europe & N Africa • 100 kW
	MALAWI	
	MALAWI BC CORP, Limbe	Irr • ENGLISH, ETC • DS • 10 kW • ALT. FREQ. TO 5993v kHz
	ROMANIA	
	†R ROMANIA INTL, Bucharest	S • S Europe • 50 kW
	R ROMANIA INTL, Galbeni	W • W Europe • 250 kW
	RUSSIA	
	†VOICE OF RUSSIA, Samara	W • S America • 500 kW
	TURKEY	
	VOICE OF TURKEY, Ankara-Emirler	S • S Asia, SE Asia & Australasia • 500 kW
	UNITED KINGDOM	
	†BBC, Via Thailand	W • S Asia • 250 kW
	UNITED NATIONS	
	UNITED NATIONS R, Via Meyerton, S Af	W M-F • E Africa • 100 kW
		W M-F • S Africa • 100 kW
	USA	
	†RFE-RL, Via Udon Thani, Thailand	S • W Asia & C Asia • 250 kW
	†VOA, Via Wertachtal, Germany	S • W Asia • 250 kW
7175	**CHINA**	
	†CHINA R INTL, Via Cerrik, Albania	S • W Europe • 150 kW
	CHINA R INTL, Via Moscow, Russia	S • N Europe • 250 kW
	GERMANY	
	†DEUTSCHE WELLE, Nauen	W • N Europe • 500 kW
	IRAN	
	VO THE ISLAMIC REP, Ahvāz	S • W Asia & C Asia • 250 kW
	VO THE ISLAMIC REP, Sirjan	S • E Europe • 500 kW
	ITALY	
	RAI INTERNATIONAL, Rome	S • N Africa • 100 kW
	OMAN	
	†R SULTANATE OF OMAN, Sīb	W • Mideast • DS • 100 kW • ALT. FREQ. TO 6085 kHz
	ROMANIA	
	†R ROMANIA INTL, Bucharest	W • W Europe • 250 kW
		S • E Europe • 250 kW
		S • E Europe • 50 kW
	RUSSIA	
	†VOICE OF RUSSIA, Vladivostok	S • E Asia • 250 kW
	USA	
	†ADVENTIST WORLD R, Via South Africa	S • W Africa • 250 kW
	†RFE-RL, Via Briech, Morocco	E Europe • 250 kW
	RFE-RL, Via Lampertheim, Germany	W • E Europe & W Asia • 100 kW
	†VOA, Via Biblis, Germany	S • S Europe • 100 kW
	VOA, Via Udon Thani, Thailand	W • E Asia • 250 kW
7180	**AUSTRALIA**	
	CVC, Darwin	S • SE Asia • 250 kW
	CHINA	
	†CHINA R INTL, Beijing	S Asia • 500 kW
(con'd)	†CHINA R INTL, Jinhua	SE Asia • 500 kW S Europe • 500 kW

World Time	0 1 2 3 4 5 6 7 8 9 10 11 12 13 14 15 16 17 18 19 20 21 22 23 24

ENGLISH ▬   ARABIC ▨   CHINESE ▢▢▢   FRENCH ▤   GERMAN ▬   RUSSIAN ═   SPANISH ▬   OTHER ▬

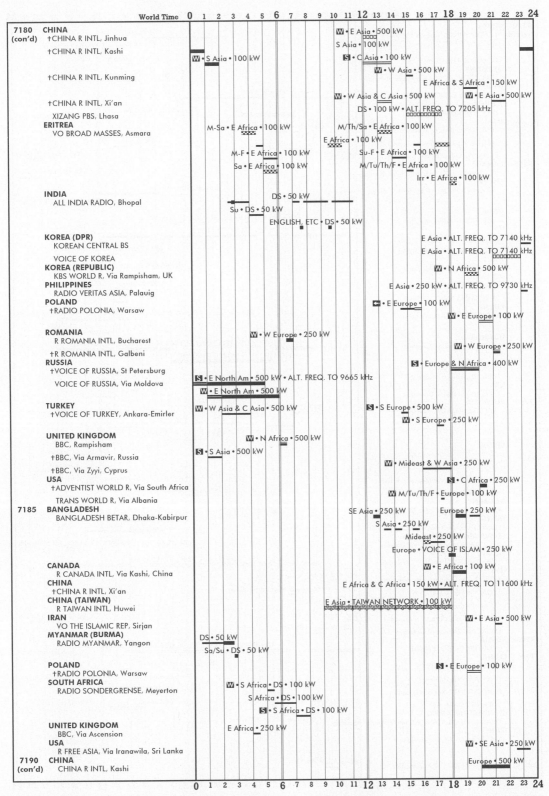

World Time 0 1 2 3 4 5 6 7 8 9 10 11 12 13 14 15 16 17 18 19 20 21 22 23 24

7180
(con'd) **CHINA**
†CHINA R INTL, Jinhua — W • E Asia • 500 kW / S Asia • 100 kW
†CHINA R INTL, Kashi — W • S Asia • 100 kW / S • C Asia • 100 kW / W • W Asia • 500 kW / E Africa & S Africa • 150 kW
†CHINA R INTL, Kunming — W • W Asia & C Asia • 500 kW / W • E Asia • 500 kW
†CHINA R INTL, Xi'an — DS • 100 kW • ALT. FREQ. TO 7205 kHz
XIZANG PBS, Lhasa
ERITREA
VO BROAD MASSES, Asmara — M-Sa • E Africa • 100 kW / M/Th/Sa • E Africa • 100 kW / E Africa • 100 kW / M-F • E Africa • 100 kW / Su-F • E Africa • 100 kW / Sa • E Africa • 100 kW / M/Tu/Th/F • E Africa • 100 kW / Irr • E Africa • 100 kW

INDIA
ALL INDIA RADIO, Bhopal — DS • 50 kW / Su • DS • 50 kW / ENGLISH, ETC • DS • 50 kW

KOREA (DPR)
KOREAN CENTRAL BS — E Asia • ALT. FREQ. TO 7140 kHz
VOICE OF KOREA — E Asia • ALT. FREQ. TO 7140 kHz
KOREA (REPUBLIC)
KBS WORLD R, Via Rampisham, UK — W • N Africa • 500 kW
PHILIPPINES
RADIO VERITAS ASIA, Palauig — E Asia • 250 kW • ALT. FREQ. TO 9730 kHz
POLAND
†RADIO POLONIA, Warsaw — ⇄ • E Europe • 100 kW / W • E Europe • 100 kW

ROMANIA
R ROMANIA INTL, Bucharest — W • W Europe • 250 kW
†R ROMANIA INTL, Galbeni — W • W Europe • 250 kW
RUSSIA
†VOICE OF RUSSIA, St Petersburg — S • Europe & N Africa • 400 kW
VOICE OF RUSSIA, Via Moldova — S • E North Am • 500 kW • ALT. FREQ. TO 9665 kHz / W • E North Am • 500 kW

TURKEY
†VOICE OF TURKEY, Ankara-Emirler — W • W Asia & C Asia • 500 kW / S • S Europe • 500 kW / W • S Europe • 250 kW

UNITED KINGDOM
BBC, Rampisham — W • N Africa • 500 kW
†BBC, Via Armavir, Russia — S • S Asia • 500 kW
†BBC, Via Zyyi, Cyprus — W • Mideast & W Asia • 250 kW
USA
†ADVENTIST WORLD R, Via South Africa — S • C Africa • 250 kW
TRANS WORLD R, Via Albania — W M/Tu/Th/F • Europe • 100 kW

7185 **BANGLADESH**
BANGLADESH BETAR, Dhaka-Kabirpur — SE Asia • 250 kW / Europe • 250 kW / S Asia • 250 kW / Mideast • 250 kW / Europe • VOICE OF ISLAM • 250 kW

CANADA
R CANADA INTL, Via Kashi, China — W • E Africa • 100 kW
CHINA
†CHINA R INTL, Xi'an — E Africa & C Africa • 150 kW • ALT. FREQ. TO 11600 kHz
CHINA (TAIWAN)
R TAIWAN INTL, Huwei — E Asia • TAIWAN NETWORK • 100 kW
IRAN
VO THE ISLAMIC REP, Sirjan — W • E Asia • 500 kW
MYANMAR (BURMA)
RADIO MYANMAR, Yangon — DS • 50 kW / Sa/Su • DS • 50 kW

POLAND
†RADIO POLONIA, Warsaw — S • E Europe • 100 kW
SOUTH AFRICA
RADIO SONDERGRENSE, Meyerton — W • S Africa • DS • 100 kW / S Africa • DS • 100 kW / S • S Africa • DS • 100 kW

UNITED KINGDOM
BBC, Via Ascension — E Africa • 250 kW
USA
R FREE ASIA, Via Iranawila, Sri Lanka — W • SE Asia • 250 kW
7190 **CHINA**
(con'd) CHINA R INTL, Kashi — Europe • 500 kW

0 1 2 3 4 5 6 7 8 9 10 11 12 13 14 15 16 17 18 19 20 21 22 23 24

SEASONAL S OR W   1-HR TIMESHIFT MIDYEAR ⇄ OR ⇉   JAMMING / OR /\   EARLIEST HEARD ◁   LATEST HEARD ▷   NEW FOR 2007 †

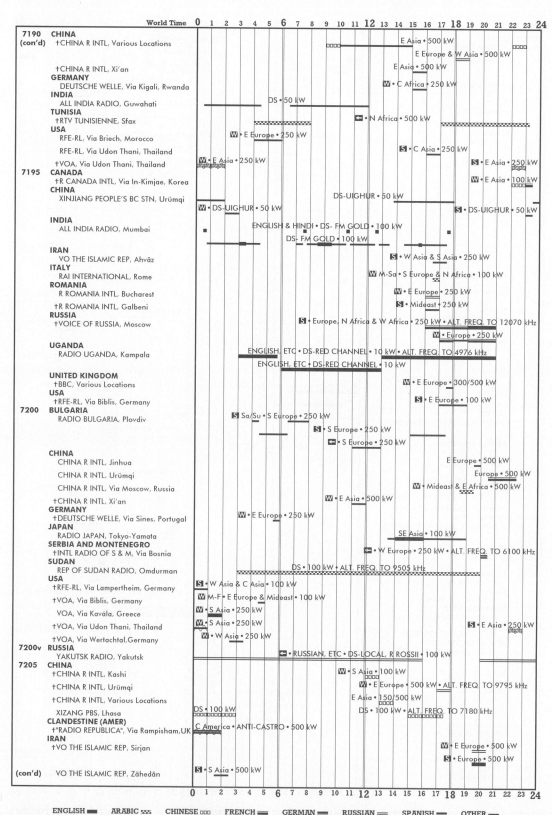

7190	**CHINA**	
(con'd)	†CHINA R INTL, Various Locations	E Asia • 500 kW
		E Europe & W Asia • 500 kW
	†CHINA R INTL, Xi'an	E Asia • 500 kW
	GERMANY	
	DEUTSCHE WELLE, Via Kigali, Rwanda	W • C Africa • 250 kW
	INDIA	
	ALL INDIA RADIO, Guwahati	DS • 50 kW
	TUNISIA	
	†RTV TUNISIENNE, Sfax	N Africa • 500 kW
	USA	
	RFE-RL, Via Briech, Morocco	W • E Europe • 250 kW
	RFE-RL, Via Udon Thani, Thailand	S • C Asia • 250 kW
	†VOA, Via Udon Thani, Thailand	W • E Asia • 250 kW / S • E Asia • 250 kW
7195	**CANADA**	
	†R CANADA INTL, Via In-Kimjae, Korea	W • E Asia • 100 kW
	CHINA	
	XINJIANG PEOPLE'S BC STN, Urümqi	DS-UIGHUR • 50 kW / W • DS-UIGHUR • 50 kW / S • DS-UIGHUR • 50 kW
	INDIA	
	ALL INDIA RADIO, Mumbai	ENGLISH & HINDI • DS- FM GOLD • 100 kW / DS- FM GOLD • 100 kW
	IRAN	
	VO THE ISLAMIC REP, Ahvāz	S • W Asia & S Asia • 250 kW
	ITALY	
	RAI INTERNATIONAL, Rome	W M-Sa • S Europe & N Africa • 100 kW
	ROMANIA	
	R ROMANIA INTL, Bucharest	W • E Europe • 250 kW
	†R ROMANIA INTL, Galbeni	S • Mideast • 250 kW
	RUSSIA	
	†VOICE OF RUSSIA, Moscow	S • Europe, N Africa & W Africa • 250 kW • ALT. FREQ. TO 12070 kHz / W • Europe • 250 kW
	UGANDA	
	RADIO UGANDA, Kampala	ENGLISH, ETC • DS-RED CHANNEL • 10 kW • ALT. FREQ. TO 4976 kHz / ENGLISH, ETC • DS-RED CHANNEL • 10 kW
	UNITED KINGDOM	
	†BBC, Various Locations	W • E Europe • 300/500 kW
	USA	
	†RFE-RL, Via Biblis, Germany	S • E Europe • 100 kW
7200	**BULGARIA**	
	RADIO BULGARIA, Plovdiv	S Sa/Su • S Europe • 250 kW / S • S Europe • 250 kW / S Europe • 250 kW
	CHINA	
	CHINA R INTL, Jinhua	E Europe • 500 kW
	CHINA R INTL, Urümqi	Europe • 500 kW
	CHINA R INTL, Via Moscow, Russia	W • Mideast & E Africa • 500 kW
	†CHINA R INTL, Xi'an	W • E Asia • 500 kW
	GERMANY	
	†DEUTSCHE WELLE, Via Sines, Portugal	W • E Europe • 250 kW
	JAPAN	
	RADIO JAPAN, Tokyo-Yamata	SE Asia • 100 kW
	SERBIA AND MONTENEGRO	
	†INTL RADIO OF S & M, Via Bosnia	W Europe • 250 kW • ALT. FREQ. TO 6100 kHz
	SUDAN	
	REP OF SUDAN RADIO, Omdurman	DS • 100 kW • ALT. FREQ. TO 9505 kHz
	USA	
	†RFE-RL, Via Lampertheim, Germany	S • W Asia & C Asia • 100 kW
	†VOA, Via Biblis, Germany	W M-F • E Europe & Mideast • 100 kW
	VOA, Via Kavála, Greece	W • S Asia • 250 kW
	†VOA, Via Udon Thani, Thailand	W • S Asia • 250 kW / S • E Asia • 250 kW
	†VOA, Via Wertachtal, Germany	W • W Asia • 250 kW
7200v	**RUSSIA**	
	YAKUTSK RADIO, Yakutsk	RUSSIAN, ETC • DS-LOCAL, R ROSSII • 100 kW
7205	**CHINA**	
	†CHINA R INTL, Kashi	W • S Asia • 100 kW
	†CHINA R INTL, Urümqi	W • E Europe • 500 kW • ALT. FREQ. TO 9795 kHz
	†CHINA R INTL, Various Locations	E Asia • 150/500 kW
	XIZANG PBS, Lhasa	DS • 100 kW / DS • 100 kW • ALT. FREQ. TO 7180 kHz
	CLANDESTINE (AMER)	
	†"RADIO REPUBLICA", Via Rampisham, UK	C America • ANTI-CASTRO • 500 kW
	IRAN	
	†VO THE ISLAMIC REP, Sirjan	W • E Europe • 500 kW / S • Europe • 500 kW
(con'd)	VO THE ISLAMIC REP, Zāhedān	S • S Asia • 500 kW

ENGLISH ▬▬   ARABIC ▨▨▨   CHINESE □□□   FRENCH ▬▬   GERMAN ▬▬   RUSSIAN ══   SPANISH ▬▬   OTHER ▬

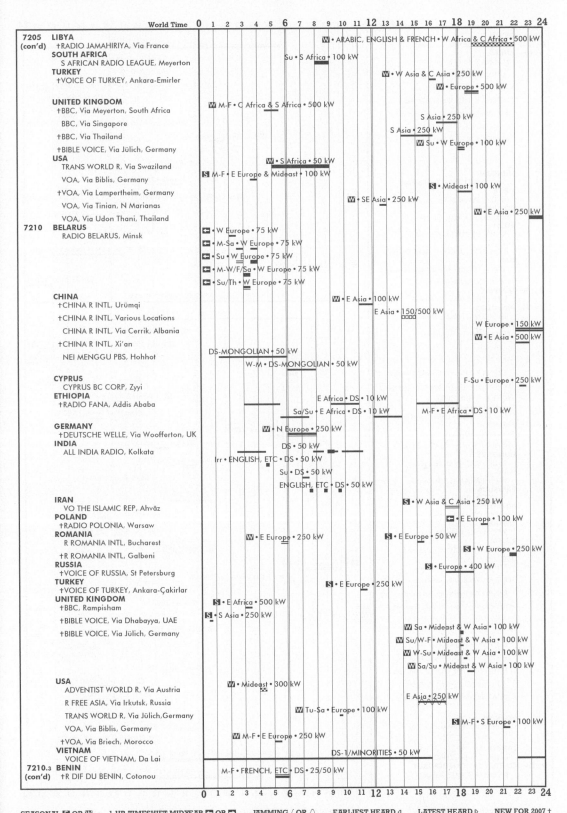

World Time · 0 1 2 3 4 5 6 7 8 9 10 11 12 13 14 15 16 17 18 19 20 21 22 23 24

7205 **LIBYA**
(con'd) †RADIO JAMAHIRIYA, Via France — W • ARABIC, ENGLISH & FRENCH • W Africa & C Africa • 500 kW
SOUTH AFRICA
 S AFRICAN RADIO LEAGUE, Meyerton — Su • S Africa • 100 kW
TURKEY
 †VOICE OF TURKEY, Ankara-Emirler — W • W Asia & C Asia • 250 kW
 — W • Europe • 500 kW

UNITED KINGDOM
 †BBC, Via Meyerton, South Africa — W M-F • C Africa & S Africa • 500 kW
 BBC, Via Singapore — S Asia • 250 kW
 †BBC, Via Thailand — S Asia • 250 kW
 †BIBLE VOICE, Via Jülich, Germany — W Su • W Europe • 100 kW
USA
 TRANS WORLD R, Via Swaziland — W • S Africa • 50 kW
 VOA, Via Biblis, Germany — S M-F • E Europe & Mideast • 100 kW
 †VOA, Via Lampertheim, Germany — S • Mideast • 100 kW
 VOA, Via Tinian, N Marianas — W • SE Asia • 250 kW
 VOA, Via Udon Thani, Thailand — W • E Asia • 250 kW
7210 **BELARUS**
 RADIO BELARUS, Minsk — • W Europe • 75 kW
 — • M-Sa • W Europe • 75 kW
 — • Su • W Europe • 75 kW
 — • M-W/F/Sa • W Europe • 75 kW
 — • Su/Th • W Europe • 75 kW

CHINA
 †CHINA R INTL, Urümqi — W • E Asia • 100 kW
 †CHINA R INTL, Various Locations — E Asia • 150/500 kW
 CHINA R INTL, Via Cerrik, Albania — W Europe • 150 kW
 †CHINA R INTL, Xi'an — W • E Asia • 500 kW
 NEI MENGGU PBS, Hohhot — DS-MONGOLIAN • 50 kW
 — W-M • DS-MONGOLIAN • 50 kW

CYPRUS
 CYPRUS BC CORP, Zyyi — F-Su • Europe • 250 kW
ETHIOPIA
 †RADIO FANA, Addis Ababa — E Africa • DS • 10 kW
 — Sa/Su • E Africa • DS • 10 kW — M-F • E Africa • DS • 10 kW

GERMANY
 †DEUTSCHE WELLE, Via Woofferton, UK — W • N Europe • 250 kW
INDIA
 ALL INDIA RADIO, Kolkata — DS • 50 kW
 — Irr • ENGLISH, ETC • DS • 50 kW
 — Su • DS • 50 kW
 — ENGLISH, ETC • DS • 50 kW

IRAN
 VO THE ISLAMIC REP, Ahvāz — S • W Asia & C Asia • 250 kW
POLAND
 †RADIO POLONIA, Warsaw — • E Europe • 100 kW
ROMANIA
 R ROMANIA INTL, Bucharest — W • E Europe • 250 kW
 — S • E Europe • 50 kW
 †R ROMANIA INTL, Galbeni — S • W Europe • 250 kW
RUSSIA
 †VOICE OF RUSSIA, St Petersburg — S • Europe • 400 kW
TURKEY
 †VOICE OF TURKEY, Ankara-Çakirlar — S • E Europe • 250 kW
UNITED KINGDOM
 †BBC, Rampisham — S • E Africa • 500 kW
 †BIBLE VOICE, Via Dhabayya, UAE — S • S Asia • 250 kW
 †BIBLE VOICE, Via Jülich, Germany — W Sa • Mideast & W Asia • 100 kW
 — W Su/W-F • Mideast & W Asia • 100 kW
 — W W-Su • Mideast & W Asia • 100 kW
 — W Sa/Su • Mideast & W Asia • 100 kW

USA
 ADVENTIST WORLD R, Via Austria — W • Mideast • 300 kW
 R FREE ASIA, Via Irkutsk, Russia — E Asia • 250 kW
 TRANS WORLD R, Via Jülich, Germany — W Tu-Sa • Europe • 100 kW
 VOA, Via Biblis, Germany — S M-F • S Europe • 100 kW
 †VOA, Via Briech, Morocco — W M-F • E Europe • 250 kW
VIETNAM
 VOICE OF VIETNAM, Da Lai — DS-1/MINORITIES • 50 kW
7210.3 **BENIN**
(con'd) †R DIF DU BENIN, Cotonou — M-F • FRENCH, ETC • DS • 25/50 kW

0 1 2 3 4 5 6 7 8 9 10 11 12 13 14 15 16 17 18 19 20 21 22 23 24

SEASONAL S OR W   1-HR TIMESHIFT MIDYEAR ◄▪ OR ▪► JAMMING / OR ∧ EARLIEST HEARD ◄ LATEST HEARD ▷ NEW FOR 2007 †

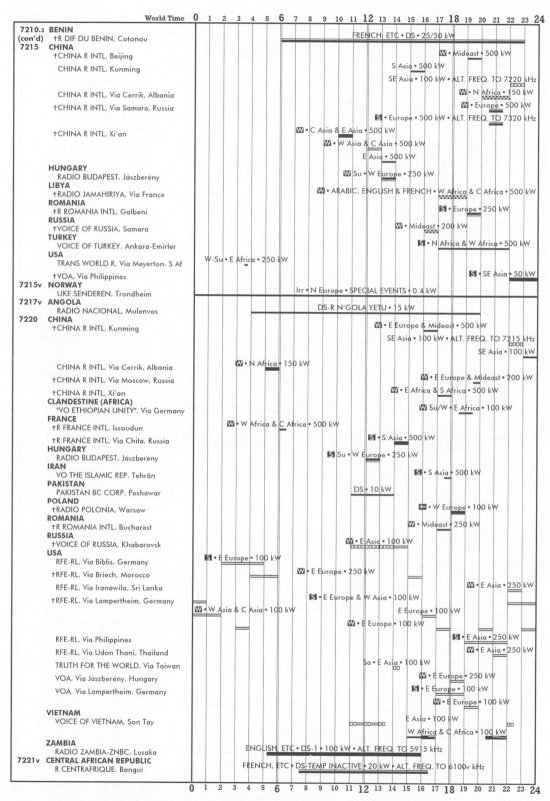

		World Time																							

7210.3 BENIN
(con'd)   †R DIF DU BENIN, Cotonou — FRENCH, ETC • DS • 25/50 kW
7215 CHINA
      †CHINA R INTL, Beijing — W • Mideast • 500 kW
      CHINA R INTL, Kunming — S Asia • 500 kW
         — SE Asia • 100 kW • ALT. FREQ. TO 7220 kHz
      CHINA R INTL, Via Cerrik, Albania — W • N Africa • 150 kW
      †CHINA R INTL, Via Samara, Russia — W • Europe • 500 kW
         — S • Europe • 500 kW • ALT. FREQ. TO 7320 kHz
      †CHINA R INTL, Xi'an — W • C Asia & E Asia • 500 kW
         — W • W Asia & C Asia • 500 kW
         — E Asia • 500 kW
      HUNGARY
      RADIO BUDAPEST, Jászberény — W Su • W Europe • 250 kW
      LIBYA
      †RADIO JAMAHIRIYA, Via France — W • ARABIC, ENGLISH & FRENCH • W Africa & C Africa • 500 kW
      ROMANIA
      †R ROMANIA INTL, Galbeni — S • Europe • 250 kW
      RUSSIA
      †VOICE OF RUSSIA, Samara — W • Mideast • 200 kW
      TURKEY
      VOICE OF TURKEY, Ankara-Emirler — S • N Africa & W Africa • 500 kW
      USA
      TRANS WORLD R, Via Meyerton, S Af — W-Su • E Africa • 250 kW
      †VOA, Via Philippines — S • SE Asia • 50 kW
7215v NORWAY
      UKE SENDEREN, Trondheim — Irr • N Europe • SPECIAL EVENTS • 0.4 kW
7217v ANGOLA
      RADIO NACIONAL, Mulenvos — DS-R N'GOLA YETU • 15 kW
7220 CHINA
      †CHINA R INTL, Kunming — W • E Europe & Mideast • 500 kW
         — SE Asia • 100 kW • ALT. FREQ. TO 7215 kHz
         — SE Asia • 100 kW
      CHINA R INTL, Via Cerrik, Albania — W • N Africa • 150 kW
      †CHINA R INTL, Via Moscow, Russia — W • E Europe & Mideast • 200 kW
      †CHINA R INTL, Xi'an — W • E Africa & S Africa • 500 kW
      CLANDESTINE (AFRICA)
      "VO ETHIOPIAN UNITY", Via Germany — W Su/W • E Africa • 100 kW
      FRANCE
      †R FRANCE INTL, Issoudun — W • W Africa & C Africa • 500 kW
      †R FRANCE INTL, Via Chita, Russia — S • S Asia • 500 kW
      HUNGARY
      RADIO BUDAPEST, Jászberény — S Su • W Europe • 250 kW
      IRAN
      VO THE ISLAMIC REP, Tehrān — S • S Asia • 500 kW
      PAKISTAN
      PAKISTAN BC CORP, Peshawar — DS • 10 kW
      POLAND
      †RADIO POLONIA, Warsaw — ◄ • W Europe • 100 kW
      ROMANIA
      †R ROMANIA INTL, Bucharest — W • Mideast • 250 kW
      RUSSIA
      †VOICE OF RUSSIA, Khabarovsk — W • E Asia • 100 kW
      USA
      RFE-RL, Via Biblis, Germany — S • E Europe • 100 kW
      †RFE-RL, Via Briech, Morocco — W • E Europe • 250 kW
      RFE-RL, Via Iranawila, Sri Lanka — W • E Asia • 250 kW
      †RFE-RL, Via Lampertheim, Germany — S • E Europe & W Asia • 100 kW
         — E Europe • 100 kW
         — W • W Asia & C Asia • 100 kW
         — W • E Europe • 100 kW
      RFE-RL, Via Philippines — S • E Asia • 250 kW
      RFE-RL, Via Udon Thani, Thailand — W • E Asia • 250 kW
      TRUTH FOR THE WORLD, Via Taiwan — Sa • E Asia • 100 kW
      VOA, Via Jászberény, Hungary — W • E Europe • 250 kW
      VOA, Via Lampertheim, Germany — S • E Europe • 100 kW
         — W • E Europe • 100 kW
      VIETNAM
      VOICE OF VIETNAM, Son Tay — E Asia • 100 kW
         — W Africa & C Africa • 100 kW
      ZAMBIA
      RADIO ZAMBIA-ZNBC, Lusaka — ENGLISH, ETC • DS-1 • 100 kW • ALT. FREQ. TO 5915 kHz
7221v CENTRAL AFRICAN REPUBLIC
      R CENTRAFRIQUE, Bangui — FRENCH, ETC • DS-TEMP INACTIVE • 20 kW • ALT. FREQ. TO 6100v kHz

ENGLISH ▬   ARABIC ▨▨▨   CHINESE □□□   FRENCH ▬▬   GERMAN ▬▬   RUSSIAN ══   SPANISH ▬▬   OTHER ▬

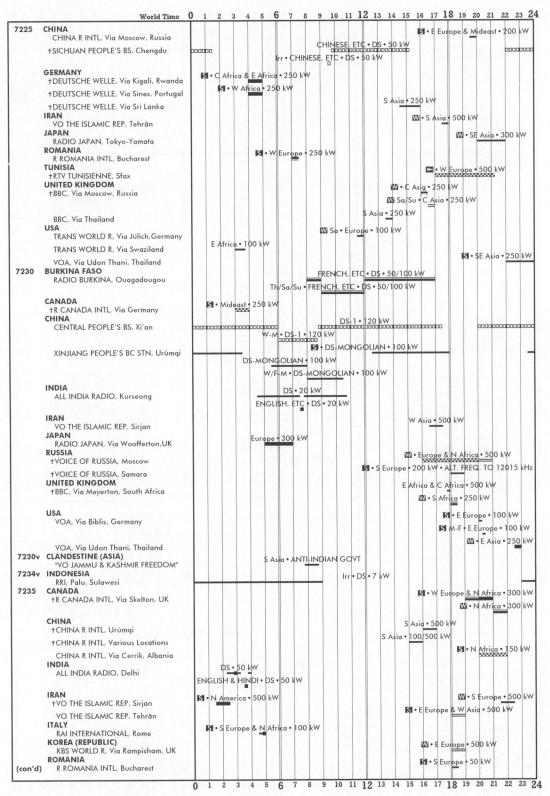

| World Time | 0 1 2 3 4 5 6 7 8 9 10 11 12 13 14 15 16 17 18 19 20 21 22 23 24 |

7225 CHINA
CHINA R INTL, Via Moscow, Russia — S • E Europe & Mideast • 200 kW
†SICHUAN PEOPLE'S BS, Chengdu — CHINESE, ETC • DS • 50 kW / Irr • CHINESE, ETC • DS • 50 kW

GERMANY
†DEUTSCHE WELLE, Via Kigali, Rwanda — S • C Africa & E Africa • 250 kW
†DEUTSCHE WELLE, Via Sines, Portugal — S • W Africa • 250 kW
†DEUTSCHE WELLE, Via Sri Lanka — S Asia • 250 kW

IRAN
VO THE ISLAMIC REP, Tehrān — W • S Asia • 500 kW

JAPAN
RADIO JAPAN, Tokyo-Yamata — W • SE Asia • 300 kW

ROMANIA
R ROMANIA INTL, Bucharest — S • W Europe • 250 kW

TUNISIA
†RTV TUNISIENNE, Sfax — ⇐ • W Europe • 500 kW

UNITED KINGDOM
†BBC, Via Moscow, Russia — W • C Asia • 250 kW / W Sa/Su • C Asia • 250 kW

BBC, Via Thailand — S Asia • 250 kW

USA
TRANS WORLD R, Via Jülich, Germany — W Sa • Europe • 100 kW
TRANS WORLD R, Via Swaziland — E Africa • 100 kW
VOA, Via Udon Thani, Thailand — S • SE Asia • 250 kW

7230 BURKINA FASO
RADIO BURKINA, Ouagadougou — FRENCH, ETC • DS • 50/100 kW / Th/Sa/Su • FRENCH, ETC • DS • 50/100 kW

CANADA
†R CANADA INTL, Via Germany — S • Mideast • 250 kW

CHINA
CENTRAL PEOPLE'S BS, Xi'an — DS-1 • 120 kW / W-M • DS-1 • 120 kW
XINJIANG PEOPLE'S BC STN, Urümqi — S • DS-MONGOLIAN • 100 kW / DS-MONGOLIAN • 100 kW / W/F·M • DS-MONGOLIAN • 100 kW

INDIA
ALL INDIA RADIO, Kurseong — DS • 20 kW / ENGLISH, ETC • DS • 20 kW

IRAN
VO THE ISLAMIC REP, Sirjan — W Asia • 500 kW

JAPAN
RADIO JAPAN, Via Woofferton, UK — Europe • 300 kW

RUSSIA
†VOICE OF RUSSIA, Moscow — W • Europe & N Africa • 500 kW
†VOICE OF RUSSIA, Samara — S • S Europe • 200 kW • ALT. FREQ. TO 12015 kHz

UNITED KINGDOM
†BBC, Via Meyerton, South Africa — E Africa & C Africa • 500 kW / W • S Africa • 250 kW

USA
VOA, Via Biblis, Germany — S • E Europe • 100 kW / S M-F • E Europe • 100 kW
VOA, Via Udon Thani, Thailand — W • E Asia • 250 kW

7230v CLANDESTINE (ASIA)
"VO JAMMU & KASHMIR FREEDOM" — S Asia • ANTI-INDIAN GOVT

7234v INDONESIA
RRI, Palu, Sulawesi — Irr • DS • 7 kW

7235 CANADA
†R CANADA INTL, Via Skelton, UK — S • W Europe & N Africa • 300 kW / W • N Africa • 300 kW

CHINA
†CHINA R INTL, Urümqi — S Asia • 500 kW
†CHINA R INTL, Various Locations — S Asia • 100/500 kW
CHINA R INTL, Via Cerrik, Albania — S • N Africa • 150 kW

INDIA
ALL INDIA RADIO, Delhi — DS • 50 kW / ENGLISH & HINDI • DS • 50 kW

IRAN
†VO THE ISLAMIC REP, Sirjan — S • N America • 500 kW / W • S Europe • 500 kW
VO THE ISLAMIC REP, Tehrān — S • E Europe & W Asia • 500 kW

ITALY
RAI INTERNATIONAL, Rome — S • S Europe & N Africa • 100 kW

KOREA (REPUBLIC)
KBS WORLD R, Via Rampisham, UK — W • E Europe • 500 kW

ROMANIA
(con'd) R ROMANIA INTL, Bucharest — S • S Europe • 50 kW

| 0 1 2 3 4 5 6 7 8 9 10 11 12 13 14 15 16 17 18 19 20 21 22 23 24 |

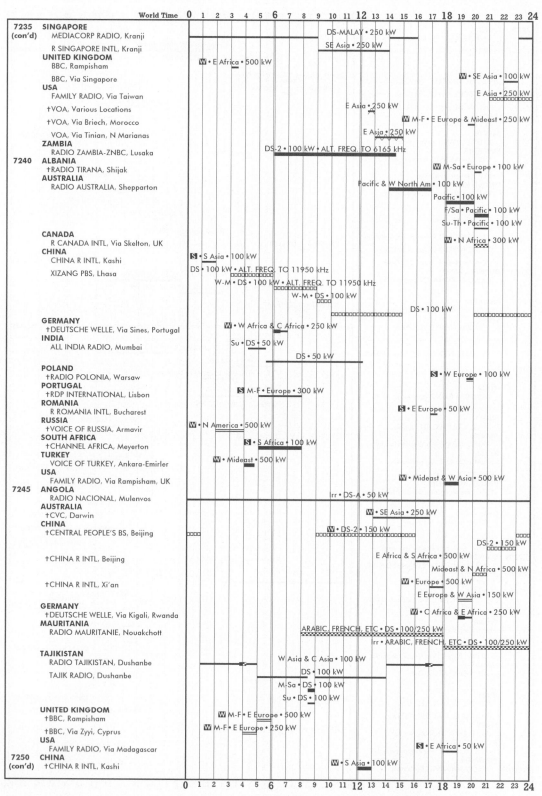

World Time 0 1 2 3 4 5 6 7 8 9 10 11 12 13 14 15 16 17 18 19 20 21 22 23 24

7235 SINGAPORE
(con'd)   MEDIACORP RADIO, Kranji — DS-MALAY • 250 kW

    R SINGAPORE INTL, Kranji — SE Asia • 250 kW
UNITED KINGDOM
    BBC, Rampisham — W • E Africa • 500 kW

    BBC, Via Singapore — W • SE Asia • 100 kW
USA
    FAMILY RADIO, Via Taiwan — E Asia • 250 kW

    †VOA, Various Locations — E Asia • 250 kW

    †VOA, Via Briech, Morocco — W • M-F • E Europe & Mideast • 250 kW

    VOA, Via Tinian, N Marianas — E Asia • 250 kW
ZAMBIA
    RADIO ZAMBIA-ZNBC, Lusaka — DS-2 • 100 kW • ALT. FREQ. TO 6165 kHz
7240 ALBANIA
    †RADIO TIRANA, Shijak — W • M-Sa • Europe • 100 kW
AUSTRALIA
    RADIO AUSTRALIA, Shepparton — Pacific & W North Am • 100 kW

    — Pacific • 100 kW

    — F/Sa • Pacific • 100 kW

    — Su-Th • Pacific • 100 kW

CANADA
    R CANADA INTL, Via Skelton, UK — W • N Africa • 300 kW
CHINA
    CHINA R INTL, Kashi — S • S Asia • 100 kW

    XIZANG PBS, Lhasa — DS • 100 kW • ALT. FREQ. TO 11950 kHz

    — W-M • DS • 100 kW • ALT. FREQ. TO 11950 kHz

    — W-M • DS • 100 kW

    — DS • 100 kW

GERMANY
    †DEUTSCHE WELLE, Via Sines, Portugal — W • W Africa & C Africa • 250 kW
INDIA
    ALL INDIA RADIO, Mumbai — Su • DS • 50 kW

    — DS • 50 kW

POLAND
    †RADIO POLONIA, Warsaw — S • W Europe • 100 kW
PORTUGAL
    †RDP INTERNATIONAL, Lisbon — S • M-F • Europe • 300 kW
ROMANIA
    R ROMANIA INTL, Bucharest — S • E Europe • 50 kW
RUSSIA
    †VOICE OF RUSSIA, Armavir — W • N America • 500 kW
SOUTH AFRICA
    †CHANNEL AFRICA, Meyerton — S • S Africa • 100 kW
TURKEY
    VOICE OF TURKEY, Ankara-Emirler — W • Mideast • 500 kW
USA
    FAMILY RADIO, Via Rampisham, UK — W • Mideast & W Asia • 500 kW
7245 ANGOLA
    RADIO NACIONAL, Mulenvos — Irr • DS-A • 50 kW
AUSTRALIA
    †CVC, Darwin — W • SE Asia • 250 kW
CHINA
    †CENTRAL PEOPLE'S BS, Beijing — W • DS-2 • 150 kW

    — DS-2 • 150 kW

    †CHINA R INTL, Beijing — E Africa & S Africa • 500 kW

    — Mideast & N Africa • 500 kW

    †CHINA R INTL, Xi'an — W • Europe • 500 kW

    — E Europe & W Asia • 150 kW

GERMANY
    †DEUTSCHE WELLE, Via Kigali, Rwanda — W • C Africa & E Africa • 250 kW
MAURITANIA
    RADIO MAURITANIE, Nouakchott — ARABIC, FRENCH, ETC • DS • 100/250 kW

    — Irr • ARABIC, FRENCH, ETC • DS • 100/250 kW

TAJIKISTAN
    RADIO TAJIKISTAN, Dushanbe — W Asia & C Asia • 100 kW

    TAJIK RADIO, Dushanbe — DS • 100 kW

    — M-Sa • DS • 100 kW

    — Su • DS • 100 kW

UNITED KINGDOM
    †BBC, Rampisham — W • M-F • E Europe • 500 kW

    †BBC, Via Zyyi, Cyprus — W • M-F • E Europe • 250 kW
USA
    FAMILY RADIO, Via Madagascar — S • E Africa • 50 kW
7250 CHINA
(con'd)   †CHINA R INTL, Kashi — W • S Asia • 100 kW

0 1 2 3 4 5 6 7 8 9 10 11 12 13 14 15 16 17 18 19 20 21 22 23 24

ENGLISH ▬   ARABIC ⌇⌇   CHINESE □□□   FRENCH ▬   GERMAN ▬   RUSSIAN ═   SPANISH ▬   OTHER ▬

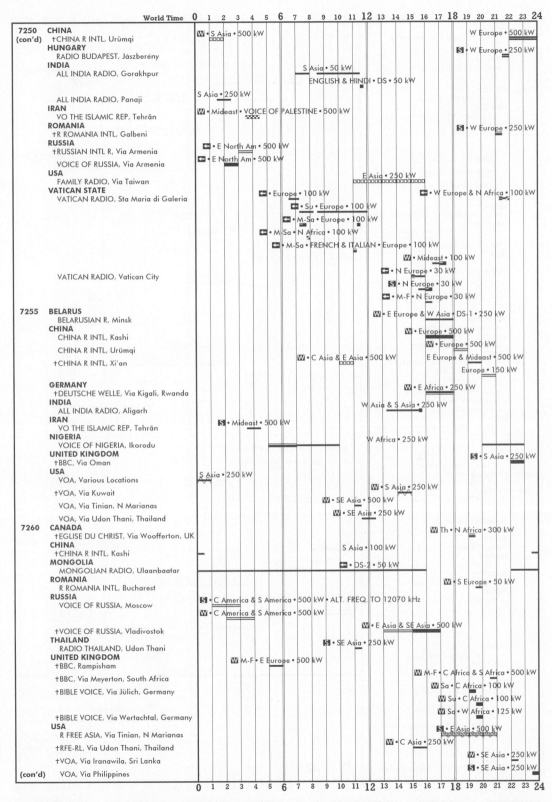

	World Time	0 1 2 3 4 5 6 7 8 9 10 11 12 13 14 15 16 17 18 19 20 21 22 23 24
7250	**CHINA**	
(con'd)	†CHINA R INTL, Urümqi	W • S Asia • 500 kW ... W Europe • 500 kW
	HUNGARY	
	RADIO BUDAPEST, Jászberény	S • W Europe • 250 kW
	INDIA	
	ALL INDIA RADIO, Gorakhpur	S Asia • 50 kW
		ENGLISH & HINDI • DS • 50 kW
	ALL INDIA RADIO, Panaji	S Asia • 250 kW
	IRAN	
	VO THE ISLAMIC REP, Tehrān	W • Mideast • VOICE OF PALESTINE • 500 kW
	ROMANIA	
	†R ROMANIA INTL, Galbeni	S • W Europe • 250 kW
	RUSSIA	
	†RUSSIAN INTL R, Via Armenia	⇦ • E North Am • 500 kW
	VOICE OF RUSSIA, Via Armenia	⇦ • E North Am • 500 kW
	USA	
	FAMILY RADIO, Via Taiwan	E Asia • 250 kW
	VATICAN STATE	
	VATICAN RADIO, Sta Maria di Galeria	⇦ • Europe • 100 kW ... ⇦ • W Europe & N Africa • 100 kW
		⇦ • Su • Europe • 100 kW
		⇦ • M-Sa • Europe • 100 kW
		⇦ • M-Sa • N Africa • 100 kW
		⇦ • M-Sa • FRENCH & ITALIAN • Europe • 100 kW
		W • Mideast • 100 kW
	VATICAN RADIO, Vatican City	⇦ • N Europe • 30 kW
		S • N Europe • 30 kW
		⇦ • M-F • N Europe • 30 kW
7255	**BELARUS**	
	BELARUSIAN R, Minsk	W • E Europe & W Asia • DS-1 • 250 kW
	CHINA	
	CHINA R INTL, Kashi	W • Europe • 500 kW
	CHINA R INTL, Urümqi	W • Europe • 500 kW
	†CHINA R INTL, Xi'an	W • C Asia & E Asia • 500 kW ... E Europe & Mideast • 500 kW
		Europe • 150 kW
	GERMANY	
	†DEUTSCHE WELLE, Via Kigali, Rwanda	W • E Africa • 250 kW
	INDIA	
	ALL INDIA RADIO, Aligarh	W Asia & S Asia • 250 kW
	IRAN	
	VO THE ISLAMIC REP, Tehrān	S • Mideast • 500 kW
	NIGERIA	
	VOICE OF NIGERIA, Ikorodu	W Africa • 250 kW
	UNITED KINGDOM	
	†BBC, Via Oman	S • S Asia • 250 kW
	USA	
	VOA, Various Locations	S Asia • 250 kW
	†VOA, Via Kuwait	W • S Asia • 250 kW
	VOA, Via Tinian, N Marianas	W • SE Asia • 500 kW
	VOA, Via Udon Thani, Thailand	W • SE Asia • 250 kW
7260	**CANADA**	
	†EGLISE DU CHRIST, Via Woofferton, UK	W Th • N Africa • 300 kW
	CHINA	
	†CHINA R INTL, Kashi	S Asia • 100 kW
	MONGOLIA	
	MONGOLIAN RADIO, Ulaanbaatar	⇦ • DS-2 • 50 kW
	ROMANIA	
	R ROMANIA INTL, Bucharest	W • S Europe • 50 kW
	RUSSIA	
	VOICE OF RUSSIA, Moscow	S • C America & S America • 500 kW • ALT. FREQ. TO 12070 kHz
		W • C America & S America • 500 kW
	†VOICE OF RUSSIA, Vladivostok	W • E Asia & SE Asia • 500 kW
	THAILAND	
	RADIO THAILAND, Udon Thani	S • SE Asia • 250 kW
	UNITED KINGDOM	
	†BBC, Rampisham	W M-F • E Europe • 500 kW
	†BBC, Via Meyerton, South Africa	W M-F • C Africa & S Africa • 500 kW
	†BIBLE VOICE, Via Jülich, Germany	W Sa • C Africa • 100 kW
		W Su • C Africa • 100 kW
		W Sa • W Africa • 125 kW
	†BIBLE VOICE, Via Wertachtal, Germany	
	USA	
	R FREE ASIA, Via Tinian, N Marianas	S • E Asia • 500 kW
	†RFE-RL, Via Udon Thani, Thailand	W • C Asia • 250 kW
	†VOA, Via Iranawila, Sri Lanka	W • SE Asia • 250 kW
(con'd)	VOA, Via Philippines	S • SE Asia • 250 kW

	0 1 2 3 4 5 6 7 8 9 10 11 12 13 14 15 16 17 18 19 20 21 22 23 24

SEASONAL S OR W   1-HR TIMESHIFT MIDYEAR ⇦ OR ⇨   JAMMING / OR ∧   EARLIEST HEARD ◁   LATEST HEARD ▷   NEW FOR 2007 †

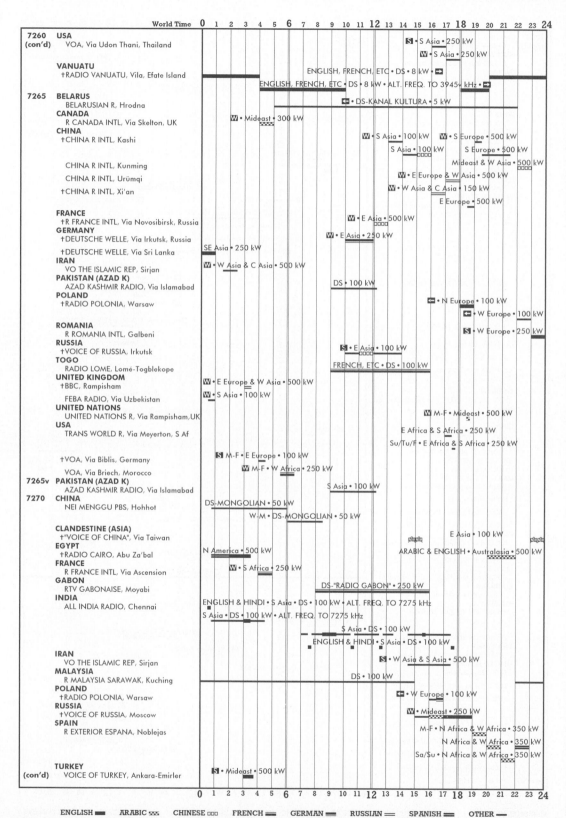

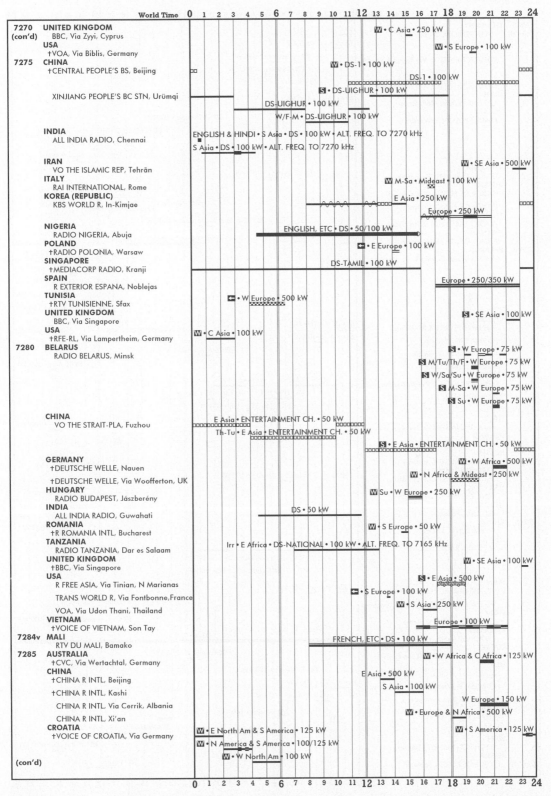

World Time 0 1 2 3 4 5 6 7 8 9 10 11 12 13 14 15 16 17 18 19 20 21 22 23 24

7270 UNITED KINGDOM	
(con'd) BBC, Via Zyyi, Cyprus	W • C Asia • 250 kW
USA	
†VOA, Via Biblis, Germany	W • S Europe • 100 kW
7275 CHINA	
†CENTRAL PEOPLE'S BS, Beijing	W • DS-1 • 100 kW / DS-1 • 100 kW
XINJIANG PEOPLE'S BC STN, Urümqi	S • DS-UIGHUR • 100 kW / DS-UIGHUR • 100 kW / W/F-M • DS-UIGHUR • 100 kW
INDIA	
ALL INDIA RADIO, Chennai	ENGLISH & HINDI • S Asia • DS • 100 kW • ALT. FREQ. TO 7270 kHz / S Asia • DS • 100 kW • ALT. FREQ. TO 7270 kHz
IRAN	
VO THE ISLAMIC REP, Tehrān	W • SE Asia • 500 kW
ITALY	
RAI INTERNATIONAL, Rome	W M-Sa • Mideast • 100 kW
KOREA (REPUBLIC)	
KBS WORLD R, In-Kimjae	E Asia • 250 kW / Europe • 250 kW
NIGERIA	
RADIO NIGERIA, Abuja	ENGLISH, ETC • DS • 50/100 kW
POLAND	
†RADIO POLONIA, Warsaw	• E Europe • 100 kW
SINGAPORE	
†MEDIACORP RADIO, Kranji	DS-TAMIL • 100 kW
SPAIN	
R EXTERIOR ESPANA, Noblejas	Europe • 250/350 kW
TUNISIA	
†RTV TUNISIENNE, Sfax	• W Europe • 500 kW
UNITED KINGDOM	
BBC, Via Singapore	S • SE Asia • 100 kW
USA	
†RFE-RL, Via Lampertheim, Germany	W • C Asia • 100 kW
7280 BELARUS	
RADIO BELARUS, Minsk	S • W Europe • 75 kW / S M/Tu/Th/F • W Europe • 75 kW / S W/Sa/Su • W Europe • 75 kW / S M-Sa • W Europe • 75 kW / S Su • W Europe • 75 kW
CHINA	
VO THE STRAIT-PLA, Fuzhou	E Asia • ENTERTAINMENT CH. • 50 kW / Th-Tu • E Asia • ENTERTAINMENT CH. • 50 kW / S • E Asia • ENTERTAINMENT CH. • 50 kW
GERMANY	
†DEUTSCHE WELLE, Nauen	W • W Africa • 500 kW
†DEUTSCHE WELLE, Via Woofferton, UK	W • N Africa & Mideast • 250 kW
HUNGARY	
RADIO BUDAPEST, Jászberény	W Su • W Europe • 250 kW
INDIA	
ALL INDIA RADIO, Guwahati	DS • 50 kW
ROMANIA	
†R ROMANIA INTL, Bucharest	W • S Europe • 50 kW
TANZANIA	
RADIO TANZANIA, Dar es Salaam	Irr • E Africa • DS-NATIONAL • 100 kW • ALT. FREQ. TO 7165 kHz
UNITED KINGDOM	
†BBC, Via Singapore	W • SE Asia • 100 kW
USA	
R FREE ASIA, Via Tinian, N Marianas	S • E Asia • 500 kW
TRANS WORLD R, Via Fontbonne, France	• S Europe • 100 kW
VOA, Via Udon Thani, Thailand	W • S Asia • 250 kW
VIETNAM	
†VOICE OF VIETNAM, Son Tay	Europe • 100 kW
7284v MALI	
RTV DU MALI, Bamako	FRENCH, ETC • DS • 100 kW
7285 AUSTRALIA	
†CVC, Via Wertachtal, Germany	W • W Africa & C Africa • 125 kW
CHINA	
†CHINA R INTL, Beijing	E Asia • 500 kW / S Asia • 100 kW
†CHINA R INTL, Kashi	W Europe • 150 kW
CHINA R INTL, Via Cerrik, Albania	W • Europe & N Africa • 500 kW
CHINA R INTL, Xi'an	
CROATIA	
†VOICE OF CROATIA, Via Germany	W • E North Am & S America • 125 kW / W • S America • 125 kW / W • N America & S America • 100/125 kW / W • W North Am • 100 kW
(con'd)	

0 1 2 3 4 5 6 7 8 9 10 11 12 13 14 15 16 17 18 19 20 21 22 23 24

SEASONAL S OR W   1-HR TIMESHIFT MIDYEAR ⊏ OR ⊐   JAMMING / OR ⋀   EARLIEST HEARD ◁   LATEST HEARD ▷   NEW FOR 2007 †

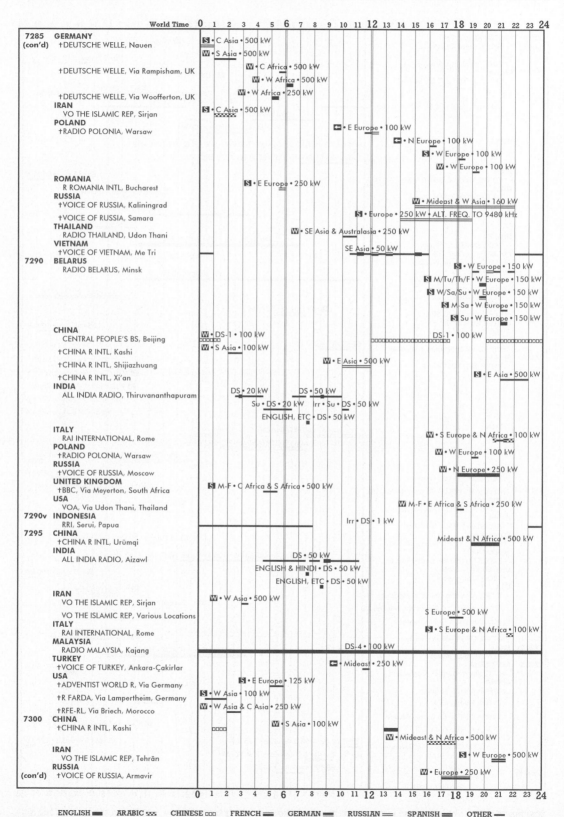

	World Time	0 1 2 3 4 5 6 7 8 9 10 11 12 13 14 15 16 17 18 19 20 21 22 23 24
7285	**GERMANY**	
(con'd)	†DEUTSCHE WELLE, Nauen	**S** • C Asia • 500 kW
		W • S Asia • 500 kW
	†DEUTSCHE WELLE, Via Rampisham, UK	**W** • C Africa • 500 kW
		W • W Africa • 500 kW
	†DEUTSCHE WELLE, Via Woofferton, UK	**W** • W Africa • 250 kW
	IRAN	
	VO THE ISLAMIC REP, Sirjan	**S** • C Asia • 500 kW
	POLAND	
	†RADIO POLONIA, Warsaw	• E Europe • 100 kW
		• N Europe • 100 kW
		S • W Europe • 100 kW
		W • W Europe • 100 kW
	ROMANIA	
	R ROMANIA INTL, Bucharest	**S** • E Europe • 250 kW
	RUSSIA	
	†VOICE OF RUSSIA, Kaliningrad	**W** • Mideast & W Asia • 160 kW
	†VOICE OF RUSSIA, Samara	**S** • Europe • 250 kW • ALT. FREQ. TO 9480 kHz
	THAILAND	
	RADIO THAILAND, Udon Thani	**W** • SE Asia & Australasia • 250 kW
	VIETNAM	
	†VOICE OF VIETNAM, Me Tri	SE Asia • 50 kW
7290	**BELARUS**	
	RADIO BELARUS, Minsk	**S** • W Europe • 150 kW
		S M/Tu/Th/F • W Europe • 150 kW
		S W/Sa/Su • W Europe • 150 kW
		S M-Sa • W Europe • 150 kW
		S Su • W Europe • 150 kW
	CHINA	
	CENTRAL PEOPLE'S BS, Beijing	**W** • DS-1 • 100 kW DS-1 • 100 kW
	†CHINA R INTL, Kashi	**W** • S Asia • 100 kW
	†CHINA R INTL, Shijiazhuang	**W** • E Asia • 500 kW
	†CHINA R INTL, Xi'an	**S** • E Asia • 500 kW
	INDIA	
	ALL INDIA RADIO, Thiruvananthapuram	DS • 20 kW DS • 50 kW
		Su • DS • 20 kW Irr • Su • DS • 50 kW
		ENGLISH, ETC • DS • 50 kW
	ITALY	
	RAI INTERNATIONAL, Rome	**W** • S Europe & N Africa • 100 kW
	POLAND	
	†RADIO POLONIA, Warsaw	**W** • W Europe • 100 kW
	RUSSIA	
	†VOICE OF RUSSIA, Moscow	**W** • N Europe • 250 kW
	UNITED KINGDOM	
	†BBC, Via Meyerton, South Africa	**S** M-F • C Africa & S Africa • 500 kW
	USA	
	VOA, Via Udon Thani, Thailand	**W** M-F • E Africa & S Africa • 250 kW
7290v	**INDONESIA**	
	RRI, Serui, Papua	Irr • DS • 1 kW
7295	**CHINA**	
	†CHINA R INTL, Urümqi	Mideast & N Africa • 500 kW
	INDIA	
	ALL INDIA RADIO, Aizawl	DS • 50 kW
		ENGLISH & HINDI • DS • 50 kW
		ENGLISH, ETC • DS • 50 kW
	IRAN	
	VO THE ISLAMIC REP, Sirjan	**W** • W Asia • 500 kW
	VO THE ISLAMIC REP, Various Locations	S Europe • 500 kW
	ITALY	
	RAI INTERNATIONAL, Rome	**S** • S Europe & N Africa • 100 kW
	MALAYSIA	
	RADIO MALAYSIA, Kajang	DS-4 • 100 kW
	TURKEY	
	†VOICE OF TURKEY, Ankara-Çakirlar	• Mideast • 250 kW
	USA	
	†ADVENTIST WORLD R, Via Germany	**S** • E Europe • 125 kW
	†R FARDA, Via Lampertheim, Germany	**S** • W Asia • 100 kW
	†RFE-RL, Via Briech, Morocco	**W** • W Asia & C Asia • 250 kW
7300	**CHINA**	
	†CHINA R INTL, Kashi	**W** • S Asia • 100 kW
		W • Mideast & N Africa • 500 kW
	IRAN	
	VO THE ISLAMIC REP, Tehrān	**S** • W Europe • 500 kW
	RUSSIA	
(con'd)	†VOICE OF RUSSIA, Armavir	**W** • Europe • 250 kW

0 1 2 3 4 5 6 7 8 9 10 11 12 13 14 15 16 17 18 19 20 21 22 23 24

ENGLISH ▬   ARABIC ⸬⸬   CHINESE □□□   FRENCH ▬▬   GERMAN ▬▬   RUSSIAN ══   SPANISH ▬▬   OTHER ▬

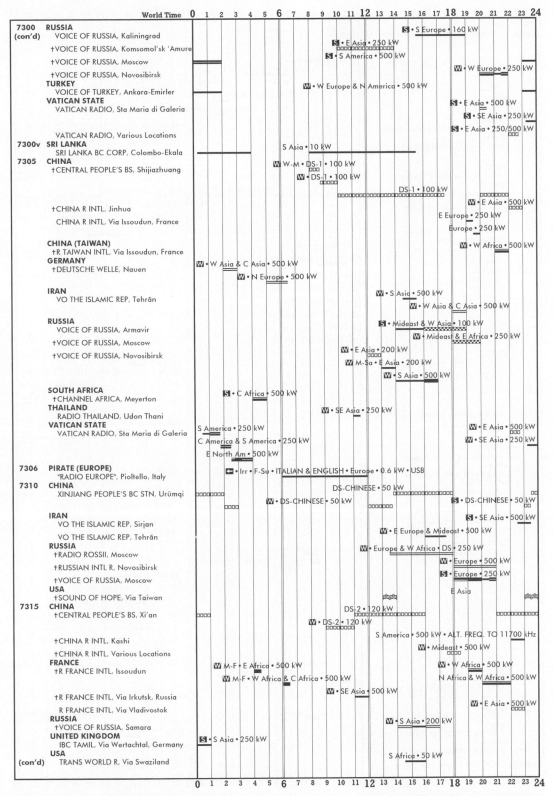

		World Time	0 1 2 3 4 5 6 7 8 9 10 11 12 13 14 15 16 17 18 19 20 21 22 23 24

7300 **RUSSIA**
(con'd)   VOICE OF RUSSIA, Kaliningrad   Ⓢ • S Europe • 160 kW
    †VOICE OF RUSSIA, Komsomol'sk 'Amure   Ⓢ • E Asia • 250 kW
    †VOICE OF RUSSIA, Moscow   Ⓢ • S America • 500 kW
    †VOICE OF RUSSIA, Novosibirsk   Ⓦ • W Europe • 250 kW
TURKEY
    VOICE OF TURKEY, Ankara-Emirler   Ⓦ • W Europe & N America • 500 kW
VATICAN STATE
    VATICAN RADIO, Sta Maria di Galeria   Ⓢ • E Asia • 500 kW
     Ⓢ • SE Asia • 250 kW
     Ⓢ • E Asia • 250/500 kW
    VATICAN RADIO, Various Locations
7300v **SRI LANKA**
    SRI LANKA BC CORP, Colombo-Ekala   S Asia • 10 kW
7305 **CHINA**
    †CENTRAL PEOPLE'S BS, Shijiazhuang   Ⓦ • W-M DS-1 • 100 kW
     Ⓦ • DS-1 • 100 kW
     DS-1 • 100 kW
    †CHINA R INTL, Jinhua   Ⓦ • E Asia • 500 kW
    CHINA R INTL, Via Issoudun, France   E Europe • 250 kW
     Europe • 250 kW
CHINA (TAIWAN)
    †R TAIWAN INTL, Via Issoudun, France   Ⓦ • W Africa • 500 kW
GERMANY
    †DEUTSCHE WELLE, Nauen   Ⓦ • W Asia & C Asia • 500 kW
     Ⓦ • N Europe • 500 kW
IRAN
    VO THE ISLAMIC REP, Tehrān   Ⓦ • S Asia • 500 kW
     Ⓦ • W Asia & C Asia • 500 kW
RUSSIA
    VOICE OF RUSSIA, Armavir   Ⓢ • Mideast & W Asia • 100 kW
    †VOICE OF RUSSIA, Moscow   Ⓦ • Mideast & E Africa • 250 kW
    †VOICE OF RUSSIA, Novosibirsk   Ⓦ • E Asia • 200 kW
     Ⓦ • M-Sa • E Asia • 200 kW
     Ⓦ • S Asia • 500 kW
SOUTH AFRICA
    †CHANNEL AFRICA, Meyerton   Ⓢ • C Africa • 500 kW
THAILAND
    RADIO THAILAND, Udon Thani   Ⓦ • SE Asia • 250 kW
VATICAN STATE
    VATICAN RADIO, Sta Maria di Galeria   S America • 250 kW   Ⓦ • E Asia • 500 kW
     C America & S America • 250 kW   Ⓦ • SE Asia • 250 kW
     E North Am • 500 kW
7306 **PIRATE (EUROPE)**
    "RADIO EUROPE", Pioltello, Italy   ⇦ • Irr • F-Su • ITALIAN & ENGLISH • Europe • 0.6 kW • USB
7310 **CHINA**
    XINJIANG PEOPLE'S BC STN, Urümqi   DS-CHINESE • 50 kW
     Ⓦ • DS-CHINESE • 50 kW   Ⓢ • DS-CHINESE • 50 kW
IRAN
    VO THE ISLAMIC REP, Sirjan   Ⓢ • SE Asia • 500 kW
    VO THE ISLAMIC REP, Tehrān   Ⓦ • E Europe & Mideast • 500 kW
RUSSIA
    †RADIO ROSSII, Moscow   Ⓦ • Europe & W Africa • DS • 250 kW
    †RUSSIAN INTL R, Novosibirsk   Ⓦ • Europe • 500 kW
    †VOICE OF RUSSIA, Moscow   Ⓢ • Europe • 250 kW
USA
    †SOUND OF HOPE, Via Taiwan   E Asia
7315 **CHINA**
    †CENTRAL PEOPLE'S BS, Xi'an   DS-2 • 120 kW
     Ⓦ • DS-2 • 120 kW
    †CHINA R INTL, Kashi   S America • 500 kW • ALT. FREQ. TO 11700 kHz
    †CHINA R INTL, Various Locations   Ⓦ • Mideast • 500 kW
FRANCE
    †R FRANCE INTL, Issoudun   Ⓦ • M-F • E Africa • 500 kW   Ⓦ • W Africa • 500 kW
     Ⓦ • M-F • W Africa & C Africa • 500 kW   N Africa & W Africa • 500 kW
    †R FRANCE INTL, Via Irkutsk, Russia   Ⓦ • SE Asia • 500 kW
    R FRANCE INTL, Via Vladivostok   Ⓦ • E Asia • 500 kW
RUSSIA
    †VOICE OF RUSSIA, Samara   Ⓦ • S Asia • 200 kW
UNITED KINGDOM
    IBC TAMIL, Via Wertachtal, Germany   Ⓢ • S Asia • 250 kW
USA
(con'd)   TRANS WORLD R, Via Swaziland   S Africa • 50 kW

		0 1 2 3 4 5 6 7 8 9 10 11 12 13 14 15 16 17 18 19 20 21 22 23 24

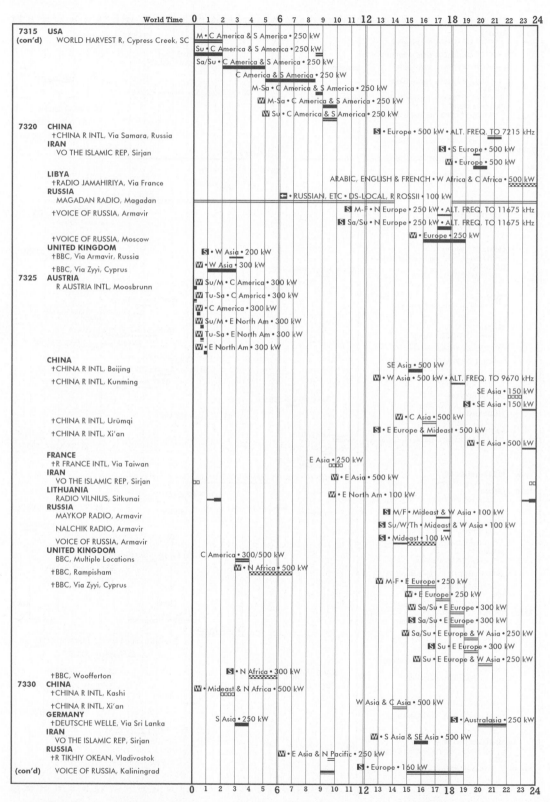

World Time 0 1 2 3 4 5 6 7 8 9 10 11 12 13 14 15 16 17 18 19 20 21 22 23 24

7315 USA
(con'd) WORLD HARVEST R, Cypress Creek, SC
  M • C America & S America • 250 kW
  Su • C America & S America • 250 kW
  Sa/Su • C America & S America • 250 kW
  C America & S America • 250 kW
  M-Sa • C America & S America • 250 kW
  W M-Sa • C America & S America • 250 kW
  W Su • C America & S America • 250 kW

7320 CHINA
  †CHINA R INTL, Via Samara, Russia   S • Europe • 500 kW • ALT. FREQ. TO 7215 kHz
  IRAN
  VO THE ISLAMIC REP, Sirjan   S • S Europe • 500 kW
         W • Europe • 500 kW
  LIBYA
  †RADIO JAMAHIRIYA, Via France   ARABIC, ENGLISH & FRENCH • W Africa & C Africa • 500 kW
  RUSSIA
  MAGADAN RADIO, Magadan   ⬅ • RUSSIAN, ETC • DS-LOCAL, R ROSSII • 100 kW
  †VOICE OF RUSSIA, Armavir   S M-F • N Europe • 250 kW • ALT. FREQ. TO 11675 kHz
         S Sa/Su • N Europe • 250 kW • ALT. FREQ. TO 11675 kHz
  †VOICE OF RUSSIA, Moscow   W • Europe • 250 kW
  UNITED KINGDOM
  †BBC, Via Armavir, Russia   S • W Asia • 200 kW
  †BBC, Via Zyyi, Cyprus   W • W Asia • 300 kW
7325 AUSTRIA
  R AUSTRIA INTL, Moosbrunn   W Su/M • C America • 300 kW
       W Tu-Sa • C America • 300 kW
       W • C America • 300 kW
       W Su/M • E North Am • 300 kW
       W Tu-Sa • E North Am • 300 kW
       W • E North Am • 300 kW

  CHINA
  †CHINA R INTL, Beijing   SE Asia • 500 kW
  †CHINA R INTL, Kunming   W • W Asia • 500 kW • ALT. FREQ. TO 9670 kHz
         SE Asia • 150 kW
         S • SE Asia • 150 kW
  †CHINA R INTL, Urümqi   W • C Asia • 500 kW
  †CHINA R INTL, Xi'an   S • E Europe & Mideast • 500 kW
         W • E Asia • 500 kW
  FRANCE
  †R FRANCE INTL, Via Taiwan   E Asia • 250 kW
  IRAN
  VO THE ISLAMIC REP, Sirjan   W • E Asia • 500 kW
  LITHUANIA
  RADIO VILNIUS, Sitkunai   W • E North Am • 100 kW
  RUSSIA
  MAYKOP RADIO, Armavir   S M/F • Mideast & W Asia • 100 kW
  NALCHIK RADIO, Armavir   S Su/W/Th • Mideast & W Asia • 100 kW
  VOICE OF RUSSIA, Armavir   S • Mideast • 100 kW
  UNITED KINGDOM
  BBC, Multiple Locations   C America • 300/500 kW
  †BBC, Rampisham   W • N Africa • 500 kW
  †BBC, Via Zyyi, Cyprus   W M-F • E Europe • 250 kW
         W • E Europe • 250 kW
         W Sa/Su • E Europe • 300 kW
         S Sa/Su • E Europe • 300 kW
         W Sa/Su • E Europe & W Asia • 250 kW
         S Su • E Europe • 300 kW
         W Su • E Europe & W Asia • 250 kW
  †BBC, Woofferton   S • N Africa • 300 kW
7330 CHINA
  †CHINA R INTL, Kashi   W • Mideast & N Africa • 500 kW
  †CHINA R INTL, Xi'an   W Asia & C Asia • 500 kW
  GERMANY
  †DEUTSCHE WELLE, Via Sri Lanka   S Asia • 250 kW   S • Australasia • 250 kW
  IRAN
  VO THE ISLAMIC REP, Sirjan   W • S Asia & SE Asia • 500 kW
  RUSSIA
  †R TIKHIY OKEAN, Vladivostok   W • E Asia & N Pacific • 250 kW
  (con'd) VOICE OF RUSSIA, Kaliningrad   S • Europe • 160 kW

0 1 2 3 4 5 6 7 8 9 10 11 12 13 14 15 16 17 18 19 20 21 22 23 24

ENGLISH ▬ ARABIC ⌇ CHINESE ▭▭▭ FRENCH ▬ GERMAN ▬ RUSSIAN ═ SPANISH ▬ OTHER ▬

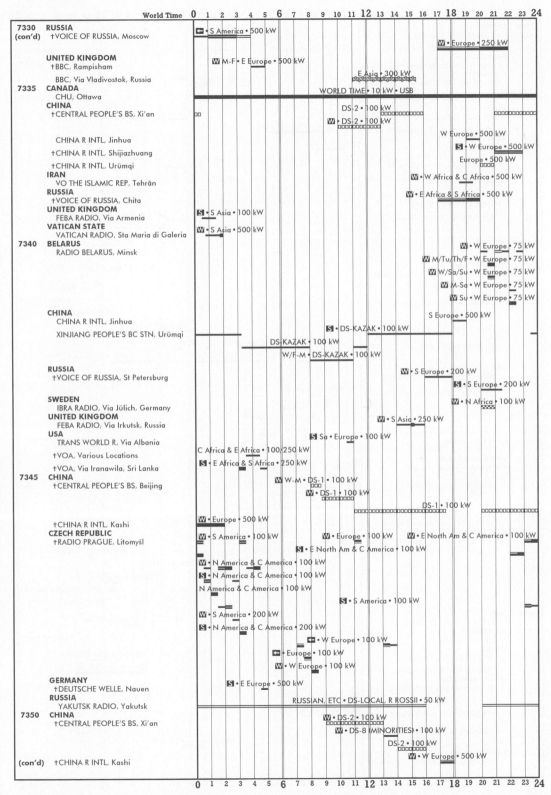

World Time 0 1 2 3 4 5 6 7 8 9 10 11 12 13 14 15 16 17 18 19 20 21 22 23 24

7330 RUSSIA
(con'd) †VOICE OF RUSSIA, Moscow
◄▪ S America • 500 kW
W • Europe • 250 kW

UNITED KINGDOM
†BBC, Rampisham
W M-F • E Europe • 500 kW

BBC, Via Vladivostok, Russia
E Asia • 300 kW

7335 CANADA
CHU, Ottawa
WORLD TIME • 10 kW • USB

CHINA
†CENTRAL PEOPLE'S BS, Xi'an
DS-2 • 100 kW
W • DS-2 • 100 kW

CHINA R INTL, Jinhua
W Europe • 500 kW

†CHINA R INTL, Shijiazhuang
S • W Europe • 500 kW

†CHINA R INTL, Urümqi
Europe • 500 kW

IRAN
VO THE ISLAMIC REP, Tehrān
W • W Africa & C Africa • 500 kW

RUSSIA
†VOICE OF RUSSIA, Chita
W • E Africa & S Africa • 500 kW

UNITED KINGDOM
FEBA RADIO, Via Armenia
S • S Asia • 100 kW

VATICAN STATE
VATICAN RADIO, Sta Maria di Galeria
W • S Asia • 500 kW

7340 BELARUS
RADIO BELARUS, Minsk
W • W Europe • 75 kW
W M/Tu/Th/F • W Europe • 75 kW
W W/Sa/Su • W Europe • 75 kW
W M-Sa • W Europe • 75 kW
W Su • W Europe • 75 kW

CHINA
CHINA R INTL, Jinhua
S Europe • 500 kW

XINJIANG PEOPLE'S BC STN, Urümqi
S • DS-KAZAK • 100 kW
DS-KAZAK • 100 kW
W/F-M • DS-KAZAK • 100 kW

RUSSIA
†VOICE OF RUSSIA, St Petersburg
W • S Europe • 200 kW
S • S Europe • 200 kW

SWEDEN
IBRA RADIO, Via Jülich, Germany
W • N Africa • 100 kW

UNITED KINGDOM
FEBA RADIO, Via Irkutsk, Russia
W • S Asia • 250 kW

USA
TRANS WORLD R, Via Albania
S • Sa • Europe • 100 kW

†VOA, Various Locations
C Africa & E Africa • 100/250 kW

†VOA, Via Iranawila, Sri Lanka
S • E Africa & S Africa • 250 kW

7345 CHINA
†CENTRAL PEOPLE'S BS, Beijing
W W-M • DS-1 • 100 kW
W • DS-1 • 100 kW
DS-1 • 100 kW

†CHINA R INTL, Kashi
W • Europe • 500 kW

CZECH REPUBLIC
†RADIO PRAGUE, Litomyšl
W • S America • 100 kW
W • Europe • 100 kW
W • E North Am & C America • 100 kW
S • E North Am & C America • 100 kW
W • N America & C America • 100 kW
S • N America & C America • 100 kW
N America & C America • 100 kW
S • S America • 100 kW
W • S America • 200 kW
S • N America & C America • 200 kW
◄▪ • W Europe • 100 kW
◄▪ • Europe • 100 kW
W • W Europe • 100 kW

GERMANY
†DEUTSCHE WELLE, Nauen
S • E Europe • 500 kW

RUSSIA
YAKUTSK RADIO, Yakutsk
RUSSIAN, ETC • DS-LOCAL, R ROSSII • 50 kW

7350 CHINA
†CENTRAL PEOPLE'S BS, Xi'an
W • DS-2 • 100 kW
W • DS-8 (MINORITIES) • 100 kW
DS-2 • 100 kW

(con'd) †CHINA R INTL, Kashi
W • W Europe • 500 kW

0 1 2 3 4 5 6 7 8 9 10 11 12 13 14 15 16 17 18 19 20 21 22 23 24

SEASONAL S OR W   1-HR TIMESHIFT MIDYEAR ◄▪ OR ▪►   JAMMING / OR ∧   EARLIEST HEARD ◄   LATEST HEARD ▷   NEW FOR 2007 †

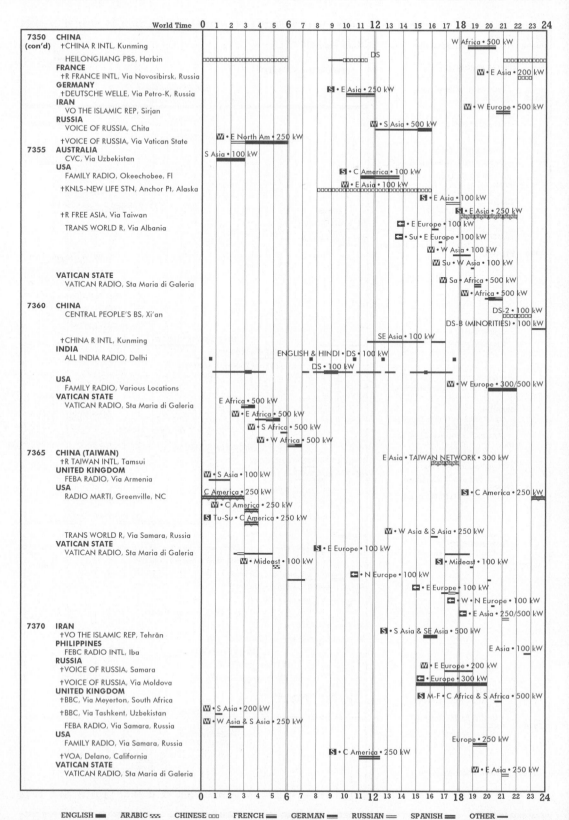

World Time 0 1 2 3 4 5 6 7 8 9 10 11 12 13 14 15 16 17 18 19 20 21 22 23 24

7350 **CHINA**
(con'd)   †CHINA R INTL, Kunming — W Africa • 500 kW
          HEILONGJIANG PBS, Harbin — DS
FRANCE
          †R FRANCE INTL, Via Novosibirsk, Russia — W • E Asia • 200 kW
GERMANY
          †DEUTSCHE WELLE, Via Petro-K, Russia — S • E Asia • 250 kW
IRAN
          VO THE ISLAMIC REP, Sirjan — W • W Europe • 500 kW
RUSSIA
          VOICE OF RUSSIA, Chita — W • S Asia • 500 kW
          †VOICE OF RUSSIA, Via Vatican State — W • E North Am • 250 kW
7355 **AUSTRALIA**
          CVC, Via Uzbekistan — S Asia • 100 kW
USA
          FAMILY RADIO, Okeechobee, Fl — S • C America • 100 kW
          †KNLS-NEW LIFE STN, Anchor Pt, Alaska — W • E Asia • 100 kW
                                             S • E Asia • 100 kW
          †R FREE ASIA, Via Taiwan — S • E Asia • 250 kW
          TRANS WORLD R, Via Albania — ↩ • E Europe • 100 kW
                                       ↩ • Su • E Europe • 100 kW
                                       W • W Asia • 100 kW
                                       W Su • W Asia • 100 kW
VATICAN STATE
          VATICAN RADIO, Sta Maria di Galeria — W Sa • Africa • 500 kW
                                                 W • Africa • 500 kW
7360 **CHINA**
          CENTRAL PEOPLE'S BS, Xi'an — DS-2 • 100 kW
                                        DS-8 (MINORITIES) • 100 kW
          †CHINA R INTL, Kunming — SE Asia • 100 kW
INDIA
          ALL INDIA RADIO, Delhi — ENGLISH & HINDI • DS • 100 kW
                                    DS • 100 kW
USA
          FAMILY RADIO, Various Locations — W • W Europe • 300/500 kW
VATICAN STATE
          VATICAN RADIO, Sta Maria di Galeria — E Africa • 500 kW
                                                 W • E Africa • 500 kW
                                                 W • S Africa • 500 kW
                                                 W • W Africa • 500 kW
7365 **CHINA (TAIWAN)**
          †R TAIWAN INTL, Tamsui — E Asia • TAIWAN NETWORK • 300 kW
UNITED KINGDOM
          FEBA RADIO, Via Armenia — W • S Asia • 100 kW
USA
          RADIO MARTI, Greenville, NC — C America • 250 kW
                                         S • C America • 250 kW
                                         W • C America • 250 kW
                                         S Tu-Su • C America • 250 kW
                                         W • W Asia & S Asia • 250 kW
          TRANS WORLD R, Via Samara, Russia — S • E Europe • 100 kW
VATICAN STATE
          VATICAN RADIO, Sta Maria di Galeria — W • Mideast • 100 kW
                                                 S • Mideast • 100 kW
                                                 ↩ • N Europe • 100 kW
                                                 ↩ • E Europe • 100 kW
                                                 ↩ • W • N Europe • 100 kW
                                                 ↩ • E Asia • 250/500 kW
7370 **IRAN**
          †VO THE ISLAMIC REP, Tehrān — S • S Asia & SE Asia • 500 kW
PHILIPPINES
          FEBC RADIO INTL, Iba — E Asia • 100 kW
RUSSIA
          †VOICE OF RUSSIA, Samara — W • E Europe • 200 kW
          †VOICE OF RUSSIA, Via Moldova — ↩ • Europe • 300 kW
UNITED KINGDOM
          †BBC, Via Meyerton, South Africa — S • M-F • C Africa & S Africa • 500 kW
          †BBC, Via Tashkent, Uzbekistan — W • S Asia • 200 kW
          FEBA RADIO, Via Samara, Russia — W • W Asia & S Asia • 250 kW
USA
          FAMILY RADIO, Via Samara, Russia — Europe • 250 kW
          †VOA, Delano, California — S • C America • 250 kW
VATICAN STATE
          VATICAN RADIO, Sta Maria di Galeria — W • E Asia • 250 kW

0 1 2 3 4 5 6 7 8 9 10 11 12 13 14 15 16 17 18 19 20 21 22 23 24

ENGLISH ▬ ARABIC ⋙ CHINESE □□□ FRENCH ▦ GERMAN ▬ RUSSIAN ═ SPANISH ▬ OTHER ▬

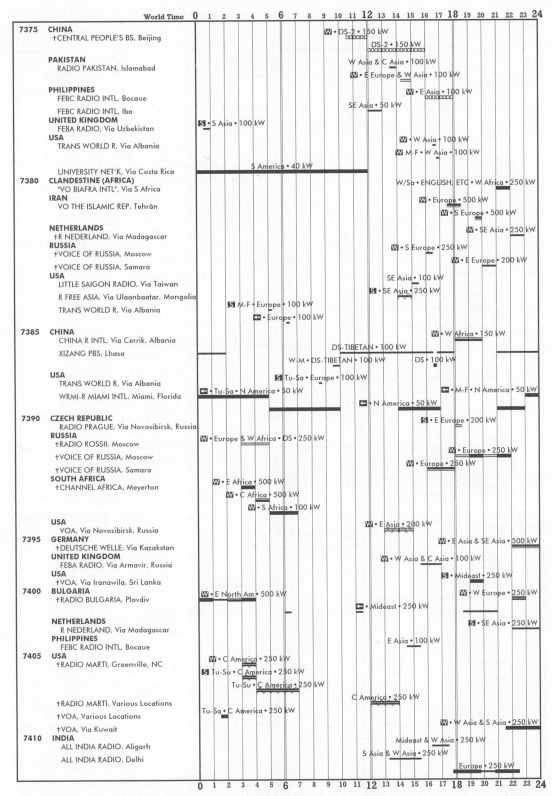

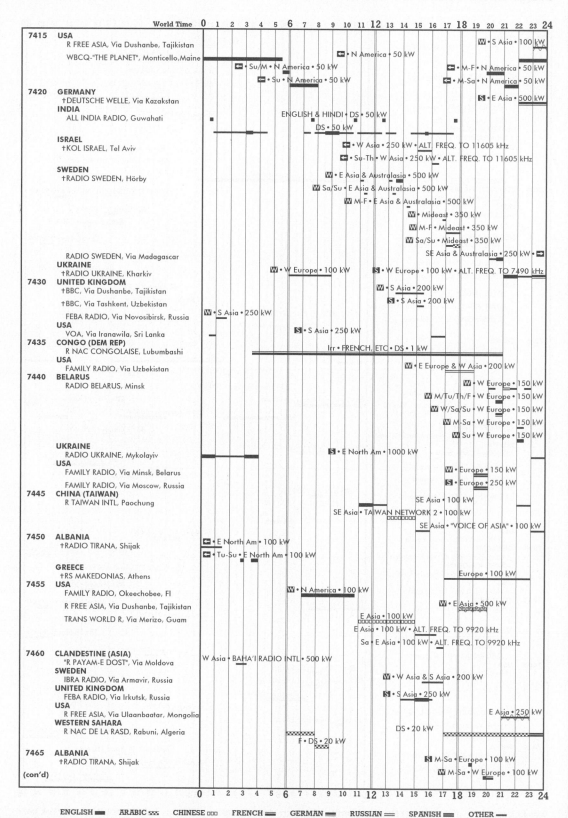

| World Time | 0 | 1 | 2 | 3 | 4 | 5 | 6 | 7 | 8 | 9 | 10 | 11 | 12 | 13 | 14 | 15 | 16 | 17 | 18 | 19 | 20 | 21 | 22 | 23 | 24 |

7415 USA
  R FREE ASIA, Via Dushanbe, Tajikistan — S Asia • 100 kW
  WBCQ-"THE PLANET", Monticello, Maine — N America • 50 kW
  — Su/M • N America • 50 kW — M-F • N America • 50 kW
  — Su • N America • 50 kW — M-Sa • N America • 50 kW

7420 GERMANY
  †DEUTSCHE WELLE, Via Kazakstan — E Asia • 500 kW
  INDIA
  ALL INDIA RADIO, Guwahati
    ENGLISH & HINDI • DS • 50 kW
    DS • 50 kW

  ISRAEL
  †KOL ISRAEL, Tel Aviv — W Asia • 250 kW • ALT. FREQ. TO 11605 kHz
    — Su-Th • W Asia • 250 kW • ALT. FREQ. TO 11605 kHz

  SWEDEN
  †RADIO SWEDEN, Hörby — E Asia & Australasia • 500 kW
    Sa/Su • E Asia & Australasia • 500 kW
    M-F • E Asia & Australasia • 500 kW
    Mideast • 350 kW
    M-F • Mideast • 350 kW
    Sa/Su • Mideast • 350 kW
    SE Asia & Australasia • 250 kW

  RADIO SWEDEN, Via Madagascar
  UKRAINE
  †RADIO UKRAINE, Kharkiv — W Europe • 100 kW — W Europe • 100 kW • ALT. FREQ. TO 7490 kHz

7430 UNITED KINGDOM
  †BBC, Via Dushanbe, Tajikistan — S Asia • 200 kW
  †BBC, Via Tashkent, Uzbekistan — S Asia • 200 kW
  FEBA RADIO, Via Novosibirsk, Russia — S Asia • 250 kW
  USA
  VOA, Via Iranawila, Sri Lanka — S Asia • 250 kW

7435 CONGO (DEM REP)
  R NAC CONGOLAISE, Lubumbashi
    Irr • FRENCH, ETC • DS • 1 kW
  USA
  FAMILY RADIO, Via Uzbekistan — E Europe & W Asia • 200 kW

7440 BELARUS
  RADIO BELARUS, Minsk — W Europe • 150 kW
    M/Tu/Th/F • W Europe • 150 kW
    W/Sa/Su • W Europe • 150 kW
    M-Sa • W Europe • 150 kW
    Su • W Europe • 150 kW

  UKRAINE
  RADIO UKRAINE, Mykolayiv — E North Am • 1000 kW
  USA
  FAMILY RADIO, Via Minsk, Belarus — Europe • 150 kW
  FAMILY RADIO, Via Moscow, Russia — Europe • 250 kW

7445 CHINA (TAIWAN)
  R TAIWAN INTL, Paochung
    SE Asia • 100 kW
    SE Asia • TAIWAN NETWORK 2 • 100 kW
    SE Asia • "VOICE OF ASIA" • 100 kW

7450 ALBANIA
  †RADIO TIRANA, Shijak — E North Am • 100 kW
    — Tu-Su • E North Am • 100 kW

  GREECE
  †RS MAKEDONIAS, Athens — Europe • 100 kW

7455 USA
  FAMILY RADIO, Okeechobee, Fl — N America • 100 kW
  R FREE ASIA, Via Dushanbe, Tajikistan — E Asia • 500 kW
  TRANS WORLD R, Via Merizo, Guam
    E Asia • 100 kW
    E Asia • 100 kW • ALT. FREQ. TO 9920 kHz
    Sa • E Asia • 100 kW • ALT. FREQ. TO 9920 kHz

7460 CLANDESTINE (ASIA)
  "R PAYAM-E DOST", Via Moldova — W Asia • BAHA'I RADIO INTL • 500 kW
  SWEDEN
  IBRA RADIO, Via Armavir, Russia — W Asia & S Asia • 200 kW
  UNITED KINGDOM
  FEBA RADIO, Via Irkutsk, Russia — S Asia • 250 kW
  USA
  R FREE ASIA, Via Ulaanbaatar, Mongolia — E Asia • 250 kW
  WESTERN SAHARA
  R NAC DE LA RASD, Rabuni, Algeria
    DS • 20 kW
    F • DS • 20 kW

7465 ALBANIA
  †RADIO TIRANA, Shijak — M-Sa • Europe • 100 kW
    — M-Sa • W Europe • 100 kW

(con'd)

ENGLISH ▬   ARABIC ⁙   CHINESE ▭▭▭   FRENCH ▬▬   GERMAN ▬▬   RUSSIAN ═   SPANISH ▬▬   OTHER ▬

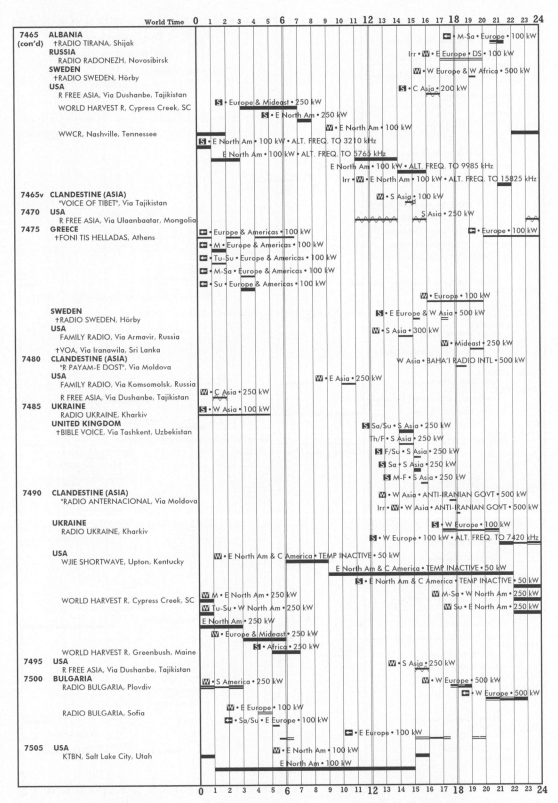

World Time | 0 1 2 3 4 5 6 7 8 9 10 11 12 13 14 15 16 17 18 19 20 21 22 23 24

7465 ALBANIA
(con'd) †RADIO TIRANA, Shijak — ☐ • M-Sa • Europe • 100 kW
RUSSIA
RADIO RADONEZH, Novosibirsk — Irr • W • E Europe • DS • 100 kW
SWEDEN
†RADIO SWEDEN, Hörby — W • W Europe & W Africa • 500 kW
USA
R FREE ASIA, Via Dushanbe, Tajikistan — S • C Asia • 200 kW
WORLD HARVEST R, Cypress Creek, SC — S • Europe & Mideast • 250 kW
S • E North Am • 250 kW
W • E North Am • 100 kW
WWCR, Nashville, Tennessee — S • E North Am • 100 kW • ALT. FREQ. TO 3210 kHz
E North Am • 100 kW • ALT. FREQ. TO 5765 kHz
E North Am • 100 kW • ALT. FREQ. TO 9985 kHz
Irr • W • E North Am • 100 kW • ALT. FREQ. TO 15825 kHz

7465v CLANDESTINE (ASIA)
"VOICE OF TIBET", Via Tajikistan — W • S Asia • 100 kW
7470 USA
R FREE ASIA, Via Ulaanbaatar, Mongolia — S Asia • 250 kW
7475 GREECE
†FONI TIS HELLADAS, Athens — ☐ • Europe & Americas • 100 kW — ☐ • Europe • 100 kW
☐ • M • Europe & Americas • 100 kW
☐ • Tu-Su • Europe & Americas • 100 kW
☐ • M-Sa • Europe & Americas • 100 kW
☐ • Su • Europe & Americas • 100 kW

SWEDEN
†RADIO SWEDEN, Hörby — W • Europe • 100 kW
S • E Europe & W Asia • 500 kW
USA
FAMILY RADIO, Via Armavir, Russia — W • S Asia • 300 kW
†VOA, Via Iranawila, Sri Lanka — W • Mideast • 250 kW
7480 CLANDESTINE (ASIA)
"R PAYAM-E DOST", Via Moldova — W Asia • BAHA'I RADIO INTL • 500 kW
USA
FAMILY RADIO, Via Komsomolsk, Russia — W • E Asia • 250 kW
R FREE ASIA, Via Dushanbe, Tajikistan — W • C Asia • 250 kW
7485 UKRAINE
RADIO UKRAINE, Kharkiv — S • W Asia • 100 kW
UNITED KINGDOM
†BIBLE VOICE, Via Tashkent, Uzbekistan — S Sa/Su • S Asia • 250 kW
Th/F • S Asia • 250 kW
S F/Su • S Asia • 250 kW
S Sa • S Asia • 250 kW
S M-F • S Asia • 250 kW

7490 CLANDESTINE (ASIA)
"RADIO ANTERNACIONAL, Via Moldova — W • W Asia • ANTI-IRANIAN GOVT • 500 kW
Irr • W • W Asia • ANTI-IRANIAN GOVT • 500 kW
UKRAINE
RADIO UKRAINE, Kharkiv — S • W Europe • 100 kW
S • W Europe • 100 kW • ALT. FREQ. TO 7420 kHz
USA
WJIE SHORTWAVE, Upton, Kentucky — W • E North Am & C America • TEMP INACTIVE • 50 kW
E North Am & C America • TEMP INACTIVE • 50 kW
S • E North Am & C America • TEMP INACTIVE • 50 kW
WORLD HARVEST R, Cypress Creek, SC — W M • E North Am • 250 kW — W M-Sa • W North Am • 250 kW
W Tu-Su • W North Am • 250 kW — W Su • E North Am • 250 kW
E North Am • 250 kW
W • Europe & Mideast • 250 kW
S • Africa • 250 kW
WORLD HARVEST R, Greenbush, Maine
7495 USA
R FREE ASIA, Via Dushanbe, Tajikistan — W • S Asia • 250 kW
7500 BULGARIA
RADIO BULGARIA, Plovdiv — W • S America • 250 kW — W • W Europe • 500 kW
☐ • W Europe • 500 kW
RADIO BULGARIA, Sofia — W • E Europe • 100 kW
☐ • Sa/Su • E Europe • 100 kW
☐ • E Europe • 100 kW
7505 USA
KTBN, Salt Lake City, Utah — W • E North Am • 100 kW
E North Am • 100 kW

| 0 1 2 3 4 5 6 7 8 9 10 11 12 13 14 15 16 17 18 19 20 21 22 23 24

World Time 0 1 2 3 4 5 6 7 8 9 10 11 12 13 14 15 16 17 18 19 20 21 22 23 24

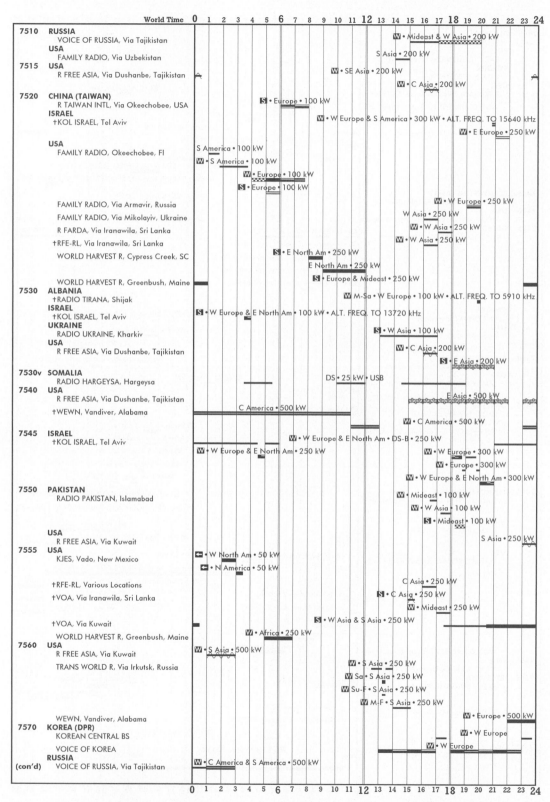

Freq	Station	
7510	**RUSSIA** VOICE OF RUSSIA, Via Tajikistan	W • Mideast & W Asia • 200 kW
	USA FAMILY RADIO, Via Uzbekistan	S Asia • 200 kW
7515	**USA** R FREE ASIA, Via Dushanbe, Tajikistan	W • SE Asia • 200 kW / W • C Asia • 200 kW
7520	**CHINA (TAIWAN)** R TAIWAN INTL, Via Okeechobee, USA	S • Europe • 100 kW
	ISRAEL †KOL ISRAEL, Tel Aviv	W • W Europe & S America • 300 kW • ALT. FREQ. TO 15640 kHz / W • E Europe • 250 kW
	USA FAMILY RADIO, Okeechobee, Fl	S America • 100 kW / W • S America • 100 kW / W • Europe • 100 kW / S • Europe • 100 kW
	FAMILY RADIO, Via Armavir, Russia	W • W Europe • 250 kW
	FAMILY RADIO, Via Mikolayiv, Ukraine	W Asia • 250 kW
	R FARDA, Via Iranwila, Sri Lanka	W • W Asia • 250 kW
	†RFE-RL, Via Iranwila, Sri Lanka	W • W Asia • 250 kW
	WORLD HARVEST R, Cypress Creek, SC	S • E North Am • 250 kW / E North Am • 250 kW
	WORLD HARVEST R, Greenbush, Maine	S • Europe & Mideast • 250 kW
7530	**ALBANIA** †RADIO TIRANA, Shijak	W M-Sa • W Europe • 100 kW • ALT. FREQ. TO 5910 kHz
	ISRAEL †KOL ISRAEL, Tel Aviv	S • W Europe & E North Am • 100 kW • ALT. FREQ. TO 13720 kHz
	UKRAINE RADIO UKRAINE, Kharkiv	S • W Asia • 100 kW
	USA R FREE ASIA, Via Dushanbe, Tajikistan	W • C Asia • 200 kW / S • E Asia • 200 kW
7530v	**SOMALIA** RADIO HARGEYSA, Hargeysa	DS • 25 kW • USB
7540	**USA** R FREE ASIA, Via Dushanbe, Tajikistan	E Asia • 500 kW
	†WEWN, Vandiver, Alabama	C America • 500 kW / W • C America • 500 kW
7545	**ISRAEL** †KOL ISRAEL, Tel Aviv	W • W Europe & E North Am • DS-B • 250 kW / W • W Europe & E North Am • 250 kW / W • W Europe • 300 kW / W • Europe • 300 kW / W • W Europe & E North Am • 300 kW
7550	**PAKISTAN** RADIO PAKISTAN, Islamabad	W • Mideast • 100 kW / W • W Asia • 100 kW / S • Mideast • 100 kW / S Asia • 250 kW
	USA R FREE ASIA, Via Kuwait	
7555	**USA** KJES, Vado, New Mexico	W North Am • 50 kW / N America • 50 kW
	†RFE-RL, Various Locations	C Asia • 250 kW / S • C Asia • 250 kW / W • Mideast • 250 kW
	†VOA, Via Iranwila, Sri Lanka	
	†VOA, Via Kuwait	S • W Asia & S Asia • 250 kW
	WORLD HARVEST R, Greenbush, Maine	W • Africa • 250 kW
7560	**USA** R FREE ASIA, Via Kuwait	W • S Asia • 500 kW
	TRANS WORLD R, Via Irkutsk, Russia	W • S Asia • 250 kW / W Sa • S Asia • 250 kW / W Su-F • S Asia • 250 kW / W M-F • S Asia • 250 kW
	WEWN, Vandiver, Alabama	W • Europe • 500 kW
7570	**KOREA (DPR)** KOREAN CENTRAL BS	W • W Europe
	VOICE OF KOREA	W • W Europe
	RUSSIA (con'd) VOICE OF RUSSIA, Via Tajikistan	W • C America & S America • 500 kW

0 1 2 3 4 5 6 7 8 9 10 11 12 13 14 15 16 17 18 19 20 21 22 23 24

ENGLISH ▪▪▪   ARABIC ░░░   CHINESE □□□   FRENCH ▬▬   GERMAN ▬▬   RUSSIAN ══   SPANISH ▬▬   OTHER ▬▬

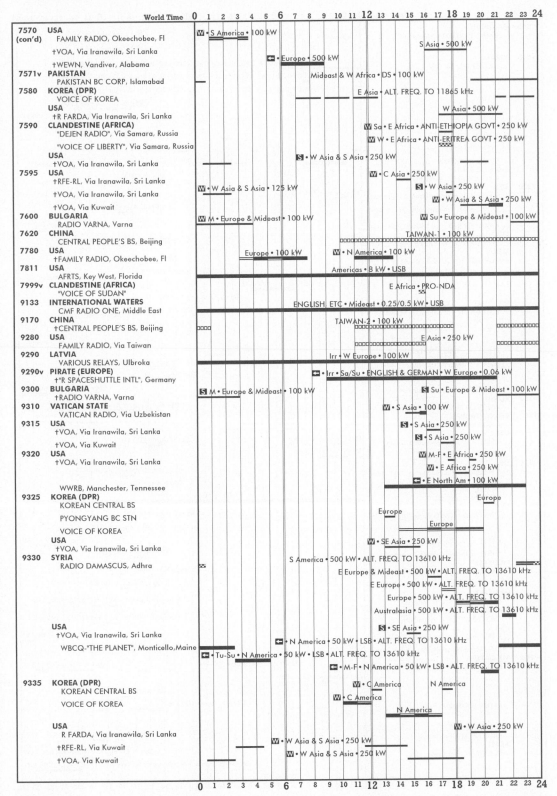

Freq	Station	Details
7570 (con'd)	**USA** FAMILY RADIO, Okeechobee, Fl	W • S America • 100 kW / S Asia • 500 kW
	†VOA, Via Iranawila, Sri Lanka	
	†WEWN, Vandiver, Alabama	⇐ • Europe • 500 kW
7571v	**PAKISTAN** PAKISTAN BC CORP, Islamabad	Mideast & W Africa • DS • 100 kW
7580	**KOREA (DPR)** VOICE OF KOREA	E Asia • ALT. FREQ. TO 11865 kHz
	USA †R FARDA, Via Iranawila, Sri Lanka	W Asia • 500 kW
7590	**CLANDESTINE (AFRICA)** "DEJEN RADIO", Via Samara, Russia	W Sa • E Africa • ANTI-ETHIOPIA GOVT • 250 kW
	"VOICE OF LIBERTY", Via Samara, Russia	W W • E Africa • ANTI-ERITREA GOVT • 250 kW
	USA †VOA, Via Iranawila, Sri Lanka	S • W Asia & S Asia • 250 kW
7595	**USA** †RFE-RL, Via Iranawila, Sri Lanka	W • C Asia • 250 kW
	†RFE-RL, Via Iranawila, Sri Lanka	W • W Asia & S Asia • 125 kW / S • W Asia • 250 kW
	†VOA, Via Kuwait	W • W Asia & S Asia • 250 kW
7600	**BULGARIA** RADIO VARNA, Varna	W M • Europe & Mideast • 100 kW / W Su • Europe & Mideast • 100 kW
7620	**CHINA** CENTRAL PEOPLE'S BS, Beijing	TAIWAN-1 • 100 kW
7780	**USA** †FAMILY RADIO, Okeechobee, Fl	Europe • 100 kW / W • N America • 100 kW
7811	**USA** AFRTS, Key West, Florida	Americas • 3 kW • USB
7999v	**CLANDESTINE (AFRICA)** "VOICE OF SUDAN"	E Africa • PRO-NDA
9133	**INTERNATIONAL WATERS** CMF RADIO ONE, Middle East	ENGLISH, ETC • Mideast • 0.25/0.5 kW • USB
9170	**CHINA** †CENTRAL PEOPLE'S BS, Beijing	TAIWAN-2 • 100 kW
9280	**USA** FAMILY RADIO, Via Taiwan	E Asia • 250 kW
9290	**LATVIA** VARIOUS RELAYS, Ulbroka	Irr • W Europe • 100 kW
9290v	**PIRATE (EUROPE)** †"R SPACESHUTTLE INTL", Germany	⇐ • Irr • Sa/Su • ENGLISH & GERMAN • W Europe • 0.06 kW
9300	**BULGARIA** †RADIO VARNA, Varna	S M • Europe & Mideast • 100 kW / S Su • Europe & Mideast • 100 kW
9310	**VATICAN STATE** VATICAN RADIO, Via Uzbekistan	W • S Asia • 100 kW
9315	**USA** †VOA, Via Iranawila, Sri Lanka	S • S Asia • 250 kW
	†VOA, Via Kuwait	S • S Asia • 250 kW
9320	**USA** †VOA, Via Iranawila, Sri Lanka	W M-F • E Africa • 250 kW
		W • E Africa • 250 kW
		⇐ • E North Am • 100 kW
	WWRB, Manchester, Tennessee	
9325	**KOREA (DPR)** KOREAN CENTRAL BS	Europe
	PYONGYANG BC STN	Europe
	VOICE OF KOREA	Europe
	USA †VOA, Via Iranawila, Sri Lanka	W • SE Asia • 250 kW
9330	**SYRIA** RADIO DAMASCUS, Adhra	S America • 500 kW • ALT. FREQ. TO 13610 kHz
		E Europe & Mideast • 500 kW • ALT. FREQ. TO 13610 kHz
		E Europe • 500 kW • ALT. FREQ. TO 13610 kHz
		Europe • 500 kW • ALT. FREQ. TO 13610 kHz
		Australasia • 500 kW • ALT. FREQ. TO 13610 kHz
	USA †VOA, Via Iranawila, Sri Lanka	S • SE Asia • 250 kW
	WBCQ-"THE PLANET", Monticello, Maine	⇐ • N America • 50 kW • LSB • ALT. FREQ. TO 13610 kHz
		⇐ • Tu-Su • N America • 50 kW • LSB • ALT. FREQ. TO 13610 kHz
		⇐ • M-F • N America • 50 kW • LSB • ALT. FREQ. TO 13610 kHz
9335	**KOREA (DPR)** KOREAN CENTRAL BS	W • C America / N America
	VOICE OF KOREA	W • C America
		N America
	USA R FARDA, Via Iranawila, Sri Lanka	W • W Asia • 250 kW
	†RFE-RL, Via Kuwait	W • W Asia & S Asia • 250 kW
	†VOA, Via Kuwait	W • W Asia & S Asia • 250 kW

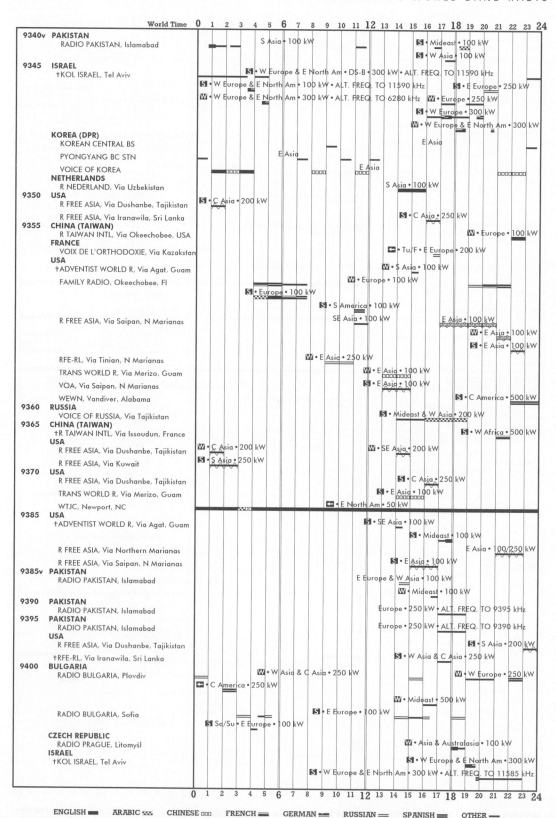

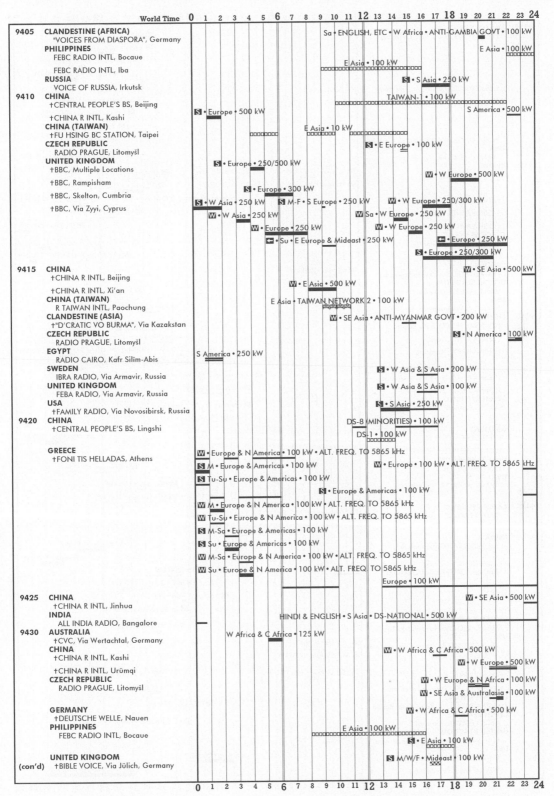

World Time

Freq	Station	
9405	**CLANDESTINE (AFRICA)**	
	"VOICES FROM DIASPORA", Germany	Sa • ENGLISH, ETC • W Africa • ANTI-GAMBIA GOVT • 100 kW
	PHILIPPINES	E Asia • 100 kW
	FEBC RADIO INTL, Bocaue	
	FEBC RADIO INTL, Iba	E Asia • 100 kW
	RUSSIA	⑤ • S Asia • 250 kW
	VOICE OF RUSSIA, Irkutsk	
9410	**CHINA**	TAIWAN-1 • 100 kW
	†CENTRAL PEOPLE'S BS, Beijing	S America • 500 kW
	†CHINA R INTL, Kashi	⑤ • Europe • 500 kW
	CHINA (TAIWAN)	E Asia • 10 kW
	†FU HSING BC STATION, Taipei	
	CZECH REPUBLIC	⑤ • E Europe • 100 kW
	RADIO PRAGUE, Litomyšl	
	UNITED KINGDOM	
	†BBC, Multiple Locations	⑤ • Europe • 250/500 kW
	†BBC, Rampisham	Ⓦ • W Europe • 500 kW
	†BBC, Skelton, Cumbria	⑤ • Europe • 300 kW
	†BBC, Via Zyyi, Cyprus	⑤ • W Asia • 250 kW Ⓦ • M-F • S Europe • 250 kW Ⓦ • W Europe • 250/300 kW
		Ⓦ • W Asia • 250 kW Ⓦ Sa • W Europe • 250 kW
		Ⓦ • Europe • 250 kW Ⓦ • W Europe • 250 kW
		⮜ Su • E Europe & Mideast • 250 kW ⮜ • Europe • 250 kW
		⑤ • Europe • 250/300 kW
9415	**CHINA**	Ⓦ • SE Asia • 500 kW
	†CHINA R INTL, Beijing	Ⓦ • E Asia • 500 kW
	†CHINA R INTL, Xi'an	
	CHINA (TAIWAN)	E Asia • TAIWAN NETWORK 2 • 100 kW
	R TAIWAN INTL, Paochung	
	CLANDESTINE (ASIA)	Ⓦ • SE Asia • ANTI-MYANMAR GOVT • 200 kW
	†"D'CRATIC VO BURMA", Via Kazakstan	
	CZECH REPUBLIC	⑤ • N America • 100 kW
	RADIO PRAGUE, Litomyšl	
	EGYPT	S America • 250 kW
	RADIO CAIRO, Kafr Silīm-Abis	
	SWEDEN	⑤ • W Asia & S Asia • 200 kW
	IBRA RADIO, Via Armavir, Russia	
	UNITED KINGDOM	⑤ • W Asia & S Asia • 100 kW
	FEBA RADIO, Via Armavir, Russia	
	USA	⑤ • S Asia • 250 kW
	†FAMILY RADIO, Via Novosibirsk, Russia	
9420	**CHINA**	DS-8 (MINORITIES) • 100 kW
	†CENTRAL PEOPLE'S BS, Lingshi	DS-1 • 100 kW
	GREECE	Ⓦ • Europe & N America • 100 kW • ALT. FREQ. TO 5865 kHz
	†FONI TIS HELLADAS, Athens	⑤ M • Europe & Americas • 100 kW Ⓦ • Europe • 100 kW • ALT. FREQ. TO 5865 kHz
		⑤ Tu-Su • Europe & Americas • 100 kW
		⑤ • Europe & Americas • 100 kW
		Ⓦ M • Europe & N America • 100 kW • ALT. FREQ. TO 5865 kHz
		Ⓦ Tu-Su • Europe & N America • 100 kW • ALT. FREQ. TO 5865 kHz
		⑤ M-Sa • Europe & Americas • 100 kW
		⑤ Su • Europe & Americas • 100 kW
		Ⓦ M-Sa • Europe & N America • 100 kW • ALT. FREQ. TO 5865 kHz
		Ⓦ Su • Europe & N America • 100 kW • ALT. FREQ. TO 5865 kHz
		Europe • 100 kW
9425	**CHINA**	Ⓦ • SE Asia • 500 kW
	†CHINA R INTL, Jinhua	
	INDIA	HINDI & ENGLISH • S Asia • DS-NATIONAL • 500 kW
	ALL INDIA RADIO, Bangalore	
9430	**AUSTRALIA**	W Africa & C Africa • 125 kW
	†CVC, Via Wertachtal, Germany	
	CHINA	Ⓦ • W Africa & C Africa • 500 kW
	†CHINA R INTL, Kashi	
	†CHINA R INTL, Urümqi	Ⓦ • W Europe • 500 kW
	CZECH REPUBLIC	Ⓦ • W Europe & N Africa • 100 kW
	RADIO PRAGUE, Litomyšl	Ⓦ • SE Asia & Australasia • 100 kW
	GERMANY	Ⓦ • W Africa & C Africa • 500 kW
	†DEUTSCHE WELLE, Nauen	
	PHILIPPINES	E Asia • 100 kW
	FEBC RADIO INTL, Bocaue	⑤ • E Asia • 100 kW
	UNITED KINGDOM	⑤ M/W/F • Mideast • 100 kW
(con'd)	†BIBLE VOICE, Via Jülich, Germany	

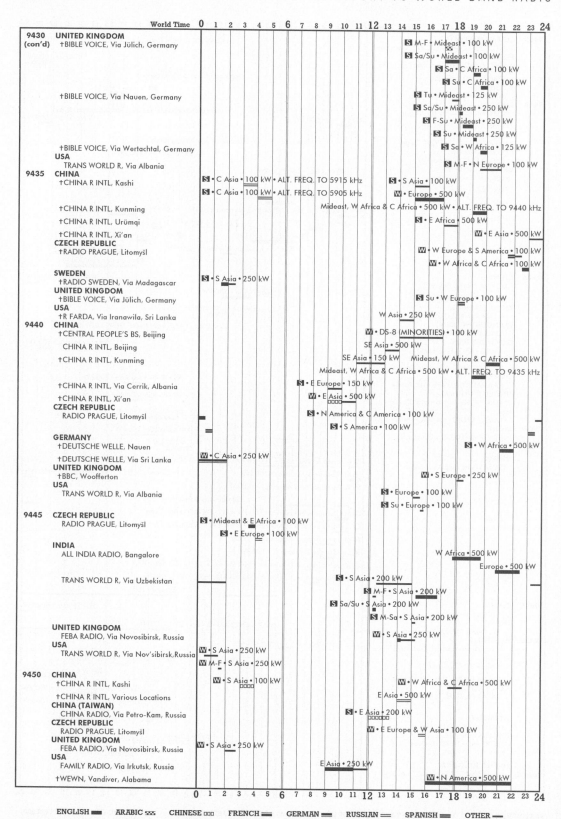

World Time 0 1 2 3 4 5 6 7 8 9 10 11 12 13 14 15 16 17 18 19 20 21 22 23 24

9430 UNITED KINGDOM
(con'd)   †BIBLE VOICE, Via Jülich, Germany   S M-F • Mideast • 100 kW
                                                    S Sa/Su • Mideast • 100 kW
                                                    S Sa • C Africa • 100 kW
                                                    S Su • C Africa • 100 kW
        †BIBLE VOICE, Via Nauen, Germany   S Tu • Mideast • 125 kW
                                                    S Sa/Su • Mideast • 250 kW
                                                    S F-Su • Mideast • 250 kW
                                                    S Su • Mideast • 250 kW
        †BIBLE VOICE, Via Wertachtal, Germany   S Sa • W Africa • 125 kW
       USA
          TRANS WORLD R, Via Albania   S M-F • N Europe • 100 kW
9435 CHINA
       †CHINA R INTL, Kashi   S • C Asia • 100 kW • ALT. FREQ. TO 5915 kHz   S • S Asia • 100 kW
                                       S • C Asia • 100 kW • ALT. FREQ. TO 5905 kHz   W • Europe • 500 kW
       †CHINA R INTL, Kunming   Mideast, W Africa & C Africa • 500 kW • ALT. FREQ. TO 9440 kHz
       †CHINA R INTL, Urümqi   S • E Africa • 500 kW
       †CHINA R INTL, Xi'an   W • E Asia • 500 kW
       CZECH REPUBLIC
       †RADIO PRAGUE, Litomyšl   W • W Europe & S America • 100 kW
                                                     W • W Africa & C Africa • 100 kW
       SWEDEN
       †RADIO SWEDEN, Via Madagascar   S • S Asia • 250 kW
       UNITED KINGDOM
       †BIBLE VOICE, Via Jülich, Germany   S Su • W Europe • 100 kW
       USA
       †R FARDA, Via Iranawila, Sri Lanka   W Asia • 250 kW
9440 CHINA
       †CENTRAL PEOPLE'S BS, Beijing   W • DS-8 (MINORITIES) • 100 kW
       CHINA R INTL, Beijing   SE Asia • 500 kW
       †CHINA R INTL, Kunming   SE Asia • 150 kW   Mideast, W Africa & C Africa • 500 kW
                                       Mideast, W Africa & C Africa • 500 kW • ALT. FREQ. TO 9435 kHz
       †CHINA R INTL, Via Cerrik, Albania   S • E Europe • 150 kW
       †CHINA R INTL, Xi'an   W • E Asia • 500 kW
       CZECH REPUBLIC
       RADIO PRAGUE, Litomyšl   S • N America & C America • 100 kW
                                            S • S America • 100 kW
       GERMANY
       †DEUTSCHE WELLE, Nauen   S • W Africa • 500 kW
       †DEUTSCHE WELLE, Via Sri Lanka   W • C Asia • 250 kW
       UNITED KINGDOM
       †BBC, Woofferton   W • S Europe • 250 kW
       USA
       TRANS WORLD R, Via Albania   S • Europe • 100 kW
                                                    S Su • Europe • 100 kW
9445 CZECH REPUBLIC
       RADIO PRAGUE, Litomyšl   S • Mideast & E Africa • 100 kW
                                       S • E Europe • 100 kW
       INDIA
       ALL INDIA RADIO, Bangalore   W Africa • 500 kW
                                                    Europe • 500 kW
       TRANS WORLD R, Via Uzbekistan   S • S Asia • 200 kW
                                       S M-F • S Asia • 200 kW
                                       S Sa/Su • S Asia • 200 kW
                                       S M-Sa • S Asia • 200 kW
       UNITED KINGDOM
       FEBA RADIO, Via Novosibirsk, Russia   W • S Asia • 250 kW
       USA
       TRANS WORLD R, Via Nov'sibirsk, Russia W • S Asia • 250 kW
                                               W M-F • S Asia • 250 kW
9450 CHINA
       †CHINA R INTL, Kashi   W • S Asia • 100 kW   W • W Africa & C Africa • 500 kW
       †CHINA R INTL, Various Locations   E Asia • 500 kW
       CHINA (TAIWAN)
       CHINA RADIO, Via Petro-Kam, Russia   S • E Asia • 200 kW
       CZECH REPUBLIC
       RADIO PRAGUE, Litomyšl   W • E Europe & W Asia • 100 kW
       UNITED KINGDOM
       FEBA RADIO, Via Novosibirsk, Russia   W • S Asia • 250 kW
       USA
       FAMILY RADIO, Via Irkutsk, Russia   E Asia • 250 kW
       †WEWN, Vandiver, Alabama   W • N America • 500 kW

0 1 2 3 4 5 6 7 8 9 10 11 12 13 14 15 16 17 18 19 20 21 22 23 24

ENGLISH ▬▬   ARABIC ⌇⌇⌇   CHINESE ▫▫▫   FRENCH ▦▦   GERMAN ▬▬   RUSSIAN ══   SPANISH ▭▭   OTHER ──

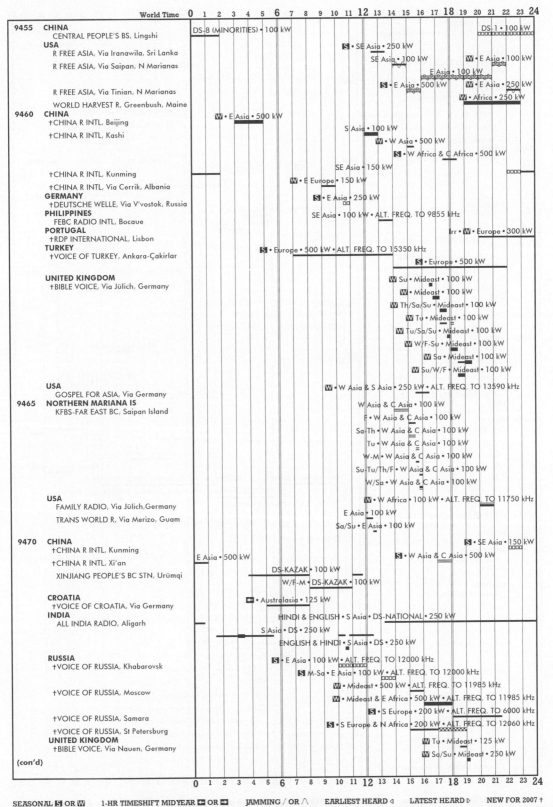

| World Time | 0 1 2 3 4 5 6 7 8 9 10 11 12 13 14 15 16 17 18 19 20 21 22 23 24 |

9455 CHINA
CENTRAL PEOPLE'S BS, Lingshi — DS-8 (MINORITIES) • 100 kW ... DS-1 • 100 kW

USA
R FREE ASIA, Via Iranawila, Sri Lanka — S • SE Asia • 250 kW
R FREE ASIA, Via Saipan, N Marianas — SE Asia • 100 kW ... W • E Asia • 100 kW
E Asia • 100 kW
R FREE ASIA, Via Tinian, N Marianas — S • E Asia • 500 kW ... W • E Asia • 250 kW
WORLD HARVEST R, Greenbush, Maine — W • Africa • 250 kW

9460 CHINA
†CHINA R INTL, Beijing — W • E Asia • 500 kW
†CHINA R INTL, Kashi — S Asia • 100 kW
W • W Asia • 500 kW
S • W Africa & C Africa • 500 kW
†CHINA R INTL, Kunming — SE Asia • 150 kW
†CHINA R INTL, Via Cerrik, Albania — W • E Europe • 150 kW

GERMANY
†DEUTSCHE WELLE, Via V'vostok, Russia — S • E Asia • 250 kW

PHILIPPINES
FEBC RADIO INTL, Bocaue — SE Asia • 100 kW • ALT. FREQ. TO 9855 kHz

PORTUGAL
†RDP INTERNATIONAL, Lisbon — Irr • W • Europe • 300 kW

TURKEY
†VOICE OF TURKEY, Ankara-Çakirlar — S • Europe • 500 kW • ALT. FREQ. TO 15350 kHz
S • Europe • 500 kW

UNITED KINGDOM
†BIBLE VOICE, Via Jülich, Germany — W Su • Mideast • 100 kW
W • Mideast • 100 kW
W Th/Sa/Su • Mideast • 100 kW
W Tu • Mideast • 100 kW
W Tu/Sa/Su • Mideast • 100 kW
W/F-Su • Mideast • 100 kW
W Sa • Mideast • 100 kW
W Su/W/F • Mideast • 100 kW

USA
GOSPEL FOR ASIA, Via Germany — W • W Asia & S Asia • 250 kW • ALT. FREQ. TO 13590 kHz

9465 NORTHERN MARIANA IS
KFBS-FAR EAST BC, Saipan Island — W Asia & C Asia • 100 kW
F • W Asia & C Asia • 100 kW
Sa-Th • W Asia & C Asia • 100 kW
Tu • W Asia & C Asia • 100 kW
W-M • W Asia & C Asia • 100 kW
Su-Tu/Th/F • W Asia & C Asia • 100 kW
W/Sa • W Asia & C Asia • 100 kW

USA
FAMILY RADIO, Via Jülich, Germany — W • W Africa • 100 kW • ALT. FREQ. TO 11750 kHz
TRANS WORLD R, Via Merizo, Guam — E Asia • 100 kW
Sa/Su • E Asia • 100 kW

9470 CHINA
†CHINA R INTL, Kunming — S • SE Asia • 150 kW
S • W Asia & C Asia • 500 kW
†CHINA R INTL, Xi'an — E Asia • 500 kW
XINJIANG PEOPLE'S BC STN, Urümqi — DS-KAZAK • 100 kW
W/F-M • DS-KAZAK • 100 kW

CROATIA
†VOICE OF CROATIA, Via Germany — ⇨ • Australasia • 125 kW

INDIA
ALL INDIA RADIO, Aligarh — HINDI & ENGLISH • S Asia • DS-NATIONAL • 250 kW
S Asia • DS • 250 kW
ENGLISH & HINDI • S Asia • DS • 250 kW

RUSSIA
†VOICE OF RUSSIA, Khabarovsk — S • E Asia • 100 kW • ALT. FREQ. TO 12000 kHz
S M-Sa • E Asia • 100 kW • ALT. FREQ. TO 12000 kHz
†VOICE OF RUSSIA, Moscow — W • Mideast • 500 kW • ALT. FREQ. TO 11985 kHz
W • Mideast & E Africa • 500 kW • ALT. FREQ. TO 11985 kHz
†VOICE OF RUSSIA, Samara — S • S Europe • 200 kW • ALT. FREQ. TO 6000 kHz
†VOICE OF RUSSIA, St Petersburg — S • S Europe & N Africa • 200 kW • ALT. FREQ. TO 12060 kHz

UNITED KINGDOM
†BIBLE VOICE, Via Nauen, Germany — W Tu • Mideast • 125 kW
W Sa/Su • Mideast • 250 kW

(con'd)

| | 0 1 2 3 4 5 6 7 8 9 10 11 12 13 14 15 16 17 18 19 20 21 22 23 24 |

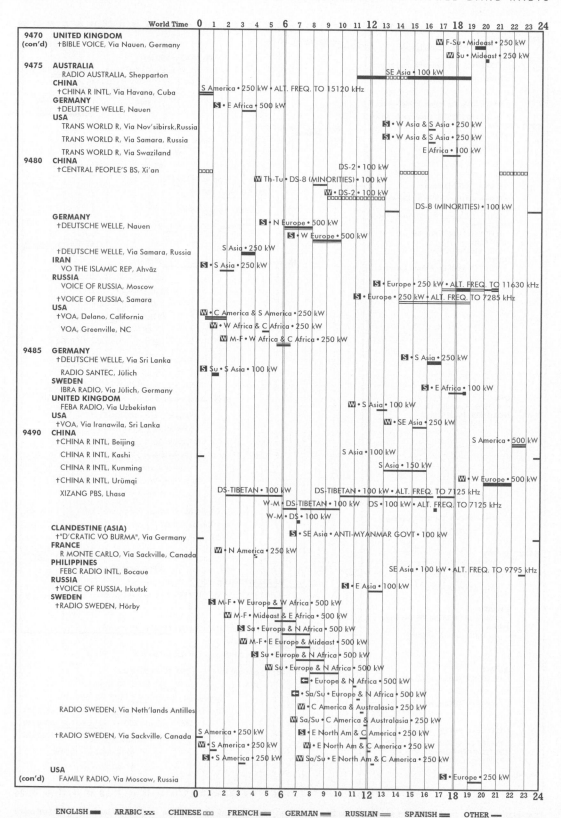

9470 **UNITED KINGDOM**	
(con'd) †BIBLE VOICE, Via Nauen, Germany	W F-Su • Mideast • 250 kW
	W Su • Mideast • 250 kW
9475 **AUSTRALIA**	
RADIO AUSTRALIA, Shepparton	SE Asia • 100 kW
CHINA	
†CHINA R INTL, Via Havana, Cuba	S America • 250 kW • ALT. FREQ. TO 15120 kHz
GERMANY	
†DEUTSCHE WELLE, Nauen	S • E Africa • 500 kW
USA	
TRANS WORLD R, Via Nov'sibirsk, Russia	S • W Asia & S Asia • 250 kW
TRANS WORLD R, Via Samara, Russia	S • W Asia & S Asia • 250 kW
TRANS WORLD R, Via Swaziland	E Africa • 100 kW
9480 **CHINA**	
†CENTRAL PEOPLE'S BS, Xi'an	DS-2 • 100 kW
	W Th-Tu • DS-8 (MINORITIES) • 100 kW
	S • DS-2 • 100 kW
	DS-8 (MINORITIES) • 100 kW
GERMANY	
†DEUTSCHE WELLE, Nauen	S • N Europe • 500 kW
	S • W Europe • 500 kW
†DEUTSCHE WELLE, Via Samara, Russia	S Asia • 250 kW
IRAN	
VO THE ISLAMIC REP, Ahvāz	S • S Asia • 250 kW
RUSSIA	
VOICE OF RUSSIA, Moscow	S • Europe • 250 kW • ALT. FREQ. TO 11630 kHz
†VOICE OF RUSSIA, Samara	S • Europe • 250 kW • ALT. FREQ. TO 7285 kHz
USA	
†VOA, Delano, California	W • C America & S America • 250 kW
VOA, Greenville, NC	W • W Africa & C Africa • 250 kW
	W M-F • W Africa & C Africa • 250 kW
9485 **GERMANY**	
†DEUTSCHE WELLE, Via Sri Lanka	S • S Asia • 250 kW
RADIO SANTEC, Jülich	S Su • S Asia • 100 kW
SWEDEN	
IBRA RADIO, Via Jülich, Germany	S • E Africa • 100 kW
UNITED KINGDOM	
FEBA RADIO, Via Uzbekistan	W • S Asia • 100 kW
USA	
†VOA, Via Iranawila, Sri Lanka	W • SE Asia • 250 kW
9490 **CHINA**	
†CHINA R INTL, Beijing	S America • 500 kW
CHINA R INTL, Kashi	S Asia • 100 kW
CHINA R INTL, Kunming	S Asia • 150 kW
†CHINA R INTL, Urümqi	W • W Europe • 500 kW
XIZANG PBS, Lhasa	DS-TIBETAN • 100 kW DS-TIBETAN • 100 kW • ALT. FREQ. TO 7125 kHz
	W-M • DS-TIBETAN • 100 kW DS • 100 kW • ALT. FREQ. TO 7125 kHz
	W-M • DS • 100 kW
CLANDESTINE (ASIA)	
†"D'CRATIC VO BURMA", Via Germany	S • SE Asia • ANTI-MYANMAR GOVT • 100 kW
FRANCE	
R MONTE CARLO, Via Sackville, Canada	W • N America • 250 kW
PHILIPPINES	
FEBC RADIO INTL, Bocaue	SE Asia • 100 kW • ALT. FREQ. TO 9795 kHz
RUSSIA	
†VOICE OF RUSSIA, Irkutsk	S • E Asia • 100 kW
SWEDEN	
†RADIO SWEDEN, Hörby	S M-F • W Europe & W Africa • 500 kW
	W M-F • Mideast & E Africa • 500 kW
	S Sa • Europe & N Africa • 500 kW
	W M-F • E Europe & Mideast • 500 kW
	S Su • Europe & N Africa • 500 kW
	W Su • Europe & N Africa • 500 kW
	• Europe & N Africa • 500 kW
	Sa/Su • Europe & N Africa • 500 kW
	W • C America & Australasia • 250 kW
	W Sa/Su • C America & Australasia • 250 kW
RADIO SWEDEN, Via Neth'lands Antilles	
†RADIO SWEDEN, Via Sackville, Canada	S America • 250 kW S • E North Am & C America • 250 kW
	W • S America • 250 kW W • E North Am & C America • 250 kW
	S • S America • 250 kW W Sa/Su • E North Am & C America • 250 kW
USA	
(con'd) FAMILY RADIO, Via Moscow, Russia	S • Europe • 250 kW

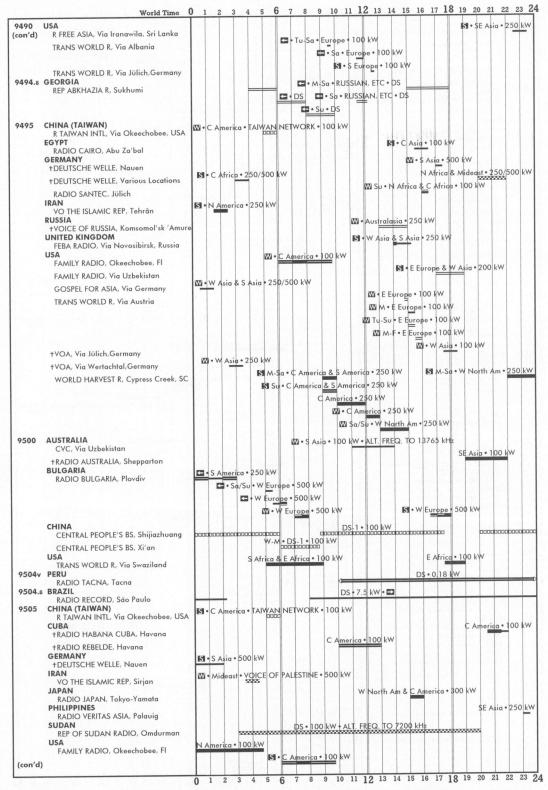

World Time		
9490 USA		
(con'd) R FREE ASIA, Via Iranawila, Sri Lanka		SE Asia • 250 kW
TRANS WORLD R, Via Albania	Tu-Sa • Europe • 100 kW	
	Sa • Europe • 100 kW	
	S Europe • 100 kW	
TRANS WORLD R, Via Jülich, Germany		
9494.8 GEORGIA		
REP ABKHAZIA R, Sukhumi	M-Sa • RUSSIAN, ETC • DS	
	DS, Sa • RUSSIAN, ETC • DS	
	Su • DS	
9495 CHINA (TAIWAN)		
R TAIWAN INTL, Via Okeechobee, USA	C America • TAIWAN NETWORK • 100 kW	
EGYPT		
RADIO CAIRO, Abu Za'bal	C Asia • 100 kW	
GERMANY	S Asia • 500 kW	
†DEUTSCHE WELLE, Nauen	C Africa • 250/500 kW	N Africa & Mideast • 250/500 kW
†DEUTSCHE WELLE, Various Locations	Su • N Africa & C Africa • 100 kW	
RADIO SANTEC, Jülich		
IRAN		
VO THE ISLAMIC REP, Tehrān	N America • 250 kW	
RUSSIA		
†VOICE OF RUSSIA, Komsomol'sk 'Amure	Australasia • 250 kW	
UNITED KINGDOM		
FEBA RADIO, Via Novosibirsk, Russia	W Asia & S Asia • 250 kW	
USA		
FAMILY RADIO, Okeechobee, Fl	C America • 100 kW	
FAMILY RADIO, Via Uzbekistan		E Europe & W Asia • 200 kW
GOSPEL FOR ASIA, Via Germany	W Asia & S Asia • 250/500 kW	
TRANS WORLD R, Via Austria	E Europe • 100 kW	
	M • E Europe • 100 kW	
	Tu-Su • E Europe • 100 kW	
	M-F • E Europe • 100 kW	
	W Asia • 100 kW	
†VOA, Via Jülich, Germany	W Asia • 250 kW	
†VOA, Via Wertachtal, Germany	M-Sa • C America & S America • 250 kW	M-Sa • W North Am • 250 kW
WORLD HARVEST R, Cypress Creek, SC	Su • C America & S America • 250 kW	
	C America • 250 kW	
	C America • 250 kW	
	Sa/Su • W North Am • 250 kW	
9500 AUSTRALIA		
CVC, Via Uzbekistan	S Asia • 100 kW • ALT. FREQ. TO 13765 kHz	
†RADIO AUSTRALIA, Shepparton		SE Asia • 100 kW
BULGARIA		
RADIO BULGARIA, Plovdiv	S America • 250 kW	
	Sa/Su • W Europe • 500 kW	
	W Europe • 500 kW	
	W Europe • 500 kW	W Europe • 500 kW
CHINA	DS-1 • 100 kW	
CENTRAL PEOPLE'S BS, Shijiazhuang	DS-1 • 100 kW	
CENTRAL PEOPLE'S BS, Xi'an	W-M • DS-1 • 100 kW	
USA		
TRANS WORLD R, Via Swaziland	S Africa & E Africa • 100 kW	E Africa • 100 kW
9504v PERU		
RADIO TACNA, Tacna		DS • 0.18 kW
9504.8 BRAZIL		
RADIO RECORD, São Paulo	DS • 7.5 kW	
9505 CHINA (TAIWAN)		
R TAIWAN INTL, Via Okeechobee, USA	C America • TAIWAN NETWORK • 100 kW	
CUBA		
†RADIO HABANA CUBA, Havana		C America • 100 kW
†RADIO REBELDE, Havana	C America • 100 kW	
GERMANY		
†DEUTSCHE WELLE, Nauen	S Asia • 500 kW	
IRAN		
VO THE ISLAMIC REP, Sirjan	Mideast • VOICE OF PALESTINE • 500 kW	
JAPAN		
RADIO JAPAN, Tokyo-Yamata	W North Am & C America • 300 kW	
PHILIPPINES		
RADIO VERITAS ASIA, Palauig		SE Asia • 250 kW
SUDAN		
REP OF SUDAN RADIO, Omdurman	DS • 100 kW • ALT. FREQ. TO 7200 kHz	
USA		
FAMILY RADIO, Okeechobee, Fl	N America • 100 kW	
(con'd)	C America • 100 kW	

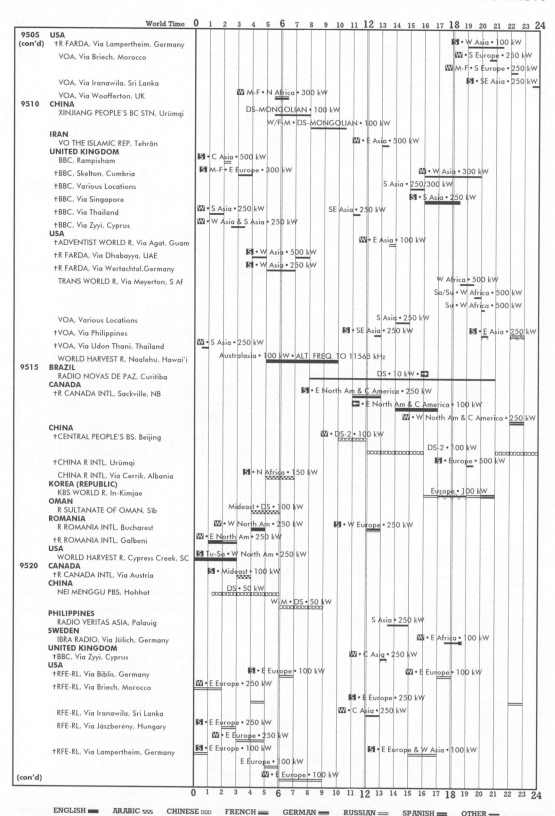

World Time 0 1 2 3 4 5 6 7 8 9 10 11 12 13 14 15 16 17 18 19 20 21 22 23 24

9505 USA
(con'd)   †R FARDA, Via Lampertheim, Germany   S • W Asia • 100 kW
          VOA, Via Briech, Morocco   W • S Europe • 250 kW
                                                                                      W M-F • S Europe • 250 kW
          VOA, Via Iranawila, Sri Lanka   S • SE Asia • 250 kW
          VOA, Via Woofferton, UK   W M-F • N Africa • 300 kW
9510 CHINA
          XINJIANG PEOPLE'S BC STN, Urümqi   DS-MONGOLIAN • 100 kW
                                                        W/F-M • DS-MONGOLIAN • 100 kW
IRAN
          VO THE ISLAMIC REP, Tehrān   W • E Asia • 500 kW
UNITED KINGDOM
          BBC, Rampisham   S • C Asia • 500 kW
          †BBC, Skelton, Cumbria   S M-F • E Europe • 300 kW   W • W Asia • 300 kW
          †BBC, Various Locations   S Asia • 250/300 kW
          †BBC, Via Singapore   S • S Asia • 250 kW
          †BBC, Via Thailand   W • S Asia • 250 kW   SE Asia • 250 kW
          †BBC, Via Zyyi, Cyprus   W • W Asia & S Asia • 250 kW
USA
          †ADVENTIST WORLD R, Via Agat, Guam   W • E Asia • 100 kW
          †R FARDA, Via Dhabayya, UAE   S • W Asia • 500 kW
          †R FARDA, Via Wertachtal, Germany   S • W Asia • 250 kW
          TRANS WORLD R, Via Meyerton, S Af   W Africa • 500 kW
                                                                                       Sa/Su • W Africa • 500 kW
                                                                                       Su • W Africa • 500 kW
          VOA, Various Locations   S Asia • 250 kW
          †VOA, Via Philippines   S • SE Asia • 250 kW   S • E Asia • 250 kW
          †VOA, Via Udon Thani, Thailand   W • S Asia • 250 kW
          WORLD HARVEST R, Naalehu, Hawai'i   Australasia • 100 kW • ALT FREQ. TO 11565 kHz
9515 BRAZIL
          RADIO NOVAS DE PAZ, Curitiba   DS • 10 kW • ▭▶
CANADA
          †R CANADA INTL, Sackville, NB   S • E North Am & C America • 250 kW
                                                          ▭▶ • E North Am & C America • 100 kW
                                                                    W • W North Am & C America • 250 kW
CHINA
          †CENTRAL PEOPLE'S BS, Beijing   W • DS-2 • 100 kW
                                                        DS-2 • 100 kW
          †CHINA R INTL, Urümqi   S • Europe • 500 kW
          CHINA R INTL, Via Cerrik, Albania   S • N Africa • 150 kW
KOREA (REPUBLIC)
          KBS WORLD R, In-Kimjae   Europe • 100 kW
OMAN
          R SULTANATE OF OMAN, Sīb   Mideast • DS • 100 kW
ROMANIA
          R ROMANIA INTL, Bucharest   W • W North Am • 250 kW   S • W Europe • 250 kW
          †R ROMANIA INTL, Galbeni   W • E North Am • 250 kW
USA
          WORLD HARVEST R, Cypress Creek, SC   S Tu-Sa • W North Am • 250 kW
9520 CANADA
          †R CANADA INTL, Via Austria   S • Mideast • 100 kW
CHINA
          NEI MENGGU PBS, Hohhot   DS • 50 kW
                                                        W M • DS • 50 kW
PHILIPPINES
          RADIO VERITAS ASIA, Palauig   S Asia • 250 kW
SWEDEN
          IBRA RADIO, Via Jülich, Germany   W • E Africa • 100 kW
UNITED KINGDOM
          †BBC, Via Zyyi, Cyprus   W • C Asia • 250 kW
USA
          †RFE-RL, Via Biblis, Germany   S • E Europe • 100 kW   W • E Europe • 100 kW
          †RFE-RL, Via Briech, Morocco   W • E Europe • 250 kW
                                                                        S • E Europe • 250 kW
                                                                        W • C Asia • 250 kW
          RFE-RL, Via Iranawila, Sri Lanka   S • E Europe • 250 kW
          RFE-RL, Via Jászberény, Hungary   W • E Europe • 250 kW
          †RFE-RL, Via Lampertheim, Germany   S • E Europe • 100 kW   S • E Europe & W Asia • 100 kW
                                               E Europe • 100 kW
                                               W • E Europe • 100 kW

(con'd)

0 1 2 3 4 5 6 7 8 9 10 11 12 13 14 15 16 17 18 19 20 21 22 23 24

ENGLISH ▬▬   ARABIC ⋙   CHINESE ▯▯▯   FRENCH ▭▭   GERMAN ▬▬   RUSSIAN ══   SPANISH ▭▭   OTHER ▬▬

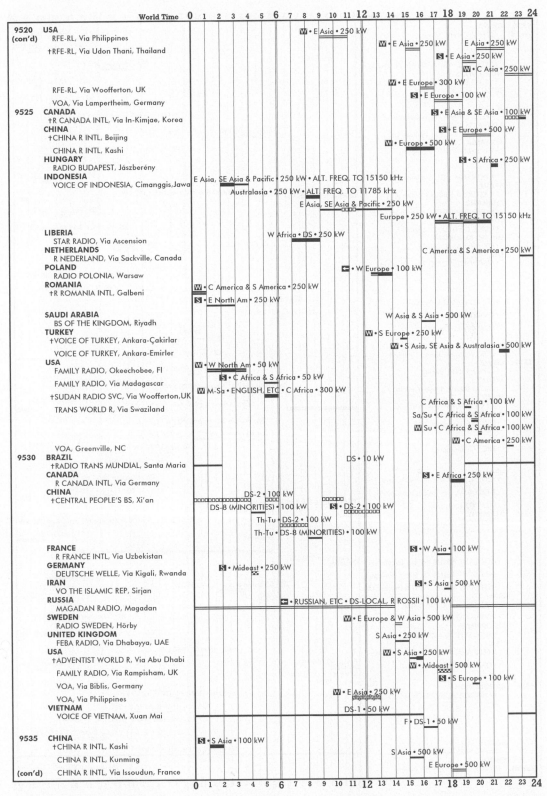

9520 (con'd)	**USA** RFE-RL, Via Philippines
	†RFE-RL, Via Udon Thani, Thailand
	RFE-RL, Via Woofferton, UK
	VOA, Via Lampertheim, Germany
9525	**CANADA** †R CANADA INTL, Via In-Kimjae, Korea
	CHINA †CHINA R INTL, Beijing
	CHINA R INTL, Kashi
	HUNGARY RADIO BUDAPEST, Jászberény
	INDONESIA VOICE OF INDONESIA, Cimanggis, Jawa
	LIBERIA STAR RADIO, Via Ascension
	NETHERLANDS R NEDERLAND, Via Sackville, Canada
	POLAND RADIO POLONIA, Warsaw
	ROMANIA †R ROMANIA INTL, Galbeni
	SAUDI ARABIA BS OF THE KINGDOM, Riyadh
	TURKEY †VOICE OF TURKEY, Ankara-Çakirlar
	VOICE OF TURKEY, Ankara-Emirler
	USA FAMILY RADIO, Okeechobee, Fl
	FAMILY RADIO, Via Madagascar
	†SUDAN RADIO SVC, Via Woofferton,UK
	TRANS WORLD R, Via Swaziland
	VOA, Greenville, NC
9530	**BRAZIL** †RADIO TRANS MUNDIAL, Santa Maria
	CANADA R CANADA INTL, Via Germany
	CHINA †CENTRAL PEOPLE'S BS, Xi'an
	FRANCE R FRANCE INTL, Via Uzbekistan
	GERMANY DEUTSCHE WELLE, Via Kigali, Rwanda
	IRAN VO THE ISLAMIC REP, Sirjan
	RUSSIA MAGADAN RADIO, Magadan
	SWEDEN RADIO SWEDEN, Hörby
	UNITED KINGDOM FEBA RADIO, Via Dhabayya, UAE
	USA †ADVENTIST WORLD R, Via Abu Dhabi
	FAMILY RADIO, Via Rampisham, UK
	VOA, Via Biblis, Germany
	VOA, Via Philippines
	VIETNAM VOICE OF VIETNAM, Xuan Mai
9535	**CHINA** †CHINA R INTL, Kashi
	CHINA R INTL, Kunming
(con'd)	CHINA R INTL, Via Issoudun, France

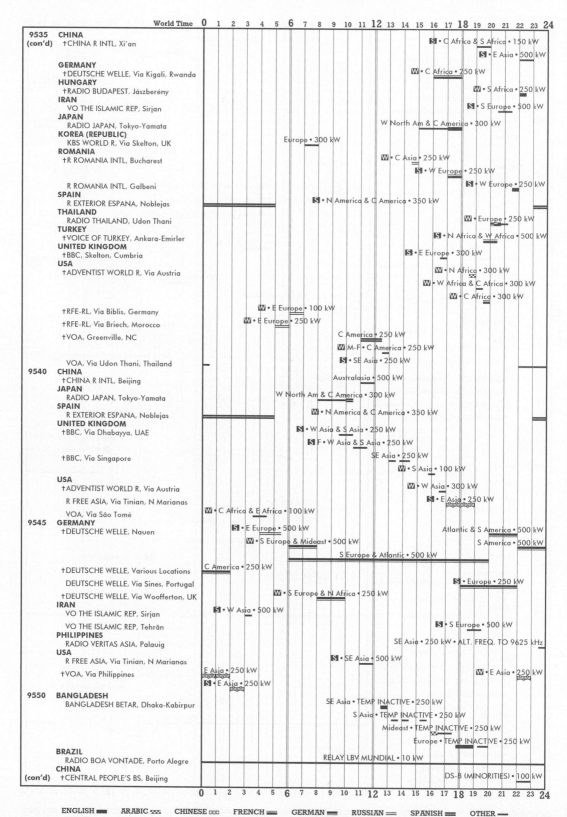

		World Time
9535 (con'd)	CHINA	†CHINA R INTL, Xi'an
	GERMANY	†DEUTSCHE WELLE, Via Kigali, Rwanda
	HUNGARY	†RADIO BUDAPEST, Jászberény
	IRAN	VO THE ISLAMIC REP, Sirjan
	JAPAN	RADIO JAPAN, Tokyo-Yamata
	KOREA (REPUBLIC)	KBS WORLD R, Via Skelton, UK
	ROMANIA	†R ROMANIA INTL, Bucharest
		R ROMANIA INTL, Galbeni
	SPAIN	R EXTERIOR ESPANA, Noblejas
	THAILAND	RADIO THAILAND, Udon Thani
	TURKEY	†VOICE OF TURKEY, Ankara-Emirler
	UNITED KINGDOM	†BBC, Skelton, Cumbria
	USA	†ADVENTIST WORLD R, Via Austria
		†RFE-RL, Via Biblis, Germany
		†RFE-RL, Via Briech, Morocco
		†VOA, Greenville, NC
		VOA, Via Udon Thani, Thailand
9540	CHINA	†CHINA R INTL, Beijing
	JAPAN	RADIO JAPAN, Tokyo-Yamata
	SPAIN	R EXTERIOR ESPANA, Noblejas
	UNITED KINGDOM	†BBC, Via Dhabayya, UAE
		†BBC, Via Singapore
	USA	†ADVENTIST WORLD R, Via Austria
		R FREE ASIA, Via Tinian, N Marianas
		VOA, Via São Tomé
9545	GERMANY	†DEUTSCHE WELLE, Nauen
		†DEUTSCHE WELLE, Various Locations
		DEUTSCHE WELLE, Via Sines, Portugal
		†DEUTSCHE WELLE, Via Woofferton, UK
	IRAN	VO THE ISLAMIC REP, Sirjan
		VO THE ISLAMIC REP, Tehrān
	PHILIPPINES	RADIO VERITAS ASIA, Palauig
	USA	R FREE ASIA, Via Tinian, N Marianas
		†VOA, Via Philippines
9550	BANGLADESH	BANGLADESH BETAR, Dhaka-Kabirpur
	BRAZIL	RADIO BOA VONTADE, Porto Alegre
	CHINA (con'd)	†CENTRAL PEOPLE'S BS, Beijing

Schedule entries (as plotted on the chart):

- CHINA R INTL, Xi'an — S · C Africa & S Africa · 150 kW; S · E Asia · 500 kW
- DEUTSCHE WELLE, Via Kigali, Rwanda — W · C Africa · 250 kW
- RADIO BUDAPEST, Jászberény — W · S Africa · 250 kW
- VO THE ISLAMIC REP, Sirjan — S · S Europe · 500 kW
- RADIO JAPAN, Tokyo-Yamata — W North Am & C America · 300 kW
- KBS WORLD R, Via Skelton, UK — Europe · 300 kW
- R ROMANIA INTL, Bucharest — W · C Asia · 250 kW; S · W Europe · 250 kW
- R ROMANIA INTL, Galbeni — S · W Europe · 250 kW
- R EXTERIOR ESPANA, Noblejas — S · N America & C America · 350 kW
- RADIO THAILAND, Udon Thani — W · Europe · 250 kW
- VOICE OF TURKEY, Ankara-Emirler — S · N Africa & W Africa · 500 kW
- BBC, Skelton, Cumbria — S · E Europe · 300 kW
- ADVENTIST WORLD R, Via Austria — W · N Africa · 300 kW; W · W Africa & C Africa · 300 kW; W · C Africa · 300 kW
- RFE-RL, Via Biblis, Germany — W · E Europe · 100 kW
- RFE-RL, Via Briech, Morocco — W · E Europe · 250 kW
- VOA, Greenville, NC — C America · 250 kW; W M-F · C America · 250 kW
- VOA, Via Udon Thani, Thailand — S · SE Asia · 250 kW
- CHINA R INTL, Beijing — Australasia · 500 kW
- RADIO JAPAN, Tokyo-Yamata — W North Am & C America · 300 kW
- R EXTERIOR ESPANA, Noblejas — W · N America & C America · 350 kW
- BBC, Via Dhabayya, UAE — S · W Asia & S Asia · 250 kW; S F · W Asia & S Asia · 250 kW
- BBC, Via Singapore — SE Asia · 250 kW
- ADVENTIST WORLD R, Via Austria — W · S Asia · 100 kW
- R FREE ASIA, Via Tinian, N Marianas — W · W Asia · 300 kW; S · E Asia · 250 kW
- VOA, Via São Tomé — W · C Africa & E Africa · 100 kW
- DEUTSCHE WELLE, Nauen — S · E Europe · 500 kW; W · S Europe & Mideast · 500 kW; Atlantic & S America · 500 kW; S America · 500 kW
- DEUTSCHE WELLE, Various Locations — S Europe & Atlantic · 500 kW; C America · 250 kW
- DEUTSCHE WELLE, Via Sines, Portugal — S · Europe · 250 kW
- DEUTSCHE WELLE, Via Woofferton, UK — W · S Europe & N Africa · 250 kW
- VO THE ISLAMIC REP, Sirjan — S · W Asia · 500 kW
- VO THE ISLAMIC REP, Tehrān — S · S Europe · 500 kW
- RADIO VERITAS ASIA, Palauig — SE Asia · 250 kW · ALT. FREQ. TO 9625 kHz
- R FREE ASIA, Via Tinian, N Marianas — S · SE Asia · 500 kW
- VOA, Via Philippines — E Asia · 250 kW; S · E Asia · 250 kW; W · E Asia · 250 kW
- BANGLADESH BETAR, Dhaka-Kabirpur — SE Asia · TEMP INACTIVE · 250 kW; S Asia · TEMP INACTIVE · 250 kW; Mideast · TEMP INACTIVE · 250 kW; Europe · TEMP INACTIVE · 250 kW
- RADIO BOA VONTADE, Porto Alegre — RELAY LBV MUNDIAL · 10 kW
- CENTRAL PEOPLE'S BS, Beijing — DS-B (MINORITIES) · 100 kW

ENGLISH ▬　ARABIC ⋈⋈⋈　CHINESE ▫▫▫　FRENCH ▭▭　GERMAN ▬▬　RUSSIAN ══　SPANISH ▬　OTHER ▬

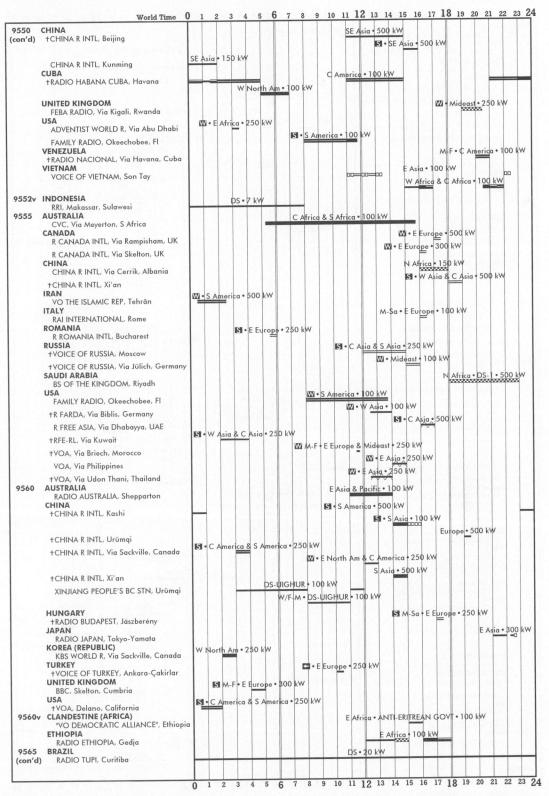

World Time

9550 (con'd)	**CHINA**
	†CHINA R INTL, Beijing
	CHINA R INTL, Kunming
	CUBA
	†RADIO HABANA CUBA, Havana
	UNITED KINGDOM
	FEBA RADIO, Via Kigali, Rwanda
	USA
	ADVENTIST WORLD R, Via Abu Dhabi
	FAMILY RADIO, Okeechobee, Fl
	VENEZUELA
	†RADIO NACIONAL, Via Havana, Cuba
	VIETNAM
	VOICE OF VIETNAM, Son Tay
9552v	**INDONESIA**
	RRI, Makassar, Sulawesi
9555	**AUSTRALIA**
	CVC, Via Meyerton, S Africa
	CANADA
	R CANADA INTL, Via Rampisham, UK
	R CANADA INTL, Via Skelton, UK
	CHINA
	CHINA R INTL, Via Cerrik, Albania
	†CHINA R INTL, Xi'an
	IRAN
	VO THE ISLAMIC REP, Tehrãn
	ITALY
	RAI INTERNATIONAL, Rome
	ROMANIA
	R ROMANIA INTL, Bucharest
	RUSSIA
	†VOICE OF RUSSIA, Moscow
	†VOICE OF RUSSIA, Via Jülich, Germany
	SAUDI ARABIA
	BS OF THE KINGDOM, Riyadh
	USA
	FAMILY RADIO, Okeechobee, Fl
	†R FARDA, Via Biblis, Germany
	R FREE ASIA, Via Dhabayya, UAE
	†RFE-RL, Via Kuwait
	†VOA, Via Briech, Morocco
	VOA, Via Philippines
	†VOA, Via Udon Thani, Thailand
9560	**AUSTRALIA**
	RADIO AUSTRALIA, Shepparton
	CHINA
	†CHINA R INTL, Kashi
	†CHINA R INTL, Urümqi
	†CHINA R INTL, Via Sackville, Canada
	†CHINA R INTL, Xi'an
	XINJIANG PEOPLE'S BC STN, Urümqi
	HUNGARY
	†RADIO BUDAPEST, Jászberény
	JAPAN
	RADIO JAPAN, Tokyo-Yamata
	KOREA (REPUBLIC)
	KBS WORLD R, Via Sackville, Canada
	TURKEY
	†VOICE OF TURKEY, Ankara-Çakirlar
	UNITED KINGDOM
	BBC, Skelton, Cumbria
	USA
	†VOA, Delano, California
9560v	**CLANDESTINE (AFRICA)**
	"VO DEMOCRATIC ALLIANCE", Ethiopia
	ETHIOPIA
	RADIO ETHIOPIA, Gedja
9565 (con'd)	**BRAZIL**
	RADIO TUPI, Curitiba

Transmission target/power notes (read from chart):

- SE Asia • 500 kW
- S • SE Asia • 500 kW
- SE Asia • 150 kW
- C America • 100 kW
- W North Am • 100 kW
- W • Mideast • 250 kW
- W • E Africa • 250 kW
- S • S America • 100 kW
- M-F • C America • 100 kW
- E Asia • 100 kW
- W Africa & C Africa • 100 kW
- DS • 7 kW
- C Africa & S Africa • 100 kW
- W • E Europe • 500 kW
- W • E Europe • 300 kW
- N Africa • 150 kW
- S • W Asia & C Asia • 500 kW
- W • S America • 500 kW
- M-Sa • E Europe • 100 kW
- S • E Europe • 250 kW
- S • C Asia & S Asia • 250 kW
- W • Mideast • 100 kW
- N Africa • DS-1 • 500 kW
- W • S America • 100 kW
- W • W Asia • 100 kW
- S • C Asia • 500 kW
- S • W Asia & C Asia • 250 kW
- W M-F • E Europe & Mideast • 250 kW
- W • E Asia • 250 kW
- W • E Asia • 250 kW
- E Asia & Pacific • 100 kW
- S • S America • 500 kW
- S • S America • 100 kW
- Europe • 500 kW
- S • C America & S America • 250 kW
- W • E North Am & C America • 250 kW
- S Asia • 500 kW
- DS-UIGHUR • 100 kW
- W/F-M • DS-UIGHUR • 100 kW
- S M-Sa • E Europe • 250 kW
- E Asia • 300 kW
- W North Am • 250 kW
- • E Europe • 250 kW
- S M-F • E Europe • 300 kW
- S • C America & S America • 250 kW
- E Africa • ANTI-ERITREAN GOVT • 100 kW
- E Africa • 100 kW
- DS • 20 kW

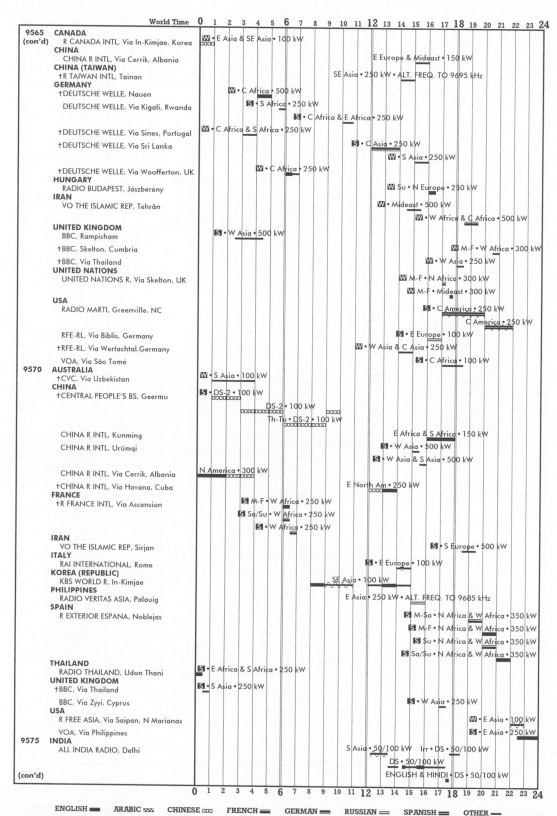

	World Time	0 1 2 3 4 5 6 7 8 9 10 11 12 13 14 15 16 17 18 19 20 21 22 23 24
9565 (con'd)	**CANADA** R CANADA INTL, Via In-Kimjae, Korea	W • E Asia & SE Asia • 100 kW
	CHINA CHINA R INTL, Via Cerrik, Albania	E Europe & Mideast • 150 kW
	CHINA (TAIWAN) †R TAIWAN INTL, Tainan	SE Asia • 250 kW • ALT. FREQ. TO 9695 kHz
	GERMANY †DEUTSCHE WELLE, Nauen	W • C Africa • 500 kW
	DEUTSCHE WELLE, Via Kigali, Rwanda	S • S Africa • 250 kW
		S • C Africa & E Africa • 250 kW
	†DEUTSCHE WELLE, Via Sines, Portugal	W • C Africa & S Africa • 250 kW
	†DEUTSCHE WELLE, Via Sri Lanka	S • C Asia • 250 kW
		W • S Asia • 250 kW
	†DEUTSCHE WELLE, Via Woofferton, UK	W • C Africa • 250 kW
	HUNGARY RADIO BUDAPEST, Jászberény	W • Su • N Europe • 250 kW
	IRAN VO THE ISLAMIC REP, Tehrān	W • Mideast • 500 kW
		W • W Africa & C Africa • 500 kW
	UNITED KINGDOM BBC, Rampisham	S • W Asia • 500 kW
	†BBC, Skelton, Cumbria	W • M-F • W Africa • 300 kW
	†BBC, Via Thailand	W • W Asia • 250 kW
	UNITED NATIONS UNITED NATIONS R, Via Skelton, UK	W • M-F • N Africa • 300 kW
		W • M-F • Mideast • 300 kW
	USA RADIO MARTI, Greenville, NC	W • C America • 250 kW
		C America • 250 kW
	RFE-RL, Via Biblis, Germany	S • E Europe • 100 kW
	†RFE-RL, Via Wertachtal, Germany	W • W Asia & C Asia • 250 kW
	VOA, Via São Tomé	S • C Africa • 100 kW
9570	**AUSTRALIA** †CVC, Via Uzbekistan	W • S Asia • 100 kW
	CHINA †CENTRAL PEOPLE'S BS, Geermu	S • DS-2 • 100 kW
		DS-2 • 100 kW
		Th-Tu • DS-2 • 100 kW
	CHINA R INTL, Kunming	E Africa & S Africa • 150 kW
	CHINA R INTL, Urümqi	S • W Asia • 500 kW
		S • W Asia & S Asia • 500 kW
	CHINA R INTL, Via Cerrik, Albania	N America • 300 kW
	†CHINA R INTL, Via Havana, Cuba	E North Am • 250 kW
	FRANCE †R FRANCE INTL, Via Ascension	S • M-F • W Africa • 250 kW
		S • Sa/Su • W Africa • 250 kW
		S • W Africa • 250 kW
	IRAN VO THE ISLAMIC REP, Sirjan	S • S Europe • 500 kW
	ITALY RAI INTERNATIONAL, Rome	S • E Europe • 100 kW
	KOREA (REPUBLIC) KBS WORLD R, In-Kimjae	SE Asia • 100 kW
	PHILIPPINES RADIO VERITAS ASIA, Palauig	E Asia • 250 kW • ALT. FREQ. TO 9685 kHz
	SPAIN R EXTERIOR ESPANA, Noblejas	S • M-Sa • N Africa & W Africa • 350 kW
		S • M-F • N Africa & W Africa • 350 kW
		S • Su • N Africa & W Africa • 350 kW
		S • Sa/Su • N Africa & W Africa • 350 kW
	THAILAND RADIO THAILAND, Udon Thani	S • E Africa & S Africa • 250 kW
	UNITED KINGDOM †BBC, Via Thailand	S • S Asia • 250 kW
	BBC, Via Zyyi, Cyprus	S • W Asia • 250 kW
	USA R FREE ASIA, Via Saipan, N Marianas	W • E Asia • 100 kW
	VOA, Via Philippines	S • E Asia • 250 kW
9575	**INDIA** ALL INDIA RADIO, Delhi	S Asia • 50/100 kW Irr • DS • 50/100 kW
		DS • 50/100 kW
(con'd)		ENGLISH & HINDI • DS • 50/100 kW

World Time	0 1 2 3 4 5 6 7 8 9 10 11 12 13 14 15 16 17 18 19 20 21 22 23 24

ENGLISH ▬   ARABIC ░░   CHINESE □□□   FRENCH ▭▭   GERMAN ▬▬   RUSSIAN ═══   SPANISH ▭▭   OTHER ▬

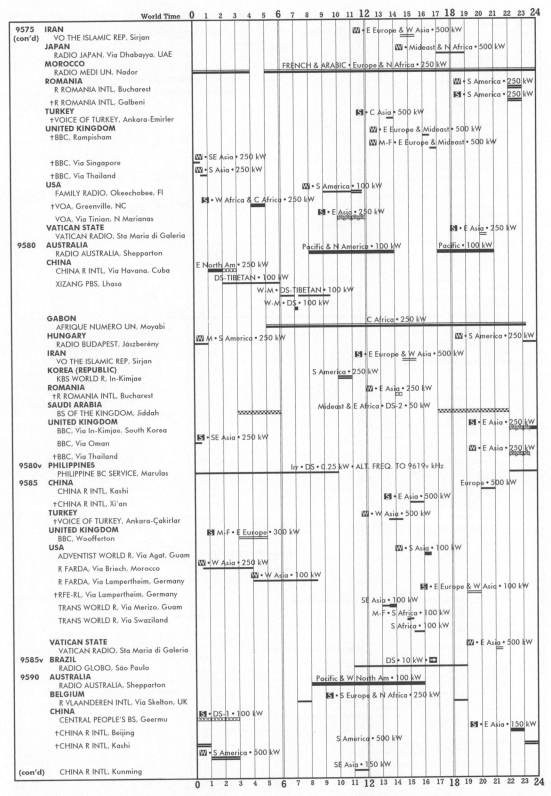

	World Time	0 1 2 3 4 5 6 7 8 9 10 11 12 13 14 15 16 17 18 19 20 21 22 23 24

9575 **IRAN**
(con'd) VO THE ISLAMIC REP, Sirjan — W • E Europe & W Asia • 500 kW
JAPAN
 RADIO JAPAN, Via Dhabayya, UAE — W • Mideast & N Africa • 500 kW
MOROCCO
 RADIO MEDI UN, Nador — FRENCH & ARABIC • Europe & N Africa • 250 kW
ROMANIA
 R ROMANIA INTL, Bucharest — W • S America • 250 kW
 †R ROMANIA INTL, Galbeni — S • S America • 250 kW
TURKEY
 †VOICE OF TURKEY, Ankara-Emirler — S • C Asia • 500 kW
UNITED KINGDOM
 †BBC, Rampisham — W • E Europe & Mideast • 500 kW
 — W M-F • E Europe & Mideast • 500 kW
 †BBC, Via Singapore — W • SE Asia • 250 kW
 †BBC, Via Thailand — W • S Asia • 250 kW
USA
 FAMILY RADIO, Okeechobee, Fl — W • S America • 100 kW
 †VOA, Greenville, NC — S • W Africa & C Africa • 250 kW
 VOA, Via Tinian, N Marianas — S • E Asia • 250 kW
VATICAN STATE
 VATICAN RADIO, Sta Maria di Galeria — S • E Asia • 250 kW
9580 **AUSTRALIA**
 RADIO AUSTRALIA, Shepparton — Pacific & N America • 100 kW — Pacific • 100 kW
CHINA
 CHINA R INTL, Via Havana, Cuba — E North Am • 250 kW
 XIZANG PBS, Lhasa — DS-TIBETAN • 100 kW
 — W-M • DS-TIBETAN • 100 kW
 — W-M • DS • 100 kW
GABON
 AFRIQUE NUMERO UN, Moyabi — C Africa • 250 kW
HUNGARY
 RADIO BUDAPEST, Jászberény — W M • S America • 250 kW — W • S America • 250 kW
IRAN
 VO THE ISLAMIC REP, Sirjan — S • E Europe & W Asia • 500 kW
KOREA (REPUBLIC)
 KBS WORLD R, In-Kimjae — S America • 250 kW
ROMANIA
 †R ROMANIA INTL, Bucharest — W • E Asia • 250 kW
SAUDI ARABIA
 BS OF THE KINGDOM, Jiddah — Mideast & E Africa • DS-2 • 50 kW
UNITED KINGDOM
 BBC, Via In-Kimjae, South Korea — S • E Asia • 250 kW
 BBC, Via Oman — S • SE Asia • 250 kW
 †BBC, Via Thailand — W • E Asia • 250 kW
9580v **PHILIPPINES**
 PHILIPPINE BC SERVICE, Marulas — Irr • DS • 0.25 kW • ALT. FREQ. TO 9619v kHz
9585 **CHINA**
 CHINA R INTL, Kashi — Europe • 500 kW
 †CHINA R INTL, Xi'an — S • E Asia • 500 kW
TURKEY
 †VOICE OF TURKEY, Ankara-Çakirlar — W • W Asia • 500 kW
UNITED KINGDOM
 BBC, Woofferton — S M-F • E Europe • 300 kW
USA
 ADVENTIST WORLD R, Via Agat, Guam — W • S Asia • 100 kW
 R FARDA, Via Briech, Morocco — W • W Asia • 250 kW
 R FARDA, Via Lampertheim, Germany — W • W Asia • 100 kW
 †RFE-RL, Via Lampertheim, Germany — S • E Europe & W Asia • 100 kW
 TRANS WORLD R, Via Merizo, Guam — SE Asia • 100 kW
 TRANS WORLD R, Via Swaziland — M-F • S Africa • 100 kW
 — S Africa • 100 kW
VATICAN STATE
 VATICAN RADIO, Sta Maria di Galeria — W • E Asia • 500 kW
9585v **BRAZIL**
 RADIO GLOBO, São Paulo — DS • 10 kW •
9590 **AUSTRALIA**
 RADIO AUSTRALIA, Shepparton — Pacific & W North Am • 100 kW
BELGIUM
 R VLAANDEREN INTL, Via Skelton, UK — S • S Europe & N Africa • 250 kW
CHINA
 CENTRAL PEOPLE'S BS, Geermu — S • DS-1 • 100 kW
 — S • E Asia • 150 kW
 †CHINA R INTL, Beijing — S America • 500 kW
 †CHINA R INTL, Kashi — W • S America • 500 kW
(con'd) CHINA R INTL, Kunming — SE Asia • 150 kW

SEASONAL S OR W   1-HR TIMESHIFT MIDYEAR ⇐ OR ⇒   JAMMING / OR ⋀   EARLIEST HEARD ◁   LATEST HEARD ▷   NEW FOR 2007 †

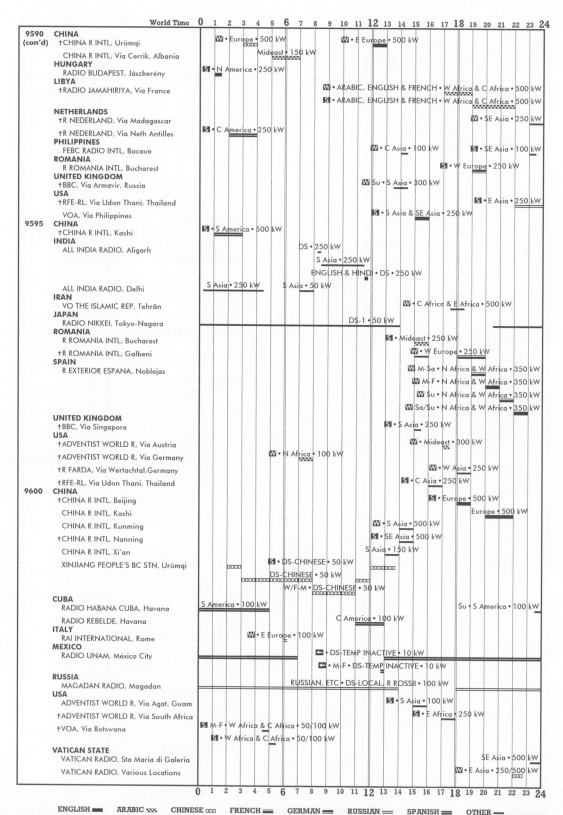

World Time | 0 1 2 3 4 5 6 7 8 9 10 11 12 13 14 15 16 17 18 19 20 21 22 23 24

9590
(con'd) **CHINA**
  †CHINA R INTL, Urümqi — W • Europe • 500 kW / W • E Europe • 500 kW
  CHINA R INTL, Via Cerrik, Albania — Mideast • 150 kW
HUNGARY
  RADIO BUDAPEST, Jászberény — S • N America • 250 kW
LIBYA
  †RADIO JAMAHIRIYA, Via France — W • ARABIC, ENGLISH & FRENCH • W Africa & C Africa • 500 kW / S • ARABIC, ENGLISH & FRENCH • W Africa & C Africa • 500 kW
NETHERLANDS
  †R NEDERLAND, Via Madagascar — W • SE Asia • 250 kW
  †R NEDERLAND, Via Neth Antilles — S • C America • 250 kW
PHILIPPINES
  FEBC RADIO INTL, Bocaue — W • C Asia • 100 kW / S • SE Asia • 100 kW
ROMANIA
  R ROMANIA INTL, Bucharest — S • W Europe • 250 kW
UNITED KINGDOM
  †BBC, Via Armavir, Russia — W Su • S Asia • 300 kW
USA
  †RFE-RL, Via Udon Thani, Thailand — S • E Asia • 250 kW
  VOA, Via Philippines — S • S Asia & SE Asia • 250 kW
9595 **CHINA**
  †CHINA R INTL, Kashi — S • S America • 500 kW
INDIA
  ALL INDIA RADIO, Aligarh — DS • 250 kW / S Asia • 250 kW / ENGLISH & HINDI • DS • 250 kW
  ALL INDIA RADIO, Delhi — S Asia • 250 kW / S Asia • 50 kW
IRAN
  VO THE ISLAMIC REP, Tehrān — W • C Africa & E Africa • 500 kW
JAPAN
  RADIO NIKKEI, Tokyo-Nagara — DS-1 • 50 kW
ROMANIA
  R ROMANIA INTL, Bucharest — S • Mideast • 250 kW
  †R ROMANIA INTL, Galbeni — W • W Europe • 250 kW
SPAIN
  R EXTERIOR ESPANA, Noblejas — W M-Sa • N Africa & W Africa • 350 kW / W M-F • N Africa & W Africa • 350 kW / W Su • N Africa & W Africa • 350 kW / W Sa/Su • N Africa & W Africa • 350 kW
UNITED KINGDOM
  †BBC, Via Singapore — S • S Asia • 250 kW
USA
  †ADVENTIST WORLD R, Via Austria — W • Mideast • 300 kW
  †ADVENTIST WORLD R, Via Germany — W • N Africa • 100 kW
  †R FARDA, Via Wertachtal, Germany — W • W Asia • 250 kW
  †RFE-RL, Via Udon Thani, Thailand — S • C Asia • 250 kW
9600 **CHINA**
  †CHINA R INTL, Beijing — S • Europe • 500 kW
  CHINA R INTL, Kashi — Europe • 500 kW
  CHINA R INTL, Kunming — W • S Asia • 500 kW
  †CHINA R INTL, Nanning — S • SE Asia • 500 kW
  CHINA R INTL, Xi'an — S Asia • 150 kW
  XINJIANG PEOPLE'S BC STN, Urümqi — S • DS-CHINESE • 50 kW / DS-CHINESE • 50 kW / W/F-M • DS-CHINESE • 50 kW
CUBA
  RADIO HABANA CUBA, Havana — S America • 100 kW / Su • S America • 100 kW
  RADIO REBELDE, Havana — C America • 100 kW
ITALY
  RAI INTERNATIONAL, Rome — W • E Europe • 100 kW
MEXICO
  RADIO UNAM, México City — • DS-TEMP INACTIVE • 10 kW / • M-F • DS-TEMP INACTIVE • 10 kW
RUSSIA
  MAGADAN RADIO, Magadan — RUSSIAN, ETC • DS-LOCAL, R ROSSII • 100 kW
USA
  ADVENTIST WORLD R, Via Agat, Guam — S • S Asia • 100 kW
  †ADVENTIST WORLD R, Via South Africa — S • E Africa • 250 kW
  †VOA, Via Botswana — S M-F • W Africa & C Africa • 50/100 kW / S • W Africa & C Africa • 50/100 kW
VATICAN STATE
  VATICAN RADIO, Sta Maria di Galeria — SE Asia • 500 kW
  VATICAN RADIO, Various Locations — W • E Asia • 250/500 kW

0 1 2 3 4 5 6 7 8 9 10 11 12 13 14 15 16 17 18 19 20 21 22 23 24

ENGLISH ▬   ARABIC ∿∿∿   CHINESE □□□   FRENCH ══   GERMAN ▬▬   RUSSIAN ══   SPANISH ══   OTHER ▬

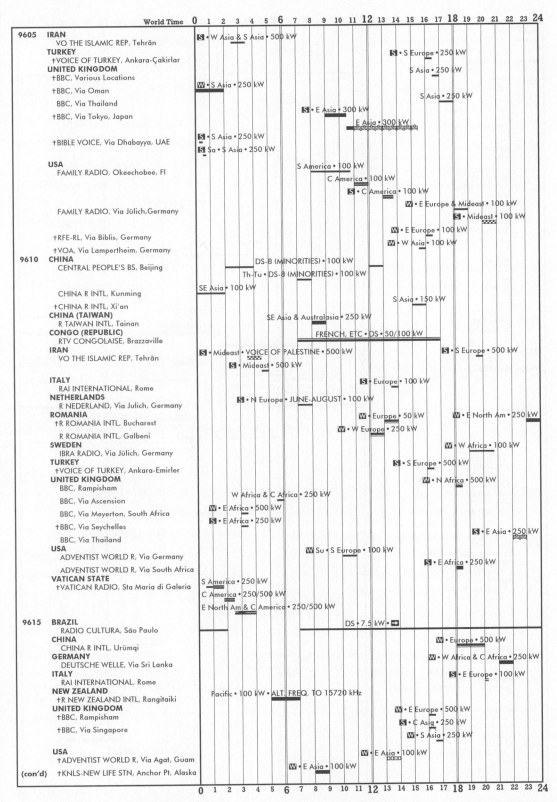

	World Time	0 1 2 3 4 5 6 7 8 9 10 11 12 13 14 15 16 17 18 19 20 21 22 23 24
9605	**IRAN**	
	VO THE ISLAMIC REP, Tehrān	⑤ • W Asia & S Asia • 500 kW
	TURKEY	
	†VOICE OF TURKEY, Ankara-Çakirlar	⑤ • S Europe • 250 kW
	UNITED KINGDOM	
	†BBC, Various Locations	S Asia • 250 kW
	†BBC, Via Oman	ⓦ • S Asia • 250 kW
	BBC, Via Thailand	S Asia • 250 kW
	†BBC, Via Tokyo, Japan	⑤ • E Asia • 300 kW
		E Asia • 300 kW
	†BIBLE VOICE, Via Dhabayya, UAE	⑤ • S Asia • 250 kW
		⑤ Sa • S Asia • 250 kW
	USA	
	FAMILY RADIO, Okeechobee, Fl	S America • 100 kW
		C America • 100 kW
		⑤ • C America • 100 kW
	FAMILY RADIO, Via Jülich, Germany	ⓦ • E Europe & Mideast • 100 kW
		⑤ • Mideast • 100 kW
	†RFE-RL, Via Biblis, Germany	ⓦ • E Europe • 100 kW
	†VOA, Via Lampertheim, Germany	ⓦ • W Asia • 100 kW
9610	**CHINA**	
	CENTRAL PEOPLE'S BS, Beijing	DS-8 (MINORITIES) • 100 kW
		Th-Tu • DS-8 (MINORITIES) • 100 kW
	CHINA R INTL, Kunming	SE Asia • 100 kW
	†CHINA R INTL, Xi'an	S Asia • 150 kW
	CHINA (TAIWAN)	
	R TAIWAN INTL, Tainan	SE Asia & Australasia • 250 kW
	CONGO (REPUBLIC)	
	RTV CONGOLAISE, Brazzaville	FRENCH, ETC • DS • 50/100 kW
	IRAN	
	VO THE ISLAMIC REP, Tehrān	⑤ • Mideast • VOICE OF PALESTINE • 500 kW ⑤ • S Europe • 500 kW
		⑤ • Mideast • 500 kW
	ITALY	
	RAI INTERNATIONAL, Rome	⑤ • Europe • 100 kW
	NETHERLANDS	
	R NEDERLAND, Via Julich, Germany	⑤ • N Europe • JUNE-AUGUST • 100 kW
	ROMANIA	
	†R ROMANIA INTL, Bucharest	ⓦ • Europe • 50 kW ⓦ • E North Am • 250 kW
	R ROMANIA INTL, Galbeni	ⓦ • W Europe • 250 kW
	SWEDEN	
	IBRA RADIO, Via Jülich, Germany	ⓦ • W Africa • 100 kW
	TURKEY	
	†VOICE OF TURKEY, Ankara-Emirler	⑤ • S Europe • 500 kW
	UNITED KINGDOM	
	BBC, Rampisham	ⓦ • N Africa • 500 kW
	BBC, Via Ascension	W Africa & C Africa • 250 kW
	BBC, Via Meyerton, South Africa	ⓦ • E Africa • 500 kW
	†BBC, Via Seychelles	⑤ • E Africa • 250 kW
	BBC, Via Thailand	⑤ • E Asia • 250 kW
	USA	
	ADVENTIST WORLD R, Via Germany	ⓦ Su • S Europe • 100 kW
	ADVENTIST WORLD R, Via South Africa	⑤ • E Africa • 250 kW
	VATICAN STATE	
	†VATICAN RADIO, Sta Maria di Galeria	S America • 250 kW
		C America • 250/500 kW
		E North Am & C America • 250/500 kW
9615	**BRAZIL**	
	RADIO CULTURA, São Paulo	DS • 7.5 kW • ➡
	CHINA	
	CHINA R INTL, Urümqi	ⓦ • Europe • 500 kW
	GERMANY	
	DEUTSCHE WELLE, Via Sri Lanka	ⓦ • W Africa & C Africa • 250 kW
	ITALY	
	RAI INTERNATIONAL, Rome	⑤ • E Europe • 100 kW
	NEW ZEALAND	
	†R NEW ZEALAND INTL, Rangitaiki	Pacific • 100 kW • ALT. FREQ. TO 15720 kHz
	UNITED KINGDOM	
	†BBC, Rampisham	ⓦ • E Europe • 500 kW
		⑤ • C Asia • 250 kW
	†BBC, Via Singapore	ⓦ • S Asia • 250 kW
	USA	
	†ADVENTIST WORLD R, Via Agat, Guam	ⓦ • E Asia • 100 kW
(con'd)	†KNLS-NEW LIFE STN, Anchor Pt, Alaska	ⓦ • E Asia • 100 kW
		0 1 2 3 4 5 6 7 8 9 10 11 12 13 14 15 16 17 18 19 20 21 22 23 24

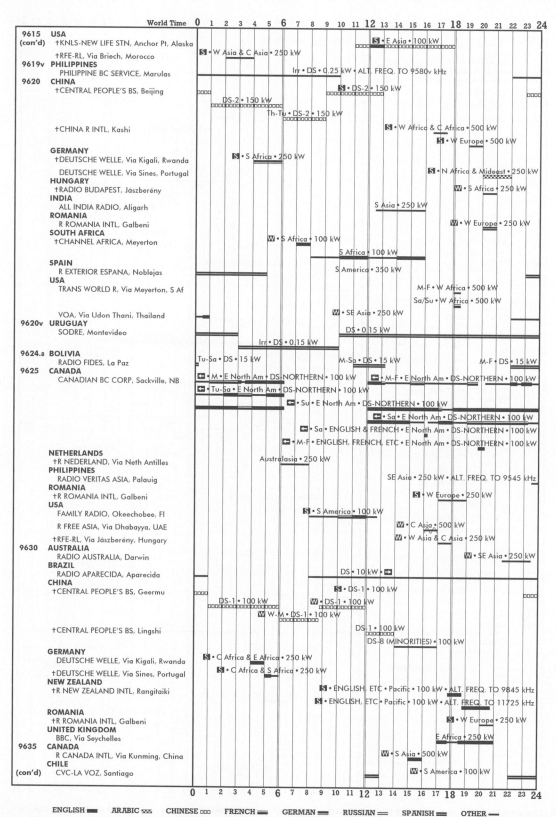

	World Time	0 1 2 3 4 5 6 7 8 9 10 11 12 13 14 15 16 17 18 19 20 21 22 23 24

9615 **USA**
(con'd)   †KNLS-NEW LIFE STN, Anchor Pt, Alaska — ⑤ • E Asia • 100 kW
         †RFE-RL, Via Briech, Morocco — ⑤ • W Asia & C Asia • 250 kW
9619v **PHILIPPINES**
         PHILIPPINE BC SERVICE, Marulas — Irr • DS • 0.25 kW • ALT. FREQ. TO 9580v kHz
9620 **CHINA**
         †CENTRAL PEOPLE'S BS, Beijing — ⑤ • DS-2 • 150 kW / DS-2 • 150 kW / Th-Tu • DS-2 • 150 kW

         †CHINA R INTL, Kashi — ⑤ • W Africa & C Africa • 500 kW / ⑤ • W Europe • 500 kW

      GERMANY
         †DEUTSCHE WELLE, Via Kigali, Rwanda — ⑤ • S Africa • 250 kW
         DEUTSCHE WELLE, Via Sines, Portugal — ⑤ • N Africa & Mideast • 250 kW
      HUNGARY
         †RADIO BUDAPEST, Jászberény — Ⓦ • S Africa • 250 kW
      INDIA
         ALL INDIA RADIO, Aligarh — S Asia • 250 kW
      ROMANIA
         R ROMANIA INTL, Galbeni — Ⓦ • W Europe • 250 kW
      SOUTH AFRICA
         †CHANNEL AFRICA, Meyerton — Ⓦ • S Africa • 100 kW / S Africa • 100 kW

      SPAIN
         R EXTERIOR ESPANA, Noblejas — S America • 350 kW
      USA
         TRANS WORLD R, Via Meyerton, S Af — M-F • W Africa • 500 kW / Sa/Su • W Africa • 500 kW

         VOA, Via Udon Thani, Thailand — Ⓦ • SE Asia • 250 kW
9620v **URUGUAY**
         SODRE, Montevideo — DS • 0.15 kW / Irr • DS • 0.15 kW

9624.8 **BOLIVIA**
         RADIO FIDES, La Paz — Tu-Sa • DS • 15 kW / M-Sa • DS • 15 kW / M-F • DS • 15 kW
9625 **CANADA**
         CANADIAN BC CORP, Sackville, NB — ← • M • E North Am • DS-NORTHERN • 100 kW / ← • M-F • E North Am • DS-NORTHERN • 100 kW
         ← • Tu-Sa • E North Am • DS-NORTHERN • 100 kW
         ← • Su • E North Am • DS-NORTHERN • 100 kW
         ← • Sa • E North Am • DS-NORTHERN • 100 kW
         ← • Sa • ENGLISH & FRENCH • E North Am • DS-NORTHERN • 100 kW
         ← • M-F • ENGLISH, FRENCH, ETC • E North Am • DS-NORTHERN • 100 kW

      NETHERLANDS
         †R NEDERLAND, Via Neth Antilles — Australasia • 250 kW
      PHILIPPINES
         RADIO VERITAS ASIA, Palauig — SE Asia • 250 kW • ALT. FREQ. TO 9545 kHz
      ROMANIA
         †R ROMANIA INTL, Galbeni — ⑤ • W Europe • 250 kW
      USA
         FAMILY RADIO, Okeechobee, Fl — ⑤ • S America • 100 kW
         R FREE ASIA, Via Dhabayya, UAE — Ⓦ • C Asia • 500 kW
         †RFE-RL, Via Jászberény, Hungary — Ⓦ • W Asia & C Asia • 250 kW
9630 **AUSTRALIA**
         RADIO AUSTRALIA, Darwin — Ⓦ • SE Asia • 250 kW
      BRAZIL
         RADIO APARECIDA, Aparecida — DS • 10 kW • →
      CHINA
         †CENTRAL PEOPLE'S BS, Geermu — ⑤ • DS-1 • 100 kW / DS-1 • 100 kW / Ⓦ • DS-1 • 100 kW / Ⓦ W-M • DS-1 • 100 kW

         †CENTRAL PEOPLE'S BS, Lingshi — DS-1 • 100 kW / DS-8 (MINORITIES) • 100 kW

      GERMANY
         DEUTSCHE WELLE, Via Kigali, Rwanda — ⑤ • C Africa & E Africa • 250 kW
         †DEUTSCHE WELLE, Via Sines, Portugal — ⑤ • C Africa & S Africa • 250 kW
      NEW ZEALAND
         †R NEW ZEALAND INTL, Rangitaiki — ⑤ • ENGLISH, ETC • Pacific • 100 kW • ALT. FREQ. TO 9845 kHz / ⑤ • ENGLISH, ETC • Pacific • 100 kW • ALT. FREQ. TO 11725 kHz

      ROMANIA
         †R ROMANIA INTL, Galbeni — ⑤ • W Europe • 250 kW
      UNITED KINGDOM
         BBC, Via Seychelles — E Africa • 250 kW
9635 **CANADA**
         R CANADA INTL, Via Kunming, China — Ⓦ • S Asia • 500 kW
      CHILE
(con'd)   CVC-LA VOZ, Santiago — Ⓦ • S America • 100 kW

	0 1 2 3 4 5 6 7 8 9 10 11 12 13 14 15 16 17 18 19 20 21 22 23 24

ENGLISH ▬▬   ARABIC ≋≋   CHINESE □□□   FRENCH ═══   GERMAN ▭▭   RUSSIAN ══   SPANISH ▭▭   OTHER ▬▬

World Time 0 1 2 3 4 5 6 7 8 9 10 11 12 13 14 15 16 17 18 19 20 21 22 23 24

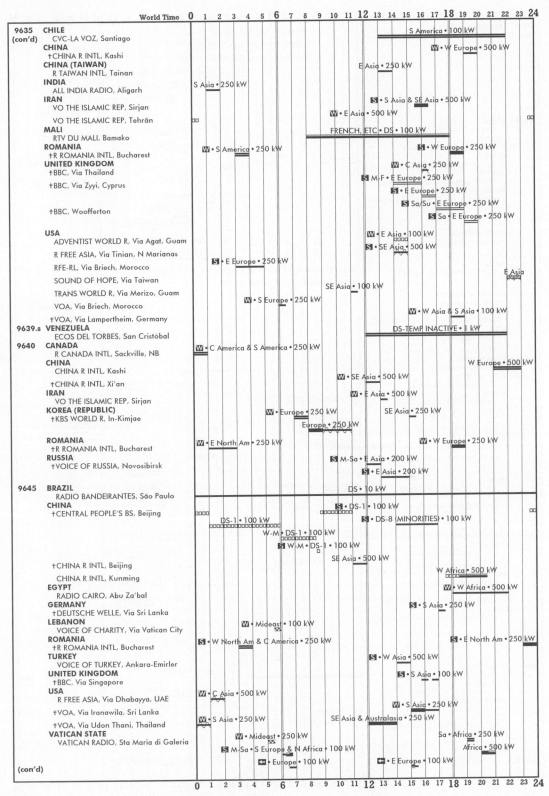

9635 **CHILE**
(con'd)   CVC-LA VOZ, Santiago — S America • 100 kW
CHINA
†CHINA R INTL, Kashi — W • W Europe • 500 kW
CHINA (TAIWAN)
R TAIWAN INTL, Tainan — E Asia • 250 kW
INDIA
ALL INDIA RADIO, Aligarh — S Asia • 250 kW
IRAN
VO THE ISLAMIC REP, Sirjan — S • S Asia & SE Asia • 500 kW
VO THE ISLAMIC REP, Tehrān — W • E Asia • 500 kW
MALI
RTV DU MALI, Bamako — FRENCH, ETC • DS • 100 kW
ROMANIA
†R ROMANIA INTL, Bucharest — W • S America • 250 kW / S • W Europe • 250 kW
UNITED KINGDOM
†BBC, Via Thailand — W • C Asia • 250 kW
— S • M-F • E Europe • 250 kW
†BBC, Via Zyyi, Cyprus — S • E Europe • 250 kW
— S • Sa/Su • E Europe • 250 kW
†BBC, Woofferton — S • Sa • E Europe • 250 kW
USA
ADVENTIST WORLD R, Via Agat, Guam — W • E Asia • 100 kW
— S • SE Asia • 500 kW
R FREE ASIA, Via Tinian, N Marianas — S • E Europe • 250 kW
RFE-RL, Via Briech, Morocco — E Asia
SOUND OF HOPE, Via Taiwan — SE Asia • 100 kW
TRANS WORLD R, Via Merizo, Guam — W • S Europe • 250 kW
VOA, Via Briech, Morocco — W • W Asia & S Asia • 100 kW
†VOA, Via Lampertheim, Germany
9639.8 **VENEZUELA**
ECOS DEL TORBES, San Cristóbal — DS-TEMP INACTIVE • 1 kW
9640 **CANADA**
R CANADA INTL, Sackville, NB — W • C America & S America • 250 kW
CHINA
CHINA R INTL, Kashi — W Europe • 500 kW
†CHINA R INTL, Xi'an — W • SE Asia • 500 kW
IRAN
VO THE ISLAMIC REP, Sirjan — W • E Asia • 500 kW
KOREA (REPUBLIC)
†KBS WORLD R, In-Kimjae — W • Europe • 250 kW / SE Asia • 250 kW
— Europe • 250 kW
ROMANIA
†R ROMANIA INTL, Bucharest — W • E North Am • 250 kW / W • W Europe • 250 kW
RUSSIA
†VOICE OF RUSSIA, Novosibirsk — S • M-Sa • E Asia • 200 kW
— S • E Asia • 200 kW
9645 **BRAZIL**
RADIO BANDEIRANTES, São Paulo — DS • 10 kW
CHINA
†CENTRAL PEOPLE'S BS, Beijing — S • DS-1 • 100 kW
— S • DS-8 (MINORITIES) • 100 kW
— DS-1 • 100 kW
— W-M • DS-1 • 100 kW
— S • W-M • DS-1 • 100 kW
— SE Asia • 500 kW
†CHINA R INTL, Beijing — W Africa • 500 kW
CHINA R INTL, Kunming — W • W Africa • 500 kW
EGYPT
RADIO CAIRO, Abu Za'bal — S • S Asia • 250 kW
GERMANY
†DEUTSCHE WELLE, Via Sri Lanka
LEBANON
VOICE OF CHARITY, Via Vatican City — W • Mideast • 100 kW
ROMANIA
†R ROMANIA INTL, Bucharest — S • W North Am & C America • 250 kW / S • E North Am • 250 kW
TURKEY
VOICE OF TURKEY, Ankara-Emirler — S • W Asia • 500 kW
UNITED KINGDOM
†BBC, Via Singapore — S • S Asia • 100 kW
USA
R FREE ASIA, Via Dhabayya, UAE — W • C Asia • 500 kW
†VOA, Via Iranawila, Sri Lanka — W • S Asia • 250 kW
†VOA, Via Udon Thani, Thailand — W • S Asia • 250 kW
— SE Asia & Australasia • 250 kW
VATICAN STATE
VATICAN RADIO, Sta Maria di Galeria — W • Mideast • 250 kW / Sa • Africa • 250 kW
— S • M-Sa • S Europe & N Africa • 100 kW / Africa • 500 kW
— ⇦ • Europe • 100 kW
— ⇦ • E Europe • 100 kW

(con'd)

0 1 2 3 4 5 6 7 8 9 10 11 12 13 14 15 16 17 18 19 20 21 22 23 24

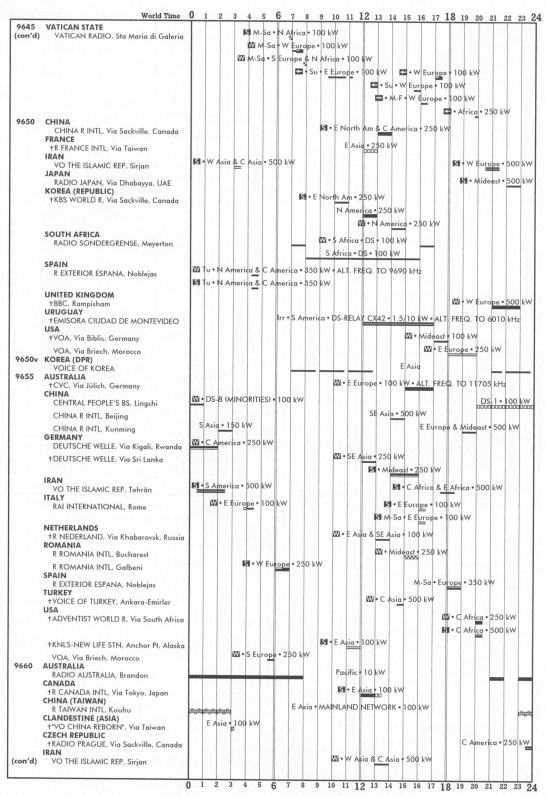

World Time	0 1 2 3 4 5 6 7 8 9 10 11 12 13 14 15 16 17 18 19 20 21 22 23 24

9645 (con'd) VATICAN STATE
VATICAN RADIO, Sta Maria di Galeria
- S • M-Sa • N Africa • 100 kW
- W • M-Sa • W Europe • 100 kW
- W • M-Sa • S Europe & N Africa • 100 kW
- ← • Su • E Europe • 100 kW   ← • W Europe • 100 kW
- ← • Su • W Europe • 100 kW
- ← • M-F • W Europe • 100 kW
- ← • Africa • 250 kW

9650 CHINA
CHINA R INTL, Via Sackville, Canada
- S • E North Am & C America • 250 kW

FRANCE
†R FRANCE INTL, Via Taiwan
- E Asia • 250 kW

IRAN
VO THE ISLAMIC REP, Sirjan
- S • W Asia & C Asia • 500 kW   S • W Europe • 500 kW

JAPAN
RADIO JAPAN, Via Dhabayya, UAE
- S • Mideast • 500 kW

KOREA (REPUBLIC)
†KBS WORLD R, Via Sackville, Canada
- S • E North Am • 250 kW
- N America • 250 kW
- W • N America • 250 kW

SOUTH AFRICA
RADIO SONDERGRENSE, Meyerton
- W • S Africa • DS • 100 kW
- S Africa • DS • 100 kW

SPAIN
R EXTERIOR ESPANA, Noblejas
- W • Tu • N America & C America • 350 kW • ALT. FREQ. TO 9690 kHz
- S • Tu • N America & C America • 350 kW

UNITED KINGDOM
†BBC, Rampisham
- W • W Europe • 500 kW

URUGUAY
†EMISORA CIUDAD DE MONTEVIDEO
- Irr • S America • DS-RELAY CX42 • 1.5/10 kW • ALT. FREQ. TO 6010 kHz

USA
†VOA, Via Biblis, Germany
- W • Mideast • 100 kW

VOA, Via Briech, Morocco
- W • E Europe • 250 kW

9650v KOREA (DPR)
VOICE OF KOREA
- E Asia

9655 AUSTRALIA
†CVC, Via Jülich, Germany
- W • E Europe • 100 kW • ALT. FREQ. TO 11705 kHz

CHINA
CENTRAL PEOPLE'S BS, Lingshi
- W • DS-8 (MINORITIES) • 100 kW   DS-1 • 100 kW

CHINA R INTL, Beijing
- SE Asia • 500 kW

CHINA R INTL, Kunming
- S Asia • 150 kW   E Europe & Mideast • 500 kW

GERMANY
DEUTSCHE WELLE, Via Kigali, Rwanda
- W • C America • 250 kW

†DEUTSCHE WELLE, Via Sri Lanka
- W • SE Asia • 250 kW
- S • Mideast • 250 kW

IRAN
VO THE ISLAMIC REP, Tehrān
- S • S America • 500 kW   S • C Africa & E Africa • 500 kW

ITALY
RAI INTERNATIONAL, Rome
- W • E Europe • 100 kW
- W • E Europe • 100 kW
- S • M-Sa • E Europe • 100 kW

NETHERLANDS
†R NEDERLAND, Via Khabarovsk, Russia
- W • E Asia & SE Asia • 100 kW

ROMANIA
R ROMANIA INTL, Bucharest
- W • Mideast • 250 kW

R ROMANIA INTL, Galbeni
- S • W Europe • 250 kW

SPAIN
R EXTERIOR ESPANA, Noblejas
- M-Sa • Europe • 350 kW

TURKEY
†VOICE OF TURKEY, Ankara-Emirler
- W • C Asia • 500 kW

USA
†ADVENTIST WORLD R, Via South Africa
- W • C Africa • 250 kW
- S • C Africa • 500 kW

†KNLS-NEW LIFE STN, Anchor Pt, Alaska
- S • E Asia • 100 kW

VOA, Via Briech, Morocco
- W • S Europe • 250 kW

9660 AUSTRALIA
RADIO AUSTRALIA, Brandon
- Pacific • 10 kW

CANADA
†R CANADA INTL, Via Tokyo, Japan
- S • E Asia • 100 kW

CHINA (TAIWAN)
R TAIWAN INTL, Kouhu
- E Asia • MAINLAND NETWORK • 100 kW

CLANDESTINE (ASIA)
†"VO CHINA REBORN", Via Taiwan
- E Asia • 100 kW

CZECH REPUBLIC
†RADIO PRAGUE, Via Sackville, Canada
- C America • 250 kW

IRAN
(con'd) VO THE ISLAMIC REP, Sirjan
- W • W Asia & C Asia • 500 kW

World Time	0 1 2 3 4 5 6 7 8 9 10 11 12 13 14 15 16 17 18 19 20 21 22 23 24

ENGLISH ▬   ARABIC ≋   CHINESE ▫▫▫   FRENCH ══   GERMAN ▬   RUSSIAN ═   SPANISH ▬   OTHER ▬

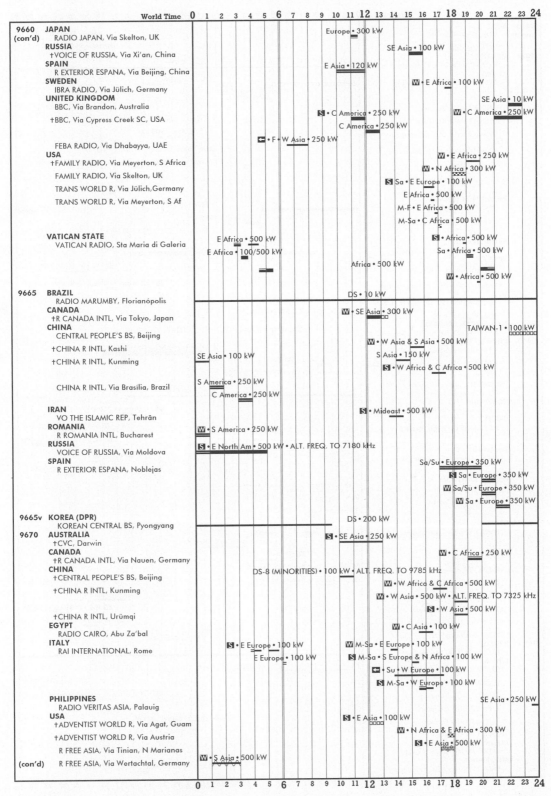

World Time 0 1 2 3 4 5 6 7 8 9 10 11 12 13 14 15 16 17 18 19 20 21 22 23 24

9660
(con'd) **JAPAN**
  RADIO JAPAN, Via Skelton, UK — Europe • 300 kW
RUSSIA
  †VOICE OF RUSSIA, Via Xi'an, China — SE Asia • 100 kW
SPAIN
  R EXTERIOR ESPANA, Via Beijing, China — E Asia • 120 kW
SWEDEN
  IBRA RADIO, Via Jülich, Germany — W • E Africa • 100 kW
UNITED KINGDOM
  BBC, Via Brandon, Australia — SE Asia • 10 kW
  †BBC, Via Cypress Creek SC, USA — S • C America • 250 kW / W • C America • 250 kW / C America • 250 kW
  FEBA RADIO, Via Dhabayya, UAE — ← • F • W Asia • 250 kW
USA
  †FAMILY RADIO, Via Meyerton, S Africa — W • E Africa • 250 kW
  FAMILY RADIO, Via Skelton, UK — W • N Africa • 300 kW
  TRANS WORLD R, Via Jülich, Germany — S • Sa • E Europe • 100 kW
  TRANS WORLD R, Via Meyerton, S Af — E Africa • 500 kW / M-F • E Africa • 500 kW / M-Sa • C Africa • 500 kW
VATICAN STATE
  VATICAN RADIO, Sta Maria di Galeria — E Africa • 500 kW / E Africa • 100/500 kW / S • Africa • 500 kW / Sa • Africa • 500 kW / Africa • 500 kW / W • Africa • 500 kW

9665 **BRAZIL**
  RADIO MARUMBY, Florianópolis — DS • 10 kW
CANADA
  †R CANADA INTL, Via Tokyo, Japan — W • SE Asia • 300 kW
CHINA
  CENTRAL PEOPLE'S BS, Beijing — TAIWAN-1 • 100 kW
  †CHINA R INTL, Kashi — W • W Asia & S Asia • 500 kW
  †CHINA R INTL, Kunming — S Asia • 150 kW / S • W Africa & C Africa • 500 kW
  CHINA R INTL, Via Brasilia, Brazil — SE Asia • 100 kW / S America • 250 kW / C America • 250 kW
IRAN
  VO THE ISLAMIC REP, Tehrān — S • Mideast • 500 kW
ROMANIA
  R ROMANIA INTL, Bucharest — W • S America • 250 kW
RUSSIA
  VOICE OF RUSSIA, Via Moldova — S • E North Am • 500 kW • ALT. FREQ. TO 7180 kHz
SPAIN
  R EXTERIOR ESPANA, Noblejas — Sa/Su • Europe • 350 kW / S • Sa • Europe • 350 kW / W • Sa/Su • Europe • 350 kW / W • Sa • Europe • 350 kW

9665v **KOREA (DPR)**
  KOREAN CENTRAL BS, Pyongyang — DS • 200 kW
9670 **AUSTRALIA**
  †CVC, Darwin — S • SE Asia • 250 kW
CANADA
  †R CANADA INTL, Via Nauen, Germany — W • C Africa • 250 kW
CHINA
  †CENTRAL PEOPLE'S BS, Beijing — DS-8 (MINORITIES) • 100 kW • ALT. FREQ. TO 9785 kHz
  †CHINA R INTL, Kunming — W • W Africa & C Africa • 500 kW / W • W Asia • 500 kW • ALT. FREQ. TO 7325 kHz
  †CHINA R INTL, Urümqi — S • W Asia • 500 kW
EGYPT
  RADIO CAIRO, Abu Za'bal — W • C Asia • 100 kW
ITALY
  RAI INTERNATIONAL, Rome — S • E Europe • 100 kW / E Europe • 100 kW / W M-Sa • E Europe • 100 kW / S M-Sa • S Europe & N Africa • 100 kW / ← • Su • W Europe • 100 kW / S M-Sa • W Europe • 100 kW
PHILIPPINES
  RADIO VERITAS ASIA, Palauig — SE Asia • 250 kW
USA
  †ADVENTIST WORLD R, Via Agat, Guam — S • E Asia • 100 kW
  †ADVENTIST WORLD R, Via Austria — W • N Africa & E Africa • 300 kW
  R FREE ASIA, Via Tinian, N Marianas — S • E Asia • 500 kW
(con'd) R FREE ASIA, Via Wertachtal, Germany — W • S Asia • 500 kW

0 1 2 3 4 5 6 7 8 9 10 11 12 13 14 15 16 17 18 19 20 21 22 23 24

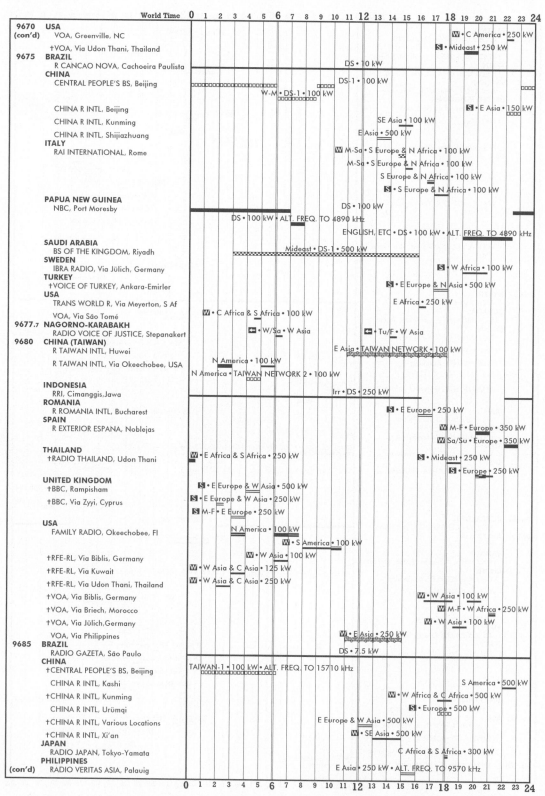

World Time 0 1 2 3 4 5 6 7 8 9 10 11 12 13 14 15 16 17 18 19 20 21 22 23 24

9670 (con'd)	**USA**
	VOA, Greenville, NC
	†VOA, Via Udon Thani, Thailand
9675	**BRAZIL**
	R CANCAO NOVA, Cachoeira Paulista
	CHINA
	CENTRAL PEOPLE'S BS, Beijing
	CHINA R INTL, Beijing
	CHINA R INTL, Kunming
	CHINA R INTL, Shijiazhuang
	ITALY
	RAI INTERNATIONAL, Rome
	PAPUA NEW GUINEA
	NBC, Port Moresby
	SAUDI ARABIA
	BS OF THE KINGDOM, Riyadh
	SWEDEN
	IBRA RADIO, Via Jülich, Germany
	TURKEY
	†VOICE OF TURKEY, Ankara-Emirler
	USA
	TRANS WORLD R, Via Meyerton, S Af
	VOA, Via São Tomé
9677.7	**NAGORNO-KARABAKH**
	RADIO VOICE OF JUSTICE, Stepanakert
9680	**CHINA (TAIWAN)**
	R TAIWAN INTL, Huwei
	R TAIWAN INTL, Via Okeechobee, USA
	INDONESIA
	RRI, Cimanggis, Jawa
	ROMANIA
	R ROMANIA INTL, Bucharest
	SPAIN
	R EXTERIOR ESPANA, Noblejas
	THAILAND
	†RADIO THAILAND, Udon Thani
	UNITED KINGDOM
	†BBC, Rampisham
	†BBC, Via Zyyi, Cyprus
	USA
	FAMILY RADIO, Okeechobee, Fl
	†RFE-RL, Via Biblis, Germany
	†RFE-RL, Via Kuwait
	†RFE-RL, Via Udon Thani, Thailand
	†VOA, Via Biblis, Germany
	†VOA, Via Briech, Morocco
	†VOA, Via Jülich, Germany
	VOA, Via Philippines
9685	**BRAZIL**
	RADIO GAZETA, São Paulo
	CHINA
	†CENTRAL PEOPLE'S BS, Beijing
	CHINA R INTL, Kashi
	†CHINA R INTL, Kunming
	CHINA R INTL, Urümqi
	†CHINA R INTL, Various Locations
	†CHINA R INTL, Xi'an
	JAPAN
	RADIO JAPAN, Tokyo-Yamata
	PHILIPPINES
(con'd)	RADIO VERITAS ASIA, Palauig

Data labels visible on chart:

- W • C America • 250 kW
- S • Mideast • 250 kW
- DS • 10 kW
- DS-1 • 100 kW
- W-M • DS-1 • 100 kW
- S • E Asia • 150 kW
- SE Asia • 100 kW
- E Asia • 500 kW
- W M-Sa • S Europe & N Africa • 100 kW
- M-Sa • S Europe & N Africa • 100 kW
- S Europe & N Africa • 100 kW
- S • S Europe & N Africa • 100 kW
- DS • 100 kW
- DS • 100 kW • ALT. FREQ. TO 4890 kHz
- ENGLISH, ETC • DS • 100 kW • ALT. FREQ. TO 4890 kHz
- Mideast • DS-1 • 500 kW
- S • W Africa • 100 kW
- S • E Europe & N Asia • 500 kW
- E Africa • 250 kW
- W • C Africa & S Africa • 100 kW
- • W/Sa • W Asia
- • Tu/F • W Asia
- E Asia • TAIWAN NETWORK • 100 kW
- N America • 100 kW
- N America • TAIWAN NETWORK 2 • 100 kW
- Irr • DS • 250 kW
- S • E Europe • 250 kW
- W M-F • Europe • 350 kW
- W Sa/Su • Europe • 350 kW
- W • E Africa & S Africa • 250 kW
- S • Mideast • 250 kW
- S • Europe • 250 kW
- S • E Europe & W Asia • 500 kW
- S • E Europe & W Asia • 250 kW
- S M-F • E Europe • 250 kW
- N America • 100 kW
- W • S America • 100 kW
- W • W Asia • 100 kW
- W • W Asia & C Asia • 125 kW
- W • W Asia & C Asia • 250 kW
- W • W Asia • 100 kW
- W M-F • W Africa • 250 kW
- W • W Asia • 100 kW
- W • E Asia • 250 kW
- DS • 7.5 kW
- TAIWAN-1 • 100 kW • ALT. FREQ. TO 15710 kHz
- S America • 500 kW
- W • W Africa & C Africa • 500 kW
- S • Europe • 500 kW
- E Europe & W Asia • 500 kW
- W • SE Asia • 500 kW
- C Africa & S Africa • 300 kW
- E Asia • 250 kW • ALT. FREQ. TO 9570 kHz

0 1 2 3 4 5 6 7 8 9 10 11 12 13 14 15 16 17 18 19 20 21 22 23 24

ENGLISH ▬▬   ARABIC ░░   CHINESE ▫▫▫   FRENCH ▬▬   GERMAN ▬▬   RUSSIAN ═══   SPANISH ▬▬   OTHER ▬

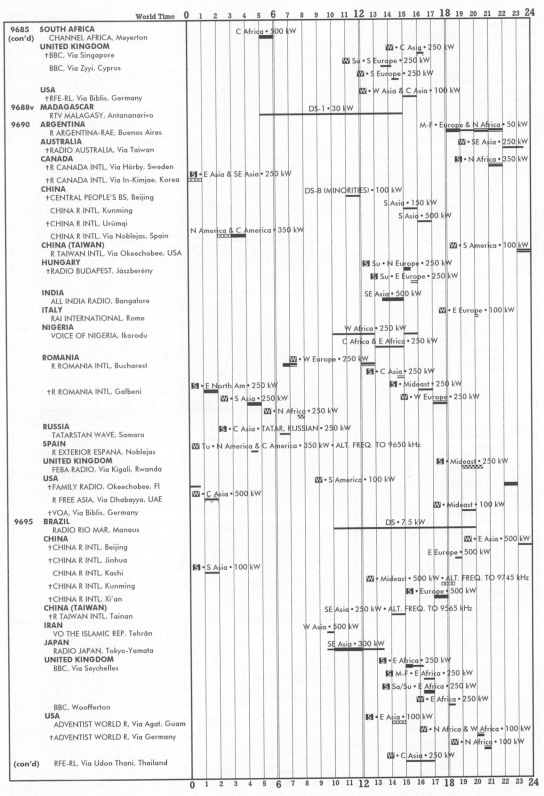

World Time 0 1 2 3 4 5 6 7 8 9 10 11 12 13 14 15 16 17 18 19 20 21 22 23 24

9685 (con'd)	SOUTH AFRICA
	CHANNEL AFRICA, Meyerton — C Africa • 500 kW
	UNITED KINGDOM
	†BBC, Via Singapore — W • C Asia • 250 kW
	— W Su • S Europe • 250 kW
	BBC, Via Zyyi, Cyprus — W • S Europe • 250 kW
	USA
	†RFE-RL, Via Biblis, Germany — W • W Asia & C Asia • 100 kW
9688v	MADAGASCAR
	RTV MALAGASY, Antananarivo — DS-1 • 30 kW
9690	ARGENTINA
	R ARGENTINA-RAE, Buenos Aires — M-F • Europe & N Africa • 50 kW
	AUSTRALIA
	†RADIO AUSTRALIA, Via Taiwan — W • SE Asia • 250 kW
	CANADA
	†R CANADA INTL, Via Hörby, Sweden — S • N Africa • 350 kW
	†R CANADA INTL, Via In-Kimjae, Korea — S • E Asia & SE Asia • 250 kW
	CHINA
	†CENTRAL PEOPLE'S BS, Beijing — DS-8 (MINORITIES) • 100 kW
	CHINA R INTL, Kunming — S Asia • 150 kW
	†CHINA R INTL, Urümqi — S Asia • 500 kW
	CHINA R INTL, Via Noblejas, Spain — N America & C America • 350 kW
	CHINA (TAIWAN)
	R TAIWAN INTL, Via Okeechobee, USA — W • S America • 100 kW
	HUNGARY
	†RADIO BUDAPEST, Jászberény — S Su • N Europe • 250 kW
	— S Su • E Europe • 250 kW
	INDIA
	ALL INDIA RADIO, Bangalore — SE Asia • 500 kW
	ITALY
	RAI INTERNATIONAL, Rome — W • E Europe • 100 kW
	NIGERIA
	VOICE OF NIGERIA, Ikorodu — W Africa • 250 kW
	— C Africa & E Africa • 250 kW
	ROMANIA
	R ROMANIA INTL, Bucharest — W • W Europe • 250 kW
	— S • C Asia • 250 kW
	— S • Mideast • 250 kW
	†R ROMANIA INTL, Galbeni — S • E North Am • 250 kW
	— W • S Asia • 250 kW — W • W Europe • 250 kW
	— W • N Africa • 250 kW
	RUSSIA
	TATARSTAN WAVE, Samara — S • C Asia • TATAR, RUSSIAN • 250 kW
	SPAIN
	R EXTERIOR ESPANA, Noblejas — W Tu • N America & C America • 350 kW • ALT. FREQ. TO 9650 kHz
	UNITED KINGDOM
	FEBA RADIO, Via Kigali, Rwanda — S • Mideast • 250 kW
	USA
	†FAMILY RADIO, Okeechobee, Fl — W • S America • 100 kW
	R FREE ASIA, Via Dhabayya, UAE — W • C Asia • 500 kW
	— W • Mideast • 100 kW
	†VOA, Via Biblis, Germany
9695	BRAZIL
	RADIO RIO MAR, Manaus — DS • 7.5 kW
	CHINA
	†CHINA R INTL, Beijing — W • E Asia • 500 kW
	†CHINA R INTL, Jinhua — E Europe • 500 kW
	CHINA R INTL, Kashi — S • S Asia • 100 kW
	†CHINA R INTL, Kunming — W • Mideast • 500 kW • ALT. FREQ. TO 9745 kHz
	†CHINA R INTL, Xi'an — S • Europe • 500 kW
	CHINA (TAIWAN)
	†R TAIWAN INTL, Tainan — SE Asia • 250 kW • ALT. FREQ. TO 9565 kHz
	IRAN
	VO THE ISLAMIC REP, Tehrān — W Asia • 500 kW
	JAPAN
	RADIO JAPAN, Tokyo-Yamata — SE Asia • 300 kW
	UNITED KINGDOM
	BBC, Via Seychelles — S • E Africa • 250 kW
	— S M-F • E Africa • 250 kW
	— S Sa/Su • E Africa • 250 kW
	— W • E Africa • 250 kW
	BBC, Woofferton
	USA
	ADVENTIST WORLD R, Via Agat, Guam — S • E Asia • 100 kW
	†ADVENTIST WORLD R, Via Germany — W • N Africa & W Africa • 100 kW
	— W • N Africa • 100 kW
(con'd)	RFE-RL, Via Udon Thani, Thailand — W • C Asia • 250 kW

0 1 2 3 4 5 6 7 8 9 10 11 12 13 14 15 16 17 18 19 20 21 22 23 24

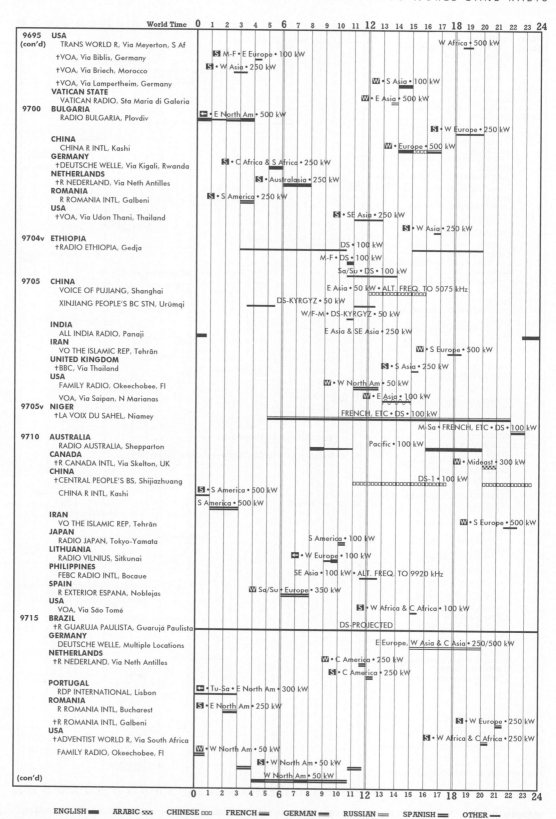

World Time | 0 1 2 3 4 5 6 7 8 9 10 11 12 13 14 15 16 17 18 19 20 21 22 23 24

9695 (con'd) USA
TRANS WORLD R, Via Meyerton, S Af — W Africa • 500 kW
†VOA, Via Biblis, Germany — S M-F • E Europe • 100 kW
†VOA, Via Briech, Morocco — S • W Asia • 250 kW
†VOA, Via Lampertheim, Germany — W • S Asia • 100 kW
VATICAN STATE
VATICAN RADIO, Sta Maria di Galeria — W • E Asia • 500 kW
9700 BULGARIA
RADIO BULGARIA, Plovdiv — E North Am • 500 kW; S • W Europe • 250 kW
CHINA
CHINA R INTL, Kashi — W • Europe • 500 kW
GERMANY
†DEUTSCHE WELLE, Via Kigali, Rwanda — S • C Africa & S Africa • 250 kW
NETHERLANDS
†R NEDERLAND, Via Neth Antilles — S • Australasia • 250 kW
ROMANIA
R ROMANIA INTL, Galbeni — S • S America • 250 kW
USA
†VOA, Via Udon Thani, Thailand — S • SE Asia • 250 kW; S • W Asia • 250 kW

9704v ETHIOPIA
†RADIO ETHIOPIA, Gedja — DS • 100 kW; M-F • DS • 100 kW; Sa/Su • DS • 100 kW

9705 CHINA
VOICE OF PUJIANG, Shanghai — E Asia • 50 kW • ALT. FREQ. TO 5075 kHz
XINJIANG PEOPLE'S BC STN, Urümqi — DS-KYRGYZ • 50 kW; W/F-M • DS-KYRGYZ • 50 kW
INDIA
ALL INDIA RADIO, Panaji — E Asia & SE Asia • 250 kW
IRAN
VO THE ISLAMIC REP, Tehrān — W • S Europe • 500 kW
UNITED KINGDOM
†BBC, Via Thailand — S • S Asia • 250 kW
USA
FAMILY RADIO, Okeechobee, Fl — W • W North Am • 50 kW
VOA, Via Saipan, N Marianas — W • E Asia • 100 kW
9705v NIGER
†LA VOIX DU SAHEL, Niamey — FRENCH, ETC • DS • 100 kW; M-Sa • FRENCH, ETC • DS • 100 kW

9710 AUSTRALIA
RADIO AUSTRALIA, Shepparton — Pacific • 100 kW
CANADA
†R CANADA INTL, Via Skelton, UK — W • Mideast • 300 kW
CHINA
†CENTRAL PEOPLE'S BS, Shijiazhuang — DS-1 • 100 kW
CHINA R INTL, Kashi — S • S America • 500 kW; S America • 500 kW
IRAN
VO THE ISLAMIC REP, Tehrān — W • S Europe • 500 kW
JAPAN
RADIO JAPAN, Tokyo-Yamata — S America • 100 kW
LITHUANIA
RADIO VILNIUS, Sitkunai — W Europe • 100 kW
PHILIPPINES
FEBC RADIO INTL, Bocaue — SE Asia • 100 kW • ALT. FREQ. TO 9920 kHz
SPAIN
R EXTERIOR ESPANA, Noblejas — W Sa/Su • Europe • 350 kW
USA
VOA, Via São Tomé — S • W Africa & C Africa • 100 kW
9715 BRAZIL
†R GUARUJA PAULISTA, Guarujá Paulista — DS-PROJECTED
GERMANY
DEUTSCHE WELLE, Multiple Locations — E Europe, W Asia & C Asia • 250/500 kW
NETHERLANDS
†R NEDERLAND, Via Neth Antilles — W • C America • 250 kW; S • C America • 250 kW
PORTUGAL
RDP INTERNATIONAL, Lisbon — Tu-Sa • E North Am • 300 kW
ROMANIA
R ROMANIA INTL, Bucharest — S • E North Am • 250 kW
†R ROMANIA INTL, Galbeni — S • W Europe • 250 kW
USA
†ADVENTIST WORLD R, Via South Africa — S • W Africa & C Africa • 250 kW
FAMILY RADIO, Okeechobee, Fl — W • W North Am • 50 kW; S • W North Am • 50 kW; W North Am • 50 kW

(con'd)

0 1 2 3 4 5 6 7 8 9 10 11 12 13 14 15 16 17 18 19 20 21 22 23 24

ENGLISH ▬ ARABIC ⋙ CHINESE □□□ FRENCH ▬ GERMAN ▬ RUSSIAN ═ SPANISH ▬ OTHER ▬

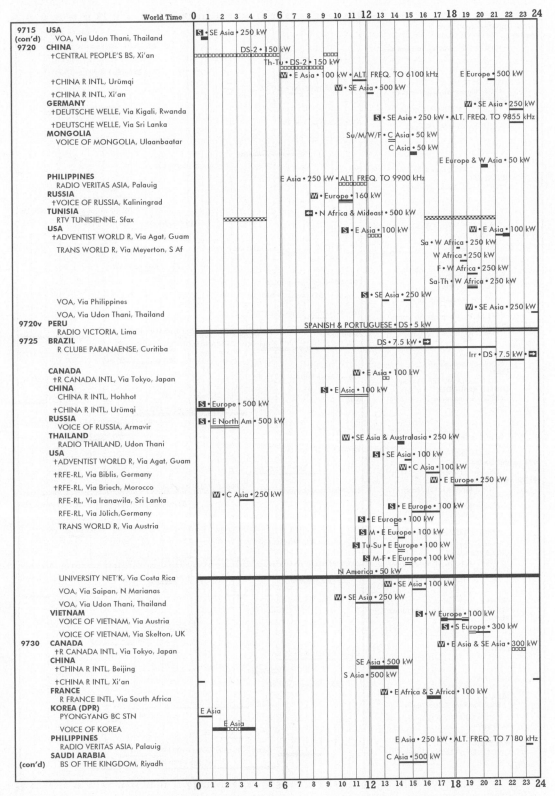

World Time

9715 (con'd)	**USA**	
	VOA, Via Udon Thani, Thailand	S • SE Asia • 250 kW
9720	**CHINA**	
	†CENTRAL PEOPLE'S BS, Xi'an	DS-2 • 150 kW
		Th-Tu • DS-2 • 150 kW
	†CHINA R INTL, Urümqi	W • E Asia • 100 kW • ALT. FREQ. TO 6100 kHz E Europe • 500 kW
	†CHINA R INTL, Xi'an	W • SE Asia • 500 kW
	GERMANY	
	†DEUTSCHE WELLE, Via Kigali, Rwanda	W • SE Asia • 250 kW
	†DEUTSCHE WELLE, Via Sri Lanka	S • SE Asia • 250 kW • ALT. FREQ. TO 9855 kHz
	MONGOLIA	
	VOICE OF MONGOLIA, Ulaanbaatar	Su/M/W/F • C Asia • 50 kW
		C Asia • 50 kW
		E Europe & W Asia • 50 kW
	PHILIPPINES	
	RADIO VERITAS ASIA, Palauig	E Asia • 250 kW • ALT. FREQ. TO 9900 kHz
	RUSSIA	
	†VOICE OF RUSSIA, Kaliningrad	W • Europe • 160 kW
	TUNISIA	
	RTV TUNISIENNE, Sfax	⇦ • N Africa & Mideast • 500 kW
	USA	
	†ADVENTIST WORLD R, Via Agat, Guam	S • E Asia • 100 kW W • E Asia • 100 kW
	TRANS WORLD R, Via Meyerton, S Af	Sa • W Africa • 250 kW
		W Africa • 250 kW
		F • W Africa • 250 kW
		Sa-Th • W Africa • 250 kW
	VOA, Via Philippines	S • SE Asia • 250 kW
	VOA, Via Udon Thani, Thailand	W • SE Asia • 250 kW
9720v	**PERU**	
	RADIO VICTORIA, Lima	SPANISH & PORTUGUESE • DS • 5 kW
9725	**BRAZIL**	
	R CLUBE PARANAENSE, Curitiba	DS • 7.5 kW • ⇨
		Irr • DS • 7.5 kW • ⇨
	CANADA	
	†R CANADA INTL, Via Tokyo, Japan	W • E Asia • 100 kW
	CHINA	
	CHINA R INTL, Hohhot	S • E Asia • 100 kW
	†CHINA R INTL, Urümqi	S • Europe • 500 kW
	RUSSIA	
	VOICE OF RUSSIA, Armavir	S • E North Am • 500 kW
	THAILAND	
	RADIO THAILAND, Udon Thani	W • SE Asia & Australasia • 250 kW
	USA	
	†ADVENTIST WORLD R, Via Agat, Guam	S • SE Asia • 100 kW
	†RFE-RL, Via Biblis, Germany	W • C Asia • 100 kW
	†RFE-RL, Via Briech, Morocco	W • E Europe • 250 kW
	RFE-RL, Via Iranawila, Sri Lanka	W • C Asia • 250 kW
	RFE-RL, Via Jülich, Germany	S • E Europe • 100 kW
	TRANS WORLD R, Via Austria	S • E Europe • 100 kW
		S • M • E Europe • 100 kW
		S Tu-Su • E Europe • 100 kW
		S M-F • E Europe • 100 kW
		N America • 50 kW
	UNIVERSITY NET'K, Via Costa Rica	
	VOA, Via Saipan, N Marianas	W • SE Asia • 100 kW
	VOA, Via Udon Thani, Thailand	W • SE Asia • 250 kW
	VIETNAM	
	VOICE OF VIETNAM, Via Austria	S • W Europe • 100 kW
	VOICE OF VIETNAM, Via Skelton, UK	S • S Europe • 300 kW
9730	**CANADA**	
	†R CANADA INTL, Via Tokyo, Japan	W • E Asia & SE Asia • 300 kW
	CHINA	
	†CHINA R INTL, Beijing	SE Asia • 500 kW
	†CHINA R INTL, Xi'an	S Asia • 500 kW
	FRANCE	
	R FRANCE INTL, Via South Africa	W • E Africa & S Africa • 100 kW
	KOREA (DPR)	
	PYONGYANG BC STN	E Asia
	VOICE OF KOREA	E Asia
	PHILIPPINES	
	RADIO VERITAS ASIA, Palauig	E Asia • 250 kW • ALT. FREQ. TO 7180 kHz
	SAUDI ARABIA	
(con'd)	BS OF THE KINGDOM, Riyadh	C Asia • 500 kW

0 1 2 3 4 5 6 7 8 9 10 11 12 13 14 15 16 17 18 19 20 21 22 23 24

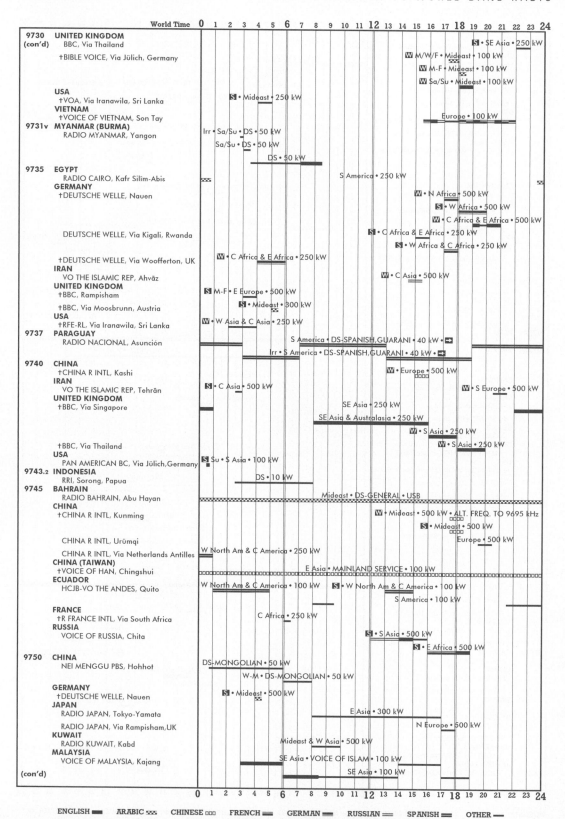

World Time

9730 UNITED KINGDOM (con'd)
BBC, Via Thailand — S • SE Asia • 250 kW
†BIBLE VOICE, Via Jülich, Germany — W M/W/F • Mideast • 100 kW / W M-F • Mideast • 100 kW / W Sa/Su • Mideast • 100 kW

USA
†VOA, Via Iranawila, Sri Lanka — S • Mideast • 250 kW
VIETNAM
†VOICE OF VIETNAM, Son Tay — Europe • 100 kW
9731v MYANMAR (BURMA)
RADIO MYANMAR, Yangon — Irr • Sa/Su • DS • 50 kW / Sa/Su • DS • 50 kW / DS • 50 kW

9735 EGYPT
RADIO CAIRO, Kafr Silīm-Abis — S America • 250 kW
GERMANY
†DEUTSCHE WELLE, Nauen — W • N Africa • 500 kW / S • W Africa • 500 kW / W • C Africa & E Africa • 500 kW
DEUTSCHE WELLE, Via Kigali, Rwanda — S • C Africa & E Africa • 250 kW / S • W Africa & C Africa • 250 kW
†DEUTSCHE WELLE, Via Woofferton, UK — W • C Africa & E Africa • 250 kW
IRAN
VO THE ISLAMIC REP, Ahvāz — W • C Asia • 500 kW
UNITED KINGDOM
†BBC, Rampisham — S M-F • E Europe • 500 kW
†BBC, Via Moosbrunn, Austria — S • Mideast • 300 kW
USA
†RFE-RL, Via Iranawila, Sri Lanka — W • W Asia & C Asia • 250 kW
9737 PARAGUAY
RADIO NACIONAL, Asunción — S America • DS-SPANISH, GUARANI • 40 kW • ➡ / Irr • S America • DS-SPANISH, GUARANI • 40 kW • ➡

9740 CHINA
†CHINA R INTL, Kashi — W • Europe • 500 kW
IRAN
VO THE ISLAMIC REP, Tehrān — S • C Asia • 500 kW / W • S Europe • 500 kW
UNITED KINGDOM
†BBC, Via Singapore — SE Asia • 250 kW / SE Asia & Australasia • 250 kW / W • S Asia • 250 kW / W • S Asia • 250 kW
†BBC, Via Thailand
USA
PAN AMERICAN BC, Via Jülich, Germany — S Su • S Asia • 100 kW
9743.2 INDONESIA
RRI, Sorong, Papua — DS • 10 kW
9745 BAHRAIN
RADIO BAHRAIN, Abu Hayan — Mideast • DS-GENERAL • USB
CHINA
†CHINA R INTL, Kunming — W • Mideast • 500 kW • ALT. FREQ. TO 9695 kHz / S • Mideast • 500 kW / Europe • 500 kW
CHINA R INTL, Urümqi
CHINA R INTL, Via Netherlands Antilles — W North Am & C America • 250 kW
CHINA (TAIWAN)
†VOICE OF HAN, Chingshui — E Asia • MAINLAND SERVICE • 100 kW
ECUADOR
HCJB-VO THE ANDES, Quito — W North Am & C America • 100 kW / S • W North Am & C America • 100 kW / S America • 100 kW
FRANCE
†R FRANCE INTL, Via South Africa — C Africa • 250 kW
RUSSIA
VOICE OF RUSSIA, Chita — S • S Asia • 500 kW / S • E Africa • 500 kW

9750 CHINA
NEI MENGGU PBS, Hohhot — DS-MONGOLIAN • 50 kW / W-M • DS-MONGOLIAN • 50 kW
GERMANY
†DEUTSCHE WELLE, Nauen — S • Mideast • 500 kW
JAPAN
RADIO JAPAN, Tokyo-Yamata — E Asia • 300 kW
RADIO JAPAN, Via Rampisham, UK — N Europe • 500 kW
KUWAIT
RADIO KUWAIT, Kabd — Mideast & W Asia • 500 kW
MALAYSIA
VOICE OF MALAYSIA, Kajang — SE Asia • VOICE OF ISLAM • 100 kW / SE Asia • 100 kW

(con'd)

ENGLISH ▬▬   ARABIC ▨▨   CHINESE ▢▢▢   FRENCH ▬▬   GERMAN ▬▬   RUSSIAN ══   SPANISH ▬▬   OTHER ▬▬

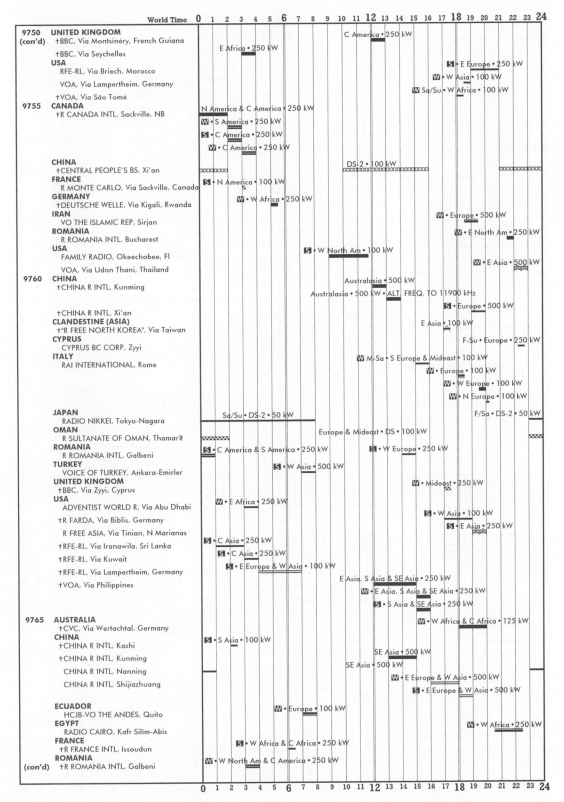

World Time	9750		
9750 (con'd)	**UNITED KINGDOM**		
	†BBC, Via Montsinéry, French Guiana	C America • 250 kW	
	†BBC, Via Seychelles	E Africa • 250 kW	
	USA		
	RFE-RL, Via Briech, Morocco	**S** • E Europe • 250 kW	
	VOA, Via Lampertheim, Germany	**W** • W Asia • 100 kW	
	†VOA, Via São Tomé	**W** Sa/Su • W Africa • 100 kW	
9755	**CANADA**		
	†R CANADA INTL, Sackville, NB	N America & C America • 250 kW	
		W • S America • 250 kW	
		S • C America • 250 kW	
		W • C America • 250 kW	
	CHINA		
	†CENTRAL PEOPLE'S BS, Xi'an	DS-2 • 100 kW	
	FRANCE		
	R MONTE CARLO, Via Sackville, Canada	**S** • N America • 100 kW	
	GERMANY		
	†DEUTSCHE WELLE, Via Kigali, Rwanda	**W** • W Africa • 250 kW	
	IRAN		
	VO THE ISLAMIC REP, Sirjan	**W** • Europe • 500 kW	
	ROMANIA		
	R ROMANIA INTL, Bucharest	**W** • E North Am • 250 kW	
	USA		
	FAMILY RADIO, Okeechobee, Fl	**S** • W North Am • 100 kW	
	VOA, Via Udon Thani, Thailand	**W** • E Asia • 500 kW	
9760	**CHINA**		
	†CHINA R INTL, Kunming	Australasia • 500 kW	
		Australasia • 500 kW • ALT. FREQ. TO 11900 kHz	
	†CHINA R INTL, Xi'an	**S** • Europe • 500 kW	
	CLANDESTINE (ASIA)		
	†"R FREE NORTH KOREA", Via Taiwan	E Asia • 100 kW	
	CYPRUS		
	CYPRUS BC CORP, Zyyi	F-Su • Europe • 250 kW	
	ITALY		
	RAI INTERNATIONAL, Rome	**W** M-Sa • S Europe & Mideast • 100 kW	
		W • Europe • 100 kW	
		W • W Europe • 100 kW	
		W • N Europe • 100 kW	
	JAPAN		
	RADIO NIKKEI, Tokyo-Nagara	Sa/Su • DS-2 • 50 kW F/Sa • DS-2 • 50 kW	
	OMAN		
	R SULTANATE OF OMAN, Thamarīt	Europe & Mideast • DS 100 kW	
	ROMANIA		
	R ROMANIA INTL, Galbeni	**S** • C America & S America • 250 kW **S** • W Europe • 250 kW	
	TURKEY		
	VOICE OF TURKEY, Ankara-Emirler	**S** • W Asia • 500 kW	
	UNITED KINGDOM		
	†BBC, Via Zyyi, Cyprus	**W** • Mideast • 250 kW	
	USA		
	ADVENTIST WORLD R, Via Abu Dhabi	**W** • E Africa • 250 kW	
	†R FARDA, Via Biblis, Germany	**S** • W Asia • 100 kW	
	R FREE ASIA, Via Tinian, N Marianas	**S** • E Asia • 250 kW	
	†RFE-RL, Via Iranawila, Sri Lanka	**S** • C Asia • 250 kW	
	†RFE-RL, Via Kuwait	**S** • C Asia • 250 kW	
	†RFE-RL, Via Lampertheim, Germany	**S** • E Europe & W Asia • 100 kW	
	†VOA, Via Philippines	E Asia, S Asia & SE Asia • 250 kW	
		W • E Asia, S Asia & SE Asia • 250 kW	
		S • S Asia & SE Asia • 250 kW	
9765	**AUSTRALIA**		
	†CVC, Via Wertachtal, Germany	**W** • W Africa & C Africa • 125 kW	
	CHINA		
	†CHINA R INTL, Kashi	**S** • S Asia • 100 kW	
	†CHINA R INTL, Kunming	SE Asia • 500 kW	
	CHINA R INTL, Nanning	SE Asia • 500 kW	
	CHINA R INTL, Shijiazhuang	**W** • E Europe & W Asia • 500 kW	
		S • E Europe & W Asia • 500 kW	
	ECUADOR		
	HCJB-VO THE ANDES, Quito	**W** • Europe • 100 kW	
	EGYPT		
	RADIO CAIRO, Kafr Silīm-Abis	**W** • W Africa • 250 kW	
	FRANCE		
	†R FRANCE INTL, Issoudun	**S** • W Africa & C Africa • 250 kW	
	ROMANIA		
(con'd)	†R ROMANIA INTL, Galbeni	**W** • W North Am & C America • 250 kW	

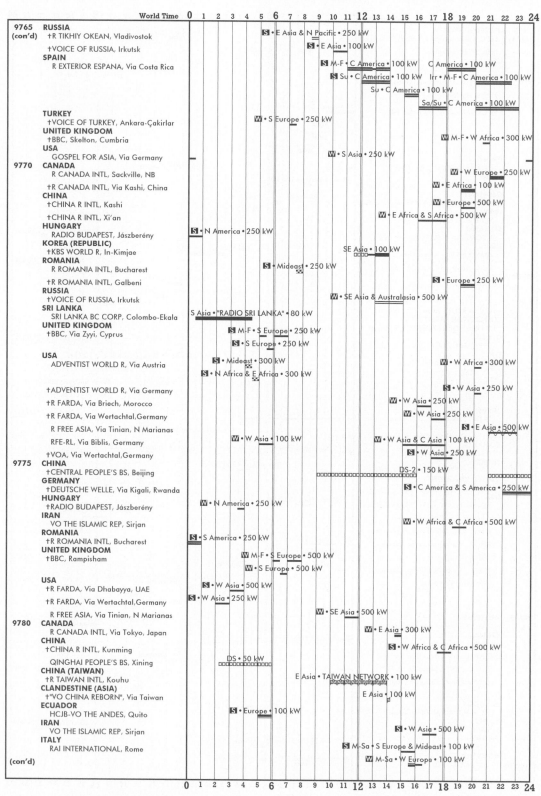

World Time		
9765 (con'd)	**RUSSIA**	
	†R TIKHIY OKEAN, Vladivostok	S • E Asia & N Pacific • 250 kW
	†VOICE OF RUSSIA, Irkutsk	S • E Asia • 100 kW
	SPAIN	
	R EXTERIOR ESPANA, Via Costa Rica	S M-F • C America • 100 kW C America • 100 kW
		S Su • C America • 100 kW Irr • M-F • C America • 100 kW
		Su • C America • 100 kW
		Sa/Su • C America • 100 kW
	TURKEY	
	†VOICE OF TURKEY, Ankara-Çakirlar	W • S Europe • 250 kW
	UNITED KINGDOM	
	†BBC, Skelton, Cumbria	W M-F • W Africa • 300 kW
	USA	
	GOSPEL FOR ASIA, Via Germany	W • S Asia • 250 kW
9770	**CANADA**	
	R CANADA INTL, Sackville, NB	W • W Europe • 250 kW
	†R CANADA INTL, Via Kashi, China	W • E Africa • 100 kW
	CHINA	
	†CHINA R INTL, Kashi	W • Europe • 500 kW
	†CHINA R INTL, Xi'an	W • E Africa & S Africa • 500 kW
	HUNGARY	
	RADIO BUDAPEST, Jászberény	S • N America • 250 kW
	KOREA (REPUBLIC)	
	†KBS WORLD R, In-Kimjae	SE Asia • 100 kW
	ROMANIA	
	R ROMANIA INTL, Bucharest	S • Mideast • 250 kW
	†R ROMANIA INTL, Galbeni	S • Europe • 250 kW
	RUSSIA	
	†VOICE OF RUSSIA, Irkutsk	W • SE Asia & Australasia • 500 kW
	SRI LANKA	
	SRI LANKA BC CORP, Colombo-Ekala	S Asia • "RADIO SRI LANKA" • 80 kW
	UNITED KINGDOM	
	†BBC, Via Zyyi, Cyprus	S M-F • S Europe • 250 kW
		S • S Europe • 250 kW
	USA	
	ADVENTIST WORLD R, Via Austria	S • Mideast • 300 kW
		S • N Africa & E Africa • 300 kW
	†ADVENTIST WORLD R, Via Germany	S • W Asia • 250 kW
	†R FARDA, Via Briech, Morocco	W • W Asia • 250 kW
	†R FARDA, Via Wertachtal, Germany	W • W Asia • 250 kW
	R FREE ASIA, Via Tinian, N Marianas	S • E Asia • 500 kW
	RFE-RL, Via Biblis, Germany	W • W Asia • 100 kW W • W Asia & C Asia • 100 kW
	†VOA, Via Wertachtal, Germany	S • W Asia • 250 kW
9775	**CHINA**	
	†CENTRAL PEOPLE'S BS, Beijing	DS-2 • 150 kW
	GERMANY	
	†DEUTSCHE WELLE, Via Kigali, Rwanda	S • C America & S America • 250 kW
	HUNGARY	
	†RADIO BUDAPEST, Jászberény	W • N America • 250 kW
	IRAN	
	VO THE ISLAMIC REP, Sirjan	W • W Africa & C Africa • 500 kW
	ROMANIA	
	†R ROMANIA INTL, Bucharest	S • S America • 250 kW
	UNITED KINGDOM	
	†BBC, Rampisham	W M-F • S Europe • 500 kW
		W • S Europe • 500 kW
	USA	
	†R FARDA, Via Dhabayya, UAE	S • W Asia • 500 kW
	†R FARDA, Via Wertachtal, Germany	S • W Asia • 250 kW
	R FREE ASIA, Via Tinian, N Marianas	W • SE Asia • 500 kW
9780	**CANADA**	
	R CANADA INTL, Via Tokyo, Japan	W • E Asia • 300 kW
	CHINA	
	†CHINA R INTL, Kunming	S • W Africa & C Africa • 500 kW
	QINGHAI PEOPLE'S BS, Xining	DS • 50 kW
	CHINA (TAIWAN)	
	†R TAIWAN INTL, Kouhu	E Asia • TAIWAN NETWORK • 100 kW
	CLANDESTINE (ASIA)	
	†"VO CHINA REBORN", Via Taiwan	E Asia • 100 kW
	ECUADOR	
	HCJB-VO THE ANDES, Quito	S • Europe • 100 kW
	IRAN	
	VO THE ISLAMIC REP, Sirjan	S • W Asia • 500 kW
	ITALY	
	RAI INTERNATIONAL, Rome	S M-Sa • S Europe & Mideast • 100 kW
		W M-Sa • W Europe • 100 kW
(con'd)		

ENGLISH ▬   ARABIC ░░░   CHINESE □□□   FRENCH ═══   GERMAN ▬▬▬   RUSSIAN ══   SPANISH ═══   OTHER ──

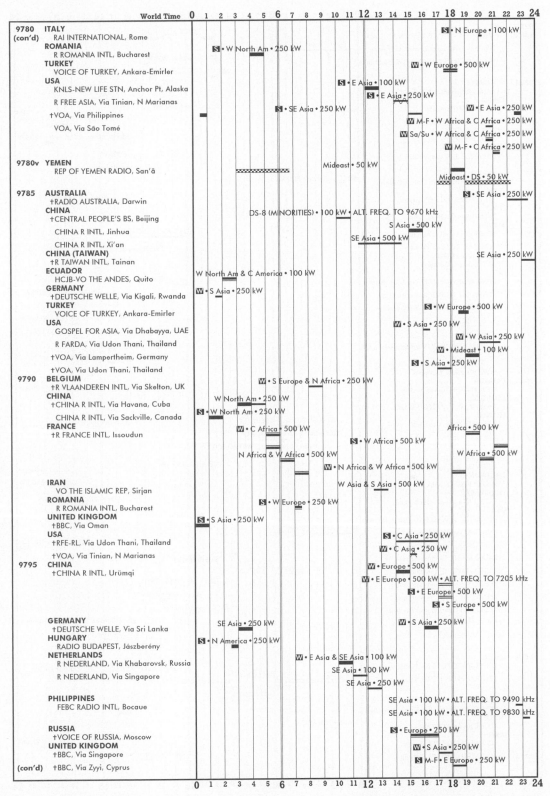

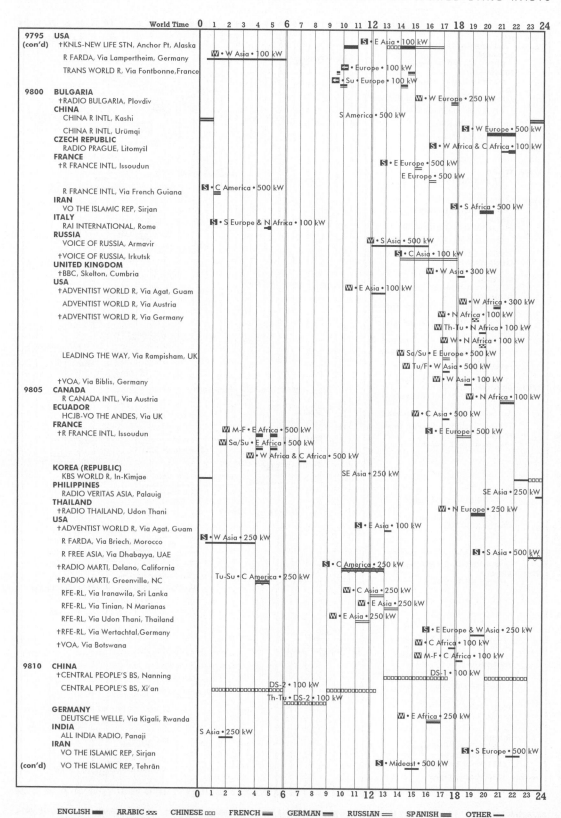

	World Time	0 1 2 3 4 5 6 7 8 9 10 11 12 13 14 15 16 17 18 19 20 21 22 23 24

9795 **USA**
(con'd) †KNLS-NEW LIFE STN, Anchor Pt, Alaska — S • E Asia • 100 kW
          R FARDA, Via Lampertheim, Germany — W • W Asia • 100 kW
          TRANS WORLD R, Via Fontbonne, France — • Europe • 100 kW / • Su • Europe • 100 kW

9800 **BULGARIA**
          †RADIO BULGARIA, Plovdiv — W • W Europe • 250 kW
          CHINA
            CHINA R INTL, Kashi — S America • 500 kW
            CHINA R INTL, Urümqi — S • W Europe • 500 kW
          CZECH REPUBLIC
            RADIO PRAGUE, Litomyšl — S • W Africa & C Africa • 100 kW
          FRANCE
            †R FRANCE INTL, Issoudun — S • E Europe • 500 kW / E Europe • 500 kW
            R FRANCE INTL, Via French Guiana — S • C America • 500 kW / S • S Africa • 500 kW
          IRAN
            VO THE ISLAMIC REP, Sirjan
          ITALY
            RAI INTERNATIONAL, Rome — S • S Europe & N Africa • 100 kW
          RUSSIA
            VOICE OF RUSSIA, Armavir — W • S Asia • 500 kW
            †VOICE OF RUSSIA, Irkutsk — S • C Asia • 100 kW
          UNITED KINGDOM
            †BBC, Skelton, Cumbria — W • W Asia • 300 kW
          USA
            †ADVENTIST WORLD R, Via Agat, Guam — W • E Asia • 100 kW
            ADVENTIST WORLD R, Via Austria — W • W Africa • 300 kW
            †ADVENTIST WORLD R, Via Germany — W • N Africa • 100 kW / W Th-Tu • N Africa • 100 kW / W W • N Africa • 100 kW
            LEADING THE WAY, Via Rampisham, UK — W Sa/Su • E Europe • 500 kW / W Tu/F • W Asia • 500 kW / W • W Asia • 100 kW
            †VOA, Via Biblis, Germany
9805 **CANADA**
            R CANADA INTL, Via Austria — W • N Africa • 100 kW
          ECUADOR
            HCJB-VO THE ANDES, Via UK — W • C Asia • 500 kW
          FRANCE
            †R FRANCE INTL, Issoudun — W M-F • E Africa • 500 kW / W Sa/Su • E Africa • 500 kW / W • W Africa & C Africa • 500 kW / S • E Europe • 500 kW
          KOREA (REPUBLIC)
            KBS WORLD R, In-Kimjae — SE Asia • 250 kW
          PHILIPPINES
            RADIO VERITAS ASIA, Palauig — SE Asia • 250 kW
          THAILAND
            †RADIO THAILAND, Udon Thani — W • N Europe • 250 kW
          USA
            †ADVENTIST WORLD R, Via Agat, Guam — S • E Asia • 100 kW
            R FARDA, Via Briech, Morocco — S • W Asia • 250 kW
            R FREE ASIA, Via Dhabayya, UAE — S • S Asia • 500 kW
            †RADIO MARTI, Delano, California — S • C America • 250 kW
            †RADIO MARTI, Greenville, NC — Tu-Su • C America • 250 kW
            RFE-RL, Via Iranawila, Sri Lanka — W • C Asia • 250 kW
            RFE-RL, Via Tinian, N Marianas — W • E Asia • 250 kW
            RFE-RL, Via Udon Thani, Thailand — W • E Asia • 250 kW
            †RFE-RL, Via Wertachtal, Germany — S • E Europe & W Asia • 250 kW
            †VOA, Via Botswana — W • C Africa • 100 kW / W M-F • C Africa • 100 kW
9810 **CHINA**
            †CENTRAL PEOPLE'S BS, Nanning — DS-1 • 100 kW
            CENTRAL PEOPLE'S BS, Xi'an — DS-2 • 100 kW / Th-Tu • DS-2 • 100 kW
          GERMANY
            DEUTSCHE WELLE, Via Kigali, Rwanda — W • E Africa • 250 kW
          INDIA
            ALL INDIA RADIO, Panaji — S Asia • 250 kW
          IRAN
            VO THE ISLAMIC REP, Sirjan — S • S Europe • 500 kW
(con'd)   VO THE ISLAMIC REP, Tehrān — S • Mideast • 500 kW

	0 1 2 3 4 5 6 7 8 9 10 11 12 13 14 15 16 17 18 19 20 21 22 23 24

ENGLISH ▬   ARABIC ∿∿   CHINESE □□□   FRENCH ═══   GERMAN ▬▬   RUSSIAN ═══   SPANISH ═══   OTHER ▬

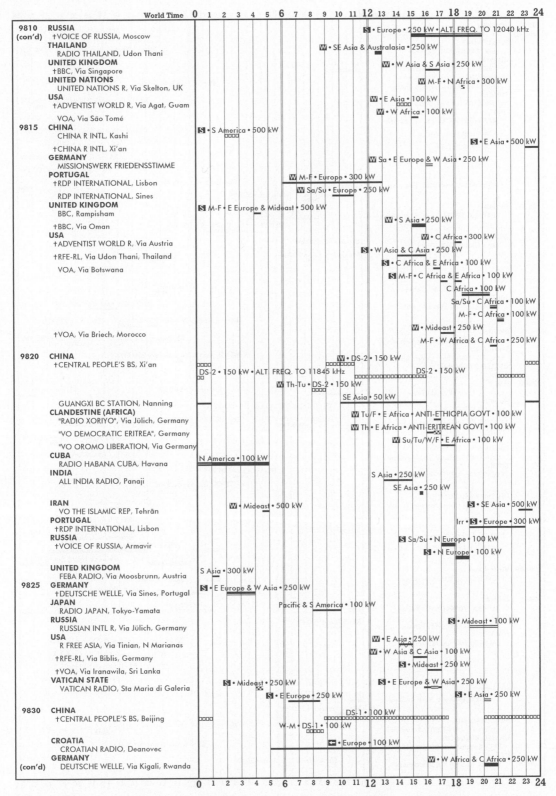

World Time	0 1 2 3 4 5 6 7 8 9 10 11 12 13 14 15 16 17 18 19 20 21 22 23 24
9810 **(con'd)** **RUSSIA** †VOICE OF RUSSIA, Moscow	S • Europe • 250 kW • ALT. FREQ. TO 12040 kHz
THAILAND RADIO THAILAND, Udon Thani	W • SE Asia & Australasia • 250 kW
UNITED KINGDOM †BBC, Via Singapore	W • W Asia & S Asia • 250 kW
UNITED NATIONS UNITED NATIONS R, Via Skelton, UK	W M-F • N Africa • 300 kW
USA †ADVENTIST WORLD R, Via Agat, Guam	W • E Asia • 100 kW
VOA, Via São Tomé	W • W Africa • 100 kW
9815 CHINA CHINA R INTL, Kashi	S • S America • 500 kW
†CHINA R INTL, Xi'an	S • E Asia • 500 kW
GERMANY MISSIONSWERK FRIEDENSSTIMME	W Sa • E Europe & W Asia • 250 kW
PORTUGAL †RDP INTERNATIONAL, Lisbon	W M-F • Europe • 300 kW
RDP INTERNATIONAL, Sines	W Sa/Su • Europe • 250 kW
UNITED KINGDOM BBC, Rampisham	S M-F • E Europe & Mideast • 500 kW
†BBC, Via Oman	W • S Asia • 250 kW
USA †ADVENTIST WORLD R, Via Austria	W • C Africa • 300 kW
†RFE-RL, Via Udon Thani, Thailand	S • W Asia & C Asia • 250 kW
VOA, Via Botswana	S • C Africa & E Africa • 100 kW
	S M-F • C Africa & E Africa • 100 kW
	C Africa • 100 kW
	Sa/Su • C Africa • 100 kW
	M-F • C Africa • 100 kW
†VOA, Via Briech, Morocco	W • Mideast • 250 kW
	M-F • W Africa & C Africa • 250 kW
9820 CHINA †CENTRAL PEOPLE'S BS, Xi'an	W • DS-2 • 150 kW
	DS-2 • 150 kW • ALT. FREQ. TO 11845 kHz DS-2 • 150 kW
	W Th-Tu • DS-2 • 150 kW
GUANGXI BC STATION, Nanning	SE Asia • 50 kW
CLANDESTINE (AFRICA) "RADIO XORIYO", Via Jülich, Germany	W Tu/F • E Africa • ANTI-ETHIOPIA GOVT • 100 kW
"VO DEMOCRATIC ERITREA", Germany	W Th • E Africa • ANTI-ERITREAN GOVT • 100 kW
"VO OROMO LIBERATION, Via Germany	W Su/Tu/W/F • E Africa • 100 kW
CUBA RADIO HABANA CUBA, Havana	N America • 100 kW
INDIA ALL INDIA RADIO, Panaji	S Asia • 250 kW
	SE Asia • 250 kW
IRAN VO THE ISLAMIC REP, Tehrān	W • Mideast • 500 kW
	S • SE Asia • 500 kW
PORTUGAL †RDP INTERNATIONAL, Lisbon	Irr • S • Europe • 300 kW
RUSSIA †VOICE OF RUSSIA, Armavir	S Sa/Su • N Europe • 100 kW
	S • N Europe • 100 kW
UNITED KINGDOM FEBA RADIO, Via Moosbrunn, Austria	S Asia • 300 kW
9825 GERMANY †DEUTSCHE WELLE, Via Sines, Portugal	S • E Europe & W Asia • 250 kW
JAPAN RADIO JAPAN, Tokyo-Yamata	Pacific & S America • 100 kW
RUSSIA RUSSIAN INTL R, Via Jülich, Germany	S • Mideast • 100 kW
USA R FREE ASIA, Via Tinian, N Marianas	W • E Asia • 250 kW
†RFE-RL, Via Biblis, Germany	W • W Asia & C Asia • 100 kW
†VOA, Via Iranawila, Sri Lanka	S • Mideast • 250 kW
VATICAN STATE VATICAN RADIO, Sta Maria di Galeria	S • Mideast • 250 kW
	S • E Europe & W Asia • 250 kW
	S • E Europe • 250 kW
	S • E Asia • 250 kW
9830 CHINA †CENTRAL PEOPLE'S BS, Beijing	DS-1 • 100 kW
	W-M • DS-1 • 100 kW
CROATIA CROATIAN RADIO, Deanovec	⇦ • Europe • 100 kW
GERMANY **(con'd)** DEUTSCHE WELLE, Via Kigali, Rwanda	W • W Africa & C Africa • 250 kW

0 1 2 3 4 5 6 7 8 9 10 11 12 13 14 15 16 17 18 19 20 21 22 23 24

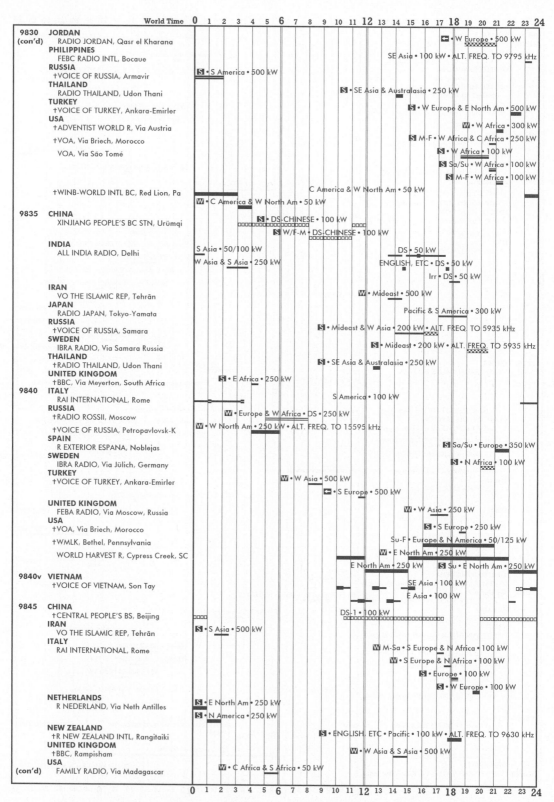

World Time 0 1 2 3 4 5 6 7 8 9 10 11 12 13 14 15 16 17 18 19 20 21 22 23 24

9830 (con'd)

JORDAN
RADIO JORDAN, Qasr el Kharana — [←] • W Europe • 500 kW

PHILIPPINES
FEBC RADIO INTL, Bocaue — SE Asia • 100 kW • ALT. FREQ. TO 9795 kHz

RUSSIA
†VOICE OF RUSSIA, Armavir — [S] • S America • 500 kW

THAILAND
RADIO THAILAND, Udon Thani — [S] • SE Asia & Australasia • 250 kW

TURKEY
†VOICE OF TURKEY, Ankara-Emirler — [S] • W Europe & E North Am • 500 kW

USA
†ADVENTIST WORLD R, Via Austria — [W] • W Africa • 300 kW
†VOA, Via Briech, Morocco — [S] M-F • W Africa & C Africa • 250 kW
VOA, Via São Tomé — [S] • W Africa • 100 kW; [S] Sa/Su • W Africa • 100 kW; [S] M-F • W Africa • 100 kW
†WINB-WORLD INTL BC, Red Lion, Pa — C America & W North Am • 50 kW; [W] • C America & W North Am • 50 kW

9835

CHINA
XINJIANG PEOPLE'S BC STN, Urümqi — [S] • DS-CHINESE • 100 kW; [S] W/F-M • DS-CHINESE • 100 kW

INDIA
ALL INDIA RADIO, Delhi — S Asia • 50/100 kW; W Asia & S Asia • 250 kW; DS • 50 kW; ENGLISH, ETC • DS • 50 kW; Irr • DS • 50 kW

IRAN
VO THE ISLAMIC REP, Tehrān — [W] • Mideast • 500 kW

JAPAN
RADIO JAPAN, Tokyo-Yamata — Pacific & S America • 300 kW

RUSSIA
†VOICE OF RUSSIA, Samara — [S] • Mideast & W Asia • 200 kW • ALT. FREQ. TO 5935 kHz

SWEDEN
IBRA RADIO, Via Samara Russia — [S] • Mideast • 200 kW • ALT. FREQ. TO 5935 kHz

THAILAND
†RADIO THAILAND, Udon Thani — [S] • SE Asia & Australasia • 250 kW

UNITED KINGDOM
†BBC, Via Meyerton, South Africa — [S] • E Africa • 250 kW

9840

ITALY
RAI INTERNATIONAL, Rome — S America • 100 kW

RUSSIA
†RADIO ROSSII, Moscow — [W] • Europe & W Africa • DS • 250 kW
†VOICE OF RUSSIA, Petropavlovsk-K — [W] • W North Am • 250 kW • ALT. FREQ. TO 15595 kHz

SPAIN
R EXTERIOR ESPANA, Noblejas — [S] Sa/Su • Europe • 350 kW

SWEDEN
IBRA RADIO, Via Jülich, Germany — [S] • N Africa • 100 kW

TURKEY
†VOICE OF TURKEY, Ankara-Emirler — [W] • W Asia • 500 kW; [←] • S Europe • 500 kW

UNITED KINGDOM
FEBA RADIO, Via Moscow, Russia — [W] • W Asia • 250 kW

USA
†VOA, Via Briech, Morocco — [S] • S Europe • 250 kW
†WMLK, Bethel, Pennsylvania — Su-F • Europe & N America • 50/125 kW
WORLD HARVEST R, Cypress Creek, SC — [W] • E North Am • 250 kW; E North Am • 250 kW; [S] Su • E North Am • 250 kW

9840v

VIETNAM
†VOICE OF VIETNAM, Son Tay — SE Asia • 100 kW; E Asia • 100 kW

9845

CHINA
†CENTRAL PEOPLE'S BS, Beijing — DS-1 • 100 kW

IRAN
VO THE ISLAMIC REP, Tehrān — [S] • S Asia • 500 kW

ITALY
RAI INTERNATIONAL, Rome — [W] M-Sa • S Europe & N Africa • 100 kW; [W] • S Europe & N Africa • 100 kW; [S] • Europe • 100 kW; [S] • W Europe • 100 kW

NETHERLANDS
R NEDERLAND, Via Neth Antilles — [S] • E North Am • 250 kW; [S] • N America • 250 kW

NEW ZEALAND
†R NEW ZEALAND INTL, Rangitaiki — [S] • ENGLISH, ETC • Pacific • 100 kW • ALT. FREQ. TO 9630 kHz

UNITED KINGDOM
†BBC, Rampisham — [W] • W Asia & S Asia • 500 kW

USA (con'd)
FAMILY RADIO, Via Madagascar — [W] • C Africa & S Africa • 50 kW

0 1 2 3 4 5 6 7 8 9 10 11 12 13 14 15 16 17 18 19 20 21 22 23 24

ENGLISH ARABIC CHINESE FRENCH GERMAN RUSSIAN SPANISH OTHER

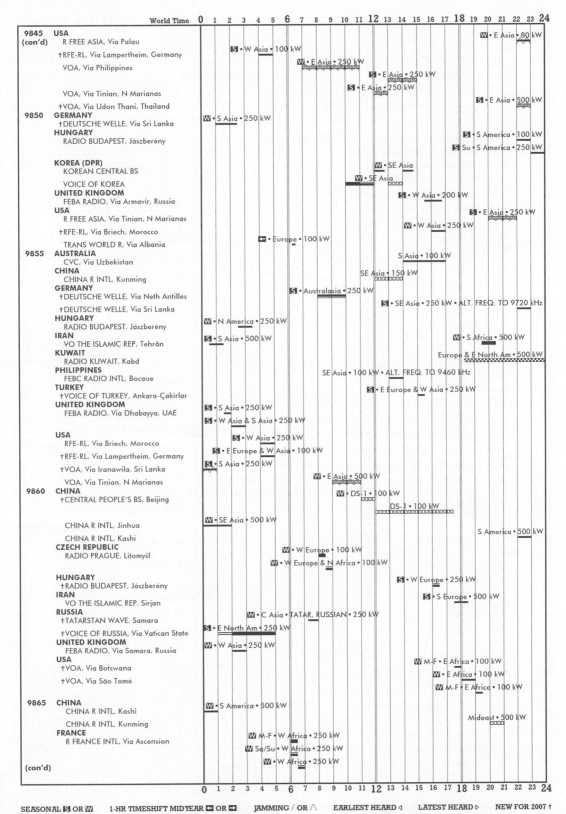

World Time 0 1 2 3 4 5 6 7 8 9 10 11 12 13 14 15 16 17 18 19 20 21 22 23 24

9845 (con'd)   **USA**
    R FREE ASIA, Via Palau — W • E Asia • 80 kW
    †RFE-RL, Via Lampertheim, Germany — S • W Asia • 100 kW
    VOA, Via Philippines — W • E Asia • 250 kW / S • E Asia • 250 kW
    VOA, Via Tinian, N Marianas — S • E Asia • 250 kW / S • E Asia • 500 kW
    †VOA, Via Udon Thani, Thailand

9850   **GERMANY**
    †DEUTSCHE WELLE, Via Sri Lanka — W • S Asia • 250 kW
    HUNGARY
    RADIO BUDAPEST, Jászberény — S • S America • 100 kW / S • Su • S America • 250 kW

    KOREA (DPR)
    KOREAN CENTRAL BS — W • SE Asia
    VOICE OF KOREA — W • SE Asia
    UNITED KINGDOM
    FEBA RADIO, Via Armavir, Russia — S • W Asia • 200 kW
    USA
    R FREE ASIA, Via Tinian, N Marianas — S • E Asia • 250 kW
    †RFE-RL, Via Briech, Morocco — W • W Asia • 250 kW
    TRANS WORLD R, Via Albania — • Europe • 100 kW

9855   **AUSTRALIA**
    CVC, Via Uzbekistan — S Asia • 100 kW
    CHINA
    CHINA R INTL, Kunming — SE Asia • 150 kW
    GERMANY
    †DEUTSCHE WELLE, Via Neth Antilles — S • Australasia • 250 kW
    †DEUTSCHE WELLE, Via Sri Lanka — S • SE Asia • 250 kW • ALT. FREQ. TO 9720 kHz
    HUNGARY
    RADIO BUDAPEST, Jászberény — W • N America • 250 kW
    IRAN
    VO THE ISLAMIC REP, Tehrān — S • S Asia • 500 kW / W • S Africa • 500 kW
    KUWAIT
    RADIO KUWAIT, Kabd — Europe & E North Am • 500 kW
    PHILIPPINES
    FEBC RADIO INTL, Bocaue — SE Asia • 100 kW • ALT. FREQ. TO 9460 kHz
    TURKEY
    †VOICE OF TURKEY, Ankara-Çakirlar — S • E Europe & W Asia • 250 kW
    UNITED KINGDOM
    FEBA RADIO, Via Dhabayya, UAE — S • S Asia • 250 kW / S • W Asia & S Asia • 250 kW
    USA
    RFE-RL, Via Briech, Morocco — S • W Asia • 250 kW
    †RFE-RL, Via Lampertheim, Germany — S • E Europe & W Asia • 100 kW
    †VOA, Via Iranawila, Sri Lanka — S • S Asia • 250 kW
    VOA, Via Tinian, N Marianas — W • E Asia • 500 kW

9860   **CHINA**
    †CENTRAL PEOPLE'S BS, Beijing — W • DS-1 • 100 kW / DS-1 • 100 kW
    CHINA R INTL, Jinhua — W • SE Asia • 500 kW
    CHINA R INTL, Kashi — S America • 500 kW
    CZECH REPUBLIC
    RADIO PRAGUE, Litomyšl — W • W Europe • 100 kW / W • W Europe & N Africa • 100 kW
    HUNGARY
    †RADIO BUDAPEST, Jászberény — S • W Europe • 250 kW
    IRAN
    VO THE ISLAMIC REP, Sirjan — S • S Europe • 500 kW
    RUSSIA
    †TATARSTAN WAVE, Samara — W • C Asia • TATAR, RUSSIAN • 250 kW
    †VOICE OF RUSSIA, Via Vatican State — S • E North Am • 250 kW
    UNITED KINGDOM
    FEBA RADIO, Via Samara, Russia — W • W Asia • 250 kW
    USA
    †VOA, Via Botswana — W • M-F • E Africa • 100 kW / W • E Africa • 100 kW
    †VOA, Via São Tomé — W • M-F • E Africa • 100 kW

9865   **CHINA**
    CHINA R INTL, Kashi — W • S America • 500 kW
    CHINA R INTL, Kunming — Mideast • 500 kW
    FRANCE
    R FRANCE INTL, Via Ascension — W • M-F • W Africa • 250 kW / W • Sa/Su • W Africa • 250 kW / W • W Africa • 250 kW

(con'd)

0 1 2 3 4 5 6 7 8 9 10 11 12 13 14 15 16 17 18 19 20 21 22 23 24

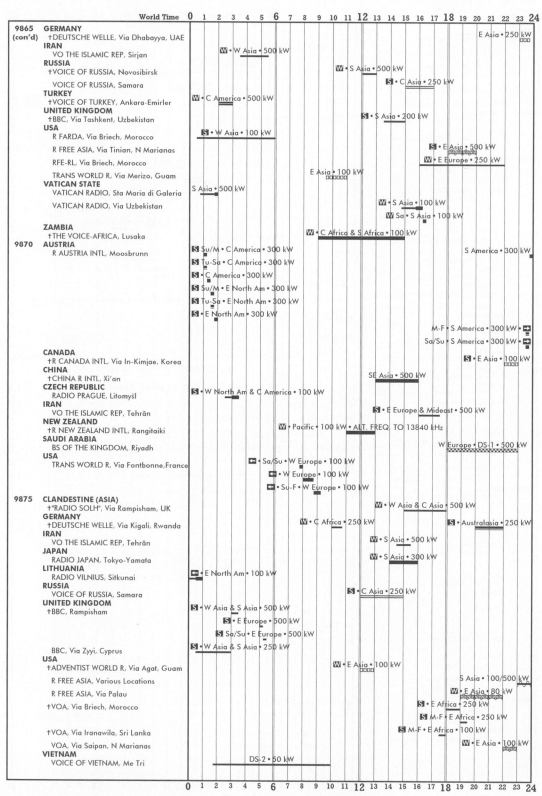

	World Time	0 1 2 3 4 5 6 7 8 9 10 11 12 13 14 15 16 17 18 19 20 21 22 23 24
9865 (con'd)	**GERMANY** †DEUTSCHE WELLE, Via Dhabayya, UAE	E Asia • 250 kW
	IRAN VO THE ISLAMIC REP, Sirjan	W • W Asia • 500 kW
	RUSSIA †VOICE OF RUSSIA, Novosibirsk	W • S Asia • 500 kW
	VOICE OF RUSSIA, Samara	S • C Asia • 250 kW
	TURKEY †VOICE OF TURKEY, Ankara-Emirler	W • C America • 500 kW
	UNITED KINGDOM †BBC, Via Tashkent, Uzbekistan	S • S Asia • 200 kW
	USA R FARDA, Via Briech, Morocco	S • W Asia • 100 kW
	R FREE ASIA, Via Tinian, N Marianas	S • E Asia • 500 kW
	RFE-RL, Via Briech, Morocco	W • E Europe • 250 kW
	TRANS WORLD R, Via Merizo, Guam	E Asia • 100 kW
	VATICAN STATE VATICAN RADIO, Sta Maria di Galeria	S Asia • 500 kW
	VATICAN RADIO, Via Uzbekistan	W • S Asia • 100 kW
		W Sa • S Asia • 100 kW
	ZAMBIA †THE VOICE-AFRICA, Lusaka	W • C Africa & S Africa • 100 kW
9870	**AUSTRIA** R AUSTRIA INTL, Moosbrunn	S Su/M • C America • 300 kW
		S Tu-Sa • C America • 300 kW
		S • C America • 300 kW
		S Su/M • E North Am • 300 kW
		S Tu-Sa • E North Am • 300 kW
		S • E North Am • 300 kW
		S America • 300 kW
		M-F • S America • 300 kW
		Sa/Su • S America • 300 kW
	CANADA †R CANADA INTL, Via In-Kimjae, Korea	S • E Asia • 100 kW
	CHINA †CHINA R INTL, Xi'an	SE Asia • 500 kW
	CZECH REPUBLIC RADIO PRAGUE, Litomyšl	S • W North Am & C America • 100 kW
	IRAN VO THE ISLAMIC REP, Tehrān	S • E Europe & Mideast • 500 kW
	NEW ZEALAND †R NEW ZEALAND INTL, Rangitaiki	W • Pacific • 100 kW • ALT. FREQ. TO 13840 kHz
	SAUDI ARABIA BS OF THE KINGDOM, Riyadh	W Europe • DS-1 • 500 kW
	USA TRANS WORLD R, Via Fontbonne, France	• Sa/Su • W Europe • 100 kW
		• W Europe • 100 kW
		• Su-F • W Europe • 100 kW
9875	**CLANDESTINE (ASIA)** †"RADIO SOLH", Via Rampisham, UK	W • W Asia & C Asia • 500 kW
	GERMANY †DEUTSCHE WELLE, Via Kigali, Rwanda	W • C Africa • 250 kW
		S • Australasia • 250 kW
	IRAN VO THE ISLAMIC REP, Tehrān	W • S Asia • 500 kW
	JAPAN RADIO JAPAN, Tokyo-Yamata	W • S Asia • 300 kW
	LITHUANIA RADIO VILNIUS, Sitkunai	• E North Am • 100 kW
	RUSSIA VOICE OF RUSSIA, Samara	S • C Asia • 250 kW
	UNITED KINGDOM †BBC, Rampisham	S • W Asia & S Asia • 500 kW
		S • E Europe • 500 kW
		S Sa/Su • E Europe • 500 kW
	BBC, Via Zyyi, Cyprus	S • W Asia & S Asia • 250 kW
	USA †ADVENTIST WORLD R, Via Agat, Guam	W • E Asia • 100 kW
	R FREE ASIA, Various Locations	S Asia • 100/500 kW
	R FREE ASIA, Via Palau	W • E Asia • 80 kW
	†VOA, Via Briech, Morocco	S • E Africa • 250 kW
		S M-F • E Africa • 250 kW
	†VOA, Via Iranawila, Sri Lanka	S M-F • E Africa • 100 kW
	VOA, Via Saipan, N Marianas	W • E Asia • 100 kW
	VIETNAM VOICE OF VIETNAM, Me Tri	DS-2 • 50 kW

0 1 2 3 4 5 6 7 8 9 10 11 12 13 14 15 16 17 18 19 20 21 22 23 24

ENGLISH ▬ ARABIC ∿∿ CHINESE □□□ FRENCH ═ GERMAN ▬ RUSSIAN ═ SPANISH ▬ OTHER ▬

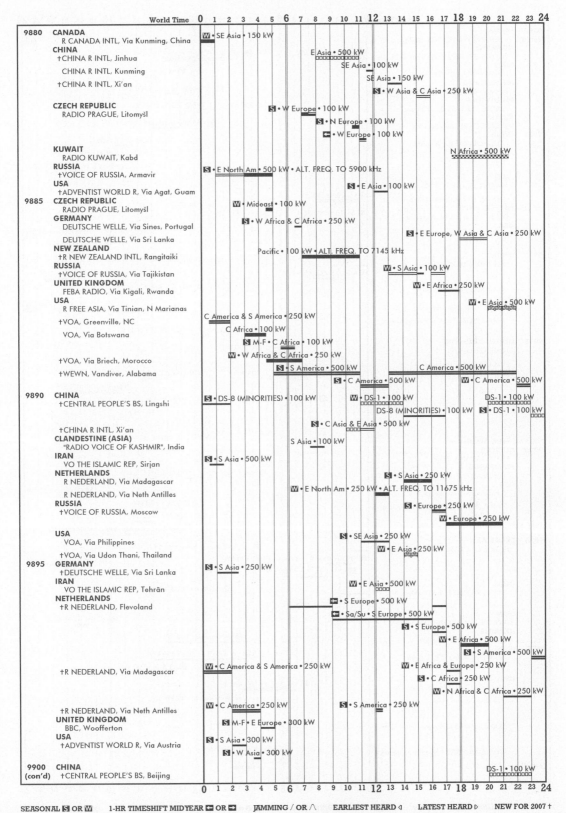

		World Time	0 1 2 3 4 5 6 7 8 9 10 11 12 13 14 15 16 17 18 19 20 21 22 23 24

9880 CANADA
R CANADA INTL, Via Kunming, China — W • SE Asia • 150 kW
CHINA
†CHINA R INTL, Jinhua — E Asia • 500 kW
CHINA R INTL, Kunming — SE Asia • 100 kW
†CHINA R INTL, Xi'an — SE Asia • 150 kW — S • W Asia & C Asia • 250 kW
CZECH REPUBLIC
RADIO PRAGUE, Litomyšl — S • W Europe • 100 kW — S • N Europe • 100 kW — ⇨ • W Europe • 100 kW
KUWAIT
RADIO KUWAIT, Kabd — N Africa • 500 kW
RUSSIA
†VOICE OF RUSSIA, Armavir — S • E North Am • 500 kW • ALT. FREQ. TO 5900 kHz
USA
†ADVENTIST WORLD R, Via Agat, Guam — S • E Asia • 100 kW

9885 CZECH REPUBLIC
RADIO PRAGUE, Litomyšl — W • Mideast • 100 kW
GERMANY
DEUTSCHE WELLE, Via Sines, Portugal — S • W Africa & C Africa • 250 kW
DEUTSCHE WELLE, Via Sri Lanka — S • E Europe, W Asia & C Asia • 250 kW
NEW ZEALAND
†R NEW ZEALAND INTL, Rangitaiki — Pacific • 100 kW • ALT. FREQ. TO 7145 kHz
RUSSIA
†VOICE OF RUSSIA, Via Tajikistan — W • S Asia • 100 kW
UNITED KINGDOM
FEBA RADIO, Via Kigali, Rwanda — W • E Africa • 250 kW
USA
R FREE ASIA, Via Tinian, N Marianas — W • E Asia • 500 kW
†VOA, Greenville, NC — C America & S America • 250 kW
VOA, Via Botswana — C Africa • 100 kW — S • M-F • C Africa • 100 kW
†VOA, Via Briech, Morocco — W • W Africa & C Africa • 250 kW
†WEWN, Vandiver, Alabama — S • S America • 500 kW — C America • 500 kW — S • C America • 500 kW — W • C America • 500 kW

9890 CHINA
†CENTRAL PEOPLE'S BS, Lingshi — S • DS-8 (MINORITIES) • 100 kW — W • DS-1 • 100 kW — DS-1 • 100 kW — DS-8 (MINORITIES) • 100 kW — S • DS-1 • 100 kW
†CHINA R INTL, Xi'an — S • C Asia & E Asia • 500 kW
CLANDESTINE (ASIA)
"RADIO VOICE OF KASHMIR", India — S Asia • 100 kW
IRAN
VO THE ISLAMIC REP, Sirjan — S • S Asia • 500 kW
NETHERLANDS
R NEDERLAND, Via Madagascar — S • S Asia • 250 kW
R NEDERLAND, Via Neth Antilles — W • E North Am • 250 kW • ALT. FREQ. TO 11675 kHz
RUSSIA
†VOICE OF RUSSIA, Moscow — S • Europe • 250 kW — W • Europe • 250 kW
USA
VOA, Via Philippines — S • SE Asia • 250 kW
†VOA, Via Udon Thani, Thailand — W • E Asia • 250 kW

9895 GERMANY
†DEUTSCHE WELLE, Via Sri Lanka — S • S Asia • 250 kW
IRAN
VO THE ISLAMIC REP, Tehrān — W • E Asia • 500 kW
NETHERLANDS
†R NEDERLAND, Flevoland — ⇨ • S Europe • 500 kW — ⇨ • Sa/Su • S Europe • 500 kW — S • S Europe • 500 kW — W • E Africa • 500 kW — S • S America • 500 kW
†R NEDERLAND, Via Madagascar — W • C America & S America • 250 kW — W • E Africa & Europe • 250 kW — S • C Africa • 250 kW — W • N Africa & C Africa • 250 kW
†R NEDERLAND, Via Neth Antilles — W • C America • 250 kW — S • S America • 250 kW
UNITED KINGDOM
BBC, Woofferton — S • M-F • E Europe • 300 kW
USA
†ADVENTIST WORLD R, Via Austria — S • S Asia • 300 kW — S • W Asia • 300 kW

9900 CHINA
(con'd) †CENTRAL PEOPLE'S BS, Beijing — DS-1 • 100 kW

	0 1 2 3 4 5 6 7 8 9 10 11 12 13 14 15 16 17 18 19 20 21 22 23 24

SEASONAL **S** OR **W**   1-HR TIMESHIFT MIDYEAR **⇦** OR **⇨**   JAMMING / OR /\   EARLIEST HEARD ◁   LATEST HEARD ▷   NEW FOR 2007 †

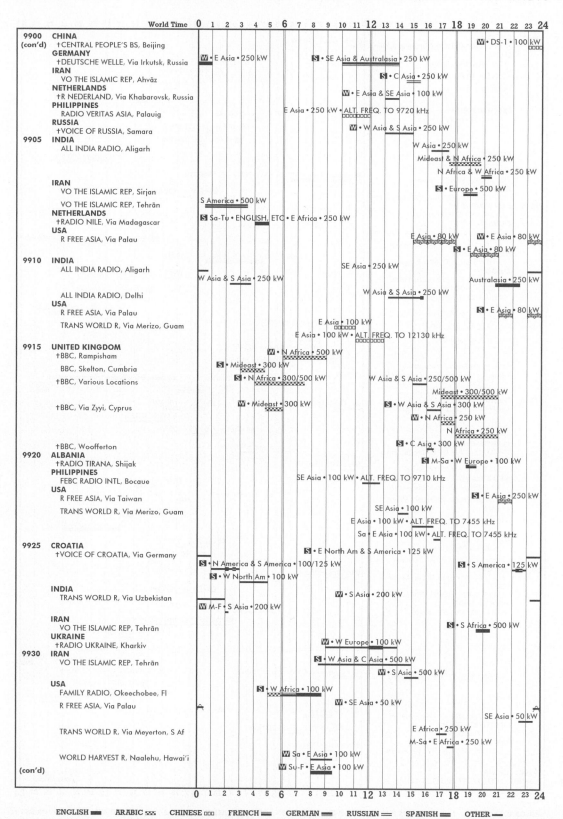

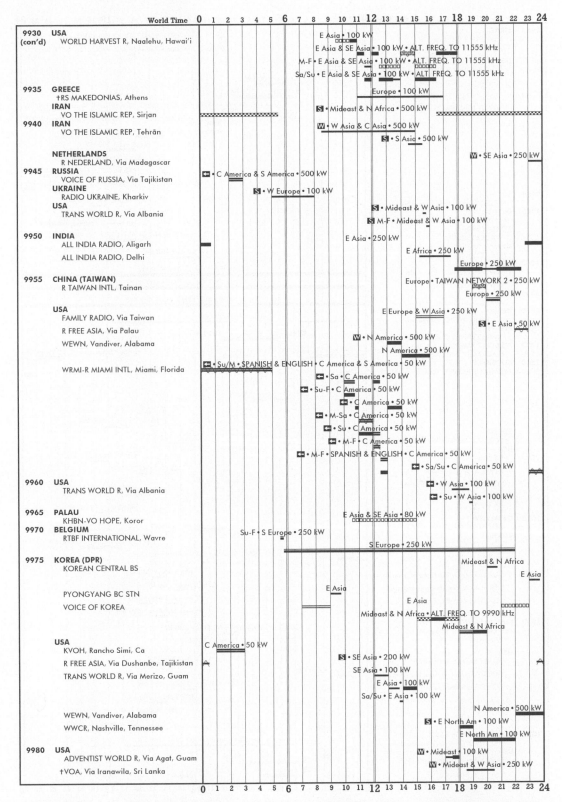

World Time   0 1 2 3 4 5 6 7 8 9 10 11 12 13 14 15 16 17 18 19 20 21 22 23 24

9930 **USA**
(con'd) WORLD HARVEST R, Naalehu, Hawai'i
- E Asia • 100 kW
- E Asia & SE Asia • 100 kW • ALT. FREQ. TO 11555 kHz
- M-F • E Asia & SE Asia • 100 kW • ALT. FREQ. TO 11555 kHz
- Sa/Su • E Asia & SE Asia • 100 kW • ALT. FREQ. TO 11555 kHz

9935 **GREECE**
†RS MAKEDONIAS, Athens
- Europe • 100 kW

IRAN
VO THE ISLAMIC REP, Sirjan
- S • Mideast & N Africa • 500 kW

9940 **IRAN**
VO THE ISLAMIC REP, Tehrān
- W • W Asia & C Asia • 500 kW
- S • S Asia • 500 kW

NETHERLANDS
R NEDERLAND, Via Madagascar
- W • SE Asia • 250 kW

9945 **RUSSIA**
VOICE OF RUSSIA, Via Tajikistan
- ⇦ • C America & S America • 500 kW

UKRAINE
RADIO UKRAINE, Kharkiv
- S • W Europe • 100 kW

USA
TRANS WORLD R, Via Albania
- S • Mideast & W Asia • 100 kW
- S • M-F • Mideast & W Asia • 100 kW

9950 **INDIA**
ALL INDIA RADIO, Aligarh
- E Asia • 250 kW

ALL INDIA RADIO, Delhi
- E Africa • 250 kW
- Europe • 250 kW

9955 **CHINA (TAIWAN)**
R TAIWAN INTL, Tainan
- Europe • TAIWAN NETWORK 2 • 250 kW
- Europe • 250 kW

USA
FAMILY RADIO, Via Taiwan
- E Europe & W Asia • 250 kW

R FREE ASIA, Via Palau
- S • E Asia • 50 kW

WEWN, Vandiver, Alabama
- W • N America • 500 kW
- N America • 500 kW

WRMI-R MIAMI INTL, Miami, Florida
- ⇦ • Su/M • SPANISH & ENGLISH • C America & S America • 50 kW
- ⇦ • Sa • C America • 50 kW
- ⇦ • Su-F • C America • 50 kW
- ⇦ • C America • 50 kW
- ⇦ • M-Sa • C America • 50 kW
- ⇦ • Su • C America • 50 kW
- ⇦ • M-F • C America • 50 kW
- ⇦ • M-F • SPANISH & ENGLISH • C America • 50 kW
- ⇦ • Sa/Su • C America • 50 kW

9960 **USA**
TRANS WORLD R, Via Albania
- ⇦ • W Asia • 100 kW
- ⇦ • Su • W Asia • 100 kW

9965 **PALAU**
KHBN-VO HOPE, Koror
- E Asia & SE Asia • 80 kW

9970 **BELGIUM**
RTBF INTERNATIONAL, Wavre
- Su-F • S Europe • 250 kW
- S Europe • 250 kW

9975 **KOREA (DPR)**
KOREAN CENTRAL BS
- Mideast & N Africa
- E Asia

PYONGYANG BC STN
- E Asia

VOICE OF KOREA
- E Asia
- Mideast & N Africa • ALT. FREQ. TO 9990 kHz
- Mideast & N Africa

USA
KVOH, Rancho Simi, Ca
- C America • 50 kW

R FREE ASIA, Via Dushanbe, Tajikistan
- S • SE Asia • 200 kW
- SE Asia • 100 kW

TRANS WORLD R, Via Merizo, Guam
- E Asia • 100 kW
- Sa/Su • E Asia • 100 kW

WEWN, Vandiver, Alabama
- N America • 500 kW

WWCR, Nashville, Tennessee
- S • E North Am • 100 kW
- E North Am • 100 kW

9980 **USA**
ADVENTIST WORLD R, Via Agat, Guam
- W • Mideast • 100 kW

†VOA, Via Iranawila, Sri Lanka
- W • Mideast & W Asia • 250 kW

0 1 2 3 4 5 6 7 8 9 10 11 12 13 14 15 16 17 18 19 20 21 22 23 24

SEASONAL S OR W   1-HR TIMESHIFT MIDYEAR ⇦ OR ⇨   JAMMING / OR ∧   EARLIEST HEARD ◁   LATEST HEARD ▷   NEW FOR 2007 †

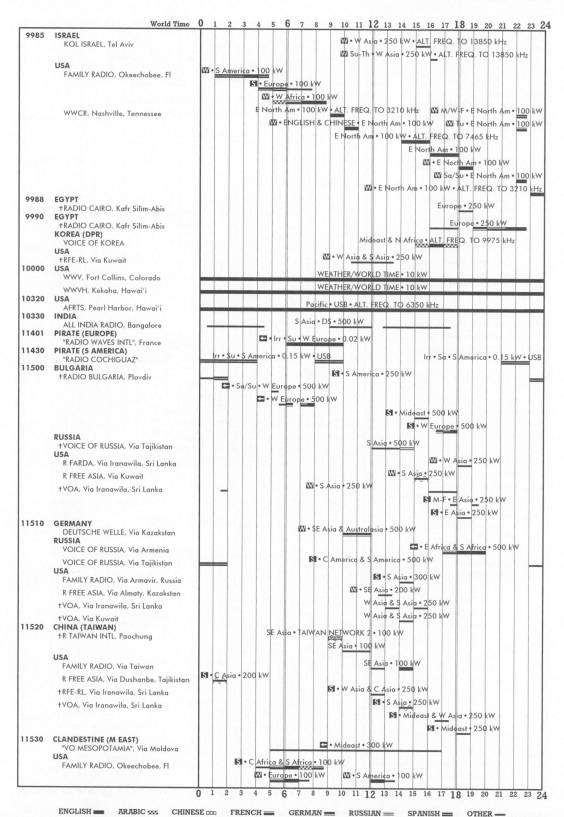

World Time 0 1 2 3 4 5 6 7 8 9 10 11 12 13 14 15 16 17 18 19 20 21 22 23 24

9985 ISRAEL
KOL ISRAEL, Tel Aviv
- W • W Asia • 250 kW • ALT. FREQ. TO 13850 kHz
- Su-Th • W Asia • 250 kW • ALT. FREQ. TO 13850 kHz

USA
FAMILY RADIO, Okeechobee, Fl
- W • S America • 100 kW
- S • Europe • 100 kW
- W • W Africa • 100 kW

WWCR, Nashville, Tennessee
- E North Am • 100 kW • ALT. FREQ. TO 3210 kHz
- M/W/F • E North Am • 100 kW
- W • ENGLISH & CHINESE • E North Am • 100 kW
- W • Tu • E North Am • 100 kW
- E North Am • 100 kW • ALT. FREQ. TO 7465 kHz
- E North Am • 100 kW
- W • E North Am • 100 kW
- W • Sa/Su • E North Am • 100 kW
- W • E North Am • 100 kW • ALT. FREQ. TO 3210 kHz

9988 EGYPT
†RADIO CAIRO, Kafr Silim-Abis
- Europe • 250 kW

9990 EGYPT
†RADIO CAIRO, Kafr Silim-Abis
- Europe • 250 kW

KOREA (DPR)
VOICE OF KOREA
- Mideast & N Africa • ALT. FREQ. TO 9975 kHz

USA
†RFE-RL, Via Kuwait
- W • W Asia & S Asia • 250 kW

10000 USA
WWV, Fort Collins, Colorado
- WEATHER/WORLD TIME • 10 kW

WWVH, Kekaha, Hawai'i
- WEATHER/WORLD TIME • 10 kW

10320 USA
AFRTS, Pearl Harbor, Hawai'i
- Pacific • USB • ALT. FREQ. TO 6350 kHz

10330 INDIA
ALL INDIA RADIO, Bangalore
- S Asia • DS • 500 kW

11401 PIRATE (EUROPE)
"RADIO WAVES INTL", France
- Irr • Su • W Europe • 0.02 kW

11430 PIRATE (S AMERICA)
"RADIO COCHIGUAZ"
- Irr • Su • S America • 0.15 kW • USB
- Irr • Sa • S America • 0.15 kW • USB

11500 BULGARIA
†RADIO BULGARIA, Plovdiv
- S • S America • 250 kW
- Sa/Su • W Europe • 500 kW
- W Europe • 500 kW
- S • Mideast • 500 kW
- S • W Europe • 500 kW

RUSSIA
†VOICE OF RUSSIA, Via Tajikistan
- S Asia • 500 kW

USA
R FARDA, Via Iranawila, Sri Lanka
- W • W Asia • 250 kW

R FREE ASIA, Via Kuwait
- W • S Asia • 250 kW

†VOA, Via Iranawila, Sri Lanka
- W • S Asia • 250 kW
- M-F • E Asia • 250 kW
- S • E Asia • 250 kW

11510 GERMANY
DEUTSCHE WELLE, Via Kazakstan
- W • SE Asia & Australasia • 500 kW

RUSSIA
VOICE OF RUSSIA, Via Armenia
- E Africa & S Africa • 500 kW

VOICE OF RUSSIA, Via Tajikistan
- S • C America & S America • 500 kW

USA
FAMILY RADIO, Via Armavir, Russia
- S • S Asia • 300 kW

R FREE ASIA, Via Almaty, Kazakstan
- W • SE Asia • 200 kW

†VOA, Via Iranawila, Sri Lanka
- W Asia & S Asia • 250 kW

†VOA, Via Kuwait
- W Asia & S Asia • 250 kW

11520 CHINA (TAIWAN)
†R TAIWAN INTL, Paochung
- SE Asia • TAIWAN NETWORK 2 • 100 kW
- SE Asia • 100 kW

USA
FAMILY RADIO, Via Taiwan
- SE Asia • 100 kW

R FREE ASIA, Via Dushanbe, Tajikistan
- S • C Asia • 200 kW

†RFE-RL, Via Iranawila, Sri Lanka
- S • W Asia & C Asia • 250 kW

†VOA, Via Iranawila, Sri Lanka
- S • S Asia • 250 kW
- S • Mideast & W Asia • 250 kW
- S • Mideast • 250 kW

11530 CLANDESTINE (M EAST)
"VO MESOPOTAMIA", Via Moldova
- Mideast • 300 kW

USA
FAMILY RADIO, Okeechobee, Fl
- S • C Africa & S Africa • 100 kW
- W • Europe • 100 kW
- W • S America • 100 kW

0 1 2 3 4 5 6 7 8 9 10 11 12 13 14 15 16 17 18 19 20 21 22 23 24

ENGLISH ▬▬   ARABIC ﹀﹀﹀   CHINESE □□□   FRENCH ═══   GERMAN ▭▭   RUSSIAN ═══   SPANISH ═══   OTHER ──

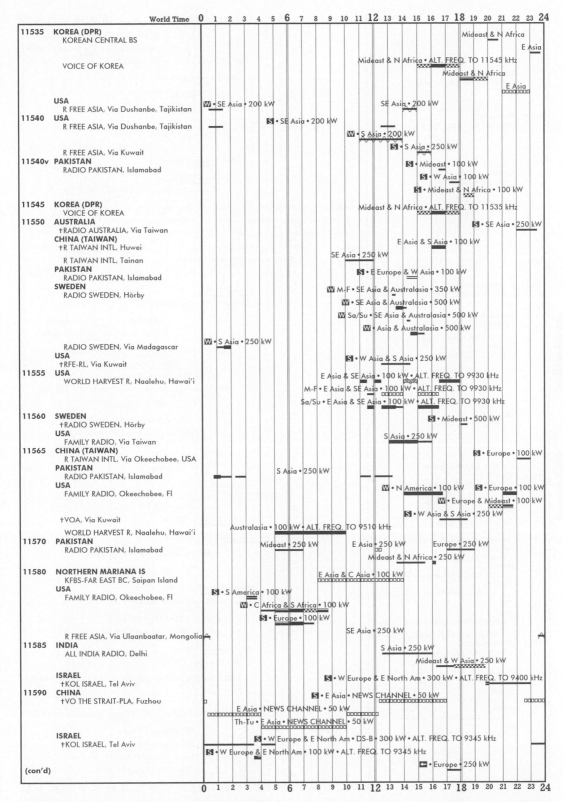

		World Time
11535	**KOREA (DPR)**	
	KOREAN CENTRAL BS	Mideast & N Africa
		E Asia
	VOICE OF KOREA	Mideast & N Africa • ALT. FREQ. TO 11545 kHz
		Mideast & N Africa
		E Asia
	USA	
	R FREE ASIA, Via Dushanbe, Tajikistan	W • SE Asia • 200 kW SE Asia • 200 kW
11540	**USA**	
	R FREE ASIA, Via Dushanbe, Tajikistan	S • SE Asia • 200 kW
		W • S Asia • 200 kW
	R FREE ASIA, Via Kuwait	S • S Asia • 250 kW
11540v	**PAKISTAN**	
	RADIO PAKISTAN, Islamabad	S • Mideast • 100 kW
		S • W Asia • 100 kW
		S • Mideast & N Africa • 100 kW
11545	**KOREA (DPR)**	
	VOICE OF KOREA	Mideast & N Africa • ALT. FREQ. TO 11535 kHz
11550	**AUSTRALIA**	
	†RADIO AUSTRALIA, Via Taiwan	S • SE Asia • 250 kW
	CHINA (TAIWAN)	
	†R TAIWAN INTL, Huwei	E Asia & S Asia • 100 kW
	R TAIWAN INTL, Tainan	SE Asia • 250 kW
	PAKISTAN	
	RADIO PAKISTAN, Islamabad	S • E Europe & W Asia • 100 kW
	SWEDEN	
	RADIO SWEDEN, Hörby	W M-F • SE Asia & Australasia • 350 kW
		W • SE Asia & Australasia • 500 kW
		W Sa/Su • SE Asia & Australasia • 500 kW
		W • Asia & Australasia • 500 kW
	RADIO SWEDEN, Via Madagascar	W • S Asia • 250 kW
	USA	
	†RFE-RL, Via Kuwait	S • W Asia & S Asia • 250 kW
11555	**USA**	
	WORLD HARVEST R, Naalehu, Hawai'i	E Asia & SE Asia • 100 kW • ALT. FREQ. TO 9930 kHz
		M-F • E Asia & SE Asia • 100 kW • ALT. FREQ. TO 9930 kHz
		Sa/Su • E Asia & SE Asia • 100 kW • ALT. FREQ. TO 9930 kHz
11560	**SWEDEN**	
	†RADIO SWEDEN, Hörby	S • Mideast • 500 kW
	USA	
	FAMILY RADIO, Via Taiwan	S Asia • 250 kW
11565	**CHINA (TAIWAN)**	
	R TAIWAN INTL, Via Okeechobee, USA	S • Europe • 100 kW
	PAKISTAN	
	RADIO PAKISTAN, Islamabad	S Asia • 250 kW
	USA	
	FAMILY RADIO, Okeechobee, Fl	W • N America • 100 kW S • Europe • 100 kW
		W • Europe & Mideast • 100 kW
	†VOA, Via Kuwait	S • W Asia & S Asia • 250 kW
	WORLD HARVEST R, Naalehu, Hawai'i	Australasia • 100 kW • ALT. FREQ. TO 9510 kHz
11570	**PAKISTAN**	
	RADIO PAKISTAN, Islamabad	Mideast • 250 kW E Asia • 250 kW Europe • 250 kW
		Mideast & N Africa • 250 kW
11580	**NORTHERN MARIANA IS**	
	KFBS-FAR EAST BC, Saipan Island	E Asia & C Asia • 100 kW
	USA	
	FAMILY RADIO, Okeechobee, Fl	S • S America • 100 kW
		W • C Africa & S Africa • 100 kW
		S • Europe • 100 kW
	R FREE ASIA, Via Ulaanbaatar, Mongolia	SE Asia • 250 kW
11585	**INDIA**	
	ALL INDIA RADIO, Delhi	S Asia • 250 kW
		Mideast & W Asia • 250 kW
	ISRAEL	
	†KOL ISRAEL, Tel Aviv	S • W Europe & E North Am • 300 kW • ALT. FREQ. TO 9400 kHz
11590	**CHINA**	
	†VO THE STRAIT-PLA, Fuzhou	S • E Asia • NEWS CHANNEL • 50 kW
		E Asia • NEWS CHANNEL • 50 kW
		Th-Tu • E Asia • NEWS CHANNEL • 50 kW
	ISRAEL	
	†KOL ISRAEL, Tel Aviv	S • W Europe & E North Am • DS-B • 300 kW • ALT. FREQ. TO 9345 kHz
		S • W Europe & E North Am • 100 kW • ALT. FREQ. TO 9345 kHz
		⇦ • Europe • 250 kW
(con'd)		

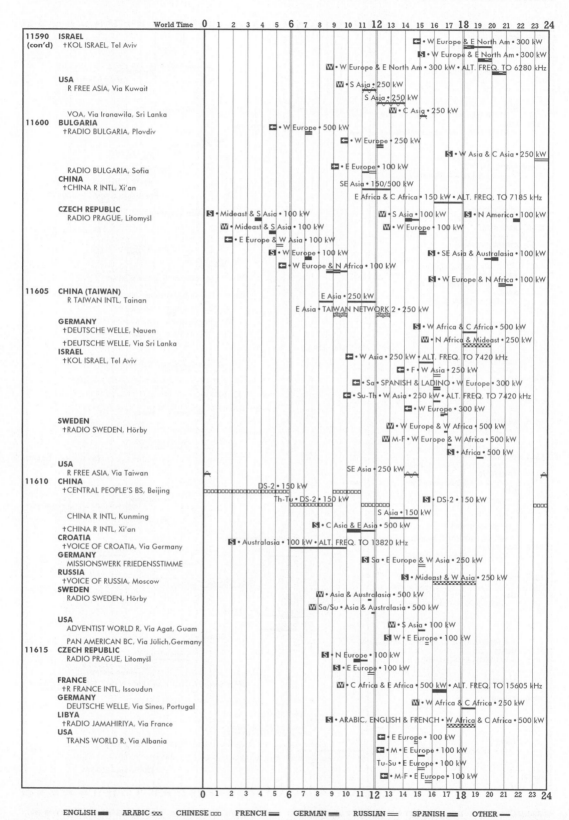

World Time	0 1 2 3 4 5 6 7 8 9 10 11 12 13 14 15 16 17 18 19 20 21 22 23 24

11590 ISRAEL (con'd) †KOL ISRAEL, Tel Aviv
- W Europe & E North Am • 300 kW
- W Europe & E North Am • 300 kW
- W Europe & E North Am • 300 kW • ALT. FREQ. TO 6280 kHz

USA R FREE ASIA, Via Kuwait
- S Asia • 250 kW
- S Asia • 250 kW

VOA, Via Iranawila, Sri Lanka
- C Asia • 250 kW

11600 BULGARIA †RADIO BULGARIA, Plovdiv
- W Europe • 500 kW
- W Europe • 250 kW
- W Asia & C Asia • 250 kW

RADIO BULGARIA, Sofia
- E Europe • 100 kW

CHINA †CHINA R INTL, Xi'an
- SE Asia • 150/500 kW
- E Africa & C Africa • 150 kW • ALT. FREQ. TO 7185 kHz

CZECH REPUBLIC RADIO PRAGUE, Litomyšl
- Mideast & S Asia • 100 kW
- S Asia • 100 kW
- N America • 100 kW
- Mideast & S Asia • 100 kW
- W Europe • 100 kW
- E Europe & W Asia • 100 kW
- W Europe • 100 kW
- SE Asia & Australasia • 100 kW
- W Europe & N Africa • 100 kW
- W Europe & N Africa • 100 kW

11605 CHINA (TAIWAN) R TAIWAN INTL, Tainan
- E Asia • 250 kW
- E Asia • TAIWAN NETWORK 2 • 250 kW

GERMANY †DEUTSCHE WELLE, Nauen
- W Africa & C Africa • 500 kW

†DEUTSCHE WELLE, Via Sri Lanka
- N Africa & Mideast • 250 kW

ISRAEL †KOL ISRAEL, Tel Aviv
- W Asia • 250 kW • ALT. FREQ. TO 7420 kHz
- F • W Asia • 250 kW
- Sa • SPANISH & LADINO • W Europe • 300 kW
- Su-Th • W Asia • 250 kW • ALT. FREQ. TO 7420 kHz
- W Europe • 300 kW

SWEDEN †RADIO SWEDEN, Hörby
- W Europe & W Africa • 500 kW
- M-F • W Europe & W Africa • 500 kW
- Africa • 500 kW

USA R FREE ASIA, Via Taiwan
- SE Asia • 250 kW

11610 CHINA †CENTRAL PEOPLE'S BS, Beijing
- DS-2 • 150 kW
- Th-Tu • DS-2 • 150 kW
- DS-2 • 150 kW

CHINA R INTL, Kunming
- S Asia • 150 kW

†CHINA R INTL, Xi'an
- C Asia & E Asia • 500 kW

CROATIA †VOICE OF CROATIA, Via Germany
- Australasia • 100 kW • ALT. FREQ. TO 13820 kHz

GERMANY MISSIONSWERK FRIEDENSSTIMME
- Sa • E Europe & W Asia • 250 kW

RUSSIA †VOICE OF RUSSIA, Moscow
- Mideast & W Asia • 250 kW

SWEDEN RADIO SWEDEN, Hörby
- Asia & Australasia • 500 kW
- Sa/Su • Asia & Australasia • 500 kW

USA ADVENTIST WORLD R, Via Agat, Guam
- S Asia • 100 kW

PAN AMERICAN BC, Via Jülich, Germany
- W • E Europe • 100 kW

11615 CZECH REPUBLIC RADIO PRAGUE, Litomyšl
- N Europe • 100 kW
- E Europe • 100 kW

FRANCE †R FRANCE INTL, Issoudun
- C Africa & E Africa • 500 kW • ALT. FREQ. TO 15605 kHz

GERMANY DEUTSCHE WELLE, Via Sines, Portugal
- W Africa & C Africa • 250 kW

LIBYA †RADIO JAMAHIRIYA, Via France
- ARABIC, ENGLISH & FRENCH • W Africa & C Africa • 500 kW

USA TRANS WORLD R, Via Albania
- E Europe • 100 kW
- M • E Europe • 100 kW
- Tu-Su • E Europe • 100 kW
- M-F • E Europe • 100 kW

	0 1 2 3 4 5 6 7 8 9 10 11 12 13 14 15 16 17 18 19 20 21 22 23 24

ENGLISH ▬ ARABIC ⌇⌇⌇ CHINESE ☐☐☐ FRENCH ══ GERMAN ▬▬ RUSSIAN ═══ SPANISH ▬▬ OTHER ▬

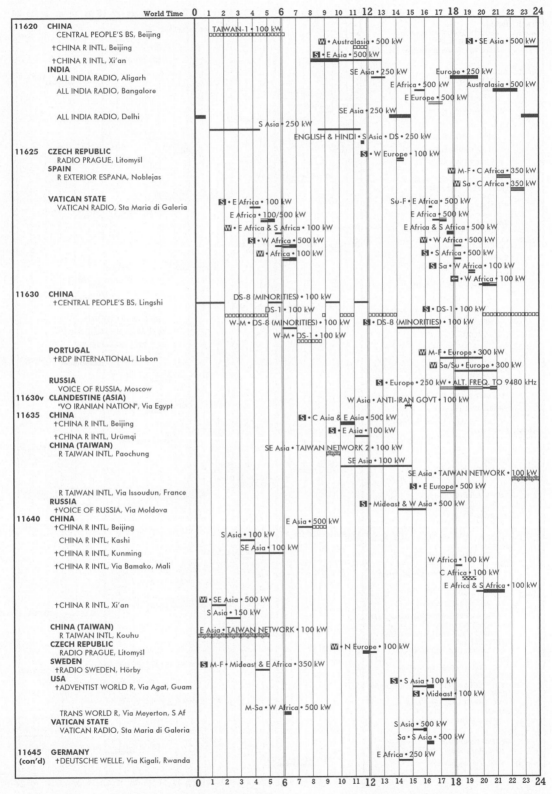

World Time 0 1 2 3 4 5 6 7 8 9 10 11 12 13 14 15 16 17 18 19 20 21 22 23 24

11620 CHINA
CENTRAL PEOPLE'S BS, Beijing — TAIWAN-1 • 100 kW
†CHINA R INTL, Beijing — W • Australasia • 500 kW / S • SE Asia • 500 kW
†CHINA R INTL, Xi'an — S • E Asia • 500 kW
INDIA
ALL INDIA RADIO, Aligarh — SE Asia • 250 kW / Europe • 250 kW
ALL INDIA RADIO, Bangalore — E Africa • 500 kW / Australasia • 500 kW / E Europe • 500 kW

ALL INDIA RADIO, Delhi — SE Asia • 250 kW
S Asia • 250 kW
ENGLISH & HINDI • S Asia • DS • 250 kW

11625 CZECH REPUBLIC
RADIO PRAGUE, Litomyšl — S • W Europe • 100 kW
SPAIN
R EXTERIOR ESPANA, Noblejas — W M-F • C Africa • 350 kW / W Sa • C Africa • 350 kW

VATICAN STATE
VATICAN RADIO, Sta Maria di Galeria
S • E Africa • 100 kW / Su-F • E Africa • 500 kW
E Africa • 100/500 kW / E Africa • 500 kW
W • E Africa & S Africa • 100 kW / E Africa & S Africa • 500 kW
S • W Africa • 500 kW / W • W Africa • 500 kW
W • Africa • 100 kW / S • S Africa • 500 kW
Sa • W Africa • 100 kW
• W Africa • 100 kW

11630 CHINA
†CENTRAL PEOPLE'S BS, Lingshi
DS-8 (MINORITIES) • 100 kW
DS-1 • 100 kW / S • DS-1 • 100 kW
W-M • DS-8 (MINORITIES) • 100 kW / S • DS-8 (MINORITIES) • 100 kW
W-M • DS-1 • 100 kW

PORTUGAL
†RDP INTERNATIONAL, Lisbon
W M-F • Europe • 300 kW / W Sa/Su • Europe • 300 kW

RUSSIA
VOICE OF RUSSIA, Moscow — S • Europe • 250 kW • ALT. FREQ. TO 9480 kHz
11630v CLANDESTINE (ASIA)
"VO IRANIAN NATION", Via Egypt — W Asia • ANTI-IRAN GOVT • 100 kW
11635 CHINA
†CHINA R INTL, Beijing — S • C Asia & E Asia • 500 kW / S • E Asia • 100 kW
†CHINA R INTL, Urümqi
CHINA (TAIWAN)
R TAIWAN INTL, Paochung
SE Asia • TAIWAN NETWORK 2 • 100 kW
SE Asia • 100 kW
SE Asia • TAIWAN NETWORK • 100 kW
S • E Europe • 500 kW

R TAIWAN INTL, Via Issoudun, France
RUSSIA
†VOICE OF RUSSIA, Via Moldova — S • Mideast & W Asia • 500 kW
11640 CHINA
†CHINA R INTL, Beijing — E Asia • 500 kW
CHINA R INTL, Kashi — S Asia • 100 kW
†CHINA R INTL, Kunming — SE Asia • 100 kW
†CHINA R INTL, Via Bamako, Mali
W Africa • 100 kW
C Africa • 100 kW
E Africa & S Africa • 100 kW

†CHINA R INTL, Xi'an — W • SE Asia • 500 kW
S Asia • 150 kW

CHINA (TAIWAN)
R TAIWAN INTL, Kouhu — E Asia • TAIWAN NETWORK • 100 kW
CZECH REPUBLIC
RADIO PRAGUE, Litomyšl — W • N Europe • 100 kW
SWEDEN
†RADIO SWEDEN, Hörby — S M-F • Mideast & E Africa • 350 kW
USA
†ADVENTIST WORLD R, Via Agat, Guam — S • S Asia • 100 kW / S • Mideast • 100 kW

TRANS WORLD R, Via Meyerton, S Af — M-Sa • W Africa • 500 kW
VATICAN STATE
VATICAN RADIO, Sta Maria di Galeria
S Asia • 500 kW
Sa • S Asia • 500 kW

11645 GERMANY
(con'd) †DEUTSCHE WELLE, Via Kigali, Rwanda — E Africa • 250 kW

0 1 2 3 4 5 6 7 8 9 10 11 12 13 14 15 16 17 18 19 20 21 22 23 24

SEASONAL **S** OR **W**   1-HR TIMESHIFT MIDYEAR ⟵ OR ⟶   JAMMING / OR /\   EARLIEST HEARD ◁   LATEST HEARD ▷   NEW FOR 2007 †

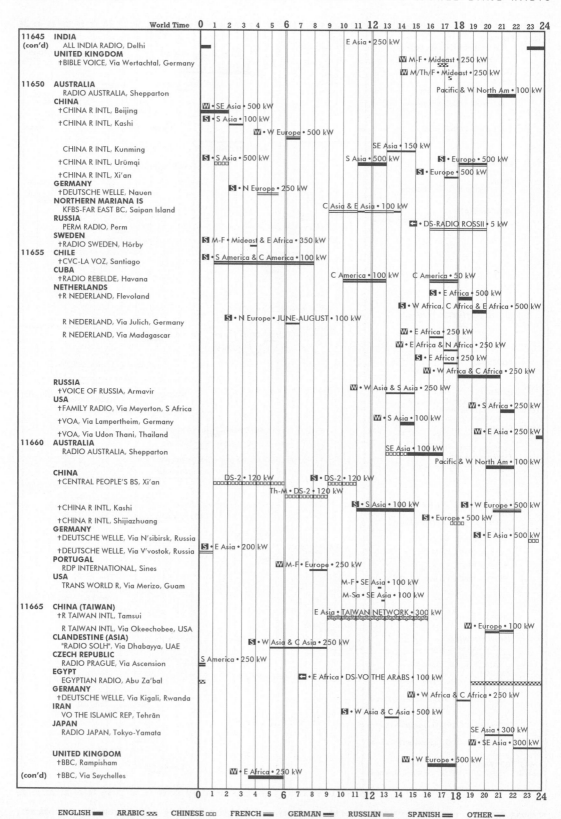

	World Time	0 1 2 3 4 5 6 7 8 9 10 11 12 13 14 15 16 17 18 19 20 21 22 23 24
11645 (con'd)	**INDIA** ALL INDIA RADIO, Delhi	E Asia • 250 kW
	UNITED KINGDOM †BIBLE VOICE, Via Wertachtal, Germany	W M-F • Mideast • 250 kW / W M/Th/F • Mideast • 250 kW
11650	**AUSTRALIA** RADIO AUSTRALIA, Shepparton	Pacific & W North Am • 100 kW
	CHINA †CHINA R INTL, Beijing	W • SE Asia • 500 kW
	†CHINA R INTL, Kashi	S • S Asia • 100 kW / W • W Europe • 500 kW
	CHINA R INTL, Kunming	SE Asia • 150 kW
	†CHINA R INTL, Urümqi	S • S Asia • 500 kW S Asia • 500 kW S • Europe • 500 kW
	†CHINA R INTL, Xi'an	S • Europe • 500 kW
	GERMANY †DEUTSCHE WELLE, Nauen	S • N Europe • 250 kW
	NORTHERN MARIANA IS KFBS-FAR EAST BC, Saipan Island	C Asia & E Asia • 100 kW
	RUSSIA PERM RADIO, Perm	• DS-RADIO ROSSII • 5 kW
	SWEDEN †RADIO SWEDEN, Hörby	S M-F • Mideast & E Africa • 350 kW
11655	**CHILE** †CVC-LA VOZ, Santiago	S • S America & C America • 100 kW
	CUBA †RADIO REBELDE, Havana	C America • 100 kW C America • 50 kW
	NETHERLANDS †R NEDERLAND, Flevoland	S • E Africa • 500 kW
		S • W Africa, C Africa & E Africa • 500 kW
	R NEDERLAND, Via Julich, Germany	S • N Europe • JUNE-AUGUST • 100 kW
	R NEDERLAND, Via Madagascar	W • E Africa • 250 kW
		W • E Africa & N Africa • 250 kW
		S • E Africa • 250 kW
		W • W Africa & C Africa • 250 kW
	RUSSIA †VOICE OF RUSSIA, Armavir	W • W Asia & S Asia • 250 kW
	USA †FAMILY RADIO, Via Meyerton, S Africa	W • S Africa • 250 kW
	†VOA, Via Lampertheim, Germany	W • S Asia • 100 kW
	†VOA, Via Udon Thani, Thailand	W • E Asia • 250 kW
11660	**AUSTRALIA** RADIO AUSTRALIA, Shepparton	SE Asia • 100 kW
		Pacific & W North Am • 100 kW
	CHINA †CENTRAL PEOPLE'S BS, Xi'an	DS-2 • 120 kW S • DS-2 • 120 kW
		Th-M • DS-2 • 120 kW
	†CHINA R INTL, Kashi	S • S Asia • 100 kW S • W Europe • 500 kW
	†CHINA R INTL, Shijiazhuang	S • Europe • 500 kW
	GERMANY †DEUTSCHE WELLE, Via N'sibirsk, Russia	S • E Asia • 500 kW
	†DEUTSCHE WELLE, Via V'vostok, Russia	S • E Asia • 200 kW
	PORTUGAL RDP INTERNATIONAL, Sines	W M-F • Europe • 250 kW
	USA TRANS WORLD R, Via Merizo, Guam	M-F • SE Asia • 100 kW
		M-Sa • SE Asia • 100 kW
11665	**CHINA (TAIWAN)** †R TAIWAN INTL, Tamsui	E Asia • TAIWAN NETWORK • 300 kW
	R TAIWAN INTL, Via Okeechobee, USA	W • Europe • 100 kW
	CLANDESTINE (ASIA) "RADIO SOLH", Via Dhabayya, UAE	S • W Asia & C Asia • 250 kW
	CZECH REPUBLIC RADIO PRAGUE, Via Ascension	S America • 250 kW
	EGYPT EGYPTIAN RADIO, Abu Za'bal	• E Africa • DS-VO THE ARABS • 100 kW
	GERMANY †DEUTSCHE WELLE, Via Kigali, Rwanda	W • W Africa & C Africa • 250 kW
	IRAN VO THE ISLAMIC REP, Tehrān	S • W Asia & C Asia • 500 kW
	JAPAN RADIO JAPAN, Tokyo-Yamata	SE Asia • 300 kW
		W • SE Asia • 300 kW
	UNITED KINGDOM †BBC, Rampisham	W • W Europe • 500 kW
(con'd)	†BBC, Via Seychelles	W • E Africa • 250 kW

ENGLISH ▬ ARABIC ⧓ CHINESE ⬚⬚⬚ FRENCH ▭▭ GERMAN ▭ RUSSIAN ══ SPANISH ══ OTHER ▬

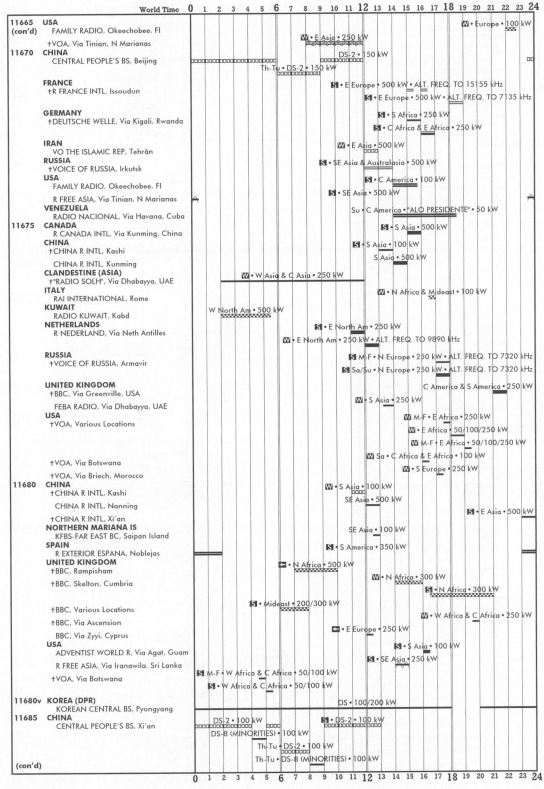

World Time

11665 (con'd)	USA
	FAMILY RADIO, Okeechobee, Fl
	†VOA, Via Tinian, N Marianas
11670	CHINA
	CENTRAL PEOPLE'S BS, Beijing
	FRANCE
	†R FRANCE INTL, Issoudun
	GERMANY
	†DEUTSCHE WELLE, Via Kigali, Rwanda
	IRAN
	VO THE ISLAMIC REP, Tehrān
	RUSSIA
	†VOICE OF RUSSIA, Irkutsk
	USA
	FAMILY RADIO, Okeechobee, Fl
	R FREE ASIA, Via Tinian, N Marianas
	VENEZUELA
	RADIO NACIONAL, Via Havana, Cuba
11675	CANADA
	R CANADA INTL, Via Kunming, China
	CHINA
	†CHINA R INTL, Kashi
	CHINA R INTL, Kunming
	CLANDESTINE (ASIA)
	†"RADIO SOLH", Via Dhabayya, UAE
	ITALY
	RAI INTERNATIONAL, Rome
	KUWAIT
	RADIO KUWAIT, Kabd
	NETHERLANDS
	R NEDERLAND, Via Neth Antilles
	RUSSIA
	†VOICE OF RUSSIA, Armavir
	UNITED KINGDOM
	†BBC, Via Greenville, USA
	FEBA RADIO, Via Dhabayya, UAE
	USA
	†VOA, Various Locations
	†VOA, Via Botswana
	†VOA, Via Briech, Morocco
11680	CHINA
	†CHINA R INTL, Kashi
	CHINA R INTL, Nanning
	†CHINA R INTL, Xi'an
	NORTHERN MARIANA IS
	KFBS-FAR EAST BC, Saipan Island
	SPAIN
	R EXTERIOR ESPANA, Noblejas
	UNITED KINGDOM
	†BBC, Rampisham
	†BBC, Skelton, Cumbria
	†BBC, Various Locations
	†BBC, Via Ascension
	BBC, Via Zyyi, Cyprus
	USA
	ADVENTIST WORLD R, Via Agat, Guam
	R FREE ASIA, Via Iranawila, Sri Lanka
	†VOA, Via Botswana
11680v	KOREA (DPR)
	KOREAN CENTRAL BS, Pyongyang
11685	CHINA
	CENTRAL PEOPLE'S BS, Xi'an
(con'd)	

W • Europe • 100 kW
W • E Asia • 250 kW
DS-2 • 150 kW
Th-Tu • DS-2 • 150 kW
S • E Europe • 500 kW • ALT. FREQ. TO 15155 kHz
S • E Europe • 500 kW • ALT. FREQ. TO 7135 kHz
S • S Africa • 250 kW
S • C Africa & E Africa • 250 kW
W • E Asia • 500 kW
S • SE Asia & Australasia • 500 kW
S • C America • 100 kW
S • SE Asia • 500 kW
Su • C America • "ALO PRESIDENTE" • 50 kW
S • S Asia • 500 kW
S • S Asia • 100 kW
S Asia • 500 kW
W • W Asia & C Asia • 250 kW
W • N Africa & Mideast • 100 kW
W North Am • 500 kW
S • E North Am • 250 kW
W • E North Am • 250 kW • ALT. FREQ. TO 9890 kHz
S M-F • N Europe • 250 kW • ALT. FREQ. TO 7320 kHz
S Sa/Su • N Europe • 250 kW • ALT. FREQ. TO 7320 kHz
C America & S America • 250 kW
W • S Asia • 250 kW
W M-F • E Africa • 250 kW
W • E Africa • 50/100/250 kW
W M-F • E Africa • 50/100/250 kW
W Sa • C Africa & E Africa • 100 kW
W • S Europe • 250 kW
W • S Asia • 100 kW
SE Asia • 500 kW
S • E Asia • 500 kW
SE Asia • 100 kW
S • S America • 350 kW
→ • N Africa • 500 kW
W • N Africa • 300 kW
S • N Africa • 300 kW
S • Mideast • 200/300 kW
W • W Africa & C Africa • 250 kW
→ • E Europe • 250 kW
S • S Asia • 100 kW
S • SE Asia • 250 kW
S M-F • W Africa & C Africa • 50/100 kW
S • W Africa & C Africa • 50/100 kW
DS • 100/200 kW
S • DS-2 • 100 kW
DS-2 • 100 kW
DS-8 (MINORITIES) • 100 kW
Th-Tu • DS-2 • 100 kW
Th-Tu • DS-8 (MINORITIES) • 100 kW

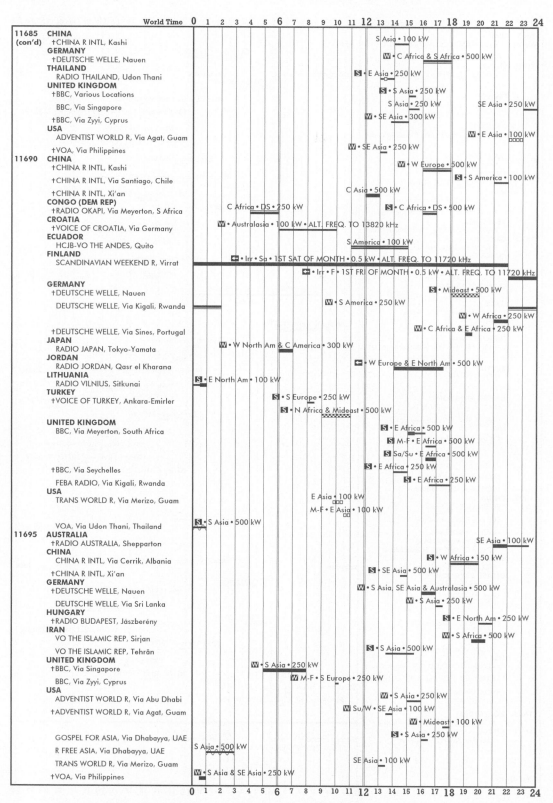

World Time 0 1 2 3 4 5 6 7 8 9 10 11 12 13 14 15 16 17 18 19 20 21 22 23 24

11685
(con'd)   **CHINA**
          †CHINA R INTL, Kashi   S Asia • 100 kW
          GERMANY
          †DEUTSCHE WELLE, Nauen   W • C Africa & S Africa • 500 kW
          THAILAND
          RADIO THAILAND, Udon Thani   S • E Asia • 250 kW
          UNITED KINGDOM
          †BBC, Various Locations   S • S Asia • 250 kW
          BBC, Via Singapore   S Asia • 250 kW   SE Asia • 250 kW
          †BBC, Via Zyyi, Cyprus   W • SE Asia • 300 kW
          USA
          ADVENTIST WORLD R, Via Agat, Guam   W • E Asia • 100 kW
          †VOA, Via Philippines   W • SE Asia • 250 kW
11690 **CHINA**
          †CHINA R INTL, Kashi   W • W Europe • 500 kW
          †CHINA R INTL, Via Santiago, Chile   S • S America • 100 kW
          †CHINA R INTL, Xi'an   C Asia • 500 kW
          CONGO (DEM REP)
          †RADIO OKAPI, Via Meyerton, S Africa   C Africa • DS • 250 kW   S • C Africa • DS • 500 kW
          CROATIA
          †VOICE OF CROATIA, Via Germany   W • Australasia • 100 kW • ALT. FREQ. TO 13820 kHz
          ECUADOR
          HCJB-VO THE ANDES, Quito   S America • 100 kW
          FINLAND
          SCANDINAVIAN WEEKEND R, Virrat   ⊡ • Irr • Sa • 1ST SAT OF MONTH • 0.5 kW • ALT. FREQ. TO 11720 kHz

                                                   ⊡ • Irr • F • 1ST FRI OF MONTH • 0.5 kW • ALT. FREQ. TO 11720 kHz
          GERMANY
          †DEUTSCHE WELLE, Nauen   S • Mideast • 500 kW
          DEUTSCHE WELLE, Via Kigali, Rwanda   W • S America • 250 kW
                                                                              W • W Africa • 250 kW
          †DEUTSCHE WELLE, Via Sines, Portugal   W • C Africa & E Africa • 250 kW
          JAPAN
          RADIO JAPAN, Tokyo-Yamata   W • W North Am & C America • 300 kW
          JORDAN
          RADIO JORDAN, Qasr el Kharana   ⊡ • W Europe & E North Am • 500 kW
          LITHUANIA
          RADIO VILNIUS, Sitkunai   S • E North Am • 100 kW
          TURKEY
          †VOICE OF TURKEY, Ankara-Emirler   S • S Europe • 250 kW
                                                  S • N Africa & Mideast • 500 kW
          UNITED KINGDOM
          BBC, Via Meyerton, South Africa   S • E Africa • 500 kW
                                                           S • M-F • E Africa • 500 kW
                                                           S Sa/Su • E Africa • 500 kW
          †BBC, Via Seychelles   S • E Africa • 250 kW
          FEBA RADIO, Via Kigali, Rwanda   S • E Africa • 250 kW
          USA
          TRANS WORLD R, Via Merizo, Guam   E Asia • 100 kW
                                                   M-F • E Asia • 100 kW
          VOA, Via Udon Thani, Thailand   S • S Asia • 500 kW
11695 **AUSTRALIA**
          †RADIO AUSTRALIA, Shepparton   SE Asia • 100 kW
          CHINA
          CHINA R INTL, Via Cerrik, Albania   S • W Africa • 150 kW
          †CHINA R INTL, Xi'an   S • SE Asia • 500 kW
          GERMANY
          †DEUTSCHE WELLE, Nauen   W • S Asia, SE Asia & Australasia • 500 kW
          DEUTSCHE WELLE, Via Sri Lanka   W • S Asia • 250 kW
          HUNGARY
          †RADIO BUDAPEST, Jászberény   S • E North Am • 250 kW
          IRAN
          VO THE ISLAMIC REP, Sirjan   W • S Africa • 500 kW
          VO THE ISLAMIC REP, Tehrān   S • S Asia • 500 kW
          UNITED KINGDOM
          †BBC, Via Singapore   W • S Asia • 250 kW
          BBC, Via Zyyi, Cyprus   W M-F • S Europe • 250 kW
          USA
          ADVENTIST WORLD R, Via Abu Dhabi   W • S Asia • 250 kW
          †ADVENTIST WORLD R, Via Agat, Guam   W Su/W • SE Asia • 100 kW
                                                          W • Mideast • 100 kW
          GOSPEL FOR ASIA, Via Dhabayya, UAE   S • S Asia • 250 kW
          R FREE ASIA, Via Dhabayya, UAE   S Asia • 500 kW
          TRANS WORLD R, Via Merizo, Guam   SE Asia • 100 kW
          †VOA, Via Philippines   W • S Asia & SE Asia • 250 kW

0 1 2 3 4 5 6 7 8 9 10 11 12 13 14 15 16 17 18 19 20 21 22 23 24

ENGLISH ▬   ARABIC ░░░   CHINESE □□□   FRENCH ══   GERMAN ▬▬   RUSSIAN ══   SPANISH ══   OTHER ──

World Time   0 1 2 3 4 5 6 7 8 9 10 11 12 13 14 15 16 17 18 19 20 21 22 23 24

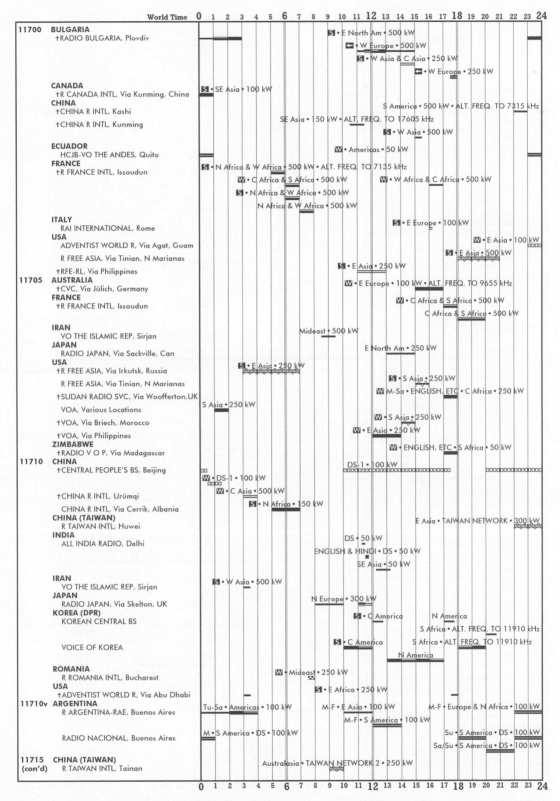

11700 BULGARIA
†RADIO BULGARIA, Plovdiv
- **S** • E North Am • 500 kW
- ⇦ • W Europe • 500 kW
- **S** • W Asia & C Asia • 250 kW
- ⇦ • W Europe • 250 kW

CANADA
†R CANADA INTL, Via Kunming, China
- **S** • SE Asia • 100 kW

CHINA
†CHINA R INTL, Kashi
- S America • 500 kW • ALT. FREQ. TO 7315 kHz

†CHINA R INTL, Kunming
- SE Asia • 150 kW • ALT. FREQ. TO 17605 kHz
- **S** • W Asia • 500 kW

ECUADOR
HCJB-VO THE ANDES, Quito
- **W** • Americas • 50 kW

FRANCE
†R FRANCE INTL, Issoudun
- **S** • N Africa & W Africa • 500 kW • ALT. FREQ. TO 7135 kHz
- **W** • C Africa & S Africa • 500 kW
- **W** • W Africa & C Africa • 500 kW
- **S** • N Africa & W Africa • 500 kW
- N Africa & W Africa • 500 kW

ITALY
RAI INTERNATIONAL, Rome
- **S** • E Europe • 100 kW

USA
ADVENTIST WORLD R, Via Agat, Guam
- **W** • E Asia • 100 kW

R FREE ASIA, Via Tinian, N Marianas
- **S** • E Asia • 500 kW

†RFE-RL, Via Philippines
- **S** • E Asia • 250 kW

11705 AUSTRALIA
†CVC, Via Jülich, Germany
- **W** • E Europe • 100 kW • ALT. FREQ. TO 9655 kHz

FRANCE
†R FRANCE INTL, Issoudun
- **W** • C Africa & S Africa • 500 kW
- C Africa & S Africa • 500 kW

IRAN
VO THE ISLAMIC REP, Sirjan
- Mideast • 500 kW

JAPAN
RADIO JAPAN, Via Sackville, Can
- E North Am • 250 kW

USA
†R FREE ASIA, Via Irkutsk, Russia
- **S** • E Asia • 250 kW

R FREE ASIA, Via Tinian, N Marianas
- **S** • S Asia • 250 kW

†SUDAN RADIO SVC, Via Woofferton, UK
- **W** M-Sa • ENGLISH, ETC • C Africa • 250 kW

VOA, Various Locations
- S Asia • 250 kW

†VOA, Via Briech, Morocco
- **W** • S Asia • 250 kW

†VOA, Via Philippines
- **W** • E Asia • 250 kW

ZIMBABWE
†RADIO V O P, Via Madagascar
- **W** • ENGLISH, ETC • S Africa • 50 kW

11710 CHINA
†CENTRAL PEOPLE'S BS, Beijing
- DS-1 • 100 kW
- **W** • DS-1 • 100 kW

†CHINA R INTL, Urümqi
- **W** • C Asia • 500 kW

CHINA R INTL, Via Cerrik, Albania
- **S** • N Africa • 150 kW

CHINA (TAIWAN)
R TAIWAN INTL, Huwei
- E Asia • TAIWAN NETWORK • 300 kW

INDIA
ALL INDIA RADIO, Delhi
- DS • 50 kW
- ENGLISH & HINDI • DS • 50 kW
- SE Asia • 50 kW

IRAN
VO THE ISLAMIC REP, Sirjan
- **S** • W Asia • 500 kW

JAPAN
RADIO JAPAN, Via Skelton, UK
- N Europe • 300 kW

KOREA (DPR)
KOREAN CENTRAL BS
- **S** • C America
- N America
- S Africa • ALT. FREQ. TO 11910 kHz

VOICE OF KOREA
- **S** • C America
- S Africa • ALT FREQ. TO 11910 kHz
- N America

ROMANIA
R ROMANIA INTL, Bucharest
- **W** • Mideast • 250 kW
- **S**

USA
†ADVENTIST WORLD R, Via Abu Dhabi
- **S** • E Africa • 250 kW

11710v ARGENTINA
R ARGENTINA-RAE, Buenos Aires
- Tu-Sa • Americas • 100 kW
- M-F • E Asia • 100 kW
- M-F • Europe & N Africa • 100 kW
- M-F • S America • 100 kW

RADIO NACIONAL, Buenos Aires
- M • S America • DS • 100 kW
- Su • S America • DS • 100 kW
- Sa/Su • S America • DS • 100 kW

11715 CHINA (TAIWAN)
(con'd)   R TAIWAN INTL, Tainan
- Australasia • TAIWAN NETWORK 2 • 250 kW

0 1 2 3 4 5 6 7 8 9 10 11 12 13 14 15 16 17 18 19 20 21 22 23 24

SEASONAL **S** OR **W**   1-HR TIMESHIFT MIDYEAR ⇦ OR ⇨   JAMMING / OR ⋀   EARLIEST HEARD ◁   LATEST HEARD ▷   NEW FOR 2007 †

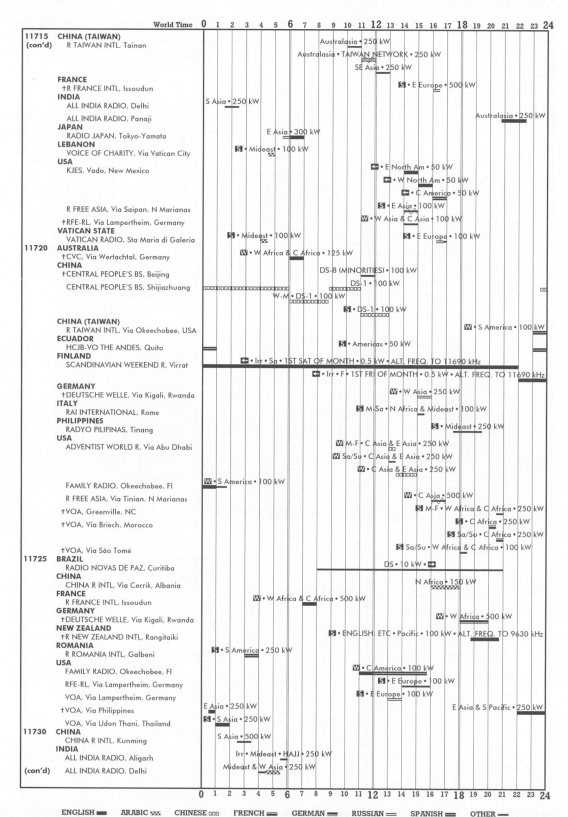

| World Time | 0 | 1 | 2 | 3 | 4 | 5 | 6 | 7 | 8 | 9 | 10 | 11 | 12 | 13 | 14 | 15 | 16 | 17 | 18 | 19 | 20 | 21 | 22 | 23 | 24 |

11715 (con'd) CHINA (TAIWAN)
R TAIWAN INTL, Tainan — Australasia • 250 kW; Australasia • TAIWAN NETWORK • 250 kW; SE Asia • 250 kW

FRANCE
†R FRANCE INTL, Issoudun — S • E Europe • 500 kW
INDIA
ALL INDIA RADIO, Delhi — S Asia • 250 kW
ALL INDIA RADIO, Panaji — Australasia • 250 kW
JAPAN
RADIO JAPAN, Tokyo-Yamata — E Asia • 300 kW
LEBANON
VOICE OF CHARITY, Via Vatican City — S • Mideast • 100 kW
USA
KJES, Vado, New Mexico — E North Am • 50 kW; W North Am • 50 kW; C America • 50 kW
R FREE ASIA, Via Saipan, N Marianas — S • E Asia • 100 kW
†RFE-RL, Via Lampertheim, Germany — W • W Asia & C Asia • 100 kW
VATICAN STATE
VATICAN RADIO, Sta Maria di Galeria — S • Mideast • 100 kW; S • E Europe • 100 kW
11720 AUSTRALIA
†CVC, Via Wertachtal, Germany — W • W Africa & C Africa • 125 kW
CHINA
†CENTRAL PEOPLE'S BS, Beijing — DS-8 (MINORITIES) • 100 kW
CENTRAL PEOPLE'S BS, Shijiazhuang — DS-1 • 100 kW; W-M • DS-1 • 100 kW; S • DS-1 • 100 kW
CHINA (TAIWAN)
R TAIWAN INTL, Via Okeechobee, USA — W • S America • 100 kW
ECUADOR
HCJB-VO THE ANDES, Quito — S • Americas • 50 kW
FINLAND
SCANDINAVIAN WEEKEND R, Virrat — Irr • Sa • 1ST SAT OF MONTH • 0.5 kW • ALT. FREQ. TO 11690 kHz; Irr • F • 1ST FRI OF MONTH • 0.5 kW • ALT. FREQ. TO 11690 kHz
GERMANY
†DEUTSCHE WELLE, Via Kigali, Rwanda — W • W Asia • 250 kW
ITALY
RAI INTERNATIONAL, Rome — S M-Sa • N Africa & Mideast • 100 kW
PHILIPPINES
RADYO PILIPINAS, Tinang — S • Mideast • 250 kW
USA
ADVENTIST WORLD R, Via Abu Dhabi — W M-F • C Asia & E Asia • 250 kW; W Sa/Su • C Asia & E Asia • 250 kW; W • C Asia & E Asia • 250 kW
FAMILY RADIO, Okeechobee, Fl — W • S America • 100 kW
R FREE ASIA, Via Tinian, N Marianas — W • C Asia • 500 kW
†VOA, Greenville, NC — S M-F • W Africa & C Africa • 250 kW
†VOA, Via Briech, Morocco — S • C Africa • 250 kW; S Sa/Su • C Africa • 250 kW
†VOA, Via São Tomé — S Sa/Su • W Africa & C Africa • 100 kW
11725 BRAZIL
RADIO NOVAS DE PAZ, Curitiba — DS • 10 kW •
CHINA
CHINA R INTL, Via Cerrik, Albania — N Africa • 150 kW
FRANCE
R FRANCE INTL, Issoudun — W • W Africa & C Africa • 500 kW
GERMANY
†DEUTSCHE WELLE, Via Kigali, Rwanda — W • W Africa • 500 kW
NEW ZEALAND
†R NEW ZEALAND INTL, Rangitaiki — S • ENGLISH, ETC • Pacific • 100 kW • ALT. FREQ. TO 9630 kHz
ROMANIA
R ROMANIA INTL, Galbeni — S • S America • 250 kW
USA
FAMILY RADIO, Okeechobee, Fl — W • C America • 100 kW
RFE-RL, Via Lampertheim, Germany — S • E Europe • 100 kW
VOA, Via Lampertheim, Germany — S • E Europe • 100 kW
†VOA, Via Philippines — E Asia • 250 kW; E Asia & S Pacific • 250 kW
VOA, Via Udon Thani, Thailand — S • S Asia • 250 kW
11730 CHINA
CHINA R INTL, Kunming — S Asia • 500 kW
INDIA
ALL INDIA RADIO, Aligarh — Irr • Mideast • HAJJ • 250 kW
(con'd) ALL INDIA RADIO, Delhi — Mideast & W Asia • 250 kW

| | 0 | 1 | 2 | 3 | 4 | 5 | 6 | 7 | 8 | 9 | 10 | 11 | 12 | 13 | 14 | 15 | 16 | 17 | 18 | 19 | 20 | 21 | 22 | 23 | 24 |

ENGLISH ▬ ARABIC ⋙ CHINESE ▫▫▫ FRENCH ▭ GERMAN ▭ RUSSIAN ═ SPANISH ▬ OTHER —

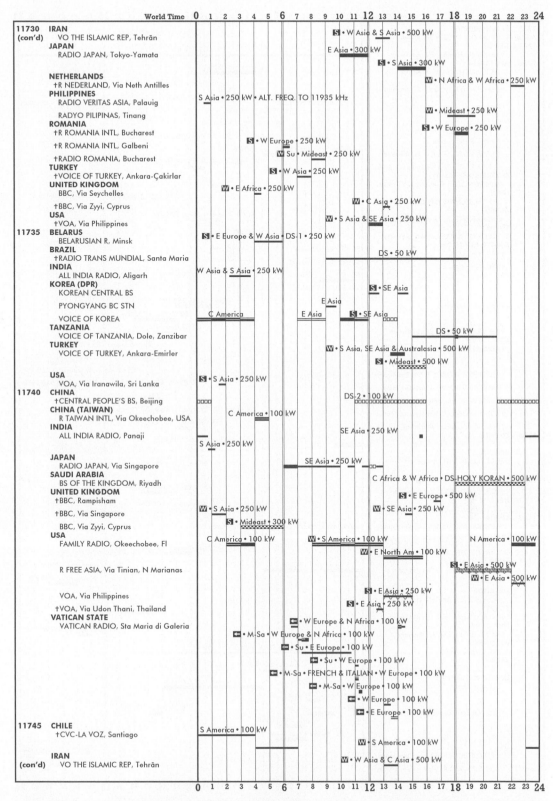

World Time																								
	0	1	2	3	4	5	6	7	8	9	10	11	12	13	14	15	16	17	18	19	20	21	22	23	24

11730 IRAN (con'd)
VO THE ISLAMIC REP, Tehrān — S • W Asia & S Asia • 500 kW

JAPAN
RADIO JAPAN, Tokyo-Yamata — E Asia • 300 kW
— S • S Asia • 300 kW

NETHERLANDS
†R NEDERLAND, Via Neth Antilles — W • N Africa & W Africa • 250 kW

PHILIPPINES
RADIO VERITAS ASIA, Palauig — S Asia • 250 kW • ALT. FREQ. TO 11935 kHz

RADYO PILIPINAS, Tinang — W • Mideast • 250 kW

ROMANIA
†R ROMANIA INTL, Bucharest — S • W Europe • 250 kW

†R ROMANIA INTL, Galbeni — S • W Europe • 250 kW

†RADIO ROMANIA, Bucharest — W • Su • Mideast • 250 kW

TURKEY
†VOICE OF TURKEY, Ankara-Çakirlar — S • W Asia • 250 kW

UNITED KINGDOM
BBC, Via Seychelles — W • E Africa • 250 kW

†BBC, Via Zyyi, Cyprus — W • C Asia • 250 kW

USA
†VOA, Via Philippines — W • S Asia & SE Asia • 250 kW

11735 BELARUS
BELARUSIAN R, Minsk — S • E Europe & W Asia • DS-1 • 250 kW

BRAZIL
†RADIO TRANS MUNDIAL, Santa Maria — DS • 50 kW

INDIA
ALL INDIA RADIO, Aligarh — W Asia & S Asia • 250 kW

KOREA (DPR)
KOREAN CENTRAL BS — S • SE Asia

PYONGYANG BC STN — E Asia

VOICE OF KOREA — C America / E Asia / S • SE Asia

TANZANIA
VOICE OF TANZANIA, Dole, Zanzibar — DS • 50 kW

TURKEY
VOICE OF TURKEY, Ankara-Emirler — W • S Asia, SE Asia & Australasia • 500 kW
— S • Mideast • 500 kW

USA
VOA, Via Iranawila, Sri Lanka — S • S Asia • 250 kW

11740 CHINA
†CENTRAL PEOPLE'S BS, Beijing — DS-2 • 100 kW

CHINA (TAIWAN)
R TAIWAN INTL, Via Okeechobee, USA — C America • 100 kW

INDIA
ALL INDIA RADIO, Panaji — SE Asia • 250 kW
S Asia • 250 kW

JAPAN
RADIO JAPAN, Via Singapore — SE Asia • 250 kW

SAUDI ARABIA
BS OF THE KINGDOM, Riyadh — C Africa & W Africa • DS-HOLY KORAN • 500 kW

UNITED KINGDOM
†BBC, Rampisham — S • E Europe • 500 kW

†BBC, Via Singapore — W • S Asia • 250 kW
— W • SE Asia • 250 kW

BBC, Via Zyyi, Cyprus — S • Mideast • 300 kW

USA
FAMILY RADIO, Okeechobee, Fl — C America • 100 kW / W • S America • 100 kW / N America • 100 kW
— W • E North Am • 100 kW

R FREE ASIA, Via Tinian, N Marianas — S • E Asia • 500 kW
— W • E Asia • 500 kW

VOA, Via Philippines — S • E Asia • 250 kW

†VOA, Via Udon Thani, Thailand — S • E Asia • 250 kW

VATICAN STATE
VATICAN RADIO, Sta Maria di Galeria — • W Europe & N Africa • 100 kW
— • M-Sa • W Europe & N Africa • 100 kW
— • Su • E Europe • 100 kW
— • Su • W Europe • 100 kW
— • M-Sa • FRENCH & ITALIAN • W Europe • 100 kW
— • M-Sa • W Europe • 100 kW
— • W Europe • 100 kW
— • E Europe • 100 kW

11745 CHILE
†CVC-LA VOZ, Santiago — S America • 100 kW
— W • S America • 100 kW

IRAN (con'd)
VO THE ISLAMIC REP, Tehrān — W • W Asia & C Asia • 500 kW

	0	1	2	3	4	5	6	7	8	9	10	11	12	13	14	15	16	17	18	19	20	21	22	23	24

SEASONAL S OR W   1-HR TIMESHIFT MIDYEAR ⊏ OR ⊐   JAMMING / OR ∧   EARLIEST HEARD ◁   LATEST HEARD ▷   NEW FOR 2007 †

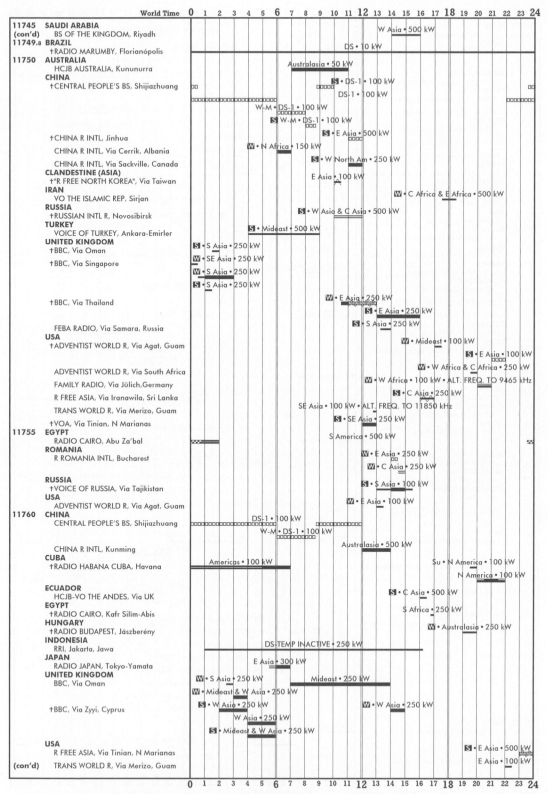

World Time 0 1 2 3 4 5 6 7 8 9 10 11 12 13 14 15 16 17 18 19 20 21 22 23 24

11745 SAUDI ARABIA	
(con'd) BS OF THE KINGDOM, Riyadh	W Asia • 500 kW
11749.8 BRAZIL	DS • 10 kW
†RADIO MARUMBY, Florianópolis	
11750 AUSTRALIA	
HCJB AUSTRALIA, Kununurra	Australasia • 50 kW
CHINA	S • DS-1 • 100 kW
†CENTRAL PEOPLE'S BS, Shijiazhuang	DS-1 • 100 kW
	W-M • DS-1 • 100 kW
	S W-M • DS-1 • 100 kW
†CHINA R INTL, Jinhua	S • E Asia • 500 kW
CHINA R INTL, Via Cerrik, Albania	W • N Africa • 150 kW
CHINA R INTL, Via Sackville, Canada	S • W North Am • 250 kW
CLANDESTINE (ASIA)	
†"R FREE NORTH KOREA", Via Taiwan	E Asia • 100 kW
IRAN	
VO THE ISLAMIC REP, Sirjan	W • C Africa & E Africa • 500 kW
RUSSIA	
†RUSSIAN INTL R, Novosibirsk	S • W Asia & C Asia • 500 kW
TURKEY	
VOICE OF TURKEY, Ankara-Emirler	S • Mideast • 500 kW
UNITED KINGDOM	
†BBC, Via Oman	S • S Asia • 250 kW
	W • SE Asia • 250 kW
†BBC, Via Singapore	W • S Asia • 250 kW
	S • S Asia • 250 kW
†BBC, Via Thailand	W • E Asia • 250 kW
	S • E Asia • 250 kW
FEBA RADIO, Via Samara, Russia	S • S Asia • 250 kW
USA	
†ADVENTIST WORLD R, Via Agat, Guam	W • Mideast • 100 kW
	S • E Asia • 100 kW
ADVENTIST WORLD R, Via South Africa	W • W Africa & C Africa • 250 kW
FAMILY RADIO, Via Jülich, Germany	W • W Africa • 100 kW • ALT. FREQ. TO 9465 kHz
R FREE ASIA, Via Iranawila, Sri Lanka	W • C Asia • 250 kW
TRANS WORLD R, Via Merizo, Guam	SE Asia • 100 kW • ALT. FREQ. TO 11850 kHz
†VOA, Via Tinian, N Marianas	S • SE Asia • 250 kW
11755 EGYPT	
RADIO CAIRO, Abu Za'bal	S America • 500 kW
ROMANIA	
R ROMANIA INTL, Bucharest	W • E Asia • 250 kW
	W • C Asia • 250 kW
RUSSIA	
†VOICE OF RUSSIA, Via Tajikistan	S • S Asia • 100 kW
USA	
ADVENTIST WORLD R, Via Agat, Guam	W • E Asia • 100 kW
11760 CHINA	
CENTRAL PEOPLE'S BS, Shijiazhuang	DS-1 • 100 kW
	W-M • DS-1 • 100 kW
CHINA R INTL, Kunming	Australasia • 500 kW
CUBA	
†RADIO HABANA CUBA, Havana	Americas • 100 kW
	Su • N America • 100 kW
	N America • 100 kW
ECUADOR	
HCJB-VO THE ANDES, Via UK	S • C Asia • 500 kW
EGYPT	
†RADIO CAIRO, Kafr Silim-Abis	S Africa • 250 kW
HUNGARY	
†RADIO BUDAPEST, Jászberény	W • Australasia • 250 kW
INDONESIA	
RRI, Jakarta, Jawa	DS • TEMP INACTIVE • 250 kW
JAPAN	
RADIO JAPAN, Tokyo-Yamata	E Asia • 300 kW
UNITED KINGDOM	
BBC, Via Oman	W • S Asia • 250 kW
	Mideast • 250 kW
	W • Mideast & W Asia • 250 kW
†BBC, Via Zyyi, Cyprus	S • W Asia • 250 kW
	W • W Asia • 250 kW
	W Asia • 250 kW
	S • Mideast & W Asia • 250 kW
USA	
R FREE ASIA, Via Tinian, N Marianas	S • E Asia • 500 kW
(con'd) TRANS WORLD R, Via Merizo, Guam	E Asia • 100 kW

0 1 2 3 4 5 6 7 8 9 10 11 12 13 14 15 16 17 18 19 20 21 22 23 24

ENGLISH ▬ ARABIC ⌇⌇⌇ CHINESE ▯▯▯ FRENCH ▭ GERMAN ▬ RUSSIAN ═ SPANISH ▬ OTHER ▬

World Time 0 1 2 3 4 5 6 7 8 9 10 11 12 13 14 15 16 17 18 19 20 21 22 23 24

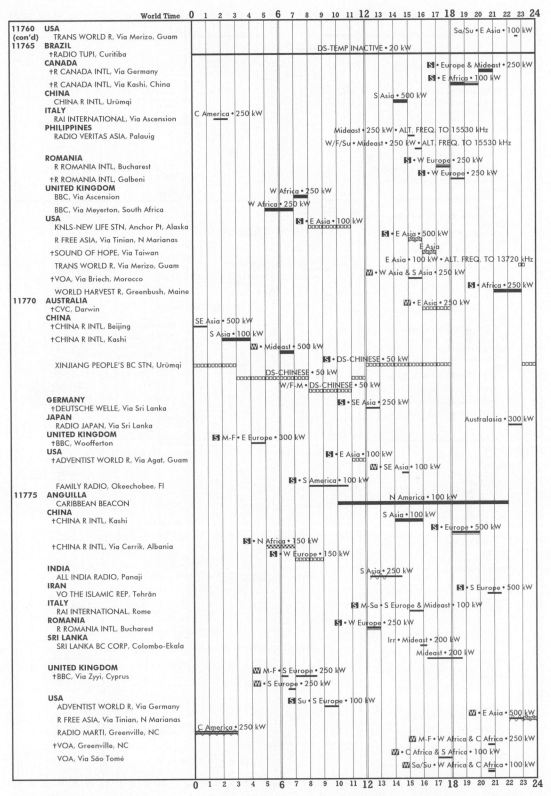

11760
(con'd) USA
  TRANS WORLD R, Via Merizo, Guam — Sa/Su • E Asia • 100 kW
11765 BRAZIL
  †RADIO TUPI, Curitiba — DS-TEMP INACTIVE • 20 kW
CANADA
  †R CANADA INTL, Via Germany — S • Europe & Mideast • 250 kW
  †R CANADA INTL, Via Kashi, China — S • E Africa • 100 kW
CHINA
  CHINA R INTL, Urümqi — S Asia • 500 kW
ITALY
  RAI INTERNATIONAL, Via Ascension — C America • 250 kW
PHILIPPINES
  RADIO VERITAS ASIA, Palauig — Mideast • 250 kW • ALT. FREQ. TO 15530 kHz
  — W/F/Su • Mideast • 250 kW • ALT. FREQ. TO 15530 kHz
ROMANIA
  R ROMANIA INTL, Bucharest — S • W Europe • 250 kW
  †R ROMANIA INTL, Galbeni — S • W Europe • 250 kW
UNITED KINGDOM
  BBC, Via Ascension — W Africa • 250 kW
  BBC, Via Meyerton, South Africa — W Africa • 250 kW
USA
  KNLS-NEW LIFE STN, Anchor Pt, Alaska — S • E Asia • 100 kW
  R FREE ASIA, Via Tinian, N Marianas — S • E Asia • 500 kW
  †SOUND OF HOPE, Via Taiwan — E Asia / E Asia • 100 kW • ALT. FREQ. TO 13720 kHz
  TRANS WORLD R, Via Merizo, Guam — W • W Asia & S Asia • 250 kW
  †VOA, Via Briech, Morocco
  WORLD HARVEST R, Greenbush, Maine — S • Africa • 250 kW
11770 AUSTRALIA
  †CVC, Darwin — W • E Asia • 250 kW
CHINA
  †CHINA R INTL, Beijing — SE Asia • 500 kW
  †CHINA R INTL, Kashi — S Asia • 100 kW / W • Mideast • 500 kW
  XINJIANG PEOPLE'S BC STN, Urümqi — S • DS-CHINESE • 50 kW / DS-CHINESE • 50 kW / W/F-M • DS-CHINESE • 50 kW
GERMANY
  †DEUTSCHE WELLE, Via Sri Lanka — S • SE Asia • 250 kW
JAPAN
  RADIO JAPAN, Via Sri Lanka — Australasia • 300 kW
UNITED KINGDOM
  †BBC, Woofferton — S • M-F • E Europe • 300 kW
USA
  †ADVENTIST WORLD R, Via Agat, Guam — S • E Asia • 100 kW / W • SE Asia • 100 kW
  FAMILY RADIO, Okeechobee, Fl — S • S America • 100 kW
11775 ANGUILLA
  CARIBBEAN BEACON — N America • 100 kW
CHINA
  †CHINA R INTL, Kashi — S Asia • 100 kW / S • Europe • 500 kW
  †CHINA R INTL, Via Cerrik, Albania — S • N Africa • 150 kW / S • W Europe • 150 kW
INDIA
  ALL INDIA RADIO, Panaji — S Asia • 250 kW
IRAN
  VO THE ISLAMIC REP, Tehrān — S • S Europe • 500 kW
ITALY
  RAI INTERNATIONAL, Rome — S • M-Sa • S Europe & Mideast • 100 kW
ROMANIA
  R ROMANIA INTL, Bucharest — S • W Europe • 250 kW
SRI LANKA
  SRI LANKA BC CORP, Colombo-Ekala — Irr • Mideast • 200 kW / Mideast • 200 kW
UNITED KINGDOM
  †BBC, Via Zyyi, Cyprus — W • M-F • S Europe • 250 kW / W • S Europe • 250 kW
USA
  ADVENTIST WORLD R, Via Germany — S • Su • S Europe • 100 kW
  R FREE ASIA, Via Tinian, N Marianas — W • E Asia • 500 kW
  RADIO MARTI, Greenville, NC — C America • 250 kW
  †VOA, Greenville, NC — W • M-F • W Africa & C Africa • 250 kW / W • C Africa & S Africa • 100 kW
  VOA, Via São Tomé — W • Sa/Su • W Africa & C Africa • 100 kW

0 1 2 3 4 5 6 7 8 9 10 11 12 13 14 15 16 17 18 19 20 21 22 23 24

SEASONAL S OR W   1-HR TIMESHIFT MIDYEAR ⬅ OR ➡   JAMMING / OR /\   EARLIEST HEARD ◁   LATEST HEARD ▷   NEW FOR 2007 †

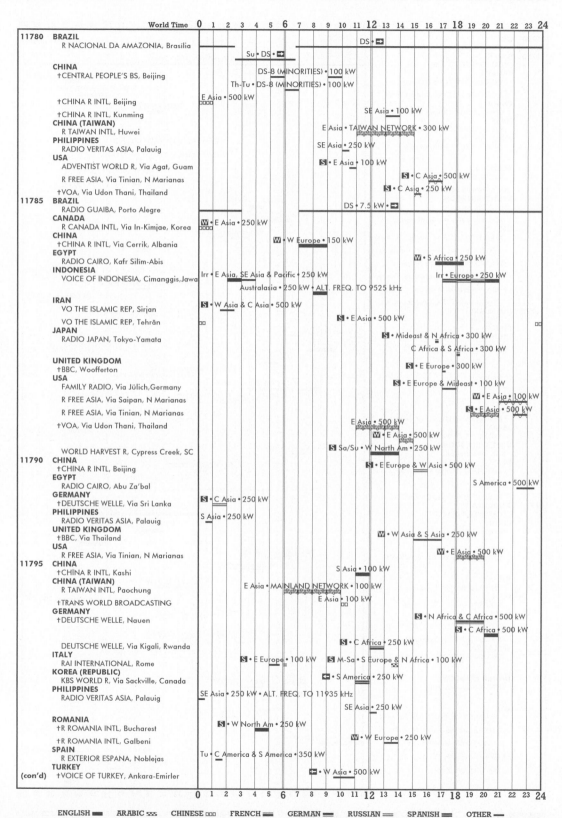

World Time 0 1 2 3 4 5 6 7 8 9 10 11 12 13 14 15 16 17 18 19 20 21 22 23 24

11780	**BRAZIL**
	R NACIONAL DA AMAZONIA, Brasilia
	DS →
	Su • DS • →
	CHINA
	†CENTRAL PEOPLE'S BS, Beijing
	DS-8 (MINORITIES) • 100 kW
	Th-Tu • DS-8 (MINORITIES) • 100 kW
	†CHINA R INTL, Beijing — E Asia • 500 kW
	†CHINA R INTL, Kunming — SE Asia • 100 kW
	CHINA (TAIWAN)
	R TAIWAN INTL, Huwei — E Asia • TAIWAN NETWORK • 300 kW
	PHILIPPINES
	RADIO VERITAS ASIA, Palauig — SE Asia • 250 kW
	USA
	ADVENTIST WORLD R, Via Agat, Guam — S • E Asia • 100 kW
	R FREE ASIA, Via Tinian, N Marianas — S • C Asia • 500 kW
	†VOA, Via Udon Thani, Thailand — S • C Asia • 250 kW
11785	**BRAZIL**
	RADIO GUAIBA, Porto Alegre — DS • 7.5 kW • →
	CANADA
	R CANADA INTL, Via In-Kimjae, Korea — W • E Asia • 250 kW
	CHINA
	†CHINA R INTL, Via Cerrik, Albania — W • W Europe • 150 kW
	EGYPT
	RADIO CAIRO, Kafr Silim-Abis — W • S Africa • 250 kW
	INDONESIA
	VOICE OF INDONESIA, Cimanggis,Jawa — Irr • E Asia, SE Asia & Pacific • 250 kW Irr • Europe • 250 kW
	Australasia • 250 kW • ALT. FREQ. TO 9525 kHz
	IRAN
	VO THE ISLAMIC REP, Sirjan — S • W Asia & C Asia • 500 kW
	VO THE ISLAMIC REP, Tehrān — S • E Asia • 500 kW
	JAPAN
	RADIO JAPAN, Tokyo-Yamata — S • Mideast & N Africa • 300 kW
	C Africa & S Africa • 300 kW
	UNITED KINGDOM
	†BBC, Woofferton — S • E Europe • 300 kW
	USA
	FAMILY RADIO, Via Jülich,Germany — S • E Europe & Mideast • 100 kW
	R FREE ASIA, Via Saipan, N Marianas — W • E Asia • 100 kW
	R FREE ASIA, Via Tinian, N Marianas — S • E Asia • 500 kW
	†VOA, Via Udon Thani, Thailand — E Asia • 500 kW
	W • E Asia • 500 kW
	WORLD HARVEST R, Cypress Creek, SC — S Sa/Su • W North Am • 250 kW
11790	**CHINA**
	†CHINA R INTL, Beijing — S • E Europe & W Asia • 500 kW
	EGYPT
	RADIO CAIRO, Abu Za'bal — S America • 500 kW
	GERMANY
	†DEUTSCHE WELLE, Via Sri Lanka — S • C Asia • 250 kW
	PHILIPPINES
	RADIO VERITAS ASIA, Palauig — S Asia • 250 kW
	UNITED KINGDOM
	†BBC, Via Thailand — W • W Asia & S Asia • 250 kW
	USA
	R FREE ASIA, Via Tinian, N Marianas — W • E Asia • 500 kW
11795	**CHINA**
	†CHINA R INTL, Kashi — S Asia • 100 kW
	CHINA (TAIWAN)
	R TAIWAN INTL, Paochung — E Asia • MAINLAND NETWORK • 100 kW
	E Asia • 100 kW
	†TRANS WORLD BROADCASTING
	GERMANY
	†DEUTSCHE WELLE, Nauen — S • N Africa & C Africa • 500 kW
	S • C Africa • 500 kW
	DEUTSCHE WELLE, Via Kigali, Rwanda — S • C Africa • 250 kW
	ITALY
	RAI INTERNATIONAL, Rome — S • E Europe • 100 kW S M-Sa • S Europe & N Africa • 100 kW
	KOREA (REPUBLIC)
	KBS WORLD R, Via Sackville, Canada — → • S America • 250 kW
	PHILIPPINES
	RADIO VERITAS ASIA, Palauig — SE Asia • 250 kW • ALT. FREQ. TO 11935 kHz
	SE Asia • 250 kW
	ROMANIA
	†R ROMANIA INTL, Bucharest — S • W North Am • 250 kW
	†R ROMANIA INTL, Galbeni — W • W Europe • 250 kW
	SPAIN
	R EXTERIOR ESPANA, Noblejas — Tu • C America & S America • 350 kW
	TURKEY
(con'd)	†VOICE OF TURKEY, Ankara-Emirler — → • W Asia • 500 kW

0 1 2 3 4 5 6 7 8 9 10 11 12 13 14 15 16 17 18 19 20 21 22 23 24

ENGLISH ▬   ARABIC ∿∿∿   CHINESE □□□   FRENCH ══   GERMAN ▬▬   RUSSIAN ══   SPANISH ▬▬   OTHER ▬

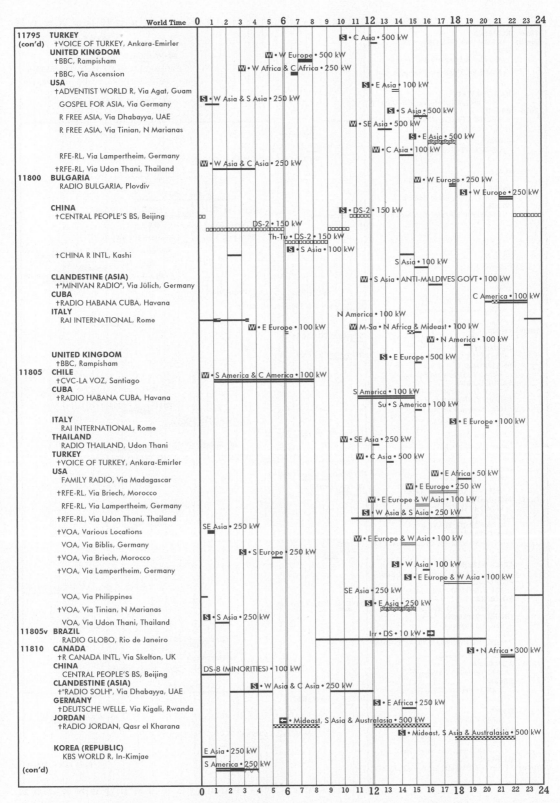

World Time · 0 1 2 3 4 5 6 7 8 9 10 11 12 13 14 15 16 17 18 19 20 21 22 23 24

11795 **TURKEY**
(con'd) †VOICE OF TURKEY, Ankara-Emirler — S • C Asia • 500 kW
UNITED KINGDOM
†BBC, Rampisham — W • W Europe • 500 kW
†BBC, Via Ascension — W • W Africa & C Africa • 250 kW
USA
†ADVENTIST WORLD R, Via Agat, Guam — S • E Asia • 100 kW
GOSPEL FOR ASIA, Via Germany — S • W Asia & S Asia • 250 kW
R FREE ASIA, Via Dhabayya, UAE — S • S Asia • 500 kW
R FREE ASIA, Via Tinian, N Marianas — W • SE Asia • 500 kW
— S • E Asia • 500 kW
— W • C Asia • 100 kW
RFE-RL, Via Lampertheim, Germany — W • W Asia & C Asia • 250 kW
†RFE-RL, Via Udon Thani, Thailand
11800 **BULGARIA**
RADIO BULGARIA, Plovdiv — W • W Europe • 250 kW
— S • W Europe • 250 kW
CHINA
†CENTRAL PEOPLE'S BS, Beijing — S • DS-2 • 150 kW
DS-2 • 150 kW
Th-Tu • DS-2 • 150 kW
— S • S Asia • 100 kW
†CHINA R INTL, Kashi
S Asia • 100 kW
CLANDESTINE (ASIA)
†"MINIVAN RADIO", Via Jülich, Germany — W • S Asia • ANTI-MALDIVES GOVT • 100 kW
CUBA
†RADIO HABANA CUBA, Havana — C America • 100 kW
ITALY
RAI INTERNATIONAL, Rome — N America • 100 kW
— W • E Europe • 100 kW
— W • M-Sa • N Africa & Mideast • 100 kW
— W • N America • 100 kW
UNITED KINGDOM
†BBC, Rampisham — S • E Europe • 500 kW
11805 **CHILE**
†CVC-LA VOZ, Santiago — W • S America & C America • 100 kW
CUBA
†RADIO HABANA CUBA, Havana — S America • 100 kW
— Su • S America • 100 kW
ITALY
RAI INTERNATIONAL, Rome — S • E Europe • 100 kW
THAILAND
RADIO THAILAND, Udon Thani — W • SE Asia • 250 kW
TURKEY
†VOICE OF TURKEY, Ankara-Emirler — W • C Asia • 500 kW
USA
FAMILY RADIO, Via Madagascar — W • E Africa • 50 kW
†RFE-RL, Via Briech, Morocco — W • E Europe • 250 kW
RFE-RL, Via Lampertheim, Germany — W • E Europe & W Asia • 100 kW
†RFE-RL, Via Udon Thani, Thailand — S • W Asia & S Asia • 250 kW
†VOA, Various Locations — SE Asia • 250 kW
VOA, Via Biblis, Germany — W • E Europe & W Asia • 100 kW
†VOA, Via Briech, Morocco — S • S Europe • 250 kW
VOA, Via Lampertheim, Germany — S • W Asia • 100 kW
— S • E Europe & W Asia • 100 kW
VOA, Via Philippines — SE Asia • 250 kW
†VOA, Via Tinian, N Marianas — S • E Asia • 250 kW
VOA, Via Udon Thani, Thailand — S • S Asia • 250 kW
11805v **BRAZIL**
RADIO GLOBO, Rio de Janeiro — Irr • DS • 10 kW •
11810 **CANADA**
†R CANADA INTL, Via Skelton, UK — S • N Africa • 300 kW
CHINA
CENTRAL PEOPLE'S BS, Beijing — DS-8 (MINORITIES) • 100 kW
CLANDESTINE (ASIA)
†"RADIO SOLH", Via Dhabayya, UAE — S • W Asia & C Asia • 250 kW
GERMANY
†DEUTSCHE WELLE, Via Kigali, Rwanda — S • E Africa • 250 kW
JORDAN
†RADIO JORDAN, Qasr el Kharana — • Mideast, S Asia & Australasia • 500 kW
— S • Mideast, S Asia & Australasia • 500 kW
KOREA (REPUBLIC)
KBS WORLD R, In-Kimjae — E Asia • 250 kW
— S America • 250 kW
(con'd)

0 1 2 3 4 5 6 7 8 9 10 11 12 13 14 15 16 17 18 19 20 21 22 23 24

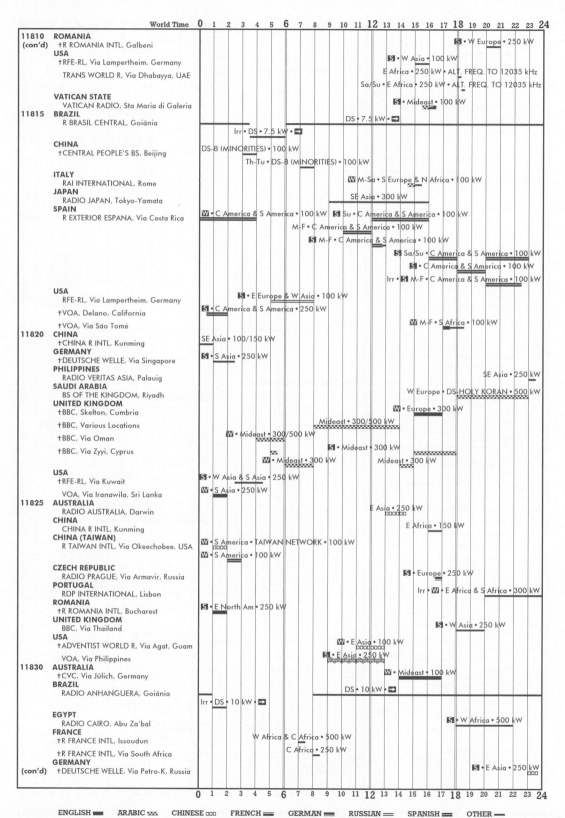

World Time   0 1 2 3 4 5 6 7 8 9 10 11 12 13 14 15 16 17 18 19 20 21 22 23 24

11810	**ROMANIA**
(con'd)	†R ROMANIA INTL, Galbeni
	USA
	†RFE-RL, Via Lampertheim, Germany
	TRANS WORLD R, Via Dhabayya, UAE
	VATICAN STATE
	VATICAN RADIO, Sta Maria di Galeria
11815	**BRAZIL**
	R BRASIL CENTRAL, Goiânia
	CHINA
	†CENTRAL PEOPLE'S BS, Beijing
	ITALY
	RAI INTERNATIONAL, Rome
	JAPAN
	RADIO JAPAN, Tokyo-Yamata
	SPAIN
	R EXTERIOR ESPANA, Via Costa Rica
	USA
	RFE-RL, Via Lampertheim, Germany
	†VOA, Delano, California
	†VOA, Via São Tomé
11820	**CHINA**
	†CHINA R INTL, Kunming
	GERMANY
	†DEUTSCHE WELLE, Via Singapore
	PHILIPPINES
	RADIO VERITAS ASIA, Palauig
	SAUDI ARABIA
	BS OF THE KINGDOM, Riyadh
	UNITED KINGDOM
	†BBC, Skelton, Cumbria
	†BBC, Various Locations
	†BBC, Via Oman
	†BBC, Via Zyyi, Cyprus
	USA
	†RFE-RL, Via Kuwait
	VOA, Via Iranawila, Sri Lanka
11825	**AUSTRALIA**
	RADIO AUSTRALIA, Darwin
	CHINA
	CHINA R INTL, Kunming
	CHINA (TAIWAN)
	R TAIWAN INTL, Via Okeechobee, USA
	CZECH REPUBLIC
	RADIO PRAGUE, Via Armavir, Russia
	PORTUGAL
	RDP INTERNATIONAL, Lisbon
	ROMANIA
	†R ROMANIA INTL, Bucharest
	UNITED KINGDOM
	BBC, Via Thailand
	USA
	†ADVENTIST WORLD R, Via Agat, Guam
	VOA, Via Philippines
11830	**AUSTRALIA**
	†CVC, Via Jülich, Germany
	BRAZIL
	RADIO ANHANGUERA, Goiânia
	EGYPT
	RADIO CAIRO, Abu Za'bal
	FRANCE
	†R FRANCE INTL, Issoudun
	†R FRANCE INTL, Via South Africa
	GERMANY
(con'd)	†DEUTSCHE WELLE, Via Petro-K, Russia

Chart entries:

- S • W Europe • 250 kW
- S • W Asia • 100 kW
- E Africa • 250 kW • ALT. FREQ. TO 12035 kHz
- Sa/Su • E Africa • 250 kW • ALT. FREQ. TO 12035 kHz
- S • Mideast • 100 kW
- DS • 7.5 kW • ➡
- Irr • DS • 7.5 kW • ➡
- DS-8 (MINORITIES) • 100 kW
- Th-Tu • DS-8 (MINORITIES) • 100 kW
- W M-Sa • S Europe & N Africa • 100 kW
- SE Asia • 300 kW
- W • C America & S America • 100 kW   S Su • C America & S America • 100 kW
- M-F • C America & S America • 100 kW
- S M-F • C America & S America • 100 kW
- S Sa/Su • C America & S America • 100 kW
- S • C America & S America • 100 kW
- Irr • S M-F • C America & S America • 100 kW
- S • E Europe & W Asia • 100 kW
- S • C America & S America • 250 kW
- W M-F • S Africa • 100 kW
- SE Asia • 100/150 kW
- S • S Asia • 250 kW
- SE Asia • 250 kW
- W Europe • DS-HOLY KORAN • 500 kW
- W • Europe • 300 kW
- Mideast • 300/500 kW
- W • Mideast • 300/500 kW
- S • Mideast • 300 kW
- W • Mideast • 300 kW
- Mideast • 300 kW
- S • W Asia & S Asia • 250 kW
- W • S Asia • 250 kW
- E Asia • 250 kW
- E Africa • 150 kW
- W • S America • TAIWAN NETWORK • 100 kW
- W • S America • 100 kW
- S • Europe • 250 kW
- Irr • W • E Africa & S Africa • 300 kW
- S • E North Am • 250 kW
- S • W Asia • 250 kW
- W • E Asia • 100 kW
- S • E Asia • 250 kW
- W • Mideast • 100 kW
- DS • 10 kW • ➡
- Irr • DS • 10 kW • ➡
- S • W Africa • 500 kW
- W Africa & C Africa • 500 kW
- C Africa • 250 kW
- S • E Asia • 250 kW

0 1 2 3 4 5 6 7 8 9 10 11 12 13 14 15 16 17 18 19 20 21 22 23 24

ENGLISH ▬   ARABIC ⠶⠶⠶   CHINESE □□□   FRENCH ▬   GERMAN ▬   RUSSIAN ══   SPANISH ▬   OTHER ▬

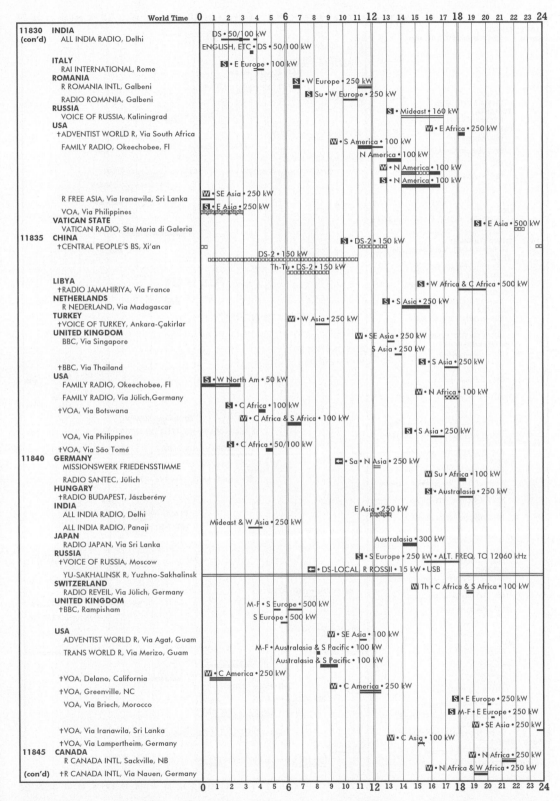

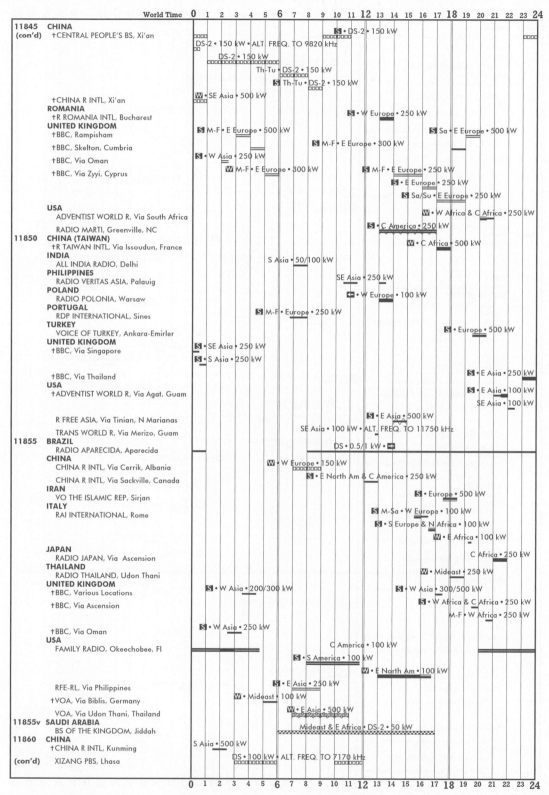

World Time 0 1 2 3 4 5 6 7 8 9 10 11 12 13 14 15 16 17 18 19 20 21 22 23 24

11845 **CHINA**
(con'd) †CENTRAL PEOPLE'S BS, Xi'an — S • DS-2 • 150 kW
DS-2 • 150 kW • ALT. FREQ. TO 9820 kHz
DS-2 • 150 kW
Th-Tu • DS-2 • 150 kW
S Th-Tu • DS-2 • 150 kW

†CHINA R INTL, Xi'an — W • SE Asia • 500 kW
ROMANIA
†R ROMANIA INTL, Bucharest — S • W Europe • 250 kW
UNITED KINGDOM
†BBC, Rampisham — S M-F • E Europe • 500 kW   S Sa • E Europe • 500 kW
†BBC, Skelton, Cumbria — S M-F • E Europe • 300 kW
†BBC, Via Oman — S • W Asia • 250 kW
†BBC, Via Zyyi, Cyprus — W M-F • E Europe • 300 kW   S M-F • E Europe • 250 kW
S • E Europe • 250 kW
S Sa/Su • E Europe • 250 kW
W • W Africa & C Africa • 250 kW

USA
ADVENTIST WORLD R, Via South Africa
RADIO MARTI, Greenville, NC — S • C America • 250 kW
11850 **CHINA (TAIWAN)**
†R TAIWAN INTL, Via Issoudun, France — W • C Africa • 500 kW
INDIA
ALL INDIA RADIO, Delhi — S Asia • 50/100 kW
PHILIPPINES
RADIO VERITAS ASIA, Palauig — SE Asia • 250 kW
POLAND
RADIO POLONIA, Warsaw — • W Europe • 100 kW
PORTUGAL
RDP INTERNATIONAL, Sines — S M-F • Europe • 250 kW
TURKEY
VOICE OF TURKEY, Ankara-Emirler — S • Europe • 500 kW
UNITED KINGDOM
†BBC, Via Singapore — S • SE Asia • 250 kW
S • S Asia • 250 kW

†BBC, Via Thailand — S • E Asia • 250 kW
USA
†ADVENTIST WORLD R, Via Agat, Guam — S • E Asia • 100 kW
SE Asia • 100 kW

R FREE ASIA, Via Tinian, N Marianas — S • E Asia • 500 kW
TRANS WORLD R, Via Merizo, Guam — SE Asia • 100 kW • ALT. FREQ. TO 11750 kHz
11855 **BRAZIL**
RADIO APARECIDA, Aparecida — DS • 0.5/1 kW •
CHINA
CHINA R INTL, Via Cerrik, Albania — W • W Europe • 150 kW
CHINA R INTL, Via Sackville, Canada — S • E North Am & C America • 250 kW
IRAN
VO THE ISLAMIC REP, Sirjan — S • Europe • 500 kW
ITALY
RAI INTERNATIONAL, Rome — S M-Sa • W Europe • 100 kW
S • S Europe & N Africa • 100 kW
W • E Africa • 100 kW

JAPAN
RADIO JAPAN, Via Ascension — C Africa • 250 kW
THAILAND
RADIO THAILAND, Udon Thani — W • Mideast • 250 kW
UNITED KINGDOM
†BBC, Various Locations — S • W Asia • 200/300 kW   S • W Asia • 300/500 kW
†BBC, Via Ascension — S • W Africa & C Africa • 250 kW
M-F • W Africa • 250 kW

†BBC, Via Oman — S • W Asia • 250 kW
USA
FAMILY RADIO, Okeechobee, Fl — C America • 100 kW
S • S America • 100 kW
W • E North Am • 100 kW

RFE-RL, Via Philippines — S • E Asia • 250 kW
†VOA, Via Biblis, Germany — W • Mideast • 100 kW
VOA, Via Udon Thani, Thailand — W • E Asia • 500 kW
11855v **SAUDI ARABIA**
BS OF THE KINGDOM, Jiddah — Mideast & E Africa • DS-2 • 50 kW
11860 **CHINA**
†CHINA R INTL, Kunming — S Asia • 500 kW

(con'd) XIZANG PBS, Lhasa — DS • 100 kW • ALT. FREQ. TO 7170 kHz

0 1 2 3 4 5 6 7 8 9 10 11 12 13 14 15 16 17 18 19 20 21 22 23 24

ENGLISH ▬   ARABIC ⁘⁘   CHINESE □□□   FRENCH ▬▬   GERMAN ▬   RUSSIAN ══   SPANISH ▬   OTHER ▬

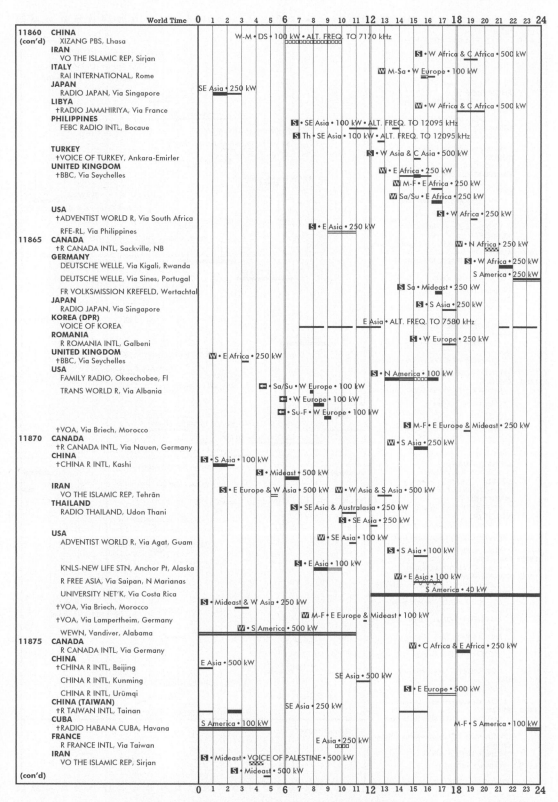

World Time	0 1 2 3 4 5 6 7 8 9 10 11 12 13 14 15 16 17 18 19 20 21 22 23 24

11860 (con'd)
CHINA
  XIZANG PBS, Lhasa — W-M • DS • 100 kW • ALT. FREQ. TO 7170 kHz
IRAN
  VO THE ISLAMIC REP, Sirjan — S • W Africa & C Africa • 500 kW
ITALY
  RAI INTERNATIONAL, Rome — W M-Sa • W Europe • 100 kW
JAPAN
  RADIO JAPAN, Via Singapore — SE Asia • 250 kW
LIBYA
  †RADIO JAMAHIRIYA, Via France — W • W Africa & C Africa • 500 kW
PHILIPPINES
  FEBC RADIO INTL, Bocaue — S • SE Asia • 100 kW • ALT. FREQ. TO 12095 kHz
  S Th • SE Asia • 100 kW • ALT. FREQ. TO 12095 kHz
TURKEY
  †VOICE OF TURKEY, Ankara-Emirler — S • W Asia & C Asia • 500 kW
UNITED KINGDOM
  †BBC, Via Seychelles — W • E Africa • 250 kW
  W M-F • E Africa • 250 kW
  W Sa/Su • E Africa • 250 kW
USA
  †ADVENTIST WORLD R, Via South Africa — S • W Africa • 250 kW
  RFE-RL, Via Philippines — S • E Asia • 250 kW

11865
CANADA
  †R CANADA INTL, Sackville, NB — W • N Africa • 250 kW
GERMANY
  DEUTSCHE WELLE, Via Kigali, Rwanda — S • W Africa • 250 kW
  DEUTSCHE WELLE, Via Sines, Portugal — S America • 250 kW
  FR VOLKSMISSION KREFELD, Wertachtal — S Sa • Mideast • 250 kW
JAPAN
  RADIO JAPAN, Via Singapore — S • S Asia • 250 kW
KOREA (DPR)
  VOICE OF KOREA — E Asia • ALT. FREQ. TO 7580 kHz
ROMANIA
  R ROMANIA INTL, Galbeni — S • W Europe • 250 kW
UNITED KINGDOM
  †BBC, Via Seychelles — W • E Africa • 250 kW
USA
  FAMILY RADIO, Okeechobee, Fl — S • N America • 100 kW
  TRANS WORLD R, Via Albania — ⇦ • Sa/Su • W Europe • 100 kW
  ⇦ • W Europe • 100 kW
  ⇦ • Su-F • W Europe • 100 kW
  S M-F • E Europe & Mideast • 250 kW
  †VOA, Via Briech, Morocco

11870
CANADA
  †R CANADA INTL, Via Nauen, Germany — W • S Asia • 250 kW
CHINA
  †CHINA R INTL, Kashi — S • S Asia • 100 kW
  S • Mideast • 500 kW
IRAN
  VO THE ISLAMIC REP, Tehrān — S • E Europe & W Asia • 500 kW   W • W Asia & S Asia • 500 kW
THAILAND
  RADIO THAILAND, Udon Thani — S • SE Asia & Australasia • 250 kW
  S • SE Asia • 250 kW
USA
  ADVENTIST WORLD R, Via Agat, Guam — W • SE Asia • 100 kW
  S • S Asia • 100 kW
  KNLS-NEW LIFE STN, Anchor Pt, Alaska — S • E Asia • 100 kW
  R FREE ASIA, Via Saipan, N Marianas — W • E Asia • 100 kW
  UNIVERSITY NET'K, Via Costa Rica — S America • 40 kW
  †VOA, Via Briech, Morocco — S • Mideast & W Asia • 250 kW
  †VOA, Via Lampertheim, Germany — W M-F • E Europe & Mideast • 100 kW
  WEWN, Vandiver, Alabama — W • S America • 500 kW

11875
CANADA
  R CANADA INTL, Via Germany — W • C Africa & E Africa • 250 kW
CHINA
  †CHINA R INTL, Beijing — E Asia • 500 kW
  CHINA R INTL, Kunming — SE Asia • 500 kW
  CHINA R INTL, Urümqi — S • E Europe • 500 kW
CHINA (TAIWAN)
  †R TAIWAN INTL, Tainan — SE Asia • 250 kW
CUBA
  †RADIO HABANA CUBA, Havana — S America • 100 kW   M-F • S America • 100 kW
FRANCE
  R FRANCE INTL, Via Taiwan — E Asia • 250 kW
IRAN
  VO THE ISLAMIC REP, Sirjan — S • Mideast • VOICE OF PALESTINE • 500 kW
  S • Mideast • 500 kW

(con'd)

	0 1 2 3 4 5 6 7 8 9 10 11 12 13 14 15 16 17 18 19 20 21 22 23 24

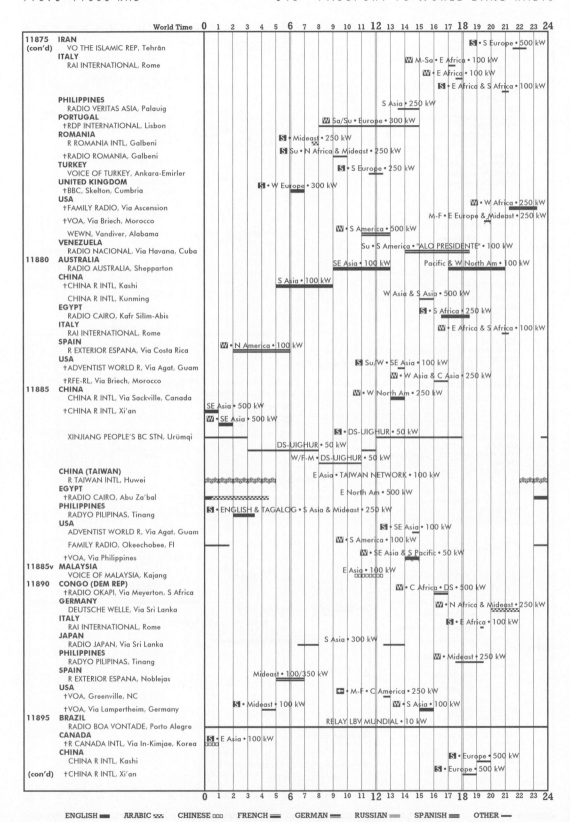

| World Time | 0 | 1 | 2 | 3 | 4 | 5 | 6 | 7 | 8 | 9 | 10 | 11 | 12 | 13 | 14 | 15 | 16 | 17 | 18 | 19 | 20 | 21 | 22 | 23 | 24 |

11875
(con'd) IRAN
VO THE ISLAMIC REP, Tehrān — S • S Europe • 500 kW
ITALY
RAI INTERNATIONAL, Rome — W • M-Sa • E Africa • 100 kW — W • E Africa • 100 kW — S • E Africa & S Africa • 100 kW

PHILIPPINES
RADIO VERITAS ASIA, Palauig — S Asia • 250 kW
PORTUGAL
†RDP INTERNATIONAL, Lisbon — W • Sa/Su • Europe • 300 kW
ROMANIA
R ROMANIA INTL, Galbeni — S • Mideast • 250 kW
†RADIO ROMANIA, Galbeni — S • Su • N Africa & Mideast • 250 kW
TURKEY
VOICE OF TURKEY, Ankara-Emirler — S • S Europe • 250 kW
UNITED KINGDOM
†BBC, Skelton, Cumbria — S • W Europe • 300 kW
USA
†FAMILY RADIO, Via Ascension — W • W Africa • 250 kW
†VOA, Via Briech, Morocco — M-F • E Europe & Mideast • 250 kW
WEWN, Vandiver, Alabama — W • S America • 500 kW
VENEZUELA
RADIO NACIONAL, Via Havana, Cuba — Su • S America • "ALO PRESIDENTE" • 100 kW

11880 AUSTRALIA
RADIO AUSTRALIA, Shepparton — SE Asia • 100 kW — Pacific & W North Am • 100 kW
CHINA
†CHINA R INTL, Kashi — S Asia • 100 kW
CHINA R INTL, Kunming — W Asia & S Asia • 500 kW
EGYPT
RADIO CAIRO, Kafr Silim-Abis — S • S Africa • 250 kW
ITALY
RAI INTERNATIONAL, Rome — W • E Africa & S Africa • 100 kW
SPAIN
R EXTERIOR ESPANA, Via Costa Rica — W • N America • 100 kW
USA
†ADVENTIST WORLD R, Via Agat, Guam — S • Su/W • SE Asia • 100 kW
†RFE-RL, Via Briech, Morocco — W • W Asia & C Asia • 250 kW

11885 CHINA
CHINA R INTL, Via Sackville, Canada — W • W North Am • 250 kW
†CHINA R INTL, Xi'an — SE Asia • 500 kW — W • SE Asia • 500 kW
XINJIANG PEOPLE'S BC STN, Urümqi — S • DS-UIGHUR • 50 kW — DS-UIGHUR • 50 kW — W/F-M • DS-UIGHUR • 50 kW
CHINA (TAIWAN)
R TAIWAN INTL, Huwei — E Asia • TAIWAN NETWORK • 100 kW
EGYPT
†RADIO CAIRO, Abu Za'bal — E North Am • 500 kW
PHILIPPINES
RADYO PILIPINAS, Tinang — S • ENGLISH & TAGALOG • S Asia & Mideast • 250 kW
USA
ADVENTIST WORLD R, Via Agat, Guam — S • SE Asia • 100 kW
FAMILY RADIO, Okeechobee, Fl — W • S America • 100 kW
†VOA, Via Philippines — W • SE Asia & S Pacific • 50 kW

11885v MALAYSIA
VOICE OF MALAYSIA, Kajang — E Asia • 100 kW

11890 CONGO (DEM REP)
†RADIO OKAPI, Via Meyerton, S Africa — W • C Africa • DS • 500 kW
GERMANY
DEUTSCHE WELLE, Via Sri Lanka — W • N Africa & Mideast • 250 kW
ITALY
RAI INTERNATIONAL, Rome — S • E Africa • 100 kW
JAPAN
RADIO JAPAN, Via Sri Lanka — S Asia • 300 kW
PHILIPPINES
RADYO PILIPINAS, Tinang — W • Mideast • 250 kW
SPAIN
R EXTERIOR ESPANA, Noblejas — Mideast • 100/350 kW
USA
†VOA, Greenville, NC — ← • M-F • C America • 250 kW
†VOA, Via Lampertheim, Germany — S • Mideast • 100 kW — W • S Asia • 100 kW

11895 BRAZIL
RADIO BOA VONTADE, Porto Alegre — RELAY LBV MUNDIAL • 10 kW
CANADA
†R CANADA INTL, Via In-Kimjae, Korea — S • E Asia • 100 kW
CHINA
CHINA R INTL, Kashi — S • Europe • 500 kW
(con'd) †CHINA R INTL, Xi'an — S • Europe • 500 kW

| 0 | 1 | 2 | 3 | 4 | 5 | 6 | 7 | 8 | 9 | 10 | 11 | 12 | 13 | 14 | 15 | 16 | 17 | 18 | 19 | 20 | 21 | 22 | 23 | 24 |

ENGLISH ▬   ARABIC ⬩⬩⬩   CHINESE □□□   FRENCH ▬   GERMAN ▬   RUSSIAN ═   SPANISH ▬   OTHER ▬

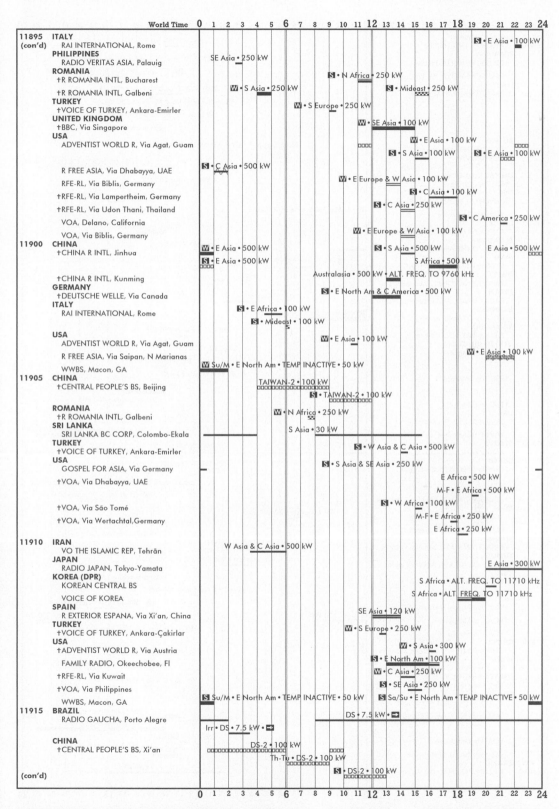

World Time 0 1 2 3 4 5 6 7 8 9 10 11 12 13 14 15 16 17 18 19 20 21 22 23 24

11895 ITALY
(con'd)   RAI INTERNATIONAL, Rome — **S** • E Asia • 100 kW
PHILIPPINES
    RADIO VERITAS ASIA, Palauig — SE Asia • 250 kW
ROMANIA
    †R ROMANIA INTL, Bucharest — **S** • N Africa • 250 kW
    †R ROMANIA INTL, Galbeni — **W** • S Asia • 250 kW   **S** • Mideast • 250 kW
TURKEY
    †VOICE OF TURKEY, Ankara-Emirler — **W** • S Europe • 250 kW
UNITED KINGDOM
    †BBC, Via Singapore — **W** • SE Asia • 100 kW
USA
    ADVENTIST WORLD R, Via Agat, Guam — **W** • E Asia • 100 kW   **S** • S Asia • 100 kW   **S** • E Asia • 100 kW
    R FREE ASIA, Via Dhabayya, UAE — **S** • C Asia • 500 kW
    RFE-RL, Via Biblis, Germany — **W** • E Europe & W Asia • 100 kW
    †RFE-RL, Via Lampertheim, Germany — **S** • C Asia • 100 kW
    †RFE-RL, Via Udon Thani, Thailand — **S** • C Asia • 250 kW
    VOA, Delano, California — **S** • C America • 250 kW
    VOA, Via Biblis, Germany — **W** • E Europe & W Asia • 100 kW

11900 CHINA
    †CHINA R INTL, Jinhua — **W** • E Asia • 500 kW   **S** • S Asia • 500 kW   E Asia • 500 kW
       S • E Asia • 500 kW   S Africa • 500 kW
    †CHINA R INTL, Kunming — Australasia • 500 kW • ALT. FREQ. TO 9760 kHz
GERMANY
    †DEUTSCHE WELLE, Via Canada — **S** • E North Am & C America • 500 kW
ITALY
    RAI INTERNATIONAL, Rome — **S** • E Africa • 100 kW
       S • Mideast • 100 kW
USA
    ADVENTIST WORLD R, Via Agat, Guam — **W** • E Asia • 100 kW
    R FREE ASIA, Via Saipan, N Marianas — **W** • E Asia • 100 kW
    WWBS, Macon, GA — **W** Su/M • E North Am • TEMP INACTIVE • 50 kW

11905 CHINA
    †CENTRAL PEOPLE'S BS, Beijing — TAIWAN-2 • 100 kW   **S** • TAIWAN-2 • 100 kW
ROMANIA
    †R ROMANIA INTL, Galbeni — **W** • N Africa • 250 kW
SRI LANKA
    SRI LANKA BC CORP, Colombo-Ekala — S Asia • 30 kW
TURKEY
    †VOICE OF TURKEY, Ankara-Emirler — **S** • W Asia & C Asia • 500 kW
USA
    GOSPEL FOR ASIA, Via Germany — **S** • S Asia & SE Asia • 250 kW
    †VOA, Via Dhabayya, UAE — E Africa • 500 kW
       M-F • E Africa • 500 kW
    †VOA, Via São Tomé — **S** • W Africa • 100 kW
    †VOA, Via Wertachtal, Germany — M-F • E Africa • 250 kW
       E Africa • 250 kW

11910 IRAN
    VO THE ISLAMIC REP, Tehrān — W Asia & C Asia • 500 kW
JAPAN
    RADIO JAPAN, Tokyo-Yamata — E Asia • 300 kW
KOREA (DPR)
    KOREAN CENTRAL BS — S Africa • ALT. FREQ. TO 11710 kHz
    VOICE OF KOREA — S Africa • ALT. FREQ. TO 11710 kHz
SPAIN
    R EXTERIOR ESPANA, Via Xi'an, China — SE Asia • 120 kW
TURKEY
    †VOICE OF TURKEY, Ankara-Çakirlar — **W** • S Europe • 250 kW
USA
    †ADVENTIST WORLD R, Via Austria — **W** • S Asia • 300 kW
    FAMILY RADIO, Okeechobee, Fl — **S** • E North Am • 100 kW
    †RFE-RL, Via Kuwait — **W** • C Asia • 250 kW
    †VOA, Via Philippines — **S** • SE Asia • 250 kW
    WWBS, Macon, GA — **S** Su/M • E North Am • TEMP INACTIVE • 50 kW   **S** Sa/Su • E North Am • TEMP INACTIVE • 50 kW

11915 BRAZIL
    RADIO GAUCHA, Porto Alegre — DS • 7.5 kW • ⇨
       Irr • DS • 7.5 kW • ⇨
CHINA
    †CENTRAL PEOPLE'S BS, Xi'an — DS-2 • 100 kW
       Th-Tu • DS-2 • 100 kW
       S • DS-2 • 100 kW

(con'd)

0 1 2 3 4 5 6 7 8 9 10 11 12 13 14 15 16 17 18 19 20 21 22 23 24

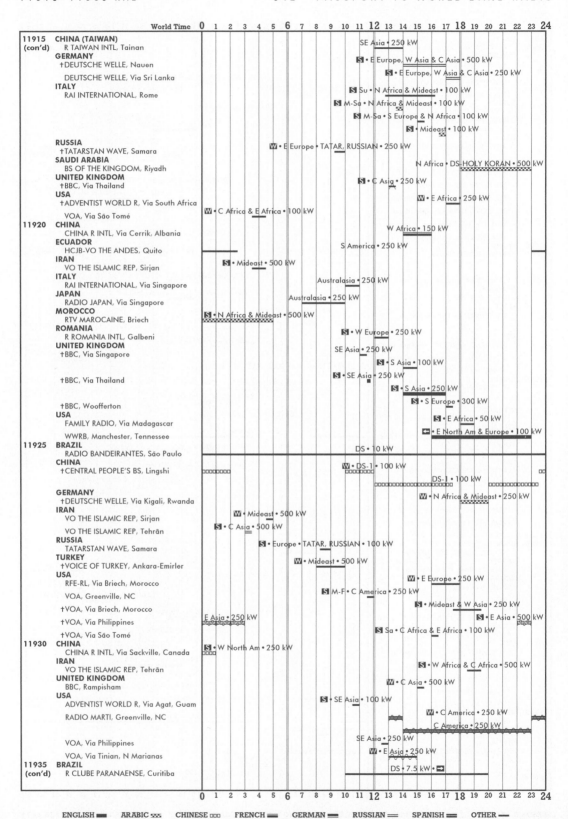

| | | World Time | 0 | 1 | 2 | 3 | 4 | 5 | 6 | 7 | 8 | 9 | 10 | 11 | 12 | 13 | 14 | 15 | 16 | 17 | 18 | 19 | 20 | 21 | 22 | 23 | 24 |

11915 (con'd)
CHINA (TAIWAN) — R TAIWAN INTL, Tainan — SE Asia • 250 kW
GERMANY — †DEUTSCHE WELLE, Nauen — S • E Europe, W Asia & C Asia • 500 kW
DEUTSCHE WELLE, Via Sri Lanka — S • E Europe, W Asia & C Asia • 250 kW
ITALY — RAI INTERNATIONAL, Rome — S • Su • N Africa & Mideast • 100 kW
S • M-Sa • N Africa & Mideast • 100 kW
S • M-Sa • S Europe & N Africa • 100 kW
S • Mideast • 100 kW
RUSSIA — †TATARSTAN WAVE, Samara — W • E Europe • TATAR, RUSSIAN • 250 kW
SAUDI ARABIA — BS OF THE KINGDOM, Riyadh — N Africa • DS-HOLY KORAN • 500 kW
UNITED KINGDOM — †BBC, Via Thailand — S • C Asia • 250 kW
USA — †ADVENTIST WORLD R, Via South Africa — W • E Africa • 250 kW
VOA, Via São Tomé — W • C Africa & E Africa • 100 kW

11920
CHINA — CHINA R INTL, Via Cerrik, Albania — W Africa • 150 kW
ECUADOR — HCJB-VO THE ANDES, Quito — S America • 250 kW
IRAN — VO THE ISLAMIC REP, Sirjan — S • Mideast • 500 kW
ITALY — RAI INTERNATIONAL, Via Singapore — Australasia • 250 kW
JAPAN — RADIO JAPAN, Via Singapore — Australasia • 250 kW
MOROCCO — RTV MAROCAINE, Briech — S • N Africa & Mideast • 500 kW
ROMANIA — R ROMANIA INTL, Galbeni — S • W Europe • 250 kW
UNITED KINGDOM — †BBC, Via Singapore — SE Asia • 250 kW
†BBC, Via Singapore — S • S Asia • 100 kW
†BBC, Via Thailand — S • SE Asia • 250 kW
S • S Asia • 250 kW
†BBC, Woofferton — S • S Europe • 300 kW
USA — FAMILY RADIO, Via Madagascar — S • E Africa • 50 kW
WWRB, Manchester, Tennessee — ← • E North Am & Europe • 100 kW

11925
BRAZIL — RADIO BANDEIRANTES, São Paulo — DS • 10 kW
CHINA — †CENTRAL PEOPLE'S BS, Lingshi — W • DS-1 • 100 kW
DS-1 • 100 kW
GERMANY — †DEUTSCHE WELLE, Via Kigali, Rwanda — W • N Africa & Mideast • 250 kW
IRAN — VO THE ISLAMIC REP, Sirjan — W • Mideast • 500 kW
VO THE ISLAMIC REP, Tehrān — S • C Asia • 500 kW
RUSSIA — TATARSTAN WAVE, Samara — S • Europe • TATAR, RUSSIAN • 100 kW
TURKEY — †VOICE OF TURKEY, Ankara-Emirler — W • Mideast • 500 kW
USA — RFE-RL, Via Briech, Morocco — W • E Europe • 250 kW
VOA, Greenville, NC — S • M-F • C America • 250 kW
†VOA, Via Briech, Morocco — S • Mideast & W Asia • 250 kW
†VOA, Via Philippines — E Asia • 250 kW
S • E Asia • 500 kW
†VOA, Via São Tomé — S • Sa • C Africa & E Africa • 100 kW

11930
CHINA — CHINA R INTL, Via Sackville, Canada — S • W North Am • 250 kW
IRAN — VO THE ISLAMIC REP, Tehrān — S • W Africa & C Africa • 500 kW
UNITED KINGDOM — BBC, Rampisham — W • C Asia • 500 kW
USA — ADVENTIST WORLD R, Via Agat, Guam — S • SE Asia • 100 kW
RADIO MARTI, Greenville, NC — W • C America • 250 kW
C America • 250 kW
VOA, Via Philippines — SE Asia • 250 kW
VOA, Via Tinian, N Marianas — W • E Asia • 250 kW

11935 (con'd)
BRAZIL — R CLUBE PARANAENSE, Curitiba — DS • 7.5 kW • →

| | | | 0 | 1 | 2 | 3 | 4 | 5 | 6 | 7 | 8 | 9 | 10 | 11 | 12 | 13 | 14 | 15 | 16 | 17 | 18 | 19 | 20 | 21 | 22 | 23 | 24 |

ENGLISH ▬   ARABIC ⋙   CHINESE ⠿   FRENCH ▦   GERMAN ▬   RUSSIAN ═   SPANISH ▭   OTHER ▬

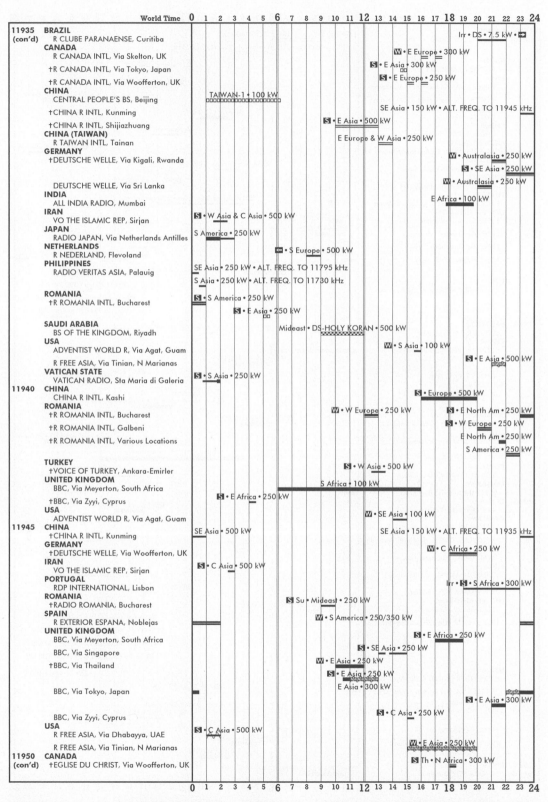

World Time   0 1 2 3 4 5 6 7 8 9 10 11 12 13 14 15 16 17 18 19 20 21 22 23 24

11935
(con'd)   **BRAZIL**
    R CLUBE PARANAENSE, Curitiba — Irr • DS • 7.5 kW • ⮕
   CANADA
    R CANADA INTL, Via Skelton, UK — W • E Europe • 300 kW
    †R CANADA INTL, Via Tokyo, Japan — S • E Asia • 300 kW
    †R CANADA INTL, Via Woofferton, UK — S • E Europe • 250 kW
   CHINA
    CENTRAL PEOPLE'S BS, Beijing — TAIWAN-1 • 100 kW
    †CHINA R INTL, Kunming — SE Asia • 150 kW • ALT. FREQ. TO 11945 kHz
    †CHINA R INTL, Shijiazhuang — S • E Asia • 500 kW
   CHINA (TAIWAN)
    R TAIWAN INTL, Tainan — E Europe & W Asia • 250 kW
   GERMANY
    †DEUTSCHE WELLE, Via Kigali, Rwanda — W • Australasia • 250 kW / S • SE Asia • 250 kW
    DEUTSCHE WELLE, Via Sri Lanka — W • Australasia • 250 kW
   INDIA
    ALL INDIA RADIO, Mumbai — E Africa • 100 kW
   IRAN
    VO THE ISLAMIC REP, Sirjan — S • W Asia & C Asia • 500 kW
   JAPAN
    RADIO JAPAN, Via Netherlands Antilles — S America • 250 kW
   NETHERLANDS
    R NEDERLAND, Flevoland — • S Europe • 500 kW
   PHILIPPINES
    RADIO VERITAS ASIA, Palauig — SE Asia • 250 kW • ALT. FREQ. TO 11795 kHz / S Asia • 250 kW • ALT. FREQ. TO 11730 kHz
   ROMANIA
    †R ROMANIA INTL, Bucharest — S • S America • 250 kW / S • E Asia • 250 kW
   SAUDI ARABIA
    BS OF THE KINGDOM, Riyadh — Mideast • DS-HOLY KORAN • 500 kW
   USA
    ADVENTIST WORLD R, Via Agat, Guam — W • S Asia • 100 kW
    R FREE ASIA, Via Tinian, N Marianas — S • E Asia • 500 kW
   VATICAN STATE
    VATICAN RADIO, Sta Maria di Galeria — S • S Asia • 250 kW

11940   **CHINA**
    CHINA R INTL, Kashi — S • Europe • 500 kW
   ROMANIA
    †R ROMANIA INTL, Bucharest — W • W Europe • 250 kW / S • E North Am • 250 kW
    †R ROMANIA INTL, Galbeni — S • W Europe • 250 kW
    †R ROMANIA INTL, Various Locations — E North Am • 250 kW / S America • 250 kW
   TURKEY
    †VOICE OF TURKEY, Ankara-Emirler — S • W Asia • 500 kW
   UNITED KINGDOM
    BBC, Via Meyerton, South Africa — S Africa • 100 kW
    †BBC, Via Zyyi, Cyprus — S • E Africa • 250 kW
   USA
    ADVENTIST WORLD R, Via Agat, Guam — W • SE Asia • 100 kW

11945   **CHINA**
    †CHINA R INTL, Kunming — SE Asia • 500 kW / SE Asia • 150 kW • ALT. FREQ. TO 11935 kHz
   GERMANY
    †DEUTSCHE WELLE, Via Woofferton, UK — W • C Africa • 250 kW
   IRAN
    VO THE ISLAMIC REP, Sirjan — S • C Asia • 500 kW
   PORTUGAL
    RDP INTERNATIONAL, Lisbon — Irr • S • S Africa • 300 kW
   ROMANIA
    †RADIO ROMANIA, Bucharest — S Su • Mideast • 250 kW
   SPAIN
    R EXTERIOR ESPANA, Noblejas — W • S America • 250/350 kW
   UNITED KINGDOM
    BBC, Via Meyerton, South Africa — S • E Africa • 250 kW
    BBC, Via Singapore — S • SE Asia • 250 kW
    †BBC, Via Thailand — W • E Asia • 250 kW / S • E Asia • 250 kW / E Asia • 300 kW
    BBC, Via Tokyo, Japan — S • E Asia • 300 kW
    BBC, Via Zyyi, Cyprus — S • C Asia • 250 kW
   USA
    R FREE ASIA, Via Dhabayya, UAE — S • C Asia • 500 kW
    R FREE ASIA, Via Tinian, N Marianas — W • E Asia • 250 kW

11950   **CANADA**
(con'd)   †EGLISE DU CHRIST, Via Woofferton, UK — S Th • N Africa • 300 kW

0 1 2 3 4 5 6 7 8 9 10 11 12 13 14 15 16 17 18 19 20 21 22 23 24

SEASONAL Ⓢ OR Ⓦ   1-HR TIMESHIFT MIDYEAR ⬅ OR ➡   JAMMING / OR ∧   EARLIEST HEARD ◁   LATEST HEARD ▷   NEW FOR 2007 †

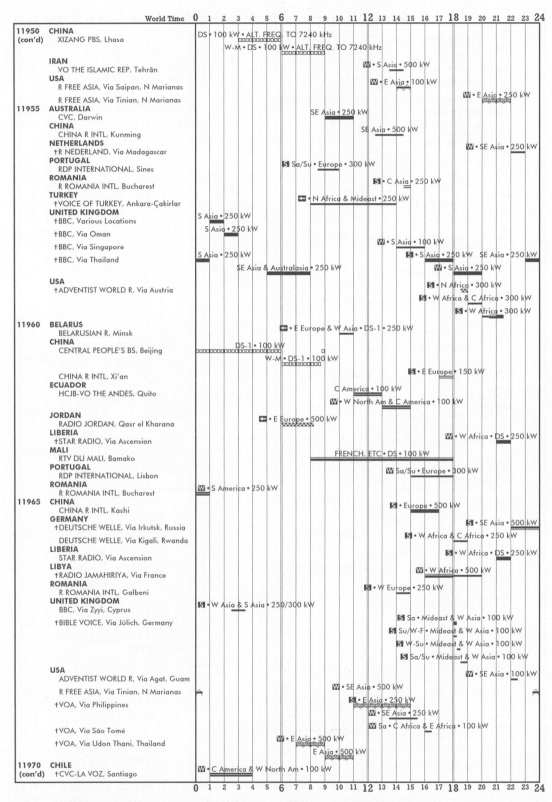

World Time   0 1 2 3 4 5 6 7 8 9 10 11 12 13 14 15 16 17 18 19 20 21 22 23 24

11950 (con'd)	**CHINA** XIZANG PBS, Lhasa	DS • 100 kW • ALT. FREQ. TO 7240 kHz / W-M • DS • 100 kW • ALT. FREQ. TO 7240 kHz
	IRAN VO THE ISLAMIC REP, Tehrān	W • S Asia • 500 kW
	USA R FREE ASIA, Via Saipan, N Marianas	W • E Asia • 100 kW
	R FREE ASIA, Via Tinian, N Marianas	W • E Asia • 250 kW
11955	**AUSTRALIA** CVC, Darwin	SE Asia • 250 kW
	CHINA CHINA R INTL, Kunming	SE Asia • 500 kW
	NETHERLANDS †R NEDERLAND, Via Madagascar	W • SE Asia • 250 kW
	PORTUGAL RDP INTERNATIONAL, Sines	S • Sa/Su • Europe • 300 kW
	ROMANIA R ROMANIA INTL, Bucharest	S • C Asia • 250 kW
	TURKEY †VOICE OF TURKEY, Ankara-Çakirlar	N Africa & Mideast • 250 kW
	UNITED KINGDOM †BBC, Various Locations	S Asia • 250 kW
	†BBC, Via Oman	S Asia • 250 kW
	†BBC, Via Singapore	W • S Asia • 100 kW
	†BBC, Via Thailand	S Asia • 250 kW / S • S Asia • 250 kW SE Asia • 250 kW / SE Asia & Australasia • 250 kW W • S Asia • 250 kW
	USA †ADVENTIST WORLD R, Via Austria	S • N Africa • 300 kW / S • W Africa & C Africa • 300 kW / S • W Africa • 300 kW
11960	**BELARUS** BELARUSIAN R, Minsk	• E Europe & W Asia • DS-1 • 250 kW
	CHINA CENTRAL PEOPLE'S BS, Beijing	DS-1 • 100 kW / W-M • DS-1 • 100 kW
	CHINA R INTL, Xi'an	S • E Europe • 150 kW
	ECUADOR HCJB-VO THE ANDES, Quito	C America • 100 kW / W • W North Am & C America • 100 kW
	JORDAN RADIO JORDAN, Qasr el Kharana	• E Europe • 500 kW
	LIBERIA †STAR RADIO, Via Ascension	W • W Africa • DS • 250 kW
	MALI RTV DU MALI, Bamako	FRENCH, ETC • DS • 100 kW
	PORTUGAL RDP INTERNATIONAL, Lisbon	W • Sa/Su • Europe • 300 kW
	ROMANIA R ROMANIA INTL, Bucharest	W • S America • 250 kW
11965	**CHINA** CHINA R INTL, Kashi	S • Europe • 500 kW
	GERMANY †DEUTSCHE WELLE, Via Irkutsk, Russia	S • SE Asia • 500 kW
	DEUTSCHE WELLE, Via Kigali, Rwanda	S • W Africa & C Africa • 250 kW
	LIBERIA STAR RADIO, Via Ascension	S • W Africa • DS • 250 kW
	LIBYA †RADIO JAMAHIRIYA, Via France	W • W Africa • 500 kW
	ROMANIA R ROMANIA INTL, Galbeni	S • W Europe • 250 kW
	UNITED KINGDOM BBC, Via Zyyi, Cyprus	S • W Asia & S Asia • 250/300 kW
	†BIBLE VOICE, Via Jülich, Germany	S • Sa • Mideast & W Asia • 100 kW / S • Su/W-F • Mideast & W Asia • 100 kW / S • W-Su • Mideast & W Asia • 100 kW / S • Sa/Su • Mideast & W Asia • 100 kW
	USA ADVENTIST WORLD R, Via Agat, Guam	W • SE Asia • 100 kW
	R FREE ASIA, Via Tinian, N Marianas	
	†VOA, Via Philippines	W • SE Asia • 500 kW / S • E Asia • 250 kW / W • SE Asia • 250 kW
	†VOA, Via São Tomé	W • Sa • C Africa & E Africa • 100 kW
	†VOA, Via Udon Thani, Thailand	W • E Asia • 500 kW / E Asia • 500 kW
11970 (con'd)	**CHILE** †CVC-LA VOZ, Santiago	W • C America & W North Am • 100 kW

0 1 2 3 4 5 6 7 8 9 10 11 12 13 14 15 16 17 18 19 20 21 22 23 24

ENGLISH ■■■   ARABIC ⋙   CHINESE ▫▫▫   FRENCH ▬   GERMAN ▬   RUSSIAN ═   SPANISH ▬   OTHER —

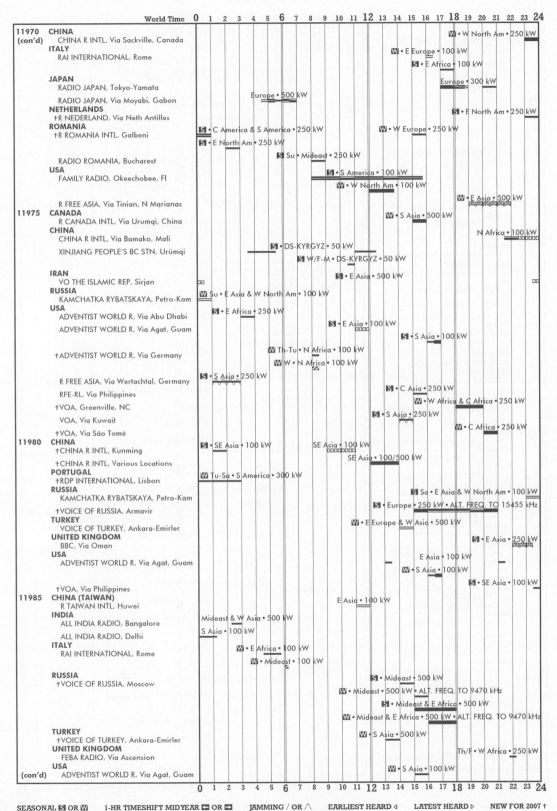

World Time 0 1 2 3 4 5 6 7 8 9 10 11 12 13 14 15 16 17 18 19 20 21 22 23 24

11970 (con'd) **CHINA**	
CHINA R INTL, Via Sackville, Canada	ⓦ • W North Am • 250 kW
ITALY	
RAI INTERNATIONAL, Rome	ⓦ • E Europe • 100 kW
	ⓢ • E Africa • 100 kW
JAPAN	
RADIO JAPAN, Tokyo-Yamata	Europe • 300 kW
RADIO JAPAN, Via Moyabi, Gabon	Europe • 500 kW
NETHERLANDS	
†R NEDERLAND, Via Neth Antilles	ⓢ • E North Am • 250 kW
ROMANIA	
†R ROMANIA INTL, Galbeni	ⓢ • C America & S America • 250 kW
	ⓦ • W Europe • 250 kW
	ⓢ • E North Am • 250 kW
RADIO ROMANIA, Bucharest	ⓢ Su • Mideast • 250 kW
USA	
FAMILY RADIO, Okeechobee, Fl	ⓢ • S America • 100 kW
	ⓦ • W North Am • 100 kW
R FREE ASIA, Via Tinian, N Marianas	ⓦ • E Asia • 500 kW
11975 CANADA	
R CANADA INTL, Via Urumqi, China	ⓦ • S Asia • 500 kW
CHINA	
CHINA R INTL, Via Bamako, Mali	N Africa • 100 kW
XINJIANG PEOPLE'S BC STN, Urümqi	ⓢ • DS-KYRGYZ • 50 kW
	ⓦ/F-M • DS-KYRGYZ • 50 kW
IRAN	
VO THE ISLAMIC REP, Sirjan	ⓢ • E Asia • 500 kW
RUSSIA	
KAMCHATKA RYBATSKAYA, Petro-Kam	ⓦ Su • E Asia & W North Am • 100 kW
USA	
ADVENTIST WORLD R, Via Abu Dhabi	ⓢ • E Africa • 250 kW
ADVENTIST WORLD R, Via Agat, Guam	ⓢ • E Asia • 100 kW
	ⓢ • S Asia • 100 kW
†ADVENTIST WORLD R, Via Germany	ⓦ Th-Tu • N Africa • 100 kW
	ⓦ W • N Africa • 100 kW
R FREE ASIA, Via Wertachtal, Germany	ⓢ • S Asia • 250 kW
RFE-RL, Via Philippines	ⓢ • C Asia • 250 kW
†VOA, Greenville, NC	ⓦ • W Africa & C Africa • 250 kW
VOA, Via Kuwait	ⓢ • S Asia • 250 kW
†VOA, Via São Tomé	ⓦ • C Africa • 250 kW
11980 CHINA	
†CHINA R INTL, Kunming	ⓢ • SE Asia • 100 kW SE Asia • 100 kW
†CHINA R INTL, Various Locations	SE Asia • 100/500 kW
PORTUGAL	
†RDP INTERNATIONAL, Lisbon	ⓦ Tu-Sa • S America • 300 kW
RUSSIA	
KAMCHATKA RYBATSKAYA, Petro-Kam	ⓢ Sa • E Asia & W North Am • 100 kW
†VOICE OF RUSSIA, Armavir	ⓢ • Europe • 250 kW • ALT. FREQ. TO 15455 kHz
TURKEY	
VOICE OF TURKEY, Ankara-Emirler	ⓦ • E Europe & W Asia • 500 kW
UNITED KINGDOM	
BBC, Via Oman	ⓢ • E Asia • 250 kW
USA	
ADVENTIST WORLD R, Via Agat, Guam	E Asia • 100 kW
	ⓦ • S Asia • 100 kW
	ⓢ • SE Asia • 100 kW
†VOA, Via Philippines	
11985 CHINA (TAIWAN)	
R TAIWAN INTL, Huwei	E Asia • 100 kW
INDIA	
ALL INDIA RADIO, Bangalore	Mideast & W Asia • 500 kW
ALL INDIA RADIO, Delhi	S Asia • 100 kW
ITALY	
RAI INTERNATIONAL, Rome	ⓦ • E Africa • 100 kW
	ⓦ • Mideast • 100 kW
RUSSIA	
†VOICE OF RUSSIA, Moscow	ⓢ • Mideast • 500 kW
	ⓦ • Mideast • 500 kW • ALT. FREQ. TO 9470 kHz
	ⓢ • Mideast & E Africa • 500 kW
	ⓦ • Mideast & E Africa • 500 kW • ALT. FREQ. TO 9470 kHz
TURKEY	
†VOICE OF TURKEY, Ankara-Emirler	ⓦ • S Asia • 500 kW
UNITED KINGDOM	
FEBA RADIO, Via Ascension	Th/F • W Africa • 250 kW
USA	
(con'd) ADVENTIST WORLD R, Via Agat, Guam	ⓦ • S Asia • 100 kW

0 1 2 3 4 5 6 7 8 9 10 11 12 13 14 15 16 17 18 19 20 21 22 23 24

SEASONAL ⓢ OR ⓦ   1-HR TIMESHIFT MIDYEAR ⇦ OR ⇨   JAMMING / OR ∧   EARLIEST HEARD ◁   LATEST HEARD ▷   NEW FOR 2007 †

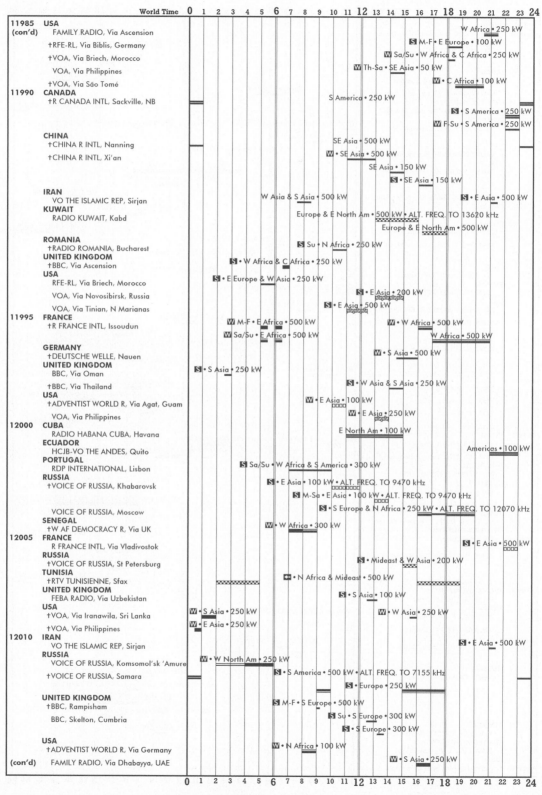

World Time 0 1 2 3 4 5 6 7 8 9 10 11 12 13 14 15 16 17 18 19 20 21 22 23 24

11985 **USA**
(con'd)   FAMILY RADIO, Via Ascension — W Africa • 250 kW
         †RFE-RL, Via Biblis, Germany — S • M-F • E Europe • 100 kW
         †VOA, Via Briech, Morocco — W • Sa/Su • W Africa & C Africa • 250 kW
         VOA, Via Philippines — W • Th-Sa • SE Asia • 50 kW
         †VOA, Via São Tomé — W • C Africa • 100 kW
11990 **CANADA**
         †R CANADA INTL, Sackville, NB — S America • 250 kW — S • S America • 250 kW — W • F-Su • S America • 250 kW

         CHINA
         †CHINA R INTL, Nanning — SE Asia • 500 kW
         †CHINA R INTL, Xi'an — W • SE Asia • 500 kW — SE Asia • 150 kW — S • SE Asia • 150 kW

         IRAN
         VO THE ISLAMIC REP, Sirjan — W Asia & S Asia • 500 kW — S • E Asia • 500 kW
         KUWAIT
         RADIO KUWAIT, Kabd — Europe & E North Am • 500 kW • ALT. FREQ. TO 13620 kHz — Europe & E North Am • 500 kW

         ROMANIA
         †RADIO ROMANIA, Bucharest — S • Su • N Africa • 250 kW
         UNITED KINGDOM
         †BBC, Via Ascension — S • W Africa & C Africa • 250 kW
         USA
         RFE-RL, Via Briech, Morocco — S • E Europe & W Asia • 250 kW
         VOA, Via Novosibirsk, Russia — S • E Asia • 200 kW
         VOA, Via Tinian, N Marianas — S • E Asia • 500 kW
11995 **FRANCE**
         †R FRANCE INTL, Issoudun — W • M-F • E Africa • 500 kW — W • W Africa • 500 kW
                                     W • Sa/Su • E Africa • 500 kW — W Africa • 500 kW

         GERMANY
         †DEUTSCHE WELLE, Nauen — W • S Asia • 500 kW
         UNITED KINGDOM
         BBC, Via Oman — S • S Asia • 250 kW
         †BBC, Via Thailand — S • W Asia & S Asia • 250 kW
         USA
         †ADVENTIST WORLD R, Via Agat, Guam — W • E Asia • 100 kW
                                              W • E Asia • 250 kW
         VOA, Via Philippines
12000 **CUBA**
         RADIO HABANA CUBA, Havana — E North Am • 100 kW
         ECUADOR
         HCJB-VO THE ANDES, Quito — Americas • 100 kW
         PORTUGAL
         RDP INTERNATIONAL, Lisbon — S • Sa/Su • W Africa & S America • 300 kW
         RUSSIA
         †VOICE OF RUSSIA, Khabarovsk — S • E Asia • 100 kW • ALT. FREQ. TO 9470 kHz
                                         S • M-Sa • E Asia • 100 kW • ALT. FREQ. TO 9470 kHz
                                         S • S Europe & N Africa • 250 kW • ALT. FREQ. TO 12070 kHz
         VOICE OF RUSSIA, Moscow
         SENEGAL
         †W AF DEMOCRACY R, Via UK — W • W Africa • 300 kW
12005 **FRANCE**
         R FRANCE INTL, Via Vladivostok — S • E Asia • 500 kW
         RUSSIA
         †VOICE OF RUSSIA, St Petersburg — S • Mideast & W Asia • 200 kW
         TUNISIA
         †RTV TUNISIENNE, Sfax — • N Africa & Mideast • 500 kW
         UNITED KINGDOM
         FEBA RADIO, Via Uzbekistan — S • S Asia • 100 kW
         USA
         †VOA, Via Iranawila, Sri Lanka — W • S Asia • 250 kW — W • W Asia • 250 kW
         †VOA, Via Philippines — W • E Asia • 250 kW
12010 **IRAN**
         VO THE ISLAMIC REP, Sirjan — S • E Asia • 500 kW
         RUSSIA
         VOICE OF RUSSIA, Komsomol'sk 'Amure — W • W North Am • 250 kW
         †VOICE OF RUSSIA, Samara — S • S America • 500 kW • ALT. FREQ. TO 7155 kHz
                                     S • Europe • 250 kW

         UNITED KINGDOM
         †BBC, Rampisham — S • M-F • S Europe • 500 kW
         BBC, Skelton, Cumbria — S • Su • S Europe • 300 kW
                                 S • S Europe • 300 kW

         USA
         †ADVENTIST WORLD R, Via Germany — W • N Africa • 100 kW
(con'd) FAMILY RADIO, Via Dhabayya, UAE — W • S Asia • 250 kW

0 1 2 3 4 5 6 7 8 9 10 11 12 13 14 15 16 17 18 19 20 21 22 23 24

ENGLISH ▬ ARABIC ≈≈ CHINESE □□□ FRENCH ═ GERMAN ━ RUSSIAN ═ SPANISH ═ OTHER ▬

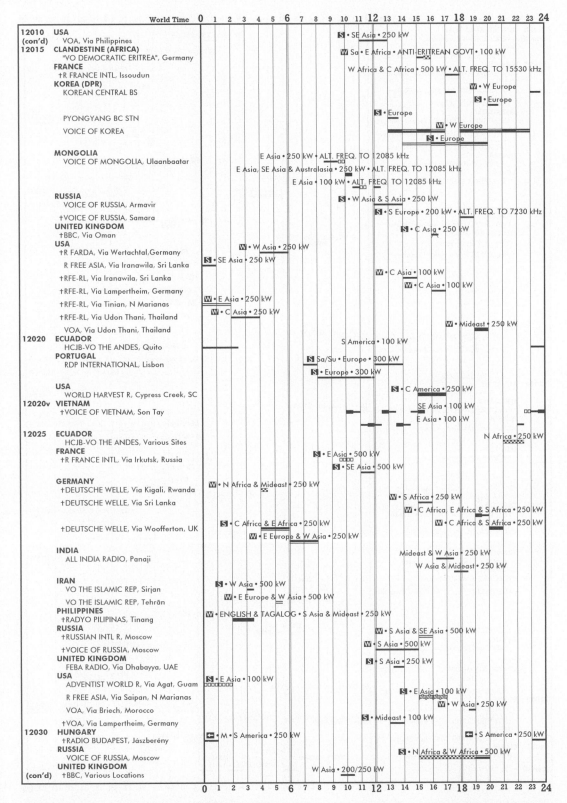

	World Time	0 1 2 3 4 5 6 7 8 9 10 11 12 13 14 15 16 17 18 19 20 21 22 23 24
12010 (con'd)	USA	VOA, Via Philippines	S • SE Asia • 250 kW
12015	CLANDESTINE (AFRICA) "VO DEMOCRATIC ERITREA", Germany	W Sa • E Africa • ANTI-ERITREAN GOVT • 100 kW
	FRANCE †R FRANCE INTL, Issoudun	W Africa & C Africa • 500 kW • ALT. FREQ. TO 15530 kHz
	KOREA (DPR) KOREAN CENTRAL BS	W • W Europe / S • Europe
	PYONGYANG BC STN	S • Europe
	VOICE OF KOREA	W • W Europe / S • Europe
	MONGOLIA VOICE OF MONGOLIA, Ulaanbaatar	E Asia • 250 kW • ALT. FREQ. TO 12085 kHz / E Asia, SE Asia & Australasia • 250 kW • ALT. FREQ. TO 12085 kHz / E Asia • 100 kW • ALT. FREQ. TO 12085 kHz
	RUSSIA VOICE OF RUSSIA, Armavir	S • W Asia & S Asia • 250 kW
	†VOICE OF RUSSIA, Samara	S • S Europe • 200 kW • ALT. FREQ. TO 7230 kHz
	UNITED KINGDOM †BBC, Via Oman	S • C Asia • 250 kW
	USA †R FARDA, Via Wertachtal, Germany	W • W Asia • 250 kW
	R FREE ASIA, Via Iranawila, Sri Lanka	S • SE Asia • 250 kW
	†RFE-RL, Via Iranawila, Sri Lanka	W • C Asia • 100 kW
	†RFE-RL, Via Lampertheim, Germany	W • C Asia • 100 kW
	†RFE-RL, Via Tinian, N Marianas	W • E Asia • 250 kW
	†RFE-RL, Via Udon Thani, Thailand	W • C Asia • 250 kW
	VOA, Via Udon Thani, Thailand	W • Mideast • 250 kW
12020	ECUADOR HCJB-VO THE ANDES, Quito	S America • 100 kW
	PORTUGAL RDP INTERNATIONAL, Lisbon	S Sa/Su • Europe • 300 kW / S • Europe • 300 kW
	USA WORLD HARVEST R, Cypress Creek, SC	S • C America • 250 kW
12020v	VIETNAM †VOICE OF VIETNAM, Son Tay	SE Asia • 100 kW / E Asia • 100 kW
12025	ECUADOR HCJB-VO THE ANDES, Various Sites	N Africa • 250 kW
	FRANCE †R FRANCE INTL, Via Irkutsk, Russia	S • E Asia • 500 kW / S • SE Asia • 500 kW
	GERMANY †DEUTSCHE WELLE, Via Kigali, Rwanda	W • N Africa & Mideast • 250 kW
	†DEUTSCHE WELLE, Via Sri Lanka	W • S Africa • 250 kW / W • C Africa, E Africa & S Africa • 250 kW
	†DEUTSCHE WELLE, Via Woofferton, UK	S • C Africa & E Africa • 250 kW / W • C Africa & S Africa • 250 kW
		W • E Europe & W Asia • 250 kW
	INDIA ALL INDIA RADIO, Panaji	Mideast & W Asia • 250 kW / W Asia & Mideast • 250 kW
	IRAN VO THE ISLAMIC REP, Sirjan	S • W Asia • 500 kW
	VO THE ISLAMIC REP, Tehrān	W • E Europe & W Asia • 500 kW
	PHILIPPINES †RADYO PILIPINAS, Tinang	W • ENGLISH & TAGALOG • S Asia & Mideast • 250 kW
	RUSSIA †RUSSIAN INTL R, Moscow	W • S Asia & SE Asia • 500 kW
	†VOICE OF RUSSIA, Moscow	W • S Asia • 500 kW
	UNITED KINGDOM FEBA RADIO, Via Dhabayya, UAE	S • S Asia • 250 kW
	USA ADVENTIST WORLD R, Via Agat, Guam	S • E Asia • 100 kW
	R FREE ASIA, Via Saipan, N Marianas	S • E Asia • 100 kW / W • W Asia • 250 kW
	VOA, Via Briech, Morocco	
	†VOA, Via Lampertheim, Germany	S • Mideast • 100 kW
12030	HUNGARY †RADIO BUDAPEST, Jászberény	M • S America • 250 kW / S America • 250 kW
	RUSSIA VOICE OF RUSSIA, Moscow	S • N Africa & W Africa • 500 kW
	UNITED KINGDOM	W Asia • 200/250 kW
(con'd)	†BBC, Various Locations	

SEASONAL S OR W   1-HR TIMESHIFT MIDYEAR ⇆ OR ⇉   JAMMING / OR ∧   EARLIEST HEARD ◁   LATEST HEARD ▷   NEW FOR 2007 †

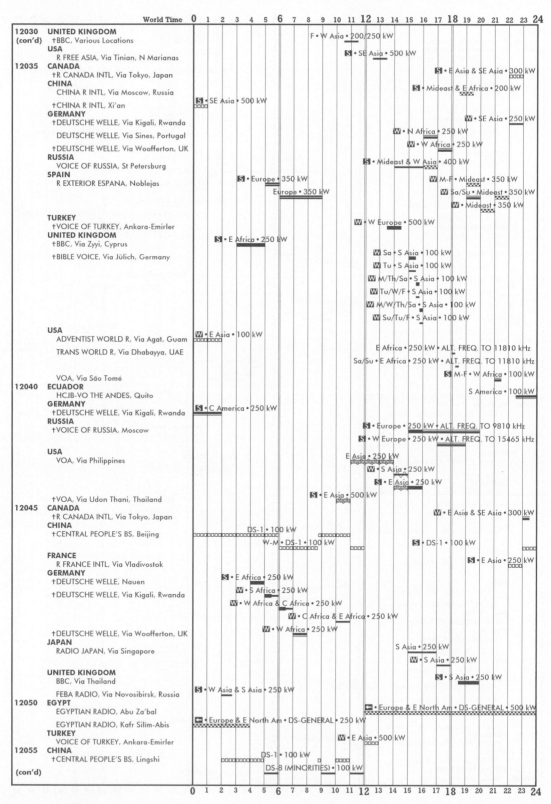

World Time 0 1 2 3 4 5 6 7 8 9 10 11 12 13 14 15 16 17 18 19 20 21 22 23 24

12030 UNITED KINGDOM
(con'd)   †BBC, Various Locations — F • W Asia • 200/250 kW
USA
R FREE ASIA, Via Tinian, N Marianas — S • SE Asia • 500 kW
12035 CANADA
†R CANADA INTL, Via Tokyo, Japan — S • E Asia & SE Asia • 300 kW
CHINA
CHINA R INTL, Via Moscow, Russia — S • Mideast & E Africa • 200 kW
†CHINA R INTL, Xi'an — S • SE Asia • 500 kW
GERMANY
†DEUTSCHE WELLE, Via Kigali, Rwanda — W • SE Asia • 250 kW
DEUTSCHE WELLE, Via Sines, Portugal — W • N Africa • 250 kW
†DEUTSCHE WELLE, Via Woofferton, UK — W • W Africa • 250 kW
RUSSIA
VOICE OF RUSSIA, St Petersburg — S • Mideast & W Asia • 400 kW
SPAIN
R EXTERIOR ESPANA, Noblejas — S • Europe • 350 kW
Europe • 350 kW
W • M-F • Mideast • 350 kW
W • Sa/Su • Mideast • 350 kW
W • Mideast • 350 kW
TURKEY
†VOICE OF TURKEY, Ankara-Emirler — W • W Europe • 500 kW
UNITED KINGDOM
†BBC, Via Zyyi, Cyprus — S • E Africa • 250 kW
†BIBLE VOICE, Via Jülich, Germany — W Sa • S Asia • 100 kW
W Tu • S Asia • 100 kW
W M/Th/Sa • S Asia • 100 kW
W Tu/W/F • S Asia • 100 kW
W M/W/Th/Sa • S Asia • 100 kW
W Su/Tu/F • S Asia • 100 kW
USA
ADVENTIST WORLD R, Via Agat, Guam — W • E Asia • 100 kW
TRANS WORLD R, Via Dhabayya, UAE — E Africa • 250 kW • ALT. FREQ. TO 11810 kHz
Sa/Su • E Africa • 250 kW • ALT. FREQ. TO 11810 kHz
VOA, Via São Tomé — S • M-F • W Africa • 100 kW
12040 ECUADOR
HCJB-VO THE ANDES, Quito — S America • 100 kW
GERMANY
†DEUTSCHE WELLE, Via Kigali, Rwanda — S • C America • 250 kW
RUSSIA
†VOICE OF RUSSIA, Moscow — S • Europe • 250 kW • ALT. FREQ. TO 9810 kHz
S • W Europe • 250 kW • ALT. FREQ. TO 15465 kHz
USA
VOA, Via Philippines — E Asia • 250 kW
W • S Asia • 250 kW
S • E Asia • 250 kW
†VOA, Via Udon Thani, Thailand — S • E Asia • 500 kW
12045 CANADA
†R CANADA INTL, Via Tokyo, Japan — W • E Asia & SE Asia • 300 kW
CHINA
†CENTRAL PEOPLE'S BS, Beijing — DS-1 • 100 kW
W-M • DS-1 • 100 kW
S • DS-1 • 100 kW
FRANCE
R FRANCE INTL, Via Vladivostok — S • E Asia • 250 kW
GERMANY
†DEUTSCHE WELLE, Nauen — S • E Africa • 250 kW
†DEUTSCHE WELLE, Via Kigali, Rwanda — W • S Africa • 250 kW
W • W Africa & C Africa • 250 kW
W • C Africa & E Africa • 250 kW
†DEUTSCHE WELLE, Via Woofferton, UK — W • W Africa • 250 kW
JAPAN
RADIO JAPAN, Via Singapore — S Asia • 250 kW
W • S Asia • 250 kW
UNITED KINGDOM
BBC, Via Thailand — S • S Asia • 250 kW
FEBA RADIO, Via Novosibirsk, Russia — S • W Asia & S Asia • 250 kW
12050 EGYPT
EGYPTIAN RADIO, Abu Za'bal — Europe & E North Am • DS-GENERAL • 500 kW
EGYPTIAN RADIO, Kafr Silim-Abis — Europe & E North Am • DS-GENERAL • 250 kW
TURKEY
VOICE OF TURKEY, Ankara-Emirler — W • E Asia • 500 kW
12055 CHINA
†CENTRAL PEOPLE'S BS, Lingshi — DS-1 • 100 kW
DS-8 (MINORITIES) • 100 kW

(con'd)

0 1 2 3 4 5 6 7 8 9 10 11 12 13 14 15 16 17 18 19 20 21 22 23 24

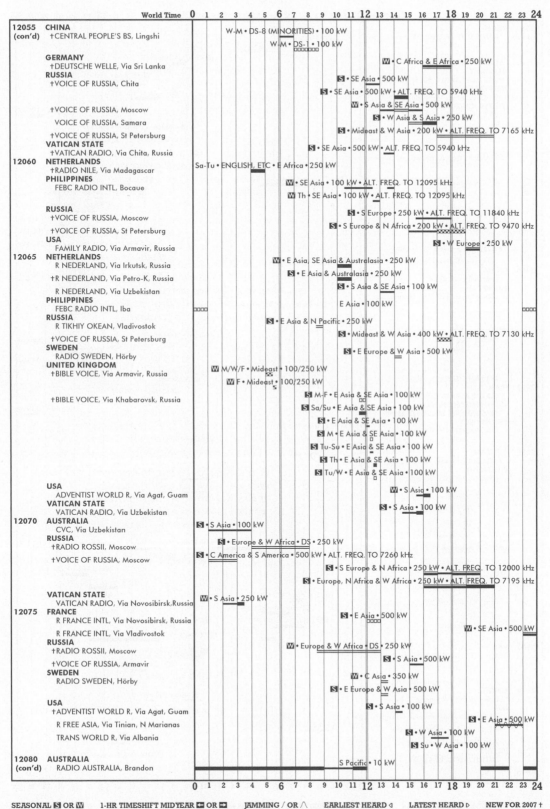

World Time 0 1 2 3 4 5 6 7 8 9 10 11 12 13 14 15 16 17 18 19 20 21 22 23 24

12055 **CHINA**
(con'd) †CENTRAL PEOPLE'S BS, Lingshi
      W-M • DS-8 (MINORITIES) • 100 kW
      W-M • DS-1 • 100 kW

GERMANY
  †DEUTSCHE WELLE, Via Sri Lanka   W • C Africa & E Africa • 250 kW
RUSSIA
  †VOICE OF RUSSIA, Chita   S • SE Asia • 500 kW
    S • SE Asia • 500 kW • ALT. FREQ. TO 5940 kHz
  †VOICE OF RUSSIA, Moscow   W • S Asia & SE Asia • 500 kW
  VOICE OF RUSSIA, Samara   S • W Asia & S Asia • 250 kW
  †VOICE OF RUSSIA, St Petersburg   S • Mideast & W Asia • 200 kW • ALT. FREQ. TO 7165 kHz
VATICAN STATE
  †VATICAN RADIO, Via Chita, Russia   S • SE Asia • 500 kW • ALT. FREQ. TO 5940 kHz
12060 **NETHERLANDS**
  †RADIO NILE, Via Madagascar Sa-Tu • ENGLISH, ETC • E Africa • 250 kW
PHILIPPINES
  FEBC RADIO INTL, Bocaue   W • SE Asia • 100 kW • ALT. FREQ. TO 12095 kHz
    W Th • SE Asia • 100 kW • ALT. FREQ. TO 12095 kHz

RUSSIA
  †VOICE OF RUSSIA, Moscow   S • S Europe • 250 kW • ALT. FREQ. TO 11840 kHz
  †VOICE OF RUSSIA, St Petersburg   S • S Europe & N Africa • 200 kW • ALT. FREQ. TO 9470 kHz
USA
  FAMILY RADIO, Via Armavir, Russia   S • W Europe • 250 kW
12065 **NETHERLANDS**
  R NEDERLAND, Via Irkutsk, Russia   W • E Asia, SE Asia & Australasia • 250 kW
  †R NEDERLAND, Via Petro-K, Russia   S • E Asia & Australasia • 250 kW
  R NEDERLAND, Via Uzbekistan   S • S Asia & SE Asia • 100 kW
PHILIPPINES
  FEBC RADIO INTL, Iba   E Asia • 100 kW
RUSSIA
  R TIKHIY OKEAN, Vladivostok   S • E Asia & N Pacific • 250 kW
  †VOICE OF RUSSIA, St Petersburg   S • Mideast & W Asia • 400 kW • ALT. FREQ. TO 7130 kHz
SWEDEN
  RADIO SWEDEN, Hörby   S • E Europe & W Asia • 500 kW
UNITED KINGDOM
  †BIBLE VOICE, Via Armavir, Russia W M/W/F • Mideast • 100/250 kW
    W F • Mideast • 100/250 kW
  †BIBLE VOICE, Via Khabarovsk, Russia   S M-F • E Asia & SE Asia • 100 kW
    S Sa/Su • E Asia & SE Asia • 100 kW
    S • E Asia & SE Asia • 100 kW
    S M • E Asia & SE Asia • 100 kW
    S Tu-Su • E Asia & SE Asia • 100 kW
    S Th • E Asia & SE Asia • 100 kW
    S Tu/W • E Asia & SE Asia • 100 kW

USA
  ADVENTIST WORLD R, Via Agat, Guam   W • S Asia • 100 kW
VATICAN STATE
  VATICAN RADIO, Via Uzbekistan   S • S Asia • 100 kW
12070 **AUSTRALIA**
  CVC, Via Uzbekistan S • S Asia • 100 kW
RUSSIA
  †RADIO ROSSII, Moscow S • Europe & W Africa • DS • 250 kW
  †VOICE OF RUSSIA, Moscow S • C America & S America • 500 kW • ALT. FREQ. TO 7260 kHz
    S • S Europe & N Africa • 250 kW • ALT. FREQ. TO 12000 kHz
    S • Europe, N Africa & W Africa • 250 kW • ALT. FREQ. TO 7195 kHz

VATICAN STATE
  VATICAN RADIO, Via Novosibirsk,Russia W • S Asia • 250 kW
12075 **FRANCE**
  R FRANCE INTL, Via Novosibirsk, Russia   S • E Asia • 500 kW
  R FRANCE INTL, Via Vladivostok   W • SE Asia • 500 kW
RUSSIA
  †RADIO ROSSII, Moscow W • Europe & W Africa • DS • 250 kW
  †VOICE OF RUSSIA, Armavir   S • S Asia • 500 kW
SWEDEN
  RADIO SWEDEN, Hörby   W • C Asia • 350 kW
    S • E Europe & W Asia • 500 kW

USA
  †ADVENTIST WORLD R, Via Agat, Guam   S • S Asia • 100 kW
  R FREE ASIA, Via Tinian, N Marianas   S • E Asia • 500 kW
  TRANS WORLD R, Via Albania   S • W Asia • 100 kW
    S Su • W Asia • 100 kW
12080 **AUSTRALIA**
(con'd) RADIO AUSTRALIA, Brandon   S Pacific • 10 kW

0 1 2 3 4 5 6 7 8 9 10 11 12 13 14 15 16 17 18 19 20 21 22 23 24

SEASONAL S OR W   1-HR TIMESHIFT MIDYEAR ⟵ OR ⟶   JAMMING / OR ∧   EARLIEST HEARD ◁   LATEST HEARD ▷   NEW FOR 2007 †

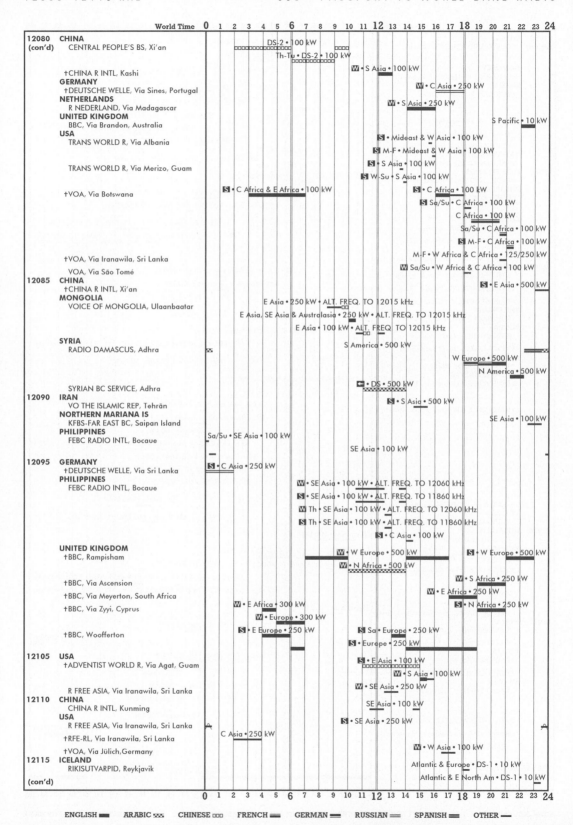

World Time 0 1 2 3 4 5 6 7 8 9 10 11 12 13 14 15 16 17 18 19 20 21 22 23 24

12080 CHINA
(con'd)   CENTRAL PEOPLE'S BS, Xi'an — DS-2 • 100 kW
          Th-Tu • DS-2 • 100 kW

          †CHINA R INTL, Kashi — W • S Asia • 100 kW
GERMANY
          †DEUTSCHE WELLE, Via Sines, Portugal — W • C Asia • 250 kW
NETHERLANDS
          R NEDERLAND, Via Madagascar — W • S Asia • 250 kW
UNITED KINGDOM
          BBC, Via Brandon, Australia — S Pacific • 10 kW
USA
          TRANS WORLD R, Via Albania — S • Mideast & W Asia • 100 kW
                                        S M-F • Mideast & W Asia • 100 kW
          TRANS WORLD R, Via Merizo, Guam — S • S Asia • 100 kW
                                            S W-Su • S Asia • 100 kW
          †VOA, Via Botswana — S • C Africa & E Africa • 100 kW
                               S • C Africa • 100 kW
                               S Sa/Su • C Africa • 100 kW
                               C Africa • 100 kW
                               Sa/Su • C Africa • 100 kW
                               S M-F • C Africa • 100 kW
          †VOA, Via Iranawila, Sri Lanka — M-F • W Africa & C Africa • 125/250 kW
          VOA, Via São Tomé — W Sa/Su • W Africa & C Africa • 100 kW
12085 CHINA
          †CHINA R INTL, Xi'an — S • E Asia • 500 kW
MONGOLIA
          VOICE OF MONGOLIA, Ulaanbaatar — E Asia • 250 kW • ALT. FREQ. TO 12015 kHz
                                           E Asia, SE Asia & Australasia • 250 kW • ALT. FREQ. TO 12015 kHz
                                           E Asia • 100 kW • ALT. FREQ. TO 12015 kHz
SYRIA
          RADIO DAMASCUS, Adhra — S America • 500 kW
                                  W Europe • 500 kW
                                  N America • 500 kW
          SYRIAN BC SERVICE, Adhra — • DS • 500 kW
12090 IRAN
          VO THE ISLAMIC REP, Tehrān — S • S Asia • 500 kW
NORTHERN MARIANA IS
          KFBS-FAR EAST BC, Saipan Island — SE Asia • 100 kW
PHILIPPINES
          FEBC RADIO INTL, Bocaue — Sa/Su • SE Asia • 100 kW
                                    SE Asia • 100 kW
12095 GERMANY
          †DEUTSCHE WELLE, Via Sri Lanka — S • C Asia • 250 kW
PHILIPPINES
          FEBC RADIO INTL, Bocaue — W • SE Asia • 100 kW • ALT. FREQ. TO 12060 kHz
                                    S • SE Asia • 100 kW • ALT. FREQ. TO 11860 kHz
                                    W Th • SE Asia • 100 kW • ALT. FREQ. TO 12060 kHz
                                    S Th • SE Asia • 100 kW • ALT. FREQ. TO 11860 kHz
                                    S • C Asia • 100 kW
UNITED KINGDOM
          †BBC, Rampisham — W • W Europe • 500 kW
                            S • W Europe • 500 kW
                            W • N Africa • 500 kW
          †BBC, Via Ascension — W • S Africa • 250 kW
          †BBC, Via Meyerton, South Africa — W • E Africa • 250 kW
          †BBC, Via Zyyi, Cyprus — W • E Africa • 300 kW
                                   S • N Africa • 250 kW
                                   W • Europe • 300 kW
          †BBC, Woofferton — S • E Europe • 250 kW
                             S Sa • Europe • 250 kW
                             S • Europe • 250 kW
12105 USA
          †ADVENTIST WORLD R, Via Agat, Guam — S • E Asia • 100 kW
                                               W • S Asia • 100 kW
          R FREE ASIA, Via Iranawila, Sri Lanka — W • SE Asia • 250 kW
12110 CHINA
          CHINA R INTL, Kunming — SE Asia • 100 kW
USA
          R FREE ASIA, Via Iranawila, Sri Lanka — S • SE Asia • 250 kW
          †RFE-RL, Via Iranawila, Sri Lanka — C Asia • 250 kW
          †VOA, Via Jülich, Germany — W • W Asia • 100 kW
12115 ICELAND
          RIKISUTVARPID, Reykjavik — Atlantic & Europe • DS-1 • 10 kW
                                     Atlantic & E North Am • DS-1 • 10 kW
(con'd)

0 1 2 3 4 5 6 7 8 9 10 11 12 13 14 15 16 17 18 19 20 21 22 23 24

ENGLISH ▬   ARABIC ░░   CHINESE □□□   FRENCH ▬   GERMAN ▬   RUSSIAN ═   SPANISH ═   OTHER ▬

World Time   0 1 2 3 4 5 6 7 8 9 10 11 12 13 14 15 16 17 18 19 20 21 22 23 24

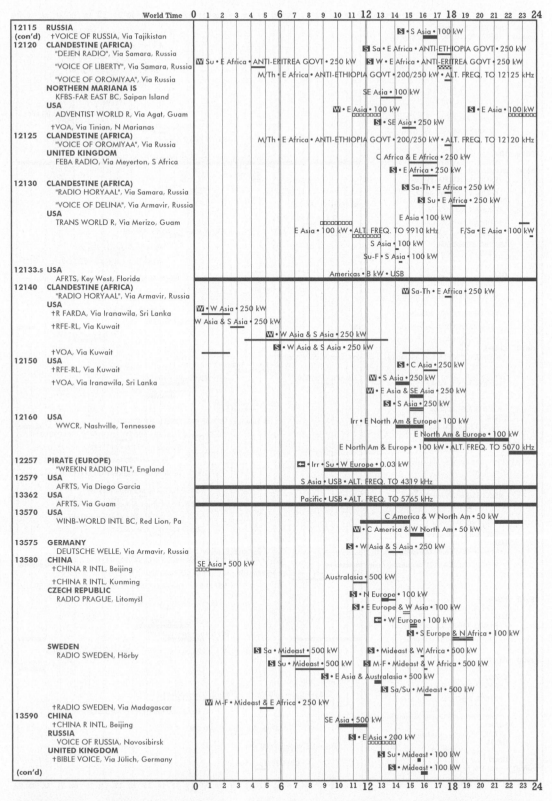

Freq	Station	Details
12115 (con'd)	**RUSSIA** †VOICE OF RUSSIA, Via Tajikistan	S • S Asia • 100 kW
12120	**CLANDESTINE (AFRICA)**	Sa • E Africa • ANTI-ETHIOPIA GOVT • 250 kW
	"DEJEN RADIO", Via Samara, Russia	W Su • E Africa • ANTI-ERITREA GOVT • 250 kW S W • E Africa • ANTI-ERITREA GOVT • 250 kW
	"VOICE OF LIBERTY", Via Samara, Russia	M/Th • E Africa • ANTI-ETHIOPIA GOVT • 200/250 kW • ALT. FREQ. TO 12125 kHz
	"VOICE OF OROMIYAA", Via Russia	
	NORTHERN MARIANA IS KFBS-FAR EAST BC, Saipan Island	SE Asia • 100 kW
	USA ADVENTIST WORLD R, Via Agat, Guam	W • E Asia • 100 kW S • E Asia • 100 kW
	†VOA, Via Tinian, N Marianas	S • SE Asia • 250 kW
12125	**CLANDESTINE (AFRICA)** "VOICE OF OROMIYAA", Via Russia	M/Th • E Africa • ANTI-ETHIOPIA GOVT • 200/250 kW • ALT. FREQ. TO 12120 kHz
	UNITED KINGDOM FEBA RADIO, Via Meyerton, S Africa	C Africa & E Africa • 250 kW S • E Africa • 250 kW
12130	**CLANDESTINE (AFRICA)** "RADIO HORYAAL", Via Samara, Russia	S Sa-Th • E Africa • 250 kW
	"VOICE OF DELINA", Via Armavir, Russia	S Su • E Africa • 250 kW
	USA TRANS WORLD R, Via Merizo, Guam	E Asia • 100 kW
		E Asia • 100 kW • ALT. FREQ. TO 9910 kHz F/Sa • E Asia • 100 kW
		S Asia • 100 kW
		Su-F • S Asia • 100 kW
12133.5	**USA** AFRTS, Key West, Florida	Americas • 8 kW • USB
12140	**CLANDESTINE (AFRICA)** "RADIO HORYAAL", Via Armavir, Russia	W Sa-Th • E Africa • 250 kW
	USA †R FARDA, Via Iranawila, Sri Lanka	W • W Asia • 250 kW
	†RFE-RL, Via Kuwait	W Asia & S Asia • 250 kW
		W • W Asia & S Asia • 250 kW
	†VOA, Via Kuwait	S • W Asia & S Asia • 250 kW
12150	**USA** †RFE-RL, Via Kuwait	S • C Asia • 250 kW
	†VOA, Via Iranawila, Sri Lanka	W • S Asia • 250 kW
		W • E Asia & SE Asia • 250 kW
		S • S Asia • 250 kW
12160	**USA** WWCR, Nashville, Tennessee	Irr • E North Am & Europe • 100 kW
		E North Am & Europe • 100 kW
		E North Am & Europe • 100 kW • ALT. FREQ. TO 5070 kHz
12257	**PIRATE (EUROPE)** "WREKIN RADIO INTL", England	← • Irr • Su • W Europe • 0.03 kW
12579	**USA** AFRTS, Via Diego Garcia	S Asia • USB • ALT. FREQ. TO 4319 kHz
13362	**USA** AFRTS, Via Guam	Pacific • USB • ALT. FREQ. TO 5765 kHz
13570	**USA** WINB-WORLD INTL BC, Red Lion, Pa	C America & W North Am • 50 kW
		W • C America & W North Am • 50 kW
13575	**GERMANY** DEUTSCHE WELLE, Via Armavir, Russia	S • W Asia & S Asia • 250 kW
13580	**CHINA** †CHINA R INTL, Beijing	SE Asia • 500 kW
	†CHINA R INTL, Kunming	Australasia • 500 kW
	CZECH REPUBLIC RADIO PRAGUE, Litomyšl	S • N Europe • 100 kW
		S • E Europe & W Asia • 100 kW
		← • W Europe • 100 kW
		S • S Europe & N Africa • 100 kW
	SWEDEN RADIO SWEDEN, Hörby	S Sa • Mideast • 500 kW S • Mideast & W Africa • 500 kW
		S Su • Mideast • 500 kW S M-F • Mideast & W Africa • 500 kW
		S • E Asia & Australasia • 500 kW
		S Sa/Su • Mideast • 500 kW
	†RADIO SWEDEN, Via Madagascar	W M-F • Mideast & E Africa • 250 kW
13590	**CHINA** †CHINA R INTL, Beijing	SE Asia • 500 kW
	RUSSIA VOICE OF RUSSIA, Novosibirsk	S • E Asia • 200 kW
	UNITED KINGDOM †BIBLE VOICE, Via Jülich, Germany	S Su • Mideast • 100 kW
		S • Mideast • 100 kW
(con'd)		

0 1 2 3 4 5 6 7 8 9 10 11 12 13 14 15 16 17 18 19 20 21 22 23 24

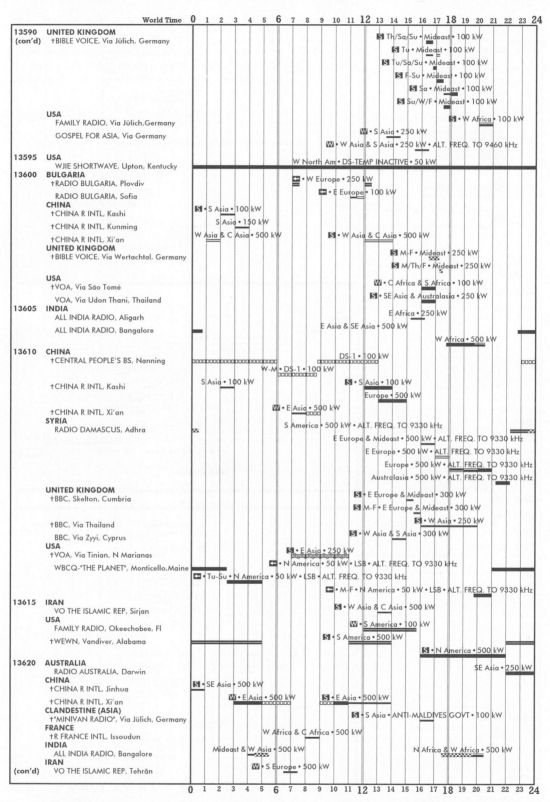

World Time 0 1 2 3 4 5 6 7 8 9 10 11 12 13 14 15 16 17 18 19 20 21 22 23 24

13590 UNITED KINGDOM
(con'd) †BIBLE VOICE, Via Jülich, Germany
- S Th/Sa/Su • Mideast • 100 kW
- S Tu • Mideast • 100 kW
- S Tu/Sa/Su • Mideast • 100 kW
- S F-Su • Mideast • 100 kW
- S Sa • Mideast • 100 kW
- S Su/W/F • Mideast • 100 kW
- S • W Africa • 100 kW

USA
FAMILY RADIO, Via Jülich, Germany
- W • S Asia • 250 kW
GOSPEL FOR ASIA, Via Germany
- W • W Asia & S Asia • 250 kW • ALT. FREQ. TO 9460 kHz

13595 USA
WJIE SHORTWAVE, Upton, Kentucky
- W North Am • DS-TEMP INACTIVE • 50 kW

13600 BULGARIA
†RADIO BULGARIA, Plovdiv
- W Europe • 250 kW
RADIO BULGARIA, Sofia
- E Europe • 100 kW
CHINA
†CHINA R INTL, Kashi
- S • S Asia • 100 kW
†CHINA R INTL, Kunming
- S Asia • 150 kW
†CHINA R INTL, Xi'an
- W Asia & C Asia • 500 kW
- S • W Asia & C Asia • 500 kW
UNITED KINGDOM
†BIBLE VOICE, Via Wertachtal, Germany
- S M-F • Mideast • 250 kW
- S M/Th/F • Mideast • 250 kW

USA
†VOA, Via São Tomé
- W • C Africa & S Africa • 100 kW
VOA, Via Udon Thani, Thailand
- S • SE Asia & Australasia • 250 kW

13605 INDIA
ALL INDIA RADIO, Aligarh
- E Africa • 250 kW
ALL INDIA RADIO, Bangalore
- E Asia & SE Asia • 500 kW
- W Africa • 500 kW

13610 CHINA
†CENTRAL PEOPLE'S BS, Nanning
- DS-1 • 100 kW
- W-M • DS-1 • 100 kW
†CHINA R INTL, Kashi
- S Asia • 100 kW
- S • S Asia • 100 kW
- Europe • 500 kW
†CHINA R INTL, Xi'an
- W • E Asia • 500 kW
SYRIA
RADIO DAMASCUS, Adhra
- S America • 500 kW • ALT. FREQ. TO 9330 kHz
- E Europe & Mideast • 500 kW • ALT. FREQ. TO 9330 kHz
- E Europe • 500 kW • ALT. FREQ. TO 9330 kHz
- Europe • 500 kW • ALT. FREQ. TO 9330 kHz
- Australasia • 500 kW • ALT. FREQ. TO 9330 kHz

UNITED KINGDOM
†BBC, Skelton, Cumbria
- S • E Europe & Mideast • 300 kW
- S M-F • E Europe & Mideast • 300 kW
†BBC, Via Thailand
- S • W Asia • 250 kW
BBC, Via Zyyi, Cyprus
- S • W Asia & S Asia • 300 kW
USA
†VOA, Via Tinian, N Marianas
- S • E Asia • 250 kW
WBCQ-"THE PLANET", Monticello, Maine
- N America • 50 kW • LSB • ALT. FREQ. TO 9330 kHz
- Tu-Su • N America • 50 kW • LSB • ALT. FREQ. TO 9330 kHz
- M-F • N America • 50 kW • LSB • ALT. FREQ. TO 9330 kHz

13615 IRAN
VO THE ISLAMIC REP, Sirjan
- S • W Asia & C Asia • 500 kW
USA
FAMILY RADIO, Okeechobee, Fl
- W • S America • 100 kW
†WEWN, Vandiver, Alabama
- S • S America • 500 kW
- S • N America • 500 kW

13620 AUSTRALIA
RADIO AUSTRALIA, Darwin
- SE Asia • 250 kW
CHINA
†CHINA R INTL, Jinhua
- S • SE Asia • 500 kW
†CHINA R INTL, Xi'an
- W • E Asia • 500 kW
- S • E Asia • 500 kW
CLANDESTINE (ASIA)
†"MINIVAN RADIO", Via Jülich, Germany
- S • S Asia • ANTI-MALDIVES GOVT • 100 kW
FRANCE
†R FRANCE INTL, Issoudun
- W Africa & C Africa • 500 kW
INDIA
ALL INDIA RADIO, Bangalore
- Mideast & W Asia • 500 kW
- N Africa & W Africa • 500 kW
IRAN
(con'd) VO THE ISLAMIC REP, Tehrān
- W • S Europe • 500 kW

0 1 2 3 4 5 6 7 8 9 10 11 12 13 14 15 16 17 18 19 20 21 22 23 24

ENGLISH ▬ ARABIC ▨ CHINESE ▫▫▫ FRENCH ═ GERMAN ▭ RUSSIAN ═ SPANISH ═ OTHER ▬

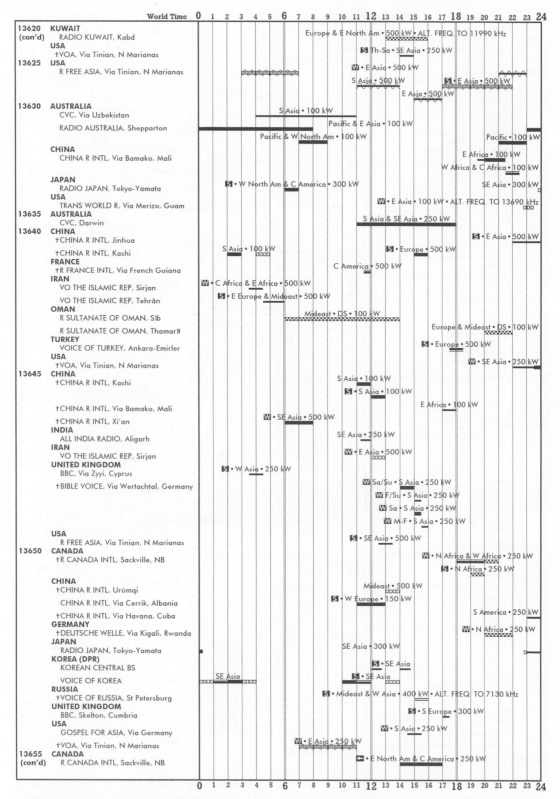

World Time 0 1 2 3 4 5 6 7 8 9 10 11 12 13 14 15 16 17 18 19 20 21 22 23 24

13620
(con'd) KUWAIT
  RADIO KUWAIT, Kabd — Europe & E North Am • 500 kW • ALT. FREQ. TO 11990 kHz
  USA
  †VOA, Via Tinian, N Marianas — S • Th-Sa • SE Asia • 250 kW
13625 USA
  R FREE ASIA, Via Tinian, N Marianas — W • E Asia • 500 kW
    S Asia • 500 kW
    S • E Asia • 500 kW
    E Asia • 500 kW

13630 AUSTRALIA
  CVC, Via Uzbekistan — S Asia • 100 kW
  RADIO AUSTRALIA, Shepparton — Pacific & E Asia • 100 kW
    Pacific & W North Am • 100 kW
    Pacific • 100 kW
  CHINA
  CHINA R INTL, Via Bamako, Mali — E Africa • 100 kW
    W Africa & C Africa • 100 kW
  JAPAN
  RADIO JAPAN, Tokyo-Yamata — S • W North Am & C America • 300 kW
    SE Asia • 300 kW
  USA
  TRANS WORLD R, Via Merizo, Guam — W • E Asia • 100 kW • ALT. FREQ. TO 13690 kHz
13635 AUSTRALIA
  CVC, Darwin — S Asia & SE Asia • 250 kW
13640 CHINA
  †CHINA R INTL, Jinhua — S • E Asia • 500 kW
  †CHINA R INTL, Kashi — S Asia • 100 kW
    S • Europe • 500 kW
  FRANCE
  †R FRANCE INTL, Via French Guiana — C America • 500 kW
  IRAN
  VO THE ISLAMIC REP, Sirjan — W • C Africa & E Africa • 500 kW
  VO THE ISLAMIC REP, Tehrān — S • E Europe & Mideast • 500 kW
  OMAN
  R SULTANATE OF OMAN, Sīb — Mideast • DS • 100 kW
  R SULTANATE OF OMAN, Thamarīt — Europe & Mideast • DS • 100 kW
  TURKEY
  VOICE OF TURKEY, Ankara-Emirler — S • Europe • 500 kW
  USA
  †VOA, Via Tinian, N Marianas — W • SE Asia • 250 kW
13645 CHINA
  †CHINA R INTL, Kashi — S Asia • 100 kW
    S • S Asia • 100 kW
    E Africa • 100 kW
  †CHINA R INTL, Via Bamako, Mali
  †CHINA R INTL, Xi'an — W • SE Asia • 500 kW
  INDIA
  ALL INDIA RADIO, Aligarh — SE Asia • 250 kW
  IRAN
  VO THE ISLAMIC REP, Sirjan — W • E Asia • 500 kW
  UNITED KINGDOM
  BBC, Via Zyyi, Cyprus — S • W Asia • 250 kW
  †BIBLE VOICE, Via Wertachtal, Germany — W • Sa/Su • S Asia • 250 kW
    W • F/Su • S Asia • 250 kW
    W • Sa • S Asia • 250 kW
    W • M-F • S Asia • 250 kW
  USA
  R FREE ASIA, Via Tinian, N Marianas — S • SE Asia • 500 kW
13650 CANADA
  †R CANADA INTL, Sackville, NB — W • N Africa & W Africa • 250 kW
    S • N Africa • 250 kW
  CHINA
  †CHINA R INTL, Urümqi — Mideast • 500 kW
  CHINA R INTL, Via Cerrik, Albania — S • W Europe • 150 kW
  †CHINA R INTL, Via Havana, Cuba — S America • 250 kW
  GERMANY
  †DEUTSCHE WELLE, Via Kigali, Rwanda — W • N Africa • 250 kW
  JAPAN
  RADIO JAPAN, Tokyo-Yamata — SE Asia • 300 kW
  KOREA (DPR)
  KOREAN CENTRAL BS — S • SE Asia
  VOICE OF KOREA — SE Asia
    S • SE Asia
  RUSSIA
  †VOICE OF RUSSIA, St Petersburg — S • Mideast & W Asia • 400 kW • ALT. FREQ. TO 7130 kHz
  UNITED KINGDOM
  BBC, Skelton, Cumbria — S • S Europe • 300 kW
  USA
  GOSPEL FOR ASIA, Via Germany — W • S Asia • 250 kW
  †VOA, Via Tinian, N Marianas — W • E Asia • 250 kW
13655 CANADA
(con'd) R CANADA INTL, Sackville, NB — E North Am & C America • 250 kW

0 1 2 3 4 5 6 7 8 9 10 11 12 13 14 15 16 17 18 19 20 21 22 23 24

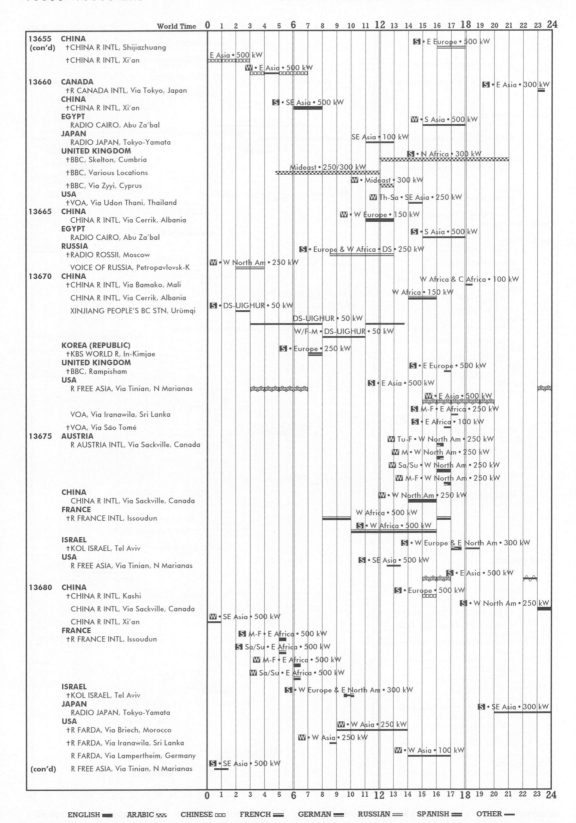

13655	**CHINA**	
(con'd)	†CHINA R INTL, Shijiazhuang	S • E Europe • 500 kW
	†CHINA R INTL, Xi'an	E Asia • 500 kW W • E Asia • 500 kW
13660	**CANADA**	
	†R CANADA INTL, Via Tokyo, Japan	S • E Asia • 300 kW
	CHINA	
	†CHINA R INTL, Xi'an	S • SE Asia • 500 kW
	EGYPT	
	RADIO CAIRO, Abu Za'bal	W • S Asia • 500 kW
	JAPAN	
	RADIO JAPAN, Tokyo-Yamata	SE Asia • 100 kW
	UNITED KINGDOM	
	†BBC, Skelton, Cumbria	S • N Africa • 300 kW
	†BBC, Various Locations	Mideast • 250/300 kW
	†BBC, Via Zyyi, Cyprus	W • Mideast • 300 kW
	USA	
	†VOA, Via Udon Thani, Thailand	W Th-Sa • SE Asia • 250 kW
13665	**CHINA**	
	CHINA R INTL, Via Cerrik, Albania	W • W Europe • 150 kW
	EGYPT	
	RADIO CAIRO, Abu Za'bal	S • S Asia • 500 kW
	RUSSIA	
	†RADIO ROSSII, Moscow	S • Europe & W Africa • DS • 250 kW
	VOICE OF RUSSIA, Petropavlovsk-K	W • W North Am • 250 kW
13670	**CHINA**	
	†CHINA R INTL, Via Bamako, Mali	W Africa & C Africa • 100 kW
	CHINA R INTL, Via Cerrik, Albania	W Africa • 150 kW
	XINJIANG PEOPLE'S BC STN, Urümqi	S • DS-UIGHUR • 50 kW DS-UIGHUR • 50 kW W/F-M • DS-UIGHUR • 50 kW
	KOREA (REPUBLIC)	
	†KBS WORLD R, In-Kimjae	S • Europe • 250 kW
	UNITED KINGDOM	
	†BBC, Rampisham	S • E Europe • 500 kW
	USA	
	R FREE ASIA, Via Tinian, N Marianas	S • E Asia • 500 kW W • E Asia • 500 kW
	VOA, Via Iranawila, Sri Lanka	S M-F • E Africa • 250 kW
	†VOA, Via São Tomé	S • E Africa • 100 kW
13675	**AUSTRIA**	
	R AUSTRIA INTL, Via Sackville, Canada	W Tu-F • W North Am • 250 kW W M • W North Am • 250 kW W Sa/Su • W North Am • 250 kW W M-F • W North Am • 250 kW
	CHINA	
	CHINA R INTL, Via Sackville, Canada	W • W North Am • 250 kW
	FRANCE	
	†R FRANCE INTL, Issoudun	W Africa • 500 kW S • W Africa • 500 kW
	ISRAEL	
	†KOL ISRAEL, Tel Aviv	S • W Europe & E North Am • 300 kW
	USA	
	R FREE ASIA, Via Tinian, N Marianas	S • SE Asia • 500 kW S • E Asia • 500 kW
13680	**CHINA**	
	†CHINA R INTL, Kashi	S • Europe • 500 kW S • W North Am • 250 kW
	CHINA R INTL, Via Sackville, Canada	W • SE Asia • 500 kW
	CHINA R INTL, Xi'an	
	FRANCE	
	†R FRANCE INTL, Issoudun	S M-F • E Africa • 500 kW S Sa/Su • E Africa • 500 kW W M-F • E Africa • 500 kW W Sa/Su • E Africa • 500 kW
	ISRAEL	
	†KOL ISRAEL, Tel Aviv	S • W Europe & E North Am • 300 kW
	JAPAN	
	RADIO JAPAN, Tokyo-Yamata	S • SE Asia • 300 kW
	USA	
	†R FARDA, Via Briech, Morocco	W • W Asia • 250 kW
	†R FARDA, Via Iranawila, Sri Lanka	W • W Asia • 250 kW
	R FARDA, Via Lampertheim, Germany	W • W Asia • 100 kW
(con'd)	R FREE ASIA, Via Tinian, N Marianas	S • SE Asia • 500 kW

World Time: 0 1 2 3 4 5 6 7 8 9 10 11 12 13 14 15 16 17 18 19 20 21 22 23 24

ENGLISH ▬   ARABIC ⌇⌇⌇   CHINESE □□□   FRENCH ▭▭   GERMAN ▬▬   RUSSIAN ═══   SPANISH ▭▭   OTHER ▬▬

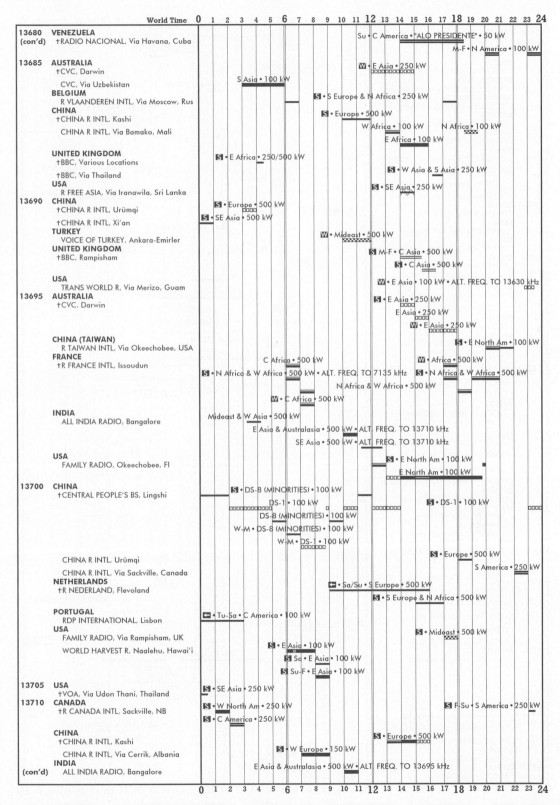

	World Time	0	1	2	3	4	5	6	7	8	9	10	11	12	13	14	15	16	17	18	19	20	21	22	23	24

13680 VENEZUELA
(con'd) †RADIO NACIONAL, Via Havana, Cuba
- Su • C America • "ALO PRESIDENTE" • 50 kW
- M-F • N America • 100 kW

13685 AUSTRALIA
†CVC, Darwin
- W • E Asia • 250 kW
CVC, Via Uzbekistan
- S Asia • 100 kW
BELGIUM
R VLAANDEREN INTL, Via Moscow, Rus
- S • S Europe & N Africa • 250 kW
CHINA
†CHINA R INTL, Kashi
- S • Europe • 500 kW
CHINA R INTL, Via Bamako, Mali
- W Africa • 100 kW   N Africa • 100 kW
- E Africa • 100 kW

UNITED KINGDOM
†BBC, Various Locations
- S • E Africa • 250/500 kW
†BBC, Via Thailand
- S • W Asia & S Asia • 250 kW
USA
R FREE ASIA, Via Iranawila, Sri Lanka
- S • SE Asia • 250 kW

13690 CHINA
†CHINA R INTL, Urümqi
- S • Europe • 500 kW
†CHINA R INTL, Xi'an
- S • SE Asia • 500 kW
TURKEY
VOICE OF TURKEY, Ankara-Emirler
- W • Mideast • 500 kW
UNITED KINGDOM
†BBC, Rampisham
- S • M-F • C Asia • 500 kW
- S • C Asia • 500 kW

USA
TRANS WORLD R, Via Merizo, Guam
- W • E Asia • 100 kW • ALT. FREQ. TO 13630 kHz
13695 AUSTRALIA
†CVC, Darwin
- S • E Asia • 250 kW
- E Asia • 250 kW
- W • E Asia • 250 kW

CHINA (TAIWAN)
R TAIWAN INTL, Via Okeechobee, USA
- S • E North Am • 100 kW
FRANCE
†R FRANCE INTL, Issoudun
- C Africa • 500 kW
- W • Africa • 500 kW
- S • N Africa & W Africa • 500 kW • ALT. FREQ. TO 7135 kHz   S • N Africa & W Africa • 500 kW
- N Africa & W Africa • 500 kW
- W • C Africa • 500 kW

INDIA
ALL INDIA RADIO, Bangalore
- Mideast & W Asia • 500 kW
- E Asia & Australasia • 500 kW • ALT. FREQ. TO 13710 kHz
- SE Asia • 500 kW • ALT. FREQ. TO 13710 kHz

USA
FAMILY RADIO, Okeechobee, Fl
- S • E North Am • 100 kW
- E North Am • 100 kW

13700 CHINA
†CENTRAL PEOPLE'S BS, Lingshi
- S • DS-8 (MINORITIES) • 100 kW
- DS-1 • 100 kW
- S • DS-1 • 100 kW
- DS-8 (MINORITIES) • 100 kW
- W-M • DS-8 (MINORITIES) • 100 kW
- W-M • DS-1 • 100 kW

CHINA R INTL, Urümqi
- S • Europe • 500 kW
CHINA R INTL, Via Sackville, Canada
- S America • 250 kW
NETHERLANDS
†R NEDERLAND, Flevoland
- ⇦ • Sa/Su • S Europe • 500 kW
- S • S Europe & N Africa • 500 kW

PORTUGAL
RDP INTERNATIONAL, Lisbon
- ⇦ • Tu-Sa • C America • 100 kW
USA
FAMILY RADIO, Via Rampisham, UK
- S • Mideast • 500 kW
WORLD HARVEST R, Naalehu, Hawai'i
- S • E Asia • 100 kW
- S • Sa • E Asia • 100 kW
- S • Su-F • E Asia • 100 kW

13705 USA
†VOA, Via Udon Thani, Thailand
- S • SE Asia • 250 kW
13710 CANADA
†R CANADA INTL, Sackville, NB
- S • W North Am • 250 kW
- S • F-Su • S America • 250 kW
- S • C America • 250 kW

CHINA
†CHINA R INTL, Kashi
- S • Europe • 500 kW
CHINA R INTL, Via Cerrik, Albania
- S • W Europe • 150 kW
INDIA
(con'd) ALL INDIA RADIO, Bangalore
- E Asia & Australasia • 500 kW • ALT. FREQ. TO 13695 kHz

	0	1	2	3	4	5	6	7	8	9	10	11	12	13	14	15	16	17	18	19	20	21	22	23	24

SEASONAL **S** OR **W**   1-HR TIMESHIFT MIDYEAR ⇦ OR ⇨   JAMMING / OR ∧   EARLIEST HEARD ◁   LATEST HEARD ▷   NEW FOR 2007 †

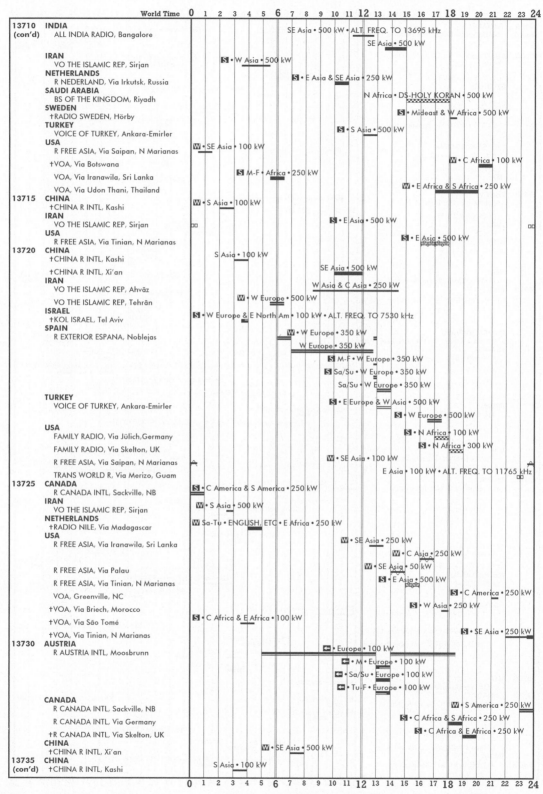

World Time | 0 1 2 3 4 5 6 7 8 9 10 11 12 13 14 15 16 17 18 19 20 21 22 23 24

13710 INDIA
(con'd) ALL INDIA RADIO, Bangalore — SE Asia • 500 kW • ALT. FREQ. TO 13695 kHz / SE Asia • 500 kW

IRAN
VO THE ISLAMIC REP, Sirjan — S • W Asia • 500 kW

NETHERLANDS
R NEDERLAND, Via Irkutsk, Russia — S • E Asia & SE Asia • 250 kW

SAUDI ARABIA
BS OF THE KINGDOM, Riyadh — N Africa • DS-HOLY KORAN • 500 kW

SWEDEN
†RADIO SWEDEN, Hörby — S • Mideast & W Africa • 500 kW

TURKEY
VOICE OF TURKEY, Ankara-Emirler — S • S Asia • 500 kW

USA
R FREE ASIA, Via Saipan, N Marianas — W • SE Asia • 100 kW

†VOA, Via Botswana — W • C Africa • 100 kW

VOA, Via Iranawila, Sri Lanka — S • M-F • Africa • 250 kW

VOA, Via Udon Thani, Thailand — W • E Africa & S Africa • 250 kW

13715 CHINA
†CHINA R INTL, Kashi — W • S Asia • 100 kW

IRAN
VO THE ISLAMIC REP, Sirjan — S • E Asia • 500 kW

USA
R FREE ASIA, Via Tinian, N Marianas — S • E Asia • 500 kW

13720 CHINA
†CHINA R INTL, Kashi — S Asia • 100 kW

†CHINA R INTL, Xi'an — SE Asia • 500 kW / W Asia & C Asia • 250 kW

IRAN
VO THE ISLAMIC REP, Ahvāz — W • W Europe • 500 kW

VO THE ISLAMIC REP, Tehrān

ISRAEL
†KOL ISRAEL, Tel Aviv — S • W Europe & E North Am • 100 kW • ALT. FREQ. TO 7530 kHz

SPAIN
R EXTERIOR ESPANA, Noblejas — W • W Europe • 350 kW / W Europe • 350 kW / S • M-F • W Europe • 350 kW / S • Sa/Su • W Europe • 350 kW / Sa/Su • W Europe • 350 kW

TURKEY
VOICE OF TURKEY, Ankara-Emirler — S • E Europe & W Asia • 500 kW / S • W Europe • 500 kW

USA
FAMILY RADIO, Via Jülich, Germany — S • N Africa • 100 kW

FAMILY RADIO, Via Skelton, UK — S • N Africa • 300 kW

R FREE ASIA, Via Saipan, N Marianas — W • SE Asia • 100 kW

TRANS WORLD R, Via Merizo, Guam — E Asia • 100 kW • ALT. FREQ. TO 11765 kHz

13725 CANADA
R CANADA INTL, Sackville, NB — S • C America & S America • 250 kW

IRAN
VO THE ISLAMIC REP, Sirjan — W • S Asia • 500 kW

NETHERLANDS
†RADIO NILE, Via Madagascar — W Sa-Tu • ENGLISH, ETC • E Africa • 250 kW

USA
R FREE ASIA, Via Iranawila, Sri Lanka — W • SE Asia • 250 kW

R FREE ASIA, Via Palau — W • C Asia • 250 kW / W • SE Asia • 50 kW

R FREE ASIA, Via Tinian, N Marianas — S • E Asia • 500 kW

VOA, Greenville, NC — S • C America • 250 kW

†VOA, Via Briech, Morocco — S • W Asia • 250 kW

†VOA, Via São Tomé — S • C Africa & E Africa • 100 kW

†VOA, Via Tinian, N Marianas — S • SE Asia • 250 kW

13730 AUSTRIA
R AUSTRIA INTL, Moosbrunn — ◄ • Europe • 100 kW / ◄ • M • Europe • 100 kW / ◄ • Sa/Su • Europe • 100 kW / ◄ • Tu-F • Europe • 100 kW

CANADA
R CANADA INTL, Sackville, NB — W • S America • 250 kW

R CANADA INTL, Via Germany — S • C Africa & S Africa • 250 kW

†R CANADA INTL, Via Skelton, UK — S • C Africa & E Africa • 250 kW

CHINA
†CHINA R INTL, Xi'an — W • SE Asia • 500 kW

13735 CHINA
(con'd) †CHINA R INTL, Kashi — S Asia • 100 kW

World Time | 0 1 2 3 4 5 6 7 8 9 10 11 12 13 14 15 16 17 18 19 20 21 22 23 24

ENGLISH ▬   ARABIC ░   CHINESE ▫▫▫   FRENCH ▭   GERMAN ▬   RUSSIAN ═   SPANISH ═   OTHER ─

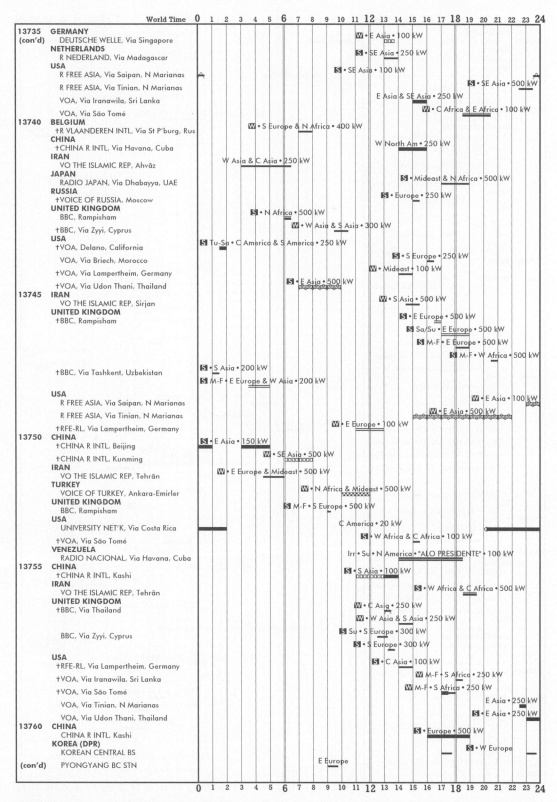

World Time 0 1 2 3 4 5 6 7 8 9 10 11 12 13 14 15 16 17 18 19 20 21 22 23 24

13735 (con'd)

GERMANY
  DEUTSCHE WELLE, Via Singapore — **W** • E Asia • 100 kW

NETHERLANDS
  R NEDERLAND, Via Madagascar — **S** • SE Asia • 250 kW

USA
  R FREE ASIA, Via Saipan, N Marianas — **S** • SE Asia • 100 kW
  R FREE ASIA, Via Tinian, N Marianas — **S** • SE Asia • 500 kW
  VOA, Via Iranawila, Sri Lanka — E Asia & SE Asia • 250 kW
  VOA, Via São Tomé — **W** • C Africa & E Africa • 100 kW

13740

BELGIUM
  †R VLAANDEREN INTL, Via St P'burg, Rus — **W** • S Europe & N Africa • 400 kW

CHINA
  †CHINA R INTL, Via Havana, Cuba — W North Am • 250 kW

IRAN
  VO THE ISLAMIC REP, Ahvāz — W Asia & C Asia • 250 kW

JAPAN
  RADIO JAPAN, Via Dhabayya, UAE — **S** • Mideast & N Africa • 500 kW

RUSSIA
  †VOICE OF RUSSIA, Moscow — **S** • Europe • 250 kW

UNITED KINGDOM
  BBC, Rampisham — **S** • N Africa • 500 kW
  †BBC, Via Zyyi, Cyprus — **W** • W Asia & S Asia • 300 kW

USA
  †VOA, Delano, California — **S** Tu-Sa • C America & S America • 250 kW
  VOA, Via Briech, Morocco — **S** • S Europe • 250 kW
  †VOA, Via Lampertheim, Germany — **W** • Mideast • 100 kW
  †VOA, Via Udon Thani, Thailand — **S** • E Asia • 500 kW

13745

IRAN
  VO THE ISLAMIC REP, Sirjan — **W** • S Asia • 500 kW

UNITED KINGDOM
  †BBC, Rampisham — **S** • E Europe • 500 kW
    S Sa/Su • E Europe • 500 kW
    S M-F • E Europe • 500 kW
    S M-F • W Africa • 500 kW
  †BBC, Via Tashkent, Uzbekistan — **S** • S Asia • 200 kW
    S M-F • E Europe & W Asia • 200 kW

USA
  R FREE ASIA, Via Saipan, N Marianas — **W** • E Asia • 100 kW
  R FREE ASIA, Via Tinian, N Marianas — **W** • E Asia • 500 kW
  †RFE-RL, Via Lampertheim, Germany — **W** • E Europe • 100 kW

13750

CHINA
  †CHINA R INTL, Beijing — **S** • E Asia • 150 kW
  †CHINA R INTL, Kunming — **W** • SE Asia • 500 kW

IRAN
  VO THE ISLAMIC REP, Tehrān — **W** • E Europe & Mideast • 500 kW

TURKEY
  VOICE OF TURKEY, Ankara-Emirler — **W** • N Africa & Mideast • 500 kW

UNITED KINGDOM
  BBC, Rampisham — **S** M-F • S Europe • 500 kW

USA
  UNIVERSITY NET'K, Via Costa Rica — C America • 20 kW
  †VOA, Via São Tomé — **S** • W Africa & C Africa • 100 kW

VENEZUELA
  RADIO NACIONAL, Via Havana, Cuba — Irr • Su • N America • "ALO PRESIDENTE" • 100 kW

13755

CHINA
  †CHINA R INTL, Kashi — **S** • S Asia • 100 kW

IRAN
  VO THE ISLAMIC REP, Tehrān — **S** • W Africa & C Africa • 500 kW

UNITED KINGDOM
  †BBC, Via Thailand — **W** • C Asia • 250 kW
    W • W Asia & S Asia • 250 kW
  BBC, Via Zyyi, Cyprus — **S** Su • S Europe • 300 kW
    S • S Europe • 300 kW

USA
  †RFE-RL, Via Lampertheim, Germany — **S** • C Asia • 100 kW
  †VOA, Via Iranawila, Sri Lanka — **W** M-F • S Africa • 250 kW
  †VOA, Via São Tomé — **W** M-F • S Africa • 250 kW
  VOA, Via Tinian, N Marianas — E Asia • 250 kW
  VOA, Via Udon Thani, Thailand — **S** • E Asia • 250 kW

13760

CHINA
  CHINA R INTL, Kashi — **S** • Europe • 500 kW

KOREA (DPR)
  KOREAN CENTRAL BS — **S** • W Europe

(con'd) PYONGYANG BC STN — E Europe

World Time 0 1 2 3 4 5 6 7 8 9 10 11 12 13 14 15 16 17 18 19 20 21 22 23 24

SEASONAL **S** OR **W**   1-HR TIMESHIFT MIDYEAR ⇐ OR ⇒   JAMMING / OR /\   EARLIEST HEARD ◁   LATEST HEARD ▷   NEW FOR 2007 †

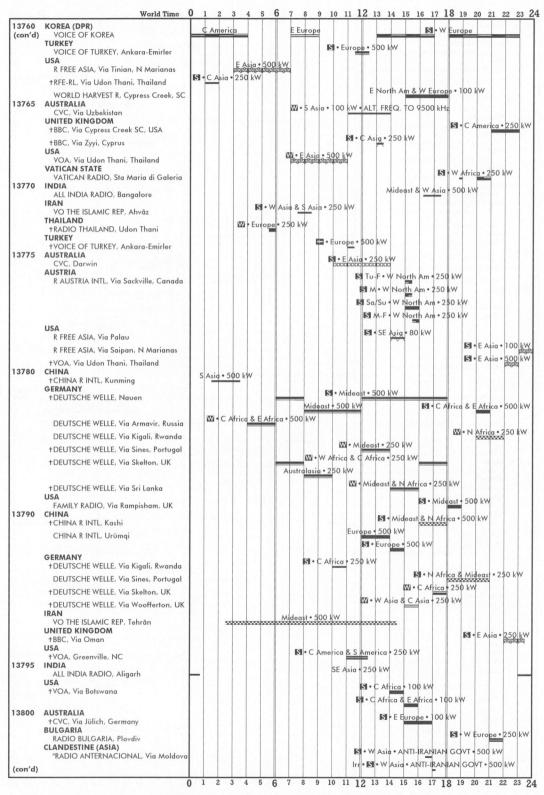

World Time 0 1 2 3 4 5 6 7 8 9 10 11 12 13 14 15 16 17 18 19 20 21 22 23 24

Frequency	Station
13760 (con'd)	KOREA (DPR)
	VOICE OF KOREA — C America / E Europe / S • W Europe
	TURKEY
	VOICE OF TURKEY, Ankara-Emirler — S • Europe • 500 kW
	USA
	R FREE ASIA, Via Tinian, N Marianas — E Asia • 500 kW
	†RFE-RL, Via Udon Thani, Thailand — S • C Asia • 250 kW
	WORLD HARVEST R, Cypress Creek, SC — E North Am & W Europe • 100 kW
13765	AUSTRALIA
	CVC, Via Uzbekistan — W • S Asia • 100 kW • ALT. FREQ. TO 9500 kHz
	UNITED KINGDOM
	†BBC, Via Cypress Creek SC, USA — S • C America • 250 kW
	†BBC, Via Zyyi, Cyprus — S • C Asia • 250 kW
	USA
	VOA, Via Udon Thani, Thailand — W • E Asia • 500 kW
	VATICAN STATE
	VATICAN RADIO, Sta Maria di Galeria — S • W Africa • 250 kW
13770	INDIA
	ALL INDIA RADIO, Bangalore — Mideast & W Asia • 500 kW
	IRAN
	VO THE ISLAMIC REP, Ahvāz — S • W Asia & S Asia • 250 kW
	THAILAND
	†RADIO THAILAND, Udon Thani — W • Europe • 250 kW
	TURKEY
	†VOICE OF TURKEY, Ankara-Emirler — • Europe • 500 kW
13775	AUSTRALIA
	CVC, Darwin — S • E Asia • 250 kW
	AUSTRIA
	R AUSTRIA INTL, Via Sackville, Canada — S Tu-F • W North Am • 250 kW
	— S M • W North Am • 250 kW
	— S Sa/Su • W North Am • 250 kW
	— S M-F • W North Am • 250 kW
	USA
	R FREE ASIA, Via Palau — S • SE Asia • 80 kW
	R FREE ASIA, Via Saipan, N Marianas — S • E Asia • 100 kW
	†VOA, Via Udon Thani, Thailand — S • E Asia • 500 kW
13780	CHINA
	†CHINA R INTL, Kunming — S Asia • 500 kW
	GERMANY
	†DEUTSCHE WELLE, Nauen — S • Mideast • 500 kW
	— Mideast • 500 kW
	DEUTSCHE WELLE, Via Armavir, Russia — W • C Africa & E Africa • 500 kW
	— S • C Africa & E Africa • 500 kW
	DEUTSCHE WELLE, Via Kigali, Rwanda — W • N Africa • 250 kW
	DEUTSCHE WELLE, Via Sines, Portugal — W • Mideast • 250 kW
	†DEUTSCHE WELLE, Via Skelton, UK — W • W Africa & C Africa • 250 kW
	— Australasia • 250 kW
	†DEUTSCHE WELLE, Via Sri Lanka — W • Mideast & N Africa • 250 kW
	USA
	FAMILY RADIO, Via Rampisham, UK — S • Mideast • 500 kW
13790	CHINA
	†CHINA R INTL, Kashi — S • Mideast & N Africa • 500 kW
	CHINA R INTL, Urūmqi — Europe • 500 kW
	— S • Europe • 500 kW
	GERMANY
	†DEUTSCHE WELLE, Via Kigali, Rwanda — S • C Africa • 250 kW
	DEUTSCHE WELLE, Via Sines, Portugal — S • N Africa & Mideast • 250 kW
	†DEUTSCHE WELLE, Via Skelton, UK — W • C Africa • 250 kW
	†DEUTSCHE WELLE, Via Woofferton, UK — W • W Asia & C Asia • 250 kW
	IRAN
	VO THE ISLAMIC REP, Tehrān — Mideast • 500 kW
	UNITED KINGDOM
	†BBC, Via Oman — S • E Asia • 250 kW
	USA
	†VOA, Greenville, NC — S • C America & S America • 250 kW
13795	INDIA
	ALL INDIA RADIO, Aligarh — SE Asia • 250 kW
	USA
	†VOA, Via Botswana — S • C Africa • 100 kW
	— S • C Africa & E Africa • 100 kW
13800	AUSTRALIA
	†CVC, Via Jülich, Germany — S • E Europe • 100 kW
	BULGARIA
	RADIO BULGARIA, Plovdiv — S • W Europe • 250 kW
	CLANDESTINE (ASIA)
	"RADIO ANTERNACIONAL, Via Moldova — S • W Asia • ANTI-IRANIAN GOVT • 500 kW
	Irr • S • W Asia • ANTI-IRANIAN GOVT • 500 kW
(con'd)	

0 1 2 3 4 5 6 7 8 9 10 11 12 13 14 15 16 17 18 19 20 21 22 23 24

ENGLISH ▬ ARABIC ▨ CHINESE ▢▢▢ FRENCH ▬▬ GERMAN ▬▬ RUSSIAN ══ SPANISH ▬▬ OTHER ▬

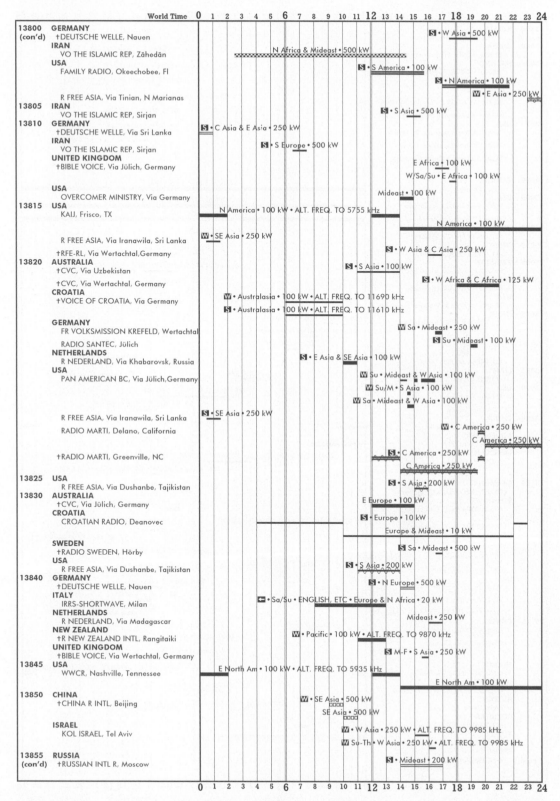

World Time		
13800 (con'd)	**GERMANY** †DEUTSCHE WELLE, Nauen	S • W Asia • 500 kW
	IRAN VO THE ISLAMIC REP, Zāhedān	N Africa & Mideast • 500 kW
	USA FAMILY RADIO, Okeechobee, Fl	S • S America • 100 kW
		S • N America • 100 kW
	R FREE ASIA, Via Tinian, N Marianas	W • E Asia • 250 kW
13805	**IRAN** VO THE ISLAMIC REP, Sirjan	S • S Asia • 500 kW
13810	**GERMANY** †DEUTSCHE WELLE, Via Sri Lanka	S • C Asia & E Asia • 250 kW
	IRAN VO THE ISLAMIC REP, Sirjan	S • S Europe • 500 kW
	UNITED KINGDOM †BIBLE VOICE, Via Jülich, Germany	E Africa • 100 kW / W/Sa/Su • E Africa • 100 kW
	USA OVERCOMER MINISTRY, Via Germany	Mideast • 100 kW
13815	**USA** KAIJ, Frisco, TX	N America • 100 kW • ALT. FREQ. TO 5755 kHz / N America • 100 kW
	R FREE ASIA, Via Iranwila, Sri Lanka	W • SE Asia • 250 kW
	†RFE-RL, Via Wertachtal, Germany	S • W Asia & C Asia • 250 kW
13820	**AUSTRALIA** †CVC, Via Uzbekistan	S • S Asia • 100 kW
	†CVC, Via Wertachtal, Germany	S • W Africa & C Africa • 125 kW
	CROATIA †VOICE OF CROATIA, Via Germany	W • Australasia • 100 kW • ALT. FREQ. TO 11690 kHz / S • Australasia • 100 kW • ALT. FREQ. TO 11610 kHz
	GERMANY FR VOLKSMISSION KREFELD, Wertachtal	W Sa • Mideast • 250 kW
	RADIO SANTEC, Jülich	S Su • Mideast • 100 kW
	NETHERLANDS R NEDERLAND, Via Khabarovsk, Russia	S • E Asia & SE Asia • 100 kW
	USA PAN AMERICAN BC, Via Jülich, Germany	W Su • Mideast & W Asia • 100 kW / W Su/M • S Asia • 100 kW / W Sa • Mideast & W Asia • 100 kW
	R FREE ASIA, Via Iranwila, Sri Lanka	S • SE Asia • 250 kW
	RADIO MARTI, Delano, California	W • C America • 250 kW / C America • 250 kW
	†RADIO MARTI, Greenville, NC	S • C America • 250 kW / C America • 250 kW
13825	**USA** R FREE ASIA, Via Dushanbe, Tajikistan	S • S Asia • 200 kW
13830	**AUSTRALIA** †CVC, Via Jülich, Germany	E Europe • 100 kW
	CROATIA CROATIAN RADIO, Deanovec	S • Europe • 10 kW / Europe & Mideast • 10 kW
	SWEDEN †RADIO SWEDEN, Hörby	S Sa • Mideast • 500 kW
	USA R FREE ASIA, Via Dushanbe, Tajikistan	S • S Asia • 200 kW
13840	**GERMANY** †DEUTSCHE WELLE, Nauen	S • N Europe • 500 kW
	ITALY IRRS-SHORTWAVE, Milan	← • Sa/Su • ENGLISH, ETC • Europe & N Africa • 20 kW
	NETHERLANDS R NEDERLAND, Via Madagascar	Mideast • 250 kW
	NEW ZEALAND †R NEW ZEALAND INTL, Rangitaiki	W • Pacific • 100 kW • ALT. FREQ. TO 9870 kHz
	UNITED KINGDOM †BIBLE VOICE, Via Wertachtal, Germany	S M-F • S Asia • 250 kW
13845	**USA** WWCR, Nashville, Tennessee	E North Am • 100 kW • ALT. FREQ. TO 5935 kHz / E North Am • 100 kW
13850	**CHINA** †CHINA R INTL, Beijing	W • SE Asia • 500 kW / SE Asia • 500 kW
	ISRAEL KOL ISRAEL, Tel Aviv	W • W Asia • 250 kW • ALT. FREQ. TO 9985 kHz / W Su-Th • W Asia • 250 kW • ALT. FREQ. TO 9985 kHz
13855 (con'd)	**RUSSIA** †RUSSIAN INTL R, Moscow	S • Mideast • 200 kW

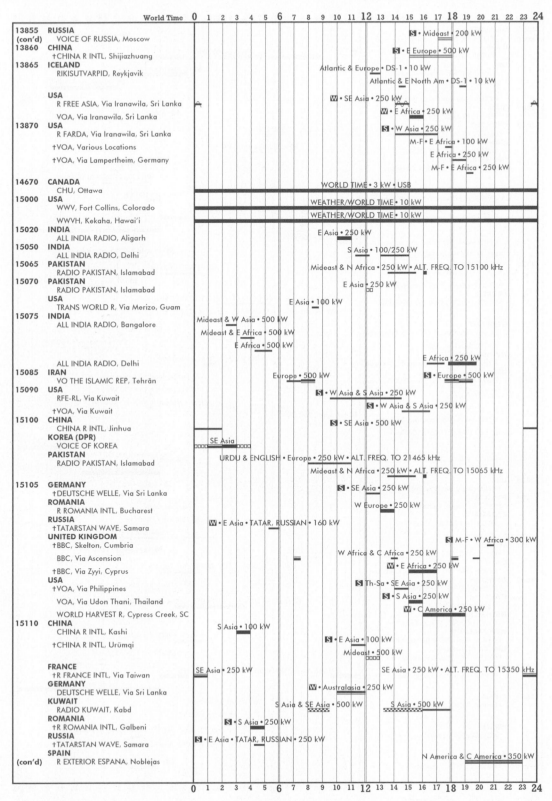

	World Time	0 1 2 3 4 5 6 7 8 9 10 11 12 13 14 15 16 17 18 19 20 21 22 23 24
13855 (con'd)	RUSSIA	
	VOICE OF RUSSIA, Moscow	S • Mideast • 200 kW
13860	CHINA	
	†CHINA R INTL, Shijiazhuang	S • E Europe • 500 kW
13865	ICELAND	
	RIKISUTVARPID, Reykjavik	Atlantic & Europe • DS-1 • 10 kW
		Atlantic & E North Am • DS-1 • 10 kW
	USA	
	R FREE ASIA, Via Iranawila, Sri Lanka	W • SE Asia • 250 kW
	VOA, Via Iranawila, Sri Lanka	W • E Africa • 250 kW
13870	USA	
	R FARDA, Via Iranawila, Sri Lanka	S • W Asia • 250 kW
	†VOA, Various Locations	M-F • E Africa • 100 kW
	†VOA, Via Lampertheim, Germany	E Africa • 250 kW
		M-F • E Africa • 250 kW
14670	CANADA	
	CHU, Ottawa	WORLD TIME • 3 kW • USB
15000	USA	
	WWV, Fort Collins, Colorado	WEATHER/WORLD TIME • 10 kW
	WWVH, Kekaha, Hawai'i	WEATHER/WORLD TIME • 10 kW
15020	INDIA	
	ALL INDIA RADIO, Aligarh	E Asia • 250 kW
15050	INDIA	
	ALL INDIA RADIO, Delhi	S Asia • 100/250 kW
15065	PAKISTAN	
	RADIO PAKISTAN, Islamabad	Mideast & N Africa • 250 kW • ALT. FREQ. TO 15100 kHz
15070	PAKISTAN	
	RADIO PAKISTAN, Islamabad	E Asia • 250 kW
	USA	
	TRANS WORLD R, Via Merizo, Guam	E Asia • 100 kW
15075	INDIA	
	ALL INDIA RADIO, Bangalore	Mideast & W Asia • 500 kW
		Mideast & E Africa • 500 kW
		E Africa • 500 kW
	ALL INDIA RADIO, Delhi	E Africa • 250 kW
15085	IRAN	
	VO THE ISLAMIC REP, Tehrān	Europe • 500 kW
		S • Europe • 500 kW
15090	USA	
	RFE-RL, Via Kuwait	S • W Asia & S Asia • 250 kW
	†VOA, Via Kuwait	S • W Asia & S Asia • 250 kW
15100	CHINA	
	CHINA R INTL, Jinhua	S • SE Asia • 500 kW
	KOREA (DPR)	
	VOICE OF KOREA	SE Asia
	PAKISTAN	
	RADIO PAKISTAN, Islamabad	URDU & ENGLISH • Europe • 250 kW • ALT. FREQ. TO 21465 kHz
		Mideast & N Africa • 250 kW • ALT. FREQ. TO 15065 kHz
15105	GERMANY	
	†DEUTSCHE WELLE, Via Sri Lanka	S • SE Asia • 250 kW
	ROMANIA	
	R ROMANIA INTL, Bucharest	W Europe • 250 kW
	RUSSIA	
	†TATARSTAN WAVE, Samara	W • E Asia • TATAR, RUSSIAN • 160 kW
	UNITED KINGDOM	
	†BBC, Skelton, Cumbria	S M-F • W Africa • 300 kW
	BBC, Via Ascension	W Africa & C Africa • 250 kW
	†BBC, Via Zyyi, Cyprus	W • E Africa • 250 kW
	USA	
	†VOA, Via Philippines	S Th-Sa • SE Asia • 250 kW
	VOA, Via Udon Thani, Thailand	S • S Asia • 250 kW
	WORLD HARVEST R, Cypress Creek, SC	W • C America • 250 kW
15110	CHINA	
	CHINA R INTL, Kashi	S Asia • 100 kW
	†CHINA R INTL, Urümqi	S • E Asia • 100 kW
		Mideast • 500 kW
	FRANCE	
	†R FRANCE INTL, Via Taiwan	SE Asia • 250 kW
		SE Asia • 250 kW • ALT. FREQ. TO 15350 kHz
	GERMANY	
	DEUTSCHE WELLE, Via Sri Lanka	W • Australasia • 250 kW
	KUWAIT	
	RADIO KUWAIT, Kabd	S Asia & SE Asia • 500 kW
		S Asia • 500 kW
	ROMANIA	
	†R ROMANIA INTL, Galbeni	S • S Asia • 250 kW
	RUSSIA	
	†TATARSTAN WAVE, Samara	S • E Asia • TATAR, RUSSIAN • 250 kW
	SPAIN	
(con'd)	R EXTERIOR ESPANA, Noblejas	N America & C America • 350 kW

World Time	0 1 2 3 4 5 6 7 8 9 10 11 12 13 14 15 16 17 18 19 20 21 22 23 24

ENGLISH ▬   ARABIC ⠶⠶   CHINESE ☐☐☐   FRENCH ▬   GERMAN ▬   RUSSIAN ═   SPANISH ═   OTHER ─

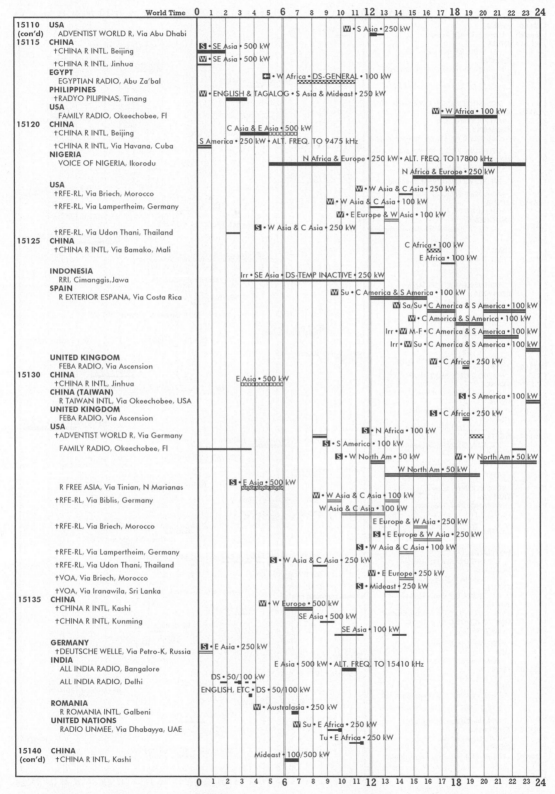

World Time		
15110 (con'd)	**USA**	
	ADVENTIST WORLD R, Via Abu Dhabi	W • S Asia • 250 kW
15115	**CHINA**	
	†CHINA R INTL, Beijing	S • SE Asia • 500 kW
	†CHINA R INTL, Jinhua	W • SE Asia • 500 kW
	EGYPT	
	EGYPTIAN RADIO, Abu Za'bal	⬅ • W Africa • DS-GENERAL • 100 kW
	PHILIPPINES	
	†RADYO PILIPINAS, Tinang	W • ENGLISH & TAGALOG • S Asia & Mideast • 250 kW
	USA	
	FAMILY RADIO, Okeechobee, Fl	W • W Africa • 100 kW
15120	**CHINA**	
	†CHINA R INTL, Beijing	C Asia & E Asia • 500 kW
	†CHINA R INTL, Via Havana, Cuba	S America • 250 kW • ALT. FREQ. TO 9475 kHz
	NIGERIA	
	VOICE OF NIGERIA, Ikorodu	N Africa & Europe • 250 kW • ALT. FREQ. TO 17800 kHz
		N Africa & Europe • 250 kW
	USA	
	†RFE-RL, Via Briech, Morocco	W • W Asia & C Asia • 250 kW
	†RFE-RL, Via Lampertheim, Germany	W • W Asia & C Asia • 100 kW
		W • E Europe & W Asia • 100 kW
	†RFE-RL, Via Udon Thani, Thailand	S • W Asia & C Asia • 250 kW
15125	**CHINA**	
	†CHINA R INTL, Via Bamako, Mali	C Africa • 100 kW
		E Africa • 100 kW
	INDONESIA	
	RRI, Cimanggis, Jawa	Irr • SE Asia • DS-TEMP INACTIVE • 250 kW
	SPAIN	
	R EXTERIOR ESPANA, Via Costa Rica	W Su • C America & S America • 100 kW
		W Sa/Su • C America & S America • 100 kW
		W • C America & S America • 100 kW
		Irr • W M-F • C America & S America • 100 kW
		Irr • W Su • C America & S America • 100 kW
	UNITED KINGDOM	
	FEBA RADIO, Via Ascension	W • C Africa • 250 kW
15130	**CHINA**	
	†CHINA R INTL, Jinhua	E Asia • 500 kW
	CHINA (TAIWAN)	
	R TAIWAN INTL, Via Okeechobee, USA	S • S America • 100 kW
	UNITED KINGDOM	
	FEBA RADIO, Via Ascension	S • C Africa • 250 kW
	USA	
	†ADVENTIST WORLD R, Via Germany	S • N Africa • 100 kW
	FAMILY RADIO, Okeechobee, Fl	S • S America • 100 kW
		S • W North Am • 50 kW	W • W North Am • 50 kW
		W North Am • 50 kW
	R FREE ASIA, Via Tinian, N Marianas	S • E Asia • 500 kW
	†RFE-RL, Via Biblis, Germany	W • W Asia & C Asia • 100 kW
		W Asia & C Asia • 100 kW
	†RFE-RL, Via Briech, Morocco	E Europe & W Asia • 250 kW
		S • E Europe & W Asia • 250 kW
	†RFE-RL, Via Lampertheim, Germany	S • W Asia & C Asia • 100 kW
	†RFE-RL, Via Udon Thani, Thailand	S • W Asia & C Asia • 250 kW
	†VOA, Via Briech, Morocco	W • E Europe • 250 kW
	†VOA, Via Iranawila, Sri Lanka	S • Mideast • 250 kW
15135	**CHINA**	
	†CHINA R INTL, Kashi	W • W Europe • 500 kW
	†CHINA R INTL, Kunming	SE Asia • 500 kW
		SE Asia • 100 kW
	GERMANY	
	†DEUTSCHE WELLE, Via Petro-K, Russia	S • E Asia • 250 kW
	INDIA	
	ALL INDIA RADIO, Bangalore	E Asia • 500 kW • ALT. FREQ. TO 15410 kHz
	ALL INDIA RADIO, Delhi	DS • 50/100 kW
		ENGLISH, ETC • DS • 50/100 kW
	ROMANIA	
	R ROMANIA INTL, Galbeni	W • Australasia • 250 kW
	UNITED NATIONS	
	RADIO UNMEE, Via Dhabayya, UAE	W Su • E Africa • 250 kW
		Tu • E Africa • 250 kW
15140 (con'd)	**CHINA**	
	†CHINA R INTL, Kashi	Mideast • 100/500 kW

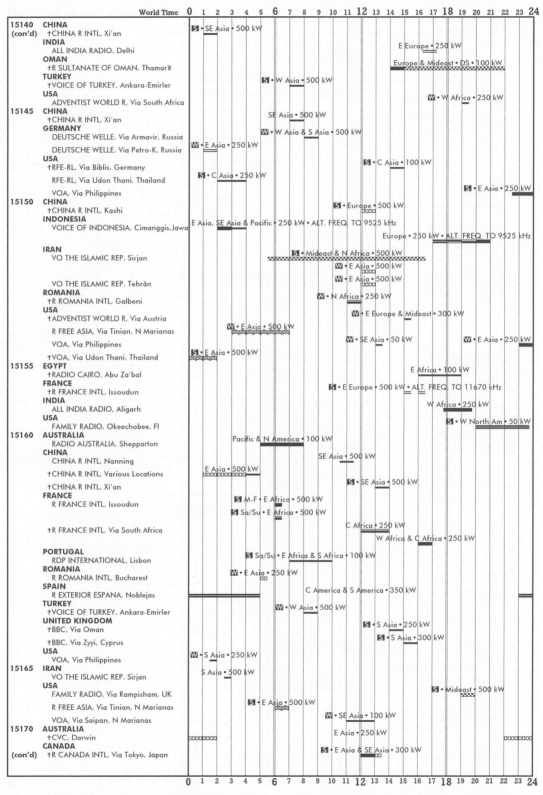

15140	
(con'd)	**CHINA**
	†CHINA R INTL, Xi'an
	INDIA
	ALL INDIA RADIO, Delhi
	OMAN
	†R SULTANATE OF OMAN, Thamarīt
	TURKEY
	†VOICE OF TURKEY, Ankara-Emirler
	USA
	ADVENTIST WORLD R, Via South Africa
15145	**CHINA**
	†CHINA R INTL, Xi'an
	GERMANY
	DEUTSCHE WELLE, Via Armavir, Russia
	DEUTSCHE WELLE, Via Petro-K, Russia
	USA
	†RFE-RL, Via Biblis, Germany
	RFE-RL, Via Udon Thani, Thailand
	VOA, Via Philippines
15150	**CHINA**
	†CHINA R INTL, Kashi
	INDONESIA
	VOICE OF INDONESIA, Cimanggis,Jawa
	IRAN
	VO THE ISLAMIC REP, Sirjan
	VO THE ISLAMIC REP, Tehrān
	ROMANIA
	†R ROMANIA INTL, Galbeni
	USA
	†ADVENTIST WORLD R, Via Austria
	R FREE ASIA, Via Tinian, N Marianas
	VOA, Via Philippines
	†VOA, Via Udon Thani, Thailand
15155	**EGYPT**
	†RADIO CAIRO, Abu Za'bal
	FRANCE
	†R FRANCE INTL, Issoudun
	INDIA
	ALL INDIA RADIO, Aligarh
	USA
	FAMILY RADIO, Okeechobee, Fl
15160	**AUSTRALIA**
	RADIO AUSTRALIA, Shepparton
	CHINA
	CHINA R INTL, Nanning
	†CHINA R INTL, Various Locations
	†CHINA R INTL, Xi'an
	FRANCE
	R FRANCE INTL, Issoudun
	†R FRANCE INTL, Via South Africa
	PORTUGAL
	RDP INTERNATIONAL, Lisbon
	ROMANIA
	R ROMANIA INTL, Bucharest
	SPAIN
	R EXTERIOR ESPANA, Noblejas
	TURKEY
	†VOICE OF TURKEY, Ankara-Emirler
	UNITED KINGDOM
	†BBC, Via Oman
	†BBC, Via Zyyi, Cyprus
	USA
	VOA, Via Philippines
15165	**IRAN**
	VO THE ISLAMIC REP, Sirjan
	USA
	FAMILY RADIO, Via Rampisham, UK
	R FREE ASIA, Via Tinian, N Marianas
	VOA, Via Saipan, N Marianas
15170	**AUSTRALIA**
	†CVC, Darwin
	CANADA
(con'd)	†R CANADA INTL, Via Tokyo, Japan

Time bar annotations:
- †CHINA R INTL, Xi'an: S • SE Asia • 500 kW
- ALL INDIA RADIO, Delhi: E Europe • 250 kW
- †R SULTANATE OF OMAN, Thamarīt: Europe & Mideast • DS • 100 kW
- †VOICE OF TURKEY, Ankara-Emirler: S • W Asia • 500 kW
- ADVENTIST WORLD R, Via South Africa: W • W Africa • 250 kW
- †CHINA R INTL, Xi'an: SE Asia • 500 kW
- DEUTSCHE WELLE, Via Armavir, Russia: W • W Asia & S Asia • 500 kW
- DEUTSCHE WELLE, Via Petro-K, Russia: W • E Asia • 250 kW
- †RFE-RL, Via Biblis, Germany: S • C Asia • 100 kW
- RFE-RL, Via Udon Thani, Thailand: S • C Asia • 250 kW
- VOA, Via Philippines: S • E Asia • 250 kW
- †CHINA R INTL, Kashi: S • Europe • 500 kW
- VOICE OF INDONESIA: E Asia, SE Asia & Pacific • 250 kW • ALT. FREQ. TO 9525 kHz; Europe • 250 kW • ALT. FREQ. TO 9525 kHz
- VO THE ISLAMIC REP, Sirjan: S • Mideast & N Africa • 500 kW; W • E Asia • 500 kW
- VO THE ISLAMIC REP, Tehrān: W • E Asia • 500 kW
- †R ROMANIA INTL, Galbeni: W • N Africa • 250 kW
- †ADVENTIST WORLD R, Via Austria: W • E Europe & Mideast • 300 kW
- R FREE ASIA, Via Tinian, N Marianas: W • E Asia • 500 kW
- VOA, Via Philippines: W • SE Asia • 50 kW; W • E Asia • 250 kW
- †VOA, Via Udon Thani, Thailand: S • E Asia • 500 kW
- †RADIO CAIRO, Abu Za'bal: E Africa • 100 kW
- †R FRANCE INTL, Issoudun: S • E Europe • 500 kW • ALT. FREQ. TO 11670 kHz
- ALL INDIA RADIO, Aligarh: W Africa • 250 kW
- FAMILY RADIO, Okeechobee, Fl: S • W North Am • 50 kW
- RADIO AUSTRALIA, Shepparton: Pacific & N America • 100 kW
- CHINA R INTL, Nanning: SE Asia • 500 kW
- †CHINA R INTL, Various Locations: E Asia • 500 kW
- †CHINA R INTL, Xi'an: S • SE Asia • 500 kW
- R FRANCE INTL, Issoudun: S M-F • E Africa • 500 kW; S Sa/Su • E Africa • 500 kW
- †R FRANCE INTL, Via South Africa: C Africa • 250 kW; W Africa & C Africa • 250 kW
- RDP INTERNATIONAL, Lisbon: S Sa/Su • E Africa & S Africa • 100 kW
- R ROMANIA INTL, Bucharest: W • E Asia • 250 kW
- R EXTERIOR ESPANA, Noblejas: C America & S America • 350 kW
- †VOICE OF TURKEY, Ankara-Emirler: W • W Asia • 500 kW
- †BBC, Via Oman: S • S Asia • 250 kW
- †BBC, Via Zyyi, Cyprus: S • S Asia • 300 kW
- VOA, Via Philippines: W • S Asia • 250 kW
- VO THE ISLAMIC REP, Sirjan: S Asia • 500 kW; S • Mideast • 500 kW
- R FREE ASIA, Via Tinian, N Marianas: S • E Asia • 500 kW
- VOA, Via Saipan, N Marianas: W • SE Asia • 100 kW
- †CVC, Darwin: E Asia • 250 kW
- †R CANADA INTL, Via Tokyo, Japan: S • E Asia & SE Asia • 300 kW

ENGLISH ▬   ARABIC ⁓⁓⁓   CHINESE ▫▫▫   FRENCH ▭▭   GERMAN ▭   RUSSIAN ═   SPANISH ═   OTHER ▬

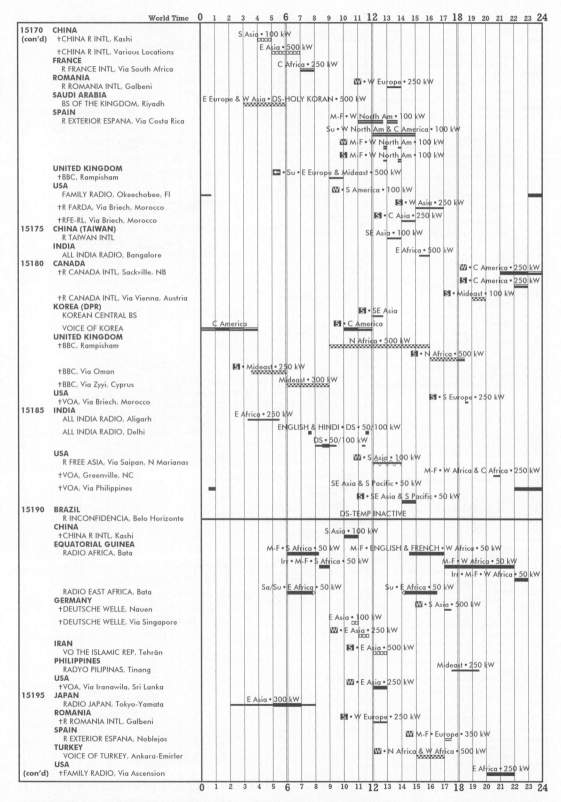

World Time 0 1 2 3 4 5 6 7 8 9 10 11 12 13 14 15 16 17 18 19 20 21 22 23 24

15170 (con'd)	CHINA	
	†CHINA R INTL, Kashi	S Asia • 100 kW
	†CHINA R INTL, Various Locations	E Asia • 500 kW
	FRANCE	
	R FRANCE INTL, Via South Africa	C Africa • 250 kW
	ROMANIA	
	R ROMANIA INTL, Galbeni	W • W Europe • 250 kW
	SAUDI ARABIA	
	BS OF THE KINGDOM, Riyadh	E Europe & W Asia • DS-HOLY KORAN • 500 kW
	SPAIN	
	R EXTERIOR ESPANA, Via Costa Rica	M-F • W North Am • 100 kW
		Su • W North Am & C America • 100 kW
		W M-F • W North Am • 100 kW
		S M-F • W North Am • 100 kW
	UNITED KINGDOM	
	†BBC, Rampisham	⇔ • Su • E Europe & Mideast • 500 kW
	USA	
	FAMILY RADIO, Okeechobee, Fl	W • S America • 100 kW
	†R FARDA, Via Briech, Morocco	S • W Asia • 250 kW
	†RFE-RL, Via Briech, Morocco	S • C Asia • 250 kW
15175	CHINA (TAIWAN)	
	R TAIWAN INTL	SE Asia • 100 kW
	INDIA	
	ALL INDIA RADIO, Bangalore	E Africa • 500 kW
15180	CANADA	
	†R CANADA INTL, Sackville, NB	W • C America • 250 kW
		S • C America • 250 kW
	†R CANADA INTL, Via Vienna, Austria	S • Mideast • 100 kW
	KOREA (DPR)	
	KOREAN CENTRAL BS	S • SE Asia
	VOICE OF KOREA	C America
		S • C America
	UNITED KINGDOM	
	†BBC, Rampisham	N Africa • 500 kW
		S • N Africa • 500 kW
	†BBC, Via Oman	S • Mideast • 250 kW
	†BBC, Via Zyyi, Cyprus	Mideast • 300 kW
	USA	
	†VOA, Via Briech, Morocco	S • S Europe • 250 kW
15185	INDIA	
	ALL INDIA RADIO, Aligarh	E Africa • 250 kW
	ALL INDIA RADIO, Delhi	ENGLISH & HINDI • DS • 50/100 kW
		DS • 50/100 kW
	USA	
	R FREE ASIA, Via Saipan, N Marianas	W • S Asia • 100 kW
	†VOA, Greenville, NC	M-F • W Africa & C Africa • 250 kW
	†VOA, Via Philippines	SE Asia & S Pacific • 50 kW
		S • SE Asia & S Pacific • 50 kW
15190	BRAZIL	
	R INCONFIDENCIA, Belo Horizonte	DS-TEMP INACTIVE
	CHINA	
	†CHINA R INTL, Kashi	S Asia • 100 kW
	EQUATORIAL GUINEA	
	RADIO AFRICA, Bata	M-F • S Africa • 50 kW M-F • ENGLISH & FRENCH • W Africa • 50 kW
		Irr • M-F • S Africa • 50 kW M-F • W Africa • 50 kW
		Irr • M-F • W Africa • 50 kW
	RADIO EAST AFRICA, Bata	Sa/Su • E Africa • 50 kW Su • E Africa • 50 kW
	GERMANY	
	†DEUTSCHE WELLE, Nauen	W • S Asia • 500 kW
	†DEUTSCHE WELLE, Via Singapore	E Asia • 100 kW
		W • E Asia • 250 kW
	IRAN	
	VO THE ISLAMIC REP, Tehrān	S • E Asia • 500 kW
	PHILIPPINES	
	RADYO PILIPINAS, Tinang	Mideast • 250 kW
	USA	
	†VOA, Via Iranawila, Sri Lanka	W • E Asia • 250 kW
15195	JAPAN	
	RADIO JAPAN, Tokyo-Yamata	E Asia • 300 kW
	ROMANIA	
	†R ROMANIA INTL, Galbeni	S • W Europe • 250 kW
	SPAIN	
	R EXTERIOR ESPANA, Noblejas	M-F • Europe • 350 kW
	TURKEY	
	VOICE OF TURKEY, Ankara-Emirler	W • N Africa & W Africa • 500 kW
	USA	
(con'd)	†FAMILY RADIO, Via Ascension	E Africa • 250 kW

0 1 2 3 4 5 6 7 8 9 10 11 12 13 14 15 16 17 18 19 20 21 22 23 24

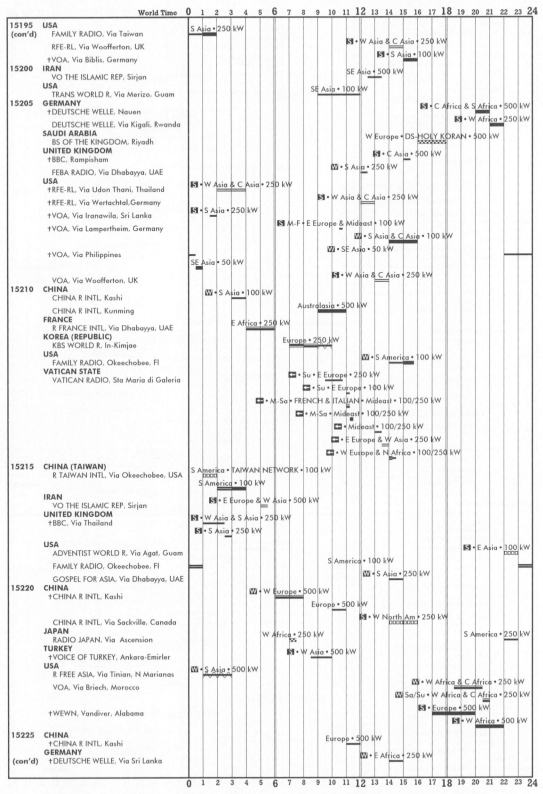

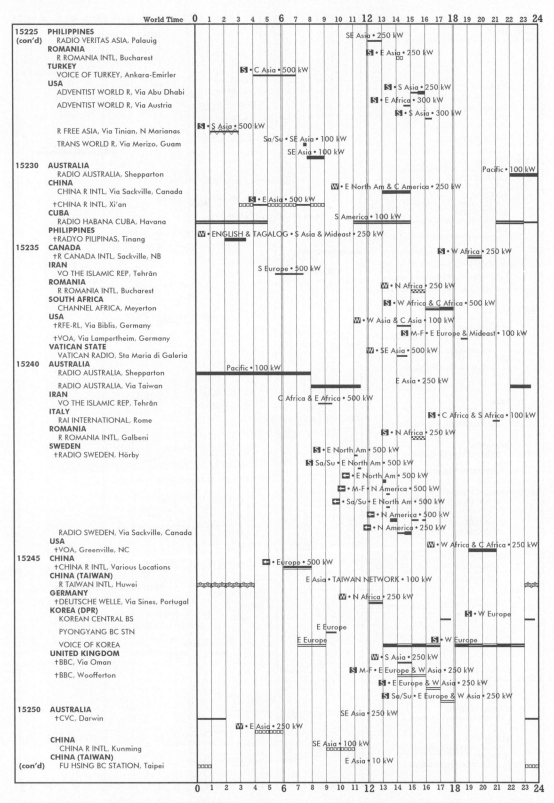

World Time

15225 (con'd)	**PHILIPPINES**
	RADIO VERITAS ASIA, Palauig	SE Asia • 250 kW
	ROMANIA
	R ROMANIA INTL, Bucharest	S • E Asia • 250 kW
	TURKEY
	VOICE OF TURKEY, Ankara-Emirler	S • C Asia • 500 kW
	USA
	ADVENTIST WORLD R, Via Abu Dhabi	S • S Asia • 250 kW
	ADVENTIST WORLD R, Via Austria	S • E Africa • 300 kW
		S • S Asia • 300 kW
	R FREE ASIA, Via Tinian, N Marianas	S • S Asia • 500 kW
	TRANS WORLD R, Via Merizo, Guam	Sa/Su • SE Asia • 100 kW
		SE Asia • 100 kW
15230	**AUSTRALIA**
	RADIO AUSTRALIA, Shepparton	Pacific • 100 kW
	CHINA
	CHINA R INTL, Via Sackville, Canada	W • E North Am & C America • 250 kW
	†CHINA R INTL, Xi'an	S • E Asia • 500 kW
	CUBA
	RADIO HABANA CUBA, Havana	S America • 100 kW
	PHILIPPINES
	†RADYO PILIPINAS, Tinang	W • ENGLISH & TAGALOG • S Asia & Mideast • 250 kW
15235	**CANADA**
	†R CANADA INTL, Sackville, NB	S • W Africa • 250 kW
	IRAN
	VO THE ISLAMIC REP, Tehrān	S Europe • 500 kW
	ROMANIA
	R ROMANIA INTL, Bucharest	W • N Africa • 250 kW
	SOUTH AFRICA
	CHANNEL AFRICA, Meyerton	S • W Africa & C Africa • 500 kW
	USA
	†RFE-RL, Via Biblis, Germany	W • W Asia & C Asia • 100 kW
	†VOA, Via Lampertheim, Germany	S M-F • E Europe & Mideast • 100 kW
	VATICAN STATE
	VATICAN RADIO, Sta Maria di Galeria	W • SE Asia • 500 kW
15240	**AUSTRALIA**
	RADIO AUSTRALIA, Shepparton	Pacific • 100 kW
	RADIO AUSTRALIA, Via Taiwan	E Asia • 250 kW
	IRAN
	VO THE ISLAMIC REP, Tehrān	C Africa & E Africa • 500 kW
	ITALY
	RAI INTERNATIONAL, Rome	S • C Africa & S Africa • 100 kW
	ROMANIA
	R ROMANIA INTL, Galbeni	S • N Africa • 250 kW
	SWEDEN
	†RADIO SWEDEN, Hörby	S • E North Am • 500 kW
		S Sa/Su • E North Am • 500 kW
		⟵ • E North Am • 500 kW
		⟵ • M-F • N America • 500 kW
		⟵ • Sa/Su • E North Am • 500 kW
		⟵ • N America • 500 kW
		⟵ • N America • 250 kW
	RADIO SWEDEN, Via Sackville, Canada
	USA
	†VOA, Greenville, NC	W • W Africa & C Africa • 250 kW
15245	**CHINA**
	†CHINA R INTL, Various Locations	⟵ • Europe • 500 kW
	CHINA (TAIWAN)
	R TAIWAN INTL, Huwei	E Asia • TAIWAN NETWORK • 100 kW
	GERMANY
	†DEUTSCHE WELLE, Via Sines, Portugal	W • N Africa • 250 kW
	KOREA (DPR)
	KOREAN CENTRAL BS	S • W Europe
	PYONGYANG BC STN	E Europe
	VOICE OF KOREA	E Europe / S • W Europe
	UNITED KINGDOM
	†BBC, Via Oman	W • S Asia • 250 kW
	†BBC, Woofferton	S M-F • E Europe & W Asia • 250 kW
		S • E Europe & W Asia • 250 kW
		S Sa/Su • E Europe & W Asia • 250 kW
15250	**AUSTRALIA**
	†CVC, Darwin	SE Asia • 250 kW
		W • E Asia • 250 kW
	CHINA
	CHINA R INTL, Kunming	SE Asia • 100 kW
	CHINA (TAIWAN)
(con'd)	FU HSING BC STATION, Taipei	E Asia • 10 kW

SEASONAL S OR W   1-HR TIMESHIFT MIDYEAR ⟵ OR ⟶   JAMMING / OR /\   EARLIEST HEARD ◁   LATEST HEARD ▷   NEW FOR 2007 †

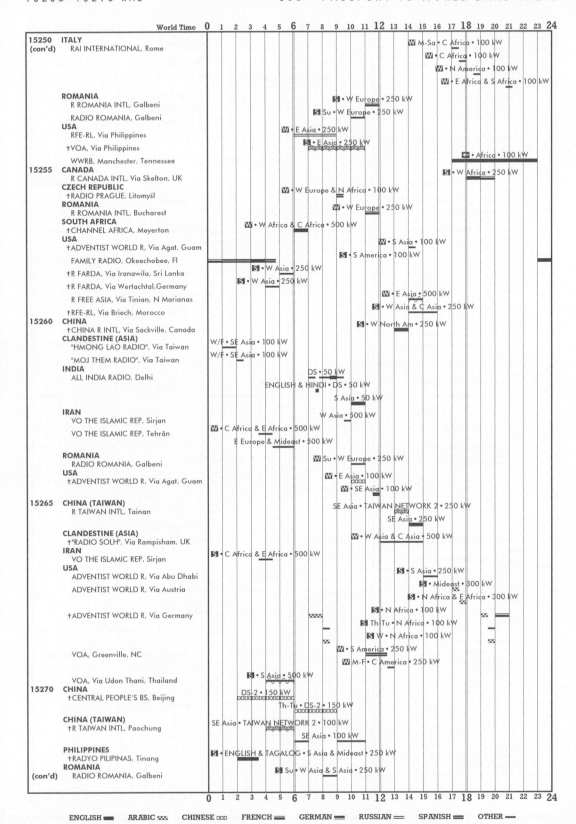

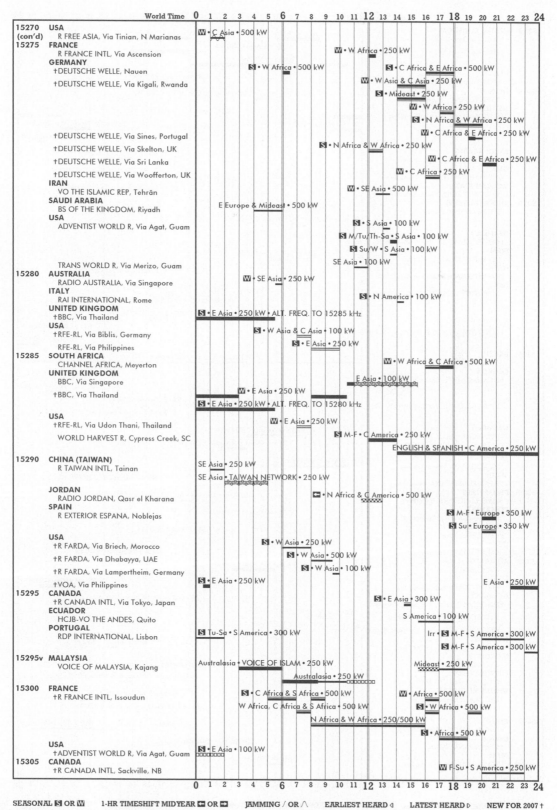

World Time   0 1 2 3 4 5 6 7 8 9 10 11 12 13 14 15 16 17 18 19 20 21 22 23 24

Freq	Country / Station	Schedule
15270 (con'd)	**USA** — R FREE ASIA, Via Tinian, N Marianas	W • C Asia • 500 kW
15275	**FRANCE** — R FRANCE INTL, Via Ascension	W • W Africa • 250 kW
	GERMANY — †DEUTSCHE WELLE, Nauen	S • W Africa • 500 kW S • C Africa & E Africa • 500 kW
	†DEUTSCHE WELLE, Via Kigali, Rwanda	W • W Asia & C Asia • 250 kW S • Mideast • 250 kW W • W Africa • 250 kW S • N Africa & W Africa • 250 kW W • C Africa & E Africa • 250 kW
	†DEUTSCHE WELLE, Via Sines, Portugal	S • N Africa & W Africa • 250 kW
	†DEUTSCHE WELLE, Via Skelton, UK	W • C Africa & E Africa • 250 kW
	†DEUTSCHE WELLE, Via Sri Lanka	W • C Africa • 250 kW
	†DEUTSCHE WELLE, Via Woofferton, UK	W • SE Asia • 500 kW
	IRAN — VO THE ISLAMIC REP, Tehrān	
	SAUDI ARABIA — BS OF THE KINGDOM, Riyadh	E Europe & Mideast • 500 kW
	USA — ADVENTIST WORLD R, Via Agat, Guam	S • S Asia • 100 kW S M/Tu/Th-Sa • S Asia • 100 kW S Su/W • S Asia • 100 kW SE Asia • 100 kW
15280	**AUSTRALIA** — RADIO AUSTRALIA, Via Singapore	W • SE Asia • 250 kW
	ITALY — RAI INTERNATIONAL, Rome	S • N America • 100 kW
	UNITED KINGDOM — †BBC, Via Thailand	S • E Asia • 250 kW • ALT. FREQ. TO 15285 kHz
	USA — †RFE-RL, Via Biblis, Germany	S • W Asia & C Asia • 100 kW
	RFE-RL, Via Philippines	S • E Asia • 250 kW
15285	**SOUTH AFRICA** — CHANNEL AFRICA, Meyerton	W • W Africa & C Africa • 500 kW
	UNITED KINGDOM — BBC, Via Singapore	E Asia • 100 kW
	†BBC, Via Thailand	W • E Asia • 250 kW S • E Asia • 250 kW • ALT. FREQ. TO 15280 kHz
	USA — †RFE-RL, Via Udon Thani, Thailand	W • E Asia • 250 kW
	WORLD HARVEST R, Cypress Creek, SC	S M-F • C America • 250 kW ENGLISH & SPANISH • C America • 250 kW
15290	**CHINA (TAIWAN)** — R TAIWAN INTL, Tainan	SE Asia • 250 kW SE Asia • TAIWAN NETWORK • 250 kW
	JORDAN — RADIO JORDAN, Qasr el Kharana	⇔ • N Africa & C America • 500 kW
	SPAIN — R EXTERIOR ESPANA, Noblejas	S M-F • Europe • 350 kW S Su • Europe • 350 kW
	USA — †R FARDA, Via Briech, Morocco	S • W Asia • 250 kW
	†R FARDA, Via Dhabayya, UAE	S • W Asia • 500 kW
	†R FARDA, Via Lampertheim, Germany	S • W Asia • 100 kW
	†VOA, Via Philippines	S • E Asia • 250 kW E Asia • 250 kW
15295	**CANADA** — †R CANADA INTL, Via Tokyo, Japan	S • E Asia • 300 kW
	ECUADOR — HCJB-VO THE ANDES, Quito	S America • 100 kW
	PORTUGAL — RDP INTERNATIONAL, Lisbon	S Tu-Sa • S America • 300 kW Irr • S M-F • S America • 300 kW S M-F • S America • 300 kW
15295v	**MALAYSIA** — VOICE OF MALAYSIA, Kajang	Australasia • VOICE OF ISLAM • 250 kW Mideast • 250 kW Australasia • 250 kW
15300	**FRANCE** — †R FRANCE INTL, Issoudun	S • C Africa & S Africa • 500 kW W • Africa • 500 kW W Africa, C Africa & S Africa • 500 kW S • W Africa • 500 kW N Africa & W Africa • 250/500 kW S • Africa • 500 kW
	USA — †ADVENTIST WORLD R, Via Agat, Guam	S • E Asia • 100 kW
15305	**CANADA** — †R CANADA INTL, Sackville, NB	W F-Su • S America • 250 kW

0 1 2 3 4 5 6 7 8 9 10 11 12 13 14 15 16 17 18 19 20 21 22 23 24

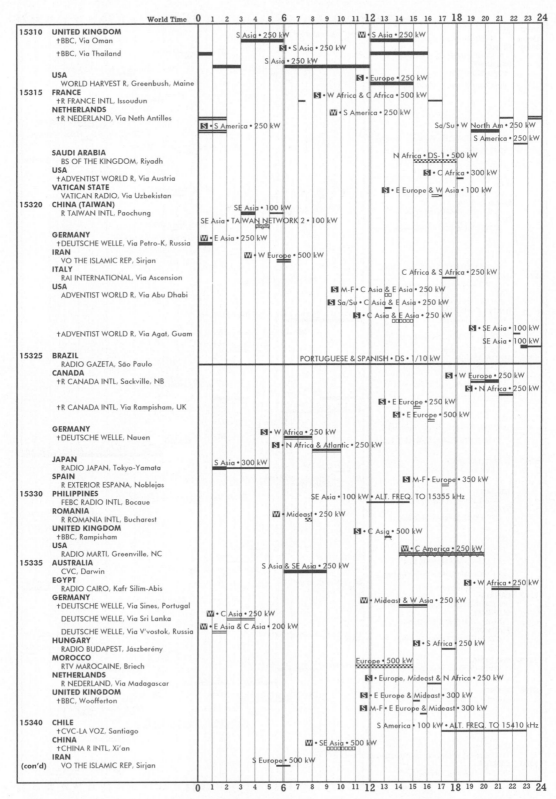

World Time 0 1 2 3 4 5 6 7 8 9 10 11 12 13 14 15 16 17 18 19 20 21 22 23 24

15310 UNITED KINGDOM
†BBC, Via Oman — S Asia • 250 kW — W • S Asia • 250 kW
†BBC, Via Thailand — S • S Asia • 250 kW — S Asia • 250 kW

USA
WORLD HARVEST R, Greenbush, Maine — S • Europe • 250 kW
15315 FRANCE
†R FRANCE INTL, Issoudun — S • W Africa & C Africa • 500 kW
NETHERLANDS
†R NEDERLAND, Via Neth Antilles — W • S America • 250 kW
S • S America • 250 kW — Sa/Su • W North Am • 250 kW
S America • 250 kW

SAUDI ARABIA
BS OF THE KINGDOM, Riyadh — N Africa • DS-1 • 500 kW
USA
†ADVENTIST WORLD R, Via Austria — S • C Africa • 300 kW
VATICAN STATE
VATICAN RADIO, Via Uzbekistan — S • E Europe & W Asia • 100 kW
15320 CHINA (TAIWAN)
R TAIWAN INTL, Paochung — SE Asia • 100 kW
SE Asia • TAIWAN NETWORK 2 • 100 kW

GERMANY
†DEUTSCHE WELLE, Via Petro-K, Russia — W • E Asia • 250 kW
IRAN
VO THE ISLAMIC REP, Sirjan — W • W Europe • 500 kW
ITALY
RAI INTERNATIONAL, Via Ascension — C Africa & S Africa • 250 kW
USA
ADVENTIST WORLD R, Via Abu Dhabi — S • M-F • C Asia & E Asia • 250 kW
S • Sa/Su • C Asia & E Asia • 250 kW
S • C Asia & E Asia • 250 kW
S • SE Asia • 100 kW
†ADVENTIST WORLD R, Via Agat, Guam — SE Asia • 100 kW

15325 BRAZIL
RADIO GAZETA, São Paulo — PORTUGUESE & SPANISH • DS • 1/10 kW
CANADA
†R CANADA INTL, Sackville, NB — S • W Europe • 250 kW
S • N Africa • 250 kW
†R CANADA INTL, Via Rampisham, UK — S • E Europe • 250 kW
S • E Europe • 500 kW

GERMANY
†DEUTSCHE WELLE, Nauen — S • W Africa • 250 kW
S • N Africa & Atlantic • 250 kW

JAPAN
RADIO JAPAN, Tokyo-Yamata — S Asia • 300 kW
SPAIN
R EXTERIOR ESPANA, Noblejas — S M-F • Europe • 350 kW
15330 PHILIPPINES
FEBC RADIO INTL, Bocaue — SE Asia • 100 kW • ALT. FREQ. TO 15355 kHz
ROMANIA
R ROMANIA INTL, Bucharest — W • Mideast • 250 kW
UNITED KINGDOM
†BBC, Rampisham — S • C Asia • 500 kW
USA
RADIO MARTI, Greenville, NC — W • C America • 250 kW
15335 AUSTRALIA
CVC, Darwin — S Asia & SE Asia • 250 kW
EGYPT
RADIO CAIRO, Kafr Silim-Abis — S • W Africa • 250 kW
GERMANY
†DEUTSCHE WELLE, Via Sines, Portugal — W • Mideast & W Asia • 250 kW
DEUTSCHE WELLE, Via Sri Lanka — W • C Asia • 250 kW
DEUTSCHE WELLE, Via V'vostok, Russia — W • E Asia & C Asia • 200 kW
HUNGARY
RADIO BUDAPEST, Jászberény — S • S Africa • 250 kW
MOROCCO
RTV MAROCAINE, Briech — Europe • 500 kW
NETHERLANDS
R NEDERLAND, Via Madagascar — S • Europe, Mideast & N Africa • 250 kW
UNITED KINGDOM
†BBC, Woofferton — S • E Europe & Mideast • 300 kW
S M-F • E Europe & Mideast • 300 kW

15340 CHILE
†CVC-LA VOZ, Santiago — S America • 100 kW • ALT. FREQ. TO 15410 kHz
CHINA
†CHINA R INTL, Xi'an — W • SE Asia • 500 kW
IRAN
(con'd) VO THE ISLAMIC REP, Sirjan — S Europe • 500 kW

0 1 2 3 4 5 6 7 8 9 10 11 12 13 14 15 16 17 18 19 20 21 22 23 24

ENGLISH ▬ ARABIC ⋙ CHINESE ▫▫▫ FRENCH ═ GERMAN ▬ RUSSIAN ═ SPANISH ═ OTHER ▬

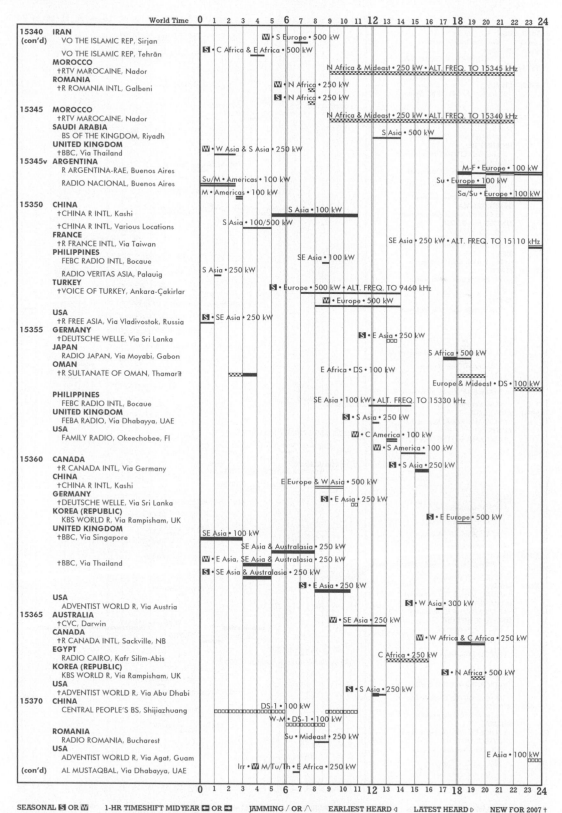

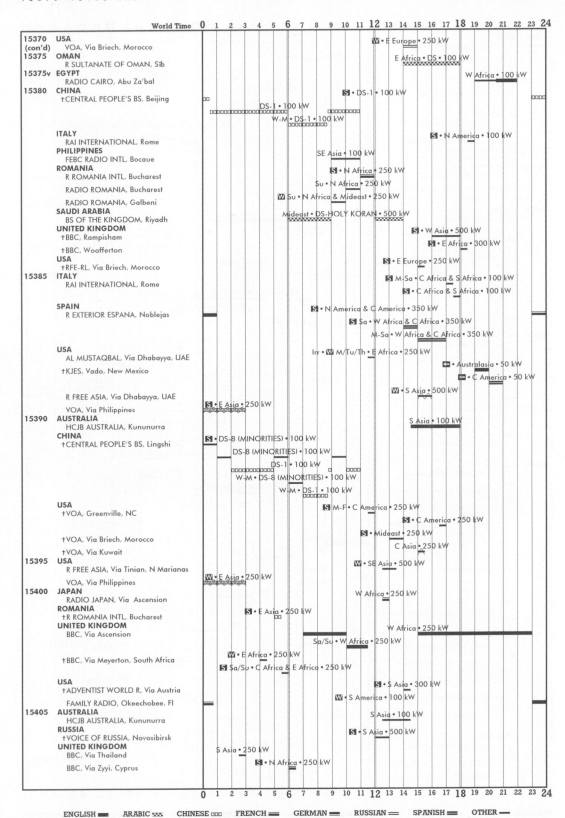

| | World Time | 0 | 1 | 2 | 3 | 4 | 5 | 6 | 7 | 8 | 9 | 10 | 11 | 12 | 13 | 14 | 15 | 16 | 17 | 18 | 19 | 20 | 21 | 22 | 23 | 24 |

15370 **USA**
(con'd)   VOA, Via Briech, Morocco — Ⓦ • E Europe • 250 kW
15375 **OMAN**
R SULTANATE OF OMAN, Sīb — E Africa • DS • 100 kW
15375v **EGYPT**
RADIO CAIRO, Abu Za'bal — W Africa • 100 kW
15380 **CHINA**
†CENTRAL PEOPLE'S BS, Beijing — Ⓢ • DS-1 • 100 kW / DS-1 • 100 kW / W-M • DS-1 • 100 kW

ITALY
RAI INTERNATIONAL, Rome — Ⓢ • N America • 100 kW
PHILIPPINES
FEBC RADIO INTL, Bocaue — SE Asia • 100 kW
ROMANIA
R ROMANIA INTL, Bucharest — Ⓢ • N Africa • 250 kW
RADIO ROMANIA, Bucharest — Su • N Africa • 250 kW
RADIO ROMANIA, Galbeni — Ⓦ Su • N Africa & Mideast • 250 kW
SAUDI ARABIA
BS OF THE KINGDOM, Riyadh — Mideast • DS-HOLY KORAN • 500 kW
UNITED KINGDOM
†BBC, Rampisham — Ⓢ • W Asia • 500 kW
†BBC, Woofferton — Ⓢ • E Africa • 300 kW
USA
†RFE-RL, Via Briech, Morocco — Ⓢ • E Europe • 250 kW
15385 **ITALY**
RAI INTERNATIONAL, Rome — Ⓢ • M-Sa • C Africa & S Africa • 100 kW / Ⓢ • C Africa & S Africa • 100 kW

SPAIN
R EXTERIOR ESPANA, Noblejas — Ⓢ • N America & C America • 350 kW / Ⓢ Sa • W Africa & C Africa • 350 kW / M-Sa • W Africa & C Africa • 350 kW

USA
AL MUSTAQBAL, Via Dhabayya, UAE — Irr • Ⓦ M/Tu/Th • E Africa • 250 kW
†KJES, Vado, New Mexico — ◁ • Australasia • 50 kW / ◁ • C America • 50 kW

R FREE ASIA, Via Dhabayya, UAE — Ⓦ • S Asia • 500 kW
VOA, Via Philippines — Ⓢ • E Asia • 250 kW
15390 **AUSTRALIA**
HCJB AUSTRALIA, Kununurra — S Asia • 100 kW
CHINA
†CENTRAL PEOPLE'S BS, Lingshi — Ⓢ • DS-8 (MINORITIES) • 100 kW / DS-8 (MINORITIES) • 100 kW / DS-1 • 100 kW / W-M • DS-8 (MINORITIES) • 100 kW / W-M • DS-1 • 100 kW

USA
†VOA, Greenville, NC — Ⓢ M-F • C America • 250 kW / Ⓢ • C America • 250 kW
†VOA, Via Briech, Morocco — Ⓢ • Mideast • 250 kW
†VOA, Via Kuwait — C Asia • 250 kW
15395 **USA**
R FREE ASIA, Via Tinian, N Marianas — Ⓦ • SE Asia • 500 kW
VOA, Via Philippines — Ⓦ • E Asia • 250 kW
15400 **JAPAN**
RADIO JAPAN, Via Ascension — W Africa • 250 kW
ROMANIA
†R ROMANIA INTL, Bucharest — Ⓢ • E Asia • 250 kW
UNITED KINGDOM
BBC, Via Ascension — W Africa • 250 kW / Sa/Su • W Africa • 250 kW
†BBC, Via Meyerton, South Africa — Ⓦ • E Africa • 250 kW / Ⓢ Sa/Su • C Africa & E Africa • 250 kW

USA
†ADVENTIST WORLD R, Via Austria — Ⓢ • S Asia • 300 kW
FAMILY RADIO, Okeechobee, Fl — Ⓦ • S America • 100 kW
15405 **AUSTRALIA**
HCJB AUSTRALIA, Kununurra — S Asia • 100 kW
RUSSIA
†VOICE OF RUSSIA, Novosibirsk — Ⓢ • S Asia • 500 kW
UNITED KINGDOM
BBC, Via Thailand — S Asia • 250 kW
BBC, Via Zyyi, Cyprus — Ⓢ • N Africa • 250 kW

| | | 0 | 1 | 2 | 3 | 4 | 5 | 6 | 7 | 8 | 9 | 10 | 11 | 12 | 13 | 14 | 15 | 16 | 17 | 18 | 19 | 20 | 21 | 22 | 23 | 24 |

ENGLISH ▬   ARABIC ⋙   CHINESE ⬚⬚⬚   FRENCH ▬▬   GERMAN ▬▬   RUSSIAN ═══   SPANISH ▬▬   OTHER ▬

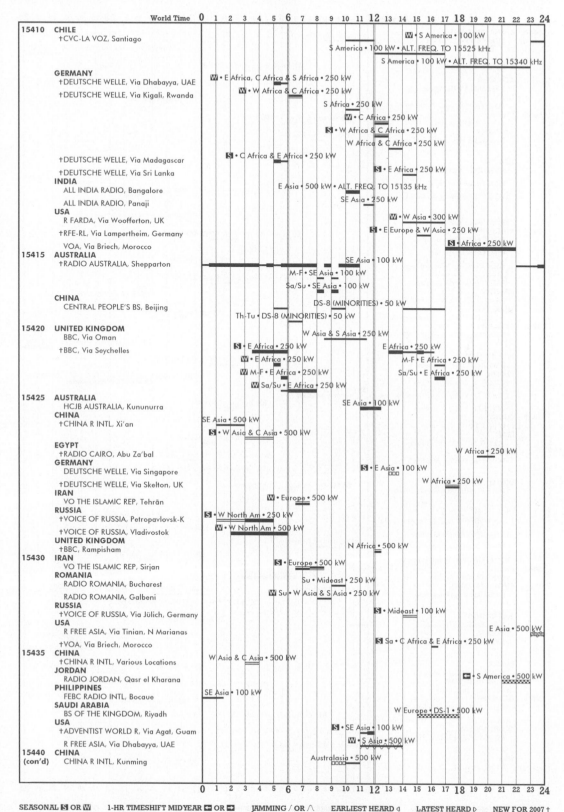

World Time 0 1 2 3 4 5 6 7 8 9 10 11 12 13 14 15 16 17 18 19 20 21 22 23 24

| 15410 | CHILE |
| | †CVC-LA VOZ, Santiago |

W • S America • 100 kW
S America • 100 kW • ALT. FREQ. TO 15525 kHz
S America • 100 kW • ALT. FREQ. TO 15340 kHz

GERMANY
†DEUTSCHE WELLE, Via Dhabayya, UAE — **W** • E Africa, C Africa & S Africa • 250 kW
†DEUTSCHE WELLE, Via Kigali, Rwanda — **W** • W Africa & C Africa • 250 kW
S Africa • 250 kW
W • C Africa • 250 kW
S • W Africa & C Africa • 250 kW
W Africa & C Africa • 250 kW
†DEUTSCHE WELLE, Via Madagascar — **S** • C Africa & E Africa • 250 kW
†DEUTSCHE WELLE, Via Sri Lanka — **S** • E Africa • 250 kW

INDIA
ALL INDIA RADIO, Bangalore — E Asia • 500 kW • ALT. FREQ. TO 15135 kHz
ALL INDIA RADIO, Panaji — SE Asia • 250 kW

USA
R FARDA, Via Woofferton, UK — **W** • W Asia • 300 kW
†RFE-RL, Via Lampertheim, Germany — **S** • E Europe & W Asia • 250 kW
VOA, Via Briech, Morocco — **S** • Africa • 250 kW

| 15415 | AUSTRALIA |
| | †RADIO AUSTRALIA, Shepparton |

SE Asia • 100 kW
M-F • SE Asia • 100 kW
Sa/Su • SE Asia • 100 kW

CHINA
CENTRAL PEOPLE'S BS, Beijing — DS-8 (MINORITIES) • 50 kW
Th-Tu • DS-8 (MINORITIES) • 50 kW

| 15420 | UNITED KINGDOM |
| | BBC, Via Oman |

W Asia & S Asia • 250 kW
†BBC, Via Seychelles — **S** • E Africa • 250 kW
E Africa • 250 kW
W • E Africa • 250 kW
M-F • E Africa • 250 kW
W M-F • E Africa • 250 kW
Sa/Su • E Africa • 250 kW
W Sa/Su • E Africa • 250 kW

| 15425 | AUSTRALIA |
| | HCJB AUSTRALIA, Kununurra |

SE Asia • 100 kW
CHINA
†CHINA R INTL, Xi'an — SE Asia • 500 kW
S • W Asia & C Asia • 500 kW

EGYPT
†RADIO CAIRO, Abu Za'bal — W Africa • 250 kW
GERMANY
DEUTSCHE WELLE, Via Singapore — **S** • E Asia • 100 kW
†DEUTSCHE WELLE, Via Skelton, UK — W Africa • 250 kW
IRAN
VO THE ISLAMIC REP, Tehrān — **W** • Europe • 500 kW
RUSSIA
†VOICE OF RUSSIA, Petropavlovsk-K — **S** • W North Am • 250 kW
†VOICE OF RUSSIA, Vladivostok — **W** • W North Am • 500 kW
UNITED KINGDOM
†BBC, Rampisham — N Africa • 500 kW

| 15430 | IRAN |
| | VO THE ISLAMIC REP, Sirjan |

S • Europe • 500 kW
ROMANIA
RADIO ROMANIA, Bucharest — Su • Mideast • 250 kW
RADIO ROMANIA, Galbeni — **W** Su • W Asia & S Asia • 250 kW
RUSSIA
†VOICE OF RUSSIA, Via Jülich, Germany — **S** • Mideast • 100 kW
USA
R FREE ASIA, Via Tinian, N Marianas — E Asia • 500 kW
†VOA, Via Briech, Morocco — **S** Sa • C Africa & E Africa • 250 kW

| 15435 | CHINA |
| | †CHINA R INTL, Various Locations |

W Asia & C Asia • 500 kW
JORDAN
RADIO JORDAN, Qasr el Kharana — **↔** • S America • 500 kW
PHILIPPINES
FEBC RADIO INTL, Bocaue — SE Asia • 100 kW
SAUDI ARABIA
BS OF THE KINGDOM, Riyadh — W Europe • DS-1 • 500 kW
USA
†ADVENTIST WORLD R, Via Agat, Guam — **S** • SE Asia • 100 kW
R FREE ASIA, Via Dhabayya, UAE — **W** • S Asia • 500 kW

| 15440 (con'd) | CHINA |
| | CHINA R INTL, Kunming |

Australasia • 500 kW

0 1 2 3 4 5 6 7 8 9 10 11 12 13 14 15 16 17 18 19 20 21 22 23 24

SEASONAL **S** OR **W**   1-HR TIMESHIFT MIDYEAR **↔** OR **➡**   JAMMING / OR /\   EARLIEST HEARD ◁   LATEST HEARD ▷   NEW FOR 2007 †

World Time 0 1 2 3 4 5 6 7 8 9 10 11 12 13 14 15 16 17 18 19 20 21 22 23 24

15440 (con'd)	**CHINA (TAIWAN)** R TAIWAN INTL, Via Okeechobee, USA	W North Am • 100 kW ... W • E North Am • 100 kW ... W North Am • TAIWAN NETWORK • 100 kW
	IRAN VO THE ISLAMIC REP, Ahvāz	W • W Asia & S Asia • 250 kW
	ROMANIA †R ROMANIA INTL, Bucharest	S • Australasia • 250 kW
	USA ADVENTIST WORLD R, Via Austria	W • S Asia • 300 kW
15445	**CHINA** †CHINA R INTL, Kashi	E Europe & W Asia • 500 kW
	GERMANY †DEUTSCHE WELLE, Via Sri Lanka	S • C Africa • 250 kW ... C Africa & E Africa • 250 kW
	USA ADVENTIST WORLD R, Via Taiwan	Sa • SE Asia • 100 kW
	VOA, Greenville, NC	S • W Africa & C Africa • 250 kW
	†VOA, Via Iranawila, Sri Lanka	W • C Africa & E Africa • 250 kW
	†VOA, Via Lampertheim, Germany	W • C Africa & E Africa • 500 kW ... W • W Asia & S Asia • 100 kW
15450	**PHILIPPINES** FEBC RADIO INTL, Bocaue	SE Asia • 100 kW • ALT. FREQ. TO 15455 kHz
	FEBC RADIO INTL, Iba	E Asia • 100 kW
	RADIO VERITAS ASIA, Palauig	SE Asia • 250 kW
	ROMANIA RADIO ROMANIA, Galbeni	S Su • N Africa & Mideast • 250 kW
	SWEDEN IBRA RADIO, Via Wertachtal, Germany	S • E Africa • 125 kW
	TURKEY †VOICE OF TURKEY, Ankara-Emirler	S • W Europe • 500 kW
15455	**CANADA** †R CANADA INTL, Sackville, NB	S • F-Su • S America • 250 kW ... S • C America & S America • 250 kW
	PHILIPPINES FEBC RADIO INTL, Bocaue	SE Asia • 100 kW • ALT. FREQ. TO 15450 kHz
	RUSSIA †VOICE OF RUSSIA, Armavir	S • Europe • 250 kW • ALT. FREQ. TO 11980 kHz
	†VOICE OF RUSSIA, Komsomol'sk 'Amure	S • W North Am • 250 kW
	†VOICE OF RUSSIA, Samara	S • Europe • 250 kW
15460	**CHINA** †CHINA R INTL, Kunming	S • Australasia • 500 kW
	IRAN VO THE ISLAMIC REP, Tehrān	W • S Asia • 500 kW
	RUSSIA VOICE OF RUSSIA, Moscow	W • SE Asia • 500 kW • ALT. FREQ. TO 17570 kHz ... W • S Asia & SE Asia • 500 kW • ALT. FREQ. TO 17570 kHz
	UNITED KINGDOM †BIBLE VOICE, Via Armavir, Russia	S M/W/F • Mideast • 100/250 kW ... S F • Mideast • 100/250 kW
	USA ADVENTIST WORLD R, Via Abu Dhabi	S • E Africa • 250 kW
	†RFE-RL, Via Briech, Morocco	S • W Asia & C Asia • 250 kW
	RFE-RL, Via Udon Thani, Thailand	S • C Asia • 250 kW
	†VOA, Via Udon Thani, Thailand	W • SE Asia & Australasia • 250 kW
15465	**CHINA** †CHINA R INTL, Kashi	S Asia • 100 kW
	CHINA (TAIWAN) R TAIWAN INTL, Paochung	E Asia • 100 kW ... SE Asia • 100 kW ... SE Asia • TAIWAN NETWORK 2 • 100 kW
	PHILIPPINES FEBC RADIO INTL, Bocaue	SE Asia • 100 kW
	ROMANIA †R ROMANIA INTL, Bucharest	S • W Europe • 250 kW ... S • E North Am • 250 kW
	RUSSIA †VOICE OF RUSSIA, Moscow	S • W Europe • 250 kW • ALT. FREQ. TO 12040 kHz
	UNITED KINGDOM †BBC, Skelton, Cumbria	W M-F • S Europe • 300 kW
15470	**GERMANY** †DEUTSCHE WELLE, Via Sri Lanka	S • S Asia • 250 kW
	†DEUTSCHE WELLE, Via Woofferton, UK	S • W Africa & C Africa • 250 kW
	SAUDI ARABIA BS OF THE KINGDOM, Riyadh	E Africa • 500 kW • ALT. FREQ. TO 17760 kHz ... E Africa, C Africa & S Africa • 500 kW • ALT. FREQ. TO 17760 kHz
(con'd)	**USA** R FREE ASIA, Via Tinian, N Marianas	W • SE Asia • 500 kW

0 1 2 3 4 5 6 7 8 9 10 11 12 13 14 15 16 17 18 19 20 21 22 23 24

ENGLISH ▬▬ ARABIC ▨▨ CHINESE □□□ FRENCH ═══ GERMAN ▬▬ RUSSIAN ══ SPANISH ▬▬ OTHER ──

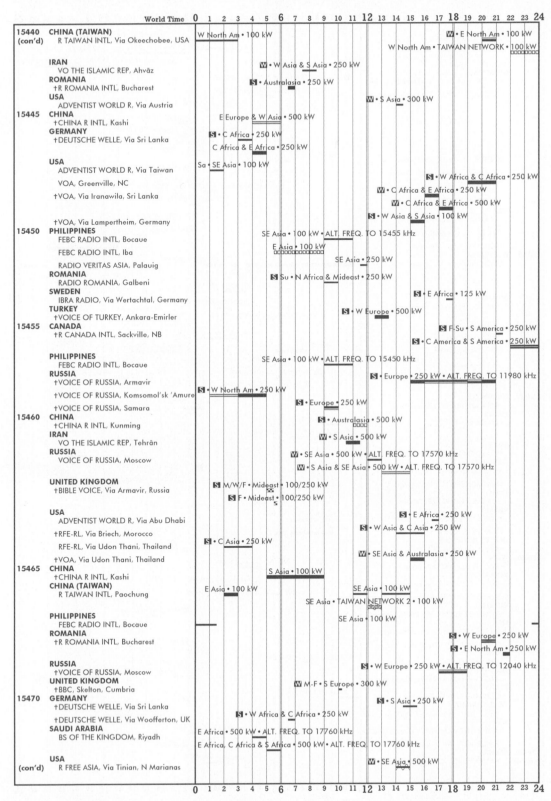

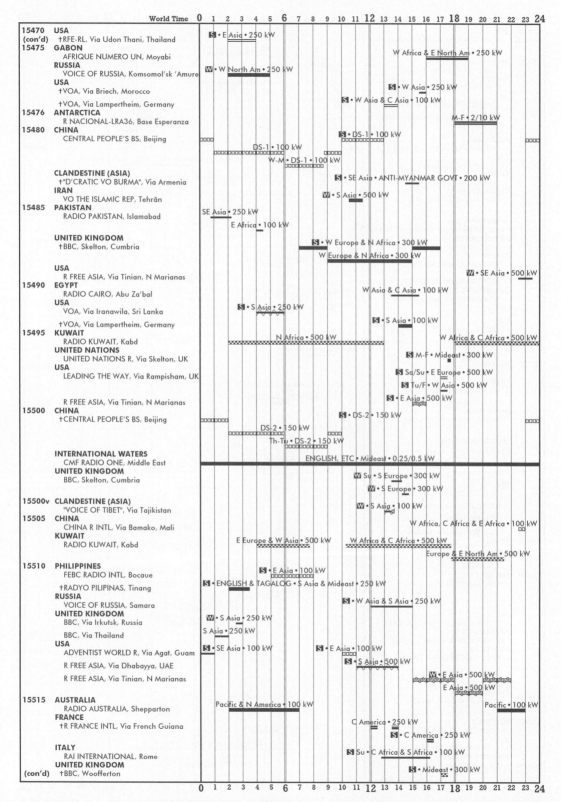

World Time

15470	USA	
(con'd)	†RFE-RL, Via Udon Thani, Thailand	**S** • E Asia • 250 kW
15475	GABON	
	AFRIQUE NUMERO UN, Moyabi	W Africa & E North Am • 250 kW
	RUSSIA	
	VOICE OF RUSSIA, Komsomol'sk 'Amure	**W** • W North Am • 250 kW
	USA	
	†VOA, Via Briech, Morocco	**S** • W Asia • 250 kW
	†VOA, Via Lampertheim, Germany	**S** • W Asia & C Asia • 100 kW
15476	ANTARCTICA	
	R NACIONAL-LRA36, Base Esperanza	M-F • 2/10 kW
15480	CHINA	
	CENTRAL PEOPLE'S BS, Beijing	**S** • DS-1 • 100 kW
		DS-1 • 100 kW
		W-M • DS-1 • 100 kW
	CLANDESTINE (ASIA)	
	†"D'CRATIC VO BURMA", Via Armenia	**S** • SE Asia • ANTI-MYANMAR GOVT • 200 kW
	IRAN	
	VO THE ISLAMIC REP, Tehrãn	**W** • S Asia • 500 kW
15485	PAKISTAN	
	RADIO PAKISTAN, Islamabad	SE Asia • 250 kW
		E Africa • 100 kW
	UNITED KINGDOM	
	†BBC, Skelton, Cumbria	**S** • W Europe & N Africa • 300 kW
		W Europe & N Africa • 300 kW
	USA	
	R FREE ASIA, Via Tinian, N Marianas	**W** • SE Asia • 500 kW
15490	EGYPT	
	RADIO CAIRO, Abu Za'bal	W Asia & C Asia • 100 kW
	USA	
	VOA, Via Iranawila, Sri Lanka	**S** • S Asia • 250 kW
	†VOA, Via Lampertheim, Germany	**S** • S Asia • 100 kW
15495	KUWAIT	
	RADIO KUWAIT, Kabd	N Africa • 500 kW W Africa & C Africa • 500 kW
	UNITED NATIONS	
	UNITED NATIONS R, Via Skelton, UK	**S** M-F • Mideast • 300 kW
	USA	
	LEADING THE WAY, Via Rampisham, UK	**S** Sa/Su • E Europe • 500 kW
		S Tu/F • W Asia • 500 kW
		S • E Asia • 500 kW
15500	R FREE ASIA, Via Tinian, N Marianas	
	CHINA	
	†CENTRAL PEOPLE'S BS, Beijing	**S** • DS-2 • 150 kW
		DS-2 • 150 kW
		Th-Tu • DS-2 • 150 kW
	INTERNATIONAL WATERS	
	CMF RADIO ONE, Middle East	ENGLISH, ETC • Mideast • 0.25/0.5 kW
	UNITED KINGDOM	
	BBC, Skelton, Cumbria	**W** Su • S Europe • 300 kW
		W • S Europe • 300 kW
15500v	CLANDESTINE (ASIA)	
	"VOICE OF TIBET", Via Tajikistan	**W** • S Asia • 100 kW
15505	CHINA	
	CHINA R INTL, Via Bamako, Mali	W Africa, C Africa & E Africa • 100 kW
	KUWAIT	
	RADIO KUWAIT, Kabd	E Europe & W Asia • 500 kW W Africa & C Africa • 500 kW
		Europe & E North Am • 500 kW
15510	PHILIPPINES	
	FEBC RADIO INTL, Bocaue	**S** • E Asia • 100 kW
	†RADYO PILIPINAS, Tinang	**S** • ENGLISH & TAGALOG • S Asia & Mideast • 250 kW
	RUSSIA	
	VOICE OF RUSSIA, Samara	**S** • W Asia & S Asia • 250 kW
	UNITED KINGDOM	
	BBC, Via Irkutsk, Russia	**W** • S Asia • 250 kW
	BBC, Via Thailand	S Asia • 250 kW
	USA	
	ADVENTIST WORLD R, Via Agat, Guam	**S** • SE Asia • 100 kW **S** • E Asia • 100 kW
	R FREE ASIA, Via Dhabayya, UAE	**S** • S Asia • 500 kW
	R FREE ASIA, Via Tinian, N Marianas	**W** • E Asia • 500 kW
		E Asia • 500 kW
15515	AUSTRALIA	
	RADIO AUSTRALIA, Shepparton	Pacific & N America • 100 kW Pacific • 100 kW
	FRANCE	
	†R FRANCE INTL, Via French Guiana	C America • 250 kW
		S • C America • 250 kW
	ITALY	
	RAI INTERNATIONAL, Rome	**S** Su • C Africa & S Africa • 100 kW
	UNITED KINGDOM	
(con'd)	†BBC, Woofferton	**S** • Mideast • 300 kW

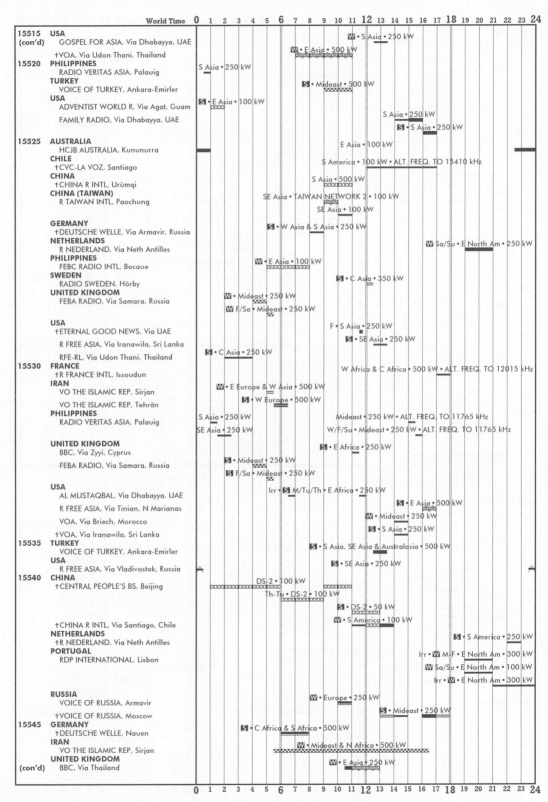

| | World Time | 0 | 1 | 2 | 3 | 4 | 5 | 6 | 7 | 8 | 9 | 10 | 11 | 12 | 13 | 14 | 15 | 16 | 17 | 18 | 19 | 20 | 21 | 22 | 23 | 24 |

15515 **USA**
(con'd) GOSPEL FOR ASIA, Via Dhabayya, UAE — W • S Asia • 250 kW
†VOA, Via Udon Thani, Thailand — W • E Asia • 500 kW
15520 **PHILIPPINES**
RADIO VERITAS ASIA, Palauig — S Asia • 250 kW
TURKEY
VOICE OF TURKEY, Ankara-Emirler — S • Mideast • 500 kW
USA
ADVENTIST WORLD R, Via Agat, Guam — S • E Asia • 100 kW
FAMILY RADIO, Via Dhabayya, UAE — S Asia • 250 kW / S • S Asia • 250 kW
15525 **AUSTRALIA**
HCJB AUSTRALIA, Kununurra — E Asia • 100 kW
CHILE
†CVC-LA VOZ, Santiago — S America • 100 kW • ALT. FREQ. TO 15410 kHz
CHINA
†CHINA R INTL, Urümqi — S Asia • 500 kW
CHINA (TAIWAN)
R TAIWAN INTL, Paochung — SE Asia • TAIWAN NETWORK 2 • 100 kW / SE Asia • 100 kW
GERMANY
†DEUTSCHE WELLE, Via Armavir, Russia — S • W Asia & S Asia • 250 kW
NETHERLANDS
R NEDERLAND, Via Neth Antilles — W Sa/Su • E North Am • 250 kW
PHILIPPINES
FEBC RADIO INTL, Bocaue — W • E Asia • 100 kW
SWEDEN
RADIO SWEDEN, Hörby — S • C Asia • 350 kW
UNITED KINGDOM
FEBA RADIO, Via Samara, Russia — W • Mideast • 250 kW / W F/Sa • Mideast • 250 kW
USA
†ETERNAL GOOD NEWS, Via UAE — F • S Asia • 250 kW
R FREE ASIA, Via Iranawila, Sri Lanka — S • SE Asia • 250 kW
RFE-RL, Via Udon Thani, Thailand — S • C Asia • 250 kW
15530 **FRANCE**
†R FRANCE INTL, Issoudun — W Africa & C Africa • 500 kW • ALT. FREQ. TO 12015 kHz
IRAN
VO THE ISLAMIC REP, Sirjan — W • E Europe & W Asia • 500 kW
VO THE ISLAMIC REP, Tehrān — S • W Europe • 500 kW
PHILIPPINES
RADIO VERITAS ASIA, Palauig — S Asia • 250 kW / Mideast • 250 kW • ALT. FREQ. TO 11765 kHz
— SE Asia • 250 kW / W/F/Su • Mideast • 250 kW • ALT. FREQ. TO 11765 kHz
UNITED KINGDOM
BBC, Via Zyyi, Cyprus — S • E Africa • 250 kW
FEBA RADIO, Via Samara, Russia — S • Mideast • 250 kW / S F/Sa • Mideast • 250 kW
USA
AL MUSTAQBAL, Via Dhabayya, UAE — Irr • S M/Tu/Th • E Africa • 250 kW
R FREE ASIA, Via Tinian, N Marianas — S • E Asia • 500 kW
VOA, Via Briech, Morocco — W • Mideast • 250 kW
†VOA, Via Iranawila, Sri Lanka — S • S Asia • 250 kW
15535 **TURKEY**
VOICE OF TURKEY, Ankara-Emirler — S • S Asia, SE Asia & Australasia • 500 kW
USA
R FREE ASIA, Via Vladivostok, Russia — S • SE Asia • 250 kW
15540 **CHINA**
†CENTRAL PEOPLE'S BS, Beijing — DS-2 • 100 kW / Th-Tu • DS-2 • 100 kW
— S • DS-2 • 50 kW
†CHINA R INTL, Via Santiago, Chile — W • S America • 100 kW
NETHERLANDS
†R NEDERLAND, Via Neth Antilles — S • S America • 250 kW
PORTUGAL
RDP INTERNATIONAL, Lisbon — Irr • W M-F • E North Am • 300 kW
— W Sa/Su • E North Am • 100 kW
— Irr • W • E North Am • 300 kW
RUSSIA
VOICE OF RUSSIA, Armavir — W • Europe • 250 kW
†VOICE OF RUSSIA, Moscow — S • Mideast • 250 kW
15545 **GERMANY**
†DEUTSCHE WELLE, Nauen — S • C Africa & S Africa • 500 kW
IRAN
VO THE ISLAMIC REP, Sirjan — W • Mideast & N Africa • 500 kW
UNITED KINGDOM
(con'd) BBC, Via Thailand — W • E Asia • 250 kW

| | World Time | 0 | 1 | 2 | 3 | 4 | 5 | 6 | 7 | 8 | 9 | 10 | 11 | 12 | 13 | 14 | 15 | 16 | 17 | 18 | 19 | 20 | 21 | 22 | 23 | 24 |

ENGLISH ▬ ARABIC ⬚⬚⬚ CHINESE ▫▫▫ FRENCH ═ GERMAN ▬ RUSSIAN ▬ SPANISH ▬ OTHER ▬

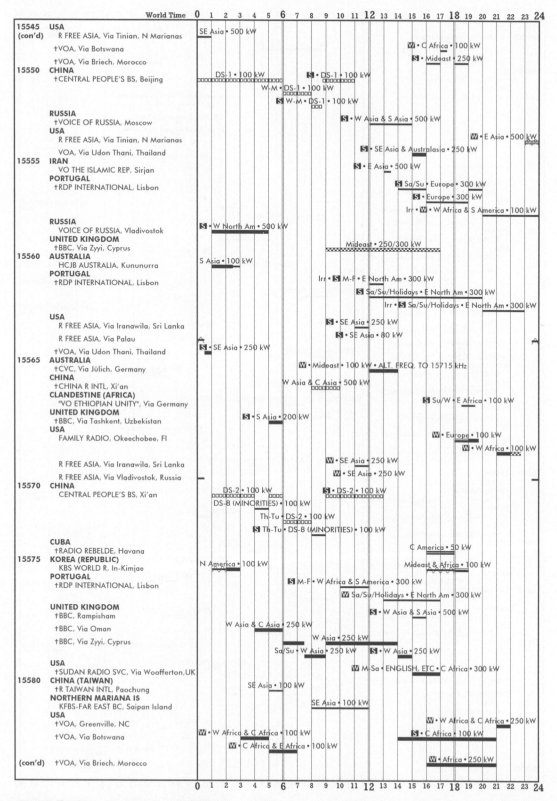

World Time 0 1 2 3 4 5 6 7 8 9 10 11 12 13 14 15 16 17 18 19 20 21 22 23 24

15545	USA	
(con'd)	R FREE ASIA, Via Tinian, N Marianas	SE Asia • 500 kW
	†VOA, Via Botswana	ⓦ • C Africa • 100 kW
	†VOA, Via Briech, Morocco	ⓢ • Mideast • 250 kW
15550	CHINA	
	†CENTRAL PEOPLE'S BS, Beijing	DS-1 • 100 kW ⓢ • DS-1 • 100 kW
		W-M • DS-1 • 100 kW
		ⓢ W-M • DS-1 • 100 kW
	RUSSIA	
	†VOICE OF RUSSIA, Moscow	ⓢ • W Asia & S Asia • 500 kW
	USA	
	R FREE ASIA, Via Tinian, N Marianas	ⓦ • E Asia • 500 kW
	VOA, Via Udon Thani, Thailand	ⓢ • SE Asia & Australasia • 250 kW
15555	IRAN	
	VO THE ISLAMIC REP, Sirjan	ⓢ • E Asia • 500 kW
	PORTUGAL	
	†RDP INTERNATIONAL, Lisbon	ⓢ Sa/Su • Europe • 300 kW
		ⓢ • Europe • 300 kW
		Irr • ⓦ • W Africa & S America • 100 kW
	RUSSIA	
	VOICE OF RUSSIA, Vladivostok	ⓢ • W North Am • 500 kW
	UNITED KINGDOM	
	†BBC, Via Zyyi, Cyprus	Mideast • 250/300 kW
15560	AUSTRALIA	
	HCJB AUSTRALIA, Kununurra	S Asia • 100 kW
	PORTUGAL	
	†RDP INTERNATIONAL, Lisbon	Irr • ⓢ M-F • E North Am • 300 kW
		ⓢ Sa/Su/Holidays • E North Am • 300 kW
		Irr • ⓢ Sa/Su/Holidays • E North Am • 300 kW
	USA	
	R FREE ASIA, Via Iranawila, Sri Lanka	ⓢ • SE Asia • 250 kW
	R FREE ASIA, Via Palau	ⓢ • SE Asia • 80 kW
	†VOA, Via Udon Thani, Thailand	ⓢ • SE Asia • 250 kW
15565	AUSTRALIA	
	†CVC, Via Jülich, Germany	ⓦ • Mideast • 100 kW • ALT. FREQ. TO 15715 kHz
	CHINA	
	†CHINA R INTL, Xi'an	W Asia & C Asia • 500 kW
	CLANDESTINE (AFRICA)	
	"VO ETHIOPIAN UNITY", Via Germany	ⓢ Su/W • E Africa • 100 kW
	UNITED KINGDOM	
	†BBC, Via Tashkent, Uzbekistan	ⓢ • S Asia • 200 kW
	USA	
	FAMILY RADIO, Okeechobee, Fl	ⓦ • Europe • 100 kW
		ⓦ • W Africa • 100 kW
	R FREE ASIA, Via Iranawila, Sri Lanka	ⓦ • SE Asia • 250 kW
	R FREE ASIA, Via Vladivostok, Russia	ⓦ • SE Asia • 250 kW
15570	CHINA	
	CENTRAL PEOPLE'S BS, Xi'an	DS-2 • 100 kW ⓢ • DS-2 • 100 kW
		DS-8 (MINORITIES) • 100 kW
		Th-Tu • DS-2 • 100 kW
		ⓢ Th-Tu • DS-8 (MINORITIES) • 100 kW
	CUBA	
	†RADIO REBELDE, Havana	C America • 50 kW
15575	KOREA (REPUBLIC)	
	KBS WORLD R, In-Kimjae	N America • 100 kW Mideast & Africa • 100 kW
	PORTUGAL	
	†RDP INTERNATIONAL, Lisbon	ⓢ M-F • W Africa & S America • 300 kW
		ⓦ Sa/Su/Holidays • E North Am • 300 kW
	UNITED KINGDOM	
	†BBC, Rampisham	ⓢ • W Asia & S Asia • 500 kW
	†BBC, Via Oman	W Asia & C Asia • 250 kW
	†BBC, Via Zyyi, Cyprus	W Asia • 250 kW
		Sa/Su • W Asia • 250 kW ⓢ • W Asia • 250 kW
	USA	
	†SUDAN RADIO SVC, Via Woofferton, UK	ⓦ M-Sa • ENGLISH, ETC • C Africa • 300 kW
15580	CHINA (TAIWAN)	
	†R TAIWAN INTL, Paochung	SE Asia • 100 kW
	NORTHERN MARIANA IS	
	KFBS-FAR EAST BC, Saipan Island	SE Asia • 100 kW
	USA	
	†VOA, Greenville, NC	ⓦ • W Africa & C Africa • 250 kW
	†VOA, Via Botswana	ⓢ • C Africa • 100 kW
		ⓦ • W Africa & C Africa • 100 kW
		ⓦ • C Africa & E Africa • 100 kW
(con'd)	†VOA, Via Briech, Morocco	ⓦ • Africa • 250 kW

0 1 2 3 4 5 6 7 8 9 10 11 12 13 14 15 16 17 18 19 20 21 22 23 24

SEASONAL ⓢ OR ⓦ   1-HR TIMESHIFT MIDYEAR ⇆ OR ⇒   JAMMING / OR ⋀   EARLIEST HEARD ◁   LATEST HEARD ▷   NEW FOR 2007 †

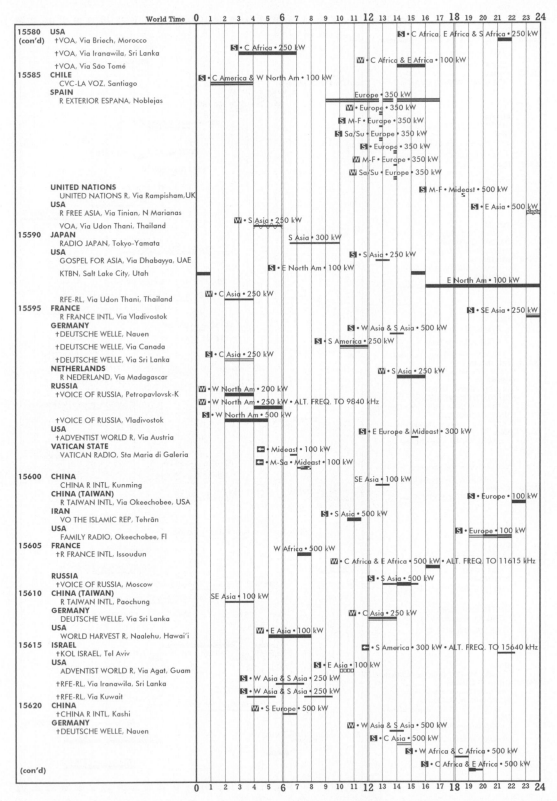

World Time	0 1 2 3 4 5 6 7 8 9 10 11 12 13 14 15 16 17 18 19 20 21 22 23 24
15580 USA	
(con'd) †VOA, Via Briech, Morocco	Ⓢ • C Africa, E Africa & S Africa • 250 kW
†VOA, Via Iranawila, Sri Lanka	Ⓢ • C Africa • 250 kW
†VOA, Via São Tomé	Ⓦ • C Africa & E Africa • 100 kW
15585 CHILE	
CVC-LA VOZ, Santiago	Ⓢ • C America & W North Am • 100 kW
SPAIN	
R EXTERIOR ESPAÑA, Noblejas	Europe • 350 kW; Ⓦ • Europe • 350 kW; Ⓢ M-F • Europe • 350 kW; Ⓢ Sa/Su • Europe • 350 kW; Ⓢ • Europe • 350 kW; Ⓦ M-F • Europe • 350 kW; Ⓦ Sa/Su • Europe • 350 kW
UNITED NATIONS	
UNITED NATIONS R, Via Rampisham, UK	Ⓢ M-F • Mideast • 500 kW
USA	
R FREE ASIA, Via Tinian, N Marianas	Ⓢ • E Asia • 500 kW
VOA, Via Udon Thani, Thailand	Ⓦ • S Asia • 250 kW
15590 JAPAN	
RADIO JAPAN, Tokyo-Yamata	S Asia • 300 kW
USA	
GOSPEL FOR ASIA, Via Dhabayya, UAE	Ⓢ • S Asia • 250 kW
KTBN, Salt Lake City, Utah	Ⓢ • E North Am • 100 kW; E North Am • 100 kW
RFE-RL, Via Udon Thani, Thailand	Ⓦ • C Asia • 250 kW
15595 FRANCE	
R FRANCE INTL, Via Vladivostok	Ⓢ • SE Asia • 250 kW
GERMANY	
†DEUTSCHE WELLE, Nauen	Ⓢ • W Asia & S Asia • 500 kW
†DEUTSCHE WELLE, Via Canada	Ⓢ • S America • 250 kW
†DEUTSCHE WELLE, Via Sri Lanka	Ⓢ • C Asia • 250 kW
NETHERLANDS	
R NEDERLAND, Via Madagascar	Ⓦ • S Asia • 250 kW
RUSSIA	
†VOICE OF RUSSIA, Petropavlovsk-K	Ⓦ • W North Am • 200 kW; Ⓦ • W North Am • 250 kW • ALT. FREQ. TO 9840 kHz
†VOICE OF RUSSIA, Vladivostok	Ⓢ • W North Am • 500 kW
USA	
†ADVENTIST WORLD R, Via Austria	Ⓢ • E Europe & Mideast • 300 kW
VATICAN STATE	
VATICAN RADIO, Sta Maria di Galeria	⬅ • Mideast • 100 kW; ⬅ • M-Sa • Mideast • 100 kW
15600 CHINA	
CHINA R INTL, Kunming	SE Asia • 100 kW
CHINA (TAIWAN)	
R TAIWAN INTL, Via Okeechobee, USA	Ⓢ • Europe • 100 kW
IRAN	
VO THE ISLAMIC REP, Tehrān	Ⓢ • S Asia • 500 kW
USA	
FAMILY RADIO, Okeechobee, Fl	Ⓢ • Europe • 100 kW
15605 FRANCE	
†R FRANCE INTL, Issoudun	W Africa • 500 kW; Ⓦ • C Africa & E Africa • 500 kW • ALT. FREQ. TO 11615 kHz
RUSSIA	
†VOICE OF RUSSIA, Moscow	Ⓢ • S Asia • 500 kW
15610 CHINA (TAIWAN)	
R TAIWAN INTL, Paochung	SE Asia • 100 kW
GERMANY	
DEUTSCHE WELLE, Via Sri Lanka	Ⓦ • C Asia • 250 kW
USA	
WORLD HARVEST R, Naalehu, Hawai'i	Ⓦ • E Asia • 100 kW
15615 ISRAEL	
†KOL ISRAEL, Tel Aviv	⬅ • S America • 300 kW • ALT. FREQ. TO 15640 kHz
USA	
ADVENTIST WORLD R, Via Agat, Guam	Ⓢ • E Asia • 100 kW
†RFE-RL, Via Iranawila, Sri Lanka	Ⓢ • W Asia & S Asia • 250 kW
†RFE-RL, Via Kuwait	Ⓢ • W Asia & S Asia • 250 kW
15620 CHINA	
†CHINA R INTL, Kashi	Ⓦ • S Europe • 500 kW
GERMANY	
†DEUTSCHE WELLE, Nauen	Ⓦ • W Asia & S Asia • 500 kW; Ⓢ • C Asia • 500 kW; Ⓢ • W Africa & C Africa • 500 kW; Ⓢ • C Africa & E Africa • 500 kW
(con'd)	

ENGLISH ▬ ARABIC ⸬ CHINESE □□□ FRENCH ▬ GERMAN ▬ RUSSIAN ═ SPANISH ▬ OTHER ▬

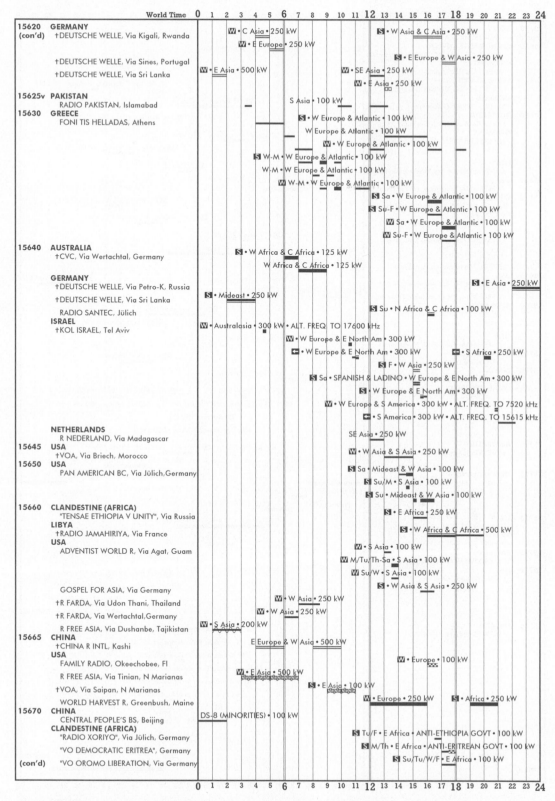

World Time 0 1 2 3 4 5 6 7 8 9 10 11 12 13 14 15 16 17 18 19 20 21 22 23 24

15620 (con'd)	GERMANY	
	†DEUTSCHE WELLE, Via Kigali, Rwanda	W • C Asia • 250 kW / S • W Asia & C Asia • 250 kW
		W • E Europe • 250 kW
	†DEUTSCHE WELLE, Via Sines, Portugal	S • E Europe & W Asia • 250 kW
	†DEUTSCHE WELLE, Via Sri Lanka	W • E Asia • 500 kW / W • SE Asia • 250 kW
		W • E Asia • 250 kW
15625v	PAKISTAN	
	RADIO PAKISTAN, Islamabad	S Asia • 100 kW
15630	GREECE	
	FONI TIS HELLADAS, Athens	S • W Europe & Atlantic • 100 kW
		W Europe & Atlantic • 100 kW
		W • W Europe & Atlantic • 100 kW
		S • W-M • W Europe & Atlantic • 100 kW
		W-M • W Europe & Atlantic • 100 kW
		W • W-M • W Europe & Atlantic • 100 kW
		S Sa • W Europe & Atlantic • 100 kW
		S Su-F • W Europe & Atlantic • 100 kW
		W Sa • W Europe & Atlantic • 100 kW
		W Su-F • W Europe & Atlantic • 100 kW
15640	AUSTRALIA	
	†CVC, Via Wertachtal, Germany	S • W Africa & C Africa • 125 kW
		W Africa & C Africa • 125 kW
	GERMANY	
	†DEUTSCHE WELLE, Via Petro-K, Russia	S • E Asia • 250 kW
	†DEUTSCHE WELLE, Via Sri Lanka	S • Mideast • 250 kW
	RADIO SANTEC, Jülich	S Su • N Africa & C Africa • 100 kW
	ISRAEL	
	†KOL ISRAEL, Tel Aviv	W • Australasia • 300 kW • ALT. FREQ. TO 17600 kHz
		W • W Europe & E North Am • 300 kW
		• W Europe & E North Am • 300 kW / • S Africa • 250 kW
		S F • W Asia • 250 kW
		Sa • SPANISH & LADINO • W Europe & E North Am • 300 kW
		S • W Europe & E North Am • 300 kW
		W • W Europe & S America • 300 kW • ALT. FREQ. TO 7520 kHz
		• S America • 300 kW • ALT. FREQ. TO 15615 kHz
	NETHERLANDS	
	R NEDERLAND, Via Madagascar	SE Asia • 250 kW
15645	USA	
	†VOA, Via Briech, Morocco	W • W Asia & S Asia • 250 kW
15650	USA	
	PAN AMERICAN BC, Via Jülich, Germany	S Sa • Mideast & W Asia • 100 kW
		S Su/M • S Asia • 100 kW
		S Su • Mideast & W Asia • 100 kW
15660	CLANDESTINE (AFRICA)	
	"TENSAE ETHIOPIA V UNITY", Via Russia	S • E Africa • 250 kW
	LIBYA	
	†RADIO JAMAHIRIYA, Via France	S • W Africa & C Africa • 500 kW
	USA	
	ADVENTIST WORLD R, Via Agat, Guam	W • S Asia • 100 kW
		W M/Tu/Th-Sa • S Asia • 100 kW
		W Su/W • S Asia • 100 kW
		S • W Asia & S Asia • 250 kW
	GOSPEL FOR ASIA, Via Germany	W • W Asia • 250 kW
	†R FARDA, Via Udon Thani, Thailand	W • W Asia • 250 kW
	†R FARDA, Via Wertachtal, Germany	
	R FREE ASIA, Via Dushanbe, Tajikistan	W • S Asia • 200 kW
15665	CHINA	
	†CHINA R INTL, Kashi	E Europe & W Asia • 500 kW
	USA	
	FAMILY RADIO, Okeechobee, Fl	W • Europe • 100 kW
	R FREE ASIA, Via Tinian, N Marianas	W • E Asia • 500 kW
	†VOA, Via Saipan, N Marianas	S • E Asia • 100 kW
	WORLD HARVEST R, Greenbush, Maine	W • Europe • 250 kW / S • Africa • 250 kW
15670	CHINA	
	CENTRAL PEOPLE'S BS, Beijing	DS-8 (MINORITIES) • 100 kW
	CLANDESTINE (AFRICA)	
	"RADIO XORIYO", Via Jülich, Germany	S Tu/F • E Africa • ANTI-ETHIOPIA GOVT • 100 kW
	"VO DEMOCRATIC ERITREA", Germany	S M/Th • E Africa • ANTI-ERITREAN GOVT • 100 kW
(con'd)	"VO OROMO LIBERATION, Via Germany	S Su/Tu/W/F • E Africa • 100 kW

0 1 2 3 4 5 6 7 8 9 10 11 12 13 14 15 16 17 18 19 20 21 22 23 24

SEASONAL S OR W   1-HR TIMESHIFT MIDYEAR ⮂ OR ⮂   JAMMING / OR /\   EARLIEST HEARD ◁   LATEST HEARD ▷   NEW FOR 2007 †

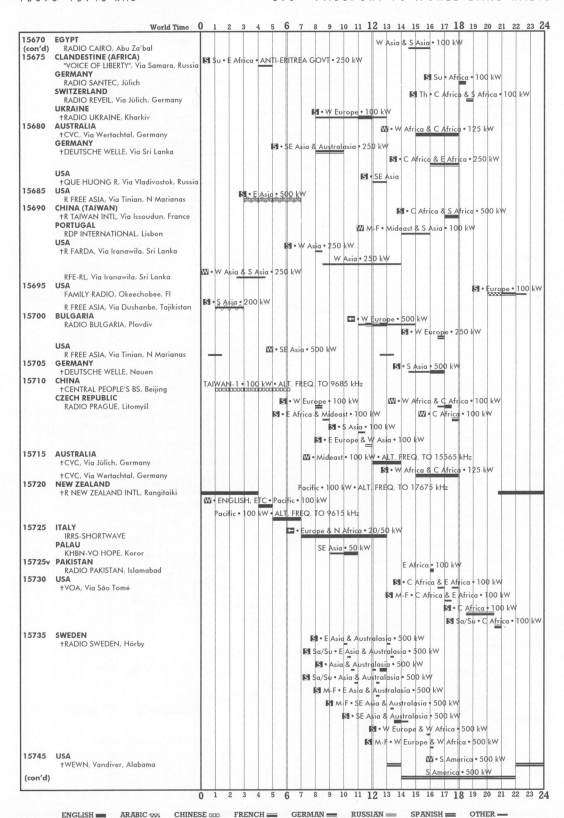

World Time		0 1 2 3 4 5 6 7 8 9 10 11 12 13 14 15 16 17 18 19 20 21 22 23 24
15670 (con'd)	**EGYPT** RADIO CAIRO, Abu Za'bal	W Asia & S Asia • 100 kW
15675	**CLANDESTINE (AFRICA)** "VOICE OF LIBERTY", Via Samara, Russia	S Su • E Africa • ANTI-ERITREA GOVT • 250 kW
	GERMANY RADIO SANTEC, Jülich	S Su • Africa • 100 kW
	SWITZERLAND RADIO REVEIL, Via Jülich, Germany	S Th • C Africa & S Africa • 100 kW
	UKRAINE †RADIO UKRAINE, Kharkiv	S • W Europe • 100 kW
15680	**AUSTRALIA** †CVC, Via Wertachtal, Germany	W • W Africa & C Africa • 125 kW
	GERMANY †DEUTSCHE WELLE, Via Sri Lanka	S • SE Asia & Australasia • 250 kW
		S • C Africa & E Africa • 250 kW
	USA †QUE HUONG R, Via Vladivostok, Russia	S • SE Asia
15685	**USA** R FREE ASIA, Via Tinian, N Marianas	S • E Asia • 500 kW
15690	**CHINA (TAIWAN)** †R TAIWAN INTL, Via Issoudun, France	S • C Africa & S Africa • 500 kW
	PORTUGAL RDP INTERNATIONAL, Lisbon	W M-F • Mideast & S Asia • 100 kW
	USA †R FARDA, Via Iranawila, Sri Lanka	S • W Asia • 250 kW
		W Asia • 250 kW
	RFE-RL, Via Iranawila, Sri Lanka	W • W Asia & S Asia • 250 kW
15695	**USA** FAMILY RADIO, Okeechobee, Fl	S • Europe • 100 kW
	R FREE ASIA, Via Dushanbe, Tajikistan	S • S Asia • 200 kW
15700	**BULGARIA** RADIO BULGARIA, Plovdiv	← • W Europe • 500 kW
		S • W Europe • 250 kW
	USA R FREE ASIA, Via Tinian, N Marianas	W • SE Asia • 500 kW
15705	**GERMANY** †DEUTSCHE WELLE, Nauen	S • S Asia • 500 kW
15710	**CHINA** †CENTRAL PEOPLE'S BS, Beijing	TAIWAN-1 • 100 kW • ALT. FREQ. TO 9685 kHz
	CZECH REPUBLIC RADIO PRAGUE, Litomyšl	S • W Europe • 100 kW W • W Africa & C Africa • 100 kW
		S • E Africa & Mideast • 100 kW W • C Africa • 100 kW
		S • S Asia • 100 kW
		S • E Europe & W Asia • 100 kW
15715	**AUSTRALIA** †CVC, Via Jülich, Germany	W • Mideast • 100 kW • ALT. FREQ. TO 15565 kHz
	†CVC, Via Wertachtal, Germany	S • W Africa & C Africa • 125 kW
15720	**NEW ZEALAND** †R NEW ZEALAND INTL, Rangitaiki	Pacific • 100 kW • ALT. FREQ. TO 17675 kHz
		W • ENGLISH, ETC • Pacific • 100 kW
		Pacific • 100 kW • ALT. FREQ. TO 9615 kHz
15725	**ITALY** IRRS-SHORTWAVE	← • Europe & N Africa • 20/50 kW
	PALAU KHBN-VO HOPE, Koror	SE Asia • 50 kW
15725v	**PAKISTAN** RADIO PAKISTAN, Islamabad	E Africa • 100 kW
15730	**USA** †VOA, Via São Tomé	S • C Africa & E Africa • 100 kW
		S M-F • C Africa & E Africa • 100 kW
		S • C Africa • 100 kW
		S Sa/Su • C Africa • 100 kW
15735	**SWEDEN** †RADIO SWEDEN, Hörby	S • E Asia & Australasia • 500 kW
		S Sa/Su • E Asia & Australasia • 500 kW
		S • Asia & Australasia • 500 kW
		S Sa/Su • Asia & Australasia • 500 kW
		S M-F • E Asia & Australasia • 500 kW
		S M-F • SE Asia & Australasia • 500 kW
		S • SE Asia & Australasia • 500 kW
		S • W Europe & W Africa • 500 kW
		S M-F • W Europe & W Africa • 500 kW
15745	**USA** †WEWN, Vandiver, Alabama	W • S America • 500 kW
(con'd)		S America • 500 kW

	0 1 2 3 4 5 6 7 8 9 10 11 12 13 14 15 16 17 18 19 20 21 22 23 24

ENGLISH ▬ ARABIC ⌇⌇⌇ CHINESE □□□ FRENCH ▭▭ GERMAN ▬▬ RUSSIAN ══ SPANISH ▭▭ OTHER ▬

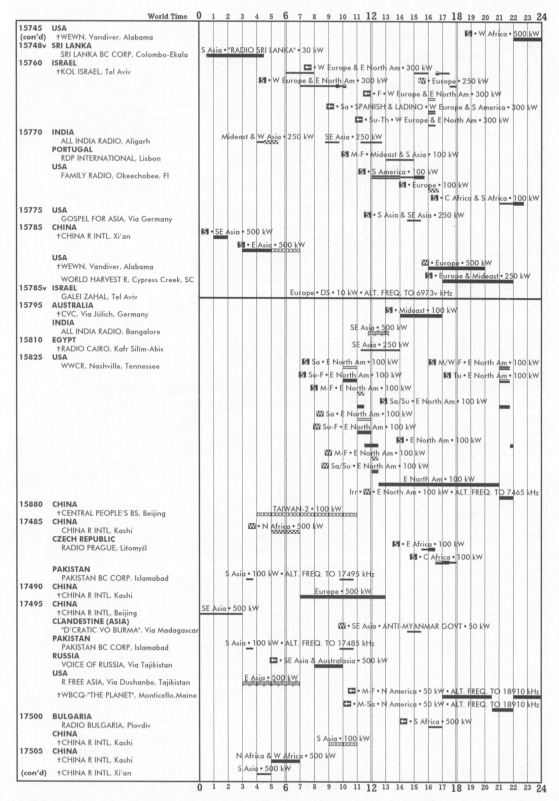

World Time

Freq	Country / Station	
15745 (con'd)	**USA** †WEWN, Vandiver, Alabama	S • W Africa • 500 kW
15748v	**SRI LANKA** SRI LANKA BC CORP, Colombo-Ekala	S Asia • "RADIO SRI LANKA" • 30 kW
15760	**ISRAEL** †KOL ISRAEL, Tel Aviv	⇄ • W Europe & E North Am • 300 kW; S • W Europe & E North Am • 300 kW; W • Europe • 250 kW; ⇄ • F • W Europe & E North Am • 300 kW; ⇄ • Sa • SPANISH & LADINO • W Europe & S America • 300 kW; ⇄ • Su-Th • W Europe & E North Am • 300 kW
15770	**INDIA** ALL INDIA RADIO, Aligarh	Mideast & W Asia • 250 kW; SE Asia • 250 kW
	PORTUGAL RDP INTERNATIONAL, Lisbon	S • M-F • Mideast & S Asia • 100 kW
	USA FAMILY RADIO, Okeechobee, Fl	S • S America • 100 kW; S • Europe • 100 kW; S • C Africa & S Africa • 100 kW
15775	**USA** GOSPEL FOR ASIA, Via Germany	S • S Asia & SE Asia • 250 kW
15785	**CHINA** †CHINA R INTL, Xi'an	S • SE Asia • 500 kW; S • E Asia • 500 kW
	USA †WEWN, Vandiver, Alabama	W • Europe • 500 kW
	WORLD HARVEST R, Cypress Creek, SC	S • Europe & Mideast • 250 kW
15785v	**ISRAEL** GALEI ZAHAL, Tel Aviv	Europe • DS • 10 kW • ALT. FREQ. TO 6973v kHz
15795	**AUSTRALIA** †CVC, Via Jülich, Germany	S • Mideast • 100 kW
	INDIA ALL INDIA RADIO, Bangalore	SE Asia • 500 kW
15810	**EGYPT** †RADIO CAIRO, Kafr Silim-Abis	SE Asia • 250 kW
15825	**USA** WWCR, Nashville, Tennessee	S • Sa • E North Am • 100 kW; S • M/W-F • E North Am • 100 kW; S • Su-F • E North Am • 100 kW; S • Tu • E North Am • 100 kW; S • M-F • E North Am • 100 kW; S • Sa/Su • E North Am • 100 kW; W • Sa • E North Am • 100 kW; W • Su-F • E North Am • 100 kW; S • E North Am • 100 kW; W • M-F • E North Am • 100 kW; W • Sa/Su • E North Am • 100 kW; E North Am • 100 kW; Irr • W • E North Am • 100 kW • ALT. FREQ. TO 7465 kHz
15880	**CHINA** †CENTRAL PEOPLE'S BS, Beijing	TAIWAN-2 • 100 kW
17485	**CHINA** CHINA R INTL, Kashi	W • N Africa • 500 kW
	CZECH REPUBLIC RADIO PRAGUE, Litomyšl	S • E Africa • 100 kW; S • C Africa • 100 kW
	PAKISTAN PAKISTAN BC CORP, Islamabad	S Asia • 100 kW • ALT. FREQ. TO 17495 kHz
17490	**CHINA** †CHINA R INTL, Kashi	Europe • 500 kW
17495	**CHINA** †CHINA R INTL, Beijing	SE Asia • 500 kW
	CLANDESTINE (ASIA) "D'CRATIC VO BURMA", Via Madagascar	W • SE Asia • ANTI-MYANMAR GOVT • 50 kW
	PAKISTAN PAKISTAN BC CORP, Islamabad	S Asia • 100 kW • ALT. FREQ. TO 17485 kHz
	RUSSIA VOICE OF RUSSIA, Via Tajikistan	⇄ • SE Asia & Australasia • 500 kW
	USA R FREE ASIA, Via Dushanbe, Tajikistan	E Asia • 500 kW; ⇄ • M-F • N America • 50 kW • ALT. FREQ. TO 18910 kHz
	†WBCQ-"THE PLANET", Monticello, Maine	⇄ • M-Sa • N America • 50 kW • ALT. FREQ. TO 18910 kHz
17500	**BULGARIA** RADIO BULGARIA, Plovdiv	⇄ • S Africa • 500 kW
	CHINA †CHINA R INTL, Kashi	S Asia • 100 kW
17505	**CHINA** †CHINA R INTL, Kashi	N Africa & W Africa • 500 kW
(con'd)	†CHINA R INTL, Xi'an	S Asia • 500 kW

SEASONAL S OR W   1-HR TIMESHIFT MIDYEAR ⇄ OR ⇄   JAMMING / OR ∧   EARLIEST HEARD ◁   LATEST HEARD ▷   NEW FOR 2007 †

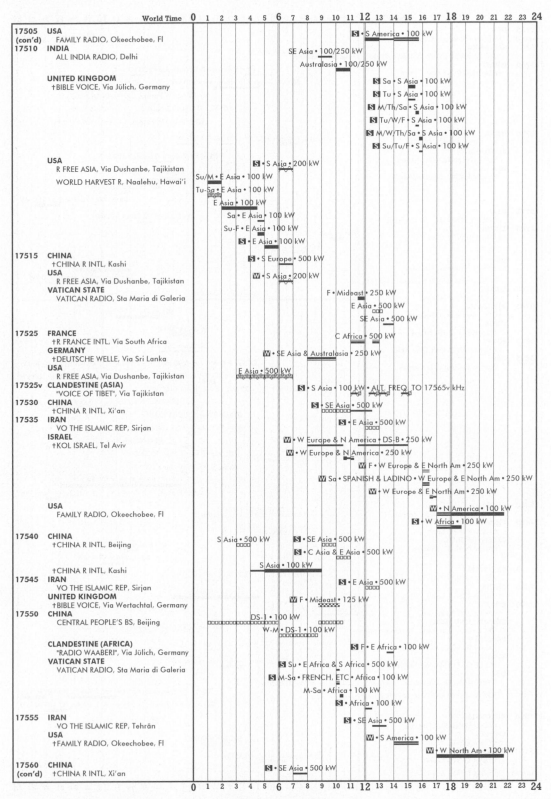

World Time		0 1 2 3 4 5 6 7 8 9 10 11 12 13 14 15 16 17 18 19 20 21 22 23 24
17505 (con'd)	USA FAMILY RADIO, Okeechobee, Fl	S • S America • 100 kW
17510	INDIA ALL INDIA RADIO, Delhi	SE Asia • 100/250 kW
		Australasia • 100/250 kW
	UNITED KINGDOM †BIBLE VOICE, Via Jülich, Germany	S Sa • S Asia • 100 kW
		S Tu • S Asia • 100 kW
		S M/Th/Sa • S Asia • 100 kW
		S Tu/W/F • S Asia • 100 kW
		S M/W/Th/Sa • S Asia • 100 kW
		S Su/Tu/F • S Asia • 100 kW
	USA R FREE ASIA, Via Dushanbe, Tajikistan	S • S Asia • 200 kW
	WORLD HARVEST R, Naalehu, Hawai'i	Su/M • E Asia • 100 kW
		Tu-Sa • E Asia • 100 kW
		E Asia • 100 kW
		Sa • E Asia • 100 kW
		Su-F • E Asia • 100 kW
		S • E Asia • 100 kW
17515	CHINA †CHINA R INTL, Kashi	S • S Europe • 500 kW
	USA R FREE ASIA, Via Dushanbe, Tajikistan	W • S Asia • 200 kW
	VATICAN STATE VATICAN RADIO, Sta Maria di Galeria	F • Mideast • 250 kW
		E Asia • 500 kW
		SE Asia • 500 kW
17525	FRANCE †R FRANCE INTL, Via South Africa	C Africa • 500 kW
	GERMANY †DEUTSCHE WELLE, Via Sri Lanka	W • SE Asia & Australasia • 250 kW
	USA R FREE ASIA, Via Dushanbe, Tajikistan	E Asia • 500 kW
17525v	CLANDESTINE (ASIA) "VOICE OF TIBET", Via Tajikistan	S • S Asia • 100 kW • ALT. FREQ TO 17565v kHz
17530	CHINA †CHINA R INTL, Xi'an	S • SE Asia • 500 kW
17535	IRAN VO THE ISLAMIC REP, Sirjan	S • E Asia • 500 kW
	ISRAEL †KOL ISRAEL, Tel Aviv	W • W Europe & N America • DS-B • 250 kW
		W • W Europe & N America • 250 kW
		W F • W Europe & E North Am • 250 kW
		W Sa • SPANISH & LADINO • W Europe & E North Am • 250 kW
		W • W Europe & E North Am • 250 kW
	USA FAMILY RADIO, Okeechobee, Fl	W • N America • 100 kW
		S • W Africa • 100 kW
17540	CHINA †CHINA R INTL, Beijing	S Asia • 500 kW
		S • SE Asia • 500 kW
		S • C Asia & E Asia • 500 kW
	†CHINA R INTL, Kashi	S Asia • 100 kW
17545	IRAN VO THE ISLAMIC REP, Sirjan	S • E Asia • 500 kW
	UNITED KINGDOM †BIBLE VOICE, Via Wertachtal, Germany	W F • Mideast • 125 kW
17550	CHINA CENTRAL PEOPLE'S BS, Beijing	DS-1 • 100 kW
		W-M • DS-1 • 100 kW
	CLANDESTINE (AFRICA) "RADIO WAABERI", Via Jülich, Germany	S F • E Africa • 100 kW
	VATICAN STATE VATICAN RADIO, Sta Maria di Galeria	S Su • E Africa & S Africa • 500 kW
		S M-Sa • FRENCH, ETC • Africa • 100 kW
		M-Sa • Africa • 100 kW
		S • Africa • 100 kW
17555	IRAN VO THE ISLAMIC REP, Tehrān	S • SE Asia • 500 kW
	USA †FAMILY RADIO, Okeechobee, Fl	W • S America • 100 kW
		W • W North Am • 100 kW
17560 (con'd)	CHINA †CHINA R INTL, Xi'an	S • SE Asia • 500 kW

| 0 1 2 3 4 5 6 7 8 9 10 11 12 13 14 15 16 17 18 19 20 21 22 23 24 |

ENGLISH ▬ ARABIC ⟩⟩⟩ CHINESE □□□ FRENCH ▭▭ GERMAN ═ RUSSIAN ══ SPANISH ═ OTHER ▬

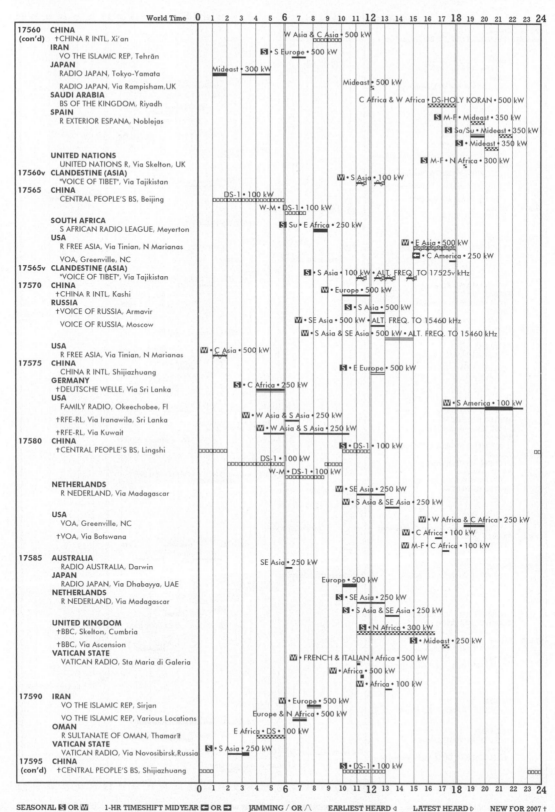

| World Time | 0 | 1 | 2 | 3 | 4 | 5 | 6 | 7 | 8 | 9 | 10 | 11 | 12 | 13 | 14 | 15 | 16 | 17 | 18 | 19 | 20 | 21 | 22 | 23 | 24 |

17560 CHINA
(con'd) †CHINA R INTL, Xi'an — W Asia & C Asia • 500 kW
IRAN
  VO THE ISLAMIC REP, Tehrān — S • S Europe • 500 kW
JAPAN
  RADIO JAPAN, Tokyo-Yamata — Mideast • 300 kW

  RADIO JAPAN, Via Rampisham, UK — Mideast • 500 kW
SAUDI ARABIA
  BS OF THE KINGDOM, Riyadh — C Africa & W Africa • DS-HOLY KORAN • 500 kW
SPAIN
  R EXTERIOR ESPANA, Noblejas — S M-F • Mideast • 350 kW
  — S Sa/Su • Mideast • 350 kW
  — S • Mideast • 350 kW

UNITED NATIONS
  UNITED NATIONS R, Via Skelton, UK — S M-F • N Africa • 300 kW
17560v CLANDESTINE (ASIA)
  "VOICE OF TIBET", Via Tajikistan — W • S Asia • 100 kW
17565 CHINA
  CENTRAL PEOPLE'S BS, Beijing — DS-1 • 100 kW
  — W-M • DS-1 • 100 kW

SOUTH AFRICA
  S AFRICAN RADIO LEAGUE, Meyerton — S Su • E Africa • 250 kW
USA
  R FREE ASIA, Via Tinian, N Marianas — W • E Asia • 500 kW

  VOA, Greenville, NC — C America • 250 kW
17565v CLANDESTINE (ASIA)
  "VOICE OF TIBET", Via Tajikistan — S • S Asia • 100 kW • ALT. FREQ. TO 17525v kHz
17570 CHINA
  †CHINA R INTL, Kashi — W • Europe • 500 kW
RUSSIA
  †VOICE OF RUSSIA, Armavir — S • S Asia • 500 kW

  VOICE OF RUSSIA, Moscow — W • SE Asia • 500 kW • ALT. FREQ. TO 15460 kHz
  — W • S Asia & SE Asia • 500 kW • ALT. FREQ. TO 15460 kHz

USA
  R FREE ASIA, Via Tinian, N Marianas — W • C Asia • 500 kW
17575 CHINA
  CHINA R INTL, Shijiazhuang — S • E Europe • 500 kW
GERMANY
  †DEUTSCHE WELLE, Via Sri Lanka — S • C Africa • 250 kW
USA
  FAMILY RADIO, Okeechobee, Fl — W • S America • 100 kW

  †RFE-RL, Via Iranawila, Sri Lanka — W • W Asia & S Asia • 250 kW

  †RFE-RL, Via Kuwait — W • W Asia & S Asia • 250 kW
17580 CHINA
  †CENTRAL PEOPLE'S BS, Lingshi — S • DS-1 • 100 kW
  — DS-1 • 100 kW
  — W-M • DS-1 • 100 kW

NETHERLANDS
  R NEDERLAND, Via Madagascar — W • SE Asia • 250 kW
  — W • S Asia & SE Asia • 250 kW

USA
  VOA, Greenville, NC — W • W Africa & C Africa • 250 kW

  †VOA, Via Botswana — W • C Africa • 100 kW
  — W M-F • C Africa • 100 kW

17585 AUSTRALIA
  RADIO AUSTRALIA, Darwin — SE Asia • 250 kW
JAPAN
  RADIO JAPAN, Via Dhabayya, UAE — Europe • 500 kW
NETHERLANDS
  R NEDERLAND, Via Madagascar — S • SE Asia • 250 kW
  — S • S Asia & SE Asia • 250 kW

UNITED KINGDOM
  †BBC, Skelton, Cumbria — S • N Africa • 300 kW

  †BBC, Via Ascension — S • Mideast • 250 kW
VATICAN STATE
  VATICAN RADIO, Sta Maria di Galeria — W • FRENCH & ITALIAN • Africa • 500 kW
  — W • Africa • 500 kW
  — W • Africa • 100 kW

17590 IRAN
  VO THE ISLAMIC REP, Sirjan — W • Europe • 500 kW

  VO THE ISLAMIC REP, Various Locations — Europe & N Africa • 500 kW
OMAN
  R SULTANATE OF OMAN, Thamarīt — E Africa • DS • 100 kW
VATICAN STATE
  VATICAN RADIO, Via Novosibirsk, Russia — S • S Asia • 250 kW
17595 CHINA
(con'd) †CENTRAL PEOPLE'S BS, Shijiazhuang — S • DS-1 • 100 kW

| | 0 | 1 | 2 | 3 | 4 | 5 | 6 | 7 | 8 | 9 | 10 | 11 | 12 | 13 | 14 | 15 | 16 | 17 | 18 | 19 | 20 | 21 | 22 | 23 | 24 |

SEASONAL **S** OR **W**   1-HR TIMESHIFT MIDYEAR **⇦** OR **⇨**   JAMMING / OR /\   EARLIEST HEARD ◁   LATEST HEARD ▷   NEW FOR 2007 †

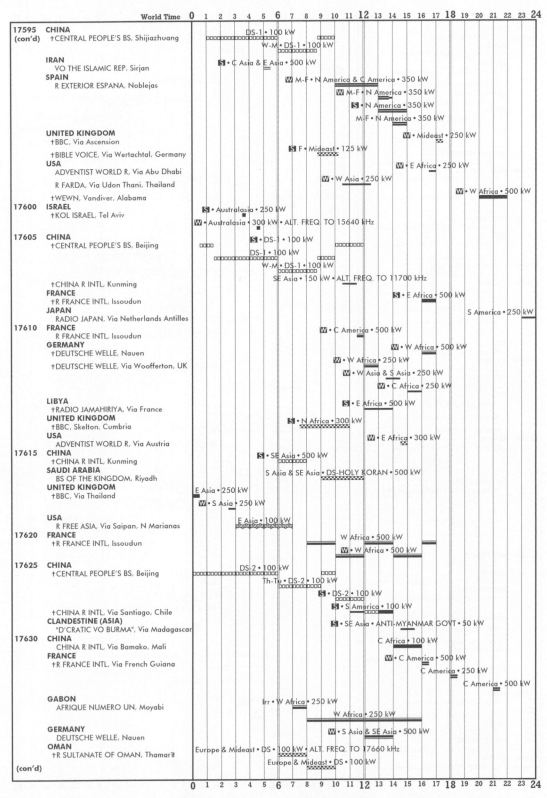

| World Time | 0 | 1 | 2 | 3 | 4 | 5 | 6 | 7 | 8 | 9 | 10 | 11 | 12 | 13 | 14 | 15 | 16 | 17 | 18 | 19 | 20 | 21 | 22 | 23 | 24 |

17595 CHINA
(con'd) †CENTRAL PEOPLE'S BS, Shijiazhuang
DS-1 • 100 kW
W-M • DS-1 • 100 kW

IRAN
VO THE ISLAMIC REP, Sirjan
S • C Asia & E Asia • 500 kW

SPAIN
R EXTERIOR ESPANA, Noblejas
W M-F • N America & C America • 350 kW
W M-F • N America • 350 kW
S • N America • 350 kW
M-F • N America • 350 kW

UNITED KINGDOM
†BBC, Via Ascension
W • Mideast • 250 kW

†BIBLE VOICE, Via Wertachtal, Germany
S F • Mideast • 125 kW

USA
ADVENTIST WORLD R, Via Abu Dhabi
W • E Africa • 250 kW

R FARDA, Via Udon Thani, Thailand
W • W Asia • 250 kW

†WEWN, Vandiver, Alabama
W • W Africa • 500 kW

17600 ISRAEL
†KOL ISRAEL, Tel Aviv
S • Australasia • 250 kW
W • Australasia • 300 kW • ALT. FREQ. TO 15640 kHz

17605 CHINA
†CENTRAL PEOPLE'S BS, Beijing
S • DS-1 • 100 kW
DS-1 • 100 kW
W-M • DS-1 • 100 kW

†CHINA R INTL, Kunming
SE Asia • 150 kW • ALT. FREQ. TO 11700 kHz

FRANCE
†R FRANCE INTL, Issoudun
S • E Africa • 500 kW

JAPAN
RADIO JAPAN, Via Netherlands Antilles
S America • 250 kW

17610 FRANCE
R FRANCE INTL, Issoudun
W • C America • 500 kW

GERMANY
†DEUTSCHE WELLE, Nauen
W • W Africa • 500 kW

†DEUTSCHE WELLE, Via Woofferton, UK
W • W Africa • 250 kW
W • W Asia & S Asia • 250 kW
W • C Africa • 250 kW

LIBYA
†RADIO JAMAHIRIYA, Via France
S • E Africa • 500 kW

UNITED KINGDOM
†BBC, Skelton, Cumbria
S • N Africa • 300 kW

USA
ADVENTIST WORLD R, Via Austria
W • E Africa • 300 kW

17615 CHINA
†CHINA R INTL, Kunming
S • SE Asia • 500 kW

SAUDI ARABIA
BS OF THE KINGDOM, Riyadh
S Asia & SE Asia • DS-HOLY KORAN • 500 kW

UNITED KINGDOM
†BBC, Via Thailand
E Asia • 250 kW
W • S Asia • 250 kW

USA
R FREE ASIA, Via Saipan, N Marianas
E Asia • 100 kW

17620 FRANCE
†R FRANCE INTL, Issoudun
W Africa • 500 kW
W • W Africa • 500 kW

17625 CHINA
†CENTRAL PEOPLE'S BS, Beijing
DS-2 • 100 kW
Th-Tu • DS-2 • 100 kW
S • DS-2 • 100 kW

†CHINA R INTL, Via Santiago, Chile
S • S America • 100 kW

CLANDESTINE (ASIA)
"D'CRATIC VO BURMA", Via Madagascar
S • SE Asia • ANTI-MYANMAR GOVT • 50 kW

17630 CHINA
CHINA R INTL, Via Bamako, Mali
C Africa • 100 kW

FRANCE
†R FRANCE INTL, Via French Guiana
W • C America • 500 kW
C America • 250 kW
C America • 500 kW

GABON
AFRIQUE NUMERO UN, Moyabi
Irr • W Africa • 250 kW
W Africa • 250 kW

GERMANY
DEUTSCHE WELLE, Nauen
W • S Asia & SE Asia • 500 kW

OMAN
†R SULTANATE OF OMAN, Thamarit
Europe & Mideast • DS • 100 kW • ALT. FREQ. TO 17660 kHz
Europe & Mideast • DS • 100 kW

(con'd)

| | 0 | 1 | 2 | 3 | 4 | 5 | 6 | 7 | 8 | 9 | 10 | 11 | 12 | 13 | 14 | 15 | 16 | 17 | 18 | 19 | 20 | 21 | 22 | 23 | 24 |

ENGLISH ▬ ARABIC ⸎⸎⸎ CHINESE □□□ FRENCH ▬ GERMAN ▬ RUSSIAN ═ SPANISH ▬ OTHER ▬

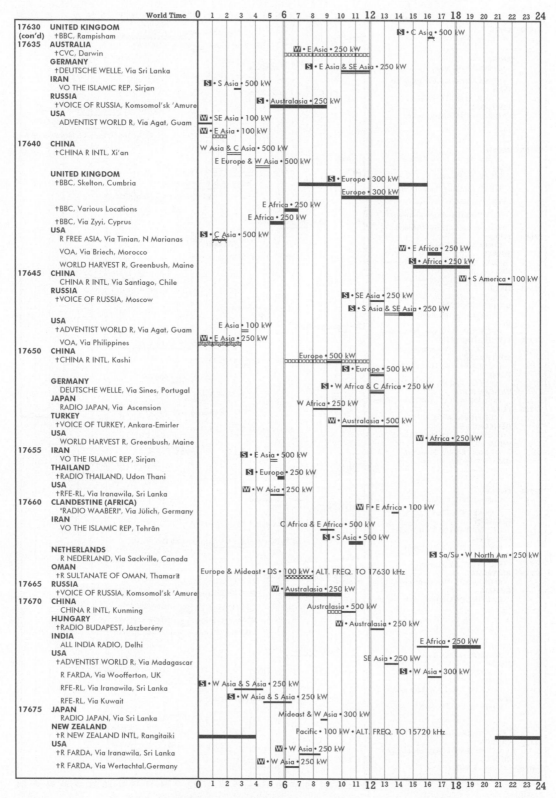

World Time

kHz	Country / Station	Target • Power
17630 (con'd)	**UNITED KINGDOM** †BBC, Rampisham	S • C Asia • 500 kW
17635	**AUSTRALIA** †CVC, Darwin	W • E Asia • 250 kW
	GERMANY †DEUTSCHE WELLE, Via Sri Lanka	S • E Asia & SE Asia • 250 kW
	IRAN VO THE ISLAMIC REP, Sirjan	S • S Asia • 500 kW
	RUSSIA †VOICE OF RUSSIA, Komsomol'sk 'Amure	S • Australasia • 250 kW
	USA ADVENTIST WORLD R, Via Agat, Guam	W • SE Asia • 100 kW
		W • E Asia • 100 kW
17640	**CHINA** †CHINA R INTL, Xi'an	W Asia & C Asia • 500 kW
		E Europe & W Asia • 500 kW
	UNITED KINGDOM †BBC, Skelton, Cumbria	S • Europe • 300 kW
		Europe • 300 kW
	†BBC, Various Locations	E Africa • 250 kW
	†BBC, Via Zyyi, Cyprus	E Africa • 250 kW
	USA R FREE ASIA, Via Tinian, N Marianas	S • C Asia • 500 kW
	VOA, Via Briech, Morocco	W • E Africa • 250 kW
	WORLD HARVEST R, Greenbush, Maine	S • Africa • 250 kW
17645	**CHINA** CHINA R INTL, Via Santiago, Chile	W • S America • 100 kW
	RUSSIA †VOICE OF RUSSIA, Moscow	S • SE Asia • 250 kW
		S • S Asia & SE Asia • 250 kW
	USA †ADVENTIST WORLD R, Via Agat, Guam	E Asia • 100 kW
	VOA, Via Philippines	W • E Asia • 250 kW
17650	**CHINA** †CHINA R INTL, Kashi	Europe • 500 kW
		S • Europe • 500 kW
	GERMANY DEUTSCHE WELLE, Via Sines, Portugal	S • W Africa & C Africa • 250 kW
	JAPAN RADIO JAPAN, Via Ascension	W Africa • 250 kW
	TURKEY †VOICE OF TURKEY, Ankara-Emirler	W • Australasia • 500 kW
	USA WORLD HARVEST R, Greenbush, Maine	W • Africa • 250 kW
17655	**IRAN** VO THE ISLAMIC REP, Sirjan	S • E Asia • 500 kW
	THAILAND †RADIO THAILAND, Udon Thani	S • Europe • 250 kW
	USA †RFE-RL, Via Iranawila, Sri Lanka	W • W Asia • 250 kW
17660	**CLANDESTINE (AFRICA)** "RADIO WAABERI", Via Jülich, Germany	W F • E Africa • 100 kW
	IRAN VO THE ISLAMIC REP, Tehrān	C Africa & E Africa • 500 kW
		S • S Asia • 500 kW
	NETHERLANDS R NEDERLAND, Via Sackville, Canada	S Sa/Su • W North Am • 250 kW
	OMAN †R SULTANATE OF OMAN, Thamarīt	Europe & Mideast • DS • 100 kW • ALT. FREQ. TO 17630 kHz
17665	**RUSSIA** †VOICE OF RUSSIA, Komsomol'sk 'Amure	W • Australasia • 250 kW
17670	**CHINA** CHINA R INTL, Kunming	Australasia • 500 kW
	HUNGARY †RADIO BUDAPEST, Jászberény	W • Australasia • 250 kW
	INDIA ALL INDIA RADIO, Delhi	E Africa • 250 kW
	USA †ADVENTIST WORLD R, Via Madagascar	SE Asia • 250 kW
	R FARDA, Via Woofferton, UK	S • W Asia • 300 kW
	RFE-RL, Via Iranawila, Sri Lanka	S • W Asia & S Asia • 250 kW
	RFE-RL, Via Kuwait	S • W Asia & S Asia • 250 kW
17675	**JAPAN** RADIO JAPAN, Via Sri Lanka	Mideast & W Asia • 300 kW
	NEW ZEALAND †R NEW ZEALAND INTL, Rangitaiki	Pacific • 100 kW • ALT. FREQ. TO 15720 kHz
	USA †R FARDA, Via Iranawila, Sri Lanka	W • W Asia • 250 kW
	†R FARDA, Via Wertachtal, Germany	W • W Asia • 250 kW

SEASONAL S OR W   1-HR TIMESHIFT MIDYEAR ⮂ OR ⮀   JAMMING / OR ∧   EARLIEST HEARD ◁   LATEST HEARD ▷   NEW FOR 2007 †

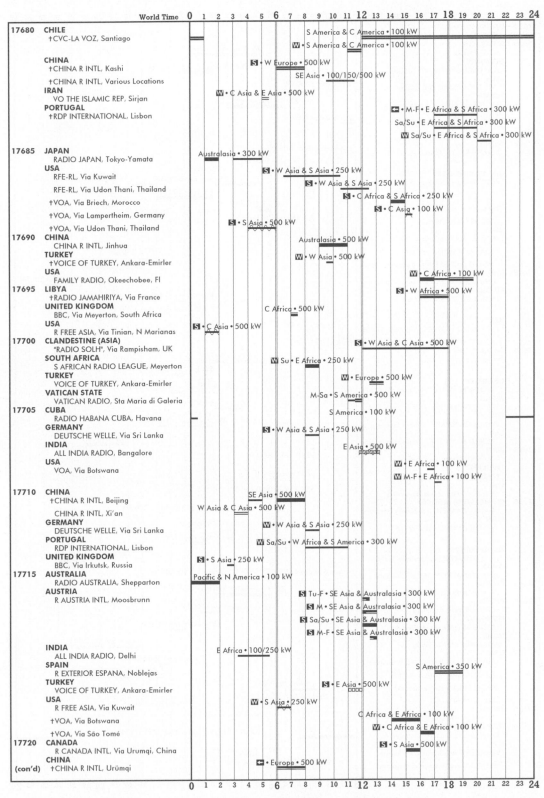

17680	**CHILE**	
	†CVC-LA VOZ, Santiago	S America & C America • 100 kW
		W • S America & C America • 100 kW
	CHINA	
	†CHINA R INTL, Kashi	S • W Europe • 500 kW
	†CHINA R INTL, Various Locations	SE Asia • 100/150/500 kW
	IRAN	
	VO THE ISLAMIC REP, Sirjan	W • C Asia & E Asia • 500 kW
	PORTUGAL	
	†RDP INTERNATIONAL, Lisbon	◘ • M-F • E Africa & S Africa • 300 kW
		Sa/Su • E Africa & S Africa • 300 kW
		W Sa/Su • E Africa & S Africa • 300 kW
17685	**JAPAN**	
	RADIO JAPAN, Tokyo-Yamata	Australasia • 300 kW
	USA	
	RFE-RL, Via Kuwait	S • W Asia & S Asia • 250 kW
	RFE-RL, Via Udon Thani, Thailand	S • W Asia & S Asia • 250 kW
	†VOA, Via Briech, Morocco	S • C Africa & S Africa • 250 kW
	†VOA, Via Lampertheim, Germany	S • C Asia • 100 kW
	†VOA, Via Udon Thani, Thailand	S • S Asia • 500 kW
17690	**CHINA**	
	CHINA R INTL, Jinhua	Australasia • 500 kW
	TURKEY	
	†VOICE OF TURKEY, Ankara-Emirler	W • W Asia • 500 kW
	USA	
	FAMILY RADIO, Okeechobee, Fl	W • C Africa • 100 kW
17695	**LIBYA**	
	†RADIO JAMAHIRIYA, Via France	S • W Africa • 500 kW
	UNITED KINGDOM	
	BBC, Via Meyerton, South Africa	C Africa • 500 kW
	USA	
	R FREE ASIA, Via Tinian, N Marianas	S • C Asia • 500 kW
17700	**CLANDESTINE (ASIA)**	
	"RADIO SOLH", Via Rampisham, UK	S • W Asia & C Asia • 500 kW
	SOUTH AFRICA	
	S AFRICAN RADIO LEAGUE, Meyerton	W Su • E Africa • 250 kW
	TURKEY	
	VOICE OF TURKEY, Ankara-Emirler	W • Europe • 500 kW
	VATICAN STATE	
	VATICAN RADIO, Sta Maria di Galeria	M-Sa • S America • 500 kW
17705	**CUBA**	
	RADIO HABANA CUBA, Havana	S America • 100 kW
	GERMANY	
	DEUTSCHE WELLE, Via Sri Lanka	S • W Asia & S Asia • 250 kW
	INDIA	
	ALL INDIA RADIO, Bangalore	E Asia • 500 kW
	USA	
	VOA, Via Botswana	W • E Africa • 100 kW
		W M-F • E Africa • 100 kW
17710	**CHINA**	
	†CHINA R INTL, Beijing	SE Asia • 500 kW
	CHINA R INTL, Xi'an	W Asia & C Asia • 500 kW
	GERMANY	
	DEUTSCHE WELLE, Via Sri Lanka	W • W Asia & S Asia • 250 kW
	PORTUGAL	
	RDP INTERNATIONAL, Lisbon	W Sa/Su • W Africa & S America • 300 kW
	UNITED KINGDOM	
	BBC, Via Irkutsk, Russia	S • S Asia • 250 kW
17715	**AUSTRALIA**	
	RADIO AUSTRALIA, Shepparton	Pacific & N America • 100 kW
	AUSTRIA	
	R AUSTRIA INTL, Moosbrunn	S Tu-F • SE Asia & Australasia • 300 kW
		S M • SE Asia & Australasia • 300 kW
		S Sa/Su • SE Asia & Australasia • 300 kW
		S M-F • SE Asia & Australasia • 300 kW
	INDIA	
	ALL INDIA RADIO, Delhi	E Africa • 100/250 kW
	SPAIN	
	R EXTERIOR ESPANA, Noblejas	S America • 350 kW
	TURKEY	
	VOICE OF TURKEY, Ankara-Emirler	S • E Asia • 500 kW
	USA	
	R FREE ASIA, Via Kuwait	W • S Asia • 250 kW
	†VOA, Via Botswana	C Africa & E Africa • 100 kW
	†VOA, Via São Tomé	W • C Africa & E Africa • 100 kW
17720	**CANADA**	
	R CANADA INTL, Via Urumqi, China	S • S Asia • 500 kW
	CHINA	
(con'd)	†CHINA R INTL, Urümqi	◘ • Europe • 500 kW

ENGLISH ▬   **ARABIC** ⌇⌇⌇   **CHINESE** □□□   **FRENCH** ═   **GERMAN** ▬   **RUSSIAN** ═   **SPANISH** ▬   **OTHER** ▬

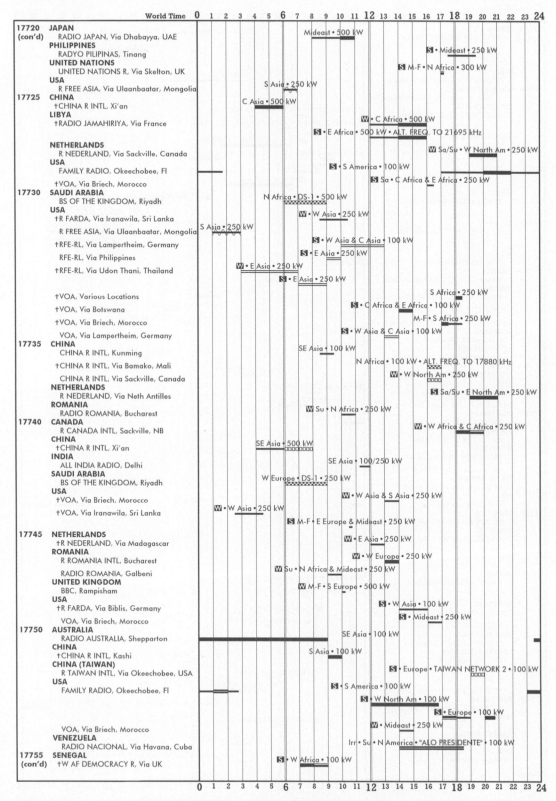

World Time 0 1 2 3 4 5 6 7 8 9 10 11 12 13 14 15 16 17 18 19 20 21 22 23 24

Freq	Country / Station	Details
17720 (con'd)	JAPAN — RADIO JAPAN, Via Dhabayya, UAE	Mideast • 500 kW
	PHILIPPINES — RADYO PILIPINAS, Tinang	S • Mideast • 250 kW
	UNITED NATIONS — UNITED NATIONS R, Via Skelton, UK	S M-F • N Africa • 300 kW
	USA — R FREE ASIA, Via Ulaanbaatar, Mongolia	S Asia • 250 kW
17725	CHINA — †CHINA R INTL, Xi'an	C Asia • 500 kW
	LIBYA — †RADIO JAMAHIRIYA, Via France	W • C Africa • 500 kW / S • E Africa • 500 kW • ALT. FREQ. TO 21695 kHz
	NETHERLANDS — R NEDERLAND, Via Sackville, Canada	W Sa/Su • W North Am • 250 kW
	USA — FAMILY RADIO, Okeechobee, Fl	S • S America • 100 kW
	†VOA, Via Briech, Morocco	S Sa • C Africa & E Africa • 250 kW
17730	SAUDI ARABIA — BS OF THE KINGDOM, Riyadh	N Africa • DS-1 • 500 kW
	USA — †R FARDA, Via Iranawila, Sri Lanka	W • W Asia • 250 kW / S Asia • 250 kW
	R FREE ASIA, Via Ulaanbaatar, Mongolia	S • W Asia & C Asia • 100 kW
	†RFE-RL, Via Lampertheim, Germany	S • E Asia • 250 kW
	RFE-RL, Via Philippines	W • E Asia • 250 kW
	†RFE-RL, Via Udon Thani, Thailand	S • E Asia • 250 kW
	†VOA, Various Locations	S Africa • 250 kW
	†VOA, Via Botswana	S • C Africa & E Africa • 100 kW
	†VOA, Via Briech, Morocco	M-F • S Africa • 250 kW
	VOA, Via Lampertheim, Germany	S • W Asia & C Asia • 100 kW
17735	CHINA — CHINA R INTL, Kunming	SE Asia • 100 kW
	†CHINA R INTL, Via Bamako, Mali	N Africa • 100 kW • ALT. FREQ. TO 17880 kHz
	CHINA R INTL, Via Sackville, Canada	W • W North Am • 250 kW
	NETHERLANDS — R NEDERLAND, Via Neth Antilles	S Sa/Su • E North Am • 250 kW
	ROMANIA — RADIO ROMANIA, Bucharest	W Su • N Africa • 250 kW
17740	CANADA — R CANADA INTL, Sackville, NB	W • W Africa & C Africa • 250 kW
	CHINA — †CHINA R INTL, Xi'an	SE Asia • 500 kW
	INDIA — ALL INDIA RADIO, Delhi	SE Asia • 100/250 kW
	SAUDI ARABIA — BS OF THE KINGDOM, Riyadh	W Europe • DS-1 • 250 kW
	USA — †VOA, Via Briech, Morocco	W • W Asia & S Asia • 250 kW
	†VOA, Via Iranawila, Sri Lanka	W • W Asia • 250 kW
		S M-F • E Europe & Mideast • 250 kW
17745	NETHERLANDS — †R NEDERLAND, Via Madagascar	W • E Asia • 250 kW
	ROMANIA — R ROMANIA INTL, Bucharest	W • W Europe • 250 kW
	RADIO ROMANIA, Galbeni	W Su • N Africa & Mideast • 250 kW
	UNITED KINGDOM — BBC, Rampisham	W M-F • S Europe • 500 kW
	USA — †R FARDA, Via Biblis, Germany	S • W Asia • 100 kW
	VOA, Via Briech, Morocco	S • Mideast • 250 kW
17750	AUSTRALIA — RADIO AUSTRALIA, Shepparton	SE Asia • 100 kW
	CHINA — †CHINA R INTL, Kashi	S Asia • 100 kW
	CHINA (TAIWAN) — R TAIWAN INTL, Via Okeechobee, USA	S • Europe • TAIWAN NETWORK 2 • 100 kW
	USA — FAMILY RADIO, Okeechobee, Fl	S • S America • 100 kW
		S • W North Am • 100 kW
		S • Europe • 100 kW
	VOA, Via Briech, Morocco	W • Mideast • 250 kW
	VENEZUELA — RADIO NACIONAL, Via Havana, Cuba	Irr • Su • N America • "ALO PRESIDENTE" • 100 kW
17755 (con'd)	SENEGAL — †W AF DEMOCRACY R, Via UK	S • W Africa • 100 kW

0 1 2 3 4 5 6 7 8 9 10 11 12 13 14 15 16 17 18 19 20 21 22 23 24

SEASONAL S OR W   1-HR TIMESHIFT MIDYEAR ⇦ OR ⇨   JAMMING / OR /\   EARLIEST HEARD ◁   LATEST HEARD ▷   NEW FOR 2007 †

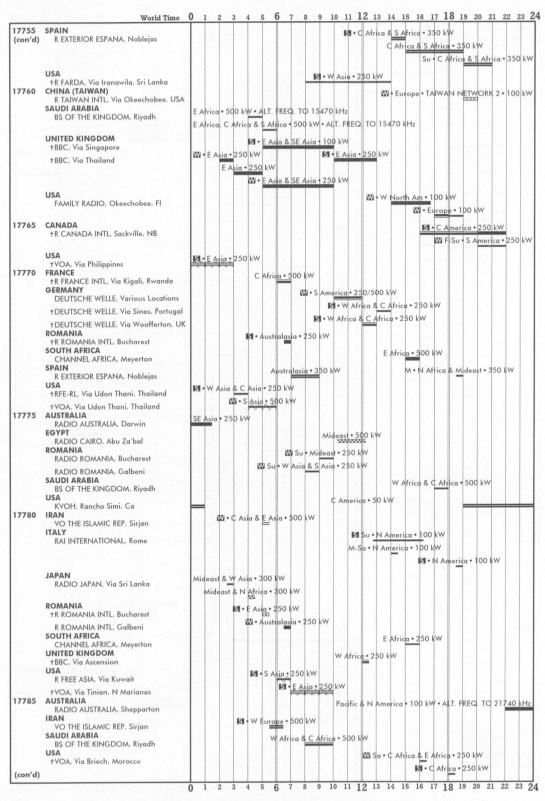

World Time 0 1 2 3 4 5 6 7 8 9 10 11 12 13 14 15 16 17 18 19 20 21 22 23 24

17755 SPAIN
(con'd)   R EXTERIOR ESPANA, Noblejas
    S • C Africa & S Africa • 350 kW
    C Africa & S Africa • 350 kW
    Su • C Africa & S Africa • 350 kW

USA
   †R FARDA, Via Iranawila, Sri Lanka
    S • W Asia • 250 kW

17760 CHINA (TAIWAN)
   R TAIWAN INTL, Via Okeechobee, USA
    W • Europe • TAIWAN NETWORK 2 • 100 kW

SAUDI ARABIA
   BS OF THE KINGDOM, Riyadh
    E Africa • 500 kW • ALT. FREQ. TO 15470 kHz
    E Africa, C Africa & S Africa • 500 kW • ALT. FREQ. TO 15470 kHz

UNITED KINGDOM
   †BBC, Via Singapore
    S • E Asia & SE Asia • 100 kW
   †BBC, Via Thailand
    W • E Asia • 250 kW
    S • E Asia • 250 kW
    E Asia • 250 kW
    W • E Asia & SE Asia • 250 kW

USA
   FAMILY RADIO, Okeechobee, Fl
    W • W North Am • 100 kW
    W • Europe • 100 kW

17765 CANADA
   †R CANADA INTL, Sackville, NB
    S • C America • 250 kW
    W F-Su • S America • 250 kW

USA
   †VOA, Via Philippines
    S • E Asia • 250 kW

17770 FRANCE
   †R FRANCE INTL, Via Kigali, Rwanda
    C Africa • 500 kW

GERMANY
   DEUTSCHE WELLE, Various Locations
    W • S America • 250/500 kW
   †DEUTSCHE WELLE, Via Sines, Portugal
    S • W Africa & C Africa • 250 kW
   †DEUTSCHE WELLE, Via Woofferton, UK
    S • W Africa & C Africa • 250 kW

ROMANIA
   †R ROMANIA INTL, Bucharest
    S • Australasia • 250 kW

SOUTH AFRICA
   CHANNEL AFRICA, Meyerton
    E Africa • 500 kW

SPAIN
   R EXTERIOR ESPANA, Noblejas
    Australasia • 350 kW
    M • N Africa & Mideast • 350 kW

USA
   †RFE-RL, Via Udon Thani, Thailand
    S • W Asia & C Asia • 250 kW
   †VOA, Via Udon Thani, Thailand
    W • S Asia • 500 kW

17775 AUSTRALIA
   RADIO AUSTRALIA, Darwin
    SE Asia • 250 kW

EGYPT
   RADIO CAIRO, Abu Za'bal
    Mideast • 500 kW

ROMANIA
   RADIO ROMANIA, Bucharest
    W Su • Mideast • 250 kW
   RADIO ROMANIA, Galbeni
    W Su • W Asia & S Asia • 250 kW

SAUDI ARABIA
   BS OF THE KINGDOM, Riyadh
    W Africa & C Africa • 500 kW

USA
   KVOH, Rancho Simi, Ca
    C America • 50 kW

17780 IRAN
   VO THE ISLAMIC REP, Sirjan
    W • C Asia & E Asia • 500 kW

ITALY
   RAI INTERNATIONAL, Rome
    S Su • N America • 100 kW
    M-Sa • N America • 100 kW
    S • N America • 100 kW

JAPAN
   RADIO JAPAN, Via Sri Lanka
    Mideast & W Asia • 300 kW
    Mideast & N Africa • 300 kW

ROMANIA
   †R ROMANIA INTL, Bucharest
    S • E Asia • 250 kW
   R ROMANIA INTL, Galbeni
    W • Australasia • 250 kW

SOUTH AFRICA
   CHANNEL AFRICA, Meyerton
    E Africa • 250 kW

UNITED KINGDOM
   †BBC, Via Ascension
    W Africa • 250 kW

USA
   R FREE ASIA, Via Kuwait
    S • S Asia • 250 kW
   †VOA, Via Tinian, N Marianas
    S • E Asia • 250 kW

17785 AUSTRALIA
   RADIO AUSTRALIA, Shepparton
    Pacific & N America • 100 kW • ALT. FREQ. TO 21740 kHz

IRAN
   VO THE ISLAMIC REP, Sirjan
    S • W Europe • 500 kW

SAUDI ARABIA
   BS OF THE KINGDOM, Riyadh
    W Africa & C Africa • 500 kW

USA
   †VOA, Via Briech, Morocco
    W Sa • C Africa & E Africa • 250 kW
    S • C Africa • 250 kW

(con'd)

0 1 2 3 4 5 6 7 8 9 10 11 12 13 14 15 16 17 18 19 20 21 22 23 24

ENGLISH ▬   ARABIC ⩥   CHINESE ▢▢▢   FRENCH ▬   GERMAN ▬   RUSSIAN ═   SPANISH ═   OTHER ▬

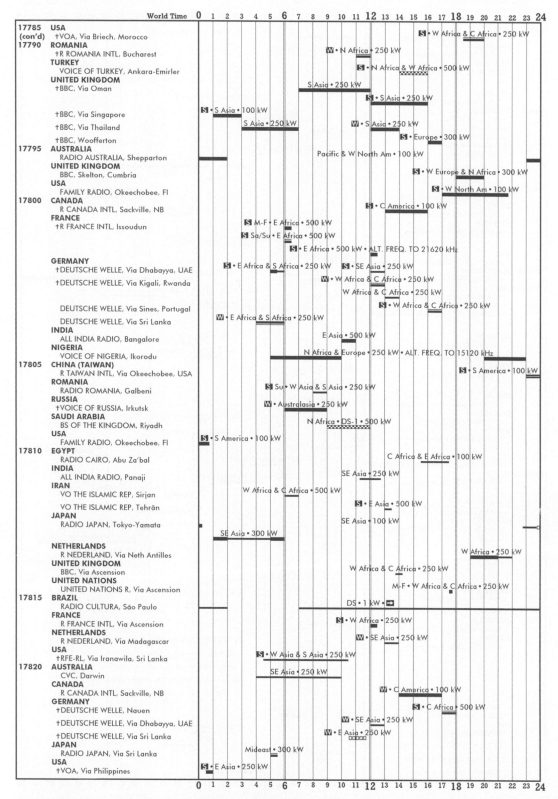

Freq	Country / Station	Schedule
17785 (con'd)	**USA** †VOA, Via Briech, Morocco	☒ • W Africa & C Africa • 250 kW
17790	**ROMANIA** †R ROMANIA INTL, Bucharest	☒ • N Africa • 250 kW
	TURKEY VOICE OF TURKEY, Ankara-Emirler	☒ • N Africa & W Africa • 500 kW
	UNITED KINGDOM †BBC, Via Oman	S Asia • 250 kW
		☒ • S Asia • 250 kW
	†BBC, Via Singapore	☒ • S Asia • 100 kW
	†BBC, Via Thailand	S Asia • 250 kW ☒ • S Asia • 250 kW
	†BBC, Woofferton	☒ • Europe • 300 kW
17795	**AUSTRALIA** RADIO AUSTRALIA, Shepparton	Pacific & W North Am • 100 kW
	UNITED KINGDOM BBC, Skelton, Cumbria	☒ • W Europe & N Africa • 300 kW
	USA FAMILY RADIO, Okeechobee, Fl	☒ • W North Am • 100 kW
17800	**CANADA** R CANADA INTL, Sackville, NB	☒ • C America • 100 kW
	FRANCE †R FRANCE INTL, Issoudun	☒ M-F • E Africa • 500 kW
		☒ Sa/Su • E Africa • 500 kW
		☒ • E Africa • 500 kW • ALT. FREQ. TO 21620 kHz
	GERMANY †DEUTSCHE WELLE, Via Dhabayya, UAE	☒ • E Africa & S Africa • 250 kW ☒ • SE Asia • 250 kW
	†DEUTSCHE WELLE, Via Kigali, Rwanda	☒ • W Africa & C Africa • 250 kW
		W Africa & C Africa • 250 kW
	DEUTSCHE WELLE, Via Sines, Portugal	☒ • W Africa & C Africa • 250 kW
	DEUTSCHE WELLE, Via Sri Lanka	☒ • E Africa & S Africa • 250 kW
	INDIA ALL INDIA RADIO, Bangalore	E Asia • 500 kW
	NIGERIA VOICE OF NIGERIA, Ikorodu	N Africa & Europe • 250 kW • ALT. FREQ. TO 15120 kHz
17805	**CHINA (TAIWAN)** R TAIWAN INTL, Via Okeechobee, USA	☒ • S America • 100 kW
	ROMANIA RADIO ROMANIA, Galbeni	☒ Su • W Asia & S Asia • 250 kW
	RUSSIA †VOICE OF RUSSIA, Irkutsk	☒ • Australasia • 250 kW
	SAUDI ARABIA BS OF THE KINGDOM, Riyadh	N Africa • DS-1 • 500 kW
	USA FAMILY RADIO, Okeechobee, Fl	☒ • S America • 100 kW
17810	**EGYPT** RADIO CAIRO, Abu Za'bal	C Africa & E Africa • 100 kW
	INDIA ALL INDIA RADIO, Panaji	SE Asia • 250 kW
	IRAN VO THE ISLAMIC REP, Sirjan	W Africa & C Africa • 500 kW
	VO THE ISLAMIC REP, Tehrān	☒ • E Asia • 500 kW
	JAPAN RADIO JAPAN, Tokyo-Yamata	SE Asia • 100 kW
		SE Asia • 300 kW
	NETHERLANDS R NEDERLAND, Via Neth Antilles	W Africa • 250 kW
	UNITED KINGDOM BBC, Via Ascension	W Africa & C Africa • 250 kW
	UNITED NATIONS UNITED NATIONS R, Via Ascension	M-F • W Africa & C Africa • 250 kW
17815	**BRAZIL** RADIO CULTURA, São Paulo	DS • 1 kW • ➡
	FRANCE R FRANCE INTL, Via Ascension	☒ • W Africa • 250 kW
	NETHERLANDS R NEDERLAND, Via Madagascar	☒ • SE Asia • 250 kW
	USA †RFE-RL, Via Iranawila, Sri Lanka	☒ • W Asia & S Asia • 250 kW
17820	**AUSTRALIA** CVC, Darwin	SE Asia • 250 kW
	CANADA R CANADA INTL, Sackville, NB	☒ • C America • 100 kW
	GERMANY †DEUTSCHE WELLE, Nauen	☒ • C Africa • 500 kW
	†DEUTSCHE WELLE, Via Dhabayya, UAE	☒ • SE Asia • 250 kW
	†DEUTSCHE WELLE, Via Sri Lanka	☒ • E Asia • 250 kW
	JAPAN RADIO JAPAN, Via Sri Lanka	Mideast • 300 kW
	USA †VOA, Via Philippines	☒ • E Asia • 250 kW

SEASONAL ☒ OR ☒   1-HR TIMESHIFT MIDYEAR ⬅ OR ➡   JAMMING / OR ∧   EARLIEST HEARD ◁   LATEST HEARD ▷   NEW FOR 2007 †

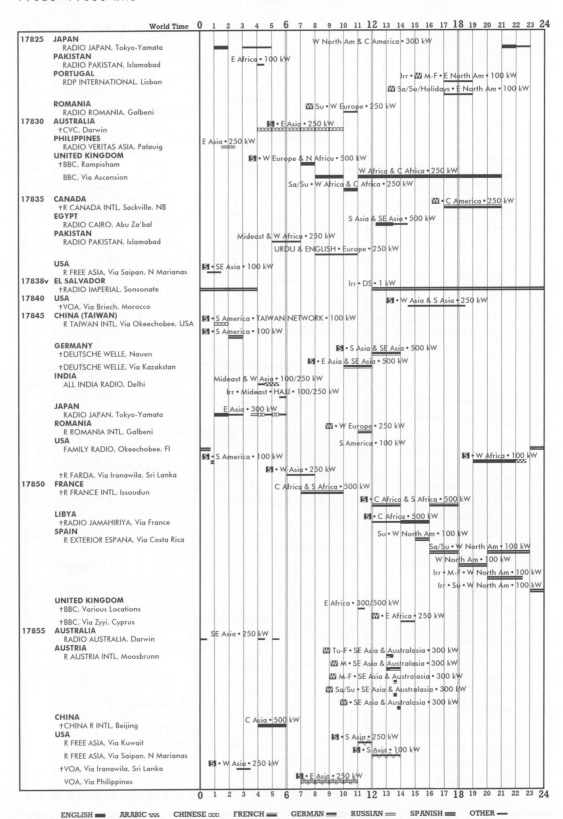

World Time 0 1 2 3 4 5 6 7 8 9 10 11 12 13 14 15 16 17 18 19 20 21 22 23 24

17825 JAPAN
RADIO JAPAN, Tokyo-Yamata — W North Am & C America • 300 kW

PAKISTAN
RADIO PAKISTAN, Islamabad — E Africa • 100 kW

PORTUGAL
RDP INTERNATIONAL, Lisbon — Irr • Ⓦ M-F • E North Am • 100 kW
Ⓦ Sa/Su/Holidays • E North Am • 100 kW

ROMANIA
RADIO ROMANIA, Galbeni — Ⓦ Su • W Europe • 250 kW

17830 AUSTRALIA
†CVC, Darwin — Ⓢ • E Asia • 250 kW

PHILIPPINES
RADIO VERITAS ASIA, Palauig — E Asia • 250 kW

UNITED KINGDOM
†BBC, Rampisham — Ⓢ • W Europe & N Africa • 500 kW
BBC, Via Ascension — W Africa & C Africa • 250 kW
Sa/Su • W Africa & C Africa • 250 kW

17835 CANADA
†R CANADA INTL, Sackville, NB — Ⓦ • C America • 250 kW

EGYPT
RADIO CAIRO, Abu Za'bal — S Asia & SE Asia • 500 kW

PAKISTAN
RADIO PAKISTAN, Islamabad — Mideast & W Africa • 250 kW
URDU & ENGLISH • Europe • 250 kW

USA
R FREE ASIA, Via Saipan, N Marianas — Ⓢ • SE Asia • 100 kW

17838v EL SALVADOR
†RADIO IMPERIAL, Sonsonate — Irr • DS • 1 kW

17840 USA
†VOA, Via Briech, Morocco — Ⓢ • W Asia & S Asia • 250 kW

17845 CHINA (TAIWAN)
R TAIWAN INTL, Via Okeechobee, USA — Ⓢ • S America • TAIWAN NETWORK • 100 kW
Ⓢ • S America • 100 kW

GERMANY
†DEUTSCHE WELLE, Nauen — Ⓢ • S Asia & SE Asia • 500 kW
†DEUTSCHE WELLE, Via Kazakstan — Ⓢ • E Asia & SE Asia • 500 kW

INDIA
ALL INDIA RADIO, Delhi — Mideast & W Asia • 100/250 kW
Irr • Mideast • HAJJ • 100/250 kW

JAPAN
RADIO JAPAN, Tokyo-Yamata — E Asia • 300 kW

ROMANIA
R ROMANIA INTL, Galbeni — Ⓦ • W Europe • 250 kW

USA
FAMILY RADIO, Okeechobee, Fl — S America • 100 kW
Ⓢ • S America • 100 kW
Ⓢ • W Africa • 100 kW

†R FARDA, Via Iranawila, Sri Lanka — Ⓢ • W Asia • 250 kW

17850 FRANCE
†R FRANCE INTL, Issoudun — C Africa & S Africa • 500 kW
Ⓢ • C Africa & S Africa • 500 kW

LIBYA
†RADIO JAMAHIRIYA, Via France — Ⓢ • C Africa • 500 kW

SPAIN
R EXTERIOR ESPANA, Via Costa Rica — Su • W North Am • 100 kW
Sa/Su • W North Am • 100 kW
W North Am • 100 kW
Irr • M-F • W North Am • 100 kW
Irr • Su • W North Am • 100 kW

UNITED KINGDOM
†BBC, Various Locations — E Africa • 300/500 kW
†BBC, Via Zyyi, Cyprus — Ⓦ • E Africa • 250 kW

17855 AUSTRALIA
RADIO AUSTRALIA, Darwin — SE Asia • 250 kW

AUSTRIA
R AUSTRIA INTL, Moosbrunn — Ⓦ Tu-F • SE Asia & Australasia • 300 kW
Ⓦ M • SE Asia & Australasia • 300 kW
Ⓦ M-F • SE Asia & Australasia • 300 kW
Ⓦ Sa/Su • SE Asia & Australasia • 300 kW
Ⓦ • SE Asia & Australasia • 300 kW

CHINA
†CHINA R INTL, Beijing — C Asia • 500 kW

USA
R FREE ASIA, Via Kuwait — Ⓢ • S Asia • 250 kW
R FREE ASIA, Via Saipan, N Marianas — Ⓢ • S Asia • 100 kW
†VOA, Via Iranawila, Sri Lanka — Ⓢ • W Asia • 250 kW
VOA, Via Philippines — Ⓢ • E Asia • 250 kW

0 1 2 3 4 5 6 7 8 9 10 11 12 13 14 15 16 17 18 19 20 21 22 23 24

ENGLISH ▬ ARABIC ⋙ CHINESE ▭▭▭ FRENCH ▭▭ GERMAN ▬▬ RUSSIAN ══ SPANISH ▭▭ OTHER ▬

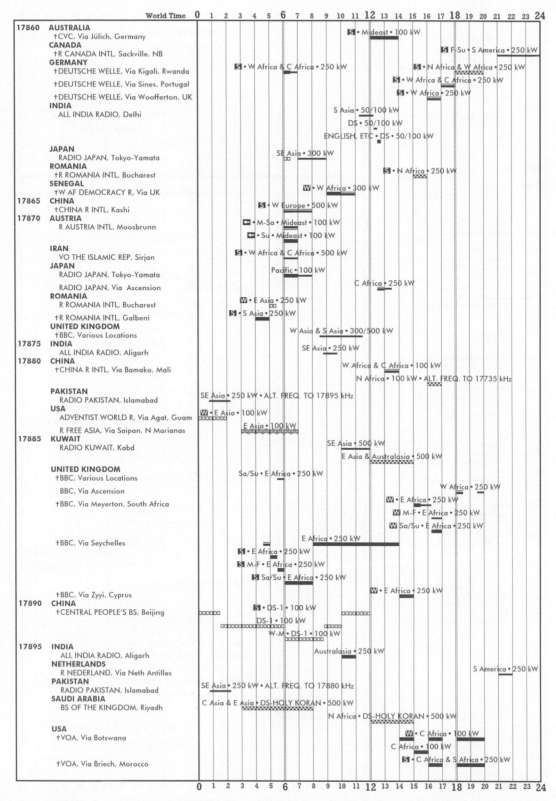

World Time 0 1 2 3 4 5 6 7 8 9 10 11 12 13 14 15 16 17 18 19 20 21 22 23 24

Freq	Station	Details
17860	**AUSTRALIA** †CVC, Via Jülich, Germany	S • Mideast • 100 kW
	CANADA †R CANADA INTL, Sackville, NB	F-Su • S America • 250 kW
	GERMANY †DEUTSCHE WELLE, Via Kigali, Rwanda	S • W Africa & C Africa • 250 kW / N Africa & W Africa • 250 kW
	†DEUTSCHE WELLE, Via Sines, Portugal	S • W Africa & C Africa • 250 kW
	†DEUTSCHE WELLE, Via Woofferton, UK	S • W Africa • 250 kW
	INDIA ALL INDIA RADIO, Delhi	S Asia • 50/100 kW
		DS • 50/100 kW
		ENGLISH, ETC • DS • 50/100 kW
	JAPAN RADIO JAPAN, Tokyo-Yamata	SE Asia • 300 kW
	ROMANIA †R ROMANIA INTL, Bucharest	S • N Africa • 250 kW
	SENEGAL †W AF DEMOCRACY R, Via UK	W • W Africa • 300 kW
17865	**CHINA** †CHINA R INTL, Kashi	S • W Europe • 500 kW
17870	**AUSTRIA** R AUSTRIA INTL, Moosbrunn	M-Sa • Mideast • 100 kW
		Su • Mideast • 100 kW
	IRAN VO THE ISLAMIC REP, Sirjan	S • W Africa & C Africa • 500 kW
	JAPAN RADIO JAPAN, Tokyo-Yamata	Pacific • 100 kW
	RADIO JAPAN, Via Ascension	C Africa • 250 kW
	ROMANIA R ROMANIA INTL, Bucharest	W • E Asia • 250 kW
	†R ROMANIA INTL, Galbeni	S • S Asia • 250 kW
	UNITED KINGDOM †BBC, Various Locations	W Asia & S Asia • 300/500 kW
17875	**INDIA** ALL INDIA RADIO, Aligarh	SE Asia • 250 kW
17880	**CHINA** †CHINA R INTL, Via Bamako, Mali	W Africa & C Africa • 100 kW
		N Africa • 100 kW • ALT. FREQ. TO 17735 kHz
	PAKISTAN RADIO PAKISTAN, Islamabad	SE Asia • 250 kW • ALT. FREQ. TO 17895 kHz
	USA ADVENTIST WORLD R, Via Agat, Guam	W • E Asia • 100 kW
	R FREE ASIA, Via Saipan, N Marianas	E Asia • 100 kW
17885	**KUWAIT** RADIO KUWAIT, Kabd	SE Asia • 500 kW
		E Asia & Australasia • 500 kW
	UNITED KINGDOM †BBC, Various Locations	Sa/Su • E Africa • 250 kW
	BBC, Via Ascension	W Africa • 250 kW
	†BBC, Via Meyerton, South Africa	W • E Africa • 250 kW
		W M-F • E Africa • 250 kW
		W Sa/Su • E Africa • 250 kW
	†BBC, Via Seychelles	E Africa • 250 kW
		S • E Africa • 250 kW
		S M-F • E Africa • 250 kW
		S Sa/Su • E Africa • 250 kW
	†BBC, Via Zyyi, Cyprus	W • E Africa • 250 kW
17890	**CHINA** †CENTRAL PEOPLE'S BS, Beijing	S • DS-1 • 100 kW
		DS-1 • 100 kW
		W-M • DS-1 • 100 kW
17895	**INDIA** ALL INDIA RADIO, Aligarh	Australasia • 250 kW
	NETHERLANDS R NEDERLAND, Via Neth Antilles	S America • 250 kW
	PAKISTAN RADIO PAKISTAN, Islamabad	SE Asia • 250 kW • ALT. FREQ. TO 17880 kHz
	SAUDI ARABIA BS OF THE KINGDOM, Riyadh	C Asia & E Asia • DS-HOLY KORAN • 500 kW
		N Africa • DS-HOLY KORAN • 500 kW
	USA †VOA, Via Botswana	W • C Africa • 100 kW
		C Africa • 100 kW
	†VOA, Via Briech, Morocco	S • C Africa & S Africa • 250 kW

0 1 2 3 4 5 6 7 8 9 10 11 12 13 14 15 16 17 18 19 20 21 22 23 24

SEASONAL S OR W   1-HR TIMESHIFT MIDYEAR ⇦ OR ⇨   JAMMING / OR /\   EARLIEST HEARD ◁   LATEST HEARD ▷   NEW FOR 2007 †

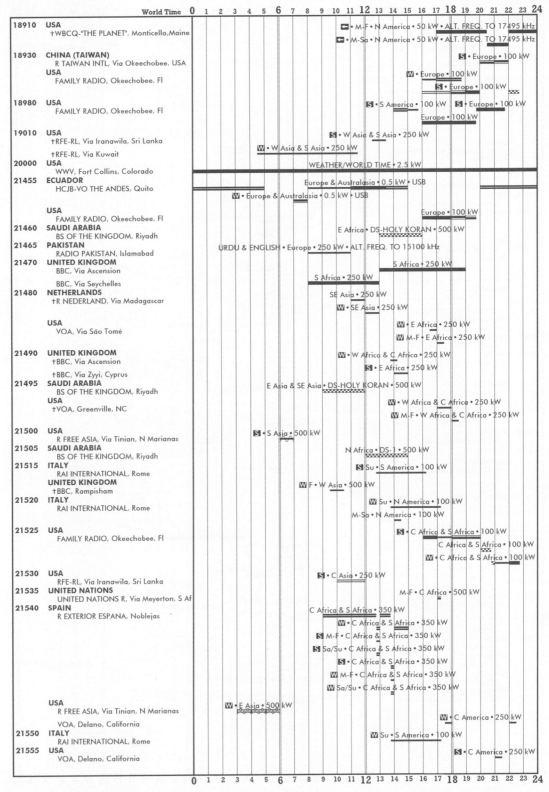

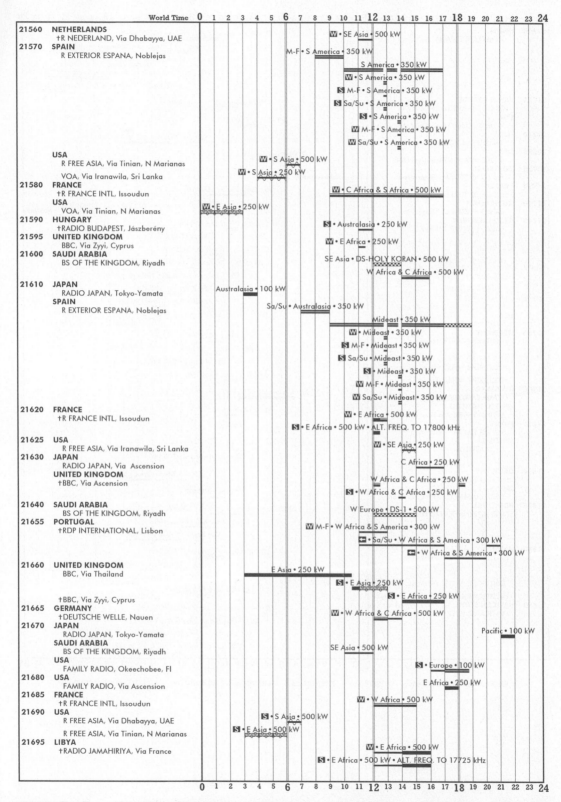

| | World Time | 0 | 1 | 2 | 3 | 4 | 5 | 6 | 7 | 8 | 9 | 10 | 11 | 12 | 13 | 14 | 15 | 16 | 17 | 18 | 19 | 20 | 21 | 22 | 23 | 24 |

21560 **NETHERLANDS**
  †R NEDERLAND, Via Dhabayya, UAE — W • SE Asia • 500 kW
21570 **SPAIN**
  R EXTERIOR ESPANA, Noblejas — M-F • S America • 350 kW
  S America • 350 kW
  W • S America • 350 kW
  S M-F • S America • 350 kW
  S Sa/Su • S America • 350 kW
  S • S America • 350 kW
  W M-F • S America • 350 kW
  W Sa/Su • S America • 350 kW

USA
  R FREE ASIA, Via Tinian, N Marianas — W • S Asia • 500 kW
  VOA, Via Iranawila, Sri Lanka — W • S Asia • 250 kW
21580 **FRANCE**
  †R FRANCE INTL, Issoudun — W • C Africa & S Africa • 500 kW
USA
  VOA, Via Tinian, N Marianas — W • E Asia • 250 kW
21590 **HUNGARY**
  †RADIO BUDAPEST, Jászberény — S • Australasia • 250 kW
21595 **UNITED KINGDOM**
  BBC, Via Zyyi, Cyprus — W • E Africa • 250 kW
21600 **SAUDI ARABIA**
  BS OF THE KINGDOM, Riyadh — SE Asia • DS-HOLY KORAN • 500 kW
  W Africa & C Africa • 500 kW

21610 **JAPAN**
  RADIO JAPAN, Tokyo-Yamata — Australasia • 100 kW
SPAIN
  R EXTERIOR ESPANA, Noblejas — Sa/Su • Australasia • 350 kW
  Mideast • 350 kW
  W • Mideast • 350 kW
  S M-F • Mideast • 350 kW
  S Sa/Su • Mideast • 350 kW
  S • Mideast • 350 kW
  W M-F • Mideast • 350 kW
  W Sa/Su • Mideast • 350 kW

21620 **FRANCE**
  †R FRANCE INTL, Issoudun — W • E Africa • 500 kW
  S • E Africa • 500 kW • ALT. FREQ. TO 17800 kHz

21625 **USA**
  R FREE ASIA, Via Iranawila, Sri Lanka — W • SE Asia • 250 kW
21630 **JAPAN**
  RADIO JAPAN, Via Ascension — C Africa • 250 kW
UNITED KINGDOM
  †BBC, Via Ascension — W Africa & C Africa • 250 kW
  S • W Africa & C Africa • 250 kW

21640 **SAUDI ARABIA**
  BS OF THE KINGDOM, Riyadh — W Europe • DS-1 • 500 kW
21655 **PORTUGAL**
  †RDP INTERNATIONAL, Lisbon — W M-F • W Africa & S America • 300 kW
  ⇆ • Sa/Su • W Africa & S America • 300 kW
  ⇆ • W Africa & S America • 300 kW

21660 **UNITED KINGDOM**
  BBC, Via Thailand — E Asia • 250 kW
  S • E Asia • 250 kW
  S • E Africa • 250 kW
  †BBC, Via Zyyi, Cyprus
21665 **GERMANY**
  †DEUTSCHE WELLE, Nauen — W • W Africa & C Africa • 500 kW
21670 **JAPAN**
  RADIO JAPAN, Tokyo-Yamata — Pacific • 100 kW
SAUDI ARABIA
  BS OF THE KINGDOM, Riyadh — SE Asia • 500 kW
USA
  FAMILY RADIO, Okeechobee, Fl — S • Europe • 100 kW
21680 **USA**
  FAMILY RADIO, Via Ascension — E Africa • 250 kW
21685 **FRANCE**
  †R FRANCE INTL, Issoudun — W • W Africa • 500 kW
21690 **USA**
  R FREE ASIA, Via Dhabayya, UAE — S • S Asia • 500 kW
  R FREE ASIA, Via Tinian, N Marianas — S • E Asia • 500 kW
21695 **LIBYA**
  †RADIO JAMAHIRIYA, Via France — W • E Africa • 500 kW
  S • E Africa • 500 kW • ALT. FREQ. TO 17725 kHz

| | World Time | 0 | 1 | 2 | 3 | 4 | 5 | 6 | 7 | 8 | 9 | 10 | 11 | 12 | 13 | 14 | 15 | 16 | 17 | 18 | 19 | 20 | 21 | 22 | 23 | 24 |

SEASONAL S OR W   1-HR TIMESHIFT MIDYEAR ⇆ OR ⇒   JAMMING / OR ∧   EARLIEST HEARD ◁   LATEST HEARD ▷   NEW FOR 2007 †

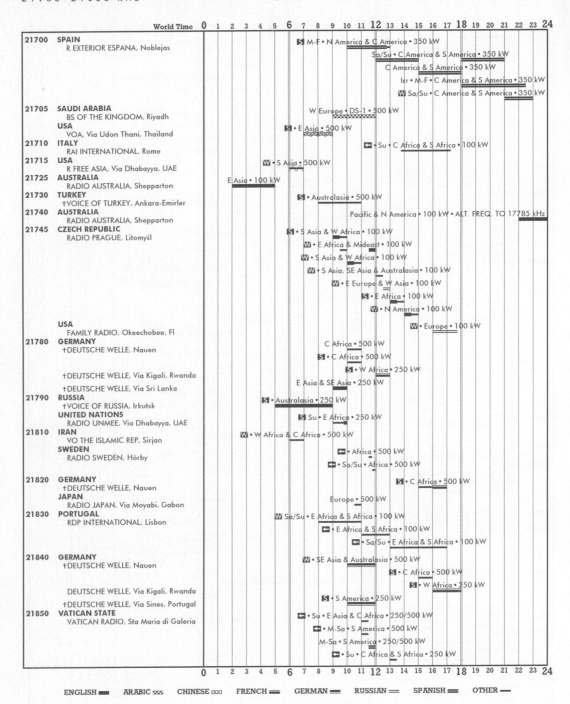

	World Time	0 1 2 3 4 5 6 7 8 9 10 11 12 13 14 15 16 17 18 19 20 21 22 23 24

21700 **SPAIN**
R EXTERIOR ESPANA, Noblejas
- **S** • M-F • N America & C America • 350 kW
- Sa/Su • C America & S America • 350 kW
- C America & S America • 350 kW
- Irr • M-F • C America & S America • 350 kW
- **W** Sa/Su • C America & S America • 350 kW

21705 **SAUDI ARABIA**
BS OF THE KINGDOM, Riyadh
- W Europe • DS-1 • 500 kW
USA
VOA, Via Udon Thani, Thailand
- **S** • E Asia • 500 kW

21710 **ITALY**
RAI INTERNATIONAL, Rome
- • Su • C Africa & S Africa • 100 kW

21715 **USA**
R FREE ASIA, Via Dhabayya, UAE
- **W** • S Asia • 500 kW

21725 **AUSTRALIA**
RADIO AUSTRALIA, Shepparton
- E Asia • 100 kW

21730 **TURKEY**
†VOICE OF TURKEY, Ankara-Emirler
- **S** • Australasia • 500 kW

21740 **AUSTRALIA**
RADIO AUSTRALIA, Shepparton
- Pacific & N America • 100 kW • ALT. FREQ. TO 17785 kHz

21745 **CZECH REPUBLIC**
RADIO PRAGUE, Litomyšl
- **S** • S Asia & W Africa • 100 kW
- **W** • E Africa & Mideast • 100 kW
- **W** • S Asia & W Africa • 100 kW
- **W** • S Asia, SE Asia & Australasia • 100 kW
- **W** • E Europe & W Asia • 100 kW
- **S** • E Africa • 100 kW
- **W** • N America • 100 kW

USA
FAMILY RADIO, Okeechobee, Fl
- **W** • Europe • 100 kW

21780 **GERMANY**
†DEUTSCHE WELLE, Nauen
- C Africa • 500 kW
- **S** • C Africa • 500 kW

†DEUTSCHE WELLE, Via Kigali, Rwanda
- **S** • W Africa • 250 kW

†DEUTSCHE WELLE, Via Sri Lanka
- E Asia & SE Asia • 250 kW

21790 **RUSSIA**
†VOICE OF RUSSIA, Irkutsk
- **S** • Australasia • 250 kW

UNITED NATIONS
RADIO UNMEE, Via Dhabayya, UAE
- **S** Su • E Africa • 250 kW

21810 **IRAN**
VO THE ISLAMIC REP, Sirjan
- **W** • W Africa & C Africa • 500 kW

SWEDEN
RADIO SWEDEN, Hörby
- • Africa • 500 kW
- • Sa/Su • Africa • 500 kW

21820 **GERMANY**
†DEUTSCHE WELLE, Nauen
- **S** • C Africa • 500 kW

JAPAN
RADIO JAPAN, Via Moyabi, Gabon
- Europe • 500 kW

21830 **PORTUGAL**
RDP INTERNATIONAL, Lisbon
- **W** Sa/Su • E Africa & S Africa • 100 kW
- • E Africa & S Africa • 100 kW
- • Sa/Su • E Africa & S Africa • 100 kW

21840 **GERMANY**
†DEUTSCHE WELLE, Nauen
- **W** • SE Asia & Australasia • 500 kW
- **S** • C Africa • 500 kW
- **S** • W Africa • 250 kW

DEUTSCHE WELLE, Via Kigali, Rwanda
- **S** • S America • 250 kW

†DEUTSCHE WELLE, Via Sines, Portugal

21850 **VATICAN STATE**
VATICAN RADIO, Sta Maria di Galeria
- • Su • E Asia & C Africa • 250/500 kW
- • M-Sa • S America • 500 kW
- M-Sa • S America • 250/500 kW
- • Su • C Africa & S Africa • 250 kW

	0 1 2 3 4 5 6 7 8 9 10 11 12 13 14 15 16 17 18 19 20 21 22 23 24

ENGLISH ▬   ARABIC ▨▨▨   CHINESE ▫▫▫   FRENCH ▭▭   GERMAN ▬▬   RUSSIAN ══   SPANISH ▬▬   OTHER —